Sentencing and Penal Policy in Canada

in Canada

Cases, Materials, and Commentary

Allan Manson

Faculty of Law
Queen's University

Patrick Healy

Faculty of Law
McGill University

Gary Trotter

Faculty of Law
Queen's University

2000
EMOND MONTGOMERY PUBLICATIONS LIMITED
TORONTO, CANADA

Printed in Canada.

Edited, designed, and typeset by WordsWorth Communications of Toronto, Canada.

We acknowledge the financial support of the Government of Canada through the Book Publishing Industry Development Program (BPIDP) for our publishing activities.

Canadian Cataloguing in Publication Data

Manson, Allan
    Sentencing and penal policy in Canada : cases, materials, and commentary

ISBN 1-55239-080-2

1. Sentences (Criminal procedure)—Canada.   2. Sentences (Criminal procedure)—Canada—Cases.   3. Alternatives to imprisonment—Canada.   I. Healy, Patrick. II. Trotter, Gary T., 1961-   .   III. Title.

KE9355.M35 2000   345.71′0772   C00-932662-6
KF9685.M35 2000

Preface

This book can be traced to the tradition at Queen's University of attempting to bridge the disciplines of criminal law, criminology, and penology. In 1988, to encourage the development and expansion of courses dealing with sentencing, the federal government offered research grants to university teachers to prepare new courses and course materials. With this assistance, Allan Manson assembled a new set of materials for his course on "Sentencing and Imprisonment." This was the first version of this book. A few years later, Gary Trotter was invited to come to Queen's to continue offering the sentencing course. He substantially revised the materials and made important contributions to their breadth and depth. At McGill, Patrick Healy starting using the "Trotter revision" in his sentencing course. He added, edited, and rearranged the materials in an effort to make them current and to improve their effectiveness as teaching tools. From then on, we worked cooperatively on annual revisions. In 1998, with the encouragement of Emond Montgomery, we began to consider how the text could be reworked to produce a set of materials that would be useful to teachers with various interests and accessible to students from different backgrounds. This published text represents a collaboration that progressed chapter by chapter and issue by issue. Each author has contributed to the selection and editing of materials and to the writing of the notes and commentary.

It is has been our goal to develop a set of materials that can be used principally by law teachers but also by other teachers in areas related to criminal justice. The 19 chapters canvass a broad array of issues, and we do not anticipate that all chapters will be used in every course. Particular interests and perspectives will shape course content. Still, we are optimistic that we have provided a sufficiently broad and diverse collection to be useful generally to teachers offering courses dealing with sentencing and imprisonment issues.

We would like to acknowledge the support of Emond Montgomery and especially the help of Nora Rock and Jim Lyons.

A.M.
P.H.
G.T.

Acknowledgments

This book, like others of its nature, contains extracts from published materials. We have attempted to request permission from and to acknowledge in the text all sources of such material. We wish to make specific reference here to the authors, publishers, journals, and institutions that have been generous in giving their permission to reproduce works in this text. If we have inadvertently overlooked any acknowledgment, we offer our sincere apologies and undertake to rectify the omission in any further editions.

Canada Law Book. M. Mandel, "Democracy, Class and the National Parole Board" (1984-1985), 27 Cr. LQ 159.

Canadian Criminal Justice Association. A. Doob, "Community Sanctions and Imprisonment: Hoping for a Miracle but Not Bothering To Pay for It" (1990), 32 *Canadian Journal of Criminology* 429.

Canadian Criminal Justice Association. F.E. Gibson, "The Renewal of Parole" (1990), 32 *Canadian Journal of Criminology* 487.

Carswell. D. Cole and A. Manson, *Release from Imprisonment: The Law of Sentencing, Parole and Judicial Review* (Toronto: Carswell, 1990), 17-18.

Clarendon Press. J. Braithwaite and P. Pettit, *Not Just Deserts: A Republican Theory of Criminal Justice* (Oxford: Clarendon Press, 1990).

Clarendon Press. C.L. Ten, *Crime, Guilt and Punishment* (Oxford: Clarendon Press, 1987).

Correctional Service Canada. "Recidivism Among Homicide Offenders" (1992), 4 *Forum on Corrections Research* 7.

Irwin. A. Manson, "Mitigating Factors," in *The Law of Sentencing* (Toronto: Irwin, 2000), 64-79.

Kluwer Academic Publishing. J. Bonta and P. Gendreau, "Re-examining the Cruel and Unusual Punishment of Prison Life" (1990), 14 *Law and Human Behavior* 347.

Kluwer Academic Publishing. J.V. Roberts and M. Jackson, "Boats Against the Current: A Note on the Effects of Imprisonment" (1991), 15 *Law and Human Behavior* 557.

Manchester University Press. M. Tonry, "Proportionality, Parsimony, and Interchangeability of Punishments," in R.A. Duff, S. Marshall, R. Dobash, and R. Dobash, eds., *Penal Theory and Practice: Tradition and Innovation in Criminal Justice* (Manchester: Manchester University Press, 1994).

Oxford University Press. H.L.A. Hart, "Prolegomenon to the Principles of Punishment," in *Punishment and Responsibilty: Essays in the Philosophy of Law* (Oxford: Oxford University Press, 1968), 11-19.

Purich Publishing. R.G. Green, *Justice in Aboriginal Communities: Sentencing Alternatives* (Saskatoon: Purich Publishing, 1998), 199-245.

Queen's Printer for Ontario. Report of the Attorney General's Advisory Committee on Charge Screening, Disclosure, and Resolution Discussions (Honourable G.A. Martin, QC, Chair) (Toronto: Queen's Printer for Ontario, 1993).

Routledge. N. Lacey, *State Punishment: Political Principles and Community Values* (London: Routledge, 1988).

Statistics Canada, Licensing Services. S. Mihorean and S. Lipinski, "International Incarceration Patterns, 1980-1990" (1992), vol. 12, no. 3 *Juristat* 1 (Canadian Centre for Justice Statistics).

Supply and Services Canada. Canadian Sentencing Commission, *Sentencing Reform: A Canadian Approach* (Ottawa: Supply and Services Canada, 1987).

Supply and Services Canada. Law Reform Commission of Canada, Report #34, *Aboriginal Peoples and Criminal Justice* (Ottawa: Supply and Services Canada, 1992).

Supply and Services Canada. Royal Commission on Aboriginal Peoples, *Bridging the Cultural Divide: A Report on Aboriginal People and Criminal Justice in Canada* (Ottawa: Supply and Services Canada, 1996).

Sweet & Maxwell. E. Erez, "Who's Afraid of the Big Bad Victim? Victim Impact Statements and Victim Empowerment *and* Enhancement of Justice" [1999] Crim. LR 545.

University of Cambridge Press. R.A. Duff, *Trials and Punishments* (Cambridge: University of Cambridge Press, 1986), 195-204.

University of Chicago Press. A. Doob and V. Marinos, "Reconceptualizing Punishment: Understanding the Limitations on the Use of Intermediate Sanctions" (1995), 2 *University of Chicago Law School Roundtable* 413.

University of Chicago Press. D. Garland, *Punishment and Modern Society: A Study in Social Theory* (Chicago: University of Chicago Press, 1990), 165-77, 204-6.

University of Chicago Press. A. von Hirsch, "Proportionality in the Philosophy of Punishment," in M. Tonry, ed. *Crime and Justice—A Review of Research, XVI* (Chicago: University of Chicago Press, 1992), 3, 6-8.

University of Ottawa, Common Law Department, Criminal Reports.
R.J. Delisle, "Annotation to *Lawrence*" (1987), 58 CR (3d) 71.

University of Ottawa, Common Law Department, Criminal Reports.
A. Manson, "The Easy Acceptance of Long Term Confinement" (1990),
79 CR (3d) 265.

University of Toronto Press. J.V. Roberts and D.P. Cole, "Sentencing and Early
Release for Offenders Convicted of Murder," in J.V. Roberts and D.P. Cole, eds.,
Making Sense of Sentencing (Toronto: University of Toronto Press, 1999).

University of Victoria, Journals of the Law Students of Victoria.
C.S. Lewis, "The Humanitarian Theory of Punishment" (1953), 6 *Res Judicatae* 224.

Table of Contents

Detailed Table of Contents

Table of Cases

A page number in boldface type indicates that the text of the case or a portion thereof is reproduced. A page number in lightface type indicates that the case is merely quoted briefly or discussed by the authors. Cases mentioned within excerpts are not listed.

CHAPTER ONE

The Philosophical Dimensions of Punishment

I. INTRODUCTION

This chapter introduces the philosophical foundations of punishment. The body of litera-ture concerning the philosophy of punishment is vast. The readings that follow provide a glimpse into this debate by illustrating some of the major theoretical themes.

The materials in this chapter consider why we have the institution of punishment. That is, from a philosophical perspective, how can the imposition of punishment by the state be justified? When the state intentionally inflicts an unwanted deprivation—that is, the imposition of physical and emotional pain or the loss of liberty—on its citizens, this is an act that demands a justification. A variety of philosophical justifications have been devel-oped, but the two main philosophical traditions in this area are utilitarian and retributive.

Utilitarian or reductive theories of punishment are rooted in the work of British philosophers Jeremy Bentham and J.S. Mill. Like utilitarianism as a general moral theory, the main premise of this approach to punishment is that the infliction of pain by the state is justified only insofar as it promotes favourable consequences. In this context, the desired favourable consequence is the reduction of crime through the "mechanisms" of deterrence, denunciation, incapacitation, and/or rehabilitation.

Retributive theories of punishment, which can be traced back to the works of I. Kant and G.W.F. Hegel (and perhaps back to biblical times), approach the problem from a completely different perspective. Punishment is imposed simply because it is *deserved* by an offender for the commission of an offence. When the state punishes an individual for the commission of an offence, the state is merely visiting on that person what he or she *deserves*.

The excerpts that are reproduced in this chapter elaborate on these philosophical traditions and consider their respective shortcomings. They provide some context for the debate. In this introductory section, the following excerpt from R.A. Duff plots the contours or boundaries of this philosophical debate. The portion of H.L.A. Hart's famous essay introduces the notion of how both philosophical traditions may operate at different levels in analyzing why we punish. Essentially, it ponders a blended or "hybrid" philo-sophical approach to punishment. Thereafter, separate sections are devoted to a consid-eration of utilitarian and retributive approaches to punishment.

Before delving into the philosophical debate, it is important to recognize the limita-tions of the scope of inquiry that we have framed for consideration. As the excerpt from

1

David Garland (infra) reminds us, the "utilitarian vs. retributivism" debate is rather one-dimensional. That is, it fails to take into account other social phenomena that might better explain the persistence of the institution of punishment in our society. We may discover, for one reason or another, that neither philosophical tradition provides an adequate justification for punishment, yet the thought of jettisoning the institution is untenable to most people. As Garland observes, the institution of punishment accommodates a complex set of social values and embodies social meaning that extends beyond the philosophical dimension considered here. Although it is not possible here to explore the large body of literature that probes the sociological aspects of punishment, it is a dimension that ought to be kept in mind. We return to Garland and his notion of "penal significantion" at the end of this chapter.

D. Garland, *Punishment and Modern Society: A Study in Social Theory*
(Chicago: University of Chicago Press, 1990) (footnotes omitted)

The philosophies of punishment, at least in their traditional form, are based upon a rather idealized and one-dimensional image of punishment: an image which poses the problem of punishment as a variant of the classic liberal conundrum of how the state should relate to the individual. But if, as I suspect, this image is an impoverished one, and fails to capture the full dimensions and complexities of punishment, then the solutions offered by philosophy are unlikely to match up to the problems of the institution. What is needed now is really a preliminary to philosophy—a descriptive prolegomenon which sets out the social foundations of punishment, its characteristic modern forms, and its social significance. Only on this basis can philosophies be developed which adequately address the normative problems of this complex institution. Quite simply, we need to know what punishment is in order to think what it can and should be. ...

Although legal punishment is understood to have a variety of aims, its primary purpose is usually represented as being the instrumental one of reducing or containing rates of criminal behaviour. It is thus possible to conceive of punishment as being simply a means to a given end to think of it as a legally approved method designed to facilitate the task of crime control. Nor is this an uncommon or particularly inadequate perception of punishment. Crime control is indeed a determinant of penal practice and this ends–means conception is widely adopted both by penologists and by philosophers of punishment. This instrumental, punishment-as-crime-control conception has, however, been unattractive to sociologists of punishment. These sociologists have usually perceived a sense in which punishment's significance or social function runs beyond the narrow realm of crime control, and they consider such an instrumentalist conception to be an unjustified narrowing of the field of study. Indeed, in some instances, certain theorists have gone so far as to deny punishment's crime-control function altogether, arguing that penality is not well adapted to this particular end, and that therefore some other end must be posited to explain its character. The most celebrated instance of this is Émile Durkheim's declaration that "if crime is not pathological then the purpose of punishment cannot be to cure it," but similar positions are adopted by writers such as Mead, Rusche and Kirchheimer, and, more recently, Michel Foucault.

Each of these writers point to the "failure" of punishment as a method of crime control and argues that it is badly adapted to this end, before going on to discuss alternative ways of understanding the phenomenon.

In a sense, this kind of approach is liberating for anyone who wishes to think about punishment, since it frees us from the need to think of punishment in "penological" terms and opens up the question of penality's other social functions. There are, however, serious problems with such a position, despite its obvious attractions. For one thing, it continues to think of punishment as a means to an end: if not now the end of "crime control" then some alternative tools, such as social solidarity (Durkheim) or political domination (Foucault). But this "purposive" or teleological conception of a social institution makes for bad sociology. Not only is it quite possible, as Nietzsche points out, for a single, historically developed institution to condense a whole series of separate ends and purposes within its sphere of operation. It is also the case that institutions are never fully explicable purely in terms of their "purposes." Institutions like the prison, or the fine, or the guillotine, are social artefacts, embodying and regenerating wider cultural categories as well as being means to serve particular penological ends. Punishment is not wholly explicable in terms of its purposes because no social artefact can be explained in this way. Like architecture or diet or clothing or table manners, punishment has an instrumental purpose, but also a cultural style and an historical tradition, and a dependence upon "institutional, technical and discursive conditions." If we are to understand such artefacts we have to think of them as social and cultural entities whose meanings can only be unravelled by careful analysis and detailed examination. As in all spheres of life, a specific need may call forth a technical response, but a whole process of historical and cultural production goes into the shaping of that "technique."

The need to control crime in its various forms, and to respond to the depredations of law-breakers is thus only one of the factors which helps shape the institutions of penality. It is, no doubt, an important one, and it would make little sense, for example, to analyse US penal policy without bearing in mind the levels of crime experienced in the USA, and the social and political consequences which follow from this. But even if one could disentangle "real" crime rates from the processes of policing, criminalizing, and punishing (through which we generate most of our knowledge of crime and at least some of its actuality), it is clear enough that criminal conduct does not determine the kind of penal action that society adopts. For one thing, it is not "crime" or even criminological knowledge about crime which most affects policy decisions, but rather the ways in which "the crime problem" is officially perceived and the political positions to which these perceptions give rise. For another, the specific forms of policing, trial, and punishment, the severity of sanctions and the frequency of their use, institutional regimes, and frameworks of condemnation are all fixed by social convention and tradition rather than by the contours of criminality. Thus to the extent that penal systems adapt their practices to the problems of crime control, they do so in ways which are heavily mediated by independent considerations such as cultural conventions, economic resources, institutional dynamics, and political arguments.

Thinking of punishment as a social artefact serving a variety of purposes and premised upon an ensemble of social forces thus allows us to consider punishment in sociological terms without dismissing its penological purposes and effects. It avoids the absurdity of thinking about punishment as if it had nothing to do with crime, without falling into the trap of thinking of it solely in crime-control terms. We can thus accept that punishment is indeed oriented towards the control of crime and so partly determined by that orientation but insist that it has other determinants and other dynamics which have to be considered if punishments is to be fully understood.

Punishment, then, is a delimited legal process, but its existence and operation are dependent upon a wide array of other social forces and conditions. These conditioning circumstances take a variety of forms some of which have been explicated by historical and sociological work in this field. Thus, for example, modern prisons presuppose definite architectural forms, security devices, disciplinary technologies, and developed regimes which organize time and space as well as the social means to finance, construct, and administer such complex organizations. And as recent work has shown, specific forms of punishment are also dependent for their support upon less obvious social and historical circumstances including political discourses and specific forms of knowledge, legal, moral, and cultural categories, and specific patterns of psychic organization or sensibility. Punishment may be a legal institution, administered by state functionaries, but it is necessarily grounded in wider patterns of knowing, feeling, and acting, and it depends upon these social roots and supports for its continuing legitimacy and operation. It is also grounded in history, for, like all social institutions, modern punishment is a historical outcome which is only imperfectly adapted to its current situation. It is a product of tradition as much as present policy: hence the need for a developmental as well as a functional perspective in the understanding of penal institutions. It is only by viewing punishment against the background of these wider forms of life and their history that we can begin to understand the informal logic which underpins penal practice. In consequence, we should be prepared to find that this "logic" is the social logic of a complex institution built upon an ensemble of conflicting and co-ordinating forces, rather than the purely instrumental logic of a technical means adapted to a given end.

R.A. Duff, *Trials and Punishments*
(Cambridge: University of Cambridge Press, 1986) (footnotes omitted)

Philosophical discussions of the meaning and justification of criminal punishment tend to move along familiar and well-worn paths. It is agreed that a system of criminal punishment stands in need of some strenuous and persuasive justification: the briefest examination of our actual penal institutions confronts us forcibly with the question of how we can justifiably subject people to such treatment; and even a more abstract or idealised account of what punishment could or should be must recognise that any punitive practice will require powerful justification. But different moral perspectives generate different accounts of why it is that punishment needs justification—of what it is about punishment that makes it morally problematic: for some it is the fact that punishment inflicts, indeed is designed to inflict, pain or suffering that most forcibly raises the issue of justification; for others it is the coercive character of punishment—the fact that it is imposed on people against their express will, thus apparently infringing their freedom and autonomy—which is most disturbing. Such different perceptions of the problem of punishment are themselves related to quite different accounts of what does or could justify a system of criminal punishment.

Consequentialists, who have been for many years the predominant party in these discussions, insist that the point of a system of criminal punishment must lie in its beneficial effects (most obviously in the reduction of harmful modes of conduct by the deterrence, reform or incapacitation of those who do or might engage in them), and its justification in the extent to which these benefits outweigh the system's costs (the harm caused by punishment; the resources needed to identify and deal with those who are to be punished). Consequentialist accounts of punishment are as diverse as the ends which consequentialists may value and which punishment may serve: but I take it to be a common and defining feature of such accounts that they require punishment to be justified by reference to benefits to which it is *contingently* related as a means to a further end. Our initial specification of the ends which we are to pursue leaves open the question of the means by which they are to be pursued, since those ends, do not of their nature require any particular method of attaining them: so we must go on to ask which methods are in facta likely to be most economically efficacious. To justify a system of punishment it is therefore not enough to show that it pursues ends which are worth pursuing, nor indeed that its benefits outweigh its costs: we must also show, by an empirical inquiry into the likely effects of actual or possible social institutions, that this way of dealing with disvalued conduct is more economically effective than other possible methods of achieving our desired ends—than, for instance, a system of "social hygiene" which regards such conduct as symptomatic of a condition which needs curative treatment rather than as an instance of criminality requiring punishment.

This contingent relation between punishment and its justifying aims generates familiar objections to such consequentialist accounts. For the whole-hearted pursuit of such aims would surely sanction the imposition of manifestly unjust punishments: the punishment of innocent scapegoats; excessively harsh punishments for relatively trivial offences; a refusal to accept excusing-conditions which should in justice be accepted. It is at best a contingent truth that just punishments are consequentially efficient; and it may sometimes be true that unjust punishments are more efficient.

A consequentialist might respond to such objections by arguing that an adequately detailed consequentialist account, which attends to *all* the likely effects of particular kinds or systems of punishment, will not in fact have such disturbing implications; that it will come closer to an extensional equivalence which "ordinary moral views" than its critics may suppose. She may also try to provide a role for, and an explanation of, the principles of justice which her critics regard as morally significant; by arguing, for instance, that we have good consequentialist reasons to obey strict rules which forbid the punishment of the innocent or the unduly harsh punishment of the guilty. But she will still face some familiar objections; that she is relying on large and unsubstantiated empirical claims about the likely effects of different kinds of practice; that her reductive and instrumental account of the principles of justice fails to capture the sense and significance of those principles, or the role which they properly play in our moral thought; and that she "begs the institution" by assuming without adequate argument that a consequentialist concern to prevent harmful conduct will generate something like a system of criminal punishment, rather than some quite different system of social hygiene or behaviour-control. Some moral radical consequentialists have indeed taken this last route, and argued that a proper concern for the appropriate consequentialist ends should lead us to abandon punishment altogether.

An alternative response to these criticisms has been to insist that the positive justifying aims of punishment must indeed lie in its consequential benefits, but to allow that our pursuit of those aims is and should be limited by other considerations or side-constraints. Such limits may be set by our concern for ends other than, and conflicting with, those which provide the justifying aims of punishment; a concern to maximise the citizen's freedom in and control over his own life may set limits on who may be punished, and how, which are not dictated by the aim of preventing disvalued conduct: but they may also be set by an avowedly non-consequentialist concern for justice which forbids us to punish the innocent, and limits the kind or amount of punishment which may be attached to different offences. Punishment which efficiently serves its justifying aims may thus still be unjustified, if it fails to satisfy these further moral constraints—constraints which are independent of the consequential ends which punishment is to serve, and which focus on its intrinsic character.

It is here that retributivist ideas are allowed to play a part in an account of punishment. Traditional attempts to find the *positive* justification of punishment in its relation to a past offence are, their critics claim, unable to explain that justificatory relationship: insofar as they have any tolerably clear meaning they are seen to depend on an unargued and unarguable intuition that "the guilty deserve to suffer" (itself perhaps reflecting a desire for revenge which hardly deserves our moral respect); or on a covertly consequentialist appeal to some particular, and arbitrarily selected, kind of beneficial effect. But we need not therefore eliminate all notions of retribution: we can deal with them (and defuse them) by allowing that they do, once properly understood, have a role in an adequate account of punishment—though not the dominant role which their traditional proponents claimed for them. Ideas of retribution and desert are now to play an etiolated and negative role, setting constraints on our pursuit of the consequentialist goals which provide the positive justifying aim of punishment: they express independent principles of justice; or logical principles involved in the meaning of "punishment"; or subordinate principles within a Rule-Utilitarian system.

Retributivists, however, are unlikely to be satisfied with this subordinate role within a fundamentally consequentialist framework: and recent years have seen a revival of full-blooded retributivist attempts to locate the meaning of punishment, not in its contingent and instrumental contribution to some further end, but in its internal relationship to a past offence; and its justification in its intrinsic character as a response to that offence. This revival, involving both academic philosophers and more practically oriented legal theorists, has been motivated in part by the manifest failure of systems constructed or reformed along purportedly consequentialist lines to achieve their avowed ends, as well as by a more theoretical dissatisfaction with consequentialist accounts of punishment; and it has led to new attempts to explicate and defend the idea that punishment is justified as merited retribution for a past offence.

We can usefully talk of the common features, and the common logical structure, of consequentialist accounts of punishment: but can we usefully talk of retributivist accounts in this way; or has the label "retributivist" been applied to such a diversity of views and principles that it now lacks any unambiguous or unitary meaning? We must indeed distinguish retributivist accounts of the justifying purpose of punishment from those which seek only to set limits on our pursuit of consequentialist aims; and amongst the former we find a notable diversity of explanations of how it is that punishment is an appropriate response to crime. Some talk of the payment of a debt incurred by crime, or of the restoration of a balance disturbed by crime; others of the expiation, atonement, or annulment of crime; others of the denunciation of crime; and we cannot suppose that these are simply different ways of expressing the same idea. But such accounts do share what can usefully be called a retributivist perspective on punishment: for they all find the sense and the justification of punishment in its relation to a past offence.

A retributivist must explain the meaning of this justificatory relationship, and the values on which it depends. She must defend herself against the accusation that her account amounts at best to a distortion of logical or moral principles which have their proper and subordinate place within a consequentialist account of the justifying aims of punishment; and at worse to a piece of metaphysical mystery-mongering which conceals a desire for revenge or retaliation behind such opaque and unilluminating metaphors as "restoring the balance" or "annulling the crime." She must meet the claim that a coercive institution like punishment can be justified only by showing that it does some significant consequential good; and she may do this by arguing that the justification of punishment has, and need have, nothing to do with its consequences, and everything to do with its intrinsic character as a response to crime: the imposition of punishment on criminals is right independently of its consequences— even, perhaps, whatever its consequences.

The range of familiar accounts of punishment thus offers us three models for its justification. A consequentialist model justifies punishment by reference to further ends to which it is contingently and instrumentally related as a means; an intrinsicalist or retributivist model justifies it by reference to its intrinsic character as distinct form, and rather than, its consequences; and a "consequentialism with side-constraints" model seeks to combine these two modes of justification by insisting that a justified system of punishment must be an efficient method of pursuing the further ends which provide its justifying aims, whilst also satisfying the independent and intrinsicalist demands of justice.

H.L.A. Hart, "Prolegomenon to the Principles of Punishment"
in *Punishment and Responsibility: Essays in the Philosophy of Law*
(Oxford: Oxford University Press, 1968), 11-19 (footnotes omitted)

I. *Introductory*

The main object of this paper is to provide a framework for the discussion of the mounting perplexities which now surround the institution of criminal punishment, and to show that any morally tolerable account of this institution must exhibit it as a compromise between distinct and partly conflicting principles.

General interest in the topic of punishment has never been greater than it is at present and I doubt if the public discussion of it has ever been more confused. The interest and the confusion are both in part due to relatively modern scepticism about two elements which have figured as essential parts of the traditionally opposed "theories" of punishment. On the one hand, the old Benthamite confidence in fear of the penalties threatened by the law as a powerful deterrent, has waned with the growing realization that the part played by calculation of any sort in anti-social behaviour has been exaggerated. On the other hand a cloud of doubt has settled over the keystone of "retributive" theory. Its advocates can no longer speak with the old confidence that statements of the form "This man who has broken the law could have kept it" had a univocal or agreed meaning; or where scepticism does not attach to the *meaning* of this form of statement, it has shaken the confidence that we are generally able to distinguish the cases where a statement of this form is true from those where it is not.

Yet quite apart from the uncertainty engendered by these fundamental doubts, which seem to call in question the accounts given of the efficacy, and the morality of punishment by all the old competing theories, the public utterances of those who conceive themselves to be expounding, as plain men for other plain men, orthodox or commonsense principles (untouched by modern psychological doubts) are uneasy. Their words often sound as if the authors had not fully grasped their meaning or did not intend the words to be taken quite literally. A glance at the parliamentary debates or the *Report of the Royal Commission on Capital Punishment* shows that many are now troubled by the suspicion that the view that there is just one supreme value or objective (e.g. Deterrence, Retribution or Reform) in terms of which *all* questions about the justification of punishment are to be answered, is somehow wrong; yet, from what is said on such occasions no clear account of what the different values or objectives are, or how they fit together in the justification of punishment, can be extracted.

No one expects judges or statesmen occupied in the business of sending people to the gallows or prison, or in making (or unmaking) laws which enable this to be done, to have much time for philosophical discussion of the principles which make it morally tolerable to do these things. A judicial bench is not and should not be a professional chair. Yet what is said in public debates about punishment by those specially concerned with it as judges or legislators is important. Few are likely to be more circumspect, and if what they say seems, as it often does, unclear, one-sided and easily refutable by pointing to some aspect of things which they have overlooked, it is likely that in our inherited ways of talking or thinking about punishment there is some persistent drive towards an over-simplification of multiple issues which require separate consideration. To counter this drive what is most needed is *not* the simple admission that instead of a single value or aim (Deterrence, Retribution, Reform or any other) a plurality of different values and aims should be given as a conjunctive answer to some *single* question concerning the justification of punishment. What is needed is the realization that different principles (each of which may in a sense be called a "justification") are relevant at different points in any morally acceptable account of punishment. What we should look for are answers to a number of different questions such as: What justifies the general practice of punishment? To whom may punishment be applied? How severely may we punish? In dealing with these and other questions concerning punishment we should bear in mind that in this, as in most other social institutions, the pursuit of one aim may be qualified by or provide an opportunity, not to be missed, for the pursuit of others. Till we have developed this sense of the complexity of punishment (and this prolegomenon aims only to do this) we shall be in no fit state to assess the extent to which the whole institution has been eroded by, or needs to be adapted to, new beliefs about the human mind.

2. Justifying Aims and Principles of Distribution

There is, I think an analogy worth considering between the concept of punishment and that of property. In both cases we have to do with a social institution of which the centrally important form is a structure of *legal* rules, even if it would be dogmatic to deny the names of punishment or property to the similar though more rudimentary rule-regulated practices within groups such as a family, or a school, or in customary societies whose customs may lack some of the standard or salient features of law (e.g. legislation, organized sanctions, courts). In both cases we are confronted by a complex institution presenting different inter-related features calling for separate explanation; or, if the morality of the institution is challenged, for separate justification. In both cases failure to distinguish separate questions or attempting to answer them all by reference to a single principle ends in confusion. Thus in the case of property we should distinguish between the question of the *definition* of property, the question why and in what circumstances it is a *good* institution to maintain, and the questions in what ways individuals may become *entitled* to acquire property and *how much* they should be allowed to acquire. These we may call questions of *Definition*, *General Justifying Aim*, and *Distribution* with the last subdivided into question of *Title* and *Amount*. It is salutary to take some classical exposition of the idea of property, say Locke's chapter "Of Property" in the *Second Treatise*, and to observe how much darkness is spread by the use of a single notion (in this case "the labour of (a man's) body and the work of his hands") to answer all these different questions which press upon us when we reflect on the institution of property. In the case of punishment the beginning of wisdom (though by no means its end) is to distinguish similar questions and confront them separately.

(a) Definition

Here I shall simply draw upon the recent admirable work scattered through English philosophical journals and add to it only an admonition of my own against the abuse of definition in the philosophical discussion of punishment. So with Mr. Benn and Professor Flew I shall define the standard or central case of "punishment" in terms of five elements:

  (i) It must involve pain or other consequences normally considered unpleasant.
  (ii) It must be for an offence against legal rules.

   (iii) It must be of an actual or supposed offender for his offence.
   (iv) It must be intentionally administered by human beings other than the offender.
   (v) It must be imposed and administered by an authority constituted by a legal
      system against which the offence is committed.

In calling this the standard or central case of punishment I shall relegate to the position of sub-standard or secondary cases the following among many other possibilities:

   (a) Punishments for breaches of legal rules imposed or administered otherwise
      than by officials (decentralised sanctions).
   (b) Punishments for breaches of non-legal rules or orders (punishments in a
      family or school).
   (c) Vicarious or collective punishment of some member of a social group for
      actions done by others without the former's authorization, encouragement,
      control or permission.
   (d) Punishment of persons (otherwise than under (c)) who neither are in fact nor
      supposed to be offenders.

The chief importance of listing these sub-standard cases is to prevent the use of what I shall call the "definitional stop" in discussions of punishment. This is an abuse of definition especially tempting when use is made of conditions (ii) and (iii) of the standard case in arguing against the utilitarian claim that the practice of punishment is justified by the beneficial consequences resulting from the observance of the laws which it secures. Here the stock "retributive" argument is: If *this* is the justification of punishment, why not apply it, when it pays to do so, to those innocent of any crime, chosen at random, or to the wife and children of the offender? And here the wrong reply is: *That*, by definition, would not be "punishment" and it is the justification of punishment which is in issue. Not only will this definitional stop fail to satisfy the advocate of "Retribution," it would prevent us from investigating the very thing which modern scepticism most calls in question: namely the rational and moral status of our preference for a system of punishment under which measures painful to individuals are to be taken against them only when they have committed an offence. Why do we prefer this to other forms of social hygiene which we might employ to prevent anti-social behaviour and which we do employ in special circumstances, sometimes with reluctance? No account of punishment can afford to dismiss this question with a definition.

(b) The Nature of an Offence

Before we reach any question of justification we must identify a preliminary question to which the answer is so simple that the question may not appear worth asking; yet it is clear that some curious "theories" of punishment gain their only plausibility from ignoring it, and others from confusing it with other questions. This question is: Why are certain kinds of action forbidden by law and so made crimes or offences? The answer is: To announce to society that these actions are not to be done and to secure that fewer of them are done. These are the common immediate aims of making any conduct a criminal offence and until we have laws made with these primary aims we shall lack the notion of a "crime" and so of a "criminal." Without recourse to the simple idea that the criminal law sets up, in its rules, standards of behaviour to encourage certain types of conduct and discourage others we cannot distinguish a punishment in the form of a fine from a tax on a course of conduct. This indeed is one grave objection to those theories of law which in the interests of simplicity or uniformity obscure the distinction between primary laws setting standards for behaviour and secondary laws specifying what officials must or may do when they are broken. Such theories insist that all legal rules are "really" directions to officials to exact "sanctions" under certain conditions, e.g. if people kill. Yet only if we keep alive the distinction (which such theories thus obscure) between the primary objective of the law in encouraging or discouraging certain kinds of behaviour, and its merely ancillary sanction or remedial steps, can we give sense to the notion of a crime or offence.

It is important however to stress the fact that in thus identifying the immediate aims of the criminal law we have not reached the stage of justification. There are indeed many forms of undesirable behaviour which it would be foolish (because ineffective or too costly) to attempt to inhibit by use of the law and some of these may be better left to educators, trades unions, churches, marriage guidance councils or other non-legal agencies. Conversely there are some forms of conduct which we believe cannot be effectively inhibited without use of the law. But it is only too plain that in fact the law may make activities criminal which it is morally important to promote and the suppression of these may be quite unjustifiable. Yet confusion between the simple immediate aim of any criminal legislation and the justification of punishment seems to be the most charitable explanation of the claim that punishment is *justified* as an "emphatic denunciation by the community of a crime." Lord Denning's dictum that this is the ultimate justification of punishment can be saved from Mr. Benn's criticism, noted above, only if it is treated as a blurred statement of the truth that the aim not of punishment, but of criminal legislation is indeed to denounce certain types of conduct as something not to be practised. Conversely the immediate aim of criminal legislation cannot be any of the things which are usually mentioned as justifying punishment: for until it is settled what conduct is to be legally denounced and discouraged we have not settled from what we are to *deter* people, or who are to be considered *criminals* from whom we are to exact *retribution*, or on whom we are to wreak *vengeance*, or whom we are to *reform*.

Even those who look upon human law as a mere instrument for enforcing "morality as such" (itself conceived as the law of God or Nature) and who at the stage of justifying punishment wish to appeal not to socially beneficial consequences but simply to the intrinsic value of inflicting suffering on wrongdoers who have disturbed by their offence the moral order, would not deny that the aim of criminal legislation is to set up types of behaviour (in this case conformity with a pre-existing moral law) as legal standards of behaviour and to secure conformity with them. No doubt in all communities certain moral offences, e.g. killing, will always be selected for suppression as crimes and it is conceivable that this may be done not to protect human beings from being killed but to save the potential murderer from sin; but it would be paradoxical to look upon the law as designed not to discourage murders at all (even conceived as sin rather than harm) but simply to extract the penalty from the murderer.

(c) General Justifying Aim

I shall not here criticize the intelligibility or consistency or adequacy of those theories that are united in denying that the practice of a system of punishment is justified by its beneficial consequences and claim instead that the main justification of the practice lies in the fact that when breach of the law involves moral guilt the application to the offender of the pain of punishment is itself a thing of value. A great variety of claims of this character, designating "Retribution" or "Expiation" or "Reprobation" as the justifying aim, fall in spite of differences under this rough general description. Though in fact I agree with Mr. Benn in thinking that these all either avoid the question of justification altogether or are in spite of their protestations disguised forms of Utilitarianism, I shall assume that Retribution, defined simply as the application of the pains of punishment to an offender who is morally guilty, may figure among the conceivable justifying aims of a system of punishment. Here I shall merely insist that it is one thing to use the word Retribution *at this point* in an account of the principle of punishment in order to designate the General Justifying Aim of the system, and quite another to use it to secure that to the question "To whom may punishment be applied?" (the question of Distribution), the answer given is "Only to an offender for an offence." Failure to distinguish Retribution as a General Justifying Aim from retribution as the simple insistence that only those who have broken the law—and voluntarily broken it—may be punished, may be traced in many writers: even perhaps in Mr. J.D. Mabbott's otherwise most illuminating essay. We shall distinguish the latter from Retribution in General Aim as "retribution in Distribution." Much confusing shadow-fighting between utilitarians and their opponents may be avoided if it is recognized that it is perfectly consistent to assert *both* that the General Justifying Aim of the practice of punishment is its beneficial consequences *and* that the pursuit of this General Aim should be qualified or restricted out of deference to principles of Distribution which require that punishment should be only of an offender for an offence. Conversely it does not in the least follow from the admission of the latter principle of retribution in Distribution that the General Justifying Aim of punishment is Retribution though of course Retribution in General Aim entails retribution in Distribution.

We shall consider later the principles of justice lying at the root of retribution in Distribution. Meanwhile it is worth observing that both the old fashioned Retributionist (in General Aim) and the most modern sceptic often make the same (and, I think, wholly mistaken) assumption that sense can only be made of the restrictive principle that punishment be applied only to an offender for an offence if the General Justifying Aim of the practice of punishment is Retribution. The sceptic consequently imputes to all systems of punishment (when they are restricted by the principle of retribution in Distribution) all the irrationality he finds in the idea of Retribution as a General Justifying Aim; conversely the advocates of the latter think the admission of retribution in Distribution is a refutation of the utilitarian claim that the social consequences of punishment are its Justifying Aim.

The most general lesson to be learnt from this extends beyond the topic of punishment. It is, that in relation to any social institution, after stating what general aim or value its maintenance fosters we should enquire whether there are any and if so what principles limiting the unqualified pursuit of that aim or value. Just because the pursuit of any single social aim always has its restrictive qualifier, our main social institutions always possess a plurality of features which can only be understood as a compromise between partly discrepant principles. This is true even of relatively minor legal institutions like that of a contract. In general this is designed to enable individuals to give effect to their wishes to create structures of legal rights and duties, and so to change, in certain ways, their legal position. Yet at the same time there is need to protect those who, in good faith, understand a verbal offer made to them to mean what it would ordinarily mean, accept it, and then act on the footing that a valid contract has been concluded. As against them, it would be unfair to allow the other party to say that the words he used in his verbal offer or the interpretation put on them did not express his real wishes or intention. Hence principles of "estoppel" or doctrines of the "objective sense" of a contract are introduced to prevent this and to qualify the principle that the law enforces contracts in order to give effect to the joint wishes of the contracting parties.

(d) Distribution

This as in the case of property has two aspects: (i) Liability (Who may be punished?) and (ii) Amount. In this section I shall chiefly be concerned with the first of these.

From the foregoing discussions two things emerge. First, though we may be clear as to what value the practice of punishment is to promote, we have still to answer as a question of Distribution "Who may be punished?" Secondly, if in answer to this question we say "only an offender for an offence" this admission of retribution in Distribution is not a principle from which anything follows as to the severity or amount of punishment; in particular it neither licenses nor requires, as Retribution in General Aim does, more severe punishments than deterrence or other utilitarian criteria would require.

The root question to be considered is, however, why we attach the moral importance which we do to retribution in Distribution. Here I shall consider the efforts made to show that restriction of punishment to offenders is a simple consequence of whatever principles (Retributive or Utilitarian) constitute the Justifying Aim of punishment.

The standard example used by philosophers to bring out the importance of retribution in Distribution is that of a wholly innocent person who has not even unintentionally done anything which the law punishes if done intentionally. It is supposed that in order to avert some social catastrophe officials of the system fabricate evidence on which he is charged, tried, convicted and sent to prison or death. Or it is supposed that without resort to any fraud more persons may be deterred from crime if wives and children of offenders were punished vicariously for their crimes. In some forms this kind of thing may be ruled out by a consistent sufficiently comprehensive utilitarianism. Certainly expedients involving fraud or faked charges might be very difficult to justify on utilitarian grounds. We can of course imagine that a negro might be sent to prison or executed on a false charge of rape in order to avoid widespread lynching of many others; but a *system* which openly empowered authorities to do this kind of thing, even if it is succeeded in averting specific evils like lynching, would awaken such apprehension and insecurity that any gain from the exercise of these powers would be any utilitarian calculation be offset by the misery caused by their existence. But official resort to this kind of fraud on a particular occasion in breach of the rules and the subsequent indemnification of the officials responsible might save many lives and so be thought to yield a clear surplus of value. Certainly vicarious punishment of an offender's family might do so and legal systems have occasionally though exceptionally resorted to this. An example of it is the Roman *Lex quisquis* providing for the punishment of the children of those guilty of *majestas*. In extreme cases many might still think it right to resort to these expedients but we should do so with the sense of sacrificing an important principle. We should be conscious of choosing the lesser of two evils, and this would be inexplicable if the principle sacrificed to utility were itself only a requirement of utility.

Similarly the moral importance of the restriction of punishment to the offender cannot be explained as merely a consequence of the principle that the General Justifying Aim is Retribution for immorality involved in breaking the law. Retribution in the Distribution of punishment has a value quite independent of Retribution as Justifying Aim. This is shown by the fact that we attach importance to the restrictive principle that only offenders may be punished, even where breach of this law might not be thought immoral. Indeed even where the laws themselves are hideously immoral as in Nazi Germany, e.g. forbidding activities (helping the sick or destitute of some racial group) which might be thought morally obligatory, the absence of the principle restricting punishment to the offender would be a further *special* iniquity; whereas admission of this principle would represent some residual respect for justice shown in the administration of morally bad laws.

II. UTILITARIAN THEORIES OF PUNISHMENT

As discussed in the introduction to this chapter, utilitarian or consequentialist theories of punishment justify the imposition of punishment in terms of the benefits that it achieves. The main benefit that consequentialist theories aspire to achieve is the reduction of crime. In *An Introduction to the Principles of Morals and Legislation* (1789), Jeremy Bentham wrote:

> Pain and pleasure are the great springs of human action. When a man perceives or supposes pain to be the consequences of an act, he is acted upon in such a manner as tends, with a certain force, to withdraw him, as it were, from the commission of that act. If the apparent magnitude of that pain be greater than the apparent magnitude of the pleasure or good he expects to be the consequence of the act, he will be absolutely prevented from performing it. The mischief which would have ensued from the act, if performed, will also by that means be prevented.
>
> With respect to a given individual, the recurrence of an offence may be provided against in three ways:—
>
> 1. By taking from him the physical power of offending.
> 2. By taking away the desire of offending.
> 3. By making him afraid of offending.

In the first case, the individual can no more commit the offence; in the second, he no longer desires to commit it; in the third, he may still wish to commit it, but he longer dares to do it. In the first case, there is a physical incapacity; in the second, a moral reformation; in the third, there is intimidation or terror of the law.

More traditionally, the language of these objectives is that punishment seeks to deter (either specifically or generally), incapacitate, or rehabilitate offenders. Moreover, punishment is said to have a denunciatory or expressive function, whereby the imposition of punishment is considered to be a symbolic reflection of society's abhorrence or abject disavowal of particular crimes.

The basic features of the utilitarian approach to punishment are explored in the following excerpts by C.L. Ten and C.S. Lewis. For another interesting discussion of these issues, see, generally, Nigel Walker, *Why Punish?* (Oxford: Oxford University Press, 1991).

As the readings below demonstrate, the utilitarian approach to punishment is vulnerable to attack on two levels. First, the goals that consequentialist theories seek to achieve are not met; that is, punishment is ineffective as a means of reforming offenders, deterring others, and generally reducing crime. This argument is rooted in a rather impressive body of empirical literature that bemoans the fact that social science has not been able to validate the efficacy of utilitarian claims. For a collection of a number of readings that address this issue, see Andrew von Hirsch and Andrew Ashworth (eds.), *Principled Sentencing* (Boston: Northeastern University Press, 1992).

The second level of attack is from a moral perspective. A theory of punishment that is founded on consequentialist notions has little regard for human dignity or autonomy in that it permits using individuals as a means to more collectivist ends. An example of this shortcoming that is popularized in the literature is the claim that a utilitarian theory of punishment authorizes the punishment of an innocent person if, in all of the circumstances, utility were to be maximized by such a practice. If this argument is valid, must we abandon our utilitarian notions *completely*, or can the point be dismissed as a fanciful complaint that occupies the most peripheral edges of an otherwise venerable philosophical tradition?

C.L. Ten, *Crime, Guilt and Punishment*
(Oxford: Clarendon Press, 1987) (footnotes omitted)

2.1. The Effects of Punishment

The utilitarian theory justifies punishment solely in terms of the good consequences produced. There are disagreements among utilitarians about the nature of the good consequences which punishment is supposed to produce. Some utilitarians may even believe that the harm done by punishment outweighs the good, and hence punishment is not justified. But many utilitarians see the main beneficial effects of punishment in terms of the *reduction of crime*, and believe that punishing offenders will have at least some, if not all, of the following good effects. First, punishment acts as a deterrent to crime. The deterrent effects can be both individual and general. Punishment deters the offender who is punished from committing similar offences in future, and it also deters potential offenders. The offender who is punished is supposed to be deterred by his experience of punishment and the threat of being punished again if he re-offends and is convicted. This is the individual deterrent effect. The general deterrent effect of punishment on potential offenders works through the threat of their being subjected to the same kind of punishment that was meted out to the convicted offender.

Secondly, punishment is supposed to have reformative or rehabilitative effects. This is confined to the offender who is punished. He is reformed in the sense that the effect of punishment is to change his values so that he will not commit similar offences in future because he believes such offences to be wrong. But if he abstains from criminal acts simply because he is afraid of being caught and punished again, then he is deterred rather than reformed and rehabilitated by punishment. So the effects of individual deterrence and rehabilitation are the same. What distinguishes them is the difference in motivation.

The third good consequence of punishment is its incapacitative effect. When an offender is serving his sentence in prison, he is taken out of general social circulation and is therefore prevented from committing a variety of offences, even though he may neither be deterred nor reformed by punishment. Of course punishment would not have an overall incapacitative effect if the offender would not have re-offended even if he were free, or if his incarceration led someone else, who would not other-wise have done so, to engage in criminal activity, perhaps as his replacement in a gang. While in prison, the offender might still commit certain offences: he might assault a fellow prisoner or a prison guard. But his opportunities are generally reduced. In some cases, however, his contacts with other prisoners would create opportunities for further involvement in crime when he is released. The incapacitative effect, though perhaps most likely in the case of imprisonment, may also be present in other forms of punishment. For example, parole may have some incapacitative effect in that although the offender is free, the fact that he is under supervision may restrict his opportunities for criminal activities.

The empirical evidence of the effects of punishment is very complex, but a brief survey will be of some use.

It looks as if the present state of our knowledge provides no basis for claiming that punishment by imprisonment reforms or rehabilitates the criminal, or that it is an individual deterrent. The position is well summed up by the Report of the Panel of the National Research Council in the United States on Research on Deterrent and Incapacitative Effects, hereafter referred to as the Panel:

> The available research on the impact of various treatment strategies both in and out of prison seems to indicate that, after controlling for initial selection differences, there are generally no statistically significant differences between the subsequent recidivism of offenders, regardless of the form of "treatment." This suggests that neither rehabilita-tive nor criminogenic effects operate very strongly. Therefore, at an aggregate level, these confounding effects are probably safely ignored.

By "criminogenic effects" the Panel refers to the undesirable effects of imprison-ment in either increasing the criminal's propensity to commit crimes or to extend the duration of his criminal career. Such effects are the opposite of the rehabilitative effects. So the present evidence seems to suggest that in general the effect of imprisonment, or of the various programmes for rehabilitation which accompany imprisonment, is neither to make the criminal a better nor a worse person with respect to the standards of behaviour set by the criminal law.

The evidence also suggests that in general punishment has no individual deterrent effect. Daniel Nagin points out that at the observational level it is difficult to distinguish between individual (or what he calls special) deterrence and rehabilitation. He concludes that, "The figures suggest that recidivism rates cannot be affected by varying the severity of the punishment, at least within acceptable limits." But Nagin cautiously adds that the evidence is only preliminary.

In a few specific cases there is indeed some evidence of the individual deterrent effect of punishment. Thus Johannes Andenaes draws attention to a study of amateur shoplifters which shows that detection and arrest, even without prosecution, produces serious shock. There is little or no recidivism among those who are apprehended and interrogated by the store police and then set free without being formally charged. A study of drunk driving in Sweden also shows that those drivers who had been arrested estimated the risk of being arrested as many times higher than other drivers.

There is disagreement about the general deterrent effects of punishment. Johannes Andenaes believes that, "In general terms it can only be stated that general deterrence works well in some fields and works poorly or not at all in other fields." But in 1974 Gordon Tullock published an article, "Does Punishment Deter Crime?" in which he surveyed the work done by economists and sociologists. Tullock points out that economists began their work under the impression that punishment would deter crime because demand curves slope downwards showing that if the cost of a good is increased then less of it will be consumed. So if the cost of committing crime is increased by more severe punishment, then there will be fewer crimes. Sociologists, on the other hand, started out with the intention of confirming what was then the accepted view in their discipline that punishment would not deter crime. But Tullock argues that, although their starting points and assumptions were radically different, both economists and sociologists, after analysing the evidence, came to the same conclusion that punishment did indeed deter crime. After surveying their studies Tullock himself is convinced that "the empirical evidence is clear," and he states his conclusions unequivocally: "Even granting the fact that most potential criminals have only a rough idea as to the frequency and severity of punishment, multiple regression studies show that increasing the frequency or severity of the punishment does reduce the likelihood that a given crime will be committed."

However, Tullock's confidence about the clarity of the empirical evidence is not shared by the Panel. The Panel argues that although the evidence consistently establishes a negative association between crime rates and sanctions (as measured by the risks of apprehension, conviction, or imprisonment), that is higher crime rates are associated with lower sanctions and vice versa, this does not necessarily sow the general deterrent effect of sanctions. The negative association may be partly or wholly explained in terms of lower sanctions being the effect rather than the cause of higher crime rates. Higher crime rates may so overburden the resources of the criminal justice system that they reduce its ability to deal with new offenders. Overburdened judges and prosecutors may use their discretion to dismiss or reduce charges, or to offer attractive plea bargains. Overcrowding of prisons may lead to a reduction in the time served in prison as more prisoners are released early on parole. The sanctions imposed on certain crimes may be reduced. So unless one can separate out the effect of higher crime rates on sanctions from the deterrent effect of sanctions on crime, one cannot interpret the evidence as establishing the presence of the general deterrent effect of punishment. The Panel's cautious assessment of the evidence is summed up in its remark that "we cannot yet assert that the evidence warrants an affirmative conclusion regarding deterrence" but the Panel adds that "the evidence certainly favours a proposition supporting deterrence more than it favours one asserting that deterrence is absent." On the other hand, the Panel believes that the evidence does not even show a significant negative association between crime rates and the severity of punishment as measured by the time served in prison, but suggests that this may partly be accounted for in terms of various distortions.

Moving from the analysis of statistics to the experimental evidence, the Panel identifies three studies which are not methodologically flawed. Of these, two show that the level of crime decreased significantly with increases in the level of sanctions, while one showed that the removal of criminal sanctions for abortions in Hawaii did not affect the incidence of abortions. So it looks as if the present experimental evidence does not permit the drawing of general conclusions. But much of the experimental evidence is consistent with the operation of deterrence, as has been noted by Nigel Walker.

Finally, we turn to the incapacitative effect of punishment. In her review of the literature for the Panel, Jacqueline Cohen suggests that disagreements about the magnitude of that effect can be attributed almost entirely to the different estimates of the average crime rate of prisoners. The estimate of the increase in crime if current prison use were reduced or eliminated has been as low as five per cent. Estimating the incapacitative effect of present prison policies is one thing. There is also the different question as to what we can expect the incapacitative effect to be if present policies are changed. Here one estimate is of a five fold decrease in crime, but Cohen points out that this can only be achieved by increasing the prison population by between 355 per cent and 567 per cent. The incapacitative effect will not be the same for all crimes. Cohen points out that using the assumptions made by the available models, the increase in prison population required to reduce violent crimes is much less than the increases needed for similar reductions in other crimes. Violent crimes can be reduced by 10 per cent with less than 30 per cent increase in prison population. This kind of consideration has led to an increasing interest in the use of selective incapacitation in which the focus of imprisonment is on certain types of offenders who are identified as having a high rate of committing crimes.

We see that the evidence is perhaps more hospitable to the claim that punishment has some general deterrent effect and some incapacitative effect than it is to the claim that it has individual deterrent effect or that it rehabilitates offenders. This will no doubt be puzzling to some, but it provides a basis for caution in responding to a high rate of recidivism. Where there is such a high rate, it shows that punishment does not deter those who are punished. But it does not show that potential offenders are not in fact deterred by punishment, or that punishment does not incapacitate.

2.2. *Punishing the Innocent*

Let us now assume that the beneficial consequences of punishment outweigh the suffering that it inflicts on offenders. Critics of the utilitarian theory argue that if punishment is to be justified solely in terms of its good consequences, then punishment cannot be confined to offenders. There might be situations in which punishing an innocent person would produce better consequences that alternative courses of action. The utilitarian is therefore committed to punishing the innocent person. This objection has played an important role in the rejection of the utilitarian theory.

Let us consider an example made famous in the literature by H.J. McCloskey. Suppose that in a particular town with a mixed population a man from one racial group rapes a woman from the other group. Because of existing racial tensions the crime is likely to produce racial violence with many people being injured, unless the guilty man is apprehended quickly. Suppose further that the sheriff of the town can prevent the violence by framing an innocent man who was near the scene of the crime, and who will be accepted by the community as the guilty person. Surely, it is argued, the best consequences will be produced by the sheriff's fabrication of evidence against him which will result in his conviction and severe punishment. But the critics maintain that the sheriff's act and the subsequent punishment of the innocent man are both wrong.

There are many ways in which utilitarians, or those sympathetic to them, can respond to this objection, and I shall consider some of their main arguments. First, it is argued that "punishing the innocent" is a logical contradiction because punishment implies guilt. Secondly, the premises of the objection are challenged. It is suggested that punishing the innocent man will not in fact produce the best consequences if we take into account all the consequences of such punishment including the long-term and less obvious consequences. Thirdly, it is claimed that the only situations in which punishing the innocent is optimistic are hypothetical and "fantastic" situations rather than situations which arise, or are likely to occur, in the real word. It is then argued that for a variety of reasons, utilitarians should not be worried by what they are committed to in such fantastic situations. In discussing this third response, I shall also consider the views of those utilitarians who maintain that the punishment of the innocent would indeed be justified in situations where it produces the best consequences. If "commonsense morality" or our intuition disagree, so much the worse for them.

2.3. *Punishment and Guilt*

In his well-known paper, "On Punishment," Anthony Quinton argues that the notion of "punishment" implies guilt in the sense that "punishment" is defined in part as the infliction of suffering on the guilty. So when suffering is inflicted on innocent people, this cannot be properly described as punishment but as something else—judicial terrorism or social surgery. If we inflict suffering on an innocent man and try to pass it off as punishment, we are guilty of lying since we make a lying imputation that he is guilty and responsible for an offence. Part of Quinton's argument seems to rest on the importance of distinguishing between, for example, typhoid carriers and criminals even though both may sometimes be treated in rather similar ways. Thus a typhoid carrier, or a person with an infectious disease, will be quarantined. He will lose his freedom in much the same way that a criminal is deprived of his freedom when he is jailed. And yet we do not call quarantine a form of punishment precisely because the disease carrier is not guilty of an offence.

It is certainly true that in the typical cases of punishment it is inflicted on a person guilty of an offence. But the crucial issue is whether we can extend the notion of punishment to the infliction of suffering on the innocent without at the same time losing the distinction between punishment and various activities like the quarantine of disease carriers and certain kinds of medical or dental treatment which are painful.

In all these cases there is the infliction of some unpleasantness or suffering, but it is only in the case of punishment that the unpleasantness is essential to what is to be done. As Wasserstrom puts it "the point of the imposition of a deprivation when it is unmistakably a punishment is that it is being imposed because it is a deprivation, because the person upon whom it is being imposed should thereby be made to suffer and in that respect be worse off than before." On the other hand, the unpleasantness experienced by those who are quarantined, or by those undergoing medical treatment, is only incidental, and not essential to what needs to be done. Advances in medical technology may lead to the replacement of painful forms of treatment by pleasant, but still effective, treatment. Medical treatment does not have to be painful at all: a sweet pill is as much a medicine as a bitter pill. Similarly, quarantine implies a degree of isolation to prevent the spread of the infection, and that in itself will be unpleasant. But it can, if resources permit, be greatly outweighed by the pleasures of the surroundings in which one is put. But punishment implies at least an overall degree of unpleasantness. So we can distinguish between punishment and quarantine without falling back on the notion that the person who is punished must be guilty, or must at least be supposed to be guilty, of an offence.

However, the truth of the matter seems to be a bit more complex than we have so far acknowledged, and Quinton's argument, though mistaken, is interesting because it gestures towards that truth. Consider the difference between a monetary fine, which is a form of punishment, and a tax which is not. Arguably both are essentially unpleasant although both may be accepted or approved of as fully justified. What then is the difference between them? In *The Concept of Law* H.L.A. Hart points out that punishment involves "an offence or breach of duty in the form of violation of a rule set up to guide the conduct of ordinary citizens." When someone is punished, he has violated a standard of conduct to which he is supposed to conform. But when he pays a tax, he has not breached any such standard of conduct. The main purpose of taxes is to raise revenue and not to set up a standard of correct conduct. Indeed the revenue-raising function of a tax would be defeated if people generally reacted to income tax by not working, or to Value Added Tax by not eating in restaurants. On the other hand, the purpose of punishment is not defeated if, as a result of it, people cease to breach the relevant standard of conduct. On the contrary, the threat of punishment is most effective when it is unnecessary to carry it out. This important difference between punishment and a tax can be blurred, as Hart acknowledges, when, for example, those running a business simply assimilate the relatively small fines for breaches of rules into the costs of the goods they produce, and pass them on to their consumers. It is also blurred in the other direction when a government imposes a tax on luxury goods partly in order to discourage their use.

A related difference between punishment and other forms of deprivation or unpleasant treatment is that punishment expresses condemnation or disapproval of the conduct punished. The person punished is blamed for what he did, and this explains the peculiar unfairness of punishing the innocent who are of course blameless.

But now, if we accept the idea that punishment involves the breach of a standard of conduct, how is this different from Quinton's point that punishment is always for an offence? The element of truth in Quinton's position is that there must be some wrongdoing or some offence for there to be punishment. But this is not to say that the person punished must be the offender. An innocent person can be punished for an offence committed by someone else. This can happen not only when the legal authority makes a mistake and punishes the wrong person, but also when it deliberately frames an innocent person.

But suppose now that my arguments fail, and Quinton's analysis of the concept of punishment is correct. It certainly does not follow that it is wrong to imprison innocent people or even to execute them. What follows is merely that we cannot *describe* these acts as *punishing* the innocent. But the real issue is a moral issue as to whether we are justified in inflicting suffering on innocent persons. Admittedly this is not exactly the same issue as whether we should *punish* the innocent which raises the additional problem of whether we may unjustly blame the blameless, but none the less it is a serious moral issue. Quinton argues that "the suffering associated with punishment *may* not be inflicted on them, firstly, as brutal and secondly, if it is represented as punishment, as involving a lie." The second objection does not hold if we do not represent the infliction of suffering on the innocent as a form of punishment. And the first objection is not one of which utilitarians can avail themselves if the brutal treatment of the innocent will in fact produce the best consequences. So the argument against the utilitarian can now be reformulated as follows: why should we confine ourselves to punishment in those cases where the infliction of suffering on the innocent will produce the best consequences?

The objection to the utilitarian position is clearly moral, and hence it cannot be evaded by appealing even to a correct definition of the notion of punishment. A proper regard for the way in which terms are used will enable us to describe correctly the moral problem which confronts us, but it cannot solve that problem for us.

2.4. *The Disutility of Punishing the Innocent*

The second utilitarian response to the charge that utilitarians are committed to punishing the innocent draws our attention to the less obvious bad consequences of punishing innocent persons, and argues that on balance the punishment of the innocent will always produce worse consequences than the failure to do so. For example, it is claimed that the fact that an innocent man has been punished will soon leak out, and when that happens, there will be a loss of confidence in the sheriff and widespread fear among the population that any one of them might be the next innocent victim of the sheriff's attempt to prevent similar violence in future. Furthermore, the sheriff himself will have his sensibilities blunted once the barrier against framing and punishing the innocent has been removed. He is more likely to adopt a similar policy the next time he faces a problem of maintaining order, and on that occasion, there may be no strong utilitarian as for punishing an innocent person. It is also not certain that there will in fact be racial violence if an innocent person is not punished. On the other hand, the suffering of the innocent person who is punished is very real. The suffering of the innocent man is likely to be greater than that of the guilty. The punishment will come as a big shock to the innocent man, and he will be angered and distressed in a way that the guilty person will not be.

But at each point of this utilitarian response, the critic can counter by tightening up the description of the example under consideration. Thus the sheriff suffers from a sudden fatal illness soon after the punishment of the innocent man, and he makes no death-bed confessions. No one else knows about the fabrication of evidence and the secret is buried with the sheriff. The innocent man who is punished has no relatives or close friends, and he himself is well endowed with an unusual temperament which faces unexpected disaster with calm resignation. We must not forget the unconvicted real offender who is still free and conceivably could give the whole show away. So he dies unexpectedly when he is run over by a bus on his way to the sheriff's funeral. Now we are back where we started with an example in which the punishment of an innocent person produces the best consequences and so should be accepted by the utilitarian. ...

I have so far assumed, for the sake of argument, that it is only in fantastic situations that utilitarians are committed to punishing the innocent. But it is now time to say something about this assumption. Most utilitarians seem to make the assumption. Thus Hare writes: "The retributivists are right at the intuitive level, and the utilitarians at the critical level." But contrast this with David Richards's claim in *The Moral Criticism of Law* that the utilitarian theory of punishment "clearly seems to allow and even require the punishment of the innocent, since it is very plausible that a higher degree of criminal deterrence would be achieved by punishing the children or relatives or friends or lovers of criminals in addition to or even in place of the criminal. Primitive systems of law often do exactly this, ..." In the face of these conflicting claims, two remarks are appropriate. First, no one can claim with confidence that, on the balance of probabilities, there are no actual cases in which punishing the innocent will produce the best consequences. But secondly, the strength of our conviction, which is shared by many utilitarians, that punishing the innocent in the real world is unjustified, cannot be accounted for simply on the basis of utilitarian considerations. If we were guided by purely utilitarian considerations, we would not be entitled to be as confident as we in fact are that such punishment in the real world is wrong, and we should indeed be prepared to experiment with limited proposals for the punishment of the innocent.

Indeed we can go further and argue that in the present state of our knowledge, surveyed earlier, the evidence of the desirable effects of punishment is not always as firmly based as is often assumed, and this presents some difficulties for a purely utilitarian justification of punishment. From the utilitarian point of view punishing offenders produces bad consequences which are certain and not speculative, namely the suffering inflicted directly by punishment on offenders and indirectly on their friends and relatives. Against this, there is no equally firm evidence, in all cases where punishment is thought to be justified, of its countervailing good effects. There is some evidence of incapacitative effects although the extent of these effects varies with different types of offences, and the evidence is also consistent with there being some general dete. rent effect. Again, there is good reason to think that the total abandonment of the practice of punishment would have unfortunate results. But there are specific crimes in which the utilitarian case for punishment, while not ruled out, is not particularly strong. It is then unclear what we should do in the present state of our knowledge if we were guided by purely utilitarian considerations. In fact our thinking on these matters is also guided by non-utilitarian considerations. Other things being equal, we think it better that the guilty should suffer through punishment than that there should be similar suffering by the innocent victims of crime. Again, given that the practice of punishment has some utilitarian justification, there will also be offenders who may justifiably be punished by appealing to non-utilitarian considerations. For example, if the punishment for some offences can be justified on utilitarian grounds in terms of the general deterrent effect and the incapacitative effect of such punishment, then it is unfair to allow those who have committed more serious offences to go unpunished even if in these latter cases the existing evidence is inadequate to show that punishment has similar good effects.

I do not believe that the practice of punishment would be justified if there were a decisive utilitarian case against it, or if it did not at least have some utilitarian support. But this is not to say that all desirable aspects of that practice can be justified in purely utilitarian terms.

C.S. Lewis, "The Humanitarian Theory of Punishment"
(1953), 6 *Res Judicatae* 224 (footnotes omitted)

In England we have lately had a controversy about Capital Punishment. I do not know whether a murderer is more likely to repent and make a good end on the gallows a few weeks after his trial or in the prison infirmary thirty years later. I do not know whether the fear of death is an indispensable deterrent. I need not, for the purpose of this article, decide whether it is a morally permissible deterrent. Those are questions which I propose to leave untouched. My subject is not Capital Punishment in particular, but that theory of punishment in general which the controversy sowed to be almost universal among my fellow-countrymen. It may be called the Humanitarian theory. Those who hold it think that it is mild and merciful. In this I believe that they are seriously mistaken. I believe that the "Humanity" which it claims is a dangerous illusion and disguises the possibility of cruelty and injustice without end. I urge a return to the traditional or Retributive theory not solely, not even primarily, in the interests of society, but in the interests of the criminal.

According to the Humanitarian theory, to punish a man because he deserves it, and as much as he deserves, is mere revenge, and therefore, barbarous and immoral. It is maintained that the only legitimate motives for punishing are the desire to deter others by example or to mend the criminal. When this theory is combined, as frequently happens, with the belief that all crime is more or less pathological, the idea of mending tails off into that of healing or curing and punishment becomes therapeutic. Thus it appears at first sight that we have passed from the harsh and self-righteous notion of giving the wicked their deserts to the charitable and enlightened one of tending the psychologically sick. What could be more amiable? One little point which is taken for granted in this theory needs, however, to be made explicit. The things done to the criminal, even if they are called cures, will be just as compulsory as they were in the old days when we called them punishments. If a tendency to steal can be cured by psychotherapy, the thief will no doubt be forced to undergo the treatment. Otherwise, society cannot continue.

My contention is that this doctrine, merciful though it appears, really means that each one of us, from the moment he breaks the law, is deprived of the rights of a human being.

The reason is this. The Humanitarian theory removes from Punishment the concept of Desert. But the concept of Desert is the only connecting link between punishment and justice. It is only as deserved or undeserved that a sentence can be just or unjust. I do not here contend that the question "Is it deserved?" is the only one we can reasonably ask about a punishment. We may very properly ask whether it is likely to deter others and to reform the criminal. But neither of these two last questions is a question about justice. There is no sense in talking about a "just deterrent" or a "just cure." We demand of a deterrent not whether it is just but whether it will deter. We demand of a cure not whether it is just but whether it succeeds. Thus when we cease to consider what the criminal deserves and consider only what will cure him or deter others, we have tacitly removed him from the sphere of justice altogether; instead of a person, a subject of rights, we now have a mere object, a patient, a "case."

The distinction will become clearer if we ask who will be qualified to determine sentences when sentences are no longer held to derive their propriety from the criminal's deservings. On the old view the problem of fixing the right sentence was a moral problem. Accordingly, the judge who did it was a person trained in jurisprudence; trained, that is, in a science which deals with rights and duties, and which, in origin at least, was consciously accepting guidance from the Law of Nature, and from Scripture. We must admit that in the actual penal code of most countries at most times these high originals were so much modified by local custom, class interests, and utilitarian concessions, as to be very imperfectly recognizable. But the code was never in principle, and not always in fact, beyond the control of the conscience of the society. And when (say, in eighteenth-century England) actual punishments conflicted too violently with the moral sense of the community, juries refused to convict and reform was finally brought about. This was possible because, so long as we are thinking in terms of Desert, the propriety of the penal code, being a moral question, is a question on which every man has the right to an opinion, not because he follows this or that profession, but because he is simply a man, a rational animal enjoying the Natural

Light. But all this is changed when we drop the concept of Desert. The only two questions we may now ask about a punishment are whether it deters and whether it cures. But these are not questions on which anyone is entitled to have an opinion simply because he is a man. He is not entitled to an opinion even if, in addition to being a man, he should happen also to be a jurist, a Christian, and a moral theologian. For they are not questions about principle but about matter of fact; and for such *cuiquam in sua arte credendum*. Only the expert "penologist" (let barbarous things have barbarous names), in the light of previous experiment, can tell us what is likely to deter: only the psychotherapist can tell us what is likely to cure. It will be in vain for the rest of us, speaking simply as men, to say, "but this punishment is hideously unjust, hideously disproportionate to the criminal's deserts." The experts with perfect logic will replay, "but nobody was talking about deserts. No one was talking about *punishment* in your archaic vindictive sense of the word. Here are the statistics proving that this treatment deters. Here are the statistics proving that this other treatment cures. What is your trouble?"

The Humanitarian theory, then, removes sentences from the hands of jurists whom the public conscience is entitled to criticize and places them in the hands of technical experts whose special sciences do not even employ such categories as rights or justice. It might be argued that since this transference results from an abandonment of the old idea of punishment, and, therefore, of all vindictive motives, it will be safe to leave our criminals in such hands. I will not pause to comment on the simple-minded view of fallen human nature which such a belief implies. Let us rather remember that the "cure" of criminals is to be compulsory; and let us then watch how the theory actually works in the mind of the Humanitarian. The immediate starting point of this article was a letter I read in one of our Leftist weeklies. The author was pleading that a certain sin, now treated by our laws as a crime, should henceforward be treated as a disease. And he complained that under the present system the offender, after a term in gaol, was simply let out to return to his original environment where he would probably relapse. What he complained of was not the shutting up but the letting out. On his remedial view of punishment the offender should, of course, be detained until he was cured. And of course the official straighteners are the only people who can say when that is. The first result of the Humanitarian theory is, therefore, to substitute for a definite sentence (reflecting to some extent the community's moral judgment on the degree of ill-desert involved) an indefinite sentence terminable only by the word of those experts and they are not experts in moral theology nor even in the Law of Nature who inflict it. Which of us, if he stood in the dock, would not prefer to be tried by the old system?

It may be said that by the continued use of the word punishment and the use of the verb "inflict" I am misrepresenting Humanitarians. They are not punishing, not inflicting, only healing. But do not let us be deceived by a name. To be taken without consent from my home and friends; to lose my liberty; to undergo all those assaults on my personality which modern psychotherapy knows how to deliver; to be re-made after some pattern of "normality" hatched in a Viennese laboratory to which I never professed allegiance; to know that this process will never end until either my captors have succeeded or I grown wise enough to cheat them with apparent success who cares whether this is called Punishment or not? That it includes most of the elements for which any punishment is feared shame, exile, bondage, and years eaten by the locust is obvious. Only enormous ill-desert could justify it; but ill-desert is the very conception which the Humanitarian theory has thrown overboard.

If we turn from the curative to the deterrent justification of punishment we shall find the new theory even more alarming. When you punish a man *in terrorem*, make of him an "example" to others, you are admittedly using him as a means to an end; someone else's end. This, in itself, would be a very wicked thing to do. On the classical theory of Punishment it was of course justified on the ground that the man deserved it. That was assumed to be established before any question of "making him an example" arose. You then, as the saying is, killed two birds with one stone; in the process of giving him what he deserved you set an example to others. But take away desert and the whole morality of the punishment disappears. Why, in Heaven's name, am I to be sacrificed to the good of society in this way? Unless, of course, I deserve it.

But that is not the worst. If the justification of exemplary punishment is not to be based on desert but solely on its efficacy as a deterrent, it is not absolutely necessary that the man we punish should even have committed the crime. The deterrent effect demands that the public should draw the moral, "If we do such an act we shall suffer like that man." The punishment of a man actually guilty whom the public think innocent will not have the desired effect; the punishment of a man actually innocent will, provided the public think him guilty. But every modern State has powers which make it easy to fake a trial. When a victim is urgently needed for exemplary purposes and a guilty victim cannot be found, all the purposes of deterrence will be equally served by the punishment (call it "cure" if you prefer) of an innocent victim, provided that the public can be cheated into thinking him guilty. It is no use to ask me why I assume that our rulers will be so wicked. The punishment of an innocent, that is, an undeserving, man is wicked only if we grant the traditional view that righteous punishment means deserved punishment. Once we have abandoned that criterion, all punishments have to be justified, if at all, on other grounds that have nothing to do with desert. Where the punishment of the innocent can be justified on those grounds (and it could in some cases be justified as a deterrent) it will be no less moral than any other punishment. Any distaste for it on the part of a Humanitarian will be merely a hang-over from the Retributive theory.

It is, indeed, important to notice that my argument so far supposes no evil intentions on the part of the Humanitarian and considers only what is involved in the logic of his position. My contention is that good men (not bad men) consistently acting upon that position would act as cruelly and unjustly as the greatest tyrants. They might in some respects act even worse. Of all tyrannies a tyranny sincerely exercised for the good of its victims may be the most oppressive. It may be better to live under robber barons than under omnipotent moral busybodies. The robber baron's cruelty may sometimes sleep, his cupidity may at some point be satiated; but those who torment us for our own good will torment us without end for they do so with the approval of their own conscience. They may be more likely to go to Heaven yet at the same time likelier to make a Hell of earth. Their very kindness stings with intolerable insult. To be "cured" against one's will and cured of states which we may not regard as disease is to be put on a level with those who have not yet reached the age of reason or those who never will; to be classed with infants, imbeciles, and domestic animals. But to be punished, however severely, because we have deserved it, because we "ought to have known better," is to be treated as a human person made in God's image.

In reality, however, we must face the possibility of bad rulers armed with a Humanitarian theory of punishment. A great many popular blue prints for a Christian society are merely what the Elizabethans called "eggs in moonshine" because they assume that the whole society is Christian or that the Christians are in control. This is not so in most contemporary States. Even if it were, our rulers would still be fallen men, and, therefore, neither very wise nor very good. As it is, they will usually be unbelievers. And since wisdom and virtue are not the only or the commonest qualifications for a place in the government, they will not often be even the best unbelievers. The practical problem of Christian politics is not that of drawing up schemes for a Christian society, but that of living as innocently as we can with unbelieving fellow-subjects under unbelieving rulers who will never be perfectly wise and good and who will sometimes be very wicked and very foolish. And when they are wicked the Humanitarian theory of punishment will put in their hands a finer instrument of tyranny than wickedness ever had before. For if crime and disease are to be regarded as the same thing, it follows that any state of mind which our masters choose to call "disease" can be treated as crime; and compulsorily cured. It will be vain to plead that states of mind which displease government need not always involve moral turpitude and do not therefore always deserve forfeiture of liberty. For our masters will not be using the concepts of Desert and Punishment but those of disease and cure. We know that one school of psychology already regards religions as a neurosis. When this particular neurosis becomes inconvenient to government, what is to hinder government from proceeding to "cure" it? Such "cure" will, of course, be compulsory; but under the Humanitarian theory it will not be called by the shocking name of Persecution. No one will blame us for being Christian, no one will hate us, no one will revile us. The new Nero will approach us with the silky manners of a doctor, and though all will be in fact as compulsory as the *tunica molesta* or Smithfield or Tyburn, all will go on within the unemotional therapeutic sphere where words like "right" and "wrong" or "freedom" and "slavery" are never heard. And thus when the command is given, every prominent Christian in the land may vanish overnight into Institutions for the Treatment of the Ideologically Unsound, and it will rest with the expert gaolers to say when (if ever) they are to re-emerge. But it will not be persecution. Even if the treatment is painful, even if it is life-long, even if it is fatal, that will be only a regrettable accident; the intention was purely therapeutic. Even in ordinary medicine there were painful operations and fatal operations; so in this. But because they are "treatment," not punishment, they can be criticized only by fellow-experts and on technical grounds, never by men as men and on grounds of justice.

This is why I think it essential to oppose the Humanitarian theory of punishment, root and branch, wherever we encounter it. It carries on its front a semblance of mercy which is wholly false. That is how it can deceive men of good will. The error began, perhaps, with Shelley's statement that the distinction between mercy and justice was invented in the courts of tyrants. It sounds noble, and was indeed the error of a noble mind. But the distinction is essential. The older view was that mercy "tempered" justice, or (on the highest level of all) that mercy and justice had met and kissed. The essential act of mercy was to pardon; and pardon in its very essence involves the recognition of guilt and ill-desert in the recipient. If crime is only a disease which needs cure, not sin which deserves punishment, it cannot be pardoned. How can you pardon a man for having a gumboil or a club foot? But the Humanitarian theory wants simply to abolish Justice and substitute Mercy for it. This means that you start being "kind" to people before you have considered their rights, and then force upon them supposed kindnesses which they in fact had a right to refuse, and finally kindnesses which no one but you will recognize as kindnesses and which the recipient will feel as abominable cruelties. You have overshot the mark. Mercy, detached from Justice, grows unmerciful. That is the important paradox. As there are plants which will flourish only in mountain soil, so it appears that Mercy will flower only when it grows in the crannies of the rock of Justice: transplanted to the marshlands of mere Humanitarianism, it becomes a man-eating weed, all the more dangerous because it is still called by the same name as the mountain variety. But we ought long ago to have learned our lesson. We should be too old now to be deceived by those humane pretensions which have served to usher in every cruelty of the revolutionary period in which we live. These are the "precious balms" which will "break our heads." There is a fine sentence in Bunyan: "It came burning hot into my mind, whatever he said, and however he flattered, when he got me home to his house, he would sell me for a slave." There is a fine couplet, too, in John Ball:

> Be ware ere ye be woe
> Know your friend from your foe.

One last word. You may ask why I send this to an Australian periodical. The reason is simple and perhaps worth recording: I can get no hearing for it in England.

NOTE

Another empirical problem that haunts the utilitarian tradition is the inefficacy of risk predictions concerning dangerousness. That is, when an individual is sentenced in a manner that focuses on his or her perceived dangerousness in the future, there can be no confidence that the person has been properly identified as a dangerous individual. The social science literature generally conveys great pessimism with regard to the ability of psychiatrists and actuaries to predict dangerousness. Even more disturbing is that psychiatrists tend to overpredict dangerousness. In "Preventive Detention and Execution: The Constitutionality of Punishing Future Crimes" (1991), 15 *Law & Human Behavior* 139, Patrick Ewing provides a gloomy account of the literature:

> While there is disagreement among researchers, clinicians and legal scholars and professionals about the accuracy of predictions of dangerousness, few knowledgeable observers would disagree with the conclusion that dangerousness cannot be predicted very accurately. Some claim that predictions of dangerousness (i.e., predictions that a given individual will, at some later time, engage in violent conduct toward others) prove to be wrong ... in virtually all cases. Others suggest that the "false positive" rate for such predictions is closer

to two out of three—two wrong predictions for every right one. Even the most optimistic behavioral scientists and legal commentators now seem to believe that the accuracy of predictions of dangerousness, whether made clinically or statistically, is "probably no better than one valid assessment out of two."

See, however, Webster, Harris, Rice, Cormier, and Quinsey, *The Violence Prediction Scheme: Assessing Dangerousness in High Risk Men* (Toronto: Centre of Criminology, University of Toronto, 1994), which argues for the use of actuarial prediction and provides a framework for developing an actuarial assessment. This framework can then be integrated with a clinical assessment to produce a final score that categorizes the person into one of nine groups based on probability of violent recidivism. The authors observe that clinical assessments should not alter the actuarial judgment by more than 10 percent in either direction. It seems that a number of professionals involved in the correctional field have been impressed by this model, although many, especially lawyers, are disturbed by it. Perhaps the reason for this concern is premised on one of the authors' own conclusions (at 65):

> The present VPS (violence prediction scheme) embodies within it a good deal of current knowledge and experience. No one claims that its use will guarantee "fairness," "accuracy," and "absence of bias" in each and every case.

Certainly it is true that there has been substantial optimistic risk-assessment research since the early studies that found the rate of false positives to be 60 percent or more. But even in light of this optimism, the two most prominent Americans in the field, Monahan and Steadman, in reporting on recent research in 1994, observed that "an increase in predictive accuracy would not obviate the profound questions of social policy and professional ethics that attend any preventive use of the state's police power" (see J. Monahan and H. Steadman, "Towards a Rejuvenation of Risk Assessment Research," in J. Monahan and H. Steadman, eds., *Violence and Mental Disorder: Developments in Risk Assessment* (Chicago: University of Chicago Press, 1994), 5).

III. RETRIBUTIVE THEORIES OF PUNISHMENT

The notion of retribution as a basis for punishment is rooted in the works of Kant and Hegel. This theory holds that punishment ought to be (or must be) imposed when it is deserved. In its purest form, retribution is reflected in the ancient *lex talionis* (that is, "an eye for an eye"). The question whether any beneficial consequences will result from the imposition of punishment is irrelevant. Indeed, an uncompromising retributivist would argue that if punishment is in fact deserved, it ought to be imposed, notwithstanding the possibility of disastrous consequences.

In the excerpts that follow (Braithwaite and Pettit and Lacey), the main features and criticisms of "classical" retributivism are explored. Classical retributivism is criticized for being intuitive or transcendental at its base and dependent on metaphor for its explanation. Retributivists attempt to justify the imposition of punishment by asserting that punishment "restores the balance," "annuls the crime," or "repays a debt to society." Do these expressions lend any force to retributivism, or do they merely restate its elemental content—that is, that the guilty *deserve* to suffer? Retributive approaches to punishment are also criticized for being nothing more than institutional revenge. Are there meaningful differences between personal revenge and a system of state punishment predicated on retributive notions?

Retributive theories of punishment have seen a revival of sorts in the last couple of decades. Some of the more positive features of retributivism have been resurrected under the banner of a "just deserts" theory (or the "new retributivism," as it is sometimes called). "Just deserts" theorists rely on retributive notions to justify proportionate sentencing. This notion should have a ring of familiarity, as the earlier excerpt from H.L.A. Hart refers to the use of retributive reasoning in the "distribution" of sanctions. Just deserts theorists, such as Andrew von Hirsch, have invoked retributive theory to construct a sentencing regime committed to the idea of proportionality. Variations of this regime found their way into the United States when a number of states adopted determinate sentencing guidelines. The excerpts from von Hirsch and Tonry debate the value of this retributive dimension of sentencing.

J. Braithwaite and P. Pettit, *Not Just Deserts: A Republican Theory of Criminal Justice*
(Oxford: Clarendon Press, 1990) (references omitted)

The Resurgence of Retributivism

Until the 1970s retributivism, the idea that criminals should be punished because they deserve it, was something of a dead letter in criminology; there were a few scholars in jurisprudence and philosophy who continued to dabble with retributive theories but they did so in ways that had little impact on public policy. During and since the Victorian era retributivism had become increasingly disreputable, probably unfairly, as an unscientific indulgence of emotions of revenge.

In that period a descendant of utilitarianism dominated criminal justice policymaking. This is the theory we call "preventionism." Preventionist criminologists were motivated by the search for ways of sentencing criminals that would incapacitate them from continuing to offend (as by locking them away from potential victims), that would give the healing and helping professions opportunities to rehabilitate them, and that would deter both those convicted (specific deterrence) and others who became aware of the punishment (general deterrence).

In that same period, ironically, positive criminology accumulated masses of evidence testifying to the failures of such utilitarian doctrines. All manner of rehabilitation programmes for offenders were tried without any producing consistent evidence that they reduce reoffending rates. The deterrence literature also failed to produce the expected evidence that more police, more prisons, and more certain and severe punishment made a significant difference to the crime rate. Since the literature we are referring to here is massive, and the conclusion we reach fairly uncontroversial within criminology, we will not delay the reader by reviewing it.

The evidence on incapacitation, as distinct from rehabilitation or deterrence, was not so clear. There is no doubt that we can prevent bank robbers from robbing banks by incarcerating or executing them. However, we cannot rely on incarceration to prevent assaulters or rapists from committing their type of offence; nor by such measures can we stop drug dealers from selling drugs or organized crime figures from running criminal empires. And while there is a minority of criminologists who think that if we can lock up enough of the right offenders for long enough we can have a substantial impact on the crime rate, most evidence suggests that with the best techniques available we are wrong about twice as often as we are right in predicting serious reoffending. The evidence is that we can never catch enough criminals to reduce crime substantially through incapacitation, or at least that the costs of locking up enough criminals to make a real difference to crime is beyond the fiscal capacities of even the wealthiest countries in the world. Moreover, there are questions about whether imprisonment does not actually worsen the problem in some ways: the convict often learns new illegal skills in "schools for crime" and criminal groups may recruit new members to fill the gap while colleagues are incarcerated.

The flight to retributivism was not only fuelled by the realization that utilitarian and preventionist criminology had failed to deliver on its promises. There was also growing documentation of the injustices perpetrated in the name of preventionist criminal justice. Indeterminate sentences, on the grounds of rehabilitation or incapacitation, allowed offenders to be locked up until they were "safe" to be returned to the community. Many offenders were locked up for extremely long periods for minor crimes; others got very short terms for serious crimes, thanks to their acting skills in feigning rehabilitation. This disparity was often the product of genuine but misguided utilitarian beliefs that certain minor offenders could be prevented from a downward spiral into more serious crime if only psychologists had long enough to work on their rehabilitation. But it also happened that rehabilitation and incapacitation were used to excuse locking up indefinitely some minor offenders who were regarded as subversive or insolent. At the other extreme, bribes were sometimes paid to secure the early release of serious offenders, ostensibly on grounds of their remarkable rehabilitation.

These indeed were good reasons for the retributivists to reject utilitarianism and preventionism. Furthermore, the new retributivists rightly accused preventionists of denying the human dignity of offenders by treating them as determined creatures whose behaviour could not be accounted for by their own choices to break the law. Preventionists tended to back off from blaming offenders; instead of holding them responsible for their wrongdoing, they sought to manipulate them by curing their sickness (rehabilitation), changing the reward–cost calculations that determined their offending (deterrence), and keeping them away from criminal opportunities (incapacitation). The retributivists were struck by the injustice, not to mention the futility, of this. So they called for punishment of offenders in proportion to their desert; mostly this meant in proportion to the harmfulness and blameworthiness of their actions. Criminals should get what they deserve—no more, no less.

By and large, then, the new retributivists who gained the ascendency in the punishment debate during the 1970s were responding to what they correctly identified as the failures, the excesses, the injustices, and the denigration of human agency of utilitarianism and preventionism. The retributivists, we will argue, were moved by the right reasons but took the wrong turn. In particular, they turned too sharply away from the positive, caring strands in the utilitarian and preventionist traditions. Tony Bottoms made the point well when he remarked: "The rehabilitative ethic, and perhaps still more the liberal reformism which preceded it, was an ethic of coercive caring, but at least there was caring."

Why the Debate Matters

For most of its history criminology has played a significant role in legitimating state intrusions into the lives and liberties of citizens. In the 1990s it is now playing this role again, thanks in part to the revival of retributivism. Yet in the 1960s and 1970s mainstream criminology began to delegitimate punitive crime control and intrusive police powers. It did this because by then criminology had shown that increased investment in deterrence, rehabilitation, and incapacitation made little or no difference to the crime rate and cost the taxpayer a fortune. The conventional wisdom of criminology was that imprisonment was a discredited institution and the less we had of it the better, that police were necessary but that attempts to give them more powers and resources should be resisted because it could not be demonstrated that doing this would reduce crime.

In some crucial respects criminologists still play this role. In Australia, for example, public opinion polls consistently show a community where those who support capital punishment outnumber those who oppose it. Most expert criminological opinion sits on the side of the opponents, from time to time trotting out evidence in public debates that where capital punishment has been reintroduced crime rates have not fallen. If expert opinion shifted to support for the view that crime could be reduced by capital punishment, the balance in the debate would probably tip, and the noose return.

But this is a vestige of the 1960s and 1970s when mainstream criminology was more consistently delegitimating of punishment. Instead of continuing to contribute to a healthy scepticism about the rationality of punishment, many of the brightest and best criminologists have now begun to cast around for alternative justifications for maintaining punishment as the pre-eminent response to crime. Retributivism serves them well, for the community can be assured that it matters not whether acts of punishment protect them from crime; we do right when we punish because we give people their just deserts. Even scholars who are anything but law and order conservatives have caught the enthusiasm: There is a feeling of a Kantian imperative behind the word "deserts." Certain things are simply wrong and ought to be punished. And this we do believe."

It follows from the theory we defend, which we will summarize in a moment, that it is good when societies feel uncomfortable about punishment, when people see punishment as a necessary evil rather than a good in itself. Just as it is healthy for citizens to be uncomfortable rather than morally smug about the rightness of killing others in war, so too with punishing criminals. Wilkins reminds us that: "if freedom is to be protected, it must be protected at its frontiers," by which he means that if we are to respect freedom, we must be particularly watchful for the freedom of those who seem least deserving of our concern. A society which feels morally comfortable about sending thousands of terrified young men and women to institutions in which they are bashed, raped, and brutalized, stripped of human dignity, denied freedom of speech and movement, has a doubtful commitment to freedom. A theory which assures us that any human being can deserve these things is subversive of that commitment.

In contending that the new retributivism has provided this assurance, we are not accusing its adherents of necessarily wanting to increase the oppressiveness of the criminal justice system. A good number of the new retributivists, especially some of the more influential among them, are liberals, even radicals, and they see the punishments deserved as much less than those currently administered by criminal justice systems. But liberal versions of just deserts inevitably reduce, in the realities of table-thumping politics, to a strategy of "getting tough."

When you play the game of criminal justice on the field of retribution, you play it on the home ground of conservative law-and-order politicians. You give full rein to those who play to the sense of normality of the majority, urging them to tyrannize the minority. Once all the players agree that retribution, or giving people what they deserve, is the rationale for punishment, the genteel visions of liberal retributivists count for nought. Some of the left retributivists now concede that they may have been co-opted into playing on the conservatives' home ground. Complicated notions like the balancing of benefits and burdens which can underpin liberal egalitarian versions of retributivism are quickly discarded by law-and-order politicians who find that their press releases are most likely to get a run by appealing to simple-minded vengeance. The long-term effect of the new retributivism in criminal justice theory will be to make the community feel more comfortable with punishment, encouraging prisons which are even more overcrowded and more brutal than at present.

None of this proves that retributivism is wrong or inadequate as a theory. It is perhaps just another illustration of Thorsten Sellin's dictum on criminal justice reform that "beautiful theories have a way of turning into ugly practices." All we have wanted to show in this section is that the debate is one that matters. Whether for good or ill, whether in the way they would have wanted or not, the new retributivists have certainly changed both the punishment debate and criminal justice policy. The long list of American states that have shifted to "flat," "determinate," or "presumptive" sentencing codes since the mid-1970s—Illinois, California, Connecticut, Colorado, Alaska, Arizona, Maine, Indiana, Minnesota, and others—is sufficient testimony to that.

N. Lacey, *State Punishment: Political Principles and Community Values*
(London: Routlege, 1988) (footnotes omitted)

Backward-Looking Justifications

The central case of an exclusively backward-looking justification is that of classical retributivism in its strong form. I take this theory to be making the claim that the state has both a right and a duty to punish, in the sense of inflicting unpleasant consequences upon an offender in response to her offence to the extent that, and by reason of that fact that, she deserves that punishment. Desert thus operates as both a necessary and a sufficient condition for justified punishment. Theories which present desert as a necessary but not a sufficient condition will be considered as mixed theories.

Thus the key notion employed by backward-looking theories is that of desert. Some writers treat desert as an axiomatic or self-evident moral principle, assuming that it needs no further explanation. Others, however (the present writer included), whilst acknowledging the place of desert in our moral intuitions and reactive attitudes, find the concept puzzling when they attempt further to analyze its normative appeal, at least in the context of punishment. Indeed, it has been argued that the apparent irreducibility of the notion gives rise to suspicions that the claim that X ought to be punished because she deserves to be punished merely amounts to the claim that X ought to be punished because she ought to be punished. If the intuition is not shared, it seems impossible to push the argument further—so this is hardly a helpful contribution to the complex debate about the justifiability of punishment. Thus many writers have acknowledged the necessity of further unpacking the notion of desert, and we need to examine some of these attempts in order to fairly evaluate the adequacy of backward-looking justifications of punishment.

The Lex Talionis

Perhaps the crudest yet the most fundamental attempt is represented by the ancient lex talionis: an eye for any eye, a life for a life, and so on. This principle, if it merits the name, certainly has the attraction of simplicity: unfortunately this is all that can be said for it. Two devastating objections eliminate it from the list of possible candidates as adequate explications of the desert principle. Most obviously, in terms of the question of how much punishment is inflicted, it supplies clear practical guidance as to the proper measure only in a selective number of cases. The penalty for murder or mutilation may seem clear, but what punishment ought to be inflicted for fraud, perjury or blackmail? The indeterminancy of the principle in these cases ought to make us wary of the status of its apparent clarity in others. And any subtler reinterpretation, such as the argument that murderers simply lose their right not to be killed, or thieves not to be stolen from, hardly generates a morally adequate or even clear set of prescriptions for a criminal justice system. Secondly, and more importantly, this principle fails to capture one of the greatest strengths of the retributivist tradition: that is, its accommodation of a strong principle of responsibility generating limitations on who may properly be punished. It is generally claimed that no punishment is deserved unless the offence is committed by an agent who is responsible in the sense of having a certain degree of knowledge of relevant circumstances and capacity for control of her actions. [As for the] significance and meaning of the principle of responsibility … for the moment it is sufficient to recall that our moral response appears to differ enormously according to whether a killing is intentional or accidental; a wounding deliberate or negligent. This commonly acknowledged moral distinction between responsibility based merely on causation—strict liability—and that based on "mental elements"—such as intent or recklessness—is ignored by the lex talionis, which directs the same response in each case. Added to the fact that the lex talionis offers no real arguments about why we should punish in the first place, these defects make it clear that we shall have to look further afield for an adequate explanation of the principle of desert central to the retributivist tradition.

The Culpability Principle

A more promising account explicates the idea of desert in terms of culpability, using this notion not only to identify the justifying reasons for punishment and those who may properly be punished, but also to fix the proper measure of punishment, in terms of a relationship of commensurability or proportionality between the offence and the punishment inflicted. Culpability is generally explained as a function of the gravity of the harm caused (such as death, injury or damage to property) combined with the degree of responsibility (intent, recklessness, negligence or mere inadvertence) of the actor. But the notion of culpability also enshrines, as indeed it must if it is to count as a justifying argument for punishment, a moral judgment about the wrongfulness of the behaviour in question. Cuplability, in other words, is equated with blameworthiness, and blameworthiness is equated in turn with punishment-worthiness. This does seem to reflect an important aspect of our entrenched habits and attitudes of praising and blaming, and in a more accurate way than does the lex talionis. However, as a normative theory of punishment, this approach too has its difficulties. Some of these, which I shall call internal criticisms, take the form of problems thrown up by the argument from culpability on its own terms: if we were to accept the principle, what would its implications be? Others, which I shall call external criticisms, cast doubt more fundamentally on the adequacy of the principle itself: does it offer an adequate explication of the content and normative force of arguments from desert? Both kinds of difficulty will have to be addressed in order to give a fair appraisal of the culpability principle. ...

Finally, and most importantly, however, serious external criticisms can be made of the culpability principle's account of why it is that we should punish. For it is not clear that the move from a judgment of blameworthiness to one of punishment–worthiness should be made so lightly. Even though our desert-based reactive attitudes may be firmly held, surely we should reflect carefully and seek further reasons before we take the additional step of deliberately acting in a harmful way against a particular individual on the basis of them? A judgment that someone has behaved wrongly does not involve or justify the further judgment that they should be punished. Ultimately, the culpability principle seems to give us no explanation of why we should think it right to punish offenders merely by reason of their past culpable actions. By what means does such an argument, if argument it is, distinguish itself from a principle of vengeance? By what moral alchemy does the prima facie wrong of punishment following on the wrong of the offence create a morally preferable situation? Why should an offence alone generate a moral reason for punitive action? None of these issues is demystified by the culpability principle.

Forfeiture of Rights, Unfair Advantages and the Restoration of a Moral Equilibrium

Given what has been said of the failure of these first two models of desert theory to generate a satisfactory justification of punishment, it makes sense to attempt further to explicate the desert principle within the context of some wider, compatible, background political philosophy. Thus the other attempts I shall consider explore the links between the concept of desert and those of justice, fairness and equality. The concepts of justice and fairness have indeed been central to the desert tradition, and it is thus with these that I shall begin.

The first of the more sophisticated versions of the desert principle which I shall consider may conveniently be labeled the forfeiture of rights view. On this view, the meaning of the claim that an offender deserves to be punished is explained within the context of the existence of a legal system which generates reciprocal political obligations upon citizens to obey its norms. Thus by virtue of a voluntarily committed offence an individual violates here obligations not only to the state but also to all other citizens, and the state is justified in depriving her of her civil rights. The thesis can be put in an extreme and a moderate form. In its extreme form it claims that an offender forfeits all her civil rights by virtue of any voluntarily committed offence. This seems on the face of it to be an implausible claim, generating as it does no limit on the amount or type of justifiable punishment and thus abandoning the proportionality principle central to the retributive tradition. A more plausible version is that which argues that the offender only forfeits a set of rights equivalent to these which she has violated: once the proportionate set of rights has been forfeited, the offender can re-enter political society on fair terms with the law-abiding.

Thus on the moderate view a full set of political rights is due to a citizen so long as she meets her political and legal obligations. This argument does generate a clear principle identifying who may be punished, but doubts remain about just what the argument amounts to as a set of positive justifying reasons for punishment. *Why* should an offender forfeit any civil rights? What does the argument add to the blank, mysterious claim that she deserves it? A further refinement argues that a voluntary offence is taken to show that the offender in a sense chose or willed her own punishment, or at least consented to it, where she was responsible for the offence, aware of its normative consequences, and acting within a fair system of rules. The punishment therefore respects the autonomy of the agent, treating her as an end in herself rather than as a means to some diffused social good. Again, this argument has some appeal as a claim about who should be punished, but as an account of why they should be punished it is inadequate: it can hardly be claimed that offenders consent to their disadvantaging punitive treatment in anything like the strong sense of consent which we generally take to be necessary to justify harsh treatment of one person by another. We can easily imagine an offender who meets the conditions of the principle yet who states in committing her offence that she does not consent to any punishment: the only way in which such an offender can be brought within the ambit of the principle is through some form of social contract argument. I shall consider the difficulties with this approach in commenting on the second sophisticated version of the desert principle, which raises a similar issue. Before moving on, however, it is worth raising the question of whether in any case the consent argument for punishment could count as a genuinely desert-based principle. In attempting to unpack that idea, we seem to have moved a considerable distance from our unreconstructed starting point.

The second version may be called the unfair advantage view. Again, we are to imagine a background system of reciprocal political obligations, and we are invited to take the view that the essence of a voluntary offence is the taking by the offender of an unfair advantage: in failing to restrain herself, the offender has had the advantage of fulfilling choices forbidden to others. The purpose and justification of punishment is, in effect, to remove that unfair advantage and to restore the "moral equilibrium" or relationships of justice that existed prior to the offence. On one extreme version of the view, until punishment is inflicted, all members of society are in some way implicated in the moral disequilibrium created by the crime, which they have failed to redress. It is presumably this type of thought which prompts Kant to say that even on the dissolution of society all murderers held in the jails ought to be executed. There is perhaps a connection between such views about the value to be attached to the restoration of the oral equilibrium and the argument that punishment "reaffirms the right"— both in terms of the rightness of the standards breached by the offence and in terms of the pre-existing relationships of justice between the members of political society. Here at last we have not only an argument about who may properly be punished, but also a positive claim about the reasons for that punishment—although reasons which, as I shall argue, are at such a high level of abstraction that their contribution to de-mystification of the desert principle is limited.

These two versions of desert theory have the important advantage over those so far considered of locating principles of punishment in their proper context—that is, within a general set of political principles. Indeed, these views are probably best understood within the social contract tradition in political philosophy, which asks us to imagine some hypothetical initial agreement upon a certain system of rules and methods of enforcement which can and must then fairly be administered by means of imposition of the agreed sanctions. But these views are not without their practical and theoretical difficulties. In the first place, neither of them gives very clear practical guidance about the fair measure of punishment in particular cases. What actual punishment would forfeit a set of rights equivalent to those violated by a rapist, a petty thief, a reckless driver? What sanction would be sufficient to remove the unfair advantage gained by the provoked manslaughterer, the tax evader or the burglar? As in the case of the law of the talion and the culpability principle, resort to arguments from conventionality agreed, customary or consequence-based penalty scales seem hard to avoid. Secondly, real difficulties have been raised about the social contract tradition itself; in what sense can a *fictitious* agreement generate obligations for release people? This subject will have to be taken up in detail in later chapters. Furthermore, these views are dependent for their force, as we have already noted, on the existence of a fair set of rules. This is not fatal in itself, but the criteria which dictate that there is indeed a just equilibrium which can be restored are not generated by the forfeiture of rights or unfair advantage principles alone. The views do presuppose an independent account of what counts as an unfair advantage and a just equilibrium.

Finally, it seems legitimate to ask whether the metaphorical ideas of restoring relationships of justice or moral equilibria outweigh the obvious disvalues attached to the suffering and other costs of punishment. Do these theories really ignore such cost completely? If not, what weight do they accord them? In what real sense does punishment "restore the right"? Do these theories really remove the mystery attaching to the original, simple desert principle, or are they, too, a form of moral alchemy? Or, in trying to avoid the mystery, do they not collapse into versions of utilitarian or other consequentialist justification? Is the real reason for punishment underlying these

theories the need to uphold a just and effective legal system, to prevent private vengeance, to remove feelings of unfairness on the parts of victims? Can any account of
punishment which ignores these factors generate a satisfactory justification? And if
so many questions crucial to the justification of punishment can only be answered by
looking beyond the desert principle, how strong a claim can that principle make to
constitute *the* justification of punishment?

Let us turn finally to a version of the desert principle which explores its links with
a principle of equality. On this view, to punish someone who deserves punishment is
to act in accordance with a principle of equal treatment: treat like cases alike, and
different ones differently. Through her voluntary offence, the offender has singled
herself out from other citizens: offenders and non-offenders ought to be treated differently. But this will not do as a theory of desert, let alone as a theory of punishment.
First of all, it is too minimal: on this basis alone it might justify treating the offender
better than the non-offender, so long as this was done consistently. In addition, the
principle generates no answer to the question of how much we ought to punish. Finally, the principle tells us nothing about why an offence makes the offender rel-
evantly different in a way which justifies punitive treatment. Not every type of voluntary differentiating action, even one affecting others, justifies a punitive response.
Thus the principle of equal treatment cannot explain the principle of desert, although
it may form an important part of that principle.

Retributive Theory

We are now in a position to evaluate the question of whether any of the arguments we
have considered as possible explications of the idea of desert makes sense of the
puzzle of the justification of punishment. This can best be done by means of a summary of the answers generated by those arguments to the three questions originally
imposed. First of all, why should we punish? It is really in answering this fundamental question that the arguments associated with desert are at their most deficient. Even
the more sophisticated versions barely rise above the level of metaphor, and leave us
with the suspicion that the idea of desert cannot be distinguished from a principle of
vengeance or the unappealing assertion that two wrongs somehow make a right.
Within the context of a general set of political principles, arguments such as that from
unfair tax advantage can answer this question, but when such a supplementation is
made, it is no longer clear that what we have is a desert theory at all, rather than a
consequence-based account. In addition, the possibility of a background system which
is not universally just complicates the force of the claim that punishment aims to
restore a moral equilibrium. Moreover, why should we necessarily give absolute priority to the demands of this narrow retributive conception of justice as opposed to
those of mercy, forgiveness and humanity?

Secondly, how much ought we to punish? This is the question to which the idea of
desert promises us a clear and determinate answer, yet on analysis it fails to fulfill that
promise. Without supplementation by either conventionally agreed scales of punishment
or arguments from consequences, arguments from desert tell us very little about what
punishments we ought to inflict. Thirdly, many of the arguments closely associated

with the retributive tradition do generate a determinate answer to the question of whom we should punish: we should only punish those who have responsibly committed offences. It is perhaps in this area that the tradition really does encompass a principle which will be fundamental to the justification of punishment, and one which is indeed reflected in our differing response to the accidental, the negligent and the deliberate offence. Yet it is not clear why these arguments need employ the concept of desert: they can be developed perfectly adequately in terms of responsibility, fairness and other arguments from distributive as opposed to retributive justice, as we shall see. And in the absence of any adequate explanation of what the desert principle amounts to, let alone of a desert-based answer to the central question of why we should punish, the responsibility principle in any case only operates as a limiting one which would have to be combined with some other arguments to generate a justification of punishment. In addition, with respect to the broader aspect of the third question, that is, what kinds of actions ought to be punished, the principles we have considered have to be supplemented by a set of general, consistent yet independent political principles in order to give any complete guidance.

Negatively, then, the retributive tradition seems accurately to reflect our considered judgment about excuses, justifications and mitigating principles: it can tell us why not to punish certain categories of person; but it fails to tell us why we should punish any persons, and in what sorts of circumstances. In addition, consistent adherence to the main purported arguments from desert would issue in a criminal justice system in some respects radically more extensive, in others greatly less so, than those generally acknowledged to be acceptable. This last factor is of course not decisive, but we may use our intuitions where they are reflected in the shape of current systems as at least pointers to the need for modification of possible theories.

A. von Hirsch, "Proportionality in the Philosophy of Punishment"
in M. Tonry, ed., *Crime and Justice—A Review of Research, XVI*
(Chicago: University of Chicago Press, 1992) (references omitted)

The last two decades have witnessed continuing debate over the rationales for allocating sanctions among convicted offenders. Various guiding theories or strategies have been put forward: "just deserts," "limiting retributivism," "selective incapacitation." The choice among them is sometimes treated as a matter of deciding allegiances: one adheres to "just deserts" or not, just as one decides to be a Democrat or a Red Sox fan or not. If one opts for just deserts, then one must worry about the scaling of penalties. If one does not, then perhaps one can disregard such issues.

Such a perspective is, I think, misleading. Sanctioning rationales differ from one another largely in the emphasis they give the principle of proportionality that is, the requirement that sanctions be proportionate in their severity to the seriousness of offenses. A desert rationale is one that gives the principle a dominant role. Other viewpoints permit proportionality to be trumped, to a greater or a lesser degree, by ulterior concerns such as those of crime control. ...

B. Desert Theories

Traditional retributive theories, such as Kant's, were sketchy. While contending that justice calls for deserved punishments, they seldom explored the grounds of penal desert claims: namely, *why* wrongdoers deserve punishment. Recently, philosophers have been looking for explanations. The two leading accounts today are, respectively, the "benefits and burdens" theory and "expressive" desert theories.

1. *Benefits and Burdens.* The benefits and burdens theory originated in the writings of two contemporary philosophers, Herbert Morris and Jeffrie Murphy. Both have recently questioned the theory, but a number of other philosophers continue to support it.

The theory offers a retrospectively oriented account of why offenders should be made to suffer punishment. The account focuses on the law as a jointly beneficial enterprise: it requires each person to desist from predatory conduct; by desisting, the person not only benefits others but is benefited by their reciprocal self-restraint. The person who victimizes others while still benefiting from their self-restraint thus obtains an unjust advantage. Punishment's function is to impose an offsetting disadvantage.

The theory has some attractions. It goes beyond fuzzy notions of "paying back" wrongdoing or "righting" the moral balance. It points to a particular unwarranted advantage the wrongdoer obtains: namely, that of benefiting from others' self-restraint while not reciprocally restraining himself. The rationale for the penalty is retrospective in focus, as a desert-oriented account should be: to offset, through punishment, the unjustly obtained benefit.

The theory has difficulties, however. One problem is that it requires a heroic belief in the justice of the underlying social arrangements. Unless it is true that our social and political systems succeed in providing mutual support for all members, including criminal offenders, then the offender has not necessarily benefited from others' law-abiding behavior.

The theory also becomes awkward when one uses it to try to decide the quantum of punishments. One difficulty is assessing benefits and burdens. The theory cannot focus on literal benefits the offender obtains as some of the worst assaultive crimes can be quite unprofitable whereas other (apparently less serious) theft crimes may provide the offender with a considerable profit. What thus must matter, instead, is the additional degree of freedom the offender has unfairly appropriated. But notions of degrees of freedom are unhelpful in making comparisons among crimes. It is one thing to say the armed robber or burglar permits himself actions that others refrain from taking and thereby unfairly obtains a liberty that others have relinquished in their (and his) mutual interest. It is different, and far more obscure, to say the robber deserves more punishment than the burglar because, somehow, he has arrogated to himself a greater degree of unwarranted freedom than the burglar has.

The theory would also seem to distort the way the gravity of crimes is assessed. R.A. Duff has pointed out the artificiality of treating victimizing crimes, such as armed robbery, in terms of the "freedom-of-action" advantage the robber gains over uninvolved third parties, rather than in terms of the intrusion into the interests or rights of actual or potential victims. Perhaps, tax evasion can be explained in terms of unjustified advantage: the tax evader refuses to pay his or her own tax, yet benefits from others' payments through the services he or she receives. Tax evasion, however, is scarcely the paradigm criminal offense, and it is straining to try to assess the heinousness of common offences such as robbery in similar fashion.

2. *"Expressive" Theories.* "Expressive" theories are those that base desert claims on the censuring aspects of punishment. Punishing someone consists of doing something painful or unpleasant to him, because he has committed a wrong, under circumstances and in a manner that conveys disapprobation of the offender for his wrong. Treating the offender as a wrongdoer, Richard Wasserstrom has pointed out, is central to the idea of punishment. The difference between a tax and a fine, for example, does not rest in the kind of material deprivation imposed: it is money, in both cases. It consists, rather, in the fact that with a fine the money is taken in a manner that conveys disapproval or censure; whereas with a tax no disapproval is implied.

A sanction that treats conduct as wrong that is, not a "neutral" sanction has two important moral functions that, arguably, are not reducible to crime prevention. One is to recognize the importance of the rights that have been infringed. Joel Feinberg has argued that the censure in punishment conveys to victims and potential victims that the state recognizes they are wronged by criminal conduct, that rights to which they are properly entitled have been infringed.

The other role of censure, discussed by R.A. Duff, is to address the wrongdoer as a moral agent, by appealing to his or her sense of right or wrong. This, Duff suggests, is not just a preventive strategy. While it is hoped that the actor will reconsider his actions and desist from wrongdoing in the future, the censure is not merely a means of changing his behavior otherwise, there would be no point in censuring actors who are repentant already (since they need no blame to make the effort to desist) or who are seemingly incorrigible (since they will not change despite the censure). Any human actor, the theory suggests, is a moral agent, capable (unless clearly incompetent) of evaluating others' assessment of their conduct. The repentant actor has his own assessment of the conduct confirmed through the disapproval of others; the defiant actor is made to understand and feel others' disapproval, even if he refuses to desist. Such communication of judgement and feeling, Duff argues, is what moral discourse among rational agents is about. What a purely "neutral" sanction not embodying blame would deny even if no less effective in preventing crime is precisely that essential status of the person as a moral agent. A neutral sanction would treat potential offenders much as beasts in a circus as beings that must be restrained, intimidated, or conditioned into submission because they are incapable of understanding that harmful conduct is wrong.

Such censure-oriented desert theories have some potential advantages. They are less dependent on the supposition that the underlying social system is wholly just: an actor with cause for complaint against the social system may still be to blame, for example, if he knowingly injures those who have done him no wrong. Moreover, the theory is more easily squared with notions of proportionality. If punishment is seen as an expression of blame for reprehensible conduct, then the quantum of punishment should depend on how reprehensible the conduct is. The punishment for typical victimizing crimes would depend on how much harm the conduct does, and how culpable the actor is for the harm and no longer on how much extra freedom of action the actor has arrogated to himself vis-à-vis third parties. …

V. The Desert Model

A desert model is a sentencing scheme that observes the proportionality principle: punishments are scaled according to the seriousness of crimes. While speaking of a "desert model" might suggest a unique scale, that is not the intent. A variety of scales of differing overall severity and differing sanctions might satisfy the requirements of this model. It is the core elements of a desert model that are sketched here. Fuller accounts of the model and its rationale are available elsewhere, as are discussions of the use of the model in scaling noncustodial sanctions.

A. Ordinal Proportionality

Ordinal proportionality is the requirement that penalties be scaled according to the comparative seriousness of crimes. Two main sub-requirements are involved. First, parity. The proportionality principle permits differences in severity of punishments only to the extent these differences reflect variations in the degree of blameworthiness of the conduct. Accordingly, when offenders have been convicted of crimes of similar seriousness, they deserve punishment of similar severity unless special circumstances (i.e., of aggravation of mitigation) can be identified that render the offense, in the particular context, more or less deserving of blame than would normally be the case. Second, rank ordering. Punishing one crime more than another expresses more disapproval for the former crime, so that it is justified only if that crime is more serious. Punishments thus are to be ordered on a penalty scale so that their relative severity reflects the seriousness rankings of the crimes involved. This restricts the extent to which the arrangement of penalties on the scale can be varied internally for crime preventive purposes. Imposing exemplary penalties for a given type of offense to halt a recent upswing in its incidence, for example, would throw the ranking of offenses out of kilter unless other penalties are adjusted accordingly. ...

B. Scale Anchoring and Cardinal Proportionality

Cardinal proportionality requires that a reasonable proportion be maintained between overall levels of punitiveness and the gravity of the criminal conduct. The scale should not, for example, be so inflated that even lesser criminal conduct is penalized with substantial deprivations.

Since cardinal proportionality places only broad and imprecise constraints on how much the penalty scale can be escalated or deflated, substantial leeway remains for locating the scale's anchoring points. What other factors would be relevant?

The penal traditions of the jurisdiction would be a starting point. Since the censure expressed through punishment is a convention, it, like any other convention, will be influenced by tradition. Normative considerations, however, may justify altering this convention. One such consideration is the goal of reducing the suffering visited on offenders.

Should crime prevention also be considered in setting the anchoring points? Certain preventive strategies would alter the comparative rankings of punishments and thus infringe ordinal proportionality. Selective incapacitation, for example, calls for the unequal punishment of offenders convicted of similar offenses on the basis of predictive criteria that do not reflect the seriousness of the criminal conduct.

Other preventive strategies, however, would not necessarily be open to this objection. Consider general deterrence. Were the penalties for particular offense categories to be set by reference to those penalties' expected deterrent effects, it would infringe ordinal proportionality, as it would no longer be the seriousness of crimes that determined the ordering of sanctions. Suppose, instead, that deterrence were used differently: penalties might be ordered according to the crimes' seriousness on the scale, with the scale's overall magnitude being decided (in part by its expected net impact on crime. Were the requisite empirical knowledge available (which it is not today), it might be possible to compare the overall deterrent impacts of alternative scale magnitudes. That information could then be used to help anchor the scale, without disturbing the ordering of penalties. Moreover, this approach would not necessarily lead to increases in severity. Penalties might be cut back below their historical levels, on grounds that no significant loss of deterrence would occur.

...

A desert-based scheme is necessarily somewhat confining in its requirement that offense seriousness, and not a variety of possible other considerations, should decide comparative punishment. Its confining character makes it easier to scale penalties in a coherent fashion, but it also limits the possibilities of achieving various other goals or objectives. Moreover, the proportionality principle rests on a particular value that of equity. Other values of various sorts might be thought to override equity considerations, in at least some situations. Hence, we need to consider the "hybrid" models: those that, to a lesser or greater extent, allow departures from ordinal desert requirements in order to achieve other purposes. ...

There is also the question of the degree of guidance a theory provides for the scaling of penalties. The proportionality principle, we have seen, offers no unique solutions, particularly because of the leeway it allows in the setting of a scale's anchoring points. However, the principle does offer considerable structure (although not unique solutions) for the comparative ordering of penalties. If proportionality is dislodged from this central, organizing role, it may not be easy to develop alternative (e.g., prevention-based) rationales that can provide much guidance. While a considerable body of theory exists concerning the principle of proportionality, lacunae remain. More thought needs to be given to the following topics, among others.

The Criteria for Gauging the Seriousness of Crimes, Particularly the Harm Dimension of Seriousness. A "living-standard" conception of harm may be a start, but it requires further scrutiny and elaboration.

Spacing. Proportionality calls not only for penalties ranked according to the gravity of crimes but also for spacing among penalties that reflects degrees of difference in crime seriousness. The spacing question, however, has received little attention.

Anchoring the Scale. If penalties are graded according to offense seriousness and the scale as a whole is not inflated or deflated unduly, the requirements of ordinal and cardinal proportionality have been satisfied, and one must look elsewhere for grounds for anchoring the scale. What these grounds might be remains largely to be explored.

There are also a number of practical issues needing further thought. One concerns back-up sanctions. Under any punishment theory emphasizing proportionality, non-custodial sanctions (rather than the severe penalty of imprisonment) should be employed for crimes other than serious ones. Using such sanctions raises the question of what should befall defendants if they violate the terms of the penalty or example, if they refuse to pay a fine or complete a stint of community service. How much added punitive bite may the back-up sanction legitimately entail?

M. Tonry, "Proportionality, Parsimony, and Interchangeability of Punishments"
in R.A. Duff, S. Marshall, R. Dobash, and R. Dobash, eds.,
Penal Theory and Practice: Tradition and Innovation in Criminal Justice
(Manchester: Manchester University Press, 1994) (references omitted)

Critique of Principle of Proportionality

Efforts to apply philosophers' distinctions to policy-makers' decisions necessarily raise different concerns that do disagreements among philosophers. Current initiatives to increase use of "non-custodial" penalties in the United Kingdom and "intermediate" sanctions in the United States necessarily require translation of theorists' distinctions into practitioners' realities.

It is at this point of translation that the case for strong proportionality conditions breaks down. There are at least five major difficulties. First, strong proportionality conditions require objectification of categories of offenders and offenses that are oversimplified and overinclusive. Second, proportionality arguments are often premised on objective legal measures of desert, typically current and past crimes, other than on the subjective degree of moral culpability expressed by the offender, under particular circumstances and conditions. Third, strong proportionality conditions run head-on into "just deserts in an unjust society." Fourth, strong proportionality conditions violate notions of parsimony by requiring imposition of unnecessarily severe punishments in individual cases in order to assure formal equivalence of suffering. Fifth, strong proportionality conditions presuppose that imposition of offenders' deserved punishments is an overriding moral imperative rather than one of several competing ethical considerations.

The Illusion of "Like-Situated Offenders"

If recent efforts in the United Kingdom and the United States to increase use of intermediate sanctions are to succeed, the appropriateness of different punishments for "like-situated offenders" must be recognised.

"Like-situated offender" is nested in quotation marks to express the artificiality of notions of like-situated offenders, comparable crimes, and generic punishments. A strong proportionality-in-punishment argument insists on equal treatment of like-situated offenders and proportionately different treatment of differently situated offenders. A fundamental difficulty is that this assumes that offenders can conveniently and justly be placed into a manageable number of more-or-less dessert categories and that standard punishments can be prescribed for each category. Unfortunately, neither side of the desert–punishment equation lends itself to standardization.

Neither offenders nor punishments come in standard cases. The practice of dividing offenders and punishments into generic categories produces much unnecessary suffering and provides only illusory proportionality. A look at Minnesota's sentencing guidelines shows why. …

Problems of objectification of crimes, offenders, and punishments are especially stark in a numerical guidelines system. In systems that feature written policy guidelines, they lurk beneath the surface. The Minnesota illustration is generally relevant to analysis of proportionality in punishment, however, because it makes real world implications of strong proportionality conditions starkly apparent. If proportionality is an, or the, overriding principle in the distribution of punishment in practice, then the imperfections of objectification that I describe are presumably regrettable but acceptable costs to be paid for a principled punishment system. If they appear unacceptable, the problem may be that the principle of proportionality offers less helpful guidance than its proponents urge.

Objective Measure of Responsibility

Von Hirsch's proportionality argument relies on objective measures of penal deservedness. This is curious. Desert theories, especially blaming theories, are premised on notions of individual blameworthiness, which seem inexorably linked to particularised judgments about moral responsibility. Objective measures of harm are seldom sufficient for conviction in the criminal law: that is why doctrines of competency, *mens rea*, and affirmative defense exist and why doctrines like strict liability and felony-murder are disfavored. If individualised moral judgments are germane to conviction, it is not obvious why they are not also germane to punishment.

If punishment is principally about blaming, surely it is relevant whether the offender was mentally impaired, socially disadvantaged, a reluctant participant, or moved by humane motives. Surely it is morally relevant, whatever the path to conviction, what the offender did, with what *mens rea*, and under what circumstances. Surely it is morally relevant whether a particular punishment will be more intensely experienced by one person than by another. In other words, the three subjective considerations that Minnesota's guidelines ignore—what did he really do, what will the conditions of his sanction really be, will he suffer more intensely than others—are relevant to moral judgments of blameworthiness and proportionate punishments. Nigel Walker expresses this when he observes: "Retributive reasoning would lead instead to a 'personal price list' which would take into account not only gradations of harm but offenders' culpability and sensibility."

The failure of von Hirsch's arguments to take account of individualised differences in culpability and individual effects of punishment looks strange when we recall that von Hirsch's is a retributive theory. Utilitarian theories reject interpersonal comparisons of utility, as Lionel Robbins' classic essay explains, either on measurement grounds (variable intensity of satisfactions, utility monsters, and so on), or on normative grounds (no individual's satisfactions *should* count for more). However, utilitarian theories are concerned with general policies and aggregate social measures and not with fine-tuned moral judgments.

An Unjust Society

Punishment schemes that attach high value to proportionality necessarily ignore the differing material conditions of life, including poverty, social disadvantage, and bias, in which human personalities and characters take form. The substantive criminal law rejects motive for intention and in the English-speaking countries allows no formal excusing or mitigating defense of social disadvantage. Yet in both the United Kingdom and the United States, most common law offenders are products of disadvantaged and deprived backgrounds and in both countries vastly disproportionate numbers of alleged, convicted, and imprisoned offenders are members of racial and ethnic minorities. The likelihood, for example, that a black American male is in prison today is eight times greater than that a white American male is in prison.

The problem of "just deserts in an unjust world" is a fundamental problem for a strong proportionality constraint. Whether retributive theories are rationalised in terms of benefits and burdens, or equilibrium, or blaming, or condemnation, or penance, they must presume equal opportunities for all to participate in society. when some are disabled from full participation by discrimination, disability, or exclusion, by denial of access to public goods, by the burdens of social and economic disadvantage, it is difficult to claim that they enjoy the benefits of autonomy that produce obligation. To take just one example, proponents of benefits and burdens theories are hard pressed to explain how a person who is denied society's benefits deserves to be burdened by social obligation. ...

Parsimony

Proponents of strong proportionality conditions necessarily prefer equality over minimization of suffering. For nearly two decades in the United States, Andrew von Hirsch and Norval Morris have been disagreeing over the role of parsimony in punishment. Von Hirsch has argued for strong desert limits on punishment and high priority to pursuit of equality and proportionality in punishment. Morris has argued that desert is a limiting, not a defining, principle of punishment and that policy should prescribe imposition of the least severe "not undeserved" sanction that meets legitimate policy ends. Within these outer bounds of "not undeserved" punishments Morris has consistently argued for observance of a principle of parsimony.

To some extent Morris and von Hirsch have argued past each other. Morris argues that a desert approach is unnecessarily harsh and von Hirsch responds by noting that he personally favors relatively modest punishments and, in any case, desert schemes are not inherently more severe than other schemes. In turn, von Hirsch argues that Morris's "not undeserved" proportionality constraints are vague, the breadth of allowable ranges of sentencing discretion is never specified, and Morris responds by noting that absolute measures of deserved punishment are unknowable and that his aim is to minimise imposition of penal suffering within bounds that any given community finds tolerable.

The problem is that they start from different major premises—von Hirsch's is the "principle of proportionality," Morris's the "principle of parsimony." The difference between them can be seen by imagining a comprehensive punishment scheme, perhaps resembling Minnesota's. Imagine that policy makers have conscientiously classified all offenders into ten categories and, using von Hirsch's ordinal/cardinal magnitude and anchoring points approach, have decided that all offenses at level VII deserve twenty-three- to twenty-five-month prison terms. Imagine further that reliable public opinion surveys have shown that 90 per cent of the general public would find a restrictive non-custodial punishment, "not unduly lenient" and a 36-month prison term "not unduly severe" for level VII offenses.

...

Sorting Out Principles

Disagreements about just punishments, like disagreements about the death penalty or abortion, are often in the end disagreements about powerful intuitions or deeply embedded values. It may be that differences in view between those who give primacy to proportionality and those who give primacy to parsimony cannot be bridged.

The burden of persuasion should rest, however, it seems to me on those who reject Isaiah Berlin's observations that "not all good things are compatible, still less all the ideals of mankind" and that "the necessity of choosing between absolute claims is then an inescapable characteristic of the human condition."

Punishment raises at least two important conflicts between ideals—between the principles of proportionality and parsimony, between the quests for criminal justice and social justice. ...

If we were single-mindedly devoted to equal opportunity, then, we should view equalization of life chances as an overriding goal of social policy. However, Fishkin argues, efforts to equalize life chances run head on into another powerful principle, that the value of autonomy in a private sphere of liberty encompasses a principle of family autonomy, of non-intrusion by the state into the family's sphere of private liberty.

In other words, equal opportunity and family autonomy conflict fundamentally. Full respect for equal opportunity would involve intrusion into the family that would widely be seen as objectionably intrusive. Full respect for family autonomy would widely be seen as cruel disregard for children's basic needs.

And so it may be with punishment. Principles of proportionality and parsimony may simply conflict, with resolutions between them necessarily partial and provisional.

IV. TRANSCENDING THE PHILOSOPHICAL DEBATE

In the introduction to this chapter, we sounded the warning that the philosophical debate framed here for consideration might be unsatisfying in certain respects. David Garland and Peter Young (in "Towards a Social Analysis of Penalty," in Garland and Young, eds., *The Power To Punish: Contemporary Penality and Social Analysis* (Aldershot: Gower Publishing Company, 1983), explain the shortcomings of this debate in the following way:

> But the important point for our purposes is that within all of these philosophical tests, "punishment" is presented and discussed as a singular, unitary phenomenon. The actual practices, institutions and sanctions are disregarded as mere empirical "accidents" and manifestations—the object of the analysis is seen as "punishment itself." A whole tradition

of philosophical writing and debate conspires to present "punishment" as something we can talk of and refer to in the singular, whilst disregarding the plurality and complexity of its empirical supports. Indeed, the fact that we continue to talk of the realm of penal sanctions in the singular term "punishment" (and not "corrections" or social defence) not only signifies the influence of penal philosophy in shaping our attitudes to the phenomenon, but also indicates which strand of philosophical argument has prevailed in British culture.

In his more recent work, David Garland has attempted to construct an original social theory of punishment. Garland examines and critiques the major sociological paradigms of punishment (including Marx, Weber, Durkheim, and Foucault) and finds each lacking in a similar way: none of these theories focuses beyond a particular cultural trait or characteristic of modern society. In the excerpt below, Garland describes how cultural mentalities and sensibilities influence the shape of penal institutions and how punishment, as a social artefact, in turn contributes to the formation of culture.

D. Garland, *Punishment and Modern Society: A Study in Social Theory*
(Chicago: University of Chicago Press, 1990) (footnotes omitted)

1. Punishment and the Production of Culture

In my discussion of punishment and culture up to this point I have stressed the ways in which penal practices and discourses have been shaped by changing forms of mentality and sensibility. My concern has been to show how society's cultural patterns come to be imprinted upon its penal institutions, so that punishment becomes a practical embodiment of some of the symbolic themes, constellations of meaning, and particular ways of feeling which constitute the wider culture. Much of my argument has been cast in historical terms, seeking to show that the sources of penal change and the determinants of penal form are to be located not just in penological reasoning, or economic interest, or strategies of power, but also in the configurations of value, meaning, and emotion which we call "culture." In other words, and with due consideration to the interplay of variables and the multiplicity of determinants, the concerns of the last two chapters has been to show "culture" as a "determinant" of punishment.

At a time when certain sociological theories and historical interpretations threaten to reduce the phenomenon of punishment to a matter of power-plays or stripped-down strategies of control, there is some value in stressing the causal formulation implied above, even if it does seem hopelessly self-evident when pronounced in general terms. (Would anyone really deny that culture helps shape punishment?) But as a description of the relations which hold between "punishment" and "culture" this formulation tells only half of the story and perhaps the less interesting half at that. In truth, the broad patterns of cultural meaning undoubtedly influence the forms of punishment. But it is also the case that punishments and penal institutions help shape the overarching culture and contribute to the generation and regeneration of its terms. It is a two-way process—an interactive relationship—and if one is to think in terms of cause and effect or vectors of determination, then the arrows must run in both directions simultaneously (though they need not be of equal magnitude nor drawn on the same plane). Like any major social institution, punishment is shaped by broad cultural patterns which have their origins elsewhere, but it also generates its own local meanings, values, and sensibilities which contribute in a small but significant way to the *bricolage* of the dominant culture. Penal institutions are thus "cause" as well as "effect" with regard to culture.

This two-way relationship which seems to confound the mechanical notions of causality which still sometimes prevail in social science is nothing other than the constitutive interplay between the general and the particular: in this case, the local culture of penality and the generic cultural patterns of society. Foucault has captured something of the sense of this when he insists that penal relations are not just an expression of governmental power but are also a positive enactment and extension of it. In much the same way, I wish to argue that penal institutions positively construct and extend cultural meanings as well as repeating or "reaffirming" them. Instead of thinking of punishment as a passive "expression" or "reflection" of cultural patterns established elsewhere, we must strive to think of it as an active generator of cultural relations and sensibilities. The aim [here], then, is to indicate just how penal practices contribute to the making of the larger culture, and to suggest the nature and significance of that contribution.

Like all social practices, punishment can be viewed from the point of view of social action or of cultural signification. It can be approached in cause-and-effect terms as an institution which "does things" or in interpretative what-does-it-mean terms as an institution which "says things." (The distinction which this implies is undoubtedly analytical rather than real, and may obscure more than it reveals, but it does describe different modes of analysis which currently exist.) To a large extent, penologists have tended to analyse punishment in terms of social action and have been concerned to trace the impact of its practices in terms of its direct effects upon those immediately affected by its activities. Punishment is viewed as a set of practices which incarcerate, supervise, deprive of resources, or otherwise regulate and control offenders, and the task of the penologist is to measure the direct effects of these actions, tracing the reformative, deterrent, or incapacitative consequences of penal measure upon the population of offenders who have undergone sanctions. Penological research is thus typically the measurement and assessment of punishment conceived as a form of direct social action.

Even within conventional penology, however, it is recognized that punishment is also intended to address a wider population to speak to potential offenders and to the public at large and that in this respect it operates not by behavioural methods or physical action but instead by means of symbols, signs, declarations, and rhetorical devices. A few penologists have set about tracing these wider effects of penality, looking for evidence of "general deterrence" or for indications that sentencing decisions affect levels of public satisfaction or insecurity but, on the whole, penologists have been unhappy with the unavoidable imprecision involved in research of this kind. The difficulties of accurate measurement, the lack of reliable data, and the impossibility of isolating penal variables from other attitude-forming forces, have led most penologists and criminologists to limit their research to more immediate and more tangible penological effects. ...

2. Penality Communicates Meaning

The suggestion that will be pursued [here] is that penal practices, discourses, and institutions play an active part in the generative process through which shared meaning, value, and ultimately culture are produced and reproduced in society. Punishment, among other things, is a communicative and didactic institution. Through the media of its practices and declarations it puts into effect and into cultural circulation some of the categories and distinctions through which we give meaning to our world.

Values, conceptions, sensibilities, and social meanings—culture, in short—do not just exist in the form of a natural atmosphere which envelopes social action and makes it meaningful. Rather, they are actively created and recreated by our social practices and institutions and punishment plays its part in this generative and regenerative process. Punishment is one of the many institutions which helps construct and support the social world by producing the shared categories and authoritative classifications through which individuals understand each other and themselves. In its own way, penal practice provides an organizing cultural framework whose declarations and actions serve as an interpretative grid through which people evaluate conduct and make moral sense of their experience. Penality thus acts as a regulatory social mechanism in two distinct respects: it regulates conduct directly through the physical medium of social action, but it also regulates meaning, thought, attitude and hence conduct through the rather different medium of signification. ...

The suggestion which I wish to make here, and to explore in the pages that follow, is that penality communicates meaning not just about crime and punishment but also about power, authority, legitimacy, normality, morality, personhood, social relations, and a host of other tangential matters. Penal signs and symbols are one part of an authoritative, institutional discourse which seeks to organize our moral and political understanding and to educate our sentiments and sensibilities. They provide a continuous, repetitive set of instructions as to how we should think about good and evil, normal and pathological, legitimate and illegitimate, order and disorder. Through their judgments, condemnations, and classifications they teach us (and persuade us) how to judge, what to condemn, and how to classify, and they supply a set of languages, idioms, and vocabularies with which to do so. These signifying practices also tell us where to locate social authority, how to preserve order and community, where to look for social dangers, and how to feel about these matters, while the evocative effect of penal symbols sets off chains of reference and association in our minds, linking the business of punishment into questions of politics, morality, and social order. In short, the practices, institutions, and discourses of penality all *signify*, and the meanings which are conveyed thereby tend to outrun the immediacies of crime and punishment and "speak of" broader and more extended issues. Penality is thus a cultural text or perhaps better, a cultural performance which communicates with a variety of social audiences and conveys an extended range of meanings. No doubt it is "read" and understood in very different ways by different social groups and the data we have on this crucial issue of "reception" (as the literary critics call it) are woefully inadequate. But if we are to understand the social effects of punishment then we are obliged to trace this positive capacity to produce meaning and create "normality" as well as its more negative capacity to suppress and silence deviance. ...

In order to deal with these important issues clearly and without unnecessary restriction, I have chosen to take up this question of penal signification and deal with it explicitly, using concepts which are appropriate to the problem at hand. And rather than assume as do the functionalist accounts of Durkheim and certain Marxists that one already knows how penality communicates and with what effects, I will be addressing the issues in a way which is appropriate to the state of our knowledge, which is to say by means of some very basic enquiries. To that end, I will raise the following simple questions: how, and by what means, do penal practices signify and communicate meaning? What are punishment's social audiences? What kinds of meanings and categories do penal practices convey? How have these meanings varied over time? And finally why, if the foregoing is true, is punishment such a resonant and expressive social institution?

3. How Does Penality Signify?

When we inspect the varied activities which make up the penal complex with a view to investigating its communicative or signifying aspects, our attention is immediately drawn to the more public and declaratory practices of the institution. In the past, these would have included all those sanctions which were executed in public, before a watching crowd such as the pillory, the whipping cart, the stocks, the scaffold, or the various kinds of public works and public humiliations. Included too would be the rituals of public confession and the semi-official printed broadsheets which were sold to the public, both of which articulated in more explicit terms the moral message which these public punishments sought to convey. Nowadays, of course, penal sanctions are rarely executed in public, but there are still elements of penal practice which are deliberately designed for public consumption and which are communicated to a social audience. One thinks particularly of the judicial declaration of sentence, and any remarks which the judge chooses to append to this crucial speech-act: a declaration or performative statement which is directed not just at the offender but also via the press and the public gallery to victims, to potential offenders, and to the public at large. In the late twentieth century, as in the eighteenth, the moment of sentencing is understood as "an occasion for addressing the multitude" and there is seldom a newspaper which appears without carrying an account of some judge's remarks and the circumstances which prompted them.

There are also other occasions and other ways in which our penal institutions set about addressing a wide audience. Government policy statements are written to describe and justify penal practice to the public. The same is true of all the annual reports produced by the many agencies involved in the criminal justice process, and of the reports of commissions of enquiry set up to investigate specific scandals or to provide a basis for new reforms. An equally prolific, though less authoritative, form of penological representation derives from the work of penal reformers, critics, and, nowadays, academics, whose accounts of the penal system, its philosophical basis, or its inherent problems and need for change often reach a wide audience, and occasionally attain a semi-official status especially if the authorities choose to accept their findings or their recommendations for reform. These documents, and others, provide a public representation of penal practice, in an orthodox textual form, often composed in equal part of factual description, persuasive rhetoric, and institutional propaganda. And to the extent that historians and sociologists have examined the signifying (or "ideological") aspects of punishment, it is usually to these texts that they have first turned.

However, to confine our analysis to the speech-acts, performances, and publications which are officially intended for public consumption would be to ignore some of the most important signifying aspects of penality. In particular, it would neglect all those practices and discourses which function as instrumental, operative elements of the sanctioning process but which also perform a crucial rhetorical or representational role at the same time. If we wish to understand the cultural messages conveyed by punishment we need to study not just the grandiloquent public statements which are occasionally made but also the pragmatic repetitive routines of daily practice, for these routines contain within them distinctive patterns of meaning and symbolic forms which are enacted and expressed every time a particular procedure is adopted, a technical language used, or a specific sanction imposed. Despite the attention given to policy documents, commission reports, and philosophical statements, it is the daily routine of sanctioning and institutional practice which does most to create a particular framework of meaning (Foucault would say a "regime of truth") in the penal realm, and it is to these practical routines that we should look first of all to discover the values, meanings, and conceptions which are embodied and expressed in penality.

It would seem, then, that the conventional distinctions drawn between instrumental activities and symbolic activities, or between "social action" and "cultural meaning" are of little use here. For these analytical divisions imply a separation which in reality does not exist as we have seen, in penality the instrumental *is* symbolic and the social act of punishment, however mundane, is at the same time an expression of cultural meaning. Perhaps a better set of terms to use in this context would be the notion of a "signifying practice" (which can be discursive or non-discursive) and of a "practical rhetoric" both of which have the advantage of traversing the artificial divide between language and action, the mental and the physical, the ideal and the real. In any case, the important thing to realize is that *all* practices, of whatever kind, are potentially signifying practices. Whatever else it does, even the most mundane form of conduct in the social world is also a possible source of expression, of symbolization, and of meaningful communication—every action is also a gesture. And as I shall argue in a moment, official penal practice is particularly laden with social and cultural significance.

The presence of symbolic meaning within the everyday forms of pragmatic penal action is most easily observed if we consider the practice of sentencing. In "passing sentence" the sentencer performs a routine, instrumental action which has the effect of activating a subsequent legal process. He or she performs a speech-act "I sentence you to three years imprisonment" which has the practical effect of authorizing and setting in motion a procedure of incarceration. The activity of sentencing is thus an operative element in an instrumental process of dealing with offenders. But the declaration of sentence also conveys a symbolic statement which may be read and understood by a wide audience (or audiences) beyond the court-room.

At the minimum, the sentence may be repeating a message which is already well known for example, that the legal system condemns acts of criminal violence, and will punish them severely. In such cases, the sanction of "three years imprisonment" signals a particular level of social censure, and fixes the meaning of that censure in a way that will be conventionally understood. Thus "imprisonment" signifies the stigma or infamy of true criminality; "three years" further qualifies the message, showing the censure to be of medium severity, pitched somewhere between the maximum and minimum available. If this kind of sentence is the standard tariff for the offence in question, then the symbolic statement which it contains is likely to occur without comment or analysis on the part of the public, and so the significance of the message will be merely reaffirmative. But the importance of the communication is dramatically heightened if the symbolic message which it contains is unexpected or in some way controversial. So, for example, if the three years imprisonment was imposed for a particularly heinous rape, its comparative leniency might be taken to symbolize a denigration of women's rights, or a demeaning of the particular victim involved, and might seem to imply (or "symbolize") a particular understanding of the relations between men and women, and their relative worth, which resonates with patriarchal attitudes and traditions. On the other hand, if the same sentence was given to a drunk driver or someone found guilty of insider trading on the stock market, then a very different political and social message would be implied which would, in present circumstances, disturb the taken-for-granted evaluations of such conduct and the state's attitude towards it.

It seems clear from this example that as well as being a cog in an instrumental process, sentencing is a signifying practice of some importance. The various sanctions available to the court are not merely a repertoire of techniques for handling offenders, they are also a system of signs which are used to convey specific meanings in terms which are generally understood by the social audience. Each specific sanction has attached to it a recognizable symbolism, so that, in any particular context, imprisonment means one thing, a fine another, probation something else, and so on. Thus whenever a sentence is passed, the sentencer knowingly deploys a conventional device for the expression of meaning, and engages in a symbolic communication of greater or lesser significance.

...

When the penal system adopts a particular conception of criminals and criminality, or a specific way of classifying prisoners, or a particular psychology of motivation and reform; or when it begins to use a particular vocabulary to describe offenders and to characterize their conduct, such conceptions and vocabularies are never confined to the in-house activities of expert practitioners. Instead they feed back into the wider society, and frequently enter into conventional wisdom and general circulation. Terms such as "degenerate," "feeble-minded" "imbecile," "delinquent," "kleptomaniac," "psychopath," and "career criminal" quickly became common currency after only a few years of official use, as did the associated vocabularies of "treatment" and "rehabilitation." Nor are these merely disembodied words, used without meaningful consequence, for their adoption in common use brings with it a whole way of thinking which slowly changes social attitudes, or at least makes available new vocabularies of motive and new explanatory languages with which to think about crime and human conduct. Moreover, as we will see, to represent the business of punishment in quasi-scientific terms, and to organize penal practices accordingly, promotes a particular image of the state and of its authority, and of its relationship to offenders and other citizens. Indeed, it has been argued with some force that the official adoption of scientific languages and rehabilitative forms in modern penal institutions has sometimes had more to do with the cultural symbolism involved than with the desire fully to implement the practices that they imply. As anyone who has compared official rhetoric to the actualities of institutions will know, many "policies" exist more at the level of public representation than of operational practice.

So penal practices and discourses, however workaday or instrumental they may seem, tend simultaneously to signify in ways which connect with the wider culture. Indeed, what information we have about the formulation of penal policy and the management of institutional regimes strongly suggests that penal functionaries are conscious of this symbolic resonance and take pains to control the way in which their practices will be interpreted. A crucial intermediary here is, however, the various media which relay and represent penal events to the public. And since these media have their own dynamics and commercial concerns, it is generally the case that news values and editorial interests restrict and select the penal messages that are effectively conveyed to a wide public audience.

...

6. The Significance of Punishment

Why is this? Why is punishment apparently capable of such symbolic resonance and force? What makes it an area of social life to which people attend and from which they draw meaning?

Sociologists such as Georges Gurvitch or Mary Douglas might attribute this symbolizing powers to punishment's status as an arena of social tension and social conflict. It is, after all, the site at which law and deviance are brought most visibly together, where social anomalies and contradictions are directly addressed, the point at which purity and danger dramatically intersect. Penal institutions deal with human and moral problems of a profound and intractable kind with the fragility of social relations, the limits of socialization, the persistence of human evil, and the insecurity of social life. And as anthropologists have shown, the intractable problems of social and human existence provide a rich soil for the development of myths, rites, and symbols as cultures strive to control and make sense of these difficult areas of experience. Punishment as an archetypal feature of human existence figures prominently in some of the most important cultural artefacts of Western society, including classical drama, traditional cosmologies, religions such as Christianity, and heresies such as psychoanalysis. The practical business of punishing offenders thus takes place within a cultural space which is already laden with meaning and which lends itself easily to symbolic use.

Moreover, ... the institutions of punishment connect directly into other major social realms and institutions, linking up with the circuits of power, exchange, morality, and sensibility which hold society together. In this sense punishment has some of the qualities of what Marcel Mauss described as a "total social fact." It is an area of social life which spills over into other areas and which takes its social meaning as much from these connections as from itself, thus accumulating a symbolic depth and richness which go beyond its immediate functioning.

Punishment also seems to fit the description of what Shils has called a societal "center," which is to say it forms a key point in the social universe, a strategic location where power is expressed, identities created, social relations forged, and life or death decisions made. As we saw earlier, the nature of such "centers" their intrinsic importance as foundations for social order makes them charismatic. They attract the attention and the imagination of members of society by virtue of their key place in the order of things and their capacity to make things happen in an authoritative way. Thus it is something more than mere entertainment that draws attention to the process of punishing much of which is routine in the extreme. Rather it is the perceived importance of the institution and its ability to draw upon the drama of large events. One might even use this explanation to help account for the "anti-charisma" of certain notorious criminals, whose personal encounters with these forces of social order seem to lend their lives a fascination which they would otherwise entirely lack.

No doubt, too, there is a psychological dimension to this phenomenon. As I have already suggested, the socialized members of a society have usually experienced an emotional training in punishment and the threat of punishment which leaves them with a lasting emotional investment in the matter. The drama of crime and punishment acts out "for real" a psychic conflict between instinctive drives and their repression which most adults experience to some degree. This being the case, the symbols of penality seem to resonate with the personal memories and associations of individuals in particular ways, producing attitudes and involvements which would not otherwise arise. As politicians have frequently discovered, penal rhetoric can be "good for persuading with" precisely because it touches upon some of the deep-seated anxieties and ambivalences which individuals commonly experience.

The meanings projected by penality today or indeed at any time are many and varied. Its rhetorics and signifying practices combine to form a dense cacophony of sounds and images rather than a carefully orchestrated message, although here and there clear patterns emerge and dominant themes are sounded. Even the basic representations which I have discussed are often, in practice, confusingly mixed up together. At various points in the penal realm one sees the imagery of "moral man," "economic man," and "psychological man" fleetingly appear as different procedures or agencies reflect disparate conceptions of human nature and its workings. In one court-room a social-contract state may be punishing while in another the welfare state is dispensing help. Penal rhetoric, like penality itself, is the living embodiment of a long historical tradition within which arguments have occurred and differences remain. Its multiplicity of meaning is thus a reflection of its historical development, in which our strategy, vocabulary, or conception has been laid upon another, without expunging all traces of the earlier style. The result is a kind of mosaic or palimpsest in which the archaic and the contemporary are able to coexist.

NOTE

The interest in expressive or communicative theories has grown and Garland can claim no monopoly: see the thoughtful article by R.A. Duff, "Penal Communications: Recent Work in the Philosophy of Punishment" (1996), 20 *Crime and Justice* 1. Also, Anthony

Bottoms has suggested that von Hirsch's recent emphasis on censure as exemplified by his book *Censure and Sanctions* (Oxford: Oxford University Press, 1993) has moved his basic theoretical approach close to a communicative theory: see A. Bottoms, "Five Puzzles in von Hirsch's Theory of Punishment," in A. Ashworth and M. Wasik, eds., *Fundamentals of Sentencing Theory: Essays in Honour of Andrew von Hirsch* (Oxford: Clarendon Press, 1998), at 84-89.

At the end of this introductory chapter, it is important to note that the chapter's initial focus was on punishment and the traditional debate between retributivist and utilitarian justifications for punishment. When we moved into the more recent period, we observed how contemporary thinkers have wrestled with issues that go beyond any general justifications and attempt to provide theoretical explanations for how punishments ought to be allocated across a range of offences. In other words, the debate shifted from punishment to the more pragmatic institution of sentencing and its distribution of punishments. The next chapter continues in this direction but moves from theory to the set of concepts and methodologies that Canadian judges have used to decide which sentencing option should be used in a particular case.

ADDITIONAL READING

Canadian Sentencing Commission (Hon. O. Archambault, Chair), *Sentencing Reform—A Canadian Approach: Report of the Canadian Sentencing Commission* (Ottawa: the commission, 1987).

Andrew von Hirsch, *Censure and Sanctions* (Oxford: Oxford University Press, 1993).

Andrew von Hirsch and Andrew Ashworth, eds., *Principled Sentencing* (Boston: Northeastern University Press, 1992).

Ted Honderich, *Punishment: The Supposed Justifications* (London: Hutchison & Co., 1969).

Igor Primoratz, *Justifying Legal Punishment* (London: Humanities Press International, Inc., 1989).

A. John Simmons, Marshall Cohen, Joshua Cohen, and Charles Beitz, eds., *Punishment— A Philosophy and Public Affairs Reader* (Princeton: Princeton University Press, 1995).

Michael Tonry, *Sentencing Matters* (New York: Oxford University Press, 1996)

Nigel Walker, *Why Punish?* (Oxford: Oxford University Press, 1991).

CHAPTER TWO

Judicial Aims and the Legislated Context

I. INTRODUCTION

This chapter traces the evolution of judicial attitudes toward sentencing and the changing statutory framework, especially the 1996 amendments to the *Criminal Code*, RSC 1985, c. C-46, as amended.

The previous chapter illustrates the divergence of philosophical views about punishment. The vigourous debate is understandable given that it encompasses fundamental questions about the relationship between the state and its citizens. Punishment is, after all, about the application of coercive force. Of course, punishment and sentencing are not synonymous or congruent concepts. Sentencing involves considerations and objectives that are not purely punitive.

Aside from controversies about the premises of sentencing, there is also considerable debate about the efficacy of sentencing within the administration of criminal justice. This is primarily the domain of modern criminology, which is concerned with not only theoretical aspects of sentencing, but empirical assessments of the administration of criminal justice. This chapter continues the examination of themes initiated in Chapter 1 but shifts the focus to the positive law as stipulated by Parliament and applied by judges. The primary purpose of this chapter is to examine sources of positive law in order to identify the aims of sentencing that are formally recognized in Canada. The secondary purpose is to consider whether Canadian law reveals any discernible ranking or priority among recognized aims of sentencing. In this chapter, we begin to examine whether there is any more consistency or coherence in Canadian law on sentencing than there is in debates concerning the philosophical dimensions of the subject.

II. THE IMPORTANCE OF JUDICIAL DISCRETION

Until 1996, the *Criminal Code* did not provide any guidance as to the objectives of sentencing or its relevant principles. Judges filled in the conceptual blanks as part of a discretionary exercise. Most jurists agree that the chief aim of sentencing is the protection of society. But the interpretation of this principle has often been uncertain or contradictory, partly because it is inherently unclear and partly because it allows for conflicting views about appropriate outcomes. For example, in one case protection may point to incarceration, while in another case it may mean enhancing the offender's rehabilitative prospects. The scope for debate and disagreement has produced a degree of disparity in sentencing that may be inevitable.

It is self-evident that a proper and just sentence must be a fit sentence. Perhaps it is also self-evident that two reasonable people could reach different conclusions about what is a fit sentence in a given case and, moreover, that neither of them need necessarily have made an error of judgment. Sentencing, by definition, requires flexibility to ensure a result that is fit for the offender and, more broadly, fit for the administration of criminal justice. In Canada, it has always been thought that the best mechanism for ensuring this result is the trained use of judicial discretion. Parliament has rarely prescribed sentences that must be imposed following a finding of guilt. In some exceptional instances, Parliament has declared penalties that must be imposed, such as a minimum term of imprisonment, but the norm is that each offence allows a sentence within a maximum term of imprisonment or an alternative to imprisonment.

Although the 1996 amendments (discussed later in this chapter) have refined the debate, judicial discretion continues to play the central role in sentencing, and its importance is acknowledged in the *Criminal Code* in much the same form as it appeared in the 1892 legislation:

> 718.3(1) Where an enactment prescribes different degrees or kinds of punishment in respect of an offence, the punishment to be imposed is, subject to the limitations prescribed in the enactment, in the discretion of the court that convicts a person who commits the offence.
>
> (2) Where an enactment prescribes punishment in respect of an offence, the punishment to be imposed is, subject to the limitations prescribed in the enactment, in the discretion of the court that convicts a person who commits the offence, but no punishment is a minimum punishment unless it is declared to be a minimum punishment.

The breadth of the discretion recognized in the law of sentencing should be immediately apparent. Judges are empowered not only to determine what is a fit sentence in the individual case, but they also have a discretion to determine the proper aims of sentencing decisions in the general run of cases. Wherever there is such discretion, there is also the possibility of disparity in approach and in result.

The Amalgam or "Wise Blending" of Values

Canadian courts have adopted an approach that allows judges to recognize and weigh various aims of sentencing, including rehabilitation, incapacitation, retribution, denunciation and deterrence. In *R v. Lyons* (1987), 61 CR (3d) 1 (SCC), a dangerous offender case, La Forest J said (at 24):

> In a rational system of sentencing, the respective importance of prevention, deterrence, retribution and rehabilitation will vary according to the nature of the crime and the circumstances of the offence.

This approach has made individualization the key perspective for judicial decision making. The following two cases show how broadly defined judicial discretion has been applied with respect to both the identification of, and choice between, competing objectives.

R v. Willaert
(1953), 105 CCC 172 (Ont. CA)

MACKAY JA: The appellant was tried at Sarnia on September 16, 17, 18, 19 and 22, 1952, before Barlow J and a jury, on an indictment charging that he on May 2, 1952, committed rape on one Shirley Post, and was found guilty. The learned trial Judge sentenced the appellant to imprisonment for life. This application is taken for leave to appeal against the length of sentence.

By s. 299 of the *Cr. Code*, a person guilty of rape may be sentenced "to suffer death or to imprisonment for life, and to be whipped." …

A useful statement of the policy of the law as administered in England is set forth in 9 Hals, 2nd ed., pp. 254-5, para. 362: "The policy of the law is, as regards most crimes, to fix a maximum penalty, which is intended only for the worst cases, and to leave to the discretion of the judge to determine to what extent in a particular case the punishment awarded should approach to or recede from the maximum limit. The exercise of this discretion is a matter of prudence and not of law."

There is little in the record itself to mitigate the gravity of the crime; nevertheless, in measuring sentence, every circumstance should be taken into consideration, and in the exercise of judicial discretion regard should be had to: the age of the prisoner; his past and present condition of life; the nature of the crime; whether the prisoner previously had a good character; whether it is a first offence; whether he has a family dependent upon him, the temptation; whether the crime was deliberate or committed on momentary impulse; the penalty provided by the Code or statute; whether the offence is one for which under the code the offender is liable to corporal punishment and, if so, whether corporal punishment should be imposed.

I am respectfully of opinion that there are three principles of criminal justice requiring earnest consideration in the determination of punishment, *viz.*, deterrence, reformation and retribution.

The governing principle of deterrence is, within reason and common sense, that the emotion of fear should be brought into play so that the offender may be made afraid to offend again and also so that others who may have contemplated offending will be restrained by the same controlling emotion. Society must be reasonably assured that the punishment meted out to one will not actually encourage others, and when some form of crime has become widespread the element of deterrence must look more to the restraining of others than to the actual offender before the Court.

Reformation is the most hopeful element in the question of punishment in most cases, and it is in that direction that the efforts of those concerned with criminal justice will be more and more directed. But reformation, too, has its distinct limitations. It has been found in England that many who have passed through all the stages of binding over to keep the peace, probation, approved school, Borstal institution, and prison, have yet become habitual criminals. They appear to be beyond all human reformative agencies.

The underlying and governing idea in the desire for retribution is in no way an eye for an eye or a tooth for a tooth, but rather that the community is anxious to express its repudiation of the crime committed and to establish and assert the welfare of the community against the evil in its midst. Thus, the infliction of punishment becomes a source of security to all and "is elevated to the first rank of benefits, when it is regarded not as an act of wrath or vengeance against a guilty or unfortunate individual who has given way to mischievous inclinations, but as an indispensable sacrifice to the common safety": See Bentham, Rationale of Punishment, p. 20, quoted at p. 255 of Halsbury *loc. cit.*

I am respectfully of opinion that the true function of criminal law in regard to punishment is in a wise blending of the deterrent and reformative, with retribution not entirely disregarded, and with a constant appreciation that the matter concerns not merely the Court and the offender but also the public and society as a going concern. Punishment is, therefore, an art—a very difficult art—essentially practical, and directly related to the existing needs of society. A punishment appropriate today might have been quite unacceptable 200 years ago and probably would be absurd 200 years hence. It is therefore impossible to lay down hard and fast and permanent rules.

• • •

The tendency in recent years has been to impose more moderate sentences. At one time it was commonly assumed that the only purpose of punishment was to punish, but today its function is conceived in very different terms. It may be to try to reclaim the offender for society, to induce and stimulate habits of regularity and reliability even to compensate partially for an education that ended prematurely, and generally to try to awaken in the mind of the vicious and irresponsible a sense of the obligations of life and citizenship. Such moderation in sentence may not be warranted in the case of confirmed criminals but in that of the first offender an effort at reclamation is surely the part of wisdom and prudence in judicial discretion.

NOTE

The general principle stated in *Willaert* remains good law: a proper sentence requires a wise blending of penal aims to be "fit" for the offence and the offender. Some of the more specific assertions made by Mackay JA have been eclipsed by later developments.

The discretion of the sentencing judge includes specific options that might be considered, but it also extends to a determination of what are "fit" or appropriate aims in sentencing. The scope of discretion, in both senses, might be constrained by the guidance of appellate courts or, in some instances, by legislative directive, but it is clear that policy considerations are central to the evolution of the law on sentencing. With *Willaert* in mind, examine the declaration of principles and objectives in the following opinion.

R v. Preston
(1990), 79 CR (3d) 61 (BC CA)

WOOD JA: The Crown applies for leave to appeal, and if leave is granted, appeals from the sentences imposed with respect to each of three convictions recorded against the respondent for possession of the narcotic diacetylmorphine (heroin). In each case the passing of sentence was suspended for a period of two years, and the respondent was ordered to be released on the terms and conditions contained in three separate probation orders.

The matter first came before three judges of this court on 22nd November 1989, at which time after hearing from counsel it was adjourned for reargument before a division of five judges. In the interim counsel were advised that the court wished to take this opportunity to reconsider, free from the constraints that may be seen to be imposed by any of its previous decisions, certain questions which seem pertinent to the issues raised on these appeals. Following the very full submissions of counsel, during which there was much helpful discussion, those questions can properly be restated as follows:

(a) Whether either general or specific deterrence must necessarily outweigh reha-bilitation as a factor in the sentencing of a non-violent addicted substance abuse;

(b) Under what circumstances should this court interfere with the exercise of judgment by a trial judge who has concluded that the offender is a reason-able risk for rehabilitation; and

(c) Whether or not it is appropriate, from time to time, for this court to re-examine the policies which underlie its previous decisions touching upon the issues raised in the first two questions.

II

The respondent is now 41 years old. She has been a heroin addict for over 20 years. In that time she has made a number of unsuccessful attempts to overcome her addic-tion. As a result of her lack of skills and education, her addiction, and poor health brought on by the self-abuse associated with that addiction, she has not worked for most of that time. She has been on social assistance continuously since 1974.

Up to the time of the matters now before the court, she has amassed at total record of 23 convictions, including eight for narcotics offences, four of which were for trafficking in heroin, five soliciting or other prostitution related convictions, and an assortment of escape, unlawfully at large, failing to appear and breach of probation convictions. Apart from concurrent sentences of two years less one day on three counts of traffick-ing in heroin, imposed in 1976, her longest sentences have been 18 months on a charge of confinement, also in 1976, and 18 months for another heroin trafficking conviction in 1985. All other sentences imposed upon her have been for 90 days or less.

...

While conceding that the prospect of full and complete rehabilitation was not assured, counsel for the respondent pointed out to the trial judge that whatever hope there was would be destroyed by a term of imprisonment. Counsel for the Crown, stressing the importance of deterrence and the protection of the public, submitted that in light of the nature of the offence and her previous criminal record the respondent ought to be sentenced to a term of imprisonment.

The trial judge gave lengthy reasons for making the orders he did. He was clearly aware of the many decisions of this court, which have either upheld or imposed sub-stantial periods of imprisonment for similar offences committed by similar offenders. In the end he took the view that he ought to order a disposition of these charges which would encourage what he saw as a genuine motivation for rehabilitation on the part of the respondent.

···

There is no doubt that heroin addicts present as poor candidates for rehabilitation, if such is measured only in terms of the number who successfully overcome their addiction. Little in the way of reliable statistics is available, but what information there is suggests that it is unrealistic to talk of a "cure" for heroin addiction. Success is measured by the extent to which the addiction is controlled, often by substitute drugs which can be legally prescribed. Some of these substitutes, like methadone, are themselves highly addictive, but their pharmacological properties are such that the addict can, if willing, maintain a relatively normal and even useful lifestyle, free from the need to commit crimes to support the craving for heroin.

···

The role of incarceration in this cycle not only fails to achieve its ultimate goal which is the protection of society, but it also costs society a great deal of money, which might better be spent elsewhere. Statistics Canada reports that during the 1988/1989 fiscal year the cost of maintaining a prisoner in a custodial facility averaged $46,282 in a federal penitentiary and $36,708 in a provincial jail.

The object of the entire criminal justice system, of course, is the protection of society, and I say at once that if incarceration is the only way of protecting society from a particular offender then, transitory and expensive though it may be, that form of protection must be invoked. But where, as in this case, the danger to society results from the potential of the addict to commit offences to support her habit, and it appears to the court that there is a reasonable chance that she may succeed in an attempt to control her addiction, then it becomes necessary to consider the ultimate benefit to society if that chance becomes a reality.

···

With respect, that benefit seems obvious. If the chance for rehabilitation becomes a reality, society will be permanently protected from the danger which she otherwise presents in the fashion described above. As well, the cost associated with her frequent incarceration will be avoided.

Without making any real effort to draw a distinction between cases of possession on the one hand, and those of trafficking or possession for the purpose of trafficking on the other, this court and other courts of appeal across the country have repeatedly stressed the need to impose deterrent sentences in drug cases. Where the drug is heroin, and in particular where there is a prior criminal record, adherence to this principle has usually led to a sentence of incarceration: see *R v. Ross* (1955), 21 CR 141, 15 WWR 1 34 (BC CA); *R v. Rogers* (1965), 46 CR 309, 52 WWR 423 (BC CA); *R v. Spicer*, 28 CCC (2d) 334, [1976] WWD 32 (Alta. CA); *R v. Spreckley*, [1984] BCWLD 2519, BC CA, Vancouver No. CA000579, 8th February 1984 (unreported); and *R v. McMorland*, [1985] BCWLD 2098, BC CA, Vancouver No. CA002700, 26th April 1985 (unreported).

···

What then is the proper approach for the court to take when sentencing in a case such as this? When the benefit to be derived to society as a whole, as a result of the successful rehabilitation of a heroin addict, is balanced against the ultimate futility of the short-term protection which the community enjoys from a sentence of incarceration, I believe it is right to conclude that the principle of deterrence should yield to any reasonable chance of rehabilitation which may show itself to the court imposing sentence. To give the offender a chance to successfully overcome his or her addiction, in such circumstances, is to risk little more than the possibility of failure, with the result that the cycle of addiction leading to crime leading to incarceration will resume, something that is inevitable, in any event, if the chance is not taken. On the other hand, as has already been pointed out, if the effort succeeds the result is fundamentally worthwhile to society as a whole.

I am not persuaded that the trial judge erred in principle in this case when he considered the rehabilitation of the respondent to be of greater importance than any deterrent value that a sentence of incarceration might have. Indeed, I am of the view that he was right in the approach that he took.

Underlying much of the argument of counsel for the Crown was the suggestion that to approve the disposition of the trial judge in this case would be to "decriminalize" heroin. Nothing could be further from the truth. A court would only be justified in giving more weight to the possibility of rehabilitation, rather than deterrence, where there is a reasonable basis for believing that the motivation for such change is genuine and there is a reasonable possibility that it will succeed. There will undoubtedly be many cases in which no such prospect exists, and in such cases it would be an error in principle to allow the factor of deterrence to be overshadowed by the illusion of rehabilitation. I have every confidence in the ability of the trial judges in this province to successfully separate fact from fiction in such matters.

...

It is also worth noting that the report of the Canadian Sentencing Commission (the "Archambault" Commission), *Sentencing Reform: A Canadian Approach* (1987), recommends that possession of a narcotic carry a maximum sentence of six months, together with an unqualified presumption that such sentence be served in the community, rather than in a custodial facility. While the recommendations of the commission do not have the force of law, and cannot therefore be said, in that sense, to represent the will of either Parliament or the people, they are nonetheless the end product of a process which included over two years of extensive public hearings held all across the country. In making its recommendations the commission recognized and took into account the fact that one of the goals of sentencing is to preserve the authority of, and to promote respect for, the law through the public's perception that the commission of offences will be met by the imposition of just sanctions.

To the extent that this goal must be considered by the court when imposing sentence, it may be, and often is, referred to as a "factor" of sentencing. In *R v. Pettigrew*, [1990] BCWLD 1260, BC CA, Vancouver No. CA011983, 12th April 1990 [now reported 56 CCC (3d) 390], Taylor JA referred to it, at p. 5 [p. 3 94 (CCC)], as:

... the elusive "fifth factor" of the sentencing system—the imposition of punishment, so as [sic] to speak, "for its own sake," rather than for isolation of the offender, rehabilitation, deterrence of the offender or deterrence of others.

As Taylor JA pointed out, this factor has been given different labels over the years, as its role in the rationale of sentencing has undergone at least the perception, if not the reality, of change. Retribution was one of its earlier titles. This court rejected retribution per se as a legitimate goal of sentencing in *R v. Hinch*, 62 WWR 205, 2 CRNS 350, [1968] 3 CCC 39. Denunciation has been used as a descriptive term for this factor as well. This court has from time to time upheld or imposed sentences designed to express society's abhorrence of the crime committed. Another, more recent, perception is that the punishment imposed ought to represent "just deserts" for the crime committed, thus suggesting a proportionality between the moral blame-worthiness of the offender and the sanction imposed.

It is this factor of sentencing which the Crown urged upon us in this case as requir-ing that a sentence of incarceration be imposed upon the respondent.

Pettigrew was a case of manslaughter. In describing the limits within which this elusive fifth factor has application, Taylor JA said this at p. 6 of the unreported rea-sons [p. 395 (CCC)]:

> In the absence of any prescribed minimum penalty, imprisonment can be imposed on this ground only if the circumstances of the case and of the offender call for such a response. In weighing the matter the court must consider, among other things, whether any adverse effects which a denunciatory punishment would have on the rehabilitation of the offender can be justified in the over-all interests of the protection and advance-ment of society.

As things presently stand, and have stood for almost 30 years, there is no statutory minimum penalty which must be imposed on a person convicted of the offence of possession of a prohibited substance, irrespective of whether the proceedings are launched by way of indictment or by summary conviction. Furthermore, nothing was put before us by the Crown to suggest an overwhelming perception on the part of the public that persons who are convicted of such an offence must be sent to jail if the authority of and respect for the law is to be maintained.

In light of everything that has been said so far about the benefit to society if the respondent succeeds in her efforts to control her addiction to heroin, I am of the view that a sentence of imprisonment could not be justified or imposed in this case on the basis of the so-called fifth factor of sentencing.

It is important to recognize that, in the case of most offences, apart from setting the maximum punishment which can be imposed upon conviction, Parliament has consistently and deliberately avoided any involvement in setting the "policy" to be applied in matters of sentencing. Thus all policy in the law of sentencing is judge-made and it is quite incorrect to say that any change in such policy ought to be left for Parliament.

It is the courts, including this court, in decisions such as those cited above, and others, which have set the policy here being re-examined, namely that as a general rule an addicted substance abuser, who is a repeat offender and who has an extensive record, must be sentenced to jail as a consequence of a conviction for possession of a prohibited narcotic. It can hardly be suggested that we are not free to re-examine that policy form time to time. Indeed, I believe it is our duty to do so.

···

With respect to the two matters properly before us, I would grant leave to appeal. Because it has not been shown that the trial judge erred in principle, or that the sentences imposed were wrong in law, I would dismiss the appeals from the suspended sentences ordered in respect of those two convictions. I would not interfere with the terms of probation ordered, except that I would add a further term requiring the respondent to submit to random urinalysis testing for traces of heroin use, as directed by her probation officer.

NOTE

The openness and flexibility of the "amalgam" or "wise blending" approach was discussed by Cole and Manson in *Release from Imprisonment: The Law of Sentencing, Parole and Judicial Review* (Toronto: Carswell, 1990), at 16-17:

> While this blending of penal objectives permeates the sentencing process and provides both systemic and individual justifications, it generates its own inevitable tensions due to the inherent contradictory nature of some objectives. At the same time, it hides the uncomfortable observation that precision and consistency may be unattainable goals.
>
> Added to this calculus we see judicial recognition of particular factors which highlight the influence of one or another of the principles of sentencing. Cases involving youthful offenders, mentally ill offenders or recidivists, and cases arising from violence against children, women or racial minorities have provoked judges to emphasize particular principles. Thus, notwithstanding the general acceptance of the amalgam approach, the existence of some distinctive features highlights the significance of protection of the public, rehabilitation, deterrence or denunciation in direct response to the category of case.

The amalgam approach allows judges to determine sentences by referring to a range of different considerations. This approach does not assert a priority among the aims of sentencing, although the courts of the various provinces tend to develop their own rules of practice under the guidance of the Court of Appeal. The amalgam approach does not prevent the courts of different provinces from adopting different approaches, nor does it prevent judges within a single court from disagreeing among themselves. An interesting example of a conflict in perspective within a court can be seen in *R v. McGinn* (1989), 75 Sask. R 161 (CA), where the majority allowed a Crown appeal against a non-custodial sentence for possession for the purposes of trafficking that arose from the seizure of one-quarter of an ounce of marijuana. It imposed in its place a six-month period of incarceration. Vancise JA, in dissent, supported the trial judge's conclusion that a period of probation and a $300 fine was appropriate. At the heart of the opinion of Vancise JA was his view that the efficacy of general deterrence had been overemphasized for many offences where a non-custodial alternative was both reasonable and justifiable. By itself, the fundamental nature of the debate in *R v. McGinn* shows how the scope of judicial discretion can easily produce disparate results.

III. SHIFTING PRIORITIES IN JUDICIAL DISCRETION

Over time, the amalgam approach has made protection of society, deterrence, denunciation, rehabilitation, and reparation the major objectives of sentencing. These objectives are often referred to as the principles of sentencing, but that is an erroneous characterization. Principles are substantive rules that shape how judicial discretion is applied to assign priority to these objectives and to determine the relevant sentencing choices. Currently, the most important principles are proportionality, parity, and restraint. However, judicial attitudes toward sentencing objectives and the applicable principles have not always been consistent, and certainly have not been static. When reading the following cases, try to assess whether the decision reflects a change in judicial attitude and, if so, consider what may have motivated it.

A. Proportionality, Culpability, and Driving Offences Causing Death or Bodily Harm

R v. Sweeney, infra, was one of a series of cases involving penitentiary sentences for driving offences where bodily harm or death had resulted. The British Columbia Court of Appeal decided to hear the group of cases together so that it could assess whether the level of sentencing had been creeping upward and, if so, whether the increased penalties were justified or not. Wood JA considers the the relative weight that should, in his view, be given to the different aims in sentencing decisions. However, there is another point that runs through the opinion—that a fit sentence must reflect the blameworthiness of the offender as it is defined by the substantive criminal law.

R v. Sweeney
(1992), 11 CR (4th) 1 (BC CA) (footnotes omitted)

WOOD JA (concurring in the result) McEACHERN CJBC (concurring): These appeals presented the court with a rare opportunity to undertake a thorough re-examination of the principles governing the imposition of sanctions in our criminal justice system. We sat five judges so that we could embark upon that exercise free from the constraints imposed by previous decisions. I believe that it is important, not only for the guidance of trial judges, but also for the information of the public, that such an opportunity not be missed.

II

While the proper role of this court on a sentence appeal is to determine the fitness of the sentence imposed in the court below according to the application of recognized legal principles, we do not perform that function in a legal vacuum devoid of any understanding of the realities of life to which our decisions must be applied. In order to understand the approach which I have taken on these appeals, it is necessary to consider some of those realities which cannot be ignored while en route to a principled determination of the fitness of the sentences imposed below.

I start with the fact that the drinking driver is an enormous social problem. The numbers alone tell us that. Every year over 10,000 convictions are recorded in this province for drinking/driving offences. The experts agree that these numbers represent only a fraction of the number of such offences actually committed. While only a small number of those who are caught have caused death or bodily harm, it is beyond dispute that in most cases that is more the result of good luck than it is an accurate reflection of the risk or danger created by such an offender.

Words alone cannot adequately describe the havoc caused by the drinking driver who is not caught in time. Beyond acknowledging the tragic and utterly futile human loss which lies in the scattered wake of such an offender's path, it is impossible to measure the consequences of his crime other than through the heartache and suffering of the surviving victims.

Yet notwithstanding our alarm over the death and destruction caused on our highways by drinking drivers, we are reluctant, as a society, to impose an absolute prohibition on drinking and driving. By setting the legal blood alcohol limit at 80 mg of alcohol in 100 ml of blood, rather than at zero, we do, in fact, permit some drinking and driving, and because the social use of alcohol is so widespread, we therefore accept the certainty that many of those who drink will also drive. Thus as a society we have clearly opted to accept the risk that there will be those who drink more than the law permits and then drive, either because they do not care, because they think they will not be caught or because they are chronic alcohol abusers whose illness destroys both the ability to know when the line has been crossed and the fear of getting caught.

...

Ordinary, reasonable and fair-minded people expect that any punishment meted out under criminal law will bear some direct proportionality to the moral culpability of the offence for which it is imposed. For reasons which I will explain more fully later, the moral culpability of the offence of impaired driving simpliciter is the same as that of the same offence, committed by the same individual, which causes either death or bodily harm to an innocent victim, irrespective of whether the latter offence is characterized as impaired, dangerous or criminally negligent driving. That is because, apart from the personal circumstances relating to that offender, the moral culpability of both offences lies in the intention to drive a motor vehicle after having voluntarily consumed more alcohol than the law permits, together with a reckless disregard for the foreseeable consequences of such driving.

...

(a) Parliamentary Direction—The 1985 Amendments

Prior to 1985, at the discretion of Crown counsel, an impaired driver who caused death could face a charge of either criminal negligence causing death (s. 203, for which the maximum penalty was life imprisonment; manslaughter (s. 219), for which the maximum sentence was also life imprisonment; or criminal negligence in the operation of a motor vehicle (s. 233(1)), for which the maximum penalty was imprisonment for five years. By virtue of s. 589(5) of the *Criminal Code*, RSC 1970, c. C-34, dangerous driving (which was also an offence under s. 233(4), and punishable as an indictable offence by imprisonment for up to two years) was an included offence of all three charges. For the impaired driver who caused bodily harm, the only available charge was criminal negligence causing bodily harm, for which the maximum punishment was imprisonment for 10 years.

The 1985 amendments, which did away with the offence of criminal negligence in the operation of a motor vehicle, increased the range of charges that can now be laid in a drinking/driving case resulting in either death or bodily harm:

s. 2230	Criminal Negligence Causing Death	Life
s. 236	Manslaughter	Life
s. 221	Criminal Negligence Causing Bodily Harm	10 years
s. 249(4)	Dangerous Driving Causing Death	14 years
s. 249(3)	Dangerous Driving Causing Bodily Harm	10 years
s. 255(3)	Impaired Driving Causing Death	14 years
s. 255(2)	Impaired Driving Causing Bodily Harm	10 years

The stated purpose of this Parliamentary initiative was to enhance the role of the criminal justice system in the war against the drinking driver. Thus it is important to note that the maximum sentences set for the offences created to address that specific problem, i.e., impaired driving causing death and impaired driving causing bodily harm, were 14 years and 10 years respectively.

···

Much has been written in recent years about the purpose of sentencing. In February of 1987 the Canadian Sentencing Commission, under the chair of Judge J.R. Omer Archambault, published its report entitled *Sentencing Reform: A Canadian Approach* (Ottawa: Supply and Services, 1987). That study was devoted to recommending legislative initiatives designed to correct perceived inadequacies in the existing sentencing process. While it would not be proper for the courts to implement specific legislative proposals, particularly when Parliament has chosen not to do so, the report nonetheless contains much information and learned discussion which is of assistance when searching for a principled judicial approach to sentencing within the existing legislative framework. Although I do not accept all of the commission's conclusions, much of what I have to say in this part of my reasons borrows heavily from the theoretical content and the informational material contained in its report.

At p. 153 of that report, the commission suggested the following "Fundamental Purpose of Sentencing":

"It is further recognized and declared that in a free and democratic society peace and security can only be enjoyed through the due application of the principles of fundamental justice. In furtherance of the overall purpose of the criminal law of maintaining a just, peaceful and safe society, the fundamental purpose of sentencing is to preserve the authority of and promote respect for the law through the imposition of just sanctions."

This philosophical statement, which I adopt, finds a more practical equivalent in the simple proposition that the purpose of sentencing is to enhance the protection of society. That purpose is achieved if the imposition of legal sanctions discourages both convicted offenders from re-offending and those who have yet to offend from doing so at all. Overlying and influencing the ability of the legal sanction or sentencing process to achieve this purpose, however, is the extent to which that process enjoys the acceptance and respect of the community at large.

A number of factors govern the community's acceptance of the sentencing process. There is a prevailing belief that sentences should reflect, and be proportionate to, both "the gravity of the offence and the degree of responsibility of the offender." In my view, the gravity of the offence and the degree of responsibility of the offender are determined by the moral culpability of the offender's conduct.

As a society, we long ago opted for a system of criminal justice in which the moral culpability of an offence is determined by the state of mind which accompanies the offender's unlawful act. Thus the consequences of an unlawful act when either intended, or foreseen and recklessly disregarded, aggravate its moral culpability. But consequences which are neither intended nor foreseen and recklessly ignored cannot aggravate the moral culpability of an unlawful act, except and to the extent that Parliament so decrees.

As I noted earlier, for the same offence committed by the same offender, the moral culpability of the offence of impaired driving simpliciter is the same as that of impaired driving causing either death or bodily harm. That is because in both cases the mental element of the crime consists of the intention to drive with a reckless disregard for foreseeable consequences. The fact that death or bodily harm does or does not result when any such offence is committed is more likely to be due to chance than to any circumstance of foreseeability, for such consequences are always foreseeable whenever a person impaired by alcohol gets behind the wheel of a car and drives.

The degree of moral culpability will, of course, vary from offender to offender according to a number of factors which will be discussed later in these reasons, all of which relate in some way to that person's state of mind. But, except to the extent that Parliament has made the consequences of impaired driving part of the actus reus of the offences under consideration, I do not accept that the moral culpability of an impaired driver who unintentionally, albeit recklessly, causes either death or bodily harm is greater than it would otherwise have been if he had been caught before such tragic consequences occurred.

...

Another factor which enhances community acceptance of the sentencing process is the extent to which it reflects consistency in the ultimate sanctions imposed upon like offenders for similar offences. However, while consistent treatment of like cases is an important goal in a principled approach to sentencing, the principle of accountability requires that the aggravating and mitigating circumstances peculiar to each offence and each offender be taken into account. Therefore, each sentence must, to some extent, be tailor-made for the circumstances peculiar to its own case. Any adherence to the principle of consistency which denies such legitimate variation would necessarily result in the imposition of arbitrary sanctions.

The respect which the community at large has for the sentencing process will also depend on the extent to which the specific goals of any sanction imposed can be seen to serve the ultimate purpose of sentencing. Those goals have traditionally been described as (i) general deterrence, (ii) specific deterrence, (iii) isolation, and (iv) rehabilitation. In recent years some cases and literature on the subject have suggested a fifth, which has come to be known as "denunciation." The Archambault Commission suggested a sixth called "just deserts." Each of these goals must be examined more closely, with particular reference to the offences under consideration in these appeals.

The theory behind the general deterrence goal of sentencing is that the legal sanction imposed on actual offenders will discourage potential offenders. While there is little empirical evidence to support such a theory, common sense tells us that to some extent, that must be so. Indeed, there can be little doubt but that the very existence of a criminal justice system acts as a deterrent which prevents many people from engaging in criminal conduct.

The problem with the theory lies in its extension to the conclusion, which I believe has been too easily accepted in the past, that the greater the sanction imposed in any given case, the greater will be its general deterrent effect. There is an increasingly persuasive body of evidence and learned opinion to the contrary.

In its report, at p. 136, the Archambault Commission noted:

"With regard to general deterrence, the overall assessment of the deterrent effects of criminal sanctions ranges from an attitude of great caution in expressing an opinion to outright scepticism."

One of the many studies referred to by the commission dealt specifically with the deterrent effect of long sentences on the rate of drinking/driving offences: A.C. Donelson, *Impaired Driving Report No. 4. Alcohol and Road Accidents in Canada: Issues Related to Future Strategies and Priorities* (Ottawa: Department of Justice, 1985). The author asserts that

"law-based, punitive measures alone cannot produce large, sustained reductions in the magnitude of the problem." …

In a follow-up study in 1989, after analyzing the statistical data and other materials available, the same author concluded that the persistence of serious drinking/driving offences as a social and criminal justice problem is due largely to the significant number of drivers with serious alcohol abuse problems. These, Donelson concludes, are the persons least likely to be deterred by the threat of arrest or punishment.

Counsel presented a considerable amount of published research material at the hearing of these appeals, most of it dedicated to an examination of the drinking and driving problem specifically. It is impossible to summarize all of that material in detail. Suffice it to say that none of it supports the argument that the imposition of severe sanctions, specifically, lengthy sentences of imprisonment, will produce a proportionate general deterrent effect on potential drinking/driving offenders.

What is clear from this material is that more education, greater enforcement, more media coverage and longer licence suspensions represent the best hopes for lessening the incidence of drinking and driving offences.

In considering this difficult subject, of course, it must be kept in mind that we are dealing with a theory, the ultimate proof or disproof of which probably lies beyond human ingenuity, for we are not likely ever to know with certainty who has, or who has not, been deterred by the imposition of a specific legal sanction. That being the case, we must not ignore any reasonable possibility that a particular sanction will deter a potential offender. But the key word in that precaution is "reasonable" and, when considering the general deterrent effect of sentences of imprisonment in respect of drinking/driving offences causing death or bodily harm, the material presented on this appeal establishes that it would be unreasonable to conclude that a sentence of five or six years' imprisonment will deter where one or two years will not.

(ii) Specific Deterrence

While it is easier, from a historical vantage, to determine whether any particular sanction has been successful in persuading an individual not to re-offend, there are also reasonable limits to the specific deterrent effect which can be expected from a sentence of imprisonment in connection with the offences under discussion. In many cases, of course, imprisonment will not be necessary to ensure that the individual does not re-offend. But in those cases where the court finds that such a sanction is necessary to meet the goal of specific deterrence, it would be unreasonable, in the absence of any cogent evidence to the contrary, to conclude that the specific deterrent value of a sentence of imprisonment will be any greater than its overall general deterrent effect. Any person who would not likely be deterred by such a sentence falls into the category of offender for whom an isolative sentence must be considered.

Isolation is achieved primarily by a sentence of imprisonment. It is justified as a "goal" of sentencing by the simple proposition that so long as an offender is sepa-rated from society, he or she cannot re-offend. In terms of the protection of society, it is the option of last resort. Even as such, it suffers from the ultimate weakness that if the fundamental requirement of proportionality is observed, the individual concerned must eventually be released from jail. Experience teaches us that most people emerge from prison a worse threat to society than when they entered. Thus care and restraint must be exercised when imposing a sentence of imprisonment even when the goal is to isolate the offender.

In relation to the offences under consideration, of course, the chronic alcohol abuser, whose inability to refrain from driving a motor vehicle while intoxicated is demonstrated by a number of previous convictions for drinking/driving-related offenc-es, presents as a candidate for an isolative sentence unless the court is persuaded that rehabilitative treatment can and will be undertaken with a reasonable prospect of success. Even in such cases, however, the fundamental requirement of proportional-ity must be observed.

...

(iv) Rehabilitation

It has long been recognized that rehabilitation, as a goal of the sentencing process, cannot be achieved through the imposition of custodial sentences. That does not mean that rehabilitation should be regarded as a less important goal of sentencing. Indeed, in my view it is self-evident that rehabilitation remains the only certain way of per-manently protecting society from a specific offender.

Thus if the rehabilitation of a specific offender remains a reasonable possibility, that is a circumstance which requires the sentencing court to consider seriously a non-custodial form of disposition. In some cases, even those involving serious criminal offences, where the chances of rehabilitation are significant, or its benefits to society substantial, the importance of imposing a rehabilitative non-custodial form of sentence may outweigh the perceived general deterrent advantages of a custodial sentence. If so, a court should not hesitate to impose the former, for in such circumstances the requirements of accountability and proportionality can be met with carefully crafted terms and conditions which both restrict the individual's freedom and enhance super-vision of the rehabilitative process.

I have previously noted that while minimum penalties are provided in the *Criminal Code* for simple impaired driving and its related offences, Parliament has so far seen fit not to impose any such requirement on drinking and driving offences which result in death or bodily harm. Thus it clearly remains open to a court to impose a non-custodial sentence upon conviction for offences of this sort where the circumstances in favour of such a disposition are sufficiently compelling to overcome the need for a sentence of imprisonment, which would otherwise be required to meet the other goals of sentencing.

(v) Denunciation

This court first gave formal recognition to the denunciation as a goal of sentencing in *R v. Oliver*, [1977] 5 WWR 344, a case in which a lawyer was convicted of converting trust funds to his own benefit with the intent of defrauding his clients. Chief Justice Farris, speaking for the court, said at p. 346 of the report:

> Courts do not impose sentences in response to public clamour, nor in a spirit of revenge. On the other hand, justice is not administered in a vacuum. Sentences imposed by courts for criminal conduct by and large must have the support of concerned and thinking citizens. If they do not have such support, the system will fail. There are cases, as Lord Denning has said, where the punishment inflicted for grave crimes should reflect the revulsion felt by the majority of citizens for them. In his view, the objects of punishment are not simply deterrent or reformative. The ultimate justification of punishment is the emphatic denunciation by the community of a crime.

In its *Report on Dispositions and Sentences in the Criminal Process: Guidelines*, published in 1976, the Law Reform Commission of Canada made the following recommendation with respect to denunciation and imprisonment, at p. 27 of the text:

> The court should not use imprisonment as a means of denouncing unlawful behaviour, except where it is convinced that no other sanction is sufficiently strong to underline the seriousness of the harm done. In determining this the court should consider:
>
> 1. the nature, seriousness and circumstances of the offence;
> 2. the social reprobation associated with the offence.

In *R v. Pettigrew* (1990), 56 CCC (3d) 390, a case of manslaughter, Taylor JA, speaking for a majority of this court, concluded, at p. 395 of the report:

> "Yet even where, as here, the crime involved is regarded as one of particular gravity—the careless taking of a life—the extent to which it should be considered morally reprehensible, so as to call for 'denunciatory' punishment, can still be assessed only on the basis of the circumstances of the particular case and offender. *In the absence of any prescribed minimum penalty, imprisonment can be imposed on this ground only if the circumstances of the case and of the offender call for such a response. In weighing the matter the court must consider, among other things, whether any adverse effects which a denunciatory punishment would have on the rehabilitation of the offender can be justi-*

fied in the over-all interests of the protection and advancement of society." [Emphasis added.]

As pointed out in the report of the Archambault Commission, the notion of denunciation as a goal of sentencing is one associated with the retributive theory of sentencing as declared in *R v. Hinch*, supra. That means that denunciation as a goal of sentencing must be strictly limited to ensuring that sentences imposed for criminal convictions are proportionate to the moral culpability of the offender's unlawful act.

...

For the reasons to which I have already referred I do not accept that the consequences of the offences under discussion can be an aggravating circumstance except to the extent that Parliament has mandated by including those consequences as part of the actus reus of the offence. Thus, for example, I do not accept the proposition ... that the offence of the impaired driver who has caused the death of one innocent victim is any less culpable than it would be if he had instead caused the death of two or three innocent victims.

While on the subject of the important principle of proportionality between any sentence imposed and the moral culpability of the offence for which it is imposed, a special note of caution is necessary in those cases where the proper application of the sentencing goals indicates that imprisonment is necessary. In those cases it is important to ensure that the court's consideration of such a sentence be removed from the abstract realm of numbers to the reality of what those numbers mean when they refer to years of real-life experience in one of our jails. Numbers such as 2, 3, 4 and 5, are low numbers, particularly when viewed through the eyes of a society which has been ravaged by inflationary pressures of one kind or another for over 50 years. But when they refer to, and define the years of, a sentence of imprisonment, they represent a very significant deprivation of freedom for the offender, during which all semblance of a normal life-style is withdrawn, dignity and self-esteem are suppressed, and little, if any, chance for reformation exists.

(vi) Just Deserts

Notwithstanding the efforts of the authors of the Archambault Commission report to distinguish this "goal" of sentencing from that of retribution, I am of the view that from a practical as opposed to a theoretical viewpoint, they are indistinguishable. Accordingly, I am of the view that it has no place in a principled approach to sentencing.

NOTE

Mr. Justice Wood concluded in *Sweeney*, and also in *Preston*, that rehabilitation cannot be achieved through incarceration. Not long after *Sweeney*, a different panel of the British Columbia Court of Appeal decided in *R v. Robitaille*, [1993] BCJ No. 1404 (BC CA), released May 19, 1993, that rehabilitative concerns must give way when protection of the public demands a lengthy custodial sentence. The accused challenged a sentence of seven years for armed robbery and two years, consecutive, for use of a firearm while committing an indictable offence. Among the relevant factors were the following: the accused was on parole at the time of the offence, and had a criminal record dating to 1974 that included many robbery offences and several violent offences, including armed robbery. He argued in the Court of Appeal that the sentence did not give adequate consideration to deterrence and rehabilitation. The appeal was dismissed with the following statements:

> [T]he theory that sentences should go up only in moderate steps is a theory which rests on the sentencing principles of rehabilitation. It should be only in cases where rehabilitation is a significant sentencing factor.
>
> So the conclusion ... that the increase in sentence should not be too large rests on a consideration of the circumstance of the particular offender and a desire not to discourage any effort he may be making to rehabilitate himself by the imposition of a sentence that may be seen by him to be a dead weight on his future life. ...
>
> In order to protect the public from someone who has demonstrated that he will persist it is unrealistic to think that a nicely stepped up sentence to five years from three years will accomplish the sentencing goal of protection of the public. Only putting him away will accomplish that goal.

Does a decision such as this conflict with the approach taken by Wood JA in *Preston* and *Sweeney*?

B. Retribution and Denunciation in Relation to Serious Offences Against the Person

Although trial judges are the primary instruments of sentencing, there are many sentence appeals each year to provincial and territorial appellate courts. Accordingly, these courts have an opportunity to make a substantial impact on judicial thinking about sentencing. For example, we look later at the efforts of the Alberta Court of Appeal to affect the results of sentencing by imposing a new methodology of sentencing—the starting point.

But the saga of sentencing does not end with provincial or territorial appellate courts. The Supreme Court of Canada has jurisdiction to entertain sentence appeals with leave: see *R v. Gardiner* (1982), 68 CCC (2d) 477 (SCC). However, the Supreme Court rarely granted leave on legal issues in sentencing cases—until recently. Since 1996, there has been a small number of sentencing decisions, some of which have had dramatic effects. For example, the Supreme Court has articulated a standard of deference to determine the threshold for appellate intervention. In a series of cases (see *R v. C.A.M.* and *R v. McDonnell*, infra, and *R v. Shropshire* (1996), 43 CR (4th) 269), the court held that an appellate court should vary a sentence only if the original sentence involved an error of law or the application of wrong principles or if the sentence is demonstrably unfit. We will return to the issue of deference later in this chapter. For now, the issue to consider in the following case is retribution and its role within the sentencing process.

R v. C.A.M.
(1996), 46 CR (4th) 269 (SCC)

[The Crown appealed a decision of the British Columbia Court of Appeal that had reduced a 25-year sentence to a sentence of 18 years and 8 months. The accused had pleaded guilty to numerous counts of sexual assault, incest, assault with a weapon, and other offences, establishing a pattern of sexual, emotional, and physical abuse inflicted on his children over a period of years. The trial judge described the offences "as egregious as any" he had ever seen in the courts, transcending "the parameters of the worst case." None of the offences carried a maximum penalty of life imprisonment. In the Court of Appeal, the accused's counsel successfully argued that where a life sentence cannot be imposed, the maximum fixed-term sentence available to a sentencing judge is 20 years. Part of the argument relied on the parole eligibiity rules under the *Corrections and Conditional Release Act*, which allow a person serving life as a maximum sentence to be eligible for parole after serving seven years, but a person serving a fixed sentence to be eligible after serving one-third of his or her sentence. The Supreme Court reversed. Speaking for a unanimous court, the decision of Lamer CJC is interesting in a number of respects, particularly for his discussion of the distinction between legitimate retributive goals and vengeance.]

...

In summary, I find no evidence from the parole eligibility rules under the *Corrections Act* that Parliament intended to impose a qualified ceiling on numerical sentences under the Code. A numerical sentence beyond 20 years may still significantly advance the traditional continuum of sentencing goals ranging from deterrence, denunciation, rehabilitation to the protection of society, notwithstanding the fact that an offender is eligible for review of the conditions of his or her incarceration after seven years (absent an order extending the period of ineligibility under s. 741.2 of the Code). Accordingly, I remain thoroughly unpersuaded that Parliament intended to preclude such numerical sentences through the adoption of the *Corrections Act* and its legislative predecessors. The very purpose of the *Corrections Act* was to enable a trial judge's sentencing discretion under the Code rather than to hobble it. In the absence of a clearer expression of legislative intent on such an important subject implicating the basic structure of our criminal justice system, I decline to read such a dramatic restriction on the sentencing discretion of judges into the *Criminal Code*.

In my view, within the broad statutory maximum and minimum penalties defined for particular offences under the Code, trial judges enjoy a wide ambit of discretion under s. 717 in selecting a "just and appropriate" fixed-term sentence which adequately promotes the traditional goals of sentencing, subject only to the fundamental principle that the global sentence imposed reflect the overall culpability of the offender and the circumstances of the offence. As such, I decline to delineate any pre-fixed outer boundary to the sentencing discretion of a trial judge, whether at 20 years, or even at 25 years as suggested by Seaton JA in dissent at the Court of Appeal. Similarly, I see no reason why numerical sentences in Canada ought to be de facto limited at 20 years as a matter of judicial habit or convention. Whether a fixed-term sentence beyond 20 years is imposed as a sentence for a single offence where life imprisonment is available but not imposed, or as a cumulative sentence for multiple offences where life imprisonment is not available, there is no a priori ceiling on fixed-term sentences under the Code.

The bastion which protects Canadians from unduly harsh fixed-term sentences is not found in the mechanics of the *Corrections Act* but rather in the good sense of our nation's trial judges. For many of the lesser crimes presently before our courts, a single or cumulative sentence beyond 20 years would undoubtedly be grossly excessive, and probably cruel and unusual. In other circumstances, such a stern sentence would be both fitting and appropriate. In our system of justice, the ultimate protection against excessive criminal punishment lies within a sentencing judge's overriding duty to fashion a "just and appropriate" punishment which is proportional to the overall culpability of the offender.

However, in the process of determining a just and appropriate fixed-term sentence of imprisonment, the sentencing judge should be mindful of the age of the offender in applying the relevant principles of sentencing. After a certain point, the utilitarian and normative goals of sentencing will eventually begin to exhaust themselves once a contemplated sentence starts to surpass any reasonable estimation of the offender's remaining natural life span. Accordingly, in exercising his or her specialized discretion under the Code, a sentencing judge should generally refrain from imposing a fixed-term sentence which so greatly exceeds an offender's expected remaining life span that the traditional goals of sentencing, even general deterrence and denunciation, have all but depleted their functional value. But with that consideration in mind, the governing principle remains the same: Canadian courts enjoy a broad discretion in imposing numerical sentences for single or multiple offences, subject only to the broad statutory parameters of the Code and the fundamental principle of our criminal law that global sentences be "just and appropriate."

Pursuant to the foregoing discussion, I conclude that the British Columbia Court of Appeal erred in applying as a principle of sentencing that fixed-term sentences under the *Criminal Code* ought to be capped at 20 years, absent special circumstances. However, the Court of Appeal also justified its reduction of the respondent's sentence on the grounds that the sentence imposed by Filmer Prov. Ct. J was unfit under the particular circumstances. Accordingly, it is still necessary to examine whether the Court of Appeal erred in law in its review of the fitness of the respondent's sentence. But before turning to that question, I intend to deal briefly with the Crown's two remaining grounds of appeal.

B. Did the Court of Appeal Err in Holding that Retribution Is Not a Legitimate Principle of Sentencing?

As a second and independent ground of appeal, the Crown argues that the Court of Appeal erred in law by relying on the proposition that "retribution is not a legitimate goal of sentencing" (p. 116) in reducing the sentence imposed by Filmer Prov. Ct. J to 18 years and 8 months. In my reading of the judgment of the Court of Appeal below, I find little evidence that the passing remarks of Wood JA in relation to the legitimacy of retribution played a significant role in his conclusion that the respondent's sentence ought to be reduced to 18 years and 8 months' imprisonment. It should be noted that Rowles JA, in her concurring reasons, did not even discuss retribution as a principle of sentencing. Similarly, there is no evidence that Filmer Prov. Ct. J placed any explicit reliance on the objective of "retribution" in initially rendering his stern sentence. Accordingly, whether or not Wood JA erred as a strict matter of law in his discussion of the philosophical merits of retribution as a principle of sentencing, I conclude that Wood JA's discussion of retribution was not a decisive element in the majority of the Court of Appeal's conclusion that the sentence of the respondent ought to be reduced to below 19 years. Therefore, I am persuaded that the remarks of Wood JA in relation to retribution did not constitute a reversible error. However, given the continued judicial debate over this issue, particularly in recent judgments of the BC Court of Appeal (see, e.g., *R v. Hicks* (1995), 56 BCAC 259, at para. 14 (rejecting retribution); *R v. Eneas*, [1994] BCJ No. 262, at paras. 45 and 46 (endorsing retribution); *R v. M.(D.E.S.)* (1993), 80 CCC (3d) 371, at p. 376 (rejecting retribution); *R v. Hoyt*, [1992] BCJ No. 2315 [reported at 17 CR (4th) 338], at paras. 21 and 22 (rejecting retribution); *R v. Pettigrew* (1990), 56 CCC (3d) 390, at pp. 394-95 (endorsing retribution)), it would be prudent for this Court to clarify briefly the existing state of Canadian law in this important area.

It has been recognized by this Court that retribution is an accepted, and indeed important, principle of sentencing in our criminal law. As La Forest J acknowledged in discussing the constitutionality of the dangerous offender provisions of the *Criminal Code* in *R v. L.(T.P.)*, (sub nom. *R v. L.*) [1987] 2 SCR 309, at p. 329:

> In a rational system of sentencing, the respective importance of prevention, deterrence, retribution and rehabilitation will vary according to the nature of the crime and the circumstances of the offender. No one would suggest that any of these functional considerations should be excluded from the legitimate purview of legislative or judicial decisions regarding sentencing.

This Court has since re-endorsed this passage on a number of occasions as a proper articulation of some of the guiding principles of sentencing in a number of subsequent cases. See *Luxton*, supra, at p. 721; *Goltz*, supra, at p. 503; and *Shropshire*, supra, at para. 23.

The Canadian Sentencing Commission in its 1987 Report on Sentencing Reform also endorsed retribution as a legitimate and relevant consideration in the sentencing process. While the Commission noted that strict retributivist theory on its own fails to provide a general justification for the imposition of criminal sanctions, the Commission argued that retribution, in conjunction with other utilitarian justifications of punishment (i.e., deterrence and rehabilitation), contributes to a more coherent theory of punishment (supra, at pp. 141-42, 143-45). More specifically, the Commission argued that a theory of retribution centred on "just deserts" or "just sanctions" provides a helpful organizing principle for the imposition of criminal sanctions (at p. 143). Indeed, as the Commission noted, retribution frequently operates as a principle of restraint, as utilitarian principles alone may direct individualized punishments which unfairly exceed the culpability of the offender. As the Report stated at pp. 133-34:

> The ethical foundation of retributivism lies in the following principle: it is immoral to treat one person as a resource for others. From this principle it follows that the only legitimate ground for punishing a person is the blameworthiness of his or her conduct. It also follows that sanctions must be strictly proportionate to the culpability of a person and to the seriousness of the offence for which that person has been convicted. ... According to these principles, all exemplary sentences (i.e. the imposition of a harsher sanction on an individual offender so that he or she may be made an example to the community) are unjustified, because they imply that an offender's plight may be used as a means or as a resource to deter potential offenders.

See, similarly, B.P. Archibald, *Crime and Punishment: The Constitutional Requirements for Sentencing Reform in Canada* (August 1988), at p. 18. With these considerations in mind, the Commission explicitly defined the fundamental purpose of sentencing with reference to the normative goal of imposing "just sanctions." As the Commission cast the guiding purpose of criminal sentencing, at p. 153:

> In furtherance of the overall purpose of the criminal law of maintaining a just, peaceful and safe society, the fundamental purpose of sentencing is to preserve the authority of and promote respect for the law through the imposition of just sanctions.

A majority of this Court has since expressed approval of this passage as an accurate statement of the essential goals of sentencing. See *R v. Jones*, [1994] 2 SCR 229, at p. 291 (although I dissented on the merits of the case).

Retribution, as an objective of sentencing, represents nothing less than the hallowed principle that criminal punishment, in addition to advancing utilitarian considerations related to deterrence and rehabilitation, should also be imposed to sanction the moral culpability of the offender. In my view, retribution is integrally woven into the existing principles of sentencing in Canadian law through the fundamental requirement that a sentence imposed be "just and appropriate" under the circumstances. Indeed, it is my profound belief that retribution represents an important unifying principle of our penal law by offering an essential conceptual link between the attribution of criminal liability and the imposition of criminal sanctions. With regard to the attribution of criminal liability, I have repeatedly held that it is a principle of "fundamental justice" under s. 7 of the Charter that criminal liability may only be imposed if an accused possesses a minimum "culpable mental state" in respect of the ingredients of the alleged offence. See *R v. Martineau*, [1990] 2 SCR 633, at p. 645. See, similarly, *Motor Vehicle Act* (British Columbia), supra; *R v. Vaillancourt*, [1987] 2 SCR 636. It is this mental state which gives rise to the "moral blameworthiness" which justifies the state in imposing the stigma and punishment associated with a criminal sentence. See *Martineau*, at p. 646. I submit that it is this same element of "moral blameworthiness" which animates the determination of the appropriate quantum of punishment for a convicted offender as a "just sanction." As I noted in *Martineau* in discussing the sentencing scheme for manslaughter under the Code, it is a recognized principle of our justice system that "punishment be meted out with regard to the level of moral blameworthiness of the offender" (p. 647). See the similar observations of W.E.B. Code in "Proportionate Blameworthiness and the Rule against Constructive Sentencing" (1992), 11 CR (4th) 40, at pp. 41-42.

However, the meaning of retribution is deserving of some clarification. The legitimacy of retribution as a principle of sentencing has often been questioned as a result of its unfortunate association with "vengeance" in common parlance. See, e.g., *R v. Hinch*, supra, at pp. 43-44; *R v. Calder* (1956), 114 CCC 155 (Man. CA), at p. 161. But it should be clear from my foregoing discussion that retribution bears little relation to vengeance, and I attribute much of the criticism of retribution as a principle to this confusion. As both academic and judicial commentators have noted, vengeance has no role to play in a civilized system of sentencing. See Ruby, *Sentencing*, supra, at p. 13. Vengeance, as I understand it, represents an uncalibrated act of harm upon another, frequently motivated by emotion and anger, as a reprisal for harm inflicted upon oneself by that person. Retribution in a criminal context, by contrast, represents an objective, reasoned and measured determination of an appropriate punishment which properly reflects the moral culpability of the offender, having regard to the intentional risk-taking of the offender, the consequential harm caused by the offender, and the normative character of the offender's conduct. Furthermore, unlike vengeance, retribution incorporates a principle of restraint; retribution requires the imposition of a just and appropriate punishment, and nothing more. As R. Cross has noted in *The English Sentencing System* (2nd ed. 1975), at p. 121: "The retributivist insists that the punishment must not be disproportionate to the offender's deserts."

Retribution, as well, should be conceptually distinguished from its legitimate sibling, denunciation. Retribution requires that a judicial sentence properly reflect the moral blameworthiness of that particular offender. The objective of denunciation mandates that a sentence should also communicate society's condemnation of that particular offender's conduct. In short, a sentence with a denunciatory element represents a symbolic, collective statement that the offender's conduct should be punished for encroaching on our society's basic code of values as enshrined within our substantive criminal law. As Lord Justice Lawton stated in *R v. Sargeant* (1974), 60 Cr. App. Rep. 74 (CA), at p. 77: "society, through the courts, must show its abhorrence of particular types of crime, and the only way in which the courts can show this is by the sentences they pass." The relevance of both retribution and denunciation as goals of sentencing underscores that our criminal justice system is not simply a vast system of negative penalties designed to prevent objectively harmful conduct by increasing the cost the offender must bear in committing an enumerated offence. Our criminal law is also a system of values. A sentence which expresses denunciation is simply the means by which these values are communicated. In short, in addition to attaching negative consequences to undesirable behaviour, judicial sentences should also be imposed in a manner which positively instills the basic set of communal values shared by all Canadians as expressed by the *Criminal Code*.

As a closing note to this discussion, it is important to stress that neither retribution nor denunciation alone provides an exhaustive justification for the imposition of criminal sanctions. Rather, in our system of justice, normative and utilitarian considerations operate in conjunction with one another to provide a coherent justification for criminal punishment. As Gonthier J emphasized in *Goltz*, supra, at p. 502, the goals of the penal sanction are both "broad and varied." Accordingly, the meaning of retribution must be considered in conjunction with the other legitimate objectives of sentencing, which include (but are not limited to) deterrence, denunciation, rehabilitation and the protection of society. Indeed, it is difficult to perfectly separate these inter-related principles. And as La Forest J emphasized in *L.(T.P.)*, the relative weight and importance of these multiple factors will frequently vary depending on the nature of the crime and the circumstances of the offender. In the final analysis, the overarching duty of a sentencing judge is to draw upon all the legitimate principles of sentencing to determine a "just and appropriate" sentence which reflects the gravity of the offence committed and the moral blameworthiness of the offender.

...

In the case at hand, the majority of the Court of Appeal reduced the sentence of the respondent primarily as a result of the framework of sentencing principles the court inherited from the previous cases of *Rooke* and *D.(G.W.)*, supra. As I have argued previously, I believe that this framework was incorrect in law. But the Court of Appeal also justified its reduction of sentence with reference to a contextual application of the accepted principles of sentencing to this case. More specifically, the majority concluded that the goals of deterrence and denunciation do not support a sentence of 25 years in this case, because both of these sentencing goals experience sharply diminishing returns following 20 years. On the subject of deterrence, Wood JA pointed to the empirical studies he outlined in his concurring judgment in *Sweeney*, supra, which question the deterrent effect of criminal sanctions. The majority also concluded that the protection of society would not be advanced by such a sentence; as Wood JA argued, as a result of the parole eligibility rules, an increase of sentence of 5 years to 25 years is potentially limited to an additional 4 months of imprisonment.

With the greatest respect, I believe the Court of Appeal erred in this instance by engaging in an overly interventionist mode of appellate review of the "fitness" of sentence which transcended the standard of deference we articulated in *Shropshire*. Notwithstanding the existence of some empirical studies which question the general deterrent effect of sentencing, it was open for the sentencing judge to reasonably conclude that the particular blend of sentencing goals, ranging from specific and general deterrence, denunciation and rehabilitation to the protection of society, required a sentence of 25 years in this instance. Moreover, on the facts, the sentencing judge was entitled to find that an overall term of imprisonment of 25 years represented a "just sanction" for the crimes of the respondent.

The respondent committed a vile pattern of physical and sexual abuse against the very children he was entrusted to protect. The degree of violence exhibited in these crimes was disturbingly high, and the respondent's children will undoubtedly be scarred for life. The psychiatrist and psychologist who examined the respondent agree that he faces dim prospects of rehabilitation. Without doubt, the respondent deserves a severe sentence which expresses the society's revulsion at his crimes.

After taking into account all the circumstances of the offence, the trial judge sentenced the respondent to 25 years' imprisonment. In imposing that term of imprisonment, Filmer Prov. Ct. J was at liberty to incorporate credit for time served in custody pursuant to s. 721(3) of the Code, but chose not to. I see no reason to believe that the sentencing order of Filmer Prov. Ct. J was demonstrably unfit.

C. General Deterrence and Drug Offences

There are many factors that can influence judicial attitudes toward sentencing: legislative amendments, perceptions of public opinion, empirical evidence, and the results of official studies. In *R v. McLeod*, infra, Vancise JA brings a fresh consideration of the efficacy of general deterrence to the decision to incarcerate in a case involving a 31-year-old offender with a lengthy record who had been convicted of trafficking in 50 tablets of Xanax, contrary to s. 31 of the *Food and Drugs Act*, RSC 1985, c. F-27, as it then existed. The trial judge had placed the offender on intensive probation for two years, including an initial period of electronic monitoring for six months. The judge had been impressed by the progress made by the offender during the 13 months on bail between the charge and the sentencing, especially with respect to his alcohol- and drug-abuse problems and his educational upgrading. For the majority of the Court of Appeal, Vancise JA dismissed the Crown appeal.

R v. McLeod
(1993), 81 CCC (3d) 83 (Sask. CA)

VANCISE JA:

...

The issue here is whether the Provincial Court judge erred in imposing the alternate sentence of intensive probation of two years, with a term which requires that the accused be confined to his residence for the first six months and that his whereabouts for that period of confinement be electronically monitored, instead of a custodial sentence. It is not necessary for me to repeat what I said in *R v. McGinn* (1989), 49 CCC (3d) 137, 75 Sask. R 161, 7 WCB (2d) 338, concerning the historical development and purpose of custodial sentences. Suffice it to say, imprisonment began as an alternative to harsher punishment and with the hope that hard work served in isolation would reform the offender. The concept has not been an overwhelming success.

A number of inquiries (the latest being in 1987) have examined the use of incarceration as a sanction when sentencing offenders. They all say, without exception, that the use of incarceration has failed and should be used with restraint. As the Ouimet Report noted, the object of the Canadian judicial system is to protect society from crime in a manner commanding public support while avoiding needless injury to the offender. The Ouimet Report proposed that incarceration be used with restraint and proposed the following all-encompassing sentencing policy:

> ... segregate the dangerous, deter and retrain the rationally motivated professional criminal, deal as constructively as possible with every offender as the circumstances of the case permit, release the harmless, imprison the casual offender not committed to a criminal career only where no other disposition is appropriate. In every disposition, the possibility of rehabilitation should be taken into account.

The committee concluded that, in so far as minor offences are concerned, all non-carceral options should be exhausted before there is recourse to incarceration. No one, or at least few, would disagree with lengthy prison terms for violent offences. I agree with the committee that a strong case can be made for alternate forms of sentences for offenders who do not pose a threat of physical violence or harm or endanger the safety of others. In determining whether a custodial term should be imposed it is necessary to examine a number of concepts which are inherent in the sentencing process. One must examine, first, the definition and purpose of sentencing; secondly, the principles or factors which determine what constitutes a fit sentence; thirdly, the effectiveness of custodial sentences as deterrence; fourthly, the role of appellate courts in developing sentencing guidelines, fifthly, alternate sanctions, and finally, public confidence in the administration of justice which includes disparity in sentences.

Prior to embarking on such an examination it is worth repeating that sentencing does and must take place within a framework of principles wherein the courts seek to impose a fit sentence having regard to the offence and the offender. As noted, the real problem is not enumerating the factors or stating the principles but rather, the emphasis to be accorded to the factors (about which I will have more to say) in each case.

The Definition and Purpose of Sentencing

The Law Reform Commission of Canada defines sentencing as:

> Sentencing is used to refer to that process in which the court or officials, having inquired into an alleged offence, give a reasoned statement making clear what values are at stake and what is involved in the offence. As the sentence is carried out, it may be necessary from time to time, as in probation, to change or amend conditions relating to the sentence.

There are two distinct elements in sentencing: punishment, and the determination or expression of the sanction. As Culliton CJS noted in *R v. Morrissette* (1970), 1 CCC (2d) 307 at pp. 309-10, 12 CRNS 392, 75 WWR 644 (Sask. CA):

> Both trial and appellate Judges must be ever mindful of the fact that the principal purpose of the criminal process, of which sentencing is an important element, is the protection of society.
>
> From time to time, Courts have reviewed the principles to be considered in the determination of proper sentences. This Court recently did so in *R v. Kissick* (1969), 70 WWR 365. As has been stated many times, the factors to be considered are:
>
> (1) punishment;
> (2) deterrence;
> (3) protection of the public; and
> (4) the reformation and rehabilitation of the offender.
>
> The real problem arises in deciding the factor to be emphasized in a particular case. Of necessity, the circumstances surrounding the commission of an offence differ in each case so that even for the same offence sentences may justifiably show a wide variation.

Fit Sentences

It is therefore within this broad framework that a Provincial Court of Appeal must deal with appeals in respect of sentencing in an effort to give guidelines which will as much as possible permit the courts to achieve uniformity of sentencing. One must, however, recognize that uniformity is the ideal and that its achievement is impossible given the need to consider the individual circumstances of accused persons. The appellate court must, when discrepancies occur, ensure that the disparate sentences for similar offences can be distinguished and rationalized.

Effectiveness of Custodial Sentences as Deterrence

General deterrence has been defined as the "inhibiting effect of sanctions." Deterrence is but one of a number of factors in determining a fit sentence. It has, as Culliton CJS stated in *Morrissette*, at p. 310, two aspects, general and specific. It must be considered from an objective point of view if the purpose is to deter others. If the purpose is to deter the accused then greater consideration must be given to the individual, his record, attitude and possibility of rehabilitation and reformation. If both general and specific deterrence are important then all factors must be weighed and a sentence fixed which properly balances the two.

Having said that, one must ask whether general deterrence is effective in reducing the crime rate because it is this factor on which the Crown relies, above all others, for the imposition of a carceral sentence. The appellant Crown contends that general deterrence is necessary to control and reduce crime in seeking to justify a custodial sentence.

There is no empirical evidence that general deterrence as it relates to length of sentences is effective in reducing the crime rate. There is no evidence that higher sentences are effective in reducing the crime rate.

A study done for the US National Academy of Science stated:

> In summary ... we cannot yet assert that the evidence warrants an affirmative conclusion regarding deterrence. We believe scientific caution must be exercised in interpreting the limited validity of the available evidence and the number of competing explanations for the results. Our reluctance to draw stronger conclusions does not imply support for a position that deterrence does not exist, since the evidence certainly favors a proposition supporting deterrence more than it favors one asserting that deterrence is absent. The major challenge for future research is to estimate the magnitude of the effects of different sanctions on various crime types, an issue on which none of the evidence available thus far provides very useful guidance.

Daniel Nagin makes the same point concisely in a separate study made for the US panel:

> ... despite the intensity of the research effort, the empirical evidence is still not sufficient for providing a rigorous confirmation of the existence of a deterrent effect. Perhaps more important, the evidence is woefully inadequate for providing a good estimate of the magnitude of whatever effect may exist.
>
> Policy makers in the criminal justice system are done a disservice if they are left with the impression that the empirical evidence, which they themselves are frequently unable to evaluate, strongly supports the deterrence hypothesis.

Professor Cousineau, after reviewing the research on this issue for the Canadian Sentencing Commission (1984), stated:

> Drawing upon some nine bodies of research addressing the deterrence question, we contend that there is little or no evidence to sustain an empirically justified belief in the deterrent efficacy of legal sanctions. However, to go beyond a review of this literature and set out several arguments which document the mitigation of deterrent oriented legal sanctions [sic].
>
> Our thesis, however, is not confined to deterrence oriented legal sanctions. We suggest that many factors mitigate the effects of any legal sanctions intended to produce specific uniform outcomes.

That is not say that deterrence is not, as Culliton CJS noted, a factor to be taken into account. The research referred to emphasizes that there is no evidence to indicate that the level of sentence is effective in reducing the crime rate and that its importance has been overstated. The best evidence in support of general deterrence is that the likelihood of apprehension is important in reducing the crime rate. That seems to suggest that society would be better served by directing more resources towards prevention and rehabilitation rather than building prisons to house people who are not in any way deterred by longer sentences.

It would appear that general deterrence has a limited effect on criminal activity. To conclude that longer sentences have a greater deterrent effect than shorter sentences one must demonstrate that:

1. the public is aware of the sentence (a somewhat dubious proposition);
2. the offender will perceive the likelihood of apprehension (a dubious proposition);
3. the offender, being aware of the likelihood of apprehension, would commit the offence for the lower penalty, say one month, but not for the higher penalty, say six months (a very dubious proposition).

Viewed in this way, is it any wonder that increases in penalties have had little effect on the crime rate. If upward variations are not effective are there other things that can be done? With an abundance of evidence available to demonstrate that carceral sentences do not curb the crime rate should alternatives not be examined? I believe the answer to both questions is yes. I believe that the answer lies with the greater use of alternate sanctions, sanctions that are somewhere between probation and incarceration. I propose to deal with some of those alternatives

Role of Appellate Courts in Developing Guidelines

The right to appellate review of sentences was introduced in Canada in 1921, but no consistent principles of sentencing have resulted from such right of review. The role of the appellate court is to "[state] the principles underlying the imposition of sentences so that at least a uniformity of approach [to the imposition of sentences] may be achieved": *R v. Morrissette*, at p. 311. There are, however, no absolutes in the matter of sentences and while, as Culliton CJS stated in *Morrissette*, there can be no such thing as a uniform sentence, the court has an obligation to ensure that the disparities between sentences can be rationalized.

Within this broad mandate, should the appellate courts, in the absence of specific legislative directives, not be examining the fundamental issue of when non-carceral sentences ought to be used? Put another way, should the appellate courts not, in a principled way, identify those offences which ought not to attract a custodial sentence and provide guidelines to the trial courts. I believe that they should and I believe that such an approach is consistent with the role of an appellate court. It is consistent with the approach described by Culliton CJS in *Morrissette*, where after dealing with the principles of sentencing he stated (at pp. 309-10):

> There is as well, as there should be, a constant changing of approach to the problem of sentencing. This changing attitude, in my opinion, was properly expressed by Ernest A. Cote, QC, who, in an address to the John Howard Society of Alberta, said:
>
> > "Perhaps the principal difference between criminal justice in the past and today is that the concepts of retribution, deterrence, and denunciation of evil are slowly

being abandoned and gradually being replaced by what are considered to be realistic, social science concepts."

Such a changing attitude requires, from time to time, a review and reappraisal of both
the elements underlying an appropriate sentence and the emphasis to be placed on thereon.

Given that there are no legislative guidelines, it is for the appellate courts to develop
and articulate guidelines. There have been a number of suggestions from the Canadian
Sentencing Commission and parliamentary committees but no legislation has been
enacted. Parliament attempted to establish principles with respect to the use of incarceration in the *Criminal Law Reform Act*, 1984 (Bill C-19), which died on the order
paper. That Act sought to limit incarceration to cases where the protection of the
public was necessary and where it was necessary to punish an offender because of
non-compliance with an order or sentence imposed by the court. In other words,
restraint was urged. As long ago as 1975 in *R v. Wood* (1975), 26 CCC (2d) 100,
[1976] 2 WWR 135, the Alberta Court of Appeal stated (at p. 107): "... offences
which require a prison sentence ... grow fewer and fewer as more humane and varied
types of punishment are developed." Unfortunately, some 18 years later, we are still
not using those forms of punishment to advantage and are still sending people to
prison when an alternate sanction would be more effective.

In my opinion, a strong case can be made out for developing guidelines for the use
of alternate forms of sentencing for the majority of non-violent crimes. I say this,
notwithstanding the presumption that seems to exist that incarceration is the norm
and that non-carceral sentences are exceptions to the norm. The custodial presumption has been expressed in a number of ways but it is usually expressed under the
guise of a public interest requirement for certain offences. Professor Allan Young, in
his research entitled: *The Role of an Appellate Court in Developing Sentencing Guidelines*, which was prepared for the Canadian Sentencing Commission (1984), noted
that an examination of the list of offences caught by the custodial presumption reveals
that it encompasses almost every offence except obscenity, gambling and some property offences that are neither repetitive nor involve a breach of trust. Those offences
caught by the presumption include theft by a person in a position of trust, drug trafficking, crimes of violence, perjury and related offences against the administration of
justice, repetitive break and enters, extortion and sophisticated commercial crime.
An offender has a difficult task in displacing the presumption of incarceration and in
most cases the presumption is displaced by factors peculiar to the accused and not by
an overriding principle.

The fundamental question to be answered here is whether incarceration is an appropriate sanction. The courts must determine whether the offence is one which requires
that the public be protected and that the offender be removed from society in order to
ensure that protection. In deciding whether a non-custodial sentence should be
imposed, the court should take into account the following factors:

(a) whether the accused's conduct caused or threatened serious harm to another
person or his property;
(b) whether the act was planned or the resultant harm was planned;
(c) the conduct of the offender during the commission of the offence;

(d) whether the victim's conduct facilitated the commission of the offence;

(e) the likelihood of reoffending;

(f) the possibility of the offender responding positively to probationary treatment; and

(g) the record of the offender.

This list is not exhaustive but contains a number of factors which I believe should be considered in deciding whether or not a non-custodial sentence should be imposed. There are certain categories of offences which, prima facie, require incarceration, for example, trafficking in heroin or cocaine. The presumption of incarceration should remain when dealing with hard drugs where the social costs and the potential for enormous profit in the retailing and wholesaling of the drug exists. Offences such as possession, possession for the purpose of trafficking and even trafficking in small amounts of drugs ought not to attract the presumption of incarceration. Trafficking in and possession of commercial quantities as retailer, wholesaler, importer or courier should carry the presumption of incarceration.

NOTE

The views of the Supreme Court of Canada on the role of retribution and the meaning of denunciation are a guide for all sentencing courts. The remarks in *C.A.M.* are conceptual and do not dictate particular sentencing results as much as they add content to the sentencing analysis. Although the views expressed in *Sweeney* and *McLeod* come from provincial appellate courts, do you not find the arguments compelling? Are there counterarguments worthy of attention? Later, we discuss the 1996 amendments. Keep these cases in mind and consider whether the insertion of a statement of purpose, objectives, and principles into the *Criminal Code* has affected the impact or legitimacy of the views expressed.

IV. DISPARITY AND THE DESIRE FOR UNIFORMITY OF APPROACH

In *McLeod*, supra, Vancise JA argued that it is the role of the appellate courts to "develop and articulate guidelines." Without guidance, the scope of judicial discretion in sentencing matters places the sentencer in a difficult position. Clearly, there are diverse views and controversies about issues as fundamental as the underlying philosophy of sentencing, the efficacy of various sentences, and the legitimacy of certain factors such as public opinion. One would hope that a principled approach exists so that the intrusive impact of sentences is not left entirely to the predilections of a particular judge or the extent to which a judge is able to rise above public uproar. But so far, we have not been able to discern a clear and easily applicable set of principles that has garnered the unequivocal support of either philosophers or jurists.

For many years, disparity in sentencing decisions has been regarded as an issue that requires attention by the courts and, perhaps, by Parliament. Disparity, however, can mean different things. The importance of judicial discretion and a "fit" sentence necessarily means in Canadian law that there cannot be identical cases or identical sentences. That is, a measure of disparity is inherent in Canadian sentencing law. Moreover, many practitioners claim that this element of disparity is the strongest virtue of a system that seeks to ensure the protection of society through fit sentences. They argue that a sentence cannot be fit unless it can be justified as an appropriate response to the individual offence and the individual offender. This approach certainly acknowledges that every case is in some sense unique because the sentencer is charged with the responsibility of pronouncing the law's response to an unlawful act committed by a specific person in particular circumstances. In a broader sense, however, disparity is understood to mean the absence of prescriptive certainty in the law of sentencing. It is clear that the priority of principles and objectives in sentencing vary over time. It is also clear that the principles of sentencing in Canada vary from place to place. The Supreme Court of Canada has steadily refused over many years to entertain appeals concerned with the quantum of sentence, and it has rarely asserted its jurisdiction to clarify principles of general importance in sentencing matters. For practical purposes, then, the provincial courts of appeal have primary responsibility for providing guidance to trial judges in sentencing matters. Variations in sentencing practice can therefore be found in different parts of the country. One of the issues that divides the courts is the proper approach to the issue of disparity.

In considering this issue, imagine a spectrum of approaches. At each end of that spectrum are positions that can, for convenience only, be described as "subjective" and "objective." The essential characteristic of "subjective" sentencing is the individualized decision, determined in the discretion of the judge, within a set of principles that are established and agreed by reference to practice and the authoritative decisions of appellate courts. By contrast, an "objective" approach to the sentencing decision eliminates or suppresses the exercise of judicial discretion, and thus denies the need for sentencing decisions to be individualized. A central feature in such decision making is the prescription of fixed sentences. This conceptual spectrum obviously allows for various models of sentencing that lie somewhere between a purely subjective and purely objective model. The imperfections of purely subjective or purely objective models of sentencing are immediately apparent. Both would be unjust—the former because discretion would be unconstrained by principle and the latter because principle could not bend to ensure that justice is done in the individual case.

The natural tendency of a system that emphasizes the need for individualized sentencing is to construct a range of sentencing options that are considered appropriate for the offence and the offender. This range emerges from continued practice and periodic review by appellate courts. Although the individualized approach to sentencing and the "wise blending" of principles are well established in Canadian law, there are some provinces in which the appellate courts have attempted to introduce a greater measure of objectivity in sentencing decisions so as to enhance consistency and reduce disparity. The crux of these initiatives is to identify a "starting point" for sentences in a given class of offences. As the label implies, the starting point is not a fixed tariff that denies any scope for the adjustment of the sentence.

D. Cole and A. Manson, *Release from Imprisonment:*
The Law of Sentencing, Parole and Judicial Review
(Toronto: Carswell, 1990), 17-18

...

Once we begin talking about distinctive features and the notion of categories of offenders, we enter the controversy over whether the sentencing process should reflect an individualized response to the offender and the offence or whether, in fact or theory, a "tariff" approach is more appropriate. Commonly, an individualized sentence means one which gives primary effect to the principles of punishment, individual deterrence and rehabilitation without regard to symbolic impact on the community. Thus, the circumstances and conduct of the specific offender provide the essential framework for sentencing. In many cases, the offender's rehabilitative prospects will play a dominant role. In some cases, incapacitation to protect the community will receive the highest attention. A tariff, in its manifold guises, pushes the issue of rehabilitation into the background in order that a message of denunciatory or generally deterrent nature be broadcast to the community. A useful example of the "tariff" approach in its most rigid form is the mandatory life sentence required by the *Criminal Code* in cases of murder. The stipulated response is a function of the intrinsic gravity and harm entailed by acts which satisfy the elements of the offence of murder. The impact on the offender, whether with reference to individual deterrence or rehabilitative prospects, is deemed irrelevant. Within the realm of judicial sentencing, the "tariff" approach suggests that some offences necessarily are sufficiently grave and generate such harm or threat as to warrant a pre-articulated penal response. That is, intrinsic blameworthiness justifies a particular deterrent and denunciatory sentence in order to leave no doubt in the community's mind about the values which have been threatened and the extent to which the State will respond to that threat.

As an explanation of judicial sentencing, the notion of a tariff has been generated by David A. Thomas' analysis of sentencing and appellate review in England. In his view, the tariff takes the form of a range within which sentences are considered fit. Another form of tariff might involve a norm or starting point to which aggravating or mitigating factors can be applied. Clearly, tariffs can be imposed explicitly or implicitly.

The extent to which some form of tariff has crept into Canadian sentencing is debatable. As the Code provides no formulaic equation or methodology for producing a fit sentence, the resolution of what constitutes a fit sentence is ultimately determined by our provincial appellate courts. In an effort to inject uniformity, at least within an individual province, some appellate courts have begun to consider new methods of structuring discretion including the idea of a judicially imposed tariff.

The decision that follows illustrates the starting-point approach to sentencing as developed by the Alberta Court of Appeal and later followed in other provinces, at least with respect to sexual-assault cases. Consider whether this approach is consistent or inconsistent with the "amalgam" or "wise blending" of sentencing principles discussed earlier.

R v. Sandercock
(1985), 22 CCC (3d) 79 (Alta. CA)

KERANS JA: This is a Crown appeal from a sentence of three years on a charge of sexual assault. Judgment was reserved to consider the general idea of the starting-point approach to sentencing, as well as the appropriate starting-point for a major sexual assault and, of course, to consider the fitness of the sentence under review. All members of the court were consulted about the first two issues and we are authorized to say that the conclusions in these reasons were approved by a majority of all of the judges of the court, as well as this panel, and are to be considered as a guideline.

I

We first reaffirm the commitment of this court to the "starting-point approach" to sentencing. This approach, first expressed by this court in *R v. Johnas et al.* (1982), 2 CCC (3d) 490, 32 CR (3d) 1, 41 AR 183, has been criticized as a euphemism for a mandated minimal sentence. Also, Crown counsel often make that suggestion. These interpretations misunderstand that approach. On the contrary, it does not arbitrarily confine the discretion of the sentencing court. Rather, it offers a rational structure for its exercise, and a structure which is just because it guards against both disparity and inflexibility.

At the risk of stressing the obvious, we will consider these twin difficulties (disparity and inflexibility) in detail. On the one hand, appellate guidance offered cannot be so vague as to permit unjustified disparity of sentences. The discretion of sentencing judges is wide, but is not unfettered. Each sentence must, in the words of the *Criminal Code*, be "fit," and a significantly disparate sentence is not a fit sentence unless there is a reason for the disparity. Justice requires that two offenders in identical life circumstances who commit identical crimes should receive identical sentences. Such a twinning is rare, but the sentence process must be such that the reason for any apparent disparity is clear.

On the other hand, the guidance offered should not be too rigid. A fixed guideline, or tariff (or, indeed, even an "approved range"), fails to take into account the immense variety of circumstances which can be found in different cases involving a conviction for the same offence. Even putting aside the offender's circumstances, those who advocate some form of fixed sentences fail to appreciate that the definitions of the crimes in the *Criminal Code* contain only certain key elements required for guilt. For example, the definition of robbery requires only the taking of the property of another accompanied by an act of violence. The elements for guilt are the same whether the offence involves an elaborate bank hold-up or, literally, taking candy from a baby. The category of "robbery" is simply too broad for any meaningful sentence regime. The manifest object of the *Criminal Code* is that the sentencing process will adjust for the other important factors, whether aggravating or mitigating. This is why the sentencing judge is given a wide scope of terms of possible sentences.

The crime of sexual assault, like the crime of robbery, is so broadly defined that it encompasses all manner of crimes, some serious, some not so serious. A rational sentencing structure segregates them into meaningful categories. The minimal and maximal sentences permitted by law remain possible, although to be sure the former is unlikely for the serious categories and the latter for the less serious.

The sentencing process now adopted by this court is to state atypical categories with precision, and to acknowledge at the same time that each actual case presents differences from the archetypical case. These differences might mitigate or aggravate. Nevertheless, the idea of a typical case affords a starting-point for sentencing because one can state a precise sentence for that precise category. An actual sentence in a real case will vary upwards or downwards from that depending upon the balance of the factors present in the actual case. Many archetypes already exist, of which "bank hold-up" is a good example. What cannot always be found in the cases is a precise definition of such typical cases, and this imprecision can lead to confusion. Nor can a precise starting-point always be found.

This, then, is the starting-point approach: first, a categorization of a crime into "typical cases," second, a starting sentence for each typical case, third, the refinement of the sentence to the very specific circumstances of the actual case.

This court has a duty to offer guidance in the form of a statement of typical cases and starting-points. Sentencing courts, in turn, are asked to acknowledge the starting-point and then summarize the relevant factors before passing sentence. We thus have not the injustice of uniform sentences but the justice of a uniform approach. Dangerous rigidity is avoided because there are no arbitrary end-points. Nor is there real disparity, because all sentences of the same genre start at the same point and differences are rationally explained.

This is the sentencing policy adopted by this court.

II

The second issue is to describe a fit starting-point for offences under s. 246.1 of the *Criminal Code*.

The crime of sexual assault covers the huge spectrum of cases from a stolen kiss to the worst forms of human degradation: see *R v. Taylor* (1985), 19 CCC (3d) 156, 44 CR (3d) 263, 36 Alta. LR (2d) 275. The first step, as with robbery, is to describe some "typical" cases. Several will probably appear, and a starting-point be found. There is no magic in this; it is simply a description of the basic elements of a meaningful category of crimes which fall within the broadly defined code offence: see, for example, *R v. R.P.T.* (1983), 7 CCC (3d) 109, [1983] 5 WWR 558, 46 AR 87.

Sometimes, the crime is not serious: see, for example, *R v. Croft* (1979), Alta. D 7505-02. It is not, however, the purpose of these reasons to deal with minor sexual assaults.

One archetypical case of sexual assault is where a person, by violence or threat of violence, forces an adult victim to submit to sexual activity of a sort or intensity such that a reasonable person would know beforehand that the victim likely would suffer lasting emotional or psychological injury, whether or not physical injury occurs. The injury might come from the sexual aspect of the situation or from the violence used or from any combination of the two. This category, which we would describe as major sexual assault, includes not only what we suspect will continue to be called rape, but obviously also many cases of attempted rape, *fellatio*, *cunnilingus*, and buggery where the foreseeable major harm which we later describe more fully is present.

The paramount sentencing factors for a major sexual assault must be deterrence and what has been called denunciation. In *R v. Wood* (1975), 26 CCC (2d) 100 at p. 107, [1976] 2 WWR 135 at p. 143 McDermid JA adopts these words from a Law Reform Commission paper to explain the denunciatory effect of sentencing:

Assuming that one of the purposes of the criminal law is the protection of certain core values in society, is it not an important function of sentencing and dispositions to assist in making clear what those values are? The educative effect of the sentencing process cannot be lost sight of. Through the sentence the courts may influence the behavior of others by confirming for them that their law abiding conduct is approved and that it is still worthwhile to resist temptation.

The key, then, to a major sexual assault is the evident blameworthiness of the offender, which was described by Laycraft JA (as he then was) in *R v. Fait* (1982), 68 CCC (2d) 367, 20 Alta. LR (2d) 90 *sub nom. R v. F.*, 37 AR 273, as [at p. 374] "… contemptuous disregard for the feelings and personal integrity of the victim." It is sometimes said that we live in a sexually permissive era, the age of the liberated libido. Many believe that gratification of sexual desire by almost any means is not only normal but "healthy." This attitude unsurprisingly has led to some confusion, and the belief by some that society also permits the use of others as objects for sexual gratification. It does not, and denunciatory sentences are needed to reinforce the point.

The other aspect which creates a major sexual assault is the effect on the victim. Notwithstanding statements in some authorities to the contrary, the tradition is to assume, in the case of a rape for example, that the victim has suffered notable psychological or emotional harm aside entirely from any physical injury. Of course, once this assumption is brought into question, the Crown must prove it. Nevertheless, harm generally is inferred from the very nature of the assault. This harm includes not just the haunting fear of another attack, the painful struggle with a feeling that somehow the victim is to blame, and the sense of violation or outrage, but also a lingering sense of powerlessness. What we mean by his last is that, while we all are aware in an intellectual way about the fragility of normal existence, to experience a sudden and real threat to one's well-being, a threat so intense that one must beg to be spared, tends to destroy that sense of personal security which modern society strives to offer and humanity so obviously wants. It matters little in this respect whether that threat comes from a robber, a rapist, or any swaggering bully.

The starting-point to sentencing for a major sexual assault is three years, assuming a mature accused with previous good character and no criminal record. On the other hand, we emphasize that the typical case just described does not include a major aggravating factor which is present sufficiently often that it could almost be called a secondary category: this is where the attack is planned and deliberate, whether the offender has stalked his victim or chosen her at random: see, by way of example, *R v. Cardinal* (1983), Alta. D 7515-01 [summarized 9 WCB 118]. …

Before turning to the facts of the appeal before us, we propose to discuss the last step in this sentencing approach, a consideration of the many aggravating and mitigating factors which often arise and which must be weighed in fixing a fit sentence in a specific case.

…

In the circumstances of this case, it could be said that the victim was imprudent as to her own safety. This does not, however, offer the slightest mitigation. Nor is the drunkenness of the accused relevant except in support of the argument that the attack was spontaneous. Nor can Sandercock claim that he previously had good character, nor that he spared the victim the added pain of offering testimony. In the circumstances, any claim of remorse rings hollowly. The most that can be said for him is that he did offer a plea of guilty and thereby waived some of his constitutional rights in deference to the expeditious administration of justice.

In my view, on a balance of all the factors here, I would allow the Crown leave to appeal, allow the appeal, and substitute a sentence of four and one-half years for the sentence of three years imposed by the learned trial judge.

NOTE

Subsequently, the Alberta Court of Appeal extended the starting-point or tariff approach to sentencing by applying it to a number of offences. In *R v. S.(W.B.)* (1992), 73 CCC (3d) 530 (Alta. CA), the court established a starting point of four years for sexual offences against children in the context of a trust or "near-trust" relationship. Similarly, in *R v. Brown et al.* (1992), 73 CCC (3d) 242 (Alta. CA), a starting point for interspousal assaults was established and subsequently confirmed in *R v. Ollenberger* (1994), 29 CR (4th) 166 (Alta. CA). With respect to manslaughter, however, the variety of ways in which the offence can be committed persuaded the Alberta Court of Appeal that it was not amenable to the starting-point approach (see *R v. Tallman* (1989), 68 CR (3d) 367). The Manitoba Court of Appeal has applied the starting-point analysis to this type of case. In *R v. C.D.* (1991), 75 Man. R (2d) 14 (CA) and *R v. M.F.D.* (1991), 75 Man. R (2d) 21 (CA), the court established a four- to five-year starting point for sexual assaults perpetrated by family members where the victim is a young child and the sexual abuse extends over a period of time. The Nova Scotia Court of Appeal has also adopted the starting-point approach in a number of different types of cases (see *R v. Owen* (1982), 50 NSR (2d) 696 (CA) and *R v. Boutilier* (1985), 66 NSR (2d) 310 (CA)).

The Court of Appeal for Ontario refused to follow the starting-point approach established in *Johnas* and *Sandercock*. In *R v. Glassford* (1988), 42 CCC (3d) 259 (Ont. CA), a case involving a sexual assault on a woman, the court reiterated this position (at 265):

> As in the past, this court declines to follow and apply the judgment in *Sandercock*. A review of the other cases cited reveals that primarily each case must be decided on its own facts. Further, the cases reflect a trend in recent years towards longer sentences for offences of this character.

However, consider the judgment of the Court of Appeal for Ontario in the following case, *R v. Joseph B.* (1990), 36 OAC 307 (Ont. CA). Does this case not establish a stratified tariff of sorts? The Alberta Court of Appeal in *R v. S.(W.B.)*, supra, made the following observations about the *Joseph B.* case (at 551):

> The view we take of the matter is consistent with that expressed by the Ontario Court of Appeal in *R v. B.(J.)* and by this court in *R v. Jankovik*. To state that the "usual range" of sentence in cases of sexual abuse of children by a person who stands *in loco parentis* in cases of sexual intercourse will be three to five years (as the Ontario Court of Appeal said), is not far different from saying that the starting point is four to five years.

R v. Joseph B.
(1990), 36 OAC 307 (Ont. CA)

BLAIR JA: The appellant appeals against concurrent sentences of eight years for sexual assault and five years for indecent assault upon his stepdaughter imposed after conviction by Byers DCJ, sitting with a jury. The offences were committed between 1978 and 1988. The earlier period from 1978 to 1983 was covered by the court for indecent assault under the former s. 149(1) of the *Criminal Code*, RSC 1970, c. C-34, which provided for a maximum sentence of five years. It was repealed by SC 1980-81-82-83, c. 125, s. 8. The latter period, from 1983 to 1987, was covered by the count for sexual assault under s. 246.1 (now s. 271 of the *Criminal Code*, RSC 1985, c. C-46) which was enacted by s. 19 of the 1980-81-82-83 amendments. It provides for a maximum sentence of ten years' imprisonment.

The appellant commenced having sexual intercourse with his stepdaughter when she was only six years of age. Except for the periods he was in prison, he had intercourse with her almost every week and sometimes more frequently until well after her fourteenth birthday. The intercourse was mainly vaginal but occasionally oral. Except for one occasion when the appellant put the stepdaughter's head in a sink, there was no violence, apart from the acts of indecent and sexual assault. However, at all times the victim was threatened with punishment if she did not comply with the appellant's demands or if she informed anyone of the assaults. Very late in the sequence of assaults she complained to her mother who disbelieved her and, indeed, testified on behalf of her husband at the trial. The assaults only came to light when the victim complained to a neighbour who called the police.

The learned trial judge described the appellant as a "violent man." He was a heavy drinker. On a number of occasions, the wife, the victim and the one son of the marriage had to seek refuge from his violence in a neighbour's house.

The appellant has a significant criminal record. His most serious conviction was for attempted rape in 1982 arising from a sexual attack on an eight year old girlfriend of the stepdaughter who was staying in his house overnight, for which he was sentenced to imprisonment for two years less one day. His other convictions included two for assault, two for drinking and driving offences and single convictions for wilful damage, theft and failure to comply with a probation order. For these offences he was twice sentenced to a fine and for the others, to short sentences the longest of which was three months' imprisonment.

The decisions of provincial appellate courts establish that, except in usual circumstances, a penitentiary sentence is called for in all cases of sexual abuse of children to whom the convicted person stands in loco parentis if the abuse involves sexual intercourse. Such sentences reflect society's denunciation of this abhorrent conduct and the breach of trust reposed on parents or guardians of children. Both counsel agreed that the usual range of sentences for this type of offence is from three to five years. The length of sentence within the range of three to five years depends on a number of factors. These include the age of the victim, the duration and frequency of the sexual assaults, the criminal record of the offender, the effects on the victim and the presence or absence of collateral violence or remorse.

Substantially the same cases were referred to by both counsel and no useful purpose would be served by a detailed analysis to illustrate how the sentencing factors enumerated above were applied to particular situations. It may be of assistance for future reference to categorize the severity of the decisions. Sentences of five years, the high end of the range, were imposed in *R v. Issler* (1976), 1 AR 27 (Alta. CA); *R v. R.P.T.* (1983), 46 AR 87; 7 CCC (3d) 109 (Alta. CA); *R v. Deley* (1988), 27 OAC 287 (Ont. CA); and *R v. Mino* (1985), 9 OAC 81 (Ont. CA). Sentences of four years, the middle of the range, were imposed in *R v. Watson* (1987), 22 OAC 239 (Ont. CA.); *R v. R.J.S.* (1985), 8 OAC 241; 45 CR (3d) 161 (Ont. CA); and *R v. E.G.* (1987), 20 OAC 378 (Ont. CA). Sentences of three years, the low end of the range, were imposed in *R v. K.S.L.*, unreported, May 5, 1987 (BC CA), and *R v. Pearson*, unreported, October 5, 1981 (Que. CA)). This court's decision in *R v. Tomigo*, unreported, June 30, 1981, demonstrates that the ordinary range will be exceeded where the circumstances cry out for a more severe penalty. In that case, the convicted person had engaged for a period of approximately ten years in vaginal and anal intercourse routinely and frequently with his three stepdaughters commencing, in each case, when they were very young. This court increased a sentence of four years imposed by the trial judge to twelve years.

In this case, Byers DCJ stated in imposing sentence that he was "dealing … with crimes of violence and power." He found several aggravating factors in the conduct of the appellant. The chief one was that the sentence in 1982 "had apparently no effect whatsoever on him" as he continued his assaults on his stepdaughter immediately upon his release. There was no evidence of remorse or of any effort by the appellant to understand or to restrain his sexual behaviour. Because he pleaded not guilty, the stepdaughter was required to testify and be cross-examined both at the preliminary inquiry and at trial where the appellant did not testify. In the trial judge's opinion, the stepdaughter would "carry the scars … forever" and the appellant had "robbed her of her childhood." The offences, in his view, involved a gross breach of parental trust. Rather than protect his stepdaughter the appellant preyed upon her.

The trial judge also expressed concern about the effect of the appellant's conduct on his family and he strongly recommended that the Children's Aid Society should be prepared to assist them. He concluded by stating that general deterrence was the sole principle of punishment applicable to this type of offence. He questioned whether his sentence would have any deterrent effect on the offender but it would accomplish the purpose of removing him "from any opportunity for some time of preying on another young lady."

No expert psychiatric or psychological evidence was given as to the effect of the appellant's conduct on his stepdaughter. How profound it must have been is illustrated by the evidence of her mother. Her daughter failed her physical education class at school, even though it was a class which everyone usually passed, because she refused to take her clothes off in front of other girls. Even when she was with her mother, she would go into a different room to change clothes. She habitually wore a lot of clothes in layers over her body.

Mr. O'Connor, in his able argument, referred to the appellant's background as a mitigating factor. It was similar to that of many offenders of this type—residence in a remote community, low social standing, and limited education. With his usual frankness, however, he acknowledged that this was not a justification for the appellant's conduct. He conceded that a sentence beyond the usual five year range was called for because the appellant had persisted in the sexual abuse of his stepdaughter after serving his sentence for attempted rape. He suggested that six years' imprisonment would be an appropriate sentence and advanced two arguments in support of his proposal.

His first submission was that the trial judge erred in stating that general deterrence is the sole principle of punishment applicable to this case. In my respectful opinion, this constitutes an error in principle and resulted in the trial judge excluding the possibility of reform and rehabilitation when imposing sentence. All these factors must be considered in sentencing for this type of offence as Tallis JA said in *R v. Gordon* (1984), 34 Sask. R 232, at p. 233:

> The principle of sentencing which emphasizes the need generally to express society's revulsion for crimes of this kind by the imposition of a lengthy custodial sentence is not a principle which demands a rigid and inflexible adherence to it in all cases involving the commission of such offences, regardless of the circumstances. The factors of deterrence and denunciation which the court must apply should be balanced against all other considerations properly taken into account in the sentencing process.

The main aim of sentencing is the protection of society which is more likely to be accomplished by the rehabilitation of the appellant than by an overly severe denunciatory sentence. Nevertheless, in view of the appellant's background and the gravity of his offence, the sentence of eight years cannot be considered to have been unfit when it was imposed.

NOTE

Is the starting-point approach radically different from or inconsistent with the idea of an appropriate range? Does it do more than define a starting point within a range and compel trial judges to have good reasons for departing from the starting point?

The rationale for the starting-point approach is obvious, but whether it provides a net improvement in sentencing is contentious. One weakness in this approach is suggested by *Johnas* and *Sandercock*. The appropriate starting point must be stated for a defined class of offences but, as the court makes clear, a "class of offences" is not a broad abstraction but a comparatively narrow category, such as break and enter committed by youthful offenders in an urban setting. In *Sandercock* and *Ollenberger*, the court notes that the class of sexual assault and domestic assault must be significantly subdivided before it can determine a suitable starting point. Some of these subdivisions are concerned with characteristics pertaining to the mode of committing the offence while others are concerned with characteristics of offenders. These subdivisions assume that the Court of Appeal is competent to make legislative decisions that distinguish not only in degree but in kind between different classes of offences. Unless it can be shown that the appellate courts have this skill, it is far from evident that the starting-point approach marks a net improvement over the more flexible "range" approach. This is a distinct issue from whether appellate courts have the power to subdivide offences for sentencing purposes: see the comments of the trial judge reported in *R v. Jackson* (1993), 87 CCC (3d) 56 (Sask. CA). As a practical matter, the multiplication of subdivided classes only multiplies the possibilities for arguing that a stated starting point should not apply in the individual case.

In 1997, the Supreme Court of Canada heard an appeal in a starting-point case from Alberta where the trial judge had imposed two sentences of 12 months each, to be served concurrently, for sexual assaults on a 16-year-old foster child and a 14-year-old babysitter. The Alberta Court of Appeal, applying *Sandercock*, held that the judge erred in not characterizing the offences as major sexual assaults and raised the sentences to four years and one year consecutive. On appeal to the Supreme Court of Canada, a majority of five to four reversed the Court of Appeal decision and restored the original sentence.

R v. McDonnell
(1997), 6 CR (5th) 231 (SCC)

Per SOPINKA J (LAMER CJC, CORY, IACOBUCCI, and MAJOR JJ concurring): The deferential approach set out in *Shropshire* was confirmed and refined in *M.(C.A.)*. In that case, Lamer CJ, on behalf of the Court, stated at paras. 90-92:

> Put simply, absent an error in principle, failure to consider a relevant factor, or an overemphasis of the appropriate factors, a court of appeal should only intervene to vary a sentence imposed at trial if the sentence is demonstrably unfit. Parliament explicitly vested sentencing judges with a discretion to determine the appropriate degree and kind of punishment under the *Criminal Code*. As s. 717(1) reads:
>
>> 717(1) Where an enactment prescribes different degrees or kinds of punishment in respect of an offence, the punishment to be imposed is, subject to the limitations prescribed in the enactment, in the discretion of the court that convicts the person who commits the offence.
>
> This deferential standard of review has profound functional justifications. As Iacobucci J explained in *Shropshire*, at para. 46, where the sentencing judge has had the benefit of presiding over the trial of the offender, he or she will have had the comparative advantage of having seen and heard the witnesses to the crime. But in the absence of a full trial, where the offender has pleaded guilty to an offence and the sentencing judge has only enjoyed the benefit of oral and written sentencing submissions (as was the case in both *Shropshire* and this instance), the argument in favour of deference remains compelling. A sentencing judge still enjoys a position of advantage over an appellate judge in being able to directly assess the sentencing submissions of both the Crown and the offender. A sentencing judge also possesses the unique qualifications of experience and judgment from having served on the front lines of our criminal justice system. Perhaps most importantly, the sentencing judge will normally preside near or within the community which has suffered the consequences of the offender's crime. As such, the sentencing judge will have a strong sense of the particular blend of sentencing goals that will be "just and appropriate" for the protection of that community. The determination of a just and appropriate sentence is a delicate art which attempts to balance carefully the societal goals of sentencing against the moral blameworthiness

of the offender and the circumstances of the offence, while at all times taking into account the needs and current conditions of and in the community. The discretion of a sentencing judge should thus not be interfered with lightly.

Appellate courts, of course, serve an important function in reviewing and minimizing the disparity of sentences imposed by sentencing judges for similar offenders and similar offences committed throughout Canada. ... But in exercising this role, courts of appeal must still exercise a margin of deference before intervening in the specialized discretion that Parliament has explicitly vested in sentencing judges. It has been repeatedly stressed that there is no such thing as a uniform sentence for a particular crime. ... Sentencing is an inherently individualized process, and the search for a single appropriate sentence for a similar offender and a similar crime will frequently be a fruitless exercise of academic abstraction. As well, sentences for a particular offence should be expected to vary to some degree across various communities and regions in this country, as the "just and appropriate" mix of accepted sentencing goals will depend on the needs and current conditions of and in the particular community where the crime occurred. For these reasons, consistent with the general standard of review we articulated in *Shropshire*, I believe that a court of appeal should only intervene to minimize the disparity of sentences where the sentence imposed by the trial judge is in substantial and marked departure from the sentences customarily imposed for similar offenders committing similar crimes.

[para17] I have included extensive references to these cases because in my view they are highly significant to the case at bar. *M.(C.A.)* set out that, in the absence of an error of principle, failure to consider a relevant factor, or overemphasis of the appropriate factors, a sentence should only be overturned if the sentence is demonstrably unfit. The respondent submitted that the sentencing judge in the present case failed to consider relevant factors and that the sentence was demonstrably unfit. Moreover, both the respondent and the Court of Appeal appear to have treated the failure of the sentencing judge to characterize the offence as a major sexual assault as an error in principle. I will discuss these contentions in turn.

B. Relevant Factors and Demonstrable Unfitness

[para18] *Sandercock*, supra, established in Alberta the notion of a "major sexual assault," which carried with it a presumptive sentence ("starting point") of three years. *Sandercock* stated at p. 84 that the key to a major sexual assault is the "evident blameworthiness of the offender" as reflected in the extent to which the offender's actions demonstrated a "contemptuous disregard for the feelings and personal integrity of the victim." The Court of Appeal held in the present case that the sentencing judge erred in failing to find that the first offence amounted to a major sexual assault.

[para19] In concluding that the sentencing judge had mischaracterized the nature of the assault which was the subject of the first offence, the Court of Appeal relied on several factors. First, the court stated (at p. 173):

One salient fact cannot be overlooked. This was not, despite the defence suggestion, a case of "fondling." It was a case of penile penetration of the vagina. The fact that

McDonnell only succeeded in partially penetrating the complainant's vagina with his penis because of the complainant's efforts to resist him does not make this any less a major sexual assault. Partial penetration will suffice. Accordingly, this assault falls squarely within what is described in Sandercock as one of the archetypical cases of major sexual assault.

Second, the court did not accept the submission of the defence, which the court stated (at p. 173) the "trial judge appears to have implicitly accepted," that the first offence could not constitute major sexual assault because of the absence of psychological harm. The court held that non-consensual intercourse leads to a very high likelihood of trauma, which likelihood is one of the indicia of a major sexual assault according to Sandercock. In any event, the court concluded based on viva voce evidence and the victim impact statement that the complainant in the first case did suffer psychological harm. On the basis of these factors, the court concluded that the first offence was a major sexual assault and that the sentence ordered by the sentencing judge was insufficient.

[para20] In my view, the Court of Appeal fails to point to a relevant factor not considered by the sentencing judge that would give rise to appellate review of the sentence. The first factor emphasized by the Court of Appeal, partial penetration, was explicitly cited by the sentencing judge. She stated:

> The assault, while reprehensible, was an isolated one, and it was a situation of far more than fondling as the accused attempted penetration. However, in that case, there was no involvement of violence nor of threats. It did not involve oral sex nor anal intercourse, and there was only partial penetration.

Clearly, the sentencing judge did consider penetration as a factor in reaching a sentence. Thus, consideration of this factor fails to give grounds to alter the sentence.

[para21] The second factor alluded to by the Court of Appeal, psychological trauma, was also considered by the sentencing judge. The judge stated:

> It was a traumatic experience for the victim, but she was already 16 years old and was having other problems which may have contributed to her subsequent state of mind.

The judge later stated:

> In sentencing Terry McDonnell, I take into account his strong family support, the strong community support, his remorse and his desire to quit drinking, but also the trauma suffered by the victim at a time when she was already troubled, and the fact that FACS doesn't see counselling as being of any use to prevent re-offending, for Mr. McDonnell might simply re-offend if drunk again.

It is clear, in my view, that the sentencing judge did not fail to consider the trauma to the complainant in the first assault.

[para22] Finally, the Court of Appeal stated (at p. 175) that it was "perverse" for the sentencing judge to treat the other personal problems the first complainant had been having around the time of the assault as a mitigating factor. I disagree with this characterization of the sentencing judge's views in the matter. It appears to me that in the first statement above the sentencing judge noted the problems the complainant

had been having as a partial explanation of her personal problems after the assault; that is, not all her problems after the assault were attributable to the assault. The second statement by the sentencing judge indicates that while there were mitigating factors, the complainant's personal problems actually made the assault more serious. The Court of Appeal did not interpret the judge correctly, in my view, in reaching its conclusion that the sentencing judge had misused the evidence of the problems that the first complainant had been having.

[para23] The respondent's submission that the judge failed to consider relevant factors in my view cannot succeed with respect to the first offence. The respondent also submits that the sentence imposed was demonstrably unfit. The sentence originally imposed for the first offence was one year, whereas the Court of Appeal imposed a four-year sentence. The "starting point" as set out in *Sandercock* for a major sexual assault was three years. These differences in themselves provide me no basis to conclude that the judge's sentence originally passed was demonstrably unfit.

[para24] *Sandercock* does not purport to create a rigid tariff. At pp. 82-83 the Alberta Court of Appeal stated:

> … the [sentencing] guidance offered should not be too rigid. A fixed guideline, or tariff (or, indeed, even an "approved range"), fails to take into account the immense variety of circumstances which can be found in different cases involving a conviction for the same offence. Even putting aside the offender's circumstances, those who advocate some form of fixed sentences fail to appreciate that the definitions of the crimes in the *Criminal Code* contain only certain key elements required for guilt. … The manifest object of the *Criminal Code* is that the sentencing process will adjust for the other important factors, whether aggravating or mitigating. This is why the sentencing judge is given a wide scope of terms of possible sentences.

Indeed, for reasons which follow, I conclude that it would be inappropriate to do so. Faithful to this instruction, the sentencing judge took into account all relevant mitigating and aggravating circumstances and arrived at what she considered was an appropriate sentence. Accordingly, the sentence's departure from the Court of Appeal's view of the appropriate starting point does not in itself imply that the sentence was demonstrably unfit.

[para25] Moreover, I note that in a case not dissimilar to the present case, the Alberta Court of Appeal imposed a custodial sentence of one year. In *R v. A.B.C.* (1991), 120 AR 106, the accused had sexually assaulted his sedated 16-year-old daughter, fondling her breasts and vagina and possibly penetrating her vagina with his penis. The Court of Appeal vacated the two-year suspended sentence and imposed a custodial sentence of one year. The respondent submitted in oral argument, and my colleague McLachlin J appears to have accepted this submission, that *A.B.C.* was decided on the basis of procedural delays and other particular facts and should not affect the present analysis. On the contrary, to the extent that the particular facts in *A.B.C.* determined the sentence in that case, it may also be equally argued that the particular facts of the present case determined the one-year sentence meted out by the sentencing judge for a sexual assault similar in nature to that in *A.B.C.* It is difficult to conclude that a sentence of one year in the present case, given the similarities to

A.B.C., was demonstrably unfit. While this sentence is at the bottom of the scale, this does not make it demonstrably unfit. I note that in both *Shropshire* and *M.(C.A.)*, two recent, unanimous decisions, this Court refused on the basis of deference to reduce sentences that were clearly at the high end of the spectrum.

[para26] In summary, with respect to the first assault, the trial judge did not fail to consider relevant factors, nor was the sentence demonstrably unfit.

[para27] With respect to the second offence, the same conclusion applies: the judge did not ignore the factors raised by the Court of Appeal, nor is there any indication that the sentence was demonstrably unfit. The sentencing judge did, as the Court of Appeal acknowledged (at p. 176), consider the trauma to the complainant, stating:

> Regarding the charges of assault against [the second complainant], the victim in this case has been traumatized, but the acts of the accused were very much in the "less grave" category. Mr. McDonnell is a man of otherwise good character and is a strong member of his community. He has always maintained employment and supported his family. An additional lengthy consecutive custodial sentence to the custodial sentence imposed on the first charge would only seek to destroy the accused and his family and is not necessary to deter others from committing such an offence.
>
> I will thus sentence him to six months in jail concurrent to the first sentence, plus probation for the same period of time.

Neither the Court of Appeal nor the respondent points out a factor ignored by the sentencing judge in reaching her conclusion of a sentence of six months for the second offence. Nor is there any reason given by either the respondent or the Court of Appeal to conclude that a six-month sentence was demonstrably unfit. The Court of Appeal simply disagreed with the sentence ordered and substituted its own opinion for that of the sentencing judge.

[para28] My colleague McLachlin J disagrees with this analysis and states that the sentences imposed by the sentencing judge were outside the acceptable range. While the above analysis generally addresses her reasoning, I add here that I disagree with her conclusion that a variety of past cases reveals that the sentence in the present case was demonstrably unfit. McLachlin J provides at para. 110 a lengthy list of cases which she contends support the conclusion that a sentence under two years in the present case was inappropriate. While I will not review each case upon which she relies, I will note that, in my view, many of the cases provided are inappropriate cases to consider in the present context. For example, in *R v. S.G.O.R.* (1991), 113 AR 36 (CA), aside from other sexual offences involved in the case, the accused raped his daughter over 20 times from when she was four years old until she was 12. In *R v. S.(W.B.)*; *R v. P.(M.)* (1992), 73 CCC (3d) 530 (Alta. CA), the accused S. engaged repeatedly in anal intercourse with his six-year-old stepdaughter and his stepson, who was initially in grade three, over a period of two years. The accused P. committed both anal and vaginal rape of a seven-year-old child, physically beating her head and body. *R v. Spence* (1992), 78 CCC (3d) 451 (Alta. CA), involved an accused raping his 15-year-old cousin and physically beating and threatening her. *R v. Nicholson* (1993), 145 AR 262 (CA), involved 20 to 30 acts of intercourse starting when the complainant was 12 years old; associated with this abuse, the accused, amongst other

things, discharged a rifle in the direction of the complainant as she attempted to escape his residence. Other cases cited by McLachlin J involved children much younger than the complainants in the present case, such as *R v. Lapatak* (1995), 169 AR 385 (CA), which involved a three-year-old victim.

[para29] In my view, many of the cases cited by McLachlin J involved offences considerably more serious than the present case. While any sexual offence is serious, particularly on young people, the violence of the offences, the repetition of the offences, and the extreme youth of the victims in the cases cited above clearly distinguish them from the present case. Indeed, contrary to supporting McLachlin J's position, in my view the variable circumstances in the cases she cites highlight the importance of individualized sentencing. In any event, in my respectful view, the sentences in the cases she cites do not lead to the conclusion that the sentences in the present case were demonstrably unfit. The sentences in the present case, while low, were not demonstrably unfit.

C. Error in Principle

[para30] While I have concluded that the sentencing judge did not ignore factors and that the sentences were not demonstrably unfit, according to *M.(C.A.)* and *Shropshire*, appellate review of a sentence is also appropriate if the sentencing judge committed an error in principle. Both the Court of Appeal and the respondent appear to treat the alleged departure from *Sandercock* as an error in principle. For example, the Court of Appeal found and the respondent submitted that the first assault was a "major sexual assault" in contradiction to the finding of the sentencing judge. The Court of Appeal stated (at pp. 172-73):

> We have concluded that the trial judge erred in finding that this was not a major sexual assault. This court made it clear in *R v. Sandercock* … , that the key to a major sexual assault is the "evident blameworthiness of the offender" as reflected in the extent to which the offender's actions demonstrated a "contemptuous disregard for the feelings and personal integrity of the victim." Here, McDonnell's actions in the first case clearly fall within the category of a major sexual assault.

The court then treated the error as one which justified alteration of the sentence, which implicitly treated the failure to find the major sexual assault as an error in principle. The Court of Appeal concluded that the sentencing judge wrongly declined to find a major sexual assault in part on the basis of what the court viewed as a misapprehension of the requirements for a major sexual assault. The court stated that the sentencing judge appeared to accept the argument of the defence that there was no significant psychological harm in the first case, and therefore there was no major sexual assault. The court stated (at p. 173) that while actual psychological harm may generally be presumed from non-consensual intercourse, it is not the actual harm, but the high likelihood of harm from the nature of the assault that gives rise to a major sexual assault.

[para31] I disagree with the Court of Appeal that the sentencing judge accepted the argument of the defence that there was no psychological harm. As noted above,

the sentencing judge specifically found psychological harm to the complainants in both cases. In my view, even if the sentencing judge required proof of such harm before finding a major sexual assault, the sentencing judge appeared to find such harm so any "error" in this regard did not affect the outcome.

[para32] In any event, in my view it can never be an error in principle in itself to fail to place a particular offence within a judicially created category of assault for the purposes of sentencing. There are two main reasons for this conclusion. First, *Shropshire* and *M.(C.A.)*, two recent and unanimous decisions of this Court, clearly deference should be shown to a lower court's sentencing decision. If an appellate court could simply create reviewable principles by creating categories of offences, deference is diminished in a manner that is inconsistent with *Shropshire* and *M.(C.A.)*. In order to circumvent deference and to enable appellate review of a particular sentence, a court may simply create a category of offence and a "starting point" for that offence, and treat as an error in principle any deviation in sentencing from the category so created. Indeed, that is what the Court of Appeal in Alberta has done in the present case. If the categories are defined narrowly, and deviations from the categorization are generally reversed, the discretion that should be left in the hands of the trial and sentencing judges is shifted considerably to the appellate courts.

[para33] Second, there is no legal basis for the judicial creation of a category of offence within a statutory offence for the purposes of sentencing. As has been true since *Frey v. Fedoruk*, [1950] SCR 517, it is not for judges to create criminal offences, but rather for the legislature to enact such offences. By creating a species of sexual assault known as a "major sexual assault," and by basing sentencing decisions on such a categorization, the Alberta Court of Appeal has effectively created an offence, at least for the purposes of sentencing, contrary to the spirit if not the letter of Frey.

[para34] The danger of courts encroaching into the realm of Parliament by creating offences is illustrated by the present case. The Court of Appeal appeared to base its conclusion that the first assault was a "major sexual assault" on the likelihood of psychological harm and indeed on the existence of actual harm. The court thus concluded that the sentence should be based on the existence of such harm. There is, however, a specific offence that deals with sexual assault causing bodily harm within the *Criminal Code*, namely s. 272(c). I note that *R v. McCraw*, [1991] 3 SCR 72, established that psychological harm from a sexual assault may be considered bodily harm. Given Parliament's intention to treat sexual assaults causing bodily harm under s. 272(c), it is particularly inappropriate to create a "major sexual assault," which is based at least in part on the existence of harm to the complainant pursuant to s. 271. While the Court of Appeal at times appeared to rely simply on the likelihood of harm in the present case, in *Sandercock* itself, actual harm was contemplated. *Sandercock* stated at p. 85, "[t]he other aspect which creates a major sexual assault is the effect on the victim." In my view, if the prosecution is to be based on the harm to the victim, the accused should be charged under the appropriate section, s. 272(c). It is not for the courts to establish a subset of offence within s. 271 that is based on harm.

[para35] There is a further problem with the treatment of harm by the Court of Appeal in the present case in that it appeared at times to establish a presumption of psychological harm from a sexual assault. Admittedly, at other times the Court

discussed the likelihood of psychological harm from an offence as illustrating the seriousness of the offence, rather than actual harm itself. To illustrate this ambiguity, consider the following passage (at p. 173):

> The first point we wish to make is that we cannot envision a situation where non-consensual intercourse—vaginal, anal or oral—would not fall into the major sexual assault category. … In addition, in each case, there also exists a very real likelihood of psychological harm. Therefore, what must be understood is that it is not necessary that the Crown prove the existence of this kind of harm as a condition precedent to the courts classifying a sexual assault as a major one. Psychological harm is presumed in the absence of evidence to the contrary.

The court later stated (at p. 174):

> To put the matter another way, the offender is being sentenced on the basis of a major sexual assault, not because any specific psychological consequences have flowed from the attack but rather because of the nature of the attack and the fact that it poses the very real likelihood of long-term emotional or psychological harm. The fact that no such harm may materialize, a fact one could not possibly know until the victim's life had been lived in its entirety, is not a mitigating factor. However, that said, this does not mean that the consequences of the sexual assault are irrelevant. The degree of seriousness of the actions may be measured against the likely long-term consequences of the prohibited act. In other words, where the psychological harm has been severe, that may well be an aggravating factor. Of course, where harm beyond that which would be normally presumed is claimed in a case, the Crown must lead evidence to substantiate it.

[para36] These passages are somewhat unclear. At one point it appears that the court presumes that psychological harm would result from a sexual assault, while at another point it appears that the court is not presuming psychological harm, but rather is simply noting, correctly in my view, the likelihood of psychological harm resulting from the actions of the accused. *McCraw*, supra, established that a threat to commit sexual assault amounted to a threat to commit assault causing bodily harm because of the high likelihood of psychological harm resulting from a sexual assault, a likelihood recognized by the Court of Appeal in the present case. Such a likelihood does not, however, establish a legal presumption of harm in cases involving an actual assault, as opposed to a threat. If harm is an element of the offence, the Crown must prove its existence beyond a reasonable doubt.

[para37] To the extent that the Court of Appeal held that the Crown need not prove psychological harm in some instances, but rather such harm may be presumed, it was in error. As stated above, if the Crown wishes to rely upon the existence of psychological harm, in my view the Crown should charge under the section set out in the Code that contemplates harm, s. 272(c), and prove the offence. If an element of the offence, bodily (psychological) harm, is presumed, the Crown is improperly relieved of part of the burden of proof, which is contrary to the presumption of innocence. Accepting that harm may be an aggravating factor under s. 271, *R v. Gardiner*, [1982] 2 SCR 368, held that each aggravating factor in a sentencing hearing must be proved beyond a reasonable doubt. Such an approach is confirmed by Parliament in the new

s. 724(3)(e) of the *Criminal Code* (as amended by SC 1995, c. 22, s. 6). If psychological harm may be presumed, the burden of proving harm as an aggravating factor is improperly lifted from the Crown and shifted to the accused to disprove harm.

[para38] In the present case, a presumption of harm is unnecessary. The sentencing judge found as a fact that each complainant in the present case was traumatized. The sentence was reached after considering the harm that resulted from the offences. Thus, the Court of Appeal's discussion of the presumption of harm was, in my view, both erroneous and unnecessary; harm existed and was considered in setting the sentence.

[para39] The Court of Appeal appeared to make two other suggestions of errors in principle by the trial judge. I note that the respondent did not specifically raise these alleged errors in written argument before this Court, but raised them specifically only in oral argument. One error alleged by the Court of Appeal was that the trial judge improperly relied on *R v. R.P.T.* (1983), 7 CCC (3d) 109 (Alta. CA). The court stated that, notwithstanding that the principles it set out were revisited in *R v. S.(W.B.)*; *R v. P.(M.)*, supra, *R.P.T.* was factually inapplicable because in the present case there was no family that might be restored. In my view, the court erred in finding that the trial judge relied on *R.P.T.* with respect to the restoration of the family. *R.P.T.* held at p. 114 that even where there is a family to restore, if the sexual assault by a person in loco parentis on a family member were serious, "[t]he only solution, however imperfect ... must be to graft a rehabilitative sentence to a denunciatory sentence." If the assault were less serious and if there were a family to restore, a lesser sentence may be imposed; indeed, if the circumstances were "less significant" (p. 115), a suspended sentence may be appropriate.

[para40] In the present case, the sentencing judge stated that while she was cognizant of *R.P.T.*, "this is not a case where simple rehabilitation will suffice." She stated that a rehabilitative sentence must be grafted to a denunciatory sentence. She thus apparently relied on the aspect of *R.P.T.* which held that despite the existence of a family, both a denunciatory and a rehabilitative sentence are required where the assault is serious. Contrary to the position of the Court of Appeal, she did not rely on the aspect of *R.P.T.* which stated that restoration of the family should be a mitigating consideration in cases where the assault is less serious. Given that the sentencing judge did not follow *R.P.T.* to rely on family restoration to mitigate the sentence, the Court of Appeal failed to point out an error in principle by the sentencing judge with respect to *R.P.T.*

[para41] Another error suggested by the Court of Appeal was that the sentencing judge improperly relied upon the passage of time "between the first and second offence (and sentencing)" (p. 177). The sentencing judge did not in any way rely upon the passage of time between the first offence and the second offence. Neither did the sentencing judge rely upon the passage of time between the first offence and sentencing per se, but rather the judge stated that "the time elapsed since the offence has relevance in relation to the relative effect of this on both the accused and the victim." I presume that the sentencing judge was referring to effect of the actions on the accused since the offence, which included, for example, remorse and a desire to quit drinking, and to the effect of the actions on the victim since the offence, which included the psychological harm that the victim had displayed since the offence. These

factors may be relevant considerations and the sentencing judge did not err in principle in referring to them.

[para42] I note that my colleague McLachlin J states that she agrees that failing to characterize the offence into a particular, judicially created category of assault is not an error in principle which would justify appellate review. However, I am concerned that while she states she does not view it as such an error, she effectively treats it, if not as an error in principle, then otherwise as an error giving rise to appellate review. She states at para. 109:

> As indicated earlier, the "starting point" is not a principle of law, but rather a tool to determine the proper range of sentence for a certain type of offence. Failure to allude to the appropriate starting point or range is not an error of principle as that term is used in *M.(C.A.)*, supra. If the trial judge fails to refer to the appropriate starting point or range but in the end imposes a sentence within the acceptable range of sentence for the offence as adjusted for the particular circumstances of the offender, a court of appeal should not interfere. On the other hand, if the sentence falls outside the appropriate range, the court of appeal must interfere: *Shropshire*, supra.

This statement, combined with her emphasis on starting points in her analysis of demonstrable unfitness in the present case, suggests to me that McLachlin J in effect treats the failure to characterize an assault properly as an error permitting appellate intervention on sentencing. That is, the failure to characterize the assault properly is not an error in principle, but if the sentence reached as a result of that error is not very similar or identical to the sentence that would have been reached had the mischaracterization not occurred, appellate courts may intervene. In my view, this effectively states that while appellate courts must permit sentencing judges to err in characterizing the offence, appellate courts may intervene, notwithstanding deference, if the trial judge's mischaracterization affected significantly the sentence ordered. Given that different views of the nature of the assault would almost inevitably lead to different sentences, in my view, mischaracterization is treated by McLachlin J as an error which will often lead to appellate intervention. In my view, as stated, mischaracterization of the offence according to judicially created categories is not an error in principle, nor should it be treated as one. In my respectful opinion, McLachlin J takes an overly permissive approach to appellate intervention that is inconsistent with both *Shropshire* and *M.(C.A.)*.

[para43] I add that I do not disagree with McLachlin J that appellate courts may set out starting-point sentences as guides to lower courts. Moreover, the starting point may well be a factor to consider in determining whether a sentence is demonstrably unfit. If there is a wide disparity between the starting point for the offence and the sentence imposed, then, assuming that the Court of Appeal has set a reasonable starting point, the starting point certainly suggests, but is not determinative of, unfitness. In my view, however, the approach taken by McLachlin J in the present case places too great an emphasis on the effect of deviation from the starting point. Unless there otherwise is a reason under *Shropshire* or *M.(C.A.)* to interfere with the sentence, a sentence cannot be altered on appeal, notwithstanding deviation from a starting point. Deviation from a starting point may be a factor in considering demonstrable unfitness, but does not have the significance McLachlin J gives it.

D. Concurrent or Consecutive Sentences

[para44] The Court of Appeal not only substituted its view of the appropriate sentence for each offence in the present case, but also held that the sentences should be served consecutively, not concurrently as had been ordered by the sentencing judge. The Court of Appeal stated (at p. 177):

> Nor was this a case where concurrent sentences were appropriate. … These two offences were totally unrelated. There were two different victims and the offences were separated by a period of seven years.

[para45] The sentencing judge considered whether to order consecutive and concurrent sentences and concluded that concurrent sentences were appropriate, stating:

> An additional lengthy consecutive custodial sentence to the custodial sentence imposed on the first charge would only seek to destroy the accused and his family and is not necessary to deter others from committing such an offence.

[para46] In my opinion, the decision to order concurrent or consecutive sentences should be treated with the same deference owed by appellate courts to sentencing judges concerning the length of sentences ordered. The rationale for deference with respect to the length of sentence, clearly stated in both *Shropshire* and *M.(C.A.)*, applies equally to the decision to order concurrent or consecutive sentences. In both setting duration and the type of sentence, the sentencing judge exercises his or her discretion based on his or her first-hand knowledge of the case; it is not for an appellate court to intervene absent an error in principle, unless the sentencing judge ignored factors or imposed a sentence which, considered in its entirety, is demonstrably unfit. The Court of Appeal in the present case failed to raise a legitimate reason to alter the order of concurrent sentences made by the sentencing judge; the court simply disagreed with the result of the sentencing judge's exercise of discretion, which is insufficient to interfere.

···

McLACHLIN J dissenting (LaForest, L'Heureux-Dubé, and Gonthier JJ concurring):

···

[para57] My difficulty with the position of the appellant and the reasons of Sopinka J stems mainly from a different understanding of the nature and effect of the "starting-point" approach to sentencing. It is therefore necessary to set out my conception of that approach at the outset.

[para58] The starting-point approach to sentencing involves two steps. First, the judge determines the range of sentence for a typical case. Using that range as a starting point, a trial judge then adjusts the sentence upward or downward on the basis of factors relating to the particular offence and offender: *R v. Hessam* (1983), 43 AR 247 (CA), *R v. Sandercock* (1985), 22 CCC (3d) 79 (Alta. CA). This approach is distinguished from the tariff approach to sentencing which takes no account of the individual circumstances of the offender: C.C. Ruby, *Sentencing* (4th ed. 1994), at p. 479. The tariff approach looks only at the nature of the offence. In contrast, the starting-point approach mandates consideration of specific aggravating and mitigating factors directly relevant to the individual accused. In this way, the starting-point

approach combines general considerations relating to the crime committed with personalized considerations relating to the particular offender and the unique circumstances of the assault.

[para59] The first step on the starting-point approach consists of determining the appropriate range of sentence for an offence of this type in a typical case, assuming an offender of good character with no criminal record. In the case of sexual assault, the judge looks at the manner in which the assault was committed (e.g., by violence or threats or trickery), the nature of the sexual activity, and, most importantly, whether or not this sort of offence is likely to cause lasting emotional or psychological injury. The "key ... to a major sexual assault is the evident blameworthiness of the offender," the "contemptuous disregard for the feelings and personal integrity of the victim": *Sandercock*, supra, at p. 84. The inquiry at this stage, to repeat, is generalized and objective. The task of the judge at this stage is to determine the blameworthiness of an offender who commits the type of offence at issue in a typical case. Because the inquiry at this point is general, it proceeds on certain assumptions. The issue, on harm, is not whether actual trauma occurred, but whether this sort of criminal act would be likely to cause lasting emotional or psychological trauma. As to the offender, it is assumed that the offender is of good character and has no criminal record. See *Sandercock*, supra.

[para60] The exercise of choosing a starting point in this way resembles the longstanding practice of setting a range of sentence as a tool to arrive at a just and appropriate sentence that reflects both the crime and the individual circumstances of the offence and the offender. As Ruby, supra, at p. 482, notes, "[i]t certainly is not a new method of sentencing." The starting point may be viewed as the mid-point in the traditional range of sentences for a particular sort of crime.

[para61] The choice of a starting point is only—as the phrase makes clear—a starting point. Based as it is on assumptions as to the harm likely to flow from a typical case of the type of criminal act and the good character of the accused, it could not in fairness or principle serve as a final indication of the appropriate sentence in a particular case. As noted in *Sandercock*, supra, every case has its own unique characteristics, and every offender his or her own unique history. The goals of sentencing—deterrence, retribution and rehabilitation—play out differently depending on the peculiar concatenation of circumstances presented in each case. In short, the sentence must be individualized to the particular crime and the particular offender before the court. Having determined a starting point, the judge must go on to consider these factors and their effect on the appropriate sentence. The factors peculiar to the particular case and offender before the court may mitigate, resulting in a lower sentence than the typical case reflected by the starting point. Or they may exacerbate, resulting in a higher sentence than would prevail in the typical case.

(2) Why Was the Starting-Point Approach Developed?

[para62] The starting-point approach was developed as a way of incorporating into the sentencing process the dual perspectives of the seriousness of the offence and the need to consider the individual circumstances of the offender. It represents a restatement

of the long-standing practice of sentencing judges of beginning by considering the range of sentence that has been posed for similar criminal acts followed by consideration of factors peculiar to the case and offender before them.

[para63] Despite the common practice of first determining a range and then individualizing the sentence, the jurisprudence dealing with the proper approach to sentencing is not as clear as might be desired. Professor A. Young, *The Role of an Appellate Court in Developing Sentencing Guidelines* (1988), a report written for the Canadian Sentencing Commission, offers a useful history of sentencing theory in Canada and the failure of the courts to adequately meet the challenge of devising a principled and consistent approach to sentencing.

[para64] Appellate review of sentences was initiated only in 1921, explaining the absence of long-standing principles to guide trial judges. Prior to 1921, trial judges gave the sentence they saw fit and that was the end of the matter. Nor, in the years after 1921, were the courts instrumental "in designing relevant sentencing principles to assist lower-courts. ... Only in recent years have the appellate courts begun to express dissatisfaction with the impressionistic nature of sentencing decisions" (Young, supra, at p. 6). The maxim "Let the punishment fit the crime" might rule on Gilbert and Sullivan's stage, but in the courts the theme was "that the punishment should fit the offender" (Young, at p. 8). Precedents and theory played little part in the sentencing process. "In a sentencing model based upon the primacy of the individual there is little need for precedents that can extend beyond the characteristics of the offender in any given case" (Young, at p. 8). The Saskatchewan Court of Appeal (*R v. Natanson* (1927), 49 CCC 89) put the conventional wisdom this way (at p. 90):

> It would be impossible, and if possible it would be undesirable to lay down any general rule as to the punishment to be inflicted for any particular class of offence. Every case must be dealt with on its own facts and circumstance[s].

Similarly, in *R v. Connor and Hall* (1957), 118 CCC 237, the Ontario Court of Appeal opined (at p. 238):

> It serves little useful purpose and affords little assistance to the Court to know what sentences have beenimposed in other countries or jurisdictions or by other Courts.

[para65] The traditional notion that sentencing is primarily a matter of impression for the sentencing judge and only secondarily a matter of principle began to be questioned by the courts in the mid-60s. Behind the challenge lay increasing recognition that some measure of uniformity was essential in a sentencing process that not only was just, but was perceived to be just. In *R v. Baldhead*, [1966] 4 CCC 183 (Sask. CA), it was held that a sentence could be reviewed if it represented "a marked departure from the sentences customarily imposed in the same jurisdiction for the same or similar crimes" (p. 187).

[para66] *Baldhead* did no more than confer judicial respectability on an emerging general consensus that the law should award similar sentences for similar crimes, subject to adjustment for factors peculiar to each case. Sentences may properly vary somewhat from case to case to reflect factors peculiar to the particular act and offender on trial. But it affronts common-sense notions of justice if people who have committed the same criminal act receive wildly disparate sentences. It is neither fair nor just that

one person languish in prison years after another, who committed a similar act, is released to liberty. *Baldhead* expressed the growing view that a measure of uniformity, tempered but not obliterated by considerations particular to each case, must stand as a fundamental goal of sentencing law.

[para67] Many courts since *Baldhead* have embraced the objective of uniformity as a factor to be considered in sentencing. However, the relationship between the goal of sentencing uniformity and the goal of reflecting in a sentence the circumstances of the particular case and offender remained largely ill-defined up until the jurisprudence advocating a starting-point approach. Alongside decisions advocating the need for a measure of uniformity, stand other decisions evincing reluctance to commit it to principle. As Young, supra, puts it: "The courts have not wholly embraced the notion of uniformity for fear that broad, general principles will fail to take into account the unique characteristics of every offender" (pp. 9-10). By contrast, the starting-point approach represents an attempt to marry in one sentencing principle the values of uniformity and individualization.

[para68] It was no accident that the starting-point approach was eventually applied in the context of the crime of sexual assault. The wide spectrum of conduct embraced by the crime of "sexual assault" and the disparate views different judges may take with respect to the gravity of particular types of sexual assaults give rise to wide variations in sentences for offences that seem quite similar. See P. Marshall, "Sexual Assault, The Charter and Sentencing Reform" (1988), 63 CR (3d) 216. Depending on where a particular judge placed a particular type of sexual assault on the spectrum of severity and the seriousness with which he or she regarded that assault, a sentence might be high or low or anywhere in between. The disparities between sentences threatened to go beyond the legitimate area of divergence represented by the individual circumstances of a particular offender and offence, to a more generalized divergence based on judicial views of the seriousness of the offence. This called for judicial action. As the Manitoba Court of Appeal put it in *R v. Jourdain and Kudyba* (1958), 121 CCC 82, at p. 87:

> It is the duty not only of this Court but of all the Courts of the Province and the Crown to do whatever is possible to bring about uniformity and equalization of sentences for crimes of the same or similar gravity.

The response of courts, charged as they were with maintaining reasonable uniformity of sentences, was to introduce the concept of the "starting point."

(3) In What Jurisdictions Has the Starting-Point Approach Been Adopted?

[para69] The Courts of Appeal for Alberta, Nova Scotia (*R v. Zong* (1986), 173 APR 432), Manitoba (*R v. Muswagon* (1993), 88 Man. R (2d) 319), British Columbia (*R v. Post* (1996), 72 BCAC 312) and Saskatchewan (*R v. Jackson* (1993), 87 CCC (3d) 56) have applied the starting-point approach to sentencing to deal with marked disparities in sentences for certain crimes. The Ontario Court of Appeal in *R v. Glassford* (1988), 27 OAC 194 explicitly rejected the starting-point approach to sentencing articulated in *Sandercock*, supra. However, that same court has recently adopted the approach in narcotics cases. See *R v. Cunningham* (1996), 104 CCC (3d) 542.

[para70] In addition to the Canadian examples, the English Court of Appeal also appears to have adopted this approach. In *R v. Edwards*; *R v. Brandy*, the English Court of Appeal, Criminal Division, suggested that "[a]n appropriate level of sentencing for serious dwelling house burglary where the house was unoccupied was three years on a conviction, with variations either way to reflect the particular circumstances of the case" (*The Times*, July 1, 1996). In fact, it appears that the starting-point concept is not of recent origin in England. Cross, *The English Sentencing System* (2nd ed. 1975), states at p. 148:

> The statement of 1900 is contained in a Memorandum produced by Lord Alveston (the then Lord Chief Justice) in an effort to get agreement among the Queen's Bench Judges about the normal punishment of offences. It was sent to the Home Office and no further action appears to have been taken on it; but it is now printed as Appendix 5 of *Enforcing the Law* by Professor Jackson of Cambridge. The Memorandum states that it is not possible to do more than recommend "a range of punishments within certain limits" and throughout it speaks of periods such as three to five years penal servitude as the "correct range."

When dealing with rape, for instance, the Memorandum mentions five to seven years penal servitude as giving:

> a reasonable range of punishment to be increased if there are accompanying circumstances of aggravation, such, for example, as rape by a gang or by a parent or master, or with brutal violence, and to be reduced if there are extenuating circumstances.

[para71] The Australian courts appear to follow a similar approach. In *R v. Jabaltjari* (1989), 46 A Crim. R 47, the Court of Criminal Appeal (Northern Territory) did not interfere with the trial judge's approach described as follows: "Having fixed on the objective sentence his Honour then made appropriate adjustments downward to give effect to the mitigating circumstances personal to the respondent" (p. 64). Although the approach is referred to by the Court as the "tariff" approach, it seems to be identical to the starting-point approach.

NOTE

The practical result of the majority's decision in this case is to restore the concurrent sentences of 12 months' imprisonment. Do you think this is appropriate or "fit" for these offences? Does the majority decision signal the end of starting points, or does it merely reduce them to guides for sentencing judges? See the decision in *R v. Waldner* (1998), 15 CR (5th) 159 (Alta. CA) per Berger JA at 169, where he distills the following principles from *McDonnell*:

1. Appellate courts may set out starting points as guides to lower courts;
2. The starting point set by a Court of Appeal must be reasonable;
3. If the starting point is reasonable, it *may* be a factor to consider in determining whether a sentence is demonstrably unfit;
4. A *wide disparity* between the starting point and the sentence imposed suggests unfitness; it is not determinative of unfitness;
5. Unless there is a reason under *Shropshire* or *M.(C.A.)* to interfere with the sentence, a sentence cannot be altered on appeal, notwithstanding deviation from a starting point.

V. THE 1996 AMENDMENTS AND THE INTRODUCTION OF LEGISLATIVE GUIDANCE

In 1996, the *Criminal Code* was amended to provide a legislative statement of the aims of sentencing in Canadian law. The absence of such a statement until that date underscores the importance of judicial decision making as the primary source of guidance. For many years, however, it has been argued that Canadian law needs a statutory statement of the aims of sentencing. This point was made forcefully in the studies of several committees and commissions working under the authority of the government or parliament, including the Ouimet committee, the Law Reform Commission of Canada, and the Royal Commission on Sentencing. The same idea was endorsed by a standing committee of the House of Commons (see *Taking Responsibility*, Report of the House of Commons Standing Committee on Justice and Solicitor General on Its Review of Sentencing, Conditional Release, and Related Aspects of Corrections (Ottawa: 1988).

The government of Canada introduced legislation in 1984 that would have included a statutory statement of aims in sentencing, but this bill died. Another attempt was made with Bill C-41 in 1994, which was passed by Parliament in 1995 as SC 1995, c. 22. It came into force on September 3, 1996. This legislation was heralded by the minister of justice as instigating major reform of the law of sentencing in Canada.

An important aspect of Bill C-41 is the statement of the "Purpose and Principles of Sentencing" in s. 718. This provision was the subject of considerable controversy during consultations respecting the bill:

> 718. The fundamental purpose of sentencing is to contribute, along with crime prevention initiatives, to respect for the law and the maintenance of a just, peaceful and safe society by imposing just sanctions that have one or more of the following objectives:
>
>   (a) to denounce unlawful conduct;
>
>   (b) to deter the offender and other persons from committing offences;
>
>   (c) to separate offenders from society, where necessary;
>
>   (d) to assist in rehabilitating offenders;
>
>   (e) to provide reparations for harm done to victims or to the community; and
>
>   (f) to promote a sense of responsibility in offenders, and acknowledgment of the harm done to victims and to the community.
>
> 718.1 A sentence must be proportionate to the gravity of the offence and the degree of responsibility of the offender.

To what extent does the statement of principles in s. 718 respond to the issues raised in this chapter? Is it possible to discern in s. 718 any statement of the priority that should be given among the principles identified? Will it resolve the weaknesses of the amalgam approach, or does it merely codify that approach and all of its problems?

Some commentators have already identified some deficiencies in s. 718. In "Statutory Sentencing Reform: The Purpose and Principles of Sentencing" (1995), 37 *CLQ* 220, Julian Roberts and Andrew von Hirsch state that s. 718 is not sufficiently detailed to provide prescriptive guidance for judges. They favour the implementation of specific sentencing guidelines. They write:

> The challenge to drafters of a statement of sentencing purpose and principle is to reconcile diverse and frequently conflicting sentencing aims. The task is not impossible, and nor does

it necessarily mean promoting a single sentencing purpose at the expense of all the others. Multi-purpose statements can still offer guidance and affect sentencing practices at the trial court level but they must specify the conditions under which certain aims are favoured over others. This section of the article will also necessitate some discussion of the utility of sentencing guidelines, for guidelines are the means by which a statement of purpose effects changes in sentencing practices. *The statement of purpose is the compass and guidelines the road map. Without the guidelines, judges know roughly where they are going but not necessarily how to get there. Without the statement judges would be following instructions in the absence of a clear sense of over-all direction.* [Emphasis added.]

We will examine sentencing guidelines in a subsequent chapter.

In addition to the statement of purpose and objectives is the following statement of principle is stated in the legislation:

> 718.2. A court that imposes a sentence shall also take into consideration the following principles:
>
>   (a) a sentence should be increased or reduced to account for any relevant aggravating or mitigating circumstances relating to the offence or the offender, and, without limiting the generality of the foregoing,
>
>   (i) evidence that the offence was motivated by bias, prejudice or hate based on race, national or ethnic origin, language, colour, religion, sex, age, mental or physical disability, sexual orientation or any other similar factor,
>
>   (ii) evidence that the offender, in committing the offence, abused the offender's spouse or child,
>
>   (iii) evidence that the offender, in committing the offence, abused a position of trust or authority in relation to the victim, or
>
>   (iv) evidence that the offence was committed for the benefit of, at the direction of or in association with a criminal organization
>
> shall be deemed to be aggravating circumstances;
>
>   (b) a sentence should be similar to sentences imposed on similar offenders for similar offences committed in similar circumstances;
>
>   (c) where consecutive sentences are imposed, the combined sentence should not be unduly long or harsh;
>
>   (d) an offender should not be deprived of liberty, if less restrictive sanctions may be appropriate in the circumstances; and
>
>   (e) all available sanctions other than imprisonment that are reasonable in the circumstances should be considered for all offenders, with particular attention to the circumstances of aboriginal offenders.

What does this statement achieve? Does it effectively entrench the principle of restraint? If so, what is the relationship between restraint and proportionality referred to in s. 718.1?

By the end of the 1990s, two appeals were heard by the Supreme Court that addressed the effect of the 1996 amendments. *R v. Gladue*, infra, dealt specifically with the application of s. 718.2(e), and *R v. Proulx*, infra, involved the interpretation of s. 742.1, the conditional sentence provision. For a fuller discussion of *Proulx*, see Chapter 12, Conditional Sentence of Imprisonment.

R v. Gladue
(1999), 133 CCC (3d) 385 (SCC)

[The offender had pleaded guilty to manslaughter in the stabbing death of her husband. The trial judge sentenced her to three years' imprisonment. He remarked that although she was an aboriginal person, s. 718.2(e) could not apply because she did not reside in an aboriginal community. On appeal, the BC Court of Appeal disagreed with this narrow application of s. 718.2(e) but the majority (Rowles JA dissenting) did not vary the sentence. She appealed to the Supreme Court. Notwithstanding the court's important examination of overincarceration in Canada, particularly in relation to the sentencing of aboriginal offenders (a topic discussed in detail in Chapter 16), it dismissed the appeal. In this regard, it must be noted that the offender was on day parole by the time the case was heard. In the course of dealing with s. 718.2(e), the court considered the 1996 amendments in general to provide a context for its decision.]

CORY and IACOBUCCI JJ:

...

The interpretation of s. 718.2(e) must begin by considering its words in context. Although this appeal is ultimately concerned only with the meaning of the phrase "with particular attention to the circumstances of aboriginal offenders," that phrase takes on meaning from the other words of s. 718.2(e), from the purpose and principles of sentencing set out in ss. 718-718.2, and from the overall scheme of Part XXIII.

The respondent observed that some caution is in order in construing s. 718.2(e), insofar as it would be inappropriate to prejudge the many other important issues which may be raised by the reforms but which are not specifically at issue here. However, it would be equally inappropriate to construe s. 718.2(e) in a vacuum, without considering the surrounding text which gives the provision its depth of meaning. To the extent that the broader scheme of Part XXIII informs the proper construction to be given to s. 718.2(e), it will be necessary to draw at least some general conclusions about the new sentencing regime.

A core issue in this appeal is whether s. 718.2(e) should be understood as being remedial in nature, or whether s. 718.2(e), along with the other provisions of ss. 718 through 718.2, are simply a codification of existing sentencing principles. The respondent, although acknowledging that s. 718.2(e) was likely designed to encourage sentencing judges to experiment to some degree with alternatives to incarceration and to be sensitive to principles of restorative justice, at the same time favours the view that ss. 718-718.2 are largely a restatement of existing law. Alternatively, the appellant argues strongly that s. 718.2(e)'s specific reference to aboriginal offenders can have no purpose unless it effects a change in the law. The appellant advances the view that s. 718.2(e) is in fact an "affirmative action" provision justified under s. 15(2) of the *Canadian Charter of Rights and Freedoms*.

Section 12 of the Interpretation Act deems the purpose of the enactment of the new Part XXIII of the *Criminal Code* to be remedial in nature, and requires that all of the provisions of Part XXIII, including s. 718.2(e), be given a fair, large and liberal construction and interpretation in order to attain that remedial objective. However, the existence of s. 12 does not answer the essential question of what the remedial purpose of s. 718.2(e) is. One view is that the remedial purpose of ss. 718, 718.1 and 718.2 taken together was precisely to codify the purpose and existing principles of sentencing to provide more systematic guidance to sentencing judges in individual cases. Codification, under this view, is remedial in and of itself because it simplifies and adds structure to trial level sentencing decisions: see, e.g., *McDonald* [(1997), 113 CCC (3d) 418 (Sask. CA), at pp. 460-64], per Sherstobitoff JA.

In our view, s. 718.2(e) is more than simply a re-affirmation of existing sentencing principles. The remedial component of the provision consists not only in the fact that it codifies a principle of sentencing, but, far more importantly, in its direction to sentencing judges to undertake the process of sentencing aboriginal offenders differently, in order to endeavour to achieve a truly fit and proper sentence in the particular case. It should be said that the words of s. 718.2(e) do not alter the fundamental duty of the sentencing judge to impose a sentence that is fit for the offence and the offender. For example, as we will discuss below, it will generally be the case as a practical matter that particularly violent and serious offences will result in imprisonment for aboriginal offenders as often as for non-aboriginal offenders. What s. 718.2(e) does alter is the method of analysis which each sentencing judge must use in determining the nature of a fit sentence for an aboriginal offender. In our view, the scheme of Part XXIII of the *Criminal Code*, the context underlying the enactment of s. 718.2(e) and the legislative history of the provision, all support an interpretation of s. 718.2(e) as having this important remedial purpose.

In his submissions before this Court, counsel for the appellant expressed the fear that s. 718.2(e) might come to be interpreted and applied in a manner which would have no real effect upon the day-to-day practice of sentencing aboriginal offenders in Canada. In light of the tragic history of the treatment of aboriginal peoples within the Canadian criminal justice system, we do not consider this fear to be unreasonable. In our view, s. 718.2(e) creates a judicial duty to give its remedial purpose real force.

Let us consider now the wording of s. 718.2(e) and its place within the overall scheme of Part XXIII of the *Criminal Code*.

Section 718.2(e) directs a court, in imposing a sentence, to consider all available sanctions other than imprisonment that are reasonable in the circumstances for all offenders, "with particular attention to the circumstances of aboriginal offenders." The broad role of the provision is clear. As a general principle, s. 718.2(e) applies to all offenders, and states that imprisonment should be the penal sanction of last resort. Prison is to be used only where no other sanction or combination of sanctions is appropriate to the offence and the offender.

The next question is the meaning to be attributed to the words "with particular attention to the circumstances of aboriginal offenders." The phrase cannot be an instruction for judges to pay "more" attention when sentencing aboriginal offenders. It would be unreasonable to assume that Parliament intended sentencing judges to prefer certain categories of offenders over others. Neither can the phrase be merely an instruction to a sentencing judge to consider the circumstances of aboriginal offenders just as she or he would consider the circumstances of any other offender. There would be no point in adding a special reference to aboriginal offenders if this was the case. Rather, the logical meaning to be derived from the special reference to the circumstances of aboriginal offenders, juxtaposed as it is against a general direction to consider "the circumstances" for all offenders, is that sentencing judges should pay particular attention to the circumstances of aboriginal offenders because those circumstances are unique, and different from those of non-aboriginal offenders. The fact that the reference to aboriginal offenders is contained in s. 718.2(e), in particular, dealing with restraint in the use of imprisonment, suggests that there is something different about aboriginal offenders which may specifically make imprisonment a less appropriate or less useful sanction.

The wording of s. 718.2(e) on its face, then, requires both consideration of alternatives to the use of imprisonment as a penal sanction generally, which amounts to a restraint in the resort to imprisonment as a sentence, and recognition by the sentencing judge of the unique circumstances of aboriginal offenders. The respondent argued before this Court that this statutory wording does not truly effect a change in the law, as some courts have in the past taken the unique circumstances of an aboriginal offender into account in determining sentence. The respondent cited some of the recent jurisprudence dealing with sentencing circles, as well as the decision of the Court of Appeal for Ontario in *R v. Fireman* (1971), 4 CCC (2d) 82, in support of the view that s. 718.2(e) should be seen simply as a codification of the state of the case law regarding the sentencing of aboriginal offenders before Part XXIII came into force in 1996. In a similar vein, it was observed by Sherstobitoff JA in *McDonald*, supra, at pp. 463-64, that it has always been a principle of sentencing that courts should consider all available sanctions other than imprisonment that are reasonable in the circumstances. Thus the general principle of restraint expressed in s. 718.2(e) with respect to all offenders might equally be seen as a codification of existing law.

With respect for the contrary view, we do not interpret s. 718.2(e) as expressing only a restatement of existing law, either with respect to the general principle of restraint in the use of prison or with respect to the specific direction regarding aboriginal offenders. One cannot interpret the words of s. 718.2(e) simply by looking to past cases to see if they contain similar statements of principle. The enactment of the new Part XXIII was a watershed, marking the first codification and significant reform of sentencing principles in the history of Canadian criminal law. Each of the provisions of Part XXIII, including s. 718.2(e), must be interpreted in its total context, taking into account its surrounding provisions.

It is true that there is ample jurisprudence supporting the principle that prison should be used as a sanction of last resort. It is equally true, though, that the sentencing amendments which came into force in 1996 as the new Part XXIII have changed the range of available penal sanctions in a significant way. The availability of the conditional sentence of imprisonment, in particular, alters the sentencing landscape in a manner which gives an entirely new meaning to the principle that imprisonment should be resorted to only where no other sentencing option is reasonable in the circumstances. The creation of the conditional sentence suggests, on its face, a desire to lessen the use of incarceration. The general principle expressed in s. 718.2(e) must be construed and applied in this light.

Further support for the view that s. 718.2(e)'s expression of the principle of restraint in sentencing is remedial, rather than simply a codification, is provided by the articulation of the purpose of sentencing in s. 718.

Traditionally, Canadian sentencing jurisprudence has focussed primarily upon achieving the aims of separation, specific and general deterrence, denunciation and rehabilitation. Sentencing, like the criminal trial process itself, has often been understood as a conflict between the interests of the state (as expressed through the aims of separation, deterrence and denunciation) and the interests of the individual offender (as expressed through the aim of rehabilitation). Indeed, rehabilitation itself is a relative late-comer to the sentencing analysis, which formerly favoured the interests of the state almost entirely.

...

Clearly, s. 718 is, in part, a restatement of the basic sentencing aims, which are listed in paras. (a) through (d). What are new, though, are paras. (e) and (f), which along with para. (d) focus upon the restorative goals of repairing the harms suffered by individual victims and by the community as a whole, promoting a sense of responsibility and an acknowledgment of the harm caused on the part of the offender, and attempting to rehabilitate or heal the offender. The concept of restorative justice which underpins paras. (d), (e), and (f) is briefly discussed below, but as a general matter restorative justice involves some form of restitution and reintegration into the community. The need for offenders to take responsibility for their actions is central to the sentencing process: D. Kwochka, "Aboriginal Injustice: Making Room for a Restorative Paradigm" (1996), 60 *Sask. L Rev.* 153 at p. 165. Restorative sentencing goals do not usually correlate with the use of prison as a sanction. In our view, Parliament's choice to include (e) and (f) alongside the traditional sentencing goals must be understood as evidencing an intention to expand the parameters of the sentencing analysis for all offenders. The principle of restraint expressed in s. 718.2(e) will necessarily be informed by this reorientation.

Just as the context of Part XXIII supports the view that s. 718.2(e) has a remedial purpose for all offenders, the scheme of Part XXIII also supports the view that s. 718.2(e) has a particular remedial role for aboriginal peoples. The respondent is correct to point out that there is jurisprudence which predates the enactment of s. 718.2(e) in which aboriginal offenders have been sentenced differently in light of their unique circumstances. However, the existence of such jurisprudence is not, on its own, especially probative of the issue of whether s. 718.2(e) has a remedial role. There is also sentencing jurisprudence which holds, for example, that a court must consider the unique circumstances of offenders who are battered spouses, or who are mentally disabled. Although the validity of the principles expressed in this latter jurisprudence is unchallenged by the 1996 sentencing reforms, one does not find reference to these principles in Part XXIII. If Part XXIII were indeed a codification of principles regarding the appropriate method of sentencing different categories of offenders, one would expect to find such references. The wording of s. 718.2(e), viewed in light of the absence of similar stipulations in the remainder of Part XXIII, reveals that Parliament has chosen to single out aboriginal offenders for particular attention.

C. Legislative History

Support for the foregoing understanding of s. 718.2(e) as having the remedial purpose of restricting the use of prison for all offenders, and as having a particular remedial role with respect to aboriginal peoples, is provided by statements made by the Minister of Justice and others at the time that what was then Bill C-41 was before Parliament. Although these statements are clearly not decisive as to the meaning and purpose of s. 718.2(e), they are nonetheless helpful, particularly insofar as they corroborate and do not contradict the meaning and purpose to be derived upon a reading of the words of the provision in the context of Part XXIII as a whole: *Rizzo & Rizzo Shoes*, supra, at paras. 31 and 35.

For instance, in introducing second reading of Bill C-41 on September 20, 1994 (House of Commons Debates, vol. IV, 1st sess., 35th Parl., at pp. 5871 and 5873), Minister of Justice Allan Rock made the following statements regarding the remedial purpose of the bill:

> Through this bill, Parliament provides the courts with clear guidelines … .
>
> The bill also defines various sentencing principles, for instance that the sentence must be proportionate to the gravity of the offence and the offender's degree of responsibility. When appropriate, alternatives must be contemplated, especially in the case of Native offenders. …
>
> A general principle that runs throughout Bill C-41 is that jails should be reserved for those who should be there. Alternatives should be put in place for those who commit offences but who do not need or merit incarceration. …
>
> Jails and prisons will be there for those who need them, for those who should be punished in that way or separated from society. … [T]his bill creates an environment which encourages community sanctions and the rehabilitation of offenders together with reparation to victims and promoting in criminals a sense of accountability for what they have done. It is not simply by being more harsh that we will achieve more effective criminal justice. We must use our scarce resources wisely.

The Minister's statements were echoed by other Members of Parliament and by Senators during the debate over the bill: see, e.g., House of Commons Debates, vol. V, 1st sess., 35th Parl., September 22, 1994, at p. 6028 (M.P. M. Bodnar); Debates of the Senate, vol. 135, No. 99, 1st sess., 35th Parl., June 21, 1995, at p. 1871 (Sen. D.J. Jessiman).

In his subsequent testimony before the House of Commons Standing Committee on Justice and Legal Affairs (Minutes of Proceedings and Evidence, Issue No. 62, November 17, 1994, at p. 62:15), the Minister of Justice addressed the specific role the government hoped would be played by s. 718.2(e):

> [T]he reason we referred specifically there to aboriginal persons is that they are sadly overrepresented in the prison populations of Canada. I think it was the Manitoba justice inquiry that found that although aboriginal persons make up only 12% of the population of Manitoba, they comprise over 50% of the prison inmates. Nationally aboriginal persons represent about 2% of Canada's population, but they represent 10.6% of persons in prison. Obviously there's a problem here.

What we're trying to do, particularly having regard to the initiatives in the aboriginal communities to achieve community justice, is to encourage courts to look at alternatives where it's consistent with the protection of the public—alternatives to jail—
and not simply resort to that easy answer in every case.

It can be seen, therefore, that the government position when Bill C-41 was under
consideration was that the new Part XXIII was to be remedial in nature. The proposed
enactment was directed, in particular, at reducing the use of prison as a sanction, at
expanding the use of restorative justice principles in sentencing, and at engaging in
both of these objectives with a sensitivity to aboriginal community justice initiatives
when sentencing aboriginal offenders.

D. The Context of the Enactment of Section 718.2(e)

Further guidance as to the scope and content of Parliament's remedial purpose in
enacting s. 718.2(e) may be derived from the social context surrounding the enactment of the provision. On this point, it is worth noting that, although there is quite a
wide divergence between the positions of the appellant and the respondent as to how
s. 718.2(e) should be applied in practice, there is general agreement between them,
and indeed between the parties and all interveners, regarding the mischief in response
to which s. 718.2(e) was enacted.

The parties and interveners agree that the purpose of s. 718.2(e) is to respond to
the problem of overincarceration in Canada, and to respond, in particular, to the more
acute problem of the disproportionate incarceration of aboriginal peoples. They also
agree that one of the roles of s. 718.2(e), and of various other provisions in Part
XXIII, is to encourage sentencing judges to apply principles of restorative justice
alongside or in the place of other, more traditional sentencing principles when making
sentencing determinations. As the respondent states in its factum before this Court,
s. 718.2(e) "provides the necessary flexibility and authority for sentencing judges to
resort to the restorative model of justice in sentencing aboriginal offenders and to
reduce the imposition of jail sentences where to do so would not sacrifice the traditional goals of sentencing."

The fact that the parties and interveners are in general agreement among themselves
regarding the purpose of s. 718.2(e) is not determinative of the issue as a matter of
statutory construction. However, as we have suggested, on the above points of agreement the parties and interveners are correct. A review of the problem of overincarceration in Canada, and of its peculiarly devastating impact upon Canada's aboriginal
peoples, provides additional insight into the purpose and proper application of this
new provision.

(1) The Problem of Overincarceration in Canada

Canada is a world leader in many fields, particularly in the areas of progressive social
policy and human rights. Unfortunately, our country is also distinguished as being a
world leader in putting people in prison. Although the United States has by far the

highest rate of incarceration among industrialized democracies, at over 600 inmates per 100,000 population, Canada's rate of approximately 130 inmates per 100,000 population places it second or third highest: see First Report on Progress for Federal/ Provincial/Territorial Ministers Responsible for Justice, Corrections Population Growth (1997), Annex B, at p. 1; Bulletin of US Bureau of Justice Statistics, "Prison and Jail Inmates at Midyear 1998" (1999); The Sentencing Project, Americans Behind Bars: US and International Use of Incarceration, 1995 (1997), at p. 1. Moreover, the rate at which Canadian courts have been imprisoning offenders has risen sharply in recent years, although there has been a slight decline of late: see Statistics Canada, Infomat: A Weekly Review (February 27, 1998), at p. 5. This record of incarceration rates obviously cannot instill a sense of pride.

The systematic use of the sanction of imprisonment in Canada may be dated to the building of the Kingston Penitentiary in 1835. The penitentiary sentence was itself originally conceived as an alternative to the harsher penalties of death, flogging, or imprisonment in a local jail. Sentencing reformers advocated the use of penitentiary imprisonment as having effects which were not only deterrent, denunciatory and pre-ventive, but also rehabilitative, with long hours spent in contemplation and hard work contributing to the betterment of the offender: see Law Reform Commission of Canada, Working Paper 11, *Imprisonment and Release* (1975), at p. 5.

Notwithstanding its idealistic origins, imprisonment quickly came to be condemned as harsh and ineffective, not only in relation to its purported rehabilitative goals, but also in relation to its broader public goals. The history of Canadian commentary regard-ing the use and effectiveness of imprisonment as a sanction was recently well sum-marized by Vancise JA, dissenting in the Saskatchewan Court of Appeal in *McDonald*, supra, at pp. 429-30:

> A number of inquiries and commissions have been held in this country to examine, among other things, the effectiveness of the use of incarceration in sentencing. There has been at least one commission or inquiry into the use of imprisonment for each decade in this century since 1914. ...
>
> An examination of the recommendations of these reports reveals one constant theme: imprisonment should be avoided if possible and should be reserved for the most seri-ous offences, particularly those involving violence. They all recommend restraint in the use of incarceration and recognize that incarceration has failed to reduce the crime rate and should be used with caution and moderation. Imprisonment has failed to sat-isfy a basic function of the Canadian judicial system which was described in the Report of the Canadian Committee on Corrections entitled: "Toward Unity: Criminal Justice and Corrections" (1969) as "to protect society from crime in a manner commanding public support while avoiding needless injury to the offender."

In a similar vein, in 1987, the Canadian Sentencing Commission wrote in its report entitled *Sentencing Reform: A Canadian Approach*, at pp. xxiii-xxiv:

> Canada does not imprison as high a portion of its population as does the United States. However, we do imprison more people than most other western democracies. The *Crimi-nal Code* displays an apparent bias toward the use of incarceration since for most offences

the penalty indicated is expressed in terms of a maximum term of imprisonment. A number of difficulties arise if imprisonment is perceived to be the preferred sanction for most offences. Perhaps most significant is that although we regularly impose this most onerous and expensive sanction, it accomplishes very little apart from separating offenders from society for a period of time. In the past few decades many groups and federally appointed committees and commissions given the responsibility of studying various aspects of the criminal justice system have argued that imprisonment should be used only as a last resort and/or that it should be reserved for those convicted of only the most serious offences. However, although much has been said, little has been done to move us in this direction.

...

With equal force, in *Taking Responsibility* (1988), at p. 75, the Standing Committee on Justice and Solicitor General stated:

It is now generally recognized that imprisonment has not been effective in rehabilitating or reforming offenders, has not been shown to be a strong deterrent, and has achieved only temporary public protection and uneven retribution, as the lengths of prison sentences handed down vary for the same type of crime.

Since imprisonment generally offers the public protection from criminal behaviour for only a limited time, rehabilitation of the offender is of great importance. However, prisons have not generally been effective in reforming their inmates, as the high incidence of recidivism among prison populations shows.

The use of imprisonment as a main response to a wide variety of offences against the law is not a tenable approach in practical terms. Most offenders are neither violent nor dangerous. Their behaviour is not likely to be improved by the prison experience. In addition, their growing numbers in jails and penitentiaries entail serious problems of expense and administration, and possibly increased future risks to society. Moreover, modern technology may now permit the monitoring in the community of some offenders who previously might have been incarcerated for incapacitation or denunciation purposes. Alternatives to imprisonment and intermediate sanctions, therefore, are increasingly viewed as necessary developments.

The Committee proposed that alternative forms of sentencing should be considered for those offenders who did not endanger the safety of others. It was put in this way, at pp. 50 and 54:

[O]ne of the primary foci of such alternatives must be on techniques which contribute to offenders accepting responsibility for their criminal conduct and, through their subsequent behaviour, demonstrating efforts to restore the victim to the position he or she was in prior to the offence and/or providing a meaningful apology. [E]xcept where to do so would place the community at undue risk, the "correction" of the offender should take place in the community and imprisonment should be used with restraint.

Thus, it may be seen that although imprisonment is intended to serve the traditional sentencing goals of separation, deterrence, denunciation, and rehabilitation, there is widespread consensus that imprisonment has not been successful in achieving some of these goals. Overincarceration is a long-standing problem that has been many times publicly acknowledged but never addressed in a systematic manner by Parliament. In recent years, compared to other countries, sentences of imprisonment in Canada have increased at an alarming rate. The 1996 sentencing reforms embodied in Part XXIII, and s. 718.2(e) in particular, must be understood as a reaction to the overuse of prison as a sanction, and must accordingly be given appropriate force as remedial provisions.

R v. Proulx
(2000), 140 CCC (3d) 449 (SCC)

[Along with a number of companion cases, the Supreme Court in *Proulx* articulated its view of the new conditional sentence. This concept is discussed in detail in Chapter 11, Imprisonment. Before dealing with that sanction, Lamer CJC for a unanimous court addressed some comments about the thrust of the 1996 amendments.]

• • •

Parliament has sought to give increased prominence to the principle of restraint in the use of prison as a sanction through the enactment of s. 718.2(d) and (e). Section 718.2(d) provides that "an offender should not be deprived of liberty, if less restrictive sanctions may be appropriate in the circumstances," while s. 718.2(e) provides that "all available sanctions other than imprisonment that are reasonable in the circumstances should be considered for all offenders, with particular attention to the circumstances of aboriginal offenders." Further evidence of Parliament's desire to lower the rate of incarceration comes from other provisions of Bill C-41: s. 718(c) qualifies the sentencing objective of separating offenders from society with the words "where necessary," thereby indicating that caution be exercised in sentencing offenders to prison; s. 734(2) imposes a duty on judges to undertake a means inquiry before imposing a fine, so as to decrease the number of offenders who are incarcerated for defaulting on payment of their fines; and of course, s. 742.1, which introduces the conditional sentence. In *Gladue*, at para. 40, the Court held that "the creation of the conditional sentence suggests, on its face, a desire to lessen the use of incarceration."

(2) Expanding the Use of Restorative Justice Principles in Sentencing

Restorative justice is concerned with the restoration of the parties that are affected by the commission of an offence. Crime generally affects at least three parties: the victim, the community, and the offender. A restorative justice approach seeks to remedy the adverse effects of crime in a manner that addresses the needs of all parties involved. This is accomplished, in part, through the rehabilitation of the offender, reparations to the victim and to the community, and the promotion of a sense of responsibility in the offender and acknowledgment of the harm done to victims and to the community.

Canadian sentencing jurisprudence has traditionally focussed on the aims of denunciation, deterrence, separation, and rehabilitation, with rehabilitation a relative latecomer to the sentencing analysis: see *Gladue*, at para. 42. With the introduction of Bill C-41, however, Parliament has placed new emphasis upon the goals of restorative justice. Section 718 sets out the fundamental purpose of sentencing, as well as the various sentencing objectives that should be vindicated when sanctions are imposed.

QUESTIONS

What do you think will be the impact of these general comments about restorative justice? In what practical circumstances can you envisage the conceptual analysis in *Gladue* and *Proulx* playing an important role in future cases?

VI. DEFERENCE AND APPELLATE REVIEW

While trial judges are the principle instruments of sentencing, cases involving arguments of principle or disputes over quantum are appealed to provincial appellate courts. Recently, the Supreme Court of Canada articulated a concept of deference that is intended to limit the degree of appellate intervention.

R v. C.A.M.
(1996), 46 CR (4th) 269 (SCC)

LAMER CJC:

...

In *Shropshire*, supra, this Court recently articulated the appropriate standard of review that a court of appeal should adopt in reviewing the fitness of sentence under s. 687(1). In the context of reviewing the fitness of an order of parole ineligibility, Iacobucci J described the standard of review as follows, at para. 46:

> An appellate court should not be given free reign to modify a sentencing order simply because it feels that a different order ought to have been made. The formulation of a sentencing order is a profoundly subjective process; the trial judge has the advantage of having seen and heard all of the witnesses whereas the appellate court can only base itself upon a written record. A variation in the sentence should only be made if the court of appeal is convinced it is not fit. That is to say, that it has found the sentence to be clearly unreasonable.

As my learned colleague noted, this standard of review traces part of its lineage to the jurisprudence of the British Columbia Court of Appeal. As Bull JA described the nature of a trial judge's sentencing discretion in *R v. Gourgon* (1981), 58 CCC (2d) 193, at p. 197:

> ... the matter is clearly one of discretion and unless patently wrong, or wrong principles applied, or correct principles applied erroneously, or proper factors ignored or overstressed, an appellate Court should be careful not to interfere with the exercise of that discretion of a trial Judge.

Put simply, absent an error in principle, failure to consider a relevant factor, or an overemphasis of the appropriate factors, a court of appeal should only intervene to vary a sentence imposed at trial if the sentence is demonstrably unfit. Parliament explicitly vested sentencing judges with a discretion to determine the appropriate degree and kind of punishment under the *Criminal Code*.

...

This deferential standard of review has profound functional justifications. As Iacobucci J explained in *Shropshire*, at para. 46, where the sentencing judge has had the benefit of presiding over the trial of the offender, he or she will have had the comparative advantage of having seen and heard the witnesses to the crime. But in the absence of a full trial, where the offender has pleaded guilty to an offence and the sentencing judge has only enjoyed the benefit of oral and written sentencing submissions (as was the case in both *Shropshire* and this instance), the argument in favour of deference remains compelling. A sentencing judge still enjoys a position of advantage over an appellate judge in being able to directly assess the sentencing submissions of both the Crown and the offender. A sentencing judge also possesses the unique qualifications of experience and judgment from having served on the front lines of our criminal justice system. Perhaps most importantly, the sentencing judge will normally preside near or within the community which has suffered the consequences of the offender's crime. As such, the sentencing judge will have a strong sense of the particular blend of sentencing goals that will be "just and appropriate" for the protection of that community. The determination of a just and appropriate sentence is a delicate art which attempts to balance carefully the societal goals of sentencing against the moral blameworthiness of the offender and the circumstances of the offence, while at all times taking into account the needs and current conditions of and in the community. The discretion of a sentencing judge should thus not be interfered with lightly.

Appellate courts, of course, serve an important function in reviewing and minimizing the disparity of sentences imposed by sentencing judges for similar offenders and similar offences committed throughout Canada. See, e.g., *R v. Knife* (1982), 16 Sask. R 40 (CA), at p. 43; *R v. Wood* (1979), 21 Crim. LQ 423 (Ont. CA), at p. 424; *R v. Mellstrom* (1975), 22 CCC (2d) 472 (Alta. CA), at p. 485; *R v. Morrissette* (1970), 1 CCC (2d) 307 (Sask. CA), at pp. 311-12; *R v. Baldhead*, [1966] 4 CCC 183 (Sask. CA) at p. 187. But in exercising this role, courts of appeal must still exercise a margin of deference before intervening in the specialized discretion that Parliament has explicitly vested in sentencing judges. It has been repeatedly stressed that there is no such thing as a uniform sentence for a particular crime. See *Mellstrom*, *Morrissette* and *Baldhead*. Sentencing is an inherently individualized process, and the search for a single appropriate sentence for a similar offender and a similar crime will frequently be a fruitless exercise of academic abstraction. As well, sentences for a particular offence should be expected to vary to some degree across various communities and regions in this country, as the "just and appropriate" mix of accepted sentencing goals will depend on the needs and current conditions of and in the particular community where the crime occurred. For these reasons, consistent with the general standard of review we articulated in *Shropshire*, I believe that a court of appeal should only intervene to minimize the disparity of sentences where the sentence imposed by the trial judge is in substantial and marked departure from the sentences customarily imposed for similar offenders committing similar crimes.

NOTE

Does this mean that a sentence at the high end of a generally accepted range will not be reviewed unless an error in principle can be identified in the sentencing judge's reasons? What if the appellate panel would have imposed a lighter sentence? Can appellate judges intervene without an error in principle if the sentence falls within the usual range, even if it is at the high end of the range?

Certainly, the justifications for deference have merit, but they are not always opera-tive. In some cases, a trial will provide a full picture of the offender and the offence, but the majority of cases proceed by way of guilty plea and the sentencing judge does not have more than a glimpse of the offender. Similarly, not all sentencing judges have the benefit of local knowledge, especially with respect to sentencing resources and options. Usually, the judge must rely on what counsel provides. Are the justifications for defer-ence offered by the Supreme Court adequate to support a standard of general application? Is there, perhaps, an underlying interest in discouraging appeals by announcing that only errors in principle or demonstrably unfit sentences will be reviewed?

Recently, some appellate courts have raised questions about the extent to which defer-ence has impeded review. *R v. Mafi* (2000), 31 CR (5th) 60 (BC CA) involved an appeal against a 20-year period of parole ineligibility for two counts of second-degree murder. In the course of his decision, McEachern CJBC commented on the standard of deference:

> Parliament has provided both the Crown and the accused with a right of appeal with leave of this Court which is rarely refused, against sentence. It must, however, be recognized and accepted that a reasonable measure of deference should be given to trial sentences. The Supreme Court of Canada has endorsed this view on a number of occasions, a fact which we must keep very much in mind. As will be seen, however, undue deference carries the risk of depriving an appellant of an effective right of appeal. In my respectful view, the present jurisprudence unduly limits the proper exercise of this right of appeal and often operates in such a way that an unfair and sometimes unjust sentence cannot always be adjusted on appeal because of the expectations of deference.

Is this accurate? Does deference preclude appellate review to the extent that some offenders are denied a right of appeal?

A recent Saskatchewan Court of Appeal decision, *R v. Laliberte*, infra, case sheds light on how appellate courts are responding to the issue of deference and the scope of appellate review of sentences.

R v. Laliberte
(2000), 31 CR (5th) 1 (Sask. CA)

[A conditional sentence was imposed at trial on an aboriginal offender with substance abuse problems who had been convicted of trafficking in small quantities of dilaudid tablets. The Crown appealed seeking a jail term in conformity with previous traffick-ing decisions. In a detailed examination of the potential role of conditional sentences in drug cases and the current application of parity, Vancise JA concluded that the appeal should be dismissed. Jackson JA concurred.]

JACKSON JA, concurring:

...

The Crown has appealed the sentence on the basis that the sentencing judge made certain errors resulting in demonstrably unfit sentences. Relying on other decisions of this Court, eg., *R v. Faubert* (1997), 152 Sask. R 228 and *R v. Englesman*, [1999] SJ No. 455 (unreported Sask. CA) and extrapolating certain principles from them, Crown counsel argued that this Court had already spoken on the fitness of conditional sentences for trafficking in "hard" drugs and should, therefore, grant leave and set aside the conditional sentence imposed. Defence counsel took issue with this. He said recent decisions of the Supreme Court of Canada require this Court to reconsider its role in reviewing sentences and to provide guidance with respect to the use of conditional sentences. These opposing positions raise squarely the proper approach to be taken in imposing a conditional sentence and this Court's role when reviewing such a sentence to determine its fitness under s. 687 of the *Criminal Code*. Moreover, this appeal was argued with two others (Keepness and Cappo) in the hope, if not the expectation, that the Court would speak on what has become an issue of some controversy. All of this has been rendered more acute since the Supreme Court of Canada has provided its opinion in *R v. Proulx*, (2000), 30 CR (5th) 1 (SCC); *R v. L.F.W.* (2000), 30 CR (5th) 73 (SCC); *R v. R.N.S.* (2000), 30 CR (5th) 63 (SCC); *R v. R.A.R.* (2000), 30 CR (5th) 49 (SCC); and *R v. Bunn* (2000), 30 CR (5th) 86 (SCC).

As a matter of practice, when this Court refuses leave to appeal a sentence, the decision to do so is not reported in the Sentencing Digest, and the refusal of leave is recorded only on the court file. Since in-depth reasons are not given, the public does not know the basis upon which the Court decided to refuse leave. This means that the fact of refusing leave has no precedential value. In the instant appeal, it appears that we are all of one mind that the sentence imposed on Ms. Laliberte was fit when imposed, but if we were simply to deny leave, an important part of the continuum of fit sentences would be missed. That is to say, conditional sentencing for a hard drug at the lower end of the spectrum would not form part of the cases cited to the Court on a regular basis. To be more precise, if we were to deny leave in this appeal, Crown and defence counsel and the public would not know that this Court is of the view that a conditional sentence imposed on an accused with these personal circumstances for trafficking in thirteen tablets of Dilaudid is not demonstrably unfit.

In my respectful opinion, a Court of Appeal has the authority to grant leave not only when there is an arguable case for intervention but also to settle an issue of significance either in practice or law. The onus on counsel seeking leave is to demonstrate a case of sufficient merit and importance to warrant intervention or review. *R v. Horvath* (1997), 152 Sask. R 277 is a case in point. *Horvath* was a Crown appeal where this Court dismissed the appeal from the imposition of a conditional sentence. Other examples exist.

Crown counsel has met the onus of persuading me that leave should be granted. Accordingly, I would grant leave.

My colleagues have taken different approaches to arrive at what is the same result. My colleague Vancise has provided a detailed analysis of the case law and statutory provisions and developed a framework for when and how courts should determine the applicability of a conditional sentence. I agree with his analysis and framework. It accords with that which was recently pronounced by the Supreme Court of Canada. He has also provided an analysis of the application of s. 718.2(e) dealing with aboriginal offenders. As he makes clear, he is able to find Ms. Laliberte's sentence to be fit without resorting to her aboriginal status. On that basis, I prefer to withhold comment on his analysis of this latter issue until it is directly engaged.

As to disparity, I will add my own thoughts. My colleague Vancise states that the principle of parity does not preclude a finding by this Court that the conditional sentence in this case is a fit sentence for two principal reasons. First, he writes that our earlier decisions relied on pre-May 1, 1997 decisions or did not refer to the pronouncements contained in *R v. Gladue*, [1999] 1 SCR 688. Secondly, the standard of appellate review as articulated in recent Supreme Court cases including *Gladue* and now *Proulx* requires this Court to give greater deference to sentencing judges such that where we might once have intervened, we are now precluded from doing so. I subscribe to that part of his reasoning which focuses on the standard of appellate review which I will now amplify.

Vancise JA traces the recent cases stating and interpreting the standard of appellate review beginning with *R v. Morrisette* (1971), 1 CCC (2d) 307 through *R v. Wenarchuk* (1982), 15 Sask. R 240, *R v. Shropshire*, [1995] 4 SCR 227, *R v. M.(C.A.)*, [1996] 1 SCR 500, *R v. McDonnell*, [1997] 1 SCR 948, *Horvath*, *Gladue* and concluding with *Proulx*, *R v. L.F.W.*, *R v. R.N.S.*, *R v. R.A.R.* and *R v. Bunn*. In my mind this review demonstrates a narrowing of the aperture of intervention for an appellate court particularly as it relates to conditional sentences.

· · ·

It is significant that the Court in *Proulx* did not indicate what will constitute an error in principle or when a sentence imposed by a trial or sentencing judge is demonstrably unfit. The realm of conditional sentencing is full of many rules—some more important than others. If the Supreme Court of Canada had said that this or that rule or factor is more or less important, appellate courts could, in an effort to fulfill its reviewing function, maintain reliance on incarceration by setting aside conditional sentences. But the Supreme Court did not. Instead, the Court speaking with one voice in *Proulx* gave extensive guidelines to trial judges to assist them in determining when to impose a conditional sentence while at the same time advising appellate courts to be chary about intervening.

As a further message to appellate courts, we can look at exactly what the Supreme Court did in *Proulx*, *L.F.W.*, *R.N.S.*, *R.A.R.* and *Bunn*. In all but one of these cases, the Supreme Court of Canada upheld the decision of the trial judge. In the one case where the Supreme Court did not uphold the decision of the trial judge (*Bunn*), the Supreme Court of Canada must be taken as expanding the use of conditional sentences. What the Court actually did is a powerful statement of the application of the standard of appellate review and the use of conditional sentences.

It should also be pointed out that in those cases where the Supreme Court set aside an appeal court's conditional sentence, it usually gave guidance to a future sentencing judge. The nature of this advice makes it clear that the Supreme Court's decision is not intended to preclude the use of a conditional sentence for a future offence of the same nature. (This also speaks to the diminishing role of parity of sentencing.) For example, in *Proulx* the Court set aside the conditional sentence imposed by the Manitoba Court of Appeal for dangerous driving causing death and restored the decision of the trial judge sentencing the accused to custody. But in doing so the Court said this:

> I hasten to add that these comments should not be taken as a directive that conditional sentences can never be imposed for offences such as dangerous driving or impaired driving. In fact, were I a trial judge, I might have found that a conditional sentence would have been appropriate in this case. The respondent is still very young, he had no prior record and no convictions since the accident, he seems completely rehabilitated, he wants to go back to school, he has already suffered a lot by causing the death of a friend and was himself in a coma for some time. To make sure that the objectives of denunciation and general deterrence would have been sufficiently addressed, I might have imposed conditions such as house arrest and a community service order requiring the offender to speak to designated groups about the consequences of dangerous driving, as was the case in *Parker*, supra, at p. 239, and *R v. Hollinsky* (1995), 103 CCC (3d) 472 (Ont. CA).
>
> However, trial judges are closer to their community and know better what would be acceptable to their community. Absent evidence that the sentence imposed by the trial judge was demonstrably unfit, the Court of Appeal should not have interfered to substitute its own opinion for that of the sentencing judge. The trial judge did not commit a reversible error in principle and she appropriately considered all the relevant factors.
>
> Although the Court of Appeal's decision is entitled to some deference (see the companion appeal *R v. R.A.R.*, 2000 SCC 8, at paras. 20-21), in my opinion it erred in holding that the sentencing judge had given undue weight to the objective of denunciation. I see no ground for the Court of Appeal's intervention.

These comments provide further guidance to an appellate court regarding the standard of appellate review. No aspect of the weighing process which led the trial judge in *Proulx* to select custody over a conditional sentence constituted reversible error. Instead, the Court assessed whether the ultimate result was demonstrably unfit. As soon as the Court reached this stage of its analysis, the standard of appellate review precluded intervention. The decision to impose or not to impose a custodial as opposed to a conditional sentence did not result, on the facts of that case, in a reversible error.

This does not mean that the Court of Appeal has no role in sentencing. Parliament has given appellate courts the obligation to review appealed sentences to determine their fitness, but this role must be fulfilled while giving great deference to sentencing judges.

That brings us specifically to the role of parity. A necessary corollary of a narrow standard of appellate review is that the emphasis on that principle of sentencing known as parity contained in s. 718.2(b) is diminished.

NOTE

The ongoing debate about deference and the threshold for appellate review raises important questions. Given that s. 687(1) of the *Criminal Code* requires appellate courts to "consider the fitness of the sentence appealed against," has the Supreme Court effectively rewritten this provision by articulating the deference standard? In *Laliberte*, supra, Jackson JA quoted an excerpt from *Proulx* in which Lamer CJC suggested that it is valuable that the trial judge knows what is "acceptable to their community." Is this an appropriate consideration? See the discussion of judicial notice in Chapter 4, Facts of the Offence for Sentencing.

CHAPTER THREE

Aggravating and Mitigating Factors

I. INTRODUCTION

The Canadian approach to sentencing requires the judge to impose a sentence that reflects the relevant objectives and emphasizes any that, in the circumstances, are predominant. Section 718.2(e) of the *Criminal Code*, RSC 1985, c. C-46, as amended, requires the judge to consider all available sanctions that are reasonable. These two exercises may point to a specific sanction or subset of available sanctions. Moreover, it may suggest a quantum band for specific sanctions. The ultimate decision, however, is refined by factors that are more discriminating than the broadly conceived objectives. Traditionally, judges have recognized sets of factors that affect the gravity of the offence and the court's perception of the offender and then have applied them to make the ultimate decisions about which sanction to impose and its quantum. Depending on the nature of the consequential effect, these are known as either mitigating or aggravating factors. Section 718.2(a) now entrenches the common law by requiring judges to increase or reduce a sentence by taking into account aggravating or mitigating circumstances, relevant to the offence or the offender. The Code lists a few examples of aggravating circumstances, some of which were clearly encompassed by the common law and others that were being applied in some cases but were also, to some extent, controversial. There are no examples of mitigating factors in the Code.

Virtually every written or oral decision includes some characterization of the relevant factors into these two categories. Over the years, the common law has recognized dozens of factors that can have a mitigating or aggravating effect. Interestingly, most of these factors are rarely examined and courts seem to accept their aggravating or mitigating effect. Of course, some are self-evident but others are not so clear. There can be legitimate debates about their relation to the sentencing function. For the most part, the underlying premises that explain the applicability of an aggravating or mitigating factor seem to relate to one of two things:

1. The gravity of the offence as defined by the offender's culpability and the consequential harm that was caused.

2. The ways in which character and conduct relate to applicable objectives of sentencing and thereby are relevant in choosing the sanction and determining its quantum. This includes the ever-expanding categories of pro-social and anti-social conduct that courts assimilate into this function.

In *R v. Sandercock* (discussed in Chapter 2 as it relates to starting points), the Alberta Court of Appeal included a brief discussion of some of the relevant and irrelevant factors that were apparent in the case. Read the following excerpt and consider whether you agree with the court's assessment of what should or should not be taken into account.

R v. Sandercock
(1985), 22 CCC (3d) 79 (Alta. CA)

KERANS JA:

...

Before turning to the facts of the appeal before us, we propose to discuss the last step in this sentencing approach, a consideration of the many aggravating and mitigating factors which often arise and which must be weighed in fixing a fit sentence in a specific case.

In recent years, great emphasis has been put on a prompt guilty plea as a special and major mitigating factor. It used to be said that this was relevant only to show remorse. Aside entirely from any remorse, however, an accused should receive substantial recognition either for sparing the victim the need to testify or to wait to testify, or for waiving some of his constitutional rights in deference to expeditious justice.

Many other mitigating and aggravating factors are often present. It is impossible to offer a complete catalogue. We can, however, mention some. (We cite reports of actual cases at this point simply to illustrate that the sentence can increase markedly when aggravating factors shift the balance.) Some involve protracted forcible confinement or kidnapping: *R v. Craig* (1975), 28 CCC (2d) 311; others include repeated assaults or other acts of degradation: *R v. Beauregard* (1982), 38 AR 350; others, further acts of horror or degradation: *R v. Sweitzer*, [1982] 5 WWR 552, 26 AR 208; others, the invasion of the sanctity of the home: see *R v. Henry* (1983), 44 AR 242; others, the display or use of a weapon: *R v. Sinitoski*, [1983] 6 WWR 247, 27 Alta. LR (2d) 141, 46 AR 206; others, several offenders acting together: *R v. Brown and Murphy* (1982), 41 AR 69; others, more than one victim: *R v. Brandon*, November 8, 1983, Edmonton 16807. It is even possible for almost all these factors to be present in one case: see *R v. Graham* (1984), Alta. D 7515-01. Mitigating factors often present include remorse, immaturity, and the global effect of several sentences for several matters.

Most actual cases show a mix of aggravating and mitigating factors. The sentencing process involves noting and weighing each and settling upon a sentence which reflects that balancing. As a result, the presence of most of the mitigating factors just mentioned and the absence of any aggravating factor might lead to a sentence of less than penitentiary time: see, for example, *R v. Harper* (1982), Alta. D 7515-02 [summarized 8 WCB 281]; *R v. Clay* (1984), Alta. D 7517-04 [reported 35 Alta. LR (2d) 20]; *R v. Frand* (unreported October 8, 1980, Edmonton 13108); or the recent case of *R v. Kergan* (unreported as yet, published August 9, 1985) [since reported 21 CCC (3d) 549, 62 AR 161]. It is unthinkable, however, that a substantial jail sentence would not be imposed in the face of the blameworthiness and harm I have described, in other words, so long as the offence remains within the category of "major sexual assault." At the other end of the scale, the presence of certain aggravating factors now justify the laying of a charge under ss. 246.2 or 246.3 of the *Criminal Code* or additional charges such as breaking and entering, kidnapping, forcible confinement, or attempted murder. Such charges, which might well have been considered redundant for a crime which carries a maximum penalty of life imprisonment, will no doubt now be seen more often. As the majority for this court said in *Kergan* and *R v. Daychief* (published the same day) [summarized 14 WCB 449] nothing in the recent statutory changes justifies the view that Parliament now views any particular sexual assault as less serious than it once did. The recent legislative changes, however, also now require that if the accused is a dangerous offender, an application for preventive detention must be made by the Crown under s. 687 of the *Criminal Code*: see *R v. Hastings*. In the past, this court has imposed life sentences on rapists who will reoffend: see, for example, *R v. Leech* (1972), 10 CCC (2d) 149, 21 CRNS 1, [1973] 1 WWR 744, and *R v. Brandon* (unreported) November 8, 1983, Edmonton, No. 16807.

We will conclude by reference to factors sometimes offered in mitigation but which are often suspect: those cases where the offender says he was drunk, or the victim of cultural conflict, or where the victim was allegedly negligent as to his or her own safety, or provoked the assault, or where the victim is of bad character.

Drunkenness generally should not be a mitigating factor. Nevertheless, the fact that an assault is totally spontaneous can offer mitigation, and sometimes drunkenness is a factor in determining whether the attack is spontaneous or whether the likely consequences were fully appreciated.

The circumstances in life of the victim, if known to the offender, can affect the assessment of the foreseeable pain to the victim: see, for example, *R v. Ricketts* (unreported, May 31, 1985, Calgary Appeal No. 17000) [since reported 61 AR 175]. Ricketts, in breach of his earlier agreement with a prostitute to pay her for an act of fellatio, suddenly demanded it free at knife-point. Her sense of outrage and fear should not be minimized, but I am sure that she would agree that the foreseeable risk of psychological shock to her was not as great as would be, say, a similar threat to somebody who had led a sheltered life: see *R v. Marsh* (unreported February 4, 1980, 12641). In this limited sense, the life-circumstances, or "character," of the victim might be relevant to sentencing. This is because these factors alter the level of reasonably foreseeable harm, which is the test, and not because grave consequences chanced to happen. In general terms, an accused is punished for blameworthiness and not for the actual consequences of the crime, although these are not to be disregarded: see *R v. Jacobs* (1982), 70 CCC (2d) 569, 16 MVR 15, 39 AR 391.

Provocation of the offender by the victim is an obvious mitigating factor. More difficult to decide is whether, in a given case, there has been provocation. It is surely not provocation, for example, simply to be a woman, or to be attractive, or to be prettily attired. Sexual arousal is not the same thing as the arousal of a desire to seek sexual satisfaction by violence to another, and provocation of the first is not necessarily provocation of the second.

Negligence of the victim as to his or her own safety is generally not relevant. The blameworthiness of the offender is not in the least diminished because the victim imprudently provides the offender with an opportunity for crime, nor does it necessarily follow that such imprudence lessens the likely pain, outrage and indignity which then visits the victim.

II. THE MENU OF RELEVANT MITIGATING FACTORS

The case law dealing with aggravating and mitigating factors is vast. Many of the commonly accepted factors are discussed in Allan Manson's *Essentials of the Law of Sentencing*. When you are reviewing the factors included in the following excerpt, consider whether and how they relate to the objectives of sentencing in s. 718.

A. Manson, "Mitigating Factors"
in *The Law of Sentencing* (Toronto: Irwin, 2000), 64-79
(footnotes omitted)

First offender: The status of being a first offender is a significant mitigating factor. The fact that the offender has not been found guilty by the criminal process before generates a number of favourable inferences, with rehabilitative prospects always at the forefront of consideration. First, being a first offender suggests that the conviction itself constitutes a punishment. It is assumed that the offender will respond positively to the deterrent effects of the process of arrest, charging, finding of guilt and imposition of sanction. This discounts any special need for individual deterrence and suggests that a lenient response is in order. Being a first offender is also consistent with demonstrating good character prior to the offence. Although it does not guarantee a non-custodial sentence, there is both a presumption against custody and a significant reducing effect if custody is mandated.

...

Prior good character: Good character evidence during a trial when responsibility is at stake is usually limited to reputation in the community. For sentencing purposes, character is much broader and will often include achievements and opinions attributed to relatives, friends, associates and acquaintances. It is usually directed to showing that the offence is out of character. In this way, evidence of conduct which shows values antithetical to those which ordinarily underlie the particular offence will be helpful. Accordingly, evidence of honesty and generosity will be relevant to a crime of dishonesty. Similarly, evidence of compassion will be relevant to a crime of violence.

Claims of prior good character are often misconceived. For example, it is often confused with a claim about standing in the community. While this is often put forward, it has a nebulous and questionable basis as a mitigating factor, more suited to showing re-integrative potential. For some offences, evidence of a person's pro-social community commitment through volunteer work is not mitigating when the offence arises from those activities. Assaulting children involved in the volunteer activity is an obvious example. In general, courts have found that good character claims are inappropriate when dealing with offences committed in the dark corners of people's lives. With respect to sexual offences, the Supreme Court has recognized that they are usually perpetrated in private, out of sight and knowledge of friends and associates. Accordingly, evidence of good community reputation has little probative value. While this conclusion was directed to the use of character evidence at trial, it applies equally to sentencing issues.

Guilty plea and remorse: The reason that a guilty plea is usually considered to be a mitigating factor is because it implies remorse and an acknowledgement of responsibility by the offender. The extent of the mitigating value is affected by the timing of the guilty plea: the earlier, the better. This is especially true if one intends to include consideration for the victims as an added element. Avoiding the need to have a victim testify is a legitimate dimension of remorse but gets little credence if a guilty plea is entered only after hearing the witness at preliminary hearing. Convenience to the court by saving its time is not a reason for mitigation. While this is a systemic benefit, it would be wrong to give the impression that foregoing the constitutional right to plead not guilty will garner credit simply because it makes the judge's life easier. The court is a public institution exercising an important public function and a guilty plea must reflect more than time-saving to support mitigation. In this sense, it ought to be communicated as an acceptance of responsibility.

Of course, a guilty plea is not the only way to show remorse. Sincere apologies and other efforts at reparation can convey a stronger message than simply the guilty plea. Moreover, remorse can be indicated even after a trial. The right to compel the Crown to prove its case does not entirely remove the opportunity to show remorse although it may diminish it.

Evidence of impairment: Impairment of judgement can be a mitigating circumstance. Sentencing ought to respond proportionately to culpability; intended consequences should be treated more severely than those caused negligently. This is a principle of fundamental justice. Accordingly, evidence that an accused was suffering from impaired judgment can be very significant.

Within the criminal law generally, voluntary intoxication has been the subject of variable and inconsistent treatment. In the 19th century, it was not considered a factor that could mitigate fault but, in this century, it became an accepted defence to a crime of specific intent. During the same period, it was accepted as a mitigating factor on sentencing. However, this has changed. Kerans JA has said:

> Drunkenness generally should not be a mitigating factor. Nevertheless, the fact that an assault is totally spontaneous can offer mitigation, and sometimes drunkenness is a factor in determining whether the attack is spontaneous or whether the likely consequences were fully appreciated.

This puts intoxication in its proper place as a factor that can distinguish between a planned offence and one generated spontaneously with little regard for consequences. Moreover, with respect to crimes of violence where there is a history of drunken violence, intoxication is an aggravating circumstance.

However, there are other situations where emotional, physical and psychological impairment can mitigate culpability because they affect judgment. Cool and deliberate choices are more culpable than those clouded by depression, medication, and extraordinary stress. Gambling addiction has been recognized as a mitigating background factor especially with respect to thefts and frauds. In *R v. Horvath*, a former bank manager was convicted of thefts totalling almost $200,000 from her employer and fraud in the amount of $35,000 from another financial institution. She was a 36 year old married woman with a child. She had become pathologically addicted to video lottery terminals and would leave work at the end of the day to gamble until late at night. She lost money and incurred huge debts. Then, she started stealing from her employer using an elaborate scheme involving fictitious and actual accounts. The trial judge heard expert evidence about her gambling addiction and her efforts to deal with it, and sentenced her to a conditional sentence of two years less a day in duration. The Crown appealed arguing that the amount stolen and the breach of trust required a custodial sentence. For the court, Bayda CJS dismissed the appeal. He said:

> Perhaps the factor that carries most weight in assessing the gravity of the offences in the particular case is the one that generated those offences. The offences were the products of a distorted mind—a mind seriously diseased by a disorder now recognized by the medical community as a mental disorder. The acts committed at the command of that mind were not acts of free choice in the same sense as are the acts of free choice of a normal mind. A pathological gambler does not have the same power of control over his or her acts as one who does not suffer from that complex disease. Accordingly, where those acts constitute criminal offences, the moral culpability—moral blameworthiness—and responsibility are not of the same order as they would be in those cases where the mind is not so affected.

Horvath highlights the ability of an addiction to reduce culpability to warrant a conditional sentence even in a case aggravated by a breach of trust. Of course, this mitigating effect of a gambling addiction has its limits. The offender in *Horvath* had no prior record and was making serious efforts to address her problem. In cases where there is a prior record, courts have not been so sympathetic to the gambling addiction factor.

While many courts have followed the *Horvath* approach to proven gambling addictions for breach of trust thefts and even for robbery, the Alberta Court of Appeal has rejected conditional sentences in cases of substantial thefts from employers. It has held that the proven gambling addiction did not constitute an exceptional circumstance that warranted a conditional sentence. This view does not seem to give proper weight to the basis for using a gambling addiction in mitigation. The gambling addiction does not serve as an excuse but it does diminish culpability if it has affected the offender to the point where there is little or no free will, as described in *Horvath*. Then, blameworthiness has been substantially reduced and this should be reflected in the sentence.

Employment record: A good employment record is always a mitigating factor although its impact may be diminished or even superceded by the nature of the offence. The reason why courts respond favourably to a good work record is because it demonstrates pro-social responsibility and conformity to community norms which are the antithesis of crime. Accordingly, the offender is considered to be more redeemable with more promising rehabilitative prospects particularly if the record is consistent over a long period of time. However, courts should be careful not to turn the absence of a good work record into an aggravating factor. Many offenders, especially those with little training and education, have diminished opportunities for work. Moreover, many offences are committed in places with high unemployment. In these situations, offenders should not be prejudiced. However, lawyers should consider finding out about community volunteer work or even a pattern of assistance to family and friends. These facts can serve the same mitigating purpose.

Collateral or indirect consequences: As a result of the commission of an offence, the offender may suffer physical, emotional, social or financial consequences. While not punishment in the true sense of pains or burdens imposed by the state after a finding of guilt, they are often considered in mitigation. However, careful distinctions need to be made.

When an offender suffers physical injury as a result of an offence, this may be relevant for sentencing purposes especially if there will be long-lasting effects. This kind of consequence may bear on a number of sentencing goals like individual and general deterrence. Certainly, this is the result when an offender is seriously injured after a driving offence. Given the general familiarity with automobiles as part of modern life, the direct conduct/consequence image plays a communicative role consistent with traditional sentencing objectives. This is not the case when the personal injury arises from uncommon conduct that is purely criminal such as might occur during a robbery.

The loss of employment or professional qualifications will often be raised as relevant collateral consequences. However, there is a distinction between situations where the specific criminal act results in disqualification from a profession or employment, and those situations where employment is lost as a result of personal or community response that stigmatizes the offender. The latter should be taken into account because it flows from the criminal process while disqualification is a more difficult issue. Careful distinctions are required. Some mitigation may be available if the disqualification arises from an offence which is not centrally related to professional responsibility. For example, there is a difference between a surgeon who is struck off the professional roll for criminal negligence causing death after performing surgery while intoxicated, and a physician who commits an offence of dishonesty in his billing practise. The former receives no sympathy for losing a profession which his conduct shows he was ill-suited to perform while the loss of livelihood for the latter is not directly related to professional qualities. Another example is a police officer who is convicted of an offence related to policing. A conviction for assaulting a prisoner will likely end a career and should not generate any mitigation when being sentenced for the assault. An off-duty offence may also end a law enforcement career but this factor would be viewed in a different light depending on the nature of the offence.

The mitigating effect of indirect consequences must be considered in relation both to future re-integration and to the nature of the offence. Burdens and hardships can flow from a conviction which are relevant because they make the rehabilitative path harder to travel. Here, one can include loss of financial or social support. People lose jobs, families are disrupted, sources of assistance disappear. Notwithstanding a need for denunciation, there are indirect consequences which arise from stigmatization and they cannot be isolated from the sentencing matrix if they will have bearing on the offender's ability to live productively in the community. The mitigation will depend on the weighing of these obstacles against the degree of denunciation appropriate to the offence.

Some indirect consequences are so inevitably linked to an offence that they seem to be part of the punishment and cannot be considered mitigating. Some realism has to be brought to the analysis. For example, losing a year in school is a relevant mitigating indirect consequence when it is put in the context of a short custodial sentence but if the exclusion from school arises from an assault on a teacher, it has no mitigating effect. The point is simply that indirect consequences must be viewed in the light of the offence itself. Where the consequence is so directly linked to the nature of an offence as to be almost inevitable, its role as a mitigating factor is greatly diminished.

Post-offence rehabilitative efforts: Progress in dealing with personal problems, and efforts to improve or repair one's social situation are always given mitigating credit. There may be concerns that such efforts are self-serving but they warrant credit because they show both a recognition of personal difficulties and a commitment to remedying them. Of course, one needs to show sincerity and motivation which can usually be done through material from a treatment programme, job, family or friends. At the sentencing stage, some credit will be given for rehabilitative plans but it is always preferable if an offender is already participating and achieving some degree of progress than simply explaining the plan for the future. Regrettably, not all communities have appropriate resources available locally. Moreover, not all treatment facilities are available at public expense. Accordingly, there is a real opportunity for the privileged offender to gain an advantage over the non-privileged. This does not diminish the mitigating effect of an offender's sincere rehabilitative efforts. However, it does mean that courts should be sensitive to these resource difficulties and be prepared to credit time and energy spent looking for appropriate resources and attempting to qualify for them as important factors. These efforts are a first step to reform since they reflect introspection and a commitment to change. The extent of the mitigating effect of post-offence efforts will depend on sincerity, actual progress and relevance to the offence. In cases of drug and alcohol abuse where the offence is closely linked to the addiction, courts should be cautious about imposing a sentence which may disrupt the rehabilitative progress. More to the point, the absence of progress is not as critical as the fact that efforts at treatment show some interest in change. It is an accepted part of dealing with drug addiction that hard-core addicts will fail a number of times along the road to recovery.

Unrelated meritorious conduct: Some courts have accepted the mitigating effect of acts of charity or bravery unrelated to the offence. The basis is that such conduct suggests something positive about the offender which should enhance the court's view of rehabilitative prospects. Also, this conduct is the kind of community involvement which one wants to encourage. This is sometimes referred to as "moral credit." Examples are saving a child from drowning or attempting to rescue people trapped in a fire. Such conduct can have taken place before or after the offence.

Acts of reparation or compensation: Reflecting the common law, two of the potential objectives of a sentence are now described in s. 718(e) and (f) as:

(e) to provide reparations for harm done to victims or to the community; and

(f) to promote a sense of responsibility in offenders, and acknowledgment of the
harm done to victims and to the community

For the same reasons that a sentence may be directed to these ends, an offender is
entitled to some mitigating credit for acts of reparation or compensation done prior to
sentencing. It may be impossible to know whether an act is purely self-interested or
really reflects remorse and a concern to rectify harm done. Absent contradictory evidence, the benefit of any doubt should always go to the offender. Obviously, some
harm is more easily rectified and some offenders are in a better position to take steps
to repair damage. Still, these are steps which should be encouraged. While lawyers
may want to encourage the repair of a broken window, they should exercise some
caution in advising offenders. A victim may harbour some residual fear of the offender. In the absence of an organized and responsible attempt at reconciliation, damage
should be repaired by a third party and not the offender personally.

Provocation and duress: Any situations which reduce the degree of culpability or
moral blameworthiness present relevant mitigating circumstances. The defence of duress
or compulsion is limited by s. 17 of the Code both in terms of qualifying offences and
factual pre-conditions. Accordingly, there will be situations where there is evidence
of compulsion but no defence to the charge. Because it can be considered less blameworthy to act under threat than of one's own initiative, these situations can mitigate a
sentence. The common case is a drug courier who argues that a threat was made to
encourage his or her participation. If there is no defence of duress, there may still be
facts that support its use for sentencing purposes.

Acts or words which provoke a violent response are in the same category. In cases
of murder, provocation under s. 232 reduces the offence to manslaughter. For all
other forms of assault, provocation is not a partial defence but can provide mitigation
on sentencing. Again, the premise is straight-forward. Punching someone is an assault
but it is a less blameworthy assault if it was provoked by an insult, threat, violent
gesture or other form of offensive or wrongful conduct. At some point, the response
is so disproportionate to the provocation that the provocation becomes irrelevant.
Conversely, the provocation may have been so severe and the retaliation so slight
that the mitigating effect produces a discharge.

In *R v. Stone*, the offender was convicted of manslaughter after being charged with
the murder of his wife. Evidence of provocation had been placed before the jury. In
imposing a sentence of seven years for manslaughter, the trial judge took into account
the provocation evidence. On appeal, it was argued by the Crown that this constituted
a double counting since the provocation evidence had already resulted in mitigating
the offence from murder to manslaughter. For the court, Bastarache J rejected this
argument and commented:

> In reaching a sentence which accurately reflects a particular offender's moral culpabil-
> ity, the sentencing judge must consider all of the circumstances of the offence, includ-
> ing whether it involved provocation. Indeed ... to ignore the defence of provocation
> accepted by the jury and the evidence upon which that defence was based, would be to
> ignore probative evidence of an offender's mental state at the time of the killing.

Accordingly, provocation was relevant in determining the level of moral culpability. At the same time, the fact that the killing occurred in the context of a spousal relationship was a relevant aggravating factor.

Delay in prosecution: Before discussing delay by authorities, it is necessary to say something about delays by victims in coming forward. It is not uncommon to find a case on a docket alleging an offence that was committed decades before, usually a serious charge involving physical or sexual abuse of the victim when the victim was a child. Regardless of the attitude at the time of the offence towards assaults on children, these are matters which are taken very seriously today. Often these offences involve a breach of trust which is now recognized in the Code as an aggravating factor and a custodial sentence of some length is usually sought for denunciatory and deterrent purposes. But what about the delay in bringing the charges forward? By itself, the intervening period does not mean very much and will not be considered as a mitigating factor. However, delay may present corollaries which can be mitigating. They are often raised in the context of submissions for a conditional sentence. For example, a lengthy period with no repetition of offending is an important mitigating factor. This, of course, is enhanced to some extent by evidence of productive social integration in terms of employment and family life during that period. The extent of its influence is affected by the gravity of the offence and is diminished by a lack of remorse or denial that the offence was a serious matter. The age of the offender can play a role. On the one hand, through the passage of time, the offender may have become elderly. While this is not mitigating, it may be accompanied by ill-health or infirmity which ought to be considered because of the inherent hardships of incarceration. From a different perspective, the offences may have been committed when the offender was very young and exemplary conduct during adulthood will be a serious mitigating factor. These examples demonstrate how the passage of time may produce changes that are relevant mitigating factors. While the ability of the justice system to reach back into time for the subject matter of prosecutions may cause some to grimace, we do not have limitations on prosecutions and there is no automatic benefit that accrues to offenders because of the passage of time.

There are Charter issues arising from delay. A prosecution may have moved slowly but not slow enough to constitute a violation of s. 11(b) and support a stay. Some courts have held that excessive delay which can be attributed to either the police or the prosecution may be a mitigating factor even if it was insufficient to produce a s. 11(b) breach. To some extent, this question is enmeshed in the debate about whether a Charter breach that does not produce a stay as a remedy can be resurrected at the sentencing stage in mitigation. However, given the recognition that any prosecution produces burdens and stress, and impinges on liberty, it is not necessary to engage in that controversy to argue that a deliberate or unnecessary expansion of the period during which these factors operate is akin to added punishment. Accordingly, it is appropriate to give it a mitigating effect.

The second issue is whether delay in sentencing can produce a s. 11(b) breach which leads to a stay rather than simply a mitigating consideration. The Supreme Court has concluded that s. 11(b) includes the right to be sentenced within a reasonable time. McLachlin J, as she then was, noted the potential adverse effects of living in "suspense" pending sentencing, and held:

> Delay in sentencing extends the time during which these constraints on an individual's liberty are imposed. While the sentencing judge may take these into account, there is no guarantee that this will occur. It follows that delay in sentencing may prejudice the accused's liberty interest.

For the purpose of s. 11(b), she applied the usual tests and concluded that, in the absence of any indicia of prejudice, the bulk of the delay occasioned by judicial illness could not be considered unreasonable. Accordingly, stays were not warranted. What is significant, however, is the recognition that delay can be an appropriate mitigating factor since it extends the ordinary impact of a sentence. Regardless of a s. 11(b) claim, one can argue that any delay that is deliberate, unnecessary or unreasonable ought to be a mitigating factor.

While pre-charge delay has no bearing on an accused's s. 11(b) rights to a speedy trial, some courts have taken deliberate delay into account in mitigation of sentence. The basis flows from the proposition that it is in everyone's interests, including the offender's, to proceed expeditiously to determine responsibility and impose a fair sanction. This kind of claim usually occurs when an offender is already serving a sentence of imprisonment and needs to resolve an outstanding charge before proceeding with release plans. From the offender's perspective, the authorities should not be able to arbitrarily postpone release by sitting on a warrant or evidence. Given the recognized interest in sentencing within a reasonable time, an example of deliberate or negligent delay which may prolong a term of imprisonment should generate mitigating consideration, including the possibility of a concurrent sentence even if otherwise not warranted.

Gap in criminal record and the intermediate recidivist: These are related factors which serve to place an offender's record into a context which has bearing on rehabilitative prospects. By definition, a recidivist is someone with a long record of previous convictions. A significant gap in that record, especially one that occurs just prior to the instant offence, indicates an ability to conform to legal norms for a substantial period of time. Notwithstanding the cynical view that a charge-free period does not mean a crime-free period, a significant gap shows a rehabilitative potential. Of course, the effect of the gap is relative but it would be enhanced if it included a period of good employment or responsible domestic relations. How the mitigation is applied depends on the nature of the offence. Where it can legitimately be concluded that imprisonment is the only reasonable alternative, a significant gap should be an important argument against an automatic escalation of the duration of imprisonment.

The "intermediate recidivist" is a category described by D.A. Thomas which includes an offender with a record who has arguably reached a point in life where a corner can be turned. For example, there may be a recent record of constructive employment with good prospects, a new domestic relationship, long-awaited success in dealing with an addiction or other personal difficulty, or a combination of these kinds of significant and potentially reformative life events. Notwithstanding the record, and depending on the nature of the instant offence, a court should give very serious consideration to a non-custodial sanction that will enhance the prospect of solid rehabilitation rather than frustrate it. One vehicle which may be particularly well-suited to this category of offender is the conditional sentence ... . There may be serious factual issues about the extent to which these significant life events have occurred, but courts are equipped to deal with issues of disputed fact and credibility. While sincerity may be a hard issue, courts should not be shy to address it.

A good example of the intermediate recidivist, although that label was not used, can be found in the case of *R v. McLeod*, an offender with a long criminal record and a long-standing problem with prescription drugs. At the age of 30, facing another drug offence and a charge of breach of probation, he experienced a number of positive changes. He returned to school and finished grades 11 and 12 before entering a college program. He attended church and AA, and did volunteer work at his school. The trial judge imposed a non-custodial sentence consisting of a two year probation period with electronic monitoring for the first six months. The Crown appealed seeking a term of imprisonment in light of the offences and the offender's record. Vancise JA wrote a lengthy decision supporting the non-custodial sentence. Recognizing the apparent change in the offender's life, he held that a fit sentence is one that is neither excessive nor inadequate judged on the merits of the particular case taking into account the circumstances of the offence and the characteristics of the offence. In his view, intensive probation supervision aided by a period of electronic monitoring was a sufficient and appropriate sanction.

Test case: Legislative provisions which have novel or ambiguous dimensions can generate good faith attempts to test their scope. With respect to non-violent crimes, an effort to create a test case for adjudicative purposes can result in a mitigated sentence. Of course, just being one of the first individuals prosecuted is not the same as an offence which was the product of a will to test the legislation. However, given the costs, rigours and uncertainties of protracted litigation, there can be a mitigating effect for an accused who decides to carry a case forward even if this decision arose after the charge.

Disadvantaged background: There is little doubt that much of crime can be traced back to histories of poverty, abuse and family dysfunction. While we applaud those who rise above the limiting and even crippling circumstances of their impoverished backgrounds, it is obvious that many cannot. The community must bear responsibility for its schools, hospitals, children's aid agencies and other social institutions which intervene in the lives of young people. When these efforts do not succeed, some recognition to disadvantaged background must be paid within the sentencing process. Of course, the impact will depend on the gravity of the offences for which the offender is being sentenced. Still, it is incumbent on courts to consider the real life-experience of the offender and put the offences into context . For example, in *R v. George*, a dangerous offender case, the British Columbia Court of Appeal had to consider the "pattern of aggressive behaviour" test in s. 753(a)(ii). In doing so, it observed:

> The dangerous offender provisions may fall more heavily on the poor and disadvantaged members of our society if their childhood conduct is counted against them. This

appellant had to face school as an aboriginal foster child living in a non-aboriginal culture with an IQ at or near the retarded level. It is understandable that any child with this background would get into a lot of trouble by lashing out aggressively when challenged by his or her environment.

This demonstrates the importance of placing relevant factors into the proper light: prior record both as a young offender and adult, employment record, educational record, family contacts. All of these factors need to be contextualized by taking into account the impact on them of the offender's disadvantaged background. It is not that difficult beginnings provide some kind of sentencing credit, but they do often explain other factors which are relevant to sentencing in an aggravating way.

A history of abuse to the offender is a controversial factor. The New Brunswick Court of Appeal has rejected the mitigating effect of an offender's "personal tragedy" in relation to a sentence for sexual assault causing bodily harm. The offender had been the victim of sexual abuse as a boy in the care of provincial institutions. The offender had a long record and the assault, inflicted on the woman he had been living with, was described as a "prolonged and vicious sexual assault which included acts of cruelty and sadism. ...." It is within this context, that the history of abuse as a youth was not given a mitigating role.

Recently, the Ontario Court of Appeal considered an offender who had received two consecutive sentences of 3½ and 2½ years for two counts of aggravated sexual assault. On top of this six year sentence he had served 19 months in pre-sentence custody. The offender was a young aboriginal man from Moose Factory and the case illustrates the important role that s. 718.2(e) can play. It also has broader impact because the court relied on the nexus between the circumstances of the offences and the disadvantaged history which the offender presented. He was a drug addict who had committed two violent assaults on the same evening while in a continuous state of intoxication. The appeal was allowed and the two sentences made concurrent for a total of 3½ years.

Mistaken belief in the nature of a prohibited substance: Currently, substantive criminal law has produced some complicated and sometimes contradictory ruling about when a mistaken belief can exonerate. For example, with drug offences, knowledge of the general nature of a substance as an illicit drug is sufficient for culpability even if the offender believes the substance was a less serious drug. There is still a controversy over whether the offence committed is the factually completed offence or an attempt at the intended offence. For sentencing purposes, it is important to remember the central role of culpability as measured by blameworthiness. As a result, the offender's mental state should be the focus of sentencing attention. While the factual context cannot be ignored, a belief that a less serious offence was in progress is a mitigating factor. Accordingly, a belief that a transaction involved only a substance held out to be heroin should be distinguished between knowledge that a substance was heroin. The Ontario Court of Appeal reached a different conclusion in an importing case where the offender believed the substance involved to be marijuana but, in fact, it was cocaine. Finlayson JA concluded that the offender should be sentenced on the basis of participation in cocaine importing. This is inconsistent with the principle of fundamental justice that recognizes greater blameworthiness in intended consequences compared to those which are negligently produced. Some mitigating distinction should be drawn to reflect the mistaken belief. Even if it has no impact on criminal responsibility, it does reflect a reduced level of blameworthiness. More recently, in *R v. Sagoe* the same court considered a situation where the offender had been convicted of possession of heroin for the purposes of trafficking. She maintained that she did not know that the substance was heroin. The court, in reducing the sentence from two years to six months, commented:

> The trial judge appears to have thought that it was irrelevant that the appellant was wilfully blind to the nature of the narcotic involved, as opposed to having knowledge that it was heroin. This is not correct. Although the appellant had to be sentenced as being in possession of heroin for the purpose of trafficking, the fact that she did not know it was heroin was a mitigating factor.

Combined with her passive role in the offence and the absence of any personal benefit, the original two year sentence was reduced to six months. This case reflects a recognition that the proper basis for assessing culpability for sentencing purposes is the factual context known to the offender.

III. STATUTORY AGGRAVATING FACTORS

A. Criminal Code, Section 718.2

718.2. A court that imposes a sentence shall also take into consideration the following principles:

(a) a sentence should be increased or reduced to account for any relevant aggravating or mitigating circumstances relating to the offence or the offender, and, without limiting the generality of the foregoing,

(i) evidence that the offence was motivated by bias, prejudice or hate based on race, national or ethnic origin, language, colour, religion, sex, age, mental or physical disability, sexual orientation or any other similar factor,

(ii) evidence that the offender, in committing the offence, abused the offender's spouse or child,

(iii) evidence that the offender, in committing the offence, abused a position of trust or authority in relation to the victim, or

(iv) evidence that the offence was committed for the benefit of, at the direction of or in association with a criminal organization

shall be deemed to be aggravating circumstances.

NOTE

Clearly, ss. 718.2(a)(i)–(iii) were recognized by the common law before statutory entrenchment. Their inclusion in the Code emphasizes the aggravating role that these factors play. Underlying these provisions are two unifying themes: the promotion of equality and the recognition of power imbalances as an aggravating context. The gravity of an offence is increased when it manifests a rejection of equal respect or an abuse of power against a vulnerable individual, or when it is motivated by a wrongful assertion of power. For an example of the role of s. 718.2(a)(i), see *R v. Miloszewski*, [1999] BCJ no. 2710 (Prov. Ct.), where sentences of 12 to 15 years were imposed on relatively young offenders for manslaughter. A caretaker at a Sikh temple had been brutally beaten to death.

B. Controlled Drugs and Substances Act

This statute, enacted in 1996 by SC 1996, c. 19 to replace the *Narcotic Control Act*, contains its own statement of purpose and a list of applicable aggravating factors:

> 10(1) Without restricting the generality of the *Criminal Code*, the fundamental purpose of any sentence for an offence under this Part is to contribute to the respect for the law and the maintenance of a just, peaceful and safe society while encouraging rehabilitation, and treatment in appropriate circumstances, of offenders and acknowledging the harm done to victims and to the community.
>
> (2) If a person is convicted of a designated substance offence, the court imposing sentence on the person shall consider any relevant aggravating factors including that the person
>
> (a) in relation to the commission of the offence,
>
> (i) carried, used or threatened to use a weapon,
>
> (ii) used or threatened to use violence,
>
> (iii) trafficked in a substance included in Schedule I, II, III or IV or possessed such a substance for the purpose of trafficking, in or near a school, on or near school grounds or in or near any other public place usually frequented by persons under the age of eighteen years, or
>
> (iv) trafficked in a substance included in Schedule I, II, III or IV, or possessed such a substance for the purpose of trafficking, to a person under the age of eighteen years;
>
> (b) was previously convicted of a designated substance offence; or
>
> (c) used the services of a person under the age of eighteen years to commit, or involved such a person in the commission of, a designated substance offence.
>
> (3) If, under subsection (1), the court is satisfied of the existence of one or more of the aggravating factors enumerated in paragraphs (2)(a) to (c), but decides not to sentence the person to imprisonment, the court shall give reasons for that decision.

IV. JUDICIALLY RECOGNIZED AGGRAVATING FACTORS

As with mitigating factors, there are numerous references in the case law to factors that courts have considered to be aggravating. Most of these bear on the gravity of the offence: the extent of harm caused, number of victims, use of weapons, infliction of brutal injury, etc. They are, for the most part, self-evident. They describe characteristics that necessarily place an offence at the more serious end of the gravity spectrum. However, the accepted aggravating circumstances that are personal characteristics of the offender are not always so self-evident in the sense that it can be difficult to articulate why they should result in a harsher penalty. There is ample case law that accepts the following list of aggravating factors as being relevant to sentencing:

- previous convictions
- actual or threatened violence or use of weapon
- cruelty or brutality

- substantial physical injuries or psychological harm
- offence committed while subjected to judicially imposed conditions
- multiple victims or multiple incidents
- group or gang activity
- impeding victim's access to the justice system
- substantial economic loss
- planning and organization
- vulnerability of victim
- deliberate risk taking

Consider this list and try to explain exactly why the particular circumstance or characteristic should be aggravating. How does it increase culpability or make the offender more blameworthy? Should there be any limits on the applicability of any of these factors? Are there other factors that you would consider aggravating? If so, can you articulate why they warrant a more severe penalty?

V. FACTORS NOT TO BE TREATED AS AGGRAVATING

There are also some factors that, at first blush, may appear relevant to sentencing but on closer analysis cannot be logically or fairly linked to the proper set of considerations that should bear on the sentencing function. Courts of appeal have identified a small number of factors that sentencing judges should not consider to be aggravating. The fact that the offender pleaded not guilty should not be used to aggravate the sanction. Otherwise, an accused is being penalized for exercising the constitutional right to be presumed innocent until the Crown has proven the case beyond a reasonable doubt. Similary, courts of appeal have held that the conduct of the defence at trial should not be held against an offender: see *R v. Kozy* (1990), 80 CR (3d) 59 (Ont. CA).

A harder issue is the absence of evidence of remorse. Although a guilty plea and other indicia of remorse are considered to be mitigating factors, does this mean that an absence of remorse is an aggravating factor? If it did, it would mean that anyone who did not accept guilt at the time of sentencing would be subjected to an increased sentence. Given that convictions are subject to appeal, and convicted persons are entitled to continue to deny guilt, should an absence of evidence of remorse be treated as a neutral factor? Of course, this does not include conduct that demonstrates callousness or actual absence of remorse.

A similar issue arises with respect to cooperation with authorities. Evidence of assistance is often considered to be mitigating. What about the converse? That is, a situation where the authorities want information and the offender refuses to assist. Remember that the law does not require confessions and it does not compel an accused person to divulge information about accomplices.

In *R v. Wristen* (1999), 47 OR (3d) 66 (Ont. CA), a second-degree murder case, the Ontario Court of Appeal said:

> The appellant was not legally obliged to assist the police. He was entitled to exercise his right to silence and require the prosecution to prove the case against him beyond a reasonable doubt. Exercising this right is not an aggravating consideration on sentence.

However, after accepting that principle, the court upheld the increase in parole eligibility to 17 years even though the trial judge was influenced by the convicted man's efforts to conceal the killing of his wife. It held that it was proper that the judge consider the efforts to hide the offence and the refusal to provide any information about the location of the body. The defence was that the woman had just disappeared and that the husband was not responsible for her death. This position was maintained throughout the appeal. Given the accused's denial of responsibility, can he be expected to disclose the location of the body? Is this different from a situation where the failure to cooperate with authorities can be characterized as callous disregard for the survivors or a victim, which is legitimately aggravating?

VI. ASSESSING RELEVANT FACTORS IN CASES OF SEXUAL ABUSE

One of the difficult areas of sentencing arises when there are convictions for sexual abuse of children. Such cases often involve a panoply of aggravating factors: extensive harm, multiple victims, abuse of position of trust. Many cases, however, are the result of old offences. What is the impact of the passage of time? Does it produce a mitigating effect if there has been no repetition of offending? Does it mitigate only if conduct has been exemplary? What is the relevance of indicia of good character in business or civic circumstances?

R v. Gordon M.
(1992), 11 OR (3d) 225 (CA)

ABELLA JA: This is an appeal by the Crown from a suspended sentence and one year's probation following a guilty plea by Gordon M., the respondent in this appeal, to twelve charges of indecently assaulting his two daughters. The charges relate to assaults which occurred from 1973 until 1979, starting when the girls were eleven or twelve years old. They stopped, as did the marriage, when the oldest daughter in 1980 disclosed the assaults to her mother. The incidents involved extensive touching, digital penetration and cunnilingus. The Crown submits that the trial judge, Misener J, erred in failing to apply principles of general deterrence and denunciation when he imposed a non-custodial sentence.

The trial judge characterized the conduct as "an extremely serious breach of trust"; "systematic," "gross," and "outrageous" misconduct; and a "serious ... and a continuing trauma" to the daughters.

The trial judge rejected the application of specific deterrence because the respondent needed no further personal deterrence, having acknowledged, apologized for, and medically treated his former behaviour, and having remarried in 1988. Nor, for the same reasons, was the principle of rehabilitation of any relevance to the respondent, there being no indication that the possibility of recidivism or anti-social conduct existed. The trial judge then considered whether the principle of general deterrence applied, and concluded that it did not. In his words:

> I have the greatest difficulty understanding sexual assault in the context of the family. I wish I knew more about it, I wish I knew why it occurs. But I'm pretty certain of one thing, I'm pretty certain that the concept of general deterrence as I've just defined it has no part to play in fashioning a sentence for those who sexually assault members of their family. Or, to be specific about it, for cases such as this. I cannot believe, indeed, I

think it very insulting to the human race for me to say that there is a given body of
fathers out there who are going to weigh the penalty and decide whether or not they
will abuse their daughters or their children. I just can't believe that that concept
expressed in such basic terms as I've just expressed it—and that's how it should be
expressed, it seems to me—I just can't believe that concept has any significance, any
part, any relevance at all to this type of case. ...

I simply cannot believe that in all the circumstances of this case the right thing to do
is to send [the respondent] to jail.

In the end, of course, the sentence must attempt to blend a particular accused with
the gravity of his or her offence. Aggravating and mitigating circumstances are
weighed, with the objective of arriving at a disposition which is, to the extent that
such a thing is humanly achievable, let alone universally accepted as such, reasonable and just in all the circumstances.

Looking at the circumstances in the respondent's case, the trial judge, in my view,
placed inappropriate reliance on several factors he characterized as mitigating.

He identified the following as mitigating factors:

a) the respondent was 51 years of age;
b) he was a well-respected, successful and accomplished businessman;
c) the respondent had the respect of the community;
d) there was a breakdown in intimacy and sexual relations between the respond-
    ent and his first wife which, in part, was a cause of the misconduct;
e) there were no threats or violence involved;
f) the respondent "fully disclosed" his misconduct to all concerned in 1980;
g) he sought treatment after the initial disclosure and was successful in his
    rehabilitation; and
h) the respondent "fully and generously" supported his wife and children until 1988.

While aspects of character are of varying relevance in sentencing depending on
the offence (see *R v. R.S.* (1985), 19 CCC (3d) 115 (Ont. CA), at p. 127, per
Lacourcière JA), I have difficulty seeing how someone who is accomplished and
successful in business is entitled to any more consideration from a court for an offence
of this kind, than someone with less business acumen or fewer resources.

Nor is it clear to me why the breakdown of "the sexual part" of the relationship
between the respondent and his wife, for whatever reason is in any way relevant to his
having abused his daughters. It suggests either that the daughters were understandable substitutes in the same home, or that the wife was in some way morally culpable
for the father assaulting their daughters, both completely untenable suggestions.

Nor do I accept that the absence of tangible violence makes the offence less worthy
of censure, since in my view "the offence of sexual assault is an inherently violent
crime": *R v. Khan*, a decision of the Ontario Court (General Division), released June
5, 1991, per Moldaver J at p. 4. There is no doubt, however, that there are escalating
degrees of violence and that these degrees are undoubtedly relevant as aggravating
factors where they exist.

Nor, in my view, do threats have to be articulated for a situation such as this to be
deemed threatening. The dimensional harm of this offence when it occurs between

parent and child is in its exploitation of the trust the child is entitled to place in a person upon whom she is dependent. While the conduct may often be explained by reference either to personal or social pathologies, it cannot ever be, or be seen to be, excused. The child is always, by virtue of the power imbalance inherent in his or her status as a child, in a more vulnerable position than the parent. In *Norberg v. Wynrib*, a decision of the Supreme Court of Canada, released June 18, 1992 [now reported [1992] 2 SCR 226; 92 DLR (4th) 449], La Forest J at p. 23 cites with approval the observations of one writer who refers to relationships where there is the capacity to "dominate and influence" as "power dependency" relationships [at 255 SCR; 463 DLR]:

> Professor Coleman outlines a number of situations which she calls "power dependency" relationships; see Coleman, "Sex in Power Dependency Relationships: Taking Unfair Advantage of the 'Fair' Sex," 53 Alb. L Rev. 95. Included in these relationships are parent–child, psychotherapist–patient, physician–patient, clergy–penitent, professor–student, attorney–client, and employer–employee. She asserts that "consent" to a sexual relationship in such relationships is inherently suspect.

(See also the opinion in *Norberg* of McLachlin J, who discusses such power imbalances and the duty they create at pp. 6-8 [at 271-74 SCR; 486-88 DLR].)

If consent is inherently suspect in these relationships, then while degrees of violence or threats may undoubtedly be considered as more or less aggravating factors in sentencing, it does not necessarily follow that their absence operates to reduce the seriousness of the offence. The status of parent–child, the dependency and vulnerability which flow from that status, and the trust the child is entitled to presume, all underscore that the relationship between parents and their children is a fiduciary one. The trust is offended no less when exploited in what appears otherwise to be a warm relationship between father and daughter, where the love a child feels for her father may generate acquiescence on her part without his subjecting her to additional physical or verbal victimization. It may even be seen, as it was by these two victims, as a greater and more traumatic invasion of their trust when it comes from a loved parent whom they are anxious to please.

I agree that the respondent acknowledged and apologized for his assaults, but only after his older daughter disclosed them to her mother. His "fully and generously" complying with his legal obligation to pay financial support to his wife and children after the disclosure resulted in their separation is, it seems to me, a neutral factor, as is his age in this case.

But while a custodial term is clearly warranted in this case, there are some mitigating factors which should be considered. From the evidence, the trial judge correctly concluded that neither specific deterrence nor rehabilitation applied. The respondent, after acknowledging the assaults, immediately sought and successfully completed counselling and therapeutic psychiatric care when his daughters disclosed his behaviour. He has consistently shown genuine remorse for his conduct. He has, according to a medical report filed with the court at sentencing, completely rehabilitated himself. The high regard and respect he enjoyed in his community have undoubtedly been irrevocably and profoundly impaired. And finally, it has been well over a year between the suspension of the respondent's sentence in May 1991, and the imposition of this custodial term on appeal.

The factors the trial judge accepted as aggravating are the following:

a) exploitation of the vulnerability of children;
b) "extremely serious" breach of parental trust or duty;
c) two victims;
d) number of offences, which the learned sentencing judge described as "gross" or "outrageous" systematic misconduct;
e) nature of the misconduct; and
f) victim impact.

Having identified them, however, he none the less found them to be worthy of less consideration than the factors he identified as mitigating. In my view, his emphasis was misplaced.

In erroneously concluding that general deterrence has no application in cases of this kind, the trial judge relied exclusively on whether there was any value of imprisonment for the particular accused, rather than taking into account any potential impact on the public perception of a father indecently assaulting two daughters over a six-year period. This court rejected that approach in *R v. Palmer* (1985), 7 OAC 348 (CA), where MacKinnon AJCO said, at p. 350:

> The learned trial judge seemed to have only the welfare and rehabilitation of the accused in mind when he imposed the sentence he did. While it is a consideration and an important consideration, it is obviously not the only consideration. The sexual abuse of a child by one *in loco parentis* is a very serious crime. It is a gross abuse of trust and power which society does not tolerate. It warrants, absent quite exceptional circumstances, a denunciatory sentence which reflects society's revulsion at this type of conduct and at the same time has regard to the possibility of rehabilitation of the offender. It is not unusual that such offenders have steady work; that it is their first brush with the criminal law; and that they express remorse when their activities are discovered. There is also an aspect of general deterrence to such a sentence which should not be ignored.

Counsel for the respondent conceded before this court that the principle of general deterrence is not only applicable but paramount in cases involving the personal sexual abuse of children. But he submits that the mitigating circumstances in this case are sufficiently exceptional that no custodial term is required. I disagree both with the proposition that the mitigating circumstances are exceptional and with the submission that a custodial term is not justified in this case.

In *R v. Clayton* (1982), 69 CCC (2d) 81 (Ont. CA), at p. 83, Cory JA stated:

> Incest is a serious crime. Although performed without violence, it may well leave lasting scars. The crime is one which often has terrible consequences for the victim. It constitutes a breach of the greatest trust that can be bestowed on a man, the trust of his children. ... It is appropriate that in most cases of incest involving young children that a term of imprisonment should be imposed.

More recently, this court confirmed that view in *R v. Fraser* (1987), 20 OAC 78 (CA). Lacourcière JA, in language directly apposite to this case, stated at p. 80:

> We are, nonetheless, all of the view that the sentence imposed failed totally to reflect the gravity of the offence and society's abhorrence with the conduct of the respondent.

This court has on many previous occasions set out the principles which should be applied in determining the sentence in these and similar cases. Those principles establish that, in the absence of exceptional circumstances, the imposition of a suspended sentence in such cases is inappropriate. Sexual abuse of children cannot be tolerated and must be denounced so that society will be made aware of the court's revulsion for such conduct which, in this case, involved a serious breach of trust.

General deterrence was not referred to in the reasons for sentence and does not seem to have been considered. The trial judge emphasized the voluntary interruption of the sexual activity as well as the rehabilitation of the offender. In our view, however, the extremely serious nature of the offence which, in itself continued over a lengthy period of time, requires a substantial period of incarceration in a reformatory. ...

In the circumstances, I would grant leave to appeal, allow the appeal, and vary the sentence to a term of 12 months. But for the mitigating factors, a heavier penalty would clearly have been justified. I can see no basis for ordering a term of probation.

PROBLEMS

Consider the following problems and select those factors that you believe should be mitigating and those that are aggravating.

1. Green was convicted of three counts of assault causing bodily harm that occurred in 1977 and 1978. In 1975, Green and his spouse adopted the two young daughters of her sister. The two girls, Helen and Doris, were five and seven at the time. Their parents had been killed in an automobile collision. For the next 10 years, the girls led terrible lives within the Green household. Essentially, they were family slaves performing all the washing, cleaning, and meal preparation for the Greens and their three sons. Their days were marked with abuse. Helen was so damaged by the experience that it took her 10 years to move from kindergarten to grade 6. She left school in grade 7 and ran away.

The offences consisted of: (1) Helen being beaten with the cord from the iron; (2) Helen being struck with a broom handle; and (3) Doris being punched and kicked, resulting in a broken nose and bruises. While there was a suggestion that Green would often walk into the bathroom when the girls were naked, Green denied these events and any voyeuristic or other illicit purpose.

Green is now 63 years old. He owned a successful hardware store in a small town from 1974 to his retirement in 1994. He was a hockey coach, a member of the Rotary, and a supporter of local charities. In 1986 he was selected as Man of the Year for his work on the new hospital wing. Although it is not well known, Green has had an alcohol problem all his adult life. When Doris first advised Green in 1994 that she had talked to the police about these events, he sought psychiatric help and began attending AA. Green's counsel has advised the court that the beatings occurred when Green was drunk. He has a previous record of two common assaults, one in 1954 and one in 1956 for which he received a $25 and $50 fine, respectively. In 1988, he was convicted of impaired driving.

After the preliminary inquiry, Green wrote a lengthy letter of apology to both Helen and Doris. Doris does not want to see Green go to jail but only wants the community "to know Green for the cruel man he is." Helen, who has had a very difficult life, has written that "Green should pay for the harm he has caused. Only a long jail term will be sufficient." Green pleaded guilty at trial.

2. Smith has been convicted of two counts of fraud that occurred in 1979, and one in 1981. Each offence involved $10,000. The victims were Mrs. Wilson and Mrs. Stein. In 1979, Smith was involved in a large land development project. He had been promised substantial financing from ABC Investments Inc. and was very optimistic that everyone who participated in his project would earn a lot of money. To raise the small amount not covered by ABC, he started to sell units at $10,000 each. In 1979, he approached Mrs. Wilson and Mrs. Stein, two of his clients. They were both widows in their late 60s. When they expressed concern about the risk, Smith told them that the investments were insured and that the principal could always be recovered. He sold them each one unit for $10,000. Although Smith believed the investment was safe because of ABC's backing, there was no insurance. That was a lie. In 1980, the president of ABC died before providing the capital. Smith approached Mrs. Wilson in 1981 and sold her another unit, repeating that the investment was insured. The project failed in 1983 and all funds were lost.

Mrs. Stein died in 1986. She had been living on her old-age pension and the $10,000 was her entire life savings. When Mrs. Stein's daughter learned of the fraud, she told the police that, because of the investment, her mother had to discontinue her July vacations to Lake Simcoe, where she had been going for the past 15 years to escape the city heat. She said, "Smith should be in jail for robbing my mother." Mrs. Wilson was still alive and was a wealthy woman. She advised that the $20,000 meant nothing to her. Smith had been a "good lad, always ready with a joke to warm a dull day" and she did not want to see him hurt.

Smith entered guilty pleas shortly after the preliminary inquiry. He voluntarily sent payments of $2,000 each to Mrs. Wilson and to Mrs. Stein's daughter. He explained that, at the time of the offence, he had many projects on the go and many debts. He was shocked that the project failed and never intended to harm anyone. At the time he was drinking heavily but in 1985 sought help for his alcohol problem.

Smith is now 58 years old. He had been a good father to his four children. He had a career as a lawyer and financial adviser, which was sometimes successful but was now over. After the charges, he resigned from the Law Society and now works as the night manager of a hotel. Smith had been involved with his community throughout his life. He volunteered with local sports leagues and gave to local charities. Now, his counsel argued, "his good deeds were forgotten and his reputation was ruined."

In 1969, before he entered law school, Smith was charged with trafficking in narcotics and conspiracy to traffick along with a number of other people. The serious charges were withdrawn when a major prosecution witness disappeared. Smith pleaded guilty to possession of a narcotic (marijuana) and was fined $500. In 1982, his name was publicly linked to various municipal politicians by journalists who tried to show that Smith had been extending various gifts to them. No charges were laid but two politicians resigned their offices.

3. Ferris has pleaded guilty to assaulting his estranged spouse. They had agreed to meet to discuss financial arrangements for their two children. While having a cup of

coffee, his spouse told him she needed more money. Ferris said that he would talk to his lawyer but that business had been bad. (He was an electrician who had become an electrical contractor.) As they were leaving the coffee shop an altercation took place. According to Frank, he removed his wallet to pay the bill and she grabbed for the wallet saying, "Do you still carry wads of money?" Her account was that she asked to see his wallet and did not make a grab for it. Frank grabbed her by the shoulders and threw her down.

Ferris is 38 years old with no prior record. He was charged with assaulting an employee in 1997, but the charge was withdrawn when the employee did not attend for his trial.

Since the assault, he attempted to persuade his spouse not to proceed with the charges but she refused. He threatened to stop making his maintenance payments but, in fact, has continued them at an increased level. A few weeks ago, he jumped into a creek to rescue an infant who had fallen in. This kind of heroic behaviour is not new. He received a civic medal for rescuing a man from a burning car in 1996.

Although he and his wife are separated, he has continued his relationship with his children. He went to a psychologist for anger-management counselling once. Since the offence, he has been charged with another assault arising from an argument over a parking space. (It is alleged that he jumped from his truck and punched a driver who had taken a space that he was waiting for.)

CHAPTER FOUR

Facts of the Offence for Sentencing

I. INTRODUCTION

The sentencing hearing follows a finding of guilt. That finding might be the result of a trial in which the trier of fact has found that the guilt of the accused has been proved beyond reasonable doubt. Alternatively, and this covers most cases, a finding of guilt is made after the accused enters a plea of guilty. In either case, once there is a finding of guilt, the trial judge must consider and pronounce sentence. However, this cannot be done unless the judge has factual information about the offender and the offence. This chapter primarily considers the manner in which facts about the commission of an offence are put in evidence at the time of sentence, but it also considers more broadly the manner in which disputed facts are put in evidence at the sentencing hearing.[1]

Where a finding of guilt is made following a guilty plea, there has been no trial of the general issue. The plea is a formal admission of the averments in the information or indictment.[2] These averments typically disclose little more than the name of the offender, the offence, and the event to which it relates. Thus it is incumbent on the court to inquire into the facts concerning the offence and the offender. Where there has been a trial, most relevant facts will have emerged in evidence already, although there might yet be information relevant to sentence that has not been adduced. Further difficulties can arise in cases of trial by jury. The trial judge, of course, is bound to impose a sentence that is consistent with the jury's verdict. The verdict typically leaves no doubt about the relevant findings, but there are cases where the findings underlying the verdict are ambiguous.

II. THE SENTENCING HEARING

A judge who is properly seized of jurisdiction to record a finding of guilt is compelled to pronounce sentence and until then there is no final judgment in the matter.[3] Although this principle applies in all cases, sentencing hearings can take different forms. There are many high-volume courts where the disposition of cases, including sentencing hearings that follow guilty pleas, appears almost perfunctory. Pleas are recorded at speed; sentences

---

1 With respect to fact finding concerning the offender and the victim, see Chapter 5.

2 Guilty pleas are discussed in Chapter 7.

3 See *Criminal Code*, RSC 1985, c. C-46, as amended, s. 720, reproduced later in this chapter.

are pronounced quickly and with a minimum of reflection. So, too, in straightforward cases, where the parties have nothing to add following the production of evidence at trial, the judge will often proceed directly to sentence unless counsel seek a postponement in order to prepare submissions. In other cases, at the request of counsel or the judge, a future date might be set for a sentencing hearing in which the parties may present evidence and submissions that are relevant to an appropriate disposition.

A conviction is not perfected until and unless there has been both a recorded finding of guilt and the pronouncement of a lawful sentence. The Code provides basic principles of law and procedure, but sentencing practice also varies from jurisdiction to jurisdiction. The significance of this point is not merely formal or technical. A finding of guilt is a necessary condition for the imposition of a sentence but, excepting mandatory minimum sentences, the finding does not of itself determine a sentence, let alone a fit sentence, for the offence or the offender. The determination of a sentence is an integral but distinct aspect of judgment in criminal cases. In this aspect of adjudication, the law requires judges to respond to the offender's wrongdoing in a manner that reflects accepted principles of sentencing.

III. THE FACTUAL BASIS OF SENTENCING

Although a judge cannot sentence without sufficient information about the offence and the offender, a guilty plea or the evidence adduced in a trial might not be adequate for sentencing purposes.

R v. Gardiner
(1982), 30 CR (3d) 289 (SCC)

[Gardiner pleaded guilty to a charge of assault causing bodily harm to his wife. At the sentencing hearing, Gardiner's testimony conflicted with that of the victim as to the circumstances of the offence. The trial judge accepted the evidence of the victim and held that the standard of proof was that of a balance of probabilities.]

DICKSON J (Martland, Ritchie and Chouinard JJ concurring):

...

In *Principles of Sentencing*, 2nd ed. (1970), Professor D.A. Thomas speaks at pp. 366-7 of an "evolving body of principle designed to ensure that the version of the facts adopted for the purpose of sentence is supported by evidence and reached according to appropriate procedural standards." One of those evolving principles, lying at the heart of this appeal, concerns the standard of proof to be applied for establishing aggravating facts which, while not affecting guilt or innocence, do have a critical effect on the length of sentence.

...

The Burden of Proof

A. Introduction

The question now to be addressed is this: What burden of proof must the Crown sustain in advancing contested aggravating facts in a sentencing proceeding, for the purpose of supporting a lengthier sentence; is the standard that of the criminal law, proof beyond a reasonable doubt, or that of the civil law, proof on a balance of probabilities?

The Crown [appellant] argues for the acceptance of a lesser onus of proof at sentencing than the traditional criminal onus of beyond a reasonable doubt, which applies at trial to the determination of guilt.

Relying heavily on American authorities, the Crown suggests that there is a sharp demarcation between the trial process and the sentencing process. Once a plea or finding of guilty is entered, the presumption of innocence no longer operates and the necessity of the full panoply of procedural protection for the accused ceases. Sentencing is a discretionary and highly subjective exercise on the part of the trial judge. The primary concern at a sentencing hearing is the availability of accurate information upon which the trial judge can rely in determining an appropriate sentence in the particular circumstances of the offender. For this reason the strict rules on the admissibility of evidence are relaxed. The trial judge is no longer confined to the narrow issue of guilt but is engaged in the difficult task of fitting the punishment to the person convicted. To require that the Crown prove contested issues beyond a reasonable doubt would be to complicate and extend sentencing hearings and convert the sentencing process into a second trial, with a resultant loss of economy.

In the event that the essentially civil onus of preponderance of evidence is rejected, the Crown proposes, in the alternative, an "intermediate" standard of "clear and convincing" evidence to apply to sentencing hearings.

The respondent [accused], on the other hand, argues for the application of the reasonable doubt standard to sentencing hearings. The "bifurcation" between trial and sentencing, proposed by the Crown, the respondent finds artificial and against the authorities. From the offender's point of view, sentencing is the most critical part of the whole trial process, it is the "gist of the proceeding," and the standard of proof required with respect to controverted facts should not be relaxed at this point. To do so is prejudicial to the accused. Administrative efficiency is insufficient justification for so radical a departure from the traditional criminal onus of beyond a reasonable doubt.

•••

[Dickson J then reviewed authorities in Canada, England, the United States and elsewhere.]

•••

F. The Principles

Sentencing is part of a fact-finding, decision-making process of the criminal law. Sir James Fitzjames Stephen, writing in 1863 [in "The Punishment of Convicts," *Cornhill Magazine* 189], said (quoted in Olah, "Sentencing: The Last Frontier of the Criminal

Law" (1980), 16 CR (3d) 97, at p. 98) that: "the sentence is the gist of the proceeding. It is to the trial what the bullet is to the powder." The statement is equally true today.

One of the hardest tasks confronting a trial judge is sentencing. The stakes are high for society and for the individual. Sentencing is the critical stage of the criminal justice system, and it is manifest that the judge should not be denied an opportunity to obtain relevant information by the imposition of all the restrictive evidential rules common to a trial. Yet the obtaining and weighing of such evidence should be fair. A substantial liberty interest of the offender is involved and the information obtained should be accurate and reliable.

It is a commonplace that the strict rules which govern at trial do not apply at a sentencing hearing and it would be undesirable to have the formalities and technicalities characteristic of the normal adversary proceeding prevail. The hearsay rule does not govern the sentencing hearing. Hearsay evidence may be accepted where found to be credible and trustworthy. The judge traditionally has had wide latitude as to the sources and types of evidence upon which to base his sentence. He must have the fullest possible information concerning the background of the accused if he is to fit the sentence to the offender rather than to the crime.

It is well to recall in any discussion of sentencing procedures that the vast majority of offenders plead guilty. Canadian figures are not readily available but American statistics suggest that about 85 *percent* of the criminal defendants plead guilty or *nolo contendere*. The sentencing judge therefore must get his facts after plea. Sentencing is, in respect of most offenders, the only significant decision the criminal justice system is called upon to make.

It should also be recalled that a plea of guilty, in itself, carries with it an admission of the essential legal ingredients of the offence admitted by the plea, and no more. Beyond that, any facts relied upon by the Crown in aggravation must be established by the Crown. If undisputed, the procedure can be very informal. If the facts are contested, the issue should be resolved by ordinary legal principles governing criminal proceedings, including resolving relevant doubt in favour of the offender.

To my mind, the facts which justify the sanction are no less important than the facts which justify the conviction: both should be subject to the same burden of proof. Crime and punishment are inextricably linked. "It would appear well established that the sentencing process is merely a phase of the trial process.": Olah, at p. 107. Upon conviction the accused is not abruptly deprived of all procedural rights existing at trial: he has a right to counsel, a right to call evidence and cross-examine prosecution witnesses, a right to give evidence himself and to address the court.

· · ·

In my view, both the informality of the sentencing procedure as to the admissibility of evidence and the wide discretion given to the trial judge in imposing sentence are factors militating *in favour of* the retention of the criminal standard of proof beyond a reasonable doubt at sentencing. Olah at p. 121:

> because the sentencing process poses the ultimate jeopardy to an individual enmeshed in the criminal process, it is just and reasonable that he be granted the protection of the reasonable doubt rule at this vital juncture of the process.

The rationale of the argument of the Crown for the acceptance of a lesser standard of proof is administrative efficiency. In my view, however, the administrative efficiency argument is not sufficient to overcome such a basic tenet suffusing our entire criminal justice system as the standard of proof beyond a reasonable doubt. I am by no means convinced that, if the standard of proof were lowered, conservation of judicial resources would be enhanced. In the event of a serious dispute as to facts, it would be in the interests of the accused to plead not guilty in order to benefit at trial from the higher standard of reasonable doubt. This would be not only destructive of judicial economy but at the same time prejudicial to whatever mitigating effect might have come from a guilty plea, as evidence of remorse.

[Dickson J then rejected a lesser standard than proof beyond reasonable doubt in respect of aggravating facts.]

Appeal dismissed.

Not all cases involve a formal sentencing hearing. In many instances, especially in cases before judge alone, the trial judge will proceed informally to hear submissions on sentence once a finding of guilt has been made. The following case illustrates the risk when conflicts arise as to the factual basis of a sentence and no evidence has been called on the points in dispute.

R v. Poorman
(1991), 6 CR (4th) 364 (Sask. CA)

VANCISE JA: The appellant was charged with assault causing bodily harm, entered a plea of guilty and was sentenced to 9 months consecutive to any sentence currently being served.

He appeals, contending that the sentence was excessive in the circumstances.

During the oral sentencing presentation by the Crown and defence, the trial Judge was presented with conflicting statements of the circumstances surrounding the offence: the circumstances alleged by the Crown which, if accepted, must be considered as aggravating; and the circumstances alleged by the defence which, if accepted, would be mitigating. No sentencing hearing was held to resolve this apparent conflict.

Thus, this Court is once again called upon to comment upon and set out the procedure to be followed by trial judges during oral informal sentencing submissions when confronted with conflicting submissions, material, or assertions surrounding the commission of the offence or the personal circumstances of the accused. The issue encompasses not only the procedures to follow but the power of the trial judge to resolve conflicting assertions and facts which do not go to guilt or innocence but which have or could have a critical effect on the length of the sentence.

Facts

Mr. Poorman and the victim, Mr. Elaschuk, were serving prisoners in the Regina Correctional Centre at the time of the offence. On the day in question, Mr. Poorman was in a common area of the Correctional Centre watching television when Mr. Elaschuk and some other inmates entered the area. The Crown prosecutor contends that Mr. Poorman got up from his chair, walked to where he, the victim, and his friends were seated, and for no reason and without any warning or provocation struck the victim in the face, breaking his glasses and inflicting a 1-inch-long wound which bled profusely. As noted, both counsel gave conflicting versions of the circumstances surrounding the events which took place. In order to appreciate the degree of conflict between the two versions, it is necessary to set out specifically the submissions made by both sides.

The Crown, after narrating the facts in the previous paragraph, stated that Mr. Elaschuk then asked the appellant why he hit him and continued with the following submission:

> What he describes following that is the Accused grabbing him and holding what the victim called a knife, a butter knife that they use in their eating routine, holding this thing into his back and forcing him from the common area into a cell, delivering to him a Kleenex, or having someone deliver Kleenex or toilet paper or something like that to him, telling him "close up the bleeding and don't say anything of this to the guards or—" He threatened to stick him with the knife. And stated that, you know, that he had done this before and he'd be prepared to do it again.
>
> •••

There had been no communication between these persons even as acquainted residents in the unit, and the victim has testified that there was no oral or gesturing provocation whatever to this. There appears to have been no reason for this.

He submitted:

> In sentencing, the Court is asked to consider the particular circumstances as between victim and Accused here being, in essence, strangers, the absence of anything provocative on the part of the victim orally or in gesture, the apparent absence of any reason for the—the assault, the potential danger that could have resulted from the location of the assault, the location of the injury from the assault. It's fortunate that he is not injured more so from the blow in the glasses that were worn. I believe the glasses were filed in exhibit at Preliminary Hearing and should be here at Court.
>
> The Court is also asked to consider significant, very significant, the setting in which this occurs; at the correctional centre as—between inmates.

The appellant's counsel also made oral submissions. The relevant portion is as follows:

> MS. MALONEY: First of all, My Lord, with respect to the circumstances of the offence I wish to emphasize that this assault is a single blow, minor injuries. There were no stitches or anything of that sort required, no effect on this person's eyesight or anything of that nature, and that Mr. Poorman was acting alone. He had not ganged upon this person, so to speak, by means of acting in concert with anyone else.

Mr. Poorman has maintained from the outset that there was never any knife involved, never any weapon of any sort involved. What he does indicate is that there is some background to this assault, to this single blow that he administered to the complainant in the area where they were all watching television.

My client indicates that there was some provocation, or at least some—

THE COURT: Now, whoa.

MS. MALONEY: ... some situation that resulted in him being angry.

THE COURT: I'm wondering, then, whether—are you so questioning the facts given to me by the Crown that perhaps we should vacate the not guilty plea.

MS. MALONEY: No, My Lord.

THE COURT: Excuse me, the guilty plea.

MS. MALONEY: It's not my intention to dispute that Mr. Poorman is guilty of an assault causing bodily harm in this situation. There is some background, though, that should have some bearing. I would suggest, in terms of trying to afford the Court some understanding—

THE COURT: Okay.

MS. MALONEY: ... of the context in which to place its sentencing.

My client indicates that the complainant had made an advance to him by touching him in a way that Mr. Poorman perceived as a sexual touching and as a result he flared up in anger and struck the person the single blow. It was impulsive and in some anger, certainly. But the situation was not prolonged. As I indicated it was a single striking motion.

The Crown replied to the issue of the knife and the provocation as follows:

If I may respond to some of my friend's comments, My Lord, before filing the record. Concerning the knife, I don't think anything significant turns on the Crown's submission concerning the knife aspect of this, and my friend's response is that that is not the item for sentencing before the Court, that aspect is—was stayed this morning, *there is that dimension to the story, though, and it is in opposition. There is issue on the fact there.*

Concerning the item of provocation that my friend raises there is issue in that regard. The Crown represents there was nothing provocative said or done prior to this. If that causes the Court a distress in considering sentence the victim is present and prepared to testify, as is the Accused present and able to testify if he chooses. [Emphasis added]

The Crown prosecutor went on to state on issue of provocation:

I invite the Court to hear evidence on the issue of provocation (inaudible—not near microphone). If it is not a matter of distress to the Court in sentencing then certainly the Crown will not proffer the evidence.

There was an adjournment, and when the proceedings resumed, and before sentencing, the appellant, in response to an invitation from the trial Judge to speak, again raised the issue of provocation in these terms:

Yes, Your Honour. Yes, I do. This assault wasn't (inaudible—not near microphone) mention a few facts about what I told that evolved around the assault. (Inaudible—not near microphone) time the assault happened we were sitting around the TV area and the victim was sitting behind me talking to somebody and they were talking about the use of jails (inaudible—not near microphone) and I turned around and told them "You guys want to keep it down." And I got up and I walked away and then (inaudible—not near microphone) I was leaving he touched me. That's when I blew up, you know. And that's what—that's what provoked me.

Thus there is a clear contradiction on two issues: (A) the presence of a knife; and (b) provocation. The trial Judge was invited to order a hearing on the issue of provocation but declined. It is not clear from the transcript whether he declined because he had resolved the issue contrary to the interests of the appellant or whether he considered it was not relevant in the circumstances.

Disposition

There are two questions raised here: (1) the power of the trial judge to resolve conflicting oral submissions on informal sentencing presentations; and (2) the procedure to be followed in informal sentencing hearings. Dickson J (as he then was) considered the standard of proof which is applicable on a sentencing hearing in *R v. Gardiner*, [1982] 2 SCR 368, 30 CR (3d) 289, 140 DLR (3d) 612, 68 CCC (2d) 477, 43 NR 361. In that case, he was dealing with a formal sentencing hearing and considered the onus and standard of proof.

···

The Court was not required to consider the procedure where there is a conflict between the Crown and the defence version of facts which are not crucial for the determination of guilt or innocence in an informal sentencing hearing. Bayda CJS considered the issue at length in *Canada (Attorney General) v. Boulet (sub nom. R v. Boulet)* (1990), 78 CR (3d) 309, 58 CCC (3d) 178, 85 Sask. R 93 (CA) (in dissent on other issues). The other two members of the panel disagreed with the result reached by the Chief Justice respecting the fitness of the sentence under appeal and specifically stated that they found it unnecessary to consider the principles stated by him respecting the rules, power of the trial judge to resolve questions of dispute, and the procedure to be followed in a sentencing hearing. In this case, it is not necessary to consider the issue in as detailed a fashion as did the Chief Justice, but it is useful to refer to some of the cases and comments that he referred to. The Chief Justice referred to the English cases of *R v. Newton* (1982), 77 Cr. App. R 13; and *Williams v. R* (1984), 77 Cr. App. R 329 (Div. Ct.) which set out the law of England as it relates to the powers of a trial judge to resolve conflicting versions of fact made during an informal sentencing hearing.

In *Newton*, the Lord Chief Justice of England set out the choices available to a trial in similar circumstances. Two of the three choices he commented upon are relevant in Canada. He stated at p. 15:

The second method which would be adopted by the judge in these circumstances is himself to hear the evidence on one side and another, and come to his own conclusion, acting so to speak as his own jury on the issue which is the root of the problem.

The third option he described as follows:

The third possibility in these circumstances is for him to hear no evidence but to listen to the submissions of counsel and then come to a conclusion. But if he does that, then ... where there is a substantial conflict between the two sides, he must come down on the side of the defendant. In other words where there has been a substantial conflict, the version of the defendant must so far as possible be accepted.

Thus in this case, if the trial Judge was of the opinion that the matter should have been resolved, his choice was to "so far as possible accept" the version of the accused and sentence him on that version of the facts, or, if he was not of the opinion that he could resolve the matter on that basis, he would hear the sworn evidence, resolve the dispute, and then sentence the accused. In *Williams*, supra, the Crown made certain statements not proved by evidence nor admitted by the accused, and the accused declined an invitation to have the disputed issues tried. The Crown submitted that because the accused had failed to call evidence as was suggested by the Crown, the version of the Crown should be accepted. Lord Justice Goff, in dealing with the procedures suggested by the Crown, said the following:

[I]n my judgment, following the principles stated by the Lord Chief Justice in *Newton* ... the Court had really only two courses open to it, assuming, as I do, that there has been a sharp divergence or substantial conflict: either to listen to submissions on both sides and proceed on the basis that the version the defendant should, as far as possible, be accepted or, if the court was not prepared to do that, then to hear evidence. It may be that such evidence, when called, will be very slight; it may be that it will be the subject of cross-examination and no evidence will be called in contradiction. But even so, given the sharp divergence or substantial conflict and given the fact that the court is not prepared to proceed on the basis that the defendant's version is substantially correct, the Court must, it seems to me, hear the evidence before forming its own view in respect of the matter which is in dispute.

As did Bayda CJS, we adopt these principles and hold that where there is a divergence of opinion or conflict of evidence not proven, the trial judge must not accept the Crown's version of the unproven facts as related at an informal hearing. If there is substantial conflict he must either: (1) hold a formal sentencing hearing at which time the Crown must prove the facts alleged on the criminal standard of proof, that is, beyond a reasonable doubt; or, (2) "so far as possible," accept the accused's version of the facts stated at the informal hearing, at which there is no evidence.

In this case, there were two disputed issues surrounding the circumstances of the offence which do not bear on the guilt or innocence of the appellant but which could affect the length of the sentence: the possession of the knife by the appellant at the time of the commission of the offence and the threat to use it if the victim "ratted"; and, whether the appellant was provoked as a result of the overtures of a homosexual nature which he alleges were made by the victim before he, the appellant, smacked him in the face.

The trial Judge, in sentencing the appellant to 9 months imprisonment consecutive to any other sentence he is currently serving, did not accept the version of the facts of the appellant. In our view, in circumstances such as this he should have ordered a sentencing hearing, at which point the Crown could call evidence on the disputed facts and appellant could call evidence or at the very least cross-examine the witnesses proffered by the Crown.

The sentence of 9 months consecutive is therefore set aside and the matter is remitted to the trial Judge for the holding of a sentencing hearing to determine the proper sentence to be imposed.

NOTE

Part XXIII of the *Criminal Code* now includes a partial codification of the procedure that should be followed to establish the factual basis for sentencing. Sections 720-726.2 of the Code (as amended by SC 1995, c. 22) read as follows:

• • •

720. A court shall, as soon as practicable after an offender has been found guilty, conduct proceedings to determine the appropriate sentence to be imposed.

• • •

723(1) Before determining the sentence, a court shall give the prosecutor and the offender an opportunity to make submissions with respect to any facts relevant to the sentence to be imposed.

(2) The court shall hear any relevant evidence presented by the prosecutor or the offender.

(3) The court may, on its own motion, after hearing argument from the prosecutor and the offender, require the production of evidence that would assist it in determining the appropriate sentence.

(4) Where it is necessary in the interests of justice, the court may, after consulting the parties, compel the appearance of any person who is a compellable witness to assist the court in determining the appropriate sentence.

(5) Hearsay evidence is admissible at sentencing proceedings, but the court may, if the court considers it to be in the interests of justice, compel a person to testify where the person

(a) has personal knowledge of the matter;

(b) is reasonably available; and

(c) is a compellable witness.

724(1) In determining a sentence, a court may accept as proved any information disclosed at the trial or at the sentencing proceedings and any facts agreed on by the prosecutor and the offender.

(2) Where the court is composed of a judge and jury, the court

(a) shall accept as proven all facts, express or implied, that are essential to the jury's verdict of guilty; and

(b) may find any other relevant fact that was disclosed by evidence at the trial to be proven, or hear evidence presented by either party with respect to that fact.

(3) Where there is a dispute with respect to any fact that is relevant to the determination of a sentence,

(a) the court shall request that evidence be adduced as to the existence of the fact unless the court is satisfied that sufficient evidence was adduced at the trial;

(b) the party wishing to rely on a relevant fact, including a fact contained in a presentence report, has the burden of proving it;

(c) either party may cross-examine any witness called by the other party;

(d) subject to paragraph (e), the court must be satisfied on a balance of probabilities of the existence of the disputed fact before relying on it in determining the sentence; and

(e) the prosecutor must establish, by proof beyond a reasonable doubt, the existence of any aggravating fact or any previous conviction by the offender.

• • •

726.1. In determining the sentence, a court shall consider any relevant information placed before it, including any representations or submissions made by or on behalf of the prosecutor or the offender.

726.2. When imposing a sentence, a court shall state the terms of the sentence imposed, and the reasons for it, and enter those terms and reasons into the record of the proceedings.

These provisions restate the conclusions of the Supreme Court in *Gardiner* in general terms. There are, however, some novelties or unresolved ambiguities in these provisions that demand attention, especially s. 724(3)(d). What is meant by the requirement that disputed, but non-aggravating facts, need only be proved to a balance of probabilities? If it means that disputed mitigating facts must be proved by the offender on a balance of probabilities, does this not diminish the principle that underlies *Gardiner*? It may be argued that *Gardiner* was concerned specifically with aggravating factors but that the court's observations concerning the application of the higher criminal standard addressed all situations. Moreover, in *R v. Pearson* (1992), 77 CCC (3d) 124, at 136-39 (SCC), Lamer CJC suggested that the Crown's obligation was a principle of fundamental justice within the meaning of s. 7 of the *Canadian Charter of Rights and Freedoms*, part I of the *Constitution Act, 1982*, RSC 1985, app. II, no. 44. Query: does this mean that s. 724(3)(d) is unconstitutional?

As noted in *Gardiner*, the courts have long held that the strict rules of admissibility at trial do not apply in the sentencing hearing. There is some analogy, therefore, to principles that apply in bail hearings. Section 723(5) expressly allows the judge to receive and consider hearsay, thus relaxing an exclusionary principle that has greater force at trial. Section 726.1 allows the court to consider "any relevant information that is placed before it." Information in this context is a broader concept than evidence that is admissible under strict rules of admissibility at trial. Although the range of information that may be considered at the sentencing hearing is broad, it is not without constraint.[4] A heightened degree of reliability and persuasiveness is necessary, obviously, where aggravating factors are in dispute. Furthermore, no degree of reliability or persuasiveness would entitle a judge to consider information that tends only to support conclusions expressly rejected in

---

4 In *R v. Hunter* (1997), 11 CR (5th) 156 (Alta. QB) the court noted, too, that the power to compel the production of information in a sentencing hearing requires some "logical nexus" between what is ordered and issues that are properly before the sentencing judge.

determining the finding of guilt. Finally, the requirement to give reasons (s. 726.2) will also force judges to note the factual considerations that are the basis for sentencing decisions. Indeed, this might be one of the most important effects of this requirement.

IV. FACT FINDING FOR SENTENCE AFTER A JURY'S VERDICT

R v. Brown
(1991), 6 CR (4th) 353 (SCC)

STEVENSON J: The accused appeals, by leave, a sentence of 12 months' imprisonment for dangerous driving imposed at trial and affirmed on appeal by a divided Court of Appeal [reported (1990), 75 CR (3d) 76; 23 MVR (2d) 89; 53 CCC (3d) 521; 81 Sask. R 295]. The issue is whether the trial Judge and the majority of the Court of Appeal erred in considering the consequences of death and bodily injury when the jury had acquitted the accused of dangerous driving causing death and bodily injury.

The accused was the driver of a motor vehicle involved in a collision with another motor vehicle. As a result of the collision, two passengers in the other vehicle died and two others were injured.

The accused was initially charged with two counts of causing death by criminal negligence. This was reduced by the preliminary inquiry Judge to dangerous driving causing death. Shortly before the trial, a new indictment was filed, adding two additional counts of dangerous driving causing bodily injury.

At the trial, the Crown argued that the accused was speeding and had driven through a red light, that this manner of driving was dangerous, and that the dangerous driving had caused the collision and resulted in death and injuries. The defence argued that the appellant was not exceeding the speed limit by an excessive amount, nor did he disobey the traffic light. Moreover, the defence urged that the manner of the appellant's driving was not causally connected to the collision or the deaths or the injuries.

The jury found the accused not guilty of causing death or bodily injury by dangerous driving but guilty of the included offences of dangerous driving, simpliciter.

On sentencing, the trial Judge noted that deterrence was the element that was most significant in this case and then turned to various relevant facts. The appellant's traffic infractions, he said, "do reflect some disregard for the rules to be obeyed in driving a vehicle." He then commented that:

> Now in this case, under the jury, they found you guilty of dangerous driving alone. And it's probably fortunate for you that they did. But the facts still are that two people died as the result—or following that collision. And two others suffer injuries that they are still being treated for today.

Included in the case on appeal was a letter or report written by the trial Judge to the Court of Appeal, which contains the following statement:

> Nothing is clearer than the death and injuries to the four victims arose directly from that collision. It was a flagrant example of dangerous driving taking all the circumstances into account.

Before the Court of Appeal, the accused argued that the sentence was excessive for dangerous driving, simpliciter. The majority of the Court of Appeal noted that, "If the [accused] is correct, the sentence here does not bear an acceptable comparison [to other cases]."

In the Court of Appeal, the majority upheld the trial Judge's sentence. In the course of his majority judgment Wakeling JA said:

> The appellant suggests that the trial judge's right is restricted severely because if he goes too far he is basing the sentence on facts which must have been rejected by the jury, otherwise the lesser verdict of dangerous driving would not have been rendered. The Crown says the trial judge not only can but has a duty to consider all of the evidence in order to determine a proper sentence, which evidence includes the fact the accused is at least partly to blame for a serious accident which took two lives. If the appellant is correct, the sentence here does not bear an acceptable comparison to such cases. ... If the Crown is correct, then the sentence is not exceptional when compared to cases in which the consequences are similar to those involved in this case.

In dissent, Tallis JA noted the Judge's obligation to respect the jury verdict, which expressly rejected any causal connection between the way he was driving and the deaths and injuries, and concluded the sentence should have been reduced to 6 months' imprisonment.

The majority referred to an apparent divergence between English and Australian courts on the position to be taken regarding findings of fact by a sentencer when the determination of guilt has been made by a jury. Clayton C. Ruby, *Sentencing*, 3d ed. (Toronto: Butterworths, 1987), at pp. 61-62; D.A. Thomas, *Principles of Sentencing*, 2d ed. (London: Heinemann, 1979), at p. 367; and *Tremblay v. R* (1969), 7 CRNS 315 (Que. CA), were cited.

The divergence to which the majority of the Court of Appeal referred centres on the question of whether the judge is bound to assume that the jury took the most lenient view of the facts which would support the verdict. That issue does not arise here because the only factual question relates to the consequences, and on that factual question the jury's decision is not in doubt. Thomas makes it clear that subject to the jury's express and implied factual findings, the judge must make the necessary sentencing findings. He or she must, of course, make those findings in keeping with the law relating to the finding of facts on sentencing set out in *R v. Gardiner*, [1982] 2 SCR 368, 30 CR (3d) 289, 140 DLR (3d) 612, 68 CCC (2d) 477, 43 NR 361, which establishes that while all credible and trustworthy evidence may be accepted, disputed facts relied upon by the Crown in aggravation must be established beyond a reasonable doubt.

In *Tremblay*, supra, the trial Judge, in sentencing for a manslaughter conviction, expressed his opinion that the accused was guilty of deliberate murder. The majority of the Court of Appeal decided not to interfere with the sentence on the basis that rid of references or expressions of opinion to give the accused's acts the character of murder, the acts were sufficiently grave to justify the sentence (a maximum). The dissenting Judge found that the sentence was not fit and that it was influenced by the conclusion that the acts were murder. The majority thus found the sentence was "fit," untainted by impermissible considerations.

Before us, the parties were agreed that there is no relevant difference between the English and Australian positions. In its factum filed here, the Crown set out the English position, again quoting Thomas from an article, "Establishing a Factual Basis for Sentencing" [1970] Crim. LR 80, at p. 82, where he says:

> [T]he Court of Appeal has developed the principle that where the factual implication of the jury's verdict is clear, the sentencer is bound to accept it and a sentence which is excessive in the light of the facts implied in the verdict will be reduced. ... This principle can only apply however where the factual implication of the jury's verdict is clear; where ... the factual implication is ambiguous, the court has held that the sentencer should not attempt to follow the logical process of the jury, but may come to his own independent determination of the relevant facts.

This statement reflects the correct principle, namely, that the sentencer is bound by the express and implied factual implications of the jury's verdict. There are other authorities to the same effect: *R v. Speid* (1985), 46 CR (3d) 22, 9 OAC 237, 20 CCC (3d) 534 (CA) at p. 47 [CR]; Kevin Boyle and M.J. Aiken, *Sentencing Law and Practice* (London: Sweet & Maxwell, 1985), at pp. 225, 227 and 229; Richard George Fox and Arie Freiberg, *Sentencing: State & Federal Law in Victoria* (Melbourne: Oxford University Press, 1985), at p. 48; Eric Stockdale and Keith Devlin, *Sentencing* (London: Waterloo, 1987), at p. 62.

The Crown, here, took a different position, namely, that the "narrow question" was whether the jury's verdict was ambiguous, leaving the sentencing Judge free to make an independent determination. The argument is that the Judge did not adequately describe the test for causation set out in *R. v. Smithers*, [1978] 1 SCR 506, 40 CRNS 79, 15 NR 287, 34 CCC (2d) 427, 75 DLR (3d) 321; *R v. Pinske* (1988), 6 MVR (2d) 19, 30 BCLR (2d) 114 (CA), affirmed orally by this Court, [1989] 2 SCR 979, 18 MVR (2d) xxxiv, 100 NR 399, 40 BCLR (2d) 1515. Counsel for the Crown analyzed the jury charge and argued that questions that were asked by the jury indicated that it may not have been properly instructed or that it had misunderstood the law on causation. Those are arguments against the jury's acquittal on the more serious charges and, if correct, would found an appeal of the acquittal. The Crown did not appeal the acquittals for dangerous driving causing death and bodily injury and must accept the verdicts.

The findings of dangerous driving, simpliciter, in the face of the more serious charges leaves no room for speculation. The jury has negated the factor of causation. This verdict was unambiguous and the trial Judge was bound by it. So was the Court of Appeal.

Since Parliament has chosen to make dangerous driving a consequence-related crime, the consequence of death or bodily injury must be taken to be excluded under a determination of guilt of dangerous driving, simpliciter. The Crown, here, conceded that had the accused entered a guilty plea to dangerous driving, simpliciter, it could not argue a more serious sentence based upon these consequences: *R v. Doerksen* (1990), 19 MVR (2d) 16, 62 Man. R (2d) 259, 53 CCC (3d) 509 (CA). There is, in my view, no valid distinction between the two situations.

It follows that the appeal must be allowed. The appellant invites us to substitute an appropriate sentence. The determination of a fit sentence for an offence is generally to be determined by the provincial appellate courts. In my view, Tallis JA has fully considered the matter and determined the fit sentence in Saskatchewan in the circumstances of this offence. I would adopt his conclusion and impose a sentence of 6 months' imprisonment and affirm the driving prohibition of 3 years imposed at trial.

Appeal allowed.

At issue in *Brown* was whether the trial judge imposed sentence on an improper factual basis. The Supreme Court leaves no doubt that it is an error of law for the trial judge to take into consideration factors that were specifically rejected by the jury in reaching their verdict. But a more frequent issue in jury trials arises when the jury's findings cannot be identified precisely. In such circumstances, the trial judge must make his or her own findings of fact for the purpose of sentencing. These matters are now partly covered in s. 724 of the *Criminal Code*, but the following cases and discussion remain useful.

R v. Lawrence
(1987), 58 CR (3d) 71 (Ont. HC)

CAMPBELL J: The jury had a choice of two different bases of manslaughter. The first basis was that the accused shook the child to death. The second basis was that McLeod shook the child to death and he was criminally negligent in failing to prevent her. In *R v. Speid* (1985), 46 CR (3d) 22, 20 CCC (3d) 534, 9 OAC 237 (CA), the learned trial judge in a similar case asked the jury to indicate on which basis they found manslaughter. In that case, the evidence of the second kind of manslaughter arose from the testimony of the accused himself, and the jury after deliberating for some time had asked for clarification of the difference between the two kinds of manslaughter. In this case there was no such basis to penetrate the deliberations of the jury by asking how they had reached their conclusion. I did not do so. I must therefore determine the findings of fact upon which the accused must be sentenced.

I am satisfied, beyond a reasonable doubt, that Lawrence shook the little girl to death. McLeod testified that he picked up the little girl or knelt or crouched beside her and grabbed her about 9:30 a.m. on 7th March 1986, because she was crying. McLeod testified that he shook her back and forth violently for minutes, despite the baby's crying, despite McLeod's pleas to stop, despite McLeod's threats to call the police and despite her warnings that something would happen to the baby if Lawrence did not stop shaking her. McLeod said that Lawrence shook and shook and kept shaking until the little girl went limp, "like a rag doll," her head flopping back and forth, her feet dragging back and forth across the floor. The baby lapsed into a final and fatal coma, from which she never emerged. She died in hospital some two or three days later, after being on life support machines for some time.

Lawrence testified that he was in the next room within earshot, heard nothing unusual, then was called in, to find the baby in the fatal coma. His testimony that he heard no noise from the next room while Jade Wilson suddenly and silently went into her fatal coma, with no crying from her and no noise from McLeod, is not worthy of belief and does not give rise to a reasonable doubt, in light of the testimony of the sustained and savage violence that was necessary to kill the little girl.

There is evidence, independent of McLeod, of admissions by Lawrence that he shook the child. Even more importantly, there is a powerful body of medical evidence about the cause of death. That evidence, which I accept, is consistent only with McLeod's evidence and is completely inconsistent with the evidence of Lawrence. The medical evidence of the degree of force necessary to cause the fatal injuries, together with the respective versions of McLeod and Lawrence, other pieces of evidence and all the surrounding circumstances, satisfies me beyond a reasonable doubt that the prisoner before the bar, Lawrence, killed the child in essentially the manner described by McLeod.

Dr. Gregory Wilson, the pathologist who conducted the post mortem examination at the Hospital for Sick Children, testified that the cause of death was "shaken child syndrome," in this case a violent shaking that made the brain move back and forth within the bony vault of the skull, causing fatal injuries to the brain. The shaking was so severe that the tissues leading from the eye to the brain were damaged by the force imposed upon the child. Dr. Wilson said that Jade's death could not have been caused by a few shakes. He said that the shaking would have to be extremely forceful, ranging through 100 to 200, or even more, back-and-forth motions of the head. He said that the brain injuries which he saw were even more severe than the injuries of a child thrown 40 feet to 50 feet from a car onto concrete. He said the least number of shakes he could give credit to is 50 or 60 shakes, and it could have been 200 or more.

While Dr. Jaffe questioned those conclusions or opinions of Dr. Wilson, the evidence of Dr. Smith, another eminently qualified pathologist, was very definite about the kind of force used. He described as "tremendous" the force that must have been used to kill the little girl. The degree of force required to produce lesser injuries in animals involves forces of 13 to 15 times the force of gravity. Dr. Smith also used the comparison of children who had fallen from a three-story building. He said it would more likely take minutes than seconds to administer the amount of shaking that was required to kill the child. He described various experiments with model dummies made to simulate children and talked about the kind of violent shaking that would be required to kill Jade Wilson. He thought that there would be 25 or 30 shakes, probably more than that, and more likely much more than that. He described how bizarre it was during the experiments to shake the model of the child that so resembled a living child and how hard one would have to work at shaking the child to deliver the actual force that was needed to kill Jade. He testified as to how much violent and repeated directed energy would be required to deliver the fatal shaking.

I conclude, on this evidence, that the shaking administered by Lawrence to the little girl was violent and sustained and pitiless. The extreme violence of the attack on the child is difficult to visualize, let alone to understand. It is only after some reflection on the evidence of Dr. Wilson and Dr. Smith, together with the evidence of McLeod, that one can develop a picture of the prolonged and unremitting savagery of that attack.

This was not the first time that the accused had attacked the little girl. Her body was covered with bruises. McLeod testified as to a systematic series of assaults by the prisoner on the child over a period of some weeks before the culminating and final assault. There were various bruises on the child's arms, corresponding bruises on the left and right side of her abdomen, bruises on the buttocks, bruises on the tops and very significant bruises on the bottom of both feet. There was an abrasion on the big toe of the right foot and an abrasion on the child's hand. There were two head injuries, reflecting a subdural haemorrhage about three weeks old and a subarachnoid haemorrhage about one week old.

I cannot be satisfied on all of the evidence that all of these previous injuries were caused by Lawrence. I am, however, satisfied, beyond a reasonable doubt, that a significant number of them are his work, including the bite mark on the toe and the hand, the bruises on the arms and chest and abdomen, where he held the child at various times while assaulting her, and particularly the bruises on the soles of the feet, caused by his repeated and forceful pounding of the child on the floor on a number of separate occasions when she would not, at his direction, remain quiet or when she would not stay in the corner for hours at a time, as he directed.

R.J. Delisle, "Annotation to *Lawrence*"
(1987), 58 CR (3d) 71

The prescribed penalty for manslaughter ranges from probation to life imprisonment, and the sentencing judge must assess the gravity of his individual case and fashion the appropriate punishment within a broad range. In this case the trial judge saw that the evidence led could support two quite different theses to account for the jury's verdict of guilt. Either the accused, by his own hand, killed the little girl, or he failed to prevent the killing and so failed in his obligation as parent to protect the child in his care. Although the legislature calls each by the same name of "manslaughter," it is obvious that the measure of guilt is different. In each case it's a matter of criminal negligence, in one case by commission, in the other omission. In an earlier case cited by the court, *R v. Speid* (1985), 46 CR (3d) 72, 20 CCC (3d) 534, 9 OAC 237 (HC), the evidence indicated the same two theories capable of supporting a manslaughter conviction in the death of a child. There, after the jury returned a verdict of guilty, the trial judge asked them to indicate which theory they had adopted. The jury deliberated and returned to announce that they believed the accused had himself killed the child, and the judge sentenced him accordingly.

The accused on a charge of manslaughter is given his choice of how he wants to be tried, by judge alone or by judge and jury. The accused in this case opted to be tried by judge and jury. The accused thus asked for the facts to be assessed by a jury: Section 11(f) of the *Canadian Charter of Rights and Freedoms* says that he is entitled to a jury assessment, and yet the judge here substitutes his own view of the facts on a most critical issue, instead of canvassing the jury. In a civil suit for negligence it is common for the judge to ask the jury to decide: first, whether the defendant was negligent; second, in what his negligence consisted; and third, whether the plaintiff was contributorily negligent and, if so, to what extent. The judge is then better able to determine his award. So too in a criminal case, when the evidence discloses alternate theories of guilt, the judge would be better equipped to determine the proper punishment if he asked the jury for a special rather than a general verdict. The accused would then be tried on the facts by a jury and the judge could then determine the best sentence to fit those facts and society's needs.

A special verdict would not be new to the criminal law, of course, although, to be fair it did fall into disuse in the 19th century. More recently, English and Canadian jurisprudence has condemned special verdicts in criminal cases: see *R v. Solomon* (1984), 6 Cr. App. R (S) 120 at 126, and *R v. Tuckey; R v. Baynham; R v. Walsh* (1985), 46 CR (3d) 97 at 110, 9 OAC 218 (CA). In the English case cited, the court allowed, however:

> The only instance we have been able to find in which it might be said to be common practice to go behind the general verdict and to enquire from the jury the basis upon which it was reached is in the case of a verdict of manslaughter, when the jury may have reached their decision on alternative grounds which have been left to them by the judge. ... This court [has] said that in such circumstances the judge may, and generally should, seek guidance from the jury concerning the basis of their verdict.

In the Ontario case cited, the court referred to the English exception but said:

> In our view, such an inquiry after the verdict and for the purpose of sentence can raise more difficulties than it solves, in that the jury may not be unanimous on the evidential basis of the verdict. ... The jury are entitled to arrive at a unanimous verdict for different reasons and on separate evidential bases. They need not be unanimous in anything but the actual verdict. To require them to state particulars of the offence found is a practice fraught with potential danger and contrary to traditional practice.

Is this a satisfactory reason for failing to follow the English practice in manslaughter cases? That the jury need not be unanimous was confirmed by the Supreme Court of Canada in *Thatcher v. R*, [1987] 1 SCR 652, 57 CR (3d) 97, [1987] 4 WWR 193 [Sask.]. Since it's perfectly proper to find guilt along different paths, what's wrong with disclosing that fact? What is the "potential danger"? If six jurymen joined in the unanimous verdict of guilt but were persuaded only of the lesser form of guilt, shouldn't that be known and shouldn't the sentence then be limited to the lesser version?

NOTE

The question of consequences is a recurring issue in sentencing. This was addressed in Chapter 2 in the context of assessing culpability for driving offences that cause death or bodily harm (see *R v. Sweeney*). Another example of a related issue arose in *R v. Petrovic* (1984), 41 CR (3d) 275 (Ont. CA) (leave to appeal refused), where the appellant was convicted of assault causing bodily harm and sentenced to five years' imprisonment. After being abused and assaulted, Petrovic's spouse took her life by jumping from the balcony of their apartment. For the court, Lacourcière JA made the following observations (at 290-91):

> It was not part of the Crown's case that the appellant drove his wife to commit suicide. If that had been the case, the charge laid would have involved culpable homicide. The severity of a five-year sentence which the Crown concedes has to be reviewed, was no doubt

considerably influenced by this factor. The appellant's punishment was increased for an intent which was not alleged against him and which he did not possess. In fact, the appellant was found guilty of assault causing bodily harm. The conduct causing injury to the victim was callous and not an isolated impulsive act but part of a long-standing pattern of physical abuse. However, the circumstances of the assault do not support an inference that the appellant intended or even contemplated the tragic result of his wife's death. To paraphrase the language of Chief Justice Trainor, delivering the judgment of the Prince Edward Island Supreme Court in *R v. Griffin* (1975), 23 CCC (2d) 11 at p. 15, 7 Nfld. & PEIR 139, it would appear that the learned trial judge gave undue weight to the actual result of the assault rather than to the probable result.

The appellant is a first offender. He is 35 years of age and trained as a musician in Yugoslavia. He has since formed a new relationship, and married again on 16th March 1984. At the time of the sentence hearing, the Crown's position was that an early parole for purposes of deportation be recommended. The learned trial judge made this recommendation.

Mr. Ruby's submission is that the appellant should be treated as a first offender and released on the basis of "time served" which is the equivalent of four and a half months. This would not, in my view, give sufficient weight to the necessity of general deterrence in cases involving callous and repeated acts of violence against a vulnerable victim belonging to a class requiring this court's protection. However, the sentence of five years was disproportionate to the gravity of the offence.

I would allow the appeal from sentence and substitute a sentence of two years in the penitentiary.

See also the annotation to *Petrovic* by Price at (1984), 41 CR (3d) 276-78.

In *R v. Tempelaar* (1995), 37 CR (4th) 91 (SCC), the accused was charged with sexual assault. The complainant testified as to the nature of the assault. The accused called no evidence and the trial judge instructed the jury that any of three stages in the complainant's version of events could constitute the offence charged, namely (1) the accused's touching of the victim's breast, (2) his touching of her crotch, and (3) his act of non-consensual intercourse with the victim. After deliberating for approximately two hours, the jury returned a verdict of guilty. After the jury was excused, the accused's counsel expressed concern that the verdict was unclear for the purposes of sentencing. As a result, the judge held the jury back, and after consultation with counsel, asked the jury to determine whether their verdict was based on the sexual touching or on the unwanted act of intercourse. About 15 minutes later, the jury returned and asked the judge whether the court required "a unanimous decision on each of the three separate incidents." The judge replied that they should be unanimous with regard to each of the incidents. In response to a further question from the jury, the judge told them to determine whether or not the accused had penetrated the victim.

One hour later, the judge informed the jury that he had erred in asking them to particularize their verdict, and he discharged them. The trial judge sentenced the accused to 30 months' imprisonment. The Ontario Court of Appeal dismissed the accused's appeal against conviction and sentence, holding that, on the authority of their decision in *Tuckey*, "the trial judge was entitled to make up his own mind on disputed questions of fact which were relevant to sentence."

On further appeal to the Supreme Court, the accused argued that his right to the benefit of a trial by jury guaranteed by s. 11(f) of the Charter, as well as his right to be presumed innocent under s. 11(d), had been compromised when the trial judge failed to pass sentence on the basis of the least aggravating set of facts that would support a finding of guilt. He argued that when the Crown exercised its discretion to rely on alternative bases of liability, he should have been entitled, as a matter of principle, to be sentenced on the basis of the least aggravating theory of liability unless the Crown had particularized its theories in separate counts. The court summarily rejected the appeal:

> LAMER CJC (orally): We find no reason to depart from the law as regards sentencing as it now stands, and has for many years. The appeal is accordingly dismissed.

For examples of how this line of cases is applied, see *R v. Cooney* (1995), 98 CCC (3d) 196 (Ont. CA); *R v. Gauthier (No. 2)* (1996), 108 CCC (3d) 231 (BC CA); *R v. Holder* (1998), 21 CR (5th) 277 (Ont. Ct. (Gen. Div.)); and *R v. Englehart* (1998), 124 CCC (3d) 505 (NB CA). See also Downes, "Findings of Fact for Sentencing in Jury Trials" (1995), 37 CR (4th) 93. In *R v. Braun* (1995), 95 CCC (3d) 443, the Manitoba Court of Appeal ruled that a person who has been found guilty after a trial in which he did not testify cannot later testify at the sentencing hearing in a manner that contradicts the clear findings of the jury.

Notwithstanding suggestions such as those made by Professor Delisle in his annotation to *Lawrence*, supra, one effect of *Tempelaar* is the rejection of the proposal for the use of special verdicts to aid sentencing decisions.

V. SELF-INCRIMINATION AND SILENCE AT THE SENTENCING HEARING

As the sentencing process only begins after a finding of guilt has been registered, does this mean that the presumption of innocence is not applicable? We have seen that with respect to factors raised to aggravate the sentence, the Crown must prove them beyond a reasonable doubt if they are contested. (This is subject to the judge's ability in a jury trial to make findings of fact so long as they are consistent with the verdict.) Accordingly, allegations are not sufficient; there must be a satisfactory factual foundation for the sentencing process even though the accused has been found guilty. What about silence? It is now clear that for purposes of determining criminal responsibility, the accused's silence cannot be considered (see *R v. Noble* (1997), 6 CR (5th) 1 (SCC)). Can the absence of an explanation for the conduct that comprises the offence be considered and used as an aggravating factor?

R v. Shropshire
(1995), 43 CR (4th) 269 (SCC)

[The accused pleaded guilty to second-degree murder after shooting the deceased in the chest three times. He offered no explanation for the killing. The trial judge sentenced him to life imprisonment and set the parole ineligibility period at 12 years. On appeal, the British Columbia Court of Appeal reduced the period to 10 years on the basis that, *inter alia*, there were no unusual circumstances to warrant an increase beyond the minimum of 10 years. The Supreme Court of Canada reversed and restored the 12-year period. Iacobucci J spoke for the court.]

IACOBUCCI J:

...

I do not see any error on the part of the trial judge. He adverted to the fact that the respondent had pleaded guilty and was only 23 years old. He recognized that the Crown was not seeking a period of parole ineligibility beyond the minimum. Nevertheless, in a legitimate exercise of his discretionary power, and after correctly reviewing the factors set out in s. 744, he imposed a 12-year period of parole ineligibility. He referred to the following factors as specifically justifying the 12-year period of parole ineligibility:

    (a) the circumstances of the killing were strange in that they provided no real answer to why it took place, and the respondent was unwilling or unable to explain his actions;

    (b) the murder was committed during the course of committing another offence, namely a drug transaction; and

    (c) the respondent has a record for both narcotic offences and violence.

Factors (b) and (c) clearly fall within the categories ("character," "nature" and "circumstances surrounding") established by s. 744. As to factor (b), I further note that the Manitoba Court of Appeal, in *R v. Ly* [(1992) 72 CCC (3d) 57], held that the period of parole ineligibility could be increased when the murder is committed in the course of another crime, particularly a crime of violence.

Factor (a), however, presents some difficulty. The respondent raises the question whether the trial judge erred in interpreting the respondent's silence in such a manner as to justify extending the period of parole ineligibility.

In response, I would affirm the analysis of Goldie JA in the court below and would hold that this silence is readily assimilable within the "circumstances surrounding the offence" criterion. The crux of Goldie JA's comments is that, in the absence of any explanation for a random and seemingly senseless killing, the trial judge was correct in sentencing the respondent in light of his refusal to offer an explanation. It was found that his refusal was deliberate and in and of itself unusual. After all, the respondent, a drug dealer with previous convictions for robbery and armed robbery, shot the victim Buffam in cold blood without provocation of any kind.

It is not for the trial judge to speculate what the respondent might have said to mitigate the severity of the offence. I quite agree with Goldie JA that the right to silence, which is fully operative in the investigative and prosecutorial stages of the criminal process, wanes in importance in the post-conviction phase when sentencing is at issue. However, in so agreeing, I emphasize that the respondent pleaded guilty; I leave for future consideration the question of drawing a negative inference from the silence of the accused when he or she has pleaded not guilty and wishes to appeal the conviction. In the case at bar, the trial judge even went so far as to invite the accused to suggest why he may have committed the offence, but no response was forthcoming.

As held by Goldie JA, the respondent "cannot expect to be rewarded for remaining silent in the circumstances." The court and the public clearly have an interest in knowing why a human life was taken by an offender.

Goldie JA's comments and the decision of the trial judge on the "silence" issue are fully consonant with the position taken by the Ontario Court of Appeal. In *R v. Able* [(1993), 65 OAC 37 (CA)], the Court of Appeal increased two co-accused's periods of parole ineligibility. At p. 39 it was held:

> No explanation has been forthcoming from either of the appellants with respect to the reason for the killing ... [which] can be best described as a callous, brutal, pointless, execution-style killing of a helpless victim.

I conclude that in certain circumstances, such as those presented in this case, it is proper to take into account the absence of an explanation of attenuating factors.

The respondent suggests that Goldie JA's comments and the decision of the trial judge contravene the pronouncements of this court in *R v. Gardiner*, [1982] 2 SCR 368. I recognize that, in *Gardiner*, this court extended certain procedural rights to sentencing proceedings. However, these were limited to the right to counsel, the right to call evidence, the right to cross-examine and the right to address the court. There is no mention made of the creation in its identical form of a substantive right such as the right to silence.

At the sentencing stage, the Crown has already proved beyond a reasonable doubt that the accused has committed the crime for which he or she stood charged or, as in this appeal, the accused has pleaded guilty to the offence; if the accused then seeks to receive the least severe sentence commensurate with his or her conviction (*i.e.* for second degree murder, life imprisonment with eligibility for parole after 10 years have elapsed) it is incumbent upon the accused to play a somewhat active role in the process. I note that the right to silence is a manifestation of the presumption of innocence: *R v. Broyles*, [1991] 3 SCR 595; *R v. Hebert*, [1990] 2 SCR 151; *R v. Chambers*, [1990] 2 SCR 1293. The presumption of innocence flows to those "charged with an offence" or suspected of having committed one; once an individual has been convicted of an offence he or she is no longer simply "charged."

Appeal allowed; parole ineligibility set at twelve years.

Can these comments be reconciled with *Gardiner* and *Noble*? Is the court converting an absence of evidence into an aggravating factor?

Once there is a finding of guilt, it is true that the presumption of innocence is spent to the extent that the prosecution is relieved of further obligation to prove the offence beyond reasonable doubt. If the burden and standard of proof are all that is meant by the presumption of innocence, it would seem to follow that there is no scope for its application in the sentencing hearing. But this might be an unduly hasty conclusion because there is a meaningful way in which the presumption of innocence can apply in sentencing. It is clear that the prosecutor must prove disputed facts beyond reasonable doubt if those facts are aggravating. Thus the higher standard of proof is required to establish heightened culpability. The rationale for this standard might not flow directly from the presumption of innocence, but it serves a purpose that is entirely consistent with that principle.[5] Similarly, the conclusion in *Brown*, supra, can be explained in an analogous fashion. The court concluded that the accused could not properly be sentenced with reference to elements of culpability that were rejected by the jury. What is this at the sentencing stage if not some vestigial protection of the principle against self-incrimination?

For general discussions of *Shropshire*, see Trotter, "Murder, Sentencing and the Supreme Court of Canada" (1996), 43 CR (4th) 288 and Norris, "Sentencing for Second-Degree Murder" (1996), 1 *Can. Crim. LR* 199.

VI. JUDICIAL NOTICE OF RELEVANT FACTS

To what extent may a judge take judicial notice of facts relevant to sentencing? This question arose incidentally in *Gladue* and has been posed also in several other cases. It is a question that affects fact finding not only in relation to the particular offender but to the nature and incidence of the offence. At least part of the answer would seem to be obvious. If the facts in question are in dispute between the parties, they must be proved by affirmative evidence. If there is no direct dispute on the facts between the parties, might it be argued nonetheless that the principle of judicial notice is inapplicable to facts that are contentious in themselves—that is, facts that are a matter of dispute?

R v. Gladue
(1999), 23 CR (5th) 197 (SCC)

[This case is considered more fully in Chapter 16, which is concerned with the sentencing of aboriginal offenders. The Supreme Court of Canada considered a wide range of issues relevant to the determination of a fit sentence for an aboriginal offender. Reference to judicial notice was made toward the end of the opinion of Cory and Iacobucci JJ.]

CORY AND IACOBUCCI JJ:

...

The foregoing discussion of guidelines for the sentencing judge has spoken of that which a judge must do when sentencing an aboriginal offender. This element of duty is a critical component of s. 718.2(e). The provision expressly provides that a court that imposes a sentence *should* consider all available sanctions other than imprisonment that are reasonable in the circumstances, and *should* pay particular attention to the circumstances of aboriginal offenders. There is no discretion as to whether to consider the unique situation of the aboriginal offender; the only discretion concerns the determination of a just and appropriate sentence.

---

5 See *R v. Pearson* (1992), 17 CR (4th) 1, at 54-55 (SCC), per Lamer CJC.

How then is the consideration of s. 718.2(e) to proceed in the daily functioning of the courts? The manner in which the sentencing judge will carry out his or her statutory duty may vary from case to case. In all instances it will be necessary for the judge to take judicial notice of the systemic or background factors and the approach to sentencing which is relevant to aboriginal offenders. However, for each particular offence and offender it may be that some evidence will be required in order to assist the sentencing judge in arriving at a fit sentence. Where a particular offender does not wish such evidence to be adduced, the right to have particular attention paid to his or her circumstances as an aboriginal offender may be waived. Where there is no such waiver, it will be extremely helpful to the sentencing judge for counsel on both sides to adduce relevant evidence. Indeed, it is to be expected that counsel will fulfil their role and assist the sentencing judge in this way.

However, even where counsel do not adduce this evidence, where for example the offender is unrepresented, it is incumbent upon the sentencing judge to attempt to acquire information regarding the circumstances of the offender as an aboriginal person. Whether the offender resides in a rural area, on a reserve or in an urban centre the sentencing judge must be made aware of alternatives to incarceration that exist whether inside or outside the aboriginal community of the particular offender. The alternatives existing in metropolitan areas must, as a matter of course, also be explored. Clearly the presence of an aboriginal offender will require special attention in pre-sentence reports. Beyond the use of the pre-sentence report, the sentencing judge may and should in appropriate circumstances and where practicable request that witnesses be called who may testify as to reasonable alternatives.

Similarly, where a sentencing judge at the trial level has not engaged in the duty imposed by s. 718.2(e) as fully as required, it is incumbent upon a court of appeal in considering an appeal against sentence on this basis to consider any fresh evidence which is relevant and admissible on sentencing. In the same vein, it should be noted that, although s. 718.2(e) does not impose a statutory duty upon the sentencing judge to provide reasons, it will be much easier for a reviewing court to determine whether and how attention was paid to the circumstances of the offender as an aboriginal person if at least brief reasons are given.

NOTE

The allusion to judicial notice is not developed further in *Gladue*. In this context, it means clearly that judges should take judicial notice of facts relating to systemic and background characteristics of aboriginal communities. It obviously does not mean that the sentencing of aboriginal offenders only would raise this concern about judicial notice because there might be many other sentencing contexts in which systemic or background factors would be material. The extent to which judicial notice should be permitted with respect to such issues is a matter that requires caution. Is it possible, for example, for a judge to take judicial notice of the incidence or prevalence of a certain type of offence within a community? For these purposes, what are the differences among evidence, notice, and mere anecdote or hearsay?

R v. Laliberte
(2000), 31 CR (5th) 1 (Sask. CA) (footnotes omitted)

[The accused, an aboriginal woman, pleaded guilty to two counts of trafficking in a controlled substance and two counts of possession of the proceeds of trafficking. She was sentenced to a conditional sentence of 12 months' imprisonment, including 4 months of electronically monitored house arrest, two years' probation, and restitution in the amount of $120. The Crown sought leave to appeal. It was granted, and the appeal was dismissed. The opinion of Vancise JA is more fully reproduced in Chapter 16. In the course of his judgment Vancise JA refers to the question of judicial notice.]

VANCISE JA:

•••

[60] The sentencing judge must also be provided with general information concerning systemic poverty, alcohol and substance abuse, cultural and racial bias in the community at large. As well, the sentencing judge must receive information concerning the particular circumstances surrounding the offence.

[61] The Supreme Court suggested [in *Gladue*] that to accomplish the sentencing task, it would be necessary for the sentencing judge to "take judicial notice of the systemic or background factors and the approach to sentencing which is relevant to aboriginal offenders." [[1999] 1 SCR 688, 731-32 (para. 83).] This raises an evidentiary issue which is problematic. Surely in the context of this judgment Justices Cory and Iacobucci are not suggesting that the systemic or background factors are so "notorious" in general as to be capable of proof without evidence or that they can be verified by resort to reports of indisputable accuracy and applied to the particular facts.

[62] The systemic cultural and background factors to which Justices Cory and Iacobucci refer are set out in great detail in *Gladue*. All the factors described are conclusions of fact taken from texts, articles, studies, or commissions of inquiry on aboriginal problems, including the *Report of the Aboriginal Justice Inquiry of Manitoba*, and *The Justice System and Aboriginal People*. Those factors were described as:

> Years of dislocation and economic development have translated, for many aboriginal peoples, into low incomes, high unemployment, lack of opportunities and options, lack or irrelevance of education, substance abuse, loneliness, and community fragmentation. These and other factors contribute to a higher incidence of crime and incarceration.

It will be necessary for the sentencing judge to take into account those factors which have been demonstrated as having caused or contributed to the aboriginal offender being before the court.

[63] The issue of how to deal with discrimination of aboriginal peoples was examined by the Supreme Court in *R v. Williams* [[1998] 1 SCR 1128] in the context of a challenge for cause, where the issue was widespread bias or prejudice in the community which had the potential to impact on the impartiality of a jury. McLachlin J concluded *on the evidence* of that case that there was widespread bias against aboriginal peoples in Canada and there is evidence that this widespread racism has translated

into systemic discrimination in the criminal justice system [at para. 58]. McLachlin J did not take judicial notice of that fact.

[64] In *Williams*, the accused called witnesses and tendered evidence to establish widespread prejudice and bias in the community against aboriginal people. This evidence demonstrated there was a reasonable possibility of bias or a realistic potential of racial bias or prejudice on the part of jurors in the context of challenge for cause in the selection of a jury. McLachlin J stated it might not be necessary to duplicate that effort in future cases to establish racial prejudice in the community because the potential for racial prejudice could be demonstrated either by evidence or by judicial notice or by proving facts capable of immediate and accurate verification.

[65] In *R v. Fleury* [[1999] 3 WWR 62 (Sask. QB)] Barclay J considered whether widespread bias or prejudice existed in Saskatchewan which might impact on the impartiality of a jury in the context of a challenge for cause. Again, after hearing evidence from an expert in the field and examining reports of commissions of inquiries, he concluded on the evidence that there was systemic racism sufficient to permit the accused to challenge jurors for cause.

[66] Klebuc J in *R v. Carratt* [[1999] SJ No. 626 (QB)] refused to take judicial notice of racial bias in the context of a sentencing hearing held to determine whether to impose a conditional sentence on an aboriginal offender. He was unwilling to accept the finding made by Barclay J in *Fleury* that systemic racism exists in Saskatchewan. He found he could not make such a finding in the absence of evidence on that issue in the particular community where the offence occurred. He was unable to determine on the evidence before him whether anti-aboriginal racism existed and had materially affected the particular offender's ability to obtain employment for example, and was the cause of the offender being before the Court.

[67] Klebuc J was satisfied on the evidence of Professor Quigley of the Faculty of Law of the University of Saskatchewan, that aboriginal peoples suffered from poverty, substance abuse and racism and were overrepresented in the prison population. At the end of the day, however, he was unable to find that those factors were the cause of the particular aboriginal offender's criminal conduct and he refused to impose a community-based sentence. I agree generally with the approach he used in attempting to comply with the directives in *Gladue*.

[68] The evidentiary question is thus reduced to: are the systemic or background matters so "notorious" that a sentencing judge can take judicial notice of them without further evidence when deciding whether to apply a restorative approach to sentencing so as to make the system more relevant to aboriginal peoples?

[69] Justices Cory and Iacobucci seem to have provided at least a partial answer to that evidentiary question by stating, immediately after their comments on judicial notice, that it will probably be necessary for some evidence to be adduced to assist the sentencing judge to decide these issues. In my opinion, evidence will be required on the "*Gladue* sentencing hearing" to establish the systemic factors referred to by the Supreme Court as well as to demonstrate how those factors have contributed to the offender being before the court and how those factors should influence the type of sentence to be imposed on the particular aboriginal offender. No operation of the principle of judicial notice will provide enough specific relevant evidence about the

particular systemic or background factors which exist in the offender's community. Nor will it provide specific evidence as to how those factors have affected the particular aboriginal offender and whether they resulted in him being before the Court. It will be necessary for the accused to call some evidence to assist the sentencing judge in determining whether, in the particular community where the offender resides, there are systemic or other background factors which have had an influence on how this particular offender came before the court with the result that there will be a different approach to sentencing and the kind of sentence to be imposed.

If the Supreme Court intended in *Gladue* to approve the use of official reports or social science data as sources of information, further clarification will be required on this point because, as Vancise JA observes in *Laliberte*, the statement by Cory and Iacobucci JJ concerning judicial notice is broad and problematic. For example, what about the personal experience of the judge, a matter that raised controversy when it was considered (in another context) in *R v. R.D.S.* (1997), 10 CR (5th) 1 (SCC)? No one expects a judge to dissociate herself from her entire experience as a citizen, a lawyer, or a judge, but personal experience is not always reliable—and might be positively unreliable—as a basis for making decisions on sentence. A judge should be able to rely on her knowledge of local sentencing practices or treatment options, but this should also be expressed in open court and put on the record so that the parties know the basis of the decision. The statutory requirement that the sentencing judge provide reasons for her decision is consistent with this.

Judicial notice dispenses with the need for proof of relevant facts, and it is problematic, to say the least, where those facts are complex and contentious. The personal experience of the judge as a source of relevant factual information is also problematic, either because it might be unreliable or because it might induce the judge to ignore relevant evidence. Some issues require a firm evidentiary foundation before they can affect a sentencing decision. One way of accomplishing this is to produce expert evidence, as was done in *Laliberte*. An issue that illustrates the need for firm evidence is the prevalence or incidence of an offence in the local community. Reliance on such information for stronger sentences is controversial because it is a form of exemplary justice. Nonetheless, a marked increase in the incidence of an offence or the recognition of a substantial rate of occurrence has been accepted by the courts as a relevant aggravating factor. But a judge cannot rely on her personal experience or observations concerning the court's recent cases as a basis for this decision. See, for example, *R v. Priest* (1996), 110 CCC (3d) 289, 293 (Ont. CA). Moreover, courts have demanded solid evidence and not just anecdotal accounts from local police officers. See, for example, *R v. Petrovic* (1984), 41 CR (3d) 275 (Ont. CA) and *R v. Edwards* (1996), 105 CCC (3d) 21 (Ont. CA).

PROBLEMS

1. The accused has been found guilty of five counts of fraud on the government, including fraud on the scheme for social assistance and fraud on a program for the creation of jobs. The facts disclose that these fraudulent activities occurred over a period

of seven years and the amounts gained, in total, exceeded $85,000. At trial, the accused raised a defence of necessity that was based on the theory that there was no other source of income for the accused and the accused's child. The defence was expressly rejected by the judge, who said that even if the accused was experiencing extremely hard times, there could still be no defence of necessity in law.

The accused intends at the sentencing hearing to raise again the issue of necessitous circumstances—that is, having no source of income.

The prosecution intends to adduce evidence of a previous conviction of trafficking in marijuana that was recorded some 15 years ago. It intends to show the existence of an outstanding support order that the accused has done nothing to enforce. The prosecution also wishes to put in evidence the fact that the accused faces a pending charge of possession of stolen goods. Finally, the prosecution seeks to prove that despite the absence of a regular and legitimate income, the accused's standard of living is relatively high, not least because she lives with others who have been charged with unrelated, but similar, offences of fraud.

What difference would it make if the finding of guilt were based on a plea of guilty?

2. Small was charged with two counts of sexual assault, both allegedly committed during the summer of 1988 when he was the manager of a resort hotel in Muskoka. The Crown's disclosure indicates that the two victims will say:

Count 1: V was a 17-year-old maid at the hotel. One morning, Small walked into a room where she was cleaning. He spoke with her for a while and offered her a better job if she was "friendlier" to him. She quickly left the room. The next day, he followed her into a room and locked the door. He began talking about how difficult it was to get employment that summer and what a shame it would be if she lost her job. He started rubbing her arm and then grabbed her toward him. She fought with him and he threatened her if she didn't "shut up." After the rape, he avoided her and never spoke to her again.

Count 2: B was a 15-year-old babysitter hired to look after Small's young son while he and his wife worked. He returned to his apartment one day when his son was asleep. He and B had a cup of tea together. After the tea, Small began asking questions about B's boyfriends and the level of sexual activity among her peers. B was uncomfortable with the conversation and started to leave. Small grabbed her shoulders and threw her onto a sofa. He pinned her down and tried to removed her shirt, but she screamed. This woke up his son and Small ran out of the apartment.

a. Assume that the Crown elects to proceed summarily, and Small enters guilty pleas. When the facts, as above, are read in, Small's counsel says:

The essential elements of the offence of sexual assault are admitted with respect to both counts. However, the accused does not admit that the interaction in count one included sexual intercourse. Also, the involvement in count two did not extend beyond touching.

b. Assume that the Crown elects to proceed by indictment and Small elects trial by judge and jury. At his trial, V and B testify as above. On the witness stand, Small denies count one. He says that he and V had a consensual sexual relationship that continued all summer. With respect to B and count two, he testified that one day she sat beside him on a sofa when his son was asleep. She started asking him about V and made some suggestive comments to him. He interpreted these as a "come on," and he touched her breast. When she backed away, he jumped from the sofa. He never went close to her again. The jury found him guilty on both counts.

How should the judge determine the factual basis for sentencing in (a) and (b)?

CHAPTER FIVE

Sources of Information
Relating to the Offender

Because of the relaxed rules of evidence at a sentencing hearing, an offender may participate in the process in a number of ways. Witnesses, such as family members, friends, or
employers, may be called to give evidence about the offender's character and employment record. The offender's counsel may submit expert evidence from a physician, psychiatrist, or psychologist to offer an explanation for the offender's conduct or place it in a
behavioural context. Usually, however, information from these sources is tendered by way
of written report or letter.

There are two codified aspects of the sentencing hearing that bear directly on the
offender's participation:

1. Section 726 gives the offender the right to speak personally at the hearing; and
2. Section 721 empowers the court to order a pre-sentence report.

Both of these provisions generate some interesting questions about the manner in which
information from and about the offender enters the sentencing process.

I. THE RIGHT TO SPEAK TO SENTENCE

By virtue of s. 726 of the *Criminal Code*, RSC 1985, c. C-46, as amended, the offender is
given the opportunity to address the judge before sentence is imposed. This section provides as follows:

> 726. Before determining the sentence to be imposed, the court shall ask whether the
> offender, if present, has anything to say.

This section was placed in the Code in 1996, but must be considered within the context
of the Code's sentencing scheme. Section 723 secures the right of an offender and the
prosecutor to make submissions on the issue of sentence and to adduce "any relevant
evidence." This is consistent with the long-held recognition of the need to provide some
degree of fairness at the sentencing hearing. What, then, is the role of s. 726? Does it
confer a further, personal right on the offender to address the court?

The following two cases (*R v. Schofield* and *R v. Dennison*) were decided under the
predecessor provision, s. 668. This section provided as follows:

668. Where a jury finds an accused guilty ... the judge presiding at the trial shall ask the accused whether he has anything to say before sentence is passed on him, but an omission to comply with this section does not affect the validity of the proceedings.

Note that the current Code provisions do not include the caution that an omission does not affect validity. The two cases below address the consequences of failing to provide the offender with an opportunity to speak before sentence is passed. Given the important differences in the wording of the two provisions, is the same type of remedy (that is, the reduction of sentence) still appropriate when there is non-compliance with s. 726? When an offender is represented by counsel, should any remedy flow from a failure to observe s. 726 if counsel has made sentencing submissions?

R v. Schofield
(1976), 36 CRNS 135 (NB CA)

BUGOLD JA: The appellant was charged with unlawfully driving a motor vehicle having consumed alcohol in such a quantity that the proportion thereof in his blood exceeded 80 milligrams of alcohol in 100 millilitres of blood contrary to s. 236 of the *Criminal Code* of Canada, RSC 1970, c. C-34, and was found not guilty following a trial before a deputy judge of the Provincial Court.

· · ·

The second and the third alternative grounds of appeal relate to the fact that the appellant was denied the right to be heard before sentence was imposed. It is evident that the sentence imposed by the trial de novo court does not form part of the written judgment dated and delivered on 3rd December 1975. The appellant contends that the failure of the County Court Judge to adjourn the case to a fixed time and place for imposing sentence constitutes a loss of jurisdiction. The appellant was given no opportunity to make, or to have made on his behalf, any submissions to the trial de novo court with respect to sentence or the time for payment of any fine imposed.

With the greatest respect it was improper for the judge of the trial de novo court to impose sentence without giving the appellant an opportunity to make submissions as to sentence. The appellant was denied the right of a fair trial. A fair hearing of a criminal trial includes the matter of sentence. The right to a fair hearing in accordance with the principles of fundamental justice for the determination of rights and obligations, provided for in s. 2(c) of the *Canadian Bill of Rights*, RSC 1970, App. III, includes the right to a fair hearing in criminal proceedings: *Lowry v. The Queen*, 19 CRNS 315, [1972] 5 WWR 229, [1974] SCR 195, 6 CCC (2d) 531, 26 DLR (3d) 244.

The *Lowry* case was an appeal by two accused from the judgment of the Manitoba Court of Appeal allowing an appeal by the Crown from the judgment at trial acquitting the appellants on charges of unlawfully assaulting peace officers in the execution of their duty, convicting the appellants and imposing upon each a sentence of six months' imprisonment. The supreme Court of Canada held, *inter alia*, that before a court of appeal proceeds to impose sentence, it must by virtue of s. 2(e) of the *Canadian Bill of Rights*, requiring "a fair hearing in accordance with ... fundamental justice," ensure that an accused be given an opportunity:

... to make, or to have made on his behalf any submission on this matter. A "fair hearing" of a criminal trial includes the matter of sentence, and, accordingly, the power to pass sentence is a power which can only be exercised after a fair hearing on that issue. This Court has jurisdiction to deal with this matter. The case should therefore be remitted to the Court of Appeal to pass sentence, after the appellants have been given the opportunity to make submissions to that Court on that matter.

The County Court Judge having imposed sentence without giving the appellant the opportunity to be heard exceeded his jurisdiction and the sentence, therefore, cannot stand.

The appeal against conviction is dismissed. The appeal against sentence is allowed and the sentence set aside.

R v. Dennison
(1990), 80 CR (3d) 78 (NB CA), leave to appeal refused 3 CR (3d) 276 (SCC)

RYAN JA (Ayles JA concurring): After an accused has been found guilty, the trial judge shall ask the accused if the accused has anything to say before sentence is passed. So says s. 668 of the *Criminal Code* of Canada.

This court has held on a number of occasions that the failure on the part of the sentencing judge to give a convicted person the right to address the court with respect to sentence will result in an automatic grant of leave to appeal sentence. In this case, after Crown counsel brought the provisions of s. 668 of the *Criminal Code* to the attention of the judge, the judge refused to ask the appellant, Ralph Leonard Dennison, whether he had anything to say before sentence was passed upon him. The sentencing judge then proceeded to impose a sentence of 12 years imprisonment for attempted murder and five years for possession of a restricted weapon. The 66-year-old appellant has appealed his convictions and seeks leave to appeal his sentence. ...

The appellant submits that his rights have been violated because he was not given an opportunity to address the court with respect to sentence before the judge imposed a penalty of imprisonment upon him. Earlier, both counsel had addressed the court with respect to sentence. Section 668 of the *Criminal Code* provides:

> 668. Where a jury finds an accused guilty ... the judge presiding at the trial shall ask the accused whether he has anything to say before sentence is passed on him, but an omission to comply with this section does not affect the validity of the proceedings.

A refusal by the trial judge to allow a convicted person to address the court with respect to sentence is a serious error, even though the Code provides that an omission to do so does not affect the validity of the proceedings. This provision first found its way into the *Criminal Code* in 1892. A failure to follow it is a violation of the accused's rights under s. 668 of the *Criminal Code*. It also violates his right to a fair trial, since the sentencing procedure is included in the trial process. Is there a Charter violation as well?

The appellant claims relief under s. 24 of the *Canadian Charter of Rights and Freedoms*. The pertinent section in his case would be s. 7, and possibly s. 11(d), if broadly interpreted with respect to the words "fair hearing" and "impartial tribunal." I preface my remarks with this: the Charter was not meant to be an innovative document, but rather a statement of traditional rights drawn from human and civil rights movements, the common law, United States constitutional law and international human rights law: see Jerome Atrens, *The Charter and Criminal Procedure* (1988), pp. 1.2 and 1.18-1.22. These fundamental rights and freedoms have, as a result of the Charter being a part of our Constitution, an entrenched status.

First of all, I will consider s. 7

> 7. Everyone has the right to life, liberty and security of the person and the right not to be deprived thereof except in accordance with the principles of fundamental justice.

as it relates to s. 668, where the judge "shall ask the accused whether he has anything to say before sentence is passed on him."

It is clear to me that a conscious decision by the trial judge to take away this right of the accused to be heard before sentence is passed on him is contrary to s. 7. The accused has a right to be heard and the judge has a corresponding duty to let him be heard and to actually call upon him to be heard before sentence is passed on him. This is irrespective of the fact that counsel for an accused has already spoken to sentence. It is at this penultimate point in the jury trial process that the reality of imprisonment squarely faces the accused. It is the final opportunity to convince the judge why the deprivation of the accused's liberty should be minimal. Denying the accused the right to speak, thus taking away from him a legitimate expectation, infringes the liberty of the accused because of the possible or probable consequences of imprisonment.

Section 668 includes wording that "an omission to comply with this section does not affect the validity of the proceedings." One must read these words with the wording in Charter s. 7 that one cannot be deprived of the right to liberty "except in accordance with the principles of fundamental justice." The question I put is whether the validity of the proceedings is affected by the conscious act of the judge in not asking the accused if he had anything to say before sentence was passed on him. I conclude three things. First of all, the earlier trial process is in no way invalidated; secondly, the saving provision of the section applies to inadvertent acts of the trial judge; and thirdly, any deliberate act of denial of a codified right relating to imprisonment is an infringement of the accused's constitutional right to liberty under s. 7 and should bear consequences in the sentencing process.

There is no principle of fundamental justice in the facts of this case that would deprive the present appellant of his right to speak to the restrictions which were about to be imposed on his liberty. It is not enough, in the case of an advertent act by the judge, to give an accused an automatic leave to appeal and ask him what he would have or might have said. That is simply too artificial. The consequences of inadvertence and advertence should not be identical. The right to a fair trial and all the guarantees contained in the Charter are basic tenets of our legal system. As such, they must be protected by the judiciary.

Writing for a majority court in the Supreme Court of Canada, Dickson J said in *R v. Gardiner*, [1982] 2 SCR 368, 30 CR (3d) 289, 68 CCC (2d) 477 at 513, 140 DLR (3d) 612, 43 NR 361 [Ont.]:

Sentencing is part of a fact-finding, decision-making process of the criminal law. Sir James Fitzjames Stephen, writing in 1863 said that "the sentence is the gist of the proceeding. It is to the trial what the bullet is to the powder" (quoted in Olah, "Sentencing: The Last Frontier of the Criminal Law," 16 CR (3d) 97 (1980), at p. 98). The statement is equally true today.

I return to my original theme. Whether I rely on the Charter or the *Criminal Code*, or a combination of them, the rights in question are all traditional rights emanating from the principle of a fair trial. The sentence imposed by the Court of Appeal must therefore reflect the trial judge's failure to conclude the sentencing process justly.

In *R v. Matthews* (1983), 45 NBR (2d) 265, 118 APR 265, this court reduced a sentence for armed robbery from five years to three year when the judge inadvertently failed to give the convicted person the opportunity to address the court with respect to sentence. In the *Matthews* case, however, there were other errors in sentencing that influenced the court in reducing the sentence so markedly. Another example may be found in *R v. MacKinnon* (1984), 56 NBR (2d) 103, 146 APR 103, a case of escaping custody. This court promptly granted leave to appeal because of the inadvertent error on the part of the trial judge. After hearing MacKinnon with respect to sentence, the Court of Appeal ordered a reduction in sentence from nine months to three months.

Here, the failure to accord the right to speak was deliberate. Because of the express infringement of the appellant's rights, the appropriate and just remedy in the circumstances is that the sentence for attempted murder should be reduced meaningfully. It must also reflect the fact that the infringement was deliberate, so as to distinguish it from a mere omission. However, the remedy must not be disproportionate to the infringement.

I would grant leave to appeal the sentences and I would allow the appeal against sentence with respect to the charge of attempted murder under s. 239 of the *Criminal Code* of Canada. I would vary the sentence from a term of imprisonment of 12 years to one of nine years in penitentiary. I would not disturb the sentence imposed for possession of a restricted weapon.

Except for the Charter violation, I would not have otherwise disturbed the sentence, in view of the jury's finding of guilty, the planning of the intended murder as evidence in tape-recorded conversations, the actions of the appellant, the criminal record of the appellant, dating back to the Second World War, and the fact that he was on probation at the time of these offences.

HOYT JA (dissenting): I have read the decision of my colleague Ryan JA and I agree with him that the appeal against conviction should be dismissed and that leave to appeal sentence should be granted. As he pointed out, this court has adopted the practice of granting leave to appeal sentence when a trial judge fails, as he is obliged to do by s. 668 of the *Criminal Code* of Canada, to ask an accused whether he has anything to say before sentence is passed upon him. In my view, unlike that of my colleague, that omission, whether accidental or deliberate, does not amount to a violation of the accused's *Canadian Charter of Rights and Freedoms* rights. The failure to provide the accused with an opportunity to speak may be remedied by granting leave to appeal and permitting the accused to make representations to this court. The court takes such representations into account when determining whether the sentence imposed by the trial judge is fit.

···

Section 668 provides that failure to comply with the section does not affect the validity of the proceedings. The courts, however, as shown above, have constructed a remedy when an accused is not permitted to speak before sentencing. In my opinion, where, as here, counsel for the accused has made representations on behalf of the accused prior to sentencing, there is no violation of s. 7 of the Charter. An accused's right to speak to sentence, provided his counsel has spoken on his behalf, is not, in my opinion, a right protected by s. 7 of the Charter.

The Court of Appeal for Ontario rejected the argument that a breach of the *Canadian Charter of Rights and Freedoms*, part I of the *Constitution Act, 1982*, RSC 1985, app. II, no. 44, should mitigate the sentence (see *R v. Glykis* (1995), 41 CR (4th) 311 (Ont. CA) and the analysis of this issue in A. Manson, "Charter Violations in Mitigation of Sentence" (1995), 41 CR (4th) 318). See, however, the subsequent decision in *R v. Leaver* (1996), 3 CR (5th) 138 (Ont. CA), where the Ontario Court of Appeal affirmed the trial judge's sentencing decision that took into account trial delay insufficient to justify a violation of s. 11(b). The court said that

the sentence imposed by the trial judge reflected an appropriate mitigation of sentence in the circumstances of this case.

The following case of *R v. Senek* was decided under the new legislation. Does the Manitoba Court of Appeal (particularly the concurring reasons of Philp JA) go too far in limiting the right contained in s. 726?

R v. Senek
(1998), 130 CCC (3d) 473 (Man. CA)

LYON JA (Monnin JA concurring): The appellant pled guilty to a count of break, enter and theft of commercial premises and was sentenced by Swail PJ to nine months in jail. He appeals from this sentence on the principal ground that the trial judge erred in failing, before passing sentence, to ask the appellant if he had anything to say on his own behalf pursuant to s. 726 of the *Criminal Code* (the Code).

The facts in brief are that on April 29, 1996, the appellant and a co-accused formulated a plan to break into the Riverboat Restaurant in Selkirk. They gained entry through the roof of the mall by prying off a hot water tank ventilation door and then entered the business premises. Once inside, they broke into a kiosk that held a small safe which they also broke open and from which stole $3,000 in one dollar coins. For the next three days the appellant and a friend went to Winnipeg, stayed at a local hotel, and spent the money buying clothing, drinking and eating in restaurants.

···

At trial, counsel for the Crown, after relating the facts of the charge, suggested a sentence of 9 to 12 months in jail. Thereafter Mr. Sawchuk, counsel for the accused, made a lengthy submission (9½ pages in the 20-page transcript of the proceedings) urging the court that any sentence imposed be a conditional one.

At the conclusion of counsel's address, the trial judge proceeded immediately to thank counsel and to deal with the question of whether or not there should be a conditional sentence pursuant to s. 742.1 of the Code. He did not ask the offender if he had anything to say as required by s. 726 of the Code, which states as follows:

Offenders May Speak To Sentence
    726. Before determining the sentence to be imposed, the court shall ask whether the offender, if present, has anything to say.

He correctly observed that the Crown's recommended sentence of 9 months to one year fell within the maximum sentence of two years, thereby making a conditional sentence eligible for consideration; that he must be satisfied that the serving of the sentence in the community would not endanger the safety of the community; and that such a sentence would be consistent with the fundamental purpose and principles of sentencing. He concluded that this was not a case for a conditional sentence. He said, taking into account the record of the accused, it would endanger the safety of the community.

We are not persuaded by counsel for the appellant that the trial judge erred in principle in exercising his discretion to deny the appellant a conditional sentence. Accordingly, the appeal on that question is dismissed.

Of the several grounds of appeal cited by the appellant, the only remaining one requiring consideration relates to the trial judge's failure to ask the appellant if he had anything to say.

Defence counsel submits that the sentencing hearing was invalidated by this error and asks this Court to vacate the trial judge's sentence and substitute for it a 9-month sentence to be served conditionally. Counsel relies primarily on *R v. Dennison* (1990), 80 CR (3d) 78, 60 CCC (3d) 342 (NB CA). *Dennison* was decided under the predecessor of this section (formerly s. 668) which contained a proviso that the failure to give the accused an opportunity to make a statement before sentencing did not affect the validity of the proceedings. That proviso was removed by amendment in 1995.

In *Dennison*, both Crown and defence counsel addressed the court with respect to sentence following the appellant's conviction by a jury on a charge of attempted murder. Ryan JA, for the majority, said (at p. 84) that the trial judge made "... a conscious decision ... to take away this right of the accused to be heard ... ." It was not a matter of inadvertence but was a (at pp. 84-85):

... [D]eliberate act of denial of a codified right relating to imprisonment ...
    It is not enough, in the case of an advertent act by the judge, to give an accused an automatic leave to appeal and ask him what he would have or might have said. ... The consequences of inadvertence and advertence should not be identical.

In the result, the majority of the court reduced the sentence from 12 years to 9 years. It is to be noted, of course, that *Dennison* is clearly distinguishable from the case at bar in that the trial judge here merely proceeded inadvertently to pass sentence after an extended plea by defence counsel for a conditional sentence.

Significantly in *Dennison*, Hoyt JA (as he then was) in his dissenting opinion noted that Ryan JA in his reasons had indicated that the majority was following a practice which had developed in the New Brunswick court of granting leave and reducing the original sentence. Hoyt JA submitted that the New Brunswick practice differed from that adopted in other provinces and in the Supreme Court, citing authorities where the courts had fashioned a remedy for failure to permit an accused to speak before sentence. He also stated (at p. 80), in support of his dissent, "… that omission, whether accidental or deliberate, does not amount to a violation of the accused's Canadian Charter of Rights and Freedoms rights."

A more recent example of this approach is found in *R v. Gorrill* (1995), 139 NSR (2d) 191 (CA), where the accused was convicted by a jury of infanticide. The trial judge inadvertently failed to ask the accused if she wished to speak to sentence. The Nova Scotia Court of Appeal held that the failure was overcome by permitting the accused to submit a written statement. Pugsley JA, speaking for the unanimous court, said (at p. 204):

> The failure of the trial judge to comply with s. 668 (supra) was inadvertent. The failure has been remedied by the acceptance of the written statement prepared by LG [the accused] (*R v. Lowry*, [1974] SCR 195). This was not a case where there was a conscious decision by a trial judge to take away the right of the accused to be heard before sentence and, accordingly, a violation of LG's Charter rights resulted (*R v. Dennison* (1991), 109 NBR (2d) 388; 273 APR 388; 60 CCC (3d) 342 (CA)). It is also pertinent that the representations to the trial judge from LG's counsel respecting sentence were thorough and covered all of the issues, lasting the best part of one hour. [My emphasis.]

> •••

In *Lowry and Lepper v. The Queen*, [1974] SCR 195, 6 CCC (2d) 531, the appellants were acquitted at trial of assaulting peace officers in the execution of their duty. The Crown appealed and the Manitoba Court of Appeal allowed the appeal, set aside the acquittals, entered convictions and sentenced the appellants to six months' imprisonment. The appellants were not present at the hearing of the appeal and had no opportunity to make submissions in respect of sentence. They appealed to the Supreme Court of Canada which held that the appeal should be dismissed on the merits, but the case should be remitted to the Court of Appeal for re-sentencing after receiving any submissions which the appellants wished to make or have made on their behalf with respect to sentence.

In the course of his judgment, Martland J said (at p. 199):

> The next question which arises is as to the power of the Court of Appeal to impose sentence without having given to the appellants an opportunity to make, or to have made on their behalf, any submission on this matter.

After determining that the imposition of sentence should be remitted to the Court of Appeal, Martland J continued (at p. 204):

> … [A]fter the appellants have been given the opportunity to make submissions to that Court on that matter.

In the result, I would dismiss this appeal on the merits, but remit the case to the Court of Appeal to pass sentence, after receiving any submissions which the appellants wish to make, or to have made on their behalf, with respect to that matter.

In the case at bar, it is worthwhile to note that no objection was made by defence counsel to the trial judge's failure to ask the accused if he had anything to say. Indeed the record discloses that there was no comment or objection before or after sentencing about this oversight on the part of the trial judge. Similarly, on the hearing of the appeal, counsel for the accused admitted that the 9-month sentence was within the appropriate range but should have been a conditional one. The only error the trial judge made was his failure to ask the accused if he had anything to say, a matter that was not raised until the notice of appeal was filed.

In summary, on the hearing of the appeal, no affidavit evidence was submitted on behalf of the accused, nor was there any indication by the accused or his counsel that he had anything to say either to the trial court or to the appellate court beyond what his counsel had said in extenso at trial and on appeal. Practice indicates that an accused sometimes wishes to correct the record given by the Crown or to supplement or correct his counsel's submissions. There was no indication of such a desire by the appellant either at trial or on appeal. The appellant was well represented by counsel both at trial and on appeal who, on both occasions, set forth his argument thoroughly and at length. In the words of Martland J in *Lowry*, counsel's submissions which the appellant had "made on his behalf" constituted the accused's best hope for the conditional sentence he sought.

This pure, inadvertent oversight by the trial judge resulted in no disadvantage or unfairness to the accused, nor did the trial judge's error constitute a substantial wrong or miscarriage of justice. In my opinion, it was simply a procedural oversight which had no bearing either on the trial judge's sentence or on our determination of the fitness of that sentence on appeal. At best, this ground of appeal could aptly be described as an afterthought advanced in support of an appeal which otherwise was without merit.

Accordingly, I would dismiss the appeal.

PHILP JA: I am in complete agreement with the analysis and disposition of this appeal by my colleague, Justice Lyon. The accused was represented by counsel at his sentencing hearing and on his appeal in this Court. Complete and thorough submissions were made on his behalf in mitigation of his sentence. The omission of the sentencing judge to ask the accused whether he had anything to say had no effect on the validity of the proceedings.

In my view, s. 726 of the *Criminal Code* should not be interpreted so as to accord to a convicted person the right to address the court personally at his sentencing hearing when his counsel has made a submission on his behalf in mitigation of sentence.

The legislative history of s. 726 suggests that the origins of the provision have long since been obscured and forgotten. Originally, the provision applied only to jury trials. It had no application to offenders who were tried for indictable offences without a jury.

And until the 1953-54 re-enactment of the *Criminal Code*, SC 1953-54, c. 51, the provision was directed to whether the accused had "anything to say why sentence should not be passed upon him according to law." The provision had nothing to do with the mitigation of the sentence that was to be passed.

The provision may well be a vestige of the "benefit of clergy" privilege that existed into the 19th century and which "operated greatly to mitigate the extreme rigor of the criminal laws." (See *Black's Law Dictionary* (6th ed. 1990), at pp. 158-59.) The privilege did not mitigate the sentence to be imposed, but rather, its application exempted the person claiming the privilege after his conviction from the punishment of death.

Appeal dismissed.

NOTE

Philp JA might be right that the "origins of the provision have long since been obscured and forgotten" in Canada, but this is not the case in the United States. The right to speak to one's sentencer, historically known as the right of allocution, has been traced back to the period in England when capital penalties were common and an accused person had no ability to give evidence.[1] Not surprisingly, the issue has been given new life south of the border with the proliferation of capital punishment and the use of juries within the capital phase of sentencing. It has been argued that the ancient right of allocution permits the prisoner to seek leniency by speaking directly to the jury without cross-examination. Some circuit courts of appeal have held allocution to be a constitutional[2] right, but the issue has not yet been addressed by the US Supreme Court. In *Green v. United States*, 365 US 301 (1961), a case that did not deal with capital punishment, the Supreme Court was unanimous in accepting the proposition that an offender should be entitled to speak to the sentencing judge even if represented by counsel who has made a sentencing submission. Frankfurter J noted that even "the most persuasive counsel may not be able to speak for a defendant as the defendant might, with halting eloquence, speak for himself."

If s. 726 creates an entitlement, is there a difference between an inadvertent failure to ask whether the offender has anything to say and a deliberate refusal to hear from an offender, as occurred in *Dennison*, supra?

Another issue that arises when an offender chooses to speak is whether the remarks must be given under oath and the accused can be cross-examined. This proposal, of course, is inconsistent with the right of allocution. But if the offender's comments are given informally, is there any limit on the subject matter? Surely, the offender cannot attempt to relitigate guilt or rebut factual evidence adduced in the usual manner, but must restrict the comments to personal attitudes, beliefs, or commitments that have some bearing on the sentencing.[3]

---

1 See *Green v. United States*, 365 US 301 (1961) and P. Barrett, "Allocution" (1944), 9 *Missouri L Rev.* 115 and 232.

2 For example, see *Badman v. Estelle*, 957 F2d 1253 (9th Cir. 1992) and *United States v. Moree*, 928 F2d 654 (5th Cir. 1991).

3 See *R v. Izzard*, [1999] NSJ No. 18 (NS CA) for an example of the difficulties that a judge can get into if the conversation with an offender moves into factual issues about the offence.

II. PRE-SENTENCE REPORTS

Pre-sentence reports are provided for in s. 721 of the *Criminal Code* as follows:

721(1) Subject to regulations made under subsection (2), where an accused, other than a corporation, pleads guilty to or is found guilty of an offence, a probation officer shall, if required to do so by a court, prepare and file with the court a report in writing relating to the accused for the purpose of assisting the court in imposing a sentence or in determining whether the accused should be discharged pursuant to section 730.

(2) The lieutenant governor in council of a province may make regulations respecting the types of offences for which a court may require a report, and respecting the content and form of the report.

(3) Unless otherwise specified by the court, the report must, wherever possible, contain information on the following matters:

(a) the offender's age, maturity, character, behaviour, attitude and willingness to make amends;

(b) the history of previous dispositions under the Young Offenders Act and of previous findings of guilt under this Act and any other Act of Parliament;

(c) the history of any alternative measures used to deal with the offender, and the offender's response to those measures; and

(d) any matter required, by any regulation made under subsection (2), to be included in the report.

(4) The report must also contain information on any other matter required by the court, after hearing argument from the prosecutor and the offender, to be included in the report, subject to any contrary regulation made under subsection (2).

(5) The clerk of the court shall provide a copy of the report, as soon as practicable after filing, to the offender or counsel for the offender, as directed by the court, and to the prosecutor.

The cases that follow were decided under the predecessor provisions, which did not include any indication of what a pre-sentence report should contain. However, these cases illustrate what courts considered appropriate in terms of the content of a pre-sentence report. It is important to realize that although counsel may make submissions to the sentencing judge on the issue whether a pre-sentence report ought to be prepared, it is a matter that falls within the (unreviewable) discretion of the sentencing judge. Accordingly, in some circumstances, ordering a pre-sentence report coerces the offender and his or her family to participate in the sentencing process. This is why it is important to ensure that only appropriate information finds its way into these reports.

R v. Dolbec and *R v. Arsenault* illustrate the problem of unnecessary and prejudicial information appearing in a pre-sentence report.

R v. Dolbec
[1963] 2 CCC 87 (BC CA)

BIRD JA: Dolbec and one Olson were involved in the theft of a motor car over the value of $50 on July 29, 1962, for which offence Dolbec was charged and convicted on July 30, 1962, on a plea of guilty entered before Magistrate J.J. Lye at Port Coquitlam, British Columbia. He was then remanded for sentence to August 7, 1962.

Meantime a pre-sentence report required by the learned Magistrate was prepared by an officer of the Provincial Probation Branch which was considered by the Magistrate prior to the imposition of the sentence.

It is apparent from comparison of the pre-sentence report and the report of the learned Magistrate made to this Court, pursuant to *Criminal Code*, 1953-54 (Can.), c. 51, s. 588(1) that the learned Magistrate in imposing a sentence of nine months' imprisonment on this 19-year-old youth, whose record showed no prior convictions, was strongly influenced in determining sentence by the information furnished in the pre-sentence report.

Regrettably that report was not furnished to the appellant before sentence was imposed, nor was he given any information relative to the contents of the report which was highly prejudicial to the appellant. Dolbec was not represented by counsel either at the time of his conviction or sentence.

It is evident from examination of the report that the Probation Officer had formed a poor opinion of the appellant based to a substantial degree upon information received from other persons, none of whom are named therein, nor does the report otherwise disclose the source of any such information or the grounds for the officer's belief in its validity. The Probation Officer closes the report with the following comment and recommendation:

"Comment:

"Subject is a 19 year old single male presently facing sentence on a charge of car theft. He is intelligent and seeks to blame his accomplice. Although chronologically he is 19, emotionally he is much less—he has never grown up, shows a marked degree of immaturity and irresponsibility. Locally he is described as a smart alec, lippy punk who frequents all the questionable cafes and hangouts. His earnings come from the pool cue and part time work at Fraser Mills (he has lost the latter source of income). Exacerbating the above is his love of alcohol and it is suggested that has a greater hold on him than he is prepared to admit.

"This is the first criminal offence on his record but he is certainly heading for serious trouble. An extremely doubtful candidate for probation because of his irresponsibility and also that placing him on Probation would bring pressures to bear that he probably couldn't stand thereby forcing him into a worse situation than at present. He has been getting away with so much for so long that Probation to him would probably mean he had once again 'beat the rap.' The strong point in this whole situation is the family rallying to keep closer tabs on him but unfortunately there seems no motivation from within himself to lead a different life. Institutionalization would assist him in forming definite living habits and may exercise a stabilizing influence on a lad who has been drifting from some time."

On the hearing of the appeal counsel for the appellant filed affidavits of Dolbec, as well as of the principal of the High School attended by him in 1961, and of his parish priest.

The appellant in his affidavit questions the factual accuracy of the probation report in many respects. He deposes further to the following

(a) "The Magistrate did not ask me if I had anything to say before sentence or suggest that I was permitted to say anything.

(b) "The Magistrate was incorrect in stating in his report that my brother-in-law was in Court and addressed the Magistrate regarding probation. In fact my brother, Roger Dolbec was in Court as well as my sister Theresa O'Bray and neither were asked whether they had anything to say on my behalf nor did either of them address the Magistrate before sentence was passed upon me. My sister Theresa informs me she did have a conversation with the Magistrate after the sentence was imposed."

The appellant's school principal in his affidavit deposed in substance as follows: The appellant

(a) "was keenly interested in his studies, was an intelligent student who showed maturity beyond the majority of students in his class.

(b) "I found Dolbec pleasant, cheerful and cooperative. He was one of the best and most pleasant students of his class.

(c) "I found him to be no discipline problem and his manners and cooperation were better than the majority of his fellow students."

The parish priest, Father A. Frechette, in his affidavit, deposes to the fact that he has known the appellant for some nine years. "He was a very good student." "I found him helpful and cooperative. He has constantly attended church and to the best of my recollection the first time he missed Sunday service was when the said charge of theft was laid against him."

In my judgment this appeal from sentence must be allowed for the following reasons:

1. The appellant was seriously prejudiced by the fact that the Magistrate took into account when sentence was imposed the contents of the probation report, no part of which was communicated to the appellant and of which he had no knowledge and, consequently, no opportunity to refute factual statements contained therein which he now says were untrue.

In *R v. Benson & Stevenson* (1951), 100 CCC 247, 13 CR 1, 3 WWR (NS) 29, the late Chief Justice Sloan, speaking for this court, laid down the following principles in respect of the use to be made of pre-sentence reports, and I quote from the [WWR] headnote which is fully supported by the text of the reasons:

"In so far as a pre-sentence report from a probation officer contains factual allegations prejudicial to the prisoner it cannot be placed in a higher or different category than a pre-sentence statement made by a police officer and the same principles must be applied to both. Therefore a convicted man ought to be informed of the substance of a probation officer's report, in so far as it is detrimental to him, so that he may have an opportunity to agree therewith or deny it if he chooses so to do. If the report contains prejudicial observations which the court considers relevant and likely to influence the sentence and this material is denied by the prisoner then proof of it, if required, should be given in open court when its accuracy may be tested by cross-examination. Alternatively, if the court does not consider it of sufficient importance to justify formal proof then such matters should be ignored as factors influencing sentence."

The foregoing decision has been constantly applied by this Court from the date of its pronouncement to the present time in relation to the use of probation reports as a factor in determining sentence.

2. The prejudicial comments contained in the probation report as to the character and conduct of the appellant are so greatly at variance with the depositions made by the appellant's high school principal in 1961, and by his parish priest, as to arouse a doubt of the validity of the information obtained by the Probation Officer.

At the conclusion of the appeal, counsel for the Crown declared that in the circumstances outlined to the Court he could not oppose a reduction of sentence and the release of the appellant on probation.

For the foregoing reasons the appeal from sentence is allowed and the sentence imposed below set aside. There will be substituted a direction that upon entering into a recognizance in Form 28 under the *Criminal Code*, without surety, before the Registrar of this Court at Vancouver, British Columbia, in the sum of Five Hundred Dollars ($500) to keep the peace and be of good behaviour during the term of one year from the date of this judgment, namely October 9, 1962, and to appear and receive judgment when called upon during the same period, the appellant shall be released on probation, the recognizance to incorporate the usual terms.

R v. Arsenault
(1981), 21 CR (3d) 269 (PEI SC)

MacDONALD J: The appellant applies for leave to appeal against the sentence imposed on the respondent and, if this is granted, appeals the decision of Carruthers C Prov. J. I would grant leave to appeal.

The facts are not in dispute. The respondent, who is 19 years of age, has no criminal record. On 22nd March 1980 he entered a liquor store and was told that because he was drunk he would not be served. He continued on into the store, picked up a case of beer and presented himself at the checkout counter, where the beer was taken from him by a store employee. Upon this occurring the respondent became very abusive, using coarse and foul language toward a female cashier. Mr. Arthur Clarke, a man standing behind him in the checkout line-up, told him to watch his language. The respondent, who was wearing a cast on his arm, swung with the arm bearing the cast and struck Mr. Clarke in the face. As a result of the blow Mr. Clarke, who was 70 years of age, fell and broke his hip and had to have two teeth removed. The respondent was charged pursuant to s. 245(2)(a) [en. 1974-75-76, c. 93, s. 22] of the *Criminal Code*, RSC 1970, c. C-34, with the indictable offence of assault.

On the above facts the trial judge fined the respondent $500 or, in default, sentenced him to 45 days' imprisonment, and placed him on probation for 18 months. In addition he was required to abstain from alcohol and obtain treatment for his alcohol problem if so required by his probation officer.

...

I wish to make a short comment on the contents of the pre-sentence report that was prepared in this matter. In *R v. Bartkow* (1978), 24 NSR (2d) 518, 1 CR (3d) S-36, 35 APR 518 (CA), MacKeigan CJNS at p. 522 stated:

"I wish those who prepare such reports would realize that it is no part of their job to give any information, whether inculpatory or exculpatory, respecting offences which the accused committed, especially ones for which he has not been convicted. Their function is to supply a picture of the accused as a person in society—his background, family, education, employment record, his physical and mental health, his associates and social activities, and his potentialities and motivations. Their function is not to supply evidence of criminal offences or details of a criminal record or to tell the court what sentence should be imposed."

This court has never made any comment on the contents of a pre-sentence report. However, I have noted that over the past few years an increasing amount of information, some of which was of the sort disapproved of in *R v. Bartkow*, has found its way into reports submitted to this court. In the present case the report contains information relating to the respondent in the following manner:

(1) Extensive reference is made to the respondent's becoming involved in fights at various branches of the Royal Canadian Legion. As these altercations involve offences for which the respondent has not been convicted, there should be no reference to them. Neither should the appellant have directly referred to them in an attempt to show the respondent as an aggressive and violent person.

(2) The probation officer gave his opinion concerning the respondent's conduct, stating it was "uncalled for."

(3) The report dealt extensively with the injuries sustained by Mr. Clarke. Information of this nature should be submitted to the court only by counsel.

(4) The report dealt with the matter of restitution to Mr. Clarke.

(5) A great number of facts concerning the commission of the offence are related in the report.

(6) The report mentions Mr. Clarke's sentiments concerning the assault and his hope that there should be "a fair measure of justice."

The report should not have dealt with any of these listed items. It is not enough to say that neither the respondent nor his counsel objected to the contents of the pre-sentence report. The report dealt with matters which the court should not have been made aware of; or, if they were properly admissible, they were not presented in the correct manner. Again, I wish to emphasize that I attach no blame to the probation officer who prepared the report in question as he merely was following a practice that has evolved over the years. This practice should now be discontinued.

The following two cases (*R v. Rudyk* and *R v. Urbanovich and Brown*) present a different problem. In these cases, exculpatory information from the offenders found its way into their pre-sentence reports. What use should sentencing judges make of this type of information? Should it make any difference if the offender testified at trial?

R v. Rudyk
(1975), 1 CR (3d) S-26 (NB CA)

MacKEIGAN CJNS: The Crown has appealed herein from the sentences imposed on the respondent by His Honour Judge P.J.T. O'Hearn in the County Court Judge's Criminal Court District No. 1 at Halifax following conviction of the respondent on two charges:

> "That he did at Halifax, on the 30th day of April, 1974, unlawfully steal from Richard's Grocery a sum of money while armed with an offensive weapon, to wit, a knife, contrary to Section 303 of the *Criminal Code*.
> "That he did at Halifax, on the 30th day of April, 1974, unlawfully steal from Jasmet Morar a sum of money while armed with an offensive weapon, to wit, a knife, contrary to Section 303 of the *Criminal Code*."

The learned trial judge sentenced the respondent to 14 days' imprisonment to be served intermittently and, in addition, to pay a $500 fine (or 60 days in default of payment), together with a period of probation of one year. In a report to this court under s. 609(1) of the *Criminal Code*, RSC 1970, c. C-34, he stated:

> "My intention ... was that the 14 days would apply concurrently to the two offences as would the probation period of one year, but that the fine of $500.00 would be an aggregate amount to be divided equally between the two offences as would the sixty days imprisonment to be served in default of payment of the fine."

Leave to appeal should be granted.

The respondent Rudyk was originally charged with both offences jointly with one Nelson Michael Lawlor. Following a preliminary inquiry in May 1974, both were committed for trial. On 10th October 1974 Lawlor pleaded guilty to both offences before O'Hearn Co. Ct. J who, on 25th October 1974, sentenced him to four years' imprisonment on each count, to run concurrently.

Rudyk was tried on both charges jointly before O'Hearn Co. Ct. J. After most of the Crown's case had been presented Rudyk changed his plea to guilty and, after an adjournment for a pre-sentence report, was sentenced by O'Hearn Co. Ct. J on 25th January 1975.

The facts disclosed by the Crown evidence are as follows. At about 11:40 p.m. on 30th April 1974 Rudyk, accompanied by Lawlor, parked his car in front of Richard's Grocery, a small corner shop in south-end Halifax. Lawlor entered the shop and, at knife-point, robbed the female clerk of over $200. Rudyk meanwhile got out of the car, stood near the trunk and glanced several times at a witness who was parked across the street. Lawlor ran from the shop and shouted, "Let's go!" Both men jumped in the car and drove away.

Driving directly to the scene of the second crime, a small shop in north-end Halifax, Rudyk stopped and Lawlor entered the shop at about 11:55 p.m. Holding a knife to the shopkeeper's stomach, he robbed him of about $93. Afterward Rudyk's car, a bright yellow Toyota, was seen driving away.

Only a few minutes later the car containing the pair was stopped on the approaches to the Angus L. Macdonald Bridge. Rudyk, the driver, had about $240 of the stolen money in his jacket. Lawlor, in the passenger's seat, had the rest of the money in his possession.

Neither Lawlor nor Rudyk gave evidence. Rudyk also did not testify at the time of sentencing.

The pre-sentence report, however, contained a version of the events quite different from that recounted above, one which, if true, would make one wonder why Rudyk pleaded guilty. I set it forth in full:

> "He had been drinking with a friend, his girlfriend, and the friend's wife. His friend suggested the two of them go for a drive. Along the way, the friend told the accused to stop the car, whereupon he entered a store and came running back to the car and stuffed something into the accused's pockets. The accused drove on and was again asked to stop for cigarettes at another store. The friend entered this store, and re-entering the car, told the accused to get moving. Shortly afterward, they were apprehended by the police.
>
> "The accused stated that it was the police who had informed him that a knife had been used in the robberies, and that when he later searched for the knife in the glove compartment of his car, it was missing. He stated that ordinarily when he drinks, he gives his car keys to a reliable person, or else takes a taxi home. He described his condition as one of inebriation for he had few recollections of the offence, apart from what the co-accused and the police had informed him."

The probation officer who prepared the report stated that the Halifax police inspector who had investigated the crimes said that "although the accused had been drinking, he was fully aware of what he was doing at the time."

The respondent was 24 years old at the time of the offence. He has a good family and employment background and no criminal record. He has been employed in the navy for over five years. All his superior officers spoke very well of him. He had performed his work satisfactorily and had never been in trouble.

The learned trial judge in imposing sentence said:

> "... I am not satisfied that it was your initiative, but I think that at some point in the thing you understood what was going on and went along with it, through, probably through weakness more than anything else and possibly because of intoxication. In other words, I don't accept the theory that you were the initiator of it, or the prime mover and I don't necessarily accept the theory that you knew how it was being done ... So, I am giving you the benefit of considerable amount of doubt."

In this report to this court, he said:

"On the day fixed for sentencing I heard counsel for the Crown and for the accused and did not accept the theory of the prosecution that the accused was more aware of the offences than he pretended to be because of the evidence I had heard and *because of the contents of the pre-sentence report.*" (The italics are mine.)

He said further that he imposed the sentence he did:

"As there appeared to be a very real prospect of public benefit from the rehabilitation of the accused in this case and as his participation appeared to be relatively minor."

I respectfully think that the learned judge should not have been influenced, as he obviously was, by the story which Rudyk told the probation officer. That self-serving story was not given to the court by Rudyk himself, when he could have been cross-examined by the Crown. It was inconsistent with the guilty plea. It strains one's credulity. It is quite conceivable that Rudyk had no prior knowledge that Lawlor as going to rob the first store. But how could he, after having $200 placed in his jacket following Lawlor's hasty departure from the first store, have believed that Lawlor's visit to the second store was an innocent search for cigarettes?

I would here urge that a pre-sentence report be confined to its very necessary and salutary role of portraying the background, character and circumstances of the person convicted. It should not, however, contain the investigator's impressions of the facts relating to the offence charged, whether based on information received from the accused, the police or other witnesses, and whether favourable or unfavourable to the accused. And if the report contains such information the trial judge should disregard it in considering sentence.

In the present case, putting aside the pre-sentence report, I can find nothing in the evidence before the learned trial judge to support the theory that the respondent did not know what was going on and was thus an innocent dupe who was, at worst, party after the fact. The best one can say is that some slight doubt may exist as to whether Rudyk knew beforehand that Lawlor was going to rob the first store. No doubt is possible, however, about his immediate acceptance of the fruits of that robbery and his knowing participation in the second robbery.

These facts make it impossible to reconcile the sentence imposed on the respondent with the four years' imprisonment meted out to his companion Lawlor. Both men were equally guilty of the offences of armed robbery which they admitted having committed.

Lawlor is twenty-five, about the same age as Rudyk, and is married with two children. He has a less favourable educational, family and employment background and was unemployed at the time of the offences. In Newfoundland he was convicted in February 1971 on 15 break and enter charges and was sentenced to a total of five months' imprisonment. He has had trouble with alcohol and was a mental patient at the Nova Scotia Hospital for two weeks in 1974. His criminal record and the fact that he undoubtedly is a poorer prospect for rehabilitation than is Rudyk, coupled with his more active part in the crimes, would undoubtedly justify a materially heavier sentence for Lawlor but hardly seem to justify the extreme disparity between their sentences.

...

Having regard to all the circumstances, and giving the respondent the benefit of all doubts that the evidence permits, I would allow the Crown's appeal and vary the sentence imposed on the respondent to one of two years' imprisonment in a federal institution on each charge, to run concurrently, without probation. Any time already served by him will, of course, be credited to him and the fine imposed, if paid, will be refunded to him.

R v. Urbanovich and Brown
(1985), 19 CCC (3d) 43 (Man. CA)

MATAS JA:

...

Tracie Marie Urbanovich and Robin Harold Brown have appealed from conviction and sentence on a joint charge of causing the death by criminal negligence of Lee Anna Brown, between March 1st and May 29, 1981 (*Criminal Code*, s. 203). Each appellant was sentenced to seven years' incarceration. (I will refer to the parties as the appellants or the accused.)

The appellants had been living together for some time prior to January, 1981, and continued their relationship during the material time. The victim was the appellants' four-month-old daughter. She was born on January 24, 1981.

The appellants had been charged with causing death by criminal negligence, causing bodily harm by criminal negligence and assault causing bodily harm. On their preliminary hearing the accused were committed to trial on the criminal negligence charges but were discharged on the charge of assault.

The trial was held before Lockwood Co. Ct. J (as he then was) sitting without a jury. The appellants were separately represented. They did not testify but their lengthy voluntary statements were admitted in evidence. At the conclusion of submissions of counsel on June 10, 1983, the proceedings were adjourned to June 30, 1983, when Lockwood Co. Ct. J delivered judgment [22 Man. R (2d) 166].

Lockwood Co. Ct. J reviewed the evidence of Dr. Hwang, a pathologist, Dr. Duncan, director of the intensive care unit at Children's Hospital and section head of paediatric anaesthesia at the hospital, Dr. Sehia, a paediatric neurologist, Dr. Reed, a radiologist specializing in X-rays of children, Dr. Kowall, the infant's paediatrician, Dr. Nigam, who had a rotation arrangement with Dr. Kowall, Dr. Ferguson, a child care specialist who is the director of ambulatory and community paediatrics at the Children's Hospital, Mrs. Askew, a registered nurse at the Misericordia Hospital who had contact with the parents and infant on May 20, 1981, at the hospital, and Mrs. Bailey, a sister of Mr. Brown. Lockwood Co. Ct. J mentioned the evidence of Mrs. Urbanovich (the mother of the female appellant) and said that [at p. 171] "In the light of the medical evidence little weight should be attached" to her evidence.

Lockwood Co. Ct. J relied on the definition of criminal negligence in s. 202 of the *Code* and the provisions of s. 197 prescribing the duty to provide necessaries of life, which would include medical treatment: *R v. Popen* (1981), 60 CCC (2d) 232 at p. 240

(Ont. CA). Lockwood Co. Ct. J found that the infant sustained a series of serious injuries caused by the acts of Mr. Brown and that the inference to be drawn from all the evidence is that the child was a victim of deliberately applied trauma. Lockwood Co. Ct. J held that Mr. Brown committed all the acts, including the act or acts which resulted in the brain injuries that led to the infant's death, and held as well that Mr. Brown was liable for depriving the child of the opportunity of receiving proper medical treatment.

Lockwood Co. Ct. J held that Ms. Urbanovich was not directly responsible for the injuries to the infant but that she failed to take reasonable steps to protect the infant from the violence which caused the injuries. Lockwood Co. Ct. J held as well that Ms. Urbanovich had deprived the infant of necessary medical attention. ...

The proceedings were adjourned to September 28, 1983, for submissions on sentence. In the meantime, separate pre-sentence reports for each appellant were prepared and a psychiatric assessment was prepared in respect of Mr. Brown by Dr. I.J. Kowalchuk. The learned trial judge made extensive references to the pre-sentence reports in giving his reasons for imposition of the sentence. At the conclusion of his remarks, Lockwood Co. Ct. J said [24 Man. R (2d) 189 at pp. 191-92]:

> At trial I drew the inference from the evidence that "the child was a victim of deliberately applied trauma." However, the new evidence introduced at the sentencing hearing, by way of pre-sentence reports, bears out what Dr. Ferguson said [at the trial] about the acts not being "committed." He testified:
>
>> "I have never stated that I felt that these were committed acts, but I nevertheless feel that the onus on individuals as parents is grave to protect children and to admit to a string of events of this nature resulting in a child's death, to me, is a very serious matter."
>
> It now seems clear from this further evidence that the acts of the accused Brown were probably not consciously deliberate, but rather took place when his mind was besotted by the effects of the consumption of alcohol, or drugs, or both. Seen in this light, the acts were not any less criminal. They do however, fall into a different category for the purposes of determining sentence. Deliberate acts of violence over a period of time resulting in death, in my view, should attract a higher range of sentence than acts which are not deliberate in the strict sense of the word.

In my view, Lockwood Co. Ct. J was right in convicting the appellants. The evidence at the trial amply supported the convictions. But, in my opinion, Lockwood Co. Ct. J erred in the way he treated the material presented at the sentencing hearing.

...

Pre-Sentence Reports

Because of the comment made by Lockwood Co. Ct. J in his sentencing judgment about the new information he had gained from the pre-sentence reports, it is necessary to examine the use which may be made of those reports.

In *Criminal Pleadings and Practice in Canada* (1983), Eugene Ewaschuk QC (now Ewaschuk J) summarized the principles applicable to the contents of a report, at p. 497, as follows:

> A pre-sentence report should be confined to the background, character and circumstances of the accused but not the accused's nor the investigator's version of the facts relating to the offence.

In Nadin-Davis, *Sentencing in Canada* (1982), pp. 524-5, reference is made to *Bernier v. The Queen* (1978), 5 CR (3d) S-1, which cited with approval a statement of MacKeigan CJNS in *R v. Bartkow* (1978), 1 CR (3d) S-36, 24 NSR (2d) 518, 35 APR 518 (NSSCAD). At p. 525 the following comment appears:

> The decision is typical of a growing trend across the country to confine the ambit of reports to personal, family, educational and employment information and similar matters. The emphasis, reading between the lines, appears to be on factual rather than opinion evidence.

To the same effect is the comment in Ruby on *Sentencing*, 2nd ed. (1980), p. 254, where the learned author says:

> It is quite often the case, especially when probation is a possible part of a sentence, that the trial judge will call for a presentence report in order to assist him in assessing the proper sentence. In *R v. Rudyk* (1975), 11 NSR (2d) 541 at p. 544 (CA)), the probation officer prepared a report which elicited from the accused his version of the facts of the case. As it turned out that version contradicted the guilty plea. The Court of Appeal said:
>
> > "I would here urge that a presentence report be confined to its very necessary and salutary role of portraying the background, character and circumstances of the person convicted. It should not, however, contain the investigator's impressions of the facts relating to the offence charged, whether based on information received from the accused, the police, or other witnesses, and whether favourable or unfavourable to the accused. And if the report contains such information the trial judge should disregard it in considering sentence."

> The reasoning involved was that any story given to the probation officer may well be self-serving, and in any event was not subject to cross-examination by counsel for the Crown. The proper place for the facts of the offence to be investigated is in open court.

In the pre-sentence report with respect to Mr. Brown, the author of the report began by saying: "In view of the evidence presented at this trial, the circumstances of this offence will not be mentioned here." However, under the heading of "Attitude Towards This Offence," Mr. Brown is quoted as referring to the "accidents" and to his criticism of the medical authorities for not being diligent enough in their examination, observation and treatment. Mr. Brown also denied any assaults. Later in the report, under the heading "Children," Mr. Brown is quoted extensively on his consumption of drugs and alcohol and on a description of several incidents involving the infant.

With respect to Ms. Urbanovich, the author of the pre-sentence report also said that since evidence was presented to the court on the circumstances of the offence it would not be presented in the report. Under the heading "Attitude Toward Offence," Ms. Urbanovich is quoted as maintaining innocence and as being critical of the paediatrician. She also referred to the consumption of alcohol and/or marijuana and referred to having been present on at least "four accidents that Brown had with the baby." Ms. Urbanovich is quoted as repeating her innocence. Throughout the report references are found to the kind of care the infant was receiving by the parents.

In my respectful opinion, none of this evidence was admissible in so far as the conviction was concerned and should have been disregarded by the learned trial judge.

In my view, the decision in *R v. Lessard* (1976), 30 CCC (2d) 70, 33 CRNS 16 (Ont. CA), does not change these well-established principles. In *Lessard*, the court held that a judge sitting without a jury is not *functus officio* following a finding of guilt, until he has imposed sentence or otherwise finally disposed of the case. The accused did not testify at the trial. The trial judge entered a conviction after hearing evidence for the Crown and submissions of counsel. The case was adjourned to permit the preparation of a pre-sentence report. When the hearing resumed counsel for the accused moved to reopen to call evidence. The trial judge granted the motion subject to the right of the Crown to call evidence in rebuttal. The accused testified at the reopening. It was not suggested by the Court of Appeal that the conviction could have been impugned by anything which appeared in the pre-sentence report. On the contrary, the court was critical of reliance by the trial judge on a psychiatric report in reasons for acquitting the accused. The psychiatrist had not testified; his report was hearsay. However, the court held that there was no substantial wrong in the circumstances.

And see *R v. Hunter* (1980), 58 CCC (2d) 190 (Ont. CA), where a motion to reopen a *voir dire* to call evidence was refused by the trial judge on the ground that he was *functus officio*. The Court of Appeal held that the trial judge was not *functus officio* in the matter and had power to reopen the *voir dire*.

With respect, I agree that a trial judge is not *functus officio* until the completion of the sentencing process and that it would have been open to Lockwood Co. Ct. J, had he felt it necessary, to permit the reopening of the trial for the calling of further evidence by the defence. What was not open to him was to consider self-serving statements by the accused as affecting the conclusions he arrived at after hearing the evidence called by the Crown and the submissions of counsel on conviction.

I think we would be opening the door to a very difficult procedure if we were to permit persons accused of crime to await the conclusion of all the evidence, decide not to give evidence as it is their right to do, and to provide information helpful to themselves, with respect to the conviction, through the medium of a pre-sentence report.

One of the questions which arises in this case is whether the change in the determination by the trial judge of the "deliberate" aspect of the appellants' conduct, even though based on inadmissible evidence, would warrant a new trial. On examination of the record I am satisfied beyond a reasonable doubt that the evidence at the trial amply supports the conclusion of Lockwood Co. Ct. J at the trial that the parties were guilty of the charges and that a new trial should not be ordered.

CHAPTER SIX

Victim Participation in the Sentencing Process

I. INTRODUCTION AND BACKGROUND

The role of the victim in the sentencing process has always been controversial and, until recently, somewhat uncertain. Controversy and uncertainty still characterize the role of the victim at other critical junctures of the criminal process as victims' rights continue to crystallize.[1] The sentencing process is the only juncture in the criminal prosecution where the participation of victims is formalized. Section 722 of the *Criminal Code*, RSC 1985, c. C-46, as amended, allows for the introduction of victim impact statements (VIS) at the sentencing hearing.

In this chapter, we address the modern approach to victim participation in the sentencing process in Anglo-Canadian law. However, it is necessary to step back and consider historical developments in this area. The participatory rights of victims in the sentencing process have not always been so accommodating. Criminal prosecutions evolved from a system of "blood feuds" in which wrongful acts that we now characterize as "criminal" were considered merely "tortious." This gave considerable power to the aggrieved person (and/or his or her family) to control the process that brought redress. Apparently, this "golden age" of the victim lasted into medieval times.[2] In the 13th century, when certain wrongs were considered a breach of or an affront to the King's Peace, the victim started to fade from the forefront of the legal process. The law relating to the redress of criminal wrongs was arrogated by the state.[3]

Until very recently, the criminal justice system was reluctant to afford the victim any formal rights of participation in the sentencing process. Research suggested that victims of crime were "re-victimized" because they were disempowered by the criminal process.[4]

---

1 See, generally, Kent Roach, *Due Process and Victims' Rights—The New Law and Politics of Criminal Justice* (Toronto: University of Toronto Press, 1999).

2 Alan Young, "Two Scales of Justice—A Reply" (1993), 35 CLQ 355, at 364-67.

3 Sociologist Nils Christie argues that the historical record of criminal prosecutions is an example of the state "stealing the conflict" from the real parties—that is, the wronged and the wrongdoer. See N. Christie, "Conflicts as Property" (1975), 17 *British Journal of Criminology* 1.

4 See the *Canadian Federal-Provincial Task Force on Justice for Victims of Crime Report* (Ottawa: Solicitor General, 1983), 60.

As a result, victims felt alienated from the criminal justice system. This alienation sometimes manifested itself in the victim's lack of confidence in the process and his or her withdrawal of cooperation with criminal justice officials.[5] The organization of the so-called victims' rights movement and the use made of this movement by law-and-order crime-control politics[6] has generated a renewed interest in the role of victims in the criminal process. The enactment of legislation permitting the introduction of VIS is one concrete reform in this area. The enactment of various victims bills of rights (mentioned infra under the heading "Looking to the Future") is another result of this movement.

The following article by Edna Erez provides a context for the discussion of the use of VIS in Canada. Erez discusses the empirical research in this area and relates it to the arguments for and against victim participation in sentencing.

E. Erez, "Who's Afraid of the Big Bad Victim? Victim Impact Statements as Victim Empowerment *and* Enhancement of Justice"
[1999] Crim. LR 545 (footnotes omitted)

Victim-oriented reforms have been adopted in numerous countries with different legal systems. Many jurisdictions have passed legislation providing for restitution from the offender, compensation from the state and various services to victims who have been impacted by a crime. Whereas most of these reforms have been accepted and welcomed, the reform providing victims with a voice, most commonly in the form of victim impact statements (VIS), has been very controversial. As recently as last summer, Andrew Ashworth, in a conference on "Integrating the Victim Perspective in Criminal Justice," warned against two dangers inherent in current practices of victim integration in criminal justice: "victims in the service of severity" and "victims in the service of offenders." According to Ashworth, the movement to incorporate victim perspectives has sometimes coincided with the movement toward greater penal severity. Ashworth echoes concerns, raised previously by others, that the use of victim impact statements in criminal justice decision making may cause increases in sentence severity. He further claims that submission of victim impact statements (VIS) to the court may be detrimental to procedural and substantive justice, as well as to the victims

---

5 See Alan Young, supra note 2, at 375. See also Edna Erez, "Victim Participation in Sentencing: Rhetoric and Reality" (1990), 18 *Journal of Criminal Justice* 19.

6 See, generally, Roach, supra note 1. See also Leslie Sebba, *Third Parties—Victims and the Criminal Justice System* (Columbus: Ohio State University Press, 1996), who reminds us that the study of social movements like the victims' rights movement is complex. Nevertheless, Sebba notes seven sociolegal/historical developments that are relevant to the renewed interest in victims: (1) the rise of victimology as a subdiscipline of criminology; (2) the results of victimization surveys in many countries; (3) the rise of "law-and-order" politics; (4) the role of feminist and other grassroots movements; (5) the alignment of the victim movement with political and social radicalism; (6) the resurgence of just deserts theory in the current dialogue on the philosophy of punishment; and (7) the development of "informalist" approaches to punishment that attempt to reconcile the victim with the offender (at 2-10).

who provide input. Using victims to accomplish the goal of harsher sentences, according to Ashworth, amounts to "victim prostitution."

This line of thinking is a continuation and expansion of Ashworth's earlier article on victim impact statements ["Victim Impact Statements and Sentencing," [1993] Crim. LR 498] in which he offered several legally based arguments against the use of victim impact statements in court. In this earlier article, Ashworth also examined the available social science evidence on the effect of VIS on criminal procedure, sentencing, and victims, and concluded, for a variety of reasons discussed below, that VIS is not a desirable practice to adopt.

This article is a response to the objections to the use of VIS in criminal justice and to concerns about the presumed detrimental effects of incorporating victim perspectives as expressed in Ashworth's earlier and more recent writing. It examines the arguments against the use of VIS in court and presents recent research findings on the effects of VIS on substantive and procedural justice, and on victims. The article then discusses the policy implications of recent research for victims' perspectives in adversarial legal systems, and concludes with a call for reconsidering the usefulness of VIS for criminal justice.

Definition and Practices of Victim Input

Victim impact statements address the effects of the crime on the victim, in terms of the victim's perceptions and expressions of the emotional, physical or economic harm he or she sustained as a result of the crime. The information for the VIS is collected, depending on the country, by justice agents such as the police (in Canada, Australia and New Zealand), or by probation officers, victim assistance or prosecution staff (in the USA). There is an agreement that the preparation of VIS should preferably be conducted by an agency that is not associated with offenders' information, such as a probation department. In a minority of jurisdictions victims prepare the statements themselves, without the assistance of any agency assigned to the task.

There is also a consensus that victim statements should ideally be contemporaneous, that is, describe the physical and emotional status of the victim at the time of sentencing. VIS, therefore, need to be updated prior to sentencing, usually by the agency responsible for the initial preparation of the VIS.

Cynicism and Research: The Use of VIS in Sentencing

The major arguments raised by Ashworth against the use of victim impact statements in sentencing revolve around three distinct issues: preservation of defendants' rights, or guarding against the erosion of the adversarial legal system, the question of sentencing for unforeseen results, and the difficulties of raising expectations. A separate issue (relevant only for those endorsing the VIS as a tool designed to better inform the court about victim harm) is whether the VIS should be read only by the prosecutor when he or she prepares the case for prosecution, or whether the VIS should be tendered to the court and available to the judge.

Procedural Issues, Sentencing Aims and Defendant Rights

Most commentators and practitioners view the provision of victim impact information as important and generally consider victim input on the harm they suffered a step
toward improving criminal justice procedures and goals. However, some observers
are concerned about the potential of VIS negatively to affect defendant rights in
adversarial legal systems. They also highlight the presumed incongruence between
the concept of VIS, which implies a restitutive model of justice, and the conventional
approach to justice. Under the restitutive model, calls for punishment that satisfies or
restores the victim are inconsistent with conventional visions of justice, which view
crime as a violation against the State, not a specific victim. Critics also view VIS as
undermining consistent and "proportionate" treatment of offenders, and the penological system which views the "public interest" as the only justification for increased
severity of penalties. Lastly, the practice of victim input could provide victims with
an opportunity to subject offenders to "unfounded or excessive allegations, made
from the relative security of VIS."

     Research suggests that the concerns expressed by opponents of the VIS concern-
ing possible erosion of adversarial criminal justice principles, rights of defendants
and imposition of harsher sentences have not materialised. Studies conducted in the
USA and in Australia comparing sentencing outcomes of cases with and without VIS,
and research in Australia on sentencing trends and comparison of sentence outcomes
before and after the VIS reform, suggest that sentence severity has not increased
following the passage of VIS legislation. Nor has the VIS affected sentencing patterns
or outcomes in the majority of the cases. The findings of qualitative research shed a
better light on these "no difference" aggregate patterns. For instance, based on in-
depth interview data of legal professionals in Australia, judges and prosecutors (and
some defence lawyers) recognised that the information available from the VIS shed
new light in a few cases, and assisted in imposing a more commensurate sentence.
Although they stated that VIS were sometimes redundant or the harm was inferentially available from other documents in the file, they also described in detail a few
cases they tried in which the content of VIS caused them to rethink the penalty they
had in mind prior to reading the VIS. In this minority of cases in which VIS made a
difference, the data revealed that the sentence was as likely to be more lenient as it
was to be more severe than initially thought. For example, if the offence was perpetrated in an unusually cruel manner, or with disregard to special vulnerability of the
victim, then the sentence was likely to be higher. The practitioners likewise provided
instances of cases they tried where the VIS led to the imposition of a more lenient
sentence than would have been indicated. For example, cases in which the victim's
statement disclosed that the victim had made a complete recovery or in circumstances
where certain injury had been mistakenly attributed to the crime. These kinds of qualitative findings provide a more textured account of the apparent pattern of "no difference" findings in quantitative studies of sentencing outcomes: some changes in outcomes do occur, but they are hidden as in the aggregate they offset each other. Without
victim input, sentences might well have been too high or too low. In other words,

contrary to the suggestions of Ashworth and others, it seems that VIS make an important contribution to proportionality rather than to severity of sentencing.

The concern that victims would use the VIS as an opportunity to subject offenders to unfounded accusations has also not materialised. In most jurisdictions currently practising VIS, victims do not prepare their own statement but it is filtered or "edited" by the specific agency responsible for the preparation of VIS. Moreover, "retelling" victims' stories often "sterilizes" them to such an extent that judges noted that the VIS was mild compared to what would have been expected in the light of the offence involved. VIS therefore turns out to be an understatement rather than an overstatement of the harm sustained in the particular offence. The recent pilot project in England confirms that victim statements tend to understate the impact of offences, and that the VIS scheme does not encourage exaggeration, inflammatory input or vindictiveness.

Concern that defendants would challenge the content of VIS thereby subjecting victims to unpleasant cross-examination on their statements has also not materialised. Legal professionals have stated that challenges to VIS in court are quite rare. According to these professionals, there are strategic disincentives militating against calling victims to the witness stand and cross-examining them on the content of their statements. There was an agreement among the legal professionals that a good defence attorney would not challenge the VIS directly and would not call victims to be cross-examined because of the adverse effects it may have on the sentence. Decision makers who hear and observe victims testifying about the impact of the crime on them may be affected by the testimony and therefore more inclined, according to the legal professionals, to impose a harsher sentence. In this respect, the concern about protecting victims from unnecessary and possibly degrading questioning regarding the content of their VIS (as distinguished from cross-examining victims about their testimony in the trial) seems to be unwarranted.

The Optimal Procedure for Bringing the VIS to the Court's Attention

There is a disagreement about whether VIS should be presented directly to the court. Some suggest that VIS should only assist prosecutors in the preparation of the case, and should not be available for the court to read. The rationale is that prosecutors represent both the victim and "the public interest," and they are charged with preparing and presenting the case. The recent report by JUSTICE, as well as a position paper by Victim Support, recommend that victims only provide details of the relevant harm they suffered to the prosecution, for preparation of the case. Prosecutors then will present the harm to the court, using their discretion as to what and how it should be presented.

This strategy, however, warrants closer examination in the light of the research on the effects of "retelling" on the content of the resulting story. This "construction of stories" or "retelling" of facts for legal consumption is often affected by various resource considerations and by the priorities of the collecting agency. When information is mediated through justice agents, there is a higher likelihood of loss or distortion of critical details. Also, research suggests that stories are often constructed to suit the goals and objectives of the mediating agency.

The Effects of VIS on Victims

Another argument against the use of VIS in sentencing is that it has harmful effects on victims. Some argued that VIS subject victims to pressures, and that victims may feel burdened by the responsibility for deciding the penalty.

This argument is empirically inaccurate, and does not represent the majority of victims who get involved in criminal justice proceedings. The cumulative knowledge acquired from research in various jurisdictions, in countries with different legal systems, suggests that victims often benefit from participation and input. With proper safeguards, the overall experience of providing input can be positive and empowering. Research conducted in the United States and Australia on victims of various crimes, where a VIS is relevant (i.e. a personal harm or loss was suffered by a specific victim), suggests that victims are interested in having a voice. These studies indicate that by and large victims do not feel burdened by being heard, nor do they feel pressured by knowing that their input has been conveyed to decision makers. The English victim statements pilot project confirms this finding. In fact, victims in continental legal systems who served as a party to the prosecution (as continental legal procedures allow) were highly satisfied with this role in the proceedings, and their level of satisfaction with justice was positively correlated with the amount of their participation. The literature on procedural justice provides theoretical explanations for these findings. According to procedural justice theories, litigants' satisfaction with justice and sense of fairness of the outcome is more affected by the procedures in which decisions were made rather than by the outcomes. Proceedings which provide victims with a voice or "process control" enhance their satisfaction with justice and sense of fair treatment.

Research in adversarial legal systems also suggests that the majority of victims of personal crimes wished to participate and provide input, even when they thought their input was ignored or did not affect the outcome of their case. Victims have multiple motives for providing input, and having a voice serves several functions for them. For some, input restores the unequal balance between themselves and the offender, particularly in cases in which the victim did not have an opportunity to testify or be heard because they were resolved by a plea. Others wanted "to communicate the impact of the offense to the offender." For the majority of the victims, filling out a VIS was a forum to formally express the crime impact on them, a civil duty they considered important for reaching a just sentence.

Providing input for VIS also helps victims to cope with the victimisation and the criminal justice experience. Many victims who filled out VIS claimed that they felt relieved or satisfied after providing the information. The recent English pilot project found that for the majority of the victims filing the statement was a worthwhile therapeutic experience, and the cathartic effect of recording the impact of the offence had been an end in itself. In-depth interviews of rape victims in the United States about their reasons for participation in criminal justice provide textured insights into the psychological, internally oriented benefits for victims' voices. Over half of the victims felt that input will assist with achieving substantive justice, and almost three quarters sought procedural justice. Through participation and input, victims wanted to engage the criminal justice process and, in the words of Nils Christie, to assert "ownership of the conflict" which they felt was misappropriated from them in the name of the state. Others wanted to reduce the power imbalance they felt with the defendant, resolve the emotional aspects of the rape, achieve emotional recovery, or achieve formal closure. This was particularly true for victims who never had the chance to be involved in the justice process because of a plea. Many victims also wanted to remind judges of the fact that behind the crime is a real person who is a victim.

The literature in the growing field of therapeutic jurisprudence provides support to the proposition that having a voice may improve victims' mental condition and welfare. Scholars in this area have discussed in length the therapeutic advantages of having a voice, and the harmful effects that feeling silenced and external to the process may have on victims.

Research further suggests that the overwhelming majority of the victims want their VIS to be used in sentencing, and many of them seek to influence the sentence imposed on the offender via the input. Although some of those who thought their input was ignored showed a lower level of satisfaction with justice because of raised expectations, this issue need not be used as an argument against the proposition that VIS can increase victim satisfaction with justice. First, the potential problem of heightening victim expectations can be resolved by explaining to victims that the VIS is only *one* of the factors judges use to determine the type and severity of penalties. As Ashworth recognises, research has shown that victims who receive explanations of the proceedings throughout the process tend to be satisfied with the outcome. Further, explanations may enhance victim satisfaction even when the outcome does not reflect victims' conception of a deserved sentence. There is no reason to suspect that explanations about the multiple factors that affect sentencing decisions will not be effective in preventing heightened expectations. One of the major aims of the victim movement, and the driving force behind it, was to help victims overcome their sense of powerlessness and reduce their feelings that the system is uncaring. Properly administered VIS schemes may be an effective way of achieving this objective, as well as creating realistic expectations.

Victims can also receive indirect benefits from providing input. A major source of satisfaction for victims is when judges pay attention to their input by citing victims' own phrases from impact statements in judicial sentencing comments. Victims feel gratified when their sense of harm is validated in judges' remarks. Victim advocates in Australia as well as in the United States indicate that victims who have heard or read sentencing comments in which judges quote their impact statements in sentencing remarks often say, "I could not believe the judge has actually listened to what I had to say."

Research also confirms that judges are sometimes unaware of victim suffering and injuries resulting from crime, because the information did not find its way into the file, either intentionally (due to bargaining considerations, or because of priorities of agencies charged with receiving the information and preparing the statements) or accidentally (due to agents underestimating the importance of the information, lack of resources to do the job, or mere incompetence or laziness). In the past, judges and other legal professionals had little opportunity to receive direct detailed input from victims and become acquainted with short and long-term effects of various crimes. Research shows that legal professionals who have been exposed to VIS have commented on how uninformed they were about the extent, variety and longevity of various victimisations, and how much they have learned from VIS about the impact of crime on victims from properly prepared VIS.

Sentencing, Unforeseen Results and the "Normal" Victim

One of the major challenges in criminal justice sentencing is forming a fair and accurate picture of crime and its consequences to guide decision makers in their difficult task. As I have argued elsewhere, being regularly exposed to victim input may provide a more balanced notion of the "normal" victim and the boundaries of harm and injury in criminal victimisation. The prosecution has its priorities and constraints in addressing the task of prosecuting offenders. More often than not, its organisational interests are in opposition to those of the victim, and they may not be interested in disclosing the full scope of the crime impact. Research also suggests that judges employ several justifications in discarding victim input, including its subjective or emotional nature, or its alleged unreliability due to victims' motives to lie or exaggerate. To resist victims' input because, for instance, it is subjective (the most common reason judges offer for objecting to VIS) is to suggest that there is an objective way to measure harm, or to experience loss, damage and injury. Yet, harm is perceived and experienced differently, according to victims' demographic and personal attributes as well as their prior experiences. Research about the relativity of harm questions the notion of the "normal" victim, and highlights legal professionals' resistance to consider victim input which differs from their own assessment of "appropriate" level of suffering and hence a "believable VIS." As feminists have shown in the context of rape and sexual harassment, the subjectivity of harm (or for that matter any personal experience) cannot be transformed to, or be judged by, "objective" measures without doing injustice to the experience and the person reporting it. Many recent legislative acts include what has been defined in the past as "merely" subjective experience. Research has also documented that harm descriptions which legal professionals have considered exaggerated or unbelievable are indeed common experiences which those acquainted with crime's impact on victims view as within the range of "normal" reactions to victimisation.

Conclusion

The purpose of instituting VIS was to provide victims a voice, not to restructure sentencing priorities. The legislation concerning victim input was not intended to substitute harm for culpability, nor to consider harm as the overriding criterion in sentencing. Providing victims with a voice has not only many therapeutic advantages and related fairness considerations, it also ensures that sentencing judges become aware of the extent of harm suffered by victims. Incorporation of victim statements also enhances sentence proportionality rather than harshness. Although it might be argued that the number of cases in which VIS make a difference in the outcome (i.e. result in either lower or higher penalty) is relatively low, to the individuals involved, and to the justice system as it whole, this makes all the difference.

To institute a meaningful reform in the area of victim participation, it is important to win the co-operation of all parties involved: prosecutors, judges and defence attorneys. These players have various professional and organisational incentives to oppose the introduction of victim input in proceedings. To date, legal professionals have had ample substantive and procedural reasons to excuse or justify their reluctance to comply with the VIS reform. The purpose of this paper was to expose these unsubstantiated justifications, and to oppose the use of research findings, which are taken out of context, to buttress what is essentially a political stand against victim integration in criminal justice.

In the light of recent evidence which challenges the traditional legal arguments against the VIS, it is time to re-evaluate the legal profession's approach to the concept and practice of victim input. Researchers in this area have pointed out that the problem of VIS has not been the instrument itself or its effect on proceedings, defendants and victims, but rather the hostile environment in which VIS has been implemented. Comparativists encourage us to increase appropriate legal transplants and decrease inappropriate ones. There is sufficient evidence at this point to suggest that VIS (among other victim-oriented reforms) is an appropriate transplant. VIS can hardly be considered a form of "victim prostitution" which "ought to be exposed and opposed." Rather, it needs to be redefined and viewed as a useful vehicle to enhance justice in adversarial criminal justice systems while it simultaneously helps and empowers victims. To approach victims in a paternalistic manner, and ignore victims' wishes to be heard, is to continue past approaches to victims as the "forgotten persons" of the system, and perpetuate the time-honoured tradition of treating victims as invisible. The social science evidence clearly suggests that we have no reason to fear, and every reason to include, victims in the criminal justice process.

II. THE TRADITIONAL APPROACH OF THE COURTS IN CANADA

The following two cases exemplify the early judicial approach to VIS in the Canadian criminal process, before the enactment of any provisions allowing for their admissibility. In *Antler*, McLachlin J (as she then was) denies relief to the victim by applying the traditional conception of the criminal prosecution as a matter between the state and the accused.

R v. Antler
(1982), 29 CR (3d) 283 (BC SC)

McLACHLIN J: On 13th April 1982, Lawrence Douglas Antler pleaded guilty to two counts of having sexual intercourse with a female person under the age of 14. The victim of the offences was [TF]. On 18th June 1982, when Mr. Antler was before a Provincial Judge for sentencing, counsel for [TF] applied to make submissions with respect to the emotional effect upon her client of the offences. The Provincial Judge denied her application, and adjourned the sentencing to 7th July 1982 in order to permit an application on the issue to this court. Counsel for [TF] now seeks an order compelling the Provincial Judge to receive her submission. Both the Crown and the accused oppose her petition.

I have concluded that the petitioner has no *locus standi* which would authorize her to invoke this court's jurisdiction to compel the Provincial Judge to receive her submission. The conduct of criminal trials in Canada is governed by the *Criminal Code*, RSC 1970, c. C-34. The *Criminal Code* contemplates prosecution of the accused by the Crown. It does not accord to persons affected by an offence status as parties to the proceeding against the accused, apart from the provisions relating to restitution of property found in ss. 654 to 657. Nor does it grant to them the right to make representations against the accused independent of those which the Crown chooses to put forward. This court cannot accord status which the *Criminal Code* does not accord; that must be left to Parliament.

· · ·

The petition is dismissed. Costs will follow the event.

In *Robinson*, the trial judge considered the request of the deceased victim's father to address the court on the sentencing hearing. The court refused the request, relying on basic principles of evidence admissibility on sentencing.

R v. Robinson
(1983), 38 CR (3d) 255 (Ont. HC, per Reid J)

THE COURT: I wish to deal first, before asking Mr. Robinson if he has anything to say, with an issue that arose earlier today. That was what I was told about the desire of Mr. Nairn to make an informal statement to the court.

· · ·

Mr. Nairn [the victim's father] appears to have indicated to Mr. Macdougall [the Crown] that he wished to make a statement and that he had already prepared something in writing which he wished me to see, but it was clear that he did not wish to be called as a witness and it was clear that Mr. Macdougall was not offering him as a witness.

Dealing first with the suggestion that something might be, in effect, handed to me, with a copy for the Crown attorney, I would like to say, it would be improper, in my opinion, for me to accept anything related to this hearing for my own private viewing. I am not expected, nor do I believe I would be permitted, to make private inquiries on my own. I must make my decision on what has been placed before me in this court.

I am, of course, entitled to take into consideration what I heard during the trial and I expect to hear counsel's submissions or any evidence that counsel see fit to put forward to assist me with this task. But anything that might affect my decision must, of course, be displayed to both sides so that the side that might be prejudiced has an adequate opportunity of defending against or explaining or confronting the source of that possible prejudice.

Consequently, it would not be appropriate for me to accept, in effect, a private communication.

As to the alternative means which I understand Mr. Nairn had in mind, that of his standing up in court and making a statement or perhaps reading what he had prepared, I will turn to that in a moment. But may I say that it was not merely the informality of the written statement that caused the problem about receiving the written statement. The fact that it was apparently not sworn, or tendered in any way as evidence is usually tendered, was not the principal reason for its rejection, because, as anyone sitting here today would realize, some informality is appropriate to these proceedings. On sentence hearings rules of evidence are frequently relaxed and more informal evidence than would be proper in respect of the issues before the jury is permitted and, indeed, encouraged. The pre-sentence report itself, which people in court will have heard referred to by both counsel, is an example of the relaxation of the strict rules of evidence and the receipt of informal evidence on such a hearing.

If, however, the pre-sentence report was found in any way objectionable by defence counsel, then defence counsel, having had a copy of it beforehand, would be given an appropriate opportunity to deal with it, to confront what was not accepted, to call evidence to challenge it or to deal with it in other ways.

So, even though informal, it would be a public document and its mere informality would not prevent its reception into evidence.

Turning, however, to the other alternative proposed by Mr. Nairn, that he might make an oral statement in court, not as a witness, but simply because as the parent of the dead child, he wished to say something, I have no doubt at all of the sincerity of his desire. No normal person could fail to have the deepest sympathy for Mr. Nairn and his wife and any member of the family of this child. They have had to face and live with what can only be described as a dreadful tragedy, and one cannot but sympathize with their desire to participate in some way in these proceedings.

But I must, as the judge, confine myself to what is relevant to the decision that I face. My sympathy for the parents must be obvious. The consequences for them, I accept, must be and have been dreadful, but I must be concerned more with the nature and quality of the act which caused the death than with its consequences for those who are left behind to grieve. My decision must be the same whether the victim was, as I have suggested here, a beloved daughter whose death is a tragedy that time alone can diminish or if she was alone and friendless with no one to mourn her loss. I must be concerned principally with other things than the effect upon those who remain.

Now, I understand from what counsel have said to me in the course of submissions that my colleague, Henry J, recently permitted a parent, in what I understand was a similar type of hearing, to make such a statement. Nothing that I have said in any way is critical of him. This proposal is, in my experience, a novel one. I have not been faced with it before.

Henry J dealt with the proposal in the circumstances before him by allowing the statement to be made. I am not informed that there was any objection to that proposal at that time. I observe also that I do not know what was the purpose of that statement.

I do not know what were the contents of the statement. Indeed, in the cases that counsel referred to in the course of their submissions to me, there is one case in which the family of the deceased asked for the minimum penalty to be imposed that could be imposed. I can therefore imagine circumstances in which a statement made by the friends or parents of the deceased might be useful and helpful.

Judges must deal with these situations as they arise, in the light of the circumstances before them. The fact that Henry J admitted it is some indication to me that both sides thought it would be helpful to him and that he had the impression that it would be helpful.

I do not consider that permitting the statement proposed in this case to be made would be helpful. As I have said, it is not for any lack of concern or sympathy for the victim or for her family. I do not think it is relevant. I do not think it would help me with the task that most judges, in my experience, agree is the most difficult that they face as judges, and that is to establish a fair and just sentence. "Fair" in the circumstances means fair to all, not merely to the victim or to the victim's family, but also to the accused in this case, the convicted man, and his family.

Principles of sentencing have been established as guidelines for me and other judges in these circumstances, and they do not, in my experience, include consideration of the effect of a tragic death such as this upon the survivors.

QUESTIONS

How did the traditional paradigm construct the role of the victim? Was the victim treated as a mere interloper? Did this model afford *any* vehicle for placing the victim's interests or concerns before the court?

III. THE CURRENT LEGAL FRAMEWORK

The first formal statutory provision for the admission of VIS was enacted by *An Act To Amend the Criminal Code (Victims of Crime)*, RSC 1985, c. 23 (4th Supp.), s. 7 (passed in 1988). This provision has been amended from time to time[7] and now appears as s. 722 of the *Criminal Code*, set out below. It is important that s. 722 be read and interpreted in its proper statutory context in conjunction with the purposes and principles of sentencing in ss. 718 to 718.2 of the *Criminal Code*. In particular, "providing reparations for harm done to victims or to the community" (s. 718(d)) and promoting "a sense of responsibility in offenders ... and acknowledgment of the harm done to victims and to the community" (s. 718(e)) are identified as objectives of the sentencing function.[8]

---

7 The section was re-enacted in Bill C-41, *An Act To Amend the Criminal Code (Sentencing)*, SC 1995, c. 22 and most recently by *An Act To Amend the Criminal Code (Victims of Crime)*, 1999, c. 25, ss. 17 and 18. This Act made changes throughout the *Criminal Code* to recognize victims explicitly. An example of these types of changes is seen in the bail provisions.

8 See the discussion of these issues in Chapter 2. Also, note that s. 718.2 identifies certain victim features or characteristics that are relevant for sentencing purposes.

The current version of s. 722 of the *Criminal Code* provides as follows:

722(1) For the purpose of determining the sentence to be imposed on an offender or whether the offender should be discharged pursuant to section 730 in respect of any offence, the court may consider a statement, prepared in accordance with subsection (2), of a victim of the offence describing the harm done to, or loss suffered by, the victim arising from the commission of the offence.

(2) A statement referred to in subsection (1) shall be

(a) prepared in writing in the form and in accordance with the procedures established by a program designated for the purpose by the Lieutenant Governor in Council of the province in which the court is exercising its jurisdiction; and

(b) filed with the court.

(2.1) The court shall, on the request of a victim, permit the victim to read a statement prepared and filed in accordance with subsection (2), or to present the statement in any other manner that the court considers appropriate.

(3) Whether or not a statement has been prepared and filed in accordance with subsection (2), the court may consider any other evidence concerning any victim of the offence for the purpose of determining the sentence to be imposed on the offender or whether the offender should be discharged pursuant to section 730.

(4) For the purpose of this section, "victim," in relation to an offence,

(a) means a person to whom harm was done or who suffered physical or emotional loss as a result of the commission of the offence, and

(b) where the person described in paragraph (a) is dead, ill or otherwise incapable of making a statement referred to in subsection (1.1), includes the spouse or any relative of that person, anyone who has in law or in fact the custody of that person or is responsible for the care or support of that person or any dependant of that person.

722.1. The clerk of the court shall provide a copy of a statement referred to in subsection 722(1), as soon as practicable after a finding of guilty, to the offender or counsel for the offender, and to the prosecutor.

722.2(1) As soon as practicable after a finding of guilt and in any event before imposing sentence, the court shall inquire of the prosecutor or a victim of the offence, or any person representing a victim of the offence, whether the victim or victims have been advised of the opportunity to prepare a statement referred to in subsection 722(1).

(2) On application of the prosecutor or a victim or on its own motion, the court may adjourn the proceedings to permit the victim to prepare a statement referred to in subsection 722(1) or to present evidence in accordance with subsection 722(3), if the court is satisfied that the adjournment would not interfere with the proper administration of justice.

Following the enactment of this legislation, the courts grappled with the question of who is a victim within the meaning of this provision. The restrictive approach to the role of victims is perpetuated in *Curtis*, a case that interpreted the original version of the provision (s. 735). Note that the original version of the legislation referred to "*the* person to whom harm is done or who suffers physical or emotional loss as a result of the commission of the offence." The amended and broader version of the section (see s. 722(4) above, amended by SC 1999, c. 25, s. 17(3)) contemplates a wider class of persons affected by a crime.

R v. Curtis
(1992), 69 CCC (3d) 385 (NB CA)

STRATTON CJNB: The appellant, Randolph Hayward Curtis, raises two issues on this appeal: (1) Did the trial judge err in admitting into evidence a victim impact statement from a person who, it is alleged, was not a victim as defined in s. 735(1.4) of the *Criminal Code*, and which, it is further alleged, contained information contrary to s. 735(1.1)? (2) Leave to appeal having previously been granted, was the sentence imposed on Mr. Curtis excessive in the circumstances?

The Facts

Mr. Curtis pleaded guilty to the offence of assault causing bodily harm to Mr. George MacMullin contrary to s. 267(1)(b) of the Code. Following receipt of a pre-sentence report, Mr. Curtis was sentenced to a term of imprisonment of nine months with probation to follow for a term of two years. The Crown agrees that the assault occurred as the result of the breakdown of Mr. Curtis' marriage and the resulting frustration which he experienced.

On November 25, 1982, Mr. Curtis married Kimberley Ann Wilson. They have one child, Kathleen Ann Curtis, who was born July 31, 1988. On March 9, 1990, the parties separated. Subsequently, Mr. Curtis and his wife appeared before the court of Queen's Bench, Family Division, on a number of occasions concerning the custody of and access to the child, support for the child and the division of marital property. On August 27, 1990, the parties settled these various issues by a consent order. By the terms of the consent order, Mrs. Curtis was to have custody of the child while Mr. Curtis was given access. Mr. Curtis also agreed to pay $200 per month for child support and he retained ownership of the marital home. On August 24, 1990, just prior to the consent order, Mr. Curtis entered into a peace bond. The peace bond was part of the over-all settlement of the domestic dispute.

In late November, 1990, Mrs. Curtis made an application to family court to restrict Mr. Curtis' access to the child. The application was granted *ex parte*. At a hearing in early January, 1991, however, Mr. Curtis was once again granted access on terms similar to those contained in the original consent order of August 27, 1990.

In March, 1991, Mrs. Curtis commenced divorce proceedings. Mr. Curtis, however, continued to hope for reconciliation. shortly after the commencement of the divorce proceedings, Mrs. Curtis began seeing the victim of the assault, Mr. George MacMullin, Mrs. Curtis advised her husband that this was not a romantic relationship. In any event, Mr. Curtis approached Mr. MacMullin and requested that he have no involvement with his wife until after the divorce hearing which was scheduled for June 26, 1991.

On Sunday morning, May 26, 1991, Mr. Curtis went to his wife's residence and in the parking-lot of her apartment he met Mrs. Curtis, his daughter Kathleen and Mr. MacMullin. All of them, including Mr. Curtis, were on their way to church. Mr. Curtis voiced his objection to his daughter going to church with Mr. MacMullin. Mr. Curtis followed the MacMullin vehicle from Mrs. Curtis' residence to the church. After the parties had parked their vehicles, Mr. Curtis approached Mr. MacMullin and threatened him. Mr. Curtis then proceeded to punch and kick Mr. MacMullin a number of times. All of this happened in front of the church and in the presence of a number of witnesses including Mrs. Curtis and the daughter Kathleen.

As a result of the assault, Mr. MacMullin suffered serious injuries including a broken nose, a fractured jaw and two broken ribs. Mr. MacMullin was hospitalized for a period of time and required surgery to repair the fractures.

As noted above, Mr. Curtis pleaded guilty to assault causing bodily harm. At the sentencing hearing, the judge received into evidence a pre-sentence report and a victim impact statement from Mr. MacMullin. Over the objection of counsel for Mr. Curtis, the judge also accepted into evidence a victim impact statement from Mrs. Curtis on behalf of herself and her daughter, Kathleen. In her statement, Mrs. Curtis relates her recollection of the assault and its effect upon her and her daughter and her future relationship with the victim's mother. It is the acceptance of Mrs. Curtis' statement which is raised as one of the two issues in this appeal.

The Legislation

Section 735(1.1) to (1.4) of the *Criminal Code* authorizes the preparation and reception of victim impact statements. Section 735(1.1) permits a sentencing court to consider a statement made by a victim of an offence which describes the harm done to or the loss suffered by the victim arising from the commission of the offence.

...

The Judgment at Trial

In his reasons for decision, the judge appears to have accepted the Crown's submission that a victim impact statement was similar to a pre-sentence report. According to the Crown, pre-sentence reports often contain hearsay evidence. If so, the defence is entitled to object to the hearsay matter and require proof of that which is alleged. The Crown submits that the procedure would be the same for victim impact statements.

In dismissing Mr. Curtis' contention that Mrs. Curtis was not a "victim" within the meaning of s. 735(1.4) of the Code, the judge said:

> As far as the Victim Impact statement itself is concerned, victims as defined under the Code are certainly defined very broadly. And my understanding of what I've heard today is that the wife, still a wife I believe, of Randolph Hayward Curtis and the girlfriend of the victim in this matter, George MacMullin, certainly suffered emotional harm. She was there when it happened. I understand again just briefly of what has been said that the daughter was also there when this assault took place. Chances are that the daughter as well suffered emotionally, emotional harm from that.
>
> And again on the broad definition of a victim under the Code I hold that in this case the wife of Randolph Hayward Curtis and the now girlfriend of the victim George MacMullin would be entitled to present to the Court a Victim Impact Statement. The contents of which are again disputable by the Defense and there is an avenue open to you in that regard.

It should also be noted in passing that Mr. Curtis raised an argument before the trial judge that ss. 7 and 24(2) of the *Canadian Charter of Rights and Freedoms* applied. The argument was not accepted by the trial judge and was abandoned on the hearing of the appeal.

The Victim Impact Statement

The Submissions

As noted, counsel for Mr. Curtis objected to the reception into evidence of Mrs. Curtis' victim impact statement. He did so on two bases: that Mrs. Curtis was not a "victim" as defined in s. 735(1.4) of the Code, and in the alternative, if she was a victim, that the statement contained information that should not have been part of a victim impact statement.

Mr. Curtis submits that the definition of "victim" contained in s. 735(1.4) refers to "the person" and is intended to be singular, *i.e.*, the actual victim. Only the "direct" victim of an offence qualifies so as to be able to submit a victim impact statement. This, he says, is made obvious when one reads the entire section. He points out that s. 735(1.4)(b) is the only exception. Section 735(1.4)(b) provides for a statement by a spouse or relative where the actual victim is dead or otherwise incapable of providing a statement. Thus, he argues, only one victim impact statement may be admissible and that one must be made by the direct victim of the offence unless that person is "dead, ill or otherwise incapable of making a statement." It is only in the latter case that a person other than the victim can provide a statement and that only as a result of s. 735(1.4)(b) which expands the definition of victim. Further, even if Mr. MacMullin had been unable to provide such a statement, Mr. Curtis submits that it is questionable whether Mrs. Curtis would fall within the expanded definition of "victim." She was neither Mr. MacMullin's spouse, relative nor his dependent.

In the alternative, Mr. Curtis contends that if Mrs. Curtis was a "victim" as contemplated by s. 735(1.4) of the Code, this particular statement should not have been admitted because it contains inadmissible information. Specifically, he submits, the statement contains details of her involvement in the offence, details as to domestic issues between she and her husband as well as statements as to the harm done to her, her two-year-old daughter and to Mr. MacMullin's mother. Thus, Mr. Curtis contends, the statement went far beyond describing "the harm done to, or loss suffered by, the victim arising from the commission of the offence" which is permitted by s. 735(1) of the Code.

The Crown, on the other hand, points out that pursuant to s. 33(2) of the *Interpretation Act*, RSC 1985, c. I-21, words in the singular include the plural and therefore the reference to "person" in s. 735(1.4)(a) of the Code was not intended to be confined to one person alone. Moreover, the Crown submits that the definition of "victim" contained in s. 735(1.4)(a) should be given a large and liberal interpretation to include any person to whom harm is done or who suffers physical or emotional loss as a result of the commission of an offence. The Crown further submits that Mrs. Curtis' statement does describe the harm done to and the loss suffered by her as a result of the offence by her husband.

Discussion

1.(a) Who Is a "Victim"?

As mentioned previously, the trial judge concluded that the word "victim" as used in ss. 735(1.1) to (1.4) of the Code should be given a broad meaning so as to include persons other than the person that one might call the direct victim. I have looked, unsuccessfully, for assistance in the case-law. While there are many cases in which victim impact statements are mentioned, in no case did I find a court that considered directly the meaning of the word "victim." A survey of the reported decisions shows, however, that in general it is the direct victim whose statement is introduced and used.

There have, however, been a number of exceptions to the general rule of receiving only the statements of "direct" victims. Impact statements have been received from an aunt (*R v. H.(A.)* (1991), 65 CCC (3d) 116, 13 WCB (2d) 49 (BC CA)); a mother (*R v. Melville*, New Westminster Registry, No. X019013, January 13, 1989); a maternal grandmother (*R v. McMurrer* (1990), 84 Nfld. & PEIR 248, 10 WCB (2d) 381 (SC); reversed on appeal, PEI CA, No. AD-0230, January 28, 1991 [reported 89 Nfld. & PEIR 36, 12 WCB (2d) 168]; leave to appeal to SCC refused, No. 22378, June 20, 1991); the members of families of the victim (*R v. Poole*, Ont. Dist. Ct. Thunder Bay District, No. 1216-88 [summarized 7 WCB (2d) 51]; *R v. Lecaine* (1990), 105 AR 261 (Alta. CA), and *R v. Black* (1990), 110 NBR (2d 208, 11 WCB (2d) 324); "many people," referring to people in the community (*R v. Sousa*, BC CA, Vancouver Registry, No. CA 12625, September 27, 1991 [summarized 14 WCB (2d) 111]), and from a series of physicians and psychiatrists who had worked with the victim: *R v. S.(C.C.)* (1990), 81 Nfld. & PEIR 81, 9 WCB (2d) 558 (SC). In *R v. McMurrer*, the case involving the statement from the maternal grandmother, the court mentioned that there was "no indication that the statement complied with s. 735(1.4)(*b*); however, the accused did not object to it." One court did say that it had concerns with respect to the introduction of the statements in general: *R v. K.(S.A.)*, BC CA, Vancouver Registry, No. CA011597, November 5, 1990 [summarized 11 WCB (2d) 484]. An Ontario court manifested "critical scepticism about unsworn testimony": see *R v. Scott*, Ont. Ct. (Gen. Div.), Hamilton, No. 1183/90, January 4, 1991 [summarized 13 WCB (2d) 394].

It is to be observed that the definition of "victim" contained in s. 735(1.4)(a) refers to "*the* person" to whom harm is done or who suffers loss. In my opinion, the use of the definite article in the definition section restricts the meaning of the word "victim" to the "direct" victim of the offence.

In addition to the use of the definite article in para. (a) of s. 735(1.4), support for a restricted meaning of the word "victim" can be found in para. (b) of s. 735(1.4) which permits certain other persons to submit a victim impact statement where "the person" referred to in para. (a) is dead, ill or otherwise incapable of making a statement. From this it would seem to follow that if the direct victim is not dead, ill or otherwise incapable, these other persons would not be allowed to submit a victim impact statement. Moreover, one of these other persons is a victim's spouse. If it was intended to allow anybody affected by an offence to submit a victim impact statement, surely one such person would be the spouse of the direct victim. Yet it appears that she or he is excluded unless the "victim" is incapacitated.

Furthermore, it is to be noted that s. 735(1.2) of the Code directs that a victim impact statement shall be prepared in accordance with procedures established by the Lieutenant-Governor in Council of the province in which the court is exercising jurisdiction. On August 23, 1990, the Lieutenant-Governor in Council of New Brunswick by OC 90-721, designated a program for the preparation and submission of victim impact statements in the province. The designated program refers specifically and repeatedly to victim impact statements describing the harm done to, or the loss suffered by, "*the* victim of a criminal offence." The program also directs that a statement should state only the effect on "*the* victim of the crime for which the offender could be sentenced." Additionally, the "guiding principles" of the program refer to "the direct victim of the offence." Thus, in my opinion, the words used in the approved program for New Brunswick support the conclusion that a restricted meaning should be given to the word "victim" under the existing legislation.

While an argument can perhaps be made that the definition of "victim" in s. 735(1.4)(a) could be read to include not only the direct victim of an offence but also a person who suffers physical or emotional loss as the result of the commission of an offence, I am not persuaded that this would be a proper reading of the legislative intent as expressed in the definition. In this respect, it is to be noted that prior to the amendment of s. 735, the Code did not allow for the introduction of victim impact statements. If Parliament had intended to permit courts to receive statements from anyone other than a direct victim, it is my opinion it could more clearly have made provision for the reception into evidence of multiple victim impact statements.

In summary, it is my opinion that even though there appears to be a tendency to relax the rules of evidence with respect to the introduction of evidence at the sentencing hearing (see, for example, the decision of the Supreme Court of Canada in *R v. Albright* (1987), 37 CCC (3d) 105, 45 DLR (4th) 11, [1987] 2 SCR 383), of the legislation in question here, given their plain and ordinary meaning, do not permit the introduction of victim impact statements except from the direct victim. If, however, the direct victim is dead, ill or otherwise incapable of making a statement, others may be permitted to do so pursuant to s. 735(1.4)(b). In the result, I have concluded that Mrs. Curtis' statement should not have been admitted into evidence.

The following case of *Phillips* addresses the same issue raised in *Curtis*, but reaches a different conclusion. Phillips was convicted of second-degree murder in the killing of a police officer. The Crown tendered victim impact statements from the deceased's fiance, his partner on the force, and a representative of a local police–community association. The latter statement spoke of the impact that the death had on the small community where he lived and served. Note that this decision was also decided before the 1999 amendments to s. 722. The revised version of the provision, s. 722(4), undoubtedly supports the *Phillips* approach.

R v. Phillips
(1995), 26 OR (3d) 522 (Gen. Div.)

...

McISAAC J: With the greatest of respect to the New Brunswick Court of Appeal [in *Curtis*], I am unable to accept this interpretation which I find would unreasonably limit the ambit of this provision in the *Criminal Code*. I do so for two reasons. They both relate to the application of the *Interpretation Act*, RSC 1985, c. I-21.

First, s. 33(2) of that Act states that words in the singular include the plural. Accordingly, there is no reason to restrict the definition of "victim" in s. 735(1.4)(a) to the singular. I find nothing in para. (b) thereof to lead me to the conclusion that it was in any way intended to, or in fact, has the effect of limiting the definition of "victim" in para. (a). This proposition would appear to be directly contrary to the legislative intent of the amendment which was adopted by the House of Commons Legislative Committee prior to the third reading of Bill C-89. See "Two Scales of Justice: The Victim as Adversary" (1993), 35 CLQ 334, an article by Mr. Steven Skurka, at p. 344 (footnote 27):

> It would appear that s. 735(1.4)(b) was adopted by the legislative committee without much, if any, discussion prior to the third reading of Bill C-89. The proposer of the amendment was moved by a particular case in British Columbia where a court had refused to accept a victim impact statement from a member of the family of a deceased victim even though other members of the family suffered from that particular crime: Commons Debates, 3rd Reading, May 3, 1988, at p. 15086.

My second concern related to the *Interpretation Act* involves s. 12 thereof which states:

> 12. Every enactment is deemed remedial, and shall be given such fair, large and liberal construction and interpretation as best ensures the attainment of its object.

As I read *R v. Curtis*, supra, Stratton CJNB was unable to find any case-law to support the submission advocating a broad interpretation of "victim" that was made by the Crown in that case: see pp. 390-91. However, the Supreme Court of Canada subsequently had occasion to assess the interplay of the principle of broad and liberal interpretation as provided for by s. 12 of the *Interpretation Act* with the rule of strict interpretation of penal statutes: see *R v. Hasselwander*, [1993] 2 SCR 398, 81 CCC (3d) 471. In considering the meaning of the term "capable of firing bullets in rapid succession" based on competing interpretation of either "immediately capable" or "readily capable," Cory J for the majority of the court in that case had occasion to turn to an examination of the purpose and goals of the provisions of the *Criminal Code* relating to prohibited weapons, specifically firearms. Simply put, Parliament intended to severely restrict the possession of instruments that were designed to kill people so that the safety of society could be advanced. From that viewpoint, an interpretation of "immediately capable" would frustrate the obvious intent to limit access to these lethal weapons. Accordingly, "capable" included a potential for conversion in a relatively short period of time with relative ease. In the result, it can be seen that the Supreme Court of Canada rejected an interpretation based on the principle of strict interpretation of a penal statute for a broad and remedial interpretation based on social policy grounds.

Applying that approach to the issue at bar, I have to consider the policy that motivated Parliament to permit consideration of a VIS and then apply those principles to the definition of "victim" in s. 735(1.4). In *R v. Nelson*, Stuart TCJ of the Yukon Territorial Court, unreported, April 13, 1992, outlined the purpose of this 1988 amendment (quoted in "Two Scales of Justice: A Reply" (1993), 35 CLQ 355, an article by Professor Alan N. Young at pp. 362-63):

> The victim impact statement accords the victim an opportunity to ensure that their concerns are incorporated in the sentencing process without being exposed to the trauma of testifying ... Sentencing, among its many objectives, aspires to impose a sentence that the victim will regard as just. Ensuring that their concerns are heard creates the basis for victims to accept and believe in the fairness of the process ... Finally, without the victim's impact, the seriousness of the crime cannot be fully appreciated. What may be viewed from the bench as trivial, may in fact be serious, and conversely what may be generally regarded as a serious crime may not be if the full story was before the court ... Victim impact statements can help offenders appreciate the ramifications of their conduct on others and thereby add an awareness essential to promote and sustain genuine contrition and the will to change their behaviour.

The same article refers to the judgment of the Supreme Court of the United States where the justices reversed themselves and ruled that VIS's were admissible on a capital sentence hearing: see *Payne v. Tennessee*, 111 S Ct. 2597 (1991), overruling *Booth v. Maryland*, 107 S Ct. 2529 (1988). In *Payne*, Souter J, concurring, focused on the balance that a VIS provided, especially in cases of homicide (at pp. 2615-16):

> Murder has foreseeable consequences. When it happens, it is always to distinct individuals, and after it happens other victims are left behind. Every defendant knows, if endowed with the mental competence for criminal responsibility, that the life he will take by his homicidal behavior is that of a unique person, like himself, and that the person to be killed probably has close associates, "survivors" who will suffer harms and deprivations from the victim's death. Just as defendants know that they are not faceless human ciphers, they know that their victims are not valueless fungibles and just as defendants appreciate the web of relationships and dependencies in which they live. They know that their victims are not human islands, but individuals with parents or children, spouses or friends or dependants. Thus, when a defendant chooses to kill, or to raise the risk of a victim's death, this choice necessarily relates to a whole human being and threatens an association of others, who may be distinctly hurt. The fact that the defendant may not know the details of a victim's life and characteristics, or the exact identities and needs of those who may survive, should not in any way obscure the further facts that death is always to a "unique" individual, and harm to some groups of survivors is a consequence of a successful homicidal act so foreseeable as to be virtually inevitable.

Both of these comments reflect the virtual flood of victims' rights initiatives that have been undertaken in the common law jurisdictions in the last decade: see pp. 359-61 of Professor Young's article, supra. As well, they confirm the fact that retribution continues to be a valid consideration in the sentencing process: see *R v. Lyons*, [1987] 2 SCR 309 at p. 329, 32 CRR 41, where La Forest J for the majority of the court stated:

> Preventative detention in the context of Part XXI, however, simply represents a judgment that the relative importance of the objectives of rehabilitation, deterrence and retribution are greatly attenuated in the circumstances of the individual case, and that of prevention, correspondingly increased.

Even though this comment may be categorized as obiter dicta, it is still binding on me: see *Sellars v. R*, [1980] 1 SCR 527, 52 CCC (2d) 345. My experience has not been that victims wish to monopolize the sentencing process; they merely want to be able to participate in it in a meaningful way.

The provision of the three contested VIS herein will assist me in lifting the character of P.C. Nystedt from the status of a "faceless human cipher." I see no potential for them to distort the sentencing hearing into an exclusive process to rectify the purely private interests of their authors. They will merely provide a balance to the anticipated evidence that will be advanced on behalf of the offender in mitigation of sentence. Accordingly, both sides will be afforded a hearing that reflects the principles of fundamental justice: see *R v. Cunningham*, [1993] 2 SCR 143, 14 CRR (2d) 234. I am persuaded that the definition of "victim" in s. 735(1.4) should be given a broad and liberal interpretation.

V. Conclusion

For these reasons, I am compelled to the conclusion that I should not follow the judgment of the New Brunswick Court of Appeal in *R v. Curtis*, supra. Based upon rules of judicial comity, I do so reluctantly. Accordingly, the VIS of PC Mike Landry, Joanne McPhee and Ms. Presley will be admitted and considered in this sentencing hearing.

Statements admissible.

The following judgment in *Gabriel* looks at the role of VIS from a functional perspective within the sentencing process. Hill J focuses on the content of VIS and how they relate to the aims and principles of sentencing in ss. 718 to 718.2 of the *Criminal Code*.

R v. Gabriel
(1999), 26 CR (5th) 364 (Ont. Ct. (Gen. Div.))

HILL J: On May 31st, 1999, Raymond Gabriel was sentenced to a term of imprisonment of 2 years less 1 day following his guilty plea to the charge of criminal negligence causing death. This disposition was imposed allowing the offender a 7-month credit for pre-sentence custody. In addition, Mr. Gabriel was made the subject of a 2-year probationary term with special conditions and a 5-year driving prohibition.

During the sentencing hearing, counsel acknowledged a general lack of direction or guidance respecting victim impact statements in particular relating to the permissible limits of content subject matter.

•••

The Victim Impact Statements

The victim impact statements filed in the *Gabriel* case included documents authored by the deceased's parents, grandparents, aunts, uncles, cousins, fiancé, and employer. As well, some statements were filed by authors whose relation to the victim could not be determined. As well, a statement was filed by the stepmother of Ms. Hunt's best friend.

As one would expect, given the number of statements, there existed considerable repetition in content within the population of documents filed.

Almost without exception, the victim impact statements were titled "Auto Accident by Raymond Gabriel Killing Samantha Hunt."

Some of the victim impact statements were in the form of letters. The majority of the statements, however, were set out in a form entitled, Victim Impact Statement, with the following subtitles:

(1) My Name
(2) Address
(3) Phone Number
(4) Relationship to Samantha Hunt
(5) Description of Impact (including emotional, psychological, social and financial loss)
(6) Date; Signature.

Some of the statements appended photographs of the deceased or poetry.

More than half of the victim impact statements contained references to one or more of the following topics:

(1) the facts of the offence,
(2) the character of the offender,
(3) the punishment Mr. Gabriel deserved.

•••

Analysis

Victim Impact Statements

Prior to codification, there existed mixed judicial reaction to the admissibility of victim impact statements. However, the trend was toward acceptance of evidence, at least from the direct victim of the offence. In *Swietlinski v. Attorney-General of Ontario* (1994), 92 CCC (3d) 449 (SCC) at 465, Lamer CJC observed: "It is well known that the victim's testimony is admissible at a hearing on sentencing ..."

As a general rule, in criminal cases, harm cannot be presumed. As an aggravating feature of sentencing, loss or harm is to be established by the prosecution: *McDonnell v. The Queen* (1997), 114 CCC (3d) 436 (SCC) at para. 22-38 per Sopinka J; *Criminal Code*, s. 724(3).

Assessment of the harm caused by a crime has long been an important concern of the law of sentencing and evidence of specific harm relates to assessment of an offender's moral culpability and blameworthiness: *Payne v. Tennessee*, 501 US 808 (1991) at 2605-6, 2608 per Rehnquist CJ […].

The victim impact statement regime was first introduced into the *Criminal Code* in 1988 (section 735). The sentencing court was afforded a discretion as to whether it would consider any tendered victim impact statements.

. . .

Accordingly, the following essential features should exist in order for a victim impact statement (the statement) to be admissible:

(1) the statement is to be prepared in writing,
(2) the statement is to be in the form and in accordance with procedures established by a program designated for that purpose by the province,
(3) the statement is to be authored by a person meeting the definition of "victim" (s. 722(4) of the Code),
(4) the statement is to describe the harm done to, or loss suffered by, the victim arising from the commission of the offence,
(5) the statement is to be filed with the court,
(6) the clerk of the court is to provide a copy of the statement to the prosecution and the defence (s. 722.1 of the Code).

Where a statement is admissible, it "shall" be considered by the sentencing court acting under Part XXIII of the *Criminal Code*.

Section 722(3) of the Code affords the sentencing court a discretion to consider other evidence concerning the victim of an offence beyond that contained in a victim impact statement.

The victim impact statement serves a number of purposes, including:

(1) Nature of the Offence   The court receives relevant evidence as to the effect or impact of the crime from the person(s) able to give direct evidence on the point. The evidence is not filtered through a third party reporter. The evidence is relevant to the seriousness of the offence which in turn assists the court in imposing proportionate punishment (s. 718.1 of the Code).
(2) Victim Reparation   Sections 718(e) and (f) recognize that a just sanction by the court should have amongst its objectives reparation for harm done to victims and the promotion of acknowledgement by the offender of harm done to a victim. Resort to the best evidence on the subject of victim loss, the victim himself or herself, not only assures an accurate measure of any necessary compensation but also serves to bring home to the offender the consequences of the criminal behaviour.

(3) Repute of the Administration of Criminal Justice   Victim participation in the trial process serves to improve the victim's perception of the legitimacy of the process. The satisfaction of being heard, in the sense of a direct submission to the court, enhances respect for the justice system on the part of the harmed individual, and over time, the community itself. Incidental to the victim impact statement process is the ability of the victim to secure a sense of regaining control over his or her life and the alleviation of the frustration of detachment which can arise where the victim perceives that he or she is ignored and uninvolved in the process.

(4) Parity of Identity   A significant concern of the sentencing hearing is finding a disposition tailored to the individual offender in an effort to ensure long range protection of the public. As a consequence, much becomes known about the accused as a person. In this process, there is a danger of the victim being reduced to obscurity—an intolerable departure from respect for the personal integrity of the victim. The victim was a special and unique person as well—information revealing the individuality of the victim and the impact of the crime on the victim's survivors achieves a measure of balance in understanding the consequences of the crime in the context of the victim's personal circumstances, or those of survivors.

The victim impact statement is not, however, the exclusive answer to the civilized treatment of victims within the criminal process. Communication with victims of crime by prosecutorial authorities, victim/offender reconciliation projects, and community support initiatives for victims, are as, or more, essential.

Victim impact statements contribute significantly to a just sentencing process. Sentencing is a reasoned, not an arbitrary, exercise. Context remains important. It is to be remembered that there is a civil justice system to address actionable wrongs between individual citizens. The criminal court is "not a social agency" (*R v. M.(E.)* (1992), 76 CCC (3d) 159 (Ont. CA) at 164 per Finlayson JA, in dissent in the result).

Without, in any fashion, diminishing the significant contribution of victim impact statements to providing victims a voice in the criminal process, it must be remembered that a criminal trial, including the sentencing phase, is not a tripartite proceeding. A convicted offender has committed a crime—an act against society as a whole. It is the public interest, not a private interest, which is to be served in sentencing.

The historic lack of legislative codification, and a similar silence in Bill C-79—*An Act to Amend the Criminal Code (Victims of Crime)* [now SC 1995, c. 22], as to the procedural circumstances of the introduction of a victim impact statement tends to foster a victim's expectations that he or she is a party to the proceeding and not a witness. Who is responsible for identifying the victim of the crime? What searches ought to be made to provide notice to all victims of the crime? Is there judicial authority to limit the number of statements filed, or which may be read under the pending amendments? It is implicit that a victim statement constitutes evidence to be considered in arriving at a fit and just sentence. Accordingly, is the statement, where written, or if read in court, under oath? subject to cross-examination? subject, to the introduction of extrinsic contradictory evidence adduced by the offender? In the court's exercise of its supervisory jurisdiction to ensure a fair trial and to control its own proceedings, can the court edit an impact statement in terms of inflammatory, overly prejudicial or irrelevant content? Should the court not be able to intercede to halt what is in effect a mini-trial within the sentencing hearing designed to supplement the record in parallel civil proceedings between victim and offender?

The dangers of a runaway model for victim participation in the sentencing process can, in the long run, serve to defeat the very objectives of victim input.

Retribution remains an important sentencing objective in sanctioning the moral culpability of the offender: *The Queen v. M.(C.A.)* (1996), 105 CCC (3d) 327 (SCC) at 365-369 per Lamer CJC. Vengeance, however, has no place in a humane sentencing regime: *The Queen v. M.(C.A.)*, supra at 368-370; *R v. Sweeney* (1992), 71 CCC (3d) 82 (BC CA) at 95 per Wood JA; *R v. Lauzon* (1940), 74 CCC 37 (Que. CA) at 52 per Walsh JA.

...

Accordingly, the victim impact statement regime should not be structured so as to foster or encourage any element of personal revenge on the part of a victim. This is a very real danger. In "Two Scales of Justice: The Victim as Adversary" (1993), 35 CLQ 334, Steven Skurka observed at pages 340 and 341:

> By asking a victim to express his comments and concerns without any further guidance, invariably this category will be used by many victims to vent their feelings about such matters as the nature of the crime, the offender, the failings of the criminal justice system and the appropriate sentence to be imposed on the offender. ...

Equally, it cannot be denied that many victims, perceiving themselves as real adversaries, will use such an opportunity as a platform for revenge against the accused. ...

There must be guidelines to ensure that victim statements "only contain relevant information": *Swietlinski v. Attorney-General of Ontario*, supra at 465. The guidelines need to limit the statements to what the Code authorizes: *R v. Barling*, [1995] BCJ No. 2225 (CA) at para. 9 per McEachern CJBC.

In Ontario, under the prior discretionary scheme, it was recognized that it was proper to consider a victim impact statement in sentencing: *R v. W.(H.W.)*, [1992] OJ No. 2407 (CA) at 2 per curiam. Concern was expressed that undue reliance not be placed upon such material: *R v. Smith*, [1994] OJ No. 3899 (CA) at para. 1 per Lacourcière JA. Improper statement contents have led to partial consideration of submitted victim impact materials: *R v. Barling*, supra at para. 7-9; *R v. Ohlenschlager*, [1994] AJ No. 510 (CA) at para. 3 per MacKenzie JA.

Impact statements should describe "the harm done to, or loss suffered by, the victim arising from the commission of the offence." The statements should not contain criticisms of the offender, assertions as to the facts of the offence, or recommendations as to the severity of punishment.

Criticism of the offender tilts the adversary system and risks the appearance of revenge motivation.

Attempts to state, or presumably to restate, the facts of the offence usurp the role of the prosecutor and risk inconsistency with, or expansion of, prior trial testimony, or facts read in, and agreed to, on the guilty plea appearance. Such was the case in

R v. McAnespie (1993), 82 CCC (3d) 527 (Ont. CA) (reversed (1994), 86 CCC (3d) 191 (SCC)) where additional disclosure by the complainant, relating to the offence, was made by the complainant in her victim impact statement.

The Attorney General represents the public interest in the prosecution of crime.

Recommendations as to penalty must be avoided, absent exceptional circumstances, i.e. a court-authorized request, an aboriginal sentencing circle, or as an aspect of a prosecutorial submission that the victim seeks leniency for the offender which might not otherwise reasonably be expected in the circumstances. The freedom to call for extraordinary sentences, beyond the limits of appellate tolerance, unjustifiably raises victim expectations, promotes an appearance of court-acceptance of vengeful submissions, and propels the system away from necessary restraint in punishing by loss of liberty (s. 718.2(d) of the Code; *Gladue v. The Queen*, supra at para. 40, 41, 57, 93). It has been suggested that frequently the victim's limited knowledge of available sentencing options may lead the victim to rely on more severe options: H.C. Rubel, "Victim Participation in Sentencing Proceedings" (1985-86), 28 CLQ 226 at 240-241. The independent neutrality of the judiciary requires that the court not react to public opinion as to the severity of sentences: *R v. Porter* (1976), 33 CCC (2d) 215 (Ont. CA) at 220 per Arnup JA.

Some mention is necessary as to circumstances where the written impact statement can be presented orally. In Mr. Gabriel's sentencing hearing, leave was given to two of the "victims" to read their victim impact statements in the courtroom. There is a discretion to do so: *R v. Selig* (1994), 134 NSR (2d) 385 (CA) at 391 per Roscoe JA. There is, however, at present, no statutory or constitutional obligation to permit this: *R v. Coelho* (1995), 41 CR (4th) 324 (BC SC) at 327-330 per Saunders J. Indeed, it is not infrequent, in this courthouse, that a victim has emotionally disintegrated while reading his or her statement or has improvised beyond the four corners of the statement directing accusations and personal invectives toward the offender. In yet other instances of victim allocution, disturbances have erupted in the public area of the courtroom. However, a sensible exercise of discretion is warranted, having regard to the totality of the circumstances, including the health and stability of the victim, the nature of the crime(s) committed, concerns as to control of the courtroom, and the number of statements filed.

The statute does not directly speak to the mechanism by which a victim impact statement is filed. Since s. 722.1 of the Code refers to the clerk of the court providing a copy of a filed victim impact statement to the "prosecutor," there is some parallel to the pre-sentence report which is submitted directly to the court with copies to the parties. The tradition has generally been that Crown counsel tenders the victim impact statement(s) on the sentencing hearing as opposed to direct line access to the court for a victim. Regardless of whether the prosecution office, or the personnel administering the program designated by the Province of Ontario (under s. 722(2)(a) of the Code), is principally involved with the victim(s), there should be some pre-filing gatekeeper function exercised in terms of ensuring that victim impact statements comply with the *Criminal Code* requirements. In this way, victim disappointment will be avoided.

The Ontario Program

Section 722(2) of the Code requires that, to be admissible, a victim impact statement "must be prepared in writing in the form and in accordance with the procedures established by a program designated for that purpose" by the province.

In Ontario, the designated program is the Victim Witness Assistance Program (VWAP) of the Ministry of the Attorney General.

By virtue of this approach, the written victim impact statement is not itself a prescribed form—it is the program (responsible for designing the form) which is designated.

The established form in Ontario mandated by the VWAP is appended to these reasons together with the government-generated Information for Victims instruction sheet provided to victims.

The February, 1994 form, apparently still in use, is not the form employed by any of the "victims" in the *Gabriel* case. I will return to this observation in due course.

The VWAP documentation is disturbing in several respects, including:

(1) The form requests information relating to physical injuries and to financial impact resulting from the crime. No reference is made to emotional loss (s. 722(4)(a)) or to other forms of harm done to the victim (ss. 722(1), 722(4)(1)) i.e. psychological or social impacts or effects.

(2) The form invites, through broad and open-ended titlage (Personal Reaction; Other Comments), statements by the victim relating to the offender, the facts of the offence, and the suggested punishment. Despite the admonition in the information circular: "Please avoid recommending a sentence," the form is cast in very broad terms. I agree with Steven Skurka's observations ("Two Scales of Justice: The Victim as Adversary," supra at pages 340-341) that this type of unfocused direction leads to improper material in victim impact statements.

(3) The accompanying information sheet, also of 1994 origin, states:

> The judge will decide whether or not to consider the Victim Impact Statement when determining the sentence.

While this statement was a correct description of the 1994 legislation, specifically s. 735(1.1) of the Code ("… the court may consider a statement …"), the amendment proclaimed September 3, 1996 (SC 1995, c. 22), s. 722(1), assures judicial consideration of an otherwise admissible victim impact statement ("… the court shall consider any statement …").

In some instances, along with the victim impact statement form, a victim may receive a two-page document entitled, Victim Impact Statement An Information Guide, also appended to these reasons. For those who receive this additional material, the following advice is provided:

> Please remember that the Victim Impact Statement is about you, not the accused. Please avoid vengeful comments; instead, concentrate on providing a description of the impact of the crime on your life. Suggestions about the penalty are not helpful since it is entirely up to the judge to make that decision. You may, however, wish to express any concerns

you have about probation conditions. For example, it may be important for you to say whether you do or don't want contact with the accused.

It would appear that many of the victims in this case were not provided, or failed to abide by, this direction.

As to the non-compliance in the Gabriel case with use of the very form utilized by the VWAP, s. 722(2)(a) speaks in mandatory terms requiring the designated program form to be the one filed with the court—in this instance, the established form which, apart from accompanying informational supplements, invites the inadmissible contents encountered in the sentencing hearing. This point was not argued by the defence. Accordingly, whether on the basis of substantial compliance with the designated form, waiver, or receipt through the vehicle of s. 722(3) of the Code, the statements are admissible subject to excision of some of their contents.

Application of Principles to This Case

Much can be said for an interpretation of "victim" in s. 722 of the Code which limits the production of a victim impact statement to the direct victim of the crime: see *R v. Curtis* (1992), 69 CCC (3d) 385 (NS CA) at 391-393 per Stratton JA. Similarly, a restrictive view is warranted regarding s. 722(4)(b) of the Code where a victim impact statement is received in a case where the crime has caused death.

In this case, statements were filed beyond the category of "spouse" or "relative" as "victim" is defined in s. 722(4)(b) of the Code. "Victim" is likely to be interpreted in the plural: *Interpretation Act*, RSC 1985, c. I-21, s. 33(2); *R v. Phillips* (1996), 26 OR (3d) 522 (Gen. Div.). Assuming that more than one relative of the deceased is authorized to file a victim impact statement pursuant to s. 722(4)(b) of the Code, it does not assist the court to have 20 relatives do so. I note that in at least one case the court considered a joint victim impact statement: *R v. F.(R.)*, [1994] OJ No. 2101 (CA) at para. 3 per curiam. While some discretion exists, by virtue of section 722(3) of the Code, to expand the receivable scope of victim impact statements, the number filed here far surpassed what was helpful to the court.

In a case of a crime resulting in death, human experience, logic and common sense surely go some distance to presuming the existence of profound grief, loss and despair. It has been observed that "the criminal law does not value one life over another" (*R v. M.(E.)*, supra at 164 per Finlayson JA) and that "A consideration of the measure of loss of a human life is not only a demeaning process but also leads to a potentially egregious weighing of the worth of an individual's life" (S. Skurka, "Two Scales of Justice: The Victim as Adversary," supra at page 343).

Also, with respect to the statements, authors, either unidentified in their connection to the deceased, or remote in connection, are not of assistance.

Statements purporting to refer to the facts of the offence were inaccurate.

Statements speaking of the offender were not informed views of the background circumstances of the offender.

Suggested penalties were made without regard to the "worst offence/worst offender" sentencing principle.

A number of statements promoted eye-for-an-eye retributive justice only, without regard to other overarching principles and objectives of sentencing.

The labelling of the impact statements as involving a "killing" is inflammatory and jeopardizes the desired restraint of the sentencing hearing.

In a couple of instances, the offender's crime was wrongfully equated to "murder." A similar problem arose in *R v. Lecaine*, [1990] AJ No. 360 (CA) drawing disapproval from the court. Stevenson JA (as he then was) stated at page 2:

> Those statements feelingly portray the grief of the mother and brother of the victim at the loss of the victim. One cannot help but have very great sympathy for these people, for their loss. We point out, however, that these statements show an understandable misapprehension of the function of the criminal law in the punishment process. The mother says that her son's life was worth "a twelve month sentence to his murderer." This accused was not his murderer. The brother says "Thou shall not kill." This accused was not a killer in the sense of being a murderer. Murder is intentional killing and this accused was not convicted of intentional killing.

In the end result, the court considered only the contents of victim impact statements which described the harm done to, or loss suffered by, the identifiable victims in this case.

NOTE

Given the wording of s. 722 and the comments of Hill J, what do you think about the following excerpts from actual VISs filed in *Gabriel*?

> Raymond Gabriel made choices on the night of July 1st that have serious consequences. His mockery of the law resulted in Samantha's death. We have a judicial system in place in Canada that states there are now consequences that he must pay for disobeying the law and taking someone's life. I expect that system to work as the court determines Raymond's consequence. He has taken every future choice that should have existed for Samantha and me and the rest of her family and friends as far as our relationship with her. ...

> It terrifies me to think that Raymond Gabriel may be back on the streets in short time and be in a position to cause more harm to other innocent people in this or some other manner. Based on his prior offences, it's obvious he shuns the law. So if his punishment is deemed to be removal of his license, he's the type that would drive anyway without one. I have worked hard all my life and I've paid my taxes faithfully—I contribute financially into this country in order that among other things, I and my family can be protected. The judicial system exists to protect those who honour it, not those who shun it. Let's not make a mockery of our system and Samantha's life by not allowing Raymond to pay the true debt he owes. ...

> I trust that you will show Raymond Gabriel the same regard that he showed for our dear Samantha.

> I am distressed that in spite of a huge publicity campaign against drinking & driving that there are still criminals that ignore these laws. To be so intoxicated and consciously decide to drive a motor vehicle is the same as pointing a loaded gun at a crowd and firing. I would request that a maximum sentence be imposed to help deter others from considering such actions. I do not feel safe on the roads with drivers like this on the road. ...

Those who breach the law are irresponsible and don't deserve the privilege of driving. I abhor the fact that so much leniency is shown for alcohol abusers. Everyone who was with this man or who served him drinks is responsible for Sam's death. At every family get together we've missed her, at Christmas, her birthday, mother's day. Please help stop this type of crime happening to another family. ...

Your Honourable Judge, as a distraught family member, as a concerned teacher and as a law abiding member of our society, I implore that you will use your authority to uphold the law and send an indisputable message to Mr. Gabriel and others who choose to drink and drive that with every choice comes a proper consequence and equally important—that the worth of a soul is great! ...

No sentence for Mr. Gabriel can bring Samantha back to us—this we know. But we want to know that the forces of justice in Canada are prepared to make a strong statement. We pray that Canada will declare that it is NOT prepared to allow itself to become a place where decent human lives are fair game, to be destroyed by careless and criminally irresponsible people, with no fear of consequence. If Mr. Gabriel is not punished to the maximum allowed by the law, it will demonstrate that the suffering he has caused— suffering which will continue for many years—means nothing. It will show that Canada does not care about the fate of its brightest and most promising asset—its youth! ...

The lesson, that the crime he has committed will not be tolerated in a decent society, must be fully impressed upon him with a just, and adequately severe sentence.

Clearly, a VIS must be relevant to issues that are properly before the court and should not cross into extraneous areas. However, the demarcation lines are not easy to draw and maintain given the personal nature of the victim's input. There can be particular problems related to the oral presentation of a VIS. Although it is relatively easy to vet the contents of a prepared written statement in advance, must the victim be warned not to stray beyond its wording? What if the victim engages in impromptu additions? How should the judge intervene? For an example of the personal and visceral kinds of comments that victims may deliver when given an opportunity to make an oral statement, see *R v. K.L.*, [1999] OJ no. 5085 (SC, per Kurisko J), where one of the victims launched into a personal attack on the offender.

In *Gabriel*, Hill J noted that the 1999 amendments, specifically new s. 722(2.1), would "remove the court's ability to prevent a victim reading an impact statement." Is this correct?

Certainly, the amendments are directed at giving victims a greater role in the decisions about whether and how to present a VIS. But do they have the effect of entirely precluding the judge's discretion to rule that a written statement is the proper manner of presentation? Hill J identified some reasons why a victim should, in specific cases, present a written rather than an oral VIS. Principally, the reasons relate to the health and stability of the victim and the need to ensure security in the courtroom. Can a judge no longer respond to these concerns by requiring a written VIS only? Has s. 722(2.1) elevated the victim's status to almost that of a party? Surely, all Code provisions must be interpreted in the manner that best preserves the integrity and fairness of the judicial process. Does s. 722 (2.1) go too far?

IV. LOOKING TO THE FUTURE

As noted at the beginning of the chapter, the sentencing process is the only juncture in the criminal process where the role of victims has been articulated. The preceding case excerpts demonstrate that the courts still adhere to the traditional dualistic models of criminal justice that do not afford a great role for victims. Nevertheless, Parliament has sought to amplify the voices of victims by amending s. 722 to permit greater knowledge of the rights they have in the process. It seems likely that the next locus of debate will revolve around how the courts interpret s. 722(2.1), which requires a court to permit a victim to read a VIS or present it "in any other manner the court considers appropriate." This right of allocution, which exists in many US jurisdictions, may have a serious, and perhaps undesirable, effect on the tone and mood of Canadian sentencing hearings.

Not all reforms in the name of victims' rights have come from Parliament. As noted in the introduction to this chapter, most provinces and territories have proclaimed victims' bills of rights. These pieces of legislation are largely declaratory and informational. First and foremost, they declare the importance of victims to the criminal process. The rights of victims are also part of Parliament's amendments to the *Criminal Code* in SC 1999, c. 25. This legislation contains the following preamble:

Preamble

Whereas the Parliament of Canada continues to be gravely concerned about the incidence of crime in Canada and its impact on society, particularly on persons who are the victims of offences;

Whereas the Parliament of Canada recognizes that the co-operation of victims of and witnesses to offences is essential to the investigation and prosecution of offences, and wishes to encourage the reporting of offences, and to provide for the prosecution of offences within a framework of laws that are consistent with the principles of fundamental justice;

Whereas the Parliament of Canada recognizes and is committed to ensuring that all persons have the full protection of the rights guaranteed by the *Canadian Charter of Rights and Freedoms* and, in the event of a conflict between the rights of accused persons and victims of and witnesses to offences, that those rights are accommodated and reconciled to the greatest extent possible;

Whereas the Parliament of Canada supports the principle that victims of and witnesses to offences should be treated with courtesy, compassion and respect by the criminal justice system, and should suffer the least amount of inconvenience necessary as a result of their involvement in the criminal justice system;

Whereas the Parliament of Canada, while recognizing that the Crown is responsible for the prosecution of offences, is of the opinion that the views and concerns of the victims should be considered in accordance with prevailing criminal law and procedure, particularly with respect to decisions that may have an impact on their safety, security or privacy;

Whereas the Parliament of Canada wishes to encourage and facilitate the provision of information to victims of and witnesses to offences regarding the criminal justice system and their role in it, and regarding specific decisions that have an impact on them;

Whereas the Parliament of Canada wishes to encourage and facilitate the participation in the criminal justice system of victims of and witnesses to offences in accordance with prevailing criminal law and procedure;

And whereas the Parliament of Canada acknowledges the fundamental importance of an open justice system that treats all persons who come before it with dignity and respect;

Provincial bills of rights also entitle victims to information from police and prosecutors at each stage of the criminal process. However, there is no formal mechanism by which these rights may be enforced against those who fail to measure up to the requirements of the statute.[9] These bills also contain provisions that are relevant to civil litigation.

Because they are provincial enactments, these bills have no *direct* bearing on the participatory rights of victims in criminal proceedings. However, they provide a rich context of victim empowerment in which s. 722 must be interpreted. Thus, these types of enactments and other societal recognition of victims' rights may well have considerable *indirect* impact on the criminal process. Indeed, they may lend legitimacy to the evolution of criminal justice models from dualistic paradigms (accused vs. the state) to more encompassing models that recognize broader victims' interests.

The legitimate needs of victims who have suffered physical injury, personal loss, or financial loss likely extend beyond the criminal justice system, which has a narrower focus and limited resources and is circumscribed by the limits of federal jurisdiction. The practical operation of schemes for the compensation, counselling, and rehabilitation of victims is best dealt with by agencies designed specifically for those purposes. These agencies are often under provincial and territorial jurisdiction. Provincial and territorial statutes that address the role of victims are typically drafted in broad terms that, at least symbolically, champion the rights of victims. The preamble reproduced above is a good example of this approach. However, it is important to ask what resources and/or concrete ameliorative steps, if any, accompany the grand claims made by provincial and territorial legislation bearing upon victims' rights.

---

9 For example, note two limiting provisions in Ontario's *Victims' Bill of Rights, 1995* (SO 1995, c. 6, as amended by SO 1999, c. 6, s. 65). Section 2(1) establishes the basic rights of victims. Section 2(2) provides that the principles set out in s. 2(1) are "subject to the availability of resources and information, what is reasonable in the circumstances of the case, what is consistent with the law and the public interest and what is necessary to ensure that the resolution of criminal proceedings is not delayed." Section 2(5) provides that "no new cause of action, right of appeal, claim or other remedy exists in law because of this section or anything done or omitted to be done under this section."

CHAPTER SEVEN

Plea Discussions and Joint Submissions

I. INTRODUCTION

The preceding chapters on procedure and evidence portray the sentencing process as primarily adversarial in nature. Indeed, it is when matters are in dispute in the criminal justice process that the parties must resort to the rules of evidence and procedure. However, at the sentencing stage, there may be little dispute between the prosecutor and the offender. Although estimates vary, it is beyond dispute that the overwhelming majority of cases are resolved by a guilty plea.[1] Often, guilty pleas follow discussion between the prosecutor and defence counsel about what sentence ought to be imposed. This same process can occur when sentencing follows a finding of guilt at trial.

The practice of plea bargaining continues to be the subject of great controversy both in the legal profession and in the public at large.[2] Every aspect of the practice was considered in the *Report of the Attorney General's Advisory Committee on Charge Screening, Disclosure and Resolution Discussions* (Toronto: Queen's Printer for Ontario, 1993), chaired by the Honourable G.A. Martin ("the Martin report"). This chapter does not retrace the contours of this elaborate debate. Instead, we take as our starting point the Martin report's statement in recommendation 46 (at 281):

> 46. The Committee is of the opinion that resolution discussions are an essential part of the criminal justice system in Ontario, and, when properly conducted, benefit not only the accused, but also victims, witnesses, counsel, and the administration of justice.

This chapter focuses on the extent to which prior arrangements made by counsel can constrain the discretion of the sentencing judge in his or her approach to the sentencing function. As we shall see, the boundaries of these constraints are often elucidated in situations where the sentencing judge rejects the arrangements presented by counsel. It then falls to the appellate courts to unravel what happened and decide whether the judge should have taken the joint submission more seriously.

---

1 See Report of the Canadian Sentencing Commission, *Sentencing Reform: A Canadian Approach* (Ottawa: the commission, 1987), 406.

2 See S.A. Cohen and A.N. Doob, "Public Attitudes to Plea Bargaining" (1989-90), 32 *Crim. LQ* 85.

II. THE JOINT SUBMISSION

A. Definitions

Discussions surrounding joint submissions are often encumbered by problems of nomenclature. Thus, it is important to define relevant terms.

Plea bargains may take many forms. A joint submission is really just one method of plea bargaining.[3] The Canadian Sentencing Commission defines a plea bargain as "any agreement by the accused to plead guilty in return for the promise of some benefit."[4] A plea bargain or plea arrangement may take the form of the Crown's withdrawal of one or more charges in exchange for the accused's guilty plea to one or more charges.[5] There need be no further agreement about the type or quantum of punishment that ought to follow. Similarly, a plea bargain may involve a plea of not guilty to the charge as laid, but a plea of guilty to a lesser and included offence. A good example of this type of arrangement is when an accused person who is charged with murder enters a plea of guilty to the lesser and included offence of manslaughter.

Both of these aspects of the plea-bargaining process are engaged largely without the sentencing judge's input. That is, these types of arrangements are conceived of and driven by counsel, and do not depend on the assent of the sentencing judge.[6] There is little that a sentencing judge can do to upset this type of "charge-bargaining" arrangement. This is not to say, however, that these types of arrangements ought to be shrouded in secrecy. On the contrary, the public interest is better served by the public disclosure of any agreement in open court.[7]

---

3 See S. Verdun-Jones and A. Hatch, *Plea Bargaining and Sentencing Guidelines* (Ottawa: Canadian Sentencing Commission, 1985), 3, where the authors list 13 forms of plea bargaining. These are reproduced in the Report of the Canadian Sentencing Commission, supra note 1, at 404-5.

4 Report of the Canadian Sentencing Commission, ibid., at 404.

5 The plea of guilty may be taken into account as a mitigating factor: see *R v. Johnston and Tremayne*, [1970] 4 CCC 64 (Ont. CA). See *R v. Fegan* (1993), 80 CCC (3d) 356 (Ont. CA), where Finlayson JA (at 8), in discussing the guilty plea, made the following statement: "It is considered by the sentencing judge as an expression of remorse. By expressing finality to the conviction process, it invites leniency in the sentencing portion of the trial." However, this is not always the case. See *Report of the Attorney General's Advisory Committee on Charge Screening, Disclosure and Resolution Discussions* (Toronto: Queen's Printer for Ontario) ("the Martin report"), 310, which emphasizes that the earlier the guilty plea is entered, the greater the mitigation that may be enjoyed. This principle is exemplified in *R v. Pitkeathly* (1994), 29 CR (4th) 182 (Ont. CA).

6 See s. 606(4) of the *Criminal Code*, RSC 1985, c. C-46, as amended. It is recognized that the trial judge is granted the discretion to reject a plea to a lesser offence if the facts do not support such a reduction, although the Court of Appeal for Ontario in *R v. Naraindeen* (1990), 80 CR (3d) 66 (Ont. CA) suggests that some deference ought to be afforded to prosecutorial discretion in this context. The potential for a clash between a judge's discretion and prosecutorial discretion may be avoided if, instead of relying on s. 606(4) to facilitate a plea to a lesser offence, the prosecutor has a new information laid (or a new indictment drafted) to charge the specific offence for which the guilty plea is offered.

7 See the Martin report, supra note 5, at 315-17, where the virtues of openness and accountability of this aspect of the process are discussed. This view is also shared by the Canadian Sentencing Commission, supra note 1, at 422-23. Of course, there will be exceptions to openness where the exigencies of unique circumstances dictate.

The joint submission may be a subset of the broader category of plea bargains or may follow a finding of guilt. There is no magic in the term "joint submission." It simply reflects a process whereby both counsel advocate the same disposition for the offender. Such an arrangement may be attached to other arrangements like those discussed above, or it may be the only aspect of the case on which counsel agree. However, it is unique in that it takes effect only on the assent of the sentencing judge. The following discussion of what consideration must be given to joint submissions centres on the judicial role. What is the test for rejecting a joint submission? If the sentencing judge decides to reject a joint submission, what are the offender's options (if any)?

B. The Treatment of the Joint Submission: Sentencing Judge Not Bound

The practice of Canadian courts has been somewhat inconsistent in dealing with the treatment of joint submissions. On the one hand, the courts have recognized the value of plea arrangements and demonstrated concern for the consequences that would accrue if judges were to give them little consideration. On the other hand, it is vital to preserve judicial independence and integrity by allowing sentencing judges to refuse to accede to a joint submission when circumstances dictate.

In the following case of *R v. Rubenstein*, the offender entered a plea of guilty to two fraud charges. After the pleas of guilty, the facts were conveyed to the court along with a joint submission whereby it was agreed that Rubenstein would receive a suspended sentence and would be placed on probation. Rubenstein was also prepared to consent to a sizable compensation order. During the presentation of submissions, it became clear that the sentencing judge would not accede to the joint submission. Rubenstein sought to withdraw his pleas of guilty. The trial judge refused, and sentenced Rubenstein to five years' imprisonment. Rubenstein appealed his conviction and sentence to the Court of Appeal for Ontario.

R v. Rubenstein
(1987), 41 CCC (3d) 91 (Ont. CA)

ZUBER JA:

...

Judge Draper concluded his remarks in which he refused to allow the withdrawal of the guilty pleas as follows:

> I'm certainly not going to allow a procedure in which you make a ... in which defence counsel makes a proposal, and when the Judge indicates it's unacceptable wishes to withdraw his plea. That would result in Judge shopping in the worst reprehensible way. That application to withdraw the plea is denied.

...

It is not argued that the trial judge was in any way bound by the joint submissions. He was obliged to give serious consideration to the joint submission and he did so, but in the end he plainly and strongly disagreed with the joint submission.

It is argued in this court that when a trial judge regards the joint submission with respect to sentence as unreasonable or in error he should so inform an accused and give that accused an opportunity to withdraw the plea. It is argued that to do otherwise would be fundamentally unfair since an accused in the position of an appellant offers the plea in the expectation that the joint submission will be followed. It was further argued that the joint submission was the *quid pro quo* for the pleas of guilty and therefore the failure of the trial judge to heed the joint submission entitled the accused to be restored to his original position, i.e., he could force the Crown to prove its case against him in full.

I disagree with this proposition. The power of the trial Judge to impose a sentence cannot be limited to a joint submission, and the joint submission cannot be the basis upon which to escape the sentencing judge when it appears that he chooses to reject the joint submission. As Judge Draper observed, an accused who could thus withdraw his plea could simply keep doing so until he found a trial judge who would accept a joint submission. A plea of guilty in the same way as a finding of guilt after trial exposes an accused to a proper sentence to be determined by the trial judge. In the case on appeal the difference between the sentence sought by the joint submission and that imposed by the trial judge was stark but that does not affect the principle involved. To permit an accused to withdraw his plea when the sentence does not suit him puts the court in the unseemly position of bargaining with the accused.

While a judge has a discretion to allow the withdrawal of a plea of guilty, Judge Draper was right in refusing to allow the withdrawal of the pleas of guilty in this case. The appeal against conviction is dismissed.

In *Rubenstein*, the court did allow the appeal against sentence, and imposed a sentence of two years less a day and a $25,000 fine. Consider the more exacting standard articulated by the Martin committee in its recommendation in this area.

Report of the Attorney General's Advisory Committee on Charge Screening, Disclosure, and Resolution Discussions
(Honourable G.A. Martin, QC, Chair)
(Toronto: Queen's Printer for Ontario, 1993)

...

58. The Committee is of the opinion that a sentencing judge should not depart from a joint submission unless the proposed sentence would bring the administration of justice into disrepute, or is otherwise not in the public interest.

As discussed above, the law is clear that a joint submission as to sentence is entitled to great weight, but does not bind the sentencing judge, who is the ultimate arbiter of what sentence should be imposed at first instance. See *R v. Rubenstein*, supra. (Ont. CA). This rule ensures that sentences will always be meted out by an impartial decision-maker, and prevents inappropriate inducements to an accused person to plead guilty in exchange for a promise of a given sentence. However, in light of the recommendations that the Committee has made on both the practice and procedure respecting resolution discussions, the Committee thinks it appropriate to comment on what it means to give a joint submission great weight in the context of resolution discussions conducted in accordance with those recommendations.

The Committee has, for the reasons discussed above at some length, concluded that resolution discussions are inherently desirable, and of considerable practical benefit to the administration of criminal justice in Ontario. Recognizing that the practice of resolution discussions, even though inherently desirable, is open to some misuse and to some misunderstanding by the public at large, the Committee has formulated a series of recommendations aimed at eradicating the problems, both real and perceived, that are associated with unrestrained resolution discussions. Accordingly, if the recommendations of the Committee are followed in their entirety, there will be in place in Ontario, in the Committee's view, a regime whereby the benefits of resolution discussions and the resolution agreements they lead to can be enjoyed without any residual concern that the resolutions arrived at are the product of a flawed process. It is in the context of this state of affairs that the Committee recommends that a sentencing judge should depart from the joint submission offered only where it would bring the administration of justice into disrepute or would otherwise be contrary to the public interest.

The Committee recognizes that an important, sometimes the most important, factor in counsel's ability to conclude resolution agreements, thereby deriving the benefits that such agreements bring, is that of certainty. Accused persons are, in the Committee's experience, prepared to waive their right to a trial far more readily if the outcome of such a waiver is certain, than they are for the purely speculative possibility that the outcome will bear some resemblance to what counsel have agreed to. And likewise, from the perspective of Crown counsel, agreed upon resolutions that have a stronger, rather than weaker sense of certainty to them, are more desirable because there is less risk that what Crown counsel concludes is an appropriate resolution of the case in the public interest will be undercut.

Since certainty of outcomes facilitates resolution discussions and agreements, and since resolution agreements, as the Committee views them, are beneficial and fair, it follows, in the Committee's view, that certainty in outcomes of resolution discussions should be promoted. Naturally, the outcomes of resolution discussions would be perfectly certain if there were a rule that a judge could not depart from them. As discussion above in the introduction to this chapter, other jurisdictions approach this state of affairs by permitting the plea to be struck if the sentencing judge does not accept the joint submission. But this is not the law in Ontario, nor, in the Committee's view, should it be. It is fundamental to our system of justice that the courts, not the parties, have the last word.

While the presiding judge cannot have his or her sentencing discretion removed by the fact of there being a joint submission, it is none the less appropriate, in the Committee's view, for the sentencing judge to have regard to the interest of certainty in resolution discussions when faced with a joint submission. Accordingly, where there is no reason in the public interest or in the need to preserve the repute of the administration of justice to depart from a joint submission, the sentencing judge should, in the Committee's opinion, give effect to the need for certainty in agreed upon resolutions by accepting the joint submission of counsel.

In *R v. Wood*, supra, at 574, the Ontario Court of Appeal noted that serious consideration should be given to recommendations of Crown counsel "where the facts outlined, following a guilty plea, are sparse." The Court went on to observe that the sentencing Court "has to recognize that Crown counsel is more familiar than itself with the extenuating or aggravating circumstances of the offence which may not be fully disclosed in the summary of the facts." The Committee wishes to emphasize that it is not making the present recommendation in order to increase such reliance by the Court upon counsel's bare recommendation as to sentence. The Committee is of the view that the record created in sentencing proceedings should not be sparse, but, rather, must always fully support the submissions made. The Committee so recommends below, where the issue is discussed in greater detail. In encouraging the sentencing judge to place appropriate emphasis upon a joint submission, the Committee is thereby placing a corollary obligation upon counsel to amply justify their position on the facts of the case as presented in open court.

Proceeding in a manner consistent with the present recommendation at a sentencing hearing where a joint submission is proposed accords, in the Committee's view, appropriate weight to the "ample" discretion possessed by the Crown as to the conduct of any given prosecution. The Court of Appeal has recognized in *R v. Naraindeen*, supra, at 72, that sentencing courts should not be "gratuitously interfering with a prosecutorial decision." Yet, proceeding in this manner also continues to ensure that the sentencing judge remains the ultimate arbiter of the propriety of the sentence, and that the sentence is demonstrated to be fit in the circumstances. The sentencing judge will not, in the Committee's view, have committed any error in principle in accepting a joint submission, as recommended above, provided he or she arrives, at the independent conclusion, based upon an adequate record, that the sentence proposed does not bring the administration of justice into disrepute and is otherwise not contrary to the public interest. Indeed, this recommendation embodies the essence of the sentencing judge's obligations in passing sentence. In so recommending, the Committee has endeavoured to define the discretion of the sentencing judge in sufficiently broad terms to ensure that the sentence imposed is ultimately just, but at the same time has accorded the parties as much assurance as can be had that their agreed-upon resolutions will find favour with the Court. In this way, it is hoped that the justice system and the community as a whole can profit to the greatest extent possible from the benefits of resolution discussions.

For another example of a situation where the sentencing judge refused to accept a joint submission, see *R v. Winn* (1995), 43 CR (4th) 71 (Ont. Ct. (Prov. Div.)). The accused entered a plea of guilty to an extremely serious sexual assault. A joint submission of 7 years' imprisonment was presented to the sentencing judge. In rejecting this submission and imposing a sentence of 12 years' imprisonment, Fairgrieve Prov. Ct. J articulated the following test:

The Court of Appeal has made it clear that a trial judge is obliged to give serious consideration to a joint submission: *R v. Rubenstein*. ... More recently it has been stated that a joint submission can properly be rejected only where a court is of the view that the proposed sentence is so unreasonable or contrary to the public interest that its acceptance would bring the administration of justice into disrepute: see, for example, *R v. Kirisit* (Ont. CA, August 11, 1993, unreported). I accept as well the principle that a trial court should not impose a sentence which exceeds that sought by the Crown unless there is a valid and compelling reason to do so: see *R v. Farizeh* [reported at 78 OAC 399]; *R v. Bahati* [reported at 78 OAC 397].[8]

Is there a qualitative difference in the various standards expressed by the courts and in the Martin report? Given the difficulty in applying standards such as the "public interest" (see *R v. Morales* (1992), 77 CCC (3d) 91 (SCC)), are these standards satisfactory?

III. SENTENCE APPEALS AND JOINT SUBMISSIONS

Appellate review of sentencing decisions is a complex aspect of the law. Although it has inspired a great deal of activity over the last number of years, it is beyond the scope of this chapter to delve into the nuances of this area.[9] However, it is important to examine the impact of joint submissions in the appellate sphere. As discussed in previous chapters, the sentencing judge at first instance is granted substantial discretion in determining an appropriate sentence. The power of the courts of appeal to review sentencing decisions is found in s. 687 of the *Criminal Code*. This section provides as follows:

> 687(1) Where an appeal is taken against sentence, the court of appeal shall, unless the sentence is one fixed by law, consider the fitness of sentence appealed against, and may on such evidence, if any, as it thinks fit to require or to receive,
>
> (a) vary the sentence within the limits prescribed by law for the accused was convicted; or
>
> (b) dismiss the appeal.

Although this appellate power appears to be quite broad on its face, recent cases from the Supreme Court of Canada have narrowed the scope of review considerably. The Supreme Court has sent a clear message that the decisions of sentencing judges must be approached with great deference. Now courts of appeal may intervene only if there was an error in principle or if the sentence imposed at first instance was "demonstrably unfit" or "clearly unreasonable." See *R v. Shropshire* (1995), 102 CCC (3d) 193 (SCC); *R v. C.A.M.* (1996), 46 CR (4th) 269 (SCC); and *R v. McDonnell* (1997), 114 CCC (3d) 436 (SCC).

---

8 The decision of Fairgrieve Prov. Ct. J was upheld by the Court of Appeal for Ontario (see (1998), 38 OR (3d) 159 (CA)). A similar approach to joint submissions was demonstrated by Fairgrieve Prov. Ct. J in *R v. Artinian* (1995), 25 CR (3d) 433 (Ont. Ct. (Prov. Div.)). However, in this case, the sentencing judge's rejection of the joint submission was overturned on appeal (see (1995), 26 OR (3d) 640 (Gen. Div.)).

9 See A. Manson, "The Supreme Court Intervenes in Sentencing" (1996), 43 CR (4th) 306 and G. Trotter, "Appellate Review of Sentencing Decisions," in J.V. Roberts and D.P. Cole, eds., *Making Sense of Sentencing* (Toronto: University of Toronto Press, 1999).

A. Appeals by the Offender

The appropriateness of a joint submission can arise in two situations when the offender launches an appeal. First, the offender may appeal on the basis that the sentencing judge erred in failing to abide by a joint submission. The other situation is where the sentencing judge imposes a sentence in accordance with the joint submission but, on appeal, the offender disavows the joint submission and contends that the sentence is unfit.

In the cases that follow, consider whether the interests that are said to be recognized by joint submissions are respected. In *R v. Wood*, the offender was charged with second-degree murder in the stabbing death of his spouse. The Crown agreed to accept a plea of manslaughter, but only on the condition that the offender join in a submission that he be sentenced to 14 years' imprisonment. The sentencing judge acceded to the joint submission and imposed the sentence suggested. However, he also made a recommendation that the offender not be released on parole until at least one half of his sentence had been served. The offender appealed.

R v. Wood
(1988), 43 CCC (3d) 570 (Ont. CA)

LACOURCIÈRE JA:

...

It is trite law that the court always retains an overriding discretion to accept or reject any recommendations of counsel with respect to the quantum of sentence, even where a joint submission is made by experienced counsel: *R v. Simoneau* (1978), 40 CCC (2d) 307 (Man. CA). But, it is also clear that serious consideration should be given by the court to recommendations of Crown counsel, particularly where the facts outlined, following a guilty plea, are sparse. The court then has to recognize that Crown counsel is more familiar than itself with the extenuating or aggravating circumstances of the offence which may not be fully disclosed in the summary of facts: see *R v. Fleury* (1971), 23 CRNS 164 (Que. CA).

While the Crown generally will not be a allowed to repudiate a position taken at trial where the accused has relied on his position before entering a guilty plea, Crown counsel has no authority to bind the Attorney-General in the exercise of his discretion to appeal. The ultimate responsibility to determine the fitness of sentence is on the Court of Appeal: *R v. Simoneau*, supra. ... Certainly the accused is given greater latitude than the Crown on an appeal of this kind in that he is generally not bound to the same extent by the submissions of his counsel as to sentence.

...

In *R v. Head* [(1985), 10 OAC 87], this court reduced a sentence of 11 years imposed after a plea of guilty to manslaughter, following a charge of second degree murder. The reduction to seven years was made notwithstanding a joint submission by defence and Crown counsel at trial that the proper range was between 10 and 15 years, a range which the Court of Appeal found to be in error.

In the present case, the learned trial judge indicated his awareness of the case-law with respect to joint submissions and, in agreeing with the joint submission, he said:

> The problem for any trial judge in sentencing is to decide on the fitness of the sentence to be imposed and I am always prepared to consider the recommendations of counsel as to their views on the range of sentence, particularly when their observations fall within the range which is normally imposed for offences of this kind, but there is a duty on the judge to ignore such recommendations if, in his view, they are improper, because a sentence is a matter of public interest and should be consistent with the gravity of the offence and the relevant facts and all the cogent surrounding circumstances. I may say that I am in accord with the sentence proposed of 14 years. I think it falls within the reasonable range for a crime of this nature and the circumstances under which it was committed.

However, in analyzing the competing principles to be considered in determining the fitness of sentence, we believe that the learned trial judge over-emphasized the incidence of violent crimes in the community and the need for general deterrence for the protection of society. In doing so, in our view, he failed to give sufficient weight to the appellant's obvious remorse and to his incipient rehabilitation. In addition, no reference was made on the available record, or in the reasons for sentence, to the 16-month period of pre-trial incarceration.

The facts disclose a spontaneous stabbing following a family quarrel in circumstances where both the appellant and the victim had ingested alcohol and drugs. There was room for doubt as to the requisite intent for murder. In our view, it was appropriate for Crown counsel to consent to the plea of manslaughter. But, in our view, the Crown overreached in attaching a condition of a joint submission to a sentence which was far in excess of the usual range of sentences for manslaughter in the circumstances of the present case. The condition placed the accused, as well as experienced defence counsel, in a difficult position and to some extent may have hampered the trial judge. It would have been preferable to submit an appropriate range of sentence and to let the trial judge determine the sentence.

· · ·

Having regard to the gravity of the offence, the mitigating circumstances, the appellant's pre-trial custody, his sincere remorse and his exemplary institutional record and notwithstanding the joint submission at trial, we think an appropriate and fit sentence would be eight years. The trial judge's recommendation to the Parole Board should be disregarded, but the s. 98 order for a period of 10 years will stand.

Was it fair for Lacourcière JA to conclude that the joint submission "may have hampered" the trial judge? Should the Court of Appeal have so easily disregarded the opinion (reflected in the agreement to the joint submission) of very experienced defence counsel as to Wood's chances of being convicted of second-degree murder?

Consider the following case of *R v. Sriskanthararjah*, in which the offender pleaded not guilty to two counts of first-degree murder in the deaths of her two daughters. After the trial started, the offender entered pleas of guilty to two counts of manslaughter. In accordance with a joint submission, the trial judge imposed sentences of six years' imprisonment, to be served concurrently on each count. In acceding to the joint submission, the trial judge recounted a litany of mitigating factors. The offender was depressed, virtually abandoned by her husband (who otherwise abused her), and left to raise her two young children (one of whom had been brain damaged) in a country where she did not speak the language of the dominant culture. The trial judge stated that "Ms Sriskantharajah progressively regressed into a state of chronic depression of crippling and monumental proportions." The offender appealed her sentence.

R v. Sriskantharajah
(1994), 90 CCC (3d) 559 (Ont. CA)

FINLAYSON JA:

...

It was conceded that there is no danger of the appellant re-offending and she is not a risk to society. As counsel for the Crown put it, she is a greater risk to herself than to anyone else.

The court received fresh evidence which supports counsel for the appellant's submission that the cultural and linguistic isolation of the appellant, a Tamil from Sri Lanka, would be alleviated to some extent if she could be incarcerated in Toronto where she would be in contact with Parkdale Community Legal Services, the South Asian Women's Centre, and the Elizabeth Fry Society of Toronto, all of which have agreed to co-operate in a program directed to teaching her English and assisting her in re-integrating into the community. These facilities are not available to the same extent in the Kingston Prison for Women.

This court has stated repeatedly that it will not lightly interfere with a sentence imposed following a joint recommendation, but I do not agree with the submission of the Crown that the burden rests upon the appellant to demonstrate that the sentence imposed would bring the administration of justice into disrepute. In this case, it is worth noting that the sentence imposed amounts really to 10 years, which was reduced by the trial judge to six years in order to give the appellant credit for two years of pretrial custody. I note also that the trial judge stated that in ordinary circumstances he would have considered the recommend range of sentence (10 to 12 years) to be markedly excessive.

In support of her contention that this court must be satisfied that the sentence imposed by the trial judge would bring the administration of justice into disrepute, counsel for the Crown referred the court to *the Report of the Attorney General's Advisory Committee on Charge Screening, Disclosure and Resolution Discussions* (chaired by the Honourable G. Arthur Martin, QC) [excerpt contained in passage reproduced above].

...

I acknowledge the appropriateness of this recommendation, especially as an admonition against imposing sentences that are too lenient, but, as stated in the excerpt, the sentence must be in the public interest, embracing a variety of concerns. Certainly, there can be no suggestion that review of these arrangements by this court is not to be exercised in an appropriate case. Deference to this court in these matters appears to be accepted by the Martin Report (at p. 332):

> Appellate review is essential to ensure that sentences imposed following resolution discussions are, at all times, within an appropriate range. Permitting Crown counsel in the appellate courts to take a position that need not necessarily accord with the position taken by the Crown at trial, permits the Crown to assist the appellate courts as fully as possible in discharging their duty to ensure that the trial courts have resolved cases in a manner that is fit and just.

The Committee notes that the rule permitting Crown appeals from joint submissions is complemented by a similar rule benefitting an accused. Indeed, the Ontario Court of Appeal has stated in *R v. Wood* that:

> "Certainly the accused is given greater latitude than the Crown on an appeal of this kind in that he is generally not bound to the same extent by the submissions of his counsel as to sentence."

The Court went on to observe that, ultimately, the fitness of the sentence imposed, not the positions of the parties, is the dominant consideration.

This case is exceptional. The appellant was diagnosed at the Clarke Institute of Psychiatry as suffering from a major depression combined with a mixed personality disorder. This depression significantly impacted upon the appellant's judgment. Her perception of life, its reality and future prospects were negatively or fatalistically skewed by this depression. Suicide became the only logical solution to her problems. In the circumstances of this crime and this particular accused, a plea bargain made eminent sense and was in the best interest of justice. However, the sentence recommended in the joint submission was simply too long.

A non-penitentiary sentence is justified where, as here, the case demonstrates that the offence arose from the compulsion of mental illness, the offender poses little or no risk to the community, there is no significant risk of re-offence and an appropriate treatment and rehabilitation is available.

...

Accordingly, leave to appeal is granted, the appeal is allowed and the sentence is reduced to a reformatory term of two years less one day to be followed by a period of probation for three years. In addition to the usual terms of probation, such as an undertaking to be of good peace and be of good behaviour, it is recommended that the appellant seek and continue to receive treatment and counselling as recommended by her probation officer. The order prohibiting the appellant from possessing any firearm, ammunition or explosive for life pursuant to s. 100 of the *Criminal Code* ... is undisturbed.

What was the precise basis upon which the Court of Appeal intervened in this case? Given the more deferential standard of review signalled by the Supreme Court of Canada in the *Shropshire* line of cases, would *Sriskantharajah* be decided differently today?

It is fair to say that the overwhelming majority of joint submissions are accepted by sentencing judges and left undisturbed by courts of appeal. The decisions reproduced in this chapter are therefore atypical. Still, these are the cases that find their way into the law reports and attract considerable attention. What effect do cases like *Rubenstein*, *Wood*, and *Sriskantharajah* have on plea bargaining in general?

Another issue that sometimes arises in appeals against sentence by the offender (where the trial judge imposes a sentence in excess of the joint submission) is whether the Crown is duty-bound to maintain the "agreement" on appeal. The range of possible answers to this question is apparent in the discussion of the limits on the Crown in the next section.

B. Appeals by the Crown

Cases involving joint submissions may sometimes result in an appeal by the Crown. Situations where the sentencing judge disregards a joint submission and imposes a more *lenient* sentence are straightforward and would seem to call into play the principles reflected in the cases cited above. However, what principles apply when the sentencing judge accepts the joint submission, but the Crown appeals in any event?

Consider the scenario in the leading case of *R v. Dubien*. Dubien was charged with raping a 14-year-old girl. During the trial, a discussion about a possible plea transpired between the accused, the Crown, and the trial judge. The accused offered to plead guilty to attempted rape because the Crown had stated that if the accused were found guilty of rape at the conclusion of trial, it would seek to have the accused declared a dangerous offender. The trial judge indicated that he would sentence the accused to 5 years in prison, even though the Crown indicated that it would submit that an appropriate sentence was 7 to 10 years. The Crown also indicated that it would not recommend an appeal if 5 years were imposed. The trial judge imposed a sentence of 5 years' imprisonment. The attorney general for Ontario launched an appeal against the sentence.

R v. Dubien
(1982), 67 CCC (2d) 341 (Ont. CA)

MacKINNON ACJO: This is an application by the Crown for leave to appeal and, if leave be granted, an appeal from a sentence imposed of five years after a plea of guilty to a charge of rape.

The application for leave to appeal is strenuously opposed on the ground that the Crown is "estopped" from appealing as, it is argued, the respondent relied on the position taken by Crown counsel at the trial and changed his plea to guilty on the basis of that "position."

· · ·

Crown counsel restated his intention to seek a sentence of seven to ten years upon a plea of guilty to rape. The trial judge indicated that he would give a sentence of five years in any event. The Crown further indicated that he felt that a term of five years was lenient, but not so lenient as to be likely to be appealed. The Crown indicated to defence counsel that in the event the respondent now pleaded guilty to rape, and in the event that the respondent was sentenced to a term of five years, Crown counsel would not recommend to the Crown law office that the sentence be appealed. He further expressed the opinion that in the absence of such a recommendation from the Assistant Crown Attorney who prosecuted the case no appeal as to sentence would be launched. *It was stated and understood, however, that the Assistant Crown Attorney in charge of the prosecution of the trial had no power to bind the Attorney General on matters of appeal and that the ultimate decision would be his* (emphasis added).

Counsel again withdrew so that defence counsel might receive further instructions from his client. Defence counsel subsequently indicated in chambers that based upon the above discussions he had received written instructions from his client that his client was prepared to change his plea to guilty of rape on the understanding that he would be sentenced to five years with a recommendation that the sentence would be served in a hospital setting.

...

The Assistant Crown Attorney did not recommend an appeal; the matter came to the attention of the office of the Attorney General independently of the Crown Attorney's office and this application for leave to appeal resulted.

...

Counsel for the respondent argues that the whole system of "plea bargaining" will collapse if leave to appeal is given. It was an *in terrorem* submission that has little relevance to the facts of this case. The Attorney General's hands cannot be tied because counsel for the respondent failed to give his client a complete exposition of the Crown's position, namely, that Crown counsel could not and was not purporting to bind the Attorney General's exercise of his authority to decide whether an appeal should or should not be taken from the sentence imposed in the instant case.

On reviewing the material filed on the appeal one cannot help feeling that even if counsel had fully explained to the respondent the Crown's position as to the rights and duties of the Attorney General, it would have made no difference to his decision to plead guilty. He had succeeded in having the threat of an application to have him declared a dangerous offender withdrawn and he knew that he was going to receive a five year sentence whether he pleaded guilty to rape or attempted rape and he knew that counsel for the Crown would not recommend an appeal no matter how upset he was at that sentence. When the trial was completed with the sentencing there was no repudiation by Crown counsel of any of his "undertakings" to which he attached the caveat already noted.

Counsel for the respondent submitted that to grant the Attorney General leave to appeal would bring the whole administration of justice into question and destroy the necessary trust which must exist between the Crown and defence counsel. I do not agree. Of course discussions between counsel can be appropriate and helpful in certain Cases and I can think of many situations where there is an "understanding," based on many relevant factors and experience, between counsel, which the Attorney General would not seek to repudiate. But that is not this case. Counsel for the Crown made it quite clear that the Attorney General could still exercise his discretion in the matter of an appeal, and that he (Crown counsel) was "upset" (to use the terminology of the respondent in his affidavit) about the proposed sentence of five years, even though he would not recommend an appeal if such a sentence were imposed. Even if he had not "conditioned" his understanding, counsel for the Crown could not take away the discretion vested in the Attorney General to determine whether an appeal should or should not be taken or the obligation imposed on this court to consider the fitness of the sentence when the matter is before us.

With great deference to the very experienced and able trial judge, I am of the view that it is not advisable for a judge to take any active part in discussions as to sentence before a plea has been taken, nor to encourage indirectly a plea of guilty by indicating what his sentence will be. It was apparent in the instant case that the sentence was going to be the same whether the respondent changed his plea or not, and there was no suggestion or implication so far as the trial judge was concerned, that the sentence would be lighter if the respondent changed his plea to guilty. A trial judge can only determine what a just sentence should be after he has heard all relevant evidence in open court on that subject and listened to the submissions of counsel.

One would expect that if there was essential agreement between counsel in their submissions as to the "usual" sentence, that would carry weight, and the Crown's position at trial would be a circumstance for an appeal court to consider in considering the fitness of the sentence appealed against: *R v. Wood* (1975), 26 CCC (2d) 100 (Alta. CA). In *R v. Turner*, [1970] 2 QB 321 at p. 327, Lord Parker CJ stated that the only exception to the rule that the judge should never indicate the sentence he has in mind to impose is where it may be helpful to indicate, "whether the accused pleads guilty or not guilty, the sentence will or will not take a particular form, e.g., a probation order or a fine, or a custodial sentence."

It seems to me that the failure of the Attorney General to raise the question of the fitness of the sentence under the circumstances of this case would be more likely to bring the administration of justice into disrepute than otherwise. There was an error, in my view, in the sentence imposed of such a nature as to require the Attorney General, in the discharge of his duty, to appeal that sentence to ensure that the administration of justice is fairly and properly carried out. The appeal, as I have stated, is not a repudiation of the Crown's qualified position at trial. I would grant leave to appeal.

In *Dubien*, the Court of Appeal allowed the appeal and substituted a sentence of nine years' imprisonment. In a sense, the court was not required to address squarely the issue of the Crown repudiating an agreement. Had the assistant Crown attorney in *Dubien* recommended an appeal to the attorney general, how might this have altered the court's response? See *R v. Agozzino*, [1970] 1 CCC 380 (Ont. CA) and *Attorney General of Canada v. Roy* (1972), 18 CRNS 89 (Que. QB). Is it a relevant consideration that the position of Crown counsel at trial "induced" or "encouraged" a plea of guilty? If it did not, should a court of appeal feel less constrained to assess the fitness of sentence? See *R v. Dubuc* (1998), 131 CCC (3d) 250 (Que. CA) and *R v. Neale*, [2000] BCJ no. 668 (CA), which contain the suggestion that the contingency of a guilty plea is a very important consideration whether a joint submission on appeal is enforceable. In other words, is there a qualitative difference between a joint submission that essentially induces a guilty plea and one that does not? Is one entitled to more deference than the other?

Consider whether the position expressed in the following excerpt from the Martin report strikes a balance that is fair.

Report of the Attorney General's Advisory Committee on Charge Screening, Disclosure, and Resolution Discussions
(Honourable G.A. Martin, QC, Chair)
(Toronto: Queen's Printer for Ontario, 1993)

...

59. The Committee observes that Crown counsel at trial cannot bind the Attorney General's discretion to appeal. The Committee recommends that where Crown counsel at trial agrees to a joint submission which the sentencing judge accepts, the Attorney General should appeal only where the sentence is so wrong as to bring the administration of justice into disrepute.

While it is clear that neither Crown nor defence counsel on appeal is bound in law by the position of the Crown at trial, the Committee recognizes that such a rule has great potential to undermine the finality of resolution agreements. This in turn may reduce the tendency for resolution agreements to be pursued, thereby diminishing the advantages which they offer, as discussed above. There is an important need for certainty in resolution agreement outcomes that appellate counsel must respect, in the same manner as a sentencing judge should respect the need for certainty when imposing sentence following a joint submission. Accordingly, the Committee has recommended that where Crown counsel at trial has agreed to a joint submission which the sentencing judge has accepted, that sentence should be appealed by the Crown only where the sentence is so wrong as to bring the administration of justice into disrepute. Much like the balance struck in the Committee's recommendation with respect to sentencing on a joint submission at the trial level, the Committee is of the view that this recommendation strikes the appropriate balance at the appellate level between ensuring resolution agreement outcomes are final, and preserving the role of the Attorney General's appellate counsel in ensuring the due administration of criminal justice. The Committee also observes that in may be undesirable for an accused person to appeal as a matter of course from a sentence imposed that is in accordance with a joint submission.

It is important to note that, while the present recommendation is similar in some respects to the recommendation concerning sentencing on a joint submission at trial, it does have a significant difference. The Committee has recommended that the sentencing judge may depart from a joint submission if the sentence proposed would bring the administration of justice into disrepute or if the sentence is not in the public interest. However, the Committee has recommended that the Crown should appeal from an accepted joint submission only if the sentence imposed would bring the administration of justice into disrepute. Thus, in the Committee's view, the circumstances in which it is appropriate for the Crown to appeal against a joint submission sentence are more limited than the circumstances in which it is appropriate for the sentencing judge to depart from a joint submission. The Crown's right to appeal from a joint submission sentence should not be exercised simply to seek minor adjustments or refinements to a sentence. Rather, the Crown should appeal only where the sentence imposed pursuant to a joint submission represents an error so grave as to bring the administration of justice into disrepute.

There are few common law jurisdictions that accord the Crown rights of appeal as broad as those found in the *Criminal Code*. The Committee's recommendation with respect to launching Crown appeals following a sentence imposed in accordance with a joint submission is therefore consistent with traditional notions of restraint which should invariably accompany the exercise of the Crown's right of appeal. Such restraint recognizes the importance for preserving, to the greatest extent possible, the finality of resolution agreements entered into by the Crown. It also recognizes that both the joint submission itself and the fact that it was accepted by the sentencing judge as not being contrary to the public interest, must be accorded due weight by appellate Crown counsel considering an appeal.

This chapter has addressed several aspects of plea bargaining in the sentencing process. There are, however, many other aspects of plea bargaining that are worthy of discussion, especially those that are practical in nature. Some issues that have not been addressed relate to matters such as the judge's role in resolution discussions, the prospect of counsel approaching judges in chambers to discuss a proposed resolution, the obligation to explain bargains on the public record, and a lawyer's duty to another lawyer when disavowing a plea bargain entered into by previous counsel. Local plea-bargaining practices vary so significantly that it is not possible to canvass them here. However, the Martin report is a good place to start any assessment of the procedural aspects of plea bargaining and joint submissions.

CHAPTER EIGHT

Diversion and Discharges

Sentencing options are set out in part XXIII of the *Criminal Code*, RSC 1985, c. C-46, as amended, starting with discharges—the least intrusive—and moving to imprisonment—the most serious and restrictive sanction available under Canadian law. Most dispositions follow conviction. Two forms of disposition, diversion and discharges, do not follow conviction. Diversion is concerned with the removal of a case from prosecution. A discharge may be given after a finding of guilt. This chapter and subsequent chapters will discuss these options following the order in which they appear in the Code.

I. DIVERSION

Section 717 provides statutory authorization for "alternative measures" for adults. Both the term and the specific provision were taken from s. 4 of the *Young Offenders Act*, RSC 1985, c. Y-1. Of course, offenders had been diverted from prosecution informally through the exercise of police or prosecutorial discretion long before s. 717 was enacted in 1996. Warnings by a police officer are a form of diversion. Similarly, taking steps to place a person under a mental health regime rather than the criminal process is a form of diversion. Some communities have developed volunteer diversion programs that work with offenders after they have been diverted from prosecution.

The Code provides a framework for diversion programs that are expressly authorized by the attorney general of a province. In a case governed by the *Young Offenders Act*, the Crown prosecutor determines whether the offender will be admitted into such a program, which requires the offender's consent and acceptance of responsibility. The requirement for a decision by the Crown prosecutor is not stated expressly in s. 717 but s. 717(1)(f) precludes the admission of an offender to alternative measures unless the prosecutor is satisfied that there is sufficient evidence for prosecution. Thus, even in jurisdictions where charges are authorized by police officers rather than Crown prosecutors, the Code seems to imply that any case where diversion is considered must be reviewed by a Crown prosecutor. There is no obvious reason why this should be required in every case, although there is merit in the notion that diversion schemes should be monitored for consistency, effectiveness, and accountability. If it is Parliament's intention in paragraph (f) to require the participation of prosecutors in individual decisions concerning diversion, it follows that the successful operation of diversion programs will require specialized teams of prosecutors. Some provinces have provided for this already, but others have not. A complicating factor in these matters is that, by its nature, diversion typically works best before a charge is contemplated.

A more perplexing question about the operation of diversion schemes lies in the requirement of approval by the attorney general or his delegate (s. 717(1)(a)). At a broad level of abstraction, it makes sense that if offenders may be diverted from prosecution, there should be some assurance that programs of alternative measures should be approved by a responsible public authority. There are also technical questions that might be raised concerning the manner in which such approval is given and publicized. But the most pressing question, and one that carries the greatest uncertainty across Canada, is whether diversion is *unavailable* in the absence of formal approval. The ramifications of this issue are significant. If formal approval is required for any program of alternative measures, it follows that the mechanism of approval will determine whether diversion will exist at all in a given jurisdiction, the type of diversion that is permitted, and the geographical distribution of such programs within the jurisdiction. The approval of the attorney general or his or her delegate, of course, will extend not only to specific programs of alternative measures; he or she can also issue administrative directives that *disapprove* the use of diversion for certain classes of offenders or offences.

With respect to programs of alternative measures authorized by s. 4 of the *Young Offenders Act*, the Supreme Court of Canada affirmed in *R v. S.(S.)* (1990), 77 CR (3d) 273 (SCC) and *R v. S.(G.)* (1990), 77 CR (3d) 303 (SCC) that the provincial authority is granted a discretion to decide whether there will be such programs within that jurisdiction and, if so, on what terms or conditions they will operate. This means, as the court stated, that there might be wide disparity among provinces with respect to the existence of diversion schemes and the manner in which they work. It should be no surprise that provinces, like people, differ in their enthusiasm for diversion schemes. Some are opposed to them on principle. Some recoil at the administrative burden of supervision they entail. Some are concerned about the fiscal implications involved in providing financial support for the operation of diversion schemes.

Many offences and offenders do not warrant full prosecution and diversion is often a useful and cost-effective alternative. Indeed, in many cases, the aims of rehabilitation and restorative justice find full expression in diversion rather than prosecution. Still, questions remain: Who should qualify for alternative measures? Are there offences, such as those involving domestic assault, for which diversion should not be a viable alternative? How can we ensure that offenders are not coerced into alternative measures when they might not be guilty? If alternative measures programs are run by volunteers, how can an acceptable level of accountability be ensured? What measures can be taken to ensure that programs operate fairly and do not impose obligations that are unduly onerous, disproportionate, or otherwise inappropriate?

Alternative measures are defined in the Code as measures other than judicial proceedings "used to deal with a person who is eighteen years of age or over and alleged to have committed an offence." The relevant provisions are as follows:

> 717(1) Alternative measures may be used to deal with a person alleged to have committed an offence only if it is not inconsistent with the protection of society and the following conditions are met:

(a) the measures are part of a program of alternative measures authorized by the Attorney General or the Attorney General's delegate or authorized by a person, or a person within a class of persons, designated by the lieutenant governor in council of a province;

(b) the person who is considering whether to use the measures is satisfied that they would be appropriate, having regard to the needs of the person alleged to have committed the offence and the interests of society and of the victim;

(c) the person, having been informed of the alternative measures, fully and freely consents to participate therein;

(d) the person has, before consenting to participate in the alternative measures, been advised of the right to be represented by counsel;

(e) the person accepts responsibility for the act or omission that forms the basis of the offence that the person is alleged to have committed;

(f) there is, in the opinion of the Attorney General or the Attorney General's agent, sufficient evidence to proceed with the prosecution of the offence; and

(g) the prosecution of the offence is not in any way barred at law.

(2) Alternative measures shall not be used to deal with a person alleged to have committed an offence if the person

(a) denies participation or involvement in the commission of the offence; or

(b) expresses the wish to have any charge against the person dealt with by the court.

(3) No admission, confession or statement accepting responsibility for a given act or omission made by a person alleged to have committed an offence as a condition of the person being dealt with by alternative measures is admissible in evidence against that person in any civil or criminal proceedings.

(4) The use of alternative measures in respect of a person alleged to have committed an offence is not a bar to proceedings against the person under this Act, but, if a charge is laid against that person in respect of that offence,

(a) where the court is satisfied on a balance of probabilities that the person has totally complied with the terms and conditions of the alternative measures, the court shall dismiss the charge; and

(b) where the court is satisfied on a balance of probabilities that the person has partially complied with the terms and conditions of the alternative measures, the court may dismiss the charge if, in the opinion of the court, the prosecution of the charge would be unfair, having regard to the circumstances and that person's performance with respect to the alternative measures.

(5) Subject to subsection (4), nothing in this section shall be construed as preventing any person from laying an information, obtaining the issue or confirmation of any process, or proceeding with the prosecution of any offence, in accordance with law.

Sections 717.1 to 717.4 are concerned with the use of information compiled in relation to a diversion scheme and the participation of the offender in one:

717.1. Sections 717.2 to 717.4 apply only in respect of persons who have been dealt with by alternative measures, regardless of the degree of their compliance with the terms and conditions of the alternative measures.

717.2(1) A record relating to any offence alleged to have been committed by a person, including the original or a copy of any fingerprints or photographs of the person, may be kept by any police force responsible for, or participating in, the investigation of the offence.

(2) A peace officer may disclose to any person any information in a record kept pursuant to this section that it is necessary to disclose in the conduct of the investigation of an offence.

(3) A peace officer may disclose to an insurance company any information in a record kept pursuant to this section for the purpose of investigating any claim arising out of an offence committed or alleged to have been committed by the person to whom the record relates.

717.3(1) A department or agency of any government in Canada may keep records containing information obtained by the department or agency

(a) for the purposes of an investigation of an offence alleged to have been committed by a person;

(b) for use in proceedings against a person under this Act; or

(c) as a result of the use of alternative measures to deal with a person.

(2) A person or organization may keep records containing information obtained by the person or organization as a result of the use of alternative measures to deal with a person alleged to have committed an offence.

717.4(1) Any record that is kept pursuant to section 717.2 or 717.3 may be made available to

(a) any judge or court for any purpose relating to proceedings relating to offences committed or alleged to have been committed by the person to whom the record relates;

(b) any peace officer

(i) for the purpose of investigating any offence that the person is suspected on reasonable grounds of having committed, or in respect of which the person has been arrested or charged, or

(ii) for any purposes related to administration of the case to which the record relates;

(c) any member of a department or agency of a government in Canada, or any agent thereof, that is

(i) engaged in the administration of alternative measures in respect of the person, or

(ii) preparing a report in respect of the person pursuant to this Act; or

(d) any other person who is deemed, or any person within a class of persons that is deemed, by a judge of a court to have a valid interest in the record, to the extent directed by the judge, if the judge is satisfied that the disclosure is

(i) desirable in the public interest for research or statistical purposes, or

(ii) desirable in the interest of the proper administration of justice.

(2) Where a record is made available for inspection to any person under subparagraph (1)(d)(i), that person may subsequently disclose information contained in the record, but may not disclose the information in any form that would reasonably be expected to identify the person to whom it relates.

(3) Any person to whom a record is authorized to be made available under this section may be given any information contained in the record and may be given a copy of any part of the record.

(4) Nothing in this section authorizes the introduction into evidence of any part of a record that would not otherwise be admissible in evidence.

(5) A record kept pursuant to section 717.2 or 717.3 may not be introduced into evidence, except for the purposes set out in paragraph 721(3)(c), more than two years after the end of the period for which the person agreed to participate in the alternative measures.

There is abundant literature on diversion measures in Canada and elsewhere. For some recent views on the matter, see the various papers collected in Healy and Dumont, eds., *Dawn or Dusk in Sentencing* (Montreal: Thémis, 1997).

II. ABSOLUTE AND CONDITIONAL DISCHARGES

In certain circumstances, the *Criminal Code* provides relief against the full opprobrium of criminal conviction by allowing an absolute or a conditional discharge. These sanctions are best understood by considering the registration of a conviction as a two-stage process. Typically, a conviction is considered synonymous with the finding of guilt by a judge or jury, but it is more accurate to say that a conviction is perfected when a finding of guilt and sentence are formally recorded. (See *R v. McInnis* (1973), 23 CRNS 152, at 156-63 (Ont. CA); *R v. Senior* (1996), 181 AR 1 (CA), aff'd. (1997), 116 CCC (3d) 152, at 158-59; and *R v. Pearson* (1998), 130 CCC (3d) 297 (SCC).) It is only *after* a finding of guilt that the judge considers whether a *conviction* (as opposed to a discharge) ought to be imposed. Note, however, that discharges are not available if the offence is punishable by a minimum penalty or carries a maximum penalty of more than 14 years.

The immediate effect of a discharge, whether it is absolute and immediate in effect, or conditional and thus delayed, is that there is no criminal record of conviction and sentence against the accused under the *Criminal Records Act*, RSC 1985, c. C-47, as amended. This is a matter of great importance to the offender because there are disabilities that may follow the recording of a criminal conviction, including difficulties with employment, travel, immigration, or other significant personal matters. As will be seen below, a discharge may be granted in the discretion of the court only if this disposition is in the best interests of the offender and is not contrary to the public interest. Section 730 of the Code provides as follows:

> 730(1) Where an accused, other than a corporation, pleads guilty to or is found guilty of an offence, other than an offence for which a minimum punishment is prescribed by law or an offence punishable by imprisonment for fourteen years or for life, the court before which the accused appears may, if it considers it to be in the best interests of the accused and not contrary to the public interest, instead of convicting the accused, by order direct that the accused be discharged absolutely or on the conditions prescribed in a probation order made under subsection 731(2).
>
> (2) Subject to Part XVI, where an accused who has not been taken into custody or who has been released from custody under or by virtue of any provision of Part XVI pleads guilty of or is found guilty of an offence but is not convicted, the appearance notice, promise to appear, summons, undertaking or recognizance issued to or given or entered into by the accused continues in force, subject to its terms, until a disposition in respect of the accused is made under subsection (1) unless, at the time the accused pleads guilty or is

found guilty, the court, judge or justice orders that the accused be taken into custody pending such a disposition.

(3) Where a court directs under subsection (1) that an offender be discharged of an offence, the offender shall be deemed not to have been convicted of the offence except that

(a) the offender may appeal from the determination of guilt as if it were a conviction in respect of the offence;

(b) the Attorney General and, in the case of summary conviction proceedings, the informant or the informant's agent may appeal from the decision of the court not to convict the offender of the offence as if that decision were a judgment or verdict of acquittal of the offender or a dismissal of the information against the offender; and

(c) the offender may plead autrefois convict in respect of any subsequent charge relating to the offence.

(4) Where an offender who is bound by the conditions of a probation order made at a time when the offender was directed to be discharged under this section is convicted of an offence, including an offence under section 733.1, the court that made the probation order may, in addition to or in lieu of exercising its authority under subsection 732.2(5), at any time when it may take action under that subsection, revoke the discharge, convict the offender of the offence to which the discharge relates and impose any sentence that could have been imposed if the offender had been convicted at the time of discharge, and no appeal lies from a conviction under this subsection where an appeal was taken from the order directing that the offender be discharged.

The following cases illustrate how the courts determine whether to grant a discharge. A discharge must be either absolute or conditional, not some combination of the two. In one case, the court ruled that an order of a conditional discharge that was to become absolute on completion of the conditions and the payment of an indemnity was improper (*R v. Hébert*, [1986] RJQ 236 (CA)). It should also be noted that the Code does not authorize the payment of a fine as one of the conditions in a conditional discharge (see *R v. Carroll* (1995), 38 CR (4th) 238 (BC CA).

R v. Fallofield
(1973), 22 CRNS 342 (BC CA)

FARRIS CJBC: The two questions in this appeal are:

1. Did the Provincial Court Judge err in refusing to grant an absolute or a conditional discharge; and
2. If the answer is yes, has this Court the power to make such an order?

In my opinion, the answer to both questions is yes.

The appellant pleaded guilty to a charge of being in unlawful possession of some pieces of carpet of a total value of less than $200, knowing the same to have been obtained by theft. The appellant is a corporal in the Canadian Armed Forces, aged 26, married, and with no previous record. He and his two co-accused were employed by the Fairfield Moving & Storage Company in Victoria. Apparently the appellant was supplementing his income by what is commonly known as "moonlighting."

In September last, the three men were delivering refrigerators to a new apartment building and took from the premises some left-over pieces of carpeting. The accused had five pieces of carpeting of a value of $33.07. The co-accused likewise had small quantities of carpet.

The police officer who investigated the matter said that, when he attended at the residence of the accused, the accused turned over the five pieces of carpet and stated that he thought they were scraps. The officer also testified that he found the accused to be friendly and co-operative and would agree that "rather than being a thief, was more simply a foolish individual, getting involved in something slightly more serious than a foolish prank but not really a thief at nature."

A warrant officer from the Canadian Armed Forces was called and testified that "Corporal Fallofield is one of the best men we have. He is a very good worker—a very conscientious man." He further testified that this conviction "could very possibly affect his future career in the Navy."

At the hearing in the Court below, counsel for the appellant applied under the *Criminal Code*, RSC 1970, c. C-34, s. 662.1(1) [en. 1972, c. 13, s. 57] for a conditional discharge. This section reads as follows:

> 662.1(1) Where an accused, other than a corporation, pleads guilty to or is found guilty of an offence, other than an offence for which a minimum punishment is prescribed by law or an offence punishable, in the proceedings commenced against him, by imprisonment for fourteen years or for life or by death, the court before which he appears may, if it considers it to be in the best interests of the accused and not contrary to the public interest, instead of convicting the accused, by order direct that the accused be discharged absolutely or upon the conditions prescribed in a probation order.

The trial judge declined to grant the discharge, convicted the appellant, and sentenced him to a fine of $100, or in default, 30 days in prison. It is from this disposition of the matter that the present appeal is brought.

The basis of the trial Judge's refusal to grant the discharge was that he did not think that "this was a case of strict liability or that it is a case where the offence being committed was entirely completely unintentional or unavoidable." In doing so, he relied on an extract from Devlin on *Sentencing in Magistrates' Courts* which has reference to the provisions of the English legislation.

In my respectful opinion, the trial Judge proceeded upon a wrong principle. There is nothing in the language of the section that so limits its application. In *Mark Fishing Co. v. United Fishermen and Allied Workers Union* (1968), 64 WWR 530, 68 DLR 92d) 41 (BC CA), beginning at p. 543, there is a review of a number of cases, the gist of which may be gathered from one of the expressions quoted [p. 545]: "a discretion which is unfettered by law must not be fettered by judicial interpretation of it." To the same effect, in *Ebrahimi v. Westbourne Galleries Ltd.*, [1973] AC 360—where the case turned on the application of a clause in the *Companies Act* that authorizes a court to wind up a company "if the court is of the opinion that it is just and equitable

that the company should be wound up." Lord Reid, with whose judgment other learned
Law Lords agreed, said at p. 374H:

> There are two other restrictive interpretations which I mention to reject. First, there has
> been a tendency to create categories or headings under which cases must be brought if
> the clause is to apply. This is wrong. Illustrations may be used, but general words should
> remain general and not be reduced to the sum of particular instances.

Nevertheless, it is useful to review the manner in which the Courts have dealt with
cases arising under this section in the less than two years since its enactment. In *R v.
Derkson* (1972), 20 CRNS 129, 9 CCC (2d) 97, where the accused pleaded guilty to a
charge of possession of cannabis resin, the Provincial Court refused to grant an order
of absolute or conditional discharge, notwithstanding that counsel for the Crown stated
"that the Crown will in future adopt a more tolerant posture in these cases," namely,
where the accused had no previous convictions and was of good character and reputation. The Judge held that the discharge provisions should never be applied routinely to any criminal offence.

In *R v. Stafrace* (1972), 10 CCC (2d) 181, the Court of Appeal of Ontario considered that where the appellant had been convicted of theft of two boxes of potato
chips, having a value of approximately $10, the property of his employer, it was a
proper case for the exercise of the power but that the Court of Appeal had no jurisdiction to grant the discharge.

In *R v. Campbell*, 21 CRNS 273, [1973] 2 WWR 246, 10 CCC (2d) 26 (Alta.), the
District Court Judge granted an absolute discharge where the accused was charged
with taking part in an immoral performance, after having been told that a judge had
recently held—wrongly, as was later decided on appeal—that taking part in a similar
performance was not an offence.

In *R v. Sanchez-Pino*, [1973] 2 OR 314, 11 CCC (2d) 53, the Court of Appeal
considered that a conditional or absolute discharge should not be granted in a shoplifting case, although they agreed that their decision did not mean that shoplifting could
never be an offence in respect of which s. 662.1(1) can apply.

In *R v. Millen* (1973), 21 CRNS 225, 11 CCC (2d) 70 (NS), the accused was granted
an absolute discharge where he had pleaded guilty to a charge under s. 236 of the
Code of driving with more than 80 milligrams of alcohol in 100 millilitres of blood.

In *R v. Christman*, [1973] 3 WWR 475, 11 CCC (2d) 245, a conditional discharge
was granted by the Alberta Appellate Division in respect of a charge of theft under
s. 294(b) [am. 1972, c. 13, s. 23] of the Code.

In *R v. Hampton*, an unreported judgment of this Court dated 13th February 1973,
an absolute discharge was granted in respect of a charge of shoplifting, on the ground
that there was "good reason for thinking that it will be in the public interest to grant a
discharge."

In *R v. Barrett*, an unreported judgment of the Court of Appeal for the Yukon Territory delivered on 2nd March 1973, the accused was found guilty of theft by conversion; instead of being convicted, he was granted a conditional discharge. On appeal
this disposition was set aside, a conviction was entered and a term of imprisonment

was imposed, the Court being of the opinion that the magistrate had overlooked that he could grant a discharge only if he was of the opinion that so to do was not contrary to the public interest.

In *R v. Tifenbach*, an unreported judgment of this Court dated 18th May 1973, absolute or conditional discharge was refused where the accused had been found guilty on two counts of indecent assault on a male person.

From this review of the authorities and my own view of the meaning of s. 662.1, I draw the following conclusions; subject, of course, to what I have said above as to the exercise of discretion.

(1) The section may be used in respect of *any* offence other than an offence for which a minimum punishment is prescribed by law or the offence is punishable by imprisonment for 14 years or for life or by death.

(2) The section contemplates the commission of an offence. There is nothing in the language that limits it to a technical or trivial violation.

(3) Of the two conditions precedent to the exercise of the jurisdiction, the first is that the court must consider that it is in the best interests of the accused that he should be discharged either absolutely or upon condition. If it is not in the best interests of the accused, that, of course, is the end of the matter. If it is decided that it is in the best interests of the accused, then that brings the next consideration into operation.

(4) The second condition precedent is that the court must consider that a grant of discharge is not contrary to the public interest.

(5) Generally, the first condition would presuppose that the accused is a person of good character, without previous conviction, that it is not necessary to enter a conviction against him in order to deter him from future offences or to rehabilitate him, and that the entry of a conviction against him may have significant adverse repercussions.

(6) In the context of the second condition the public interest in the deterrence of others, while it must be given due weight, does not preclude the judicious use of the discharge provisions.

(7) The powers given by s. 662.1 should not be exercised as an alternative to probation or suspended sentence.

(8) Section 662.1 should not be applied routinely to any particular offence. This may result in an apparent lack of uniformity in the application of the discharge provisions. This lack will be more apparent than real and will stem from the differences in the circumstances of cases.

Applying these conclusions, this is a case where it is appropriate to grant an absolute discharge. It is clear that it is in the best interests of the accused that such a discharge be granted. I cannot see that such a grant is contrary to the public interest. I find it difficult to believe that the deterrence of others will be in any way diminished by the failure to render a conviction against this accused.

Accordingly, if this Court has the power so to do I would grant a discharge and I see no point in imposing conditions.

...

In *R v. Stafrace* (supra), the Ontario Court of Appeal held that the power conferred upon a judge of first instance by s. 662.1 of the *Criminal Code* to order an accused discharged is to be exercised "instead of" entering the conviction and if a conviction is entered there is no power as far as an appellate court is concerned to enter a discharge unless the conviction can be vacated upon proper grounds. Thus, if the accused proceeds on an appeal from sentence alone there is no jurisdiction to grant a discharge.

In a later case of *R v. Sanchez-Pino* (supra), the Ontario Court of Appeal held that, if the Court of Appeal considered that the trial judge erred in law in entering a conviction instead of granting an order for discharge, this would enable the Court of Appeal to quash the conviction and order a new trial. At such a new trial the trial judge would then consider whether he should make an order for discharge or enter a conviction.

In *R v. Christman* (supra), the Appellate Division of the Supreme Court of Alberta reached a different conclusion. Delivering the judgment of the Court, Clement JA said in part:

> I have no doubt that the determination by the trial court whether or not it will make an order for discharge is a disposition under subs. (1) of s. 662.1 …
>
> Since it is the "disposition" that is in appeal as a matter of sentence, this Court is empowered to vary the disposition within the limits prescribed by law. Those limits range from an unfavourable exercise of the discretion (as in the present case), to an order directing an unconditional discharge. If the disposition by the trial court is varied on such an appeal against sentence, the judgment of the Court of Appeal has the same force and effect as a disposition duly made by the trial court. The consequence is that the conviction recorded against the accused must be expunged, since by statute an order directing a discharge is made *instead* of making a conviction, and in its place the order directing a discharge is recorded and, by virtue of s. 614(2), must have the same effect as if made by the trial court prior to formal conviction.
>
> I regret that the foregoing views are at variance with those expressed by the Court of Appeal of Ontario in *R v. Stafrace* (supra). Our divergence appears to arise largely because of the effect above given to the statutory definition of "sentence."

With respect, I agree with the views of the Alberta Court of Appeal and think that they are to be preferred to the views expressed in the decisions of the Ontario Court of Appeal. The line of reasoning that commends itself to me is briefly as follows. Under s. 601 the word "sentence" in Part XVIII of the Code includes a disposition made under s. 662.1(1). A determination by a trial court before which an accused pleads guilty or by which an accused is found guilty whether or not it will make an order for discharge is such a disposition. Section 603(1)(b) confers a right of appeal against a sentence and so against such a disposition. Under s. 614(1) the Court of Appeal may vary a sentence and, applying the reasoning above, may substitute for the decision to convict the accused instead of discharging him an order directing that he be discharged.

Accordingly, it is my opinion that this Court has the power to grant a discharge. The order I would make would be to allow the appeal from sentence, to quash the conviction and to order that the appellant be discharged absolutely.

Appeal allowed; absolute discharge ordered.

R v. McInnis
(1973), 23 CRNS 152 (Ont. CA)

MARTIN JA: This is an appeal by the appellant from her conviction by His Honour Provincial Court Judge R.T. Bennett on two charges of theft and from the sentence imposed, namely, suspended sentence and probation for two years.

The appeal was initially from sentence only but the Court, on the hearing of the appeal, granted leave to the appellant to amend the notice of appeal to include an appeal from conviction as well as sentence in order that the broad questions raised by the appeal might be considered fully.

The questions raised by the appeal are:

(a) Whether the Court of Appeal is empowered to direct that an accused who has been convicted by the trial Court be discharged absolutely or upon conditions pursuant to s. 662.1(1) of the *Criminal Code*.

(b) Whether, if the Court is empowered under the above circumstances to direct that the accused be discharged absolutely or upon conditions, it is appropriate in the present case to direct an absolute or conditional discharge.

...

The manifest purpose of the legislation is to enable a Court before which an accused pleads guilty to an offence or which finds an accused guilty of an offence, to make a disposition of the case, in appropriate circumstances, which will avoid ascribing a criminal record to the accused.

...

In my view, s. 662.1(1) of the *Criminal Code* which provides that, in the circumstances envisaged therein, the Court may, *instead of convicting the accused*, direct that he be discharged absolutely or upon conditions simply means that notwithstanding the plea of guilty or the finding of guilt, the Court may, instead of passing judgment, that is sentence, and recording a conviction, direct that he be discharged either absolutely or conditionally. Where the Court directs that the accused be discharged, the accused is by the section deemed not to have been convicted. It is to be observed that in many cases the finding of guilt followed by the imposition of sentence constitutes the only record of the registering of a conviction.

...

Turning now from the jurisdictional question to the merits of the appeal, I am of the view that the case is a proper one for the application of s. 662.1. The appellant was 16 years of age at the time of the commission of the offences. Both offences were committed on the same day and involved the theft by appellant and her co-accused of two sweaters from one store and another sweater from a second store. The offences were committed during a brief period when the appellant had left the family home because of a dispute with her parents. The pre-sentence report indicates that emotional stress and possibly undesirable influences may have brought about the conduct in question. The appellant at the time of the commission of the offences was, as she still is, a high school student in Grade 11. Both her academic and attendance records are satisfactory and the pre-sentence report is a favourable one.

I would dismiss the appeal from conviction, allow the appeal from sentence and in the place of the sentence imposed by the trial judge, would direct that the appellant, pursuant to s. 662.1, be discharged upon the same conditions as those set out in the probation order.

Appeal allowed.

R v. Bram
(1982), 30 CR (3d) 398 (Alta. CA)

LAYCRAFT JA: In this case the accused was convicted after trial of the offence of offering money to an employee of Edmonton Telephones to release to him the addresses and telephone numbers of persons with silent numbers. He was employed as a "skip tracer," that is, one whose job it is to trace persons who have changed their addresses for the purposes of avoiding payment of sums due on credit accounts. The accused was granted an absolute discharge and the Crown now appeals that disposition. The Crown does not seek incarceration or, indeed, any other particular sentence. It merely argues that on his conviction for this offence the accused should be left with a criminal record.

The accused is a survivor of the holocaust of World War II, in which many millions of his co-religionists were murdered. He is the only member of a family of 12 persons who survived the European death camps. At some time after World War II he arrived in Canada, where he married and raised a family. He has been an exemplary citizen and at 58 years of age has never been convicted of any offence other than the present one. In the material filed with us a wide range of citizens speak highly of him. He is described as an upright man and a citizen of exceptional quality. It is apparent that he did not for a time realize that he was doing wrong in the commission of this offence. He seemed to feel that in tracing persons who deliberately avoid obligations such conduct is permissible, though he now does realize that he was doing wrong.

Section 662.1 [en. SC 1972, c. 13, s. 57; am. SC 1974-75-76, c. 93, s. 80] of the *Criminal Code*, RSC 1970, c. C-34, authorizes an absolute discharge when, in the words of the section, the court "considers it to be in the best interest of the accused and not contrary to the public interest."

The tests for the application of this section were extensively reviewed by this court in *R v. MacFarlane*, 3 Alta. LR (2d) 341, [1976] WWD 74, in which a number of factors were listed particularizing the general words of the section. The case points out that, apart from those cases in which there is need to deter the accused himself from further offences, the absolute discharge will in almost every case be in the interests of the accused. There is no such need in the present case, and the contest is therefore whether an absolute discharge would or would not be in the public interest.

R v. MacFarlane states that the jurisdiction to grant an absolute discharge should be used sparingly in the interests of preserving the general deterrence principle of criminal sentencing. Nevertheless that is not to say that it is only in the case of trivial or unintentional offences that absolute discharges should be granted. This point is expressed in Nadin-Davis on *Sentencing in Canada* (1982), at p. 479 in these terms:

While frugality is in order in the application of discharges, the Courts have repeatedly emphasized the wide range of possible candidates and offences. In *Fallofield* [*R v. Fallofield*, 22 CRNS 342, [1973] 6 WWR 472, 13 CCC (2d) 450 (BC CA)] it was held that s. 662.1 is not limited in application to cases of strict liability, or cases where the offence was completely unintentional or unavoidable. Extending this principle, the Ontario court in *Vicente* [*R v. Vicente* (1975), 18 Cr. LQ 292 (Ont. CA)] has added that the granting of discharges should not be confined to trivial matters. In appropriate circumstances, a discharge may be granted in a case which is not trivial.

The author also notes that the seriousness of the offence is naturally a pertinent consideration, and cites the *MacFarlane* decision, supra, for this proposition.

In this case, applying the principles enunciated in *R v. MacFarlane*, we conclude that we will not interfere with the absolute discharge granted by the learned trial judge. The offence is not prevalent in the community, as the Crown readily conceded. The accused had little to gain directly from it, since his income was determined on an hourly basis and not as a percentage of recovery of unpaid accounts. For this accused in relation to this offence we see no need for deterrence, nor do we perceive that the public interest requires that persons dealing with him in the future be able to determine that the offence was committed. He has been an excellent citizen of his adopted country, of whom it may be said with a high degree of confidence that he will not offend again. That conclusion was apparently reached also by the learned trial judge, who observed him giving evidence for upwards of 1½ hours. No adequate grounds have been shown to us to interfere with the disposition by the trial judge. Accordingly the Crown is refused leave to appeal.

Leave to appeal refused.

R v. Shokohi-Manesh
(1992), 69 CCC (3d) 286 (BC CA)

TAYLOR JA: Subject to leave being granted Mehran Shokohi-Manesh appeals the suspended sentence with two years probation which was imposed on him two years ago for possession of a stolen cellular telephone.

The appellant, who is now 23, arrived in the country as a refugee some three years ago from Iran. He had at the time of trial been working part-time as a waiter while studying at Douglas College and was awaiting the processing of his application for landed immigrant status as a refugee. No previous record was alleged at his trial but Crown counsel opposed the granting of a discharge on the grounds that the property involved was of considerable value, that the accused had not assisted the police and the court, and that he showed no remorse. Crown counsel suggested that a fine should properly be imposed. The sentencing judge accepted that a discharge was not appropriate, and instead suspended sentence and imposed a two-year probation order in the standard terms requiring that the appellant report as directed to a probation officer.

The consequences for the appellant's hopes of obtaining refugee status in Canada of the refusal of a discharge were not gone into before the trial judge. Before us it was explained that the entry of a conviction on the present charge absolutely prevents consideration of the appellant's application. It is solely for this reason that he now seeks leave to appeal.

The circumstances of the offence were these. The appellant was arrested when he returned to a cellular telephone store to pick up a cellular telephone which he had taken there in order to have it "renumbered" so that he could make use of it. The manager of the store was suspicious that the phone might have been stolen and reported the matter to the police. Officers were waiting at the store when the appellant came back.

The manager testified that the appellant said the phone had been given to him by an uncle who had left the country. When questioned by the police, however, the appellant said he found it abandoned in a public phone booth late at night two or three months earlier and had taken it to a department store in an effort to locate the owner. At his trial the appellant repeated the account of finding the telephone and said that he kept it hoping that he would get a reward for its return. The judge accepted that the crime was in effect one of theft after finding, that is to say that the appellant did indeed find the telephone outside the restaurant, as he said, and that he proceeded thereafter to convert it to his own use.

After the probation order had been in effect for one year the appellant's probation officer reported to the court favourably on his conduct. The officer wrote:

> In my opinion Mehran's offence is an isolated one for him and is not part of an ongoing pattern of criminal activity. His offence is really part of "the second year syndrome," which many newcomers to Canada experience. It is characterized by loneliness, home-sickness, depression, confusion and sometimes by a foolish illegal act.
>
> All in all he has cooperated with the probation order to his benefit, and I feel the order has now served its purpose.

The sentencing judge accepted this recommendation and vacated the probation order.

It is, in effect, urged on us by Mr. Goldberg on behalf of the appellant that had the information now available been before the sentencing judge the judge might have taken a different view of the appropriateness of granting a discharge. The appellant is a first offender. It appears that despite his unfortunate lapse in the face of temptation he has come to be regarded by a skilled probation officer as a person of good character. Plainly, it would be in his best interests that the bar which the conviction creates to his prospects of receiving landed status should be removed. The remaining question under s. 736(1) is whether the granting of a discharge would be contrary to the public interest. Obviously, this is a dispensation to be used judiciously by the courts.

The fact that an accused person's immigration status will be adversely affected by a conviction does not in itself justify the granting of a discharge: see *R v. Melo* (1975), 26 CC (2d) 510, 310 CRNS 328 (Ont. CA). Clearly, the granting of a discharge will not in itself ensure that the appellant's application before the immigration authorities will in fact be approved. But I think the fact that here a refusal of a discharge would absolutely bar him from consideration for refugee status admission is a consideration that, in this particular case, can properly be given weight without offending the public interest.

Because of his age and because he has been steadily employed at all times while in Canada, because he has satisfied the probation authorities that the adverse impression created at his trial is not in fact warranted, because his crime in the end result did not cause loss to anyone, because of the nature of his apology and the rescission of the punishment imposed on him, I am of the view that this is a case in which it would not be contrary to the public interest that the relief sought be granted.

I would grant leave to appeal. I would allow the appeal against sentence and substitute for the penalty imposed an unconditional discharge.

Appeal allowed and sentence varied.

There are many cases that deal with the question of immigration status. See, for example, *R v. Mason* (1978), 6 CR (3d) 14 (Ont. CA); *R v. Elberhdadi* (1994), 58 QAC 318; and *R v. Abouabedellah* (1996), 109 CCC (3d) 447 (Que. CA).

R v. Aussem
[1997] OJ no. 5582 (Prov. Div., December 3, 1997)

KARSWICK PROV. J: David Aussem, who is 22 years old, has been found guilty of assault with a weapon, that is a hockey stick, contrary to section 267(1)(a) of the Canadian *Criminal Code*, and assault contrary to section 266 of the Canadian *Criminal Code*.

He violently cross-checked a standing opponent from behind, by striking him with his hockey stick across the back of his neck. David Aussem was skating at full speed when he struck the other player. Later, on his way to his team's dressing room, he attacked the opposing team's manager by punching him on the side of his head.

Defence counsel, Mr. Genesee, submits that a conditional discharge would be an appropriate sentence, in the interests of the offender and not contrary to the public interest. He draws attention to the offender's good reputation in the community, his commitment to the work ethic and his remorse for his actions and their serious consequences.

He concedes that general deterrence is an important consideration in the sentencing but argues that convictions for these assaults, or the incarceration of his client, will not necessarily result in a lessening of hockey violence. David Aussem has already suffered for his actions. There has been critical media and community comment about his actions and he has lost the opportunity to expand on his hockey activities since he could not play in Europe this past year. He was required to remain here in Ontario to attend at his trial. It is submitted that no harsh sentence should be imposed since David Aussem himself is not likely to repeat this kind of conduct.

However, it should be noted, that this was not some technical violation of the criminal law or some borderline act of violence. The offender skated the greater length of the ice surface before he struck his unsuspecting opponent, thereby violently throwing him to the ice. There was absolutely no provocation or excuse for this attack during the pre-game warm up.

Further, the offender needlessly assaulted a person whom he believed, at the time of the assault, to be a member of the public. Spectators are at the game to watch it and to cheer their side and perhaps jeer the opposing side. They are not to be encouraged to engage any player in any direct confrontation. Further, players, most certainly, must be discouraged from engaging in confrontations with, or attacks upon, spectators. It would be dangerous for the court to impose a sentence which may be perceived by the public and others to condone assaults of spectators.

Extreme or serious acts of hockey violence which result in serious injury, or may reasonably be expected to result in serious injury, should not be seen to be taken lightly either.

A conditional discharge would tend to diminish the serious nature of these assaults, thereby sending an incorrect message to the players, officials and spectators. In these circumstances, it would be contrary to the public interest to grant a conditional discharge.

Mr. Cantlon calls for the imposition of 60 to 90 days in jail. He submits that this excessively violent act requires the court to send out a message to all hockey players and others involved in physical contact sports activities, that such conduct will not be condoned and, indeed, will be vigorously sanctioned.

Fortunately, it should be noted, that the victim was able to return after one week to play effective hockey. He continues to pursue his promising career at Boston University and has sustained no seriously disabling injury. His potential for achieving a successful career in hockey has not been undermined.

David Aussem demonstrated early remorse for his actions. He apologized to Christopher Heron before the play-off series commenced. He arranged for an early meeting with Daniel Gale to express his regrets. Bradley Grant testified that counselling had been explored by David Aussem.

Moreover, David Aussem was not involved in either of the two earlier fights during the pre-game warm up. He remained reasonably restrained until the end.

The evidence adduced at trial and at the sentencing hearing, leads me to conclude that he is not a violent person but a talented athlete who has worked very hard at developing his hockey skills. He seems to possess a tenacity and determination which has enabled him to overcome the obstacle of a lack of size to succeed in hockey. His strength of character has also enabled him to overcome a learning disability to succeed at school and in his community.

At this sentencing, it is important to note the lack of a serious disabling injury to Christopher Heron, even though the potential for such grave injury was present. That factor, as well as the otherwise favourable and impressive personal antecedents of the offender, his early remorse, and his lack of an adult criminal court record, persuade me to conclude that the imposition of a jail term would be inappropriate, against his best interest and contrary to the public interest.

Players who engage in the game of hockey will continue to realize that their serious acts of violence committed in the course of the sports event may result in criminal charges and upon conviction, in appropriate circumstances, may still result in the imposition of jail terms.

Concurrently, on both charges, sentence is suspended and David Aussem is placed on probation for a period of 18 months.

The conditions are as follows:

1. Keep the peace and be of good behaviour.
2. Be under the supervision of a probation officer and report as required.
3. Keep the probation officer fully advised of your address and immediately notify the probation officer of any change of address.
4. Complete 100 hours of community service as directed or approved by the probation officer. Such community service to be completed within 12 months and to be related, if possible, to amateur hockey and to be directed at aspiring young hockey players, with the objective of discouraging them from engaging in undue violence in the course of the sports event.
5. Participate in such counselling for anger management as may be directed or approved by the probation officer.
6. Within three months, make a contribution of $500.00 to an accredited amateur hockey league in the Province of Ontario, such donation to be designated for use in promoting less violence in the game of hockey. The recipient to be approved by the probation officer.

Order accordingly.

The general approach in *Fallofield* and *McInnis* has been followed in subsequent cases, but the specific criteria for granting a discharge—conditional or absolute—cannot easily be enumerated. It is clear that in the absence of a prescribed minimum or a maximum of more than fourteen years, a discharge is a viable option for all offences. The courts have said repeatedly that discharges should not be routinely granted and should not be routinely refused for any class of offence or offender. For example, the courts have not precluded discharges in cases of sexual assault (see *R v. Moreau* (1992), 76 CCC (3d) 181 (Que. CA) and *R v. Rozon*, [1999] RJQ 805 (SC)). Conversely, while not excluding the possibility of a discharge, the courts have occasionally taken a firmer position against this disposition when the offence appears to be part of a growing pattern of comparable offences. This has been seen, for example, in the rejection of discharges in cases dealing with the violent behaviour of parents at their children's hockey games (see *R v. Bebis*, [1989] OJ no. 1620 (Div. Ct.) and *R v. Musselman*, [1999] OJ no. 4666 (SC)).

Courts have held that an offender who has previously been discharged is not for this reason alone ineligible for a discharge on a subsequent offence (*R v. Elsharawy* (1997), 119 CCC (3d) 565 (Nfld. CA); *R v. Tan* (1974), 74 CCC (2d) 184 (BC CA); and *R v. Drew* (1978), 45 CCC (2d) 212 (BC CA)). Recurring themes in decisions concerning discharges are the possibility that a criminal conviction would place the offender in a position of disproportionate adversity or difficulty. For further illustrations see, for example, *R v. Mullin*

(1990), 56 CCC (3d) 476 (PEI CA); *R v. Cyr*, [1992] RL 13 (Que. CA); *R v. Burke* (1996), 108 CCC (3d) 260 (Nfld. CA); *Elsharawy*, supra; and *Rozon*, supra. The offender's immigration status or consequences with regard to his employment are frequent grounds on which discharges are sought. With respect to employment, however, there are instances in which the nature of the offence, because of the offender's area of employment, militates against a discharge. This might be the case, for example, when a police officer is convicted of assault on a person in custody. Of course, the officer could attempt to distinguish between the loss of a job and the potential loss of a career. Is the question for the judge whether the consequence can be characterized as unfair or disproportionate to culpability?

NOTE

The *Criminal Records Act*, RSC 1985, c. C-47, deals with the duration of the record of the discharge. Section 6.1(1) provides that "no record of a discharge" shall be disclosed to any person, nor shall the existence of the record or the fact of the discharge be disclosed to any person if more than one year has passed since the offender was discharged absolutely or more than three years have passed "since the offender was discharged on the conditions prescribed in a probation order." Moreover, pursuant to s. 6.1(2), the commissioner of the Royal Canadian Mounted Police, who is responsible for the custody of criminal records kept in an automated retrieval system known as CPIC, must purge the record of a discharge from the system after the relevant period has expired.

CHAPTER NINE

Probation

I. INTRODUCTION

Community-based sanctions occupy a crucial position in the Canadian sentencing scheme. Most first offenders can realistically expect to be sentenced to a term of probation. Probation may be imposed on its own or in combination with a term of imprisonment or a fine (but not both). It is a sanction that is restorative and rehabilitative in focus, as emphasized by the Supreme Court of Canada in *R v. Proulx* (2000), 30 CR (5th) 1 (reproduced in Chapter 12). The nature of probation is expressed well in the following passage from Ruby, *Sentencing,* 5th ed. (Toronto: Butterworths, 1999), 331-32 (footnotes omitted):

> The object of the sections dealing with probation is to ensure that appropriate persons convicted of criminal offences be given an opportunity to rehabilitate themselves, without being sent to prison, through the supervision of probation officers and the convicting court. The value of probation lies in the fact that it is a restraint on the freedom of the accused through supervised control and the realization that the breach of probation would likely lead to a term of imprisonment. It should not be thought that a lengthy criminal record, even for serious offences, precludes the use of probation instead of imprisonment. Even where other sentencing alternatives have been tried and have failed, where circumstances indicate that success on probation is a real possibility, probation may be ordered as a "last chance" before someone is in a state where a life of crime and imprisonment seems inevitable. The interests of the public will, in the long term, be better produced by a successful probation term than by any alternate measure.
>
> It is submitted that the principal virtue of probation lies not in probation itself, but in the contrast which it provides to the inflexibility of imprisonment, and the impersonal nature of the fine.
>
> There will usually be no point in imposing a suspended sentence and probation upon an offender who rejects it.

When probation was first introduced into Canadian law (SC 1889, c. 44), it was restricted to young first offenders and relatively minor offences. Moreover, it required the offender to enter into a recognizance sometimes with sureties. Initially, there was no supervision or reporting but simply a requirement to keep the peace and be of good behaviour. In 1921, the *Criminal Code* was amended to permit forms of supervision that led eventually to an official probation service for adults. Legislation authorizing the appointment of probation officers was enacted in Ontario in 1922 and in British Columbia in 1946. See

Hamai, Ville, Harris, Hough, and Zvekic, *Probation Around the World: A Comparative Study* (London: Routledge, 1995), 36. In Jaffary, "Probation for the Adult Offender" (1949), 27 *Can. Bar Rev.* 1020, at 1036, the author speculated that there were fewer than 20 probation officers in Canada at the time and that their qualifications fell far below those recommended by the Archambault commission in 1938.

After major revision of the *Criminal Code* in 1955, two basic kinds of probation were available to sentencing judges. First, a court was allowed to order an offender to enter into a recognizance for up to two years, with or without sureties, and "to keep the peace and be of good behaviour." Such an order could be made in addition to a sentence for an indictable offence or "in addition to or in lieu of sentence" in summary conviction matters. The underlying intention seemed to be that sureties might be useful to encourage lawful behaviour. (See the notes following s. 637 in *Martin's Criminal Code*, 1955, which include a quotation from *Greaves' Consolidated Acts* explaining the English predecessor legislation.) The second form of probation empowered a court to suspend the passing of sentence and order the accused to enter into a recognizance that could include reporting conditions, conditions requiring restitution or reparation, or "such further conditions as [the court] considers desirable." Here, the person responsible for supervision could return the offender to court and, in cases of breach, the offender could be re-sentenced.

These were the provisions applicable at the time of the review conducted by the Canadian Committee on Corrections. In the committee's 1969 report, *Towards Unity*, known commonly as the Ouimet report, an entire chapter was dedicated to probation. In general, the committee supported expanded use of community sanctions. It described probation as providing

> [o]ne of the most effective means of giving expression to one of the fundamental principles on which this report is based—that, whenever feasible, efforts to rehabilitate an offender should take place in the community.

The report was critical because the only remedy for non-compliance was for the Crown to apply for forfeiture of the indebtedness created by the recognizance. Moreover, it questioned the utility of attaching probation to a sentence of imprisonment because of the degree of prediction involved. However, the report noted a "substantial rate of success" with probation and advocated expanded use of it. The committee recommended using probation orders rather than recognizances with mandatory conditions that the offender keep the peace and be of good behaviour, appear in court when required, be under the supervision of a probation officer, and report periodically to that officer. It also recommended that the Code be amended to permit discretionary conditions "to fit the needs of the individual case." The report added the following comment:

> Conditions in a probation order should be kept to a minimum. Particularly, conditions that interfere with aspects of a probationer's life that have nothing to do with his offence should be avoided.

It can readily be seen that the committee viewed probation as a rehabilitative tool that ought not to be encumbered by extraneous prohibitions.

Not all of the Ouimet report recommendations dealing with probation were adopted by Parliament. Probation continued to be available in addition to terms of imprisonment so long as the term did not exceed two years. Parliament did replace the recognizance with a probation order and a list of mandatory and discretionary conditions. (See SC 1968-69, c. 38, s. 75.) It also created a separate offence for breach of probation.

For further discussion of probation, see Ruby, supra, chapter 9; and Barnett, "Probation Orders Under the Criminal Code" (1977), 38 CRNS 165. See also the Report of the Canadian Sentencing Commission, *Sentencing Reform* (1987), chapter 12 and the Report of the Standing Committee of the House of Commons on Justice and the Solicitor General, *Taking Responsibility* (1988) ("the Daubney report"), chapter 7.

II. ALTERNATIVES TO IMPRISONMENT

A. Doob, "Community Sanctions and Imprisonment: Hoping for a Miracle but Not Bothering Even To Pray for It"
(1990), 32 *Canadian Journal of Criminology* 415 (footnotes omitted)

...

Our thinking and sometimes our laws reflect a presumption in favour of imprisonment. Our penalty structure for criminal offences is uniformly stated in terms of the maximum sentence of imprisonment that can be imposed. Other sanctions, then, become "alternatives." This is not true of the *Young Offenders Act* where a number of different dispositions are listed (in s. 20(1) of the Act), the final one being custody. The problem is that even our language tends to encourage us to think first of imprisonment, and then of "alternatives."

It was in part for these reasons that the Canadian Sentencing Commission, in its 1987 report, used the term "community sanctions" instead of the more common terms such as "non-custodial" or "non-carceral" sanctions or "alternatives" to imprisonment. The Commission wanted to get away from the dichotomy between custody and all other sanctions, and wished to emphasize that it does not view imprisonment as the pivotal sanction with all other possible sentences being measured against it.

The linguistic distinction between the term "alternatives" and some term like "community sanctions" which emphasizes the independent status of the sanction is important beyond the symbolic point that it makes. It leads one to ask the obvious and critical question: if we have "community sanctions," when should they be imposed?

This in turn forces us to ask a series of other questions including the following:

How should sentences—community sanctions included—be allocated?
What purpose or purposes should sentencing serve?
What principles should govern the determination of sentences?
What kinds of offenders convicted of what kinds of offences should normally receive community sanctions?

An Example of an Attempt To Increase the Use of Community Sanctions:
The Report of the Canadian Sentencing Commission

The formal Declaration of Purpose and Principles of Sentencing proposed by the Canadian Sentencing Commission need not be reproduced here (See Canada 1987: 152-155). For the purposes of this paper, it is sufficient to consider the following aspects of it:

a) The paramount principle determining the sentence is that the sanction be proportionate to the gravity of the offence and the degree of responsibility of the offender for the offence.

b) There is a presumption in favour of the least onerous sanction.

c) Imprisonment is to be imposed only for specific purposes.

The implications of this policy are important. First of all, since the severity of the sentence is supposed to be proportionate to the seriousness of the offence, it follows that the less serious offences—in particular the very common but less serious property offences—should predominately receive less severe sentences. Given that the Commission also endorsed the principle of restraint in the use of imprisonment, this statement could be operationalized as meaning that there should be an increased use of community sanctions.

But a statement of purpose and principles is not enough. It may tell judges what principles to follow and may give judges a fairly good idea for a particular case of the appropriate levels of sanction *in relation to* other cases. But on its own, such a statement does not tell the judge explicitly what kinds of sanctions should be imposed for particular kinds of cases. Thus a "proportionality" model such as that recommended by the Canadian Sentencing Commission is neither harsh nor lenient on its own: without further elaboration, it does not imply either an increased use of community sanctions nor an increased use of imprisonment. Principles are necessary, but they do not provide sufficient guidelines for the sentencing judge.

The Canadian Sentencing Commission went one step further in suggesting that explicit policy be made. It recommended that guidelines—created by a Commission, but assented to by Parliament—be made part of our sentencing law. Guidelines, under its recommendations, could consist of two separate parts. For all offences, there would be an explicit presumption of custody or community sanction. If the presumptive disposition were a sentence of imprisonment, the guidelines would indicate the presumptive range. If it were not, then, a community sanction would be imposed. Furthermore, the Commission recommended that specific guidance—presumably in the form of guidelines—be developed for the use of community sanctions. As von Hirsch, Wasik, and Greene (1989) have noted, explicit guidance for community sanctions can be given that is consistent with an over-riding sentencing rationale.

Conclusion

In the context of the theme of this paper, then, community sanctions should not be "alternatives," but should become sanctions in their own right. More importantly, they should be sanctions that would be described in appropriate legislation as appropriate for certain kinds of cases. In other words, they wouldn't be add-ons to the system, but would be, presumptively, the correct sanction for many offences.

According to the Canadian Sentencing Commission, community sanctions should often be used instead of imprisonment and should be designated as the appropriate sentence for many common offences. Many very common property offences (for which a sizable number of offenders are currently imprisoned) would have, as the presumptive sentence, a community sanction. It is expected that, if the Canadian

Sentencing Commission recommendations were implemented, the number of people incarcerated would drop because of the increased use of community sanctions.

Clearly, however, there can be no guarantee of success. There is a good deal of evidence that the criminal justice system is quite resistant to change. Changes cannot be made at one level of the system—in this case in the law governing sentencing—with an assurance that the changes would be implemented exactly as intended. It was for that reason, among others, that the Canadian Sentencing Commission recommended that a permanent sentencing commission be created. It could have as one of its major responsibilities the monitoring of sentencing to ensure that desired changes occurred. It would be able to recommend—and implement—changes quickly to eliminate unanticipated problems should they occur.

In Canada it would appear that a number of conditions must be met to be confident that there will be increased use of community sanctions, or "alternatives." These would include:

The presence of well-run community sanctions;
A policy that endorses the use of them;
Legal and administrative procedures that put community sanctions on an equal footing with imprisonment as sentencing choices;
Guidance to decision makers on the appropriate use of community sanctions.

Obviously it is possible to have successful "alternatives" without the policy changes I have suggested just as it might happen, to use the analogy I made earlier, that adding a third type of wine to a menu will shift customers away from the wines in short supply. However, if we want to ensure success, we probably have to work a little harder to achieve the changes we want. Those who believe in the effectiveness of prayer might try that. But Parliamentary action would seem to be a more sure bet.

The statutory provisions governing probation (*Criminal Code*, RSC 1985, c. C-46, as amended by SC 1995, c. 22) are reproduced below. When reading them, consider the following questions: When *must* and when *may* a sentencing judge impose a probation order? Can a probation order be combined with other sentencing options and, if so, which ones?

Criminal Code, Sections 731, 732.1, 732.2, 733, and 733.1

731(1) Where a person is convicted of an offence, a court may, having regard to the age and character of the offender, the commission,

(a) if no minimum punishment is prescribed by law, suspend the passing of sentence and direct that the offender be released on the conditions prescribed in a probation order; or

(b) in addition to fining or sentencing the offender to imprisonment for a term not exceeding two years, direct that the offender comply with the conditions prescribed in a probation order.

(2) A court may also make a probation order where it discharges an accused under subsection 730(1).

731.1(1) Before making a probation order, the court shall consider whether section 100 is applicable.

(2) For greater certainty, a condition of a probation order referred to in paragraph 732.1(3)(d) does not affect the operation of section 100.

· · ·

732.1(2) The court shall prescribe, as conditions of a probation order, that the offender do all of the following:

(a) keep the peace and be of good behaviour;

(b) appear before the court when required to do so by the court; and

(c) notify the court or the probation officer in advance of any change of name or address, and promptly notify the court or the probation officer of any change of employment or occupation.

(3) The court may prescribe, as additional conditions of a probation order, that the offender do one or more of the following:

(a) report to a probation officer

(i) within two working days, or such longer period as the court directs, after the making of the probation order, and

(ii) thereafter, when required by the probation officer and in the manner directed by the probation officer;

(b) remain within the jurisdiction of the court unless written permission to go outside that jurisdiction is obtained from the court or the probation officer;

(c) abstain from

(i) the consumption of alcohol or other intoxicating substances, or

(ii) the consumption of drugs except in accordance with a medical prescription;

(d) abstain from owning, possessing or carrying a weapon;

(e) provide for the support or care of dependants;

(f) perform up to 240 hours of community service over a period not exceeding eighteen months;

(g) if the offender agrees, and subject to the program director's acceptance of the offender, participate actively in a treatment program approved by the province; and

(h) comply with such other reasonable conditions as the court considers desirable, subject to any regulations made under subsection 738(2), for protecting society and for facilitating the offender's successful reintegration into the community.

(4) A probation order may be in Form 46, and the court that makes the probation order shall specify therein the period for which it is to remain in force.

(5) A court that makes a probation order shall

(a) cause to be given to the offender

(i) a copy of the order,

(ii) an explanation of the substance of subsections 732.2(3) and (5) and section 733.1, and

(iii) an explanation of the procedure for applying under subsection 732.2(3) for a change to the optional conditions; and

(b) take reasonable measures to ensure that the offender understands the order and the explanations given to the offender under paragraph (a).

732.2(1) A probation order comes into force

(a) on the date on which the order is made;

(b) where the offender is sentenced to imprisonment under paragraph 731(1)(b) or was previously sentenced to imprisonment for another offence, as soon as the offender is released from prison or, if released from prison on conditional release, at the expiration of the sentence of imprisonment; or

(c) where the offender is under a conditional sentence, at the expiration of the conditional sentence.

(2) Subject to subsection (5),

(a) where an offender who is bound by a probation order is convicted of an offence, including an offence under section 733.1, or is imprisoned under paragraph 731(1)(b) in default of payment of a fine, the order continues in force except in so far as the sentence renders it impossible for the offender for the time being to comply with the order; and

(b) no probation order shall continue in force for more than three years after the date on which the order came into force.

(3) A court that makes a probation order may at any time, on application by the offender, the probation officer or the prosecutor, require the offender to appear before it and, after hearing the offender and one or both of the probation officer and the prosecutor,

(a) make any changes to the optional conditions that in the opinion of the court are rendered desirable by a change in the circumstances since those conditions were pre-scribed,

(b) relieve the offender, either absolutely or on such terms or for such period as the court deems desirable, of compliance with any optional condition, or

(c) decrease the period for which the probation order is to remain in force,

and the court shall thereupon endorse the probation order accordingly and, if it changes the optional conditions, inform the offender of its action and give the offender a copy of the order so endorsed.

(4) All the functions of the court under subsection (3) may be exercised in chambers.

(5) Where an offender who is bound by a probation order is convicted of an offence, including an offence under section 733.1, and

(a) the time within which an appeal may be taken against that conviction has expired and the offender has not taken an appeal,

(b) the offender has taken an appeal against that conviction and the appeal has been dismissed, or

(c) the offender has given written notice to the court that convicted the offender that the offender elects not to appeal the conviction or has abandoned the appeal, as the case may be,

in addition to any punishment that may be imposed for that offence, the court that made the probation order may, on application by the prosecutor, require the offender to appear before it and, after hearing the prosecutor and the offender,

(d) where the probation order was made under paragraph 731(1)(a), revoke the order and impose any sentence that could have been imposed if the passing of sentence had not been suspended, or

(e) make such changes to the optional conditions as the court deems desirable, or extend the period for which the order is to remain in force for such period, not exceeding one year, as the court deems desirable, and the court shall thereupon endorse the probation order accordingly and, if it changes the optional conditions or extends the period for which the order is to remain in force, inform the offender of its action and give the offender a copy of the order so endorsed.

(6) The provisions of Parts XVI and XVIII with respect to compelling the appearance of an accused before a justice apply, with such modifications as the circumstances require, to proceedings under subsections (3) and (5).

733(1) Where an offender who is bound by a probation order becomes a resident of, or is convicted or discharged under section 730 of an offence including an offence under section 733.1 in, a territorial division other than the territorial division where the order was made, the court that made the order may,

(a) on the application of a probation officer, and

(b) if both such territorial divisions are not in the same province, with the consent of the Attorney General of the province in which the order was made,

transfer the order to a court in that other territorial division that would, having regard to the mode of trial of the offender, have had jurisdiction to make the order in that other territorial division if the offender had been tried and convicted there of the offence in respect of which the order was made, and the order may thereafter be dealt with and enforced by the court to which it is so transferred in all respects as if that court had made the order.

(2) Where a court that has made a probation order or to which a probation order has been transferred pursuant to subsection (1) is for any reason unable to act, the powers of that court in relation to the probation order may be exercised by any other court that has equivalent jurisdiction in the same province.

733.1(1) An offender who is bound by a probation order and who, without reasonable excuse, fails or refuses to comply with that order is guilty of

(a) an indictable offence and is liable to imprisonment for a term not exceeding two years; or

(b) an offence punishable on summary conviction and is liable to imprisonment for a term not exceeding eighteen months, or to a fine not exceeding two thousand dollars, or both.

III. A TERM NOT EXCEEDING TWO YEARS

A probation order cannot be added to a term of imprisonment that exceeds two years (see s. 731(1)(b)). Does this include a sentence arising only from the current proceedings? Does it apply when the offender is serving a term made up of more than one element that exceeds two years in the aggregate?

R v. Young
(1980), 27 CR (3d) 85 (BC CA)

LAMBERT JA: This is an application for leave to appeal against sentence imposed upon four counts in an indictment following guilty pleas on those four counts.

The four offences occurred on three separate days. Three of the counts related to the offence of buggery, under s. 155 of the *Criminal Code*, RSC 1970, c. C-34, for which the maximum sentence is 14 years.

The other count related to the offence of an indecent assault under s. 156 of the Code. The maximum sentence is 10 years.

...

Counsel for the appellant urges us to consider a sentence of two years on the first count of buggery, two years consecutive on the second count of buggery, one year concurrent for the third count of buggery, as well as the two years concurrent for indecent assault, and then to impose, consecutive to the second two year consecutive term for buggery, a term of three years' probation.

Thus at the conclusion of a total of four years' imprisonment there would be imposed three years' probation.

It was urged upon us that a sentence in those terms would be consistent with the provisions of s. 663(1)(b) of the *Criminal Code* and s. 664(2)(b) provides that no probation order shall continue in force for more than three years.

...

In my opinion, it is contrary to the intent of the Code and to the intent of Parliament when s. 663(1)(b) was enacted to contemplate imposing a period of probation following consecutive sentences which total more than two years, even if none of those sentences is in itself longer than two years.

...

Appeal dismissed.

What if the offender is serving a *remanet* from a previous sentence as a result of the revocation of parole or statutory release? See *R v. Currie* (1982), 27 CR (3d) 118 (Ont. CA), which held that the aggregate includes a *remanet*.

What if the offender receives a probation order in addition to a sentence of less than two years but subsequently receives another sentence that brings the aggregate above the two-year limit? See *R v. Miller* (1987), 36 CCC (3d) 100 (Ont. CA) and *R v. Hendrix* (1999), 137 CCC (3d) 445 (Nfld. CA), which held that the subsequent sentence renders the probation period illegal.

IV. WHEN DOES THE PROBATION PERIOD BEGIN?

If the period of probation follows a term of imprisonment, when does it begin? Provincial prisoners released by reason of remission are released without conditions and without supervision. Federal prisoners are released on statutory release subject to conditions and can be reincarcerated for breach of conditions. Before the 1996 amendments, this was a controversy. See *R v. Constant* (1978), 40 CCC (2d) 329 (Man. CA). Now see s. 732.2(1)(b), which distinguishes between the two kinds of confinement.

V. OPTIONAL CONDITIONS

What kinds of conditions can be attached to a probation order? Some of the optional conditions are clear; others are vague. Sometimes the vagueness relates to how an order should be structured or monitored. Vagueness also pervades the kinds of sanctions that may be encompassed. For example, there is a residual subcategory, s. 732.1(3)(h) that is now defined as "such other reasonable conditions as the court considers desirable ... for protecting society and for facilitating the offender's successful reintegration into the community."

The following cases, while dealing with the definitions of available conditions as they were worded before 1996, provide insights into the interpretive issues that arise from the optional condition categories.

R v. Ziatas
(1973), 13 CCC (2d) 287 (Ont. CA)

MARTIN JA: This is an application for leave to appeal and an appeal by the accused from the sentence imposed upon him by Provincial Judge Foster upon conviction of the accused on his plea of guilty to a charge of assault with intent to resist arrest contrary to s. 246(2)(b) of the *Criminal Code*.

The Provincial Judge imposed a fine of $150 and placed the appellant on probation for a term of one year. One of the conditions of the probation order was that the appellant should not operate a motor vehicle for the period of one year. Counsel for the appellant contended that, since s. 238 [am. 1972, c. 13, s. 18] of the *Criminal Code* expressly empowers a Court that convicts an offender of any of the offences enumerated in the section, to prohibit the offender from driving a motor vehicle for the period specified in the section, and since the offence of which the appellant was convicted is not one of the enumerated offences, the Court had no power to require as a condition of the probation order that the accused not operate a motor vehicle during the period of probation. Without deciding whether or not the Provincial Judge had jurisdiction to impose this condition as a term of the probation order, we are all of the view that he proceeded upon a wrong principle, inasmuch as he imposed this term of the probation order as an additional punishment to be imposed upon the accused, whereas his only power, if he had any jurisdiction to impose the condition under s. 663(2) of the *Criminal Code*, was to impose such reasonable conditions as he considered desirable for securing the good conduct of the accused and for preventing the repetition by him of the same offence or the commission of other offences.

In the circumstances the appeal is allowed and the condition that the accused not operate a motor vehicle during his term of probation is struck out of the probation order and the appeal is allowed to give effect to this variation.

Appeal allowed.

The ruling in *Ziatas* with respect to the residual subcategory has been followed in a number of cases. See *R v. Caja and Billings* (1977), 36 CCC (2d) 401 (Ont. CA); *R v. Lavender* (1981), 59 CCC (2d) 551 (BC CA); and *R v. L.* (1986), 50 CR (3d) 398 (Alta. CA).

An important term that is often included in probation orders is a provision that the accused person devote a certain amount of time to "community service." Until 1996, there was no specific authorization to impose this type of term. Courts used the residual subcategory as the authorization for community-service orders.

R v. Tanner
(1983), 36 CR (3d) 64 (Man. Prov. Ct.)

ALLEN PROV. J: The information in this case charges that:

> Dennis Nelson Tanner, at the City of Winnipeg (in Manitoba) between the 16th day of December AD 1981 and the 28th day of August in the year of Our Lord one thousand nine hundred and eighty-two, while bound by a probation order made by Judge H. Collerman on the 25th day of June 1981, in Provincial Judges Court (Criminal Division), Public Safety Building, Winnipeg, did unlawfully and wilfully fail to comply with such order to wit: to carry out ninety-six hours of community work free of charge, terms, location and type of work to be arranged by Manitoba Probation Services, and failing to carry out ninety-six hours of community work as arranged by Manitoba Probation Service.

From the representations made to me, I understand, although it is not clearly stated, that the essential ingredients of the offence are admitted for the purpose of my deciding a preliminary question raised by accused's counsel. I do not understand that he is precluded from advancing evidence or argument should the first question raised be decided contrary to submissions.

From the information quoted above, it can be seen that the learned trial judge specified that the accused perform 96 hours of community service work free of charge but left the terms, location, and type of work to be arranged by the Manitoba Probation Service. This, it is argued, is an unauthorized delegation by the learned trial judge of his judicial function; therefore, the order is void *ab initio*, and there is no basis for the present charge against the accused.

...

On the authorities cited herein and referred to by other courts, I believe my opening comment relative to the power to delegate one's judicial function is well founded.

Equally, since the decision of the Supreme Court of Canada in *R v. Sterner*, [1982] 1 SCR 173, 64 CCC (2d) 160, 14 Sask. R 79, 40 NR 423, it is established that judges can delegate administrative functions.

The task in each case is to determine whether the delegation is of a judicial or administrative function. In determining that, regard must be had to the object of the legislation under which we act, what we wish to achieve, and the practicalities of the situation. Parliament has not legislated in a vacuum and programs providing for supervised probation, community service, and other means of punishing, rehabilitating, and deterring an accused person were created under a perceived need and after much study and consideration. The purpose of probation, community service and programs of like nature is to avoid, in appropriate cases, the imposition of terms of incarceration on those who, with assistance of whatever type may be necessary, may be rehabilitated and adequately punished without incarceration. The effort is made, through the type of programs described, to solve and alleviate anti-social behaviour, upgrade skills and education, and appraise and treat a variety of problems such as drug abuse, alcoholism and even a lack of social skills. The need for such programs can be, and under our laws must be, discovered by the court, with the assistance of persons and agencies available for that purpose, and it is the court that must prescribe the nature of the program to be followed by an accused person who is placed on probation in order to achieve the desired result. That I see as part of the judicial function.

But I cannot see that the day-to-day supervision of probationers is to be considered part of the judicial function. While as judges we may be able to identify the need for a program, few, if any of us, have the training or experience to oversee such programs on a day-to-day basis; we are dependent more and more on those who are probation officers, representatives of the Alcoholism Foundation, Alcoholics Anonymous, X-Kalay, the Salvation Army, and many other groups dedicated to assisting those who require these skills. It is the workers in these fields who have the necessary knowledge, skill and training to adapt the program of rehabilitation to the needs of the subject. The programs may require revision from time to time during the period of probation to adapt to the progress, or lack of it, by the subject. Efforts at first considered appropriate may have to give way to other methods that prove more appropriate. To have to specify in detail how a particular program should be carried out may be impossible for a judge at the time of sentencing.

At the risk of being over-zealous in making my point, let me give an example. Assume, as is often the case, that the accused is one who requires counselling. To assure that counselling, he is placed on probation with directions to report to the probation officer. Must we specify the time, place, frequency and method of reporting? If we do so, the result could be that the accused does not get the counselling required and the probation officer is unable to fulfil his assigned task properly. In another instance, the accused may respond rapidly and the need for counselling diminishes and eventually disappears well before the time of the expiration of the probation. Should the requirement to report be such that the already busy time of our social workers be utilized unnecessarily? Should the accused be imposed upon to comply with the conditions which, in this case, are no longer necessary or appropriate? The answer to these rhetorical questions is, in my opinion, no. I say this not only because

I think it is the only workable answer (need and convenience do not change the law), but because, once the objective is recognized and prescribed by the court, surely the day-to-day application of the court order is administrative. Once a court has ordered, say, counselling, the manner, place, time and frequency of such counselling is surely a manner of carrying out, i.e., administering, the court's order.

This approach is, in my opinion, recognized by the legislation. So far as probation officers are concerned, they are, by virtue of s. 4(1)(a) of the *Manitoba Corrections Act*, CCSM, c. C230, officers of the court. The *Criminal Code* has, at least by implication, recognized probation officers and others as necessary adjuncts of the court: see ss. 662 [re-en. 1972, c. 13, s. 57] and 663(2) of the Code. I repeat, Parliament was not acting in a vacuum but, in providing for probation and conditions of probation, recognized the need of the court for the assistance of those usually more fitted to carry out the administrative part of probation.

I realize that community service is somewhat different from other conditions of probation in that there is an element of punishment involved. It is a program designed to impress upon offenders that they must pay to an extent for their transgressions; it also recognizes that imprisonment is not necessary. The difficulty in a judge dictating the details of such service at the time of sentencing, particularly where the period of probation is lengthy, is mind-boggling. I repeat, difficulty is not the determining factor, but surely, once the need for community service is recognized by the court, the details of the nature of that work and time and place of performance are but administrative details.

...

Under the circumstances, I am of the view that the order of Collerman Prov. J is a valid order.

R v. Richards
(1979), 11 CR (3d) 193 (Ont. CA)

HOWLAND CJO: The Attorney General of Canada applies for leave to appeal and, if leave be granted, appeals from the sentence imposed upon the respondent by Graburn Co. Ct. J on 24th October 1978, following a conviction entered the previous day on the respondent's plea of guilty to the offence of possession of diacetylmorphine (heroin), contrary to s. 3(1) of the *Narcotic Control Act*, RSC 1970, c. N-1. Although initially arraigned on an indictment charging him with the possession of heroin for the purpose of trafficking, the respondent pleaded guilty to the included offence of simple possession of heroin. This plea was accepted by the trial judge, with the concurrence of Crown counsel.

The learned trial judge suspended the passing of sentence and released the respondent on the following statutory and special conditions contained in a probation order to be in force for one year, namely:

(1) to keep the peace and be of good behaviour, and come and receive judgment when called upon;
(2) within the next 24 hours to report to a probation officer;

(3) to continue treatment for heroin addiction with Dr. Stevens at Stevens Psychiatric Centre in New York City and at such other places as she directs when elsewhere than in New York;

(4) to report to the probation officer in Toronto during the week of 7th May 1979 and 24th September 1979 and to file up-to-date reports from the Stevens Psychiatric Centre in New York City and reports from such other psychiatric facilities as Dr. Stevens or the probation officer considers necessary; and

(5) within the first six months of the probation, after making the necessary arrangements through the probation officer and with officials of the Canadian National Institute for the Blind ("CNIB") here in Toronto, either personally or with a group of musicians of choice, to the blind young people associated with the Canadian National Institute for the Blind.

This probation order was subsequently varied by Graburn Co. Ct. J on 23rd April 1979, following an application by counsel for the Crown on 4th April 1979 to vary the probation order so as to postpone the benefit performance originally ordered.

The variation which was made ordered the respondent to report to his probation officer during the week of 23rd April 1979 instead of during the week of 7th May 1979, and further provided for two benefit performances at the Oshawa Civic Centre, Oshawa, instead of the one performance at the CNIB Bayview Auditorium, Toronto.

The facts leading to the charge, so far as material, are these. On 27th February 1977 officers of the Ontario Provincial Police and the RCMP went to the Harbour Castle Hotel in Toronto to execute a warrant for the arrest of Anita Pallenberg, described as the "common law wife" of the respondent. In the course of the search of a bedroom in which the respondent was sleeping the officers found paraphernalia suitable for the administration of heroin. These items contained traces of heroin. The officers also found in the top drawer of a dresser a leather pouch, inside of which was a clear plastic bag containing a white powder; which on analysis proved to be 22 grams of heroin of 32 per cent purity.

The respondent remained asleep during the search, which lasted about half an hour. He was then awakened, arrested and charged with being in possession of heroin for the purpose of trafficking.

The respondent is a musician and is a leading member of the Rolling Stones, a well-known "rock and roll" band. The respondent gave a statement to the police in which he admitted that the heroin was his. He indicated to the police that he had been a heavy user for four years and that he had purchased a large quantity of the drug to satisfy his habit for the five to six weeks that he was going to be in Canada. (It was conceded by the Crown that the heroin was purchased in Canada.) He also told the police that he had tried to "kick" the habit several times, but that he was on tour and did not have time to complete his treatment programmes.

The normal purity of "street heroin" is between 10 and 20 per cent. Using 15 per cent as the average, the 22 grams of heroin seized were said to be equal to 44 grams of "street heroin." An extremely heavy user would use ten capsules a day. The heroin seized was said to have a wholesale value of $2,000 to $3,000. It is conceded, however, that the quantity found in the possession of the respondent is not inconsistent with the amount required by the respondent for his personal consumption during his Canadian tour.

The following facts derived from the submission of counsel, and the reports filed with the consent of both counsel on the proceedings with respect to sentence are not in dispute. The respondent is a British citizen and at the time of the imposition of sentence was 34 years of age. He received his early education at Dartford, Kent. He then attended an art school, where he studied graphic design and while there learned to play the guitar. The group known as the Rolling Stones was formed in 1962, and has been giving performances and making recordings since that time. In 1967 the respondent began to use drugs, and in 1969 he commenced to inject himself with heroin subcutaneously. Counsel for the respondent at trial attributed the respondent's experimentation with drugs to exhaustion following a gruelling schedule. Be that as it may, the respondent's use of drugs developed to the point where he was using large amounts of heroin daily. The respondent, prior to his arrest on the present charge, had made several attempts to cure his addiction. His first attempt, early in 1972, was apparently successful, but the treatment did not result in a permanent cure. The respondent also took treatment in Switzerland later in the year 1972. He was convicted in London, England, in November 1973 of the possession of heroin, for which a fine of £50 was imposed. We are informed that the conviction resulted from traces of heroin found on spoons and a syringe, and that the quantity of heroin involved was not substantial. The appellant continued to use heroin, and in 1974 was again treated unsuccessfully in Switzerland.

The respondent, following his arrest on the present charge, again sought treatment, and in the month of May 1977 he came under the care of Dr. Anita Stevens in New York City. Crown counsel at the trial filed two reports from Dr. Stevens, and defence counsel filed a number of reports from her, the latest of which was dated 21st October 1978. The reports disclosed that the respondent was receiving from Dr. Stevens psychiatric treatment for his drug addiction, on a regular basis; further, that he was receiving psychotherapy to assist him in overcoming the underlying reasons for his previous use of drugs; that he had made remarkable progress; and that he was strongly motivated to overcome his addiction. Regular laboratory tests showed that he was free from drugs and, in particular, free from heroin. In her report dated 21st October 1978 Dr. Stevens recommended that the respondent continue to receive psychotherapy without interruption for a further period of 6 to 12 months. Dr. Stevens' assessment and recommendation was supported by a letter from Dr. Lewis R. Wolberg, Clinical Professor of Psychiatry at New York University Medical School.

On the hearing of the appeal, we received additional material, including a post-sentence report dated 12th June 1979, from the respondent's probation officer, to whom Dr. Stevens has been providing periodic reports. The post-sentence report verifies that the respondent has complied with the terms of the probation order with respect to treatment, that he has remained free from drugs and that he has continued to be strongly motivated to rid himself of his previous drug dependency.

The two concerts provided for in the amended probation order were held in April 1979. 2700 blind persons and their escorts attended the concerts and were admitted without charge. Tickets were sold to the general public. The respondent and the supporting musicians received no payment for their services. In addition, the respondent and Mick Jagger, the lead singer of the group, paid their own expenses. The CNIB received a net amount of $39,000 after the payment of all its expenses in connection with the concerts.

...

The statistics to which reference has been made do not, of course, disclose the circumstances of the offence or the offender in those cases where a non-custodial sentence was imposed for possession of heroin, and undue weight should not be given to them. The high percentage of cases in which non-custodial sentences were imposed is nonetheless a fact of some significance, which the learned trial judge was entitled to take into account. Whether a non-custodial sentence is an appropriate disposition following a conviction of an addict for simple possession of heroin must of necessity depend on all the circumstances. There can be little doubt that the cure of heroin addiction is, at best, difficult, and that the offender must be strongly motivated to overcome his addiction if there is to be any chance of success. Past experience with respect to the offender may show that the offender is not likely to respond to community-based treatment, or the circumstances may be such as to require the temporary removal of the offender from his environment and to indicate that he can be assisted only in a correctional facility. In those circumstances, a custodial sentence is appropriate.

...

In *R v. Shaw* (1977), 36 CRNS 358, this court, although of the view that the trial judge had erred in not imposing a custodial sentence, declined to interfere with the sentence imposed, where the positive rehabilitation program in progress was proving effective, being of the opinion that the public interest would be best served by permitting the sentence imposed upon the respondents to stand.

We wish to make it clear that the appeal was pursued and brought on as expeditiously as the circumstances permitted, and no blame attaches to anyone in that respect. We are nonetheless of the view that at this stage of the proceedings, when the terms of the probation order with respect to treatment have been virtually completed and the prescribed community service has been performed, we ought not to vary the sentence unless we are satisfied that it is so manifestly wrong that we are required in the interest of justice to intervene.

We have not been so satisfied. To impose a custodial sentence now would impose a hardship greatly in excess of that which would have resulted from a custodial sentence in the first instance: see *R v. Bartkow* (1978), 1 CR (3d) S-36 (NS CA): and *R v. Binder*, Ont. CA, 3rd May 1979 (not yet reported).

There are two subsidiary grounds of appeal which may be dealt with quite briefly. The appellant contends that the trial judge erred in suspending the passing of sentence and releasing the respondent on probation, since, in the absence of international arrangement, the terms of the order could not be supervised or enforced. The learned trial judge was of the view that in the special circumstances the terms of the order were capable of enforcement. Even if initially it was an error in principle to make a probation order with respect to a non-resident of Canada—a question which we do not find it necessary to decide—the respondent has voluntarily complied with the terms of the order. Accordingly, we would not give effect to this ground of appeal.

Mr. Scollin also contended that the type of community service directed to be performed was wholly inappropriate—that the giving of a concert by the respondent is not seen as punishment. With respect to the desirability, in general, of imposing a requirement in a probation order that an offender perform community services, we reiterate the views of this court expressed by Dubin JA in *R v. Shaw*, supra. He said at p. 362:

> During the appeal some concern was expressed as to the validity of that term in each probation order which required both of the respondents to perform community services. The trial judge was anxious that both these two young men make amends in a positive way for the damage that they had done, not only to society, but to their own peer groups. In my opinion s. 663(2)(h) of the *Criminal Code* authorizes the imposition of such a term ...
>
> Not only do I think that the provisions in the probation orders relating to this matter are valid, but in appropriate cases should be more extensively used.

In general, it is appropriate to require an offender to perform community services of the type that he is fitted to perform. In the present case, the service performed by the respondent benefitted substantially the CNIB. In the case of another offender not possessing the advantages of the respondent, a lesser service within the abilities of the offender may count as an equivalent.

Although we are strongly of the view that the probation order should also have contained a term that, in addition to performing the concerts, the respondent should engage in a programme to point out the disastrous consequences that the drug addict faces and actively to discourage the use of drugs, we do not consider it would now be appropriate or practical to impose new terms.

Appeal dismissed.

Psychiatric treatment as a condition of probation has been the subject of some controversy, especially since the *Canadian Charter of Rights and Freedoms*, part I of the *Constitution Act, 1982*, RSC 1985, app. II, no. 44, came into force. Consider the different approaches in the two following decisions.

R v. Rogers
(1990), 61 CCC (3d) 481 (BC CA)

ANDERSON JA: This is an appeal from a sentence imposed on May 22, 1990, by McGivern Prov. Ct. J, wherein he ordered that the appellant be placed on probation for a period of 15 months. The probation order reads, in part, as follows:

> WHEREAS on May 22nd, 1990, at Vancouver, BC Donald Rogers, hereinafter called the offender, pleaded guilty to, or was tried under the *Criminal Code* and was convicted or found guilty, as the case may be, upon the charge that

On the 9th day of April, 1990, in the City of Vancouver, Province of British Columbia, did have in his possession a weapon to wit: a knife, for a purpose dangerous to the
public peace, contrary to Section 87 of the *Criminal Code* of Canada.

Pursuant to Section 606(4) CCC, with the consent of the prosecutor, the accused
pleads not guilty to the offence charged, but guilty to the offence of possession of a
concealed weapon, and find the accused not guilty of the offence charged but guilty of
the offence of possession of a concealed weapon.

AND WHEREAS on May 22nd, 1990, the Court adjudged that the offender be imprisoned in the Province of British Columbia, for the term of one (1) day, and, in addition
thereto, that the said offender comply with the conditions hereinafter prescribed:

Now, therefore, the said offender shall, for the period of fifteen (15) months from
the date of expiration of his sentence of imprisonment, comply with the following conditions, namely that the said offender shall keep the peace and be of good behaviour
and appear before the Court when required to do so by the court, and, in addition,

1. You will report today to a Probation Officer at 275 E Cordova St., Vancouver,
BC and then report to the Inter Ministerial Project at 219 Main St., Vancouver, BC.
After that you will have to go back to the Inter Ministerial Project Office whenever
they tell you to, at least once a month.

2. *You will, under their direction, seek and take whatever psychiatric assessment or treatment that can be arranged for you, and you shall do that as you are
directed by the Inter Ministerial Project Office.*

3. As directed by the Inter Ministerial Project Office you shall report to the Forensic Psychiatric Outpatient Clinic on West Broadway, Vancouver, BC.

4. You will not have any knives in your pocket; on your possession in a public
place, except while eating in a restaurant.

(Emphasis added.)

On April 9, 1990, the appellant was arrested on a charge of possession of a knife
for a purpose dangerous to the public peace.

The circumstances of the offence were described by counsel for the Crown as
follows:

Your Honour, the circumstances here, it was April 9th, 1990, at approximately three twenty
in the afternoon. A witness sees the accused cross Hornby and approaches a woman who's
standing on the corner. Apparently there's quite a few peoples standing on the corner.

He is holding what appears to be a kitchen knife in his right hand. He is described as
poking it, one of the people, one of these women who was standing there. The woman
moves. There's no contact. The light changes and people start crossing the street. The
accused then picks the knife up, puts it over his head and does really nothing with it. He
then puts the knife back into his pocket.

• • •

The appellant appeared in court on April 11, 1990, and was remanded at that time
for 30 days in order that a psychiatric assessment be obtained.

• • •

From the above assessment, the following facts may be gleaned:

(1) The appellant has been suffering from a chronic mental illness, schizophrenia, since 1982 or earlier.
(2) Since his admission to hospital, the appellant has received medication and his mental condition has greatly improved.
(3) Prior to his discharge from hospital, Dr. Levy discussed with the appellant the possibility of a "long acting," intramuscular injection but this was refused.
(4) The appellant has a past history of non-compliance with medication programs and, therefore, his future prognosis is poor.

We were informed by counsel for the appellant that he is now under the care of a private physician and that he is now, by consent, taking medication as prescribed by his physician.

The order made by McGivern Prov. Ct. J was made pursuant to s. 737(2)(h) of the *Criminal Code* reading as follows:

> (h) comply with such other reasonable conditions as the court considers desirable for securing the good conduct of the accused and for preventing a repetition by him of the same offence or the commission of other offences.

Counsel for the appellant submits that, in the circumstances of this case, a probation order compelling an accused person to "seek and take whatever psychiatric assessment or treatment that can be arranged for you" is contrary to s. 7 of the *Canadian Charter of Rights and Freedoms*.

He made reference to several reports of the Law Reform Commission of Canada in his factum as follows:

> The Law Reform Commission of Canada has considered the issue of treatment in relation to the criminal law in a number of publications. As far back as 1975, the Law Reform Commission in its working Paper number 14, "THE CRIMINAL PROCESS AND MENTAL DISORDER" [1975], indicated that probation orders which contained conditions of psychiatric treatment should only be made where the offender consents. See page 45 of the aforesaid report:

> > Probation orders with conditions of psychiatric treatment should be made only where: (1) the offender understands the kind of program to be followed, (2) he consents to the program and, (3) the psychiatric or counselling services have agreed to accept the offender for treatment.

> See also Working Paper 26, "MEDICAL TREATMENT AND CRIMINAL LAW" [1980], p. 73, where the following recommendations are contained:

> > (10) that the right of a competent adult to refuse treatment be specifically recognized by the *Criminal Code*;
> > (11) that treatment shall not be administered against an individual's refusal, unless there is a finding of incompetence or an exception recognized in law.

He also relied upon the judgment of the Supreme Court of Canada in *Reference re s. 94(2) of Motor Vehicle Act* (1985), 23 CCC (3d) 289, 24 DLR (4th) 536, 48 CR (3d) 289.

I agree with the submissions made by counsel for the appellant. In my opinion, a probation order which compels an accused person to take psychiatric treatment or medication is an unreasonable restraint upon the liberty and security of the accused person. It is contrary to the fundamental principles of justice and, save in exceptional circumstances, cannot be saved by s. 1 of the Charter. Exceptional circumstances are not present here.

While, as counsel for the Crown has stated, it is unlikely that an accused person would be subjected to unusual or dangerous medication or treatment, that risk always exists. In my opinion, it is the protection of the public which is the principal support for an order compelling the compulsory taking of treatment or medication. That is insufficient to save the order under s. 1 of the Charter. Other less drastic means are available to accomplish that purpose.

The fact that the probation order in this case is invalid, as being contrary to the Charter, does not solve the problem confronting the court. While the rehabilitation of the appellant is important, the court must consider the risks involved in permitting the appellant to be at liberty on probation. In other cases, where the trial judge finds as a fact that an accused person is suffering from schizophrenia or a like illness and refuses to consent to prescribed treatment or medication, it might very well be that the trial judge would not consider probation. The risk to society might be too great and only incarceration may afford the necessary protection.

I do not think it is possible to say that a particular form of probation order will be appropriate for all cases. The sentence to be imposed on each offender must be based on the general principles of sentencing which include a consideration of the circumstances of the offence and of the offender. The result is that different conditions may be imposed in probation orders depending on the circumstances of each case. To the extent possible, the conditions should be designed to ensure the protection of the public. However, they should not compel an offender to undergo medical treatment including the compulsory taking of medication. It is with those considerations in mind that now consider the conditions numbered one to four in the probation order in the case at bar.

In this case the appellant has a history of non-compliance with prescribed treatment and medication. However, he has now consented to, and is taking, treatment and medication under the care of a private physician. If he continues to take the advice of his physician and takes medication as prescribed, the risk of unlawful behaviour on the part of the appellant will be greatly reduced.

Having regard to the above, I would supplant conditions numbered one to four in the probation order with the following provisions:

1. You will take reasonable steps to maintain yourself in such condition that:
   (a) your chronic schizophrenia will not likely cause you to conduct yourself in a manner dangerous to yourself or anyone else; and
   (b) it is not likely you will commit further offences.
2. You will forthwith report to a Probation Officer at 275 E Cordova St., Vancouver, BC and thereafter, if directed to do so, you will forthwith report to the Inter Ministerial project at 219 Main St., Vancouver, BC.
3. You will thereafter attend as directed from time to time at the Inter Ministerial project for the purpose of receiving such medical counselling and treatment

as may be recommended except that you shall not be required to submit to any treatment or medication to which you do not consent.

4. If you do not consent to the form of medical treatment or medication which is prescribed or recommended, you shall forthwith report to your Probation Officer and thereafter report daily to your Probation Officer. If directed to do so by your Probation Officer, you shall report to the Inter Ministerial Project at 219 Main Street, Vancouver, BC for the purpose of being monitored with respect to a possible breach of Condition 1 above.

5. You shall provide your treating physician with a copy of this order and the name, address and telephone number of your Probation Officer. You shall instruct your treating physician that if you fail to take medication as prescribed by him or fail to keep any appointments made with him, he is to advise your Probation Officer immediately of any such failures.

6. Except when eating in a restaurant you will not have any knife in your possession.

Appeal allowed.

For a similar ruling, see *R v. Kieling* (1991), 64 CCC (3d) 124 (Sask. CA), where the court deleted a term of probation that required the offender to "take prescribed medication." The offender had a long history of persistently harassing entertainer Anne Murray and her family.

R v. Hynes
(1991), 64 CCC (3d) 421 (Nfld. SCAD)

GOODRIDGE CJN: The appellant, having pleaded guilty to a charge of mischief, was sentenced to the maximum term of two years in prison and placed on probation for a further period of three years. He seeks leave to appeal and, if granted, appeals from this sentence.

The charge was that he interfered with Donald Decker in the lawful use and enjoyment of his property which is located on Norman's Lane in Roddickton, Newfoundland. The offence is contrary to s. 430(1)(c) of the *Criminal Code* which provides:

430.(1) Every one commits mischief who wilfully …

(c) obstructs, interrupts or interferes with the lawful use, enjoyment or operation of property;

He was tried by indictment and the maximum sentence is prescribed by s. 430(4)(a):

430(4) Every one who commits mischief in relation to property, other than property described in subsection (3),

(a) is guilty of an indictable offence and liable to imprisonment for a term not exceeding two years;

Section 430(3) refers to property exceeding $1,000 in value.

The appellant was born on October 30, 1968.

On August 11, 1990, at approximately 10:00 p.m. the police visited the residence of Mr. Decker to discuss some problems that he was having with the appellant. The fact that Mr. Decker would talk to the police incited the appellant. As soon as the police left he attacked the Decker residence. He showered the house with "rocks" three times and each time had to be "scared away." At the time of his arrest the appellant was again in front of the Decker residence and it appeared to some that another onslaught might be forthcoming.

The appellant was under the influence of alcohol at the time. He was on probation not to drink alcohol and not to have any dealings with Mr. Decker or his family. This was a result of a previous criminal offence in relation to the family.

When arrested he kicked and punched the police car at length. He yelled and screamed for a great length of time and threatened to kill Mr. Decker and himself as soon as he was released.

The appellant has a lengthy criminal record.

...

Dr. John Henderson of the Grenfell Health Centre at Roddickton testified. He said that the appellant is a paranoid schizophrenic. The treatment for this is tranquillizers administered either orally or by injection. This illness was diagnosed in September, 1989. He was in an institution for mental and nervous diseases known as the Waterford Hospital at the time of the diagnosis.

The doctor said that there was no cure for schizophrenia but that medication helps to control behavioural problems.

Upon his release from the Waterford Hospital the appellant was given intermuscular medication at the health centre. He was subsequently placed on oral medication but apparently discontinued taking the medication and never returned to the health centre.

The appellant comes from a disturbed family background and spent about a year in Mount Cashel Orphanage. At the age of 18 he was placed in the Whitbourne Boys Home as a consequence of one of the offences above referred to. He has only grade three education and is unable to read or write. He has never worked and is dependent on social assistance. He abuses alcohol and drugs and his social interaction is extremely limited. He is paranoid, aggressive and hostile with very little insight. Mr. Decker has become the object of his hostility and paranoia. Although he is suffering from a paranoid schizophrenic illness, psychiatrists have deemed that he is fit to stand trial but that he should be regarded as being mentally ill to the point of being a danger to others. In the opinion of one psychiatrist he is certifiable under the *Mental Health Act*. The recommendation was that he should continue to receive psychiatric treatment in a controlled setting.

On clinical examination, the appellant admitted to having auditory hallucinations that commanded him to throw rocks at his neighbour's house. He responds well to a drug called piportil.

...

The problem in this case is that the appellant requires medication to abate his conduct. He is currently in Kingston Penitentiary and receiving, presumably voluntarily, medication. The indication from his counsel is that he is progressing favourably.

There is no way that the court can mandate medical treatment while a prisoner is in custody although it may be made a condition of probation. It may be, however, that if a prisoner continues to receive medication and to improve, those responsible for early release may be persuaded that he is an appropriate candidate for early release. If he does not undergo treatment or if he undergoes treatment but does not improve, then those authorities may consider that early release is inappropriate.

The problem here is that if the appellant fails to continue his medication he may revert to his former condition and continue to be a threat to the Decker family.

For this reason, whatever the custodial term may be, probation with conditions for medical treatment is a virtual requirement unless it is precluded by law.

The principle, however, seems to be established that the prison system should not be used as a health institution. A psychiatric condition may warrant a shorter term than is usual but does not justify a term that goes beyond an acceptable range.

The question before the court is whether or not the sentence imposed by Judge Baker was fit. It is for others to determine how much of that sentence should be served within the walls of a penitentiary.

Because of the record of the appellant and because of the possibility, if not probability, that he will revert to his former ways upon release, a shorter than usual term is certainly not indicated.

The trial judge was in error in sentencing the appellant to the maximum term only because other authorities had not stepped in. The sentence must be a fit one. A two-year term is not justified simply because the appellant, because of his mental condition, ought to be kept out of circulation as long as possible. However, a probation order incorporating rehabilitative measures is justified.

The penal authorities and the public health authorities must play a role in this matter. The court cannot subject a person to a longer prison term than normal because of a psychiatric problem.

The appellant, as noted, has a record. He has a propensity for drinking too much and is to some degree addicted to non-prescriptive drugs. There is in fact some indication that this addiction may in some way have induced the paranoid schizophrenic condition. His conduct has persuaded Mr. Decker that it is necessary to keep a shotgun on hand for the protection of his family. This has the potential for death or serious injury. While the measures taken by Mr. Decker are not condoned by the court, they are measures which were induced by the conduct of the appellant. The appellant is aware of his condition and of the need to take medication and has failed to do so. He has limited education and an unfortunate background but this is not necessarily a reason to give a lighter sentence. In fact, a lengthier sentence may have rehabilitative value in some cases.

Deterrence is not a pertinent factor in a case such as this; rehabilitation is. While deterrence generally indicates a longer prison term and rehabilitation a shorter prison term, rehabilitation in this case seems more readily available to the appellant in custody than out.

Given these circumstances and the pressing need for the protection of the public it is the opinion of the court that a severe custodial term is warranted but that two years is beyond the acceptable range. A one-year sentence is substituted. The three-year probation period is proper but the conditions should be varied as follows:

Upon release from custody the appellant shall be on probation for a period of three years upon the following conditions:

(a) he shall report to a probation officer once a month;

(b) he shall abstain from the consumption of alcohol;

(c) he shall abstain from the use of drugs not medically prescribed and not legally available by over the counter sales;

(d) he shall not in any way interfere with Donald Decker, his wife or children;

(e) he shall not enter upon Norman's Lane at Roddickton;

(f) he shall report to adult corrections as they shall direct and abide by conditions set up by adult corrections for taking and ensuring that he take all medically prescribed drugs;

(g) he shall abide by all directions of adult corrections given with respect to psychiatric treatment and health;

(h) he shall advise the RCMP at Roddickton and adult corrections of any change of address.

Leave to appeal is granted. The appeal is allowed and the sentence reduced to one year. The three-year probation period is confirmed upon the statutory conditions and the revised conditions stated above.

The registrar of the court will ensure that the provisions of s. 737(4) of the *Criminal Code* are complied with.

Appeal allowed.

In concluding this section, consideration is given to one of the newest community-based sanctions—electronic monitoring. Electronic monitoring is usually associated with the objective of effecting the "house arrest" of the offender or monitoring compliance with certain probation or bail conditions, such as curfews. In some Canadian jurisdictions, it has become an important aspect of conditional sentences. For reasons explored further in Chapter 12, the use of electronic monitoring in conditional sentencing is likely to increase significantly.

Electronic monitoring has been administered on a small scale in England and in some parts of Canada. See Nellis, "The Electronic Monitoring of Offenders in England and Wales" (1991), 31 *Brit. J Criminology* 165 and Mainprize, "Electronic Monitoring in Corrections: Assessing Cost Effectiveness and the Potential for Widening the Net of Social Control" (1992), 34 *Can. J Criminology* 161.

R v. Erdmann
(1991), 64 CCC (3d) 188 (Sask. CA)

WAKELING JA: The respondent pleaded guilty to two charges of trafficking in *cannabis* resin (hashish), and one charge of possession of hashish for the purpose of trafficking. It is not a case of an isolated incident, but rather a situation where the appellant acknowledges she is a user and has been trafficking for some time but thought it was safe to do so if she restricted her customers to her circle of friends and fellow users. The possession charge did not relate to a relatively trifling quantity, rather, it amounted to one-half pound, for which a price of $2,000 was being considered.

The respondent is 22 years of age and has one child which she has placed with her mother for care and upbringing. She lives common law with a man who is also a user. At the time of the offence, she was employed part time at Sears, working approximately 30 hours per week.

The trial judge felt a sentence of nine months was justified, applying the reasoning of such cases as *R v. McGinn* (1989), 49 CCC (3d) 137, 75 Sask. R 161, 7 WCB (2d) 338, emanating from this court. He, however, concluded that this was a suitable occasion to utilize an electronic monitoring device and therefore ordered a suspended sentence with six months of electronic monitoring and probation for one year.

The principal issue on this appeal was whether the use of an electronic monitoring device was appropriate in this case.

A Crown employee was present in court to answer questions regarding that program and she indicated the electronic monitoring device was being used effectively in a number of cases. When questioned about the criteria which was employed to determine which of the many convicted persons should serve their sentence in this fashion, she responded that it largely depended on the temperamental suitability of the party. In this case, Erdmann was considered a suitable candidate and this had been largely confirmed by reason of the fact she had been successfully monitored for approximately three months.

A program summary was provided and that document described the target group in this way:

> Though a wide range of offenders are eligible for consideration of this sanction, the project's primary emphasis will be on native and female offenders as well as those individuals that normally would receive a sentence of incarceration with probation to follow.
>
> The selection of cases must be done on an individualized basis and will require careful screening of the offenders. In identifying these cases, Corrections will be looking for people that rate at the very high end of the offenders classification system and are clearly candidates for incarceration.

This same issue regarding the use of an electronic monitoring device came before this court fairly recently when on a conviction for dangerous driving the trial judge imposed a sentence of 18 months' probation plus the application of the electronic monitoring program for approximately five months: *R v. Pearman*, delivered November 5, 1990 [since reported 26 MVR (2d) 1; 11 WCB (2d) 430].

In *Pearman*, it was decided that the monitoring device did not provide a suitable penalty and a term of six months should have been imposed. The concern was expressed by the court in the following manner [at 3-4 (MVR)]:

> We note at the outset that the respondent was charged with dangerous driving, a serious offence which resulted in serious injury and damage to the victim. In our opinion, a suspended sentence and imposition of terms under the intensive probation supervision/

electronic monitoring program was inappropriate in the circumstances of the case. The sentence failed to take into account the factor of deterrence and public confidence in the administration of justice. This Court recently stated in *R v. Powell* (1989), 19 MVR (2d) 36, 52 CCC (3d) 403, 81 Sask. R 301 [at 43 (MVR)]:

> "[I]n a crime of this nature, the factor of deterrence must be given adequate consideration. If the sentence adequately emphasizes community disapproval of such conduct by branding it reprehensible, one can hope that it will have a moral and educative effect on the attitude of the public. Not only will the offender refrain from repeating such conduct, but perhaps some other members of the public will appreciate the seriousness of such conduct."

In our opinion, a sentence of 6 months' imprisonment is the minimum imprisonment that should have been imposed in these circumstances.

We are obviously proceeding through the early stages of the electronic monitoring program. It is impossible to say how effective it may become and the extent of its application. It would be unfortunate for this court to set firm and absolute standards for the application of the program in its developmental stage, but at the same time it is quite appropriate to be somewhat cautious in our approach to its implementation. This is particularly so when others have incurred the penalty of institutional incarceration and no special circumstances have been shown to exist for the application of the program in this case, other than the fact the respondent is a temperamentally suitable candidate.

This court has shown its concern about the harmful social consequences of the drug trade and the need to have special concern for the concept of general deterrence in order that everyone may be aware there is no easy way to experiment with the profits available from the sale of drugs. It is not sufficiently clear that the use of this program, in circumstances such as exist here, will adequately continue that message. This concern is consistent with that expressed in *R v. Pearman*.

In the circumstances, this appeal is allowed. A sentence of nine months would ordinarily have been the minimum we would have imposed, but as a period of three months has already been spent with the program, the sentence is set at six months. The question of equivalency was discussed, and Crown counsel seemed generally to accept that it was reasonable to allow a month for a month, and we see no reason in this case to provide otherwise.

The above represents, in a general way, the oral judgment delivered after the hearing. However, upon further reflection, the panel expresses its concern that if the courts are to play the dominant role in determining when this form of punishment is to be adopted, as may well be necessary and appropriate, then more help must be provided to the courts to enable the formulation of appropriate general criteria and the application of that criteria. A decision as to the suitability of this form of punishment cannot be adequately made without some form of report, such as a pre-sentence report, outlining the basis upon which the recommendation is being made. Obviously, only a small percentage of those convicted of an offence are offered the opportunity of participating in this program. That selection must therefore, in fairness, be carefully made and should not be the result of a haphazard process. On the basis of what was before us, we cannot be assured of much more than the temperamental suitability of the respondent.

Appeal allowed.

VI. BREACH OF PROBATION

Some attention has been paid to the meaning of breaching the peace for the purposes of a probation order. In *R v. Grey* (1993), 19 CR (4th) 363 (Ont. Prov. Div.), it was held that a failure to keep the peace required at least an apprehended breach of municipal, provincial or federal law and not some lesser standard of disruption. This was also the view of the Newfoundland Court of Appeal in *R v. D.R.* (1999), 138 CCC (3d) 405. In *R v. Greco* (1999), 136 CCC (3d) 271 (Ont. CJ), it was held that an offender who breaches the peace abroad can still be tried for breach of probation in Canada. The court rejected the suggestion that keeping the peace meant the Queen's peace in Canada, but the scope of this decision might be open to debate. For comparison of procedures on breach of probation and breach of a conditional sentence, see Chapter 12.

When probation accompanies a suspended sentence, theoretically it is the passing of sentence that is suspended. Accordingly, s. 732.2(5) of the Code provides a framework for dealing with a prisoner who, while bound by a probation order, is convicted of another offence, including the offence of non-compliance with a probation order. This can include imposing "any sentence that could have been imposed if the passing of sentence had not been suspended." This procedure is rarely used in most jurisdictions. It is also skeletal in the sense that it is triggered "on application of the prosecutor." Fairness requires more.

R v. Tuckey
(1977), 34 CCC (2d) 572 (Ont. CA)

DUBIN JA: On June 26, 1974, the appellant was given a suspended sentence and placed on probation for a period of three years by His Honour Judge Street, after pleading guilty to a charge of theft. On February 12, 1976, while in custody with respect to other matters, he was brought before the trial Judge. He was given no notice as to the nature of the proceedings which were to be held on that day.

…

Although the present *Criminal Code* does not require the formalities of an information and is silent as to procedure, I am satisfied that the basic principles of natural justice must prevail; one of which principles relevant here is that no man shall be condemned unless he has been given prior notice of the allegations against him and a fair opportunity to make full answer and defence.

In a proceeding under s. 664(4), although there is no longer a requirement for an information on oath, the minimum requirement surely must be that the accused before being brought before the tribunal should be given reasonable notice in writing of the Crown's intention to take such proceedings, which notice should clearly articulate the nature of the proceedings, the grounds upon which the Crown intends to rely in support of its application, the nature of the order sought, and the hearing date. Section 664(5) provides for the procedure which may be followed in bringing the accused before the Court.

In the instant case no such notice was given. The appellant had no opportunity to defend himself. Section 664(4) gives the Court that made the probation order a broad discretion as to the appropriate order to be made on an application brought pursuant to that section. The inquiry is not limited to proof of the violation of any condition in the probation order. It follows that the trial Judge had no right in the circumstances of this case to refuse the appellant his request for an adjournment to obtain counsel. It is to be noted that the appellant's ultimate acquiescence that the proceedings should continue was given *in terrorem*.

...

The appellant had pleaded guilty to a charge of theft. He had a prior criminal record, but the trial Judge originally thought it appropriate to suspend the passing of sentence and make an order for three years' probation. The appellant breached his probation, and an application under s. 664(4) was in order. By his conduct the appellant had forfeited his right to leniency. The function of the trial Judge was then to impose a sentence proportionate to the offence which the appellant had committed. The sentence of 30 months was not proportionate to that offence, even when it was imposed upon a person who was not entitled to leniency.

Appeal allowed.

NOTE

Electronic monitoring or other forms of house arrest are not expressly authorized by any sentencing provision. Can the residual subcategory encompass this form of community sanction? See *R v. M.(D.E.S.)* (1993), 21 CR (4th) 55 (BC CA), in which the rehabilitative principle underlying probation was expanded to include maintenance of rehabilitation in a case where the offences, although serious, occurred a number of years before between a brother and sister who were children when the wrongful sexual conduct began. Now that the definition of the residual subcategory has changed, does this expand or diminish the court's ability to use electronic monitoring or house arrest? Note that the previous definition of the residual subcategory has been transplanted into the conditional sentence provisions. See s. 742.3(3)(f).

As will be seen in Chapter 12, Conditional Sentencing, the Supreme Court has characterized probation as a sanction that is restorative and rehabilitative in purpose. On this basis, it is perhaps arguable that house arrest or even electronic monitoring are inappropriate for probation orders. It is too early to determine whether this argument will gain force. If it does, one explanation might be that judges who previously granted probation orders with some form of house arrest or electronic monitoring have elected to impose conditional sentences.

In some of the materials presented in this chapter, the courts have grappled with the appropriateness of probation orders and their contents. The introduction of conditional sentences might well have a significant effect on the future use of probation orders. The relationship between the two is a matter to watch with some care.

CHAPTER TEN

Monetary Sanctions: Fines and Restitution

I. INTRODUCTION

In this chapter, we consider the use of those forms of intermediate sanctions that involve orders to pay money. A fine is a sanction that uses a monetary burden as a punitive measure. Fines are paid to the state. A fine can be imposed on its own or in conjunction with other sanctions. Although the imposition of a fine raises important procedural issues, it also raises fundamental questions about *quantum*. The amount of the monetary burden imposed depends on the financial resources and income-earning abilities of the offender.

Restitution refers to a monetary order intended to compensate for certain kinds of loss occasioned by the offence. These amounts are paid to the victims. Restitution orders are typically imposed in addition to other sanctions. As they are when imposing fines, the courts are often concerned with ensuring that any restitution order made does not exceed the offender's financial capabilities.

In reviewing the cases and materials below, consider the different penological aims of these two sanctions. In determining whether either one of these sanctions should be imposed, and the amount that is appropriate, have the courts properly distinguished between fines and restitution orders? Do ss. 718 to 718.2 of the *Criminal Code*, RSC 1985, c. C-46, as amended (neither of which the more recent decisions refer to) lend any assistance to this analysis?

II. THE FINE

A. The Public Attitude to Fines

Before examining the relevant statutory provisions, it will be useful to consider how the Canadian public views fines as a sanction. It appears that most Canadians do not believe that a monetary penalty is "punishment."

A. Doob and V. Marinos, "Reconceptualizing Punishment:
Understanding the Limitations on the Use of Intermediate Sanctions"
(1995), 2 *University of Chicago Law School Roundtable* 413 (footnotes omitted)

...

The Limits on the Use of the Fine: A Case Study
of the Limits on Interchangeability

Canada makes heavy use of fines. In fact, fines are the most heavily used disposition in Canadian Criminal Courts. The Canadian Sentencing Commission, like Morris and Tonry, recommended increased use of fines and suggested that a day or unit fine system be developed. Interestingly, however, the Canadian Sentencing Commission never addressed itself to the purposes that fines might or might not be able to serve at sentencing. In particular, it did not explore directly the limits on the use of inter-mediate punishments generally or the fine in particular. Like Morris and Tonry, the Canadian Sentencing Commission saw all punishments as more or less qualitatively similar. This view of the simplicity of punishments was consistent with some very specific Canadian data on the community service order that had been carried out a few years earlier.

In a national public opinion poll, Canadian adults were asked what they thought the most appropriate sentence was for a first-time offender convicted of breaking and entering a private home and stealing property worth $250. They were given various traditional choices: probation, fines, imprisonment, or some combination. Twenty-nine percent chose imprisonment. When these respondents were asked whether instead of imprisonment, they would favor a community service order, almost everyone (90 percent) indicated they would favor it at least sometimes. Forty-one percent would prefer the community service order in all or most cases. An additional 36 percent would want it for "some" cases, with 14 percent favoring it "only in very rare cases."

We and others interpreted these findings to mean that Canadians, in general, support the use of intermediate punishments instead of imprisonment. Perhaps we were par-tially correct. However, it may simply be wrong that one can automatically substitute any convenient intermediate punishment such as a fine or community service for imprisonment when looking for a way to avoid using prison. Even if true, presum-ably there are limits: the size of the penalty has to be appropriate, and of course, as Morris and Tonry point out, the penalty must be imposed, and not just pronounced.

Some data recently collected by one of the authors of this Article suggest that the world is not so simple. In this study, a heterogeneous sample of people in Toronto answered a series of questions about fines. A number of conceptually separate sub-studies were embedded in the survey questionnaire. First, respondents were asked to think about a sentence handed down for a minor shoplifting charge. The sentence was described, for different groups of respondents, as being either a fine of two hun-dred dollars or four hundred dollars, or a prison sentence of four or eight days. The respondents viewed imprisonment as considerably more effective than fines in "expressing society's disapproval for the harm that was caused." At least as interest-ing is that the size of the penalty (within the rather constrained limits used in this experiment) did not make any difference in the perceived denunciatory value of the penalty. However, for both fines and imprisonment, those who had the sentence described to them as involving the higher penalty rated this penalty as being more severe. The results, then, do not appear to be a product of simple differences in perceived severity; if they had been, the results of the denunciatory value of the punishment would be parallel to those of the severity of the punishment.

In the experiment, harsher penalties were seen as being more severe, but imprisonment was seen as having a greater denunciatory value than fines. There appears to be something "special" about imprisonment that fines do not possess. Nevertheless, most of the respondents favored the use of a fine as a punishment for the offense. About 19 percent of the respondents saw a fine or imprisonment as being equally appropriate; about two-thirds of those who differentiated between fines and imprisonment favored the fine. Although the two types of penalties have different denunciatory values in the eyes of the respondents, denunciation cannot be too important, since respondents favor the use of the punishment that is not as able to "express society's disapproval for the harm that was caused."

Respondents were additionally asked whether they thought that "first time offenders who have committed the following offenses [should be given] a fine instead of imprisonment." If they thought that a fine was appropriate, they were to indicate the dollar value of the fine that they would recommend. Respondents could set the fine, then, at any amount they thought appropriate. In terms of severity, the sky was the limit.

The data . . . demonstrate the limited acceptability of the fine. Even when respondents could set a fine of any size, they were generally unwilling to substitute a fine for imprisonment for minor violent offenses. They were, however, willing to suggest a fine as a substitute for imprisonment for most property offenses, even when the value of the property taken is relatively high. Imprisonment can, of course, be used to incapacitate an offender. Hence it is theoretically possible that respondents may have preferred imprisonment for those convicted of violent offenses in order to accomplish this goal. It is unlikely, however, that in the case of "touching a woman in a sexual manner without consent" incapacitation would be seen as an important goal.

There is a final piece of evidence showing that fines had a meaning different from imprisonment. Respondents answered a series of questions in which they were asked to imagine that a particular sentence of imprisonment (expressed in months) was appropriate. They were asked whether they would find a fine of so many months of take-home income as an appropriate substitute. Half of the respondents were told what the cost of imprisonment would be. The critical issue here was whether respondents were affected in their decision by having the cost of imprisonment made salient. It turns out, once again, that the results were offense-specific. For the theft that was described, but not for minor assaults, mentioning the cost of imprisonment led the respondent to favor a fine. Despite being presented with the cost of imprisonment, fines were still viewed as being more appropriate for minor property offenses rather than minor instances of violence.

B. Criminal Code, Sections 734-737

The following sections of the *Criminal Code* are concerned with the applicability of the fine. They incorporate substantial amendments made to the sentencing provisions in 1996. Although the main section relating to fines—s. 734—is quite straightforward, the provisions become complex in their response to defaults after an offender has been ordered to pay a fine.

    734(1) A court that convicts a person, other than a corporation, of an offence, except an offence that is punishable by a minimum term of imprisonment, may, in addition to or in lieu of any other sanction that the court is authorized to impose, fine the offender, subject to subsection (2), by making an order under section 734.1.

    (2) A court may fine an offender under this section only if the court is satisfied that the offender is able to pay the fine, or discharge it under section 736.

    (3) For the purposes of this section and sections 734.1 to 737, a person is in default of payment of a fine if the fine has not been paid in full by the time set out in the order made under section 734.1.

    (4) Where an offender is fined under this section, a term of imprisonment, determined in accordance with subsection (5), shall be deemed to be imposed in default of payment of the fine.

    (5) The length, in days, of the term of imprisonment referred to in subsection (4) is the lesser of

        (a) a fraction of which

           (i) the numerator is the aggregate of

              (A) the unpaid amount of the fine, and

              (B) the costs and charges of committing and conveying the defaulter to prison, calculated in accordance with regulations made under subsection (7), and

           (ii) the denominator is equal to eight times the provincial minimum hourly wage, at the time of default, in the province in which the fine was imposed, rounded down to the nearest whole number of days, and

        (b) the maximum term of imprisonment, expressed in days, that the court could itself impose on conviction.

    (6) All or any part of a fine imposed under this section may be taken out of moneys found in the possession of the offender at the time of the arrest of the offender if the court making the order, on being satisfied that ownership of or right to possession of those moneys is not disputed by claimants other than the offender, so directs.

    (7) The lieutenant governor in council of a province may make regulations respecting the calculation of the costs and charges referred to in clause (5)(a)(i)(B) and in paragraph 734.8(1)(b).

    734.1. A court that fines an offender under section 734 shall do so by making an order that clearly sets out

        (a) the amount of the fine;

        (b) the manner in which the fine is to be paid;

        (c) the time or times by which the fine, or any portion thereof, must be paid; and

        (d) such other terms respecting the payment of the fine as the court deems appropriate.

734.2. A court that makes an order under section 734.1 shall

(a) cause to be given to the offender

(i) a copy of the order,

(ii) an explanation of the substance of sections 734 to 734.8 and 736,

(iii) an explanation of available programs referred to in section 736 and of the procedure for applying for admission to such programs, and

(iv) an explanation of the procedure for applying under section 734.3 for a change in the terms of the order; and

(b) take reasonable measures to ensure that the offender understands the order and the explanations given to the offender under paragraph (a).

734.3. A court that makes an order under section 734.1, or a person designated, either by name or by title of office, by that court, may, on application by or on behalf of the offender, subject to any rules made by the court under section 482, change any term of the order except the amount of the fine, and any reference in this section and sections 734, 734.1, 734.2 and 734.6 to an order shall be read as including a reference to the order as changed pursuant to this section.

. . .

734.5. Where an offender is in default of payment of a fine,

(a) the person responsible, by or under an Act of the legislature of the province to whom the proceeds of the fine belong by virtue of subsection 734.4(1), for issuing or renewing a licence, permit or other similar instrument in relation to the offender may refuse to issue or renew the licence, permit or other instrument until the fine is paid in full, proof of which lies on the offender; or

(b) where the proceeds of the fine belong to Her Majesty in right of Canada by virtue of subsection 734.4(2), the person responsible, by or under an Act of Parliament, for issuing or renewing a licence, permit or other similar instrument in relation to the offender may refuse to issue or renew the licence, permit or other instrument until the fine is paid in full, proof of which lies on the offender.

734.6(1) Where

(a) an offender is in default of payment of a fine, or

(b) a forfeiture imposed by law is not paid as required by the order imposing it, then, in addition to any other method provided by law for recovering the fine or forfeiture,

(c) the Attorney General of the province to whom the proceeds of the fine or forfeiture belong, or

(d) the Attorney General of Canada, where the proceeds of the fine or forfeiture belong to Her Majesty in right of Canada,

may, by filing the order, enter as a judgment the amount of the fine or forfeiture, and costs, if any, in any civil court in Canada that has jurisdiction to enter a judgment for that amount.

(2) An order that is entered as a judgment under this section is enforceable in the same manner as if it were a judgment obtained by the Attorney General of the province or the Attorney General of Canada, as the case may be, in civil proceedings.

734.7(1) Where time has been allowed for payment of a fine, the court shall not issue a warrant of committal in default of payment of the fine

(a) until the expiration of the time allowed for payment of the fine in full; and

(b) unless the court is satisfied

(i) that the mechanisms provided by sections 734.5 and 734.6 are not appropriate in the circumstances, or

(ii) that the offender has, without reasonable excuse, refused to pay the fine or discharge it under section 736.

(2) Where no time has been allowed for payment of a fine and a warrant committing the offender to prison for default of payment of the fine is issued, the court shall state in the warrant the reason for immediate committal.

· · ·

735(1) A corporation that is convicted of an offence is liable, in lieu of any imprisonment that is prescribed as punishment for that offence, to be fined in an amount, except where otherwise provided by law,

(a) that is in the discretion of the court, where the offence is an indictable offence; or

(b) not exceeding twenty-five thousand dollars, where the offence is a summary conviction offence.

(2) Section 734.6 applies, with such modifications as the circumstances require, where a fine imposed under subsection (1) or under any other Act of Parliament is not paid forthwith.

736(1) An offender who is fined under section 734 may, whether or not the offender is serving a term of imprisonment imposed in default of payment of the fine, discharge the fine in whole or in part by earning credits for work performed during a period not greater than two years in a program established for that purpose by the lieutenant governor in council

(a) of the province in which the fine was imposed, or

(b) of the province in which the offender resides, where an appropriate agreement is in effect between the government of that province and the government of the province in which the fine was imposed,

if the offender is admissible to such a program.

(2) A program referred to in subsection (1) shall determine the rate at which credits are earned and may provide for the manner of crediting any amounts earned against the fine and any other matters necessary for or incidental to carrying out the program.

(3) Credits earned for work performed as provided by subsection (1) shall, for the purposes of this Act, be deemed to be payment in respect of a fine.

(4) Where, by virtue of subsection 734.4(2), the proceeds of a fine belong to Her Majesty in right of Canada, an offender may discharge the fine in whole or in part in a fine option program of a province pursuant to subsection (1), where an appropriate agreement is in effect between the government of the province and the Government of Canada.

s. 737(1) Subject to subsection (2), where an offender is convicted or discharged under section 736 of an offence under this Act or the *Controlled Drugs and Substances Act*, the court imposing sentence on or discharging the offender shall, in addition to any other punishment imposed on the offender, order the offender to pay a victim fine surcharge in an amount not exceeding

(a) fifteen per cent of any fine that is imposed on the offender for that offence or, where no fine is imposed on the offender for that offence, ten thousand dollars, or

(b) such lesser amount as may be prescribed by, or calculated in the manner prescribed by, regulations made by the Governor in Council under subsection (5), subject to such terms and conditions as may be prescribed by those regulations.

(2) Where the offender establishes to the satisfaction of the court that undue hardship to the offender or the dependants of the offender would result from the making of an order under subsection (1), the court is not required to make the order.

(3) Where the court does not make an order under subsection (1), the court shall

(a) provide the reasons why the order is not being made; and

(b) enter the reasons in the record of the proceedings or, where the proceedings are not recorded, provide written reasons.

(4) A victim fine surcharge imposed under subsection (1) shall be applied for the purposes of providing such assistance to victims of offences as the lieutenant governor in council of the province in which the surcharge is imposed may direct from time to time.

(5) The Governor in Council may, for the purposes of subsection (1), make regulations prescribing the maximum amount or the manner of calculating the maximum amount of a victim fine surcharge to be imposed under that subsection, not exceeding the amount referred to in paragraph (1)(a), and any terms and conditions subject to which the victim fine surcharge is to be imposed.

(6) Subsections 734(2) to (4) and sections 734.1, 734.3 and 734.7 apply, and section 736 does not apply, in respect of a victim fine surcharge imposed under subsection (1).

C. The 1996 Amendments to the Fine Provisions

The new statutory provisions have addressed a number of situations that presented problems in the past. One anachronism required that a fine could be imposed for a sentence punishable by more than five years' imprisonment *only* if it was imposed *in addition to* a term of imprisonment. To satisfy this peculiar requirement, the courts were forced to impose ludicrous one-day prison sentences. This charade saw the offender enter into custody, only to be released moments later. Now, s. 734(1) authorizes the use of a fine for any offence, either in addition to or in lieu of another punishment.

1. Means To Pay

Section 734(2) requires the sentencing judge to be satisfied that the offender is able to pay the fine before making the order. Before this amendment, the issue of means to pay and the need for an inquiry was a source of controversy. In *R v. Snider* (1977), 37 CCC (2d) 189 (Ont. CA), Martin JA made the following ruling in a case involving a $25,000 fine for a bookmaking offence where the offender recorded bets of $1,000,000 over a six-week period:

> Unfortunately, no inquiry was conducted by the trial Judge before imposing the fine as to the appellant's ability to pay it. We do not in any way criticize the trial Judge for failing to conduct such an inquiry in this case, as there was no indication by defence counsel (who is not the counsel for the appellant in this Court) that the appellant could not pay a substantial fine when that disposition was suggested by the Crown Attorney.

We think that in cases of this kind, substantial fines are required if they are to act as a deterrent. In our view, the trial Judge should first consider whether a fine, as opposed to a custodial sentence, is an appropriate disposition. In some cases of this kind the trial Judge might, of course, consider that the imposition of a custodial sentence, even though the offender was not a principal, was necessary. In the present case however, the trial Judge accepted the submission of Crown counsel and did not impose a custodial sentence.

Counsel for the Crown does not dispute that the appellant is unable to pay the fine imposed. Having decided that a fine is an appropriate disposition, the trial Judge should only impose a fine that is within the offender's ability to pay, bearing in mind of course, the possibility that he may extend the time for payment. Otherwise a custodial sentence results from inability to pay the fine.

We have carefully considered whether we ought in this case to substitute a custodial sentence in lieu of the fine imposed by the trial Judge on the basis that it was an inappropriate disposition, as was done in *R v. Hall* (1968), 52 Cr. App. R 736. We think, however, in the particular circumstances of this case, that we should not interfere with the trial Judge's discretion in imposing a fine. Since, however, the fine exceeds the appellant's ability to pay we have concluded that we should allow the appeal, reduce the fine to the sum of $2,400, payable over a period of two years and in default of payment the appellant is to be imprisoned for three months, and, in addition, the appellant will be placed on probation for two years on the statutory conditions. The appeal is allowed to give effect to this variation.

The importance of considering the financial means of the offender becomes apparent in the context of the enforcement provisions. Failure to pay a fine may result in a period of imprisonment. Thus, it is critical that, at the "front end" of the process—when the fine is actually imposed—it does not exceed the means of the offender. Fines that are beyond the means of an offender may turn into *de facto* prison terms due to the enforcement mechanism of imprisonment in default.

2. Enforcement: Imprisonment in Default

Until 1996, ordering imprisonment in default of payment of a fine was discretionary. However, this discretionary order was commonly made. As a result, large numbers of Canadians were incarcerated for non-payment of fines. The extent of such imprisonment raised the anachronistic spectre of imprisonment for debt. Surely, incarceration should be a response to criminal conduct, not financial status. Even small fines may be beyond the means of some people. Some courts expressed concerns about imprisonment in default.

R v. Deeb; R v. Wilson
(1986), 28 CCC (3d) 257 (Ont. Prov. Ct.)

SCULLION SENIOR PROV. CT. J: The accused, Mahmoud Ahmed Deeb, appeared before me on April 4, 1986, on a charge that on or about November 26, 1985, in the Municipality of Metropolitan Toronto in the Judicial District of York unlawfully did commit an assault on Nuccio Ferri contrary to s. 245 of the *Criminal Code*. The Crown elected to proceed summarily. The accused pleaded not guilty. After a lengthy trial the accused as found guilty and was sentenced by me on May 22, 1986.

Charles W. Wilson appeared before me on May 22, 1986, and was arraigned on a charge of mischief.

The Facts—Mahmoud Ahmed Deeb

On November 26, 1985, the accused was drinking at Pat & Mario's Tavern located at 2300 Yonge St. in the City of Toronto. He was with several friends, had been drinking prior to entering the premises and had further consumed alcohol while in the tavern. At about 11:00 p.m. he left the tavern and went down the hall to the washroom. The complainant who worked for the tavern as an assistant manager told the accused that he could not come back into the establishment because he and his friends were causing trouble. The assistant manager sent a waiter back to the accused's table. The waiter notified his friends that the accused was barred from the tavern and brought his coat back to the accused. The accused lashed out suddenly and hit the assistant manager on the right cheek and nose. A small altercation broke out and the police were called. The assistant manager received a bloody nose and swelling over the right eye. The accused, Deeb, had a prior finding of guilt from 1983 for which he received a conditional discharge.

The Facts—Charles W. Wilson

On January 6, 1986, at about 4:45 in the morning, the accused and another man went to the dwelling-house at 11 Boston Ave. in the City of Toronto. They were under the impression that the occupant of the dwelling-house, Darren Spice, whom they believed had stolen the accused's video cassette recorder (VCR), was on the premises. They had been drinking all evening and brought a piece of steel pipe along which they used to smash open the door of the premises. They smashed the window on the door and caused damage to the amount of $186.50. The actual owners of the home, Dale and Sharon Beers, confronted the accused. There was a slight scuffle and the accused threatened Mr. Beers with the pipe. The accused and the other man left the premises and were shortly [after] apprehended by the police. The accused paid $150 to the landlord for the door and $36.50 to Sharon Beers for the lock. The police are continuing their investigation regarding Darren Spice in connection with the VCR. On the above facts, I convicted the accused.

On the question of sentence on both of these matters the Crown did not ask for a period of incarceration but submitted that a substantial fine was the proper sentence. After hearing submissions from both counsel, I determined that a fine was the proper sentence in both these matters and rejected a period of incarceration. I fined Mahmoud Ahmed Deeb $300 and 60 days to pay and Mr. Wilson $500 with 90 days to pay. The Crown argues that there should be an alternative because in their view if there is no alternative the accused will not pay his fine.

On Friday, February 14, 1986, the Honourable Ian G. Scott, Attorney-General for the Province of Ontario, addressed the John Howard Society conference in Toronto.

He says, on p. 3 of his speech:

> Sentencing should reflect the social mores of the time. Questions of contemporary morality, of right and wrong, of fairness, and of deeply held beliefs about human conduct and human nature, are inevitably encountered in attempts to reform the law.
>
> Our job, the job for all of us, is not merely to follow public opinion with respect to the sentencing of offenders, but also to lead that public opinion, which may cry for revenge.

On p. 5, he says:

> I would rather rely on the discretion of the Judge and his or her balance of humanitarian values, to make these measures a condition of probation. I believe that the community has an extremely powerful influence on the positive re-integration of an offender. *I do believe that the search and identification of alternatives to incarceration must continue. This view holds true for all levels of the courts and sentencing.*
>
> • • •

I agree with the Attorney-General that we must find alternatives to incarceration. As a result, I obtained from the Ministry of Corrections a graph showing the relationship between admissions of fine defaulters and time served in provincial institutions:

• • •

It is evident from this graph that 32.4% of the admissions to our provincial institutions are fine default admissions. In fact, what the courts are doing is creating a debtors prison. In the case of *R v. Natrall* (1972), 9 CCC (2d) 390 at p. 397, 32 DLR (3d) 241, 20 CRNS 265 (BC CA), Justice Tysoe JA states: "I agree that no one should be imprisoned for non-payment of a fine if in truth he is so devoid of means that he is quite unable to pay it." Further, on p. 397:

> The spirit and intent of the section is that, when it comes to imposing a fine and imprisonment in default of payment thereof, consideration shall be given to the means of the particular accused and the amount of the fine and the terms of payment shall not be such that they are beyond his ability to meet. Indeed, in some cases the Judge may leave the matter in the position that imprisonment is not to follow default in payment but recovery of the fine is to be left to civil proceedings by the Crown. ...
>
> • • •

From the reading of this article and a review of the authorities, I am driven to the view that imprisonment in default of a fine is simply an enforcement mechanism for the collection of those unpaid fines and should not be a consideration by the court unless there are unusual and exceptional circumstances to warrant imprisonment. A judge in coming to the conclusion that a fine is the proper sentence has already rejected a period of incarceration. The mechanism for proceeding civilly is already in place in the Province of Ontario under the *Young Offenders Act* and *Provincial Offences Act*. Therefore, by proceeding through the civil court the Crown could alleviate the problems and pressures on the province's correctional institutions that were mentioned by the Attorney-General in his speech to the John Howard Society.

In addition, police departments would not have to enforce committal orders and would have more personnel available for the prosecution of criminals and the safeguarding of our streets. The actual effect of the "debtors prison" would be ended.

In summary, having considered all of the above reasons, I am in agreement with the Attorney-General when he states that the courts should look for alternatives to imprisonment and I am in agreement with the learned authors of the article, "Imprisonment in Default and Fundamental Justice," in that there should not be imprisonment in lieu of a fine at the time of sentence unless there are unusual circumstances. I leave the question of whether there is a breach of the *Charter of Rights* for another time.

Turning to the two cases at hand, I can find no unusual circumstances to indicate that these two accused will not pay their fines within the prescribed time. Both of these accused are working and if further time to pay the fines is required they can make an application for extension or in the alternative the Crown can proceed by civil process. I have therefore come to the conclusion that it is not necessary to impose a period of imprisonment as an alternative to payment of the fines and I so ordered.

For further consideration of these issues, see MacDougall, "*Hebb*: Imprisonment in Default of Fine Payment and S. 7 of the Charter" (1989), 69 CR (3d) 23; Jobson and Atkins, "Imprisonment in Default and Fundamental Justice" (1986), 28 *Crim. LQ* 251; and Kimball, "In the Matter of Judicial Discretion and the Imposition of Default Orders" (1989-90), 32 *Crim. LQ* 467.

The 1996 amendments dramatically changed the mechanism for dealing with fine defaults. First, s. 734(5) provides a formula for calculating the extent of imprisonment in default that, pursuant to s. 734(4), is "deemed to be imposed." Does this mean that a judge has no discretion to refuse to add default time?

More significantly, before a warrant for committal can issue, it must be determined that alternative collection steps have been tried and failed (see s. 734.7(1)). Are these mechanisms sufficient to ensure that people are not being incarcerated for poverty?

III. RESTITUTION

Before the 1996 amendments, the *Criminal Code* addressed the issue of making an offender reimburse his or her victims through two mechanisms. The Code contained a separate provision that permitted sentencing judges to make "compensation orders" in favour of named victims. Compensation orders could be enforced against the offender in the same way as a civil judgment. The Code also authorized the inclusion of "restitution orders" as a term of probation. Fashioned in this manner, the restitution order was enforceable, like any other term of probation, with the threat of a criminal charge under s. 733.1.

Since 1996, a discrete form of restitution order has replaced the pre-existing provisions. The new provisions, ss. 738 to 741.2, answer a number of the technical issues that plagued the earlier scheme. In considering these sections and the applicable cases, keep in mind the following two purposes of sentencing as stated in s. 718 of the *Criminal Code*:

> (e) to provide reparations for harm done to victims or to the community; and
>
> (f) to promote a sense of responsibility in offenders, and acknowledgement of the harm done to victims and to the community.

A. Criminal Code, Sections 738-741.2

738(1) Where an offender is convicted or discharged under section 730 of an offence, the court imposing sentence on or discharging the offender may, on application of the Attorney General or on its own motion, in addition to any other measure imposed on the offender, order that the offender make restitution to another person as follows:

(a) in the case of damage to, or the loss or destruction of, the property of any person as a result of the commission of the offence or the arrest or attempted arrest of the offender, by paying to the person an amount not exceeding the replacement value of the property as of the date the order is imposed, less the value of any part of the property that is returned to that person as of the date it is returned, where the amount is readily ascertainable;

(b) in the case of bodily harm to any person as a result of the commission of the offence or the arrest or attempted arrest of the offender, by paying to the person an amount not exceeding all pecuniary damages, including loss of income or support, incurred as a result of the bodily harm, where the amount is readily ascertainable; and

(c) in the case of bodily harm or threat of bodily harm to the offender's spouse or child, or any other person, as a result of the commission of the offence or the arrest or attempted arrest of the offender, where the spouse, child or other person was a member of the offender's household at the relevant time, by paying to the person in question, independently of any amount ordered to be paid under paragraphs (a) and (b), an amount not exceeding actual and reasonable expenses incurred by that person, as a result of moving out of the offender's household, for temporary housing, food, child care and transportation, where the amount is readily ascertainable.

(2) The lieutenant governor in council of a province may make regulations precluding the inclusion of provisions on enforcement of restitution orders as an optional condition of a probation order or of a conditional sentence order.

739. Where an offender is convicted or discharged under section 730 of an offence and

(a) any property obtained as a result of the commission of the offence has been conveyed or transferred for valuable consideration to a person acting in good faith and without notice, or

(b) the offender has borrowed money on the security of that property from a person acting in good faith and without notice,

the court may, where that property has been returned to the lawful owner or the person who had lawful possession of that property at the time the offence was committed, order the offender to pay as restitution to the person referred to in paragraph (a) or (b) an amount not exceeding the amount of consideration for that property or the total amount outstanding in respect of the loan, as the case may be.

740. Where the court finds it applicable and appropriate in the circumstances of a case to make, in relation to an offender, an order of restitution under section 738 or 739, and

(a) an order of forfeiture under this or any other Act of Parliament may be made in respect of property that is the same as property in respect of which the order of restitution may be made, or

(b) the court is considering ordering the offender to pay a fine and it appears to the court that the offender would not have the means or ability to comply with both the order of restitution and the order to pay the fine, the court shall first make the order of restitution and shall then consider whether and to what extent an order of forfeiture or an order to pay a fine is appropriate in the circumstances.

741(1) Where an amount that is ordered to be paid under section 738 or 739 is not paid forthwith, the person to whom the amount was ordered to be paid may, by filing the order, enter as a judgment the amount ordered to be paid in any civil court in Canada that has jurisdiction to enter a judgment for that amount, and that judgment is enforceable against the offender in the same manner as if it were a judgment rendered against the offender in that court in civil proceedings.

(2) All or any part of an amount that is ordered to be paid under section 738 or 739 may be taken out of moneys found in the possession of the offender at the time of the arrest of the offender if the court making the order, on being satisfied that ownership of or right to possession of those moneys is not disputed by claimants other than the offender, so directs.

741.1. Where a court makes an order of restitution under section 738 or 739, it shall cause notice of the content of the order, or a copy of the order, to be given to the person to whom the restitution is ordered to be paid.

741.2. A civil remedy for an act or omission is not affected by reason only that an order for restitution under section 738 or 739 has been made in respect of that act or omission.

B. The Application of the Provisions

The above provisions are new, and describe the new mechanism in detail. Accordingly, many cases dealing with the pre-existing mechanisms will have little relevance, except to show the legislative history and explain why some provisions have been enacted.

1. The Constitutionality of Restitution

It has been argued that the inclusion of restitution provisions in the *Criminal Code* is improper because reparation between offender and victim is a matter for the civil litigation process. This issue is addressed in the following decision of *Zelensky*. Although this case was decided under the pre-existing provisions, it is still relevant to the current legislative scheme. It explains the proper place and scope of restitution sanctions within the criminal law sphere.

R v. Zelensky
(1978), 41 CCC (2d) 97 (SCC)

LASKIN CJC: This appeal, brought here by leave to this Court, challenges the majority judgment of the Manitoba Court of Appeal (Matas JA, Hall and O'Sullivan JJA, concurring; Monin JA, Guy JA, concurring, dissenting) which invalidated s. 653 of the *Criminal Code* and held also, and in any event, that Provincial Court Judge Collerman erred in law in making an order for compensation under that provision and in directing restitution of stolen property under s. 655. The order for compensation and for restitution was a composite order made at the time the respondent Anne

Zelensky was sentenced to imprisonment and to a term of probation after pleading guilty to theft and was in pursuance of an application or such relief made by T. Eaton Company Limited, the victim of the theft.

The validity of s. 655 was not impeached before the Manitoba Court of Appeal or before this court, and there was nothing in the reasons of Matas JA [33 CCC (2d) 147; 73 DLR (3d) 596], which pertained particularly to the direction for restitution of the stolen goods by way of contesting that part of the trial Judge's composite order. It appears to have been swept out by reason of its association with the order for compensation. Counsel for the respondent Anne Zelensky did not complain here of the order for restitution and, in my view, it must stand as a severable order validly made under s. 655, whatever be the disposition as to the order for compensation under s. 653 and as to the validity of this last-mentioned provision.

...

Sections 653, 654 and 655 have been in the *Criminal Code* in similar but not exact formulation since the Code's enactment in 1892: see ss. 836, 837, 838. The original of the present s. 653, namely s. 836, provided for compensation not exceeding $1,000 upon the application of the person aggrieved, the amount to be deemed a judgment debt owing by the accused and enforceable in the same way as an order for costs under s. 832, which provided, *inter alia*, for satisfaction in whole or in part out of money belonging to and taken from the accused on his arrest.

The provision for compensation was not then tied expressly to the sentencing process as is now the case under s. 653. Under the original of the present s. 654, namely, s. 837, where property involved in the offence was sold to a *bona fide* purchaser and restored to the true owner, the purchaser could apply for compensation out of money of the accused taken from him on his apprehension. The present s. 654 clearly goes farther in providing for an order for a money payment, subject to the Court being able to direct that all or part of the compensation to the purchaser be paid out of money in the possession of the accused at the time of his arrest and which is indisputably his. Neither in [s.] 836 [nor] 837 was there any such express provision as now exists in ss. 653 and 654 for filing the order for compensation, with effect as a judgment enforceable as if it was a judgment in civil proceedings.

The principle of restitution under the present s. 655 is carried forward from the original s. 838, but the present provision is more explicit (if, indeed, the original provision covers the point at all) that an order will not be made if there is a dispute as to ownership of the property involved by claimants other than the accused. No such issue arose in the present case and, as I have already said, the order for restitution must stand.

It appears to me that ss. 653, 654 and 655, historically and currently, reflect a scheme of criminal law administration under which property, taken or destroyed or damaged in the commission of a crime, is brought into account following the disposition of culpability, and may be ordered by the criminal Court to be returned to the victimized owner if it is under the control of the Court and its ownership is not in dispute or that reparation be made by the offender, either in whole or in part out of money found in his possession when arrested if it is indisputably his and otherwise under an order for compensation, where the property has been destroyed or damaged.

I think s. 655(2) gives particular emphasis to the scheme in providing for an order of restitution, even if the accused has been acquitted, where the property involved in the commission of an offence is under the control of the Court. The integrity of the scheme is seen in s. 654, already mentioned, which enables the Criminal Court to tidy up a situation where stolen property has been sold to a *bona fide* purchaser and it is available for restoration to the victimized owner, the Court authorized upon such restitution to inflict upon the offender a liability to pay to the innocent purchaser what he gave for the goods.

• • •

Apart from the question of enforcement under s. 666(1) (which may be contrasted with the enforcement open under s. 653 by filing the compensation order in a superior Court with effect as a judgment thereof), I see no difference in principle between a provision for reparation in a probation order, as an additional term of what is in effect a sentence, and a direction for compensation or reparation by an order under s. 653 which, if made at all, must be made at the time sentence is imposed. I find little to choose, except on the side of formality, in the requirement of s. 653 that the compensation order must be based on an application by the person aggrieved rather than be made by the Court *suo motu* as is apparently, but only apparently, the position under s. 663(2)(e).

• • •

There is, moreover, another important aspect of s. 653 that must be kept in mind. The court's power to make a concurrent order for compensation as part of the sentencing process is discretionary. I am of the view that in exercising that discretion the Court should have regard to whether the aggrieved person is invoking s. 653 to emphasize the sanctions against the offender as well as to benefit himself. A relevant consideration would be whether civil proceedings have been taken and, if so, whether they are being pursued.

There are other factors that enter into the exercise of the discretion, such as the means of the offender, and whether the criminal Court will be involved in a long process of assessment of the loss, although I do not read s. 653 as requiring exact measurement. A plea of guilty will, obviously, make the Court's task easier where it is asked to make an order of compensation, but there is no reason why an attempt to secure agreement on the amount of loss should not be made where the conviction follows a plea of not guilty. It is probable, of course, that the likelihood of an appeal will militate against agreement but I would add that I do not regard it as a function of the criminal Court to force agreement to enable it to make an order for compensation. What all of this comes to is that I agree with Matas JA that, constitutionality apart, an order for compensation should only be made with restraint and with caution.

The present case is one in which restraint and caution should have been exercised in a refusal to make a compensation order. The aggrieved company instituted civil proceedings, for the recovery of money and merchandise stolen from it by the offenders, a day before criminal charges were brought against them. It continued with the civil proceedings, taking steps in connection therewith while the criminal proceedings were in progress, and even after the offenders had pleaded guilty to theft. The aggrieved company then decided to seek a compensation order under s. 653 and a dispute arose with respect to the amount of the loss, particularly in relation to the money that was allegedly stolen. So far as appears, the civil proceedings were maintained while the application for a compensation order was pursued. The civil proceedings were justified because of the desire to get a garnishment order. In all the circumstances, I would not interfere with that part of the judgment of the majority of the Manitoba Court of Appeal holding that the order for compensation should not have been made.

I wish to dwell further on the course of proceedings in this case in order to provide some guidance to trial Judges on the proper application of s. 653 and in order to make clear that s. 653 is not to be used *in terrorem* as a substitute for or a reinforcement for civil proceedings. Its validity is based, as I have already said, on its association with the sentencing process, and its administration in particular cases must be limited by that consideration.

What emerges from the facts here is that the T. Eaton Company sought to use the criminal process as a more expeditious means of recovering the money lost by the fraudulent activities of the accused. Its co-operation with the Crown during the early course of the criminal proceedings is understandable, but at the same time it was pursuing a civil remedy against the accused, and the civil proceedings had reached the stage of discovery when the accused came up for sentencing by the criminal Court. Eaton's then joined in the criminal proceedings as an "aggrieved person," and it became evident immediately that the amount of the loss suffered by it was in dispute. The dispute was not resolved, as it would have been under the procedures available in a civil Court, and the order for compensation made in the criminal proceedings was somewhat arbitrary as to amount.

Section 653 does not spell out any procedure for resolving a dispute as to quantum; its process is, *ex facie*, summary but I do not think that it precludes an inquiry by the trial Judge to establish the amount of compensation, so long as this can be done expeditiously and without turning the sentencing proceedings into the equivalent of a civil trial or into a reference in a civil proceeding. What is important is to contain s. 653 within its valid character as part of the sentencing process and thus avoid the allegation of intrusion into provincial legislative authority in relation to property and civil rights in the Province. Although, as I have already noted, the Courts have recognized the wide scope of the federal power in relation to criminal law and criminal procedure, and although there is now a broad range of powers in a sentencing Court to deal with offenders, it none the less remains true that the criminal law cannot be used to disguise an encroachment upon provincial legislative authority: see *Re Reciprocal Ins. Legislation* (1924), 41 CCC 336, [1924] 1 DLR 789, [1924] AC 328; *Reference re Validity of s. 5(2) of the Dairy Industry Act (Margarine Case)*, [1949] 1 DLR 433 at pp. 473-4, [1949] SCR 1 at p. 50; affirmed [1950] 4 DLR 689, [1951] AC 179 *sub nom. Canadian Federation of Agriculture v. A-G Quebec.*

It must be obvious, therefore, that s. 653 is not the platform upon which to unravel involved commercial transactions in order to provide monetary redress to those entitled thereto as against an accused. The latter, too, may have a proper interest in insisting that civil proceedings be taken against him so that he may avail himself of the procedures for discovery and production of documents, as well as of a proper trial of issues which go to the merit of monetary claims against him. Again, the criminal Court cannot be expected to nor should it act under s. 653 if it would be required to interpret written documents in order to arrive at a sum of money sought through an order of compensation. So too, it would be improper to invoke s. 653 if the effect of provincial legislation would have to be considered in order to determine what order should be made. Indeed, any serious contest on legal or factual issues, or on whether the person alleging himself to be aggrieved is so in fact, should signal a denial of recourse to an order under s. 653.

The following case of *R v. Devgan* takes *Zelensky* as a starting point, but demonstrates the problems that can occur when the criminal restitution process collides with the civil process.

R v. Devgan
(1999), 136 CCC (3d) 238 (Ont. CA)

LABROSSE JA: The appellant was convicted by German J on January 26, 1996 of one count of fraud ("count 1") and one count of making a false statement ("count 2"), contrary to sections 380(1)(a) and 362(1)(c) of the *Criminal Code*. The two counts involved different complainants. On May 17, 1996, the trial judge sentenced the appellant to ninety days in jail to be served intermittently. On application by the Crown, the trial judge made two compensation orders under s. 725(1) of the *Criminal Code*, one in favour of each complainant. This appeal is only concerned with the validity of the compensation orders.

Sections 725(1) and (2) read as follows:

> 725(1) A court that convicts or discharges under section 736 an accused of an offence may, on the application of a person aggrieved, at the time sentence is imposed, order the accused to pay to that person an amount by way of satisfaction or compensation for loss of or damage to property suffered by that person as a result of the commission of the offence.
>
> (2) Where an amount that is ordered to be paid under subsection (1) is not paid forthwith, the applicant may, by filing the order, enter as a judgment, in the superior court of the province in which the trial was held, the amount ordered to be paid, and that judgment is enforceable against the accused in the same manner as if it were a judgment rendered against the accused in that court in civil proceedings.

Section 725 (now 738) was amended on September 3, 1996. The parties agreed that the amendments are of no consequence for the purpose of this appeal.

Count 1

Count 1 related to the appellant fraudulently placing a mortgage on the complainant's business property in the amount of $425,000. The appellant misled the complainant as to the true value of the mortgage. She believed that she was renewing a mortgage for $83,000.

The complainant commenced a civil action against the appellant and others on September 26, 1988. The action was settled on March 11, 1993. The appellant consented to judgment for $110,000 with interest thereon, to be paid to the complainant on specific terms. Prior to March 11, 1993, the appellant made an assignment in bankruptcy. The minutes of settlement provided that the judgment survived the bankruptcy of the appellant. At the time of the sentencing hearing, the complainant was receiving payments pursuant to the terms of the settlement.

In support of its application for compensation under s. 725(1) of the *Criminal Code*, the Crown relied on a letter from the former solicitor for the complainant in respect of the mortgage transaction. The letter stated that, in addition to the amount of the settlement in the civil action, the complainant had sustained a loss of $78,534.83 for legal fees and disbursements related to the fraudulent mortgage. The letter also stated that the solicitor estimated that no more than $5,000 of the total fees and disbursements had been expended in the prosecution of the civil action against the appellant which ultimately settled. The balance of the legal fees and disbursements related to other proceedings against the appellant and other persons.

In her reasons for sentence, the trial judge stated that she would not make a compensation order with respect to the judgment "because it would just duplicate what she [the complainant] already has. She has a judgment for the amount that is outstanding." However, when advised that costs were never awarded to the complainant as part of the minutes of settlement, the trial judge made a compensation order for $73,534.83. This figure represented the total for legal fees and disbursements incurred by the complainant less the estimated $5,000 in costs related to the settled civil claim. Presumably, this amount was deducted because these costs could have been part of the settlement.

Count 2

Count 2 related to a loan made by the second complainant to the appellant by way of a promissory note in the amount of $100,000. The promissory note falsely indicated that the appellant had an interest in the property subject to the mortgage in count 1.

The complainant instituted a civil action against the appellant for fraud. On December 6, 1989, she recovered by way of summary judgment the principal amount of $100,000 and prejudgment interest of $28,900.

The trial judge made a compensation order in favour of the complainant in the amount of $128,900 which amount included both the principal and prejudgment interest. She saw no difficulty in awarding interest as part of the compensation order, although concerns were raised during submissions as to the propriety of including interest in a compensation order. Moreover, unlike count 1, she was not concerned with any issue of duplication in granting the second compensation order despite the existing civil judgment.

The appellant appeals from both compensation orders.

Positions of the Parties

It is the position of the appellant that the trial judge erred in issuing the compensation orders. He argues that as both complainants had obtained civil judgments against him prior to the criminal proceedings, the doctrine of *res judicata* operated to bar the granting of the compensation orders under s. 725(1) of the *Criminal Code*. If this argument fails, the appellant maintains that the granting of the compensation orders was not a proper exercise of the discretion conferred by s. 725(1).

The respondent argues that the doctrine of *res judicata* has no application to this case and that the making of the compensation orders was a proper exercise of discretion by the trial judge in sentencing the appellant.

Issues

The issues on this appeal are twofold. First, whether a civil judgment can serve as a bar to a compensation order under s. 725(1) of the *Criminal Code* on the basis of *res judicata*. Second, whether, in the circumstances of this case, the making of the compensation orders by the trial judge was a proper exercise of discretion.

Res Judicata

In *London Life Insurance Co. v. Zavitz* (1992), 12 CR (4th) 267, the British Columbia Court of Appeal addressed the issue of *res judicata* in relation to s. 725(1) of the *Criminal Code*. In that case, London Life alleged that it had been defrauded by the defendant and brought a civil action against her for the amount of its loss. The defendant also pleaded guilty to a criminal charge of fraud. As part of her sentence, London Life was granted a compensation order pursuant to s. 725(1). London Life filed its compensation order in the Supreme Court of British Columbia and sought to proceed with its civil action against the defendant. A chambers judge dismissed the action, finding that the compensation order was a complete bar on the basis of *res judicata*. In allowing an appeal from this decision, the Court of Appeal concluded that a compensation order made under s. 725(1) cannot operate as *res judicata* to bar a civil action. At p. 270, McEachern CJBC, speaking for the court, stated:

> … Chief Justice Laskin [in *R v. Zelensky* (1978), 41 CCC (2d) 97 (SCC)] concluded that Parliament has not purported to interfere with any right of civil recourse by reason of the making of a compensation order. That and the facts: (a) that compensation orders are discretionary both as to whether an order should be made and as to amount (which might be less than the amount owed); (b) they carry no interest; (c) they are doubtfully assignable; (d) they are not subject to appeal except by the accused; and, (e) they are intended for an entirely different purpose, that is, as part of the sentencing process, persuade me I should not give the compensation order the status of a judgment for the purpose of the *res judicata* doctrine. …
>
> My conclusion therefore is that the compensation order stands outside the civil law system and, except as to quantum of an ultimate judgment, does not bar or impede the

civil process. I say this because a plaintiff must, of course, give credit for any amount recovered under a compensation order.

See, also, *Williamson v. Wyton* (1984), 42 CPC 20 (Ont. Prov. Ct.); and *Hurley v. Foreman* (1962), 35 DLR (2d) 596 (NBQB).

Accordingly, the law is well-established that a compensation order cannot serve as a bar to a civil action on the basis of *res judicata*.

The appellant does not question this proposition. However, he maintains that in the reverse situation res judicata applies with the result that an existing civil judgment precludes the granting of a compensation order.

In *R v. Carter* (1990), 9 CCLS 69 (Ont. Ct. (Gen. Div.)), a decision not referred to by the parties, Borins J (as he then was) considered this very issue. In Carter, the accused was convicted of numerous fraud-related offences. On sentencing, the accused, like the appellant in the instant case, opposed the making of a compensation order under s. 725(1) because the victim had previously obtained a civil judgment against him. The application for compensation was also opposed by the accused on the ground that as an undischarged bankrupt he was unable to pay the amount of any compensation order.

Borins J rejected both arguments. At p. 4 of his reasons, he said:

> In my view, it is settled law that the granting of a compensation order is part of the sentencing process and is separate and distinct from the process of civil recovery, and that the existence of an unsatisfied civil (judgment against an accused is simply a circumstance for the sentencing judge to take into consideration in the exercise of the judge's discretion in determining whether or not a compensation order is to be granted. Similarly, the fact that an accused is bankrupt and may not have the financial ability to pay a compensation order are circumstances for the sentencing judge to consider. This conclusion is based on two decisions of the Supreme Court of Canada, *R v. Zelensky* [citations omitted]; and *R v. Fitzgibbon* [citations omitted]; and the decision of the Ontario Court of Appeal in *R v. Scherer* (1984), 16 CCC (3d) 30. In my opinion, this is a proper case in which to issue a compensation order.

The position of the appellant cannot succeed for the same reasons referred to in *Zavitz* and *Carter*. Just as s. 725 does not purport to interfere with any right of civil recourse, neither can a civil judgment purport to usurp the power given to a sentencing judge under s. 725(1). Compensation orders are discretionary, both as to whether an order should be made and as to amount. At most, the existence of a civil judgment is but a factor for the sentencing judge to consider in exercising this discretion.

I also note that certain essential requirements for the application of the doctrine of *res judicata* are not met in this case. Specifically, the availability of *res judicata* depends on identity of parties and of subject matter. The compensation orders are intended for an entirely different purpose than the civil remedies, namely as part of the sentencing process. Moreover, the Crown was a party to both compensation orders but was not involved in the civil actions. Similarly, the complainants were both parties in the civil actions but were not parties at the criminal proceedings. See

Maynard v. Maynard, [1951] SCR 346 at 358-59, [1951] 1 DLR 241; and Spencer Bower and Turner, *The Doctrine of Res Judicata* (2nd ed., 1969) at pp. 18-19.

The argument that a civil judgment operates as a bar to a compensation order under s. 725(1) of the *Criminal Code* on the basis of *res judicata* therefore fails.

Exercise of Discretion

The remaining issue is whether, in the circumstances of this case, the making of the compensation orders involved a proper exercise of discretion.

The starting point for this analysis is the decision of the Supreme Court of Canada in *R v. Zelensky* (1978), 41 CCC (2d) 97. In *Zelensky*, the accused pleaded guilty to theft. In addition to a term of imprisonment, the sentencing judge made a compensation order pursuant to s. 653(1) (s. 725(1)) of the *Criminal Code*). The victim had also instituted a civil action against the accused which was continuing at the time of the order. The principal issue was whether s. 653 was ultra vires Parliament as legislation pertaining to property and civil rights which properly fell within the legislative competence of the province. Laskin CJ, speaking for the court, reviewed the historical development of compensation orders under the *Criminal Code* and determined that s. 653 was valid legislation as part of the criminal sentencing process.

More to the point with respect to the issues raised in this appeal, Laskin CJ held that a court's power to make a compensation order as part of the sentencing process is discretionary. See, also, *R v. Fitzgibbon* (1990), 55 CCC (3d) 449 (SCC) at 453.

In *Zelensky*, Laskin CJ identified certain objectives and factors that relate to the application of s. 725(1). These considerations have been expanded upon in subsequent cases. Below, I have consolidated these objectives and factors, all of which are relevant to the issue of what constitutes a proper exercise of discretion for the purpose of s. 725(1).

1. An order for compensation should be made with restraint and caution;
2. The concept of compensation is essential to the sentencing process:

    (i) it emphasizes the sanction imposed upon the offender;
    (ii) it makes the accused responsible for making restitution to the victim;
    (iii) it prevents the accused from profiting from crime; and
    (iv) it provides a convenient, rapid and inexpensive means of recovery for the victim;

3. A sentencing judge should consider;

    (i) the purpose of the aggrieved person in invoking s. 725(1);
    (ii) whether civil proceedings have been initiated and are being pursued; and
    (iii) the means of the offender.

4. A compensation order should not be used as a substitute for civil proceedings. Parliament did not intend that compensation orders would displace the civil remedies necessary to ensure full compensation to victims.

5. A compensation order is not the appropriate mechanism to unravel involved commercial transactions;
6. A compensation order should not be granted when it would require the criminal court to interpret written documents to determine the amount of money sought through the order. The loss should be capable of ready calculation.
7. A compensation order should not be granted if the effect of provincial legislation would have to be considered in order to determine what order should be made;
8. Any serious contest on legal or factual issues should signal a denial of recourse to an order;
9. Double recovery can be prevented by the jurisdiction of the civil courts to require proper accounting of all sums recovered; and
10. A compensation order may be appropriate where a related civil judgment has been rendered unenforceable as a result of bankruptcy.

For a discussion of these factors, see *R v. Zelensky* at 111-13; *R v. Fitzgibbon* at 454-55, *London Life Insurance Co. v. Zavitz* at 270; *R v. Scherer* (1984), 16 CCC (3d) 30 (Ont. CA) at 37-38; *R v. Salituro* (1990), 56 CCC (3d) 350 (Ont. CA) at 372-73; *R v. Horne* (1996), 34 OR (3d) 142 (Gen. Div.) at 148-49; and *R v. Carter* at 75-76.

It is in light of these considerations that an exercise of discretion under s. 725(1) must be assessed. None of these considerations by themselves are determinative of whether a compensation order should be granted. The weight to be given to individual considerations will depend on the circumstances of each case. Nor is the preceding list intended to be exhaustive. Indeed, other relevant considerations may arise in future cases.

I appreciate that a reviewing court should not lightly interfere with the exercise of discretion necessarily involved in imposing a sentence. As made clear by the Supreme Court of Canada in *R v. Shropshire* (1995), 102 CCC (3d) 193 (SCC), the appropriate standard of review in this context is one of reasonableness. This court should therefore only interfere with the trial judge's exercise of discretion in granting the compensation orders under s. 725(1) if the trial judge applied wrong principles or if the sentence was excessive or inadequate. See, also, *R v. M.(C.A.)* (1996), 105 CCC (3d) 327 (SCC).

Count 1

With respect to count 1, the trial judge exercised her discretion in refusing to grant a compensation order for the amount of the civil judgment which, as she said, would only duplicate what the complainant had already received. There was no question that as a debt or liability arising out of fraud, the judgment survived the bankruptcy of the appellant under s. 178(1)(e) of the *Bankruptcy and Insolvency Act*, RSC 1985, c. B-3. In addition, as already noted, the minutes of settlement expressly provided for this outcome.

It remains to be determined whether the compensation order for legal fees and disbursements was valid.

The parties have not provided any case where legal costs were included as part of a compensation order. Whether s. 725(1) contemplates compensation for legal fees and disbursements requires a close reading of that section. For ease of reference, s. 725(1) is reproduced. It provides:

> 725(1) A court that convicts or discharges under section 736 an accused of an offence may, on the application of a person aggrieved, at the time sentence is imposed, order the accused to pay to that person an amount by way of satisfaction or compensation for loss of or damage to property suffered by that person as a result of the commission of the offence.

The wording of this section is clear and unambiguous. Under s. 725(1), the court can order the accused to pay an amount by way of satisfaction or compensation for loss or damage to property as a result of the criminal offence in question.

In *R v. Zelensky*, Laskin CJ commented on the scope of s. 725. At p. 103, he said:

> It appears to me that ss. 653, 654 and 655 [ss. 725, 726, and 727], historically and currently, reflect a scheme of criminal law administration under which property, taken or destroyed or damaged in the commission of a crime, is brought into account following the disposition of culpability, and may be ordered by the criminal Court to be returned to the victimized owner if it is under the control of the Court and its ownership is not in dispute or that reparation be made by the offender, either in whole or in part out of money found in his possession when arrested if it is indisputably his and otherwise under an order for compensation, where the property has been destroyed or damaged.

In *R v. Brunner* (1995), 27 Alta. LR (3d) 436, 97 CCC (3d) 31, Conrad JA, speaking for the Alberta Court of Appeal, relied on this same statement in concluding that s. 25 was never intended to provide compensation for loss of rents or profits from loss of property. In reaching this conclusion, he noted that the wording of s. 725(1) makes no reference to damages arising from loss of use of property.

Section 725(1) also makes no mention of compensation for legal costs arising out of loss or damage to property. This is not a question of discretion. The wording of the section does not authorize the making of a compensation order for legal fees and disbursements.

The Court in *R v. Brunner* found that s. 725(1) was never intended to confer upon the criminal courts the right to award civil loss-of-use damages to a victim. I also read this section as compelling the conclusion that it does not permit the making of a compensation order for legal costs incurred to recover property lost or damaged as a result of a criminal offence. Parliament never intended to confer upon the criminal courts the right to award compensation for legal fees and disbursements as part of a compensation order. An order under this section is limited to an amount representing the actual loss of the property.

Extending s. 725 to include recovery for incidental damages would cross the constitutional boundary of s. 725 and intrude upon the jurisdiction of the civil courts. As Laskin CJ stated in *R v. Zelensky* at p. 111:

> The constitutional basis of s. 653 must, in my opinion, be held in constant view by a Judge called upon to apply its terms. It would be wrong, therefore, to relax in any way the requirement that the application for compensation be directly associated with the sentence imposed as the public reprobation of the offence.

To paraphrase Conrad JA in *R v. Brunner*, claims for legal fees and disbursements, like claims for loss of use or profits, would change the nature of the criminal inquiry, and properly fall within the domain of the civil courts.

Accordingly, in my view, a compensation order for the complainant's legal fees and disbursements should not have been granted. This is not the proper subject matter of s. 725.

The compensation order in respect of count 1 is therefore set aside.

Count 2

Turning to count 2, the compensation order made in favour of the complainant was for the total civil judgment which included the loss suffered by the complainant of $100,000 together with interest of $28,900.

In *R v. Bordonaro* (1983), 10 WCB 353 (Ont. Co. Ct.), an application was made for a compensation order pursuant to s. 653(1) of the *Criminal Code* for an amount which included a claim for prejudgment interest. Cartwright Co. Ct. J noted that s. 653(1) permitted the making of an order "by way of satisfaction or compensation for loss of property." On this wording, he concluded that it was not within the competence of the court to include pre-judgment interest as part of a compensation order.

In *R v. Carter*, Borins J concluded that a compensation order made under s. 725(1) of the *Criminal Code* could include interest. He relied on the decision of the English Court of Appeal in *R v. Schofield*, [1978] 2 All ER 705. In that case, the court was dealing with s. 35(1) of the *Powers of Criminal Courts Act*, 1973 (UK), 1973, c. 62. The Act provided "compensation for any personal injury, loss or damage resulting from that offence." The court interpreted these words as not being limited to any particular kind of loss, provided the loss was a result of the criminal offence. Borins J applied this reasoning to his interpretation of s. 725(1) in making a compensation order that included interest.

In my view, that reasoning cannot be applied to the wording of s. 725(1). Unlike s. 35(1) of the *Powers of Criminal Courts Act*, 1973, compensation for loss under s. 725(1) of the *Criminal Code* is limited to a particular kind of loss, namely loss of or damage to property as a result of the commission of the offence. In making an order under this section, compensation is restricted to the loss of the property itself and does not extend to loss of the use of the property or interest on it. The wording of s. 725(1) does not permit the inclusion of interest in a compensation order made under this section.

The balance of the compensation order comprised the loss of the $100,000 loan with respect to which the complainant had already obtained a judgment in 1989. The trial judge did not give reasons why she was of the view that a compensation order should nonetheless be made for the same loss. Presumably, the reason the trial judge included this amount as part of the order was to address the possibility that the complainant would not be able to enforce her civil judgment against the appellant given his subsequent bankruptcy in 1993.

As indicated earlier, the $100,000 debt that formed the basis of the civil judgment was also the subject matter of the conviction on count 2 for the offence of making a false statement contrary to s. 362(1)(c) of the *Criminal Code of Canada*. Section 178(1)(e) of the *Bankruptcy and Insolvency Act* provides that an order of discharge does not release a bankrupt from any debt or liability for obtaining property by false pretenses or fraudulent misrepresentation. The complainant's civil judgment against the appellant appears to come within the wording of this section and to survive the appellant's discharge from bankruptcy. However, it is not apparent from the record whether this outcome was specifically addressed either in the civil proceedings or at the bankruptcy discharge hearing. In these circumstances, it was entirely appropriate for the trial judge to make a compensation order for the amount of $100,000 so as to obviate any necessity for further civil proceedings.

Accordingly, the appeal is allowed. The compensation order for $73,534.83 is set aside and the compensation order for $128,000 is reduced to $100,000.

Appeal allowed.

[The Supreme Court of Canada denied leave to appeal in *Devgan*.]

2. The Means To Pay a Restitution Order

Although the fine provisions make a finding about the offender's means and ability to pay a necessary part of the procedure, means is not mentioned in the new restitution provisions. With respect to the pre-existing compensation order, Martin JA in *R v. Scherer* (1984), 16 CCC (3d) 30 (Ont. CA)—a case involving a large-scale breach of trust fraud—made the following comment about compensation and means to pay:

> [S]ince a compensation order under s. 653 is enforceable as a civil judgment, entirely different considerations apply to the making of an order under s. 653 and the making of restitution or reparation a term of a probation order under s. 663 of the Code. In the latter case, it is incumbent on the sentencing tribunal before making restitution or reparation a term of probation to satisfy itself that the term is one which can reasonably be performed during the period of probation. To impose restitution or reparation as a term of a probation order which cannot realistically be complied with is to invite a breach of the probation order. No such consideration applies to an order under s. 653.
>
> Mr. Morphy for the appellant stressed that one of the factors mentioned by Chief Justice Laskin that should be taken into account by the sentencing court in exercising its discretion to make a compensation order is "the means of the offender." I do not read the Chief Justice's judgment, however, as indicating that the means of the offender is, in every case, controlling. It may be that in some cases it would be inappropriate and undesirable to make a compensation order in an amount that it is unrealistic to think the accused could ever discharge. However, in the present case, counsel stated before the trial judge and before us, and it is not in dispute, that in order to qualify for compensation the Law Society requires the victim to exhaust his remedies against an accused. The least expensive and most expeditious way for an applicant for compensation to satisfy this requirement is to obtain an order under s. 653. The Law Society accepts such an order, duly filed under s. 653(2), as a victim's obligation to proceed against an accused. In my view, where the amount lost by the victims

of the appellant's criminal conduct is admitted it would not be sensible to require them to incur the additional expense of undertaking civil proceedings to establish their loss, nor do I believe that it would assist in the appellant's rehabilitation to permit him to put his victims to this additional trouble and expense.

The trial judge in making the compensation order took into account: (a) the fact that the appellant did not dispute the amounts claimed by the victims; (b) the fact that the victims had not instituted civil proceedings, and (c) the fact that not requiring the victims to take civil proceedings did not deprive the appellant of any procedural safeguard that he wished to assert.

In making the compensation orders the trial judge also stated that because over one-half of the total amount misappropriated was misappropriated after august, 1982, it lent credence to the applicants' argument that there should be an investigation to "see if the accused is really as destitute as everyone otherwise seems to suggest." Mr. Morphy disputed this statement. He submitted that it was undisputed on the sentencing proceedings that the appellant was without means and that if this had been an issue, it could readily have been established that the appellant had no assets with which to discharge the compensation orders. In the circumstances, I am prepared to proceed on the assumption that the appellant at the time the compensation orders were made had no assets with which to discharge them and that there is little likelihood he will ever have the means to satisfy them.

In my view, however, it was appropriate having regard to the others matters that I have referred to, for the trial judge in the exercise of the discretion conferred on him by s. 653 to make the compensation orders.

R v. Biegus
(1999), 141 CCC (3d) 245 (Ont. CA)

FELDMAN JA: The appellant was involved in 7 bank thefts in 1994. The ringleader, Hornett, worked for Intercon Security and as a result had access to the Royal Bank branches. The appellant participated with Hornett in all 7 thefts, and for one of them, Hornett had recruited a third man, Vance. Hornett and a fourth man, Dobson conducted 4 other thefts in the same way.

The modus operandi for all of the thefts was similar and involved gaining access to the combination for the ATM machine in the branch and using that combination to empty the bank's ATM of its stock of $5 and $20 dollar bills. The total amount stolen in all of the thefts was $1.1 million.

Each of the 4 men pleaded guilty. The appellant's proceedings were separate from the others. He received a sentence of two years less a day and a restitution order in favour of the Royal Bank in the amount of $638,534.00. He has served his jail sentence and seeks to appeal the quantum of the restitution order.

The ringleader, Mr. Hornett was involved in all 11 of the thefts which resulted in a total loss to the Royal Bank of $1,099,622.24, of which $237,000 was recovered from the perpetrators. Mr. Hornett received a sentence of 4 years in the penitentiary as well as two restitution orders totalling $862,622.24, one in favour of the Royal Bank for $409,234.54 and the other in favour of American Home Insurance, its insurer for $453,387.70. The amount of $862,622.24 represented the entire unrecovered portion of the bank's total loss, $453,387.70 of which, relating only to the 7 Hornett/Biegus thefts, had been repaid to the bank by its insurer.

Mr. Dobson was involved in 4 of the thefts with Mr. Hornett. He received a sentence of two years in the penitentiary and a restitution order of $210,088.72 in favour of the Royal Bank. This was the amount which he and Mr. Hornett stole in the four robberies in which he participated. No part of that money had been repaid to the bank by insurance. Mr. Vance was involved in only one theft and was very co-operative with the police. He received a conditional sentence of 60 days.

Mr. Biegus was involved in 7 break-ins on three nights with Mr. Hornett. The total loss from those thefts was $652,534.12. Mr. Biegus co-operated fully with the police. He returned $14,000 which he had available in cash. The bank instituted civil proceedings against him, pursuant to which an order was obtained which froze all of his assets including a house which he had purchased and GIC's. The freeze order was put in place pending the outcome of the sentencing.

Mr. Biegus had used his share of the funds to continue his school career at Ryerson, to place a down payment on a house and to make some investments. He did not embark upon an extravagant lifestyle, in contrast with Mr. Hornett who spent the money on expensive goods.

During the sentencing proceedings, counsel for Mr. Biegus suggested to the court that the most that Mr. Biegus received as his share of the proceeds of the crimes he committed with Mr. Hornett (and Mr. Vance) was $250,000, although exact figures were not available. He indicated that Mr. Biegus was prepared to accept a restitution order in that amount.

The Crown sought a sentence of two years less a day in reformatory as well as a restitution order in the amount of $638,534 in favour of the bank. ($652,534 – $14,000). The trial judge accepted that submission.

Crown counsel on the appeal indicated that each of the restitution orders made in these cases is considered to be joint and several, the effect being that to the extent that the bank recovers from any one of the perpetrators, the amount of the recovery accrues to the benefit of the others and the principle of subrogation also applies.

In my view the sentencing judge erred in law in the imposition of the restitution order on the appellant, by failing to give any consideration to the issue of the ability of the appellant to pay the amount ordered. This resulted in an order which was excessive in the circumstances.

Furthermore, the effect of the four orders in these cases where there are multiple perpetrators and where the orders overlap in amount because they are each intended to cover the entire amount of the loss for which each was responsible, is to create an unclear legal situation on the issue of accounting and subrogation. For example, what will determine whether it is the appellant or Dobson who is able to claim the benefit of any payment which may be made by Hornett to the bank on its judgment? Or, to the extent that Hornett may make any payment to the insurance company on its judgment which represents part of the bank's loss on the Hornett/Biegus thefts, what is the legal mechanism for the appellant to obtain credit for such payment in respect of his order which is all in favour of the bank?

Ability To Pay

This court has recently addressed the proper factors which a sentencing judge is to weigh when considering whether to impose a restitution order, now under s. 738 of the *Criminal Code*, as part of a sentence: *R v. Devgan* (1999), 44 OR (3d) 161 at 168.

The issue was also recently fully canvassed by the Manitoba Court of Appeal in *R v. Siemens* (1999), 136 CCC (3d) 353.

Both courts have pointed out that one of the factors which the court is to consider is the ability of the accused to pay. A restitution order made by a sentencing court survives any bankruptcy of the accused: *Bankruptcy and Insolvency Act*, RSC 1985, c. B-3, s. 178(1)(a). Therefore, it is there for life. It is not intended to be such a burden that it may affect the prospects for rehabilitation of the accused. That is why ability to pay is one of the factors which the court must consider.

In a case such as this where the perpetrator committed crimes jointly with others and split the proceeds, no one perpetrator is in a position on his own to make good the full loss to the victim from the property stolen, even though each is fully responsible for the victim's full loss. Section 738 of the Code provides for compensation to any person for the loss of property "as a result of the commission of the offence."

Therefore where the sentencing court is considering a restitution order in these circumstances, it must give particular consideration to the source from which the convicted person is going to be able to repay the portion of the funds which went to a co-accused.

· · ·

In this case during submissions on sentence the judge had the following exchange with defense counsel:

> THE COURT: Well, let's be practical. The man is only going to live another 50 years. He won't be able to pay $600,000.
>
> Mr. McKinnon: No, he won't be.
>
> THE COURT: So I mean we're talking just hot air really that I would be talking if I imposed a restitution order for $600,000. We know he's not going to pay that.

In his reasons for sentence, the judge discussed the appellant's inability to pay in the context of remorse as follows:

> I have some difficulty with the question of restitution and the remorse other than that expressed by Mr. Biegus which was expanded upon significantly by Mr. McKinnon. In my view, if there was remorse which had commenced in the mind and heart of the accused prior to his being investigated there would be now significantly more money available to pay to the bank by way of restitution than $14,000 and the interest in a home which he apparently has purchased. In other words, if remorse had set in shortly after the commission of the offences ceased, in my view the accused would have squirrelled away certainly a larger amount of money than $14,000 in order to pay the money back to the bank which he had stolen.
>
> So with the uncertainty, and even unlikelihood of restitution anywhere near the amount that the bank has lost, being obvious from the facts which have been put before

me, I have some difficulty with the degree or the depth of the remorse with which the accused is now motivated. But I do, as I have said, pay heed to the importance of there being some consideration given the accused not only for his plea of guilty but for his co-operation with the police upon his being investigated. In my view, the sentence of two years less a day significantly reflects that advantage to the accused.

There is no other discussion of the factors to be considered in the imposition of a restitution order as part of a sentence. The judge imposed a sentence of two years less a day in jail and added that "a restitution order will go in favour of the Royal Bank for $638,534."

The sentencing judge recognized the accused's inability to pay the order imposed, but failed to address why that fact became irrelevant in ultimately imposing the order. Although the sentencing court is not required to make ability to pay the overriding consideration in respect of a restitution order, it is one of the factors which the court must consider and weigh: *R v. Fitzgibbon* (1990), 40 OAC 81 at 90 (SCC). In this case it is clear that the court was very aware of the inability to pay and appeared to therefore consider the order somewhat futile, but imposed it in any event. In my view the judge erred in that regard.

For the purpose of the appeal the appellant was cross-examined by Crown counsel as to his current income status. He is employed in a job which pays him $30,000 a year. Over time he has the potential to earn a salary of $45,000-$50,000 in a job in his field. This information does not change the conclusion of the sentencing judge that he will never be able to pay the amount of the restitution order. The appellant advised the court at the appeal that he would be prepared to accept an order in the amount of $264,000 which he believed represented his share of the proceeds of the stolen money.

The Effect of Ordering Restitution of the Full Amount Stolen Against Each of the Three Perpetrators

In this case, the effect of the restitution orders against Hornett, Dobson and Biegus works a potential unfairness to Biegus in the event that the Bank or its insurer may be able to recover any portion of the loss from Hornett.

First, on the facts presented by the Crown on the appeal $453,387.70 of the $638,534 for which the appellant is responsible has been repaid to the Bank by its insurer. Nevertheless, the appellant was ordered to pay the full amount as restitution to the Royal Bank, although at the sentencing hearing, counsel did attempt to explain the insurance involvement to the court. No issue was raised on appeal as to the propriety of the order made, and as such, I make no comment on it. However, one potential problem for the appellant is that to the extent that payment may be made by Hornett on the American Home judgment, there is no mechanism by which such payment will be treated as credit to the appellant on his judgment in favour of the Bank.

Second, because of the fact that Biegus and Dobson were involved in entirely separate thefts, neither is entitled to any credit on his judgment for a payment by the other to the Bank. However, if Hornett makes any payment, there is no mechanism for determining which thefts are to be credited and therefore whose judgment is to be reduced, Dobson's or the appellant's. Because these orders were made as restitution orders in separate criminal proceedings, instead of through the civil process where the issues of the mechanics of orderly and fair recovery could be fully canvassed and the appropriate orders or directions made, the result is that these issues have not been addressed or provided for.

In *Devgan* and *Siemens*, the courts both reiterated the long-standing principle that restitution orders are to made cautiously and with restraint and are intended to be applied where the circumstances are relatively simple and straightforward in terms of the amount to be ordered and the effect of the order. In *Siemens*, at p. 357 the court stated as the final principle that "The fact that there were multiple participants in the crimes ... is a factor which militates against a restitution order enforceable against one accused, but not against the others." This case is a variation on that fact situation, and suggests a variation on that principle: Where there are multiple perpetrators, the order must ensure not only the proper recovery for the victim, but also not work an unfairness as between the perpetrators that would not result if the matter had been left to the civil courts.

Although there is no bar which prevents a court from making an order against each co-accused for the full amount of the victim's loss if the circumstances justify such an order, because of the various complications resulting from the orders made in the separate proceedings on the guilty pleas of Hornett and Dobson, it was not appropriate for the sentencing judge in this case to make a restitution order against the appellant for the full amount stolen. However, in another case it may be possible to reconcile orders made against co-accused or in separate proceedings in a way that would not have the potential to work unfairness to any of the parties.

The issue then becomes the appropriate amount of the restitution order in this case. In all the circumstances, the amount of the order should be limited to the amount that the appellant acknowledged he received from the robbery and for which he could not seek indemnity from Hornett, nor claim credit for any amount paid by Hornett. There is no suggestion on this record that this amount is inaccurate.

Such an order would not preclude the Bank from continuing with the civil proceedings against the appellant for the higher amount if it so chose, as the doctrine of *res judicata* does not apply in respect of civil judgments and restitution orders (see *Devgan* at p. 165-67). It would also make the restitution order a fair one within the principles which are applicable for the imposition of such orders.

Conclusion

The sentencing judge erred by failing to consider the factor of ability to pay in determining the quantum of the restitution order, and by failing to take account of the potentially unfair effect of the orders already made against other accused on the execution of the restitution order for this appellant. As a result this court may assess and impose the order which it considers reasonable in the circumstances.

I would therefore grant leave to appeal sentence in respect of the restitution order, allow the appeal, set aside the restitution order in favour of the Royal Bank in the

amount of $638,534, and impose an order in favour of the Royal Bank in the amount
of $264,000.

Other cases have held that the offender's means is a relevant, but not controlling, factor.
See *R v. Shapiro* (1987), 35 CCC (3d) 364 (Ont. Dist. Ct.) (a fraud by a chartered
accountant) and *R v. Fitzgibbon* (1990), 76 CR (3d) 378 (SCC) (a fraud by a lawyer).
Fitzgibbon also held that under the pre-existing compensation provision, the Law Society
of Upper Canada qualified as an aggrieved person because its compensation fund had
made payments to the clients who had been defrauded. Could an order in favour of the
Law Society still be made under the new provisions?

Although it seems self-evident that the means of the offender ought to be relevant to
the *quantum* of a fine imposed on an offender, should it be relevant to the application of
the restitution provisions? If the amount of the restitution order is easily quantifiable,
why should a court refrain from making a restitution order if the offender demonstrates
that he is unable to pay? Inability to pay is no answer to a civil action for damages. Why
should it be relevant in the criminal law sphere?

PROBLEM

Assume that you are a trial judge. You have just convicted an offender on a charge of
"fraud over $5,000" where the loss totalled $9,000. You have decided that a conditional
sentence of 18 months is the appropriate disposition but you also want to order restitution. The offender works as an engineer and can make periodic payments. Can you order
that he pay $500 per month? How would you make this order? What if you decide that
the appropriate disposition is a suspended sentence and a probation period of 18 months?
Could you use the probation order to include a schedule for payment of the restitution?
Note that before the 1996 amendments the probation provisions contained a discrete
optional condition dealing with restitution, which was commonly used to sequence
payments over time. This provision was repealed and not replaced with one that deals
expressly with sequenced payments.

CHAPTER ELEVEN

Imprisonment

I. INTRODUCTION

Imprisonment is available as a penalty for all offences. The *Criminal Code*, RSC 1985, c. C-46, as amended, stipulates the maximum period of imprisonment that may be imposed. Only rarely does it provide for minimum penalties (see the discussion of minimum penalties below). Sentences of less than two years are served in provincial or territorial institutions (see s. 743.1(3)), while sentences that extend for two years or more, either by themselves or in the aggregate with other sentences, are served in federal penitentiaries (see ss. 743.1(1) and (5)). The structure and decision-making processes of the federal penitentiary system are determined by the *Corrections and Conditional Release Act*, SC 1992, c. 20, which replaced both the *Penitentiary Act* and the *Parole Act*. Each province and territory has its own enabling legislation. Later, in Chapter 19, we discuss judicial review of internal prison and parole decisions.

The use of incarceration in Canada is striking. The following materials place the tendency toward prison sentences in context, both internationally and historically. Imprisonment statistics can be deceiving, and comparisons should be made carefully. First, it is important to ensure that similar dates are compared. Admissions—the number of people received in custody during a period—should not be confused with an average count—the average population over a period. Second, when looking at count or population data, it is essential to segregate sentenced offenders from the total population, which, in many systems, will include remand prisoners awaiting trial. For example, the 1998-99 Statistics Canada Adult Correctional Services Survey indicates that the average "inmate count" was 19,233 provincial and territorial prisoners and 13,178 federal prisoners, for a total of 32,411 prisoners (see (June 2000), vol. 20, no. 3 *Juristat* 4). This produces an incarceration ratio of about 140 in 100,000 adults. Although all penitentiary prisoners were serving a sentence, a large number of the provincial and territorial prisoners (about one-third) were on remand pending trial. Therefore, the incarceration rate as a function of the sentencing process alone is lower than 140 in 100,000.

S. Mihorean and S. Lipinski,
"International Incarceration Patterns, 1980-1990"
(1992), vol. 12, no. 3 *Juristat* 1 (Canadian Centre for Justice Statistics)
(footnotes omitted)

Introduction

To inform the justice community and the public, the Correctional Services Program of the Canadian Centre for Justice Statistics collects and disseminates Canadian corrections data. To better assess the current state of Canadian corrections this report provides a comparison of international incarceration patterns.

A review of the literature has shown that the comparison of indicators of criminality and incarceration across nations is hindered by numerous difficulties. In many cases the problems are insurmountable, impeded by the political, social, economic and operational realities of each country. Of the studies in the available literature, few adequately contend with methodological and definitional issues which arise in international comparisons. Comparisons are often made between countries using data and methodologies that are neither appropriate nor comparable, findings are often inconclusive and difficult to interpret. To address these concerns the current trend in the international literature leans towards analyses of smaller and more manageable international data sets.

International comparisons of incarceration patterns are most useful when the denominator, on which the number of incarcerations are based, is standardized. For this reason, international comparisons of incarceration have traditionally been based on national populations. More reliable data collection procedures in the industrialized countries have now made other avenues of analysis available. This study, in addition to using the recognized population based method, utilizes a Risk Rate; a measure designed to better understand the relationship between the number of incarcerations and the number of recorded offences. This is in accordance with an emerging methodology, which involves the "normalization" of incarceration patterns using recorded offences. The Risk Rate focuses more on the population at risk of being incarcerated by using recorded offences as the denominator. The Risk Rate is more a reflection of local attitudes. The type of the crime does not impact upon the usefulness of the Risk Rate.

The major advantage to a Risk Rate is the logical relationship between the numerator (sentenced prisoners) and the denominator (recorded offences). When examining international Risk Rates one must assume that offences are processed through the respective systems in a consistent manner. Crimes which are considered significant enough to be recorded will be processed. If the number of recorded offences are known to be as reliable a denominator as population, then the Risk Rate is a superior indicator of incarceration trends. Internationally, however, offence counting practices vary considerably. The requisites for providing useful data in cross-national comparisons are too demanding for most countries to participate. The comparability and availability of information enabled the compilation of incarceration and offence data for Canada and eight other participants. Risk Rates are used here only to provide an alternative view of the incarceration trend within individual jurisdictions.

The diversity of incarceration patterns among the participants involved in this study indicate that indeed there are factors, particular to the participants, which influence the trends observed. Further investigation would be useful to explain in greater depth the relationships and variances, between the number of recorded offences and the number of sentenced prisoners, observed in these data.

Analysis

The joint analysis of international incarceration and crime data has, to-date, only begun to be investigated in any detail. Lynch (1988) has noted that most cross-national studies have acknowledged the influence of crime rates on the rate of imprisonment, but have not accounted for it. One aim of the present study is to contribute to the understanding of the relationship between sentenced prisoners, recorded offences and the risk of incarceration.

A rank ordering of incarceration rates for 1989 places Canada as third among the nine participants.

In comparison, a ranking of Risk Rates sees Canada's position changed slightly to fourth. When considering the Risk Rates of the participants it is important to realize that this measure is very much affected by the crime counting methods employed by the participating nations. The Risk Rate shows incarceration patterns in relation to criminality as defined by that jurisdiction. Therefore, the remaining analysis is confined to the comparison of incarceration patterns within individual participants over the study period.

With the exception of the United States, international incarceration patterns indicate relatively stable trends, increasing by a maximum of 20% and decreasing by no more than 15%. Of the nine participants in this study, only one registered an overall decrease in their rate of incarceration: Northern Ireland (−15%).

Canada—The Canadian incarceration rate has remained relatively constant since 1980. The overall reported increase of 14% is largely due to the sizeable growth in the number of prisoners under sentence that was recorded over the first two years of the study period. A moderate increase in Canada's national population (11%) is another factor contributing to the incarceration rate increase. Over the study period the Canadian Risk Rate trend decreased marginally by .3%, from 900 offenders sentenced to incarceration for every 100,000 recorded offences in 1980, to 897 in 1990. The relatively constant Risk Rate trend reflects Canada's consistent response to the offences recorded in Canada. This consistent response is not as evident from the population based rate.

United States—The American incarceration rate experienced a sizeable and steady increase (121%) over the study period. This represents an increase of 170 sentenced prisoners per 100,000 population, in itself greater than the 1980 figure of 140 sentenced prisoners. The Risk Rate in 1990 depicts an increase of almost 3,000 more sentenced prisoners per 100,000 recorded offences than eleven years previous.

England and Wales—The increase of 15% in the number of sentenced prisoners in England and Wales between 1980 and 1990 overshadowed the 3% increase in the national population. These changes brought about a rise in the incarceration rate of

11%. The number of recorded offences increased by more than one-half (55%). The more significant change in the number of recorded offences compared with the change in the number of sentenced prisoners, resulted in an overall decrease of 25% in the Risk Rate for England and Wales.

Scotland—Between 1980 and 1990, the Scottish incarceration rate realized a 19% increase from 53 to 63 sentenced prisoners per 100,000 population. The growth in the number of sentenced prisoners (16%) combined with the slight decrease in the national population (−1.8%) resulted in the incarceration rate increase. An increase in the number of recorded offences (47%), which more than doubled the increase in the number of sentenced prisoners, resulted in a 21% decrease in the Scottish Risk Rate.

Northern Ireland—Small growth in the national population (4%) coupled with a decrease in the number of sentenced prisoners (−13%), resulted in a 15% decline in the incarceration rate. The overall trend of the Risk Rate for Northern Ireland between 1981 and 1989 evidenced a decrease of 5%. This was due in large part to the decrease in the number of sentenced prisoners combined with little change in the number of recorded offences (1%).

Australia—Despite a moderate decline in the first half of the study period the Australian incarceration rate registered an overall increase of 20%, mostly due to the significant growth in the number of sentenced prisoners (39%). The national population experienced consistent growth for an overall increase of 16%. The growth trend in the number of recorded offenders (72%) significantly overshadowed the growth in the number of sentenced prisoners, driving the Risk Rate downwards (−26%).

Switzerland—Between 1982 and 1990 the rate of incarceration in Switzerland increased by 10%, caused by increases in both the national population and in the number of sentenced prisoners, 6% and 16% respectively. Despite several significant annual fluctuations in the nine year Risk Rate trend, it has remained relatively constant (−1%). Both the number of sentenced prisoners and the number of recorded offences have had comparable rates of increase, 16% and 17% respectively.

Denmark—The national population of Denmark remained relatively stable between 1980 and 1990, decreasing by only 2%. This, combined with a 9% increase in the number of sentenced prisoners, resulted in an increase of 10% in the Danish incarceration rate. There has been a consistent decrease in the Danish Risk Rate (−16%): largely a reflection of the increase in the number of recorded offences (29%) more than tripling the increase in the number of sentenced prisoners.

Sweden—The Swedish incarceration rate experienced a growth of 11% over the study period. An overall increase in the number of sentenced prisoners (14%), taken with less significant growth in the national population (3%), is largely responsible for this increase. From 1980 to 1990 the Risk Rate for Sweden decreased by 13%, the result of an increase in the number of recorded offences (31%) more than doubling that of the number of sentenced prisoners.

The relationships between the changes in the rates of incarceration and the actual rates of incarceration among the participants seemingly suggests that, if the trend observed over this study period were to continue, a re-ordering of the international incarceration scene would take place. For example, Northern Ireland's incarceration rate is the fourth largest of the nine participants, although it reported the only decrease in this rate (−15%) over the study period. Similarly, the increase realized in the rate of incarceration for Scotland is third largest while their actual incarceration rate, as of 1990, is the fourth smallest.

A. Doob, "Community Sanctions and Imprisonment: Hoping for a Miracle but Not Bothering To Even Pray for It"
(1990), 32 *Canadian Journal of Criminology* 415

It is unlikely that many readers of the report of the Canadian Sentencing Commission (1987) were surprised to find that the Canadian Association of Elizabeth Fry Societies, the John Howard Society of Canada, and the Quaker Committee on Jails and Justice were quoted as saying, in effect, that, in Canada, we should be more sparing in our use of imprisonment as a sanction. But belief that we overuse imprisonment is not limited to groups such as these. A case can be made that there is a consensus in Canada that more people are being imprisoned than should be. In a national poll carried out in the mid-1980, about 70% of Canadians indicated that they would rather put tax money into the development of community sanctions than into building more prisons. This opinion is not new. One can find numerous statements in official Canadian reports suggesting that dispositions other than imprisonment for our offenders should be developed.

More than half a century ago, the Report of the Royal Commission to Investigate the Penal System of Canada (the Archambault Report 1938: 100) stated that:

> The undeniable responsibility of the state to those held in its custody is to see that they are not returned to freedom worse than when they were taken in charge. This responsibility has been officially recognized in Canada for nearly a century but, although recognized, it has not been discharged.

In the 1956 report of the Committee appointed to inquire into the principles and procedures followed in the remission service of the Department of Justice of Canada (the Fauteux Report 1956: 14, 18), readers are told:

> In addition, it goes without saying that, from a financial point of view, a great saving of public moneys can be achieved by the use, in proper cases, of probation rather than imprisonment as a means of rehabilitation. ... The trend in England ... appears to be "imprisonment as a last resort." This new approach ... has probably resulted from the success of probation and parole and has not, so far as we can ascertain, resulted in any general increase in crime in that country.

In its 1969 report "Toward Unity: Criminal Justice and Corrections," the Canadian Committee on Corrections (the "Ouimet Committee") recommended an approach that should have minimized the use of imprisonment:

> The existence of [certain] restrictions upon the power of a court to sentence otherwise than to imprisonment all too frequently leads to a practice of imposing a sentence of

imprisonment in the absence of mitigating factors. (Canada, Canadian Committee on Corrections 1969: 191)

In conclusion the Committee maintains the imprisonment or confinement should be used only as an ultimate resort when all other alternatives have failed, but subject to its other recommendations concerning different types of offender and different categories of dispositions. (Canada, Canadian Committee on Corrections 1969: 204)

The Law Reform Commission of Canada, in its first report to Parliament urged that we make less use of imprisonment. It argued that even in the case of:

hard core real crimes needing traditional trials and serious punishment ... we need restraint. For one thing, the cost of the criminal law to the offender, the taxpayer and all of us must always be kept as low as possible. For another, the danger with all punishments is simply that familiarity breeds contempt. The harsher the punishments, the slower we should be to use it. This applies especially to punishments of last resort. The major punishment of last resort is prison. This is today the ultimate weapon of the criminal law. As such it must be used sparingly ... . (Law Reform Commission of Canada 1976: 24)

Restricting our use of imprisonment will allow more scope for other types of penalties. ... Positive penalties like restitution and community service orders should be increasingly substituted for the negative and uncreative warehousing of prison. (Law Reform Commission of Canada 1976: 25)

Perhaps more surprising than these statements by non-parliamentary bodies is the endorsement of the increased use of community sanctions in the August 1988 "Report of the Standing Committee on Justice and Solicitor General on its Review of Sentencing, Conditional Release and Related Aspects of Corrections" (commonly known as the "Daubney Committee"). It suggested that Canada overuses imprisonment and should make more use of community sanctions.

The Committee reached a consensus early in its deliberations about the desirability of using alternatives to incarceration as sentencing dispositions for offenders who commit non-violent offences. Using incarceration for such offenders is clearly too expensive in both financial and social terms. ... Too many people are sentenced to incarceration for non-violent offences and non-payment of fines—this creates overcrowding and results in violation of the proportionality principle in sentencing. Moreover, the growth in prison populations does not appear to have reduced crime. In the Committee's view, expensive prison resources should be reserved for the most serious cases. (Daubney Report 1988: 49-50)

Though not explicitly stating his disapproval of the relatively high level of use of imprisonment in Canada, the then Minister of Justice, Mr. Ray Hnatyshyn, in August 1988, told the Canadian Bar Association in the context of announcing plans for the reform of sentencing that,

Many sources have documented the reliance on imprisonment in this country. While this is changing, Canada still incarcerates a comparatively large number of individuals.

This is costly to the individual and to society at large, and has been the target of criticism by academics and practitioners alike. (Hnatyshyn 1988: 5)

An earlier government document, published in 1982 over the signature of the then Minister of Justice, Jean Chrétien, "sets out the policy of the Government of Canada with respect to the purpose and principles of the criminal law" (Preface to "The Criminal Law in Canadian Society"). As the then Minister notes,

As such, it is unique in Canadian history. Never before has the Government articulated such a comprehensive and fundamental statement concerning its view of the philosophical underpinnings of criminal law policy (Canada 1982: Preface).

Consistent with previous documents, the policy of the Government of Canada, apparently was (and presumably still is) that

in awarding sentences, preference should be given to the least restrictive alternative adequate and appropriate in the circumstances. (Canada 1982: 64, 65)

The policy statement goes on to note that this principle, read together with others implies that

a hierarchy of sentencing options, from the least to the most serious, should be available (at least potentially) for most offences and that in effect the use of the more serious alternatives must be justified on grounds of necessity.

A bit later in this statement of Government of Canada policy, the reader is told that guidelines applicable to sentencing should "establish that imprisonment should be used only when lesser sanctions are inadequate or inappropriate ... ."

If Canada were the only country where these kinds of concerns were being expressed, one might not be surprised to find that change had not been implemented. But Canada is not alone. In Britain, at about the same time as the Daubney Committee was making its final recommendations, a Green Paper was released with a clear anti-imprisonment tone. Entitled "Punishment, custody, and the community," the paper introduces the topic in the following way:

Last year 69,000 offenders were sentenced to custody for indictable offences in England and Wales. For many of them, this was the right punishment, because their offences were very serious. ... But for other, less serious, offenders, a spell in custody is not the most effective punishment. Imprisonment restricts offenders' liberty, but it also reduces their responsibility. ... Punishment in the community would encourage offenders to drop out of crime and to develop into responsible and law abiding citizens. (United Kingdom 1988: 1)

After noting that most inmates of British prisons were not convicted of violent offences, it points out that most are there for burglaries which are often "opportunist thefts from houses with open doors or windows, with no damage to the house or threats to the people living there. Nearly half the burglaries reported are of offices, shops and other buildings, not houses." In this context, the Green Paper asks (rhetorically, one might suggest):

"Are we sending too many people to prison? Is imprisonment the best, or only, way to deal with recidivist burglars and thieves … ?" (United Kingdom 1988: 9)

In February 1990, the Government of the United Kingdom answered its own question. Using harsh law-and-order language, Mrs. Thatcher's government's White Paper states that:

> The Government believes that more offenders should be punished in the community. … The Government believes that a new approach is needed if the use of custody is to be reduced. Punishment in the community should be an effective way of dealing with many offenders, particularly those convicted of property crimes and less serious offences of violence. … (United Kingdom 1990: 18)

Though it points out the financial savings to be realized if the Government is successful in shifting people from prison to the community, the paper concludes that:

> The proposals in this White Paper are put forward on their merits because punishment in the community is likely to be more suitable and effective than custody for offenders who have not committed the more serious offences. The proposals should increase punishment in the community and reduce the use of custody. Punishment in the community also imposes a lesser burden on the taxpayer than custody. (United Kingdom 1990: 47)

In another part of the Commonwealth, one only has to read the table of contents to infer the position being taken. The title to Chapter 3 of the 1988 report on sentencing of the Australian Law Reform Commission—"Reducing the emphasis on imprisonment"—gives the flavour of Australian (federal) concerns and approaches. That Commission notes that

> … the emphasis which the criminal justice system presently places on imprisonment as a punishment for offences must be reduced. Instead more emphasis needs to be placed on non-custodial sanctions, particularly the community based sanctions such as the community service order. … (Australia, Law Reform Commission 1988: 20)

Later in the report, it is noted that

> All Australian governments, including the federal government, are committed to reducing the emphasis on imprisonment as a sanction. This was underlined when corrections Ministers, meeting in Melbourne in 1987, endorsed a public statement that said, in part "in each jurisdiction, a review and rationalization of sentencing legislation, policies and practices should promote diversion from imprisonment and should reduce the maximum and average lengths of imprisonment." (Australia, Law Reform Commission 1988: 27)

Finally, a recent United Nations report prepared by representatives of about a dozen countries representing all parts of the world recommended that

> A range of sanctions should be available to enable the sentencing judge to choose the most appropriate one, bearing in mind [that] sentences involving imprisonment should be imposed only if there are demonstrable grounds for believing that community sanctions would be inappropriate. … Imprisonment should be used as a last resort. …

None but the most serious offences should be excluded from the application of community sanctions. ... (United Nations 1988: 8)

Apparently almost alone in its view of imprisonment is the United States Sentencing Commission. In its "Introductory Commentary" on probation, for example, the Commission notes that under US federal law "probation is a sentence in and of itself." It then goes on to note that:

Probation may be used as an alternative to incarceration, provided that the terms and conditions can be fashioned so as to meet *fully* the statutory purposes of sentencing, including promoting respect for law, providing just punishment for the offence, achieving general deterrence, and protecting the public from further crimes by the defendant. (US Sentencing Commission 1988: 5.5: emphasis added)

One does not have to be too cynical to suggest that it is unlikely that probation (or any other disposition) will ever "meet fully" all of these purposes. In any case, there are few offences covered by these guidelines where a convicted offender could completely escape custody.

Indeed, even the most trivial offences committed by someone with no criminal record include, within the guideline range, at least some time in custody. Those slightly more serious do not contain the possibility of a community sanction if sentenced within the guideline range. Under the US Sentencing Commission's guidelines, a break and enter of an unoccupied store where the total loss was minimal committed by a person with no criminal record would result in a sentence of between 10 and 16 months. Had it been a dwelling that was broken into, the guideline indicates that the sentence (for the first-time offender) should be between 24 and 30 months.

In Canada, of course, accurate sentencing statistics are not available, but it is likely that most such cases—especially where it was a non-dwelling that was burgled—would result in a community sanction. Under the guidelines proposed by the Canadian Sentencing commission, the presumptive sentence would be a community sanction for a first offender who committed a minor burglary of either a dwelling or a non-dwelling.

In the context of most civilized countries, the various recommendations made by the Canadian Sentencing Commission for a de-emphasis on imprisonment can hardly be seen as anything but the current Canadian and world wisdom. Few, then, would be expected to argue against the restrictions placed on imprisonment included in the Commission's "Principles of Sentencing."

A term of imprisonment should be imposed only (a) to protect the public from crimes of violence, (b) where any other sanction would not sufficiently reflect the gravity of the offence or the repetitive nature of the criminal conduct of an offender, or adequately protect the public or the integrity of the administration of justice, (c) to penalize an offender for willful non-compliance with the terms of any other sentence that has been imposed on the offender where no other sanction appears adequate to compel compliance. (Canada, Canadian Sentencing Commission 1987: 154)

Why then is it that we do not have the kind of increased use of community sanctions that we apparently, like much of the world, have wanted? As is implied by the subtitle, the thesis of this paper is that in many jurisdictions—and certainly in Canada—we should not have been surprised when we began creating "alternatives" to find that the effects were not as we might have wanted. We should not have been surprised if we were to find that the use of incarceration was not diminished by these new alternatives. Similarly, we would have had no valid reason to be smug if we had found that incarceration levels had decreased as a result of these new sentencing alternatives. In fact, we had no reason to expect *any* particular outcome because we did almost nothing to determine how community sanctions would be used.

NOTE

There are two recent developments worthy of note. First, consider the following comments of Cory and Iacobucci JJ in *R v. Gladue* (1999), 23 CR (5th) 197 (SCC):

> Canada is a world leader in many fields, particularly in the areas of progressive social policy and human rights.
>
> Unfortunately, our country is also distinguished as being a world leader in putting people in prison. Although the United States has by far the highest rate of incarceration among industrialized democracies, at over 600 inmates per 100,000 population, Canada's rate of approximately 130 inmates per 100,000 population places it second or third highest: See First Report on Progress for Federal/Provincial/Territorial Ministers Responsible for Justice, Corrections Population Growth (1997), Annex B, at p. 1; Bulletin of US Bureau of Justice Statistics, "Prison and Jail Inmates at Midyear 1998" (1999); The Sentencing Project, Americans Behind Bars: US and International Use of Incarceration, 1995 (1997), at p. 1.
>
> Moreover, the rate at which Canadian courts have been imprisoning offenders has risen sharply in recent years, although there has been a slight decline of late: see Statistics Canada, Infomat: A Weekly Review (February 27, 1998), at p. 5. This record of incarceration rates obviously cannot instill a sense of pride. ...
>
> Thus, it may be seen that although imprisonment is intended to serve the traditional sentencing goals of separation, deterrence, denunciation, and rehabilitation, there is widespread consensus that imprisonment has not been successful in achieving some of these goals. Overincarceration is a long-standing problem that has been many times publicly acknowledged but never addressed in a systematic manner by Parliament. In recent years, compared to other countries, sentences of imprisonment in Canada have increased at an alarming rate. The 1996 sentencing reforms embodied in Part XXIII, and s. 718.2(e) in particular, must be understood as a reaction to the overuse of prison as a sanction, and must accordingly be given appropriate force as remedial provisions.

Second, there has been a huge increase in incarceration in the United States over the past few years. Recent studies calculate the incarceration rate in 1997 at 445 sentenced prisoners per 100,000 US residents: see A. Blumstein and A.J. Beck, "Population Growth in US Prisons, 1980-1996," in Tonry and Petersilia, (1999), 26 *Crime and Justice* 17-61, at 18. Although Canada remains further behind in the imprisonment race, Canadians should reflect on the impact of such strategies as the "war on drugs" and "three strikes, you're out."

Table 1   Comparative Incarceration Rates, 1993-1997[a]

	1993	1994	1995	1996	1997
United States[b]	531	567	601	618	649
New Zealand	127	121	123	127	137
Canada[c]	131	136	133	137	129
England and Wales	89	96	99	107	120
Scotland	115	109	110	101	119
Spain	115	106	102	—	113
Northern Ireland	118	117	106	—	95
Turkey	52	72	90	87	94
Germany	81	83	81	83	90
France	86	90	89	90	90
Switzerland	81	—	81	85	88
Netherlands	51	55	—	75	87
Austria	91	85	76	84	86
Italy	89	90	87	85	86
Belgium	72	65	76	76	82
Ireland	60	59	59	62	68
Denmark	71	72	66	61	62
Sweden	66	66	66	65	59
Finland	62	59	59	58	56
Norway	60	62	56	52	53
Cyprus	30	25	26	35	40

[a] Rates are based on 100,000 population. [b] Figures for the United States are for incarcerated adults only (that is, youths are excluded). [c] Canadian youth custody figures for 1995-1997 were adjusted to represent 100% survey coverage. Canadian rates are reported on a fiscal-year basis (April 1 through March 31).

Source: Solicitor General Canada, *Corrections and Conditional Release Statistical Overview* (Ottawa: Solicitor General Canada, November 1999).

Table 1 shows comparative incarceration rates for the period 1993-1997 in 21 countries. It appears that the data in the table reflect total incarceration populations—that is, both sentenced and remanded offenders. This explains the substantial difference between the 1997 US rate shown in the table (649 per 100,000) and the one used by Blumstein and Beck (445 per 100,000).

II. THE EFFECTS OF INCARCERATION

The literature in this area is complex and vast. Imprisonment serves the twin purposes of incapacitation and separation. Certainly, incarceration provides a dramatic restriction in liberty during the period of incarceration, but whether this promotes any other anticipated goals of sentencing is controversial. Imprisonment not only separates the prisoner from the community but also places control over the environment and the daily routines of her life into the hands of the correctional system. Thus, the impact of imprisonment must be measured both in terms of its duration and its personal effects. Supporters of imprisonment assume that its rigours will produce deterrence. Also, it is expected that there may be some degree of rehabilitation. This, of course, is a function of the extent that the system provides programming directed at education, vocational training, or problems like substance abuse.

It cannot be assumed without confirming evidence that any system or institution in which a particular prisoner will eventually be confined actually provides relevant programming. There are, of course, negative consequences. Communities, families, and employment situations change over time and a prisoner does not simply return to fill the place that he previously vacated. The mere separation of the offender from his or her family and friends is often the source of both economic and emotional repercussions. Moreover, depending on the quality of the correctional system and the way in which it is manifested in a particular institution, imprisonment can produce serious negative effects: see the discussion of health risks, violence, mental health, institutionalization, and other negative effects in N. Walker and N. Padfield, *Sentencing: Theory, Law and Practice*, 2d ed. (London: Butterworths, 1996), 153-63.

One Canadian study dealing with violence in prisons concluded that a male prisoner runs a 14 times greater risk of being a victim of homicide in prison than does a man of comparable age living in the community. See F.J. Porporino and P. Doherty, *An Historical Analysis of Victims of Homicide in Canadian Penitentiaries* (Ottawa: Solicitor General Canada, 1985); also see A. Bottoms, "Interpersonal Violence and Social Order in Prisons" and A. Liebling, "Suicide and Prison Coping" (1999), 26 *Crime and Justice Review* at 205-82 and 283-360 respectively.

The following materials illustrate an ongoing debate about the potential consequences of long-term confinement. This debate is especially significant given the growing number of prisoners serving life sentences as a result of both the aggregate of people with long periods of parole ineligibility and an apparent lengthening of sentences for some offences. Combined with the claim that imprisonment is inefficacious in achieving sentencing objectives, this body of literature ought to be significant from a law reform perspective. However, substantive debate has too often been replaced by the politics of law and order.

J. Bonta and P. Gendreau, "Re-examining the Cruel and Unusual Punishment of Prison Life"
(1990), 14 *Law and Human Behavior* 347 (references omitted)

Historically, prisons have been described as barren landscapes devoid of even the most basic elements of humanity and detrimental to the humanity of the offender. Perhaps one of the best known descriptions of the inhumanity of prison is Cohen and Taylor's description of long-term inmates in a British maximum security prison. Such notions about prison life have been pervasive whether from the perspective of investigative journalists or academics writing for basic criminology texts.

Mitford (1973), in her very effective polemical style, painted a scathing indictment of prisons. Not only does imprisonment strip offenders of civil liberties, but also prison reforms are nothing but rhetoric and rehabilitation initiatives are despotic. Goffman (1961) also has been equally harsh in his assessment of the prison as a "total institution."

Careful empirical evaluations, however, have failed to uncover these pervasive negative effects of incarceration that so many have assumed. Mitford (1973) and Cohen and Taylor (1972) did not provide empirical evidence for psychological or behavioral deterioration. We need to be reminded that even Goffman (1961) did not collect data directly from prisons. His conclusions were based upon a review of the prison literature combined with data gathered from "asylums." Furthermore, earlier reviews of empirical studies also failed to uncover the widespread harm that is presumed inherent to prisons.

For some, the quantitative data, gathered as much as possible under conditions of objectivity, must not be believed. The failure of such data to confirm popular expectations has led to a number of responses. One is an increased dependence upon a phenomenological approach, or, at the very least, a shift from quantitative psychology to a process that examines prison existence in a qualitative and interpretative manner.

Another expression of disbelief in the data comes from critics who have argued that the failure to find damaging effects of incarceration has been due to the "false reality" of the researchers concerned. This false reality has apparently been ascribed to the fact that government researchers have vested interests in reporting results uncritical of the penal establishment.

A final concern, in this case emanating from researchers who have not yet embraced phenomenology, has been that much of the research has reached a "dead end." Historically, incarceration research examined informal social organizations within prisons and did not speak persuasively to the actual effects of imprisonment itself. In addition, the methodological problems in much of the early work were considerable and a number of researchers have been rather critical of the early simplistic approaches to imprisonment research. That is, much of the early research was guided by the "all or none" views of the deprivation and the early importation theorists. Thus, the complex nature of incarceration was not addressed.

In the past, most prisons were maximum security, and psychoeducational programming was minimal. Daily prison life featured 20-hour lock-up for a few and highly regimentized and monotonous work duties for the rest. Until recently, approaching the examination of prison life from a uniform perspective made eminently good sense. Now, however, the realities of prison life are far different. It is now appropriate to reexamine the effects of incarceration with special attention to the specific conditions of confinement. Although prisons may appear similar on the surface, closer examination finds them varying widely in security, living conditions, and the degree of programming.

Prison overcrowding, almost unknown in the early 1970s, is now very evident. Today, both very long-term and short-term periods of incarceration have dramatically increased. The number of offenders incarcerated is over 700,000. Current government crime control strategies, in the United States at least, will likely ensure that imprisonment will be the preferred option for the time being. In addition, one of the most extreme forms of prison life, solitary confinement, is still frequently employed.

Thus, research examining the effects of prison life is critically important. More knowledge must be generated and analyses of prison life must take into account the deprivation and importation literature, while also recognizing the great variety of structures and experiences that incarceration currently includes.

Selection and Organization of Studies

This review focuses on quantitative studies about effects of imprisonment. Qualitative or phenomenological studies were not included. To be included in the review, a study was required to employ objective measures of the variables of interest and to evaluate the relationship between them by means of statistical tests.

Thus, the majority of studies were of a correlational or quasiexperimental nature. The only truly experimental studies (i.e., random assignment) were found in the solitary confinement literature. Some studies appeared to straddle both the quantitative and qualitative camps. In these instances, we made a judgment call and only included them for discussion where appropriate.

The studies were identified with the aid of a computer search of the prison adjustment and penal literature. Other reviews and a review of recent criminological journals identified additional studies.

We viewed imprisonment as an independent variable and the behavioral and psychological observations of inmates as dependent variables. This organization appeared to work well with the studies dealing with specific conditions of confinement (e.g., solitary confinement). There is, on the other hand, a voluminous and frequently reviewed literature that has the independent variable, imprisonment, less clearly defined and investigates dependent variables, such as attitude and self-esteem changes. These later studies were not included in the present review.

Finally, a further comment on the dependent variables in the review is in order. Our interest was on the evaluation of assumed negative effects due to incarceration, and, therefore, we reviewed topics that were most likely to evidence such effects. We did not review the literature on rehabilitation and educational programs in prisons because their stated purpose is to actively promote positive behaviors. In general, *negative effects* were behaviors that threatened the physical welfare of the offender (e.g., aggressive behavior, suicide) and indicators of physiological stress levels (e.g., elevated blood pressure) and psychological distress (e.g., depression).

We examined specific aspects of confinement, namely, crowding, long-term imprisonment, solitary confinement, short-term detention, and death row. We make one departure from this format and provide a commentary on the health risks associated with imprisonment, which follows from our discussion of prison crowding. In our review of the prison crowding literature, we were able to use meta-analytic techniques because there were both an identifiable theoretical perspective and sufficient studies that could be subjected to analysis. With respect to the other aspects of confinement, either there were too few studies (e.g., death row) or they consistently failed to show negative consequences (e.g., solitary confinement), or, as in the case of long-term confinement, the cross-sectional methodology with multiple groups did not make the data amenable to meta-analytic techniques.

Crowding

Crowding is invariably perceived negatively. It is seen by many correctional managers as *the* major barrier to humane housing of offenders despite an estimated 170,000 additional new beds since 1980. This population explosion has prompted court interventions, sentencing reforms, and innovative classification systems intended to reduce prison populations.

Researchers view crowding as a complex phenomenon. Stokols (1972) distinguished *density*, a physical condition, from *crowding*, a psychological condition involving the individual's perception of constraints imposed by limited space. Loo (1973) further differentiated physical density into *spatial density* (number of people constant but the available space varies) and *social density* (space is constant but the number of people vary). For example, prison renovations might reduce the amount of space available to a number of inmates (spatial density), but the effects of this spatial rearrangement on the inmates may differ from the effects of a sudden influx of new inmates into the institution (social density).

Despite these distinctions, corrections research has been inconsistent in the use of the concepts of crowding and spatial and social density. Studies have described crowding as both an independent and dependent variable, and the distinction between social and spatial density has infrequently been noted.

Most researchers agree that crowding describes a psychological response to high population density which is often viewed as stressful. Although high population density is a necessary condition for crowding, it is not a sufficient condition, and other variables may be required to produce the perception of crowding. Sundstrom (1978) described crowding as a sequential process resulting form an interaction of person variables, high population density, correlates of high density (e.g., increased noise levels), and situational variables (e.g. duration of exposure).

Following Sundstrom's model, we would expect that the behaviors observed under high population densities would vary in intensity and variety with length of exposure. For example, under brief exposure we may see elevated blood pressure, followed by reports of anxiety as exposure increases, and ending with violent behavioral outbursts under prolonged exposures. To test this hypothesis, a longitudinal design is required, and, to the best of our knowledge, there is only one study that has approximated this goal. Indirect support of the model may be gathered from comparisons of the relative strength of the relationships between population density and a variety of outcomes. That is, we would expect that reports of physiological and psychological stress would be relatively easy to come by and that the findings would be robust, whereas observations of violent behavior would be more infrequent and equivocal.

To explore this model, we undertook both a qualitative and quantitative review of the prison crowd in literature. Studies that provided sufficient statistical information on the relationship between population density and the dependent variable were subject to a meta-analysis. The dependent variable was arranged into three categories: physiological, psychological, and behavioral. Some studies reported more than one measure within a category. In these situations, we gave priority to systolic blood pressure for the physiological category, a paper-and-pencil measure of perceived crowding described by Paulus (1988) for the psychological category, and misconduct for the behavioral category. These measures were the most frequently used. We would have liked to categorize the measures of crowding into aggregate, social, and spatial density, but to have done so would have drastically reduced our samples in each cell.

The strength of the relationship, or effect size, was measured by Cohen (1977) and calculated using the statistical conversion formulas described by Glass, McGaw, and Smith (1981). In our analysis, d indicated the size of the difference in standard units between crowded and noncrowded conditions. Standardizing the measures (d) allowed us to compare results from different studies. For studies that reported nonsignificant results, d was set at zero. ...

... [P]hysiological and psychological stress responses (Outcomes A and B) were very likely under crowded prison conditions. The majority of studies employing such measures found significant results. The one inconsistent finding was the *inverse* relationship between crowding and blood pressure ($d = -.70$) reported by McCain, Cox, and Paulus (1980). This may have been a spurious result because there was no relationship between blood pressure and crowding for the institution in question for the previous year (1978). If this size effect is removed from the calculation of the mean, then we obtain a mean of $d = .51$ for Outcome A, which is quite consistent with the model. In the case of behavioral acting-out, the strength of the relationship diminished to the point of being relatively insignificant as the studies ranged in effect size from $-.90$ to $+.87$.

While the results outlined under Outcomes A and B seem straightforward, some clarification is required. That is, although physiological stress in response to population density was the rule, reports of psychological stress concomitant with physiological stress were not always observed and, for the most part, rarely studied. When the two were observed together, the relationship was usually dependent upon other variables. In 1973, Paulus, McCain, and Cox reported (no data were presented) that social density was related to a physiological measure of stress (palmer sweat) but not to a subjective appraisal of feeling crowded. However, in a subsequent study, which considered length of exposure, there was an increased perception of feeling crowded for inmates in dormitories (high social density) but not for inmates in cells (low social density). Other studies have noted the moderating effect of length of exposure on physiological and psychological measures of stress.

In the one longitudinal study reported in the literature, Ostfield and his colleagues (1987) followed 128 inmates through their incarceration to release and postrelease. Physiological and psychological measures were taken at regular intervals and controls were introduced for other confounding variables such as weight and criminal history. They found changes in blood pressure associated with population density but no statistically significant changes for anxiety, hostility, and depression.

These studies, nevertheless, suggested a positive relationship between social density and physiological indicators of stress and subjective reports of discomfort. Indications of physiological stress appear as immediate consequences to high social density, and it is possible that with increased exposure to such a situation other cumulative consequences such as psychological distress may follow.

It is important, however, from a policy perspective, to evaluate whether or not population density is related to severe, disruptive behavior that may jeopardize the physical safety of the inmates. The findings ... do not support an overall relationship between crowding and disruptive inmate behavior.

Megargee (1977) was the first to empirically study the relationship between crowding and reported disciplinary infractions. He collected data over a 3-year span at a medium security prison for youthful offenders (aged 18 to 25). Spatial density was more highly correlated with institutional misconduct than was social density, but social interaction factors (e.g., friendship ties) may have played an important role. Density, without distinction to spatial or social density, and disciplinary infractions are, according to some investigators, positively related, but no such association was found by others.

From our appraisal of the empirical literature we cannot conclude that high population density is always associated with aggressive behavior. Most researchers agree that other variables play important moderating roles. One important moderator variable is age of the inmates. The relationship between misconduct and population density has been more pronounced in institutions housing young offenders. Even in studies that failed to uncover a general positive relationship, the introduction of age as a moderator showed a correlation between population density and misconduct. In the Ekland-Olson et al. study (1983), when institutions with a relatively young population (median age of 27) were selected for analysis, a highly significant correlation was found ($r = .58$ or a $d = 1.43$). The authors concluded that age is a much better predictor of disciplinary infractions than prison size.

Only one study discounts the importance of age. Gaes and McGuire (1985) assessed a variety of predictors along with age and under these conditions age became relatively less important. The authors observed that most studies of overcrowding and misconduct typically assess few variables and may overestimate the importance of any one variable.

Interpreting the behavioral consequences of prison overcrowding is further confounded by the use of aggregate level data. ... [A]lmost all the studies under Outcome C are aggregate level data. The problem with this level of analysis is that many other factors (e.g., age, release policies) may play more important roles than population density. Clayton and Carr (1987) have shown that aggregate data analysis overestimates the relationship between crowding and behavior (a point already made in the preceding paragraph). In their study investigating the relationship between prison overcrowding and recidivism (2 years postrelease), age was the critical variable. The only other study that used recidivism as an outcome measure was by Farringotn and Nuttall (1980), and they found a significant relationship between crowding and postrelease recidivism. However, Gaes (1983) has suggested that other extraneous variables (e.g., age, staff–inmate ratios) could better account for the results.

Although age has consistently been identified as an important moderating variable, explanations of why this is so have not been carefully researched. Are the young simply impulsive, lack coping skills, and more easily susceptible to stress? MacKenzie (1987) found oppositional or "assertive" attitudes and fear of victimization rather than coping ability as most relevant to misconducts. Clearly further research on this issue is desirable.

The identification of person variables as moderators in the experience of prison crowding raises the enduring issue of importation versus deprivation. That is, are the behaviors observed in prison reflective of behavioral patterns that were present prior to incarceration or a response to the deprivation of liberties imposed by confinement? As Freedman (1975) wrote, "crowding has neither good nor bad effects but rather serves to intensify the individual's typical reactions to a situation." Thus, the disciplinary infractions observed in crowded prisons may be the result of either high population densities or a continuation of behaviors that existed before incarceration, or both. As Ruback and Innes (1988) have remarked, there are no studies that have partitioned inmates with violent histories from nonviolent inmates. This is very important because it is usually the maximum security settings that are crowded, and they are also the settings most likely to house violent inmates. The possibility of an interaction can be seen in Smith's (1982) account of how assertive inmates became more aggressive and the passive inmates more submissive under crowded conditions.

There are other factors, besides person variables, that may influence aggressive behavior in crowded prisons. For instance, crowded prisons may be poorly managed. Although prison populations may fluctuate widely, corresponding changes in the number of supervisory staff, counselors, and programs rarely occur. When the population is large, there are fewer correctional staff to monitor behavior and provide inmates with the opportunities to learn adaptive coping skills. The management of prisons and prison systems may account for some inmate disturbances. A case in point is the occurrence of sudden changes in the population membership. Porporino and Dudley (1984), in reviewing evidence from 24 Canadian penitentiaries, found high inmate turnover more important than population density in the prediction of inmate disruptions. The authors speculated that inmates are required to deal with newly arrived inmates more frequently and this may be extremely stressful. For example, in the 1980 New Mexico prison riot, the inmate population was not at its peak but there was a sudden influx of new inmates in the months preceding the riot.

Another factor appears to be the chronicity of the situation. That is, as sentence length or exposure to crowded situations increase so does the risk for misconduct. This is a tentative conclusion because of other confounding factors such as age and type of institution.

In summary, crowded prisons may produce physiological and psychological stress among many inmates. More disruptive effects, however, depend upon moderating person variables such as age, institutional parameters (e.g., sudden shifts in the inmate membership), and the chronicity of the situation. In addition, aggressive behavior may be a cumulative effect of high population densities. More research into the parameters that govern this effect is required.

Two theoretical models have been advanced in an effort to explain the inmate's response to prison overcrowding. The social-interaction demand model favored by Paulus and his colleagues assumes that social interactions interfere with goal attainment and increase uncertainty and cognitive load. That is, it is the nature of the social interactions that may produce negative effects and high population densities are important only to the degree that they affect social interactions. The second model is based on a cognitive social-learning model.

This latter model places greater emphasis on individual differences (person variables) and stresses two processes: attribution and learned coping behavior. Increases in population density produce changes not only in social interactions but also changes in noise level, temperature, etc., and these in turn produce physiological arousal. When inmates attribute this arousal to violation of their personal space rather than some other factor they then report feeling crowded. Once the attribution is made, existing coping behaviours are activated with the goal to reduce arousal and feelings of crowding.

Except for MacKenzie's (1987) findings, penal researchers have found that coping behavior plays a significant role in the inmates' response to incarceration and that inmates vary in the effectiveness of their coping behaviors. Clements (1979) has suggested that coping behavior may be influential in the inmates' adaptation to prison overcrowding, although some of these behaviors, such as assault and suicide, are clearly not adaptive. Unfortunately, poor coping skills are all too prevalent among inmate populations and this is reflected in their disruptive behavioral responses to high population densities. However, other behaviors can alleviate crowding-induced arousal and at the same time be adaptive. For example, class-room attendance and psychological interventions have been shown to decrease feelings of being crowded. Besides searching for ways to control the prison population growth we can also develop programs to teach individual inmates more effective skills to cope with high prison populations.

Health Risks

As we have seen with the prison crowding literature, it is not uncommon to observe physiological and psychological distress associated with high population densities. Such outcomes are also commonly associated with stress and physical disorders. In fact, many studies of prison overcrowding will use illness complaints as a dependent measure. Thus, we now turn our attention to a related topic and ask ourselves if imprisonment threatens the health of the confined.

Most of the research has dealt with the identification and description of illnesses reported by prisoners. Available data fail to clearly indicate whether inmates display more or less health risks than the general population. When threats to health come from suicide and self-mutilation, then inmates are clearly at risk. Though it is widely believed that the risk of homicide is greater within prison than in the community, the evidence is mixed. In Canadian penitentiaries, the homicide rates are close to 20 times that of similar aged males in Canadian society. In the United States, deaths due to homicide are actually less likely within prison. With respect to self-injurious behavior, the results are more consistent. Inmate suicides for a 20-year period in the United States were at a rate of 17.5 per 100,000 inmates in contrast to 11 per 100,000 people in the general population. Self-mutilations are at an even higher rate.

When one examines the incidence of physical illnesses, the findings are less conclusive. One of the classic studies comes from Jones (1976) who surveyed the health risks of Tennessee prisoners and compared them where possible to probationers and data existing on the general adult male US population. The patterns of results are rather complex but, by and large, a variety of health problems, injuries, and selected symptoms of psychological distress were higher for certain classes of inmates than probationers, parolees, and, where data existed, for the general population.

In contrast to Jones (1976), a number of other researchers have failed to find deleterious effects on health. Goldsmith (1972) followed 50 inmates over a 2-month period and found no major health problems as assessed by physical examinations. On a larger inmate sample ($N = 491$), Derro (1978) found that only 12% of the symptoms reported on admission related to a significant illness. This is an important point because many studies "count" health care contacts without differentiating the nature of the contact. Inmates may seek the aid of health care professionals for reasons other than a physical illness.

Two studies also reported a significantly lower incidence of hypertension among inmates compared to the general population. Culpepper and Froom (1980) found the incidence of hypertension among a prison population at 6%. In another study, the incidence of hypertension among 1,300 inmates was 4.5%. We remind the reader, however, that this finding relates to the effects of incarceration in general and not to specific conditions such as prison crowding where the results are different (Gaes, 1985).

One of the problems with the interpretation of the above data has been that there is so little use of adequate control groups especially with respect to age and race. Also, Baird (1977) found that many prisoners with physical complaints were displaying a variety of health risks well *before* incarceration. As a case in point, Bentz and Noel (1983) found that upon entering prison, inmates were reporting a higher incidence of psychiatric disorder than a sample of a rural population in North Carolina. This finding is also of interest in light of Gibbs' (1987) claim that incarceration aggravates psychological symptomatology (we will say more about this in the discussion on short-term detention).

A final consideration is that many prisons may actually be conductive to good health. In a number of cases, illness complaints have either decreased with time served or remained unchanged. In most prisons, inmates have regular and nutritious diets, access to recreational exercise, and opportunity to sleep. Furthermore, offenders can obtain fairly immediate health care. Because of this last possibility, health risks could easily be overreported in prisons with extensive health services and thus bias some of the research findings.

In summary, the current findings recall Glueck and Glueck's (1950) comparison of 500 delinquents with 500 nondelinquents: In training school, the boys were generally healthy and physically fit, whereas in the community, as a result of their adventurous lifestyles, they were prone to more serious accidents. More than 35 years later, Ruback and Innes (1988) make this same observation based upon information from adult inmates. Thus, as far as physical health is concerned, imprisonment may have the fortuitous benefit of isolating the offender from a highly risky lifestyle in the community.

Long-Term Incarceration

In 1984 there were approximately 1,500 offenders serving life sentences in Canadian prisons and with recent legislation defining minimum sentences (25 years) without parole for first and second degree murder, those numbers are expected to increase significantly. Similar trends have also been noted in the United States, where mandatory and lengthy prison terms have been widely implemented. What happens to these people as a result of such lengthy sentences? Most of the research has focused upon time spans not longer than 2 or 3 years, and our knowledge regarding offenders serving sentences of 5, 10, or more years is less adequate.

Using cross-sectional designs, Heskin and his colleagues measured inmates' performances on cognitive tests, personality measures, and attitudinal scales. Four groups of prisoners, all sentenced to at least 10 years, were studied. The average time served was 2.5 years for the first group of inmates, 4.9 years for the second group, 6.9 years for the third, and 11.3 for the last group. No differences were found among the groups in intellectual performance, although there was a decline in perceptual motor speed on the cognitive tasks. On the personality and attitudinal tests, there were increases in hostility and social introversion and decreases in self-evaluations and evaluations of work and father.

Subsequently, Bolton, Smith, Heskin, and Banister (1976) retested 154 of the original 175 inmates in the Heskin research (average retest interval was 2 years). Their findings showed no evidence of psychological deterioration. In fact, verbal intelligence improved over time and hostility decreased. The findings with respect to hostility are in contrast to the cross-sectional studies, but, as the authors noted, there was a significant drop-out rate. Furthermore, the initial testing occurred during a period of institutional tensions, which may have produced artificially high hostility scores.

Sapsford (1978) administered a psychometric test battery to 60 prisoners sentenced to life imprisonment. The prisoners formed three groups: (1) reception (newly received), (2) middle (6th year of sentence), and (3) hard core (average sentence served was 21.4 years). Some matching was attempted but it is not clear the extent to which the procedure was successful. From the results, only three inmates could be described as having failed to cope with their sentence. The only deteriorating effects observed were increases in dependency upon staff for direction and social introversion. In fact, depression and anxiety were lower for inmates serving longer sentences.

Reed's (1978) geriatric prisoner research also has relevance to the issue. His aged prisoners (mean age of 60 years), with an average sentence served of 23 years, reported fewer life problems than their peers in the outside community. Furthermore, they reported active interests and feelings younger than their age.

Similarly, Richards (1978) also failed to note negative differences between British prisoners who had served at least 8 years of their sentences and inmates who had served more than 10 years. The two groups were matched on age at sentencing and type of offense. The inmates were asked to rate the frequency and severity of 20 different problems that may be initiated by incarceration (e.g., missing social life, sexual frustration). The results showed no differences in the perception of problems by the two groups, and there was agreement by the inmates that coping could be best accomplished by relying on "myself."

Utilizing Richard's (1978) problem-ranking task, Flanagan (1980a) assessed American inmates who had served at least 5 years and compared his results to those reported by Richards (1978). He found that the American inmates perceived similar problems to those reported by the British prisoners in that they also did not perceive the problems as particularly threatening to their mental health. Furthermore, they preferred to cope with their sentences on their own rather than seek the aid of others. In another study, Flanagan (1980b) compared misconduct rates of 701 short-term prisoners (less than 5 years) and 765 long-term inmates. Even after controlling for age, the misconduct rate among the long-term inmates was approximately half that of the short-term offenders.

Rasch (1981) assessed lifers who had served 3, 8.5, and 13.5 years and found no deterioration in health, psychiatric symptoms, or intellect. The results of MMP1 testing documented decreased pathology over time, replicating Sapsford's (1980) findings. Another German study, cited by Wormith (1984a), apparently found similar results. Moreover, when long-term inmates (20 years) displayed pathology, such behaviors were apparent long before incarceration

A series of studies conducted by Wormith (1984, 1986) observed a differential impact from long-term incarceration. In the first study, 269 inmates who had served from 1 month to 10 years were administered a psychometric test battery. Once again those inmates who had served the most time displayed significantly less deviance. This relationship remained even after the introduction of controls for sentence length, age upon admission, and race. Improvement over time was also noted on attitudinal measures and nonpathological personality characteristics. Finally, changes in intelligence did not vary with length of incarceration.

The second study by Wormith (1986) consisted of a random sample of 634 male prisoners stratified according to sentence length and time served. Long-term inmates (8 years to life), compared to short-term inmates, demonstrated better adjustment on measures of self-reports of emotions and attitudes (e.g., anger) and institution discipline. On measures of criminal sentiments, long-term offenders displayed a U-shaped function while short-term offenders became more antisocial. As expected, long-term inmates had deteriorating community relationships over time but made more use of institutional programs (e.g., education), which was likely important for a successful adaptation to prison life.

MacKenzie and Goodstein (1985) reported findings similar to those described by Wormith (1984, 1986). Long-term inmates (more than 6 years served) found the earlier portion of their sentences more stressful, but with time they learned to cope effectively. Of particular interest was their differentiation of two subgroups of long-term offenders. Using prison experience as a discriminating factor, they identified two groups, inmates with minimal prison experience (lifers) and inmates with extensive prison experience (habituals). Both groups showed the same adjustment patterns, contrary to the expectation that habituals would evidence disruptive behaviors. Similar findings with respect to female offenders have also been reported by MacKenzie, Robinson, and Campbell (1989). In fact, long-term inmates were more bothered by boredom and lack of activities than by anxiety.

Most of the above studies have been cross-sectional. A publication by Zamble and Porporino (1990) on how inmates cope with prison assumes importance for two reasons. First, it is longitudinal. Of their sample (*N* = 133), 30% were serving sentences of more than 10 years. They were assessed within 1 month of admission and 1½ years later, Zamble and Porporino found no *overall* indication of deterioration of coping skills over time, even for inmates serving their first incarceration. As well, there was no increase in identification with "criminal others" and their "view of the world" did not change. The authors surmise that as prisons, by and large, constrain behavior and do little to encourage changes in behavior one way or the other, inmates typically undergo a "behavioral deep freeze." The outside-world behaviors that led the offender into trouble prior to imprisonment remain until release.

Secondly, it is important to emphasize that Zamble and Proporino do not in the least deny the fact that individual differences are meaningful. They reported that how some inmates coped with incarceration correlated with postprison recidivism. For example, some of the significant factors were changes in perceptions of prison life, degree and type of socialization with incarcerated peers, planning for the future, and motivation regarding work and educational goals. We will return to this point later.

In summary, from the available evidence and on the dimensions measured, there is little to support the conclusion that long-term imprisonment necessarily has detrimental effects. As a caution, however, Flanagan (1982) claims that lifers may change upon other dimensions that have yet to be objectively measured. For example, family separation issues and vocational skill training needs present unique difficulties for long-term inmates. Unfortunately, cross-sectional designs and, until recently, small subject populations have been characteristic of these studies.

Solitary Confinement

Solitary confinement is "the most individually destructive, psychologically crippling and socially alienating experience that could conceivably exist within the borders of the country." So wrote Jackson (1983) in his scathing denouncement of the use of solitary confinement for prisoners. The commonly accepted definition of prison solitary confinement is maximum security lock-up, usually for punitive reasons. Sensory stimulation is very limited. The inmate may have a book to read and access to a half hour of "recreation" (alone). Conditions of prison solitary should not be confused with other forms of protective segregation where admission is usually voluntary, and the inmate has access to programming, TV, and so forth. No doubt, if any prison experience is evidence of cruel and unusual punishment, then surely that experience is prison solitary.

In contrast to the popular notions of solitary's negative effects, there exists an extensive experimental literature on the effects of placing people (usually volunteer college students) in solitary, or conditions of sensory deprivation, which has been ignored in the penology literature. It should be noted that the conditions in some of the sensory deprivation experiments are more severe than that found in prison solitary. In fact, this literature has much relevance to prison solitary confinement. Considerable research has also been undertaken with prisoners, themselves, and many of these studies are, methodologically, the most rigorous of all the prison studies. Therefore, conclusions drawn from this source are especially informative.

Experimental studies have found few detrimental effects for subjects placed in solitary confinement for periods up to 10 days. All but one of these studies employed random assignment and most employed a double blind assessment of dependent variables.

Perceptual and motor abilities were not impaired, physiological levels of stress were lower than for the control groups, and various attitudes toward the environment and the self did not worsen. Individual differences have also been observed. Experience with prison life, conceptual ability, anxiety, diurnal adrenal levels, and EEG patterns were related to some of the results reported, although it should be noted that results are based upon very small sample sizes. Some of the experimental studies even reported beneficial results. In certain respects, the prison literature is quite consistent with the experimental sensory deprivation laboratory data.

In contrast to the studies that used volunteer subjects, Weinberg (1967) looked at 20 inmates who were involuntarily placed for 5 days in solitary confinement. Using measures such as cognitive and personality tests, language usage, and time estimation, he, too, found no deleterious effects. Suedfeld, Ramirez, and Baker-Brown (1982), also studying inmates involuntarily in solitary confinement, also failed to find detrimental effects. Their data were collected from five prisons in Canada and the United States, and they found that, in general, inmates found the first 72 hours the most difficult but after that they adjusted quite well. The authors reached this conclusion: "Our data lend no support to the claim that solitary confinement … is overwhelmingly aversive, stressful, or damaging to the inmates."

In contrast, Cormiet and Williams (1966) and Grassian (1983) recorded signs of pathology for inmates incarcerated in solitary for periods up to a year. No objective measures or control groups were used. In the former study, most of the inmates exhibited substantial pathology prior to solitary. In the second study, all subjects were involved in a class action suit against their keepers at the time of the interview, and the author actively encouraged more disclosure when the inmates were not forthcoming with reports of distress. Similarly, the experimental literature on sensory deprivation demonstrates that once controls for set and expectancies are introduced, bizarre experiences, under even the most severe conditions (immobilization and sensory deprivation for 14 days, were minimal for the majority of subjects.

The real culprit may not necessarily be the condition of solitary per se but the manner in which inmates have been treated. There is evidence suggesting that this is the basis for most inmate complaints. Jackson (1983) himself acceded to this fact. When inmates are dealt with capriciously by management or individual custodial officers, psychological stress can be created even in the most humane of prison environments. Therefore, solitary confinement may not be cruel and unusual punishment under the humane and time-limited conditions investigated in experimental studies or in correctional jurisdictions that have well-defined and effectively administered ethical guidelines for its use.

We must emphasize that this is *not* an argument for employing solitary and certainly not for the absurdly lengthy periods as documented by Jackson (1983). Gendreau and Bonta (1984) have outlined several research issues that urgently need to be addressed. Some of these are studies investigating individual tolerance of solitary confinement, its possible deterrent effect, and a compelling need to find alternatives to humanely restrain those who are a danger to themselves and others while incarcerated. With rare exceptions, the necessary research has not been conducted.

Short-Term Detention

In 1972, nearly 4,000 jails in the United States processed 1 million male and female offenders per year. The offenders were charged with a variety of crimes and approximately 75% of them were awaiting trial. Despite the extensive use of jails, little is known about the effects of short-term detention. Perhaps this is the area that requires most attention, as it is the initial adjustment phases that are important in assessing the impact of incarceration. For example, 50% of suicides occur in the first 24 hours of imprisonment.

A common belief is that waiting for trial and sentencing produces a considerable amount of anxiety. More specifically, anxiety increases as the trial and sentencing dates approach and then decreases after sentencing when the uncertainty surrounding trial has passed.

A study by Dyer is difficult to evaluate because of the lack of information provided. Dyer administered an anxiety scale to adolescent females and found a decrease in anxiety over time in detention. However, no information regarding the number of subjects, the setting, and the interval between tests was provided. Oleski (1977) administered the same scale to 60 male inmates (ages 18 to 26) in a Boston city jail. All were awaiting trial and all had limited prior prison experience. The tests were administered 1 week after admission and again 8 weeks later. Anxiety levels were found to be higher at posttest.

Bonta and Nackivell (1980) administered the same anxiety scale used in the previous studies to four groups of inmates selected without age and court status limitations. Group 1 inmates were remanded into custody and sentenced by the time they were retested; Group 2 were still awaiting sentencing. Group 3 inmates entered the jail already sentenced, and Group 4 was a control group for the effects of testing. The test was administered within 1 week of reception and again 3 to 4 weeks later. No changes in anxiety over time or after sentencing were observed.

Gibbs (1987) assessed psychopathology among 339 jail inmates. The inmates were asked to rate symptoms prior to incarceration, 72 hours into confinement, and again 5 days later. He found symptoms to increase between preincarceration and 72 hours of imprisonment and interpreted this finding as showing that detention per se affects symptoms. However, the interpretation is not entirely convincing. First of all, symptomatology prior to incarceration was based upon the inmates' recollections of their difficulties before detention and thus subject to memory and reporting biases. Second, at the 5-day retest, symptoms actually diminished, and third, the finding that those without prior hospitalizations did worse was a puzzling finding and not consistent with the prison as stress model.

There is another intriguing, albeit tangential, aspect to the short-term detention literature, and that is the use of short-term detention as a deterrent. Three common strategies are "Scared Straight," "boot camp," and shock probation programs. The assumption is that prison life is aversive in some form or other and that exposure to it will decrease the probability of future criminal behavior, particularly for impressionable young offenders.

The classic evaluation of "Scared Straight" by Finckenauer and Storti (1978) found only one of nine attitudinal measures significantly changed for juveniles as a result of brief exposure to hardened prisoners and no reduction in recidivism. Other variations on the original program have also found no overall deterrent effect, although some individual differences were noted. Similarly, there is now general consensus that shock probation (i.e., short prison terms prior to probation) has also failed to demonstrate significant deterrent effects. There is even one report suggesting that shock probation for a subgroup of probationers increased recidivism!

Some jurisdictions have received media attention by employing quasimilitary, boot camp regimes for offenders. In the only evaluation with a follow-up that we are aware of—although more will be forthcoming in the near future—juveniles taking part in such a program did not have reduced reconviction rates compared to nonparticipatory youths. Curiously, older adolescents reported an easier time in the program compared to their previous experiences with incarceration.

...

Summary and Conclusion

When it comes to scholarly inquiry in the field of criminal justice, a pernicious tendency has been to invoke rhetoric over reality and affirm ideology over respect for empirical evidence. We have witnessed this sad state of affairs in the debates over the effectiveness of rehabilitation, personality and crime, and the relationship between social class and criminal behavior.

If we are to make progress in understanding what it is our prisons do to inmates, then we must respect the available evidence. We do not discount the importance of phenomenology in assessing prison life; this line of inquiry does provide valuable insight. But, if we stray too far from the epistemic values that are crucial to a vigorous social science then we run the risk of making disastrous policy decisions. Therefore, if we are to have a more constructive agenda we must face the fact that simplistic notions of the "pains of imprisonment" simply will not be instructive and will mitigate against the inmate's well-being.

The facts are that long-term imprisonment and specific conditions of confinement such as solitary, under limiting and humane conditions, fail to show any sort of profound detrimental effects. The crowding literature indicates that moderating variables play a crucial role. The health risks to inmates appear minimal. Unfortunately prisons, in a way, may minimize some stress by removing the need to make daily decisions that are important for community living.

If we approach prison life with sensitivity, however, we will foster a much more realistic and proactive research and policy agenda. Our literature review revealed considerable support for this notion. We repeatedly found that interactions between certain types of individual differences and situational components explained a meaningful percentage of the variance. To illustrate, we found that age, changes in the prison population, and the chronicity of the situation had profound influences on the responses of inmates to high population density. There also appear to be some cognitive and biological individual differences that may influence adjustment to solitary confinement.

In regard to the above, it is important that the assessment of environments reach the same level of methodological sophistication as the assessment of individuals.

There have been some promising developments toward that end. Wenk and Moos (1972) have developed the correctional Institutions Environment Scale; Toch (1977), the Prison Preference Profile; and Wright (1985), the Prison Environment Inventory. These are initial steps and it is hoped that research along these lines will continue.

Our final comments are in regard to theory development. To date, the incarceration literature has been very much influenced by a "pains of imprisonment" model. This model views imprisonment as psychologically harmful. However, the empirical data we reviewed question the validity of the view that imprisonment is *universally* painful. Solitary confinement, under limiting and humane conditions, long-term imprisonment, and short-term detention fail to show detrimental effects. From a physical health standpoint, inmates appear more healthy than their community counterparts. We have little data on the effects of death row, and the crowding literature indicates that moderating variables play a crucial role.

On a brighter note, the stress model does provide a positive agenda for ameliorative action. In the long-term incarceration literature, researchers have found that some inmates cope successfully with prison but others do not and that the type of coping is modestly related to future recidivism. Furthermore, on the basis of their analysis, if emotional distress is reported by inmates, it is more often early on in their incarceration. It is at this point that they may be receptive to treatment. The implications for the timing of prison-based treatment programs is obvious. The crucial point is that on the basis of this evidence, we can now develop a variety of cognitive-behavioral and/ or skills training programs that could assist prisoners in dealing with their experiences in the most constructive manner possible. There is accumulating and persuasive evidence, moreover, that certain types of offender programming strategies in prison can reduce subsequent recidivism. This proactive agenda, we wish to emphasize, was not forthcoming from those who viewed prisons as invariably destructive. Unfortunately, their recommendations were for almost total deinstitutionalization, which is not only an extreme view, but also one that is totally unpalatable given North American cultural values and the current sociopolitical reality.

In our view, a social learning perspective provides a more comprehensive explanation of the evidence. Social learning theory examines behavior (attitudes, motor actions, emotions) as a function of the rewards and punishments operating in a prison environment. There is an explicit acceptance of personal variables moderating the responsivity to imprisonment. Several questions emerge from this perspective: *Who* perceives prisons as stressful? *What* aspect of imprisonment shapes behavior? And *how* do individuals respond to imprisonment? Answers to these questions would provide insight into the individuals who do not perceive their environments as stressful while imprisoned and what aspects of imprisonment attenuate the prison experience. In addition, this perspective would clarify the links between emotions, attitudes, and behavior.

From this review, we also see a clear research agenda. Further efforts to understand the effects of prison overcrowding should focus on individual levels of analysis along with multiple measures of the three outcome variables (emotions, attitudes, and behavior). Longitudinal designs should be the rule. The inherent difficulties in interpreting aggregate level data appear only to confuse our understanding of the impact of crowded conditions on the individual. We need to know under what conditions an individual feels crowded, becomes emotionally distressed, and copes with this distress in a maladaptive manner. For example, Ruback, Carr, and Hopper (1986) suggested that perceived control is a possible mediator. The solution to prison overcrowding is not to embark on a prohibitively expensive prison construction program but rather to alter the rate of intake and release. One way of accomplishing this task is to increase community correctional treatment programs that would allow the diversion of inmates away from prisons. Despite the reluctance of many correctional administrators to develop such programs, there appears to be considerable public support not only for community treatment initiatives but for rehabilitation in general.

The application of longitudinal designs using data collected at the individual level is also needed in the other areas we have discussed. This is especially so with long-term imprisonment and health risks where the data suggest that if anything, the prison system may actually prevent deterioration. However, only longitudinal designs will allow us to make such a conclusion with any high degree of certainty. If future research leads us to the same conclusion, then the next step would be to identify the system contingencies that support such an environment, for certainly we can learn something positive from this type of result. Finally, and remarkably, we know so little about the psychological impact of a system that houses over a million individuals: the jails. Here, almost any type of reasoned research would be a step in the right direction.

All of the above is easier said than done. The host of issues that need to be researched seem infinite. The methodological complexities in examining both person and situation interaction are pronounced. But, it appears to us to be a positive agenda in order to gain knowledge addressing a vital question.

J.V. Roberts and M. Jackson, "Boats Against the Current: A Note on the Effects of Imprisonment"
(1991), 15 *Law and Human Behavior* 557 (footnotes and references omitted)

In their review of research on the effects of imprisonment, Bonta and Gendreau (1990) draw the rather startling conclusions that "long-term imprisonment and specific conditions of confinement such as solitary, under limiting and humane conditions, fail to show any sort of profound detrimental effects" and "many prisons may actually be conducive to good health." In light of our experience, both direct and indirect (through research as well as the sworn testimony of witnesses), we have difficulty sharing this upbeat assessment of the effects of incarceration. We feel imprisonment should be used with far more restraint than at the present, and before rejecting the view that imprisonment is intrinsically destructive, we would require evidence more compelling than that generated by contemporary social science research.

The authors assume that a sentence of custody is more punitive than, but in other ways no different from, other sanctions. In our opinion, this view fails to take into account the phenomenology of the prison as it has evolved in western society. Incarceration has acquired a significance that exceeds description as mere punishment.

This is not to say that the effects of imprisonment are impervious to scientific investigation, but simply that the experience of incarceration might not be adequately captured by the usual social science dependent variables. Can the effects of an experience such as living on death row really be captured by psychiatric interviews or the MMPI? Bonta and Gendreau state: "From the *available evidence and on the dimensions measured* there is little to support the conclusion that long-term imprisonment necessarily has detrimental effects" (emphasis added). Our point is that the available evidence does not permit one to draw a conclusion that flies in the face of centuries of human experience.

Post-Release Consequences of Imprisonment

The research reviewed focused exclusively on inmates. This eliminates from consideration consequences of imprisonment that await the inmate upon emerging from prison. These consequences have been well documented: some are psychological (including self-perceptions, self-esteem, and so on), some are related to the workplace (the absence of job skills resulting from protracted incarceration), but perhaps the most pernicious effects concern the reactions of others.

The stigmatizing effect of a prison record has, of course, long been recognized. In 1859, the report of the Board of Prison Inspectors noted that an inmate is released "with the stamp of the prison upon him" and that this fact has important consequences for the individual. The fact that an individual has served time is fraught with implication. A Harris poll in the US in 1968 found that many people would feel uneasy working with ex-inmates; a Canadian survey found that people are more at ease in the presence of an ex-mental patient than an ex-inmate. The social reaction to an individual who has spent time in prison can be as damaging as the direct effects of incarcerations. Bonta and Gendreau's review is curiously silent regarding this kind of effect.

One of us recently represented a man released from prison after serving 37 years under an indeterminate sentence. He was released on the grounds that his continued imprisonment constituted cruel and unusual punishment. From the evidence presented to the courts, this man, measured by Bonta and Gendreau's objective indices of negative effects of imprisonment—"behaviors which threaten the physical welfare of the offender (e.g., aggressive behavior, suicide) … psychological stress levels (e.g., elevated blood pressure) and psychological stress (e.g., depression)"—is in better shape after imprisonment. According to the Bonta and Gendreau approach to the scientific measurement of long-term imprisonment, there is therefore nothing cruel or unusual about 37 years in prison.

It would be a salutary exercise in scientific humility for Bonta and Gendreau to put aside their "objective measures" and to consider the effects of such a period of imprisonment in the manner in which it was described by the Supreme Court of Canada. In the words of Mr. Justice Cory: "The period of incarceration has been long indeed. … During his incarceration, governments have changed, wars have begun and ended and a generation has grown to maturity." Understanding the negative impact of 37 years of imprisonment on Mr. Steele requires an acknowledgment that he finds himself separated by an unbridgeable gap of social experience from his peers in the free community. The generation of free men and women with whom he lost contact 37 years earlier are now thinking about retirement. For his part, Mr. Steele has to think about starting a new life. While his peers reap the rewards associated with parenthood (and grandparenthood), he must confront the isolation accumulated over 37 years of separation from society. Bonta and Gendreau would argue that this is to confuse rhetoric with science. We would argue that their approach substitutes a spurious objectivity for the human dimension of punishment as it is experienced by prisoners.

Suicide: What Exactly Are the Risks?

The suicide data from Canada are far more chilling than suggested by Bonta and Gendreau. Burtch and Ericson (1979) cite rates for specific Canadian institutions that range from 164 to 528 per 100,000. In fact, the picture is bleaker still, for almost all comparisons to date between suicide rates for inmates and populations outside prison have failed to correct for critical demographic differences. Frequently the comparison is between inmates and the general public (as in Bonta and Gendreau's review). The comparison is clearly inappropriate; the two populations are still not comparable in terms of their a priori suicide risk. In the US, the modal suicide profile is of a white male, over 65, living in the western States and belonging to the upper social strata. Dunne, McIntosh, and Dunne-Maxim (1987) note that suicide rates are "directly proportional to age level." They also note the "extremely low rate for blacks." The average penitentiary inmate is young (relative to the general population), from a lower-class, urban background. As well, a disproportionate percentage are black. In short, a priori suicide rates for incarcerated men are much lower than the rates for the population at large. Thus when Coggan and Walker (1982) note that the suicide rate in British prisons is 11 times the national rate, this comparison *under*estimates considerably the risk created by prisons. (Suicide in British prisons is approaching epidemic proportions: Almost 200 inmates have killed themselves within the last 4 years—*Guardian Weekly*, 1991). An additional issue is that estimates of suicide risk due to incarceration are based upon suicides committed during imprisonment; no one has studied suicide in ex-inmate populations. Imprisonment increases the likelihood of social isolation, divorce, unemployment, and many other factors that elevate the individual's suicide risk. In addition, suicide is not a phenomenon that touches 17.5 individuals but to which the remainder are impervious: For every successful suicide there are many times more attempted suicides. And yet, Bonta and Gendreau can conclude that "the health risks to inmates [due to imprisonment] appear minimal."

Solitary Confinement: Rhetoric and Reality

Bonta and Gendreau maintain that the extensive experimental literature on the effects of placing people (usually volunteer students) in solitary or conditions of sensory deprivation is being ignored in the penology literature. They argue that "in fact, this literature has much relevance to prison solitary confinement." Suedfeld, who has written extensively in this area using the same conceptual framework as Bonta and Gendreau, argues exactly the opposite. In his most recent article, after rejecting the comparability of the experience of political prisoners (or prisoners of war) to that of convicts who have been placed in solitary, he states:

> *Even less appropriate* is the comparison between the SC (solitary confinement) condition and field or laboratory experiments on isolation and stimulus reduction. ... Significant differences between the conditions are the duration of the confinement, the amount of movement allowed inside the confinement area ... the perceived benevolence of the people in charge, and the purpose for which the individual is undergoing the experience. Furthermore, experimental subjects—unlike SC prisoners—can end their participation at will. Some of these differences may make SC less severe than the laboratory technique while others may do the opposite; their combination makes a complex pattern that *ensures non-comparability*. (emphasis added)

Bonta and Gendreau cite their own research using volunteers in solitary for periods of up to 10 days. Suedfeld et al. (1982) noted that "this literature has several major flaws" including the use of measures that lack ecological validity, brief periods of isolation, and inmate volunteer subjects.

Bonta and Gendreau, in referring to the Suedfeld et al. (1982) study, cite their conclusion in the following way: "Our data lend no support to the claim that solitary confinement is overwhelmingly aversive, stressful, or damaging to the inmates." Noticeably absent from Bonta and Gendreau's citation are the important qualifications and disclaimers made by Suedfeld et al. Thus, Suedfeld et al. pointedly noted that one of the shortcomings of their study was that "the sample is truncated. *Individuals who are completely unable to adapt to SC and become psychotic or committed suicide were obviously not included*" (emphasis added). Suedfeld et al. also acknowledge that

> there is a rather extensive autobiographical, anecdotal, and clinical literature indicating that many prisoners find long periods of SC intolerable and that for some inmates even short periods of relatively mild SC may be very stressful. *It should be clear that our data do not in any way contradict this literature, and that we do not deny its validity.* (emphasis added).

Our point here is that Bonta and Gendreau seriously overstate what their kind of empirical research can tell us about the effects of solitary confinement.

Our other major point regarding solitary confinement addresses a different issue altogether. The authors lament what they refer to as "the pernicious tendency to invoke rhetoric over reality"; yet their own conclusions reflect a disregard for the reality they admire, and they embrace the very rhetoric they disdain. They conclude that "the real culprit may not necessarily be the condition of solitary *per se* but the manner in which inmates have been treated."

Research on the Canadian federal correctional regime regarding administrative segregation reveals that over the last 20-year period there have been extensive changes in federal administrative policy and rules. The official "rhetoric" for the use of administrative segregation speaks of Bonta and Gendreau's "well-defined and effectively administered ethical guidelines for its use." The reality as reflected in these studies of what actually happens in Canadian prisons is that administrative segregation continues to be applied in an arbitrary manner that violates fundamental principles of justice. By defining empirical research in such a way as to exclude studies such as those cited here, Bonta and Gendreau reduce the horizon of empirical research relevant to the evaluation of solitary confinement to studies that are, in effect, quite irrelevant to the real-life experience of prisoners.

The Ideology of Imprisonment

Bonta and Gendreau reject the relevance of ideology to criminal justice research and policy making. They thus fail to acknowledge the extent to which a certain ideology has achieved a constitutional and legal foundation that has direct implications for the resolution of criminal justice policy questions. The report of the Fraser Commission on Prostitution and Pornography in Canada is an important case in point. Advocates of the decriminalization of pornography argued that the research in the area had failed to demonstrate the necessary causal link between increased availability of pornographic material and sexual violence toward women. Such a failure was, so the argument went, fatal to using the criminal law to prohibit material that was entitled to constitutional protection as freedom of expression. The Commission, while accepting that the evidence failed to meet the threshold of proving a causal link, nevertheless concluded that this did not resolve the issue. Referring to the ideology of equality and the manner in which this was now entrenched in Section 15 of the *Canadian Charter of Rights and Freedoms*, the Fraser Commission found compelling the argument that some pornographic material, by virtue of the way in which it portrays and demeans the common humanity and dignity of women, violates the ideology of equality and of Section 15 of the *Canadian Charter of Rights and Freedoms*.

One can and should make an analogy between this principal (rather than pernicious) application of ideology and the practice of imprisonment and the question of whether it is destructive to the psychological and emotional well-being of prisoners. No one, including Bonta and Gendreau, will argue that imprisonment does not involve a major assault on a prisoner's privacy. Bonta and Gendreau, however, maintain that it is a matter of scientific inquiry to measure the extent to which imprisonment has negative physiological, psychological, and behavioral effects. To them, without such objective measurements, no negative conclusions about the pains of imprisonment should be drawn. We maintain that this is misconceived.

Policy Implications

The policy implications that we fear will be drawn from a review of this nature is that incarceration should continue to serve as the primary response to crime. This will then impede the movement to reduce our dependence upon correctional institutions, a dependence that has been denounced by every major commission of inquiry in Canada from 1849 (the Brown Commission) to 1987 (the Canadian Sentencing Commission).

The ethos of criminal justice in the 20th century can be characterized as a movement away from punishment *per se* and toward a position that incarceration is at best a necessary evil. This movement is reflected in the conditions under which sentences of imprisonment are served. We have abandoned special diets, hard labor, corporal punishment, and other privations of mind and body. As well, we have introduced intermittent sentences, educational and employment-related programs, conjugal visits, and other such innovations that either render prison life more like life in the community or otherwise reduce the impact of prison upon the individual. Guiding this transformation is the recognition that the practice of imprisonment in contemporary society is frequently a disgrace while the underlying principle is an admission of failure, a holdover from earlier times. Articles that question the negative consequences of prison hearken back to an earlier era and can only be, in F. Scott Fitzgerald's words, "boats against the current, borne back ceaselessly into the past."

NOTE

Another interesting element to this controversy arises from a "meta-analysis" study conducted by Gendreau, Goggin, and Cullen (see "The Effects of Prison Sentences on Recidivism," *User Report 1999-24* (Ottawa: Solicitor General Canada, 1999)). They observed that (1) prison produced slight increases in recidivism; and (2) "there was some tendency for lower risk offenders to be more negatively affected by the prison sentence." Accordingly, they concluded that:

1. one should not use imprisonment "with the expectation of reducing criminal behaviour";
2. the excessive use of incarceration is very costly in the light of its perceived benefits;
3. careful and comprehensive assessments should be carried out to determine who is being adversely affected by prison; and
4. the "primary justification" for imprisonment as a sanction is incapacitation and retribution.

Criminal Code, Sections 718.3, 719, and 743.1

There are a number of technical issues that relate to where and how terms of imprisonment are served. For the most part, these are determined by the *Criminal Code*.

The ability to impose a consecutive sentence arises from s. 718.3(4):

> 718.3(4) Where an accused
>
> (a) is sentenced while under sentence for an offence, and a term of imprisonment, whether in default of payment of a fine or otherwise, is imposed,
>
> (b) is convicted of an offence punishable with both fine and imprisonment and both are imposed, or
>
> (c) is convicted of more offences than one, and
>
> (i) more than one fine is imposed,
>
> (ii) terms of imprisonment for the respective offences are imposed, or

> (iii) a term of imprisonment is imposed in respect of one offence and a fine is imposed in respect of another offence,

the court that sentences the accused may direct that the terms of imprisonment that are imposed by the court or result from the operation of subsection 734(4) shall be served consecutively.

Otherwise, a sentence commences when imposed (see s. 719(1)).

The locus of confinement depends on the length of the sentence either by itself or as an aggregate with other sentences the prisoner must serve. This is also prescribed by s. 743:

> 743.1(1) Except where otherwise provided, a person who is sentenced to imprisonment for
>> (a) life,
>> (b) a term of two years or more, or
>> (c) two or more terms of less than two years each that are to be served one after the other and that, in the aggregate, amount to two years or more,
>
> shall be sentenced to imprisonment in a penitentiary.
>
> (2) Where a person who is sentenced to imprisonment in a penitentiary is, before the expiration of that sentence, sentenced to imprisonment for a term of less than two years, the person shall serve that term in a penitentiary, but if the previous sentence of imprisonment in a penitentiary is set aside, that person shall serve that term in accordance with subsection (3).
>
> (3) A person who is sentenced to imprisonment and who is not required to be sentenced as provided in subsection (1) or (2) shall, unless a special prison is prescribed by law, be sentenced to imprisonment in a prison or other place of confinement, other than a penitentiary, within the province in which the person is convicted, in which the sentence of imprisonment may be lawfully executed.
>
> (3.1) Notwithstanding subsection (3), an offender who is required to be supervised by an order made under paragraph 753.1(3)(b) and who is sentenced for another offence during the period of the supervision shall be sentenced to imprisonment in a penitentiary.
>
> (4) Where a person is sentenced to imprisonment in a penitentiary while the person is lawfully imprisoned in a place other than a penitentiary, that person shall, except where otherwise provided, be sent immediately to the penitentiary, and shall serve in the penitentiary the unexpired portion of the term of imprisonment that that person was serving when sentenced to the penitentiary as well as the term of imprisonment for which that person was sentenced to the penitentiary.
>
> (5) Where, at any time, a person who is imprisoned in a prison or place of confinement other than a penitentiary is subject to two or more terms of imprisonment, each of which is for less than two years, that are to be served one after the other, and the aggregate of the unexpired portions of those terms at that time amounts to two years or more, the person shall be transferred to a penitentiary to serve those terms, but if any one or more of such terms is set aside or reduced and the unexpired portions of the remaining term or terms on the day on which that person was transferred under this section amounted to less than two years, that person shall serve that term or terms in accordance with subsection (3).

III. INTERMITTENT SENTENCES

A court may mitigate the full effect of a custodial sentence by ordering that it be served intermittently—that is, not continuously. This usually, but not always, means on weekends. This is made possible by s. 732 of the *Criminal Code*, which provides:

732(1) Where the court imposes a sentence of imprisonment of ninety days or less on an offender convicted of an offence, whether in default of payment of a fine or otherwise, the court may, having regard to the age and character of the offender, the nature of the offence and the circumstances surrounding its commission, and the availability of appropriate accommodation to ensure compliance with the sentence, order

(a) that the sentence be served intermittently at such times as are specified in the order; and

(b) that the offender comply with the conditions prescribed in a probation order when not in confinement during the period that the sentence is being served and, if the court so orders, on release from prison after completing the intermittent sentence.

(2) An offender who is ordered to serve a sentence of imprisonment intermittently may, on giving notice to the prosecutor, apply to the court that imposed the sentence to allow it to be served on consecutive days.

(3) Where a court imposes a sentence of imprisonment on a person who is subject to an intermittent sentence in respect of another offence, the unexpired portion of the intermittent sentence shall be served on consecutive days unless the court otherwise orders.

The original intermittent sentence provisions were enacted by SC 1972, c. 13, s. 58, along with a set of other new and revised provisions described under the subheading "Absolute and Conditional Discharge, Suspended Sentence, Intermittent Sentence and Probation." These provisions were the result of recommendations in the Ouimet report (Report of the Canadian Committee on Corrections, 1969), which discussed the utility of both weekend and nightly detention and found evidence of beneficial applications of such alternatives in European countries. It recommended that courts "be empowered to impose a sentence of imprisonment to be served intermittently, the total period of imprisonment not to exceed six months." Obviously, Parliament agreed with the Ouimet report, except that it put a 90-day cap on intermittent sentences.

In *R v. Parisian* (1993), 81 CCC (3d) 351 (Man. CA), the offender appealed against a three-month sentence for possessing cannabis resin for the purposes of trafficking. The appellant sought only to serve the sentence intermittently. For the court, Twaddle JA said:

Ordinarily the decision to allow or not to allow a convicted person to serve time intermittently is one to be made by the sentencing judge. This court will only interfere if the decision is made on a wrong principle or is clearly wrong.

In the present case, the offence involved a relatively small quantity of narcotic; the accused was a small player; the sale which the accused intended to make were to persons who frequent a beverage room. Her circumstances are such that a sentence of three months if not served intermittently will cause some hardship because she has two children whom it would be difficult to place for care if she serves her sentence other than intermittently. Additionally, she has the opportunity to take a course of education to upgrade herself if she is free to take it from Monday to Friday. The accused has no prior record.

The learned sentencing judge imposed a sentence which is within the range for this particular offence and this offender, but we think she was wrong to characterize it as one at the lower end of that range. Additionally, she placed undue emphasis on the fact that the accused was unemployed and did not need an intermittent sentence to save her job. The need for the accused to educate herself and make arrangements for her children are equally valid reasons for an intermittent sentence.

In the circumstances, we are of the view that the judge's decision not to allow the sentence to be served intermittently was clearly wrong. Accordingly, we allow the appeal, set aside the sentence of three months imprisonment and substitute one of 90 days to be served intermittently.

Since 1972, the intermittent sentence has become an important element of a fair and rational sentencing scheme that includes both statutorily mandated minimum sentences of imprisonment and judge-made presumptions of incarceration. The most common role for the intermittent sentence is with respect to impaired driving offenders. When Parliament addressed the range of penalties applicable to this kind of offence in 1985 and created new offences with substantially higher maxima when bodily harm or death had occurred, it also tailored the impaired driving simpliciter sentences to integrate them with the availability of intermittent sentences. Previously, the mandated penalty for a third conviction was three months, outside the range of an intermittent sentence. However, the 1985 amendments (SC 1985, c. 19, s. 36) reduced this threshold to 90 days. Obviously, while Parliament was concerned with enhancing the penalties for this category, especially when the consequences are death or bodily harm, it was also concerned with instilling fairness in the system by permitting a judge to consider the appropriateness of an intermittent sentence. The potential scope of this consideration can be appreciated by noting the recent statistics. In 1997, 48,318 convictions were registered for impaired driving, resulting in 9,776 sentences of imprisonment with a median length of 30 days.

The most common use of an intermittent sentence is to respond to a case where a brief period of incarceration is mandated either by the Code or by a presumption of incarceration, but imprisonment for a continuous period will risk the offender's job, schooling, or family. Without an intermittent sentence, some offenders will not be able to maintain their careers, profession, or employment. It is the lowest people on the employment ladder—those with the least marketable skills and the least vocational resources—who will be replaced first. Thus, the working poor offender will likely become even more impoverished, while the middle-class offender will likely keep his or her job. Similarly, a parent from a traditional family has a spouse to care for children during a brief period of confinement. A single parent, if not able to find a willing relative, risks losing a child to the local Children's Aid Society, even over a 14-day sentence. Students struggling to succeed in an increasingly more challenging world risk losing a school term as a consequence of a brief period of incarceration. Again, the more financially able the student is, the easier it is to overcome this obstacle, whether through extra tutoring or re-enrollment. Some may not be able to bounce back.

IV. MAXIMUM SENTENCES

With respect to maximum sentences, recall the discussion of the Supreme Court of Canada decision in *R v. M.(C.A.)* in Chapter 2. Generally, the maximum sentence is intended for the worst offence committed by the worst offender. Of course, this is an overly simplistic statement, given the infinite ways that offenders from various backgrounds commit offences. But it does indicate the necessarily high threshold for a maximum sentence. In a later chapter, we will look at the indeterminate sentence that flows from a finding that an offender is a dangerous offender pursuant to s. 753 of the *Criminal Code*. A number of appellate courts have held that a life sentence, as a maximum sentence, should not be imposed on grounds of dangerousness simply to circumvent the dangerous offender procedures. See, for example, *R v. Pontello* (1978), 38 CCC (2d) 262 (Ont. CA), a case of rape. In another rape case, a life sentence was upheld, given the planning, the brutality, and the dangerousness of the offender, who suffered from a personality disorder (see *R v. Hill* (1974), 15 CCC (2d) 145 (Ont. CA)). More recently, one rarely sees this attitude expressed by courts. The reason is likely the recognition that a dangerous offender finding can result in a longer period of incarceration than a life sentence.

V. MINIMUM SENTENCES

Minimum sentences have been challenged on Charter grounds. Essentially, the courts have held that the idea of a minimum sentence is not unconstitutional, but a specific example may violate s. 12 of the *Canadian Charter of Rights and Freedoms*, part I of the *Constitution Act, 1982*, RSC 1985, app. II, no. 44, if it imposes a sentence that is grossly disproportionate to the offence and the circumstances of the offender (see *R v. Smith*, infra, and *R v. Goltz*, [1991] 3 SCR 485).

R v. Smith
(1987), 34 CCC (3d) 97 (SCC)

LAMER J:

...

In measuring the content of the legislation, the courts are to look to the purpose and effect of the legislation. Dickson J, as he then was, in *R v. Big M Drug Mart Ltd.* (1985), 18 CCC (3d) 385 at p. 414, 18 DLR (4th) 321 at p. 350, [1985] 1 SCR 295, at p. 331, speaking for the majority of this court, stated: "In my view, both purpose and effect are relevant in determining constitutionality; either an unconstitutional purpose or an unconstitutional effect can invalidate legislation." And further, at pp. 415-6 CCC, pp. 351-2 DLR, p. 334 SCR:

> I agree with the respondent that the legislation's purpose is the initial test of constitutional validity and its effects are to be considered when the law under review has passed or, at least, has purportedly passed the purpose test. ...
>
> Thus, if a law with a valid purpose interferes by its impact, with rights or freedoms, a litigant could still argue the effects of the legislation as a means to defeat its applicability

and possibly its validity. In short, the effects test will only be necessary to defeat legislation with a valid purpose; effects can never be relied upon to save legislation with an invalid purpose.

Thus, even though the pursuit of a constitutionally invalid purpose will result in the invalidity of the impugned legislation irrespective of its effects, a valid purpose does not end the constitutional inquiry. The means chosen by Parliament to achieve that valid purpose may result in effects which deprive Canadians of their rights guaranteed under the Charter. In such a case it would then be incumbent upon the authorities to demonstrate under s. 1 that the importance of that valid purpose is such that, irrespective of the effect of the legislation, it is a reasonable limit in a free and democratic society.

The undisputed fact that the purpose of s. 5(2) of the *Narcotic Control Act* is constitutionally valid is not a bar to an analysis of s. 5(2) in order to determine if the minimum has the effect of obliging the judge in certain cases to impose a cruel and unusual punishment, and thereby is a prima facie violation of s. 12; and, if it is, to then reconsider under s. 1 that purpose and any other considerations relevant to determining whether the impugned legislation may be salvaged.

The Meaning of S. 12

It is generally accepted in a society such as ours that the State has the power to impose a "treatment or punishment" on an individual where it is necessary to do so to attain some legitimate end and where the requisite procedure has been followed. The Charter limits this power: s. 7 provides that everyone has the right not to be deprived of life, liberty and security of the person except in accordance with the principles of fundamental justice, s. 9 provides that everyone has the right not to be arbitrarily detained or imprisoned, and s. 12 guarantees the right not to be subjected to any cruel and unusual treatment or punishment.

The limitation at issue here is s. 12 of the Charter. In my view, the protection afforded by s. 12 governs the quality of the punishment and is concerned with the effect that the punishment may have on the person on whom it is imposed. I would agree with Laskin CJC in *Miller and Cockriell*, supra, where he defined the phrase "cruel and unusual" as a "compendious expression of a norm." The criterion which must be applied in order to determine whether a punishment is cruel and unusual within the meaning of s. 12 of the Charter is, to use the words of Laskin CJC in *Miller and Cockriell*, supra, at p. 183 CCC, p. 330 DLR, p. 688 SCR, "whether the punishment prescribed is so excessive as to outrage standards of decency." In other words, though the State may impose punishment, the effect of that punishment must not be grossly disproportionate to what would have been appropriate.

In imposing a sentence of imprisonment the judge will assess the circumstances of the case in order to arrive at an appropriate sentence. The test for review under s. 12 of the Charter is one of gross disproportionality, because it is aimed at punishments that are more than merely excessive. We should be careful not to stigmatize every disproportionate or excessive sentence as being a constitutional violation, and should leave to the usual sentencing appeal process the task of reviewing the fitness of a sentence. Section 12 will only be infringed where the sentence is so unfit having regard to the offence and the offender as to be grossly disproportionate.

In assessing whether a sentence is grossly disproportionate, the court must first consider the gravity of the offence, the personal characteristics of the offender and the particular circumstances of the case in order to determine what range of sentences would have been appropriate to punish, rehabilitate or deter this particular offender or to protect the public from this particular offender. The other purposes which may be pursued by the imposition of punishment, in particular the deterrence of other potential offenders, are thus not relevant at this stage of the inquiry. This does not mean that the judge or the legislator can no longer consider general deterrence or other penological purposes that go beyond the particular offender in determining a sentence, but only that the resulting sentence must not be grossly disproportionate to what the offender deserves. If a grossly disproportionate sentence is "prescribed by law," then the purpose which it seeks to attain will fall to be assessed under s. 1. Section 12 ensures that individual offenders receive punishments that are appropriate, or at least not grossly disproportionate, to their particular circumstances, while s. 1 permits this right to be overridden to achieve some important societal objective.

One must also measure the effect of the sentence actually imposed. If it is grossly disproportionate to what would have been appropriate, then it infringes s. 12. The effect of the sentence is often a composite of many factors and is not limited to the quantum or duration of the sentence but includes its nature and the conditions under which it is applied. Sometimes by its length alone or by its very nature will the sentence be grossly disproportionate to the purpose sought. Sometimes it will be the result of the combination of factors which, when considered in isolation, would not in and of themselves amount to gross disproportionality. For example, 20 years for a first offence against property would be grossly disproportionate, but so would three months of imprisonment if the prison authorities decide it should be served in solitary confinement. Finally, I should add that some punishments or treatments will always be grossly disproportionate and will always outrage our standards of decency: for example, the infliction of corporal punishment, such as the lash, irrespective of the number of lashes imposed, or, to give examples of treatment, the lobotomisation of certain dangerous offenders or the castration of sexual offenders.

The numerous criteria proposed pursuant to s. 2(b) of the *Canadian Bill of Rights* and the Eighth Amendment of the American Constitution are, in my opinion, useful as factors to determine whether a violation of s. 12 has occurred. Thus, to refer to tests listed by Professor Tarnopolsky, the determination of whether the punishment is necessary to achieve a valid penal purpose, whether it is founded on recognized sentencing principles, and whether there exist valid alternatives to the punishment imposed, are all guidelines which, without being determinative in themselves, help to assess whether the punishment is grossly disproportionate.

There is a further aspect of proportionality which has been considered on occasion by the American courts: a comparison with punishments imposed for other crimes in the same jurisdiction: see *Solem v. Helm* (1983), 463 US 277 at p. 291. Of course, the simple fact that penalties for similar offences are divergent does not necessarily mean that the greater penalty is grossly disproportionate and thus cruel and unusual. At most, the divergence in penalties is an indication that the greater penalty may be excessive, but it will remain necessary to assess the penalty in accordance with the factors discussed above. The notion that there must be a gradation of punishments according to the malignity of offences may be considered to be a principle of fundamental justice under s. 7, but, given my decision under s. 12, I do not find it necessary to deal with that issue here.

Recently, a number of appellate court decisions have dealt with the new four-year minimum penalties imposed for a variety of offences committed with a firearm and questioned the impact of s. 719(3) on a mandated minimum sentence. This provision empowers a judge to take into account pre-sentence custody. Imagine a situation where two offenders are accused of robbery, and it is alleged that a firearm was used. Section 344(a) imposes a mandatory sentence of four years. One offender is released on bail, while the other serves 12 months in custody before the trial. Both are convicted. Does fairness not require some credit for the pre-sentence custody? How can the judge give effect to both s. 719(3) and s. 344(a)? See the decision of Rosenberg JA for the Ontario Court of Appeal in *R v. McDonald* (1998), 127 CCC (3d) 57 and compare it with *R v. Lapierre* (1998), 123 CCC (3d) 332 (Que. CA). This issue has now been resolved by the Supreme Court of Canada in *R v. Wust*, infra.

R v. Wust
(2000), 143 CCC (3d) 129 (SCC)

ARBOUR J (for the court):

. . .

[para18] Mandatory minimum sentences are not the norm in this country, and they depart from the general principles of sentencing expressed in the Code, in the case law, and in the literature on sentencing. In particular, they often detract from what Parliament has expressed as the fundamental principle of sentencing in s. 718.1 of the Code: the principle of proportionality. Several mandatory minimum sentences have been challenged under s. 12 of the Charter, as constituting cruel and unusual punishment: see, for example, *R v. Smith*, [1987] 1 SCR 1045, 34 CCC (3d) 97, 40 DLR (4th) 435, *R v. Goltz*, [1991] 3 SCR 485, 67 CCC (3d) 481, and *Morrisey*, supra.

[para19] On some occasions, a mandatory minimum sentence has been struck down under s. 12, on the basis that the minimum prescribed by law was, or could be, on a reasonable hypothetical basis, grossly disproportionate to what the circumstances called for. See for example *Smith*, striking down s. 5(2) of the *Narcotic Control Act*; *R v. Bill* (1998), 13 CR (5th) 125 (BCSC), striking down the four-year minimum sentence for manslaughter with a firearm under s. 236(a) of the Code; *R v. Leimanis*, [1992] BCJ No. 2280 (QL) (Prov. Ct.), in which the s. 88(1)(c) minimum sentence of the BC *Motor Vehicle Act* for driving under a s. 85(a) prohibition was invalidated; and *R v. Pasacreta*, [1995] BCJ No. 2823 (QL) (Prov. Ct.), where the same penalty as in *Leimanis* for driving under a s. 84 prohibition was also struck down.

[para20] In other cases, courts have fashioned the remedy of a constitutional exemption from a mandatory minimum sentence, thereby upholding the enactment as valid while exempting the accused from its application: see *R v. Chief* (1989), 51 CCC (3d) 265 (YTCA), and *R v. McGillivary* (1991), 62 CCC (3d) 407 (Sask. CA). Finally, in some of the cases where the courts have upheld a minimum sentence as constitutionally valid, it has been noted that the mandatory minimum sentence was demonstrably unfit or harsh in the case before the court. See, for example, *McDonald*, at p. 85, per Rosenberg JA, and *R v. Hainnu*, [1998] NWTJ No. 101 (QL) (SC) at para. 71.

[para21] Even if it can be argued that harsh, unfit sentences may prove to be a powerful deterrent, and therefore still serve a valid purpose, it seems to me that sentences that are unjustly severe are more likely to inspire contempt and resentment than to foster compliance with the law. It is a well-established principle of the criminal justice system that judges must strive to impose a sentence tailored to the individual case: *R v. M.(C.A.)*, [1996] 1 SCR 500 at para. 92, 105 CCC (3d) 327, per Lamer CJ; *R v. Gladue*, [1999] 1 SCR 688 at para. 93, 133 CCC (3d) 385, 171 DLR (4th) 385, per Cory and Iacobucci JJ.

[para22] Consequently, it is important to interpret legislation which deals, directly and indirectly, with mandatory minimum sentences, in a manner that is consistent with general principles of sentencing, and that does not offend the integrity of the criminal justice system. This is entirely possible in this case, and, in my view, such an approach reflects the intention of Parliament that all sentences be administered consistently, except to the limited extent required to give effect to a mandatory minimum.

[para23] In accordance with the umbrella principle of statutory interpretation expressed by this Court in *Rizzo & Rizzo Shoes Ltd. (Re)*, [1998] 1 SCR 27 at paras. 20-23, 154 DLR (4th) 193, mandatory minimum sentences must be understood in the full context of the sentencing scheme, including the management of sentences provided for in the *Corrections and Conditional Release Act*, SC 1992, c. 20. Several provisions of the Code, and of other federal statutes, provide for various forms of punishment upon conviction for an offence. Most enactments providing for the possibility of imprisonment do so by establishing a maximum term of imprisonment. In deciding on the appropriate sentence, the court is directed by Part XXIII of the Code to consider various purposes and principles of sentencing, such as denunciation, general and specific deterrence, public safety, rehabilitation, restoration, proportionality, disparity, totality and restraint, and to take into account both aggravating and mitigating factors. The case law provides additional guidelines, often in illustrating what an appropriate range of sentence might be in the circumstances of a particular case. In arriving at a fit sentence, the court must also be alive to some computing rules, for example, the rule that sentences cannot normally be back- or post-dated: s. 719(1) of the Code; see also *R v. Patterson* (1946), 87 CCC 86 (Ont. CA) at p. 87, per Robertson CJ, and *R v. Sloan* (1947), 87 CCC 198 (Ont. CA) at pp. 198-99, per Roach JA, cited with approval by Rosenberg JA, in *McDonald*, at p. 71.

[para24] Rarely is the sentencing court concerned with what happens after the sentence is imposed, that is, in the administration of the sentence. Sometimes it is required to do so by addressing, by way of recommendation, or in mandatory terms, a particular form of treatment for the offender. For instance in murder cases, the sentencing

court will determine a fixed term of parole ineligibility: s. 745.4 of the Code. However, for the most part, after a sentence of imprisonment is imposed, the *Corrections and Conditional Release Act* comes into play to administer that sentence, with the almost invariable effect of reducing the amount of time actually served in detention. Under this Act, the offender earns statutory remission, that is, time that will be automatically deducted from the sentence imposed. Furthermore, he or she will become eligible for escorted and unescorted temporary absences, work releases, day parole and full parole, and statutory release. In short, it is quite possible, indeed, it is most likely, that the person sentenced will not be incarcerated for the full period of time imposed in the sentence pronounced by the court.

[para25] The *Corrections and Conditional Release Act*, in effect, "deems" the time spent lawfully at large by the offender who is released on parole, statutory release or unescorted temporary absence as a continuation of the sentence until its expiration: s. 128(1). This provision applies to all sentences, even where the term of imprisonment imposed is a statutory mandatory minimum.

[para26] The *Firearms Act* addressed the issue of the administration of mandatory minimum sentences, but in a very minimal way by amending one section of Schedule I of the *Corrections and Conditional Release Act*. Schedule I sets out the offences for which the sentencing court has power to delay eligibility for full parole to the lesser of one-half of the sentence or ten years, rather than the standard time for full parole eligibility of the lesser of one-third of the sentence or seven years: s. 120(1) of the *Corrections and Conditional Release Act*, referring to, among other sections, s. 743.6 of the Code. In s. 165, the *Firearms Act* amends Schedule I to include using an imitation firearm in the commission of an offence, as prohibited by s. 85(2) of the Code.

[para27] This slight amendment of the *Corrections and Conditional Releases Act* by the *Firearms Act* suggests that while Parliament turned its mind to the administration of sentences when it was introducing the firearms-related minimum sentences, it did not see fit to alter the general administration of sentences in a way that would distinguish the new mandatory minimums from other sentences. It therefore follows that a rigid interpretation of s. 719(3), which suggests that time served before sentence cannot be credited to reduce a minimum sentence because it would offend the requirement that nothing short of the minimum be served, does not accord with the general management of minimum sentences, which are in every other respect "reduced" like all others, even to below the minimum.

[para28] In addition, and in contrast to statutory remission or parole, pre-sentence custody is time actually served in detention, and often in harsher circumstances than the punishment will ultimately call for. In *R v. Rezaie* (1996), 112 CCC (3d) 97 (Ont. CA), to which several lower courts have referred in their consideration of pre-sentencing custody, Laskin JA succinctly summarizes the particular features of pre-trial custody that result in its frequent characterization as "dead time" at p. 104:

> ... in two respects, pre-trial custody is even more onerous than post-sentencing custody. First, other than for a sentence of life imprisonment, legislative provisions for parole eligibility and statutory release do not take into account time spent in custody before trial (or before sentencing). Second, local detention centres ordinarily do not provide educational, retraining or rehabilitation programs to an accused in custody waiting trial.

[para29] As this quotation from *Rezaie* demonstrates, pre-sentencing custody, pre-trial custody, pre-disposition custody and "dead time" are all used to refer to the time spent by an accused person in detention prior to conviction and sentencing. For the purposes of this decision, I consider all these terms to refer to the same thing; however, I prefer "pre-sentencing custody" as it most accurately captures all the time an offender may have spent in custody prior to the imposition of sentence.

[para30] Several years ago, Professor Martin L. Friedland published an important study of pre-sentencing custody in which he referred to Professor Caleb Foote's Comment on the New York Bail Study project, noting that "accused persons … are confined pending trial under conditions which are more oppressive and restrictive than those applied to convicted and sentenced felons": "Detention Before Trial: A Study of Criminal Cases Tried in the Toronto Magistrates' Courts" (1965), at p. 104. As Rosenberg JA noted in *McDonald* at p. 72: "There has been little change in the conditions under which remand prisoners are held in this province in the almost forty years since Professor Friedland did his study." Considering the severe nature of pre-sentencing custody, and that the accused person is in fact deprived of his or her liberty, credit for pre-sentencing custody is arguably less offensive to the concept of a minimum period of incarceration than would be the granting of statutory remission or parole. It is therefore ironic that the applicability of s. 719(3) has encountered such difficulties in the case of minimum sentences, simply because the "interference" with the minimum is at the initial sentence determination stage and thus more readily apparent.

[para31] As was pointed out by Rosenberg JA in *McDonald* at p. 73, Parliament enacted the forerunner to s. 719(3) of the *Criminal Code* as part of the *Bail Reform Act*, RSC 1970, c. 2 (2nd Supp.), for the very specific purpose of ensuring that the well-established practice of sentencing judges to give credit for time served while computing a sentence would be available even to reduce a sentence below the minimum fixed by law. During the second reading of what was then Bill C-218, *Amendment of Provisions of the Criminal Code* relating to Arrest and Bail, Justice Minister John Turner described Parliament's intention regarding what is now s. 719(3):

> Generally speaking, the courts in deciding what sentence to impose on a person convicted of an offence take into account the time he has spent in custody awaiting trial. However, under the present *Criminal Code*, a sentence commences only when it is imposed, and the court's hands are tied in those cases where a minimum term of imprisonment must be imposed. In such cases, therefore, the court is bound to impose not less than the minimum sentence even though the convicted person may have been in custody awaiting trial for a period in excess of the minimum sentence. The new version of the bill would permit the court, in a proper case, to take this time into account in imposing sentence. [House of Commons Debates, February 5, 1971, at p. 3118.]

[para32] Counsel for the respondent has directed this Court's attention to the remarks of then Justice Minister Allan Rock concerning Bill C-68, an Act respecting firearms and other weapons, during the House of Commons debates and before the Standing Committee on Justice and Legal Affairs. On these occasions, the Justice Minister articulated Parliament's intention that the new mandatory minimum sentences for firearms-related offences act as a strong deterrent to the use of guns in

crime. See House of Commons Debates, February 16, 1995, at pp. 9706 et seq.; House of Commons, Standing Committee on Justice and Legal Affairs, Evidence, April 24, 1995, Meeting No. 105, and May 19, 1995, Meeting No. 147. However, when Parliament enacted s. 344(a) as part of the *Firearms Act* in 1995, Parliament did not also modify s. 719(3), to exempt this new minimum sentence from its application, any more than it modified the applicability of the provisions of the *Corrections and Conditional Release Act* to mandatory minimum sentences. For the courts to exempt s. 344(a) from the application of s. 719(3), enacted specifically to apply to mandatory minimum sentences, would therefore defeat the intention of Parliament.

[para33] All of the above suggests that if indeed s. 719(3) had to be interpreted such as to prevent credit being given for time served in detention prior to sentencing under a mandatory minimum offence, the result would be offensive both to rationality and to justice. Fortunately, as was admirably explained by Rosenberg JA in *McDonald*, this result is avoided through the application of sound principles of statutory interpretation.

[para34] In his judgment, Rosenberg JA employed several well-established rules of statutory interpretation to conclude as he did, at p. 69, that s. 719(3) provides sentencing judges with a "substantive power to count pre-sentence custody in fixing the length of the sentence." I agree with his analysis. In particular, I approve of his reference to the principle that provisions in penal statutes, when ambiguous, should be interpreted in a manner favourable to the accused (see *R v. McIntosh*, [1995] 1 SCR 686 at para. 29, 95 CCC (3d) 481, per Lamer CJ); to the need to interpret legislation so as to avoid conflict between its internal provisions, to avoid absurd results by searching for internal coherence and consistency in the statute; and finally, where a provision is capable of more than one interpretation, to choose the interpretation which is consistent with the Charter: *Slaight Communications Inc. v. Davidson*, [1989] 1 SCR 1038 at p. 1078, 59 DLR (4th) 416, per Lamer J (as he then was). Without repeating Rosenberg JA's analysis here, I wish to make a few observations.

B. The Distinction Between Punishment and Sentence

[para35] Rosenberg JA relied on the distinction between the meaning of the words "punishment" and "sentence," the former being used in s. 344(a) and the latter in s. 719(3). I set out the relevant provisions again, for ease of reference:

> 344. Every person who commits robbery is guilty of an indictable offence and liable
>   (a) where a firearm is used in the commission of the offence, to imprisonment for life and to a minimum punishment of imprisonment for a term of four years ...
> 719(3) In determining the sentence to be imposed on a person convicted of an offence, a court may take into account any time spent in custody by the person as a result of the offence.

[para36] The distinction between "sentence" and "punishment" was developed by the Canadian Sentencing Reform Commission in its 1987 report, "Sentencing Reform: A Canadian Approach," at pp. 110 et seq. In summary, Rosenberg JA emphasized at pp. 76-78 that "sentencing" is a judicial determination of a legal sanction, in

contrast to "punishment" which is the actual infliction of the legal sanction. While this distinction is helpful, I do not think that it is fundamental to sustain the conclusion that s. 719(3) may be applied to s. 344(a). The French version does not employ a similar distinction in the language of the two sections. In French, the expression "la peine" is used interchangeably for "punishment" (s. 344(a)), for "sentencing" (title to s. 718.2) and for "sentence" (i.e., ss. 718.2 and 719). However, the expression "punishment" which is used twice in s. 718.3(1), is referred to in French first as "la peine" and the second time, in the same sentence, as "la punition." What is fundamental is less the words chosen, in the French or English version, but the concepts that they carry. Again, for ease of reference, I set out some of these provisions:

> 344. Quiconque commet un vol qualifié est coupable d'un acte criminel passible:
>   (a) s'il y a usage d'une arme à feu lors de la perpétration de l'infraction, de l'emprisonnement à perpétuité, la peine minimale étant de quatre ans. ...
> 718.3(1) Lorsqu'une disposition prescrit différents degrés ou genres de peine à l'égard d'une infraction, la punition à infliger est, sous réserve des restrictions contenues dans la disposition, à la discrétion du tribunal qui condamne l'auteur de l'infraction. ...
> 719(3) Pour fixer la peine à infliger à une personne déclarée coupable d'une infraction, le tribunal peut prendre en compte toute période que la personne a passée sous garde par suite de l'infraction.

[para37] Overall, both versions lead to the same conclusion, since the French phrase in s. 719(3), "pour fixer la peine" places the emphasis on the sentencing judge's role of calculating the appropriate sentence, and in doing so, provides the discretion for considering the amount of time already spent in custody by the convicted offender in relation to the offence. Since these sections refer to "la peine," it seems logical to conclude that in determining "la peine minimale" it is acceptable to apply s. 719(3), since "la peine minimale" is merely a subset of "la peine" generally, and has not been excluded expressly from the operation of s. 719(3). No violence is done to the language of the Code when the sections are read together, in French or in English, and are understood to mean, as Parliament intended, that an offender will receive a minimum sentence of four years, to commence when it is imposed, and calculated with credit given for time served.

C. The Effect of Pre-Sentencing Custody on the Legally Detained Accused

[para38] I have already commented on the usually harsh nature of pre-sentencing custody and referred to the frequent characterization of this detention as "dead time." Some further comments are required.

[para39] Counsel for the respondent urged this Court to consider the apparent fallacy of recognizing pre-sentencing custody as punishment, since it is commonly recognized that Canadian law does not punish innocent citizens. Rosenberg JA in *McDonald*, at p. 77, noted that "accused persons are not denied bail to punish them before their guilt has been determined." He referred to this Court's decision in *R v. Pearson*, [1992] 3 SCR 665 at pp. 687-88, 77 CCC (3d) 124, where Lamer CJ held that the presumption of innocence as guaranteed by s. 11(d) of the Charter has "no

application at the bail stage of the criminal process, where the guilt or innocence of the accused is not determined and where punishment is not imposed."

[para40] Counsel for the respondent also referred to this passage from Pearson to support the contention that pre-trial custody may not be considered as part of the offender's punishment. With respect, it is important to consider the broader context of Lamer CJ's comments. At that point in the Pearson judgment (at pp. 687-88), Lamer CJ was elaborating on the specific understanding of the s. 11(d) presumption of innocence in the trial context:

> Thus the effect of s. 11(d) is to create a procedural and evidentiary rule at trial that the prosecution must prove guilt beyond a reasonable doubt. This procedural and evidentiary rule has no application at the bail stage of the criminal process, where the guilt or innocence of the accused is not determined and where punishment is not imposed. Accordingly, s. 515(6)(d) does not violate s. 11(d).

Looking at this larger context, one cannot conclude that Lamer C.J. was proposing that pre-sentencing custody could never be viewed as punishment or that it could not retroactively be treated as part of the punishment, as provided for by s. 719(3).

[para41] To maintain that pre-sentencing custody can never be deemed punishment following conviction because the legal system does not punish innocent people is an exercise in semantics that does not acknowledge the reality of pre-sentencing custody so carefully delineated by Laskin JA, in *Rezaie*, supra, and by Gary Trotter in his text, *The Law of Bail in Canada* (1992), at p. 28:

> Remand prisoners, as they are sometimes called, often spend their time awaiting trial in detention centres or local jails that are ill-suited to lengthy stays. As the Ouimet Report stressed, such institutions may restrict liberty more than many institutions which house the convicted. Due to overcrowding, inmate turnover and the problems of effectively implementing programs and recreation activities, serving time in such institutions can be quite onerous.

Therefore, while pre-trial detention is not intended as punishment when it is imposed, it is, in effect, deemed part of the punishment following the offender's conviction, by the operation of s. 719(3). The effect of deeming such detention punishment is not unlike the determination, discussed earlier in these reasons, that time spent lawfully at large while on parole is considered nonetheless a continuation of the offender's sentence of incarceration.

[para42] If this Court were to conclude that the discretion provided by s. 719(3) to consider pre-sentencing custody was not applicable to the mandatory minimum sentence of s. 344(a), it is certain that unjust sentences would result. First, courts would be placed in the difficult situation of delivering unequal treatment to similarly situated offenders: for examples, see *McDonald*, at pp. 80-81. Secondly, because of the gravity of the offence and the concern for public safety, many persons charged under s. 344(a), even first time offenders, would often be remanded in custody while awaiting trial. Consequently, discrepancies in sentencing between least and worst offenders would increase, since the worst offender, whose sentence exceeded the mini-

mum would benefit from pre-sentencing credit, while the first time offender whose sentence would be set at the minimum, would not receive credit for his or her pre-sentencing detention. An interpretation of s. 719(3) and s. 344(a) that would reward the worst offender and penalize the least offender is surely to be avoided.

[para43] These examples of the absurd results we could expect from an exclusion of the application of s. 719(3) to mandatory minimum sentences, such as that provided by s. 344(a), are further indication that Parliament intended these two sections to be interpreted harmoniously and consistently within the overall context of the criminal justice system's sentencing regime.

D. Calculating the Amount of Credit for Pre-Sentence Custody

[para44] I see no advantage in detracting from the well-entrenched judicial discretion provided in s. 719(3) by endorsing a mechanical formula for crediting pre-sentencing custody. As we have re-affirmed in this decision, the goal of sentencing is to impose a just and fit sentence, responsive to the facts of the individual offender and the particular circumstances of the commission of the offence. I adopt the reasoning of Laskin JA in *Rezaie*, at p. 105, where he noted that:

> ... provincial appellate courts have rejected a mathematical formula for crediting pre-trial custody, instead insisting that the amount of time to be credited should be determined on a case by case basis. ... Although a fixed multiplier may be unwise, absent justification, sentencing judges should give some credit for time spent in custody before trial (and before sentencing). [Citations omitted]

[para45] In the past, many judges have given more or less two months credit for each month spent in pre-sentencing detention. This is entirely appropriate even though a different ratio could also be applied, for example if the accused has been detained prior to trial in an institution where he or she has had full access to educational, vocational and rehabilitation programs. The often applied ratio of 2:1 reflects not only the harshness of the detention due to the absence of programs, which may be more severe in some cases than in others, but reflects also the fact that none of the remission mechanisms contained in the *Corrections and Conditional Release Act* apply to that period of detention. "Dead time" is "real" time. The credit cannot and need not be determined by a rigid formula and is thus best left to the sentencing judge, who remains in the best position to carefully weigh all the factors which go toward the determination of the appropriate sentence, including the decision to credit the offender for any time spent in pre-sentencing custody.

V. Disposition of the Appeal

[para46] I would allow the appeal and set aside the judgment of the Court of Appeal. I would reinstate the sentence imposed on the appellant by Grist J, who granted the appellant one year credit for his seven months of pre-sentencing custody, and sentenced him under s. 344(a) to three and one half years' imprisonment. The concurrent

sentence of one year for possession of a restricted weapon would remain unaffected by these reasons.

Appeal allowed.

NOTE

Another aspect of the challenges to mandatory minimum sentences is the constitutional exemption that arose originally in the context of mandated firearms prohibitions (see the discussion in Chapter 13). Although the argument has been rejected by a number of appellate courts in the four-year minimum sentence cases discussed above, it was front and centre in *R v. Latimer* (see Chapter 14), and will inevitably be addressed by the Supreme Court in that case.

CHAPTER TWELVE

Conditional Sentence of Imprisonment

I. INTRODUCTION

The conditional sentence was created with the enactment of Bill C-41 in 1995 (SC 1995, c. 22), coming into force in 1996 with the new part XXIII of the *Criminal Code*, RSC 1985, c. C-46, as amended. The conditional sentence has proven to be the most significant and controversial aspect of the reformed part XXIII. While a clear empirical picture is not yet available, conditional sentences have been imposed in close to 50,000 cases (as of the spring of 2000). Clearly, sentencing judges have perceived a role for them. The important issue is how that role should be defined.

History of the Conditional Sentence

The idea of suspending dispositions for fixed periods of time can be traced back to the Report of the Canadian Committee on Corrections, *Toward Unity: Criminal Justice and Corrections* (Ottawa: Queen's Printer, 1969) ("the Ouimet report") and the English suspended sentence. Both examples are distinguishable from the traditional Canadian suspended sentence, where the imposition of sentence is suspended, but not its execution. In 1984, Bill C-19 was tabled for first reading. It contained proposals for sentencing reform based on *The Criminal Law in Canadian Society* (Ottawa: Supply and Services, 1982), a statement of government policy concerning the criminal law. The bill included a new option, entitled the "conditional sentence," which was to be defined in the following form:

> 661. Where an offender other than a corporation is convicted of an offence, except an offence for which a minimum punishment is prescribed by law, the court may suspend the imposition of any other sanction and direct that the offender enter into a recognizance in Form 28 without sureties to keep the peace and be of good behaviour for such period, not exceeding two years, as the court thinks fit.

This proposed option would have permitted the suspension of any kind of sentence without conditions, except to avoid further offences. It was essentially the Ouimet model. Bill C-19 died on the order paper.

The government of Canada issued a green paper on sentencing and corrections in 1990. This led in 1992 to another sentencing reform bill, C-90. Neither the term "conditional sentence" nor any mechanism that might fit that name appeared in these documents. However, that was not the end of the idea. One of the major criticisms of the green paper was the absence of new non-custodial options for sentencing judges. Around the same time as the release of that document came the publication of Morris and Tonry's "Intermediate Sanctions: Between Prison and Parole." Within this category of intermediate sanction would be included non-custodial alternatives such as intensive supervision, house arrest, electronic monitoring, day-reporting centres, and community service. The Department of Justice circulated a series of discussion papers that canvassed some of the "intermediate sanction" alternatives. One paper, dated December 9, 1991, returned to the subject of a conditional sentence but defined it as "an alternative to the suspended sentence." In other words, rather than suspending the imposition of a sentence, as has been Canada's approach, the proposal would have suspended the execution of the sentence and amended the consequential breach procedure so that failures to comply would no longer be an offence but rather trigger court intervention. In essence, this would be a revision to the probation scheme. Ultimately this proposal, for whatever reason, was rejected.

We know what was contained in Bill C-41, the conditional sentence now found in s. 742.1 of the Code. We also know what was on the table at the time Bill C-41 was drafted. This is clear both from a long view of the sentencing debate going back to Ouimet and also from the short view going back to Bill C-90. Clearly, we witnessed a combination of four factors: (1) concern about the overuse of imprisonment, (2) support for greater use of community sentences, (3) discussions around intermediate sanctions, and (4) the criticism of Bill C-90 in 1990 that it did not contain any new alternatives to imprisonment. Only one inference can reasonably be drawn from the decision made by the minister of justice not to revise probation but to use some of the proposed elements to structure a new alternative to imprisonment—the conditional sentence. One might question the statutory form of this new option, but its history and context leave little doubt about its purpose.

Aside from representing a response to concerns about the overuse of imprisonment, the manner in which the conditional sentence evolved is also important. Clearly, it was not a revision of probation. The probation provisions and the suspended sentence were continued with only minor amendments. The conditional sentence is not a free-standing, discrete sentencing option. Rather, it is available in some cases where imprisonment was previously mandated as an alternative mode of serving a sentence.

II. GENERAL PRINCIPLES

In the three years after the new part XXIII came into force on September 3, 1996, trial and appellate courts in the provinces and territories grappled with the proper interpretation of the provisions concerning conditional sentences. This jurisprudence was as much concerned with matters of methodology as with substantive principle and policy. Although discrepancies among decisions eventually diminished, there remained considerable variations in approach and results. It was clear that guidance was required from the Supreme Court of Canada. As seen in Chapter 2, Judicial Aims and the Legislated Context, that court rarely hears sentencing cases, and its practice in this regard is quite deliberate. Nevertheless, in 1999, the Supreme Court heard six cases relating to conditional sentences. The principal opinion was given by Lamer CJC for a unanimous court in *Proulx*, and it is there that readers will find the guidance given to lower courts and the practising bar. It is appropriate, however, to look also at the other cases decided by the court concerning conditional sentences, if only to consider whether or not the principles announced in *Proulx* are demonstrably at work in the other decisions.

Proulx is lengthy and is reproduced here virtually in its entirety. The relevant provisions of the Code concerned with conditional sentences are included in the opinion of Lamer CJC.

R v. Proulx
(2000), 140 CCC (3d) 449 (SCC)

LAMER CJC: By passing *An Act to amend the Criminal Code (sentencing) and other Acts in consequence thereof*, SC 1995, c. 22 ("Bill C-41"), Parliament has sent a clear message to all Canadian judges that too many people are being sent to prison. In an attempt to remedy the problem of overincarceration, Parliament has introduced a new form of sentence, the conditional sentence of imprisonment.

As a matter of established practice and sound policy, this Court rarely hears appeals relating to sentences: see *R v. Gardiner*, [1982] 2 SCR 368, at 404; *R v. Chaisson*, [1995] 2 SCR 1118, at 1123; and *R v. M.(C.A.)*, [1996] 1 SCR 500, at para. 33. However, we have decided to hear this case and four related cases because they afford the Court the opportunity to set out for the first time the principles that govern the new and innovative conditional sentencing regime. Given the inevitable length of these reasons, I have summarized the essentials at para. 127.

I. Factual Background

On the morning of November 1, 1995, after a night of partying involving consumption of some alcohol, the respondent decided to drive his friends home even though he knew that his vehicle was not mechanically sound. For a period of 10 to 20 minutes, the respondent, who had only seven weeks of experience as a licensed driver, drove erratically, weaving in and out of traffic, tailgating and trying to pass other vehicles without signalling, despite steady oncoming traffic and slippery roads. As the respondent was trying to pass another vehicle, he drove his car into an oncoming lane of traffic, side-swiped a first car and crashed into a second one. The driver of the second vehicle was seriously injured. The accident also claimed the life of a passenger in the respondent's car. The respondent was in a near-death coma for some time, but ultimately recovered from his injuries. The respondent entered guilty pleas to one count of dangerous driving causing death and one count of dangerous driving causing bodily harm.

II. Judgments Below

A. Manitoba Court of Queen's Bench

On June 5, 1997, Keyser J sentenced the respondent to 18 months of incarceration, to be served concurrently on both charges. In her reasons for sentence, the judge explained that she was not prepared to order a penitentiary term because the respondent was only 18 years old at the time of the accident, he had no prior record and he himself was seriously injured in the accident. She also noted that the respondent was now employed and expecting a first child with his girlfriend. She conceded that the amount of alcohol involved—one and a half to two beers—was probably not a major factor in the accident. However, she found that the respondent's knowledge that he was operating an unsafe vehicle, the fact that, prior to the accident, he had just barely avoided rear-ending another vehicle and his egregious driving in general that morning warranted such a sentence.

Keyser J then turned her attention to the question of whether it was appropriate to allow the respondent to serve his sentence in the community, pursuant to s. 742.1 of the *Criminal Code*, RSC 1985, c. C-46. She took notice of the May 2, 1997 amendment to s. 742.1, which added to that section an express reference to the fundamental purpose and principles of sentencing listed in ss. 718 to 718.2 of the Code. She concluded that this amendment meant that she had to refer to the fundamental purpose and principles of sentencing in deciding whether to impose a conditional sentence. In the case at hand, she found that even though the respondent would not endanger the community and a jail sentence would not be necessary to deter him from similar conduct in the future or to rehabilitate him, a conditional sentence would not be appropriate because it would be inconsistent with the objectives of denunciation and general deterrence.

Keyser J sentenced the respondent to 18 months of incarceration and, pursuant to s. 259(2) of the *Criminal Code*, she made an order prohibiting the respondent from driving for a period of five years.

B. *Manitoba Court of Appeal (1997), 123 Man. R (2d) 107*

The Court of Appeal allowed the appeal and substituted a conditional custodial sentence for the jail term. Helper JA, writing for the court, contended that the sentencing judge had erred in her application of s. 742.1 by giving undue weight to the objective of denunciation. She explained that the recent amendment to s. 742.1 had not changed the fact that Parliament had identified the safety of the community as the primary consideration when deciding whether to impose a conditional sentence. Helper JA added that the principles of sentencing played a different role in the determination of whether to impose a conditional sentence than they did in determining the length of the sentence. At pp. 111-12, she stated:

> However, in s. 742.1(b), Parliament has directed the sentencing judge to look to the principles of sentencing only for the purpose of satisfying herself that there is consistency between those principles and a conditional sentence for a particular offender. The amendment does not direct the sentencing judge to consider individually each of the principles of sentencing and determine that each is consistent with the offender's serving his sentence in the community. The sentencing judge must consider the principles of sentencing globally. It would be contrary to Parliament's intent for the sentencing judge to single out any one factor and to give it substantial weight to the exclusion of the other listed factors when she is making a decision under s. 742.1(b).

According to Helper JA, the sentencing judge's comments implied that a conditional sentence would never be appropriate for the offence of dangerous driving, even when the offender did not potentially endanger the community, because that offence required a large component of general deterrence. Helper JA found this to be an error, as it would have rendered s. 742.1 inoperable in the case of particular offences, contrary to Parliament's intention. She found that, in the instant appeal, the sentencing judge had failed to recognize that a conditional sentence had some denunciatory effect.

Helper JA concluded that generally, after the judge has attributed the appropriate weight to each relevant principle of sentencing, determined that a fit sentence would be less than two years and found that the offender would not be a danger to the community, a conditional sentence would be consistent with ss. 718 to 718.2.

III. Relevant Statutory Provisions

Criminal Code, RSC, 1985, c. C-46

...

742.1. Where a person is convicted of an offence, except an offence that is punishable by a minimum term of imprisonment, and the court
> (a) imposes a sentence of imprisonment of less than two years, and
> (b) is satisfied that serving the sentence in the community would not endanger the safety of the community and would be consistent with the fundamental purpose and principles of sentencing set out in sections 718 to 718.2,

the court may, for the purpose of supervising the offender's behaviour in the community, order that the offender serve the sentence in the community, subject to the offender's complying with the conditions of a conditional sentence order made under section 742.3.

...

742.3(1) The court shall prescribe, as conditions of a conditional sentence order, that the offender do all of the following:
> (a) keep the peace and be of good behaviour;
> (b) appear before the court when required to do so by the court;
> (c) report to a supervisor
> > (i) within two working days, or such longer period as the court directs, after the making of the conditional sentence order, and
> > (ii) thereafter, when required by the supervisor and in the manner directed by the supervisor;
> (d) remain within the jurisdiction of the court unless written permission to go outside that jurisdiction is obtained from the court or the supervisor; and
> (e) notify the court or the supervisor in advance of any change of name or address, and promptly notify the court or the supervisor of any change of employment or occupation.

(2) The court may prescribe, as additional conditions of a conditional sentence order, that the offender do one or more of the following:
> (a) abstain from
> > (i) the consumption of alcohol or other intoxicating substances, or
> > (ii) the consumption of drugs except in accordance with a medical prescription;

(b) abstain from owning, possessing or carrying a weapon;

(c) provide for the support or care of dependants;

(d) perform up to 240 hours of community service over a period not exceeding eighteen months;

(e) attend a treatment program approved by the province; and

(f) comply with such other reasonable conditions as the court considers desirable, subject to any regulations made under subsection 738(2), for securing the good conduct of the offender and for preventing a repetition by the offender of the same offence or the commission of other offences.

...

742.6. ...

(9) Where the court is satisfied, on a balance of probabilities, that the offender has without reasonable excuse, the proof of which lies on the offender, breached a condition of the conditional sentence order, the court may

(a) take no action;

(b) change the optional conditions;

(c) suspend the conditional sentence order and direct

(i) that the offender serve in custody a portion of the unexpired sentence, and

(ii) that the conditional sentence order resume on the offender's release from custody, either with or without changes to the optional conditions; or

(d) terminate the conditional sentence order and direct that the offender be committed to custody until the expiration of the sentence.

IV. Issues

This appeal concerns the proper interpretation and application of the conditional sentencing regime set out in s. 742.1 and subsequent sections of the *Criminal Code*.

Since it came into force on September 3, 1996, the conditional sentence has generated considerable debate. With the advent of s. 742.1, Parliament has clearly mandated that certain offenders who used to go to prison should now serve their sentences in the community. Section 742.1 makes a conditional sentence available to a subclass of non-dangerous offenders who, prior to the introduction of this new regime, would have been sentenced to a term of incarceration of less than two years for offences with no minimum term of imprisonment.

In my view, to address meaningfully the complex interpretive issues raised by this appeal, it is important to situate this new sentencing tool in the broader context of the comprehensive sentencing reforms enacted by Parliament in Bill C-41. I will also consider the nature of the conditional sentence, contrasting it with probationary measures and incarceration. Next, I will address particular interpretive issues posed by s. 742(1). I will first discuss the statutory prerequisites to the imposition of a conditional sentence. Thereafter, I will consider how courts should determine whether a conditional sentence is appropriate; assuming the prerequisites are satisfied, I conclude with some general comments on the deference to which trial judges are entitled in matters of sentencing and dispose of the case at hand in conformity with the principles outlined in these reasons.

V. Analysis

A. The 1996 Sentencing Reforms (Bill C-41)

In September 1996, Bill C-41 came into effect. It substantially reformed Part XXIII of the *Criminal Code*, and introduced, *inter alia*, an express statement of the purposes and principles of sentencing, provisions for alternative measures for adult offenders and a new type of sanction, the conditional sentence of imprisonment.

As my colleagues Cory and Iacobucci JJ explained in *R v. Gladue*, [1999] 1 SCR 688, at para. 39, "[t]he enactment of the new Part XXIII was a watershed, marking the first codification and significant reform of sentencing principles in the history of Canadian criminal law." They noted two of Parliament's principal objectives in enacting this new legislation: (i) reducing the use of prison as a sanction, and (ii) expanding the use of restorative justice principles in sentencing (at para. 48).

(1) Reducing the Use of Prison as a Sanction

Bill C-41 is in large part a response to the problem of overincarceration in Canada. It was noted in *Gladue*, at para. 52, that Canada's incarceration rate of approximately 130 inmates per 100,000 population places it second or third highest among industrialized democracies. In their reasons, Cory and Iacobucci JJ reviewed numerous studies that uniformly concluded that incarceration is costly, frequently unduly harsh and "ineffective, not only in relation to its purported rehabilitative goals, but also in relation to its broader public goals" (para. 54). See also Report of the Canadian Committee on Corrections, *Toward Unity: Criminal Justice and Corrections* (1969); *Canadian Sentencing Commission, Sentencing Reform: A Canadian Approach* (1987), at pp. xxiii-xxiv; Standing Committee on Justice and Solicitor General, *Taking Responsibility* (1988), at p. 75. Prison has been characterized by some as a finishing school for criminals and as ill-preparing them for reintegration into society: see generally Canadian Committee on Corrections, *supra*, at p. 314; Correctional Service of Canada, *A Summary of Analysis of Some Major Inquiries on Corrections—1938 to 1977* (1982), at p. iv. At para. 57, Cory and Iacobucci JJ held:

> Thus, it may be seen that although imprisonment is intended to serve the traditional sentencing goals of separation, deterrence, denunciation, and rehabilitation, there is widespread consensus that imprisonment has not been successful in achieving some of these goals. Overincarceration is a long-standing problem that has been many times publicly acknowledged but never addressed in a systematic manner by Parliament. In recent years, compared to other countries, sentences of imprisonment in Canada have increased at an alarming rate. *The 1996 sentencing reforms embodied in Part XXIII, and s. 718.2(e) in particular, must be understood as a reaction to the overuse of prison as a sanction, and must accordingly be given appropriate force as remedial provisions.* [Emphasis in original.]

Parliament has sought to give increased prominence to the principle of restraint in the use of prison as a sanction through the enactment of s. 718.2(a) and (e). Section 718.2(d) provides that "an offender should not be deprived of liberty, if less restrictive sanctions may be appropriate in the circumstances," while s. 718.2(e) provides that "all available sanctions other than imprisonment that are reasonable in the circumstances should be considered for all offenders, with particular attention to the circumstances of aboriginal offenders." Further evidence of Parliament's desire to lower the rate of incarceration comes from other provisions of Bill C-41: s. 718(c) qualifies the sentencing objective of separating offenders from society with the words "where necessary," thereby indicating that caution be exercised in sentencing offenders to prison; s. 734(2) imposes a duty on judges to undertake a means inquiry before imposing a fine, so as to decrease the number of offenders who are incarcerated for defaulting on payment of their fines; and of course, s. 742.1, which introduces the conditional sentence. In *Gladue*, at para. 40, the Court held that "the creation of the conditional sentence suggests, on its face, a desire to lessen the use of incarceration."

(2) Expanding the Use of Restorative Justice Principles in Sentencing

Restorative justice is concerned with the restoration of the parties that are affected by the commission of an offence. Crime generally affects at least three parties: the victim, the community, and the offender. A restorative justice approach seeks to remedy the adverse effects of crime in a manner that addresses the needs of all parties involved. This is accomplished, in part, through the rehabilitation of the offender, reparations to the victim and to the community, and the promotion of a sense of responsibility in the offender and acknowledgment of the harm done to victims and to the community.

Canadian sentencing jurisprudence has traditionally focussed on the aims of denunciation, deterrence, separation, and rehabilitation, with rehabilitation a relative latecomer to the sentencing analysis: see *Gladue*, at para. 42. With the introduction of Bill C-41, however, Parliament has placed new emphasis upon the goals of restorative justice. Section 718 sets out the fundamental purpose of sentencing, as well as the various sentencing objectives that should be vindicated when sanctions are imposed. In *Gladue*, supra, Cory and Iacobucci JJ stated (at para. 43):

Clearly, s. 718 is, in part, a restatement of the basic sentencing aims, which are listed in paras. (a) through (d). What are new, though, are paras. (e) and (f), which along with para. (d) focus upon the restorative goals of repairing the harms suffered by individual victims and by the community as a whole, promoting a sense of responsibility and an acknowledgment of the harm caused on the part of the offender, and attempting to rehabilitate or heal the offender. The concept of restorative justice which underpins paras. (a), (e), and (f) is briefly discussed below, *but as a general matter restorative justice involves some form of restitution and reintegration into the community. The need for offenders to take responsibility for their actions is central to the sentencing process ... . Restorative sentencing goals do not usually correlate with the use of prison as a sanction. In our view, Parliament's choice to include (e) and (f) alongside the traditional sentencing goals must be understood as evidencing an intention to expand the parameters of the sentencing analysis for all offenders.* [Emphasis added; citation omitted.]

Parliament has mandated that expanded use be made of restorative principles in sentencing as a result of the general failure of incarceration to rehabilitate offenders

and reintegrate them into society. By placing a new emphasis on restorative principles, Parliament expects both to reduce the rate of incarceration and improve the
effectiveness of sentencing. During the second reading of Bill C-41 on September
20, 1994 (*House of Commons Debates*, vol. IV, 1st Sess., 35th Parl., at p. 5873),
Minister of Justice Allan Rock made the following statements:

> A general principle that runs throughout Bill C-41 is that jails should be reserved for
> those who should be there. Alternatives should be put in place for those who commit
> offences but who do not need or merit incarceration. ...
>
> Jails and prisons will be there for those who need them, for those who should be
> punished in that way or separated from society. ... [T]his bill creates an environment
> which encourages community sanctions and the rehabilitation of offenders together
> with reparation to victims and promoting in criminals a sense of accountability for
> what they have done.
>
> It is not simply by being more harsh that we will achieve more effective criminal
> justice. We must use our scarce resources wisely.

B. *The Nature of the Conditional Sentence*

The conditional sentence was specifically enacted as a new sanction designed to
achieve both of Parliament's objectives. The conditional sentence is a meaningful alternative to incarceration for less serious and non-dangerous offenders. The offenders
who meet the criteria of s. 742.1 will serve a sentence under strict surveillance in the
community instead of going to prison. These offenders' liberty will be constrained by
conditions to be attached to the sentence, as set out in s. 742.3 of the *Criminal Code*.
In case of breach of conditions, the offender will be brought back before a judge,
pursuant to s. 742.6. If an offender cannot provide a reasonable excuse for breaching
the conditions of his or her sentence, the judge may order him or her to serve the
remainder of the sentence in jail, as it was intended by Parliament that there be a real
threat of incarceration to increase compliance with the conditions of the sentence.

The conditional sentence incorporates some elements of non-custodial measures
and some others of incarceration. Because it is served in the community, it will generally be more effective than incarceration at achieving the restorative objectives of
rehabilitation, reparations to the victim and community, and the promotion of a sense
of responsibility in the offender. However, *it is also a punitive sanction capable of
achieving the objectives of denunciation and deterrence*. It is this punitive aspect that
distinguishes the conditional sentence from probation, and it is to this issue that I
now turn.

(1) Comparing Conditional Sentences with Probation

There has been some confusion among members of the judiciary and the public alike
about the difference between a conditional sentence and a suspended sentence with
probation. This confusion is understandable, as the statutory provisions regarding
conditions to be attached to conditional sentences (s. 742.3) and probation orders

(s. 732.1) are very similar. Notwithstanding these similarities, there is an important distinction between the two. While a suspended sentence with probation is primarily a rehabilitative sentencing tool, the evidence suggests that Parliament intended a conditional sentence to address both punitive and rehabilitative objectives.

(a) A Comparative Reading of the Provisions

A comparative reading of the provisions governing conditional sentences and probation orders reveals three differences. First, a probation order includes only three compulsory conditions—to keep the peace and be of good behaviour, appear before the court when required, and notify the court or probation officer of any change in employment or address—whereas there are five such conditions in the case of a conditional sentence. The two additional compulsory conditions of a conditional sentence—to report to a supervisor and remain within the jurisdiction unless permission is granted to leave—are listed as optional conditions under a probation order.

The second difference concerns the power of the judge to order the offender to undergo treatment. Under a conditional sentence, the sentencing judge can order the offender to attend a treatment program, regardless of whether the offender consents. Under a probation order, the judge can only impose a treatment order with the consent of the offender (with the exception of drug or alcohol addiction programs since the 1999 amendment to s. 732.1 (SC 1999, c. 32, s. 6)). In practice, however, this difference is not very significant, since it is unlikely that an offender faced with the choice between imprisonment and a suspended sentence with treatment as a condition of probation would refuse to consent to treatment.

The third difference is in the wording of the residual clauses of the provisions governing the imposition of optional conditions. In the case of a conditional sentence, s. 742.3(2)(f) provides that the court may order that the offender comply with such other reasonable conditions as the court considers desirable "for securing the good conduct of the offender and for preventing a repetition by the offender of the same offence or the commission of other offences." By contrast, s. 732.1(3)(h) provides that the court may impose such other reasonable conditions of probation "for protecting society and for facilitating the offender's successful reintegration into the community."

On their face, these three differences do not suggest that a conditional sentence is more punitive than a suspended sentence with probation. Moreover, the penalty for breach of probation is potentially more severe than that for breach of a conditional sentence. Pursuant to s. 733.1(1), breach of probation constitutes a new offence, punishable by up to two years imprisonment, while a breach of condition does not constitute a new offence *per se*. The maximum penalties are also different. In the case of a breach of probation, the offender is subject to the revocation of the probation order and can be sentenced for the original offence (in cases where a suspended sentence was rendered): see s. 732.2(5). By contrast in the case of breaches of conditional sentences, the maximum punishment available is incarceration for the time remaining of the original sentence (s. 742.6(9)). Presumably, if a conditional sentence is more onerous than probation, the consequences of breaching a condition should be more onerous as well.

(b) Conditional Sentences Must Be More Punitive Than Probation

Despite the similarities between the provisions and the fact that the penalty for breach of probation is potentially more severe than for breach of a conditional sentence, there are strong indications that Parliament intended the conditional sentence to be more punitive than probation. It is a well accepted principle of statutory interpretation that no legislative provision should be interpreted so as to render it mere surplusage. It would be absurd if Parliament intended conditional sentences to amount merely to probation under a different name. While this argument is clearly not dispositive, it suggests that Parliament intended there to be a meaningful distinction between the two sanctions. I will now consider more specific arguments in support of this position.

The conditional sentence is defined in the Code as a sentence of imprisonment. The heading of s. 742 reads "Conditional Sentence of Imprisonment." Furthermore, s. 742.1(a) requires the court to impose a sentence of imprisonment of less than two years before considering whether the sentence can be served in the community subject to the appropriate conditions. Parliament intended imprisonment, in the form of incarceration, to be more punitive than probation, as it is far more restrictive of the offender's liberty. Since a conditional sentence is, at least notionally, a sentence of imprisonment, it follows that it too should be interpreted as more punitive than probation.

On a related note, with the enactment of s. 742.1, Parliament has mandated that certain non-dangerous offenders who would otherwise have gone to jail for up to two years now serve their sentences in the community. If a conditional sentence is not distinguished from probation, then these offenders will receive what are effectively considerably less onerous probation orders instead of jail terms. Such lenient sentences would not provide sufficient denunciation and deterrence, nor would they be accepted by the public. Section 718 provides that the fundamental purpose of sentencing is "to contribute ... to respect for the law and the maintenance of a just, peaceful and safe society." Inadequate sanctions undermine respect for the law. Accordingly, it is important to distinguish a conditional sentence from probation by way of the use of punitive conditions.

Earlier I drew attention to a subtle difference between the residual clauses in the provisions governing the imposition of optional conditions of probation orders and conditional sentences. While the difference between the two residual clauses is subtle, it is also significant. In order to appreciate this difference, it is necessary to consider the case law and practice that has developed with respect to probation.

Probation has traditionally been viewed as a rehabilitative sentencing tool. Recently, the rehabilitative nature of the probation order was explained by the Saskatchewan Court of Appeal in *R v. Taylor* (1997), 122 CCC (3d) 376. Bayda CJS wrote, at p. 394:

> Apart from the wording of the provision, the innate character of a probation order is such that it seeks to influence the future behaviour of the offender. More specifically, it seeks to secure "the good conduct" of the offender and to deter him from committing the same or other offences. *It does not particularly seek to reflect the seriousness of the offence or the offender's degree of culpability. Nor does it particularly seek to fill the need for*

denunciation of the offence or the general deterrence of others to commit the same or
other offences. Depending upon the specific conditions of the order there may well be a
punitive aspect to a probation order but punishment is not the dominant or an inherent
purpose. It is perhaps not even a secondary purpose but is more in the nature of a
consequence of an offender's compliance with one or more of the specific conditions
with which he or she may find it hard to comply. [Emphasis added.]

Many appellate courts have struck out conditions of probation that were imposed to punish rather than rehabilitate the offender: see *R v. Ziatas* (1973), 13 CCC (2d) 287 (Ont. CA), at p. 288; *R v. Caja* (1977), 36 CCC (2d) 401 (Ont. CA), at pp. 402-3; *R v. Lavender* (1981) 59 CCC (2d) 551 (BC CA), at pp. 552-53; and *R v. L.* (1986), 50 CR (3d) 398 (Alta. CA), at pp. 399-400. The impugned terms of probation in these cases were imposed pursuant to a residual clause in force at the time whose wording was virtually identical to that presently used in s. 742.3(2)(f).

Despite the virtual identity in the wording of s. 742.3(2)(f) and the old residual clause applicable to probation orders, it would be a mistake to conclude that punitive conditions cannot now be imposed under s. 742.3(2)(f). Parliament amended the residual clause for probation, s. 732.1(3)(h), to read "for protecting society and for *facilitating the offender's successful reintegration into the community*" (emphasis added). It did so to make clear the rehabilitative purpose of probation and to distinguish s. 742.3(2)(f) from s. 732.1(3)(h). The wording used in s. 742.3(2)(f) does not focus principally on the rehabilitation and reintegration of the offender. If s. 742.3(2)(f) were interpreted as precluding punitive conditions, it would frustrate Parliament's intention in distinguishing the two forms of sentence. Parliament would not have distinguished them if it intended both clauses to serve the same purpose.

In light of the foregoing, it is clear that Parliament intended a conditional sentence to be more punitive than a suspended sentence with probation, notwithstanding the similarities between the two sanctions in respect of their rehabilitative purposes. I agree wholeheartedly with Vancise JA, who, dissenting in *R v. McDonald* (1997), 113 CCC (3d) 418 (Sask. CA), stated, at p. 443, that conditional sentences were designed to "permit the accused to avoid imprisonment but not to avoid punishment."

Accordingly, conditional sentences should generally include punitive conditions that are restrictive of the offender's liberty. Conditions such as house arrest or strict curfews should be the norm, not the exception. As the Minister of Justice said during the second reading of Bill C-41 (*House of Commons Debates*, supra, at p. 5873), "[t]his sanction is obviously aimed at offenders who would otherwise be in jail but who could be in the community under *tight* controls" (emphasis added).

There must be a reason for failing to impose punitive conditions when a conditional sentence order is made. Sentencing judges should always be mindful of the fact that conditional sentences are only to be imposed on offenders who would otherwise have been sent to jail. If the judge is of the opinion that punitive conditions are unnecessary, then probation, rather than a conditional sentence, is most likely the appropriate disposition.

The punitive nature of the conditional sentence should also inform the treatment of breaches of conditions. As I have already discussed, the maximum penalty for breach of probation is potentially more severe than that for breach of a conditional sentence. In practice, however, breaches of conditional sentences may be punished more severely than breaches of probation. Without commenting on the constitutionality of these provisions, I note that breaches of conditional sentence need only be proved on a balance of probabilities, pursuant to s. 742.6(9), whereas breaches of probation must be proved beyond a reasonable doubt.

More importantly, where an offender breaches a condition without reasonable excuse, there should be a presumption that the offender serve the remainder of his or her sentence in jail. This constant threat of incarceration will help to ensure that the offender complies with the conditions imposed: see *R v. Brady* (1998), 121 CCC (3d) 504 (Alta. CA); J.V. Roberts, "Conditional Sentencing: Sword of Damocles or Pandora's Box?" (1997), 2 *Can. Crim. L Rev.* 183. It also assists in distinguishing the conditional sentence from probation by making the consequences of a breach of condition more severe.

(2) Conditional Sentences and Incarceration

Although a conditional sentence is by statutory definition a sentence of imprisonment, this Court, in *R v. Shropshire*, [1995] 4 SCR 227, at para. 21, recognized that there "is a very significant difference between being behind bars and functioning within society while on conditional release." See also *Cunningham v. Canada*, [1993] 2 SCR 143, at p. 150, per McLachlin J. These comments are equally applicable to the conditional sentence. Indeed, offenders serving a conditional sentence in the community are only partially deprived of their freedom. Even if their liberty is restricted by the conditions attached to their sentence, they are not confined to an institution and they can continue to attend to their normal employment or educational endeavours. They are not deprived of their private life to the same extent. Nor are they subject to a regimented schedule or an institutional diet.

This is not to say that the conditional sentence is a lenient punishment or that it does not provide significant denunciation and deterrence, or that a conditional sentence can never be as harsh as incarceration. As this Court stated in *Gladue*, supra, at para. 72,

> in our view a sentence focussed on restorative justice is not necessarily a "lighter" punishment. Some proponents of restorative justice argue that when it is combined with probationary conditions it may in some circumstances impose a greater burden on the offender than a custodial sentence.

A conditional sentence may be as onerous as, or perhaps even more onerous than, a jail term, particularly in circumstances where the offender is forced to take responsibility for his or her actions and make reparations to both the victim and the community, all the while living in the community under tight controls.

Moreover, the conditional sentence is not subject to reduction through parole. This would seem to follow from s. 112(1) of the *Corrections and Conditional Release Act*, SC 1992, c. 20, which gives the provincial parole board jurisdiction in respect of the parole of offenders "serving sentences of imprisonment in provincial correctional facilities" (*R v. Wismayer* (1997), 115 CCC (3d) 18 (Ont. CA), at p. 33).

I would add that the fact that a conditional sentence cannot be reduced through parole does not in itself lead to the conclusion that as a general matter a conditional sentence is as onerous as or even more onerous than a jail term of equivalent duration. There is no parole simply because the offender is never actually incarcerated and he or she does not need to be reintegrated into society. But even when an offender is released from custody on parole, the original sentence continues in force. As I stated in *M.(C.A.)*, supra, at para. 62:

> [I]n short, the history, structure and existing practice of the conditional release system collectively indicate that a grant of parole represents *a change in the conditions* under which a judicial sentence must be served, rather than *a reduction* of the judicial sentence itself. ... But even though the conditions of incarceration are subject to change through a grant of parole to the offender's benefit, the offender's sentence continues in full effect. The offender remains under the strict control of the parole system, and the offender's liberty remains significantly curtailed for the full duration of the offender's numerical or life sentence. [Emphasis in original.]

The parolee has to serve the final portion of his or her sentence under conditions similar to those that can be imposed under a conditional sentence, perhaps even under stricter conditions, as the parolee can be assigned to a "community-based residential facility": see s. 133 of the *Corrections and Conditional Release Act* and s. 161 of the *Corrections and Conditional Release Regulations*, SOR/92-620.

In light of these observations, a conditional sentence, even with stringent conditions, will usually be a more lenient sentence than a jail term of equivalent duration: see also *Gagnon c. La Reine*, [1998] RJQ 2636 (CA), at p. 2645; *Brady*, supra, at paras. 36 and 48-50. The fact that incarceration is a threatened punishment for those who breach their conditions provides further support for this conclusion. In order for incarceration to serve as a punishment for breach of a conditional sentence, logically it must be more onerous than a conditional sentence.

C. *Application of Section 742.1 of the Criminal Code*

...

[Section 742.1] lists four criteria that a court must consider before deciding to impose a conditional sentence:

(1) the offender must be convicted of an offence that is not punishable by a minimum term of imprisonment;
(2) the court must impose a term of imprisonment of less than two years;
(3) the safety of the community would not be endangered by the offender serving the sentence in the community; and
(4) a conditional sentence would be consistent with the fundamental purpose and principles of sentencing set out in ss. 718 to 718.2.

In my view, the first three criteria are prerequisites to any conditional sentence. These prerequisites answer the question of whether or not a conditional sentence is possible in the circumstances. Once they are met, the next question is whether a conditional sentence is appropriate. This decision turns upon a consideration of the fundamental purpose and principles of sentencing set out in ss. 718 to 718.2. I will discuss each of these elements in turn.

(1) The Offender Must Be Convicted of an Offence That Is Not Punishable by a Minimum Term of Imprisonment

This prerequisite is straightforward. The offence for which the offender was convicted must not be punishable by a minimum term of imprisonment. Offences with a minimum term of imprisonment are the only statutory exclusions from the conditional sentencing regime.

(2) The Court Must Impose a Term of Imprisonment of Less Than Two Years

Parliament intended that a conditional sentence be considered only for those offenders who would have otherwise received a sentence of imprisonment of less than two years. There is some controversy as to whether this means that the judge must actually impose a term of imprisonment of a *fixed* duration before considering the possibility of a conditional sentence. Far from addressing purely methodological concerns, this question carries implications as to the role of ss. 718 to 718.2 in the determination of the appropriate sentence, the duration of the sentence, its venue and other modalities.

A literal reading of s. 742.1(a) suggests that the decision to impose a conditional sentence should be made in two distinct stages. In the first stage, the judge would have to decide the appropriate sentence according to the general purposes and principles of sentencing (now set out in ss. 718 to 718.2). Having found that a term of imprisonment of less than two years is warranted, the judge would then, in a second stage, decide whether this same term should be served in the community pursuant to s. 742.1. At first sight since Parliament said: "and the court (a) imposes a sentence of imprisonment of less than two years," it seems that the sentencing judge must first impose a term of imprisonment of a fixed duration before contemplating the possibility that this term be served in the community.

This two-step approach was endorsed by the Manitoba Court of Appeal in the present appeal. However, this literal reading of s. 742.1 and the two-step approach it implies introduce a rigidity which is both unworkable and undesirable in practice.

(a) Duration and Venue Cannot Be Separated

This two-step process does not correspond to the reality of sentencing. In practice, the determination of a term of imprisonment is necessarily intertwined with the decision of where the offender will serve the sentence. A judge does not impose a fixed sentence of "x months" in the abstract, without having in mind where that sentence will be served (see *Brady*, supra, at para. 86; *R v. Pierce* (1997), 114 CCC (3d) 23 (Ont. CA), at p. 39; *R v. Ursel* (1997), 96 BCAC 241, at p. 284 (*per* Ryan JA) and pp. 291-92 (*per* Rowles JA)). Furthermore, when a conditional sentence is chosen, its duration will depend on the type of conditions imposed. Therefore, the duration of the sentence should not be determined separately from the determination of its venue.

(b) "Penalogical Paradox"

There is a contradiction embedded in this rigid two-step process. After having applied ss. 718 to 718.2 in the first stage to conclude that the appropriate sentence is a term of imprisonment of a fixed duration (in all cases less than two years), the judge would then have to decide if serving the same sentence in the community is still consistent with the fundamental purpose and principles of sentencing set out in ss. 718 to 718.2, as required by s. 742.1(b). It is unrealistic to believe that a judge would consider the objectives and principles twice or make a clear distinction in his or her mind between the application of ss. 718 to 718.2 in the first stage and in the second stage. Even if this could be done, it could lead to a "penalogical paradox," as described by J. Gemmell in "The New Conditional Sentencing Regime" (1997), 39 *Crim. LQ* 334, at p. 337:

> ... the judge must first determine that imprisonment is the only reasonable sanction in the circumstances, then decide whether the offender should nevertheless serve that sentence in the community. The decision to impose a conditional sentence is almost a kind of *reductio ad absurdum* of the original decision that called for imprisonment. [Footnote omitted.]

This second step of the analytical process would effectively compromise the principles of sentencing that led to the imposition of a sentence of imprisonment in the first place. For instance, the principle of proportionality, set out in s. 718.1 as the fundamental principle of sentencing, directs that all sentences must be proportional to the gravity of the offence and the degree of responsibility of the offender. When a judge—in the first stage decides—that a term of imprisonment of "x months" is appropriate, it means that *this* sentence is proportional. If the sentencing judge decides—in the second stage—that *the same term* can be served in the community, it is possible that the sentence is no longer proportional to the gravity of the offence and the responsibility of the offender, since a conditional sentence will generally be more lenient than a jail term of equivalent duration. Thus, such a two-step approach introduces a rigidity in the sentencing process that could lead to an unfit sentence.

(c) A Purposive Interpretation of Section 742.1(a)

These problems can be addressed by a purposive interpretation of s. 742.1. For the reasons discussed above, the requirement that the court "imposes a sentence of imprisonment of less than two years" could not have been intended to impose on judges a rigid two-step process. Rather, it was included to identify the type of offenders who could be entitled to a conditional sentence. At one end of the range, Parliament denied the possibility of a conditional sentence for offenders who should receive a penitentiary term. At the other end, Parliament intended to ensure that offenders who were entitled to a more lenient community measure—such as a suspended sentence with probation— did not receive a conditional sentence, a harsher sanction in this legislative scheme.

Section 742.1(a), when read in conjunction with ss. 718.2(d) and 718.2(e), cautions sentencing judges against "widening the net" of the conditional sentencing regime by imposing conditional sentences on offenders who would otherwise have received a non-custodial disposition (*Gagnon*, supra, at p. 2645; *Mcdonald*, supra, at pp. 437-39). As Rosenberg JA puts it in *Wismayer*, supra, at p. 42:

Parliament's goal of reducing the prison population of nonviolent offenders and increased use of community sanctions will be frustrated if the courts refuse to use the conditional sentence order for offences that normally attract a jail sentence and resort to the conditional sentence only for offences that previously would have attracted non-custodial dispositions.

Erroneously imposing conditional sentences could undermine Parliament's objective of reducing incarceration for less serious offenders.

These concerns are illustrated by the English experience with a similar sentence called a "suspended sentence." As Parker LCJ explained, writing for the Court of Appeal (Criminal Division) in *R v. O'Keefe* (1968), 53 Cr. App. R 91, at pp. 94-95:

> This Court would like to say as emphatically as they can that suspended sentences should not be given when, but for the power to give a suspended sentence, a probation order was the proper order to make. After all, a suspended sentence is a sentence of imprisonment. ...
>
> Therefore, it seems to the Court that before one gets to a suspended sentence at all, a court must go through the process of eliminating other possible courses such as absolute discharge, conditional discharge, probation order, fine, and then say to itself ... this is a case for imprisonment, and the final question, it being a case for imprisonment: is immediate imprisonment required, or can I give a suspended sentence?

A similar approach should be used by Canadian courts. Hence, a purposive interpretation of s. 742.1(a) does not dictate a rigid two-step approach in which the judge would first have to impose a term of imprisonment of a *fixed* duration and then decide if that fixed term of imprisonment can be served in the community. In my view, the requirement that the court must impose a sentence of imprisonment of less than two years can be fulfilled by a preliminary determination of the appropriate range of available sentences. Thus, the approach I suggest still requires the judge to proceed in two stages. However, the judge need not impose a term of imprisonment of a fixed duration at the first stage of the analysis. Rather, at this stage, the judge simply has to exclude two possibilities: (a) probationary measures; and (b) a penitentiary term. If either of these sentences is appropriate, then a conditional sentence should not be imposed.

In making this preliminary determination, the judge need only consider the fundamental purpose and principles of sentencing set out in ss. 718 to 718.2 to the extent necessary to narrow the range of sentence for the offender. The submissions of the parties, although not binding, may prove helpful in this regard. For example, both parties may agree that the appropriate range of sentence is a term of imprisonment of less than two years.

Once that preliminary determination is made, and assuming the other statutory prerequisites are met, the judge should then proceed to the second stage of the analysis: determining whether a conditional sentence would be consistent with the fundamental purpose and principles of sentencing set out in ss. 718 to 718.2. Unlike the first stage, the principles of sentencing are now considered comprehensively. Further, it is at the second stage that the duration and venue of the sentence should be determined, and, if a conditional sentence, the conditions to be imposed.

This purposive interpretation of s. 742.1(a) avoids the pitfalls of the literal interpretation discussed above, while at all times taking into account the principles and objectives of sentencing. As I stressed in *M.(C.A.)*, supra, at para. 82,

> In the final analysis, the overarching duty of a sentencing judge is to draw upon all the legitimate principles of sentencing to determine a "just and appropriate" sentence which reflects the gravity of the offence committed and the moral blameworthiness of the offender.

(3) The Safety of the Community Would Not Be Endangered by the Offender Serving the Sentence in the Community

This criterion, set out in s. 742.1(b), has generated wide discussion in courts and among authors. I intend to discuss the following issues:

(a) Is safety of the community a prerequisite to any conditional sentence?
(b) Does "safety of the community" refer only to the threat posed by the specific offender?
(c) How should courts evaluate danger to the community?
(d) Is risk of economic prejudice to be considered in assessing danger to the community?

(a) A Prerequisite to Any Conditional Sentence

As a prerequisite to any conditional sentence, the sentencing judge must be satisfied that having the offender serve the sentence in the community would not endanger its safety: see *Brady*, supra, at para. 58; *R v. Maheu*, [1997] RJQ 410, 116 CCC (3d) 361 (CA), at p. 368 CCC; *Gagnon*, supra, at p. 2641; *Pierce*, supra, at p. 39; *Ursel*, supra, at pp. 284-86 (*per* Ryan JA). *If the sentencing judge is not satisfied that the safety of the community can be preserved, a conditional sentence must never be imposed.*

With respect, the Manitoba Court of Appeal in the case before us erred in concluding that safety of the community was the primary consideration in the decision to impose a conditional sentence. As the Alberta Court of Appeal in *Brady*, supra, at para. 58, stated:

> So to suggest that danger is the primary consideration is tendentious. It wrongly implies that absence of danger trumps or has paramountcy over other sentencing principles. Either the offender meets the no-danger threshold, or he does not. If he does, this consideration is spent and the focus must then properly be on the other sentencing principles and objectives.

I agree. It is only once the judge is satisfied that the safety of the community would not be endangered, in the sense explained in paragraphs 66 to 76 below, that he or she can examine whether a conditional sentence "would be consistent with the fundamental purpose and principles of sentencing set out in sections 718 to 718.2." In other words, rather than being an overarching consideration in the process of determining whether a conditional sentence is appropriate, the criterion of safety of the community should be viewed as a condition precedent to the assessment of whether a conditional sentence would be a fit and proper sanction in the circumstances.

(b) "Safety of the Community" Refers to the Threat Posed by the Specific Offender

The issue here is whether "safety of the community" refers only to the threat posed by the specific offender or whether it also extends to the broader risk of undermining respect for the law. The proponents of the broader interpretation argue that, in certain cases where a conditional sentence could be imposed, it would be perceived that wrongdoers are receiving lenient sentences, thereby insufficiently deterring those who may be inclined to engage in similar acts of wrongdoing, and, in turn, endangering the safety of the community.

Leaving aside the fact that a properly crafted conditional sentence can also achieve the objectives of general deterrence and denunciation, I think the debate has been rendered largely academic in light of an amendment to s. 742.1(b) (SC 1997, c. 18, s. 107.1) which clarified that courts must take into consideration the fundamental purpose and principles of sentencing set out in ss. 718 to 718.2 in deciding whether to impose a conditional sentence. This ensures that objectives such as denunciation and deterrence will be dealt with in the decision to impose a conditional sentence. Since these factors will be taken into account later in the analysis, there is no need to include them in the consideration of the safety of the community.

In my view, the focus of the analysis at this point should clearly be on the risk posed by the individual offender while serving his sentence in the community. I would note that a majority of appellate courts have adopted an interpretation of the criterion referring only to the threat posed by the specific offender: see *Gagnon*, supra, at pp. 2640-41 (*per* Fish JA); *R v. Parker* (1997), 116 CCC (3d) 236 (NS CA), at pp. 247-48; *Ursel*, supra, at p. 260.1; *R v. Horvath*, [1997] 8 WWR 357 (Sask. CA), at p. 374; *Brady*, supra, at paras. 60-61; *Wismayer*, supra, at p. 44.

(c) How Should Courts Evaluate Danger to the Community?

In my opinion, to assess the danger to the community posed by the offender while serving his or her sentence in the community, two factors must be taken into account: (1) the risk of the offender re-offending; and (2) the gravity of the damage that could ensue in the event of re-offence. If the judge finds that there is a real risk of re-offence, incarceration should be imposed. Of course, there is always some risk that an offender may re-offend. If the judge thinks this risk is minimal, the gravity of the damage that could follow were the offender to re-offend should also be taken into consideration. In certain cases, the minimal risk of re-offending will be offset by the possibility of a great prejudice, thereby precluding a conditional sentence.

(i) RISK OF RE-OFFENCE

A variety of factors will be relevant in assessing the risk of re-offence. In *Brady*, supra, at paras. 117-27, Fraser CJA suggested that consideration be given to whether the offender has previously complied with court orders and, more generally, to whether the offender has a criminal record that suggests that the offender will not abide by the conditional sentence. Rousseau-Houle JA in *Maheu*, supra, at p. 374 CCC enumerated additional factors which may be of relevance:

> 1) the nature of the offence, 2) the relevant circumstances of the offence, which can put in issue prior and subsequent incidents, 3) the degree of participation of the accused, 4) the relationship of the accused with the victim, 5) the profile of the accused, that is, his [or her] occupation, lifestyle, criminal record, family situation, mental state, 6) his [or her] conduct following the commission of the offence, 7) the danger which the interim release of the accused represents for the community, notably that part of the community affected by the matter. [Translation.]

This list is instructive, but should not be considered exhaustive. The risk that a particular offender poses to the community must be assessed in each case, on its own facts. Moreover, the factors outlined above should not be applied mechanically. As Fraser CJA held in *Brady*, supra, at para. 124:

> Forgetting a court date once ten years ago does not automatically bar an offender from any future conditional sentence. Nor does turning up for his trial guarantee an offender a conditional sentence. The sentencing judge must of course look at all aspects of these previous disobediences of courts. That includes frequency, age, maturity, recency, seriousness of disobedience and surrounding circumstances.

The risk of re-offence should also be assessed in light of the conditions attached to the sentence. Where an offender might pose some risk of endangering the safety of the community, it is possible that this risk can be reduced to a minimal one by the imposition of appropriate conditions to the sentence: see *Wismayer*, supra, at p. 32; *Brady*, supra, at para. 62; *Maheu*, supra, at p. 374 CCC. Indeed, this is contemplated by s. 742.3(2)(f), which allows the court to include as optional conditions "such other reasonable conditions as the court considers desirable ... for securing the good conduct of the offender and for preventing a repetition by the offender of the same offence or the commission of other offences." For example, a judge may wish to impose a conditional sentence with a treatment order on an offender with a drug addiction, notwithstanding the fact that the offender has a lengthy criminal record linked to this addiction, provided the judge is confident that there is a good chance of rehabilitation and that the level of supervision will be sufficient to ensure that the offender complies with the sentence.

This last point concerning the level of supervision in the community must be underscored. As the Alberta Court of Appeal stressed in *Brady*, supra, at para. 135:

> A conditional sentence drafted in the abstract without knowledge of what actual supervision and institutions and programs are available and suitable for this offender is often worse than tokenism: it is a sham.

Hence, the judge must know or be made aware of the supervision available in the community by the supervision officer or by counsel. If the level of supervision available in the community is not sufficient to ensure safety of the community, the judge should impose a sentence of incarceration.

(ii) GRAVITY OF THE DAMAGE IN THE EVENT OF RE-OFFENCE

Once the judge finds that the risk of recidivism is minimal, the second factor to consider is the gravity of the potential damage in case of re-offence. Particularly in the case of violent offenders, a small risk of very harmful future crime may well warrant a conclusion that the prerequisite is not met: see *Brady*, supra, at para. 63.

(d) Risk of Economic Harm Can Be Taken into Consideration

The meaning of the phrase "would not endanger the safety of the community" should not be restricted to a consideration of the danger to physical or psychological safety of persons. In my view, this part of s. 742.1(b) cannot be given this narrow meaning. As Finch JA stated in *Ursel*, supra, at p. 264 (dissenting in part but endorsed by the majority on this issue, at p. 287):

> I would not give to this phrase the restricted meaning for which the defence contends. Members of our community have a reasonable expectation of safety not only in respect of their persons, but in respect as well of their property and financial resources. When homes are broken into, motor-vehicles are stolen, employers are defrauded of monies, or financial papers are forged, the safety of the community is, in my view, endangered. We go to considerable lengths to protect and secure ourselves against the losses that may result from these sorts of crimes, and I think most ordinary citizens would regard themselves as threatened or endangered where their property or financial resources are exposed to the risk of loss.

I agree with this reasoning. The phrase "would not endanger the safety of the community" should be construed broadly, and include the risk of any criminal activity. Such a broad interpretation encompasses the risk of economic harm.

(4) Consistent with the Fundamental Purpose and Principles of Sentencing Set Out in Sections 718 to 718.2

Once the sentencing judge has found the offender guilty of an offence for which there is no minimum term of imprisonment, has rejected both a probationary sentence and a penitentiary term as inappropriate, and is satisfied that the offender would not endanger the community, the judge must then consider whether a conditional sentence would be consistent with the fundamental purpose and principles of sentencing set out in ss. 718 to 718.2.

A consideration of the principles set out in ss. 718 to 718.2 will determine whether the offender should serve his or her sentence in the community or in jail. The sentencing principles also inform the determination of the duration of these sentences and, if a conditional sentence, the nature of the conditions to be imposed.

(a) Offences Presumptively Excluded from the Conditional Sentencing Regime?

Section 742.1 does not exclude any offences from the conditional sentencing regime except those with a minimum term of imprisonment. Parliament could have easily excluded specific offences in addition to those with a mandatory minimum term of imprisonment but chose not to. As Rosenberg JA held in *Wismayer*, supra, at p. 32,

Parliament clearly envisaged that a conditional sentence would be available even in cases of crimes of violence that are not punishable by a minimum term of imprisonment. Thus, s. 742.2 requires the court, before imposing a conditional sentence, to consider whether a firearms prohibition under s. 100 of the *Criminal Code* is applicable. Such orders may only be imposed for indictable offences having a maximum sentence of ten years or more "in the commission of which violence against a person is used, threatened, or attempted" (s. 100(1)) and for certain weapons and drug offences (s. 100(2)).

Thus, a conditional sentence is available in principle for *all* offences in which the statutory prerequisites are satisfied.

Several parties in the appeals before us argued that the fundamental purpose and principles of sentencing support a presumption against conditional sentences for certain offences. The Attorney General of Canada and the Attorney General for Ontario submitted that a conditional sentence would rarely be appropriate for offences such as: sexual offences against children; aggravated sexual assault; manslaughter; serious fraud or theft; serious morality offences; impaired or dangerous driving causing death or bodily harm; and trafficking or possession of certain narcotics. They submitted that this followed from the principle of proportionality as well as from a consideration of the objectives of denunciation and deterrence. A number of appellate court decisions support this position.

In my view, while the gravity of such offences is clearly relevant to determining whether a conditional sentence is appropriate in the circumstances, it would be both unwise and unnecessary to establish judicially created presumptions that conditional sentences are inappropriate for specific offences. Offence-specific presumptions introduce unwarranted rigidity in the determination of whether a conditional sentence is a just and appropriate sanction. Such presumptions do not accord with the principle of proportionality set out in s. 718.1 and the value of individualization in sentencing, nor are they necessary to achieve the important objectives of uniformity and consistency in the use of conditional sentences.

This Court has held on a number of occasions that sentencing is an individualized process, in which the trial judge has considerable discretion in fashioning a fit sentence. The rationale behind this approach stems from the principle of proportionality, the fundamental principle of sentencing, which provides that a sentence must be proportional to the gravity of the offence and the degree of responsibility of the offender. Proportionality requires an examination of the specific circumstances of both the offender and the offence so that the "punishment fits the crime." As a by-product of such an individualized approach, there will be inevitable variation in sentences imposed for particular crimes. In *M.(C.A.)*, supra, I stated, at para. 92:

> It has been repeatedly stressed that there is no such thing as a uniform sentence for a particular crime. Sentencing is an inherently individualized process, and the search for a single appropriate sentence for a similar offender and a similar crime will frequently be a fruitless exercise of academic abstraction. As well, sentences for a particular offence should be expected to vary to some degree across various communities and regions in this country, as the "just and appropriate" mix of accepted sentencing goals

will depend on the needs and current conditions of and in the particular community where the crime occurred.

My difficulty with the suggestion that the proportionality principle presumptively excludes certain offences from the conditional sentencing regime is that such an approach focuses inordinately on the gravity of the offence and insufficiently on the moral blameworthiness of the offender. This fundamentally misconstrues the nature of the principle. Proportionality requires that full consideration be given to both factors. As s. 718.1 provides,

> A sentence must be proportionate to the gravity of the offence *and* the degree of responsibility of the offender. [Emphasis added.]

Some appellate courts have held that once the statutory prerequisites are satisfied there ought to be a presumption in favour of a conditional sentence. In the instant appeal, Helper JA found at p. 112 that:

> Generally (though certainly not in all cases), it will be that, when a sentencing judge has attributed the appropriate weight to each of the relevant principles in determining that a fit sentence would be less than two years and has found that the offender would not be a danger to the community, a decision to allow the offender to serve his sentence in the community will be consistent with ss. 718 to 718.2.

It is possible to interpret these comments as implying that once the judge has found that the prerequisites to a conditional sentence are met, a conditional sentence would presumably be consistent with the fundamental purpose and principles of sentencing. Assuming that Helper JA intended to suggest that there ought to be a presumption in favour of a conditional sentence once the prerequisites are met, I respectfully disagree with her. For the same reasons that I rejected the use of presumptions against conditional sentences, I also reject presumptions in favour of them. The particular circumstances of the offender and the offence must be considered in each case.

(b) A Need for Starting Points?

An individualized sentencing regime will of necessity entail a certain degree of disparity in sentencing. I recognize that it is important for appellate courts to minimize, to the greatest extent possible, "the disparity of sentences imposed by sentencing judges for similar offenders and similar offences committed throughout Canada": *M.(C.A.)*, supra, at para. 92. Towards this end, this Court held in *R v. McDonnell*, [1997] 1 SCR 948, that "starting point sentences" may be set out as guides to lower courts in order to achieve greater uniformity and consistency. I am also acutely aware of the need to provide guidance to lower courts regarding the use of the conditional sentence, as it is a new sanction which has created a considerable amount of controversy and confusion in its short life.

That said, I do not find it necessary to resort to starting points in respect of specific offences to provide guidance as to the proper use of conditional sentences. In my view, the risks posed by starting points, in the form of offence-specific presumptions in favour of incarceration, outweigh their benefits. Starting points are most useful in circumstances where there is the potential for a large disparity between sentences imposed for a particular crime because the range of sentence set out in the Code is particularly broad. In the case of conditional sentences, however, the statutory prerequisites of s. 742.1 considerably narrow the range of cases in which a conditional sentence may be imposed. A conditional sentence may only be imposed on nondangerous offenders who would otherwise have received a jail sentence of less than two years. Accordingly, the potential disparity of sentence between those offenders who were candidates for a conditional sentence and received a jail term, and those who received a conditional sentence, is relatively small.

The minimal benefits of uniformity in these circumstances are exceeded by the costs of the associated loss of individualization in sentencing. By creating offence-specific starting points, there is a risk that these starting points will evolve into de facto minimum sentences of imprisonment. This would thwart Parliament's intention of not excluding particular categories of offence from the conditional sentencing regime. It could also result in the imposition of disproportionate sentences in some cases.

Given the narrow range of application for conditional sentences, I am of the opinion that a consideration of the principles of sentencing themselves, without offence-specific presumptions, can provide sufficient guidance as to whether a conditional sentence should be imposed. Some principles militate in favour of a conditional sentence, whereas others favour incarceration. It is the task of this Court to articulate, in general terms, which principles favour each sanction. Although it cannot ensure uniformity of result, the articulation of these principles can at least ensure uniformity in approach to the imposition of conditional sentences. It is to this task that I now turn.

(c) Principles Militating For and Against a Conditional Sentence

First, a consideration of ss. 718.2(d) and 718.2(e) leads me to the conclusion that *serious consideration* should be given to the imposition of a conditional sentence in all cases where the first three statutory prerequisites are satisfied. Sections 718.2(d) and 718.2(e) codify the important principle of restraint in sentencing and were specifically enacted, along with s. 742.1, to help reduce the rate of incarceration in Canada. Accordingly, it would be an error in principle not to consider the possibility of a conditional sentence seriously when the statutory prerequisites are met. Failure to advert to the possibility of a conditional sentence in reasons for sentence where there are reasonable grounds for finding that the first three statutory prerequisites have been met may well constitute reversible error.

I pause here to consider an interpretive difficulty posed by s. 718.2(e). By its terms, s. 718.2(e) requires judges to consider "all available sanctions *other than imprisonment* that are reasonable in the circumstances" (emphasis added). A conditional sentence, however, is defined as a sentence of imprisonment. As a sentence of imprisonment, it cannot be an alternative to imprisonment. It would therefore appear as though s. 718.2(e) has no bearing on the sentencing judge's decision as to whether a conditional sentence or a jail term should be imposed. Indeed, if interpreted in the technical sense ascribed to imprisonment in Part XXIII of the *Criminal Code*, s. 718.2(e) would only be relevant to the judge's preliminary determination as to whether a sentence of imprisonment, as opposed to a probationary measure, should be imposed. Once the sentencing judge rejects a probationary sentence as inappropriate, the legislative force of s. 718.2(e) is arguably spent.

This interpretation seems to fly in the face of Parliament's intention in enacting s. 718.2(e)—reducing the rate of incarceration. As this Court held in *Gladue*, supra, at para. 40:

> The availability of the conditional sentence of imprisonment, in particular, alters the sentencing landscape in a manner which gives an entirely new meaning to the principle that imprisonment should be resorted to only where no other sentencing option is reasonable in the circumstances. *The creation of the conditional sentence suggests, on its face, a desire to lessen the use of incarceration. The general principle expressed in s. 718.2(c) must be construed and applied in this light.* [Emphasis added.]

Moreover, if this interpretation of s. 718.2(c) were adopted, it could lead to absurd results in relation to aboriginal offenders. The particular circumstances of aboriginal offenders would only be relevant in deciding whether to impose probationary sentences, and not in deciding whether a conditional sentence should be preferred to incarceration. This would greatly diminish the remedial purpose animating Parliament's enactment of this provision, which contemplates the greater use of conditional sentences and other alternatives to incarceration in cases of aboriginal offenders.

The language used in the French version avoids this difficulty. The French version reads as follows:

> 718.2 Le tribunal détermine la peine à infliger compte tenu également des principes suivants.
>
> e) *l'examen de toutes les sanctions substitutives applicables* qui sont justifiées dans les circonstances, plus particulièrement en ce qui concerne les délinquants autochtones. [Emphasis added.]

The use of *"sanctions substitutives"* for "sanctions other than imprisonment" in the French version of this provision means that s. 718.2(e) plays a role not only in the decision as to whether imprisonment or probationary measures should be imposed (preliminary step of the analysis), but also in the decision as to whether to impose a conditional sentence of imprisonment since conditional sentences are clearly *"sanctions substitutives"* to incarceration.

The French version and the English version of s. 718.2(e) are therefore in conflict. In conformity with a long-standing principle of interpretation, to resolve the conflict between the two official versions, we have to look for the meaning common to both: see for instance *Kwiatkowsky v. Minister of Employment and Immigration*, [1982] 2 SCR 856, at pp. 863-64; *Gravel v. City of St-Léonard*, [1978] 1 SCR 660, at p. 669; *Pfizer Co. v. Deputy Minister of National Revenue for Customs and Excise*, [1977] 1 SCR 456, at pp. 464-65; *Tupper v. The Queen*, [1967] SCR 589, at p. 593; *Goodyear Tire and Rubber Co. of Canada v. T. Eaton Co.*, [1956] SCR 610, at p. 614; P.-A. Côté, *Interprétation des lois* (3rd ed. 1999), at pp. 412-15. Accordingly, the word "imprisonment" in s. 718.2(c) should be interpreted as "incarceration" rather than in its technical sense of encompassing both incarceration and a conditional sentence. Read in this light, s. 718.2(e) clearly exerts an influence on the sentencing judge's determination as to whether to impose a conditional sentence as opposed to a jail term.

Both ss. 718.2(d) and 718.2(e) seek to vindicate the important objective of restraint in the use of incarceration. However, neither seeks to do so at all costs. Section 718.2(d) provides that "an offender should not be deprived of liberty if less restrictive sanctions *may be inappropriate in the circumstances*" (emphasis added). Section 718.2(e) provides that "all available sanctions other than imprisonment *that are reasonable in the circumstances* should be considered" (emphasis added). In my view, a determination of when less restrictive sanctions are "appropriate" and alternatives to incarceration "reasonable" in the circumstances requires a consideration of the other principles of sentencing set out in ss. 718 to 718.2.

In determining which principles favour of a conditional sentence and which favour incarceration, it is necessary to consider again the nature and purpose of the conditional sentence. Through an appreciation of Parliament's intention in enacting this new sanction and the mischief it seeks to redress, trial judges will be better able to make appropriate use of this innovative tool.

The conditional sentence, as I have already noted, was introduced in the amendments to Part XXIII of the Code. Two of the main objectives underlying the reform of Part XXIII were to reduce the use of incarceration as a sanction and to give greater prominence to the principles of restorative justice in sentencing—the objectives of rehabilitation, reparation to the victim and the community, and the promotion of a sense of responsibility in the offender.

The conditional sentence facilitates the achievement of both of Parliament's objectives. It affords the sentencing judge the opportunity to craft a sentence with appropriate conditions that can lead to the rehabilitation of the offender, reparations to the community, and the promotion of a sense of responsibility in ways that jail cannot. However, it is also a punitive sanction. Indeed, it is the punitive aspect of a conditional sentence that distinguishes it from probation. As discussed above, it was not Parliament's intention that offenders who would otherwise have gone to jail for up to two years less a day now be given probation or some equivalent thereof.

Thus, a conditional sentence can achieve both punitive and restorative objectives. To the extent that both punitive and restorative objectives can be achieved in a given case, a conditional sentence is likely a better sanction than incarceration. Where the need for punishment is particularly pressing, and there is little opportunity to achieve any restorative objectives, incarceration will likely be the more attractive sanction. However, even where restorative objectives cannot be readily satisfied, a conditional sentence will be preferable to incarceration in cases where a conditional sentence can achieve the objectives of denunciation and deterrence as effectively as incarceration. This follows from the principle of restraint in s. 718.2(d) and (e), which militates in favour of alternatives to incarceration where appropriate in the circumstances.

I turn now to the question of when a conditional sentence may be appropriate having regard to the six sentencing objectives set out in s. 718.

(i) DENUNCIATION

Denunciation is the communication of society's condemnation of the offender's conduct. In *M.(C.A.)*, supra, at para. 81, I wrote:

> In short, a sentence with a denunciatory element represents a symbolic, collective statement that the offender's conduct should be punished for encroaching on our society's basic code of values as enshrined within our substantive criminal law. As Lord Justice Lawton stated in *R v. Sargeant* (1974), 60 Cr. App. R 74, at p. 77: "society, through the courts, must show its abhorrence of particular types of crime, and the only way in which the courts can show this is by the sentence they pass."

Incarceration will usually provide more denunciation than a conditional sentence, as a conditional sentence is generally a more lenient sentence than a jail term of equivalent duration. That said, a conditional sentence can still provide a significant amount of denunciation. This is particularly so when onerous conditions are imposed and the duration of the conditional sentence is extended beyond the duration of the jail sentence that would ordinarily have been imposed in the circumstances. I will discuss each point in turn.

First, the conditions should have a punitive aspect. Indeed, the need for punitive conditions is the reason why a probationary sentence was rejected and a sentence of imprisonment of less than two years imposed. As stated above, conditions such as house arrest should be the norm, not the exception. This means that the offender should be confined to his or her home except when working, attending school, or fulfilling other conditions of his or her sentence, e.g. community service, meeting with the supervisor, or participating in treatment programs. Of course, there will need to be exceptions for medical emergencies, religious observance, and the like.

Second, although a literal reading of s. 742.1 suggests that a conditional sentence must be of equivalent duration to the jail term that would otherwise have been imposed, I have explained earlier why such a literal interpretation of s. 742.1 should be eschewed. Instead, the preferred approach is to have the judge reject a probationary sentence and a penitentiary term as inappropriate in the circumstances, and then consider whether a conditional sentence of less than two years would be consistent with the fundamental purpose and principles of sentencing, provided the statutory prerequisites are met. This approach does not require that there be any equivalence between the duration of the conditional sentence and the jail term that would otherwise have been imposed. The sole requirement is that the duration and conditions of a conditional sentence make for a just and appropriate sentence: see *Brady*, supra, at para. 111; *Ursel*, supra, at pp. 284-86 and 291-92; *Pierce*, supra, at p. 39; J.V. Roberts, "The Hunt for the Paper Tiger: Conditional Sentencing after *Brady*" (1999), 42 *Crim. LQ* 38, at pp. 47-52.

The stigma of a conditional sentence with house arrest should not be underestimated. Living in the community under strict conditions where fellow residents are well aware of the offender's criminal misconduct can provide ample denunciation in many cases. In certain circumstances, the shame of encountering members of the community may make it even more difficult for the offender to serve his or her sentence in the community than in prison.

The amount of denunciation provided by a conditional sentence will be heavily dependent on the circumstances of the offender, the nature of the conditions imposed, and the community in which the sentence is to be served. As a general matter, the more serious the offence and the greater the need for denunciation, the longer and more onerous the conditional sentence should be. However, there may be certain circumstances in which the need for denunciation is so pressing that incarceration will be the only suitable way in which to express society's condemnation of the offender's conduct.

(ii) DETERRENCE

Incarceration, which is ordinarily a harsher sanction, may provide more deterrence than a conditional sentence. Judges should be wary, however, of placing too much weight on deterrence when choosing between a conditional sentence and incarceration: see *Wismayer*, supra, at p. 36. The empirical evidence suggests that the deterrent effect of incarceration is uncertain: see generally *Sentencing Reform: A Canadian Approach. Report of the Canadian Sentencing Commission* (1987) at pp. 136-37. Moreover, a conditional sentence can provide significant deterrence if sufficiently punitive conditions are imposed and the public is made aware of the severity of these sentences. There is also the possibility of deterrence through the use of community service orders, including those in which the offender may be obliged to speak to members of the community about the evils of the particular criminal conduct in which he or she engaged, assuming the offender were amenable to such a condition. Nevertheless, there may be circumstances in which the need for deterrence will warrant incarceration. This will depend in part on whether the offence is one in which the effects of incarceration are likely to have a real deterrent effect, as well as on the circumstances of the community in which the offences were committed.

(iii) SEPARATION

The objective of separation is not applicable in determining whether a conditional sentence would be consistent with the fundamental purpose and principles of sentencing because it is a prerequisite of a conditional sentence that the offender not pose a danger to the community. Accordingly, it is not necessary to completely separate the offender from society. To the extent that incarceration, which leads to the complete separation of offenders, is warranted in circumstances where the statutory prerequisites are met, it is as a result of the objectives of denunciation and deterrence, not the need for separation as such.

(iv) RESTORATIVE OBJECTIVES

While incarceration may provide for more denunciation and deterrence than a conditional sentence, a conditional sentence is generally better suited to achieving the restorative objectives of rehabilitation, reparations, and promotion of a sense of responsibility in the offender. As this Court held in *Gladue*, supra, at para. 43, "[r]estorative sentencing goals do not usually correlate with the use of prison as a sanction." The importance of these goals is not to be underestimated, as they are primarily responsible for lowering the rate of recidivism. Consequently, when the objectives of rehabilitation, reparation, and promotion of a sense of responsibility may realistically be achieved in the case of a particular offender, a conditional sentence will likely be the appropriate sanction, subject to the denunciation and deterrence considerations outlined above.

I will now consider examples of conditions that seek to vindicate these objectives. There are any number of conditions a judge may impose in order to rehabilitate an offender. Mandatory treatment orders may be imposed, such as psychological counseling and alcohol and drug rehabilitation. It is well known that sentencing an offender to a term of incarceration for an offence related to a drug addiction, without addressing the addiction, will probably not lead to the rehabilitation of the offender. *The Final Report of the Commission of Inquiry into the Non-Medical Use of Drugs* (1973) noted at p. 59 that

> These adverse effects of imprisonment are particularly reflected in the treatment of drug offenders. Our investigations suggest that there is considerable circulation of drugs within penal institutions, that offenders are reinforced in their attachment to the drug culture, and that in many cases they are introduced to certain kinds of drug use by prison contacts. Thus imprisonment does not cut off all contact with drugs or the drug subculture, nor does it cut off contact with individual drug users. Actually, it increases exposure to the influence of chronic, harmful drug users.

House arrest may also have a rehabilitative effect to a certain extent insofar as it prevents the offender from engaging in habitual anti-social associations and promotes pro-social behaviors such as attendance at work or educational institutions: see Roberts, "The Hunt for the Paper Tiger: Conditional Sentencing after *Brady*," supra, at p. 65.

The objectives of reparations to the victim and the community, as well as the promotion of a sense of responsibility in offenders and acknowledgment of the harm done to victims and to the community, may also be well served by a conditional sentence. For example, in some cases, restitution orders to compensate the victim may be made a condition. Furthermore, the imposition of a condition of community service can assist the offender in making reparations to the community and in promoting a sense of responsibility. An interesting possibility in this regard would be an order that the offender speak in public about the unfortunate consequences of his or her conduct, assuming the offender were amenable to such a condition. Not only could such an order promote a sense of responsibility and an acknowledgment of the harm done by the offender, it could also further the objective of deterrence, as I discussed above. In my view, the use of community service orders should be encouraged, provided that there are suitable programs available for the offender in the community. By increasing the use of community service orders, offenders will be seen by members of the public as paying back their debt to society. This will assist in contributing to public respect for the law.

(v) SUMMARY

In sum, in determining whether a conditional sentence would be consistent with the fundamental purpose and principles of sentencing, sentencing judges should consider which sentencing objectives figure most prominently in the factual circumstances of the particular case before them. Where a combination of both punitive and restorative objectives may be achieved, a conditional sentence will likely be more appropriate than incarceration. In determining whether restorative objectives can be satisfied in a particular case, the judge should consider the offender's prospects of rehabilitation, including whether the offender has proposed a particular plan of rehabilitation; the availability of appropriate community service and treatment programs, whether the offender has acknowledged his or her wrongdoing and expresses remorse; as well as the victim's wishes as revealed by the victim impact statement (consideration of which is now mandatory pursuant to s. 722 of the Code). This list is not exhaustive.

Where punitive objectives such as denunciation and deterrence are particularly pressing, such as cases in which there are aggravating circumstances, incarceration will generally be the preferable sanction. This may be so notwithstanding the fact that restorative goals might be achieved by a conditional sentence. Conversely, a conditional sentence may provide sufficient denunciation and deterrence, even in cases in which restorative objectives are of diminished importance, depending on the nature of the conditions imposed, the duration of the conditional sentence, and the circumstances of the offender and the community in which the conditional sentence is to be served.

Finally, it bears pointing out that a conditional sentence may be imposed even in circumstances where there are aggravating circumstances relating to the offence or the offender. Aggravating circumstances will obviously increase the need for denunciation and deterrence. However, it would be a mistake to rule out the possibility of a conditional sentence *ab initio* simply because aggravating factors are present. I repeat that each case must be considered individually.

Sentencing judges will frequently be confronted with situations in which some objectives militate in favour of a conditional sentence, whereas others favour incarceration. in those cases, the trial judge will be called upon to weigh the various objectives in fashioning a fit sentence. As La Forest J stated in *R v. Lyons*, [1987] 2 SCR 309, at p. 329, "[i]n a rational system of sentencing, the respective importance of prevention, deterrence, retribution and rehabilitation will vary according to the nature of the crime and the circumstances of the offender." There is no easy test or formula that the judge can apply in weighing these factors. Much will depend on the good judgment and wisdom of sentencing judges, whom Parliament vested with considerable discretion in making these determinations pursuant to s. 718.3.

(d) Appropriate Conditions

In the event that a judge chooses to impose a conditional sentence, there are five compulsory conditions listed in s. 742.3(1) that must be imposed. The judge also has considerable discretion in imposing optional conditions pursuant to s. 742.3(2). There are a number of principles that should guide the judge in exercising this discretion. First, the conditions must ensure the safety of the community. Second, conditions must be tailored to fit the particular circumstances of the offender and the offence. The type of conditions imposed will be a function of the sentencing judge's creativity. However, conditions will prove fruitless if the offender is incapable of abiding by them, and will increase the probability that the offender will be incarcerated as a result of breaching them. Third, punitive conditions such as house arrest should be the norm, not the exception. Fourth, the conditions must be realistically enforceable. This requires a consideration of the available resources in the community in which the sentence is to be served. I agree with Rosenberg JA, who, in "Recent Developments in Sentencing," a paper prepared for the National Judicial Institute's Supreme Court of Nova Scotia Education Seminar in Halifax, February 25-26, 1999, at p. 63, wrote that:

> the courts must be careful not to impose conditions that are purely cosmetic and are incapable of effective enforcement. For example, I would think that any condition that can only be effectively enforced through an intolerable intrusion into the privacy of innocent persons would be problematic. Conditions that impose an unacceptable burden on the supervisor might also be of dubious value. If the conditions that the court imposes are impractical, the justice system will be brought into disrepute.

D. Burden of Proof

It is submitted by the intervener the Attorney General for Ontario that the offender has the burden of proving that a conditional sentence should be imposed pursuant to s. 742.1. According to the Attorney General:

> [W]hen a sentencing court determines that a reformatory sentence of imprisonment is an appropriate sentence for an offender, there is, in effect, a *rebuttable presumption* that this custodial sentence will prevail unless the *offender* can convince the sentencing Court to make the sentence of imprisonment "conditional." [Emphasis in original]

The Attorney General for Ontario's position seems to be premised on a rigid two-step approach, which I rejected for the reasons explained earlier. The Attorney General submits that the offender has to establish that: (a) he or she would not endanger the safety of the community by serving a conditional sentence; and (b) the imposition of a conditional sentence would be consistent with the fundamental purpose and principles set out in ss. 718 to 718.2.

I disagree. The wording used in s. 742.1 does not attribute to either party the onus of establishing that the offender should or should not receive a conditional sentence. To inform his or her decision about the appropriate sentence, the judge can take into consideration all the evidence, no matter who adduces it (*Ursel*, supra, at pp. 264-65 and 287).

In matters of sentencing, while each party is expected to establish elements in support of its position as to the appropriate sentence that should be imposed, the ultimate decision as to what constitutes the best disposition is left to the discretion of the sentencing judge. This message is explicit in ss. 718.3(1) and (2):

> 718.3(1) Where an enactment prescribes different degrees or kinds of punishment in respect of an offence, the punishment to be imposed is, subject to the limitations prescribed in the enactment, in the discretion of the court that convicts a person who commits the offence.
>
> (2) Where an enactment prescribes a punishment in respect of an offence, the punishment to be imposed is, subject to the limitations prescribed in the enactment, in the discretion of the court that convicts a person who commits the offence, but no punishment is a minimum punishment unless it is declared to be a minimum punishment.

The sentencing judge can take into account the submissions and evidence presented by counsel (s. 723), but is in no way bound by them in the decision as to the sentence. Having said this, in practice, it will generally be the offender who is best situated to convince the judge that a conditional sentence is indeed appropriate. Therefore, it would be in the offender's best interests to establish those elements militating in favour of a conditional sentence: see *Ursel*, supra, at pp. 264-65; *R v. Fleet* (1997), 120 CCC 457 (Ont. CA), at para. 26. For instance, the offender should inform the judge of his or her remorse, willingness to repair and acknowledgment of responsibility, and propose a plan of rehabilitation. The offender could also convince the judge that he or she would not endanger the safety of the community if appropriate conditions were imposed. It would be to the great benefit of the offender to make submissions in this regard. I would also note the importance of the role of the supervision officer in informing the judge on these issues.

E. Deference Owed to Sentencing Judges

In recent years, this Court has repeatedly stated that the sentence imposed by a trial court is entitled to considerable deference from appellate courts: see *Shropshire*, [[1995] 4 SCR 227; 102 CCC (3d) 193], at paras. 46-50; *M.(C.A.)*, supra, at paras. 89-94; *McDonnell*, supra, at paras. 15-17 (majority); *R v. W.(G.)*, SCC, No. 26705, October 15, 1999, at paras. 18-19. In *M.(C.A.)*, at para. 90, I wrote:

> Put simply, absent an error in principle, failure to consider a relevant factor, or an over-emphasis of the appropriate factors, a court of appeal should only intervene to vary a sentence imposed at trial if the sentence is demonstrably unfit. Parliament explicitly vested sentencing judges with a *discretion* to determine the appropriate degree and kind of punishment under the *Criminal Code*. [Emphasis in original.]

Several provisions of Part XXIII confirm that Parliament intended to confer a wide discretion upon the sentencing judge. As a general rule, ss. 718.3(1) and 718.3(2) provide that the degree and kind of punishment to be imposed is left to the discretion of the sentencing judge. Moreover, the opening words of s. 718 specify that the sentencing judge must seek to achieve the fundamental purpose of sentencing "by imposing just sanctions that have *one or more* of the following objectives" (emphasis added). In the context of the conditional sentence, s. 742.1 provides that the judge "may" impose a conditional sentence and enjoys a wide discretion in the drafting of the appropriate conditions, pursuant to s. 742.3(2).

Although an appellate court might entertain a different opinion as to what objectives should be pursued and the best way to do so, that difference will generally not constitute an error of law justifying interference. Further, minor errors in the sequence of application of s. 742.1 may not warrant intervention by appellate courts. Again, I stress that appellate courts should not second-guess sentencing judges unless the sentence imposed is demonstrably unfit.

As explained in *M.(C.A.)*, supra, at para. 91:

> This deferential standard of review has profound functional justifications. As Iacobucci J explained in *Shropshire*, at para. 46, where the sentencing judge has had the benefit of

presiding over the trial of the offender, he or she will have had the comparative advantage of having seen and heard the witnesses to the crime. But in the absence of a full trial, where the offender has pleaded guilty to an offence and the sentencing judge has only enjoyed the benefit of oral and written sentencing submissions (as was the case in both *Shropshire* and this instance), the argument in favour of deference remains compelling. A sentencing judge still enjoys a position of advantage over an appellate judge in being able to directly assess the sentencing submissions of both the Crown and the offender. A sentencing judge also possesses the unique qualifications of experience and judgment from having served on the front lines of our criminal justice system. *Perhaps most importantly, the sentencing judge will normally preside near or within the community which has suffered the consequences of the offender's crime. As such, the sentencing judge will have a strong sense of the particular blend of sentencing goals that will be "just and appropriate" for the protection of that community. The determination of a just and appropriate sentence is a delicate art which attempts to balance carefully the societal goals of sentencing against the moral blameworthiness of the offender and the circumstances of the offence, while at all times taking into account the needs and current conditions of and in the community.* The discretion of a sentencing judge should thus not be interfered with lightly. [Emphasis added.]

This last justification is particularly relevant in the case of conditional sentences. Crafting appropriate conditions requires knowledge of both the needs and resources of the community.

VI. Summary

At this point, a short summary of what has been said in these reasons might be useful:

1. Bill C-41 in general and the conditional sentence in particular were enacted both to reduce reliance on incarceration as a sanction and to increase the use of principles of restorative justice in sentencing.
2. A conditional sentence should be distinguished from probationary measures. Probation is primarily a rehabilitative sentencing tool. By contrast, Parliament intended conditional sentences to include both punitive and rehabilitative aspects. Therefore, conditional sentences should generally include punitive conditions that are restrictive of the offender's liberty. Conditions such as house arrest should be the norm, not the exception.
3. No offences are excluded from the conditional sentencing regime except those with a minimum term of imprisonment, nor should there be presumptions in favour of or against a conditional sentence for specific offences.
4. The requirement in s. 742.1(a) that the judge impose a sentence of imprisonment of less than two years does not require the judge to first impose a sentence of imprisonment of a fixed duration before considering whether that sentence can be served in the community. Although this approach is suggested by the text of s. 742.1(a), it is unrealistic and could lead to unfit sentences in some cases. Instead, a purposive interpretation of s. 742.1(a) should be adopted. In a preliminary determination, the sentencing judge should reject a penitentiary

term and probationary measures as inappropriate. Having determined that the appropriate range of sentence is a term of imprisonment of less than two years, the judge should then consider whether it is appropriate for the offender to serve his or her sentence in the community.

5. As a corollary of the purposive interpretation of s. 742.1(a), a conditional sentence need not be of equivalent duration to the sentence of incarceration that would otherwise have been imposed. The sole requirement is that the duration and conditions of a conditional sentence make for a just and appropriate sentence.

6. The requirement in s. 742.1(h) that the judge be satisfied that the safety of the community would not be endangered by the offender serving his or her sentence in the community is a condition precedent to the imposition of a conditional sentence, and not the primary consideration in determining whether a conditional sentence is appropriate. In making this determination, the judge should consider the risk posed by the specific offender, not the broader risk of whether the imposition of a conditional sentence would endanger the safety of the community by providing insufficient general deterrence or undermining general respect for the law. Two factors should be taken into account: (1) the risk of the offender re-offending; and (2) the gravity of the damage that could ensue in the event of re-offence. A consideration of the risk posed by the offender should include the risk of any criminal activity, and not be limited solely to the risk of physical or psychological harm to individuals.

7. Once the prerequisites of s. 742.1 are satisfied, the judge should give serious consideration to the possibility of a conditional sentence in all cases by examining whether a conditional sentence is consistent with the fundamental purpose and principles of sentencing set out in ss. 718 to 718.2. This follows from Parliament's clear message to the judiciary to reduce the use of incarceration as a sanction.

8. A conditional sentence can provide significant denunciation and deterrence. As a general matter, the more serious the offence, the longer and more onerous the conditional sentence should be. There may be some circumstances, however, where the need for denunciation or deterrence is so pressing that incarceration will be the only suitable way in which to express society's condemnation of the offender's conduct or to deter similar conduct in the future.

9. Generally, a conditional sentence will be better than incarceration at achieving the restorative objectives of rehabilitation, reparations to the victim and the community, and promotion of a sense of responsibility in the offender and acknowledgment of the harm done to the victim and the community.

10. Where a combination of both punitive and restorative objectives may be achieved, a conditional sentence will likely be more appropriate than incarceration. Where objectives such as denunciation and deterrence are particularly pressing, incarceration will generally be the preferable sanction. This may be so notwithstanding the fact that restorative goals might be achieved. However, a conditional sentence may provide sufficient denunciation and deterrence, even in cases in which restorative objectives are of lesser importance, depending on the nature of the conditions imposed, the duration of the sentence, and the

circumstances of both the offender and the community in which the conditional sentence is to be served.

11. A conditional sentence may be imposed even where there are aggravating circumstances, although the need for denunciation and deterrence will increase in these circumstances.

12. No party is under a burden of proof to establish that a conditional sentence is either appropriate or inappropriate in the circumstances. The judge should consider all relevant evidence, no matter by whom it is adduced. However, it would be in the offender's best interests to establish elements militating in favour of a conditional sentence.

13. Sentencing judges have a wide discretion in the choice of the appropriate sentence. They are entitled to considerable deference from appellate courts. As explained in *M.(C.A.)*, supra, at para. 90: "Put simply, absent an error in principle, failure to consider a relevant factor, or an overemphasis of the appropriate factors, a court of appeal should only intervene to vary a sentence imposed at trial if the sentence is demonstrably unfit."

VII. Application to the Case at Hand

In the case at hand, Keyser J considered that a term of imprisonment of 18 months was appropriate and declined to permit the respondent to serve his term in the community. She found that, while the respondent would not endanger the safety of the community by serving a conditional sentence, such a sentence would not be in conformity with the objectives of s. 718. In her view, even if incarceration was not necessary to deter the respondent from similar future conduct or necessary for his rehabilitation, incarceration was necessary to denounce the conduct of the respondent and to deter others from engaging in similar conduct.

While Keyser J seems to have proceeded according to a rigid two-step process, in deviation from the approach I have set out, I am not convinced that an 18-month sentence of incarceration was demonstrably unfit for these offences and this offender. I point out that the offences here were very serious, and that they had resulted in a death and in severe bodily harm. Moreover, dangerous driving and impaired driving may be offences for which harsh sentences plausibly provide general deterrence. These crimes are often committed by otherwise law-abiding persons, with good employment records and families. Arguably, such persons are the ones most likely to be deterred by the threat of severe penalties: see *R v. McVeigh* (1985), 22 CCC (3d) 145 (Ont. CA), at p. 1501; *R v. Biancofiore* (1997), 119 CCC (3d) 344, at paras. 18-24; *R v. Blakely* (1998), 40 OR (3d) 541 (CA), at pp. 542-43.

I hasten to add that these comments should not be taken as a directive that conditional sentences can never be imposed for offences such as dangerous driving or impaired driving. In fact, were I a trial judge, I might have found that a conditional sentence would have been appropriate in this case. The respondent is still very young, he had no prior record and no convictions since the accident, he seems completely rehabilitated, he wants to go back to school, he has already suffered a lot by causing the death of a friend and was himself in a coma for some time. To make sure that the

objectives of denunciation and general deterrence would have been sufficiently addressed, I might have imposed conditions such as house arrest and a community
service order requiring the offender to speak to designated groups about the consequences of dangerous driving, as was the case in *Parker*, supra, at p. 239, and *R v.
Hollinsky* (1995), 103 CCC (3d) 472 (Ont. CA).

However, trial judges are closer to their community and know better what would
be acceptable to their community. Absent evidence that the sentence imposed by the
trial judge was demonstrably unfit, the Court of Appeal should not have interfered to
substitute its own opinion for that of the sentencing judge. The trial judge did not
commit a reversible error in principle and she appropriately considered all the relevant factors. Although the Court of Appeal's decision is entitled to some deference
(see the companion appeal *R v. R.A.R.*, 2000 SCC 8, at paras. 2021), in my opinion it
erred in holding that the sentencing judge had given undue weight to the objective of
denunciation. I see no ground for the Court of Appeal's intervention.

VIII. Disposition

I would allow the appeal. Accordingly, the 18-month sentence of incarceration
imposed by the trial judge should be restored. However, given that the respondent
has already served the conditional sentence imposed by the Court of Appeal in its
entirety, and that the Crown stated in oral argument that it was not seeking any further
punishment, I would stay the service of the sentence of incarceration.

NOTE

Although *Proulx* has answered a number of the controversies generated by the addition
of s. 742.1 to the *Criminal Code*, it has not made the judge's role an easy one. The
difficulty in applying these principles to the hard cases that commonly come to court is
exemplified by the results in the companion cases released the same day as *Proulx*. In *R
v. Bunn* (2000), 140 CCC (3d) 505 (SCC), a case of breach of trust theft by a lawyer, the
Supreme Court upheld the conditional sentence 5 to 3. The fact that the offender was the
sole caregiver for a disabled spouse was a significant factor militating against a custodial
term. In *R v. L.F.W.* (2000), 140 CCC (3d) 539 (SCC), the judges split evenly on whether
to uphold a conditional sentence for a man who, more than 25 years before, committed
offences of indecent assault and gross indecency on a young girl between the ages of 6
and 12. The offender had apparently committed no other offences in the interim, had
dealt successfully with an alcohol problem, and had a good work record. In *R v. R.N.S.*
(2000), 140 CCC (3d) 553 (SCC), the judges unanimously agreed that a 9-month sentence of imprisonment should be restored in a case of sexual assault and invitation to
sexual touching committed on a stepdaughter who was between the ages of 5 and 8. The
case of *R v. R.A.R.* (2000), 140 CCC (3d) 523 (SCC) involved a sexual assault conviction
and two convictions for common assault committed at a workplace by an employer on an
employee in her early 20s. L'Heureux-Dubé J and five other judges allowed the appeal,
restoring the one-year term of imprisonment. In dissent, Lamer CJC would have maintained the 9-month conditional sentence with house arrest and sex-offender treatment,
although he remarked that a lengthier conditional sentence would have been preferable.

In the result, conditional sentences were maintained only in *Bunn* and *L.F.W.*, but not without significant dissent. For the three other offenders, a sentence of imprisonment was substituted although stayed, since the conditional sentences had already been served and the Crown was not requesting additional punishments.

The effect of *Proulx* upon the practice of sentencing judges and appellate courts in the provinces and territories has yet to be settled. The following decision of the Saskatchewan Court of Appeal, by a majority, indicates that the guidance provided in *Proulx* has opened a fresh round of argument in and among various courts. Of particular note in future cases will be the attempt of the courts to situate the conditional sentence between a term of imprisonment in a provincial jail and probation. Also of note will be the effect of the Supreme Court's pronouncements concerning appellate deference upon the practice of appellate courts at lower levels, that is the provincial or territorial court of appeal or the summary-conviction appeal court.

The opinion of Cameron JA, dissenting in part, is omitted.

R v. Laliberte
(2000), 143 CCC (3d) 503 (Sask. CA) (footnotes omitted)

VANCISE JA (Cameron, Vancise, and Jackson JJA):

Application for Leave To Appeal

This is the first of two cases dealing with the principles to be applied by sentencing judges when deciding whether to impose a conditional sentence of imprisonment pursuant to s. 742.1 of the *Criminal Code*, RSC 1985, c. C-46 on offenders convicted of trafficking or possession for the purposes of trafficking in a controlled substance contrary to the provisions of the *Controlled Drugs and Substances Act*, SC 1996, c. 19.

The respondent, Monica Laliberte, pleaded guilty to two counts of trafficking in a controlled substance and two counts of possession of the proceeds of the crime of trafficking. She was sentenced to a conditional sentence of imprisonment of 12 months, which included four months of electronically monitored house arrest, two years' probation and restitution of $120. This was the money she obtained from an undercover agent.

The Crown's application for leave to appeal the conditional sentence raises a number of issues, which although not stated in precisely these terms can be summarized as follows: (1) the standard of appellate review; (2) the fundamental nature of conditional sentences of imprisonment; (3) whether a conditional sentence of imprisonment is an appropriate sentence for trafficking or possession for the purpose of trafficking; (4) disparity in sentences; and, (5) the principles to be applied in the sentencing of aboriginal offenders pursuant to s. 718.2(e) of the Code. Although from time to time addressed in the past by this Court, these issues need to be re-addressed in light of the recent decision of the Supreme Court of Canada in *R v. Gladue* [1999] 1 SCR 688; 133 CCC (3d) 385 and *R v. Proulx* [2000] SCC 5; 140 CCC (3d) 449. I would grant leave for application to appeal.

Facts

In the summer of 1998 the Prince Albert drug squad carried out an undercover drug operation. An undercover agent contacted the respondent, Monica Laliberte, to buy Dilaudid, a hydromorphone. She sold the undercover agent a total of 13 tablets of Dilaudid on September 17 for a total of $120.

Dilaudid is a hydrogenated ketone of morphine, a narcotic analgesic and a controlled drug. It is usually ingested intravenously, is approximately eight times more potent than morphine and the analgesic effect can last three to four hours. Continuous use of the drug can lead to a drug dependency.

The respondent is a user of marijuana but does not use Dilaudid. She admitted she sold the pills to make money but claims she was acting as an intermediary for a third party. She was charged and pleaded guilty to two counts of trafficking in a controlled substance contrary to s. 5(1) of the Act and two counts of possessing the proceeds of the crime of trafficking contrary to s. 8(1) of the Act.

...

General Principles

Appellate Review

Section 687(1) of the *Criminal Code* authorizes an appellate court to consider the fitness of the sentence and to vary the sentence imposed by a trial judge within the limits prescribed by law or to dismiss the appeal. In this province, the standard of appellate review in sentencing matters was established by cases like *R v. Morrissette* (1971), 1 CCC (2d) 307 and *R v. Wenarchuk* (1982), 15 Sask. R 24; 67 CCC (2d) 169 among others. The Supreme Court of Canada (hereinafter the Supreme Court) examined the standard of appellate review in sentencing matters in the late 1990s in three decisions: *R v. Shropshire*, [1995] 4 SCR 227; 102 CCC (3d) 193; *R v. M.(C.A.)*, [1996] 1 SCR 500; 105 CCC (3d) 327; and *R v. McDonnell*, [1997] 1 SCR 948; 210 NR 241; 114 CCC (3d) 436.

In *Shropshire*, Iacobucci J, speaking for the Court, made it clear that: (1) the sentencing process was a "profoundly subjective process"; (2) trial judges enjoy significant advantages over courts of appeal in sentencing matters; (3) courts of appeal should not be given free reign to modify sentences imposed by trial judges; and (4) sentences should only be disturbed if the court of appeal is convinced that the sentence imposed is not fit. He defined "not fit" as "clearly unreasonable."

Chief Justice Lamer, in *M.(C.A.)*, specifically adopted and expanded the deferential approach of appellate review developed by the Supreme Court in *Shropshire*. The Chief Justice noted that s. 717 of the Code vests trial judges with discretion to determine the appropriate degree and kind of punishment or sentence and that the deferential standard of review has "profound functional justifications." One of those functional justifications is that a sentencing judge enjoys a position of advantage over an appellate judge in being able to assess the submissions of the Crown and the offender. This is because sentencing judges possess unique qualifications of judgment and experience gained by serving in the front lines of the criminal justice system. The

Chief Justice pointed out that a sentencing judge will normally reside in or near the community which has suffered the consequences of the offenders' actions and will have a sense of the particular sentencing goals that will be "just and appropriate" for the protection of that community. The Chief Justice stated:

> The determination of a just and appropriate sentence is a delicate art which attempts to balance carefully the societal goals of sentencing against the moral blameworthiness of the offender and the circumstances of the offence, while at all times taking into account the needs and current conditions of and in the community.

He concluded the discretion of the sentencing judge should not be interfered with lightly and then only for very limited reasons. He summed up by stating that absent an error in principle, failure to consider a relevant factor or an overemphasis of the appropriate factors, a court of appeal should only intervene if the sentence is demonstrably unfit.

The Supreme Court returned to the subject in *R v. McDonnell* where the deferential approach enunciated in *Shropshire* and *M.(C.A.)* was confirmed. Mr. Justice Sopinka, writing for the majority, succinctly summarized the principles of appellate review of sentences as: error of principle by the trial judge; failure to consider a relevant factor; overemphasis of the appropriate factors; and, demonstrable unfitness of the sentence.

The effect of these three Supreme Court judgments has a profound effect on how we as a court of appeal deal with sentence appeals. Suffice it to say that prior to these decisions, this Court had not followed a "strong deferential approach" to sentence appeals. The result is, as Bayda CJS noted in *R v. Horvath* (1997), 152 Sask. R 277; 117 CCC (3d) 110 that the approach to reviewing sentences as set out by this Court in *Morrissette* and *Wenarchuk* must now be replaced by the "strong deferential" standard of appellate review as set out by the Supreme Court in *Shropshire, M.(C.A.)* and *McDonnell.* Unless the sentencing judge has erred in principle, failed to consider a relevant factor or overemphasized an appropriate factor or imposed a sentence that is demonstrably unfit this court must not intervene.

This deferential approach to sentence appeals is apt to produce more individualized sentences and consequently apt to produce a wider disparity of sentences when viewed from the perspective of the "offence" as distinct from the "offender."

Part XXIII—Codification of Sentencing Principles or a New Sentencing Regime

...

Subsections 718.2(d) and (e) and 742.1 leave no doubt that the amendments to the Code represent a fundamental shift in sentencing—a shift away from incarceration to both a wider range of punitive responses and to a restorative model involving more community-based sentencing. Those subsections provide that imprisonment is to be used as a last resort. While it has been the stated policy of the Government of Canada since 1984 that imprisonment should be used as a last resort, the reality is otherwise.

A core issue in *Gladue* was whether Part XXIII and in particular ss. 718.2(d) and (c) of Part XXIII are remedial in nature. The Supreme Court found not only that the purpose of Part XXIII was remedial but that all the provisions of Part XXIII are to be given a fair, large, and liberal interpretation in order to attain that remedial objective. The remedial component of the sentencing provisions is an endeavour to achieve a fit and proper sentence in the particular case, not only for aboriginal offenders, but for all offenders.

The Supreme Court also strongly rejected the argument that s. 718.2 is merely a restatement or codification of the existing sentencing law either with respect to the general principles of restraint on the use of imprisonment or on the specific direction regarding aboriginal offenders. The Court stated:

> In our view, s. 718.2(e) is *more* than simply a re-affirmation of existing sentencing principles. The remedial component of the provision consists not only in the fact that it codifies a principle of sentencing, but, far more importantly, in its direction to sentencing judges to undertake the process of sentencing aboriginal offenders differently, in order to endeavour to achieve a truly fit and proper sentence in the particular case. It should be said that the words of s. 718.2(e) do not alter the fundamental duty of the sentencing judge to impose a sentence that is fit for the offence and the offender. For example, as we will discuss below, it will generally be the case as a practical matter that particularly violent and serious offences will result in imprisonment for aboriginal offenders as often as for non-aboriginal offenders. What s. 718.2(e) does alter is the method of analysis which each sentencing judge must use in determining the nature of a fit sentence for an aboriginal offender. In our view, the scheme of Part XXIII of the *Criminal Code*, the context underlying the enactment of s. 718.2(e), and the legislative history of the provision all support an interpretation of s. 718.2(e) as having this important remedial purpose.

This interpretation is important to keep in mind when considering the issue of disparity of sentences.

Conditional Sentence of Imprisonment

Section 742.1 is a self-contained sentencing regime that, for the first time, introduces a provision in the Code permitting an offender in certain circumstances to serve his sentence of imprisonment in the community rather than in prison. This provision is contained within the broad remedial purpose and context of Part XXIII and was designed by Parliament to achieve the objectives of reducing the use of prisons and expanding the use of restorative justice. A conditional sentence of imprisonment incorporates some elements of a non-custodial sentence and some of a custodial sentence. It will generally be more effective in achieving restorative goals of sentencing than a carceral sentence because it is served in the community. It is however a punitive sanction and therefore capable of satisfying the objectives of denunciation and deterrence. It is this punitive aspect that distinguishes the conditional sentence from probation.

The imposition of a conditional sentence must be approached in a principled way to ensure the sanction is used as a clear alternative to incarceration and not merely as a substitute for community-based sanctions such as fines, probation, community service and absolute and conditional discharges. To do otherwise will result in net widening which occurs when an offender who would otherwise have received a community-based sanction is sentenced to a conditional sentence of imprisonment.

...

1. Are Conditional Sentences Prohibited for Any Offences?

The Supreme Court dealt with this matter extensively in *Proulx* and pointed out that s. 742.1 does not restrict the use of a conditional sentence of imprisonment to a particular class of offences. The only restrictions on the use of a conditional sentence are that there must be no minimum sentence of imprisonment mandated for the particular offence for which the offender has been convicted and the sentence must be less than two years. Thus, a conditional sentence is available for all offences in which the statutory prerequisites are satisfied.

In my opinion, a conditional sentence of imprisonment should not be restricted to minor offences or property offences. The sentence should be used in appropriate circumstances for all offences including drug offences and offences against the person. This is always subject to the qualification that the statutory prerequisites have been satisfied and that ordering the offender to serve the sentence in the community will not put the collectivity at risk and in danger. The type of offence or the gravity of the offence should not determine whether a conditional sentence of imprisonment is available. Rather, the sentence should be tailored to the offender, having regard to the principles and purposes of sentencing, the moral blameworthiness of the offender, the circumstances of the offence, the current needs of the community and the interests of public security in the same way a sentencing judge would decide any sentence of imprisonment. A conditional sentence of imprisonment is appropriate for any prison sentence of less than two years (subject to the above qualifications) and the goals of deterrence and denunciation can be met by serving the sentence in the community.

...

2. Factors To Consider in Imposing a Conditional Sentence

The Code contains no guidance as to what factors or principles are to be applied to determine whether the sentence should be served in the community. Section 742.1 provides that the court "may, for the purpose of supervising the offender's behaviour in the community, order that the offender serve the sentence in the community," subject to certain conditions. Just as there are no statutory provisions on which to rely to determine whether an accused would be a danger to the community if the sentence is served in the community, s. 742.1 does not set out what factors are to be used to decide whether a conditional sentence should be imposed. Section 742.1(b) was amended to provide that the sentencing judge, in deciding this issue, must be satisfied the decision is also consistent with the fundamental purposes and principles of sentencing set out in ss. 718 to 718.2. In *Proulx*, the Chief Justice in describing the principles to be applied for imposing a conditional sentence of imprisonment, stated that "*serious consideration* should be given to imposing a conditional sentence of imprisonment in all cases where the three statutory prerequisites are satisfied." He pointed out that "a failure to advert to the possibility of a conditional sentence where there are reason-able grounds for finding that the three statutory prerequisites have been met may well constitute reversible error." The Chief Justice concluded that s. 718(2)(e) clearly exerts an influence on a trial judge when deciding whether to impose a conditional sentence as opposed to a custodial sentence.

...

3. Can a Conditional Sentence of Imprisonment Satisfy the Objectives and Principles of Sentencing?

A. Denunciation

At this stage of the inquiry the sentence must be consistent with the principles of sentencing in ss. 718 to 718.2. In making the decision to impose a conditional sentence of imprisonment, the sentencing judge should take into account that forms of constraint or deprivation of liberty other than imprisonment can satisfy the purposes and objects of sentencing contained in ss. 718 to 718.2. The principle of denunciation, which is the communication of society's condemnation of the offender's conduct, can be achieved without a custodial sentence. Incarceration will provide more denunciation than a conditional sentence of imprisonment but a conditional sentence which deprives or restricts an offender's liberty such as electronically monitored house arrest or a curfew can effectively satisfy those principles. The Chief Justice made it clear that this is particularly true when the conditions restricting an offender's liberty are puni-tive and his liberty is severely restricted. Severe restrictions on the offender's liberty are to be the norm and not the exception.

...

The Supreme Court makes it clear that the principle of denunciation can be satis-fied by the imposition of punitive conditions in the conditional sentencing order. The Supreme Court states that these punitive orders should be the norm, not the exception (how this comports with the stated objective of encouraging the use of the principles of restorative justice is left to our imaginations). Second, a term of imprisonment which would be longer that a custodial sentence would also satisfy that requirement. Finally, the Supreme Court notes that the stigma of house arrest cannot be underestimated.

B. Deterrence

I have long questioned the effectiveness of custodial sentences as a deterrent to reducing and controlling the rate of crime. I first expressed doubts on its effect in 1989 in *R v. McGinn* (1989), 75 Sask. R 161; 49 CCC (3d) 137 (Sask. CA) and later in *R v. McLeod* (1993), 81 CCC (3d) 83 (Sask. CA). The Supreme Court has now stated in *Proulx* that "[j]udges should be wary, however, of placing too much weight on deterrence."

C. Restorative Justice Objectives

The Supreme Court makes it clear in *Proulx* that a conditional sentence is "generally better suited to achieving the restorative objectives of rehabilitation, reparations and promotion of a sense of responsibility in the offender." Prison does not normally correlate with restorative justice.

4. Where Will the Sentence Be Served—in Prison or in the Community?

In my opinion, and as the Supreme Court makes clear in *Proulx*, Parliament did not intend the offender to be liberated on a conditional sentence without the imposition of any controls or constraints. Even if his sentence is being served in the community, the offender remains under the control of the correctional system. This is made clear by s. 742.6(9)(d), which gives the court the power to terminate the conditional sentence and order the offender "be committed to custody until the expiration of the sentence." The offender's liberty is restricted for the full term of the sentence. The offender has a greater degree of freedom and liberty only because the conditions of his imprisonment have been changed from the physical confinement of a prison to the restraints imposed on the offender's movements in the community.

This changed milieu in which the offender serves the sentence is similar to conditional release. Just as in conditional release, a conditional sentence of imprisonment does not change the term of imprisonment, it represents a change in the conditions under which the sentence is served. Chief Justice Lamer described the effect of such a community-based sentence in *M.(C.A.)* when dealing with conditional release:

> But even though the conditions of incarceration are subject to change through a grant of parole to the offender's benefit, the offender's sentence continues in full effect. The offender remains under the strict control of the parole system, and the offender's liberty remains significantly curtailed for the full duration of the offender's numerical or life sentence.

Thus, the conditional sentence of imprisonment directs how, where, and under what conditions the sentence will be served.

5. Conclusion

A sentence under s. 742.1 is not just a choice between imprisonment or not. It is a community-based sentence that permits a great deal of creativity for fulfilling the objectives outlined in ss. 718 to 718.2 as well as establishing consequences for a breach of the sentence. That creativity is fostered by the element of control the offender is subjected to during his sentence under s. 742.3(1). That section of the Code specifically provides that the court shall prescribe certain mandatory conditions as a condition of the imposition of a conditional sentence. Section 742.3(2) contains optional conditions that a sentencing judge may prescribe to enhance the control. Those optional conditions are, or can be, punitive in nature and are a further measure of control such as: ordering the accused to abstain from the use of alcohol or drugs; to attend a treatment program; community service; or, intensive probation supervision, which could include electronically monitored house arrest to further the rehabilitation of the offender and to prevent the commission of similar offences. Parliament, in a typically Canadian way, has tried to blend traditional retributive goals of sentencing with concepts of restorative justice.

If one approaches the imposition of a conditional sentence in this logical manner, one is less tempted to use a sanction designed to replace imprisonment as an alternative to appropriate existing community-based sanctions or alternative measures, and net widening should be reduced if not eliminated.

Sentencing of Aboriginal Offenders

...

The sentencing judge must, as he or she would do with a non-aboriginal offender, consider the background and systemic factors which are important for sentencing the aboriginal offender. The Supreme Court made it clear that systemic and background factors are important elements in the incidence of crime and recidivism for non-aboriginal offenders and are equally important in the determination of appropriate sentences for aboriginal offenders. In the case of aboriginal offenders, those factors will include the "unique background and systemic factors" which played a part in the offender's criminal behaviour. If those factors played a significant role in the commission of the offence the sentencing judge must consider them in determining whether a sentence of imprisonment would actually deter or denounce the crime in a meaningful way.

How then does the sentencing judge determine a fit sentence under s. 718.2(e)? The role of a sentencing judge does not change when sentencing an aboriginal offender or a non-aboriginal offender. The sentencing judge must determine a fit sentence by taking into account all relevant circumstances of the offence, the offender, the victim or victims and the community. Although s. 718.2(e) requires that imprisonment be used as a last resort for all offenders in determining the appropriate penalty for an aboriginal offender, the section requires that the sentencing judge also take into account the unique systemic and background factors of the offender.

To begin with, two comments must be made. First, it is not intended as a general rule that sentences for aboriginals and non-aboriginals must necessarily be different. The Supreme Court makes it clear that it is unreasonable to assume that aboriginal peoples do not believe in the traditional sentencing goals of deterrence, denunciation and separation where necessary. A restorative approach will, therefore, not always result in a non-carceral penalty. Secondly, for serious offences where imprisonment must be considered the appropriate sentence, it is more likely that the terms of imprisonment for aboriginals and non-aboriginals will be similar if not the same, even taking into account the different concepts of sentencing. The similarities are likely to increase proportionally with the seriousness and level of violence of the offence.

It is also worth noting that the Supreme Court specifically commented that neither aboriginal offenders nor their communities have been well served by the over-incarceration of aboriginal offenders. The Court also noted that the principles of restorative justice or community-based sanctions coincide with the aboriginal concept of sentencing. Indeed, as I noted above when dealing with conditional sentences of imprisonment, serving the sentence in the community can often fulfill the denunciatory and deterrent goals of sentencing more effectively than a sentence of imprisonment. The goals of restorative justice should in appropriate cases be given at least as much and arguably more weight when sentencing an aboriginal offender than the purposes of sentencing in ss. 718 to 718.2.

What then are the procedural implications which arise as a result of *Gladue*? In my opinion, the decision has created a duty on all sentencing judges to consider the unique systemic circumstances and background of aboriginal offenders when determining the appropriate sentence. This can only happen if the Crown, the defence bar and all other agencies in the criminal justice system, such as probation officers and youth court workers, provide sentencing judges with the information necessary to enable them to make the decisions required under s. 718.2(e). In any event, the Supreme Court made it clear that there is no discretion about whether to consider the unique situation of aboriginal offenders. Those factors must be considered when deciding the appropriate sentence of an aboriginal offender.

Section 718.2(e) requires a sentencing judge to conduct a three-step inquiry to determine whether an aboriginal offender should be incarcerated. The sentencing judge must: (1) examine the unique systemic or background circumstances common to aboriginal offenders as a group; (2) consider the particular circumstances of the offender which resulted in him committing the crime for which he is before the court; and (3) then decide, having regard for the information obtained in steps (1) and (2), whether incarceration is required for the particular aboriginal offender before the court.

...

Within that framework the sentencing judge therefore must be provided with the following information on a sentencing hearing:

1) Whether the offender is aboriginal, that is, someone who comes within the scope of s. 25 of the Charter and s. 35 of the *Constitution Act, 1982*;
2) What band or community or reserve the offender comes from and whether the offender lives on or off the reserve or in an urban or rural setting. This information should also include particulars of the treatment facilities, the existence of a justice committee, and any alternative measures or community-based programs.
3) Whether the offender has been affected by:
   a) substance abuse in the community;
   b) alcohol abuse in the community;
   c) poverty;
   d) overt racism;
   e) family or community breakdown.
4) Whether imprisonment would effectively deter or denounce crime in the subject community. Within this heading it would be useful for the Court to determine whether or not crime prevention can be better served by principles of restorative justice or by imprisonment.
5) What sentencing options exist in the community at large and in the offender's community. For example, does an alternative measures program exist in the offender's community if he lives on a reserve?

The sentencing judge must also be provided with general information concerning systemic poverty, alcohol and substance abuse, cultural and racial bias in the community at large. As well, the sentencing judge must receive information concerning the particular circumstances surrounding the offence.

The Supreme Court suggested that to accomplish the sentencing task, it would be necessary for the sentencing judge to "take judicial notice of the systemic or background factors and the approach to sentencing which is relevant to aboriginal offenders." This raises an evidentiary issue which is problematic. Surely in the context of this judgment Justices Cory and Iacobucci are not suggesting that the systemic or background factors are so "notorious" in general as to be capable of proof without evidence or that they can be verified by resort to reports of indisputable accuracy and applied the particular facts.

The systemic cultural and background factors to which Justices Cory and Iacobucci refer are set out in great detail in *Gladue*. All the factors described are conclusions of fact taken from texts, articles, studies, or commissions of inquiry on aboriginal problems, including the *Report of the Aboriginal Justice Inquiry of Manitoba* and *The Justice System and Aboriginal People*. Those factors were described as:

Years of dislocation and economic development have translated, for many aboriginal peoples, into low incomes, high unemployment, lack of opportunities and options, lack or irrelevance of education, substance abuse, loneliness, and community fragmentation. These and other factors contribute to a higher incidence of crime and incarceration.

It will be necessary for the sentencing judge to take into account those factors which have been demonstrated as having caused or contributed to the aboriginal offender being before the court.

The issue of how to deal with discrimination of aboriginal peoples was examined by the Supreme Court in *R v. Williams*, [1998] 1 SCR 1128; [1999] 4 WWR 711; 124 CCC (3d) 481, in the context of a challenge for cause, where the issue was widespread bias or prejudice in the community which had the potential to impact on the impartiality of a jury. McLachlin J concluded *on the evidence* of that case that there was widespread bias against aboriginal peoples in Canada and there is evidence that this widespread racism has translated into systemic discrimination in the criminal justice system. McLachlin J did not take judicial notice of that fact.

In *Williams*, the accused called witnesses and tendered evidence to establish widespread prejudice and bias in the community against aboriginal people. This evidence demonstrated there was a reasonable possibility of bias or a realistic potential of racial bias or prejudice on the part of jurors in the context of challenge for cause in the selection of a jury. McLachlin J stated it might not be necessary to duplicate that effort in future cases to establish racial prejudice in the community because the potential for racial prejudice could be demonstrated either by evidence or by judicial notice or by proving facts capable of immediate and accurate verification.

In *R v. Fleury*, [[1999] 3 WWR 62 (Sask. QB)] Barclay J considered whether widespread bias or prejudice existed in Saskatchewan which might impact on the impartiality of a jury in the context of a challenge for cause. Again, after hearing evidence from an expert in the field and examining reports of commissions of inquiries, he concluded on the evidence that there was systemic racism sufficient to permit the accused to challenge jurors for cause.

Klebuc J in *R v. Carratt*, [1999] SJ No. 626 (QL), refused to take judicial notice of racial bias in the context of a sentencing hearing held to determine whether to impose a conditional sentence on an aboriginal offender. He was unwilling to accept the finding made by Barclay J in *Fleury* that systemic racism exists in Saskatchewan. He found he could not make such a finding in the absence of evidence on that issue in the particular community where the offence occurred. He was unable to determine on the evidence before him whether anti-aboriginal racism existed and had materially affected the particular offender's ability to obtain employment for example, and was the cause of the offender being before the Court.

Klebuc J was satisfied on the evidence of Professor Quigley of the Faculty of Law of the University of Saskatchewan, that aboriginal peoples suffered from poverty, substance abuse and racism and were overrepresented in the prison population. At the end of the day, however, he was unable to find that those factors were the cause of the particular aboriginal offender's criminal conduct and he refused to impose a community-based sentence. I agree generally with the approach he used in attempting to comply with the directives in *Gladue*.

The evidentiary question is thus reduced to: are the systemic or background matters so "notorious" that a sentencing judge can take judicial notice of them without further evidence when deciding whether to apply a restorative approach to sentencing so as to make the system more relevant to aboriginal peoples?

Justices Cory and Iacobucci seem to have provided at least a partial answer to that evidentiary question by stating, immediately after their comments on judicial notice, that it will probably be necessary for some evidence to be adduced to assist the sentencing judge to decide these issues. In my opinion, evidence will be required on the "*Gladue* sentencing hearing" to establish the systemic factors referred to by the Supreme Court as well as to demonstrate how those factors have contributed to the offender being before the court and how those factors should influence the type of sentence to be imposed on the particular aboriginal offender. No operation of the principle of judicial notice will provide enough specific relevant evidence about the particular systemic or background factors which exist in the offender's community. Nor will it provide specific evidence as to how those factors have affected the particular aboriginal offender and whether they resulted in him being before the Court. It will be necessary for the accused to call some evidence to assist the sentencing judge in determining whether, in the particular community where the offender resides, there are systemic or other background factors which have had an influence on how this particular offender came before the court with the result that there will be a different approach to sentencing and the kind of sentence to be imposed.

As a cautionary note, I would repeat that s. 718.2(e) is not to be interpreted as requiring an automatic reduction of the sentence simply because the offender is aboriginal. The Supreme Court makes it clear that the section is but one factor to be taken into account when determining an appropriate sentence. It is essential the section be read in the context of Part XXIII and the sentence depend upon all of the principles and goals of sentencing being considered.

Disparity of Sentences

...

Chief Justice Bayda (speaking for the Court) noted in *R v. Horvath* that there is a certain degree of fluidity in the principle of parity. He stated:

[I]nherent in the principle of parity is a degree of fluidity. Were this not so this Court, for example, should today be imposing similar sentences for similar offenders committing similar offences in similar circumstances, as it did 25 or 30 years ago. We know that is not taking place. Similarly if that degree of fluidity were not inherent in the principle of parity then this Court should ignore the provisions of ss. 742.1 to 742.3 on the ground that in many cases in the past (prior to 1 September 1996) this Court imposed sentences of imprisonment to be served in a prison "on similar offenders for similar offences committed in similar circumstances" and to now order that the sentence be served in the community would be to impose a sentence not "similar," a result the principle of parity precludes. In my respectful view to so ignore ss. 742.1 to 742.3 would fly in the face of Parliament's intention. I find that a sentence which requires a term of imprisonment to be served in the community does not necessarily contravene the principle of parity if prior to the passing of s. 742.1 the sentence would have to have been served in a prison. To find otherwise would be to render s. 742.1 meaningless.

Thus, in both *Taylor* and *Horvath*, this Court accepted the principle that disparity is a fluid notion, and that the changes and modifications to the law in Part XXIII have fundamentally altered how courts of appeal should view sentences imposed prior to its coming into force. Those sentences decided before the amendments to Part XXIII can no longer be regarded as establishing immutable sentencing principles or ranges against which sentences decided after the changes came into effect must be measured. They must be examined having regard to the "new sentencing regime," and the restorative paradigm adopted by Parliament as interpreted by the Supreme Court. Courts of appeal must examine the sentences imposed since September 3, 1996 through "changing lenses."

...

Parity of Sentencing

...

Since the adoption by Parliament of Part XXIII, sentencing judges and courts of appeal have a judicial duty to approach sentencing differently than they did previously. When determining whether imprisonment is an appropriate sentence the court must consider imprisonment the sanction of last resort and not the sanction of choice. A restorative paradigm has been added to the sentencing options and Parliament has expressly directed judges to take this into account when determining a fit sentence.

Thus, those cases which were decided prior to *Gladue*, such as *Faubert*, and those which were decided without taking into account the subsequent decision of the Supreme Court of Canada in *Gladue* must be read in light of this Court's decision in *R v. Taylor* and the comments of Chief Justice Bayda that:

One must not overlook that the "mix of accepted sentencing goals" now includes a sentencing objective that was not there when many of the cases cited by [the] Crown in support of [the] principle of parity were decided. I refer to the objective in s. 718(f): "to promote a sense of responsibility in offenders and acknowledgment of the harm done to victims in the community." Nor in considering the "mix of accepted goals" should one overlook the fact that Mr. Taylor is an aboriginal offender within the meaning of s. 718.2(e). Because of his ancestry, Parliament has directed that "particular attention" be given to the principle of restraint. In my respectful view, for a trial judge to "vary" the sentence [from the norm] in order to accommodate that "mix of accepted sentencing goals" fashioned by the "particular community" is not a breach of the principle of parity. ...

It is useful to remember D.A. Thomas's observation that "individualized" sentences should not be expected to conform to the application of "tariff principles." In my opinion, one must examine with care cases decided by this Court before September 3, 1996 as well as those decided subsequent thereto which did not take into account the Supreme Court's decision in *Gladue*. It is necessary to apply to those cases the principles of sentencing subsequently adopted in Part XXIII of the Code. In other words, it is not "business as usual." There is a new sentencing regime, one which must be taken into account in determining the appropriateness and fitness of sentences.

In each of *Faubert*, *Englesman* and *Neufeld*, the Court decided that a community-based sentence was not appropriate. The principal reason was that there was a disparity with sentences for similar offences which had been decided before Part XXIII had come into effect or had been decided subsequently but were compared to cases decided prior to Part XXIII coming into force. It is not possible to find, subsequent to *Gladue*, that the same approach and principles followed pre-*Gladue* should be followed post-*Gladue* to determine whether there is disparity in sentence. In *Proulx*, Chief Justice Lamer made it clear that the deferential standard of appellate review has profound functional justifications. The sentencing judge will have a strong sense of the particular blend of sentencing goals that will be appropriate for the protection of the community. This is particularly so in the case of conditional sentences where crafting appropriate conditions requires knowledge of both the needs and resources of the community.

In my opinion, these sentences must be approached on a principled basis recognizing that the law of sentencing has changed and that there is a new sentencing regime. That does not mean to say that a conditional sentence or a restorative approach to sentencing must be adopted in all cases. The sentence must be viewed having regard to the appropriate and just mix of sentencing goals to determine whether a custodial sentence is appropriate. Each case must be approached individually to determine whether the principles of restorative justice as opposed to the traditional retributive model will apply. Not every trafficking case that warrants a sentence of two years less a day will attract a conditional sentence of imprisonment. Indeed, cases where the Crown has proved a strong commercial element to the offence are unlikely to attract a community-based sentence and the appropriate sentence is likely to be a custodial sentence. It will depend in each case on the particular circumstances of the accused and of the offence.

In the circumstances of this case, I am unable to conclude, based on the principles of parity, particularly in light of the standard of appellate review, that the trial judge erred in imposing a conditional sentence of imprisonment when one overlays the principles of sentencing now contained in Part XXIII and the reasoning set out in *Gladue* and *Proulx*. It is, therefore, apparent that in the circumstances of this case, a conditional sentence of imprisonment was the appropriate sentence. It is not an unfit sentence and we should not interfere.

Since writing these reasons I have read the reasons of Jackson JA and I agree with her reasons concerning the granting of leave to appeal and her additional comments on the standard of appellate review.

For all the above reasons the appeal is dismissed.

JACKSON JA (concurring in part): Little is written in Canada about the considerations that lead a Court of Appeal to grant or refuse leave to appeal a sentence under ss. 675(1)(b) or 676(1)(a) of the *Criminal Code*. Nonetheless, to say that this Court only grants leave if it intends to intervene restricts too narrowly our role in these matters. Take the within appeal as an example.

The Crown has appealed the sentence on the basis that the sentencing judge made certain errors resulting in demonstrably unfit sentences. Relying on other decisions of this Court, e.g., *R v. Faubert* and *R v. Englesman*, and extrapolating certain principles from them, Crown counsel argued that this Court had already spoken on the fitness of conditional sentences for trafficking in "hard" drugs and should, therefore, grant leave and set aside the conditional sentence imposed. Defence counsel took issue with this. He said recent decisions of the Supreme Court of Canada require this Court to reconsider its role in reviewing sentences and to provide guidance with respect to the use of conditional sentences. These opposing positions raise squarely the proper approach to be taken in imposing a conditional sentence and this Court's role when reviewing such a sentence to determine its fitness under s. 687 of the *Criminal Code*. Moreover, this appeal was argued with two others (*Keepness* and *Cappo*) in the hope, if not the expectation, that the Court would speak on what has become an issue of some controversy. All of this has been rendered more acute since the Supreme Court of Canada has provided its opinion in *R v. Proulx*, 2000 SCC 5, 140 CCC (3d) 449; *R v. L.F.W.*, 2000 SCC 6, 140 CCC (3d) 539; *R v. R.N.S.*, 2000 SCC 7, 140 CCC (3d) 553; *R v. R.A.R.*, 2000 SCC 8, 140 CCC (3d) 523; and *R v. Bunn*, 2000 SCC 9, 140 CCC (3d) 505.

As a matter of practice, when this Court refuses leave to appeal a sentence, the decision to do so is not reported in the *Sentencing Digest*, and the refusal of leave is recorded only on the court file. Since in-depth reasons are not given, the public does not know the basis upon which the Court decided to refuse leave. This means that the fact of refusing leave has no precedential value. In the instant appeal, it appears that we are all of one mind that the sentence imposed on Ms. Laliberte was fit when imposed, but if we were simply to deny leave, an important part of the continuum of fit sentences would be missed. That is to say, conditional sentencing for a hard drug at the lower end of the spectrum would not form part of the cases cited to the Court on a regular basis. To be more precise, if we were to deny leave in this appeal, Crown and defence counsel and the public would not know that this Court is of the view that a conditional sentence imposed on an accused with these personal circumstances for trafficking in thirteen tablets of Dilaudid is not demonstrably unfit.

In my respectful opinion, a Court of Appeal has the authority to grant leave not only when there is an arguable case for intervention but also to settle an issue of significance either in practice or law. The onus on counsel seeking leave is to demonstrate a case of sufficient merit and importance to warrant intervention or review. *R v. Horvath* is a case in point. *Horvath* was a Crown appeal where this Court dismissed the appeal from the imposition of a conditional sentence. Other examples exist.

Crown counsel has met the onus of persuading me that leave should be granted. Accordingly, I would grant leave.

My colleagues have taken different approaches to arrive at what is the same result. My colleague Vancise JA has provided a detailed analysis of the case law and statutory provisions and developed a framework for when and how courts should determine the applicability of a conditional sentence. I agree with his analysis and framework. It accords with that which was recently pronounced by the Supreme Court of Canada. He has also provided an analysis of the application of s. 718.2(e) dealing with aboriginal offenders. As he makes clear, he is able to find Ms. Laliberte's sentence to be fit without resorting to her aboriginal status. On that basis, I prefer to withhold comment on his analysis of this latter issue until it is directly engaged.

As to disparity, I will add my own thoughts. My colleague Vancise JA states that the principle of parity does not preclude a finding by this Court that the conditional sentence in this case is a fit sentence for two principal reasons. First, he writes that our earlier decisions relied on pre-May 1, 1997 decisions or did not refer to the pronouncements contained in *R v. Gladue*. Secondly, the standard of appellate review as articulated in recent Supreme Court cases including *Gladue* and now *Proulx* requires this Court to give greater deference to sentencing judges such that where we might once have intervened, we are now precluded from doing so. I subscribe to that part of his reasoning which focuses on the standard of appellate review which I will now amplify.

Vancise JA traces the recent cases stating and interpreting the standard of appellate review beginning with *R v. Morrissette* through *R v. Wenarchuk*, *R v. Shropshire*, *R v. M.(C.A.)*, *R v. McDonnell*, *Horvath*, *Gladue* and concluding with *Proulx*, *R v. L.F.W.*, *R v. R.N.S.*, *R v. R.A.R.* and *R v. Bunn*. In my mind this review demonstrates a narrowing of the aperture of intervention for an appellate court particularly as it relates to conditional sentences.

· · ·

It is significant that the Court in *Proulx* did not indicate what will constitute an error in principle or when a sentence imposed by a trial or sentencing judge is demonstrably unfit. The realm of conditional sentencing is full of many rules—some more important than others. If the Supreme Court of Canada had said that this or that rule or factor is more or less important, appellate courts could, in an effort to fulfill its reviewing function, maintain reliance on incarceration by setting aside conditional sentences. But the Supreme Court did not. Instead, the Court speaking with one voice in *Proulx* gave extensive guidelines to trial judges to assist them in determining when to impose a conditional sentence while at the same time advising appellate courts to be chary about intervening.

As a further message to appellate courts, we can look at exactly what the Supreme Court did in *Proulx*, *L.F.W.*, *R.N.S.*, *R.A.R.* and *Bunn*. In all but one of these cases, the Supreme Court of Canada upheld the decision of the trial judge. In the one case where the Supreme Court did not uphold the decision of the trial judge (*Bunn*), the Supreme Court of Canada must be taken as expanding the use of conditional sentences. What the Court actually did is a powerful statement of the application of the standard of appellate review and the use of conditional sentences.

It should also be pointed out that in those cases where the Supreme Court set aside an appeal court's conditional sentence, it usually gave guidance to a future sentencing judge. The nature of this advice makes it clear that the Supreme Court's decision is not intended to preclude the use of a conditional sentence for a future offence of the same nature. (This also speaks to the diminishing role of parity of sentencing.) For example, in *Proulx* the Court set aside the conditional sentence imposed by the Manitoba Court of Appeal for dangerous driving causing death and restored the decision of the trial judge sentencing the accused to custody.

. . .

However, trial judges are closer to their community and know better what would be acceptable to their community. Absent evidence that the sentence imposed by the trial judge was demonstrably unfit, the Court of Appeal should not have interfered to substitute its own opinion for that of the sentencing judge. The trial judge did not commit a reversible error in principle and she appropriately considered all the relevant factors. Although the Court of Appeal's decision is entitled to some deference (see the companion appeal *R v. R.A.R.*), in my opinion it erred in holding that the sentencing judge had given undue weight to the objective of denunciation. I see no ground for the Court of Appeal's intervention.

These comments provide further guidance to an appellate court regarding the standard of appellate review. No aspect of the weighing process which led the trial judge in *Proulx* to select custody over a conditional sentence constituted reversible error. Instead, the Court assessed whether the ultimate result was demonstrably unfit. As soon as the Court reached this stage of its analysis, the standard of appellate review precluded intervention. The decision to impose or not to impose a custodial as opposed to a conditional sentence did not result, on the facts of that case, in a reversible error.

This does not mean that the Court of Appeal has no role in sentencing. Parliament has given appellate courts the obligation to review appealed sentences to determine their fitness, but this role must be fulfilled while giving great deference to sentencing judges.

That brings us specifically to the role of parity. A necessary corollary of a narrow standard of appellate review is that the emphasis on that principle of sentencing known as parity contained in s. 718.2(b) is diminished. (Clause 718.2(b) states "a sentence should be similar to sentences imposed on similar offenders for similar offences committed in similar circumstances.") As support for this view, I turn again to how the Supreme Court applied the principles of sentencing in each of *R v. Proulx*, *R v. L.F.W.*, *R v. R.N.S.*, *R v. R.A.R.* and *R v. Bunn*. None of the five cases refer to sentence parity in either upholding or overturning a conditional sentence.

At paras. [79] to [89] of the Supreme Court's decision in *Proulx*, Lamer CJ discusses in sequence the issues raised by "proportionality" and "the need for starting point sentences." At para. [81] he rejects the notion that there is a presumption against conditional sentences for certain offences.

. . .

Then at para. [86], Lamer CJ begins to determine whether there is a need for starting points with respect to the imposition of conditional sentences. While recognizing the utility for starting point sentences as a means of providing guides to lower courts to achieve greater uniformity and consistency, he rejects their use in respect of specific offences as a means of providing guidance as to the proper use of conditional sentences.

. . .

I take this as confirmation that an appellate court should interfere with great reluctance when a sentencing judge has imposed a conditional sentence on the basis alone that it does not conform with similar sentences given to similar offenders.

For these reasons, then, I would also dismiss the within appeal.

Application for leave to appeal granted; appeal dismissed.

III. SUPERVISION AND BREACH

Of central importance to the effectiveness of conditional sentencing are measures relating to supervision and breach. Indeed, in several jurisdictions sentencing judges have expressed reluctance to impose a conditional sentence unless and until provincial authorities invest greater resources in mechanisms for effective supervision of conditions.

The procedure and principles applicable in cases of alleged breach of conditions have already proved problematic, and ss. 742.6 and 742.7 of the Code were amended in an attempt to clarify some of the difficulties (see SC 1999, c. 5). This matter has not been considered by the Supreme Court to date, but many of the relevant questions were addressed in *Whitty*, reproduced below. At the core of the controversy is the relationship between the mechanism for considering an alleged breach of conditions and the conduct that allegedly constitutes the breach. Is there commission of a separate offence? Is the offender subject to multiple punishment for a single offence? For a fuller exposition of these issues, though written before the amendments of 1999, see the editorial "Breach of a Conditional Sentence by Allegedly Committing Another Offence" (1998), 3 *Can. Crim. LR* 1.

R v. Whitty
(1999), 135 CCC (3d) 77 (Nfld. CA)

GUSHUE JA (Gushue CJN, O'Neill and Marshall JJA) (MARSHALL JA concurring):—
The principal issue in this appeal is whether s. 742.6(9) of the *Criminal Code of Canada* violates s. 7, s. 11(d) and/or s. 11(h) of the *Canadian Charter of Rights and Freedoms*. The collateral issue raised at the trial level was whether, if s. 742.6(9) does violate any or all of the above Charter provisions, it is "saved" by s. 1 of the Charter?

Facts

Following the respondent's conviction of theft (s. 334) and of using a forged document (s. 368(1)(c)), he was sentenced on September 9, 1996 to nine months' imprisonment to be served conditionally. Included in the order was the mandatory condition requiring the respondent "to keep the peace and be of good behaviour."

On March 25, 1997 the respondent was arrested and charged with assault (s. 266) and two counts of uttering threats (s. 264.1(2)). The trial of these matters was scheduled for June 5, 1997.

On April 15, 1997 the Crown applied, pursuant to s. 742.6 of the *Criminal Code*, to have the conditional sentence varied on the ground that the respondent had breached a term or terms of that sentence. The written allegation from the complainant was attached to a "conditional sentence report," which was filed. The complainant also testified at the hearing, as did the respondent. He denied having committed the offences with which he was charged while serving the conditional sentence. Counsel for the respondent then applied to have s. 742.6(9) declared to be in contravention of ss. 7, 11(d) and 11(h) of the Charter.

Following the hearing, in a written judgment, the trial judge concluded that s. 742.6(9) violates s. 7 of the Charter, (1) by relieving the Crown of the burden of proof beyond a reasonable doubt in establishing that a breach of the conditional sentence occurred; and (2) by placing an onus on the accused to establish a reasonable excuse, once the Crown established a breach.

The Crown's s. 742.6 application was consequently dismissed and it is from that decision that this appeal is taken.

· · ·

Crown Argument

(a) Section 11

The Crown points out that s. 11(d) of the Charter protects the right of a person "charged with an offence" to be presumed innocent. Thus the section is limited to those who have been charged with a criminal offence. The Crown argues that to attempt to place a s. 742.6 hearing within this category would require considerable expansion of the wording. The respondent here was not charged with any new offence.

As to s. 11(h), the Supreme Court of Canada in *R v. Schmidt* (1987), 33 CCC (3d) 193, stated at page 211:

> The right is that of a person charged with an offence not to be tried for the offence again if he or she has already been finally acquitted of the offence.

In the present case, the Crown submits that the s. 742.6 application does not result in the respondent being charged with any offence.

Further, he would not be convicted or acquitted of any offence; nor is it proposed that he be punished or sentenced for any offence. The whole purpose of s. 742.6 is not to impose further punishment, but rather to ensure that the order that a period of imprisonment be served outside of a prison provides deterrence and protection of the public if the conditional sentence is not being complied with. The Crown relies on the case of *R v. Shubley*, [1990] 1 SCR 3, 52 CCC (3d) 481, where McLachlin J stated at p. 23:

> I conclude that the sanctions conferred on the superintendent for prison misconduct do not constitute "true penal consequences," within the Wigglesworth test. Confined as

they are to the manner in which the inmate serves his time, and involving neither punitive fines nor a sentence of imprisonment, they appear to be entirely commensurate with the goal of fostering internal prison discipline and are not of the magnitude or consequence that would be expected for redressing wrongs done to society at large. Certainly the discipline meted to the appellant in this case is not such as to attract the application of s. 11(h).

(I would interject here that *R v. Wigglesworth*, [1987] 2 SCR 541, 37 CCC (3d) 385, stated that a matter could fall within s. 11 either because by its very nature it is a criminal proceeding or because a conviction could lead to a true penal consequence. Such would apply to an offence which is criminal in nature, even if such offence might carry only relatively minor consequences, e.g. a minor traffic offence. The headnote in *Wigglesworth* states that s. 11 applies to offences which are of a public nature, intended to promote public order and welfare within a public sphere of activity, as compared to matters which are private, domestic or disciplinary, which, although regulatory, protective or corrective, are primarily intended to maintain discipline, etc. All prosecutions for criminal offences under the *Criminal Code* and for quasi-criminal offences under Provincial legislation are automatically subject to s. 11, since they are the very kind of offences to which it was intended that s. 11 apply. A true penal consequence which would attract the application of s. 11 is imprisonment or a fine imposed for the purpose of redressing the wrong done to society at large, rather than maintaining internal discipline within a limited sphere of activity.)
Madam Justice McLachlin stated also in *Shubley*:

> Forfeiture of remission does not constitute the imposition of a sentence of imprisonment by the superintendent, but merely represents the loss of a privilege dependent on good behaviour ... cancellation of earned remission does not constitute punishment, but is rather the withholding of a reward.

The Crown argues that a decision under s. 742.6, which orders that the remainder of a sentence be served in the penitentiary, is not the further imposition of a period of imprisonment. The respondent is already serving a period of imprisonment. Rather, it is the place of imprisonment which is changed. Nor should it be assumed that incarceration is a greater form of punishment than a conditional sentence. The Crown concludes on this issue that s. 11 of the Charter has no application because the respondent is not charged with an offence. Wilson J, in *Wigglesworth* is quoted [at p. 558]: "[I]t is ... preferable to restrict s. 11 to the most serious offences known to our law, i.e., criminal and penal matters, and to leave other offences subject to the more flexible criteria of fundamental justice in s. 7."

Section 7

The Crown states that while proof beyond a reasonable doubt is an immutable Charter right when a person is charged with a criminal offence, it is not an immutable principle in every context. Thus, before considering the principles of fundamental justice there must first be a deprivation of "life, liberty or security." Such is not the case in a s. 742.6 application because no additional punishment can be imposed. The Crown draws an analogy between sections of the *Parole Act*, RSC 1985, c. P-2, which give the Parole Board the power to change the degree of supervision required, and counsel quotes from *R v. Evans* (1986), 30 CCC (3d) 313 (Ont. CA), where Robins JA stated at page 316: "These sections do not change the sentence imposed on the inmate by the court that convicted him and, consequently, do not impose an additional penalty." In our opinion, they do no more than change the manner or condition under which certain inmates must serve the balance of their sentence.

The Crown's submission is that a judge acting under a s. 742.6 application cannot impose a period of imprisonment. He or she can only vary the place in which it will be served. Thus, the respondent's liberty interests as protected by s. 7 of the Charter are not affected.

The Crown, in support of the proposition that not every deprivation of liberty is a violation of s. 7 and, further, that a standard of proof below a reasonable doubt does not by itself violate the Charter, quotes from *R v. Pearson* (1992), 77 CCC (3d) 124 (SCC), where Lamer CJC stated at page 136:

> This, of course, does not mean that there can be no deprivation of life, liberty or security of the person until guilt is established beyond reasonable doubt by the prosecution at trial [...] certain deprivations of liberty and security of the person may be in accordance with the principles of fundamental justice where there are reasonable grounds for doing so, rather than only after guilt has been established beyond a reasonable doubt. [...] While the presumption is pervasive in the criminal process, its particular requirements will vary according to the context in which it comes to be applied.

Lamer CJC, at page 137, added:

> Each of these cases may be seen as an example of the broad but flexible scope of the presumption of innocence as a principle of fundamental justice under s. 7 of the Charter. The principle does not necessarily require anything in the nature of proof beyond reasonable doubt, because the particular step in the process does not involve a determination of guilt. Precisely what is required depends upon the basic tenets of our legal system as exemplified by specific Charter rights, basic principles of penal policy as viewed in the light of "an analysis of the nature, sources, rationale and essential role of that principle within the judicial process and in our legal system, as it evolves."

The Crown maintains that an allegation that a conditional sentence is not being complied with cannot be equated with a criminal charge, nor indeed is it as serious as e.g., a decision to deny bail. Not only are the potential consequences to, in this case, the respondent markedly different, society must be ensured that those "imprisoned at home" are being deterred and are no more a danger than those who receive periods of "real imprisonment." There is no question that the onus is on the Crown to establish that the conditional sentence order was breached; however, there is no onus on the respondent at this stage and he is not convicted of anything by such a finding. There is no presumption of guilt. Indeed a s. 742.6 hearing commences with a presumption that the respondent has not breached the conditional sentence. Such presumption stands until the Crown establishes (on a balance of probabilities) that a breach occurred. Constitutional standards developed in the context of criminal charges cannot be applied automatically to s. 742.6 hearings.

The Crown concludes that s. 742.6 must be read in its entirety. It allows for a quick response (within 30 days maximum) to allegations of breaches of conditional sentences. While proof beyond a reasonable doubt is not required, the trial judge is granted flexibility unheard of when a criminal charge is involved because that judge can decide to "take no action" even when he or she is persuaded that a conditional sentence has been breached and no reasonable excuse exists.

To place this "onus" (if such it can be termed) on the respondent, particularly after the Crown has established the existence of a breach, is to afford an extra or additional benefit upon the respondent—not a burden.

I do not intend to deal with the submissions made with respect to the possible application of s. 1 of the Charter because, as will be seen, it is unnecessary for the disposition of the appeal.

The Crown concludes that it was open to Parliament to have created an offence section in the *Criminal Code* for breaches of conditional sentencing orders. Such would result in a criminal record for failing to comply and would also allow for additional periods of imprisonment to be imposed. Therefore, on balance, s. 742.6 appears to be a measured response in comparison, particularly when one considers the discretion granted to the judge "to take no action." As to the means being proportional to the objective, when one considers that the alternative is to turn the procedure into a criminal trial, the means utilized in s. 742.6 are deemed by the Crown to be quite proportionate.

In summary, the Crown states that if the purpose of the legislation is to be achieved, use of the reasonable doubt standard would be totally impractical because s. 742.6 hearings would become another and further criminal trial. Apart from the fact that the administrative burden would be a heavy one to bear, conditional sentences could be completed before such a hearing could be held thereby rendering any breach moot.

Respondent's Argument

Counsel for the respondent takes a diametrically opposed position to that taken by the Crown in respect of both s. 7 and 11 of the Charter.

(a) Section 11

In considering the *Wigglesworth* test, the respondent states that s. 742.6 is an offence under the "by nature" test because its purpose is to "regulate conduct within a limited sphere of activity." As to the "true penal consequence" test, the likelihood of imprisonment results in a breach of a conditional sentence order constituting an "offence." The respondent also states that the judicial determination of "guilt" or "innocence" of the breach places s. 742.6 within the context of a criminal offence that warrants s. 11 protection. The purpose of the penalty permitted under s. 742.6 is to redress the wrong done to society at large. Counsel appears to be saying that until a breach of condition occurs (which presumably means that such breach has been established as having occurred), the safety of the public is not in jeopardy, but may be considered to be as a result of such breach. The respondent visualizes a considerable difference between serving the sentence in the community, i.e. at home, and serving the sentence "within the confines of a correctional facility." He concludes from this that this change constitutes a true penal consequence pursuant to *Wigglesworth*. It is also submitted that the finding of a breach of a conditional sentence order is a finding of "guilt" by the court; therefore, the procedures under s. 742.6 constitute the respondent being charged with an offence within the meaning of s. 11 of the Charter.

As to s. 11(d) specifically, it is clear that the respondent starts with the premise that the respondent has been charged with an offence and that the establishing of a breach of his conditional sentence order implies a finding of guilt. A conditional sentence order is analogized as being "remarkably similar" to a probation order, as well as to a suspended sentence. In the former case a breach of probation must be proved beyond a reasonable doubt and counsel argues that the only difference between a suspended sentence and a conditional sentence order is one of semantics in that Parliament has omitted to use the word "offence" for breach of a conditional sentence order.

With respect to s. 11(h) of the Charter the respondent's submission here is that s. 742.6 places him at substantial risk of being tried and punished twice for the same offence. If he was found not to have breached the conditional sentence order, at a further criminal trial he may still have been convicted of the offence which constitutes a breach. Alternatively, if there is a finding that there has been a breach of the order and he is ordered to serve a period of time in custody, but yet is acquitted at trial, he would have been punished for an offence for which he was exonerated. It is the respondent's further argument that if he was found to have breached the conditional sentence order and convicted at trial, he would be sentenced twice for the same offence inasmuch as a concurrent sentence is not available in relation to conditional sentence orders.

(b) Section 7

The respondent submits that a breach of s. 11(d) and/or s. 11(h) of the Charter violates the principle of fundamental justice, thus breaching s. 7 as well. The concept of imprisonment (by which the respondent obviously means imprisonment in a prison or correctional facility) should not be imposed unless the accused person is fully protected by the principles of fundamental justice, i.e. proof beyond a reasonable doubt that the offence was committed. Otherwise, guilt of an accused person would be determined without that person having the benefit of a presumption of innocence.

The respondent also takes issue with the position of the Crown that the conditional sentencing regime cannot logically survive unless the provisions of s. 742.6 are permitted to stand. It is denied that there will be a substantial increase in the burden on the courts in scheduling. Further, even if efficiency and usefulness are affected, they are nevertheless less pressing objectives than that of deprivation of liberty; the "rational connection" to expediency and efficiency cannot override the lack of "rational connection" to protecting the accused person.

Analysis

I am in substantial agreement with the submissions of the Crown generally, and fully subscribe to the statement that the respondent was not charged with any new offence. In order to deal with the actual issue in this matter, it is important to first understand the nature of a conditional sentence order.

...

Section 742.1 appears deceptively simple. It is not simple. It is an alternate sentencing regime. Where an offender is convicted of an offence, the trial judge must first consider whether there should be a term of imprisonment. If the judge is of the opinion that, given the principles of sentencing, the nature of the offence and the antecedents of the offender, there ought to be a fine, or a suspension of sentence, or if there should be imprisonment and that imprisonment should exceed two years, s. 742.1 has no application. If, however, the judge is of the view that there should be a sentence of imprisonment and such sentence should be less than two years, it is then incumbent upon the judge to consider whether that sentence is to be served in prison or whether, having been satisfied that the requirements of s. 742.1(b) have been met, he or she will order the offender to serve the sentence "in the community" (which would normally mean at home), subject to conditions, both mandatory and optional. While the judge obviously must take s. 742.1 into consideration, the decision as to whether or not a conditional sentence is to be imposed is solely within his or her discretion.

Several points are immediately apparent. A conditional sentence is not the same as the suspension of sentence and probation. In the latter, the judge makes a decision that there will be no period of imprisonment on the mandatory undertaking by the offender that, for a period of time of up to three years, he will comply with certain prescribed conditions. If during the probation period the Crown takes the view that a condition of probation has been breached by the offender, the separate criminal charge of breach of probation may be laid and, if established, which would have to be on the basis of proof beyond a reasonable doubt, then the original sentence is also open for reassessment and a possible term of imprisonment. It is apparent that any such breach would be one having true penal consequences, as referred to in *Wigglesworth*.

Contrary to the position put forward by the respondent, such is not the case with a conditional sentence. Section 742.1 clearly states that a conditional sentence is a term of imprisonment—one that is being served in the community rather than behind prison bars. As noted earlier, the trial judge appears also to have been of the view that a conditional sentence is not a sentence of imprisonment because there is no deprivation of the liberty of the offender. This runs counter to what has been already stated by this Court in various cases, including *R v. W.(L.F.)* (1997), 119 CCC (3d) 97, *R v. Oliver* (1997), 147 Nfld. & PEIR 210, *R v. Quilty* (1997), 156 Nfld. & PEIR 320, and *R v. M.(J.)* (1998), 160 Nfld. & PEIR 38. Indeed, these cases state that because s. 742.1 makes reference specifically to the conditional sentence being a term of imprisonment, a curtailment of the offender's liberty in some manner, e.g. house confinement, is an essential and necessary ingredient of a conditional sentence. As pointed out by Green JA in *M.(J.)*, the conditions imposed must, in the circumstances, accomplish a "roughly equivalent deterrent effect." Green JA further added that:

... a conditional sentence can have the potential of imposing greater restrictions on liberty than would a comparable term of incarceration. As such, it need not be regarded as a more lenient type of punishment in a specific case. It is, rather, a different form of punishment designed to achieve the same sentencing objectives.

Thus, the conditional sentence, when imposed, is one having true penal consequences. A sentencing judge, having been satisfied, at least at that stage, that society or the community will not be endangered if the offender is required to serve the sentence in the community, makes such a disposition and imposes certain terms and conditions which must be complied with by the offender. Apart from the compulsory conditions provided for in s. 742.3, one of which is to keep the peace and be of good behaviour, certain optional conditions may also be added to suit the circumstances.

A summary of what occurs after a breach of any condition is alleged to have occurred is set out at paragraphs 10 and 11 above. A full reading of s. 742.6 shows clearly that the offender's interests are stringently protected and that even if a breach is established, on a balance of probabilities, to have occurred, considerable discretion is afforded the judge in arriving at the remedy. Obviously, the disposition would be governed by the nature of the breach and, particularly, whether the breach leads the judge to revisit the original finding that a conditional sentence for that offender would not endanger the safety of the community and, as well, to revisit whether, in light of what has happened, a conditional sentence would continue to be consistent with general sentencing principles.

As has been stated, the aspect of s. 742.6(9)(a) with which exception is taken, and which the trial judge found to be flawed, is that the Crown need only demonstrate on a balance of probabilities that a breach has occurred.

Both the appellant and the respondent rely on *Wigglesworth* to support their respective positions and those arguments are set out above. As seen, that decision of the Supreme Court of Canada stated that a matter could fall within s. 11 of the Charter either because by its very nature it is a criminal proceeding or because a conviction could lead to a true penal consequence. It has been concluded that because a sentence in the form of a term of imprisonment has been imposed, there has already been a true penal consequence to the respondent. The original proceeding was also by its nature a criminal one. I agree with the Crown, however, that the procedure under s. 742.6 cannot be so categorized. The respondent having already been sentenced to imprisonment, this hearing is one aimed only at determining whether changed circumstances should lead to a variation of the manner in which that imprisonment should be served. It is not a further criminal charge.

The approach taken by the trial judge, however, would have the "de facto" effect of turning the s. 742.6 hearing into a criminal trial—one requiring proof beyond a reasonable doubt of the breach. Yet it is not a criminal trial. The breaching of a conditional sentence order is not a criminal offence, as a breach of a probation order would be. Obviously, the alleged breach could amount to a criminal offence, as would appear to be the case here, but it is just as obvious that a breach could (and undoubtedly usually would) be something less. It is also important to note that even if a criminal offence is alleged to have occurred as a result of the breach, something far less that the commission of such offence, e.g. preliminary acts leading up to the ultimate act, would be sufficient to establish a breach of a condition to keep the peace and be of good behaviour.

It cannot be overlooked as well that the trial judge's approach of requiring proof beyond a reasonable doubt of any breach would likely decimate the conditional sentence regime. The simple and expeditious procedure currently contained in the legislation for dealing with a breach would be replaced by what would be in effect another criminal trial—many of which trials would not be heard until after the original sentence was served.

One could well say that the sentencing process as contemplated by the conditional sentencing legislation is intended to be a continuous process, rather than an "all or nothing" approach. The sentencing court, in agreeing to impose a conditional sentence, makes the best assessment it can on the information available at the sentencing hearing, while attempting to ensure that such sentence will be consistent with general sentencing principles. However, unlike other sentences, it is not a final disposition. If, subsequently, there is a failure to abide by the conditions of the order, the court is then presented with further information on which it may make a more informed decision. Having assessed such information, the court may decide that sentencing principles can only be complied with by the serving of the remainder of the sentence in prison. Thus, that decision is reached based on actual experience, rather than speculation at the original hearing as to the likelihood of the offender complying with conditions. As stated, even if a breach is established, the court does not have to order a jail term. Even with the new information, a conditional sentence may still be consistent with sentencing principles.

In summary, the respondent was not charged with a further offence. All that was being sought by the Crown was "… a change in the form in which (his) sentence is served (which), whether it be favourable or unfavourable to the prisoner, is not, in itself, contrary to any principle of fundamental justice" (per McLachlin J in *Cunningham v. Canada* (1993), 80 CCC (3d) 492 (SCC) at p. 499). In other words, we are dealing with an application to vary a sentence. I see no breach of the respondent's rights under either s. 7 or 11 of the Charter. The guilt or innocence of the respondent was no longer at issue and no further punishment was being sought. There existed therefore no requirement for proof beyond a reasonable doubt of any breach alleged to have been committed. Emphasis must further be placed on the powers granted the judge in s. 742.6(9) to accept a "reasonable excuse" as an answer to a breach, and in subsection (a) of that section to "take no action" in any event. Such powers are not granted a judge in dealing with a criminal offence.

All of the above leads me to the conclusion that the appeal must succeed. The trial judge's order dismissing the Crown's application is set aside and the matter is remitted to Provincial Court for continuation of the hearing under s. 742.6(9) of the *Criminal Code*.

O'NEILL JA (dissenting):—I have read in draft the decision of my brother Gushue JA and, with respect, I am unable to agree with his disposition of this matter.

On September 9, 1996 the respondent was sentenced to a term of imprisonment of nine months and the trial judge, under s. 742.1 of the *Criminal Code*, ordered that the sentence be served conditionally. No conditions other than the compulsory conditions under s. 742.3(1) were prescribed.

On March 25, 1997, during the term of the conditional sentence, the respondent was charged with assault and two counts of uttering threats which were alleged to have occurred during the term of the conditional sentence. The charges were laid following a complaint by his estranged wife and her boyfriend. The trial of these matters was scheduled for June 5, 1997, at around the same time that the term of the conditional sentence would end.

On March 31, 1997, a conditional sentence report was filed alleging a breach of condition. Attached to the conditional sentence report was a statement from the complainant setting out details of the alleged offences which were alleged to constitute the breach of condition. The Crown applied to have the respondent's conditional sentence varied. At the hearing, the respondent's wife gave evidence as did the respondent. He denied having committed the offences.

The conditional sentence being served by the respondent would have ended, as already noted, in June 1997, unless, during the term of the conditional sentence, he was sentenced to a term of imprisonment for another offence, in which case the running of the conditional sentence would be suspended during the period of imprisonment for that other offence, unless otherwise ordered by the court under s. 742.4(3) or 742.6(9): see s. 742.7. Section 742.7 contemplates a situation where an offender, during the term of the conditional sentence, is convicted and imprisoned for another offence, whenever committed, which would, of course, include the period that the offender is "at large" under the conditional sentence order.

The respondent applied to the judge hearing the application to have s. 742.6(9) of the *Criminal Code* declared to be in contravention of ss. 7, 11(d) and 11(h) of the *Canadian Charter of Rights and Freedoms* and argued that s. 742.6(9) could not be saved under s. 1 of the Charter.

The judge concluded that s. 742.6(9) violated s. 7 of the Charter: (1) by relieving the Crown of the burden of proof beyond a reasonable doubt in establishing that a breach of the conditional sentence occurred, and (2) by placing an onus on the offender to establish a reasonable excuse once the Crown established the breach. He also concluded that s. 742.6(9) is not saved by s. 1 of the Charter. The Crown's application was dismissed.

The Crown appeals to this Court and seeks the allowing of the appeal, a declaration that the constitutionality of s. 742.6 of the *Criminal Code* be confirmed and an order that the matter be remitted to the Provincial Court for a new hearing.

The Issues on Appeal

The issues argued before the trial judge and on the appeal to this Court were whether the onus on the Crown being that of "on a balance of probabilities," and the onus on the offender with respect to "without reasonable excuse, the proof of which lies on the offender," violate the Charter.

The Imposition of a Conditional Sentence Under S. 742.1 and the
Nature of the Proceeding Under S. 742.6(9)

...

To have decided on a sentence of imprisonment, it must be assumed that the sentencing judge had decided that, consistent with the objectives and principles of sentencing as set out in ss. 718 and 718.2 of the *Criminal Code,* which, of course are applicable to sentencing of any type, a fit sentence is a term of imprisonment. If that sentence is less than two years, and there being no minimum term of imprisonment with respect to that offence, the sentencing judge must then consider whether he is satisfied that the sentence, if served in the community, would not endanger the safety of the community and would still be consistent with the objectives and principles in ss. 718 and 718.2 already referred to. If so satisfied, the sentencing judge may order that the offender serve the sentence in the community subject to the offender's complying with the compulsory conditions set out in s. 742.3(1) and such further optional conditions if any, under s. 742.3(2), as the judge may prescribe. At the same time, the sentencing judge will have been aware of the procedures which may become applicable under ss. 742.4 and 742.6, the former dealing with changes which may be made to the optional conditions following upon a change of circumstances, and the latter setting out the powers of the court following an allegation that there has been a breach of a condition.

It will be helpful to examine the status of the offender who has been ordered to serve his sentence in the community.

There is a body of judicial thought to the effect that the references to "serving the sentence in the community" and "serve the sentence in the community" in s. 742.1 should, in effect, be read as if the words "of imprisonment" appeared after the word "sentence" in each. With due respect to those who hold a contrary view, it is, in my view, an error to construe the status of an offender serving a conditional sentence as one serving a term of imprisonment. Indeed, the sentencing judge, in the imposition of a conditional sentence, has made a very important and far reaching decision in concluding that the offender need not serve the sentence in prison, or "in custody" as that term is used in s. 742.6(9).

Section 742.6 sets out the procedure to be followed and the powers of a court where a breach of a condition of a conditional sentence order is alleged. Section 742.6(9) is as follows:

Powers of court 742.6(9)
Where the court is satisfied, on a balance of probabilities, that the offender has without reasonable excuse, the proof of which lies on the offender, breached a condition of the conditional sentence order, the court may

    (a) take no action;

    (b) change the optional conditions;

    (c) suspend the conditional sentence order and direct

        (i) that the offender serve in custody a portion of the unexpired sentence, and

        (ii) that the conditional sentence order resume on the offender's release from custody, either with or without changes to the optional conditions; or

    (d) terminate the conditional sentence order and direct that the offender be committed to custody until the expiration of the sentence.

Counsel for the Crown argued that the onus on the Crown to establish a breach of condition only on a balance of probabilities was appropriate because, under the legislation, an offender alleged to have committed a breach of the conditional order is not charged with a criminal offence and, therefore, the criminal standard is not required nor is it appropriate. Further, the Crown argued that once the Crown has established, on the balance of probabilities, that a condition had been breached, it was not unreasonable that the onus be on the offender to establish a reasonable excuse for having committed the breach.

In support of its position, the Crown argued that s. 742.6 is designed to allow for a simple and expeditious procedure for dealing with breaches of conditional sentences. It also points to the requirement that since a hearing with respect to any allegation of a breach must be held within thirty days, then, where the conditional sentence is a short one, or where a significant period of the conditional sentence has been completed, the offender would face no penalty since a hearing based on the criminal standard of proof could not reasonably be expected to be conducted within the required time. Crown counsel argued that it is the section's simplicity and flexibility which are its keys.

The Crown argued as well that when a "conditional sentence turns out not to be appropriate," presumably when a breach has occurred, the public should know that there is a quick and expeditious procedure for dealing with it. In that context, the Crown argued that the trial judge's decision here would have a devastating effect on conditional sentence procedures and would endanger the public's acceptance of conditional sentences and the courts' ability to have confidence in ordering them.

In any consideration of s. 742.6, one must look at the very real and broad powers which the court has under s. 742.6(9)(c) and (d) which could involve the actual imprisonment of the offender for a long period of time. This power is all the more far reaching when one considers that the usual remission benefits may not be available to an offender who has been ordered, under s-ss. (c) and (d), to serve any part of the conditional sentence period in custody. Still important, but to a lesser extent, is the power given to the court under s-ss. (b) and (c) to change the optional conditions, which could result in serious restrictions on the offender's liberty such as the equivalent of house arrest or strict curfews. The powers of the court under s. 742.9 become all the more significant here where, as noted earlier, the offender, when placed on the conditional sentence, was only made subject to the compulsory conditions as set out in s. 742.3(1).

The fact that the court may "take no action," as contemplated by s. 742.6(9)(a), does not in any way take away from these broad powers. This option permits the application, in appropriate cases, of the principle of *"de minimis non curat lex"* which has been part of the criminal law in many jurisdictions for years. At the same time, s. 742.6(9)(a) permits a trial judge to conclude that, notwithstanding the breach, which may be a serious one, a court may conclude that a continuation of the conditional sentence as originally set may still be consistent with sentencing principles and can be justified in the particular circumstances.

The Applicability of S. 11 of the Charter

Sections 11(d) and (h) of the Charter are as follows:

> 11. Any person charged with an offence has the right. ...
> (d) to be presumed innocent until proven guilty according to law in a fair and public hearing by an independent and impartial tribunal; ...
> (h) if finally acquitted of the offence, not to be tried for it again and, if finally found guilty and punished for the offence, not to be tried or punished for it again.

The trial judge did not rule that s. 11 applied nor did he rely on it in reaching his decision. In fact, the trial judge concluded that "it seems doubtful that s. 11 of the Charter has application." However, the issue as to the applicability of s. 11 was argued on the appeal to this Court.

Crown counsel takes the position that Parliament has deliberately chosen not to create an offence for the breaching of a conditional sentence order. In support of this position, it was argued that a s. 742.6 hearing does not involve a decision on the guilt or innocence of an offender, nor can any additional punishment be imposed on the offender following a finding that there was a breach.

This argument has its basis in the position taken by Crown counsel that the offender is actually serving a sentence of imprisonment in the community, and, although the form of imprisonment can be changed, there can be no additional punishment imposed. Indeed, in his argument, Crown counsel, perhaps disingenuously, refers to a person serving a conditional sentence as being "an inmate." (*Black's Law Dictionary*, 6th ed., describes "inmate" as "a person confined to a prison, penitentiary or the like." There are other definitions of "inmate" in *Black's* but none is of any relevance here.)

The following excerpts are from the appellant's factum with respect to ss. 11(d) and (h) of the Charter and succinctly set out its position: ss. 11(d) and (h) of the Charter require that the person is charged with an offence. In this case that essential prerequisite is missing. Parliament has specifically chosen not to create an offence for breaching a conditional sentence order. An "inmate" who has breached a conditional sentence, unlike a person on probation, for instance, has previously been found to have committed an offence for which a period of imprisonment was deemed appropriate. The serving of the sentence in the community does not alter the nature of the sentence. Therefore, s. 742.6 of the Code creates a procedural mechanism for dealing with "inmates" who are serving their sentence in the community. The standard of reasonable doubt has no application. ... A decision under s. 742.6, ordering that the remainder of a sentence be served in a penitentiary, is not the imposition of a period of imprisonment. The Respondent is already serving the period of imprisonment. It is the place of imprisonment which is changed. It should not be assumed that incarceration is a greater form of punishment than a conditional sentence.

In the result, it was Crown counsel's position that s. 11 of the Charter has no application since it provides a right to the criminal standard and onus of proof only when a person is charged with a criminal offence and further, that an order under s. 742.6(9) of the *Criminal Code* cannot result in the imposition of a period of imprisonment.

For the respondent, it was argued that the procedure set out in s. 742.6 of the *Criminal Code* for the revocation of a conditional sentence constitutes, in effect, an offender "being charged with an offence" as that phrase is used in s. 11 of the Charter.

In his argument, counsel for the respondent referred to *R v. Wigglesworth* (1987), 60 CR (3d) 193, 37 CCC (3d) 385 (SCC), where Wilson J, for the majority in the Supreme Court of Canada, set out a two-part test to determine whether a matter constituted an offence pursuant to s. 11. At pp. 209-210 she said: "… a matter could fall within s. 11 either because by its very nature it is a criminal proceeding or because a conviction in respect of the offence may lead to a true penal consequence."

...

Although framed differently in the legislation, I have difficulty in seeing that the procedure to deal with alleged breaches of conditions of conditional sentence orders should be any different than the procedures to be applied with respect to breaches of probation, where the orders of probation in respect of same were made as part of a conditional discharge, an intermittent sentence, or a suspended sentence, or where a probation order was made along with a fine or a term of imprisonment. In each of these situations, the breach must be proved beyond a reasonable doubt just as any other criminal offence and there is no onus of any kind on the accused.

In my view, the magnitude of the options open to the court in s. 742.6(9)(c) and (d), is severe enough to warrant the protection granted by s. 11. The options include, not merely a change in the method of serving a sentence—the position argued by the Crown—but the committal of the offender to a corrections facility for all or part of the term remaining in the sentence imposed and the consequences following upon that term of imprisonment. In my view, the powers given to the judge subject the offender to "true penal consequences" and demand that the offender, following an allegation of a breach of condition, be given the full protection of s. 11(d) of the Charter which would require that the Court be satisfied beyond a reasonable doubt that a breach has occurred.

Having concluded that s. 742.6(9) is in breach of s. 11(d) of the Charter, I will not be dealing with whether it is also in breach of s. 11(h) of the Charter.

Does S. 742.6(9) Breach S. 7 of the Charter?

Section 7 of the Charter is as follows:

> 7. Everyone has the right to life, liberty and security of the person and the right not to be deprived thereof except in accordance with the principles of fundamental justice.

Clearly, inherent in the "principles of fundamental justice" is the right to be presumed innocent and only to be convicted of an offence upon proof beyond a reasonable doubt. As argued by counsel for the respondent, s. 7 defines the parameters of fundamental justice—life, liberty and security of the person—and these can only be taken away if the principles of fundamental justice are applied to the procedure which could result in any of these being taken away.

With respect to s. 7 of the Charter, the Crown repeats its position that in a s. 742.6 hearing application, no additional punishment can be imposed, and the duration of the restriction on the offender's liberty is not affected—there is no additional penalty. Crown counsel takes that argument further and says that an offender subjected to a s. 742.6 hearing faces no risk of imprisonment, since the offender is already serving the period of imprisonment that had been imposed earlier. Crown counsel, however, admits that *Cunningham v. Canada*, [1993] 2 SCR 143, 80 CCC (3d) 492, may be authority for concluding that the power of the court under s. 742.6(9)(c) and (d) to vary the place or form of imprisonment does affect the offender's liberty interests as protected by s. 7 of the Charter.

In *Cunningham*, the appellant had been serving a twelve-year term of imprisonment. Under the *Parole Act* in force at the time of his sentencing, he would be entitled to be released on mandatory supervision after serving approximately two-thirds of the sentence, provided he was of good behaviour. During his term of imprisonment, the *Parole Act* was amended to allow the Commissioner of Corrections, within six months of the "presumptive release date," to refer a case to the National Parole Board, where he has reason to believe that the inmate is likely, prior to the expiration of his sentence, to commit an offence causing death or serious harm, and the Parole Board could, if it saw fit, delay the inmate's release. The appellant was ordered to be detained until his sentence expired, subject to annual review. McLachlin J for the Court, in discussing whether the appellant had suffered a deprivation of liberty which would attract the protection of s. 7 of the Charter, said at p. 148: "In my view, the appellant has shown that he has been deprived of liberty. The argument that because the appellant was sentenced to 12 years' imprisonment there can be no further impeachment of his liberty interest within the 12-year period runs counter to previous pronouncements, and oversimplifies the concept of liberty." This and other courts have recognized that there are different types of liberty interests in the context of correctional law. In *Dumas v. Leclerc Institute*, [1986] 2 SCR 459, at p. 464, Lamer J (as he then was) identified three different deprivations of liberty: (1) The initial deprivation of liberty; (2) a substantial change in conditions amounting to a further deprivation of liberty; and (3) a continuation of the deprivation of liberty.

Later, on p. 150, McLachlin J continued: "… the manner in which he may serve a part of that sentence, the second liberty interest identified by Lamer J in *Dumas*, supra, has been affected. One has more liberty, or a better quality of liberty, when one is serving time on mandatory supervision than when one is serving time in prison."

McLachlin J concluded that the appellant by virtue of the change in the Parole Regulations had "suffered deprivation of liberty." At p. 151, she said: "The change in the manner in which the sentence was served in this case meets this test. There is a significant difference between life inside a prison versus the greater liberty enjoyed on the outside under mandatory supervision. Such a change was recognized as worthy of s. 7 protection in *Gamble* [[1988] 1 SCR 595]."

Although on the particular facts in *Cunningham*, the Court ruled that the appellant had not established that the changes to the *Parole Act* deprived him of his liberty contrary to the principles of fundamental justice, the case does make clear that a change in the way a sentence is to be served can attract s. 7 protection. This Court in *R v. Lambert* [93 CCC (3d) 88 at pp. 94–95] considered the implications of s. 743.6(1) of the *Criminal Code* which permits a judge to order that an accused serve one-half of his sentence before eligibility for parole. There, Crown counsel had argued that the making of an order under s. 741.2 was not part of the punishment or sentence imposed for the offence but was merely the fixing of the parole eligibility period. The Court stated:

[P]ostponing the eligibility date for full parole, thereby creating a veiled warning and risk of a longer period of incarceration, on any reasonable interpretation is an additional price or disadvantage for a prisoner. It is obviously an extra burden to be endured. Unquestionably, the section 741.2 order adversely affected the appellant. It is true that the four-year "sentence" remains the same, but the order giving rise to a potentially longer period of imprisonment, or at least to an extended span of strict supervision and control, means an escalation of the sanction or punishment for the offence. The variation in the "manner" in which the sentence is to be served clearly entails a more "severe treatment."

Lambert does not raise any Charter question because the order under s. 741.2 being considered was made by the sentencing judge when the sentence was imposed and he was empowered under s. 743.6(1) to make that order as part of the sentence. However, *Lambert* clearly recognizes the principle that the way in which a sentence is being served "might indicate an escalation of the sanction or punishment" and a more "severe treatment."

Here, as already noted, the respondent, on being ordered to serve his sentence conditionally, was only placed on the compulsory conditions set out in s. 742.3(1) of the *Criminal Code*.

...

I should add that no probation order was made to follow the period of the conditional sentence imposed on the offender.

Obviously, the trial judge in concluding that the conditional sentence was appropriate saw no need for any further conditions which might in any way fetter or restrict the liberty of the offender. That decision would have been made by the trial judge after a consideration of all the facts which would of course have been proved beyond a reasonable doubt.

Whether a Breach of Condition Hearing Is a Sentencing Hearing

In concluding that s. 742.6(9) breached s. 7 of the Charter, the trial judge said:

[T]he breach procedure is really a continuation of the original sentencing process and not a separate administrative procedure akin to a parole hearing. Consequently the application of a different burden of proof (balance of probabilities) and the imposition of an obligation on the accused to show reasonable excuse for the breach is not in keeping with the principles of fairness and fundamental justice. This finding is reinforced considering that the consequences to the accused can range from immediate termination of his conditional sentence to the changing of the optional conditions. The optional conditions can involve the addition of community service hours, attendance at treatment programs, or "any other reasonable conditions." It is difficult to conceive of the imposition of any of these consequences as not being an interference with the liberty of the accused. The accused serving a conditional sentence of imprisonment is more than just an extramural prisoner, he is outside the walls as a result of a judicial determination that service of his sentence can be achieved in all its aspects both denunciatory and rehabilitative without the necessity of incarcerating him. It stands to reason therefore that a change to this determination requires more than the application of a purely administrative function. I find therefore that s. 742.6(9) requirements relieving the prosecution of the burden of proof beyond a reasonable doubt and the imposition on the accused of the onus to show reasonable excuse does contravene s. 7 of the Charter.

Section 673 of the *Criminal Code* states that "sentence" includes an order made under s. 742.3. In my view, any change which may be made to a conditional sentence order, by way of: (1) a change in the optional conditions, (2) the suspension of the conditional sentence, which could direct the offender to serve in custody any part of the unexpired sentence, with or without changes to the conditions, or (3) by terminating the conditional sentence order and directing that the offender serve the balance of the sentence in custody, results in a change, and potentially, a very substantial change, in the sentence being served by the offender.

In *R v. Gardiner* (1982), 68 CCC (2d) 477 (SCC), Dickson J, in discussing the principles of sentencing, said at pp. 513-514: "One of the hardest tasks confronting a trial judge is sentencing. The stakes are high for society and for the individual. Sentencing is the critical stage of the criminal justice system, and it is manifest that the judge should not be denied an opportunity to obtain relevant information by the imposition of all the restrictive evidential rules common to a trial. Yet the obtaining and weighing of such evidence should be fair. A substantial liberty interest of the offender is involved and the information obtained should be accurate and reliable."

And later on p. 514:

To my mind, the facts which justify the sanction are no less important than the facts which justify the conviction; both should be subject to the same burden of proof. Crime and punishment are inextricably linked. "It would appear well established that the sentencing process is merely a phase of the trial process."

And later at p. 515:

In my view, both the informality of the sentencing procedure as to the admissibility of evidence and the wide discretion given to the trial judge in imposing sentence are factors militating in favour of the retention of the criminal standard of proof beyond a reasonable doubt at sentencing: "[B]ecause the sentencing process poses the ultimate jeopardy to an individual enmeshed in the criminal process, it is just and reasonable that he be granted the protection of the reasonable doubt rule at this vital juncture of the process." The rationale of the argument of the Crown for the acceptance of a lesser standard of proof is administrative efficiency. In my view, however, the administrative efficiency argument is not sufficient to overcome such a basic tenet suffusing our entire criminal justice system as the standard of proof beyond a reasonable doubt. I am by no means convinced that if the standard of proof were lowered, conservation of judicial resources would be enhanced ... . There would seem in principle no good reason why the sentencing judge in deciding disputed facts should not observe the same evidentiary standards as we demand of juries.

In my view, the same principles which governed the trial judge in considering the appropriate disposition of the matter following trial, should equally apply if any change is to be made in how the sentence is to be served. The alleged breach giving rise to the application by the Crown, whether that breach, in itself, would constitute a criminal offence, should be proved beyond a reasonable doubt as in any sentencing hearing such as this, in reality, is, albeit an extended one, but nevertheless contemplated by the legislation.

Clearly a sanction, by way of increased punishment, is being sought by the Crown and it follows, in my view, that the facts necessary to ground a change in the sentence must be proved beyond a reasonable doubt just as any facts which may be relied on by the Crown in the original sentencing hearing to support a particular sentence must be proved beyond a reasonable doubt.

Because, to use the words of Dickson J in *Gardiner,* "a substantial liberty interest of the offender is involved ... ," then any facts which may be relied on by the Crown to change the manner in which the sentence is being served, should be proved beyond a reasonable doubt.

Can S. 742.6(9) Be Saved by S. 1 of the Charter?

Section 1 of the Charter is as follows:

> 1. The *Canadian Charter of Rights and Freedoms* guarantees the rights and freedoms set out in it subject only to such reasonable limits prescribed by law as can be demonstrably justified in a free and democratic society.

In his decision, the trial judge reviewed the relevant law with respect to whether s. 742.6(9) could be saved by s. 1 of the Charter, including *R v. Laba* (1994), 34 CR (4th) 360, 94 CCC (3d) 385 (SCC), where Sopinka J set out the Oakes test (*R v. Oakes,* [1986] 1 SCR 103, 24 CCC (3d) 321) at p. 390:

> Taking into account the modification suggested by the Chief Justice in his reasons in *Dagenais v. Canadian Broadcasting Corp.* [34 CR (4th) 269 (SCC)], released concurrently herewith ... the test can be stated as follows: 1) In order to be sufficiently important to warrant overriding a constitutionally protected right or freedom the impugned provision must relate to concerns which are pressing and substantial in a free and democratic society; 2) The means chosen to achieve the legislative objective must pass a three-part proportionality test which requires that they (a) be rationally connected to the objective, (b) impair the right or freedom in question as little as possible and (c) have deleterious effects which are proportional to both their salubrious effects and the importance of the objective which has been identified as being of "sufficient importance."

The trial judge reviewed the impugned legislation in the light of that test and referred specifically to the second step in the inquiry as set out by Sopinka J at p. 392 of *Laba*:

> The second step in the inquiry into whether an impugned provision is a proportional means of achieving a given end is to determine whether the government has demonstrated that the provision impairs constitutionally protected rights or freedoms as little as possible. This usually involves determining whether alternative means of achieving the objective were available to Parliament.

The trial judge concluded that s. 742.6(9) is not saved by s. 1 of the Charter. He said:

In drafting s. 742.6(9), Parliament could have chosen to leave the burden of proof as beyond a reasonable doubt and not placed an onus on the accused to show reasonable excuse. In examining the mandatory conditions of a conditional sentence, reporting when required, remaining within the jurisdiction of the court and notifying the court of any change of address, these are clearly all matters which would seem to be easily proven in the event of a breach of any of them. Likewise, the optional conditions seem by and large the sort of allegations that would be easily proven. Consequently it is very difficult to see why there would be any logical reason to lessen the burden of proof or shift the onus to the accused. There is no obvious practical advantage in doing this and no apparent justification for the impairment of the right of the accused to the usual burden of proof in a criminal proceeding. In the case at bar, the situation is especially problematic in that what is alleged is a separate criminal offence that forms the basis for the alleged breach. In this case the accused is clearly at a severe disadvantage on the facts before me in that the Crown need only prove the allegation on a balance of probabilities and in so doing is relying on the largely uncorroborated allegation of a single witness. There is little the accused can do in the face of such a process when the threshold for the prosecution to meet is reduced to this level. The Crown has not demonstrated in this case that Parliament has chosen the alternative which impairs s. 7 as little as is reasonably possible.

I agree with the reasoning of the trial judge and in his conclusion that s. 742.6(9) contravenes s. 7 and is not saved by s. 1 of the Charter.

Conclusion

As to the disposition of the matter by the trial judge, the Crown argued that there was no basis for dismissing the Crown's application since the finding of unconstitutionality related only to the question of onus, and a consideration of the merits of the application, regardless of onus, was and is a separate issue. The Crown argued that the trial judge, having reached a decision on the constitutional issue, should still have considered the Crown's application to determine if a breach had been established and what order if any should issue. I do not deem it necessary to specifically deal with this matter in light of the decision of this Court that the matter be remitted to the Provincial Court for continuation of the hearing.

In my opinion, the trial judge was not in error in concluding that s. 742.6(9) of the *Criminal Code* contravenes s. 7 and is not saved by s. 1 of the *Canadian Charter of Rights and Freedoms*. I would dismiss the appeal.

Appeal allowed.

PROBLEMS

1. After a Sunday softball tournament, Bob Phelan stayed at the park with his team and a few cases of beer. Recognizing that he had a long drive home for dinner, he tried to be careful and stopped drinking after two cans of beer. He lost track of time and did not leave until just before dusk. While driving east on a quiet two-lane country road, he pulled out to pass a slower vehicle. The road at this point was approaching a hill and was

marked with a solid white line. Just before he reached the crest of the hill, a car driving west appeared in front of Phelan. The second car veered into the ditch but struck Phelan's car on the front driver's side and flipped over. The occupants were trapped inside the car for over an hour before being rescued.

The driver of the second car, Barbara Miller, was killed. Her children, who were in the back seat, were unharmed physically. A victim impact statement prepared by Miller's father revealed the following:

> The youngest child has suffered psychological harm since the collision, probably attribut-
> able to the experience of being trapped in the car. Both children miss their mother very
> much. They are experiencing difficulties sleeping and have been eating poorly. At school
> their behaviour has been disruptive. We all miss Barbara and the man who killed her should
> spend the rest of his life in prison.

Phelan suffered head injuries and was hospitalized for a week but seems to have recovered. At the hospital, a blood sample, which was not obtained by warrant, indicated a blood/alcohol level of 110 mg alcohol per 100 ml of blood. Phelan was charged with dangerous driving causing death and impaired driving causing death. Given the inadmissibility of the blood/alcohol reading, the latter charge was dismissed but he was convicted of dangerous driving causing death after a trial in the Provincial Division. The court found that the combination of his speed (likely 10–15 km/hr over the posted limit of 80 km/hr) and his failure to obey the solid white line constituted a marked and substantial departure from the actions of an ordinary, prudent driver.

Phelan is a 43-year-old electrician. He is married with two young children. He has a previous conviction for impaired driving in 1981. In 1983, he was convicted of speeding (20 km/hr over the limit). In 1988, he was convicted of assault after a workplace altercation and received a suspended sentence. He has been steadily employed since leaving high school.

The Crown submits that a two-year sentence is warranted by the facts of the offence, including the drinking. She argues that only the intervention of good fortune prevented more deaths. Defence counsel argues that a conditional sentence of two years less a day is appropriate. In her submission, the blood/alcohol reading cannot be considered. Given the fact that Phelan does not have a record for egregious driving, does not have a drinking problem, and thereby presents no danger to the community, she submits that his job and his family justify his serving the sentence in the community. Is a conditional sentence appropriate?

2. Smith and Jones were married in 1992. In February 1998, Jones told Smith that she had decided to leave the relationship. Although she planned to stay in the matrimonial home temporarily, Jones told Smith that she did not want to continue a sexual relationship. On April 15, 1998, Smith forced Jones into an act of sexual intercourse. Jones left the matrimonial home; Smith was charged with sexual assault. Smith subsequently persisted in his efforts to contact Jones, even though he had entered into an undertaking pursuant to s. 515(2) not to communicate with her. On one occasion, he met her on the street, and grabbed her by the shoulders and pushed her. These events were part of an

unsolicited and unwanted attempt at reconciliation and resulted in new criminal charges: two charges of breach of an undertaking, plus assault and criminal harassment. Smith pleaded guilty to all charges.

Smith has no previous record. Aside from these offences, he could be considered a person of good character. In the year prior to the end of his marriage, five close relatives had died, including his grandparents, who had raised him. He was under a great deal of stress and had no one close to him to discuss his personal problems. Smith had spent a month in pre-trial custody prior to his sentencing. A psychiatrist called by Smith testified that the period of pre-trial custody had impressed Smith with the seriousness of his conduct and its impact on Jones. The psychiatrist offered the opinion that Smith represented no danger to Jones or anyone else and proposed a treatment plan that, in his view, could be implemented in the community through regular sessions with him but that would not be available, at least through someone with his expertise, inside an institution.

Defence counsel agrees that these offences usually call for a term of imprisonment but argues for a conditional sentence of 18 months. Crown counsel agrees with the 18 months but argues that the sentence should be served in custody. How would you sentence Smith?

3. Brent Hudson began his teaching career in 1985 at Sir Sandford Fleming High School in Cobourg. He was 23 years old. He taught mathematics and physical education. He also coached various teams. He had been a sports star at university, a fact well known to all the boys, who admired him enormously. In December 1985, he took a hockey team to a four-day tournament at York University in Toronto over the Christmas holidays. Hudson and the team stayed at a university residence but he had his own room. One of the youngest players, Philip Lasky, injured his shoulder during a game. Lasky was 15 years old. That evening, Hudson asked to see him to consider whether he was well enough to play the next day. Hudson and Lasky talked for a while. Hudson wanted to examine the boy's shoulder and Lasky removed his shirt. The details of the next few hours are unclear. However, a few months later, at Hudson's invitation, the two began a sexual relationship that lasted for a number of months. It included touching, fondling, and masturbation. During this period, they would meet at least once per week. Hudson would ask Lasky to come to his office in the gym after everyone else had left and Lasky would stay until the early evening. Lasky's older brother was suspicious about Hudson and confronted him in late May 1986. As a result, Hudson stopped seeing Lasky.

In 1997, Lasky was a medical student at Queen's University but his life had started to deteriorate. He couldn't concentrate and paid little attention to how he looked or what he ate. He was a lonely and unhappy person. He took a leave from school and began seeing a psychiatrist. During a counselling session in 1997, he discussed his relationship with Hudson. His psychiatrist encouraged him to report the events to the Cobourg police. Hudson was subsequently charged with two counts of "sexual exploitation" contrary to s. 153(1) of the *Criminal Code*, one relating to the first encounter and the other to the extended relationship. The community of Cobourg had recently been shocked by a series of allegations of sexual assaults committed by a scout leader and a choir master. The Crown attorney elected to proceed against Hudson by indictment. Before the preliminary inquiry, Hudson pleaded guilty and the sentencing was adjourned to March 2000. Lasky prepared a victim impact statement. In it, he discussed his loneliness and unhappiness and attributed these to his inability to form a close relationship with anyone. He mistrusted people and blamed his mistrust on Hudson. The statement described an empty young life, filled with depression and loneliness, which Lasky attributed to the manner in which he was "used" by Hudson.

Until criminal charges were brought against him, Hudson had continued teaching in Cobourg and had risen to the position of vice-principal. He was a successful teacher and coach, and he had lived in a monogamous relationship for over 10 years. In a psychiatric report filed by his counsel, the psychiatrist found no evidence of pedophilia or other aberrant sexual predispositions. Hudson had never had another relationship with a student and spoke sadly and with regret and remorse about Lasky. The psychiatrist explained Hudson's conduct as "the unfortunate infatuation of an immature young man with a very handsome boy." The psychiatrist accepted that this was a single incident in Hudson's life. Although the Cobourg police investigated thoroughly, they found no evidence of any other crimes or improper relations between Hudson and other students. When the charges were laid, Hudson was suspended from his job and subsequently resigned.

Hudson and his partner, a dentist, have moved to Ottawa. He feels that he has no job prospects, given that his only experience is teaching and coaching young people. He has been working as a volunteer at the local food bank. On February 26, 2000, Lasky committed suicide. He left a note that said simply: "Brent, I'm sorry." Both counsel have a copy of the note.

Defence counsel is seeking a conditional sentence. What are the relevant factors in the case? What principles should you consider in dealing with the sentence?

Given that there are two counts, can you impose a sentence of imprisonment for one and a conditional sentence for the other? Can you impose two conditional sentences to be served consecutively?

4. Mary Blanchard is a 30-year-old aboriginal woman from a small northern Ontario community. She has been living in Thunder Bay for the past 10 years. On January 20, 2000, she was charged with two counts of trafficking, arising from the sale of small quantities of marijuana and cocaine to an undercover officer. On March 10, 2000, she entered guilty pleas to the two charges and the sentencing was adjourned until April 15 to allow for the preparation of a pre-sentence report.

The pre-sentence report indicates that Blanchard has a substantial record for property offences and drug possession. In 1997 and 1998, she was convicted of trafficking in small quantities of cocaine. She received short jail terms (30 and 60 days) for both offences. It is apparent that she has suffered from both alcohol and substance abuse for many years. During this time she has not been gainfully employed for any substantial period. On two occasions she entered a residential drug treatment program but both times left prematurely. She is a talented artist but has produced very little work since leaving her community in 1990.

Blanchard's counsel is seeking a conditional sentence. She has advised the court that a bed is waiting for Blanchard in a residential drug treatment centre. She has also submitted that Blanchard has been reunited with her family, who want her to return home after she has completed the treatment program. Her community, although poor, has organized an after-care schedule that involves a number of community volunteers who will be available to Blanchard on a daily basis to assist her in avoiding a relapse. They have also arranged for her to teach art part time at the local school.

The Crown has argued that trafficking requires a punitive response. Moreover, no hard evidence has been adduced about Blanchard's home community that would support reliance on s. 718.2(e).

Can the judge consider Blanchard's aboriginal background? Since most trafficking cases lead to incarceration, would a conditional sentence produce unjustifiable disparity? Can a conditional sentence be crafted that would meet the principles articulated in *Proulx* and *Wells*?

5. On January 15, 2000, Dave Rankin pleaded guilty in Windsor, Ontario to theft of $140,000 from his employer. His counsel adduced evidence that Rankin was severely depressed by his spouse's illness and, in compensation, developed a gambling addiction. As a result, he lost his savings and resorted to an ill-conceived theft from his employer, a trust company. The judge sentenced Rankin to 20 months' imprisonment to be served, pursuant to s. 742.1, in the community. Aside from the mandatory conditions, Rankin was ordered to continue with treatment for his gambling addiction and to refrain entirely from gambling or entering a casino or race track.

On April 2, 2000, Rankin was charged with "over 80" after being stopped in a holiday roadside check in London, Ontario. After consulting with his lawyer, he had agreed to a breathalyzer test and blew 130 mg alcohol/100 ml of blood. He appeared in court on April 20 and a trial date was set for August 12, 2000. In the meantime, his conditional sentence supervisor learned about this new charge on April 19 and commenced a breach application under s. 742.6 on the basis that Rankin had "failed to keep the peace and be of good behaviour as evidenced by the commission of a new offence"—namely, "impaired driving/over 80." As a result, a warrant was issued for Rankin's arrest on April 21. On May 2, 2000, he was arrested in Windsor at his home and subsequently released by the officer in charge pursuant to s. 742.6(1)(e) on a promise to appear in court on May 20 to answer the breach allegation.

Assume that Rankin appears in your court on May 20 without counsel and asks for time to retain one.

- If he has no counsel, can the matter be adjourned to June 15, even though this is more than 30 days from the date of his arrest?
- Can the court proceed to entertain the breach allegation on June 15, given that it is based on a criminal charge for which he has not been found guilty or pleaded guilty to the new charge?
- What happens to the conditional sentence pending the determination of the breach?
- At the hearing of the breach allegation, can the Crown make its case without *viva voce* evidence by filing the allegation, complete with the supervisor's report and any written statements in support plus proof of notice upon the offender?
- Assume that you ultimately hear the breach allegation on September 5, 2000. Does it matter whether Rankin was convicted or acquitted on the impaired charge?

- If you decide that the breach has been made out, what remedy under s. 742.6(9) is appropriate?
- If you are considering some time in custody short of termination, what effect will this have on the conditional sentence?
- If you are concerned about the duration of the sanction, can you give any credit for the time between the breach allegation and the breach finding?

CHAPTER THIRTEEN

Prohibitions

Various provisions in the *Criminal Code*, RSC 1985, c. C-46, as amended, either permit or require the imposition of a specific prohibition as part of a sentence. In each case, care should be taken to ensure that the applicable statutory requirements are met before a prohibition is sought or imposed. It is essential to distinguish between those situations where a prohibition *may* be imposed at the discretion of the court and those situations where the prohibition *must* be imposed. Even in the latter category, as some of the cases below demonstrate, there may be room to argue for an exemption.

I. DRIVING

The most common prohibition is found in s. 259(1) of the Code, which requires an order prohibiting the offender from operating a motor vehicle if he or she is convicted of impaired driving or driving "over 80" (with a blood alcohol level over 80 mg):

(a) for a first offence, for not more than three years and not less than three months;

(b) for a second offence, for not more than three years and not less than six months;

(c) for each subsequent offence, during a period of not more than three years and not less than one year.

As well, provincial and territorial legislation provides for a contemporaneous licence suspension for a longer period that varies across jurisdictions. Section 259(2) of the Code permits, at the discretion of the court, a driving prohibition following a conviction under s. 220, 221, 236, 249, 250, 251, 252, 255(2), 255(3), or 259 for periods that depend on the maximum sentence to which the underlying offence subjects the offender. Section 259(4) creates the offence of driving while disqualified.

II. FIREARMS PROHIBITIONS

The following provisions form part of a comprehensive reform of firearms legislation enacted by SC 1995, c. 39, s. 139, which replaced part III of the *Criminal Code* in its entirety. It contains a restructured mandatory prohibition (s. 109) and a discretionary prohibition (s. 110). The mandatory prohibition is broader in its application than were its predecessors. Beyond offences involving violence, it now applies to a number of weapons offences and to offences under ss. 6 and 7 of the *Controlled Drugs and Substances Act*, SC 1996, c. 19.

Criminal Code, Sections 109-110

109(1) Where a person is convicted, or discharged under section 730, of

(a) an indictable offence in the commission of which violence against a person was used, threatened or attempted and for which the person may be sentenced to imprisonment for ten years or more,

(b) an offence under subsection 85(1) (using firearm in commission of offence), subsection 85(2) (using imitation firearm in commission of offence), 95(1) (possession of prohibited or restricted firearm with ammunition), 99(1) (weapons trafficking), 100(1) (possession for purpose of weapons trafficking), 102(1) (making automatic firearm), 103(1) (importing or exporting knowing it is unauthorized) or section 264 (criminal harassment),

(c) an offence relating to the contravention of subsection 6(1) or (2) or 7(1) or (2) of the *Controlled Drugs and Substances Act*, or

(d) an offence that involves, or the subject-matter of which is, a firearm, a cross-bow, a prohibited weapon, a restricted weapon, a prohibited device, any ammunition, any prohibited ammunition or an explosive substance and, at the time of the offence, the person was prohibited by any order made under this Act or any other Act of Parliament from possessing any such thing,

the court that sentences the person or directs that the person be discharged, as the case may be, shall, in addition to any other punishment that may be imposed for that offence or any other condition prescribed in the order of discharge, make an order prohibiting the person from possessing any firearm, cross-bow, prohibited weapon, restricted weapon, prohibited device, ammunition, prohibited ammunition and explosive substance during the period specified in the order as determined in accordance with subsection (2) or (3), as the case may be.

(2) An order made under subsection (1) shall, in the case of a first conviction for or discharge from the offence to which the order relates, prohibit the person from possessing

(a) any firearm, other than a prohibited firearm or restricted firearm, and any cross-bow, restricted weapon, ammunition and explosive substance during the period that

(i) begins on the day on which the order is made, and

(ii) ends not earlier than ten years after the person's release from imprisonment after conviction for the offence or, if the person is not then imprisoned or subject to imprisonment, after the person's conviction for or discharge from the offence; and

(b) any prohibited firearm, restricted firearm, prohibited weapon, prohibited device and prohibited ammunition for life.

(3) An order made under subsection (1) shall, in any case other than a case described in subsection (2), prohibit the person from possessing any firearm, cross-bow, restricted weapon, ammunition and explosive substance for life.

(4) In subparagraph (2)(a)(ii), "release from imprisonment" means release from confinement by reason of expiration of sentence, commencement of statutory release or grant of parole.

(5) Sections 113 to 117 apply in respect of every order made under subsection (1).

110(1) Where a person is convicted, or discharged under section 730, of

(a) an offence, other than an offence referred to in any of paragraphs 109(1)(a), (b) and (c), in the commission of which violence against a person was used, threatened or attempted, or

(b) an offence that involves, or the subject-matter of which is, a firearm, a cross-bow, a prohibited weapon, a restricted weapon, a prohibited device, ammunition, prohibited ammunition or an explosive substance and, at the time of the offence, the person was not prohibited by any order made under this Act or any other Act of Parliament from possessing any such thing,

the court that sentences the person or directs that the person be discharged, as the case may be, shall, in addition to any other punishment that may be imposed for that offence or any other condition prescribed in the order of discharge, consider whether it is desirable, in the interests of the safety of the person or of any other person, to make an order prohibiting the person from possessing any firearm, cross-bow, prohibited weapon, restricted weapon, prohibited device, ammunition, prohibited ammunition or explosive substance, or all such things, and where the court decides that it is so desirable, the court shall so order.

(2) An order made under subsection (1) against a person begins on the day on which the order is made and ends not later than ten years after the person's release from imprisonment after conviction for the offence to which the order relates or, if the person is not then imprisoned or subject to imprisonment, after the person's conviction for or discharge from the offence.

(3) Where the court does not make an order under subsection (1), or where the court does make such an order but does not prohibit the possession of everything referred to in that subsection, the court shall include in the record a statement of the court's reasons for not doing so.

(4) In subsection (2), "release from imprisonment" means release from confinement by reason of expiration of sentence, commencement of statutory release or grant of parole.

(5) Sections 113 to 117 apply in respect of every order made under subsection (1).

The following cases deal with different forms of the firearms prohibition. While you should pay attention to the changes in statutory wording over the years, they address a number of technical and conceptual issues that relate to the mandatory prohibition. This provision applies in respect of any indictable offence in which violence was used, threatened, or attempted, and that makes the offender liable to imprisonment of 10 years or more.

R v. Keays

(1983), 10 CCC (3d) 229 (Ont. CA)

DUBIN JA: This appeal brought by the Crown raises issues with respect to the interpretation of s. 98(1) of the *Criminal Code*, which provides as follows:

98(2) Where a person is convicted of an indictable offence in the commission of which violence against a person is used, threatened or attempted and for which the offender may be sentenced to imprisonment for ten years or more or of an offence under section 83, the court shall, in addition to any other punishment that may be imposed for that offence, make an order prohibiting him from having in his possession any firearm or any ammunition or explosive substance for any period of time specified in the order that commences on the day the order is made and expires not earlier than

    (a) in the case of a first conviction for such an offence, five years, and

    (b) in any other case, ten years,

after the time of his release from imprisonment after conviction for the offence.

In this case the accused was convicted of possession of a weapon for a purpose dangerous to the public peace, and the evidence disclosed that during the commission of that offence, an act of violence occurred.

Following his conviction, the Crown introduced into evidence the criminal record of the respondent, which disclosed two prior convictions for robbery while armed. Both those convictions preceded the date of the proclamation of s. 98(1) of the *Criminal Code*.

The learned trial judge held that since the convictions for robbery while armed preceded the effective date of s. 98(1), they were irrelevant and thus treated the conviction for possession of a weapon for a purpose dangerous to the public peace as a first conviction and limited the prohibition period to that of five years.

In this respect we think that he erred. In our view, it is not a case of a first conviction under s. 98(1) if a person convicted for an offence described in s. 98(1) has been previously convicted of such an offence even though such an offence had been committed prior to the proclamation of s. 98(1) into law. To interpret the section in this manner is not giving it a retrospective effect. Retrospectivity does not occur by merely bringing into play facts which have preceded the enactment.

               ...

In responding to the appeal, counsel for the respondent supported the judgment on two alternative grounds. He first argued that s. 98(1) is only applicable if the offence for which the accused had been convicted is an offence for which a person could not be convicted without committing an act of violence. Obviously, a person who is convicted of the offence of possession of a weapon for a purpose dangerous to the public peace could do so without committing an act of violence or threatening violence. However, in this case the evidence clearly disclosed that an act of violence was committed. In our view, once it is shown that a person has been convicted of an indictable offence in the commission of which violence against the person is used, threatened or attempted and for which the offender may be sentenced to imprisonment for 10 years or more, s. 98(1) becomes applicable, notwithstanding that the offence for which the accused has been convicted could have been committed without violence. That matter has been fully resolved by the judgment of this court in *R v. Broome* (1981), 63 CCC (2d) 426, 24 CR (3d) 254, and on that ground also the respondent fails.

However, a further point was made by counsel for the respondent which was not canvassed before the trial judge in light of the ground relied on by him in disposing of this matter. As has been noted, the Crown adduced evidence that the respondent in this case had been previously convicted on two occasions for robbery while armed. If those armed robberies were accompanied by violence, then the order under s. 98(1) must be one for not less than 10 years. But to constitute a second offence under s. 98(1) the person must have been previously convicted of an indictable offence in the commission of which violence against the person was used, threatened or attempted and for which the offender could have been sentenced to imprisonment for 10 years or more. But, by definition, a person could commit robbery while armed without an act of violence. Section 302(d) provides:

> 302. Every one commits robbery who ...
>
> (d) steals from any person while armed with an offence weapon or imitation thereof.

Thus mere proof of a conviction for robbery while armed does not constitute proof that an act of violence was actually committed during the commission of the offence.

Since this matter was not canvassed before the learned trial judge, we think the Crown should be given the opportunity to prove whether, during the course of the commission of the two armed robberies upon which the Crown relies, the accused had committed any acts of violence.

In the result therefore, the appeal will be allowed, the order under appeal set aside and the matter remitted to the trial judge to afford the Crown the opportunity of adducing evidence with respect to the two prior convictions.

Appeal allowed.

R v. Avery
(1986), 30 CCC (3d) 16 (NWT CA)

HARRADENCE JA (dissenting)—The respondent Frederick Allen Avery was convicted of an offence under s. 85 of the *Criminal Code*. Following this conviction, a firearms prohibition order was entered against Mr. Avery on June 18, 1985. The order prohibited the respondent from possessing firearms, ammunition or explosive substances for a period of five years.

On August 13, 1985, the respondent was charged with violating the firearms prohibition order, contrary to s. 98(12) of the *Criminal Code*, when in an apparent attempt to comply with the order, Mr. Avery sold a rifle to one Mr. Bourque. The rifle was impounded and the respondent charged.

The trial judge dismissed the charge on the ground that the firearms prohibition order, made pursuant to s. 98(1) of the *Criminal Code*, was defective in that it did not contain the mandatory provision required by s. 98(13) specifying a reasonable period of time within which the respondent could dispose of firearms already in his possession. The Crown appeals.

· · ·

I deal first with the argument that a prosecution under s-s. (12) may be supported where the order fails to comply with s-s. (13). Such an interpretation is to construe the word "shall" as other than imperative.

Further, this construction continues to expose the person against whom the order is made to criminal prosecution, not because of wrongdoing on his part but because he has been denied the benefit of the protection Parliament has mandated he shall have. He has been denied this protection through no fault of his own but because the court failed to give effect to the mandatory provisos of s-s. (13) of the *Criminal Code* of Canada.

· · ·

I am therefore of opinion that if the period required by s-s. (13) is not contained in the order, then the legal mechanism by which s-s. (12) can be brought to bear is not in place and the section is not available to create an offence for breach of the prohibition. This in no way detracts from the validity of the order and the prohibition it contains is in full force and effect. An offence for its breach is created by another section of the *Criminal Code*. I have in mind s. 88 of the *Criminal Code* of Canada. However, a prosecution under that section would enjoy little chance of success if a firearm was in lawful possession prior to the making of the order and a reasonable time for its disposition had not expired at the time the charge was laid. The protection contained in s-s. (13) against the mischief created in the previous enactment would not be contravened.

· · ·

There is one final point to illustrate the important nexus of the reasonable disposal period in s. 98(13) to the *actus reus* in s. 98(12). The prosecution must not only prove the wrongful deed; it is legally incumbent upon the Crown at some point in the proceedings and whether or not by a primary or secondary burden of proof, to show that the crime was committed without a legal excuse. By the addition of s. 98(13), and limited to the facts of *Avery*, Parliament has pre-empted this Crown argument. This proposition is consistent with the genesis of this unique *actus reus*. As Glanville Williams explains (ibid., p. 19):

> A further step must now be taken. *Actus reus* includes, in the terminology here suggested, *not merely the whole objective situation that has to be proved by the prosecution, but also the absence of any ground of justification or excuse*, whether such justification or excuse be stated in any statute creating the crime or implied by the courts in accordance with general principles.

(Emphasis added.)

As the accused could not through his conduct have committed the wrong physical act which Parliament contemplated, dismissal of the charge under s. 98(12) was proper and the appeal will be dismissed.

KERANS JA: This is a Crown appeal from an acquittal on a charge, under s. 98(12) of the *Criminal Code*, of possession of a weapon in violation of an earlier judge's order prohibiting possession as a consequence of a conviction for violent crime.

The fact was not denied that the accused was in possession of a gun in contravention of the terms of a prohibition order made March 20, 1985, and entered June 18, 1985, pursuant to s. 98. The earlier order (which by happenstance had been made by him) was "defective." This was correct in the sense that he had failed to make any order under s. 98(13) nor indeed to address his mind to the issue posed by that subsection, which provides:

> 98(13) An order made pursuant to subsection (1), (2), (6) or (7) shall specify therein a reasonable period of time within which the person against whom the order is made may surrender to a police officer or firearm officer or otherwise lawfully dispose of any firearm or any ammunition or explosive substance lawfully possessed by him prior to the making of the order, and subsection (12) does not apply to him during such period of time.

This provision is not without relevance in this case because the offence occurred within four months after the order and came to light because the accused was trying to sell his gun in an apparent attempt to rid himself of it in rough compliance with the prohibition. The learned trial judge, admirably aware of his own earlier failing, perceived that he had unfairly exposed the accused to this charge.

· · ·

In this case the accused could have, and did not, seek relief from the original error by appeal if not writ. In the fact of his having failed to do so, he must obey the order which he chose to let stand. When he argues now that he should not be convicted for the breach of it because it is bad, he is saying he did not have to obey it. A collateral attack is nothing less than a request for an affirmation of defiance.

The reason for the rule is that the law must encourage respect for due process by itself respecting it. It is a rule of practical necessity. For example, in *R v. Adams* (1978), 45 CCC (2d) 459, 6 CR (3d) 257, [1979] 2 WWR 108 (BC CA), an accused appealed a conviction for escape from lawful custody on the ground that his original detention was illegal. Craig JA observes at p. 469:

> [i]f a trial Judge permitted an accused to go behind a warrant of committal … the judge would be holding, in effect, that the jailer had no right to detain the accused, yet the jailer would have to detain the accused because the warrant was still subsisting.

Worse, can a jailer refuse to detain because he thinks the committal bad, and wait until he is charged before demonstrating it is bad? The rule is designed to avoid an invitation to anarchy.

The great difficulty with the rule is that it can work a harsh result on an unsophisticated accused who, like the accused before us, fails to appreciate the need to make a direct attack on a bad order. His relative lack of blameworthiness cannot avoid favourable contrast, in cases of this sort, with errors by judicial officers, as often as not compounded by other errors by governmental officials. The accused's situation in such a case obviously stirs sympathy. Very often, I suspect, the Crown does not proceed with charges *ex debito justitiae*. Sometimes, as here, the Crown is less sympathetic than are the courts. Unfortunately, perhaps, the Crown discretion is not directly reviewable. Fortunately, the power to grant a discharge permits Canadian courts in most cases to offer relief where the blameworthiness of the accused is minimal: see *R v. Campbell and Mlynarchuk* (1972), 10 CCC (2d) 26, 21 CRNS 273, [1973] 2 WWR 246.

· · ·

I would allow the appeal and declare the accused guilty of a breach of the order which he indubitably breached. In the circumstances, however, I would invoke s. 662.1(1) and grant him an absolute discharge.

Appeal allowed.

NOTE

The following cases consider not only prohibitions but also a controversial remedy known as a constitutional exemption. You will see that in some cases courts have held that the effect of a sanction that is otherwise valid constitutionally might be so disproportionate in the circumstances of the particular offender that it supports a claim under s. 12 of *Canadian Charter of Rights and Freedoms*, part I of the *Constitution Act, 1982*, RSC 1985, app. II, no. 44. As a result, some courts have upheld the statutory provision but granted an exemption to the offender. Other courts have held either that the provision is valid and should be applied or that the provision should be struck down, without allowing for an intermediate remedy such as the constitutional exemption. In addition to these cases, see the opinion in *Latimer* in Chapter 14, Sentencing for Murder.

R v. Kelly
(1990), 59 CCC (3d) 497 (Ont. CA)

[Note that two of the three appellants in this case were police officers who were convicted of assault causing bodily harm arising from an incident when they were off duty.]

FINLAYSON JA:

...

Sentence

The Crown sought a custodial term for Patrick Kelly but we did not call on counsel for this respondent in the sentence appeal on this issue. A custodial term was merited for all three respondents, but we can think of no reason for singling out Patrick Kelly on appeal. In our opinion there is very little to distinguish the conduct of one respondent on the sentence appeal from that of the others.

The principal argument on sentence related to the request by the Crown that this court implement the provisions of s. 100(1) [formerly s. 98(1)] of the Code and order a firearm prohibition of five years. The relevant provisions are as follows:

> 100(1) Where an offender is convicted ... of an indictable offence in the commission of which violence against a person is used, threatened or attempted and for which the offender may be sentenced to imprisonment for ten years or more ... the court that sentences the offender shall, in addition to any other punishment that may be imposed for that offence, make an order prohibiting the offender from having in his possession any firearm or any ammunition or explosive substance for any period of time specified in the order that commences on the day the order is made and expires not earlier than
>> (a) in the case of a first conviction for such an offence, five years, and
>> (b) in any other case, ten years,
> after the time of the offender's release from imprisonment after conviction for the offence or, if the offender is not then imprisoned or subject to imprisonment, after the time of the offender's conviction ... for that offence.

There was no discussion at trial regarding the application of this section. Counsel for the Crown submits that the application of the section is mandatory in the circumstances of these convictions and that this court has no discretion but to impose the prohibition requested.

Counsel for the respondents on the sentence appeal conceded that the section is applicable but they requested a "constitutional exemption" for the Kellys, citing two justifications:

(a) while this was a crime of violence, no firearms were used in the commission of it;

(b) the two Kellys are police officers and the prohibition would effectively prevent them from carrying out their duties as police officers and in all probability lead to their discharge from the force.

It was submitted that the effect of a mandatory order would be offensive and unfair as compared to the effect the prohibition would have on other individuals and would amount to cruel and unusual treatment or punishment in their cases contrary to s. 12 of the *Canadian Charter of Rights and Freedoms*.

Despite the fact that the thrust of argument by counsel on behalf of the two Kellys was not directed to having s. 100(1) ruled unconstitutional *per se*, I think it is necessary to look at some of the decided cases on this issue in order to put their request for a constitutional exemption in perspective. The leading case is *R v. Smith* (1987), 34 CCC (3d) 97, 40 DLR (4th) 435, [1987] 1 SCR 1045. The court was dealing here with s. 5(2) of the *Narcotic Control Act*, RSC 1970, c. N-1, which provided for imprisonment for life "but not less than seven years" for any person guilty of importing into Canada or exporting from Canada any narcotic. ...

In addressing the constitutionality of s. 100 of the Code with reference to s. 12 of the Charter, the first thing that should be said is that the prohibition is not unusual. Similar legislation has been enacted in the United States of America, the United Kingdom and in Australia. (See Title VII of the *Omnibus Crime Control and Safe Streets Act*, 1968 18 USC App., s. 1202(a)(1) as amended (US); Title IV of the *Gun Control Act*, 1968, 18 USC, s-s. 992(g) and (h) as amended (US); *Firearms Act*, 1968 (UK) c. 27, s. 21 (Great Britain); *Firearms and Dangerous Weapons Act*, 1973 (NSW), No. 38 (Australia).) As to its being cruel, it can hardly be said that depriving a person of the right to possess a firearm is cruel in itself.

In any event, whether a sentence violates s. 12 does not depend on its individually meeting the tests of cruelty and unusualness. Rather, the true test is whether the sentence is grossly disproportionate to the offence in question. In the present case, far from being grossly disproportionate, the prohibition appears totally appropriate when one considers that it applies only to a person convicted of an indictable offence punishable by imprisonment for ten years or more; and only if during the commission of the offence violence was used, threatened or attempted; and even then, only if the violence was directed towards another person. In the final analysis, all that can be said against the prohibition is that it might constitute cruel and unusual treatment or punishment in the individual case where its practical effect is to preclude persons, like the Kellys in this appeal, from earning their present livelihood in its present form. ...

I have no difficulty in finding that s. 100 does not offend s. 12 of the Charter. As indicated earlier, this was not the central proposition put to us by counsel for the Kellys. It was submitted, rather, that in order to give constitutional validity to s. 100(1), one must look at the facts in each individual case. The Kellys submitted that the section is constitutionally overinclusive and the court could strike it down on that account. This echoes the language of Lamer J that the net is cast too wide. On the other hand, it was submitted, the court can read this section down selectively. Counsel for the Kellys picked up on the language of Lamer J that we must look at the effect the punishment may have upon the recipient and that in imposing a sentence, the judge will assess the circumstances of the individual case. Put another way, while the prohibition cannot be said to be cruel and unusual *per se*, the failure to provide for an adjudicative remedy in certain cases can result in the violation of an individual's Charter rights. Therefore, it was submitted, people for whom the prohibition constitutes cruel and unusual punishment or treatment should be able to ask for and receive a constitutional exemption.

With respect, while these submissions have an initial appeal, I think that they cannot withstand closer scrutiny. As Lamer J has pointed out, we should not confuse the result with the means used to achieve that result. If the complaint relates to arbitrariness or lack of due process, then the reference points should be ss. 9 and 7 of the Charter. Counsel expressly disavowed reliance upon any section of the Charter other than s. 12.

The real complaint in this case is that the penalty does not fall with equal severity on all to whom it applies. The case on appeal is as good an example as one can find. To Payne, a former policeman, the prohibition at most might be an inconvenience. To the Kellys, it may well cost them their jobs. However, there is nothing unusual about this. A conviction for impaired driving may be inconsequential to an irresponsible teenager, it may mean loss of employment to a truck driver or it may be fatal to the career of a person in public office.

As counsel for the Crown has pointed out, the prohibition we are dealing with is narrowly focused. It is directed against persons who have committed violent crimes against the person and are in consequence the very persons who should not be in possession of instruments of violence. Under the circumstances a request for a constitutional exemption is somewhat paradoxical. The only persons who would request it are those who have firearms and want to keep them. To exclude them from the prohibition would denude s. 100(1) of any utility because it would exempt from its operation the very persons who pose the greatest risk to society.

Section 100(1) is not an example of casting too wide a net. The example that Lamer J gave in *Smith*, where he contrasted the situation of an international drug dealer with that of a naive student carrying a single marijuana cigarette, both subject to a minimum seven year sentence, has no application here. There is no example that one can give under s. 100(1) where the result would be more than merely excessive and become grossly disproportionate to the offence committed. In the case of the Kellys, they may well lose their employment because of the convictions alone. If they surmount that hurdle, they may be permitted to assume other duties to accommodate the prohibition. In any event, it cannot be said that a mandatory prohibition directed towards a person convicted of a crime is unconstitutional because it precludes continued employment in a particular trade or calling.

I have considerable difficulty in contemplating a situation where it would be appropriate to grant constitutional exemptions to minimum sentences or mandatory penalties. It is to be noted that in *Smith*, where the example of the student being lumped in with the drug dealer brought home so vividly the inequality of treatment encompassed by s. 5(2) of the *Narcotic Control Act*, the use of constitutional exemptions was not considered to be the remedy. The entire section was struck down.

...

Accordingly, I would allow the Crown leave to appeal against sentence and allow the appeal in part by ordering that all three respondents on the sentence appeal be prohibited from having in their individual possessions any firearms or any ammunition or explosive substances for a period of five years from the date of their conviction. As earlier stated, the appeals against conviction are dismissed.

Appeal allowed.

R v. Netser
(1992), 70 CCC (3d) 477 (NWT CA)

McLUNG JA (orally): I will give my judgment, concurred in by Major JA. Côté JA has reasons he will deliver in dissent.

We think that the preponderance of current Canadian appellate authority does support the principle that there may be a constitutional exemption from the prohibition orders found in s. 100(1) of the *Criminal Code*. That is, in proper cases. We regard earlier opinions to the contrary, including what I said in *R v. Tobac* (1985), 20 CCC (3d) 49, [1986] 1 CNLR 138, 15 CRR 356 (NWTC), to have been overtaken by later authorities touching s. 12 of the *Canadian Charter of Rights and Freedoms*. They include *R v. Chief* (1989), 51 CCC (3d) 265, 74 CR (3d) 57, [1990] 1 CNLR 92 (YT CA), and *R v. McGillivray* (1991), 62 CCC (3d) 407, [1991] 3 CNLR 113, 89 Sask. R 289 (CA). On the other hand, Ontario has affirmed the comprehensive application of s. 100(1): *R v. Kelly* (1990), 59 CCC (3d) 497, 80 CR (3d) 185, 4 CRR (2d) 157 (Ont. CA).

What is cruel and unusual punishment depends on several factors, including whether the sentencing treatment, here the mandatory order, was grossly disproportionate to the offence. We take that to mean that the court is free to examine the particulars of the underlying offence as well as its statutory definition and maximum penalty. The sentencing consequences must be shocking and in thorough conflict with accepted standards of decency.

We will not review the significant impact of the weapons prohibition on the appellant's safety, daily life and livelihood. What is of additional concern to us is that he has never, apparently, abused firearms or weapons in the past. His offence is unrelated to firearms. It was a sexual assault, the assault being the striking of the victim on her elbow with the telephone she was attempting to use to call the police and kicking her in the head and pushing her around the room. Without minimizing it, the assault was quite divorced from the use or misuse of a firearm or explosives. The weapon sanction was supplied solely by the statute but is unrelated to the offence or the offender and, seemingly, the objects of the arms prohibition legislation itself. Here, it is unfair, beyond mere severity or excessiveness and because of its disproportionality cannot be saved by s. 1 of the Charter (*R v. Chief*, supra).

We think we are entitled to relieve against a full prohibition and, on the undisputed facts here, should do so. What we have in mind is a conditional prohibition of the type crafted by the Saskatchewan Court of Appeal in *McGillivray*. Hence we allow the appeal, vary the sentence and impose the following prohibition, in the place and stead of that imposed at trial (which we declare inoperative):

> Joe Netser shall forthwith deliver all firearms owned or possessed by him to the NCO in charge of the RCMP Detachment at Coral Harbour, NWT, or his designate, and thereafter is not to possess any firearm at any time except as specifically permitted in writing by the said officer who shall temporarily release the firearms as needed by the appellant for the sole purpose of guiding, hunting, trapping or the provision of food.

The conditional prohibition will operate for a period of five years from the date of conviction.

In this limited sense the appeal is allowed and the sentence varied.

CÔTÉ JA (dissenting) (orally): Given the view of the facts which I am about to express, it is not necessary for me to decide whether constitutional exemptions from firearms prohibitions can or do exist. I will simply assume for the sake of argument that they do.

Whether such an exemption is merited in this case is largely a question of fact, as the appellant concedes. As I understand the issues here, they involve the weight to be given to the facts. The decision appealed from was by a Territorial Court judge sitting (on two occasions) in Coral Harbour, NWT. The appellant stresses the distinctive nature of that community, and indeed asks us to take judicial notice of the polar bear situation there. All those considerations make me unwilling to assign different weights to the facts. But if I had to reweigh the facts, I would not assign to them any weight drastically different from the weight given by the sentencing judge.

In my view, the case for constitutional exemptions from firearms prohibitions rests on the suggestion that taking away a person's livelihood, or seriously endangering his life, is a drastic punishment and hence cruel and unusual. I cannot say that the facts here even approach that state. I do not view a lack of connection between the precise facts of the individual crime, or previous record, and the prohibition, as being the test. Parliament has enacted an automatic prohibition in a wide set of cases. More mildness of the crime would not be sufficient for a constitutional exemption, in my respectful view. Nor do I see the sexual assault here as being mild, though it could have been far worse.

I would have dismissed the appeal.

Appeal allowed.

III. OTHER PROHIBITION ORDERS: CRIMINAL CODE, SECTIONS 161 AND 446(5)

Two other noteworthy prohibitions may be imposed as part of a sentence. Section 161 of the Code allows a judge to include within the terms of a sentence for various sexual offences an order that prohibits the offender from being in public places where children under the age of 14 are present. The judge may also order the offender not to obtain any paid or voluntary position involving a position of trust or authority with children. Section 446(5) of the Code allows the judge to prohibit a person convicted of cruelty to animals from owning or having custody of animals for not more than two years. There are few reported cases concerning these prohibitions.

Is there any basis on which it might be argued that the orders permitted under s. 161 or 446(5) are constitutionally invalid in whole or in part?

CHAPTER FOURTEEN

Sentencing for Murder

I. INTRODUCTION

For the purposes of sentencing, murder is treated differently from all other offences under the *Criminal Code*, RSC 1985, c. C-46, as amended. On a conviction for murder (first or second degree), the sentencing judge has no discretion; the offender must be sentenced to life imprisonment. With first-degree murder, the offender must serve 25 years' imprisonment before he or she becomes eligible for parole. There is more flexibility with second-degree murder. The trial judge may set the offender's parole ineligibility between 10 and 25 years. Because of this mandated severity, many murder trials are effectively about whether the offence was murder (with the mandatory sentencing regime) or manslaughter (with a maximum sentence of life imprisonment, with no minimal parole period). As discussed later in this chapter, the constitutionality of the sentencing provisions for murder have been challenged because the lack of flexibility can sometimes lead to an injustice.

The sentencing scheme for murder is also unique because of its inclusion of jury input. As set out in ss. 745 and 746 of the *Criminal Code*, on a conviction for second-degree murder, the trial judge must seek a recommendation from the jury on the appropriate length of parole ineligibility. Moreover, after an offender has served 15 years of his or her sentence for either first- or second-degree murder (if the ineligibility period was set at more than 15 years), he or she may bring an application under s. 746 of the Code to have the period of ineligibility shortened or terminated. This provision, known colloquially as the "faint hope clause," has proven very controversial in recent years.

In the next part, we set out the *Criminal Code* provisions that are relevant to sentencing individuals convicted of murder. However, before examining this specialized sentencing regime in more detail, consider the materials under section III, "Murder in Canada: Empirical and Constitutional Considerations," which attempt to place these provisions in context.

II. CRIMINAL CODE, SECTIONS 745-745.5

Sentence of Life Imprisonment

745. Subject to section 745.1, the sentence to be pronounced against a person who is to be sentenced to imprisonment for life shall be

(a) in respect of a person who has been convicted of high treason or first degree murder, that he be sentenced to imprisonment for life without eligibility for parole until the person has served twenty-five years of the sentence;

(b) in respect of a person who has been convicted of second degree murder where that person has previously been convicted of culpable homicide that is murder, however described under this Act, that that person be sentenced to imprisonment for life without eligibility for parole until the person has served twenty-five years of the sentence;

(c) in respect of a person who has been convicted of second degree murder, that the person be sentenced to imprisonment for life without eligibility for parole until the person has served at least ten years of the sentence or such greater number of years, not being more than twenty-five years, as has been substituted therefor pursuant to section 745.4; and

(d) in respect of a person who has been convicted of any other offence, that the person be sentenced to imprisonment for life with normal eligibility for parole.

Persons Under Eighteen

745.1. The sentence to be pronounced against a person who was under the age of eighteen at the time of the commission of the offence for which the person is convicted of first degree murder or second degree murder and who is to be sentenced to imprisonment for life shall be that the person be sentenced to imprisonment for life without eligibility for parole until the person has served

(a) such period between five and seven years of the sentence as is specified by the judge presiding at the trial, or if no period is specified by the judge presiding at the trial, five years, in the case of a person who was under the age of sixteen at the time of the commission of the offence;

(b) ten years, in the case of a person convicted of first degree murder who was sixteen or seventeen years of age at the time of the commission of the offence; and

(c) seven years, in the case of a person convicted of second degree murder who was sixteen or seventeen years of age at the time of the comimission of the offence.

Recommendation by Jury

745.2. Subject to section 745.3, where a jury finds an accused guilty of second degree murder, the judge presiding at the trial shall, before discharging the jury, put to them the following question:

> You have found the accused guilty of second degree murder and the law requires that I now pronounce a sentence of imprisonment for life against the accused. Do you wish to make any recommendation with respect to the number of years that the accused must serve before the accused is eligible for release on parole? You are not required to make any recommendation but if you do, your recommendation will be considered by me when I am determining whether I should substitute for the ten year period, which the law would otherwise require the accused to serve before the accused is eligible to be considered for release on parole, a number of years that is more than ten but not more than twenty-five.

Persons Under Sixteen

745.3. Where a jury finds an accused guilty of first degree murder or second degree murder and the accused was under the age of sixteen at the time of the commission of the offence, the judge presiding at the trial shall, before discharging the jury, put to them the following question:

> You have found the accused guilty of first degree murder (or second degree murder) and the law requires that I now pronounce a sentence of imprisonment for life against the accused. Do you wish to make any recommendation with respect to the period of imprisonment that the accused must serve before the accused is eligible for release on parole? You are not required to make any recommendation but if you do, your recommendation will be considered by me when I am determining the period of imprisonment that is between five years and seven years that the law would require the accused to serve before the accused is eligible to be considered for release on parole.

Ineligibility for Parole

745.4. Subject to section 745.5, at the time of the sentencing under section 745 of an offender who is convicted of second degree murder, the judge who presided at the trial of the offender or, if that judge is unable to do so, any judge of the same court may, having regard to the character of the offender, the nature of the offence and the circumstances surrounding its commission, and to the recommendation, if any, made pursuant to section 745.2, by order, substitute for ten years a number of years of imprisonment (being more than ten but not more than twenty-five) without eligibility for parole, as the judge deems fit in the circumstances.

745.5. At the time of the sentencing under section 745.1 of an offender who is convicted of first degree murder or second degree murder and who was under the age of sixteen at the time of the commission of the offence, the judge who presided at the trial of the offender or, if that judge is unable to do so, any judge of the same court, may, having regard to the age and character of the offender, the nature of the offence and the circumstances surrounding its commission, and to the recommendation, if any, made pursuant to section 745.3, by order, decide the period of imprisonment the offender is to serve that is between five years and seven years without eligibility for parole, as the judge deems fit in the circumstances.

III. MURDER IN CANADA: EMPIRICAL AND CONSTITUTIONAL CONSIDERATIONS

In this section, we attempt to situate the murder provisions in a broader context by throwing some light on why murder continues to be treated differently for sentencing purposes. Is it because, as a group, those convicted of murder are more dangerous than other types of offenders? Do they tend to re-offend at a greater rate? Or do we hope that the stiff and relatively inflexible sentencing scheme does a good job of deterring would-be offenders? Or does the retention of the current scheme really boil down to a moral judgment? That is, do we sentence those convicted of murder so harshly because they deserve it, from a retributivist perspective? The resolution of these issues is vital to the questions surrounding the constitutionality of this sentencing scheme.

These important questions are difficult to answer. The Canadian Centre for Justice Statistics keeps track of many features of homicides committed in Canada. In its most recent report, which is current to 1998, Statistics Canada provides the following glimpse into the prevalence of homicide in Canada:

The general decline in homicides, evidenced since the mid-1970's, continued in 1998. There were 555 homicide offences reported, 31 fewer than the previous year, and well below the average of 641 for the previous decade. The 1998 homicide rate of 1.83 per 100,000 population represented a decrease of 6% from 1997, and was the lowest recorded since 1968.

Since 1961, when national homicide statistics were first collected, there have been two distinct trends. After several years of stability, the homicide rate increased steadily from 1.25 per 100,000 population in 1966 to a peak of 3.03 in 1975, an increase of 142%. From 1975 to 1998, despite yearly fluctuations, the homicide rate has gradually declined, reaching a rate of 1.83 in 1998, a decrease of 40% compared to 1975.

...

Although Canada's rate is generally three to four times lower than the USA rate, it is still higher than many European countries. For example, England and Wales reported a homicide rate of 1.30 per 100,000 population in 1998, almost 29% lower than Canada's rate.[1]

These figures represent rates of homicide in general, including murder, manslaughter, and infanticide. In terms of the focus of this chapter, Statistics Canada provides the following information about the breakdown of the global homicide rate:

First degree murder, as a proportion of all homicides, has generally been increasing since 1976, although it has declined from 58% in 1996 to 51% in 1998. Conversely, homicides classified by the police as second degree murder have generally been decreasing, and in 1998, represented a proportion of 39%. Despite annual fluctuations, around 9% of all homicides are classified as manslaughter each year, and the remaining 1% are infanticide.[2]

There are many other aspects of homicide explored in this Statistics Canada report, including use of firearms, age and sex of victims and accused, accused–victim relationships, and alcohol/drug involvement.

These statistics provide some interesting insights into the commission of murder offences in Canada, but they do not tell us a great deal about the backgrounds of the offenders who commit these offences. The following study, while somewhat dated, addresses the issue of recidivism of those convicted of homicide.

"Recidivism Among Homicide Offenders"
(1992), 4 *Forum on Corrections Research* 7

How well do murder and manslaughter offenders perform when they are finally released from federal prisons? This article presents statistics that may shed some light on the question.

---

1 O. Fedorowycz, "Homicide in Canada—1998" (1999), vol. 19, no. 10 *Juristat Service Bulletin* 3. The report also indicates that the attempted murder rate has also been declining since 1981.

2 Ibid., at 6.

Offenders Originally Incarcerated for Murder

A recent study followed murder offenders released on full parole between 1975 and 1990 to determine whether their time spent in the community on parole was successful or not. The length of the follow-up period varied—from up to 15 years for those released in 1975, to only a few months for those released in 1990.

Between 1 January 1975 and 31 March 1990, 658 murder offenders were released on full parole. Some of these offenders were released more than once for a total of 752 full-parole releases. ... [M]ore than three quarters of released murder offenders (77.5%) were not reincarcerated while on parole. Of those who were reincarcerated, 13.3% had their release revoked for a technical violation of their parole conditions and 9.2% for an indictable offence.

Of the 69 indictable offences committed by the released murder offenders, 30.4% (21) were offences against the person, 18.8% (13) were narcotics offences, 17.5% (12) were property offences, 8.7% (6) were robbery and 24.6% (17) were other *Criminal Code* offences.

Five released murder offenders (of a total of 658) were convicted of having committed a second murder while they were on full parole. Three of these were convicted of first-degree murder and two of second-degree murder. All five offenders had originally been convicted of non-capital murder. Besides these, no released murderer has been convicted of attempted murder or any other offence causing death.

Recidivism among murder offenders can be considered another way—murder offender groups can be divided into specific categories. ... [T]he outcome of the full-parole releases, as of 31 July 1990, [can be] compared among those who were convicted of capital murder, non-capital murder, first-degree murder and second-degree murder.

About one in 10 offenders convicted of second-degree murder, none convicted of first-degree murder, about one in three convicted of capital murder and one in four convicted of non-capital murder had their full parole revoked. Furthermore, 0.6% of second-degree murderers, no first-degree murderers, 2.7% of capital murderers and 3.5% of non-capital murderers committed an offence against another person while on full parole. Comparisons should not be made between these groups based on these data, since the size of some groups (e.g., first-degree murderers) is very small and the follow-up period was very brief.

Offenders Originally Convicted of Manslaughter

Between 1 January 1975 and 31 March 1990, 2,242 offenders originally convicted of manslaughter were released, either on full parole or mandatory supervision. Some of these offenders were released more than once, for a total of 3,172 releases. Of these, 222 (7%) were released at warrant expiry (i.e., at the end of their sentence) and, therefore, were not released to community supervision.

Of the 93% of manslaughter offenders who were released to community supervision, 47.7% (1,407) were released on full parole and 52.3% (1,543) on mandatory supervision. These offenders were followed until 31 July 1990 to determine whether any had been reincarcerated while on release.

Of the full-parole releases, less than one quarter (21.7%) were revoked: 14.6% for a technical violation of the condition of a parole, 6.5% for an indictable offence and 0.5% for a summary offence. About twice the proportion (41.5%) of those released on mandatory supervision were revoked: 30.6% for a technical violation of the conditions of parole, 10% for an indictable offence and 0.9% for a summary offence … .

Of the 92 (6.5%) full-parole releases of manslaughter offenders that were revoked for an indictable offence, 2.1% were revoked for offences against the person, 0.6% for robbery, 1.7% for property offences, 0.4% for narcotics offences and 1.7% for other *Criminal Code* offences.

Of the releases to mandatory supervision, 10% (154) were revoked for indictable offences: 3.2% were revoked for an offence against the person, 1.2% for robbery, 3.4% for property offences, 0.1% for narcotics offences and 2% for other *Criminal Code* offences.

Some manslaughter offenders released on full parole or mandatory

- Asiatic—1.4% of long-termers versus 0.9% of the total offender population; and
- other (including not specified)—4.7% of long-termers versus 5.4% of the total offender population.

This distribution suggests that members of diverse ethnic groups (i.e., non-Caucasians) are not overrepresented in the long-term offender population.

Marital Status

Available data indicate that about half of incarcerated offenders reported their marital status as single. Sentence length appeared to have no bearing on this finding. However, long-term offenders appeared somewhat less likely than other offenders to be involved in common-law relationships.

The breakdown of marital status, in decreasing order of frequency, is:

- single—50.5% of long-term inmates versus 47.5% of short-term inmates;
- common-law—21.5% of long-term inmates versus 28.6% of short-term inmates;
- married—13.5% of long-term inmates versus 11.9% of short-term inmates;
- separated or divorced—11.1% of long-term inmates versus 10.6% of short-term inmates; and
- other (including not specified)—3.4% of long-term inmates versus 1.4% of short-term inmates.

Summary

About one quarter of the total federal-offender population is serving a long-term sentence (i.e. 10 years or more). This is true of both male and female offender populations. Three out of five long-termers are incarcerated and two out of five are on some form of conditional release.

Quebec and the Pacific region have proportionately more long-term offenders, while the Atlantic and Prairie regions have proportionately fewer. Ontario has a more equitable proportion of long-termers.

During the past 10 years, the number of long-term offenders under federal jurisdiction increased by the same proportion as the number of federal offenders in general. During this same period, federal corrections admitted proportionately fewer long-termers, and released proportionately more long-termers, than offenders in general.

The vast majority of long-termers are Caucasian. About half of all long-term offenders are single, while about one in three is married (includes common-law). During the past 10 years, the average age of long-term offenders has increased by almost three years and is now about 38 years. Offenders serving life sentences for first-degree murder as a group, show the most dramatic increase in age.

Long- and short-term offenders have similar histories of federal incarceration, with the majority of both groups having no previous federal incarceration. After a five-year follow-up, only about one in five long-term offenders had been reconvicted of a criminal offence, while none of the 75 released offenders serving life sentences for murder had been subsequently reconvicted of murder.

In the late 1980s and early 1990s, the Supreme Court of Canada was busy shaping the contours of the constitutional requirements of fault. This was largely played out in the context of murder offences. Indeed, it was in *R v. Vaillancourt* (1987), 60 CR (3d) 289 (SCC), a murder case, that the court solidified the subjective fault requirement as a constitutional imperative. A subsequent wave of cases provided the court with an opportuntity to refine its approach. Among these cases were *Arkell* and *Luxton*. Although both cases were concerned with the constitutionality of offence-creating provisions (then s. 213 of the *Criminal Code*), they raised questions relating to the constitutionality of the sentencing provisions for first-degree murder. Given the breadth of the court's approach to these issues, *Arkell* and *Luxton* really address the constitutionality of mandatory sentencing for second-degree murder as well. As the extract by Allan Manson following these cases suggests, these issues appear to have been litigated and decided on an inadequate factual record.

R v. Arkell
(1990), 79 CR (3d) 207 (SCC)

LAMER CJC:

...

Analysis

For the reasons I have stated in *R v. Martineau* [(1990), 79 CR (3d) 129 (SCC)], released concurrently, s. 213(a) of the *Criminal Code* is of no force or effect, and the first two constitutional questions should, therefore, be answered accordingly. The third and fourth constitutional questions require an analysis of s. 214(5) of the *Criminal Code*. The main argument of the appellant, as regards his constitutional challenge of the section, is that it is arbitrary and irrational and thereby offends s. 7 of the Charter. In my view, this submission is answered by this court's judgment in *Paré* [(1987),

60 CR (3d) 346 (SCC)]. In that case a unanimous seven-person panel affirmed that s. 214 is a classification section concerned with sentencing and does not create a substantive offence. Wilson J, speaking for the court, put it this way at p. 625:

> It is clear from a reading of these provisions that s. 214 serves a different function from ss. 212 and 213. Sections 212 and 213 create the substantive offence of murder. Section 214 is simply concerned with classifying for sentencing purposes the offences created by ss. 212 and 213. It tells us whether the murder is first degree or second degree. This view of s. 214 was expressly adopted by this court in *R v. Farrant*, [1983] 1 SCR 124 (*per* Dickson J as he then was) at p. 140) and in *Droste v. The Queen*, [1984] 1 SCR 208 (*per* Dickson J as he then was) at p. 218).

Indeed, the appellant concedes that s. 214(5) is a sentencing classification provision.

The argument of the appellant suggests that the sentencing scheme is flawed and in violation of s. 7 of the Charter because it results in the punishment of individuals that is not proportionate to the seriousness of the offences giving rise to the sentences. First, I must note that as a result of this court's decision in *Martineau*, released concurrently, it can no longer be said that s. 214(5) has the potential to classify unintentional killings as first degree murder. A conviction for murder requires proof beyond a reasonable doubt of subjective foresight of death. Therefore, when we reach the stage of classifying murders as either first or second degree, we are dealing with individuals who have committed the most serious crime in our *Criminal Code*, and who have been proven to have done so with the highest level of moral culpability, that of subjective foresight. Section 214(5) represents a decision by Parliament to impose a more serious punishment on those found guilty of murder while committing certain listed offences.

This leads me to a second point, namely, a consideration of the underlying rationale of s. 214(5). Again, I refer to the decision of this court in *Paré*, at pp. 632-33:

> All murders are serious crimes. Some murders, however, are so threatening to the public that Parliament has chosen to impose exceptional penalties on the perpetrators. One such class of murders is that found in s. 214(5), murders done while committing a hijacking, a kidnapping and forcible confinement, a rape, or an indecent assault. ...
>
> The offences listed in s. 214(5) are all offences involving the unlawful domination of people by other people. Thus an organizing principle for s. 214(5) can be found. This principle is that where a murder is committed by someone already abusing his power by illegally dominating another, the murder should be treated as an exceptionally serious crime. Parliament has chosen to treat these murders as murders in the first degree.

I can find no principle of fundamental justice that prevents Parliament, guided by the organizing principle identified by this court in *Paré*, from classifying murders done while committing certain underlying offences as more serious, and thereby attaching more serious penalties to them. In the case of the distinction between first and second degree murder, the difference is a maximum extra 15 years that must be served before one is eligible for parole. This distinction is neither arbitrary nor irrational. The section is based on an organizing principle that treats murders committed while the perpetrator is illegally dominating another person as more serious than other murders. Further, the relationship between the classification and the moral blameworthiness of the offender clearly exists.

Section 214 only comes into play when murder has been proven beyond a reasonable doubt. In light of *Martineau*, this means that the offender has been proven to have had subjective foresight of death. Parliament's decision to treat more seriously murders that have been committed while the offender is exploiting a position of power through illegal domination of the victim accords with the principle that there must be a proportionality between a sentence and the moral blameworthiness of the offender and other considerations such as deterrence and societal condemnation of the acts of the offender. Therefore, I conclude that in so far as s. 214(5) is neither arbitrary nor irrational, it does not infringe upon s. 7 of the Charter. I note that in this appeal there was no argument made as regards s. 12 of the Charter, although that issue was raised in a case heard and disposed of concurrently, *R v. Luxton*.

R v. Luxton
(1990), 79 CR (3d) 193 (SCC)

LAMER CJC:

...

For the reasons stated in *R v. Martineau* [(1990), 79 CR (3d) 129 (SCC)], released concurrently, s. 213(a) of the *Criminal Code* infringes ss. 7 and 11(d) of the Charter and cannot be saved by s. 1 of the Charter. Therefore, the first constitutional question is answered in the affirmative and the second question in the negative.

The remaining questions require an examination of the combined effect of s. 214(5)(e) and s. 669 of the Code on the rights guaranteed by ss. 7, 9 and 12 of the Charter, and s. 2(e) of the *Canadian Bill of Rights*. The appellant combines his argument in respect of s. 7 of the charter and s. 2(e) of the *Canadian Bill of Rights*. He submits that the principles of fundamental justice require that differing degrees of moral blameworthiness in different offences be reflected in differential sentences, and that sentencing be individualized. The appellant cites the following judgments as support for the view that the combined effect of s. 214(5)(e) and s. 669 offends the principles that a just sentencing system contains a gradation of punishments differentiated according to the malignity of offences and that sentencing be individualized: *Re BC Motor Vehicle Act*, [1982] 2 SCR 486, per Wilson J; *R v. Smith*, [1987] 1 SCR 1045, per Lamer J and per Wilson J; and *R v. Lyons*, [1987] 2 SCR 309, per LaForest J. In my view, assuming that s. 7 incorporates the propositions cited by the appellant as principles of fundamental justice, the combined effect of s. 214(5)(e) and s. 669 is in accordance with them. Section 214(5) of the *Criminal Code* isolates a particular group of murderers, namely, those who have murdered while committing certain offences involving the illegal domination of the victim, and classifies them for sentencing purposes as murderers in the first degree. As a result of s. 669 the murderer is sentenced to life imprisonment without parole eligibility for 25 years. It is of some note that even in cases of first degree murder, s. 672 [now s. 745] of the Code provides that after serving 15 years the offender can apply to the Chief Justice in the province for a reduction in the number of years of imprisonment without eligibility for parole having regard for the character of the applicant, his conduct while serving the sentence, the nature of the offence for which he was convicted and any other matters that are relevant in the circumstances. This indicates that even in the cases of our most serious offenders, Parliament has provided for some sensitivity to the individual circumstances of each case when it comes to sentencing.

I must also reiterate that what we are speaking of here is a classification scheme for the purposes of sentencing. The distinction between first and second degree murder only comes into play when it has first been proven beyond a reasonable doubt that the offender is guilty of murder, that is, that he or she had subjective foresight of death: *R v. Martineau*, handed down this day. There is no doubt that a sentencing scheme must exhibit a proportionality to the seriousness of the offence, or to put it another way, there must be a gradation of punishments according to the malignity of the offences. However, a sentencing scheme also must take into account other factors that are of significance for the societal interest in punishing wrongdoers. In *Lyons*, supra, at pp. 328-29, La Forest J considered the dangerous offender designation in the Code and said the following in respect of the relationship between sentencing and its objectives:

> I accordingly agree with the respondent's submission that it cannot be considered a violation of fundamental justice for Parliament to identify those offenders who, in the interests of protecting the public, ought to be sentenced according to considerations which are not entirely reactive or based on a "just deserts" rationale. The imposition of a sentence which "is partly punitive but is mainly imposed for the protection of the public" ... seems to me to accord with the fundamental purpose of the criminal law generally, and of sentencing in particular, namely, the protection of society. In a rational system of sentencing, the respective importance of prevention, deterrence, retribution and rehabilitation will vary according to the nature of the crime and the circumstances of the offender.

In my view the combination of s. 214(5)(e) and s. 669 clearly demonstrates a proportionality between the moral turpitude of the offender and the malignity of the offence, and moreover it is in accord with the other objectives of a system of sentencing identified by La Forest J in *Lyons*. As I have stated, we are dealing with individuals that have committed murder and have done so with the now constitutionally mandated *mens rea* of subjective foresight of death. Parliament has chosen, once it has been proven that an offender has committed murder, to classify certain of those murders as first degree. Murders that are done while committing offences which involve the illegal domination of the victim by the offender have been classified as first degree murder. Forcible confinement is one of those offences involving illegal domination. The added element of forcible confinement, in the context of the commission of a murder, markedly enhances the moral blameworthiness of an offender. Indeed, forcible confinement is punishable by up to 10 years in prison. The decision of Parliament to elevate murders done while the offender commits forcible confinement to the level of first degree murder is consonant with the principle of proportionality between the blameworthiness of the offender and the punishment. Further, it is consistent with the individualization of sentencing especially since only those who have killed with subjective foresight of death while also committing the offence of forcible confinement are subjected to that punishment. I, therefore, can find no principle of fundamental justice that has been violated by the combination of s. 215(5)(e) and s. 669 of the *Criminal Code*. Equally, for these same reasons I conclude that there is no violation of s. 2(e) of the *Canadian Bill of Rights*.

The appellant also submits in a separate argument that the combination of s. 214(5)(e) and s. 669 contravenes s. 9 of the Charter because of the imposition of a mandatory term of imprisonment by statute for an offence that encompasses a range of moral turpitude. This argument overlaps a great deal with the appellant's s. 7 argument and I would only add the following comments to those I have already made above. The combined effect of the impugned sections do not demonstrate arbitrariness on the part of Parliament. Indeed, as I noted above, Parliament has narrowly defined a class of murderers under an organizing principle of illegal domination and has specifically defined the conditions under which the offender can be found guilty of first degree murder. In order to be found guilty of first degree murder under s. 214(5)(e), the offender must have committed murder with subjective foresight of death and must have committed the murder "while committing or attempting to commit ... forcible confinement." Where the act causing death and the acts constituting the forcible confinement "all form part of one continuous sequence of events forming a single transaction," the death is caused "while committing" an offence for the purpose of s. 214(5); see *Paré*, supra, at p. 632. To commit the underlying offence of forcible confinement, the offender must use "physical restraint, contrary to the wishes of the person restrained, but to which the victim submits unwillingly, thereby depriving the person of his or her liberty to move from one place to another": quote from *R v. Dollan* (1980), 53 CCC (2d) 146 (Ont. HC), as cited with approval in *R v. Gratton* (1985), 18 CCC (3d) 462 (CA) [at p. 473]. It is true that the definition of forcible confinement adopted by the courts allows for varying circumstances in each individual case. But this alone is not a sign of arbitrariness. The offence of forcible confinement as defined falls clearly under the rubric of the organizing principle enunciated by Wilson J in *Paré*, namely, that of the illegal domination of no person by another. The decision of Parliament to attach a minimum 25-year sentence without eligibility for parole in cases of first degree murder, having regard to all these circumstances, cannot be said to be arbitrary within the meaning of s. 9 of the Charter. The incarceration is statutorily authorized, it narrowly defines a class of offenders with respect to whom the punishment will be invoked and it prescribes quite specifically the conditions under which an offender may be found guilty of first-degree murder. Further, the policy decision of Parliament to classify these murders as first degree murders accords with the broader objectives of a sentencing scheme. The elevation of murder while committing a forcible confinement to first degree reflects a societal denunciation of those offenders who choose to exploit their position of dominance and power to the point of murder.

The appellant's final argument is that the combined effect of s. 215(5)(e) and s. 669 contravenes s. 12 of the Charter. Section 12 of the Charter protects individuals against cruel and unusual punishment. The phrase "cruel and unusual punishment" has been considered by this court in *R v. Smith*, supra. That case held that the criterion to be applied in order to determine whether a punishment is cruel and unusual is whether the punishment is so excessive as to outrage standards of decency. At pp. 1072-73 stated that:

> The test for review under s. 12 of the Charter is one of gross disproportionality, because it is aimed at punishments that are more than merely excessive. We should be careful not to stigmatize every disproportionate or excessive sentence as being a constitutional violation, and should leave to the usual sentencing appeal process the task of reviewing the fitness of a sentence. Section 12 will only be infringed where the sentence is so unfit having regard to the offence and the offender as to be grossly disproportionate.
>
> In assessing whether a sentence is grossly disproportionate, the court must first consider the gravity of the offence, the personal characteristics of the offender and the particular circumstances of the case in order to determine what range of sentences would have been appropriate to punish, rehabilitate or deter this particular offender or to protect the public from this particular offender.

In *Lyons*, supra, La Forest J addressed the meaning of the word "grossly" at pp. 344-45:

> The word "grossly" [as in "grossly disproportionate"], it seems to me, reflects this Court's concern not to hold Parliament to a standard so exacting, at least in the context of s. 12, as to require punishments to be perfectly suited to accommodate the moral nuances of every crime and every offender.

In my view, the combination of s. 214(5)(e) and s. 669 does not constitute cruel and unusual punishment. These sections provide for punishment of the most serious crime in our criminal law, that of first degree murder. This is a crime that carries with it the most serious level of moral blameworthiness, namely, subjective foresight of death. The penalty is severe and deservedly so. The minimum 25 years to be served before eligibility for parole reflects society's condemnation of a person who has exploited a position of power and dominance to the gravest extent possible by murdering the person that he or she is forcibly confining. The punishment is not excessive and clearly does not outrage our standards of decency. In my view, it is within the purview of Parliament, in order to meet the objectives of a rational system of sentencing, to treat our most serious crime with an appropriate degree of certainty and severity. I reiterate that even in the case of first degree murder, Parliament has been sensitive to the particular circumstances of each offender through various provisions allowing for the Royal prerogative of mercy, the availability of escorted absences from custody for humanitarian and rehabilitative purposes and for early parole: see s. 672, s. 674 [now s. 747] and s. 686 [now s. 751] of the *Criminal Code*. In *Smith*, supra, at p. 1070, I quoted with approval the following statement by Borins DCJ in *R v. Guiller*, Ont. Dist. Ct. [48 CR (3d) 226]:

> It is not for the court to pass on the wisdom of Parliament with respect to the gravity of various offences and the range of penalties which may be imposed upon those found guilty of committing the offences. Parliament has broad discussion in proscribing conduct as criminal and in determining proper punishment. While the final judgment as to whether a punishment exceeds constitutional limits set by the Charter is properly a judicial function the court should be reluctant to interfere with the considered views of Parliament and then only in the clearest of cases where the punishment prescribed is so

excessive when compared with the punishment prescribed for other offences as to outrage standards of decency.

Therefore, I conclude that in the case at bar the impugned provisions in combination do not represent cruel and unusual punishment within the meaning of s. 12 of the Charter.

A. Manson, "The Easy Acceptance of Long Term Confinement"
(1990), 79 CR (3d) 265 (footnotes omitted)

...

The History of Section 742(a)

The creation of two categories of murder, first and second degree, and the current punishments for these offences evolved from the debate over capital punishment which occupied Parliament and the Canadian public for over twenty years. In 1956, a joint committee of the Senate and House of Commons recommended the retention of capital punishment but suggested that the offence of murder be divided into capital and non-capital categories. In 1961, the *Criminal Code* was amended to provide for capital murder which would be punishable by hanging unless the person was under the age of 18 years: *An Act to Amend the Criminal Code* (Capital Murder), SC 1960-61, c. 44, s. 1. Capital murder consisted of a killing that was planned and deliberate, a killing resulting from the direct intervention or counselling by the accused in the course of certain stipulated crimes, or the killing of a police officer or prison guard. All other murder was characterized as non-capital and was punishable by life imprisonment. This régime continued in force until 28th December 1967, although as a result of reviews by the Cabinet for the purpose of advising the Governor-General on commutation, the last hangings in Canada took place on 11th December 1962 at the Don Jail in Toronto. In 1967 the Code was again amended, to limit capital murder to those cases where an accused, by his or her own act, caused or assisted in the causing of the death of a police officer or prison officer, or counselled or procured that death: *An Act to Amend the Criminal Code*, SC 1967-68, c. 15, s. 1. This limitation was intended to last for only five years (s. 4), but was continued for a further five years in 1972: *Criminal Law Amendment (Capital Punishment) Act*, SC 1973-74, c. 38, s. 10. During this semi-moratorium, persons who had been sentenced to death but whose sentences had been commuted could not be released from confinement without the approval of the Governor in Council. Persons who were sentenced to life imprisonment for murder could be released on parole after serving ten years, unless the trial judge increased the period of parole ineligibility. This was the statutory sentencing background against which Parliament resumed the debate on capital punishment in 1976.

The often passionate and partisan Parliamentary discussion in 1976 focussed on the fundamental issue of the legitimacy of capital punishment, and little attention was paid to the elements of the proposed alternatives. In the Standing Committee on

Justice and Legal Affairs, a clause-by-clause consideration of the new bill took place. In that committee, statistics were tabled to show the Canadian experience with life imprisonment, as well as the régimes which operated in other jurisdictions where capital punishment had been abolished. The following table indicates the average periods actually served in custody in Canada between 1961 and 1974.

	1961-68	1968-74
Capital Murder (commuted) ...	12.0	13.2
Non-Capital Murder	6.2	7.7

These figures are particularly interesting when put into a comparative context as discussed by the parliamentarians in committee at the time. A United Nations group of experts had only a few years earlier observed that, in countries which employed life imprisonment as an alternative to capital punishment, the most common median length of term served was between 10 and 15 years, and the average custodial term was about 14 years. The Solicitor General offered the committee the following examples of statutory minimum terms of incarceration for comparable offences in various American and European jurisdictions: see the minutes of the standing committee, ante, note 3, p. 72:60:

New York:	15–25 years
California:	7 years
England:	parole review after 4 years
Sweden:	10 years
Denmark:	5 years
Massachusetts: ...	15 years
Holland:	no statutory minimum

With all the data, both Canadian and comparative, pointing to a period of between 10 and 15 years, why did the proposed legislation include a minimum term for first degree of 25 years? The answer is simple: politics and expedience. Warren Allmand, the Solicitor General, who had been given the responsibility of steering the struggle to abolish capital punishment, had been told by the Canadian Association of Police Chiefs, who supported the death penalty, that only a minimum sentence as severe as 25 years could conceivably be an alternative to the rope: see the minutes of the standing committee, ante, note 3, pp. 72:60-61. In retrospect, Mr. Allmand was probably correct in responding to views of that sort in order to achieve the success of the abolition movement. Now, 15 years later, ample time has passed to assess the trade-off in the light of hard evidence about the effects of long term confinement. Instead, what was a political compromise in 1976 is now a constitutional benchmark.

The 25-Year Minimum and Sections 7 and 9 of the Charter

The appellants argued that the principles of fundamental justice, as guaranteed by s. 7 of the Charter, require a scheme of differentiated sentences which respond to varying degrees of moral blameworthiness. Accordingly, so the argument went, a mandatory long term sentence encompassing all kinds of first degree murders denied to individual convicted persons their entitlement to be sentenced according to their particular circumstances. Without confirming that s. 7 includes constitutional requirements of proportionate and individualized sentences, Lamer CJC concludes in *Lauzon* at p. 201 that the longer minimum term mandated for first degree murder by ss. 231(5)(e) and 742 "demonstrates a proportionality between the moral turpitude of the offender and the malignity of the offence." This conforms, according to Lamer CJC, with the objectives of a rational sentencing system as described in the court's earlier decision in *R v. Lyons*, [1987] 2 SCR 309, per La Forest J at pp. 328-29. He points out that, with respect to convictions pursuant to s. 231(5)(e), the longer mandatory sentence is consistent with an individualized sentencing policy, since it applies only to someone who killed with subjective foresight of death while committing the underlying offence of forcible confinement, an offence involving the illegal domination of another. For similar reasons, and in accordance with the judgment in *Lyons*, Lamer CJC finds that the sentence does not constitute arbitrary detention in breach of s. 9 of the Charter, since it is statutorily authorized and relates to a narrowly-defined class of offenders for whom specific conditions of responsibility are prescribed.

The 25-Year Minimum and Section 12 of the Charter

The manner in which the 25-year minimum term is measured against the s. 12 guarantee prohibiting cruel and unusual punishment is especially troubling. The leading case in this regard is *R v. Smith*, [1981] 1 SCR 1045, in which the court confirmed that s. 12 represents a "compendious expression of a norm" (p. 205) which prohibits grossly disproportionate punishments. The two judgments in that case offered various tests which might produce a finding of cruel and unusual punishment, including whether the punishment outrages standards of decency. Lamer J at pp. 231-32 discussed eight tests, and McIntyre J at p. 212 synthesized these tests into three categories: (1) whether the punishment outrages the public conscience or degrades human dignity; (2) whether the punishment goes beyond what is necessary to achieve its purpose; and (3) whether the punishment is imposed on a rational basis. In *Luxton*, the test of outraging decency becomes the single analytical tool used to validate the mandatory long term confinement for first degree murder.

In essence, the judgment in *Luxton* says that it is constitutionally acceptable to impose the most severe punishment for the most serious offence. No one would quarrel with the logic of this proposition. While it must be true, it nevertheless misses the point in two significant ways. First, although the reasoning justifies the imposition of a harsher sentence for first degree murder, it ignores the actual length of the term imposed. The same analysis could be applied to justify mandatory terms of 30, 40 or 50 years. Secondly, by truncating the s. 12 analysis into solely a question about societal outrage, the court either ignores the effects of the duration of the sentence or assumes that the community knows the real effects of 25-year minimum terms and accepts them as legitimate aspects of penal policy. The issue of duration and its impact is clearly part of a proper s. 12 analysis, yet no evidence was adduced about the human impact of long term confinement. Although the Supreme Court has reminded us on a number of occasions that legislation might fail to pass Charter muster by reason of either its purpose or its effects, no empirical or expert material was placed before the court to explain the effects of the punishment in question. The argument proceeded entirely on conceptual grounds, with reference primarily to the idea of a hierarchy of punishments. The actual punishment was not assessed in real, human terms.

It is not fair to suggest that Lamer CJC has ignored the question of 25 years of confinement and its relation to the personal circumstances of offenders. He observes at p. 203 that "Parliament has been sensitive to the particular circumstances of each offender through various provisions allowing for the Royal prerogative of mercy, the availability of escorted absences from custody for humanitarian and rehabilitative purposes, and for early parole." In an abstract sense, the possibility of these indulgences exists, but the reality is that they are very rarely used. Last spring, when a 70-year old woman received a pardon after serving 11 years of a first degree murder term, the newspapers announced that it was the first pardon granted to a person convicted of first degree murder, and that only nine prisoners had received pardons in the past ten years. The Royal prerogative of mercy is available to ameliorate the harshness of sentences, but it is most often used in situations where it has been established that a person was wrongly convicted. The availability of escorted temporary absence passes is another example of the sardonic gap between statutory possibility and practical reality. Passes of this sort for a lifer require the approval of the institution where the prisoner is confined, the approval of the National Parole Board and the deployment of one or two staff persons to act as escorts. The board's own manual advises that this power should be used "very sparingly" in order not to "depreciate" the seriousness of the sentence. Consequently, escorted passes are awarded principally for funerals, visits to sick relatives and other related family events. The reference to early parole must mean the parole ineligibility review pursuant to s. 745 [am. RSC 1985, c. 27 (2nd Supp.), s. 10] of the code, which a prisoner can commence after serving 15 years in custody. This process only provides a new parole eligibility date. The issue of release is then delegated to the parole board for the application of its usual criteria, typically a process which takes a minimum of three years. Again it is important to recognize that the court had no material before it demonstrating how these extraordinary processes really work. Had the court found the mandatory punishment to be illegitimate, these factors, along with issues of legislative objective and real impact, would have been relevant to the s. 1 justificatory analysis.

Conclusion

The rulings in *Luxton* and *Arkell* do not preclude any individual convicted of first degree murder from attempting to challenge the application of the mandatory sentence as it relates to his or her particular circumstances. In *Smith* it was pointed out at pp. 233-34 that the effect of an otherwise acceptable sentence in a particular, personal context might render the punishment grossly disproportionate. The Yukon Court of Appeal, relying on *Smith*, has ruled that a firearms prohibition produced a grossly disproportionate impact on a professional trapper: *R v. Chief* (1990), 74 CR (3d) 57, (YTCA); cf. *R v. Kelly*, Ont. CA, 6th September 1990 (not yet reported). Another example of an individualized inquiry is *Steele v. Mountain Inst.* (1990), 76 CR (3d) 307, affirmed by SCC, 8th November 1990 (not yet reported), in which the continued confinement of a prisoner who had been designated a "criminal sexual psychopath" in 1953 was declared to be cruel and unusual punishment. More pertinent to the issue of murder sentencing, in *R v. Daniels*, Sask. CA 15th July 1990 (not yet reported), Wedge J found that it was cruel and unusual punishment to require native women from Saskatchewan to serve a life sentence for second degree murder in the federal Prison for women at Kingston, Ontario. In that case the principal argument, also accepted by the court, was that shipping the convicted women out of the province to the Prison for Women resulted in impermissible discrimination contrary to s. 15(1) of the Charter. If one contemplates other circumstances where a sentence may be considered discriminatory in terms of its effect by reason of sex or age, extreme examples may also reach the level of gross disproportionality. Consider the sentencing of a 14-year-old girl tried and convicted as a party in adult court in Newfoundland of first degree murder. After assessing her blameworthiness, her age and the conditions of confinement at the Prison for Women, is it not a grossly disproportionate sentence? Can't a similar argument be made for a 14-year-old boy? While maturity does not lend itself so easily to a reciprocal analysis, it does lead one's mind to cases of disability where the impact of confinement, in personal and access terms, will be dramatically unfair because of the structural and programming limitations of institutions. Equally problematic are cases of special health problems which could produce a severe differential impact on the sentenced person. As time passes and lawyers are confronted with the circumstances of individual cases, other examples of differential impact will appear which arguably approach the standard of gross disproportionality.

The more important question is whether the Supreme Court will decide to reconsider the constitutionality of the mandatory sentence for first degree murder when it is provided with a full, empirical record. Certainly the court has the power to rethink an important issue of this sort, particularly if persuasive material is presented to it. The prospect, however, is doubtful, and one might wonder whether, in the wake of *Luxton* and *Arkell*, a lawyer would have the temerity to bring a new leave application on this issue. However, as discussed above, a s. 12 argument can be based on individual impact, and it may be that, in the context of an individual challenge to the application of the mandatory sentence, the Supreme Court might choose to rehear the general issue.

Given the rate at which the numbers of people serving long terms of incarceration are accumulating in our penitentiaries, it is imperative that some authority, either Parliament or the courts, address their minds to the legitimacy of long term confinement. The 25-year parole ineligibility period was created as a political expedient in the face of compelling data pointing to a lower minimum term. At the time, very little was known about the human effects of long term confinement. Now, over 15 years have passed and no effort seems to have been made to assess this harshest feature of our sentencing régime. It is beginning to dominate the penitentiary environment, and begs for serious reconsideration. While we await a new assessment of this form of long term confinement, lawyers should remember that s. 12 provides an opportunity, albeit a limited one, for justice in the individual case. The judgment in *Luxton* and *Arkell* should not discourage counsel from placing individual cases before the courts, with complete factual records.

For the time being, *Arkell* and *Luxton* effectively preclude further challenges to the legislation that creates the mandatory sentencing scheme for murder. However, as Manson points out, this does not mean that individual litigants must necessarily be deprived of a remedy in exceptional cases. Robert Latimer has litigated the purported constitutional shortcomings of the mandatory minimum by attempting to obtain a constitutional exemption from the operation of the law. The following is an excerpt from this judgment of the Saskatchewan Court of Appeal. At the time of writing, Latimer's appeal to the Supreme Court of Canada was on reserve.

R v. Latimer
(1998), 131 CCC (3d) 191 (Sask. CA)

BY THE COURT: Robert Latimer was convicted on November 5, 1997 of second degree murder in the death of his daughter, Tracey, and was afterwards sentenced to a term of imprisonment of one year to be followed by a period of probation of one year less a day. Tracey was a 12-year-old quadriplegic afflicted with severe cerebral palsy and suffering continual pain. Mr. Latimer asphyxiated her with carbon monoxide by placing her inside the cab of his truck, attaching a hose to the tailpipe of the vehicle, and diverting the exhaust into the cab.

Mr. Latimer had been convicted of the same offence three years earlier and been sentenced to the mandatory term of life imprisonment, without eligibility for parole for ten years. On that occasion he appealed to this Court against both his conviction and sentence: *R v. Latimer* (1995), 99 CCC (3d) 481 (Sask. CA) (per Bayda CJS, Tallis and Sherstobitoff JJA).

In a unanimous decision the Court dismissed the appeal against conviction. The Court rejected Mr. Latimer's contentions that the trial judge had erred in the following respects: (1) in failing to allow the jury to reach a decision on the basis of the justice of the case, rather than the letter of the law, and of the right of her father to choose death for her, given her physical and intellectual incapacity; (2) in admitting into evidence incriminating statements made by Mr. Latimer in the course of the police investigation into the death; and (3) in failing to leave the defence of necessity to the jury.

The Court went on, by majority decision, to dismiss the appeal against sentence, turning down an application by Mr. Latimer for an order exempting him from the applicable provisions of sections 235 and 745 of the *Criminal Code*. Taken together, these sections prescribe a sentence of life imprisonment for murder, subject to potential release on parole after the expiration of at least 25 years, in the case of first degree murder, and of at least 10 years in the case of second degree murder. Mr. Latimer had sought the exemption on the primary basis a sentence of life imprisonment, without eligibility for parole for 10 years, amounted in the circumstances to "cruel and unusual punishment," prohibited by section 12 of the Canadian *Charter of Rights and Freedoms*. Justices Tallis and Sherstobitoff did not agree with this proposition and dismissed the appeal in consequence. In dissent, Chief Justice Bayda expressed the opinion the sentence amounted in the circumstances to cruel and unusual punishment. In the result, he would have granted the sought-after exemption and directed that sentence be imposed without regard to sections 235 and 745 of the Code.

Following the dismissal of that appeal, two things occurred. First, it was discovered that in advance of the trial Crown counsel had had potential jurors interviewed regarding their views on subjects of significance to the cause. Second, Mr. Latimer appealed to the Supreme Court of Canada. He sought an acquittal on the basis that the Court of Appeal, along with the trial judge, had erred in law in relation to the admission of his incriminating statements. Alternatively, he sought a new trial on the basis of Crown counsel's conduct in having the potential jurors interviewed. The Supreme Court rejected the contention that Mr. Latimer's incriminating statements had been admitted in error, but ordered a new trial, the need for which had been conceded by the Attorney General, in consequence of Crown counsel's conduct: *R v. Latimer* (1997), 4 CR (5th) 1 (SCC).

The new trial was presided over by Mr. Justice Noble, sitting with a jury. As previously noted, Mr. Latimer was again convicted of second degree murder. This time, however, he was sentenced to a year in jail, to be followed by a year of probation. He then appealed, contending the conviction could not stand in the face of what had occurred at trial. The Attorney General also appealed, contending the sentence had been imposed in error and fell to be set aside in favour of the mandatory sentence of life imprisonment, without eligibility for parole for 10 years. These, of course, are the appeals now before us.

· · ·

The Jury's Question Concerning Sentencing

In the course of its deliberations, the jury sent the following note to the trial judge:

1. What is the procedure once the verdict has been reached?
2. Sergeant Conlon's testimony he advised R. Latimer to get a lawyer because he would be charged with first degree murder. Why is R. Latimer charged with second degree murder?
3. Is there any possible way we can have input into a recommendation for sentencing?

Before responding, the trial judge asked counsel for their views. A lengthy discussion followed, centred on the third question. Mr. Brayford suggested the jury be told of the sentencing provisions of the *Criminal Code* relating to second degree murder, including those of 745.2 allowing for a jury upon conviction to make a recommendation regarding the number of years the accused must serve before being eligible for release on parole. Counsel for the Crown opposed this suggestion.

Having heard from counsel, Mr. Justice Noble recalled the jury, informed them of the procedure that follows upon reaching a verdict and told them not to concern themselves with why the accused had been charged with second rather than first degree murder. He said this fell within the discretion of Crown counsel. The trial judge also told them that not to concern themselves with the penalty for the offence, saying:

> I should have told you when I charged you, because I sometimes do this, but not in every case, that the penalty in any of these charges is not the concern of the jury. Your concern is, as I said, the guilt or innocence of the accused, and you must reach—that's your job—you reach that conclusion and don't concern yourself what the penalty might be. We say that because we don't want you to be influenced one way or the other with what the penalty is.

Had Justice Noble stopped there, his response might well have gone unchallenged, because he followed the usual practice of withholding comment about sentence, by counsel and judge alike: *R v. Stevenson* (1990), 58 CCC (3d) 464 (Ont. CA); *R v. Schwartz & Schwartz* (1978), 40 CCC (2d) 161 (NSCA); *R v. Nielson & Stolar* (1984), 16 CCC (3d) 39 (Man. CA). The practice is founded on the two principles that (i) sentencing considerations are irrelevant to the determination by the jury of whether or not the elements of the offence have been proved beyond a reasonable doubt, and (ii) the jury might be improperly influenced in making that determination were it to concern itself with sentencing. Indeed counsel for Mr. Latimer conceded on the hearing of the appeal that had the trial judge said no more than this, there could have been no objection. Counsel suggested, however, that trial judges would do well in cases such as this to apprise juries of the punishment provisions of the *Criminal Code* so that juries, just as trial judges, might have a complete picture of the case.

That aside, the trial judge did not stop there, and in the submission of counsel for Mr. Latimer he made a fatal error in continuing as he did. Having reminded the jury they were not to concern themselves with penalty, because he did not want them to be influenced one way or another by such considerations, he went on to add:

> So it may be that later on, once you have reached a verdict, you—we will have some discussions about that, but not at this stage of the game. You must just carry on and answer the question that was put to you, okay?

These added remarks, it was submitted, so prejudiced Mr. Latimer's right to a fair trial as to warrant a new trial. Counsel for Mr. Latimer contended that this left the jury with the impression that it could make recommendations about penalty, should it find the accused guilty as charged, an impression that served to ease the jury's burden and deprive Mr. Latimer of a more anxiously considered and certain verdict.

By way of identifying the nature of the prejudice that was said to have flowed from this, counsel referred us to two cases: *McLean v. The King*, [1933] 1 SCR 688 and *R v. Cracknell* (1931), 56 CCC 190 (Ont. CA). In McLean's case the jury had been told by counsel that, although the sentence for murder was death, the Crown was empowered to commute the sentence to life imprisonment. This prompted the trial judge to explain the matter to the jury in the course of his charge, anxious as he was to impress upon the jurors the need to reach a verdict solely upon the evidence before them. The Supreme

Court of Canada held that the reference to executive clemency was undoubtedly unfortunate, but that it had caused no harm to the accused when viewed in the light of the charge as a whole. In explaining why it was unfortunate, the Court said this:

> Such a reference could not assist the jury in performing their duty to decide the issue of fact before them, and there is always some risk that a suggestion that a verdict is to be reviewed may result in some abatement of the deep sense of responsibility with which a jury ought to be brought to regard their duty in passing upon any criminal charge, and, preeminently, when the offence charged is murder, to which the law attaches the capital penalty [p. 693].

In Cracknell's case, the trial judge practically told the jury that, should it find the accused guilty of murder, Ottawa would reduce the sentence to life imprisonment, given the man's mental instability and the public's disapproval of hanging such persons. In consequence, the Ontario Court of Appeal set aside the accused's conviction and ordered a new trial, saying [at p. 192]:

> The statutory sentence of death which must follow a finding of guilty of murder casts upon juries the duty of exercising the greatest care in weighing the evidence and in refusing to convict unless satisfied beyond reasonable doubt of the guilt of an accused. The law entitles the accused to the protection which the proper observance of that duty affords him, and the practically telling by the Judge to the jury that, if they should bring in a verdict of murder, the sentence would be commuted, must have weakened such protection and have deprived him of a legal right, and thus … have caused a miscarriage of justice. … Nothing irrelevant or foreign to a case should be allowed to unbalance the scales of justice.

Returning with this in mind to Mr. Justice Noble's instructions to the jury, we think the import of his added remarks must be assessed in the context in which they were primarily made, namely in response to the jury's final question: "Is there any possible way we can have input into a recommendation for sentencing?" To which he replied in essence "… later on, once you have reached a verdict, we may have some discussions about that, but not at this stage of the game." This falls short of an assurance that the jury would be able to make a recommendation, which is all they had asked about, and it certainly does not amount to a suggestion that, even if they should find the accused guilty, they need not be overly concerned lest the sentence fall too heavily upon him.

Indeed, the response begs the question. And following, as it does, immediately upon the trial judge having informed the jury that they were not to concern themselves with sentence, the response does so to such a degree as to virtually leave the question unanswered. Taken at face value, there is little more to this than the jury having been told by the judge that he may discuss the subject of their question with them at a later stage. In other words, he deflected the question rather than met it head on.

He might have done otherwise by informing the jury, for example, that while it is for the judge to impose sentence in accordance with the law if the jury finds the accused guilty, the jury must nevertheless be given an opportunity to make a recommendation going to the terms of the sentence. Had he said that, there might be something more to the matter, even though he would have been quite correct. In that event, the jury might conceivably have been induced to find, more readily than otherwise, that the accused was guilty as charged. But as it is phrased, the response cannot be said to have left the jury with the understanding that the impact upon Mr. Latimer of a finding of guilt could be significantly tempered by the jury by means of a recommendation as to sentence.

Viewed in this light, it is difficult to see any real prejudice to the accused, much less prejudice to the extent of that identified in the *McLean* and *Cracknell* decisions. Indeed we cannot see how the trial judge's added remarks served to deny Mr. Latimer a fair trial by depriving him of a more deliberate and certain verdict. And so we cannot give effect to this ground of appeal.

It follows, then, that we have decided to dismiss the appeal against conviction.

The Appeal Against Sentence

Once the jury delivered its verdict, the trial judge invited them, as required by section 745.2 of the *Criminal Code*, to return to the jury room for the purposes of determining if they wished to recommend an increase in the minimum term of 10 years that Mr. Latimer would have to serve before becoming eligible for parole. Shortly afterwards the jury came back and asked the judge a question: "Can we recommend less than ten years before parole?" Mr. Justice Noble responded by saying,

> Well, on the wording of the section, not really, but I guess you can say anything you want in terms of recommendation, but on the number of years, the section doesn't permit me to go below that. So, whatever you recommend I'll take it into account.

The jury then resumed its deliberations and soon returned to express its views: "We recommend that Robert Latimer be eligible for parole after one year."

It was not, of course, open to the trial judge to act on this recommendation, having regard for the provisions of sections 235 and 745 of the *Criminal Code*. As noted above, these sections prescribe a mandatory minimum sentence of life imprisonment without eligibility for parole for at least ten years in the case of second degree murder.

Even so, Mr. Brayford suggested that some other, lesser sentence could be imposed, having regard for the *Charter of Rights and Freedoms*. He submitted that the mandatory minimum sentence amounted in the circumstances of this case to a violation of Mr. Latimer's constitutional right under section 12 of the Charter not to be subjected to any "cruel and unusual punishment." Accordingly he asked that an exemption from these provisions of the *Criminal Code* be granted to Mr. Latimer pursuant to section 24(1) of the Charter. He suggested in the alternative that these provisions of the *Criminal Code* might be seen as unconstitutional in light of section 12 of the Charter and be treated therefore as invalid pursuant to section 52(1) of the *Constitution Act, 1982*.

Counsel for the Crown opposed this. He contended that these provisions of the *Criminal Code* were not inconsistent with section 12 of the Charter and had therefore to be taken as valid. That being so, he added, the trial judge was unable to exempt Mr. Latimer from the operation of these provisions. Furthermore, counsel argued, the trial judge was foreclosed from doing so by the earlier judgment of this Court rejecting such an exemption.

Upon reflection, Noble J decided that a sentence of life imprisonment without the prospect of parole for ten years would constitute "cruel and unusual punishment" in these circumstances, having regard for section 12 of the Charter and the interpretation of this expression by the Supreme Court of Canada in such cases as *R v. Smith*, [1987] 1 SCR 1045, and *R v. Goltz*, [1991] 3 SCR 485.

That being so, he decided to grant the exemption, noting generally that such exemptions had been granted from time to time in relation to punitive statutory provisions imposing grossly disproportionate punishments. He also noted that counsel for Mr. Latimer had more or less conceded that the relevant provisions of sections 235 and 745 of the *Criminal Code* were not unconstitutional, which is to say inconsistent with section 12 of the Charter as contemplated by section 52(1) of the *Constitution Act, 1982* and therefore of no force or effect. However, he regarded this as inconsequential, for he was of the view it was unnecessary to the grant of the exemption that these provisions of the Code first be found to be inconsistent with section 12 of the Charter. And in deciding to grant the exemption, he rejected the contention of Crown counsel that the earlier judgment of this Court precluded him from doing so, saying he was not bound thereby because of differences in the two cases.

In effect, he identified three such differences: First, there was the evidence that Mr. Latimer had acted out of compassion and taken his daughter's life not because she was disabled, as was taken to have been the case in the Court of Appeal, but because she was suffering so much pain. Second, there was the additional evidence of several more witnesses, including Dr. Menzies, who confirmed that Mr. Latimer felt compelled to act out of concern for the child's present and future pain. Finally, there was the jury's recommendation that Mr. Latimer be eligible for parole after serving only a year in prison, a matter which if ignored would bring the administration of justice into disrepute in the eyes of many people.

And so Mr. Justice Noble distinguished the earlier case and departed from the judgment of this Court, although he went on to rely upon the dissenting reasons of Chief Justice Bayda in deciding to grant the exemption. In conclusion, he expressed the opinion that, if this case did not warrant the grant of such exemption, few if any such cases featuring "compassionate homicide" would qualify [121 CCC (3d) 326 at p. 347]:

> Accordingly, I find that Mr. Latimer's s. 12 Charter right has been violated and that he be granted a constitutional exemption from the sentencing prescribed by ss. 235 and 745 of the *Criminal Code*, and that pursuant to s. 24 of the Charter I must substitute a sentence which is appropriate and just in the circumstances.

The trial judge went on, as previously mentioned, to impose a sentence of one year in prison, to be followed by a one-year period of probation.

The Attorney General then appealed, stating that the trial judge had erred in four respects: (i) in failing to apply the judgment of this Court in *R v. Latimer* (1995), 99 CCC (3d) 481, disallowing Mr. Latimer's earlier claim to the exemption at issue; (ii) in granting the exemption without first finding, pursuant to 52(1) of the *Constitution Act,*

1982, that the sentencing provisions in question were inconsistent with section 12 of the Charter and therefore of no force or effect; (iii) in deciding to grant the exemption without regard for sections 748 and 749 of the *Criminal Code* by which Parliament left the Crown entirely free, acting through the Governor General in Council, to extend the royal prerogative of mercy to persons sentenced to terms of imprisonment under any Act of Parliament, including the *Criminal Code*; and (iv) in imposing an illegal sentence, contrary to sections 235 and 745 of the *Criminal Code*.

At the outset, we may say that in our respectful opinion the learned trial judge took too much upon himself in bypassing the judgment of this Court, the direction of Parliament, and the executive power of clemency referred to in section 748 of the *Criminal Code*. The section expressly recognizes that this power extends to persons sentenced to imprisonment on the authority of the Code, including those imprisoned for second degree murder and not eligible for parole for at least ten years. Indeed we are of the view the trial judge erred in not dismissing the application for an order exempting the accused from the combined operation of sections 235 and 745.2 of the *Criminal Code* and sentencing him in accordance with those sections, following this Court's earlier judgment.

As we see it, the trial judge was bound by the earlier judgment of this Court, for there was no material difference between the case before him and the previous case. Certainly there was no relevant difference in the act of the accused and his accompanying state of mind. The trial judge's suggestion that this Court had predicated its judgment upon the fact Mr. Latimer had taken the life of his child not because she was in pain but because she was disabled, is not only unrealistic, it is simply not tenable in light of the previous reasons for judgment. In delivering the judgment of the Court on the issue of sentence, Tallis JA summed up the actions of the accused in these words [at p. 520]:

> This homicide involves a significant degree of premeditation. The appellant contemplated taking Tracey's life before performing the act that caused her death. It was "intentional" in every sense of the word. Although he did so to spare her further pain, this approach ignores many other relevant considerations. As a self-appointed surrogate decision-maker, he was not entitled to take the criminal law into his own hands and terminate her life.

Nor, as suggested by the trial judge, are the two cases distinguishable on the basis additional evidence was adduced at the second trial. The evidentiary differences between the first and second trials were more quantitative than qualitative. For what it was worth in the circumstances, including the absence of testimony from the accused, even the opinion evidence of Dr. Menzies pertaining to the accused's motivation in killing his daughter served to add little to what had already been known or presumed.

Finally, the jury's recommendation that the accused be eligible for parole after spending a year in custody did not constitute a legitimate distinguishing factor. The recommendation was not only uninformed, in the sense the jury had not been informed of the purposes and principles of sentencing or the policy considerations underlying Parliament's enactment of sections 235, 745.2, and 748 of the *Criminal Code*, but it also had no legal effect. Section 745.2 only allows for a recommendation concerning "a number of years that is more than ten but no more than twenty-five."

We are therefore of the opinion that it was not open to the trial judge to depart from this Court's earlier judgment. It follows, then, that he was bound to dismiss the application for an order exempting Mr. Latimer from the operation of sections 235 and 745.2 of the Code.

Nor are we minded to depart from that judgment. Indeed, we can see no supportable basis for doing so, having regard for the reasons for judgment and the practice by which intermediate courts of appeal are bound by their previous judgments in the absence of the extraordinary.

As the reasons make clear, and as we have already said, the previous judgment was rendered upon an evidentiary base that did not differ materially from that now before us. Similarly, the defence of necessity has been rejected, meaning of course that Mr. Latimer is answerable for the inexcusable murder of Tracey Latimer, a murder that has been classified by Parliament, for sentencing purposes, as second degree. The judgment in the previous case was rendered on the assumption it was open to the Court in appropriate circumstances to grant constitutional exemptions, and as the reasons demonstrate the judgment was founded upon the application of the controlling principles found in *R v. Luxton*, [1990] 2 SCR 711.

In Luxton's case the Supreme Court of Canada decided that the mandatory sentence of life imprisonment for first degree murder, without eligibility for parole for at least twenty-five years, did not represent cruel and unusual punishment within the meaning of section 12 of the Charter. That decision was predicated at the outset upon respect for the wisdom of Parliament and its will.

···

The earlier judgment of this Court is heavily reliant upon this decision, as is apparent from the concluding paragraphs of the reasons for judgment [at p. 520]:

> The real issue for determination on this sentence appeal is whether the appellant should be held answerable for the murder of his daughter. We are asked to treat the conviction as essentially the functional equivalent of manslaughter for the purpose of determining a fit sentence. Although Parliament has not created a separate offence or sentencing regime for murder in such circumstances, we are asked to override the existing requirements by granting a constitutional exemption based on ss. 7 or 12 of the Charter.
>
> This homicide involves a significant degree of premeditation. The appellant contemplated taking Tracey's life before performing the act that caused her death. It was "intentional" in every sense of the word. Although he did so to spare her further pain, this approach ignores many other relevant considerations. As a self-appointed surrogate decision-maker, he was not entitled to take the criminal law into his own hands and terminate her life. Furthermore, society, through the operation of the criminal law is entitled to guard against potential abuses in such situations. Accordingly, statutory penalties are fashioned to meet the broad objectives and purposes of the criminal law.
>
> In the circumstances of this case we reject the appellant's request for a constitutional exemption from the prescribed sentences for second degree murder. It is open to Parliament to modify the existing law by appropriate legislation that establishes sentencing criteria for "mercy" killing. In the meantime, it is not for the court to pass on the wisdom of Parliament with respect to the range of penalties to be imposed on those found guilty of murder. Furthermore, as observed by Lamer CJC in *Luxton*, supra,

p. 460, Parliament has been sensitive to the particular circumstances of each offender, even in cases of first degree murder, through various processes allowing for the royal prerogative of mercy, the availability of escorted absences from custody for humanitarian rehabilitation purposes and for early parole.

We dismiss the appellant's application for a constitutional exemption and affirm the sentence imposed by the learned trial judge.

These references to the royal prerogative of mercy, including that appearing in Luxton's case upon which this judgment is based, bring to mind the century-old case of *The Queen v. Dudley and Stephens*, [1884-85] 14 QB Div. 273. There a man, lost at sea and starving to death along with others, turned to a weakened boy lying at the bottom of the boat, prayed for forgiveness, and killed the boy for the purpose of saving himself and the others from starvation. He was found guilty of murder, on a special verdict handed down by a reluctant jury and affirmed in law by a five-judge court, and was thereupon sentenced to death in accordance with the law. In delivering the views of the court upon the matter, Coleridge CJ noted the inherent difficulty in finding the accused guilty of murder and sentencing him accordingly [at p. 288]:

> It is not suggested that in this particular case the deeds were "devilish," but it is quite plain that such a principle [of necessity] once admitted might be made the legal cloak for unbridled passion and atrocious crime. There is no safe path for judges to tread but to ascertain the law to the best of their ability and to declare it according to their judgment; and if in any case the law appears too severe on individuals, to leave it to the Sovereign to exercise that prerogative of mercy which the Constitution has entrusted to the hands fittest to dispense it.

The sentence was afterwards commuted by the Crown to six months' imprisonment in exercise of the royal prerogative of mercy.

This is an aside, however, for the point at issue is that the law has not been changed since this Court rendered its previous judgment, and counsel could point us to no more recent authority bearing upon the case. Counsel for the Attorney General referred to some added authority on whether it is possible to grant a constitutional exemption from the operation of any of the provisions of the *Criminal Code* in the absence of a finding, pursuant to section 52(1) of the *Constitution Act, 1982*, that such provisions are inconsistent with the Charter and therefore of no force or effect to the extent of such inconsistency. This is neither here nor there, however, for the purpose at hand, and it is unnecessary to consider the matter.

Nor is it necessary to take up the submission made on behalf of the Intervenors, who stood four-square against any diminution by the courts of the consequences prescribed by Parliament for murder, including the intentional taking of the life of a disabled person, however badly disabled.

It is unnecessary to do so because we are not minded, as we have said, to depart from the previous judgment of this Court. There is no tenable basis for doing so: the circumstances remain materially the same; the previous judgment was a considered one, made upon a complete foundation, as the reasons therefor demonstrate; and the judgment has not since been affected by any change in the law or by any more recent authority than that referred to in the previous reasons for judgment.

We have decided for the above reasons to allow the appeal of the Attorney General against sentence. Accordingly the sentence imposed in the Court of Queen's Bench is set aside and in its place the minimum mandatory sentence prescribed by the combination of sections 235 and 745.2 of the *Criminal Code* is imposed.

For an interesting discussion of the issues raised by this decision, see B. Sneiderman, "The Case of Robert Latimer: A Commentary on Crime and Punishment" (1999), 37 *Alta. L Rev.* 1017. Also, for a critique of the earlier decision of the Saskatchewan Court of Appeal ((1995), 41 CR (4th) 1), see T. Quigley, "*R v. Latimer*: Hard Cases Make Interesting Law" (1995), 41 CR (4th) 89.

Eradicating the mandatory sentencing scheme for murder, whether in general or on a case-by-case basis, is no simple matter. If Parliament were to alter the present law and permit judges to sentence murderers constrained only by the maximum sentence of life imprisonment, the consequences could well be dramatic. It would have the effect of blurring the distinction between manslaughter and murder, for the purposes of sentencing. Perhaps a new offence of "culpable homicide" might emerge from this change. Although this might have the effect of inducing many more guilty pleas in homicide cases, surely the basis upon which we currently distinguish liability for murder and manslaughter—that is, the intention of the offender—will be relevant to the length of the sentence that is imposed. Collapsing the categories of homicide in order to achieve a more discretionary sentencing regime may merely result in shifting these sorts of decisions from the "trial phase" to the "sentencing phase" of the proceedings. If this happens, what will this do to the right to trial by jury in this context?

These issues were considered in the United Kingdom by the Select Committee on Murder and Life Imprisonment.[3] After careful consideration of the evidence and views of many leading experts, the committee rejected a proposal that the mandatory sentence of life imprisonment for murder be changed.

IV. APPLYING THE PROVISIONS

A. Determining Parole Eligibility for Second-Degree Murder

The sentencing provisions for second-degree murder have caused Canadian courts great difficulties. The courts have struggled to reach an appropriate interpretation of the provisions. Until recently, there was some controversy over the general approach to this sentencing function. Courts divided on the issue whether there was a general presumption in

---

3 See House of Lords, *Report of the Select Committee on Murder and Life Imprisonment* (HL-78-I) (London: HMSO, 1989). One of the most ardent and persistent critics of the life sentence for murder is the British scholar Lord Windlesham. See, in particular, "The Penalty for Murder," in *Responses to Crime* (Oxford: Clarendon Press, 1987); "Life Imprisonment: A Sentence Nobody Can Understand?" in *Responses to Crime—Penal Policy in the Making*, vol. 2 (Oxford: Clarendon Press, 1993); and "Life Sentences: The Defects of Duality" in *Responses to Crime—Legislating with the Tide* (Oxford: Clarendon Press, 1996).

favour of imposing the 10-year minimum, leaving the question of dangerousness to the parole board. This view saw increases beyond the minimum only in "unusual circumstances" (see *R v. Gourgon* (1981), 58 CCC (2d) 193 (BC CA) and *R v. Jordan* (1983), 7 CCC (3d) 143 (BC CA)). Others favoured an approach that allowed the sentencing judge to fix the period of parole eligibility at a level that he or she thought was "fit," free from presumptions of restraint (see *R v. Mitchell* (1987), 39 CCC (3d) 141 (NS SCAD) and *R v. Wenarchuk* (1982), 67 CCC (2d) 169 (Sask. CA)). After many years of (sometimes sharp) judicial debate, the Supreme Court of Canada purported to settle the issue in *R v. Shrosphire*.

R v. Shropshire
(1995), 43 CR (4th) 269 (SCC)

IACOBUCCI J: This appeal was allowed on June 15, 1995, with reasons to follow. These are those reasons.

At issue in this appeal are the factors and principles that should guide a trial judge in determining whether to extend the period of parole ineligibility on a second degree murder conviction beyond the statutory minimum of 10 years. This appeal also touches on the appropriate standard of appellate review to be exercised when considering a trial judge's decision to postpone the period of parole eligibility. Both of these issues engage the broad theme of when the discretion of a sentencing judge ought to be altered.

I. Background

The respondent, Michael Thomas Shropshire, pleaded guilty to the second degree murder of Timothy Buffam. The offence was committed at the respondent's home in Abbotsford, British Columbia, on May 26, 1992, during a marijuana transaction between the respondent, the deceased, and Lorne Lang, a third person accompanying the deceased. Lang is otherwise known as "Animal." The respondent was acquainted with Buffam and Lang as the trio had had prior narcotics dealings. Without any warning, the respondent shot Buffam three times in the chest as they were about to enter the garage to complete the marijuana deal. The respondent then chased Lang in his vehicle shouting "Hacksaw told me to do it!" Hacksaw is the nickname of another associate.

Two days later, the respondent gave himself up to the police. After a preliminary hearing, the respondent pleaded guilty to second degree murder. He professed remorse for his actions but was unwilling or unable to explain them. No motive for the killing was ever ascertained. The respondent has a prior criminal record including two convictions in Youth Court for robbery, a conviction for impaired driving, and two narcotic offences as an adult.

On June 17, 1993, McKinnon J of the Supreme Court of British Columbia sentenced the respondent to life imprisonment without eligibility for parole for 12 years. This period of non-eligibility for parole is two years more than the minimum (and most common) period of parole ineligibility for second degree murder, namely 10 years.

Trial judges are permitted, by virtue of the discretionary power accorded to them by s. 744 of the *Criminal Code*, RSC 1985, c. C-46, to extend the period of parole ineligibility beyond the statutory minimum. The respondent challenged the discretionary s. 744 decision of the trial judge.

On May 4, 1994, a majority of the Court of Appeal for British Columbia allowed the respondent's appeal against sentence, and reduced the period of parole ineligibility to 10 years: (1994) 90 CCC (3d) 234, 45 BCAC 252, 72 WAC 252. Goldie JA dissented and would have dismissed the appeal.

...

III. Judgments Below

A. Supreme Court of British Columbia

McKinnon J stated that it was the duty of a trial judge "to consider the appropriate sentence having regard to the character of the offender, the nature of the offence, and the circumstances surrounding its commission." He then concluded:

> The accused pleaded guilty to second degree murder and I have imposed the mandatory sentence of life imprisonment. It remains to determine the period he must serve before eligibility for parole.
>
> I have the joint submission of Crown and defence that it should be the minimum prescribed, namely ten years. Notwithstanding that submission it is the duty of the trial judge to consider the appropriate sentence having regard to the character of the offender, the nature of the offence, and the circumstances surrounding its commission.
>
> This offence was committed during a marijuana transaction between three people who had prior similar dealings and who were certainly known to one another. The accused was selling a quantity of marijuana to one Lang. The deceased, Buffam, was along as both driver and co-purchaser but appears to have been a minor player insofar as this transaction was concerned. It was set up between Shropshire and Lang.
>
> There is some indication that Shropshire anticipated trouble with Lang as he owed him $1,400, but the evidence is equivocal as Lang claims they were warmly greeted by Shropshire when they arrived. In any event, according to Lang, nothing transpired while there to cause Mr. Shropshire to fire three bullets into Buffam. Mr. Shropshire professes remorse for his actions but seems unwilling to explain just why he killed Mr. Buffam.
>
> Lang says that for reasons completely foreign to him, Shropshire fired three shots into Buffam as they were all about to enter the garage to complete the marijuana deal. Shropshire then chased Lang with his vehicle, and depending upon whose version you accept it was either to get him to come back to the house and phone the police or to kill him as well. Independent witnesses noted the car chase but only Lang could say that Shropshire attempted to shoot him in this chase. Various shouts by Shropshire to Lang about "Hacksaw told me to do it" were made. Hacksaw is apparently the nickname of another associate. It is all very strange, made even stranger by Mr. Shropshire's unwillingness or inability to explain his actions.
>
> Mr. Shropshire is only twenty-three years old but has a criminal record for both narcotic offences and offences of violence. He has the support of both his parents and

his wife with whom he has two children. He appears to have been involved in the criminal element for most of his young years, and while I would not want to unduly affect what must be a life that is still very much capable of reformation, given the factors which I must consider, balanced against the facts, I believe the period of ineligibility must be for twelve years. I so impose such period.

B. British Columbia Court of Appeal (1994), 90 CCC (3d) 234

The majority of the court allowed the appeal against sentence and reduced the period of parole ineligibility to 10 years.

(i) Per Lambert JA (Cumming JA concurring)

Lambert JA found it hard to conceive that "the sentencing principles of general deterrence and specific deterrence should have any application in setting a period of ineligibility of parole of longer than 10 years" (p. 237). He stated that if someone was not deterred by the thought of a life sentence coupled with ineligibility for parole for a period of 10 years, then it was hard to conceive that extending the period of ineligibility for parole would have any deterrent effect on that person.

Lambert JA found that the effect of an order imposing a period of parole ineligibility longer than 10 years was to prevent the parole board from exercising "the very function it is designed to perform" (p. 238). To this end, so as not to usurp the function of the parole board, such an order could only be issued in unusual circumstances. More specifically, the extended period of the parole ineligibility order could only be based upon two justifications. First, if "the judge forms the impression that the convicted person is dangerous if left at large and will continue to be dangerous after the passage of 10 years and that the evidence at trial is such that the judge considers that he has a clearer view of the danger of the person in question than the parole board will have in 10 years time, when the relevance of the question of danger becomes significant at all" (p. 238). Second, when denunciation is of the essence: "a conclusion that a sentence of life imprisonment coupled with parole ineligibility for a period of 10 years is an insufficient denunciation by society, having regard to the gravity of the offence" (p. 238).

Lambert JA then concluded that neither of these reasons justified McKinnon J's decision to extend the period of parole ineligibility in this case. With respect to dangerousness, Lambert JA observed that McKinnon J had failed to give sufficient reasons for forming his opinion. Regarding denunciation, Lambert JA held (at pp. 238-39):

> ... in imposing such a denunciatory sentence ... the cost of keeping him in for extra years is in excess of $50,000 a year ... and ... in imposing extra years of parole ineligibility it must be concluded that the extra denunciation is worth more than $50,000 a year to society. ...

> I cannot fit the reason given by the sentencing judge, namely, that there was no explanation given by the accused when he pleaded guilty about why he committed this

murder, within the two categories which I have mentioned. I do not think that reason comes either in the first category of dangerousness, or within the second category of denunciation.

I think it is a relevant circumstance that both Crown counsel and defence counsel, in their submissions to the sentencing judge, submitted that a period of parole ineligibility of 10 years as required by the Code was the appropriate period.

I consider in this case that a period of parole ineligibility of 10 years meets the goals of Parliament in enacting these provisions. I do not think there was any unusual circumstance in this case ... which would justify an increase.

(ii) Per Goldie JA (Dissenting)

Goldie JA held that the *Criminal Code* requires a trial judge to consider the circumstances surrounding the commission of the crime. Goldie JA stated that the effect of the respondent's refusal to disclose the circumstances surrounding the incident "blocks at the threshold a meaningful consideration of the reasons for his anti-social behaviour, that is to say, for an act the foreseeable consequence of which was death—the very epitome of anti-social behaviour" (p. 241). He concluded therefore that the respondent's silence was of relevance in justifying the imposition of a longer period of parole ineligibility (at p. 241):

> In my view, in the absence of any explanation, a virtually random, certainly irrational on the face of it, and senseless taking of a life should put this behaviour at the upper end, not the lower end of the offence of second degree murder. Furthermore, in the absence of an explanation it was entirely open to the sentencing judge to treat the earlier convictions of robbery and armed robbery, although committed six years before, as offences of violence. I take from that, he treated this offence as continuing evidence of a propensity. Indeed, there was nothing that would have allowed him to treat the killing here as the aberration of the moment.
>
> In my view, the deliberate refusal to offer an explanation for the occurrence of such a serious offence is a circumstance in itself which should be treated as sufficiently unusual as to justify an increased period of ineligibility. Silence after the plea of guilty is not the same thing as silence before conviction.

Goldie JA added that the reason for protecting the right to remain silent disappeared with the plea of guilty. The respondent could not expect to be rewarded for remaining silent in the sentencing circumstances. Goldie JA then concluded that the trial judge did not err with respect to the enhanced period of parole ineligibility (at p. 242):

> He [the trial judge] took cognizance of the factors he was bound to consider in the unusual circumstance that the [respondent] chose to create. He did not impose a period that suggested he was substituting first degree murder for what occurred. He took into account the character, lifestyle, and age of the accused so far as he could do so in the absence of any cooperation from the [respondent]. He considered the mitigating circumstances so far as he was informed of them. In my view, the added two year period was fit and I would have dismissed the appeal.

IV. Issues on Appeal

I would state the issues in the following manner:

1. What are the appropriate factors for a sentencing judge to consider in determining whether a period of parole ineligibility of longer than 10 years should be awarded for an individual convicted of second degree murder?

...

V. Analysis

A. What are the appropriate factors for a sentencing judge to consider in determining whether a period of parole ineligibility of longer than 10 years should be awarded for an individual convicted of second degree murder?

The majority of the British Columbia Court of Appeal held that there are only two factors to consider in justifying an enhanced period of parole ineligibility: (1) an assessment of future dangerousness, and (2) denunciation. With respect, I disagree. Although these factors are of relevance in justifying an extension of the period of parole ineligibility, they are by no means determinative or exclusive.

Section 744 of the *Criminal Code* authorizes a trial judge to impose a period of parole ineligibility greater than the minimum 10-year period. This provision, which governs this appeal, reads as follows:

> 744. Subject to section 744.1, at the time of the sentencing under paragraph 742(b) of an offender who is convicted of second degree murder, the judge who presided at the trial of the offender ... may, having regard to the character of the offender, the nature of the offence and the circumstances surrounding its commission ... substitute for ten years a number of years of imprisonment (being more than ten but not more than twenty-five) without eligibility for parole, as the judge deems fit in the circumstances.

The determination under s. 744 is thus a very fact-sensitive process. The factors to be considered in fixing an extended period of parole ineligibility are:

(1) the character of the offender;
(2) the nature of the offence; and
(3) the circumstances surrounding the commission of the offence;

all bearing in mind the discretionary power conferred on the trial judge.

No reference is made to denunciation or assessments of future dangerousness in the statutory language. By elevating "denunciation" and "assessment of future dangerousness" as the only criteria by which extended periods of parole ineligibility can be determined, the majority of the British Columbia Court of Appeal has, in effect, judicially amended the clear statutory language. This is not to say, however, that these two criteria should not be part of the analysis. For example, "denunciation" can fall within the statutory criterion of the "nature of the offence." Similarly, "future dangerousness" can fall within the rubric of the "character of the offender."

On the issue of denunciation, Lambert JA stated that it would not provide a valid basis for ordering a longer period of parole ineligibility unless it is "concluded that the extra denunciation is worth more than $50,000 a year to society" (p. 239). I cannot accept that position. It is entirely inappropriate to require a trial judge to engage in such a cost-benefit budgetary analysis. As submitted by the appellant before this Court:

> The question of how society allocates public resources is for Parliament to determine. By enacting s. 744, Parliament has determined that some of society's resources will be allocated to imprisoning convicted murderers beyond the ten year point. If Parliament determines that the fiscal cost of that incarceration is too high, then they can amend s. 744. It is not the task of individual judges carrying out the sentencing process to engage in that kind of budgetary analysis.

Furthermore, this sort of fiscal analysis would yield undesirable results from a policy perspective.

"Deterrence" is also a relevant criterion in justifying a s. 744 order. Parole eligibility informs the content of the "punishment" meted out to an offender: for example, there is a very significant difference between being behind bars and functioning within society while on conditional release. Consequently, I believe that lengthened periods of parole ineligibility could reasonably be expected to deter some persons from reoffending. Such is also the position of a variety of provincial appellate courts, from which the British Columbia Court of Appeal presently diverges: *R v. Wenarchuk* (1982), 67 CCC (2d) 169 (Sask. CA); *R v. Mitchell* (1987), 39 CCC (3d) 141 (NSCA); *R v. Young* (1993), 78 CCC (3d) 538 (NSCA); *R v. Able* (1993), 65 OAC 37 (CA); *R v. Ly* (1992), 72 CCC (3d) 57 (Man. CA), per Twaddle JA (Scott CJM concurring), at p. 61: "Parliament's purpose in adding a minimum period of parole ineligibility to a life sentence was, in my view, twofold. It was to deter and denounce the crime."

More importantly, the British Columbia Court of Appeal's position is also irreconcilable with the view taken by this Court of the interplay between parole eligibility and deterrence. For example, in *R v. Arkell*, [1990] 2 SCR 695, at p. 704 it was stated:

> ... the distinction between first and second degree murder ... is a maximum extra fifteen years that must be served before one is eligible for parole. ... Parliament's decision to treat more seriously murders that have been committed while the offender is exploiting a position of power through illegal domination of the victim [i.e. first degree murder] accords with the principle that there must be a proportionality between a sentence and the moral blameworthiness of the offender and other considerations such as deterrence and societal condemnation of the acts of the offender.

The only difference in terms of punishment between first and second degree murder is the duration of parole ineligibility. This clearly indicates that parole ineligibility is part of the "punishment" and thereby forms an important element of sentencing policy. As such, it must be concerned with deterrence, whether general or specific. The jurisprudence of this Court is clear that deterrence is a well-established objective of sentencing policy. In *R v. Lyons*, [1987] 2 SCR 309, La Forest J held at p. 329:

In a rational system of sentencing, the respective importance of prevention, deterrence, retribution and rehabilitation will vary according to the nature of the crime and the circumstances of the offender. No one would suggest that any of these functional considerations should be excluded from the legitimate purview of legislative or judicial decisions regarding sentencing.

Section 744 must be concerned with all of the factors cited in *Lyons*. In *R v. Luxton*, [1990] 2 SCR 711, the importance of structuring sentences to take into account the individual accused and the particular crime was emphasized. This is also a factor that any order made pursuant to s. 744 ought to take into consideration.

The exercise of a trial judge's discretion under s. 744 should not be more strictly circumscribed than the sentencing itself. The section does not embody any limiting statutory language; rather it is quite the contrary. In its terms, it is very similar to s. 745, which permits an application to be made to reduce the parole ineligibility period after 15 years of incarceration. Section 745 has recently been given judicial scrutiny by this Court in *R v. Swietlinski*, [1994] 3 SCR 481. That case involved an assessment of the relevant considerations for a jury hearing a s. 745 application; Lamer CJ concluded at p. 500:

> It is true that deterrence is one of the functions of the penalty and that it is therefore legitimate for the jury to take this factor into account when hearing an application under s. 745.

There is no reason why the functions of s. 744 should be given a more restrictive interpretation than those of s. 745.

In any event, independent of the effect that parole ineligibility may empirically have on recidivism, Lambert JA's reasoning, in both this case as well as in *R v. Hogben* (1994), 40 BCAC 257, completely precludes the concept of "deterrence" from informing the decision of whether or not to extend the period of parole ineligibility. This in my view constitutes an unduly restrictive interpretation of s. 744 and erroneously contravenes the jurisprudence of this court as well as other appellate courts.

I also find it necessary to deal with Lambert JA's conclusion that a period of parole ineligibility in excess of 10 years will not be justified unless there are "unusual circumstances." This conclusion resonates in the earlier decisions of the British Columbia Court of Appeal in *R v. Brown* (1993), 83 CCC (3d) 394, and *R v. Gourgon* (1981), 58 CCC (2d) 193. In my opinion, this is too high a standard and makes it overly difficult for trial judges to exercise the discretionary power to set extended periods of parole ineligibility. The language of s. 744 does not require "unusual circumstances." As a result, to so require by judicial pronouncement runs contrary to Parliamentary intent.

In my opinion, a more appropriate standard, which would better reflect the intentions of Parliament, can be stated in this manner: as a general rule, the period of parole ineligibility shall be for 10 years, but this can be ousted by a determination of the trial judge that, according to the criteria enumerated in s. 744, the offender should wait a longer period before having his suitability to be released into the general public assessed. To this end, an extension of the period of parole ineligibility would not be "unusual," although it may well be that, in the median number of cases, a period of 10 years might still be awarded.

I am supported in this conclusion by a review of the legislative history, academic commentary, and judicial interpretation of s. 744, and the sentencing scheme for second degree murder.

Section 742(b) of the Code provides that a person sentenced to life imprisonment for second degree murder shall not be eligible for parole "until he has served at least ten years of his sentence or such greater number of years, not being more than twenty-five years, as has been substituted therefor pursuant to section 744." In permitting a sliding scale of parole ineligibility, Parliament intended to recognize that, within the category of second degree murder, there will be a broad range of seriousness reflecting varying degrees of moral culpability. As a result, the period of parole ineligibility for second degree murder will run anywhere between a minimum of 10 years and a maximum of 25, the latter being equal to that prescribed for first degree murder. The mere fact that the median period gravitates towards the 10-year minimum does not, ipso facto, mean that any other period of time is "unusual."

I should pause to repeat that in the instant appeal we are concerned with a period of parole ineligibility for second degree murder of 12 years, this being only two years more than the minimum.

If the objective of s. 744 is to give the trial judge an element of discretion in sentencing to reflect the fact that within second degree murder there is both a range of seriousness and varying degrees of moral culpability, then it is incorrect to start from the proposition that the sentence must be the statutory minimum unless there are unusual circumstances. As discussed supra, a preferable approach would be to view the 10-year period as a minimum contingent on what the "judge deems fit in the circumstances," the content of this "fitness" being informed by the criteria listed in s. 744. As held in other Canadian jurisdictions, the power to extend the period of parole ineligibility need not be sparingly used.

For example, in *R v. Wenarchuk*, supra, the Saskatchewan Court of Appeal (per Bayda CJS for a five-judge panel) held at p. 173 that:

> [It is no longer appropriate] that the "order (increasing the parole non-eligibility period) should be sparingly made." The order should be made whenever such an order is "fit in the circumstances."

I would equally affirm the following passage from the decision of the Nova Scotia Court of Appeal in *R v. Doyle* (1991), 108 NSR (2d) 1, at p. 5, leave to appeal to this Court refused, [1992] 2 SCR vi, which I find apposite to the present discussion:

> The Code does not fix the sentence for second degree murder as life imprisonment with no parole eligibility for ten years. The discretion conferred on the sentencing judge by s. 742(b) and s. 744 is not whether to move from a prima facie period of ten years, but rather what is a fit sentence, applying the proper guidelines. Unusual circumstances are not the prerequisite for moving away from the ten year minimum, although as the cases illustrate, they certainly play a role in the proper exercise of the judicial discretion. ...
>
> It is not the law that unusual circumstances, brutality, torture or a bad record must be demonstrated before the judge may exercise his discretion to move above the ten years minimum. Nor is there any burden on the Crown to demonstrate that the period should be more than the minimum.

On another note, I do not find that permitting trial judges to extend the period of parole ineligibility usurps or impinges upon the function of the parole board. I am cognizant of the fact that, upon the expiry of the period of parole ineligibility, there is no guarantee of release into the public. At that point, it is incumbent upon the parole board to assess the suitability of such release, and in so doing it is guided by the legislative objectives of the parole system: see ss. 101 and 102 of the *Corrections and Conditional Release Act*, SC 1992, c. 20. However, it is clear that the parole board is not the only participant in the parole process. All it is designed to do is, within the parameters defined by the judiciary, decide whether an offender can be released. A key component of those parameters is the determination of when the period of parole eligibility (i.e. when the parole board can commence its administrative review function) starts to run. This is the manner in which the system is geared to function—with complementary yet distinct input from both the judiciary and the parole administrators. It is the role of the sentencing judge to circumscribe, in certain statutorily defined circumstances, the operation of the parole board. The decision of McKinnon J in the case at bar neither skews this balance nor unduly trumps the function of the parole board. As noted by the Saskatchewan Court of Appeal in *Wenarchuk*, supra, at pp. 172-73:

> The object of the provision in s. 671 [now s. 744] is not to take away from the Parole Board, or in some way diminish, the Board's function to determine whether the accused is sufficiently rehabilitated (from the standpoint of risk to and the protection of society) to permit his release into society. ... The object, rather, is to give back to the judge some of the discretion he normally has in the matter of sentencing—discretion that the statute took away from him when it provided for a life sentence [for murder]—so that the judge may do justice, not retributive or punitive justice, but justice to reflect the accused's culpability and to better express society's repudiation for the particular crime committed by the particular accused (with that repudiation's attendant beneficial consequences for society, including its protection through individual and general deterrence and, where necessary, segregation from society). ...
>
> An order under s. 671 does not impinge upon the powers of the Board. At most, it has the effect of postponing the Board's exercise of its powers—its full powers.

Applying these legal principles to the particular facts of this case, I do not see any error on the part of the trial judge. He adverted to the fact that the respondent had pleaded guilty and was only 23 years old. He recognized that the Crown was not seeking a period of parole ineligibility beyond the minimum. Nevertheless, in a legitimate exercise of his discretionary power, and after correctly reviewing the factors set out in s. 744, he imposed a 12-year period of parole ineligibility. He referred to the following factors as specifically justifying the 12-year period of parole ineligibility:

(a) the circumstances of the killing were strange in that they provided no real answer to why it took place, and the respondent was unwilling or unable to explain his actions;

(b) the murder was committed during the course of committing another offence, namely a drug transaction; and

(c) the respondent has a record for both narcotic offences and violence.

Factors (b) and (c) clearly fall within the categories ("character," "nature" and "circumstances surrounding") established by s. 744. As to factor (b), I further note that the Manitoba Court of Appeal, in *R v. Ly*, supra, held that the period of parole ineligibility could be increased when the murder is committed in the course of another crime, particularly a crime of violence.

Factor (a), however, presents some difficulty. The respondent raises the question whether the trial judge erred in interpreting the respondent's silence in such a manner as to justify extending the period of parole ineligibility.

In response, I would affirm the analysis of Goldie JA in the court below (at pp. 241-42) and would hold that this silence is readily assimilable within the "circumstances surrounding the offence" criterion. The crux of Goldie JA's comments is that, in the absence of any explanation for a random and seemingly senseless killing, the trial judge was correct in sentencing the respondent in light of his refusal to offer an explanation. It was found that his refusal was deliberate and in and of itself unusual. After all, the respondent, a drug dealer with previous convictions for robbery and armed robbery, shot the victim Buffam in cold blood without provocation of any kind.

It is not for the trial judge to speculate what the respondent might have said to mitigate the severity of the offence. I quite agree with Goldie JA that the right to silence, which is fully operative in the investigative and prosecutorial stages of the criminal process, wanes in importance in the post-conviction phase when sentencing is at issue. However, in so agreeing, I emphasize that the respondent pleaded guilty; I leave for future consideration the question of drawing a negative inference from the silence of the accused when he or she has pleaded not guilty and wishes to appeal the conviction. In the case at bar, the trial judge even went so far as to invite the accused to suggest why he may have committed the offence, but no response was forthcoming. As held by Goldie JA (at p. 242), the respondent "cannot expect to be rewarded for remaining silent in the circumstances." The court and the public clearly have an interest in knowing why a human life was taken by an offender.

Goldie JA's comments and the decision of the trial judge on the "silence" issue are fully consonant with the position taken by the Ontario Court of Appeal. In *R v. Able*, supra, the Court of Appeal increased two co-accused's periods of parole ineligibility. At page 39 it was held:

> No explanation has been forthcoming from either of the appellants with respect to the reason for the killing ... [which] can be best described as a callous, brutal, pointless, execution-style killing of a helpless victim.

I conclude that in certain circumstances, such as those presented in this case, it is proper to take into account the absence of an explanation of attenuating factors.

The respondent suggests that Goldie JA's comments and the decision of the trial judge contravene the pronouncements of this Court in *R v. Gardiner*, [1982] 2 SCR 368. I recognize that, in *Gardiner*, this Court extended certain procedural rights to sentencing proceedings. However, these were limited to the right to counsel, the right to call evidence, the right to cross-examine and the right to address the court. There is no mention made of the creation in its identical form of a substantive right such as the right to silence.

At the sentencing stage, the Crown has already proved beyond a reasonable doubt that the accused has committed the crime for which he or she stood charged or, as in this appeal, the accused has pleaded guilty to the offence; if the accused then seeks to receive the least severe sentence commensurate with his or her conviction (i.e. for second degree murder, life imprisonment with eligibility for parole after 10 years have elapsed) it is incumbent upon the accused to play a somewhat active role in the process. I note that the right to silence is a manifestation of the presumption of innocence: *R v. Broyles*, [1991] 3 SCR 595; *R v. Hebert*, [1990] 2 SCR 151; *R v. Chambers*, [1990] 2 SCR 1293. The presumption of innocence flows to those "charged with an offence" or suspected of having committed one; once an individual has been convicted of an offence he or she is no longer simply "charged."

...

VI. Conclusions and Disposition

The trial judge properly considered the relevant factors in exercising the discretionary jurisdiction given to him under s. 744. The Court of Appeal erred in postulating an unduly restrictive and narrow approach to s. 744 and by adopting a standard of appellate review that was tantamount to substituting its opinion for that of the trial judge. Consequently, I would allow the appeal, set aside the decision of the British Columbia Court of Appeal, and restore the trial judge's s. 744 order of a period of parole ineligibility of 12 years.

———————

For commentary on this case, see A. Manson, "The Supreme Court Intervenes in Sentencing" (1995), 43 CR (4th) 306; G. Trotter, "*R v. Shropshire*: Murder, Sentencing and the Supreme Court of Canada" (1995), 43 CR (4th) 288; and J. Norris, "Sentencing for Second-Degree Murder: *R v. Shropshire*" (1996), 1 *Can. Crim. LR* 199.

Despite the authoritative pronouncement in *Shropshire*, the debate about parole eligibility persists. Consider the decision of the British Columbia Court of Appeal in *R v. Mafi* (1999), 142 CCC (3d) 449. After a jury found Mafi guilty of two counts of second-degree murder, the trial judge fixed parole ineligibility at 20 years. By a two-to-one majority, the British Columbia Court of Appeal reduced parole ineligibility to 15 years. The majority (two concurring judgments of McEachern CJBC and Lambert JA) and the minority split over the fundamental approach to sentencing under the murder provisions. The majority judgments rail against the restrictive approach to appellate review of sentencing decisions articulated in *Shropshire*. In the more temperate of the concurring majority judgments, the chief justice of British Columbia suggests that strict adherence to the Supreme Court's approach may "effectively deprive an accused of an effective right of appeal" (at 467). These criticisms of *Shropshire*, which include a consideration of *Mafi*, are reviewed in Chapter 2.[4]

———————

4 The concern with *Shropshire* is not limited to British Columbia. See also *R v. McKnight* (1999), 135 CCC (3d) 41 (Ont. CA), in which the appellant was convicted of the second-degree murder of his wife

B. The Role of the Jury

Another reason why sentencing for murder is unique is the role that is given to the jury upon a conviction for second-degree murder. The jury is permitted to make a "recommendation" on the issue of parole eligibility. Murder is the only offence in the *Criminal Code* that contemplates any formal role for the jury in the sentencing process. This procedure casts the jury in an unusual role. Unlike its task in deciding guilt or innocence, in the sentencing context, the jury need not be unanimous. Indeed, it is possible (although unlikely) that each juror could come to a different conclusion on this issue. More fundamentally, the section only calls for a "recommendation." The reality is that sentencing juries often do not provide unanimous recommendations, leaving the presiding judge with several views on the appropriate period of parole eligibility.

The cases below demonstrate that the courts are ambivalent about how to integrate a jury's recommendation into the ultimate decision. Indeed, the courts cannot even agree on the proper procedure that ought to be employed in eliciting the input of the jury on this issue. Some courts have held that the offender and the Crown may address the jury before it makes its recommendation (see *R v. Atsiqtaq*, [1988] NWTR 315 (SC)). Other courts have held that there is no right to be heard on this issue (see *R v. Neposse*, infra; *R v. Okkuatsiak* (1993), 80 CCC (3d) 251 (Nfld. CA); *R v. Challice* (1994), 20 CRR (2d) 319 (Ont. Ct. (Gen. Div.)); and *R v. Cruz* (1998), 124 CCC (3d) 157 (BC CA)). As we shall see in the next section, the jury has de facto decision-making power on a review of parole eligibility after 15 years.

R v. Nepoose
(1988), 46 CCC (3d) 421 (Alta. CA)

STRATTON JA: The question raised by this appeal is the propriety of the parties adducing evidence and addressing a jury under s. 670 of the *Criminal Code* after a conviction and before the jury respond to the question of whether or not they wish to make a recommendation with respect to ineligibility for parole.

Section 670 reads as follows:

> 670. Where a jury finds an accused guilty of second degree murder, the judge who presides at the trial shall, before discharging the jury, put to them the following question:

> You have found the accused guilty of second degree murder and the law requires that I now pronounce a sentence of imprisonment for life against him. Do you wish to make any recommendation with respect to the number of years that he must serve before he is eligible for release on parole? You are not required to make any recommendation but if you do, your recommendation will be considered by me when I am

---

and sentenced to life imprisonment without parole eligibility for 17 years. On appeal, the Court of Appeal for Ontario, by a two-to-one majority, reduced the ineligibility period to 14 years. The court (McMurtry CJO dissenting) differed on the appropriate degree of deference required by *Shropshire*.

determining whether I should substitute for the ten year period, which the law would otherwise require the accused to serve before he is eligible to be considered for release on parole, a number of years that is more than ten but not more than twenty-five.

This appellant was convicted by a jury of second degree murder. Immediately following the delivery of that verdict, the trial judge informed the jury that they had one further task and he then read to them s. 670 of the Code. He then stated that the procedure he contemplated was to have counsel make submissions to the jury as to whether the 10-year period of parole ineligibility should be extended.

Upon calling for submissions from counsel, defence counsel for the trial had this to say:

Well, the jury has heard the evidence and I think that there is no need for me to make any further submission, I think they understand Mr. Nepoose's family history, his background and the milieu from which he comes. And, I would just simply remind them to or ask them to think about that and make no recommendation at all.

Crown counsel added his own explanation of s. 670 and then presented to the jury a full statement of the appellant's lengthy and serious criminal record including the sentences he received for prior convictions. Ultimately, the jury returned with a recommendation that "the sentence be served a minimum of 20 years before eligibility for parole."

The trial judge pointed out, quite correctly, that he had the responsibility to make the final decision on sentence after considering the factors set out in s. 671, including the jury's recommendation. Counsel then made further brief comments concerning the appellant's age and state of health, whereupon the trial judge ordered that the period of parole ineglibility should be 15 years.

Section 671 of the *Criminal Code* reads as follows:

671. At the time of the sentencing under paragraph 669(b) of an offender who is convicted of second degree murder, the judge who presided at the trial of the offender or, if that judge is unable to do so, and judge of the same court may, having regard to the character of the offender, the nature of the offence and the circumstances surrounding its commission, and to the recommendation, if any, made pursuant to section 670, by order, substitute for ten years a number of years of imprisonment (being more than ten but not more than twenty-five), without eligibility for parole, as he deems fit in the circumstances.

The appellant now contends that the trial judge erred in allowing counsel to adduce facts and make submissions to the jury with regard to the period of parole ineligibility. The second ground of appeal was that the 15 years imposed by the trial judge was excessive under all the circumstances.

On the first point, no cases directly on the issue were presented to us for our consideration. A case which touches upon but does not resolve the issue is *R v. Joseph* (1984), 15 CCC (3d) 314 (BC CA). In his judgment in that case, Craig JA of the British Columbia Court of Appeal says at p. 314:

There was some discussion between counsel and the trial judge with regard to the fact that counsel had not had the opportunity to address the jury regarding any possible recommendation. The trial judge indicated that in the circumstances he was going to deal with the matter on the basis of submissions made to him by counsel. Counsel made some submissions. The judge sentenced Joseph to life imprisonment with a direction that he serve 20 years before being eligible for parole.

and further at p. 316:

Counsel for Joseph, pointing out that he had not had an opportunity to address the jury, made brief submissions as to why the judge should not give effect to the jury's recommendation. The judge then said that he was going to "accede to the recommendation of the jury" and sentenced Joseph to imprisonment for life, directing that he not be eligible for parole for 20 years.

In reducing the period of ineligibility for parole to 10 years, the British Columbia Court of Appeal neither approved nor disapproved of the procedure followed by the trial judge. It is clear that the Appeal Court simply felt that the period of ineligibility pronounced by the trial judge was inappropriately long. In the result, the *Joseph* case is of little assistance in the present appeal other than to show that the court did not criticize the procedure there adopted.

Defence counsel argued strenuously that the jury's recommendation under s. 670 should be based solely on the evidence leading to the conviction and that the jury should hear no further evidence or argument for the purposes of a s. 670 recommendation.

We agree with that submission which we conclude is supported by the very words and structure of the relevant sections of the Code.

Section 670 is uniquely framed. The precise question required to be put to the jury is set out in quotations and contains within its wording a complete explanation of the jury's responsibility. It is abundantly clear that the jury's decision under s. 670 is not final. No statement whatsoever of the factors to be considered by the jury in making or declining to make such recommendation is set out.

That situation must be contrasted to s. 671, which authorizes the final sentencing decision of the judge and specifies the factors which the judge must have regard to in so doing.

Section 670 may also be compared with s. 672 which allows a jury to be empanelled for the purpose of reviewing, in certain specified circumstances, an earlier decision relating to parole ineligibility. Section 672(2) expressly states what the jury must have regard to in reaching a s. 672 decision. It is significant that a jury's decision under s. 672 is final and not a mere recommendation as in s. 670. A s. 672 jury must have regard to the character of the applicant, his conduct while serving his sentence, the nature of the offence for which he was convicted and such other matters as the judge deems relevant in the circumstances.

If Parliament had intended that a "recommending jury" under s. 670 consider factors other than the material leading to the conviction, I am satisfied it would have so specified as it did for "final" sentencing pronouncements authorized by ss. 671 and 672.

It has been suggested that it is unfair, particularly to an accused, to ask a jury for a recommendation without the benefit of counsel's arguments and the accused's record. The injury which an accused may appear to suffer is really illusory as a s. 670 decision of the jury is not final.

The person empowered to make the final parole ineligibility decision must hear full submissions and must have regard to the specifics set out in s. 671, including the jury's recommendation. With that recommendation before him, the parties may adduce additional evidence and present arguments to the trial judge with respect to the final disposition of the sentencing.

In short, we are of the view that s. 670 is a code of sorts. It is a section which is complete on its own and says with exactitude what is to be presented to the jury on this issue. We conclude that it was the intention of Parliament that a jury, acting under s. 670, should have put to them the exact question set out in the section along with whatever further explanation of the section the trial judge deems necessary. The jury should respond to the question put to it on the basis of only the evidence and arguments of counsel presented prior to and resulting in the conviction and the trial judge's instructions. To allow the jury to hear at that stage of the proceedings the full record of the accused and argument based on that record is, in our view, an error of law. Thus, the recommendation which the trial judge received from the jury was flawed and, although the learned trial judge did not follow that recommendation, we do not know the extent to which it affected his final decision.

In *R v. Walford* (1984), 12 CCC (3d) 257, Nemetz CJBC (Carrothers JA concurring), at p. 259, decided that the approach to be taken by an appellate court in considering an appeal from a period of parole ineligibility set by the trial judge pursuant to s. 671 should be the same as on a normal appeal against sentence, namely, "… to determine what is fit having regard to the facts the trial judge had before him and any relevant new facts before his court which were not before the judge." He continued as follows:

> An appellate court, in my view, has the jurisdiction to vary a sentence whether upwards or downwards despite the trial judge's advantage in seeing and hearing an accused where the appellate court concludes that the sentence imposed was not fit."

We agree with those comments.

In the present case we do not say that the ultimate disposition by the trial judge under s. 671 was not fit, but we do say that we must look at it with special care as that disposition could have been affected by the faulty procedure above mentioned. In the result, we conclude that this court must decide upon a fit parole ineligibility period from a review of the trial record and from the material placed before us at this appeal and in so doing have regard to the factors set out in s. 671 of the Code.

...

In the result, notwithstanding the faulty procedure and the consequent flawed jury recommendation, I agree that the trial judge's determination of 15 years' parole ineligibility was a fit disposition for this appellant under the circumstances of this case.

R v. Ly and Duong
(1992), 72 CCC (3d) 57 (Man. CA)

TWADDLE JA: After a joint trial on a charge of first degree murder, each of the accused was convicted of second degree murder and sentenced to the mandatory term of life imprisonment. Each now appeals from the increased period of parole ineligibility attached to his sentence.

The crime occurred in the course of a rather unsophisticated robbery at the place of Phat Ly's employment. The victim was Phat Ly's employer. Although the robbery was undoubtedly planned and deliberate, the jury by its verdict found that the murder was not.

The circumstances of the victim's death were quite appalling. He had been beaten, tied to furniture by his hands and feet, stabbed by a knife in the neck and face and shot in the head six times. The firearm which was used as most probably a starting pistol which had been bored out to accept bullets and fire them.

When the murder was committed, the offencers were both under the age of 18 years. Neither had a record as a young offender. Events subsequent to the murder, before either was apprehended for this crime, did, however, reuslt in a difference between them.

Phat Ly emigrated to Australia with his mother. He was apprehended there and returned to Canada. He admitted that he had had some involvement with gangs of youths prior to his departure for Australia, but there is nothing to suggest that he was established in a life of crime.

Ky Duong, on the other hand, went to Toronto where he became involved in criminal activity. He was found in each of several residences containing weapons. He was arrested for the crime of break, enter and theft. In August, 1988, some six months after the murder, he became embroiled in a fight between members of rival gangs. A member of the gang which was opposed to Ky Duong was killed in gun-fire. Ky Duong was convicted of manslaughter with respect to that incident and sentenced to serve a term of $6\frac{1}{2}$ years' imprisonment.

With the exception of Ky Duong's criminal activity subsequent to the murder, the jury was well aware of all the circumstances relevant to sentencing when it was asked, pursuant to the Code, whether it wished to make any recommendation with respect to the number of years each accused should serve before he became eligible for release on parole. The jury chose to make a recommendation which was in these terms: "We recommend no more than ten years."

Despite the jury's recommendation, the learned trial judge was of the view that the crime itself merited denunciation by the imposition on each accused of a longer period of parole ineligibility than the minimum. He was also of the view that an even longer period was required in the case of Ky Duong "to reflect the relative role and character of the offenders." He consequently increased the minimum period to 15 years for Phat Ly and to 20 years for Ky Duong. It is from these increased periods of parole ineglibility that the accused appeal.

...

The Jury's Recommendation

In conferring a role on the jury in the sentencing process, Parliament must surely have intended to provide the judge with one measure of the public's revulsion at the crime. The judge is not, of course, bound by what the jury recommends, but it is an indication to him of the need for denunciation beyond that inherent in the mandatory sentence.

R v. Joseph (1984), 15 CCC (3d) 314 (BC CA), was a case in which the jury recommended 20 years of parole ineligibility. The trial judge accepted the recommendation, but the British Columbia Court of Appeal reduced the period to 10 years. The Court of Appeal accepted that the circumstances of the offence did not merit additional denunciation.

It is entirely possible that there will be a case in which the opposite is true. A jury may recommend leniency where none is warranted. Ordinarily, however, a trial judge should be slow to disregard a jury's lenient recommendation where there is a mitigating feature such as the youth of the offender.

· · ·

In the result, I would allow the sentence appeal of each offender, set aside the period of parole ineligibility imposed on each and substitute, in Phat Ly's case, a period of 12 years and, in Ky Duong's case, a period of 15 years.

LYON JA (dissenting): I have had the advantage of reading the reasons for judgment of my colleague Twaddle JA in these sentence appeals. I must, with respect, disagree with the result he arrives at.

A review of a number of recent decisions on second degree murders committed in furtherance of serious crimes such as robbery and break, enter and theft, indicates sentences for parole ineligibility ranging from the minimum of 10 years to 20 years. However, the majority of the sentences for such murders are in excess of the minimum and tend to range between 14 and 20 years. That there is no uniform consistency in sentencing and that longer periods of ineligibility tend to be given for serious or aggravated murders is the main conclusion one can draw from such a review.

· · ·

Finally, the overriding by the trial judge of the jury's recommendation for minimum eligibility is commented upon by Twaddle JA as another reason for lowering the trial judge's sentences. He states: "Ordinarily, however, a trial judge should be slow to disregard a jury's lenient recommendation where there is a mitigating feature such as the youth of the offender." Again, with respect, I must disagree.

There is nothing sacrosanct about the jury's recommendation. Indeed, as I mention later, the jury's recommendation is made without their receiving any instruction on the general principles of sentencing and, additionally, it is often made without full knowledge of pertinent sentencing information. There is ample authority for the proposition that the trial judge is not bound by the jury's recommendation and that the jury's recommendation is only one of a number of equal factors which the trial judge must consider in passing sentence "as he deems fit in the circumstances" (s. 744, supra).

As Bayda CJS said in *Wenarchuk*, supra, at p. 713:

> Since the decision in *Gulash* [Sask. CA, March 24, 1976 (unreported)], the terms of s. 218 [re-enacted, 1974-75-76, c. 105, s. 5], as noted, were recast and the section has been replaced by ss. 669 to 674 of the present Code. The appearance, for the first time, in s. 671 of the words "as he deems fit in the circumstances," the provision in s. 672 for judicial review, the removal of the provisions contained in the former s. 218(5)(e), and the current provisions, generally, in ss. 669 to 674 no longer make appropriate the statement that the "order [increasing the parole non-eligibility period] should be sparingly

made." The order should be made whenever such an order is "fit in the circumstances." As explained above, it is now no longer a question (if it ever was) of curtailing the powers of the Parole Board. An order under s. 671 does not impinge upon the powers of the Board. At most, it has the effect of *postponing* the Board's exercise of its powers—its full powers.

I also agree with Laycraft CJA (as he then was) when he said in *R v. Modin* (1989), 94 AR 81 at pp. 83-4, 66 Alta. LR (2d) 1, 6 WCB (2d) 406 (CA), in reducing a trial judge's sentence of ineligibility for parole from 20 years (as recommended by the jury) to 15 years:

> We must also respectfully disagree with the test for dealing with the jury's recommen-
> dation put by the learned trial judge. In our view that recommendation is but one of the
> several factors which must be taken into account by the trial judge along with all the
> others. *It is not correct to say that it "should be followed" unless he finds that they are*
> *"manifestly in error" or that "there is no good reason why the recommendation not be*
> *followed."* The expression of that test *was, in our view, an error in law.* Each factor in
> s. 671 (now s. 744) must be weighed and none is more important than the other as the
> process of weighing the factors commences. (My emphasis.)

See also *R v. Ameeriar* (1990), 60 CCC (3d) 431, 10 WCB (2d) 640 (Que. CA). This was a case where the jury was unable to reach unanimity and therefore did not make a recommendation as to parole ineligibility. The trial judge set the period of ineligibility at 15 years. The accused appealed. In dismissing the appeal, Monet JA made the following comments at p. 434:

> The appellant submits that as a general rule the period of ineligibility is limited to 10
> years. He then continues that if the jury recommends that a longer period be substi-
> tuted, the judge would be well advised to take this into consideration and, except for
> some exceptional reason, to give effect to this recommendation. Conversely, if the jury
> does not make a recommendation, the judge errs in not applying the general rule and by
> substituting for the "10-year period," that is, for that period which, within the meaning
> of the Code, is normally 10 years, a much longer period of time.
>
> *This proposition is unfounded. In my view, the final decision in this matter is for, the*
> *judge.* (My emphasis.)

See also *R v. Jordan* (1983), 7 CCC (3d) 143 (BC CA), which also appears to indicate that the recommendation of the jury is not the overriding factor in determining parole ineligibility.

Why must the jury's recommendation be only one factor in sentencing? Simply put, because in many, if not most cases, the jury is not in possession of all of the facts; more importantly, it is never instructed in the jurisprudence which surrounds the sentencing function of a judge; and its participation in the process in the limited manner provided by Code, ss. 744 and 745 represents the only occasions when Parliament has permitted jury involvement in what is otherwise a totally judicial function. As Dr. Don Stuart has observed in his work, *Canadian Criminal Law, A Treatise* (1982), at p. 229:

> Sentencing is an onerous task and expertise in this area is elusive. The involvement of
> the jury in this matter seems anomalous and undesirable. Judges have the advantage of
> experience.

For many of the reasons given herein, the Law Reform Commission of Canada has recommended that jury involvement in the sentencing process be abolished. See Law Reform Commission of Canada, *Homicide, Working Paper 33*, pp. 79 and 116, and excerpt from the Law Reform Commission of Canada, *The Jury*, Report 16 (1982), appended hereto as Appendix "B."

As patently manifested in the case at bar, the jury's only information concerning the accused and their backgrounds was limited to the evidence adduced at trial through the Crown witnesses who dealt, quite properly, solely with matters relevant to the charge in question. The characters of the accused were not raised nor did the co-accused give evidence. Immediately after rendering their verdicts convicting the two accused, the jury made their parole eligibility recommendation and were then discharged. The following day, the trial judge heard extended representations from Crown and defence counsel, all of which contained, as is customarily the case, background and other information to which the jury was not privy. It was only after considering the totality of evidence, the submissions by counsel on sentence, and then *applying s. 774 and the general principles of sentencing* that the trial judge made his determination.

The jury's recommendation, as previously noted, was made without any knowledge whatsoever of the serious criminal activity of Ky Duong subsequent to the murder for which he was to be sentenced. Nor did they know of Ky Duong's ongoing associations with criminal groups in both Winnipeg and Toronto, matters which had been under police surveillance. Nor did the jury have the additional information which crown and defence counsel later gave the court in speaking to sentence. They did not know Ky Duong was associated with one Bau Diu described by Crown counsel as a dangerous and violent criminal living in Toronto. Nor was the jury apprised of the details of the gangland-type stabbing and shooting which resulted in Ky Duong's plea of guilty to a charge of manslaughter in Toronto.

As the trial judge noted in passing sentence (p. 1540 of the transcript):

> He is presently serving six and a half years manslaughter in Toronto, an offence which occurred after the commission of the crime presently before the court. He also had a conviction for break, enter and theft on May 30th, 1988, this offence also having occurred after the commission of this offence.
>
> Mr. Duong did not make any statements to the police as to his role in the crime.
>
> The evidence of Mr. Tong indicates that Mr. Duong bought the firearm and loaded it with bullets while he was in the car and before setting off to the Dunn-Rite plant.
>
> There is no indication of any remorse by Mr. Duong for his actions in this crime.

This information, save the evidence of Mr. Tong, was unknown to the jury. Taken together with all of the circumstances surrounding the crime itself, it represented, in my opinion, more than adequate justification for the sentence imposed on Ky Duong and for altering the jury's recommendation. The justification for the increased period of parole ineligibility for Phat Ly has earlier been reviewed.

In the result, I would dismiss the appeals against sentence.

Appendix "B": The Law Reform Commission of Canada *The Jury*
(Ottawa: Supply and Services, 1982), Report 16

The Law Reform Commission of Canada *The Jury* [Report 16] (Ottawa: Supply and Services, 1982): draft legislation section 26(1) dealing with the judge's instructions to the jury, suggests that:

> As part of his instructions on the law, the judge shall instruct the jury that, in the event of a verdict of guilty, the jury has no prerogative to make any recommendation either as a clemency or as to the severity of the sentence.

This recommendation entails the repeal of the present section 670 of the *Criminal Code*, which provides that where the jury finds an accused guilty of second degree murder, the trial judge shall, before discharging the jury, invite them to make a recommendation regarding eligibility for release on parole. The Report continues on page 70:

> The reasons for this departure are several. First, the jury's principal role is to arrive at a verdict of guilt or innocence by weighing the evidence placed before it at trial. It is no part of that role to determine what sentence is appropriate in the event of conviction. To permit the jury to make a recommendation as to clemency or severity of sentence is to confuse the proper role of the jury with the role of the trial judge, whose exclusive responsibility it is to pronounce sentence upon a finding of guilt. Second, the Commission believes that permitting the jury to recommend clemency may compromise the integrity of its verdict. The promise of a collective plea for clemency could well operate as an effective, but unconscionable, inducement to persuade a reluctant juror to vote with the majority. A recommendation for clemency which the trial judge is under no obligation to accept should play no part in a jury's deliberations about guilt or innocence. Third, because the jury will ordinarily be familiar with the facts of the particular case before them, they will not be cognizant of the several different considerations that bear on sentence the accused's prior criminal record, if any; his *reputation the community*; his antecedent and present circumstances.

Do you think we should maintain a role for the jury in second degree murder cases? If you think we should, would you change the process at all to make it more meaningful—that is, by allowing the prosecutor and the offender to make submissions?

V. JUDICIAL REVIEW AFTER 15 YEARS

The judicial review procedure set out in s. 745 has received little attention in case law and legal literature. This is because this procedure was enacted in 1975 when the penalty for murder was restructured. Given that a person convicted of murder must wait 15 years before pursuing an application for judicial review, the first applications were not heard until the early 1990s. Because the original legislation provided for no right of appeal to the provincial courts of appeal, appellate guidance was difficult to find in this area. The only case in which the Supreme Court has pronounced on these types of hearings is *Swietlinski*, infra.

Moreover, getting a feel for how this procedure should work has been disrupted by the political attention (and consequential amendments) that this procedure has received. It has been an easy target for law-and-order politicians, who have dubbed this procedure the "loophole for lifers." However, Professor Julian Roberts and Judge David Cole provide a more sober approach to the actual operation of the section in the following extract.

J.V. Roberts and D.P. Cole, "Sentencing and Early Release for Offenders Convicted of Murder"
in J.V. Roberts and D.P. Cole, eds., *Making Sense of Sentencing*
(Toronto: University of Toronto Press, 1999)

...

Results of Applications to Date

Opponents and advocates of section 745.6 have disagreed over the results of applications to date. Several facts are clear. First, only a minority of eligible lifers have applied for a reduction of their parole ineligibility. Why this is so is less clear. Defenders of the provision suggest that inmates see little point in applying for a review, as their chances of a positive response are so low. This seems implausible since results currently indicate that most applications have been successful (although this may change as a result of the reforms introduced in 1997, discussed below.) Whatever the reason, the statistics on the outcomes to date should be viewed with this initial degree of selection in mind. Parole Board statistics demonstrate that by the end of 1996 (just prior to the passage of the reform bill), sixty-nine applications had been reviewed by juries. Of these, fifty-five, or 80 percent, had resulted in some reduction in the parole ineligibility period. Of those who had been successful with a jury, almost all had received a positive response on their subsequent application to the Parole Board.

Outcomes of Releases

Statistics of those inmates granted some form of release as of October 1996 reveal the following picture. Of those on day parole, 88 per cent had either completed their day parole period without incident or were still being supervised on day parole. Three out of thirty-two inmates on day parole had had their parole status revoked for violation of conditions; none of these had been charged with a new offence. Of all inmates who were granted a positive review and eventually released on full parole, only one had had his parole status revoked for a new crime (armed robbery).

As Roberts and Cole point out, politicians who claim that parole eligibility review does not have public support seem to ignore the fact that a prisoner's application is determined by a jury, who are usually members of the community where the offence was committed. Accordingly, the prisoner obtains relief only if the jury decides in his or her favour. Does this not reflect some degree of public support for this process? As noted below, the 1997 amendments to these provisions will likely result in fewer successful applications, especially because of the new jury unanimity requirements.

A. Criminal Code, Sections 745.6-746

Application for Judicial Review

745.6(1) Subject to subsection (2), a person may apply, in writing, to the appropriate Chief Justice in the province in which their conviction took place for a reduction in the number of years of imprisonment without eligibility for parole if the person

(a) has been convicted of murder or high treason;

(b) has been sentenced to life imprisonment for life without parole until more than fifteen years of their sentence has been served; and

(c) has served at least fifteen years of their sentence.

(2) A person who has been convicted of more than one murder may not make an application under subsection (1), whether or not proceedings were commenced in respect of any of the murders before another murder was committed.

...

Judicial Screening

745.61(1) On receipt of an application under subsection 745.6(1), the appropriate Chief Justice shall determine, or shall designate a judge of the superior court of criminal jurisdiction to determine, on the basis of the following written material, whether the applicant has shown, on a balance of probabilities, that there is a reasonable prospect that the application will succeed:

(a) the application;

(b) any report provided by the Correctional Service of Canada or other correctional authorities; and

(c) any other written evidence present to the Chief Justice or judge by the applicant or the Attorney General.

(2) In determining whether the applicant has shown that there is a reasonable prospect that the application will succeed, the Chief Justice or judge shall consider the criteria set out in paragraphs 745.63(1)(a) to (e), with such modifications as the circumstances require.

(3) If the Chief Justice or judge determines that the applicant has not shown that there is a reasonable prospect that the application will succeed, the Chief Justice may

(a) set a time not earlier than two years after the date of the determination, at or after which another applicant may be made by the applicant under subsection 745.6(1); or

(b) decide that the applicant may not make another application under that subsection.

(4) If the Chief Justice or judge determines that the applicant has not shown that there is a reasonable prospect that the application will succeed but does not set a time for another application or decide that such an application may not be made, the applicant may make another application no earlier than two years after the date of the determination.

(5) If the Chief Justice or judge determines that the applicant has shown that there is a reasonable prospect that the application will succeed, the Chief Justice shall designate a judge of the superior court of criminal jurisdiction to empanel a jury to hear the application.

Appeal

745.62(1) The applicant or the Attorney General may appeal to the Court of Appeal from a determination or a decision made under section 745.61 on any question of law or fact or mixed law and fact.

(2) The appeal shall be determined on the basis of the documents presented to the Chief Justice or judge who made the determination or decision, any reasons for the determination or decision and any other document that the Court of Appeal requires.

(3) Sections 673 to 696 apply, with such modifications as the circumstances require.

Hearing of Application

745.63(1) The jury empanelled under subsection 745.61(5) to hear the application shall consider the following criteria and determine whether the applicant's number of years of imprisonment without eligibility for parole ought to be reduced:

 (a) the character of the applicant;

 (b) the applicant's conduct while serving the sentence;

 (c) the nature of the offence for which the applicant was convicted;

 (d) any information provided by a victim at the time of the imposition of the sentence or at the time of the hearing under this section; and

 (e) any other matters that the judge considers relevant in the circumstances.

(2) In paragraph (1)(d), "victim" has the same meaning as in subsection 722(4).

(3) The jury hearing an application under subsection (1) may determine that the applicant's number of years of imprisonment without eligibility for parole ought to be reduced. The determination to reduce the number of years must be by unanimous vote.

(4) The applicant's number of years of imprisonment without eligibility for parole is not reduced if

 (a) the jury hearing an application under subsection (1) determines that the number of years ought not to be reduced;

 (b) the jury hearing an application under subsection (1) concludes that it cannot unanimously determine that the number of years ought to be reduced; or

 (c) the presiding judge, after the jury has deliberated for a reasonable period, concludes that the jury is unable to unanimously determine that the number of years ought to be reduced.

(5) If the jury determines that the number of years of imprisonment without eligibility for parole ought to be reduced, the jury may, by a vote of not less than two thirds of the members of the jury,

 (a) substitute a lesser number of years of imprisonment without eligibility for parole than that then applicable; or

 (b) terminate the ineligibility for parole.

(6) If the applicant's number of years of imprisonment without eligibility for parole is not reduced, the jury may

 (a) set a time, not earlier than two years after the date of the determination or conclusion under subsection (4), at or after which another application may be made by the applicant under subsection 745.6(1); or

 (b) decide that the applicant may not make another application under that subsection.

(7) The decision of the jury under paragraph (6)(a) or (b) must be made by not less than two thirds of its members.

(8) If the jury does not set a date at or after which another application may be made or decide that such an application may not be made, the applicant may make another application no earlier than two years after the date of the determination or conclusion under subsection (4).

Rules

745.64(1) The appropriate Chief Justice in each province or territory may make such rules as are required for the purposes of sections 745.6 to 745.63.

. . .

Time Spent in Custody

746. In calculating the period of imprisonment served for the purposes of section 745, 745.1, 745.4, 745.5 or 745.6, there shall be included any time spent in custody between

(a) in the case of a sentence of imprisonment for life after July 25, 1976, the day on which that person was arrested and taken into custody in respect of the offence for which he was sentenced to imprisonment for life and the day the sentence was imposed; or

(b) in the case of a sentence of death that has been or is deemed to have been commuted to a sentence of imprisonment for life, the day on which that person was arrested and taken into custody in respect of the offence for which he was sentenced to death and the day the sentence was commuted or deemed to have been commuted to a sentence of imprisonment for life.

This version of the procedure results from a number of revisions. Because the procedure has caught the attention of the public, opportunistic politicians (federal, provincial, and territorial alike) lobbied the government to eradicate, or at least tighten up, the procedure. This lobbying resulted in the following features of the present legislation:

- the preclusion of multiple murderers from applying for relief under the provision (s. 745.6);
- the establishment of a screening process by a judge (s. 745.61); and
- the requirement that the jury be unanimous in its decision to reduce the period of parole ineligibility. Under the previous provisions, the jury was permitted to speak with a two-thirds majority voice on this issue (s. 745.63(3)).[5]

B. Applying the Provisions

The following two decisions, *Vaillancourt* and *Swietlinski*, were decided under the original formulation of the 15-year review.

---

5 This change in the legislation was made retroactive to January 6, 1997, the date that the legislation was amended. Unless an application was already under way by the time the legislation changed, the new requirement of unanimity applied. This has been held to be constitutional (see *R v. Chaudhary* (1999), 139 CCC (3d) 547 (Ont. Sup. Ct.), leave to appeal denied). Note that ss. 745.63(6) and (7) require only a two-thirds majority voice on the number of years that parole ought to be reduced or terminated. Similarly, if a jury refuses to lower or terminate parole ineligibility, the jury may, by a two-thirds majority, stipulate the amount of time that must elapse before another application may be made.

R v. Vaillancourt
(1988), 66 CR (3d) 66 (Ont. HCJ)

CALLAGHAN ACJHC: The applicant has applied pursuant to s. 672 of the *Criminal Code* ("the Code") for a reduction of the number of years of imprisonment he must serve without eligibility for parole. On 1st October 1973 he was convicted of capital murder and sentenced to hang. This sentence was commuted to a "sentence of imprisonment for life for first degree murder" by operation of s. 25(1) of the *Criminal Law Amendment Act* (No. 2), 1976, proclaimed in force effective 26th July 1976. This enactment provided that the applicant would serve a term of life imprisonment without eligibility for parole until 25 years had been served. It also provided for a review of the ineligibility period pursuant to s. 672 of the Code: see *Criminal Law Amendment Act* (No. 2), 1976. SC 1974-75-76, c. 105, ss. 25(1) and 28(2).

On 27th January 1988 the Honourable Chief Justice of this court promulgated rules of practice ("the rules") for the conduct of applications for review brought pursuant to s. 672. On 15th April 1988 the applicant, by notice of constitutional question, indicated his intention to question the constitutional validity of the interpretation of s. 672(2) of the Code as it is reflected in the rules made by the Honourable Chief Justice, and in particular RR. 6(2), 14 and 16(2).

The applicant submits that the onus of proof in determining the number of years of imprisonment without eligibility for parole under s. 672(2) of the Code must rest with the Attorney General of Ontario and that, to the extent that the aforesaid rules place a persuasive burden of proof on the applicant, they are *ultra vires* s. 672(5) of the Code. Furthermore, it is submitted that the said rules are contrary to the principles of fundamental justice to the extent that they place an obligation on the applicant to define issues in controversy, adduce evidence and address the jury before the Attorney General of Ontario on the application for review.

...

The fundamental issue on this application is the characterization of the review procedures established in s. 672.

The applicant takes the position that the procedure established under s. 672 is part of the sentencing process and involves an assessment of blameworthiness in order to determine the appropriate degree of denunciation which, in the eyes of the representatives of the community, i.e., the jury, needs to be satisfied. The applicant submits that Parliament has, by virtue of s. 672, provided a range of 15 to 25 years within which the jury may assess the degree of blameworthiness that should attach to the applicant's conduct. When blameworthiness is in issue, the applicant submits, it is a fundamental principle of justice that the state must bear the burden of establishing all matters in controversy beyond a reasonable doubt. As s. 672 is silent with respect to the issues of onus and standard of proof, the *Canadian Charter of Rights and Freedoms*, through the guarantees of s. 7 and s. 12, requires that the procedural protections which are attendant upon other proceedings under the Code be applied to a review under s. 672. It is submitted that the rules alter this substantive law and accordingly are *ultra vires* and of no force and effect.

The respondents characterize the review under s. 672 as a process entirely distinct from that of the sentencing process at trial. It is submitted that the review provided under s. 672 is an enlightened review process which seeks to provide hope of earlier release to those serving the longest possible sentences. The respondents take the position that the issue of blameworthiness was fully and finally assessed at trial, conviction and sentence, and that the determination of guilt made at that time is not subject to review under s. 672. Accordingly, the section does not contemplate a reassessment of blameworthiness. Therefore, the onus and burden of persuasion should rest with the applicant, as he is the one moving to set aside a valid judicial order and the impugned rules are not violative of any Charter rights.

. . .

In my view, the language of s. 669(a) is mandatory. From that I infer that Parliament has specified precisely the degree of denunciation consequent upon a conviction for first degree murder. Where a conviction is registered for second degree murder, a jury has the right to make a recommendation with reference to parole eligibility under s. 670 of the Code. In contrast, when the conviction is for first degree murder, no such recommendation is available. The requisite degree of denunciation is established by Parliament in very clear language.

Counsel on behalf of the applicant submitted that the Charter, through ss. 7 and 12, requires that there be a proportional relationship between blameworthiness and punishment, and in this regard referred to the decision in *R v. Smith*, [1987] 1 SCR 1045, where it was held that a punishment is unconstitutional if it is grossly disproportionate to the offence. Counsel for the applicant submitted, therefore, that, in order for the mandatory sentence for first degree murder to be upheld as constitutional, s. 672 of the Code ought to be interpreted as requiring a jury to assess the blameworthiness of the individual offender and offence in order to determine the proportional number of years of ineligibility for parole. With respect, however, I do not agree. In *Smith*, Lamer J, with whom Dickson CJC concurred, expressly stated that a minimum mandatory sentence is not in and of itself cruel and unusual. In my view, the sentence provided in s. 669 of the Code cannot be said to be grossly disproportionate to the offence of first degree murder. A planned and deliberate killing necessarily involves an offence of the most serious order. In such circumstances, a mandatory sentence of life imprisonment without eligibility for parole for 25 years cannot be characterized as being so excessive or grossly disproportionate as to outrage standards of decency.

It was submitted on behalf of the applicant that the jury's role in a review under s. 672 is to reflect the community's condemnation of the offence and repudiation of the offender. On the contrary, that role has already been performed by the trial jury in its finding of guilt and by Parliament in its determination of the mandatory sentence that must be imposed. The issue of blameworthiness was finally assessed at trial, conviction and sentence. The determination of guilt, made at trial beyond a reasonable doubt, concludes all questions of the applicant's blameworthiness in respect of that offence. Accordingly, s. 672 does not, in my view, contemplate a reassessment of blameworthiness. Instead, it strikes a balance between considerations of leniency for the well-behaved convict in the service of his sentence, which may serve to assist in his rehabilitation, and the community interest in repudiation and deterrence of the conduct that led to his incarceration.

The jury under s. 672(2) is undertaking a review process, in the course of which they must consider the applicant's good conduct, and are given specific criteria to be applied in coming to their decision. But that jury does not again determine the degree of denunciation. With reference to the character of the applicant, his conduct while incarcerated and the circumstances of the offence, the jury determines whether or not present circumstances justify leniency and an early consideration of the applicant's case by the parole board. The review contemplated under s. 672 is a process distinct and apart from the sentencing process that took place at the conclusion at the trial. It is to be noted that the jury has no power to increase the penalty imposed at trial, but has the power only to recommend a reduction in that penalty. Accordingly, I must conclude that the review process provided for in s. 672 does not contemplate a proceeding which is part of the sentencing process, nor does blameworthiness fall to be determined again in the course of that review.

...

An application under s. 672 of the Code is permissive, and it is the applicant who has the option of determining whether or not to bring the application. There is nothing compelling the applicant to bring the application. In such circumstances, to place a persuasive onus on the applicant is not in my view violative of s. 11 of the Charter. It is the applicant who is seeking to set aside an otherwise valid judicial order. Having discharged the burden of establishing the guilt of the accused at trial beyond a reasonable doubt, the state, in my view, should not again be forced to bear the high cost of the onus of proof in post-conviction review matters. Moreover, it would be highly anomalous for the persuasive burden to revert to the state in the case of a convict such as the applicant, who had years earlier unsuccessfully appealed against the parole ineligibility period determination. The protections afforded by s. 11 of the Charter are simply inapplicable on a review under s. 672.

I am not satisfied that an application under s. 672 of the Code involves a deprivation of liberty within s. 7 of the Charter. The applicant has already been deprived of his liberty by the imposition of sentence. It would *prima facie* be an enhancement of liberty, and not a further deprivation thereof, which is involved in an application for a reduction in the number of years of ineligibility for parole under s. 672. However, even if a deprivation of liberty is at issue in a s. 672 application, such that the principles of fundamental justice must be complied with, the rules impugned in these proceedings do not appear to violate those tenets. As stated by Lamer J in *Re BC Motor Vehicle Act*, [1985] 2 SCR 486 at 513, the phrase "principles of fundamental justice cannot be given an exhaustive content or simple enumeration but will take on concrete meaning as the court addresses alleged violation of s. 7."

R v. Swietlinski

(1995), 92 CCC (3d) 449 (SCC)

LAMER CJC: This case provides an opportunity for this court to consider for the first time the interpretation of s. 745 of the *Criminal Code*, RSC 1985, c. C-46, which authorizes a reduction of the period during which persons convicted of murder are ineligible for parole.

I. Facts

The appellant Roman Swietlinski was convicted of first degree murder. His conviction was upheld by the Ontario Court of Appeal, 5 CR (3d) 324, and by this court, 55 CCC (2d) 481. Since the earlier judgment of this court sets out the facts in detail, I will only give a brief description of the murder. On the night of September 18 to 19, 1976, the appellant met the victim, Mary Frances McKenna, in a bar in Toronto. Apparently, the pair left the bar about midnight on their way to the victim's apartment. The attack which followed was one of unspeakable brutality. The appellant stabbed the victim 132 times using five different knives. The force used was such that some of the knives were broken at the time the police located them.

In the course of the first two years of his sentence the appellant committed various disciplinary offences connected with smuggling and an attempted escape. Apparently, when he was placed in punitive segregation for the latter offence he underwent a complete change of heart and became a "model prisoner." In 1983, he was transferred to a medium security institution and then in 1990, to a minimum security institution. During his confinement in these various penal institutions the appellant became involved in various charitable or religious groups. He participated in work programs in the institutions. Since 1988, he has received several permits for escorted temporary absences. At various times he took part in Alcoholics Anonymous activities. He also participated in some training sessions and requested the assistance of a psychologist.

...

III. Judgment of Ontario Court of Justice (General Division)

O'Driscoll J of the Ontario Court (General Division) was designated for empanelling a jury and hearing the case.

At the preliminary hearing provided for in s. 10 of the Ontario Rules of Practice Respecting Reduction in the Number of Years of Imprisonment Without Eligibility for Parole, SOR/88-582, in effect at that time, O'Driscoll J held that statements by members of the victim's family were not admissible as evidence. He based his decision on *R v. Vaillancourt* (1989), 49 CCC (3d) 544, 71 CR (3d) 43, 43 CRR 60 (Ont. CA), in which the Ontario Court of Appeal held that a s. 745 hearing did not form part of the sentencing process. Since s. 735(1.1) of the Code made such statements admissible in order only to facilitate the determination of the sentence, they should be excluded from a s. 745 hearing. Further, O'Driscoll J considered that the statements disclosed no information relevant to the assessment of the factors listed in s. 745(2).

The hearing itself was subsequently held and the jury refused to reduce the period of the appellant's ineligibility for parole. Further, it set November 6, 2001 as the date on which the appellant could again make a similar application. Since that date corresponds to the time when the appellant will have served 25 years of his sentence, the jury's decision amounts to prohibiting the appellant from filing another application under s. 745.

The appellant sought and obtained leave to appeal directly to this court. Section 40 of the *Supreme Court Act*, RSC 1985, c. S-26, authorizes a direct appeal since the Code makes no provision for any other avenue of appeal: *R v. Vaillancourt* (1992), 76 CCC (3d) 384n, [1990] 1 SCR xii, 57 OAC 320n (SCC).

IV. Issues

The appellant raised the following grounds of appeal, most of which relate to the judge's charge to the jury:

1. the judge should not have limited consideration of the appellant's character to his character at the time of the murder: he should also have mentioned the appellant's present character;
2. the judge should not have referred to the three factors mentioned in s. 745(2) as three independent factors, each to be proved on a balance of probabilities;
3. the judge should have reread all of the agreed statement of facts: he should not have omitted the second part, relating to "extenuating circumstances";
4. the judge did not make a fair summation of the psychiatric evidence;
5. in questioning certain witnesses and in his address to the jury, counsel for the Crown introduced inflammatory and highly prejudicial matters.

I feel that the fifth ground provides a sufficient basis for allowing this appeal. Furthermore, the first, second and fourth grounds raise legitimate concerns which only aggravate the inequity resulting from the Crown counsel's inflammatory remarks.

Additionally, since I believe that a new hearing should be ordered, I will deal with the question of the admissibility of statements by the victim's family.

V. Analysis

A. General Observations on S. 745

Section 745 of the Code was adopted in 1976 in connection with the abolition of the death penalty. The compromise arrived at between the supporters and opponents of the death penalty was its replacement by long-term imprisonment without parole. Accordingly, in the case of first degree murder the penalty is life imprisonment with no eligibility for parole for 25 years. In the case of second degree murder, this time period is 10 years, but it may be extended to 25 years by the trial judge on the jury's recommendation. In both cases, however, Parliament provided that after 15 years a jury could be empanelled to reassess the period of ineligibility.

Section 745 put in place a procedure that is original in several respects. However, we need not consider all its aspects in order to deal with the case at bar. What is important is to understand that the procedure is one for reassessing long-term imprisonment imposed by law (in the case of first degree murder) or by a judge (in the case of second degree murder). The purpose of a reassessment procedure, especially when it takes place 15 years after the initial decision, is necessarily to re-examine a decision in light of new information or factors which could not have been known initially. It follows that the primary purpose of a s. 745 hearing is to call attention to changes which have occurred in the applicant's situation and which might justify imposing a less harsh penalty upon the applicant. Accordingly, the jury's decision is not essentially different from the ordinary decision regarding length of a sentence. It is similar to that taken by a judge pursuant to s. 744 of the Code as to the period of ineligibility in cases of second degree murder.

It should also be noted, in the context of an appeal to this court, that s. 745 gives the jury a broad discretionary power. This is quite different from a trial, at which the jury must choose between two options, guilt or innocence, based on very specific rules of law. Moreover, the discretionary nature of the jury's decision is made quite clear by the fact that Parliament did not see fit to grant any right of appeal to the Court of Appeal, although as I mentioned earlier that does not prevent an appeal to this court with leave. Consequently, there is no need to analyze the judge's charge to the jury in the detail that would be appropriate in the case of a trial. This court's function is essentially to determine whether the appellant was given a fair hearing at trial.

The discretionary nature of the decision also compels the jury to adopt a different analytical approach from that used in a trial. At a trial, the jury must decide whether it has been proven beyond all reasonable doubt that the accused committed the crime with which he or she is charged. In such a proceeding, the offence is generally defined by a number of elements which must all be proven for the accused to be convicted. Each element of the offence is thus a necessary condition for a conviction. At a s. 745 hearing, on the other hand, the jury does not determine whether the applicant is guilty: another jury (or, in some cases, a judge) has already performed that task. Its duty rather is to make a discretionary decision as to the minimum length of the sentence that the applicant must serve. The concept of an element of an offence cannot be transposed onto a discretionary decision. When a person makes such a decision he or she does not apply rigid logic, requiring for example that if conditions A, B and C are met, then decision X must be the result. When legislation lists various factors that a decision-maker must take into consideration, a finding reached upon one or all of the factors does not necessarily mandate a conclusion leading to a specific decision. They are instead factors, some of which may work in favour of the applicant and some against him, and which must be assessed and weighed as a whole in arriving at a conclusion. This is quite different from a trial where very strong evidence of one aspect of an offence cannot offset the weakness of evidence of another aspect.

Accordingly, the concepts of burden of proof, proof on a balance of probabilities, or proof beyond a reasonable doubt are of very limited value in a hearing pursuant to s. 745, where the decision lies exclusively in the discretion of the jury. The jury must instead make what it, in its discretion, deems to be the best decision on the evidence: On this point see also *R v. M.(S.H.)* (1989), 50 CCC (3d) 503 at pp. 547-8, [1989] 2 SCR 446, 71 CR (3d) 257 (SCC).

B. Grounds of Appeal

1. Inappropriate Language by Counsel for the Crown

The appellant objected to certain irrelevant and prejudicial language used by counsel for the Crown. Before considering the disputed remarks in detail, it should be recalled that the function of counsel for the Crown in a s. 745 hearing is no different from the function in a criminal trial. Taschereau J described his function as follows in *Boucher v. The Queen* (1954), 110 CCC 263 at p. 267 (SCC) (translation):

> The position held by counsel for the Crown is not that of a lawyer in civil litigation. His functions are quasi-judicial. His duty is not so much to obtain a conviction as to assist the judge and the jury in ensuring that the fullest possible justice is done. His conduct before the court must always be characterized by moderation and impartiality. He will have properly performed his duty and will be beyond all reproach if, eschewing any appeal to passion, and employing a dignified manner suited to his function, he presents the evidence to the jury without going beyond what it discloses.

The first category of unacceptable language had the effect of discrediting the process of reviewing ineligibility established by s. 745. Counsel for the Crown sought, in some measure, to present the procedure as fundamentally inequitable, first, because the victim had no opportunity, as the applicant did, to have her suffering reduced, and secondly, because the 25-year ineligibility period was a bargain compared with the death penalty imposed prior to 1976 and further reducing this period of time would be an additional concession to the accused.

For example, counsel began his opening statement with the following passage:

> Ladies and gentlemen of the jury, in 1976 this country, our government abolished capital punishment. Mr. Swietlinski was convicted of the worst crime known to our criminal justice system. You will hear shortly about the facts of this offence. In 1976, the same year, Mary Frances McKenna, someone that you won't hear very much about in this proceeding—this is an application brought by Mr. Swietlinski—but you won't hear much about a person by the name of Mary Frances McKenna, who was 37 years of age at the time.

He went on to add:

> ... please don't forget the victim in this case, Mary Frances McKenna. She doesn't have a chance to come before a group of people to ask for a second chance.

He concluded his opening statement by reminding the jurors that, "... Mr. Swietlinski, a few years earlier, would have been sentenced to death for this offence ... ." In his final submission to the jury he returned to the same themes:

> Mary Frances McKenna doesn't get a chance to come before a jury and ask to have her parole eligibility reduced. Mary Frances McKenna is gone.
>
> If we wanted revenge, we would have capital punishment. As I say, we don't. We have a compromise. It's a mandatory sentence, life with no eligibility for parole for 25 years, and that's the sentence that our society imposes for the taking of a human life in the manner that Mr. Swietlinski took it. To do otherwise, as Mr. Swietlinski suggested to you about the rules at Millhaven, would be anarchy.

Counsel also sought, in questioning certain witnesses, to draw attention to the fact that the victim could not obtain the second chance the appellant was seeking and to the fact that no assistance programs were available to the victim's family whereas the penitentiary system offered the appellant a vast range of services.

Counsel further sought to discredit the parole process in the following language:

> Normally, issues of parole, parole hearings, are held by, basically, a faceless group of people. They're held in secret, in private, and really all that the Parole Board hears from is the applicant and perhaps his counsel and the kind of people that you're about to hear from, the various corrections people.

Finally, in questioning certain witnesses counsel insinuated that the Beaver Creek Institution, where the appellant had spent the last two years, was too comfortable to be called a prison and that in fact some visitors confused the institution with a neighbouring campground. In his final submission, he suggested that the transfer to this institution was sufficient reward for the appellant's good conduct during his sentence.

The combined effect of these remarks was to imply that the s. 745 hearing was a proceeding unduly favourable to the applicant, even a subversion of Parliament's intent to impose a definite 25-year penalty on first degree murderers. The conclusion that emerged from these observations, and it was not a difficult one to draw, was that the jury should deal more severely with the appellant.

Nevertheless, s. 745 is as much a part of the Code as the provisions providing for no parole for 25 years in cases of first degree murder. The possible reduction of the ineligibility period after 15 years is a choice made by Parliament which the jury must accept. Clearly, the prosecution may not call this choice into question by suggesting to the jury that it is an abnormal procedure, excessively indulgent and contrary to what it argues was Parliament's intent. That amounts to urging the jurors not to make a decision in accordance with the law if they feel that it is bad law. It is clearly unacceptable for a lawyer to make such an observation to the jury: *R v. Morgentaler* (1988), 37 CCC (3d) 449 at pp. 481-3, 44 DLR (4th) 385 at pp. 417-9, [1988] 1 SCR 30 (SCC); *R v. Finta* (1994), 88 CCC (3d) 417, 112 DLR (4th) 513, [1994] 1 SCR 701 (SCC).

In the same way, counsel may not constantly repeat that imprisonment for 25 years is a substitute for the death penalty. That is an invitation to offset the alleged excessive clemency of Parliament by a severity not justified by the wording of s. 745. The jury does not have to decide whether the penalties imposed by Parliament are too severe or not severe enough. It must simply apply the Code. The Code no longer contains the death penalty: on the contrary, s. 745 gives the appellant the right to seek a reduction in his ineligibility period. No one can be permitted to undermine the fairness of the proceeding in which the appellant may obtain such a reduction by constant references to the death penalty.

Additionally, counsel for the Crown sought to draw the jury's attention to other cases of murderers who had used their parole to commit other murders. ...

Similarly, in his opening statement he invited the jury to take into consideration cases of violence other than those of the appellant:

> We read the papers. We open the headlines today and we see concerns about violence in our society, and, in particular, we hear concerns about violence against women. I want you, when you listen to that evidence, to bear in mind that you are here representing the best interests of this community as it pertains not only to Mr. Swietlinski but the broader issues that an application, such as this, brings to bear.

In his final submission he added the following:

Violence is, unfortunately, increasing in our community. Every time you turn on the news, read the headlines you hear either reports of or people worried about the issue of violence and, in particular, violence against women.

A lot of times people come into contact or read in the paper and hear, read or see on TV something that shocks them, and the facts of this case no doubt shocked you. Well, they have concerns about things going on in our society, and they think to themselves, "Someone should do something about that," and always the someone is someone off in the distance. For the purpose of this case … you are the they. Consider that when you retire to reach your determination.

It is completely improper to invite the jury to consider isolated cases in which prisoners committed murder after being paroled. Even though the rules applicable in the s. 745 hearing are not as strict as in a criminal trial, the fact remains that the jury must consider only the applicant's case. Although the temptation may sometimes be very strong, the jury must not try the cases of other inmates or determine whether the existing system of parole is doing its job. The appellant should not be punished for the weaknesses of the system.

Furthermore, the other observations I have just referred to may have suggested to the jury that its function was in some way to solve the problem of violence in society. It is true that deterrence is one of the functions of the penalty and that it is, therefore, legitimate for the jury to take this factor into account when hearing an application under s. 745. However, the approach taken by counsel for the Crown was unacceptable. The jury cannot simply be referred to headlines in newspapers, which generally concern themselves with the worst crimes. Such a course could produce a disproportionate reaction in the jury by making it believe it could solve the problem of crime at one stroke and by giving the appellant's case the odour of a general threat. Such a tactic smacks of the in terrorem arguments disapproved by the Quebec Court of Appeal in *R v. Vallieres*, [1970] 4 CCC 69. In my view, it is possible to invite the jury to take the deterrent aspect of the penalty into account, but this should be done in the context of a general submission on the various functions performed by the penalty.

In a trial by jury it is usual for the judge to indicate to the jurors that they must base their decision solely on the evidence and that they should not read the newspapers while the trial is in progress. Sometimes drastic methods such as sequestering the jury or banning publication may be used to keep the jury free from undue influence by the media. That being the case, it is astonishing that counsel for the Crown could have invited the jury to do precisely what any good judge would tell it not to do. It is still more surprising that the trial judge did not react and rectify these remarks.

To sum up, I consider that the remarks of counsel for the Crown seriously compromised the fairness of the hearing. The judge's failure to reprimand him and to tell the jury that such remarks should not be taken into account, only aggravates the lack of fairness. However, the respondent argued that this court should dismiss the appeal because counsel for the appellant did not object to these remarks at trial. I cannot accept that argument. It is true that the absence of an objection is a factor which an appellate court may take into account in deciding whether to dismiss an appeal. In the case at bar, however, the hearing was unfair. The trial judge had a duty to ensure that the hearing was fair: *R v. Potvin* (1989), 47 CCC (3d) 289 at pp. 314-5 (SCC); *R v.*

L.(D.O.) (1993), 85 CCC (3d) 289 (SCC), at p. 318. Since he did not do so, this court must intervene, whether counsel for the appellant objected or not.

I would allow the appeal for this reason alone. This conclusion is made all the more necessary when we take into account the court's errors in compartmentalizing the burden of proof and in the review of the evidence, although those errors by themselves are not sufficiently serious to justify a rehearing.

2. Distinction Between Present and Past Character: Burden of Proof

The common error disclosed by the first two grounds of appeal is an excessive compartmentalization of the various factors listed in s. 745(2) that the jury must take into account in arriving at its decision.

The judge's first error was to limit his discussion of the appellant's character to matters prior to or contemporaneous with the murder. He made no reference to the changes in the appellant's character since his imprisonment. As I mentioned, however, the purpose of the s. 745 proceeding is to reassess the penalty imposed on the offender by reference to the way his or her situation has evolved in 15 years. The judge should, therefore, have mentioned both the appellant's past and present character.

The second error results from the following observation by the judge, made at the start of the part of his charge dealing with conduct while serving sentence:

Ladies and gentlemen, it is for you to say, but it would seem that the evidence establishes for you, on the balance of probabilities, that Roman Swietlinski was a model prisoner after he emerged from the 25 days in "the hole" at Millhaven penitentiary back in 1979 or 1980.

The judge expressed no similar opinion as to the other two factors mentioned in s. 745(2).

It is true that a judge may always give his or her opinion on the facts, so long as he or she makes it clear to the jurors that the final decision is theirs. However, this comment could have led the jury to think that the three factors mentioned in s. 745(2) were separate and that each had to be "establishe[d] ... on the balance of probabilities." As I have shown, this is not a very suitable approach in the case of a discretionary decision. The jury could have thought, in reliance on this comment, that it had to arrive at a decision favourable to the appellant on each of the three criteria.

3. Summary of Psychiatric Evidence

The appellant's psychiatric condition was one of the major questions raised in the court below. The points especially in dispute were the possibility that the appellant suffers from sexual sadism and the possibility of successful psychiatric treatment. Simplifying somewhat, it can be said that Dr. Dickey's testimony was very unfavourable to the appellant while the testimony of Mr. Jean, Drs. Wood-Hill and Quirt was favourable.

The trial judge undertook a lengthy review of the psychiatric evidence. It was probably not necessary to do this in so much detail. The issues were relatively straightforward. The expert testimony was fresh in the minds of the jurors. Moreover, each juror had a copy of the written reports available to him or her. However, when the trial judge considers it necessary or desirable to make such a review, he or she should not unduly devote greater attention to the aspects of the evidence that favour one party, yet this is what the trial judge did here. The judge placed his emphasis on Dr. Dickey's testimony, noting his professional qualifications and repeating certain parts of his testimony word for word. On the other hand, the judge made no mention at all of the testimony of Mr. Jean or Drs. Wood-Hill and Quirt. He simply mentioned short extracts from the written reports of Drs. Wood-Hill and Quirt. Though I am sure it was not intentional, the judge did nevertheless favour the respondent in his summation of the evidence. As an illustration, it can be pointed out that the review of Dr. Dickey's testimony took up 15 pages of the transcript of the charge to the jury while the passage from Dr. Wood-Hill's report extended only for a page and a half.

C. Admissibility of Victim's Statements

As I feel that a rehearing should be ordered, I think it is worth dealing with the question of the admissibility of statements by members of the victim's family. The respondent will undoubtedly seek to introduce such statements at that hearing. Additionally, since there is no right of appeal to the Court of Appeal, the appeal to this court is the only opportunity to introduce uniformity into the rulings of the superior courts on this point.

In *R v. Gardiner*, [1982] 2 SCR 368 (SCC), this court set out the general rules governing evidence at a sentencing hearing. Dickson J (as he then was) noted that the rules which applied to evidence at trial had been made more flexible: now, for example, hearsay evidence can be admitted if it is credible and reliable.

A s. 745 hearing differs from an initial hearing in many respects. However, the purpose of both is to determine the length of sentence. Consequently, evidence should be governed by similar rules. It is well known that the victim's testimony is admissible at a hearing on sentencing: see, e.g., *R v. Landry* (1981), 61 CCC (2d) 317 (NSCA). Since s. 745(2) states that the nature of the offence is one of the criteria the jury must take into account, it is clear that the victim's testimony is relevant and admissible at such a hearing. Since the ordinary rules of evidence have been loosened, this testimony can be presented by means of a written statement. Of course, such a statement should only contain relevant information. Counsel for the Crown clearly cannot use it in an attempt to introduce the type of remarks which I earlier condemned.

I, therefore, consider that the trial judge made an error in refusing to admit statements by members of the victim's family.

VI. Judgment

The appellant did not get the fair hearing to which he was entitled. The appeal is, therefore, allowed and a rehearing ordered in accordance with these reasons.

MAJOR J (dissenting): I have read the reasons of the Chief Justice and agree with him except with respect to the effect of the statements made by Crown counsel and his conclusion that victim impact statements are always admissible at s. 745 hearings. As a result I would dismiss the appeal.

A s. 745 parole eligibility review hearing is neither a criminal trial nor a sentencing review hearing. The applicant's guilt has already been determined and his sentence fixed according to the mandatory penalties in the *Criminal Code* (first degree murder) or by a judge (second degree murder). Section 745 empowers 12 jurors, who represent the community and its conscience (*R v. Nichols* (1992), 71 CCC (3d) 385 (Alta. QB)), to determine whether the applicant deserves clemency or leniency in the form of a reduction in his or her parole ineligibility.

Section 745 is unique because it authorizes the modification of a provision of the law otherwise than by royal prerogative or legislative action: *R v. Nichols, supra,* at p. 386. Under its provisions, the jury is empowered to order a reduction in parole eligibility (s. 745(4)); only two-thirds of the jury need be convinced of the verdict (s. 745(2)), and the burden of proof lies with the applicant to establish that he deserves to be treated with clemency on the balance of probabilities: *R v. Vaillancourt* (1988), 66 CR (3d) 66 (Ont. HCJ).

Section 745 only entitles a successful applicant to apply to the parole board for early parole; there is no guarantee that parole will be granted. Thus, the s. 745 jury is not empowered in any respect "to determine the length of sentence" contrary to the view expressed by the Chief Justice.

A jury seised of a parole eligibility review application must consider: (1) the applicant's character; (2) the applicant's conduct while serving his or her sentence; (3) the nature of the offence for which the applicant was convicted, and (4) such other matters as the presiding judge deems relevant: Code, s. 745(2). While some sentencing principles, relating to rehabilitation and public protection will inevitably enter into the jurors' minds as they consider character, conduct and the nature of the offence, sentencing principles, e.g., rehabilitation, deterrence, denunciation—should not play any significant role at the hearing. Parliament has not seen fit to incorporate traditional principles of sentencing into s. 745, and it would be wrong for this court to read any such principles into the section.

Given the broad nature of the discretionary powers conferred upon the jury, there is little scope for this court to interfere with the jury's determination on an appeal. It may, however, review the conduct of the presiding judge in directing the proceedings and in charging the jury. I agree with the Chief Justice that the court's role in undertaking such a review must be to determine whether the applicant had a fair hearing. In view of the nature of the proceedings, and, in particular, the fact that the ultimate determination is made by the jury based on a range of open-ended factors, deficiencies that might lead to unfairness in a criminal trial will not necessarily have the same effect in a s. 745 hearing. For example, it has been held that placing the persuasive onus on an applicant under s. 745 does not violate the presumption of innocence protected in s. 11 of the *Canadian Charter of Rights and Freedoms*: *R v. Vaillancourt, supra.*

It is in light of these considerations that an analysis of the appellant's grounds of appeal should be made. I agree with the Chief Justice that standing alone the deficiencies, in the presiding judge's instructions on the burden of proof and his review of the psychiatric evidence were not sufficiently serious to justify a rehearing, and I cannot add anything to that conclusion.

However, I disagree with the conclusion that the inappropriate comments made by Crown counsel were sufficient in their cumulative effect to require a new hearing. I also disagree that the presiding judge erred in refusing to admit victim impact statements in this case.

A. Inappropriate Language by Counsel for the Crown

Evidence is admissible only if it is: (1) relevant and (2) not subject to exclusion under any other clear rule of law or policy: Sopinka, Lederman and Bryant, *The Law of Evidence in Canada*, at p. 21. However, the trier of law retains a discretion to exclude relevant and admissible evidence if its prejudicial effect exceeds its probative value, such that its admission would impact on the fairness of the trial: ibid., at pp. 28-33; *R v. Corbett* (1988), 41 CCC (3d) 385 (SCC); *R v. Potvin* (1989), 47 CCC (3d) 289 (SCC), at pp. 314-5; and *R v. L.(D.O.)* (1993), 85 CCC (3d) 289 (SCC), at p. 318.

In this case, several of the comments made by Crown counsel which are now attacked as inflammatory were relevant and substantially probative to the issues in the case. References to the relative comforts of the Beaver Creek Institution were relevant to the jury's assessment of whether the appellant's conduct varied with his institutional setting. Defence counsel took a similar tactic when she cross-examined the appellant's parole officer on the issue of the violent setting at the Millhaven and Collins Bay institutions. Additionally, the cross-examination about cases where inmates of halfway houses have killed was relevant to the jury's assessment of the accuracy of the evidence tendered by members of the correctional community and of the parole board's decision-making processes. While such a line of questioning might be inappropriate in a criminal trial, the jury at a s. 745 hearing should, in the circumstances of this case, be entitled to consider the likelihood of an error by the National Parole Board. Therefore, it cannot be said that the presiding judge had a duty to exclude Crown counsel's comments or questioning regarding the Beaver Creek institution or infamous cases of recidivism by paroled offenders nor can it be said that his failure to exclude these statements had any effect on the fairness of the hearing.

Other comments made by Crown counsel had little relevance to issues at the review hearing. In particular, Crown counsel's repeated references to the death penalty and his comments about violence in society were irrelevant to the jury's deliberations. However, the prejudicial effect of these comments was eradicated by the following statements made by the presiding judge in his charge to the jury:

> As you know, public debate on the subject of capital punishment still comes to the fore from time to time. There are those who think it should be brought back. By the same token, there are those who argue that the 25 year non-eligibility period in the *Criminal Code* is much too harsh as it destroys all hope for the convicted person. Again, there are those who argue that the 15 year judicial review is that ray of hope held out to persons convicted of first degree murder.
>
> At a different time and different place, you are entitled to hold any one or more of those views. However, in the jury room, you are to cast aside any preconceived ideas,

notions and philosophies and deal with this case as you are required to do so by law under the dictates of Section 745 of the *Criminal Code*.

In other words, in the jury room, there is no room for "soap boxes" and no one should be riding any favourite "hobby horse." The jury room is not the place for a philosophizer. You are here as judges of the facts. You are not here as law reformers.

Other comments made by Crown counsel relating to the plight of the victim's family, the fact that the victim received no second chances and the secrecy of the parole process also had minimal relevance or probative value in the proceedings. Had this been a criminal trial, these statements would have required close scrutiny as there the burden lies with the Crown to prove every element of the offence. The admission of any prejudicial evidence might render the proceedings unfair to the accused. However, in parole eligibility review proceedings, where the burden lies with the applicant to prove that he or she deserves clemency on the balance of probabilities, and where a number of factors are weighed together by the jurors in their discretion, the same danger does not exist. A discretionary decision may still provide a fair hearing even though some of the evidence relied upon was arguably unfair.

In determining whether the accused had a fair hearing in a parole eligibility application, the whole of the proceedings rather than individual aspects of evidence or incidents must be reviewed. This court's role in reviewing a s. 745 decision is to consider the cumulative effect of the impugned evidence on the fairness of the proceedings.

In the present case, the judge advised the jurors repeatedly that they were to assess only the three factors enumerated in s. 745(2) of the Code, i.e., the appellant's character, his conduct while serving his sentence, and the nature of the offence. These same factors were set out on the jury information sheet distributed to the jurors, which read:

Part I
(a) Are you satisfied by a preponderance of credible evidence, having regard to:
    (i) the character of the Applicant and
    (ii) his conduct while serving his sentence and
    (iii) the nature of the offence for which he was convicted,

that the Applicant's number of years of imprisonment without eligibility for parole should be reduced?

Please answer: "Yes" or "No"

As outlined above, the impugned comments of Crown counsel had only a limited relevance to these three enumerated factors. There was little risk that the statements relating to the victim, her family or the secrecy of the parole process, would have any significant effect on the jury's deliberations. It is clear to me that the judge's directions put the jury's obligations squarely before them. As a result, in spite of the Crown's language, there was no threat to the fairness of the hearing.

The appellant submitted before this court that the inflammatory language used by Crown counsel rendered the proceedings fundamentally unfair. Ironically, however, defence counsel did not take that position at the hearing as no objection was raised to the language of the Crown. The only objection occurred when Crown counsel began to examine plans for renovating the Beaver Creek institution, a matter that clearly had no relevance. In fact, the appellant did not even raise the "inflammatory language" issue in his application for leave to appeal. The failure to object indicates that the statements made by the Crown in the context of the hearing were not regarded as prejudicial. These isolated comments, scattered throughout the 600-page transcript, were seen at the time as not sufficient to warrant even an objection.

While a failure to object is not determinative, it is a circumstance which may be considered by an appellate court in dismissing an appeal: *Imrich v. The Queen* (1977), 34 CCC (2d) 143 (SCC); *Lewis v. The Queen* (1979), 47 CCC (2d) 24 (SCC); *R v. Lomage* (1991), 2 OR (3d) 621 (Ont. CA). In the present case, the failure to object demonstrates that the language used by Crown counsel did not have the cumulative prejudicial effect discussed by the Chief Justice.

I am satisfied that in spite of the language complained of, the jurors were made aware of their responsibility and understood the nature of what they were doing. It is difficult to conclude that the irregularities complained of had any effect on the jury's assessment of whether the accused had satisfied the jury that he was, in the circumstances, entitled to a reduction in his parole eligibility.

I would, therefore, reject the appellant's fifth ground of appeal.

B. Victim Impact Statements

The presiding judge at the appellant's s. 745 hearing held that victim impact statements were not admissible, for two reasons. First, he ruled that the victim impact statements tendered in this case did not constitute "relevant matters" within the meaning of s. 745(2) of the *Criminal Code*. He wrote at p. 380: "As I read s. 745(2), evidence by way of the proposed victim impact statements does not form part of the relevant matters enunciated by s. 745(2)."... As well, he held that victim impact statements are in all cases inadmissible in a s. 745 hearing, stating as follows:

> ... the victim impact statement is something to be presented to the judge while she/he is hearing evidence and submissions prior to the imposition of sentence. We are now 15 years after the date of the sentencing.
>
> Moreover, the Court of Appeal for Ontario in *R v. Vaillancourt*, supra, at p. 551, said: "In my opinion, the proceedings pursuant to s. 745 cannot be said to be a part of the sentencing process ... ."

In my view, the presiding judge erred in ruling that victim impact statements are at all times inadmissible at a s. 745 hearing. Evidence of the impact of a crime on the victim clearly has no relevance to a jury's assessment of an applicant's conduct while in custody or of his character under s. 745(2). To the extent that the impact on the victim is relevant to the third enumerated factor in s. 745(2)—the nature of the offence—this relevance will usually, but not always, have been exhausted at the applicant's initial sentencing hearing. The victim's suffering in the years since the crime was committed does nothing to alter the nature of the offence, and should not automatically be admitted into evidence for this purpose.

However, it would seem to be permissible for a judge presiding at a s. 745 parole eligibility hearing to receive victim impact statements in exercising the discretion to permit the jury to hear evidence of "such other matters as the judge deems relevant in the circumstances" in s. 745(2) of the Code. Whether a judge chooses to exercise the discretion to admit victim impact statements will depend on the circumstances of the particular case. A judge should be cautious in admitting such statements, for to focus the jury on the victim, some 15 years after the crime was committed, is to invite the jury to assess the appropriateness of the applicant's sentence in terms of its retribution, denunciation and punishment goals. As outlined earlier, these principles do not form the focus of a s. 745 hearing.

Victim impact statements were only recently made a part of the sentencing process, with the coming into force of an *Act to Amend the Criminal Code* (victims of crime), RSC 1985, c. 23 (4th Supp.), in 1988 (now s. 735(1.1), (1.2), (1.3) and (1.4) of the Code). More recently, victim impact statements were made a part of the parole process: *Corrections and Conditional Release Act*, SC 1992, c. 20. Legislation which would permit the introduction of victim impact statements as a matter of course in s. 745 parole eligibility review hearings is currently pending before Parliament: Bill C-41, an *Act to Amend the Criminal Code* (sentencing) and other Acts in consequence thereof, 1st Sess., 35th Parl., 1994 (1st reading June 13, 1994), ss. 745.6(2)(d), (3). In light of the current legislative debate over the issue, it would seem inappropriate for this court to adopt a blanket rule that would make victim impact statements always admissible at s. 745 hearings.

A judge presiding at a s. 745 parole eligibility hearing has a discretion to determine when victim impact statements may be relevant to the jury's deliberations. In the present case, the trial judge exercised this discretion against the admissibility of the statements stating that "the proposed victim impact statements [do] not form part of the relevant matters enunciated by s. 745(2)" (at p. 380). This ruling was an appropriate exercise of his discretion, in this particular case, and should not be interfered with by this court.

For these reasons, I would dismiss the appeal and uphold the jury's refusal to alter the date of the appellant's parole eligibility. Appeal allowed; rehearing ordered.

CHAPTER FIFTEEN

Young Offenders

I. INTRODUCTION

In Canada, a unique sentencing system deals with young persons who commit criminal offences. Since the early 1980s, young persons—that is, persons who have not reached the age of 18 years when they offended—are sentenced in accordance with the provisions of the *Young Offenders Act*, RSC 1985, c. Y-1. This regime is about to change. At the time of writing, the new *Youth Criminal Justice Act* (Bill C-3, 1999), is making its way through Parliament. When it is enacted, it will replace the *Young Offenders Act*.

Given the present legislative state of flux, there seems to be little point in addressing the provisions of the *Young Offenders Act* in a comprehensive manner. At the same time, it would be a shame to think that there is nothing to be learned from a regime that governed our manner of punishing young persons for close to 20 years. (For a comprehensive account of the *Young Offenders Act* in general, and the sentencing provisions in particular, see Nicholas Bala, *Young Offenders Law* (Concord, ON: Irwin Law, 1997). For a historical and conceptual analysis of the sentencing of young persons, see Sanjeev S. Anand, "Sentencing, Judicial Discretion and Juvenile Justice" (1998-99), 41 CLQ 318 and 485.)

In order to reach a palatable compromise, the following discussion is limited to the consideration of general principles that are relevant to the sentencing of young persons. In the next section, the general principles applicable to the *Young Offenders Act* are set out, followed by the leading Supreme Court of Canada decision in *R v. J.J.M.* This is followed by a brief look at the provisions that facilitate the trial and sentencing of young persons in adult court in accordance with adult standards (the "transfer provisions"). Given that the concept of transfer is carried through into the *Youth Criminal Justice Act*, there is value in considering the arrangements (statutory and judicial) under the old legislation. In the final section, the key sentencing provisions of the *Youth Criminal Justice Act* are set out.

II. SENTENCING PRINCIPLES UNDER THE YOUNG OFFENDERS ACT

Young Offenders Act
RSC 1985, c. Y-1, ss. 3, 4, and 20

POLICY FOR CANADA WITH RESPECT TO YOUNG OFFENDERS / Act to be liberally construed.

537

3(1) It is hereby recognized and declared that

(a) while young persons should not in all instances be held accountable in the same manner or suffer the same consequences for their behaviour as adults, young persons who commit offences should nonetheless bear responsibility for their contraventions;

(b) society must, although it has the responsibility to take reasonable measures to prevent criminal conduct by young persons, be afforded the necessary protection from illegal behaviour;

(c) young persons who commit offences require supervision, discipline and control, but, because of their state of dependency and level of development and maturity, they also have special needs and require guidance and assistance;

(d) where it is not inconsistent with the protection of society, taking no measures or taking measures other than judicial proceedings under this Act should be considered for dealing with young persons who have committed offences;

(e) young persons have rights and freedoms in their own right, including those stated in the *Canadian Charter of Rights and Freedoms* or in the *Canadian Bill of Rights*, and in particular a right to be heard in the course of, and to participate in, the processes that lead to decisions that affect them, and young persons should have special guarantees of their rights and freedoms;

(f) in the application of this Act, the rights and freedoms of young persons include a right to the least possible interference with freedom that is consistent with the protection of society, having regard to the needs of young persons and the interests of their families;

(g) young persons have the right, in every instance where they have rights or freedoms that may be affected by this Act, to be informed as to what those rights and freedoms are; and

(h) parents have responsibility for the care and supervision of their children, and for that reason, young persons should be removed from parental supervision either partly or entirely only when measures that provide for continuing parental supervision are inappropriate.

(2) This Act shall be liberally construed to the end that young persons will be dealt with in accordance with the principles set out in subsection (1).

...

Alternative Measures

4(1) Alternative measures may be used to deal with a young person alleged to have committed an offence instead of judicial proceedings under this Act only if

(a) the measures are part of a program of alternative measures authorized by the Attorney General or his delegate or authorized by a person, or a person within a class of persons, designated by the Lieutenant Governor in Council of a province;

(b) the person who is considering whether to use such measures is satisfied that they would be appropriate, having regard to the needs of the young person and the interests of society;

(c) the young person, having been informed of the alternative measures, fully and freely consents to participate therein;

(d) the young person has, before consenting to participate in the alternative measures, been advised of his right to be represented by counsel and been given a reasonable opportunity to consult with counsel;

(e) the young person accepts responsibility for the act or omission that forms the basis of the offence that he is alleged to have committed;

(f) there is, in the opinion of the Attorney General or his agent, sufficient evidence to proceed with the prosecution of the offence; and

(g) the prosecution of the offence is not in any way barred at law.

(2) Alternative measures shall not be used to deal with a young person alleged to have committed an offence if the young person

(a) denies his participation or involvement in the commission of the offence; or

(b) expresses his wish to have any charge against him dealt with by the youth court.

(3) No admission, confession or statement accepting responsibility for a given act or omission made by a young person alleged to have committed an offence as a condition of his being dealt with by alternative measures shall be admissible in evidence against him in any civil or criminal proceedings.

(4) The use of alternative measures in respect of a young person alleged to have committed an offence is not a bar to proceedings against him under this Act, but

(a) where the youth court is satisfied on a balance of probabilities that the young person has totally complied with the terms and conditions of the alternative measures, the youth court shall dismiss any charge against him; and

(b) where the youth court is satisfied on a balance of probabilities that the young person has partially complied with the terms and conditions of the alternative measures, the youth court may dismiss any charge against him if, in the opinion of the court, the prosecution of the charge would, having regard to the circumstances, be unfair, and the youth court may consider the young person's performance with respect to the alternative measures before making a disposition under this Act.

(5) Subject to subsection (4), nothing in this section shall be construed to prevent any person from laying an information, obtaining the issue or confirmation of any process or proceeding with the prosecution of any offence in accordance with law.

Since its enactment, the courts have struggled to impose order on this new regime. The caution with which the courts approached the *Young Offenders Act* is captured in the following excerpt from *R v. R.I.*, one of the first appellate decisions under the Act.

R v. R.I.
(1985), 17 CCC (3d) 523 (Ont. CA)

...

THORSON JA: The *Young Offenders Act* does indeed reflect a shift in direction of the kind indicated by [counsel]. In my opinion, this shift must be taken into account, at least to some degree, whenever a youth court is considering the imposition of a maximum custodial disposition.

In so stating my agreement, however, I would sound a note of caution. It does not follow, in my opinion, that the relativity principle referred to by counsel must now be applied to young offenders in exactly the same way as it is to adult offenders. The close correlation which is generally looked to as appropriate in the case of an adult offender, between the seriousness of the offence and the length of the sentence imposed for it, may or may not be equally as appropriate in the case of a young offender, where the task of arriving at the "right" disposition may be a considerably more difficult and complex one, given the special needs of young persons and the kind of guidance and assistance they may require. Any uncritical application of the principle to young offenders could thus run counter to the larger objectives of the new legislation. On the other hand, as a factor to be taken into account in the disposition process, the principle is one which the new legislation must be taken to implicitly recognize.

With regard to counsel's third submission as it applies to the new Act, a comment of a similar nature may be made. Where a first custodial disposition is being made, it may well be that the public interest is adequately served by a short custodial term, and if so, that will obviously be the most desirable disposition. Again, however, it cannot be the rule in all cases, regardless of the nature of the offence or the circumstances of its commission. Moreover, the reasoning which has led our courts to favour, wherever possible, a short first custodial sentence for a youthful adult offender may lose some of its force when sought to be applied to someone of lesser maturity, as, for example, where a young offender's committal to custody reflects an adjudged need to remove him from an unhappy or hostile home environment. In his case, whatever ultimate success the custodial order may expect to enjoy may have to be more directly linked to its duration than will generally need to be the case where a youthful adult offender, facing for the first time a term of incarceration in a prison or reformatory, is the subject of such an order.

What must not be lost sight of, however, is that ultimately, in all of these cases, the issue comes down to the fitness of the particular disposition, measured against all of the factors which are properly taken into account in its making. This, of course, is the test of appellate review laid down by s. 614 of the *Criminal Code*, which makes it the duty of the Court of Appeal on any appeal taken against sentence (in this context "disposition") to consider its fitness when deciding the outcome of the appeal. Whatever the factors taken into account in any sentence or disposition, therefore, the ultimate question is whether the end result is a fit one. This, therefore, is the question in these appeals, and I now turn to a consideration of it as it bears on each of the appellants individually.

A number of years later, the Supreme Court of Canada considered the proper approach to sentencing under the *Young Offenders Act* in the following decision.

R v. J.J.M.
(1993), 81 CCC (3d) 487 (SCC)

CORY J: Neither great constitutional questions nor vexing Charter problems are raised on this appeal. Yet, since it deals with the sentencing of young offenders, it is concerned with a subject of some importance that may affect the safety and future of our society.

Factual Background

On January 18, 1991, J.J.M. and another young offender broke into premises occupied by a local radio station. An expensive camera and six audio cassettes were stolen together with $120 cash. On January 28th, they broke into an office and stole some $1,200 to $1,700 from an office cabinet. On April 26th, J.J.M. and his co-accused broke into premises, which they severely damaged, and stole a camera and $324.

On June 17, 1991, J.J.M. was convicted of three counts of break, enter and theft and one count of breach of probation. Prior to that date he had already acquired a significant record. He had been found guilty of three counts of break, enter and theft between February and April, 1990, and two separate counts of taking an automobile without consent in the months of January and February of that same year. He was, as well, subject to a probation order when the offences were committed in 1991. The probation order required him to undertake community service. However, he had not co-operated with the authorities and had completed very little of it at the time of arrest.

J.J.M. is one of nine children. The family history is depressing. The parents appear to be prone to alcohol abuse. What is worse, there are reported incidents of violence not only between the parents themselves but also of violence by the parents directed against the children. On some of these occasions, J.J.M. attempted to stop the fighting. Of the nine children, no less than eight of them had been, or were at the time of sentencing, subject to probation orders. Indeed at the time J.J.M. was sentenced, one of his sisters was sentenced in connection with an unrelated offence. Of the five younger children, still living at home, three were in custody at the Manitoba Youth Centre.

His school principal observed that the appellant was a good student until his siblings were released from custody and returned to school. As soon as that happened, he became rebellious. On several occasions J.J.M. and his siblings had been apprehended by the Awasis Agency and placed in foster homes. However, they were returned to their parents when they proved to be uncontrollable.

Courts Below

At the trial, Gyles Prov. Ct. J took careful note of the prior record and the depressing family history and ordered the appellant be placed in open custody for two years.

In the Court of Appeal 6 WAC 296, 75 Man. R (2d) 296, 14 WCB (2d) 355, Huband JA, with Lyon JA concurring, found the disposition to be a fit and proper one. He found that it was appropriate for the trial judge to take into account the mandatory judicial review of the sentence after a year. Helper JA in dissent would have reduced the period of open custody to one year. She expressed the concern that in reality the disposition attempted to provide welfare assistance for the appellant rather than assessing the appropriate sentence.

Analysis

General Approach to Young Offenders' Dispositions

The approach the court should take when sentencing young offenders, is to be ascertained from s. 3 of the *Young Offenders Act*, RSC 1985, c. Y-1. That section is entitled "Declaration of Principle" and sets out a declaration of principle in s-s. (1).

A quick reading of that section indicates that there is a marked ambivalence in its approach to the sentencing of young offenders. Yet that ambivalence should not be surprising when it is remembered that the Act reflects a courageous attempt to balance concepts and interests that are frequently conflicting.

Society must be concerned with the illegal acts of young people. The wanton destruction of the contents of a home by young offenders is just as keenly felt by the victims as would be a ransacking by adult burglars. "Swarmings" by young gangs, where the victims are surrounded and their clothing or money torn from them, are a serious cause for concern since they can be the forerunner of even more violent mob action by the same offenders as adults.

Yet there must be some flexibility in the dispositions imposed on young offenders. It is not unreasonable to expect that in many cases carefully crafted dispositions will result in the reform and rehabilitation of the young person. That must be the ultimate aim of all dispositions. They may often achieve this goal if the disposition is carefully tailored to meet both the need to protect society and to reform the offender. Let us consider once again the provisions of s. 3(1).

• • •

This court has recognized the importance of this statement of principle. In *R v. T.(V.)*, [1992] 1 SCR 749, L'Heureux-Dubé J writing for the court noted that the section should not be considered as merely a preamble. Rather it should be given the force normally attributed to substantive provisions.

Section 3(1) attempts to balance the need to make the young offenders responsible for their crimes while recognizing their vulnerability and special needs. It seeks to chart a course that avoids both the harshness of a pure criminal law approach applied to minors and the paternalistic welfare approach that was emphasized in the old *Juvenile Delinquents Act*, RSC 1970, c. J-3. Society must be protected from the violent and criminal acts committed by the young just as much as from those committed by adults. The references to responsibility contained in s. 3(1)(a) and to the protection of society in paras. (b), (d) and (f) suggest that a traditional criminal law approach should be taken into account in the sentencing of young offenders. Yet, we must approach dispositions imposed on young offenders differently because the needs and requirements of the young are distinct from those of adults.

For instance, the declaration in s. 3(1)(a) and (c) notes that young offenders cannot be held accountable in the same way as adult criminals because of their dependency on others and their obvious lack of maturity. There are other elements in the declaration which suggest that there should be a departure from the strict criminal justice model in imposing penalties on young offenders. Section 3(1)(d) for example, suggests that in some circumstances, no judicial measure should be taken against the child. Paragraph (f) confirms the offender's right to the least possible interference with his or her liberty. As well, s. 3(1)(h) establishes that young people coming within the provisions of the Act are, wherever possible, to remain under parental supervision. Further, while the wardship provisions that were set out in the *Juvenile Delinquents Act* have been abolished, it is significant that s. 23(2)(f) of the *Young Offenders Act* provides for probation orders which will contain residence requirements. These probation orders may be used by correctional authorities to place children with provincial welfare agencies.

Thus, the Act does specifically recognize that young offenders have special needs and require careful guidance. Each disposition should strive to recognize and balance the interests of society and young offenders. The very fact that these are young offenders indicates that they may become long-term adult offenders unless they can be reformed to become useful and productive members of society. Thus, the disposition imposed on a young offender must seek to have a beneficial and significant effect on both the offender and the community.

Senior Judge Beaulieu (as he then was), in "From 'Challenges and Choices' to 'A Climate for Change,'" *YOA Dispositions: Challenges and Choices* (1988), aptly described the Act's approach to sentencing at p. 4:

> The YOA does not do away with looking at who the offender is; it specially directs the judge to do so, but the youth's needs must be seen in the context of his accountability and the protection of society.
>
> The YOA too, contains some blend of criminal law and protection philosophies. However, here the scales are weighted, at least at the pre-adjudicative and adjudicative stage, toward the criminal law process. The paternalistic character of the JDA is replaced by the concept of accountability of the individual, coupled with the need to ensure that individual rights are protected by proper procedure.
>
> The YOA attempts to balance the protection of society and the young offender's needs. It attempts to balance the due process and treatment approaches.

I agree with the academic writers who have observed that the Act should be seen as part of a spectrum of legislation that runs from those statutes that provide welfare care for children at one end to the strict sentencing provisions of the *Criminal Code*.

Factors To Be Considered When Imposing Custodial Sentences

Section 24(1) of the Act requires judges to consider three elements before imposing a custodial term:

(1) the protection of society;
(2) the seriousness of the offence;
(3) the needs and circumstances of the young person.

The Act empowers the judge, in those situations where it is decided that custody is required, to determine whether it should be open or closed. Section 24.1(1) defines "open custody" as a "community residential centre, group home, child care institution, or forest or wilderness camp" or other similar facilities. Certainly, places which come within the definition of "open custody" will restrict the liberty of the young offender. Yet those facilities are not simply to be jails for young people. Rather they are facilities dedicated to the long-term welfare and reformation of the young offender. Open custody facilities do not and should not resemble penitentiaries. Indeed, the courts have very properly resisted attempts to define as "open" those facilities which provide nothing but secure confinement: see for example, *Re D.B. and The Queen* (1986), 27 CCC (3d) 468 (NS SCTD), and *Re L.H.F. and The Queen* (1985), 24 CCC (3d) 152 (PEI SC).

The *Young Offenders Act* thus provides the sentencing judge with a wide latitude as to how the disposition is to be served so as to better deal with the difficult and complex problems presented by young offenders.

With that background, it may now be appropriate to consider the specific objections that were raised by the appellant to the custodial disposition imposed on J.J.M.

Child Welfare Concerns and the Proportionality Principle

The appellant contended that the trial judge erred in imposing a lengthy disposition that could only be justified as proportional on welfare grounds. It was his submission that the dreadful conditions existing in the appellant's home should not have been a factor in assessing the length of the term of open custody. It was said that this disposition was a throw-back to a type of sentence which would have been imposed under the paternalistic scheme of the *Juvenile Delinquents Act*. The appellant argued that pursuant to the provisions of the *Young Offenders Act* the disposition had to be proportional to the offence committed.

It is true that for both adults and minors the sentence must be proportional to the offence committed. But in the sentencing of adult offenders, the principle of proportionality will have a greater significance than it will in the disposition of young offenders. For the young, a proper disposition must take into account not only the seriousness of the crime but also all the other relevant factors.

For example, two years of closed custody could never be imposed on a young offender with no prior record who had stolen a pair of gloves, no matter how intolerable or how unsavoury the conditions were in the offender's home. None the less the home situation is a factor that should always be taken into account in fashioning the appropriate disposition. It is relevant in complying with the Act's requirement that an assessment must be made of the special needs and requirements for guidance of the young offender. Intolerable conditions in the home indicate both a special need for care and the absence of any guidance within the home.

The situation in the home of a young offender should neither be ignored nor made the predominant factor in sentencing. None the less, it is a factor that can properly be taken into account in fashioning the disposition.

This was very ably expressed by Thorson JA in *R v. R.I.* (1985), 17 CCC (3d) 523. At pp. 530-1 he wrote:

> ... I would sound a note of caution. It does not follow, in my opinion, that the relativity principle referred to by counsel must now be applied to young offenders in exactly the same way as it is to adult offenders. The close correlation which is generally looked to

as appropriate in the case of an adult offender, between the seriousness of the offence and the length of the sentence imposed for it, may or may not be equally as appropriate in the case of a young offender, where the task of arriving at the "right" disposition may be a considerably more difficult and complex one, given the special needs of young persons and the kind of guidance and assistance they may require. Any uncritical application of the principle to young offenders could thus run counter to the larger objectives of the new legislation. On the other hand, as a factor to be taken into account in the disposition process, the principle is one which the new legislation must be taken to implicitly recognize.

Moreover, the reasoning which has led our courts to favour, wherever possible, a short first custodial sentence for a youthful adult offender may lose some of its force when sought to be applied to someone of lesser maturity, as, for example, where a young offender's committal to custody reflects an adjudged need to remove him from an unhappy or hostile home environment.

The aim must be both to protect society and at the same time to provide the young offender with the necessary guidance and assistance that he or she may not be getting at home. Those goals are not necessarily mutually exclusive. In the long run, society is best protected by the reformation and rehabilitation of a young offender. In turn, the young offenders are best served when they are provided with the necessary guidance and assistance to enable them to learn the skills required to become fully integrated, useful members of society.

General Deterrence

The appellant submitted that it was improper for the Court of Appeal to take into account the need for general deterrence when it assessed the dispositions. Reliance was placed on the decisions of the Courts of Appeal in both Alberta and New Brunswick. In *R v. K.G.* (1986), 31 CCC (3d) 81 (Alta. CA), it was held that general deterrence did not have any place in the sentencing of young offenders. This view was adopted by a special five-member panel of the Alberta Court of Appeal in *R v. C.W.W.* (1986), 25 CCC (3d) 355. The same position was adopted by the New Brunswick Court of Appeal in *R v. R.C.S.* (1986), 27 CCC (3d) 239.

This approach was specifically disapproved by the Courts of Appeal of Ontario and Quebec: see *R v. O.(F.)* (1986), 27 CCC (3d) 376 (Ont. CA), and *R v. L.(S.)* (1990), 75 CR (3d) 94 (Que. CA).

In *R v. O.(F.)*, supra, Brooke JA writing for the Ontario Court of Appeal expressed the opinion that although the principle of general deterrence must be considered, it had diminished importance in determining the appropriate disposition in the case of a youthful offender. This, I believe, is the correct approach. This is apparent from a consideration of some of the provisions of the *Young Offenders Act*. Section 3, in emphasizing the need for the protection of society, s. 20 by its observation that dispositions should have regard to the best interest of the young person and the public, and s. 24, which provides for a disposition imposing custody if it is in the best interest of the young person and for the protection of society, all indicate that general deterrence must be taken into account.

There is reason to believe that *Young Offenders Act* dispositions can have an effective deterrent effect. The crimes committed by the young tend to be a group activity. The group lends support and assistance to the prime offenders. The criminological literature is clear that about 80% of juvenile delinquency is a group activity, whether as part of an organized gang or with an informal group of accomplices: see Maurice Cusson in *Why Delinquency?* (1983), pp. 138-9, and Franklin E. Zimring "Kids, Groups and Crime," 72 *J Crim. L* (1981), p. 867. If the activity of the group is criminal then the disposition imposed on an individual member of the group should be such that it will deter other members of the group. For example, the sentence imposed on one member of a "swarming group" should serve to deter others in the gang.

Having said that, I would underline that general deterrence should not, through undue emphasis, have the same importance in fashioning the disposition for a youthful offender as it would in the case of an adult. One youthful offender should not be obliged to accept the responsibility for all the young offenders of his or her generation.

The Availability of a Yearly Review

The appellant argued that the Court of Appeal was in error when it assessed the disposition in light of the mandatory review provided for by s. 28(1) of the *Young Offenders Act*.

Section 28(1) and (3) provide:

> 28(1) Where a young person is committed to custody pursuant to a disposition made in respect of an offence for a period exceeding one year, the provincial director of the province in which the young person is held in custody shall cause the young person to be brought before the youth court forthwith at the end of one year from the date of the most recent disposition made in respect of the offence, and the youth court shall review the disposition. ...
>
> (3) Where a young person is committed to custody pursuant to a disposition made in respect of an offence, the provincial director may, on his own initiative, and shall, on the request of the young person, his parent or the Attorney General or his agent, on any of the grounds set out in subsection (4), cause the young person to be brought before the youth court at any time after six months from the date of the most recent disposition made in respect of the offence or, with leave of a youth court judge, at any earlier time, and, where the youth court is satisfied that there are grounds for the review under subsection (4), the court shall review the disposition.

The section is obviously salutary. It provides an incentive to young offenders to perform well and to improve their behaviour significantly as quickly as possible. As well, it gives an opportunity to the court to assess the offenders again and to make certain that the appropriate treatment or assistance has been made available to them. It introduces an aspect of review and flexibility into the sentencing procedure, with the result that any marked improvement in the behaviour, outlook and performance of the offender can be rewarded and any deterioration assessed. The Act provides a system that is akin to, yet broader than, the probation review provided for adult offenders.

The appellant sought to rely upon *R v. S.(H.S.)*, Nfld. CA, June 2, 1990, unreported [summarized 16 WCB (2d) 58]. In that case the trial judge had imposed a sentence based, in part, on the fact that it would be reviewed before it had expired. The Court of Appeal disagreed and expressed the view that a disposition must be made on the basis of the facts and law as they existed at the time it was made. They held that the review of a disposition for a young offender could not be considered when a sentence is imposed any more than could be the possibility of parole for an adult. I cannot accept that position.

The *Young Offenders Act* provides for a mandatory system of review. In the case of adult offenders, the court controls neither the parole nor remission provisions. In the *Young Offenders Act* the review procedure is an integral part of the disposition. It is therefore appropriate to take it into account as a factor, albeit not a major one, in assessing the appropriateness of a disposition.

Assessment of the Disposition in This Case

The disposition of two years in open custody was appropriate. The trial judge was faced with a young offender with a significant prior record. It was obvious that he was not co-operating with the probation authorities or fulfilling his obligations with regard to community service. The offences themselves were serious. The situation in the home was intolerable. Yet, in the absence of other family members, his good work at school indicated that there was real hope for him and that there was a pressing need to provide guidance and assistance for him. The aspect of the need for general deterrence could not be overlooked since these offences had been committed with the help and assistance of others. Further it was appropriate to consider as a factor that there would be a review of the disposition. The disposition of two years' open custody was, in all the circumstances, a fit sentence in light of the offences committed and the needs and requirements of the young offender.

In the result, as this court directed at the conclusion of the hearing, the appeal is dismissed.

For a discussion of this important decision, see Nicholas Bala, "*R v. M.(J.J.)*: The Rehabilitative Ideal for Young Offenders—Back to the Past?" (1993), 20 CR (4th) 308 and Sanjeev S. Anand, "Sentencing, Judicial Discretion and Juvenile Justice" (1998-99), 41 *CLQ* 318.

III. SENTENCING PRINCIPLES UNDER THE YOUTH CRIMINAL JUSTICE ACT

Set out below are some of the key provisions of the new *Youth Criminal Justice Act*. At the time of writing, the Bill had received second reading in the House of Commons. After setting out these provisions, we pose some questions that encourage a comparison between the approaches under the *Young Offenders Act* and the *Youth Criminal Justice Act*.

Youth Criminal Justice Act
Bill C-3, 1999

Preamble

WHEREAS society should be protected from youth crime through a youth criminal justice system that commands respect, fosters responsibility and ensures accountability through meaningful consequences and effective rehabilitation and reintegration, and that reserves its most serious intervention for the most serious crimes and reduces the over-reliance on incarceration for non-violent young persons;

WHEREAS these objectives can best be achieved by replacement of the *Young Offenders Act* with a new legal framework for the youth criminal justice system;

WHEREAS members of society share a responsibility to address the developmental challenges and the needs of young persons and to guide them into adulthood;

WHEREAS communities, families, parents and others concerned with the development of young persons should, through multi-disciplinary approaches, take reasonable steps to prevent youth crime by addressing its underlying causes, to respond to the needs of young persons, and to provide guidance and support to those at risk of committing crimes;

AND WHEREAS Canada is a party to the United Nations Convention on the Rights of the Child and recognizes that young persons have rights and freedoms, including those stated in the *Canadian Charter of Rights and Freedoms* and the *Canadian Bill of Rights*, and have special guarantees of their rights and freedoms;

. . .

2. "presumptive offence" means
   (a) an offence under one of the following provisions of the *Criminal Code*:
      (i) section 231 or 235 (first degree murder or second degree murder within the meaning of section 231),
      (ii) section 239 (attempt to commit murder),
      (iii) section 232, 234 or 236 (manslaughter), or
      (iv) section 273 (aggravated sexual assault); or
   (b) a serious violent offence for which an adult could be sentenced to imprisonment for more than two years committed by a young person after the coming into force of section 61, if at the time the young person committed the offence at least two judicial determinations have been made under subsection 41(8), at different proceedings, that the young person has committed a serious violent offence.

. . .

Declaration of Principle

Policy for Canada with Respect to Young Persons

3(1) The following principles apply in this Act:
   (a) the principal goal of the youth criminal justice system is to protect the public by
      (i) preventing crime by addressing the circumstances underlying a young person's offending behaviour,
      (ii) ensuring that a young person is subject to meaningful consequences for his or her offence, and

(iii) rehabilitating young persons who commit offences and reintegrating them into society;

(b) the criminal justice system for young persons must be separate from that of adults and emphasize the following:

(i) fair and proportionate accountability that is consistent with the greater dependency of young persons and their reduced level of maturity,

(ii) enhanced procedural protection to ensure that young persons are treated fairly and that their rights, including their right to privacy, are protected, and

(iii) a greater emphasis on rehabilitation and reintegration;

(c) within the limits of fair and proportionate accountability, the measures taken against young persons who commit offences should

(i) reinforce respect for societal values,

(ii) encourage the repair of harm done to victims and the community,

(iii) be meaningful for the individual young person and, where appropriate, involve the parents, the extended family, the community and social or other agencies in the young person's rehabilitation and reintegration, and

(iv) respect gender, ethnic, cultural and linguistic differences and respond to the needs of young persons with special requirements; and

(d) special considerations apply in respect of proceedings against young persons and, in particular,

(i) young persons have rights and freedoms in their own right, such as a right to be heard in the course of and to participate in the processes, other than the decision to prosecute, that lead to decisions that affect them, and young persons have special guarantees of their rights and freedoms,

(ii) victims should be treated with courtesy, compassion and respect for their dignity and privacy and should suffer the minimum degree of inconvenience as a result of their involvement with the youth criminal justice system,

(iii) victims should be provided with information about the proceedings and given an opportunity to participate and be heard, and

(iv) parents should be informed of measures or proceedings involving their children and encouraged to support them in addressing their offending behaviour.

Act To Be Liberally Construed

(2) This Act shall be liberally construed so as to ensure that young persons are dealt with in accordance with the principles set out in subsection (1).

...

Part 1
Extrajudicial Measures

Principles and Objectives

Declaration of Principles

4. The following principles apply in this Part:

(a) extrajudicial measures are often the most appropriate and effective way to address youth crime;

(b) extrajudicial measures allow for effective and timely interventions focused on correcting offending behaviour;

(c) extrajudicial measures are presumed to be adequate to hold a young person accountable for his or her offending behaviour if the young person has committed a non-violent offence and has not previously been found guilty of an offence; and

(d) extrajudicial measures should be used if they are adequate to hold a young person accountable for his or her offending behaviour and, if the use of extrajudicial measures is consistent with the principles set out in this section, nothing in this Act precludes their use in respect of a young person who

(i) has previously been dealt with by the use of extrajudicial measures, or

(ii) has previously been found guilty of an offence.

Objectives

5. Extrajudicial measures should be designed to

(a) provide an effective and timely response to offending behaviour outside the bounds of judicial measures;

(b) encourage young persons to acknowledge and repair the harm caused to the victim and the community;

(c) encourage families of young persons—including extended families—and the community to become involved in the design and implementation of those measures;

(d) provide an opportunity for victims to participate in decisions related to the measures selected and to receive reparation; and

(e) respect the rights and freedoms of young persons and be proportionate to the seriousness of the offence.

Warnings, Cautions and Referrals

Warnings, Cautions and Referrals

6(1) A police officer shall, before starting judicial proceedings or taking any other measures under this Act against a young person alleged to have committed an offence, consider whether it would be sufficient, having regard to the principles set out in section 4, to take no further action, warn the young person, administer a caution, if a program has been established under section 7, or refer the young person to a community-based program.

Saving

(2) The failure of a police officer to consider the options set out in subsection (1) does not invalidate any subsequent charges against the young person for the offence.

Police Cautions

7. The Attorney General may establish a program authorizing the police to administer cautions to young persons instead of starting judicial proceedings under this Act.

Crown Cautions

8. The Attorney General may establish a program authorizing prosecutors to administer cautions to young persons instead of starting or continuing judicial proceedings under this Act.

...

Extrajudicial Sanctions

Extrajudicial Sanctions

10(1) An extrajudicial sanction may be used to deal with a young person alleged to have committed an offence only if the young person cannot be adequately dealt with by a warning, caution or referral mentioned in section 6, 7 or 8 because of the seriousness of the offence, the nature and number of previous offences committed by the young person or any other aggravating circumstances.

Conditions

(2) An extrajudicial sanction may be used only if

(a) it is part of a program of sanctions that may be authorized by the Attorney General or authorized by a person, or a member of a class of persons, designated by the lieutenant governor in council of the province;

(b) the person who is considering whether to use the extrajudicial sanction is satisfied that it would be appropriate, having regard to the needs of the young person and the interests of society;

(c) the young person, having been informed of the extrajudicial sanction, fully and freely consents to be subject to it;

(d) the young person has, before consenting to be subject to the extrajudicial sanction, been advised of his or her right to be represented by counsel and been given a reasonable opportunity to consult with counsel;

(e) the young person accepts responsibility for the act or omission that forms the basis of the offence that he or she is alleged to have committed;

(f) there is, in the opinion of the Attorney General, sufficient evidence to proceed with the prosecution of the offence; and

(g) the prosecution of the offence is not in any way barred at law.

Restriction on Use

(3) An extrajudicial sanction may not be used in respect of a young person who

(a) denies participation or involvement in the commission of the offence; or

(b) expresses the wish to have the charge dealt with by a youth justice court.

Admissions Not Admissible in Evidence

(4) Any admission, confession or statement accepting responsibility for a given act or omission that is made by a young person as a condition of being dealt with by

an extrajudicial sanction is inadmissible in evidence against any young person in civil or criminal proceedings.

No Bar to Judicial Proceedings

(5) The use of an extrajudicial sanction in respect of a young person alleged to have committed an offence is not a bar to judicial proceedings under this Act, but if a charge is laid against the young person in respect of the offence,

(a) the youth justice court shall dismiss the charge if it is satisfied on a balance of probabilities that the young person has totally complied with the terms and conditions of the extrajudicial sanction; and

(b) the youth justice court may dismiss the charge if it is satisfied on a balance of probabilities that the young person has partially complied with the terms and conditions of the extrajudicial sanction and if, in the opinion of the court, prosecution of the charge would be unfair having regard to the circumstances and the young person's performance with respect to the extrajudicial sanction.

...

Part 4
Sentencing

Purpose and Principles

Purpose

37(1) The purpose of sentencing under section 41 is to contribute to the protection of society by holding a young person accountable for an offence through the imposition of just sanctions that have meaningful consequences for the young person and that promote his or her rehabilitation and reintegration into society.

Sentencing Principles

(2) A youth justice court that imposes a youth sentence on a young person shall determine the sentence in accordance with the following principles:

(a) the sentence must not result in a punishment that is greater than the punishment that would be appropriate for an adult who has been convicted of the same offence committed in similar circumstances;

(b) the sentence must be similar to the sentences imposed on young persons found guilty of the same offence committed in similar circumstances;

(c) the sentence must be proportionate to the seriousness of the offence and the degree of responsibility of the young person for that offence; and

(d) subject to paragraph (c), the sentence must

(i) be the least restrictive sentence that is capable of achieving the purpose set out in subsection (1),

(ii) be the one that is most likely to rehabilitate the young person and reintegrate him or her into society, and

(iii) promote a sense of responsibility in the young person, and an acknowledgement of the harm done to victims and the community.

Factors To Be Considered

(3) In determining a youth sentence, the youth justice court shall take into account
(a) the degree of participation by the young person in the commission of the offence;
(b) the harm done to victims and whether it was intentional or reasonably foreseeable;
(c) any reparation made by the young person to the victim or the community;
(d) the time spent in detention by the young person as a result of the offence;
(e) the previous findings of guilt of the young person; and
(f) any other aggravating and mitigating circumstances related to the young person and the offence that are relevant to the purpose and principles set out in this section.

Restriction on Committal to Custody

38(1) A youth justice court shall not commit a young person to custody under section 41 unless
(a) the young person has committed a violent offence;
(b) the young person has failed to comply with previous non-custodial sentences;
(c) the young person has committed an indictable offence for which an adult could be sentenced to imprisonment for more than two years and has a history that indicates a pattern of findings of guilt under this Act or the *Young Offenders Act*, chapter Y-1 of the Revised Statutes of Canada, 1985; or
(d) the circumstances of the offence make the imposition of a non-custodial sentence inconsistent with the purpose and principles set out in section 37.

Alternatives to Custody

(2) A youth justice court shall not impose a custodial sentence under section 41 unless the court has considered all alternatives to custody raised at the sentencing hearing that are reasonable in the circumstances, and determined that there is not a reasonable alternative, or combination of alternatives, that is in accordance with the purpose and principles set out in section 37.

Factors To Be Considered

(3) In determining whether there is a reasonable alternative to custody, a youth justice court shall consider submissions relating to
(a) the alternatives to custody that are available;
(b) the likelihood that the young person will comply with a non-custodial sentence, as evidenced by his or her compliance with previous non-custodial sentences; and
(c) the alternatives to custody that have been used in respect of young persons for similar offences committed in similar circumstances.

Imposition of Same Sentence

(4) Evidence that a particular non-custodial sentence has been imposed previously on a young person does not preclude a youth justice court from imposing the same non-custodial sentence for another offence.

Custody as Social Measure Prohibited

(5) A youth justice court shall not use custody as a substitute for appropriate child protection, mental health or other social measures.

...

Length of Custody

(8) In determining the length of a youth sentence that includes a custodial portion, a youth justice court shall be guided by the purpose and principles set out in section 37, and shall not take into consideration the fact that the supervision portion of the sentence may not be served in custody and that the sentence may be reviewed by the court under section 93.

Reasons

(9) If a youth justice court imposes a youth sentence that includes a custodial portion, the court shall state the reasons why it has determined that a non-custodial sentence is not adequate to achieve the purpose set out in subsection 37(1).

...

Youth Sentences

Recommendation of Conference

40. When a youth justice court finds a young person guilty of an offence, the court may refer the matter to a conference for recommendations to the court on an appropriate youth sentence.

Considerations as to Youth Sentence

41(1) A youth justice court shall, before imposing a youth sentence, consider any recommendations submitted under section 40, any pre-sentence report, any representations made by the parties to the proceedings or their counsel or agents and by the parents of the young person, and any other relevant information before the court.

Youth Sentence

(2) When a youth justice court finds a young person guilty of an offence'and is imposing a youth sentence, the court shall, subject to this section, impose any one of the following sanctions or any number of them that are not inconsistent with each other and, if the offence is first degree murder or second degree murder within the

meaning of section 231 of the *Criminal Code*, the court shall impose a sanction set out in paragraph (p) or subparagraph (q)(ii) or (iii) and may impose any other of the sanctions set out in this subsection that the court considers appropriate:

(a) reprimand the young person;

(b) by order direct that the young person be discharged absolutely, if the court considers it to be in the best interests of the young person and not contrary to the public interest;

(c) by order direct that the young person be discharged on any conditions that the court considers appropriate and be required to report to and be supervised by the provincial director;

(d) impose on the young person a fine not exceeding $1,000 to be paid at the time and on the terms that the court may fix;

(e) order the young person to pay to any other person at the times and on the terms that the court may fix an amount by way of compensation for loss of or damage to property or for loss of income or support, or an amount for, in the Province of Quebec, pre-trial pecuniary loss or, in any other province, special damages, for personal injury arising from the commission of the offence if the value is readily ascertainable, but no order shall be made for other damages in the Province of Quebec or for general damages in any other province;

(f) order the young person to make restitution to any other person of any property obtained by the young person as a result of the commission of the offence within the time that the court may fix, if the property is owned by the other person or was, at the time of the offence, in his or her lawful possession;

(g) if property obtained as a result of the commission of the offence has been sold to an innocent purchaser, where restitution of the property to its owner or any other person has been made or ordered, order the young person to pay the purchaser, at the time and on the terms that the court may fix, an amount not exceeding the amount paid by the purchaser for the property;

(h) subject to section 53, order the young person to compensate any person in kind or by way of personal services at the time and on the terms that the court may fix for any loss, damage or injury suffered by that person in respect of which an order may be made under paragraph (e) or (g);

(i) subject to section 53, order the young person to perform a community service at the time and on the terms that the court may fix, and to report to and be supervised by the provincial director or a person designated by the youth justice court;

(j) subject to section 50, make any order of prohibition, seizure or forfeiture that may be imposed under any Act of Parliament or any regulation made under it if an accused is found guilty or convicted of that offence, other than an order under section 161 of the *Criminal Code*;

(k) place the young person on probation in accordance with section 54 for a specified period not exceeding two years;

(l) subject to subsection (3), order the young person into an intensive support and supervision program as directed by the provincial director;

(m) subject to subsection (3) and section 53, order the young person to attend a facility offering a program approved by the provincial director, at the times and on the terms that the court may fix, for a maximum of two hundred and forty hours, over a period not exceeding six months;

(n) make a custody and supervision order with respect to the young person, ordering that a period be served in custody and that a second period—which is one half as long as the first—be served, subject to sections 96 and 97, under supervision in the community subject to conditions, the total of the periods not to exceed two years from the date of the coming into force of the order or, if the young person is found guilty of an offence for which the punishment provided by the *Criminal Code* or any other Act of Parliament is imprisonment for life, three years from the date of coming into force of the order;

(o) subject to subsection (5), make a deferred custody and supervision order that is for a specified period not exceeding six months, subject to any conditions set out in section 54 that the court considers appropriate;

(p) order the young person to serve a sentence not to exceed

(i) in the case of first degree murder, ten years comprised of

(A) a committal to custody, to be served continuously, for a period that must not, subject to subsection 103(1), exceed six years from the date of committal, and

(B) a placement under conditional supervision to be served in the community in accordance with section 104, and

(ii) in the case of second degree murder, seven years comprised of

(A) a committal to custody, to be served continuously, for a period that must not, subject to subsection 103(1), exceed four years from the date of committal, and

(B) a placement under conditional supervision to be served in the community in accordance with section 104;

(q) subject to subsection (7), make an intensive rehabilitative custody and supervision order in respect of the young person

(i) that is for a specified period that must not exceed

(A) two years from the date of committal, or

(B) if the young person is found guilty of an offence for which the punishment provided by the *Criminal Code* or any other Act of Parliament is imprisonment for life, three years from the date of committal,

and that orders the young person to be committed into a continuous period of intensive rehabilitative custody for the first portion of the sentence and, subject to subsection 103(1), to serve the remainder under conditional supervision in the community in accordance with section 104,

(ii) that is for a specified period that must not exceed, in the case of first degree murder, ten years from the date of committal, comprising

(A) a committal to intensive rehabilitative custody, to be served continuously, for a period that must not exceed six years from the date of committal, and

(B) subject to subsection 103(1), a placement under conditional supervision to be served in the community in accordance with section 104, and

(iii) that is for a specified period that must not exceed, in the case of second degree murder, seven years from the date of committal, comprising

(A) a committal to intensive rehabilitative custody, to be served continuously, for a period that must not exceed four years from the date of committal, and

(B) subject to subsection 103(1), a placement under conditional supervision to be served in the community in accordance with section 104; and

(r) impose on the young person any other reasonable and ancillary conditions
that the court considers advisable and in the best interests of the young person and
the public.

Youth Justice Court Statement

(4) When the youth justice court makes a custody and supervision order with
respect to a young person under paragraph (2)(n), the court shall state the following
with respect to that order:

You are ordered to serve (state the number of days or months to be served) in custody,
to be followed by (state one-half of the number of days or months stated above) to be
served under supervision in the community subject to conditions.

If you breach any of the conditions while you are under supervision in the community, you may be brought back into custody and required to serve the rest of the second
period in custody as well.

You should also be aware that, under other provisions of the *Youth Criminal Justice
Act*, a court could require you to serve the second period in custody as well.

Deferred Custody and Supervision Order

(5) The court may make a deferred custody and supervision order under paragraph (2)(o) if

(a) the young person is found guilty of a non-violent offence; and

(b) it is consistent with the purpose and principles set out in section 37 and the
criteria set out in section 38.

Termination of Order

(6) If a young person complies with the conditions of a deferred custody and supervision order made under paragraph (2)(o), or any conditions as amended by section
56, for the entire period that the order is in force, the order is terminated.

Intensive Rehabilitative Custody and Supervision Order

(7) A youth justice court may make an intensive rehabilitative custody and supervision order under paragraph (2)(q) in respect of a young person only if

(a) the young person has been found guilty of a presumptive offence;

(b) the young person is suffering from a mental illness or disorder, a psychological disorder or an emotional disturbance;

(c) a plan of treatment and intensive supervision has been developed for the
young person, and there are reasonable grounds to believe that the plan might

reduce the risk of the young person repeating the offence or committing other presumptive offences; and

(d) the provincial director consents to the young person's participation in the program.

Are the sentencing principles in the *Youth Criminal Justice Act* substantially different from those in ss. 718 to 718.2 of the *Criminal Code*? Do they encompass general deterrence as a potential objective of young offender sentencing? Certainly, there are some substantive principles in the proposed Act that are not expressly mentioned in the *Criminal Code*— for example, s. 37(2)(A)(ii), dealing with rehabilitation, and s. 38, imposing limits on the use of custody. Do these principles have any applicability to adults? Is there any basis for arguing that these specific principles ought to apply to adults? Here, one has to be cautious about direct translation that might also support the importation of adult notions of retribution back into the youth system.

IV. TRANSFERS TO ADULT COURT

In enacting the *Young Offenders Act*, Parliament contemplated that there would be situations that could not be addressed adequately under this special legislation. Accordingly, s. 16 of the Act provides a power to transfer a case from the youth court to the adult court, thereby subjecting the young person to all of the procedures and most of the sanctions available in the *Criminal Code*.

Originally, the transfer provision was most often resorted to in homicide cases. This situation presented the judge hearing transfer applications with a difficult dilemma. Under the *Young Offenders Act*, the maximum that could be imposed was 3 years in closed custody; under the *Criminal Code*, the young person potentially faced life imprisonment with no eligibility for parole for 25 years. Under one regime (that is, the YOA), the sanction was considered to be too lenient, while under the *Criminal Code* it was considered to be too harsh. Compounding this problem is the high visibility and political malleability of transfer decisions. As Professor Nicholas Bala has said (Nicholas Bala, *Young Offenders Law* (Concord, ON: Irwin Law, 1997), at 265):

> Owing to the high public visibility of transfer issues, the transfer provisions of the YOA have been subjected to considerable public scrutiny and were substantially amended in 1992 and again in 1995. There has been very substantial variation in how courts in different provinces have applied the transfer provisions.

The present transfer provisions have been broadened so that the "typical" transfer hearing now involves offences other than homicide. Moreover, the provisions have become more complicated by virtue of the fact that, depending upon the age of the young person, the presumption differs as to whether the young person will be tried in youth court or adult court. Again, Professor Bala explains:

> The 1995 provisions that deal with tranfer are complex ... . For youths under sixteen, there is an onus under the new section 16(1) for the applicant, invariably the Crown, to apply to

the youth court for transfer and satisfy the court that transfer is necessary. Section 16(1.01) applies to youths sixteen and seventeen years old and charged with:

- murder;
- attempted murder;
- manslaughter; or
- aggravated sexual assault.

For those youths, section 16(1.01) provides that prosecutions are presumptively to be dealt with in adult court, but the youth may seek "transfer down" by applying to youth court. For any other situation, the prosecution is presumptively in youth court, with the onus on the applicant, invariably the Crown, to satisfy the youth court that transfer is appropriate. For all situations, the 1995 test for transfer is:

> s. 16(1.1) In making the determination ... [whether to transfer] the youth court ... shall consider the interest of society, which includes the objectives of affording protection to the public and rehabilitation of the young person, and determine whether those objectives can be reconciled by the youth being under the jurisdiction of the youth court, and ...
>
> (a) if the court is of the opinion that those objectives can be so reconciled, the court shall, ...
>
> (i) in the case of an application under subsection (1), refuse to make an order that the young person be proceeeded with against in ordinary court, and
>
> (ii) in the case of an application under subsection (1.01), order that the young person be proceeded against in youth court; or
>
> (b) if the court is of the opinion that those objectives cannot be so reconciled, protection of the public shall be paramount and the court shall,
>
> (i) in the case of an application under subsection (1), order that the young person be proceeded against in ordinary court in accordance with the law ordinarily applicable to an adult charged with the offence, and
>
> (ii) in the case of an application under subsection (1.01), refuse to make an order that the young person be proceeded against in youth court.

The other significant legislative intervention was the 1995 increase in sentences for young persons charged with murder. Again, the legislation is complicated. For youths who are not transferred to adult court, the maximum sentence for first-degree murder is 10 years (a maximum of 6 years in custody and the balance on conditional supervision, presumptively to be served in the community). On a finding of guilt of second-degree murder, the maximum sentence is 7 years, with a maximum of 4 years being spent in custody, and the remaining 3 years on conditional supervision. Those youths who are transferred to adult court face more lenient sentences than their adult counterparts. Sixteen- and 17-year-olds who are convicted of murder in adult court face life imprisonment with a parole eligbility set at 10 years for first-degree murder and 7 years for second-degree murder. Those transferred youths who are under the age of 16 will receive period of parole ineligibilty between 5 and 7 years. (See Chapter 14, Sentencing for Murder.)

The concept of transfer to adult court is preserved in the *Youth Criminal Justice Act.* The following provisions of the new Act address this issue.

Youth Criminal Justice Act
Bill C-3, 1999

Access to Adult Sentences

61. An adult sentence shall be imposed on a young person who is found guilty of an offence for which an adult could be sentenced to imprisonment for more than two years, committed after the young person attained the age of fourteen years, in the following cases:

(a) in the case of a presumptive offence, if the youth justice court makes an order under subsection 70(2) or paragraph 72(1)(b); or

(b) in any other case, if the youth justice court makes an order under subsection 63(5) or paragraph 72(1)(b).

Application by Young Person

62(1) A young person who is charged with, or found guilty of, a presumptive offence committed after he or she attained the age of fourteen years may, at any time before evidence is called as to sentence or submissions are made as to sentence, make an application for an order that he or she is not liable to an adult sentence and that a youth sentence must be imposed.

Application Unopposed

(2) If the Attorney General gives notice to the youth justice court that the Attorney General does not oppose the application, the youth justice court shall, without a hearing, order that the young person, if found guilty, is not liable to an adult sentence and that a youth sentence must be imposed.

Application by Attorney General

63(1) The Attorney General may, following an application under subsection 41(8), if any is made, and before evidence is called as to sentence or submissions are made as to sentence, make an application for an order that a young person is liable to an adult sentence if the young person is or has been found guilty of an offence, other than a presumptive offence, for which an adult could be sentenced to imprisonment for more than two years, that was committed after the young person attained the age of fourteen years.

Notice of Intention To Seek Adult Sentence

(2) If the Attorney General intends to seek an adult sentence for an offence by making an application under subsection (1), or by establishing that the offence is a presumptive offence within the meaning of paragraph (b) of the definition "presumptive offence" in subsection 2(1) committed after the young person attained the age of fourteen years, the Attorney General shall, before the young person enters a plea or with leave of the youth justice court before the commencement of the trial, give notice to the young person and the youth justice court of the intention to seek an adult sentence.

Included Offences

(3) A notice of intention to seek an adult sentence given in respect of an offence is notice in respect of any included offence of which the young person is found guilty for which an adult could be sentenced to imprisonment for more than two years.

Notice to Young Person

(4) If a young person is charged with an offence other than an offence set out in paragraph (a) of the definition "presumptive offence" in subsection 2(1), committed after the young person attained the age of fourteen years, and the Attorney General intends to establish, after a finding of guilt, that the offence is a serious violent offence and a presumptive offence within the meaning of paragraph (b) of the definition "presumptive offence" in subsection 2(1) for which the young person is liable to an adult sentence, the Attorney General shall, before the young person enters a plea, give notice of that intention to the young person.

Application Unopposed

(5) If the young person gives notice to the youth justice court that the young person does not oppose the application for an adult sentence, the youth justice court shall, without a hearing, order that if the young person is found guilty of an offence for which an adult could be sentenced to imprisonment for more than two years, an adult sentence must be imposed.

Presumption Does Not Apply

64. If the Attorney General gives notice to the youth justice court that an adult sentence will not be sought in respect of a young person who is alleged to have committed an offence set out in paragraph (a) of the definition "presumptive offence" in subsection 2(1), the court shall order that the young person, if found guilty, is not liable to an adult sentence, and the court shall order a ban on publication of information that would identify the young person as having been dealt with under this Act.

Procedure for Application or Notice

65. An application under subsection 62(1) or 63(1) or a notice to the court under subsection 62(2) or 63(2) or (5) must be made or given orally, in the presence of the other party, or in writing with a copy served personally on the other party.

No Election If Youth Sentence

66. If the youth justice court has made an order under subsection 62(2) or section 64 before a young person is required to be put to an election under section 67, the young person shall not be put to an election unless the young person is alleged to have committed first degree murder or second degree murder within the meaning of section 231 of the *Criminal Code*.

Election—Adult Sentence

67(1) Subject to section 66, if a young person is charged with having, after attaining the age of fourteen years, committed an offence set out in paragraph (a) of the
definition "presumptive offence" in subsection 2(1), or if the Attorney General has
given notice under subsection 63(2) of the intention to seek an adult sentence, the
youth justice court shall, before the young person enters a plea, put the young person
to his or her election in the following words:

> You have the option to elect to be tried by a youth justice court judge without a jury and
> without having had a preliminary inquiry; or you may elect to have a preliminary inquiry
> and to be tried by a judge without a jury; or you may elect to have a preliminary inquiry and
> to be tried by a court composed of a judge and jury. If you do not elect now, you shall be
> deemed to have elected to have a preliminary inquiry and to be tried by a court com-
> posed of a judge and jury. How do you elect to be tried?
>
> ...

Paragraph (a) "Presumptive Offence"—Included Offences

69(1) If a young person who is charged with an offence set out in paragraph (a) of
the definition "presumptive offence" in subsection 2(1), committed after having attained
the age of fourteen years, is found guilty of committing an included offence for which
an adult could be sentenced to imprisonment for more than two years, other than
another presumptive offence set out in that paragraph,

(a) the Attorney General may make an application under subsection 63(1)
without the necessity of giving notice under subsection 63(2), if the finding of
guilt is for an offence that is not a presumptive offence; or

(b) subsections 68(2) to (5) apply without the necessity of the Attorney General giving notice under subsection 63(2) or (4), if the finding of guilt is for an
offence that would be a presumptive offence within the meaning of paragraph (b)
of the definition "presumptive offence" in subsection 2(1) if a judicial determination is made that the offence is a serious violent offence and on proof of previous
judicial determinations of a serious violent offence.

Other Serious Offences—Included Offences

(2) If the Attorney General has given notice under subsection 63(2) of the intention to seek an adult sentence for an offence committed after the young person attained the age of fourteen years, and the young person is found guilty of committing
an included offence for which an adult could be sentenced to imprisonment for more
than two years, the Attorney General may make an application under subsection 63(1)
or seek to apply the provisions of section 68.

Inquiry by Court to Young Person

70(1) The youth justice court, after hearing an application under subsection 41(8),
if any is made, and before evidence is called or submissions are made as to sentence,

shall inquire whether a young person wishes to make an application under subsection 62(1) and if so, whether the Attorney General would oppose it, if

    (a) the young person has been found guilty of a presumptive offence committed after he or she attained the age of fourteen years;

    (b) the young person has not already made an application under subsection 62(1); and

    (c) no order has been made under section 64.

No Application by Young Person

(2) If the young person indicates that he or she does not wish to make an application under subsection 62(1), the court shall order that an adult sentence be imposed.

Hearing—Adult Sentences

71. The youth justice court shall, at the commencement of the sentencing hearing, hold a hearing in respect of an application under subsection 62(1) or 63(1), unless the court has received notice that the application is not opposed. Both parties and the parents of the young person shall be given an opportunity to be heard at the hearing.

Test—Adult Sentences

71. In making its decision on an application heard in accordance with section 71, the youth justice court shall consider the seriousness and circumstances of the offence, and the degree of responsibility, age, maturity, character, background and previous record of the young person and any other factors that the court considers relevant, and

    (a) if it is of the opinion that a youth sentence imposed in accordance with the purpose and principles set out in section 37 would be adequate to hold the young person accountable for his or her offending behaviour, it shall order that the young person is not liable to an adult sentence and that a youth sentence must be imposed; and

    (b) if it is of the opinion that a youth sentence imposed in accordance with the purpose and principles set out in section 37 would not be adequate to hold the young person accountable for his or her offending behaviour, it shall order that an adult sentence be imposed.

Onus

(2) The onus of satisfying the youth justice court as to the matters referred to in subsection (1) is with the applicant.

Pre-Sentence Reports

(3) In making its decision, the youth justice court shall consider a pre-sentence report.

Court To State Reasons

(4) When the youth justice court makes an order under this section, it shall state the reasons for its decision.

CHAPTER SIXTEEN

Aboriginal Offenders

I. INTRODUCTION

This collection of materials in this chapter only scratch the surface of a very complex issue—the suitability of invoking Anglo-Canadian criminal justice structures and precepts to deal with aboriginal offenders. Certainly, one must question how fairly our criminal justice system has responded to aboriginal offenders. Empirically, there is no doubt that aboriginal persons are overrepresented in our penal structures. The history of Canada's relationship with its First Nations and the acknowledged constitutional status of aboriginal rights create an obligation to explore the reasons for overrepresentation, to question the record of systemic unfairness, and to find new ways of applying criminal justice.

The incongruity of applying the standard methodology of sentencing to aboriginal offenders has been apparent for many years. The case of *R v. Fireman*, infra, is almost 30 years old. Similar examples can be found in many cases involving accused persons from remote communities (see *R v. Naqitarvik* (1986), 26 CCC (3d) 193 (NWT CA) and *R v. Curley, Nagmalik, and Issigaitok*, [1984] NWTR 281 (CA).

R v. Fireman
[1971] 3 OR 380 (CA)

BROOKE JA: This is an appeal by Gabriel Fireman from the sentence of 10 years' imprisonment in the penitentiary imposed upon him by Wright J, on November 19, 1969, upon the appellant's plea of guilty on his arraignment on a charge of manslaughter.

The facts are not in dispute. The appellant and his victim were cousins who lived on friendly terms in their settlement on the shores of Attawapiskat River which is on the west shore of James Bay and distant some 470 miles north-east from the Town of Sioux Lookout and 250 miles north from the Town of Moosonee. On July 30, 1969, a large shipment of liquor was delivered to the settlement at the order of two relatives of the deceased and the appellant. These two shipments were the first that size to have been received by the people of the settlement for private use, and the trial Judge was told that the 12 persons who consumed this liquor, began as the shipments were unloaded and ended some 12 hours later, when Eli Fireman was shot to death by the appellant. Both men were deeply intoxicated. There was no real reason for the shooting. All that can be said is that after a night long of drinking, petty differences spawned arguments which culminated in a fight that ended with the fatal shot being fired. For what little significance it may be, the appellant is not said to have been a cause of the fight, nor directly involved in it.

The settlement is remote. It cannot be reached by road and is visited only twice each year by ship. Recently, mail delivery by aircraft was instituted. However, uncertain weather renders this service doubtful most of the year. The only real communication between the settlement and the rest of the country is through intermittent radio-telephone communication, the control of which is not in the hands of the Indian people at the settlement. The people at the settlement are members of the Cree nation and are called the Swamp Cree. Their dialect is not widely known even amongst the people of their nation. Very few of the people of the settlement speak any English, and it is only in recent years that the children have been taken to the nearest schools which are at the railhead at Moosonee, and there they have been given the opportunity of studying English. It is clear these people have no real familiarity with our way of life.

The police visit the area rarely as there have been very few calls for their services. Heretofore, the people of the settlement have enjoyed an excellent reputation for the 30 years that the settlement's existence has been known, for there have been no previous instances of major crimes there. The affairs of the people are governed by a chief and band council who exert strong control, and who, according to the police witnesses, are respected and obeyed in the community.

The settlement, then, is a truly remote place, cut off from the rest of the country, inhabited by people who have really little contact with our way of life; although, the evidence is that some of our material things are finding their way there now.

The principal occupation of the men of the settlement is trapping. With the approach of winter the population of the settlement dwindles from 500 to 200 persons as the men (in some cases, families) go to the traplines in the wilderness, where they remain for up to six months, returning in the spring with their catch of furs which are disposed of by sale to the Hudson's Bay post at the settlement. A good trapper can net $2,500 for his furs.

At the time of his conviction Gabriel Fireman was 25 years old. He was a good trapper quite capable of carrying on his business which included scheduling arrangements with an aircraft to fly him and his skidoo in and out from the traplines along with his cargo of furs, and he was able to manage the sale of his furs. On the other hand, the appellant is almost completely without an education, having finished the equivalent of our grade five when he was 22 years old. But this is not unusual in his community. In addition, the appellant failed grade seven three times because he did not have enough English to comprehend the basic things which were a part of that course. Perhaps because of the differences in the cultures, the appellant's IQ tests were found to be below the average for our whole society, but they were average for his own community. Some indication of the basic differences may be gained from the fact that he lived in a community where time is told only by seasons, that his sentence of 10 years is something that he is not likely to fully understand for he is unfamiliar with the calendar measurement of time in terms of days, weeks, months or years.

When it was discovered that the appellant had killed his cousin, the people of the settlement, including the families of the appellant and the deceased, were shocked and they rejected the appellant. It is plain from the evidence of the police officers, that under the direction of the chief and the band council, what evidence there was of the event was gathered up and retained for the police and Gabriel Fireman was detained by the people and turned over to the police upon their arrival. He remained ostracized by the community and it was only after he had taken communion at their church that his family would look upon him. It is said that following the process of the preliminary inquiry the community was prepared to accept him.

After considering the appellant's background, some aspects of the values of the people of the settlement, including their apparent different value of death, the learned trial Judge rejected the contention that lesser punishment would suffice and, placing the emphasis on the deterrent aspect of the sentence, imposed the term of 10 years on the appellant.

The appellant's contention is that the learned trial Judge failed to give due consideration to the effect of such a sentence upon the appellant, having regard to his background and the probabilities of his rehabilitation, and that the principle of deterrence to the whole community would have been satisfied by a much shorter term.

In my opinion, one can only proceed to consider the fitness of the sentence meted out to this man upon a proper appreciation of his cultural background and of his character, as it is only then that the full effect of the sentence upon him will be clear. When one considers these things, it is my opinion that even a short term of imprisonment in the penitentiary is substantial punishment to him. In the appellant's case, despite the best efforts of those who must be responsible for his care, the effect of his removal from his environment and his imprisonment would no doubt dull every sense by which he has lived in the north.

He can speak no English. It is not the language that he will use in his daily life upon his return to his home. There is no necessity for his knowing English there. There is little likelihood that he will learn English in the institution when one considers the restrictions on his ability to learn. With the difficulty in communication it is improbable that useful instruction would be available to him and, of some importance, how frustrating his existence when all those around him do not speak his language nor he theirs. I would think his imprisonment would produce a loneliness that would be greater than that in isolation.

On the other hand, does his sentence of 10 years take into consideration the desirability of his rehabilitation? From what I have said, in my view, it follows that it does not. To borrow words from the Canadian Committee on Corrections, I think it is probable that such a term will greatly reduce the chance of this man assuming a normal tolerable role on returning to his society and may well result in the creation of a social cripple.

His sentence as a deterrent to others raises important considerations. Normally, the trial of an accused man takes place in the area where the crime is said to have been committed. Members of the community may witness the trial and some indeed participate in it, and so through witnessing the trial and by word of mouth of those who have been there, what happened is known throughout the community. In this case, while the appellant was arrested at the settlement, his trial took place a very great distance away by reasons of the provisions of the territorial divisions of this Province.

There is no indication in the record that any person from his community participated in or was present at his trial, and it seems unlikely that this was so for the
record discloses that there was difficulty in obtaining interpreters who knew the dialect of the Swamp Cree. what knowledge would his community have of the reasons
of the learned trial Judge in sentencing the appellant or, for that matter, of this Court
in dealing with his appeal? To ask the question is to answer it.

To the appellant and to the people of the settlement the deterrent value of the
disposition of this case lies in the fact that the appellant's conduct which the people
of the settlement condemned, was condemned by the rest of our society. The people
of the settlement participated in and witnessed the arrest of the appellant and they
know that he has been segregated from them by proceedings in a distant place. To the
rest of the community the deterrent lies in the fact that this unsophisticated man of
previous good character was sent to prison for his crime and surely, it is not dependent on the magnitude of the sentence for its value. I do not think it adds greatly to the
deterrent value of what has taken place that such a severe sentence be imposed. What
is important in these circumstances is that to the whole community justice appears to
have been done and that there will be respect for the law. This is best accomplished in
the case of this first offender if he is returned to his society before time makes him a
stranger and impairs his ability to live there with some dignity.

With the greatest deference to the learned trial Judge, for the above reasons in my
view the sentence is too severe and the appeal must be allowed. The determination of
the appropriate quantum of sentence is not easy. The crime for which the appellant
was convicted is a very serious one and, yet, the appellant has not by his previous
conduct indicated that he is a dangerous person from whom society must be protected. Frankly, I think it is doubtful that prison is the answer, but that is our way.
However, regard can properly be had to the institutions in our system and their flexibility for some guidance in determining and arriving at a proper conclusion. In this
case, as the dominant consideration is the reformation and rehabilitation of this man
and of course the respect of the community for our system, I think the appropriate
sentence would have been two years less one day.

However, having regard to the time that has transpired since the appellant's conviction and sentencing, there would be little benefit to him in the change required by
such a sentence and accordingly the appeal is allowed and the sentence will be reduced
to one of two years.

NOTE

The problems faced by aboriginal offenders and the need to explore different sentencing
approaches are not restricted to residents of remote communities. Later in this chapter, we
examine sentencing circles, which attempt to shift the procedural and substantive paradigm.
In *R v. Morin* (1996), 42 CR (4th) 339 (Sask. CA), a Métis with a long record of prior
convictions pleaded guilty to a robbery in Saskatoon. With the support of the local Métis
community, the judge agreed to conduct a sentencing circle. Although a sentence in the
range of four years would have been the usual result, after hearing the recommendations
of the circle, the judge sentenced the offender to 18 months' incarceration to be followed

by 18 months' intensive probation. The Crown appealed. The majority of the five-member panel of the Saskatchewan Court of Appeal allowed the appeal principally on the ground that there was no basis to give pre-eminence to rehabilitation. However, the court observed (at 375):

> From the perspective of consequences we appear to have two systems of justice. Sentencing circles have a role to play in breaking down that apparent anomaly.

II. AN OVERVIEW OF OVERREPRESENTATION

In the past two decades, a number of studies and commissions of inquiry have documented the inordinate overrepresentation of aboriginal people in Canadian jails. These studies were documented and supported by the research and conclusions of the Royal Commission on Aboriginal Peoples.

Royal Commission on Aboriginal Peoples, *Bridging the Cultural Divide: A Report on Aboriginal People and Criminal Justice in Canada*
(Ottawa: Supply and Services Canada, 1996) (footnotes omitted)

...

From our reading of these reports and from what we learned through our research and our hearings, we drew two principal conclusions. The first is that there is a remarkable consensus on some fundamental issues and, in particular, how the Canadian justice system has failed Aboriginal people; the second conclusion is that notwithstanding the hundreds of recommendations from commissions and task forces, the reality for Aboriginal people in 1996 is that the justice system is still failing them.

...

The justice inquiries that preceded our work documented extensively how this failure has affected the lives of Aboriginal men, women and young people. The clearest evidence appears in the form of the over-representation of Aboriginal people in the criminal justice system. This was first documented in 1967 by the Canadian Corrections Association report, *Indians and the Law*, and in 1974 by the Law Reform Commission of Canada in *The Native Offender and the Law*. Reports and inquiries since then have not only confirmed the fact of over-representation but, most alarmingly, have demonstrated that the problem is getting worse, not better.

...

The [Canadian Bar] Association cautioned that "absent radical change, the problem will intensify." The surest evidence that there has been no radical change, and the most damning indictment, is found in the commissions of inquiry appointed since the publication of *Locking Up Natives in Canada*. The Aboriginal Justice Inquiry of Manitoba reported that whereas Aboriginal people accounted for 33 per cent of the population at Stony Mountain Federal Penitentiary in 1984, by 1989 the figure had risen to 46 per cent. In 1983 Aboriginal people accounted for 37 per cent of the population of the provincial Headingly Correctional Institution; by 1989 they accounted for 41 per cent. By 1989 Aboriginal women accounted for 67 per cent of the prison population at the Portage Correctional Institution for Women, and in institutions for young people, the proportion of Aboriginal people was 61 per cent. All together, Aboriginal people made up 56 per cent of the population of correctional institutions (both federal and provincial) in Manitoba in 1989. Aboriginal people account for just under 12 per cent of Manitoba's total population and "thus, Aboriginal people, depending on their age and sex, are present in the jails up to five times more than their presence in the general population."

The figures received by the Task Force on the Criminal Justice System and its Impact on the Indian and Métis People of Alberta also confirmed that Aboriginal over-representation is getting worse in the province of Alberta. Indeed, because Alberta has the second highest rate of imprisonment per person charged in the whole country, over-representation has even harsher effects than elsewhere. Aboriginal men now make up 30 per cent of the male population in provincial jails and Aboriginal women 45 per cent of the female jail population. The most alarming conclusion of the task force is that for Aboriginal young offenders, "over-representation in the criminal justice system is even more dramatic" than it is for adults, and future population projections indicate that the situation will get much worse.

> Projections indicate that by the year 2011, Aboriginal offenders will account for 38.5 per cent of all admissions to federal and provincial correctional centres in Alberta, compared to 29.5 per cent of all such offenders in 1989. ... In some age categories, for example, the 12-18 years of age group, Aboriginal offenders are projected to account for 40 per cent of the admission of population to correctional facilities by the year 2011.

The fact that in some provinces the coercive intrusion of criminal laws into the lives of Aboriginal people and Aboriginal communities is increasing, not receding, is reflected in the most recent figures from Saskatchewan. John Hylton, a human justice and public policy adviser who has kept a close watch on the situation in Saskatchewan, has broken down total and Aboriginal admissions to provincial correctional centres for the years 1976-77 and compared them to the figures for 1992-93. The breakdown reveals several startling findings:

> 1. Between 1976-77 and 1992-93, the number of admissions to Saskatchewan correctional centres increased from 4,712 to 6,889, a 46 per cent increase, during a time when the provincial population remained virtually unchanged. The rate of increase was 40.7 per cent for male admissions and 111 per cent for female admissions.
> 2. During the same period, the number of Aboriginals admitted to Saskatchewan correctional centres increased from 3,082 to 4,757, an increase of 54 per cent. Male Aboriginal admissions increased by 48 per cent, while female Aboriginal admissions increased by 107 per cent.
> 3. In terms of overall rates of admission, Aboriginals were 65.4 per cent in 1976-77 and 69.1 per cent in 1992-93.
> 4. Increases in Aboriginal admissions accounted for 77 per cent of the increase in total admissions between 1976-77 and 1992-93.

These data indicate clearly that the problem of disproportionate representation of the Aboriginal people in Saskatchewan's justice system is growing worse, not better. ... Predictions that were prepared in the early 1980s and that were rejected by some as too extreme, have in some instances proven to be conservative, particularly in the case of female Aboriginal admissions.

Aboriginal over-representation in the country's prisons, while presenting the face of injustice in its most repressive form, is only part of the picture. The Aboriginal Justice Inquiry of Manitoba commissioned a great deal of research on the other parts of a system that from beginning to end treats Aboriginal people differently. The Inquiry reported that

> Aboriginal over-representation is the end point of a series of decisions made by those with decision-making power in the justice system. An examination of each of these decisions suggests that the way that decisions are made within the justice system discriminates against Aboriginal people at virtually every point. ...
>
> - More than half of the inmates of Manitoba's jails are Aboriginal
> - Aboriginal accused are more likely to be denied bail
> - Aboriginal people spend more time in pre-trial detention than do non-Aboriginal people
> - Aboriginal accused are more likely to be charged with multiple offences than are non-Aboriginal accused
> - Lawyers spend less time with their Aboriginal clients than with non-Aboriginal clients
> - Aboriginal offenders are more than twice as likely as non-Aboriginal people to be incarcerated
>
> The over-representation of Aboriginal people occurs at virtually every step of the judicial process, from the charging of individuals to their sentencing.

In a society that places a high value on equality before the law, documenting the appalling figures of over-representation might seem to be enough, without any further analysis, to place resolution of this problem at the very top of the national human rights agenda. However, as compelling as the figures are, we believe that it is equally important to understand what lies behind these extraordinary figures, which are a primary index of the individual and social devastation that the criminal justice system has come to represent for Aboriginal people. Understanding the root causes is critical to understanding what it will take by way of a national commitment to bring about real change.

Systemic Discrimination and Aboriginal Crime Rates

Over-representation of the magnitude just described suggests either that Aboriginal peoples are committing disproportionately more crimes or that they are the victims of systemic discrimination. Recent justice studies and reports provide strong confirmatory evidence that both phenomena operate in combination.

The Royal Commission on the Donald Marshall, Jr., Prosecution concluded that

> Donald Marshall, Jr.'s status as a Native contributed to the miscarriage of justice that has plagued him since 1971. We believe that certain persons within the system would

have been more rigorous in their duties, more careful, or more conscious of fairness if Marshall had been white.

A research study prepared for that commission, The Mi'Kmaq and Criminal Justice in Nova Scotia, by Scott Clark, found that

> Systemic factors in Nova Scotia's criminal justice system lead to adverse effects for Aboriginal people because they live in or come from Aboriginal communities. Policing that has been designed specifically for Aboriginal communities is relatively ineffective. Justice processing, including legal representation in courts ... [is] often at considerable distance from Native people both physically and conceptually. By the same token, a lack of understanding by many justice system personnel of Mi'Kmaq social and economic conditions and aspirations leads to differential and often inappropriate treatment. Probation and parole services apply criteria that have built-in biases against Natives by failing to allow for their unique social and economic conditions. Indigenous processes are officially by-passed, if not consciously weakened.

The Cawsey report in Alberta also concluded that "systemic discrimination exists in the criminal justice system. "The report dealt specifically with the assertion of the police that discrimination on the basis of race did not exist in Alberta.

> In their briefs, policing services in Alberta generally express the same response: we do not treat or police people differently on the basis of race, or: race is not a fact in policing functions. On the surface, this may seem satisfactory. However, it does not address systemic discrimination. Systemic discrimination involves the concept that the application of uniform standards, common rules, and treatment of people who are not the same constitutes a form of discrimination. It means that in treating unlike people alike, adverse consequences, hardship or injustice may result. ...
>
> It is clear the operational policies applied uniformly to Aboriginal people sometimes have unjust or unduly harsh results. The reasons may be geographical, economic, or cultural. However, it must be acknowledged that the application of uniform policies can have a discriminatory effect.

Before describing some of the ways systemic discrimination contributes to overrepresentation of Aboriginal people in the criminal justice system, it is important to review the available evidence on the incidence and nature of Aboriginal crime. This is because there is a significant interrelationship between systemic discrimination and crime rates that has powerful implications for the appropriate directions for change.

The available evidence confirms that crime rates are higher in Aboriginal communities than non-Aboriginal communities. Based on 1985 figures, the task force report of the Indian Policing Policy Review concluded that

- crime rates for on-reserve Indians are significantly higher than for off-reserve Indians and than the overall national crime rate; [and that] ...
- the rate of on-reserve violent crimes per 1,000 is six times the national average, for property crimes the rate is two times the national average, and for other criminal code offences the rate is four times the national average.

In urban areas, where more than 40 per cent of Aboriginal people live, the available data suggest that Aboriginal people commit more crime and disorder offences than similar groups of non-Aboriginal people but proportionately fewer violent offences than Indians living on-reserve.

The Aboriginal Justice Inquiry of Manitoba (AJI), using 1989-1990 crime rate figures for areas of Manitoba policed by the RCMP, found that the crime rate on Indian reserves was 1.5 times the rate in non-reserve areas. The AJI also found, based on its study pf provincial court data, that on the reserves surveyed, 35 per cent of crime fell into a group of four offences: common assault, break and enter, theft under $1,000, and public mischief. Aboriginal persons were charged with fewer property offences and more offences against the person and provincial statute violations than non-Aboriginal persons.

An extensive study conducted for the Grand Council of the Crees in 1991, based on information obtained from police daily reports, current files, youth and adult court files and community interviews, found a significantly higher crime rate in nine Cree communities compared to both the Quebec and the overall Canadian rate. The assault rate in the Cree communities was more than five times the Quebec average and more than three times the national average. There were, however, significant differences among the Cree communities and, as the study itself noted, there was some difficulty in interpreting these findings, owing to a lack of information about the nature and seriousness of the assaults and their degree of comparability. The Cree research also found that much of the interpersonal violence was directed against family members, often in alcohol abuse situations. The high levels of interpersonal violence, particularly family violence, and the close relationship to alcohol abuse, parallels the findings of other studies.

Having concluded that there was a higher rate of crime among Aboriginal people (but one that varied considerably from community to community), the AJI also concluded that systemic discrimination contributed greatly to this. This was also the conclusion drawn by the Cawsey task force in Alberta. Both reports identified over-policing as one of the sources of systemic discrimination. Tim Quigley has described the phenomenon of over-policing and its impact on higher Aboriginal crime rates.

> Police use race as an indicator for patrols, for arrests, detentions. ... For instance, police in cities tend to patrol bars and streets where Aboriginal people congregate, rather than the private clubs frequented by white business people. ... This does not necessarily indicate that the police are invariably racist (although some are) since there is some empirical basis for the police view that proportionately more Aboriginal people are involved in criminality. But to operate patrols or to allocate police on ... [this] basis ... can become a self-fulfilling prophecy: patrols in areas frequented by the groups that they believe are involved in crimes will undoubtedly discover some criminality; when more police are assigned to detachments where there is a high Aboriginal population, their added presence will most assuredly detect more criminal activity.
>
> Consider, for instance, the provincial offence of being intoxicated in a public place. The police rarely arrest whites for being intoxicated in public. No wonder there is resentment on the part of Aboriginal people arrested simply for being intoxicated. This situation very often results in an Aboriginal person being charged with obstruction, resisting arrest or assaulting a peace officer. An almost inevitable consequence is incarceration. ... Yet the whole sequence of events is, at least to some extent, a product of policing criteria that include race as a factor and selective enforcement of the law.

The Aboriginal Justice Inquiry of Manitoba also addressed the systemic effect of police perceptions of Aboriginal people.

Differences in crime statistics between Aboriginal and non-Aboriginal people result, at least in part, from the manner in which the behaviour of Aboriginal people becomes categorized and stigmatized. This may happen because, to a certain extent, police tend to view the world in terms of "respectable" people and "criminal" types. Criminal types are thought to exhibit certain characteristics which provide cues to the officer to initiate action. Thus, the police may tend to stop a higher proportion of people who are visibly different from the dominant society, including Aboriginal people, for minor offences, simply because they believe that such people may tend to commit more serious crimes. Members of groups that are perceived to be a danger to the public order are given much less latitude in their behaviour before the police take action. An example might be a group of Aboriginal youth who gather in a park. Because it is believed that their presence may be a precursor to more deviant action, they are subjected to controlling activities by the police.

Over-policing is not unique to Canadian police forces. A similar point is made in a New Zealand report dealing with the effect on crime control strategies of police perceptions of the high rate of Maori crime.

Individual police, both as officers and as members of society, are aware of the high rate of Maori offending. … Individual police officers, subject to those perceptions, become susceptible to beliefs that Maori men are more likely to be criminal, or that certain types of conduct are more likely to be associated with them. Such beliefs unavoidably, if often unconsciously, affect the exercise of discretionary powers. These individual perceptions and stereotypes are reinforced by the intrinsic attitudes of the police institution which is constantly aware of the wider society's concerns and values. Thus, for example, a social perception of increasing gang or street crime, apparently disproportionately committed by Maori offenders, will lead to an increased allocation of police resources to those areas of activity. Such a concentration leads to a greater number of arrests of mainly Maori people who in turn will maintain the perception of Maori criminality. The likelihood that this perception will bias future use of discretionary powers by the police is thereby increased as well. It is a cyclic process of "deviancy amplification" in which stereotypes and perceptions help stimulate policies in a self-fulfilling weave of unfairness.

Significantly, several of the studies we reviewed concluded that some Aboriginal communities experience the extremes of both over-policing and under-policing. Jean-Paul Brodeur, in his study for the Grand Council of the Crees, provided this review of the research:

In a joint study for the Government of Canada, the Government of Saskatchewan and the Indian Nations, authors Prefontaine, Opekokew and Tyler found that Native communities complained of an excessively rigorous enforcement of the law in relation to minor or petty offences. In his study on RCMP policing of Aboriginals, Loree also concluded that when compared to non-Aboriginal communities, Aboriginal communities received proportionately greater law enforcement attention and proportionately less peace-keeping and other services. The situation is best described by Depew when he states that:

Despite some similarities in Native and non-Native offender profiles, the prevalence of minor and alcohol-related offences provides the basis for Native over-
representation in the correctional system which in many areas of the country is
disturbingly high. ...

Native people also appear to be subject to the extremes of over-policing and
under-policing which can lead to disproportionate levels of Native arrests and
charges, and under-utilization of policing services, respectively.

Under-policing is an issue identified by Pauktuutit, the Inuit Women's Association
of Canada, in its report, *Inuit Women and Justice*, as one of special concern in some
smaller Inuit communities where there are no community-based police services. In an
appendix documenting the concerns of Inuit women in Labrador, the report demonstrates forcefully how this places women and children at particular risk.

The RCMP has a responsibility to protect and serve our community. Women and elders
are major consumers of police services. In order to serve all parts of the communities,
the police have to know our communities, they must be a part of our communities.
They must also understand what the life of a woman who has been beaten can be like in
the community along the Labrador coast where there are no police, or where the police
are not very supportive. Without this knowledge and understanding, the RCMP will not
be able to respond to the needs of the victims of violence. Until we have the necessary
resources in our communities to provide for protection to women on a permanent basis
(for example, police based in the community) and to provide a safe place where women
can receive counselling, support and protection, many women will not leave and can't
leave the violent home. ...

While we recognize that the realities of violence in the family translate into the need
for added resources, it is not acceptable, on the one hand, to tell us that this is a funding
problem and that there is not enough money provided by the province to provide adequate policing. Yet on the other hand, the federal government provides enough funds to
hire two police officers for Labrador and eight in Newfoundland to respond to cigarette
smuggling. The communities of Postville, Rigolet, and Makkovik, like other communities on the coast, require police based in the community. Women in these communities
are in a dangerous position.

Brodeur points out that simultaneous under- and over-policing prevail not only in
Canadian Aboriginal communities but also have characterized the style of policing in
Australian Aboriginal settlements and in inner-city areas in England where there are
significant black populations. We were struck by the relevance of the following
statement, based on the findings of Lord Scarman, who conducted a public inquiry
into the riots in Brixton, a predominately black suburb of London.

The true nature of police–black relations in the inner-cities of Britain can only be understood in terms of this simultaneous over-policing and under-policing. There is too much
policing against the community and not enough policing that answers the needs of the
community.

Brodeur concludes that

In a Canadian context, Aboriginals are submitted to over-policing for minor or petty
offences—e.g., drinking violations—and suffer from under-policing with regard to being

protected from more serious offences, such as violent assaults against persons (particularly within the family).

The Root Causes of Over-Representation and Aboriginal Crime

Although over-policing and other forms of systemic discrimination undoubtedly play their part in higher crime rates, the evidence available to us leads us to conclude that for many Aboriginal communities, crime and social disorder play more havoc in personal and community well-being than they do in the lives of non-Aboriginal people and communities. Like the figures on over-representation, the statistics on higher crime rates demand further answers to hard questions directed to the root causes. Misunderstanding the roots of the problem can lead only to solutions that provide, at best, temporary alleviation and, at worst, aggravation of the pain reflected in the faces of Aboriginal victims of crimes—in many cases women and children—and in the faces of the Aboriginal men and women who receive their "just" deserts in the form of a prison sentence.

We are not the first commission to grapple with the question of explaining and understanding the causes of Aboriginal over-representation and high crime rates. As the Aboriginal Justice Inquiry of Manitoba observed, an entire sub-specialty of criminology is devoted to determining the causes of crime, and a great deal of academic attention has been directed to the specific issue of Aboriginal over-representation. From our review and analysis of the research, we have identified three primary explanatory theories; although they have significant points of overlap, they point in different directions regarding what must be changed to stem and turn the tide.

One powerfully persistent explanation for the problems facing Aboriginal people in the justice system is cultural difference between Aboriginal people and other Canadians. This was invoked most recently by Chief Justice McEachern in his judgement in the *Gitksan and Wet'suwet'en* case, where the following explanation is offered for Indian disadvantage:

> For reasons which can only be answered by anthropology, if at all, the Indians of the colony, while accepting many of the advantages of the European civilization, did not prosper proportionately with the white community as expected. ... No-one can speak with much certainty or confidence about what really went wrong in the relations between the Indians and the colonists. ... In my view the Indians' lack of cultural preparation for the new regime was indeed the probable cause of the debilitating dependence from which few Indians in North America have not yet escaped.
>
> Being of a culture where everyone looked after himself or perished, the Indians knew how to survive (in most years) but they were not as industrious in the new economic climate as was thought to be necessary by the new-comers in the Colony. In addition, the Indians were a gravely weakened people by reason of foreign diseases which took a fearful toll, and by the ravages of alcohol. They became a conquered people, not by force of arms, for that was not necessary, but by an invading culture and a relentless energy with which they would not, or could not, compete.

A cultural explanatory model has provided the basis for a number of initiatives, referred to generically as the "indigenization" of the criminal justice system. The intent of these initiatives is to close the culture gap by adding to the existing system elements that make it more culturally appropriate for Aboriginal people. Thus, on the assumption that one of the important cultural problems facing Aboriginal people is understanding the language and formal processes of Canadian law, the introduction of Aboriginal court workers is designed to provide a cultural bridge within the existing process. Using the same cultural model, we have seen in different parts of Canada the appointment of Aboriginal police officers, probation officers and justices of the peace. We describe some of these developments in more detail in the next chapter.

There is no doubt that cultural conflict explains much of the alienation that Aboriginal people experience in the justice system, and we return to some of the fundamental cultural differences between Aboriginal and non-Aboriginal understandings of justice later in this report. The difficulty, however, with this explanation and the uses to which it has been put is that it is often based on an underlying assumption that the problem lies with the limitations of Aboriginal culture to adapt to non-Aboriginal legal culture—an assumption of inferiority reflected in the passage from Chief Justice McEachern's judgement just quoted.

Associate Chief Judge Murray Sinclair, one of the commissioners of the Aboriginal Justice Inquiry of Manitoba, recently addressed the limitations of this approach. After reviewing some of the principal conclusions of the Manitoba inquiry—including findings that Aboriginal people are less likely than non-Aboriginal people to plea bargain or to benefit from a negotiated plea, that they are more likely than non-Aboriginal people to plead guilty, even when they are not or do not believe themselves to be guilty, and that they are more likely to leave the legal process without understanding, and therefore without respecting, what has occurred to them or why—he makes the following comments:

> Many times I have heard people ask: "What is it about Aboriginal people that causes them to behave like that?" Such a question suggests the problem lies within the Aboriginal person or with his or her community. That, almost inevitably, leads one to conclude that the answer lies in trying to change the Aboriginal person or his or her community. As a result, almost all our efforts at reform have centred on informing or educating Aboriginal people about the justice system, on finding ways to get them to "connect" with the system or on finding ways to make it easier for them to find their way through it.
>
> Establishing and funding more and better Aboriginal court worker or Aboriginal paralegal programs, printing more and better Aboriginally focused information kits, making more and better audio and video tapes in Aboriginal languages about how courts and laws work, establishing Aboriginal law student programs, hiring more Aboriginal court staff with the ability to speak Aboriginal languages and recruiting or appointing more Aboriginal judges, all find their justification in such thinking.
>
> Attempts, at reforming the system itself in ways that address other, more significant, issues have not been undertaken. The main reason, I believe, is because the non-Aboriginal people who control the system have not seen the problem as lying within "the system." It is time to question whether at least some of the problem lies in the way we do business within the justice system. Perhaps the question should be restated as "what is wrong with our justice system that Aboriginal people find it so alienating?"

We agree with Judge Sinclair that asking the question in this way allows us to address the fundamental differences that Aboriginal people bring to the meaning of justice as a concept and a process.

As Judge Sinclair argues, theories of culture conflict have been applied in the past in a way that locates the source of the problem within Aboriginal culture. There is, however, a further limitation on the exclusively cultural explanation of over-representation in the criminal justice system that takes us deeper into an understanding of Aboriginal crime. This limitation is that an exclusively cultural explanation obscures structural problems grounded in the economic and social inequalities experienced by Aboriginal people. As described by Carole La Prairie,

> What the early task forces and studies failed to recognize or did not want to address, was that the disproportionate representation of Native people as offenders in the system, was not tied exclusively to culture conflict but was grounded primarily in socio-economic marginality and deprivation. ...
>
> Access to justice by way of indigenization has both strengths and weaknesses. It provides employment to a number of Aboriginal people and it may help to demystify the criminal justice process so that Aboriginal people feel less alienated and fearful. What indigenization fails to do, however, is to address in any fundamental way the criminal justice problems which result from the socio-economic marginality. The real danger of an exclusively indigenized approach is that the problems may appear to be "solved," little more will be attempted, partly because indigenization is a very visible activity.

Cast as a structural problem of social and economic marginality, the argument is that Aboriginal people are disproportionately impoverished and belong to a social underclass, and that their over-representation in the criminal justice system is a particular example of the established correlation between social and economic deprivation and criminality.

We observed in our special report on suicide that Aboriginal people are at the bottom of almost every available index of socio-economic well-being, whether they measure educational levels, employment opportunities, housing conditions, per capita incomes or any of the other conditions that give non-Aboriginal Canadians one of the highest standards of living in the world. There is no doubt in our minds that economic and social deprivation is a major underlying cause of disproportionately high rates of criminality among Aboriginal people.

We are also persuaded that some of the debilitating conditions facing Aboriginal communities daily are aggravated by the distinctive nature of Aboriginal societies. Thus, as Carole La Prairie points out in her study for the James Bay Cree, there is evidential support for a correlation between over-crowded housing conditions and interpersonal conflict and violence, which often takes place between close family members residing together. In the case of the James Bay Cree, traditional concepts of order and the cultural values placed on the way people relate to each other in a social context reflect the legacy of nomadic-hunting settlement patterns. People not only have their distinctive roles but have their distinctive places in relationship to each other. Over-crowded housing where these distinctions cannot be reflected or respected can and does exacerbate an already problematic sedentary existence in contemporary Cree communities. Thus, current housing conditions, not only in Cree but other Aboriginal people, contribute to tensions in kinship relationships that may in turn be linked to problems of interpersonal conflict, violence and crime.

Socio-economic deprivation not only has explanatory power in relation to high rates of Aboriginal crime, but it also contributes directly to the systemic discrimination that swells the ranks of Aboriginal people in prison. The most obvious and well documented example of this is the imprisonment of Aboriginal people for non-payment of fines. In a 1974 report entitled *The Native Offender and the Law*, the Law Reform Commission concluded that a large number of Aboriginal offenders were sent to jail for non-payment of fines. The advent of fine option programs, under which a person can pay off a fine through community work, has not significantly changed the fact that Aboriginal people go to prison for being poor. In Saskatchewan, in 1992-93, Aboriginal people made up almost 75 per cent of those jailed for fine default. The Cawsey report, after observing that the Canadian Sentencing Commission recommended a reduction in the use of imprisonment for fine default, concluded that there was little evidence of that recommendation, made in 1987, being implemented in Alberta. The report stated:

> A number of speakers at our community meeting spoke with disdain about a practice associated with the problem of fine default. They stated that some judges keep a "black book" on offenders. Apparently, these notations are used in determining whether an accused will be granted time to pay for fines levied. By means of the "black book" system, a judge keeps a tally on those who have failed to meet the time limits on previous occasions. When appearing in court again, accused persons do not get time to pay if their names have been entered in the "black book" previously.
>
> ...

But imprisonment for fine default is only the most obvious example of systemic discrimination built upon socio-economic deprivation. As the Aboriginal Justice Inquiry of Manitoba found, Aboriginal people are more likely to be denied bail and therefore subject to pre-trial detention. While there is certainly no evidence to suggest that judges deliberately discriminate against Aboriginal people, the factors taken into account in determining whether to subject a person to pre-trial detention relate to whether the person is employed, has a fixed address, is involved in educational programs, or has strong links with the community; as a result, social and economic disadvantage can influence the decision in a particular direction, and that direction is toward the doors of remand centres.

Pre-trial detention, once imposed, has a number of effects. It creates additional pressure to plead guilty in order to get the matter over with, it limits the accused's ability to marshal resources, whether financial or community, to put before the court a community-based sentencing plan, and it therefore increases the likelihood of a sentence of imprisonment.

The way apparently neutral and legally relevant criteria applied at various stages of the criminal justice process compound or snowball to produce systemic discrimination against Aboriginal people is described well by Quigley.

> There are also some other factors that might bear on the disproportionate rate of imprisonment and that are more directly related to the sentencing process. Some of these are presently seen as legally relevant criteria—prior criminal record, employment status,

educational level, etc. ... Prior criminal record as a factor can have an undue influence on the imprisonment rate for Aboriginal people due to the snowball effect of some of the factors listed above. If there are more young Aboriginal people, if they are disproportionately unemployed, idle and alienated, and if they are overly scrutinized by the police, it should not be surprising that frequently breaches of the law are detected and punished. Add to that the greater likelihood of being denied bail (which increases the chance of being jailed if convicted), the greater likelihood of fine default and the diminished likelihood of receiving probation, and there is a greater probability of imprisonment being imposed. Some of the same factors increase the chances of the same person re-offending and being detected once again. After that, every succeeding conviction is much more apt to be punished by imprisonment, thus creating a snowball effect: jail becomes virtually the only option, regardless of the seriousness of the offence.

Socio-economic factors such as employment status, level of education, family situation, etc. appear on the surface as neutral criteria. They are considered as such by the legal system. Yet they can conceal an extremely strong bias in the sentencing process. Convicted persons with steady employment and stability in their lives, or at least prospects of the same, are much less likely to be sent to jail for offences that are borderline imprisonment offences. The unemployed, transients, the poorly educated are all better candidates for imprisonment. Given the social, political and economic aspects of our society place Aboriginal people disproportionately within the ranks of the latter; our society literally sentences more of them to jail. This is systemic discrimination.

The Aboriginal Justice Inquiry of Manitoba came to the same conclusion. The commissioners wrote:

Historically, the justice system has discriminated against Aboriginal people by providing legal sanction for their oppression. This oppression of previous generations forced Aboriginal people into their current state of social and economic distress. Now, a seemingly neutral justice system discriminates against current generations of Aboriginal people by applying laws which have an adverse impact on people of lower socio-economic status. This is no less racial discrimination; it is merely "laundered" racial discrimination. It is untenable to say that discrimination which builds upon the effects of racial discrimination is not racial discrimination itself. Past injustices cannot be ignored or built upon.

There is no doubt in our minds that economic and social deprivation is a significant contributor to the high incidence of Aboriginal crime and over-representation in the justice system. We believe, however, that a further level of understanding is required beyond acknowledgement of the role played by poverty and debilitating social conditions in the creation and perpetuation of Aboriginal crime. We are persuaded that this further understanding comes from integrating the cultural and socio-economic explanations for over-representation with a broader historical and political analysis. We have concluded that over-representation is linked directly to the particular and distinctive historical and political processes that have made Aboriginal people poor beyond poverty.

Our analysis and conclusions parallel those set out in our special report on suicide. In that report we identified some of the risk factors that explain, in part, the high rate of Aboriginal suicide. As we have just demonstrated with respect to the high rate of Aboriginal crime, these factors include culture stress and socio-economic deprivation. We concluded, however, that

> Aboriginal people experience [these] risk factors ... with greater frequency and intensity than do Canadians generally. The reasons are rooted in the relations between Aboriginal peoples and the rest of Canadian society—relations that were shaped in the colonial era and have never been thoroughly reshaped since that time."

The relationship of colonialism provides an overarching conceptual and historical link in understanding much of what has happened to Aboriginal peoples. Its relationship to issues of criminal justice was identified clearly by the Canadian Bar Association in its 1988 report, *Locking Up Natives in Canada.*

> What links these views of native criminality as caused by poverty or alcohol is the historical process which Native people have experienced in Canada, along with indigenous people in other parts of the world, the process of colonization. In the Canadian context that process, with the advance first of the agricultural and then the industrial frontier, has left Native people in most parts of the country dispossessed of all but the remnants of what was once their homelands; that process, superintended by missionaries and Indian agents armed with the power of the law, took such extreme forms as criminalizing central Indian institutions such as the Potlatch and Sundance, and systematically undermined the foundations of many Native communities. The Native people of Canada have, over the course of the last two centuries, been moved to the margins of their own territories and of our "just" society.
>
> This process of dispossession and marginalization has carried with it enormous costs of which crime and alcoholism are but two items on a long list. ... The relationship between these indices of disorganization and deprivation and Canada's historical relationship with Native people has been the subject of intense scrutiny in the last decade. In the mid-1970s the MacKenzie Valley Pipeline Inquiry focused national attention on the implications for the Native people of the North on a rapid escalation of a large scale industrial development. Mr. Justice Berger (as he then was), in assessing the causes for the alarming rise in the incidence of alcoholism, crime, violence and welfare dependence in the North, had this to say:

> I am persuaded that the incidence of these disorders is closely bound up with the rapid expansion of the industrial system and with its persistent intrusion into every part of the Native people's lives. The process affects the complex links between Native people and their past, their culturally preferred economic life, and their individual, familial and political respect. We should not be surprised to learn that the economic forces that have broken these vital links, and that are unresponsive to the distress of those who have been hurt, should lead to serious disorders. Crimes of violence can, to some extent, be seen as expressions of frustrations, confusion and indignation, but we can go beyond that interpretation to the obvious connection between crimes of violence and the change the South has, in recent years, brought to the Native people of the North. With that obvious connection, we can affirm one simple proposition: the more the industrial frontier displaces the homeland in the North, the worse the incidence of crime and violence will be.

Important implications flow from this analysis. The idea that new programs, more planning and an increase in social service personnel will solve these problems misconstrues their real nature and cause. The high rates of social and personal breakdown in the North are, in good measure, the responses of individual families who have suffered the loss of meaning in their lives and control over their destiny.

The principal recommendations which come from the MacKenzie Valley Pipeline Inquiry were that the Native people of the North must have their right to control that destiny—their right to self-determination—recognized and that there must be a settlement of Native claims in which that right is entrenched as a lodestar. Only then could Native people chart a future responding to their values and priorities rather than living under the shadow of ours.

III. THE 1996 AMENDMENTS AND SUPREME COURT GUIDANCE

As seen in Chapter 2, the 1996 amendments added to the *Criminal Code*, RSC 1985, c. C-46, as amended, a statement of purpose and objectives for sentencing and some of the major substantive principles. Along with proportionality (s. 718.1), the Code also mandates respect for the principle of restraint in ss. 718(c), 718.2(d), and 718.2(e). The last provision makes specific reference to aboriginal offenders:

718.2. A court that imposes a sentence shall also take into consideration the following principles: ...

(e) all available sanctions other than imprisonment that are reasonable in the circumstances should be considered for all offenders, *with particular attention to the circumstances of aboriginal offenders.*

In *R v. Gladue*, below, the Supreme Court addressed the intended purpose and application of this provision.

R v. Gladue
(1999), 23 CR (5th) 197 (SCC)

[The offender, a 19-year-old woman of aboriginal background, had pleaded guilty to manslaughter as a result of the stabbing death of her common law husband. At her sentencing hearing, the judge stated that s. 718.2(e) could have no application because both parties lived in an urban environment and not in an aboriginal community. She was sentenced to three years' imprisonment. On appeal, the British Columbia Court of Appeal held that whether or not she lived in an aboriginal community could not restrict the application of s. 718.2(e), but the majority (Rowles JA dissenting) still dismissed the sentence appeal. In the Supreme Court of Canada, Cory and Iacobucci JJ writing for a unanimous court provided important guidance on the role of s. 718.2(e).]

CORY and IACOBUCCI JJ (Lamer CJC and L'Heureux-Dubé, Gonthier, Bastarache, Binnie JJ concurring):

...

Further guidance as to the scope and content of Parliament's remedial purpose in enacting s. 718.2(e) may be derived from the social context surrounding the enactment of the provision. On this point, it is worth noting that, although there is quite a wide divergence between the positions of the appellant and the respondent as to how s. 718.2(e) should be applied in practice, there is general agreement between them, and indeed between the parties and all interveners, regarding the mischief in response to which s. 718.2(e) was enacted.

The parties and interveners agree that the purpose of s. 718.2(e) is to respond to the problem of overincarceration in Canada, and to respond, in particular, to the more acute problem of the disproportionate incarceration of aboriginal peoples. They also agree that one of the roles of s. 718.2(e), and of various other provisions in Part XXIII, is to encourage sentencing judges to apply principles of restorative justice alongside or in the place of other, more traditional sentencing principles when making sentencing determinations. As the respondent states in its factum before this Court, s. 718.2(e) "provides the necessary flexibility and authority for sentencing judges to resort to the restorative model of justice in sentencing aboriginal offenders and to reduce the imposition of jail sentences where to do so would not sacrifice the traditional goals of sentencing.

The fact that the parties and interveners are in general agreement among themselves regarding the purpose of s. 718.2(e) is not determinative of the issue as a matter of statutory construction. However, as we have suggested, on the above points of agreement the parties and interveners are correct. A review of the problem of overincarceration in Canada, and of its peculiarly devastating impact upon Canada's aboriginal peoples, provides additional insight into the purpose and proper application of this new provision.

...

Thus, it may be seen that although imprisonment is intended to serve the traditional sentencing goals of separation, deterrence, denunciation, and rehabilitation, there is widespread consensus that imprisonment has not been successful in achieving some of these goals. Overincarceration is a long-standing problem that has been many times publicly acknowledged but never addressed in a systematic manner by Parliament. In recent years, compared to other countries, sentences of imprisonment in Canada have increased at an alarming rate. The 1996 sentencing reforms embodied in Part XXIII, and s. 718.2(e) in particular, must be understood as a reaction to the overuse of prison as a sanction, and must accordingly be given appropriate force as remedial provisions.

(2) The Overrepresentation of Aboriginal Canadians in Penal Institutions

If overreliance upon incarceration is a problem with the general population, it is of much greater concern in the sentencing of aboriginal Canadians. In the mid-1980s, aboriginal people were about 2 percent of the population of Canada, yet they made up 10 percent of the penitentiary population. In Manitoba and Saskatchewan, aboriginal people constituted something between 6 and 7 percent of the population, yet in Manitoba they represented 46 percent of the provincial admissions and in Saskatchewan 60 percent: see M. Jackson, "Locking Up Natives in Canada" (1988-89), 23 *UBC L Rev.* 215 (article originally prepared as a report of the Canadian Bar Association

Committee on Imprisonment and Release in June 1988), at pp. 215-16. The situation has not improved in recent years. By 1997, aboriginal peoples constituted closer to 3 percent of the population of Canada and amounted to 12 percent of all federal inmates: Solicitor General of Canada, Consolidated Report, *Towards a Just, Peaceful and Safe Society: The Corrections and Conditional Release Act—Five Years Later* (1998), at pp. 142-55. The situation continues to be particularly worrisome in Manitoba, where in 1995-96 they made up 55 percent of admissions to provincial correctional facilities, and in Saskatchewan, where they made up 72 percent of admissions. A similar, albeit less drastic situation prevails in Alberta and British Columbia: Canadian Centre for Justice Statistics, *Adult Correctional Services in Canada, 1995-96* (1997), at p. 30.

This serious problem of aboriginal overrepresentation in Canadian prisons is well documented. Like the general problem of overincarceration itself, the excessive incarceration of aboriginal peoples has received the attention of a large number of commissions and inquiries: see, by way of example only, Canadian Corrections Association, *Indians and the Law* (1967); Law Reform Commission of Canada, *The Native Offender and the Law* (1974), prepared by D. A. Schmeiser; Public Inquiry into the Administration of Justice and Aboriginal People, *Report of the Aboriginal Justice Inquiry of Manitoba*, vol. 1, *The Justice System and Aboriginal People* (1991); Royal Commission on Aboriginal Peoples, *Bridging the Cultural Divide* (1996).

...

Not surprisingly, the excessive imprisonment of aboriginal people is only the tip of the iceberg insofar as the estrangement of the aboriginal peoples from the Canadian criminal justice system is concerned. Aboriginal people are overrepresented in virtually all aspects of the system. As this Court recently noted in *R v. Williams*, [1998] 1 SCR 1128, at para. 58, there is widespread bias against aboriginal people within Canada, and "[t]here is evidence that this widespread racism has translated into systemic discrimination in the criminal justice system."

Statements regarding the extent and severity of this problem are disturbingly common. In *Bridging the Cultural Divide*, supra, at p. 309, the Royal Commission on Aboriginal Peoples listed as its first "Major Findings and Conclusions" the following striking yet representative statement:

> The Canadian criminal justice system has failed the Aboriginal peoples of Canada— First Nations, Inuit and Métis people, on-reserve and off-reserve, urban and rural—in all territorial and governmental jurisdictions. The principal reason for this crushing failure is the fundamentally different world views of Aboriginal and non-Aboriginal people with respect to such elemental issues as the substantive content of justice and the process of achieving justice.

To the same effect, the Aboriginal Justice Inquiry of Manitoba described the justice system in Manitoba as having failed aboriginal people on a "massive scale," referring particularly to the substantially different cultural values and experiences of aboriginal people: *The Justice System and Aboriginal People*, supra, at pp. 1 and 86.

These findings cry out for recognition of the magnitude and gravity of the problem, and for responses to alleviate it. The figures are stark and reflect what may fairly be termed a crisis in the Canadian criminal justice system. The drastic overrepresentation of aboriginal peoples within both the Canadian prison population and the criminal justice system reveals a sad and pressing social problem. It is reasonable to assume that Parliament, in singling out aboriginal offenders for distinct sentencing treatment in s. 718.2(e), intended to attempt to redress this social problem to some degree. The provision may properly be seen as Parliament's direction to members of the judiciary to inquire into the causes of the problem and to endeavour to remedy it, to the extent that a remedy is possible through the sentencing process.

It is clear that sentencing innovation by itself cannot remove the causes of aboriginal offending and the greater problem of aboriginal alienation from the criminal justice system. The unbalanced ratio of imprisonment for aboriginal offenders flows from a number of sources, including poverty, substance abuse, lack of education, and the lack of employment opportunities for aboriginal people. It arises also from bias against aboriginal people and from an unfortunate institutional approach that is more inclined to refuse bail and to impose more and longer prison terms for aboriginal offenders. There are many aspects of this sad situation which cannot be addressed in these reasons. What can and must be addressed, though, is the limited role that sentencing judges will play in remedying injustice against aboriginal peoples in Canada. Sentencing judges are among those decision-makers who have the power to influence the treatment of aboriginal offenders in the justice system. They determine most directly whether an aboriginal offender will go to jail, or whether other sentencing options may be employed which will play perhaps a stronger role in restoring a sense of balance to the offender, victim, and community, and in preventing future crime.

E. A Framework of Analysis for the Sentencing Judge

(1) What Are the "Circumstances of Aboriginal Offenders"?

How are sentencing judges to play their remedial role? The words of s. 718.2(e) instruct the sentencing judge to pay particular attention to the circumstances of aboriginal offenders, with the implication that those circumstances are significantly different from those of non-aboriginal offenders. The background considerations regarding the distinct situation of aboriginal peoples in Canada encompass a wide range of unique circumstances, including, most particularly:

(A) The unique systemic or background factors which may have played a part in bringing the particular aboriginal offender before the courts; and

(B) The types of sentencing procedures and sanctions which may be appropriate in the circumstances for the offender because of his or her particular aboriginal heritage or connection.

(a) Systemic and Background Factors

The background factors which figure prominently in the causation of crime by aboriginal offenders are by now well known. Years of dislocation and economic development have translated, for many aboriginal peoples, into low incomes, high unemployment, lack of opportunities and options, lack or irrelevance of education, substance abuse, loneliness, and community fragmentation. These and other factors contribute to a higher incidence of crime and incarceration. A disturbing account of these factors is set out by Professor Tim Quigley, "Some Issues in Sentencing of Aboriginal Offenders," in *Continuing Poundmaker and Riel's Quest* (1994), at pp. 269-300. Quigley ably describes the process whereby these various factors produce an overincarceration of aboriginal offenders, noting (at pp. 275-76) that "[t]he unemployed, transients, the poorly educated are all better candidates for imprisonment. When the social, political and economic aspects of our society place Aboriginal people disproportionately within the ranks of the latter, our society literally sentences more of them to jail."

It is true that systemic and background factors explain in part the incidence of crime and recidivism for non-aboriginal offenders as well. However, it must be recognized that the circumstances of aboriginal offenders differ from those of the majority because many aboriginal people are victims of systemic and direct discrimination, many suffer the legacy of dislocation, and many are substantially affected by poor social and economic conditions. Moreover, as has been emphasized repeatedly in studies and commission reports, aboriginal offenders are, as a result of these unique systemic and background factors, more adversely affected by incarceration and less likely to be "rehabilitated" thereby, because the internment milieu is often culturally inappropriate and regrettably discrimination towards them is so often rampant in penal institutions.

In this case, of course, we are dealing with factors that must be considered by a judge sentencing an aboriginal offender. While background and systemic factors will also be of importance for a judge in sentencing a non-aboriginal offender, the judge who is called upon to sentence an aboriginal offender must give attention to the unique background and systemic factors which may have played a part in bringing the particular offender before the courts. In cases where such factors have played a significant role, it is incumbent upon the sentencing judge to consider these factors in evaluating whether imprisonment would actually serve to deter, or to denounce crime in a sense that would be meaningful to the community of which the offender is a member. In many instances, more restorative sentencing principles will gain primary relevance precisely because the prevention of crime as well as individual and social healing cannot occur through other means.

(b) Appropriate Sentencing Procedures and Sanctions

Closely related to the background and systemic factors which have contributed to an excessive aboriginal incarceration rate are the different conceptions of appropriate sentencing procedures and sanctions held by aboriginal people. A significant problem experienced by aboriginal people who come into contact with the criminal justice system is that the traditional sentencing ideals of deterrence, separation, and denunciation are often far removed from the understanding of sentencing held by these offenders and their community. The aims of restorative justice as now expressed in paras. (d), (e), and (f) of s. 718 of the *Criminal Code* apply to all offenders, and not only aboriginal offenders. However, most traditional aboriginal conceptions of sentencing place a primary emphasis upon the ideals of restorative justice. This tradition is extremely important to the analysis under s. 718.2(e).

The concept and principles of a restorative approach will necessarily have to be developed over time in the jurisprudence, as different issues and different conceptions of sentencing are addressed in their appropriate context. In general terms, restorative justice may be described as an approach to remedying crime in which it is understood that all things are interrelated and that crime disrupts the harmony which existed prior to its occurrence, or at least which it is felt should exist. The appropriateness of a particular sanction is largely determined by the needs of the victims, and the community, as well as the offender. The focus is on the human beings closely affected by the crime. See generally, e.g., *Bridging the Cultural Divide*, supra, at pp. 12-25; *The Justice System and Aboriginal People*, supra, at pp. 17-46; Kwochka, supra; M. Jackson, "In Search of the Pathways to Justice: Alternative Dispute Resolution in Aboriginal Communities," [1992] *UBC L Rev.* (Special Edition) 147.

The existing overemphasis on incarceration in Canada may be partly due to the perception that a restorative approach is a more lenient approach to crime and that imprisonment constitutes the ultimate punishment. Yet in our view a sentence focused on restorative justice is not necessarily a "lighter" punishment. Some proponents of restorative justice argue that when it is combined with probationary conditions it may in some circumstances impose a greater burden on the offender than a custodial sentence. See Kwochka, supra, who writes at p. 165:

> At this point there is some divergence among proponents of restorative justice. Some seek to abandon the punishment paradigm by focusing on the differing goals of a restorative system. Others, while cognizant of the differing goals, argue for a restorative system in terms of a punishment model. They argue that non-custodial sentences can have an equivalent punishment value when produced and administered by a restorative system and that the healing process can be more intense than incarceration. Restorative justice necessarily involves some form of restitution and reintegration into the community. Central to the process is the need for offenders to take responsibility for their actions. By comparison, incarceration obviates the need to accept responsibility. Facing victim and community is for some more frightening than the possibility of a term of imprisonment and yields a more beneficial result in that the offender may become a healed and functional member of the community rather than a bitter offender returning after a term of imprisonment.

In describing in general terms some of the basic tenets of traditional aboriginal sentencing approaches, we do not wish to imply that all aboriginal offenders, victims, and communities share an identical understanding of appropriate sentences for particular offences and offenders. Aboriginal communities stretch from coast to coast and from the border with the United States to the far north. Their customs and traditions and their concept of sentencing vary widely. What is important to recognize is that, for many if not most aboriginal offenders, the current concepts of sentencing are inappropriate because they have frequently not responded to the needs, experiences, and perspectives of aboriginal people or aboriginal communities.

It is unnecessary to engage here in an extensive discussion of the relatively recent evolution of innovative sentencing practices, such as healing and sentencing circles, and aboriginal community council projects, which are available to aboriginal offenders. What is important to note is that the different conceptions of sentencing held by many aboriginal people share a common underlying principle: that is, the importance of community-based sanctions. Sentencing judges should not conclude that the absence of alternatives specific to an aboriginal community eliminates their ability to impose a sanction that takes into account principles of restorative justice and the needs of the parties involved. Rather, the point is that one of the unique circumstances of aboriginal offenders is that community-based sanctions coincide with the aboriginal concept of sentencing and the needs of aboriginal people and communities. It is often the case that neither aboriginal offenders nor their communities are well served by incarcerating offenders, particularly for less serious or non-violent offences. Where these sanctions are reasonable in the circumstances, they should be implemented. In all instances, it is appropriate to attempt to craft the sentencing process and the sanctions imposed in accordance with the aboriginal perspective.

(2) The Search for a Fit Sentence

The role of the judge who sentences an aboriginal offender is, as for every offender, to determine a fit sentence taking into account all the circumstances of the offence, the offender, the victims, and the community. Nothing in Part XXIII of the *Criminal Code* alters this fundamental duty as a general matter. However, the effect of s. 718.2(e), viewed in the context of Part XXIII as a whole, is to alter the method of analysis which sentencing judges must use in determining a fit sentence for aboriginal offenders. Section 718.2(e) requires that sentencing determinations take into account the unique circumstances of aboriginal peoples.

In *R v. M.(C.A.)*, [1996] 1 SCR 500, at p. 567, Lamer CJ restated the long-standing principle of Canadian sentencing law that the appropriateness of a sentence will depend on the particular circumstances of the offence, the offender, and the community in which the offence took place. Disparity of sentences for similar crimes is a natural consequence of this individualized focus. As he stated:

> It has been repeatedly stressed that there is no such thing as a uniform sentence for a particular crime. ... Sentencing is an inherently individualized process, and the search for a single appropriate sentence for a similar offender and a similar crime will frequently be a fruitless exercise of academic abstraction. As well, sentences for a particular offence should be expected to vary to some degree across various communities and regions of this country, as the "just and appropriate" mix of accepted sentencing goals will depend on the needs and current conditions of and in the particular community where the crime occurred.

The comments of Lamer CJ are particularly apt in the context of aboriginal offenders. As explained herein, the circumstances of aboriginal offenders are markedly different from those of other offenders, being characterized by unique systemic and background factors. Further, an aboriginal offender's community will frequently understand the nature of a just sanction in a manner significantly different from that of many non-aboriginal communities. In appropriate cases, some of the traditional sentencing objectives will be correspondingly less relevant in determining a sentence that is reasonable in the circumstances, and the goals of restorative justice will quite properly be given greater weight. Through its reform of the purpose of sentencing in s. 718, and through its specific directive to judges who sentence aboriginal offenders, Parliament has, more than ever before, empowered sentencing judges to craft sentences in a manner which is meaningful to aboriginal peoples.

In describing the effect of s. 718.2(e) in this way, we do not mean to suggest that, as a general practice, aboriginal offenders must always be sentenced in a manner which gives greatest weight to the principles of restorative justice, and less weight to goals such as deterrence, denunciation, and separation. It is unreasonable to assume that aboriginal peoples themselves do not believe in the importance of these latter goals, and even if they do not, that such goals must not predominate in appropriate cases. Clearly there are some serious offences and some offenders for which and for whom separation, denunciation, and deterrence are fundamentally relevant.

Yet, even where an offence is considered serious, the length of the term of imprisonment must be considered. In some circumstances the length of the sentence of an aboriginal offender may be less and in others the same as that of any other offender. Generally, the more violent and serious the offence the more likely it is as a practical reality that the terms of imprisonment for aboriginals and non-aboriginals will be close to each other or the same, even taking into account their different concepts of sentencing.

As with all sentencing decisions, the sentencing of aboriginal offenders must proceed on an individual (or a case-by-case) basis: For this offence, committed by this offender, harming this victim, in this community, what is the appropriate sanction under the *Criminal Code*? What understanding of criminal sanctions is held by the community? What is the nature of the relationship between the offender and his or her community? What combination of systemic or background factors contributed to this particular offender coming before the courts for this particular offence? How has the offender who is being sentenced been affected by, for example, substance abuse in the community, or poverty, or overt racism, or family or community breakdown? Would imprisonment effectively serve to deter or denounce crime in a sense that would be significant to the offender and community, or are crime prevention and other goals better achieved through healing? What sentencing options present themselves in these circumstances?

The analysis for sentencing aboriginal offenders, as for all offenders, must be holistic and designed to achieve a fit sentence in the circumstances. There is no single test that a judge can apply in order to determine the sentence. The sentencing judge is required to take into account all of the surrounding circumstances regarding the offence, the offender, the victims, and the community, including the unique circumstances of the offender as an aboriginal person. Sentencing must proceed with sensitivity to and understanding of the difficulties aboriginal people have faced with both the criminal justice system and society at large. When evaluating these circumstances in light of the aims and principles of sentencing as set out in Part XXIII of the *Criminal Code* and in the jurisprudence, the judge must strive to arrive at a sentence which is just and appropriate in the circumstances. By means of s. 718.2(e), sentencing judges have been provided with a degree of flexibility and discretion to consider in appropriate circumstances alternative sentences to incarceration which are appropriate for the aboriginal offender and community and yet comply with the mandated principles and purpose of sentencing. In this way, effect may be given to the aboriginal emphasis upon healing and restoration of both the victim and the offender.

(3) The Duty of the Sentencing Judge

The foregoing discussion of guidelines for the sentencing judge has spoken of that which a judge must do when sentencing an aboriginal offender. This element of duty is a critical component of s. 718.2(e). The provision expressly provides that a court that imposes a sentence should consider all available sanctions other than imprisonment that are reasonable in the circumstances, and should pay particular attention to the circumstances of aboriginal offenders. There is no discretion as to whether to consider the unique situation of the aboriginal offender; the only discretion concerns the determination of a just and appropriate sentence.

How then is the consideration of s. 718.2(e) to proceed in the daily functioning of the courts? The manner in which the sentencing judge will carry out his or her statutory duty may vary from case to case. In all instances it will be necessary for the judge to take judicial notice of the systemic or background factors and the approach to sentencing which is relevant to aboriginal offenders. However, for each particular offence and offender it may be that some evidence will be required in order to assist the sentencing judge in arriving at a fit sentence. Where a particular offender does not wish such evidence to be adduced, the right to have particular attention paid to his or her circumstances as an aboriginal offender may be waived. Where there is no such waiver, it will be extremely helpful to the sentencing judge for counsel on both sides to adduce relevant evidence. Indeed, it is to be expected that counsel will fulfil their role and assist the sentencing judge in this way.

However, even where counsel do not adduce this evidence, where for example the offender is unrepresented, it is incumbent upon the sentencing judge to attempt to acquire information regarding the circumstances of the offender as an aboriginal person. Whether the offender resides in a rural area, on a reserve or in an urban centre the sentencing judge must be made aware of alternatives to incarceration that exist whether inside or outside the aboriginal community of the particular offender. The alternatives existing in metropolitan areas must, as a matter of course, also be explored. Clearly the presence of an aboriginal offender will require special attention in pre-sentence reports. Beyond the use of the pre-sentence report, the sentencing judge may and should in appropriate circumstances and where practicable request that witnesses be called who may testify as to reasonable alternatives.

Similarly, where a sentencing judge at the trial level has not engaged in the duty imposed by s. 718.2(e) as fully as required, it is incumbent upon a court of appeal in considering an appeal against sentence on this basis to consider any fresh evidence which is relevant and admissible on sentencing. In the same vein, it should be noted that, although s. 718.2(e) does not impose a statutory duty upon the sentencing judge to provide reasons, it will be much easier for a reviewing court to determine whether and how attention was paid to the circumstances of the offender as an aboriginal person if at least brief reasons are given.

(4) The Issue of "Reverse Discrimination"

Something must also be said as to the manner in which s. 718.2(e) should not be interpreted. The appellant and the respondent diverged significantly in their interpretation of the appropriate role to be played by s. 718.2(e). While the respondent saw the provision largely as a restatement of existing sentencing principles, the appellant advanced the position that s. 718.2(e) functions as an affirmative action provision justified under s. 15(2) of the Charter. The respondent cautioned that, in his view, the appellant's understanding of the provision would result in "reverse discrimination" so as to favour aboriginal offenders over other offenders.

There is no constitutional challenge to s. 718.2(e) in these proceedings, and accordingly we do not address specifically the applicability of s. 15 of the Charter. We would note, though, that the aim of s. 718.2(e) is to reduce the tragic overrepresentation of aboriginal people in prisons. It seeks to ameliorate the present situation and to deal with the particular offence and offender and community. The fact that a court is called upon to take into consideration the unique circumstances surrounding these different parties is not unfair to non-aboriginal people. Rather, the fundamental purpose of s. 718.2(e) is to treat aboriginal offenders fairly by taking into account their difference.

But s. 718.2(e) should not be taken as requiring an automatic reduction of a sentence, or a remission of a warranted period of incarceration, simply because the offender is aboriginal. To the extent that the appellant's submission on affirmative action means that s. 718.2(e) requires an automatic reduction in sentence for an aboriginal offender, we reject that view. The provision is a direction to sentencing judges to consider certain unique circumstances pertaining to aboriginal offenders as a part of the task of weighing the multitude of factors which must be taken into account in striving to impose a fit sentence. It cannot be forgotten that s. 718.2(e) must be considered in the context of that section read as a whole and in the context of s. 718, s. 718.1, and the overall scheme of Part XXIII. It is one of the statutorily mandated considerations that a sentencing judge must take into account. It may not always mean a lower sentence for an aboriginal offender. The sentence imposed will depend upon all the factors which must be taken into account in each individual case. The weight to be given to these various factors will vary in each case. At the same time, it must in every case be recalled that the direction to consider these unique circumstances flows from the staggering injustice currently experienced by aboriginal peoples with the criminal justice system. The provision reflects the reality that many aboriginal people are alienated from this system which frequently does not reflect their needs or their understanding of an appropriate sentence.

(5) Who Comes Within the Purview of Section 718.2(e)?

The question of whether s. 718.2(e) applies to all aboriginal persons, or only to certain classes thereof, is raised by this appeal. The following passage of the reasons of the judge at trial appears to reflect some ambiguity as to the applicability of the provision to aboriginal people who do not live in rural areas or on a reserve:

> The factor that is mentioned in the *Criminal Code* is that particular attention to the circumstances of aboriginal offenders should be considered. In this case both the deceased and the accused were aboriginals, but they are not living within the aboriginal community as such. They are living off a reserve and the offence occurred in an urban setting. They [sic] do not appear to have been any special circumstances because of their aboriginal status and so I am not giving any special consideration to their background in passing this sentence.

It could be understood from that passage that, in this case, there were no special circumstances to warrant the application of s. 718.2(e), and the fact that the context of the offence was not in a rural setting or on a reserve was only one of those missing circumstances. However, this passage was interpreted by the majority of the Court of Appeal as implying that, "as a matter of principle, s. 718.2(e) can have no application to aboriginals 'not living within the aboriginal community'" (p. 137). This understanding of the provision was unanimously rejected by the members of the Court of Appeal. With respect to the trial judge, who was given little assistance from counsel on this issue, we agree with the Court of Appeal that such a restrictive interpretation of the provision would be inappropriate.

The class of aboriginal people who come within the purview of the specific reference to the circumstances of aboriginal offenders in s. 718.2(e) must be, at least, all who come within the scope of s. 25 of the Charter and s. 35 of the *Constitution Act, 1982*. The numbers involved are significant. National census figures from 1996 show that an estimated 799,010 people were identified as aboriginal in 1996. Of this number, 529,040 were Indians (registered or non-registered), 204,115 Métis and 40,220 Inuit.

Section 718.2(e) applies to all aboriginal offenders wherever they reside, whether on- or off-reserve, in a large city or a rural area. Indeed it has been observed that many aboriginals living in urban areas are closely attached to their culture. See the Royal Commission on Aboriginal Peoples, *Report of the Royal Commission on Aboriginal Peoples*, vol. 4, *Perspectives and Realities* (1996), at p. 521:

> Throughout the Commission's hearings, Aboriginal people stressed the fundamental importance of retaining and enhancing their cultural identity while living in urban areas. Aboriginal identity lies at the heart of Aboriginal peoples' existence; maintaining that identity is an essential and self-validating pursuit for aboriginal people in cities.

And at p. 525:

> Cultural identity for urban Aboriginal people is also tied to a land base or ancestral territory. For many, the two concepts are inseparable. ... Identification with an ancestral place is important to urban people because of the associated ritual, ceremony and traditions, as well as the people who remain there, the sense of belonging, the bond to an ancestral community, and the accessibility of family, community and elders.

Section 718.2(e) requires the sentencing judge to explore reasonable alternatives to incarceration in the case of all aboriginal offenders. Obviously, if an aboriginal community has a program or tradition of alternative sanctions, and support and supervision are available to the offender, it may be easier to find and impose an alternative sentence. However, even if community support is not available, every effort should be made in appropriate circumstances to find a sensitive and helpful alternative. For all purposes, the term "community" must be defined broadly so as to include any network of support and interaction that might be available in an urban centre. At the same time, the residence of the aboriginal offender in an urban centre that lacks any network of support does not relieve the sentencing judge of the obligation to try to find an alternative to imprisonment.

VI. Summary

Let us see if a general summary can be made of what has been discussed in these reasons.

1. Part XXIII of the *Criminal Code* codifies the fundamental purpose and principles of sentencing and the factors that should be considered by a judge in striving to determine a sentence that is fit for the offender and the offence.

2. Section 718.2(e) mandatorily requires sentencing judges to consider all available sanctions other than imprisonment and to pay particular attention to the circumstances of aboriginal offenders.

3. Section 718.2(e) is not simply a codification of existing jurisprudence. It is remedial in nature. Its purpose is to ameliorate the serious problem of overrepresentation of aboriginal people in prisons, And to encourage sentencing judges to have recourse to a restorative approach to sentencing. There is a judicial duty to give the provision's remedial purpose real force.

4. Section 718.2(e) must be read and considered in the context of the rest of the factors referred to in that section and in light of all of Part XXIII. All principles and factors set out in Part XXIII must be taken into consideration in determining the fit sentence. Attention should be paid to the fact that Part XXIII, through ss. 718, 718.2(e), and 742.1, among other provisions, has placed a new emphasis upon decreasing the use of incarceration.

5. Sentencing is an individual process and in each case the consideration must continue to be what is a fit sentence for this accused for this offence in this community. However, the effect of s. 718.2(e) is to alter the method of analysis which sentencing judges must use in determining a fit sentence for aboriginal offenders.

6. Section 718.2(e) directs sentencing judges to undertake the sentencing of aboriginal offenders individually, but also differently, because the circumstances of aboriginal people are unique. In sentencing an aboriginal offender, the judge must consider:

   (A) The unique systemic or background factors which may have played a part in bringing the particular aboriginal offender before the courts; and
   (B) The types of sentencing procedures and sanctions which may be appropriate in the circumstances for the offender because of his or her particular aboriginal heritage or connection.

7. In order to undertake these considerations the trial judge will require information pertaining to the accused. Judges may take judicial notice of the broad systemic and background factors affecting aboriginal people, and of the priority given in aboriginal cultures to a restorative approach to sentencing. In the usual course of events, additional case-specific information will come from counsel and from a pre-sentence report which takes into account the factors set out in #6, which in turn may come from representations of

the relevant aboriginal community which will usually be that of the offender. The offender may waive the gathering of that information.

8. If there is no alternative to incarceration the length of the term must be carefully considered.

9. Section 718.2(e) is not to be taken as a means of automatically reducing the prison sentence of aboriginal offenders; nor should it be assumed that an offender is receiving a more lenient sentence simply because incarceration is not imposed.

10. The absence of alternative sentencing programs specific to an aboriginal community does not eliminate the ability of a sentencing judge to impose a sanction that takes into account principles of restorative justice and the needs of the parties involved.

11. Section 718.2(e) applies to all aboriginal persons wherever they reside, whether on- or off-reserve, in a large city or a rural area. In defining the relevant aboriginal community for the purpose of achieving an effective sentence, the term "community" must be defined broadly so as to include any network of support and interaction that might be available, including in an urban centre. At the same time, the residence of the aboriginal offender in an urban centre that lacks any network of support does not relieve the sentencing judge of the obligation to try to find an alternative to imprisonment.

12. Based on the foregoing, the jail term for an aboriginal offender may in some circumstances be less than the term imposed on a non-aboriginal offender for the same offence.

13. It is unreasonable to assume that aboriginal peoples do not believe in the importance of traditional sentencing goals such as deterrence, denunciation, and separation, where warranted. In this context, generally, the more serious and violent the crime, the more likely it will be as a practical matter that the terms of imprisonment will be the same for similar offences and offenders, whether the offender is aboriginal or non-aboriginal.

NOTE

The Supreme Court dismissed Ms Gladue's appeal against the three-year sentence primarily because, by the time the decision was released, she was already in the community on day parole.

IV. CHALLENGING THE TRADITIONAL PARADIGM: THE USE OF SENTENCING CIRCLES

The traditional adversarial manner in which sentencing hearings are conducted has attracted some criticism. As a result, even before the decision in *Gladue*, much attention had been paid to alternative sentencing processes and options that are more consistent with aboriginal traditions and experience. The importance of exploring alternatives was recognized by the Law Reform Commission of Canada in 1992.

Law Reform Commission of Canada, Report #34,
Aboriginal Peoples and Criminal Justice
(Ottawa: Supply and Services Canada, 1992) (footnotes omitted)

One prevalent focus within the literature on solutions to the problem of over-representation has been on what are called "alternatives to incarceration." While even the most recent of analyses continue to support the creative use of well-designed and adequately funded alternatives to incarceration or community sanctions, we recognize that many experiments with these alternatives in recent years have been severely criticized.

Theoretically, several alternatives to imprisonment exist at the sentencing stage, such as conditional discharges, suspended sentences, community service orders, compensation, restitution and fine option programs. In addition, options such as diversion, victim–offender reconciliation programs and mediation are also alternatives to imprisonment in the sense that they do not entail resort to the ordinary process of trial and sentencing. Our Commission has long supported these alternatives, but they are underused.

Recommendation

13(1) Alternatives to imprisonment should be used whenever possible. The *Criminal Code* provisions creating such alternatives should ensure that those alternatives are given first consideration at sentencing. A judge imprisoning an Aboriginal person for an offence amenable to the use of alternative dispositions should be required to set forth the reasons for using imprisonment rather than a non-custodial option.

The case for the use of creative Aboriginal methods of dispute resolution is cogently argued and described by Jackson in our commissioned study entitled *In Search of the Pathways to Justice.* In our view, special alternative programs for Aboriginal persons are important for several reasons. First, they possess the potential to reduce the number of Aboriginal persons in prisons. Further, they could with very little adjustment incorporate customary law, thus increasing their acceptability to the affected population. Finally, they are organized around the concept of community-involvement and thus can promote social peace and a sense of community control. Alternative programs are consistent with Aboriginal values in that they seek reconciliation between an offender and the community as a whole, and pursue the goal of restoring harmony.

NOTE

In the context of criminal proceedings involving aboriginal offenders, some judges have complained that the free flow of information is hampered by the bipolar nature of adversarial proceedings. This has led to the development of the sentencing "circle," whereby the usual trappings of our criminal courts are cast aside. Instead, the judge, counsel, the offender, and significant members of his or her community form a circle and engage in a discussion about the appropriate disposition for the offender. The link between the sentencing circle and First Nations culture was discussed in *R v. Morin* (1995), 101 CCC (3d) 124 (Sask. CA), in which Bayda CJS (in dissent) made the following observations:

> In addressing the sentencing circle question it behooves one to be mindful of the origin of the sentencing circle and its underlying philosophy. The sentencing circle has its genesis in the healing circle which from time immemorial has been a part of the culture of many First Nations of Canada and of the indigenous people of other countries. The healing circle originated and developed amongst the First Nations people at a time when they lived in small relatively isolated communities. ... When a member of the community committed a wrongful act against another member, the community resorted to a healing circle to resolve the problems created by the wrongful act. The circle was premised on two fundamental notions: first, the wrongful act was a breach of the relationship between the wrongdoer and the victim and a breach of the relationship between the wrongdoer and the community; and second, the well-being of the community and consequently the protection of its members and the society generally depended not upon retribution or punishment of the wrongdoer, but upon "healing" the breaches of the two relationships. The emphasis was primarily, if not entirely, upon a restorative or healing approach as distinct from a retributive or punitive approach.

In addition to locating the origin of the sentencing circle, this passage underscores the intimate link between the use of the sentencing circle and the restorative or rehabilitative approach to sentencing in the aboriginal context. Although the sentencing circle is dealt with here—in a discussion of procedural and evidentiary sentencing matters—there is also a large "substantive" component to this issue.

The use of the sentencing circle has received wide acceptance in a number of provinces. However, there is some disagreement about when it is appropriate to construct a sentencing circle. Indeed, as McEachern CJYT held in *R v. Johnson* (1994), 91 CCC (3d) 21 (Yukon CA), the availability of this procedure, along with its precise contours, ought to be the subject of rules of court, pursuant to s. 482(2) of the *Criminal Code*. This would allow all of the parties to know what is expected of them.

R v. Moses was the seminal decision in the expansion of sentencing circles beyond a few northern communities. This case explains the purposes of sentencing circles and the process as it was practised in the town of Mayo in the Yukon in 1992. While reading it, consider how the process fits within the usual sentencing hearing process and whether it could be adapted in conditions other than small remote communities. Also, ask yourself what we learn about the usual sentencing process by examining the sentencing circle process.

R v. Moses

(1992), 71 CCC (3d) 347 (Yukon Terr. Ct.) (footnotes omitted)

STUART TERR. CT. J: The reasons for this sentence will take us on an unusual journey. Unusual, because the process was as influential in moulding the final decision as any substantive factors. Consequently, this judgment examines the process as well as the traditional stuffings of sentences, mitigating and aggravating circumstances.

...

In this case, by changing the process, the primary issues changed, and consequently, the decision was substantially different from what might have been decided had the usual process been followed.

The justice system rules and procedures provide a comfortable barrier for justice professionals from fully confronting the futility, destruction, and injustice left behind in the wake of circuit courts. For those who dared in this case to step outside this comfortable barrier, I hope these reasons capture their input and courage.

1. Process

(A) Overview

Rising crime rates, especially for violent offences, alarming recidivist rates and escalating costs in monetary and human terms have forced societies the world over to search for alternatives to their malfunctioning justice systems. In the western world much of the energy expended in this search has focused on sentencing. While the underlying problems of crime and the gross inadequacies of the justice system stem from much broader, deeper ills within society, significant immediate improvement within the court process can be achieved by changing the sentencing process.

Currently, the search for improving sentencing champions a greater role for victims of crime, reconciliation, restraint in the use of incarceration and a broadening of sentencing alternatives that calls upon less government expenditure and more community participation. As many studies expose the imprudence of excessive reliance upon punishment as the central objective in sentencing, rehabilitation and reconciliation are properly accorded greater emphasis. All these changes call upon communities to become more actively involved and to assume more responsibility for resolving conflict. To engage meaningful community participation, the sentence decision-making process must be altered to share power with the community, and where appropriate, communities must be empowered to resolve many conflicts now processed through criminal courts.

An important step towards constructive community involvement must involve significant changes to the sentencing process before, during and after sentencing.

...

(C) Sentencing Hearing

In any decision-making process, power, control, the over-all atmosphere and dynamics are significantly influenced by the physical setting, and especially by the places accorded to participants. Those who wish to create a particular atmosphere, or especially to manipulate a decision-making process to their advantage, have from time immemorial astutely controlled the physical setting of the decision-making forum. Among the great predator groups in the animal kingdom, often the place secured by each member in the site they rest or hunt, significantly influences their ability to control group decisions. In the criminal justice process (arguably one of contemporary society's great predators), the physical arrangement in a court-room profoundly affects who participates and how they participate. The organization of the court-room influences the content, scope and importance of information provided to the court. The rules governing the court hearing reinforce the allocation of power and influence fostered by the physical setting.

The combined effect of the rules and the court-room arrangements entrench the adversarial nature of the process. The judge, defence and Crown counsel, fortified by their prominent places in the court-room and by the rules, own and control the process and no one in a court-room can have any doubt about that.

For centuries, the basic organization of the court has not changed. Nothing has been done to encourage meaningful participation by the accused, the victim, or by the community; remarkable, considering how the location of a meeting, the design of the room, furniture arrangements, and the seating of participants are so meticulously considered in most decision-making processes to ensure the setting reinforce the objective of the process. If the objective of the sentencing process is now to enhance sentencing options, to afford greater concern to the impact on victims, to shift focus from punishment to rehabilitation, and to meaningfully engage communities in sharing responsibility for sentencing decisions, it may be advantageous for the justice system to examine how court procedures and the physical arrangements within court-rooms militate against these new objectives. It was in this case.

(D) Advantages of Circle

In this case, a change in the physical arrangement of the court-room produced a major change in the process.

(1) Physical Setting

For court, a circle to seat 30 people was arranged as tightly as numbers allowed. When all seats were occupied, additional seating was provided in an outer circle for persons arriving after the "hearing" had commenced.

Defence sat beside the accused and his family. The Crown sat immediately across the circle from defence counsel to the right of the judge. Officials and members from the First Nation, the RCMP officers, the probation officer and others were left to find their own "comfortable" place within the circle.

(2) Dynamics of the Circle

By arranging the court in a circle without desks or tables, with all participants facing each other, with equal access and equal exposure to each other, the dynamics of the decision-making process were profoundly changed.

Everyone around the circle introduced themselves. Everyone remained seated when speaking. After opening remarks from the judge and counsel, the formal process dissolved into an informal but intense discussion of what might best protect the community and extract Philip from the grip of alcohol and crime.

The tone was tempered by the close proximity of all participants. For the most part, participants referred to each other by name, not by title. While disagreements and arguments were provoked by most topics, posturing, pontification, and the well-worn platitudes, commonly characteristic of court-room speeches by counsel and judges, were gratefully absent.

The circle setting dramatically changed the roles of all participants, as well as the focus, tone, content and scope of discussions. The following observations denote the more obvious benefits generated by the circle setting.

(i) Challenges Monopoly of Professionals

The foreboding court-room setting discourages meaningful participation beyond lawyers and judges.

The judge presiding on high, robed to emphasize his authoritative dominance, armed with the power to control the process, is rarely challenged. Lawyers, by their deference, and by standing when addressing the judge, reinforce to the community the judge's pivotal importance. All of this combines to encourage the community to believe judges uniquely and exclusively possess the wisdom and resources to develop a just and viable result. They are so grievously wrong.

Counsel, due to the rules, and their prominent place in the court, control the input of information. Their ease with the rules, their facility with the peculiar legal language, exudes a confidence and skill that lay people commonly perceive as a prerequisite to participate.

The community relegated to the back of the room, is separated from counsel and the judge either by an actual bar or by placing their seats at a distinct distance behind counsel tables. The interplay between lawyers and the judge creates the perception of a ritualistic play. The set, as well as the performance, discourages anyone else from participating.

The circle significantly breaks down the dominance that traditional court-rooms accord lawyers and judges. In a circle, the ability to contribute, the importance and credibility of any input is not defined by seating arrangements. The audience is changed. All persons within the circle must be addressed. Equally, anyone in the circle may ask a direct question to anyone. Questions about the community and the accused force discussions into a level of detail usually avoided in the court-room by sweeping assumptions and boiler-plate platitudes. In the court-room, reliance upon technical legal language imbues the process with the air of resolutely addressing difficult issues. In fact, behind the facade of legalese, many crucial considerations are either ignored or superficially considered. The circle denies the comfort of evading difficult issues through the use of obtuse, complex technical language.

(ii) Encourages Lay Participation

The circle setting drew everyone into the discussion. Unlike the court-room, where the setting facilitates participation only by counsel and the judge, the circle prompted a natural rhythm of discussion.

The physical proximity of all participants, the ability to see the face of the person speaking, the conversational tone, the absence of incomprehensible rituals, and the intermingling of professionals and lay members of the community during breaks, all a consequence of the circle, broke down many barriers to participation.

The highly defined roles imposed upon professionals by the formal justice process creates barriers to communication. The circle drew out the person buried behind their role, and encouraged a more personal and less professional contribution. The circle, in revealing the person behind the professional facade fostered a greater sense of equality between lay and professional participants in the circle. This sense of equality and the discovery of significant common concerns and objectives is essential to sustain an effective partnership between the community and the justice system.

(iii) Enhances Information

The justice system rarely acquires adequate information to competently target the sentencing process on the underlying causes of criminal behaviour. Too often courts are forced to precariously rely upon bare-bones information, usually based on second or third-hand sources. Consequently, sentencing guided by very incomplete information places too much reliance upon mythological understandings about deterrence and punishment, and upon stereotypical categories used to describe the crime and the offender.

The rituals and specialized language of the sentencing process produce an aura of competence. Rising crime rates (especially rising recidivism) despite staggering increases in expenditures, debunk this illusory aura. Sentencing could be vastly improved by enhancing the quantity and quality of information.

The paucity and stagnancy of sentencing information severely handicaps any endeavour to purposely employ sentencing remedies. Very little is known in sentencing about offenders, victims, the crucial underlying factors causing the criminal behaviour, or about the larger context of the home and community, and almost nothing is known about how the court process affects the conflict or upon the persons involved. Acting on a woefully incomplete understanding of either the larger circumstances or of the specific life circumstances of those directly affected by crime, the court rarely appreciates whether the sentence resolves or exacerbates the fundamental problems promoting crime.

Of course, all judges and counsel know these circumstances exist, but the courtroom setting, and emphasis on getting through the docket, of processing cases as any good bureaucracy might process licence applications, encourages wilful blindness about many relevant circumstances in sentencing. The sentencing process, in searching for an effective sentence to fit the specific needs in each case, is analogous to a "fast forwarded" game of Pin the Tail on the Donkey.

Community involvement through the circle generates not only new information, but information not normally available to the court. Through the circle, participants can respond to concerns, fill in gaps, and ensure each new sentencing option is measured against a broader, more detailed base of information. In the circle, the flow of information is alive, flexible and more readily capable of assessing and responding to new ideas.

Despite psychiatric and alcohol assessments, and an extensive and exceptionally researched pre-sentence report, the circle in this case provided additional relevant and particularly valuable information to probe and assess each new creative option.

Documents, files, reports, and assessments help introduce the offender to the court, but often present a lifeless portrayal which can be easily misconstrued. The circle, by enabling Philip to speak for himself, and by enabling others who have known him all his life to share their knowledge, substantially improved the court's perception.

Court-room procedures and rules often preclude or discourage many sources from contributing crucial information. The circle removes or reduces many of the impediments blocking the flow of essential information into court.

(iv) Creative Search for New Options

Public censure often focuses on the differences in sentences meted out for the same crime. There should be more, not fewer differences in sentences. If the reasons for the differences stems from personal attitudes of judges, the inadequacy of information, an inability to appreciate the remedial impact of various sentencing options, an absence of commonly accepted objectives, or ignorance of the impact of crime on victims, then public concern is warranted. The reasons for the differences, not simply the differences themselves, determine whether the differences are laudable or condemnable.

In a multicultural society, where gross inequities in opportunities, social resources, and social conditions abound, just sentencing cannot be monolithic or measured against any standard national "typical sentence." If the predominate objectives in sentencing are protection of the community, rehabilitation of the offender, minimizing adverse impacts on victims, and particularly greater community involvement, then even greater differences in sentencing for the same crime should be expected and welcomed. In at least two significant ways, the circle will accentuate differences in sentences for the same crime. The circle, by enhancing community participation, generates a richer range of sentencing options. Secondly, the circle by improving the quality and quantity of information provides the ability to refine and focus the use of sentencing options to meet the particular needs in each case.

In this case the circle promoted among all participants a desire to find an appropriate sentence that best served all of the above objectives. Their creative search produced a sentence markedly different from customary sentences for such crimes, and radically departed from the pattern of sentences previously imposed upon Philip for similar offences. The circle forged a collective desire for something different, something unlike the sentences imposed in the past 10 years, something everyone could support, something they believed would work. Fuelled by the expanded and responsive flow of information, the circle participants worked towards a consensus, towards a unique response to a problem that had plagued the community for 10 years and had stolen 10 years of productive life from Philip.

I was surprised by the result, but the new information and the option provided by the community rendered the final sentence obvious and compelling. The combination of new information and an array of new sentencing options can dramatically change sentencing dispositions from those based on information normally available and dependant upon the limited range of conventional sentencing remedies.

...

(vi) Encouraging the Offender's Participation

Philip Moses, as is typical of most offenders, had not significantly participated in any of the previous seven sentencing hearings which had instrumentally shaped his life. Most offenders, during formal court proceedings, sit with head bowed, sometimes in fear, more often in anger as incomprehensible discussions ramble on about their life, crimes, and about how communities must be protected from such hardened criminals.

Circuit lawyers, usually different each time, carry the primary responsibility to speak on behalf of offenders such as Philip. Their knowledge of the offender is derived from a few brief interviews, police reports, criminal records and sometimes from pre-sentence reports.

However well intentioned they might be, circuit counsel can never know Philip as well as his family or others within his community. Nor can any counsel fully reflect the offender's pain, suffering, or desperate search for help. Equally, the anger, resentment and hostility of many offenders is rarely expressed, as competent counsel manage to ensure a properly contrite, dutiful face masks any burning feelings which may, if revealed, provoke a harsher sentence. Consequently, the court sentences in blissful ignorance, missing the opportunity to constructively appreciate perceptions and feelings that may perpetually frustrate rehabilitative plans.

In the circle, the police, mother, brother, Chief of the First Nation, the probation officer, and other community members expressed constructive concern about Philip. They repeatedly spoke of the need to "reintegrate" Philip with his family and his First Nation.

This was the first time Philip heard anyone from his community, or from his First Nation offer support. He could no longer believe that the police and the community were solely interested in removing him from their midst.

These comments within the circle drew Philip into the discussion. His eloquence, passion, and pain riveted everyone's attention. His contribution moved the search for an effective sentence past several concerns shared around the circle. No, he did not convince everyone, nor did he ultimately secure what he sought, but his passion and candour significantly contributed to constructing the sentence.

(vii) Involving Victims in Sentencing

Many offenders perceive only the state as the aggrieved party. They fail to appreciate the very human pain and suffering they cause. Absent an appreciation of the victim's suffering, offenders fail to understand their sentence except as the intrusion of an insensitive, oppressive state bent on punishment. An offender's remorse is more likely to be prompted by a desire to seek mercy from the state or by a recognition that they have been "bad." Only when an offender's pain caused by the oppression of the criminal justice system is confronted by the pain that victims experience from crime, can most offenders gain a proper perspective of their behaviour. Without this perspective, the motivation to successfully pursue rehabilitation lacks an important and often essential ingredient.

Much work remains to find an appropriate means of including the victim, or in the very least, including the impact on the victim in the sentencing process. The circle affords an important opportunity to explore the potential of productively incorporating the impact upon victims in sentencing.

...

(xii) Merging Values: First Nation and Western Governments

Because aboriginal people use the same language, engage in similar play and work, western society assumes similar underlying values govern and motivate their conduct. Particularly within the justice system, this widely spread erroneous assumption has had a disastrous impact on aboriginal people and their communities.

Much of the systemic discrimination against aboriginal people within the justice system stems from a failure to recognize the fundamental differences between aboriginal and western cultures. Aboriginal culture does not place as high a premium on individual responsibility or approach conflict in the direct confrontational manner championed by our adversarial process. Aboriginal people see value in avoiding confrontation and in refraining from speaking publicly against each other. In dealing with conflict, emphasis is placed on reconciliation, the restoration of harmony and the removal of underlying pressures generating conflict.

After extensive exposure to the justice system, it has been assumed too readily that aboriginal people have adjusted to our adversarial process with its obsession on individual rights and individual responsibility, another tragically wrong assumption. Similarly, we have erroneously assumed by inviting their involvement in our system they will be willing and eager participants. If we generally seek their partnership in resolving crime, a process that fairly accommodates both value systems must emerge.

The circle has the potential to accord greater recognition to aboriginal values, and to create a less confrontational, less adversarial means of processing conflict. Yet the circle retains the primary principles and protections inherent to the justice system. The circle contributes the basis for developing a genuine partnership between aboriginal communities and the justice system by according the flexibility for both sets of values to influence the decision-making process in sentencing.

(3) Safeguards: Protecting Individual Rights in Merging the Community and Justice System in the Circle

Courage, patience, and tolerance must accompany all participants in the search for a productive partnership between communities and the justice system. The search need not be foolhardy. Many safeguards can be adapted to protect individual rights while opening the process to community involvement. In this experiment with the circle, the following safeguards were used to cushion any adverse impact on individual rights. Within the justice system, a critical assessment must be made about what is truly inviolable and what has by convention been presumed to be. Many conventions have survived long past the justification for their original creation.

(i) Open Court

The court-room remained the same, only the furniture was rearranged. The door was open, the public retained free access to the room.

The long-standing reasons for open court may not be as persuasive in some sentencing hearings where privacy may be essential to precipitate frank exchanges which reveal extremely sensitive family or personal information. Normally, such information, vital to competently employing any sentencing option, is rarely available as participants are understandably reluctant to share intimate circumstances of their life in an open public court-room, especially in small communities where anonymity is impossible.

In most cases there will be no need to limit access. However, where clear advantages flow from a closed session, the longstanding reasons for open court must be dusted off and re-examined in light of the advantages derived from acquiring extremely sensitive and personal information from offenders, victims or their families and friends.

(ii) Transcripts

The court reporter remained a part of the circle.

In some cases, there are good reasons to question why a transcript embracing all circle discussions is necessary. Some aspects of the discussion may be best excluded from the transcript, or where the circle is closed to the public, the transcript retained in a confidential manner, available only if required by a court of appeal.

To establish appropriate guidelines in assessing the competing values of an open versus a closed process on a case-by-case basis, some of the ancient icons of criminal procedures need an airing and reassessment.

The tradition of a circle—"what comes out in a circle, stays in a circle"—runs counter to the justice tradition requiring both an open court and transcripts. A more flexible set of rules for exceptions must be fashioned to establish a balance in emerging First Nation, community, and justice system values in the circle.

(iii) Upper Limits to Sentence

The circle is designed to explore and develop viable sentencing options drawing upon, whenever possible, community-based resources. The circle is not designed to extract reasons to increase the severity of punishment. Accordingly, at the outset of the circle process, Crown and defence counsel were called upon to make their customary sentencing submissions. Based on these submissions, I indicated the upper-limit sentence for the offence.

By stating at the outset an upper limit to the sentence based on conventional sentencing principles and remedies, the offender enters the circle without fearing a harsher jail sentence provoked by candour or anger within the circle. This constitutes an important basis to encourage offenders to participate.

The upper limit also provides a basis for the circle to appreciate what will happen in the absence of community alternatives. The utility of the upper-limit sentence can be measured against any new information shared in the circle. Any community-based alternative developed by the circle may be substituted for part or all of this sentence.

(iv) Opportunity for Offender To Speak

The *Criminal Code*, s. 668, ensures the offender has an opportunity to speak in his own words before a sentence is imposed. This opportunity is generally offered after all submissions have been made, and the court has all but formally concluded what the sentence will be. It is generally a perfunctory step in the process, rarely used and generally of little effect.

Defence counsel bears the primary and often exclusive responsibility to represent the offender's interest. How far we have come from the time when lawyers were banned and offenders left to make their own submissions. Somewhere on this journey from exclusive reliance upon the offender to essentially exclusive reliance upon defence counsel, we passed a more fitting balance in the participatory roles of counsel and offender. It may be too cute to suggest courts currently sentence defence counsel, not offenders, but the thought does highlight how much sentencing depends upon the work, competence, knowledge, and eloquence of defence counsel.

The inequities in proceeding without counsel are staggering. Similarly, the involvement of communities creates its own inequities within the circle. In a very unequal world, no justice system can create equality, or for that matter render perfect justice. The circle improves the offender's ability to participate, and thereby reduces the obvious inequities in a process that minimizes participation by the very person who is the primary focus of the process. More thought, or innovation must be invested to extract the best from the existing justice process and from the circle to create a viable balance between individual rights and community involvement.

(v) Crown and Defence Counsel

The traditional and essential functions of Crown and defence counsel are not excluded by the circle.

The Crown at the outset placed before the circle the interests of the state in sentencing the offender. The Crown's participation through questions and by engaging in the discussions retains the circle's awareness of the larger interests of the state. Aware of community-provided alternatives, having acquired first-hand knowledge of a broad spectrum of community concerns and armed with detailed information about the offender, the Crown at the end of the circle discussions can more competently assess how the interests of the state, and the interests of the community are best addressed in sentencing.

Especially on circuit, the Crown is forced to make assumptions about what sentences protect the community. Through the circle, these assumptions are examined by members of the very community Crown submissions are designed to protect.

Defence counsel, knowing that at worst the offender faces a conventional sentence presaged at the outset of the hearing, can constructively use the circle to develop a sentencing plan to advance the immediate and long-term interests of his client. Community support generated by the circle, as it did in this case, creates viable alternatives to jail.

(vi) Disputed Facts

Any disputed fact must be proven in the customary manner. Proof of a disputed fact can be carried out in the circle by the examination of witnesses under oath. Alternatively, during a break in the circle discussions, court can be resumed and all the traditional trappings of the court-room engaged to resolve a disputed fact.

The circle moves along a different road to consensus than the adversarial character of the formal court-room hearings. The process in a circle can either resolve disputes in a less adversarial manner, or render the disputed fact irrelevant or unimportant by evolving a sentencing disposition principally relevant upon community-based alternatives. However, the formal court process provides a "safeguard" to be called upon by either counsel at any time a matter in the circle necessitates formal proof.

NOTE

Although much of the development of sentencing circles has occurred in the Yukon and northern Saskatchewan, credit for their modern introduction as a way of responding to the circumstances of aboriginal offenders should be given to Judge C.C. Barnett, formerly of the BC Provincial Court, who sat for many years in Williams Lake and the Queen Charlotte Islands.

In different communities, sentencing circles have evolved in different forms, but always with the common feature of broad-based community participation. A brief account of their development in Saskatchewan was given by Fafard Prov. Ct. J in *R v. Joseyounen*, [1995] 6 WWR 438:

> The first sentencing circle to be held in Saskatchewan took place in Sandy Bay in July of 1992. I was the presiding judge. Since then many sentencing circles have been held in Northern Saskatchewan (I estimate that I have dealt with over 60 cases in that manner myself), and out of this experience by me and my colleagues on the Provincial Court in the north, there have emerged seven criteria that we apply in deciding if a case for sentencing should go to a circle. These criteria are not carved in stone, but they provide guidelines sufficiently simple for the lay public to understand, and also capable of application so that our decisions are not being made arbitrarily.
>
> It is imperative that the public, aboriginal and others, be able to know and understand what is happening in the development of sentencing circles: the credibility of the administration of justice depends on it.

Fafard J's criteria are:

1. The accused must agree to be referred to the sentencing circle.
2. The accused must have deep roots in the community in which the circle is held and from which the participants are drawn.
3. There are elders or respected non-political community leaders willing to participate.
4. The victim is willing to participate and has been subjected to no coercion or pressure in so agreeing.
5. The court should try to determine beforehand, as best it can, if the victim is subject to battered spouse syndrome. If she is, then she should have counselling made available to her and be accompanied by a support team in the circle.
6. Disputed facts have been resolved in advance.
7. The case is one in which a court would be willing to take a calculated risk and depart from the usual range of sentencing.

These criteria were applied by the majority of the Saskatchean Court of Appeal in *R v. Morin* (1995), 101 CCC (3d) 124 (Sask. CA) to reject the appropriateness of a sentencing circle following a conviction for robbery by an aboriginal offender who lived in Saskatoon. On the facts, there was some doubt about the offender's sincerity in seeking help from the local aboriginal community.

In the Yukon, the use of circles has evolved since the decision in *Moses*, supra. In *R v. Gingell* (1996), 50 CR (4th) 32 (YTC), Lilles J described the process that has been developed by Kwanlin Dun, the aboriginal community near Whitehorse. Other alternative forms of sentencing procedure are also in use. See, for example, the decision in *R v. P.(J.A.)* (1991), 6 CR (4th) 126 (YTC) for a description of sentencing in Teslin, a community in the southern Yukon, where the clan leaders sit with the sentencing judge to offer advice on an appropriate sentence.

One of the most successful examples of a circle approach has been used in the community of Hollow Water in Manitoba. Its sentencing circle is described by Ross Gordon Green.

R.G. Green, *Justice in Aboriginal Communities: Sentencing Alternatives*
(Saskatoon: Purich Publishing, 1998) (footnotes omitted)

Hollow Water is located 190 kilometres (118 miles) northeast of Winnipeg on the east shore of Lake Winnipeg. It covers 1620 hectares (4,000 acres) of land within the Canadian Precambrian Shield. The band's native language is Ojibway. As of 1994, the on-reserve population was 490 and off-reserve was 512. This band is a signatory to Treaty 5, signed in 1875. Hollow Water is bordered by the Métis communities of Aghaming, Manigotogan, and Seymourville. The total resident population of Hollow Water and the surrounding communities is 1200. Resources at Hollow Water include a K–12 school, a convenience store, a gas bar, a community hall, a band office, and a water treatment plant. No regular court sittings are held at Hollow Water. Provincial Court for this community is held 100 kilometres (62 miles) to the south in Pine Falls. However, since December of 1993, the Provincial Court of Manitoba has convened at Hollow Water to conduct sentencing circles that have dealt with offenders charged with sexual assault.

Hollow Water represents a unique example of a community-driven approach to dispute resolution and the healing and treatment of both offenders and victims. Rupert Ross described its development:

> In 1984, a group of social service providers got together, concerned about the future of their young people. As they looked into the issues of youth substance abuse, vandalism, truancy and suicide, their focus shifted to the home life of those children and to the substance abuse and family violence that often prevailed. Upon closer examination of those issues, the focus changed again, for inter-generational sexual abuse was identified as the root problem. Other dysfunctional behaviour came to be seen primarily as symptomatic. By 1987, they began to tackle sexual abuse head on, creating what they

have called their Community Holistic Circle Healing Program [CHCH]. They presently estimate that 75 percent of the population of Hollow Water are victims of sexual abuse, and 35 percent are "victimizers."

CHCH co-ordinator Berma Bushie cited frustration with the prevailing criminal justice and child welfare systems as factors contributing to CHCH's development:

> We also studied the *Child Welfare Act*, the legal system and how it was dealing with these [child sexual abuse] cases, and we were horrified to find out that our children were further victimized. ... Child Welfare's practice at the time, and probably still is, is when a child disclosed [he or she was] ... removed from the family and, in a lot of situations, a child was removed from the community. And then there's absolutely no help offered to the offender. Everything was turned over to the legal system and charges laid, court would take place, and that's it. And the child would be expected to testify against the offender in criminal court, and to us that's not protecting our children. So based on the laws that continue to govern us, we feel that we have to ensure protection for our children. We have to have a say in what happens to them.

As of February 6, 1995, the assessment team comprised seven sexual abuse workers, the local child and family service supervisor, a support worker, a councillor from the band, two Native Alcohol (NADAP) workers, a public health nurse, a local band constable, an RCMP officer from Pine Falls, a person from the Roman Catholic church, two people from provincial Child and Family Services, and the local school principal. The procedure followed by CHCH's assessment team is complex and includes provision of support and treatment for victims and victimizers and their respective families.

After initial disclosure of sexual abuse by a child, a thirteen-step process is followed by the assessment team. These steps are: (1) effecting disclosure, (2) protecting the child/victim, (3) confronting the victimizer, (4) assisting the victimizer's spouse, (5) assisting the family or families directly affected and the community, (6) calling together the assessment team, (7) getting the victimizer to admit and accept responsibility, (8) preparing the victimizer, (9) preparing the victim, (10) preparing all family or families, (11) organizing a special gathering, (12) implementing the healing contract, and (13) conducting the cleansing ceremony.

The assessment team is divided into support teams for the victim, victimizer, and family. After ensuring the safety of the victim, the accused is confronted by a member of the assessment team, who encourages the accused to take responsibility for his or her actions and to participate in CHCH. Berma Bushie explained:

> We feel as a community it's our job to go and confront the offender and not to rely on the RCMP, because they haven't been very successful in getting people to take responsibility for what they've done. When people see the RCMP, they just clam up, won't speak, and so we feel as a community we have a better ... track record of getting people to take responsibility for what they've done. ... Nine times out of ten, the offender takes responsibility, and we inform the offender of the plan in place. We inform [him] of the community approach. We also inform him about the treatment expectations, the circles that ... he's going to have to go through. We also tell the offender that he has to go plead guilty in court.

When criminal charges follow a disclosure, the CHCH approach promotes accept-ance of responsibility by the offender through entry of an early guilty plea in court. This practice stands in sharp contrast to the presumption of innocence enjoyed by accused persons in Canadian law and their right to remain silent. In fairness, though, the goal of team members is to help both child complainants and adult accused. After entry of a guilty plea, members of the assessment team then ask the court to adjourn sentencing for at least four months to allow treatment with the offender to begin. Berma Bushie indicated that this period of time was requested so that the assessment team could be assured that the offender was committed to healing.

Offenders are expected to participate in four circles. In the first circle, the offender discloses details of his offence to the CHCH assessment team. In the second circle, the victim tells the offender how the abuse has affected his or her life. In the third circle, the offender describes his actions to his family. Finally, in the fourth circle, the offender faces his community in a sentencing circle. Prior to the introduction of cir-cle sentencing at Hollow Water in December 1993, the assessment team prepared and presented recommendations on sentence to the court sitting in Pine Falls. This proce-dure was outlined in *R v. S.(H.M.)*.

CHCH has actively opposed offender incarceration and has argued that jail cannot break the generational cycle of violence. Assessment team member Marcel Hardesty supported this analysis. He explained that he had asked a sexual offender, recently returned from jail, whether he would commit the offence again. The offender had responded that he would be sure not to get caught if he did it again. Hardesty questioned the lesson being taught by jail and suggested incarceration only reduces the chances of other victims and abusers coming forward.

CHCH focusses on restoring harmony between victims and offenders and the community-at-large through traditional holistic practices. In this process, a conjunc-tive relationship has developed between CHCH and the criminal justice system both prior to and after sentencing. A protocol between the Manitoba Department of Justice and CHCH was negotiated in 1991 in which the department recognized CHCH's program as an option for the treatment and supervision of sexual assault offenders and agreed to consider a non-custodial sentence if that was the recommendation of the assessment team. This protocol was negotiated by CHCH to give the assessment team input into sentencing and to avoid repeatedly educating Crown attorneys about the CHCH approach.

The first sentencing circle at Hollow Water occurred December 9, 1993. It involved serious sexual assaults perpetrated by two parents on their children. The assessment team foresaw dire consequences for the offenders if this case went through the conven-tional system. According to assessment team member Lorne Hagel, Judge Murray Sinclair of the Provincial Court of Manitoba had advised the team that, given the of-fences and circumstances involved, eight to ten years' incarceration would be a realis-tic sentence. Judge Sinclair advised me that the initial Crown position on sentence was five to six years' incarceration, while even defence counsel conceded that two-and-a-half to four years might be appropriate for one offender, with less jail time for the other. The CHCH assessment team made representations to the Provincial Court requesting formation of a sentencing circle and explaining the evolution of commu-nity participation in that community. The submission characterized circle sentencing as an extension of the community's role in holding offenders accountable for their actions and healing the pain they inflicted on their victims:

> Up until now the sentencing hearing has been the point at which all of the parties of the legal system (Crown, defence, judge) and the community have come together. Major differences of opinion as to how to proceed have often existed. As we see it, the legal system usually arrives with an outside agenda of punishment and deterrence of the "guilty" victimizer, and safety and protection of the victim and community; the community on the other hand, arrives with an agenda of accountability of the victimizer to the community, and restoration of balance to all parties of the victimization.
>
> As we see it, the differences in the agendas are seriously deterring the healing process of the community. We believe that the restoration of balance is more likely to occur if sentencing itself is more consistent in process and in content with the healing work of the community. Sentencing needs to become more of a step in the healing process, rather than a diversion from it. ... The sentencing circle promotes the above rationale. ... As we see it, the sentencing circle plays two primary purposes (1) it promotes the community healing process by providing a forum for the community to address the parties at the time of sentencing, and (2) it allows the court to hear directly from the people most directly affected by the pain of the victimization. In the past the Crown and defence, as well as ourselves, have attempted to portray this information. We believe that it is now time for the court to hear from the victim, the family of the victim, the victimizer, the family of the victimizer and the community-at-large.

This first sentencing circle commenced at seven o'clock in the morning with a sunrise and pipe ceremony and ended at nine o'clock that night. Winnipeg Free Press reporter Kevin Rollason described the atmosphere and process followed at this circle:

> While the smell of sweet grass filled the air, two circles were formed in the centre of the hall for the sentencing of a man and woman charged with incest. The inner circle of about 40 people held the key participants—including both offenders and victims—while the outer circle consisted of about 200 other relatives, friends and community members. ... Just before court was called to order, a man holding a tray of burning sweet grass and buffalo grass went around the inner circle, allowing each participant to "wash" the smoke over their hair, faces and clothes. Passing an eagle feather from hand to hand, each person spoke in order around the circles. The discussion went around a total of four times. During the first circle, people spoke about why they were there. During the second, participants were able to speak to the victims. The third and fourth circles were designed to be separate—one centering on the effects of the crime and the other on "restoring balance" to the offenders. However, when the proceedings threatened to extend well into the night, the last two circles had to be melded into one.

At the conclusion of the circle, all participants, with the exception of a cousin of one of the victims but including the Crown prosecutor, agreed jail would be counterproductive for these offenders. Judge Sinclair indicated to me that these offenders had progressed from a state of total denial to one of total acceptance and responsibility for their actions. In addition, the two had actively worked in convincing one hundred other sexual abusers from Hollow Water to come forward and admit their actions publicly. At the circle's conclusion, Judge Sinclair imposed a three-year suspended sentence on each offender with probation containing a condition that each offender follow the directions of the CHCH assessment team.

Despite the many disclosures of abuse heard at the initial Hollow Water sentencing circle, few subsequent sentencing circles were conducted and there was no increase in sexual assault charges laid against Hollow Water residents. This suggests that many incidents of abuse were being dealt with locally outside the conventional justice system or were not being dealt with at all. An article on Hollow Water published on April 8, 1995, in *The Globe and Mail* stated that, since 1986, only five offenders had been jailed instead of entering the CHCH program and forty-eight offenders had enrolled in the treatment program.

The limited number of offenders sentenced through sentencing circles or incarcerated outside the CHCH program suggest that many offenders in the program were not being charged. This highlights the interesting and often complex relationship between local dispute-resolution processes and the broader justice system. At one level, the community of Hollow Water was working conjunctively with the formal justice system, through the involvement of CHCH members in court assessments and circle sentencing. At another level, the community was apparently operating separately from the formal system, assuming complete control of dispute resolution. The reality across the criminal justice system in Canada is that the number of cases processed through the formal system represents only a small proportion of ongoing criminal activity. What may be different at Hollow Water is the availability of local resources to address the behaviour of offenders, while at the same time protecting victims within that community.

As part of their local system of social control, and in an effort to hold offenders responsible for their actions and encourage their active participation in treatment, a community review was held on the six-month anniversary of each sentencing circle. Berma Bushie explained:

One of the things that the community does is, after sentencing, we tell the offenders "for the next three years, you are on probation and every six months we are bringing the case back to the community, for the community to review how you are doing in treatment. ..." [The community review] is one of the ways, besides probation, ... used to make sure that people are following the [sentencing circle's] recommendation.

The review process encourages community assistance in holding offenders accountable for their victimization and promotes active participation in their treatment. As Bushie explained:

We found that after the first sentencing circle back in December 1993 ... that in the treatment area ... there was a regression on the part of the offenders. They were getting back into their denial process. They were getting back to creating negative support for their case and stuff like that. ... [W]e felt that ... [our assessment] team was not strong enough to stop the regression and to get the people [offenders] back on track with their healing. And because the community came out to speak and give recommendations to the court for their sentencing [circle] ... we felt as a team ... we needed to go back to the community to report ... what was happening. ... And as a team we felt that, before we thought about going through [the process of charging the offenders with breach of probation and bringing this case back to court, ... we felt that we ... should go back through the community. First, give all the details ... and have the community help us decide where this case should go. ... And they [the community members in attendance at the review] felt that these people should be given a chance, and that, again, they repeated their support for these people. They repeated their expectations of the kinds of treatments they wanted the offenders to take, and the work that they wanted them to do. And we said, "Okay, we'll do that and six months down the line, we'll come back and we'll report to you and see how these people are doing.

A community sentencing review held at Hollow Water on February 22, 1995 for three sexual offenders who had been sentenced through a sentencing circle was attended by approximately thirty community members including one of the victims. The victim in attendance had been victimized by two of the offenders. She was apparently sitting in a circle with her abusers for the first time, although she did not speak. The other victim had moved to Winnipeg. The assessment team members assigned to each victim and offender were present and reported to the circle.

This review followed a similar format to the sentencing circles. During successive rounds of the circle, participants in the review learned of the treatment and progress of all victims and offenders and, in turn, addressed the three offenders and one victim in attendance. Participants also developed recommendations for continued offender treatment and victim support. Comments by participants made it clear there was strong community pressure on the offenders to continue treatment. Several women, while acknowledging the progress made by each offender, openly challenged the offenders not to regress in their treatment and to assist the assessment team by naming their other victims. Berma Bushie commented to the offenders that jail "would have been the easy way out for you." She thanked them for taking responsibility for their actions and for facing their community in the circle.

NOTE

Although sentencing circles provide a more appropriate forum for the sentencing of aboriginal offenders, they raise a number of questions. Must the offender have pleaded guilty, or is it sufficient that he or she accepts guilt in the circle? Can circles be used for all cases? Can they be modified for use in non-aboriginal communities? Have they produced constructive results without diminishing the interests of the victim? With respect to the efficacy of sentencing circles, see Julian Roberts and Carole La Prairie, "Sentencing Circles: Some Unanswered Questions" (1996-97), 39 *Crim. LQ* 69.

Given the understandable divisions and loyalties that exist within communities, some observers have questioned whether a sentencing circle can transcend power imbalances inherent in certain offences. This important issue is addressed by Green.

R.G. Green, *Justice in Aboriginal Communities: Sentencing Alternatives*
(Saskatoon: Purich Publishing, 1998) (footnotes omitted)

...

Justice Co-ordinator Mary Crnkovich described an example of such a power imbalance within an Inuit sentencing circle in northern Quebec. This circle had been formed to consider the sentence of an offender who had assaulted his wife:

> Aside from the fact that the sentence was based on a proposal presented by the accused, the victim could hardly, in her position, oppose such a proposal or complain that it was not working. Again to suggest that her attendance [for counselling] would keep the accused honest, demonstrates, in the author's view, the judge's misunderstanding of the life circumstances of this woman as a victim of violence. How could this woman speak out against her husband? How could she speak out against the mayor [and] ... others in her community [who attended the sentencing circle]? Did the judge really believe she would speak out based on the history of this case to date? The victim's actions or lack thereof during the circle, demonstrated the degree of fear and deference paid to her spouse.

Rupert Ross has suggested that it might be inappropriate to conduct a sentencing circle without previously identifying and addressing power imbalances between offenders and victims. This appears not to have been done in the Inuit circle described above. Such an approach was, however, practised at Hollow Water in cases of serious child sexual abuse. At Hollow Water, each offender and victim was assigned a separate support team, and the two were not brought together until such time as they could face each other on an equal footing. When a sentencing circle was held, the victim was encouraged, but not required, to attend. If the victim chose to attend the circle, he or she was accompanied by a specific worker for support.

The Hollow Water approach brings into question the appropriateness of circle sentencing for cases involving domestic violence unless there has been prior intervention by a local justice committee or other local support personnel. Intervention prior to sentencing, however, means lengthy adjournments of sentencing by the trial court. At Hollow Water, there was a protocol in effect between the Manitoba Department of Justice and the community that recognized the propriety of such adjournments for completion of the healing program. However, the Alberta Court of Appeal, in *R v. A.B.C.*, rejected the practice of lengthy adjournments for treatment, making the Hollow Water approach unlikely to be accepted in Alberta. The Saskatchewan Court of Appeal, in *Taylor*, also rejected the trial judge's decision, following a sentencing circle, to adjourn sentencing for one year and to banish the offender to an isolated island under the terms of an undertaking. If lengthy adjournments are sought, for such purposes as facilitating victim counselling and support prior to a sentencing circle, Crown consent is essential. If this support is not forthcoming, lengthy adjournments will likely be declared unlawful if contested on appeal. In contrast to domestic assault cases, sentencing circles may be more beneficial, and potentially less threatening, when victims [are] not well acquainted with the offenders. In *Morin*, the victim and offender were strangers prior to the offence. The sentencing circle appears to have allowed the victim to confront her assailant while putting a human face to him. At the circle, she directly challenged the offender, Ivan Morin:

> Morin's victim, [a] university student ... said she didn't hate Morin and didn't appear [to be] looking for revenge. "I did not come here out of vindictiveness and I have no anger towards you. I came here to challenge you in your actions." [The victim] said what she and the rest of the community wanted was a commitment from Morin to break his cycle of crime. "I need a commitment from you to better yourself. It can't come from anyone else here," [the victim] said.

This victim also attained insight into the offender's personal situation and problems.

Although reconciliation between parties to an offence is possible during a sentencing circle, offences involving long-standing power imbalances will continue to necessitate vigilance by judges in ensuring, to the extent possible, protection of the victims. Unfortunately, such protection may be short-lived in isolated communities, where the routine departure of the court party after adjournment makes community-based support for such victims essential. Cases of domestic violence underscore the importance of ongoing resources and support at the local level for both victims and offenders. It is unrealistic to expect that a few hours in a sentencing circle will permanently alter historic patterns of offending and imbalances of power. Clearly, sentencing circles can be catalysts to start significant changes in behaviour on the part of offenders. Any chance of achieving this goal, however, depends on the availability and success of locally accessible resources, including support, treatment, and counselling for victims and offenders, and, in cases involving abuse, close supervision of offenders and protection of victims.

The appropriateness of community participation at sentencing may also bring into question the treatment of the victim by the local community as a whole. Caution respecting power imbalances between offenders and victims, in the context of a request for a community-based sentencing hearing, was expressed by the Ontario Court of Justice (General Division) in *R v. A.F.* The victim had been outcast from her community as a result of her complaint and the resulting criminal proceeding. She had moved to Southern Ontario following her disclosure. Justice Stach voiced the following caution:

> The success of a community-based sentencing approach depends very much upon the active participation of and sincere commitment of each participant. ... So too, where the nature of the crime bespeaks an imbalance of power as between the victim and the offender, great care ought to be taken. ...
>
> The perspective of the accused, the convenience of witnesses and the perspective of the community are not the only considerations. The rights of the public, the perspective of the victim, and the Court's duty to ascertain the truth are all *valid and sometime competing considerations.* In cases of sexual assault, for example, an imbalance of power as between the offender and the victim is commonplace. Where that imbalance is not offset by some other visible community support for the victim, the logic of a community-based sentencing hearing is dissipated.

Questions of power imbalance highlight the complex dynamics that may occur during a sentencing circle.

V. CONDITIONAL SENTENCES AND ABORIGINAL OFFENDERS

In Chapter 12, we discussed in detail the new sanction of a conditional sentence that was the subject of the Supreme Court's attention in *R v. Proulx*. Although a number of conditional sentence cases were argued at the same time as *Proulx*, one judgment that was not released until later was *R v. Wells*, infra. It dealt with the application of the conditional sentence regime to an aboriginal offender.

R v. Wells
(2000), 30 CR (5th) 254 (SCC)

[The offender was convicted of sexual assault involving an 18-year-old victim who was either asleep or unconsious by reason of intoxication. He was sentenced to 20 months' incarceration. Prior to the Supreme Court decision in *Gladue* dealing with s. 718.2(e), his sentence appeal was heard and dismissed. Fresh evidence was filed indicating his involvment with the aboriginal community and his efforts to deal with his alcohol abuse problem by attending an aboriginal treatment centre. On appeal to the Supreme Court, the relationship between s. 718.2(e) and conditional sentences was a central issue.]

IACOBUCCI J for the court:

...

In *Gladue*, supra, the Court concluded that, as a general principle, s. 718.2(e) indicates that a custodial sentence is the penal sanction of last resort for all offenders, to be used only where no other sanction is appropriate. As to the words "with particular attention to the circumstances of aboriginal offenders," the Court reasoned that sentencing judges should pay particular attention to the fact that the circumstances of aboriginal offenders are unique in comparison with those of non-aboriginal offenders. Section 718.2(e) has a remedial purpose for all offenders, focusing as it does on the concept of restorative justice, a sentencing approach which seeks to restore the harmony that existed prior to the accused's actions. Again, the appropriateness of the sentence will take into account the needs of the victims, the offender, and the community as a whole.

While the objective of restorative justice, by virtue of s. 718.2(e), applies to all offenders, the requirement to pay "particular attention to the circumstances of aboriginal offenders" recognizes that most traditional aboriginal conceptions of sentencing hold restorative justice to be the primary objective. In addition, s. 718.2(e) has a particular remedial purpose for aboriginal peoples, as it was intended to address the serious problem of overincarceration of aboriginal offenders in Canadian penal institutions. In singling out aboriginal offenders for distinct sentencing treatment in s. 718.2(e), it is reasonable to assume that Parliament intended to address this social problem, to the extent that a remedy was possible through sentencing procedures.

In order to provide guidance to sentencing judges as to the manner in which the remedial purpose of s. 718.2(e) could be given effect, the reasons in *Gladue* set out a framework of analysis for the sentencing judge. In considering the circumstances of aboriginal offenders, the sentencing judge must take into account, at the very least, both the unique systemic or background factors that are mitigating in nature in that they may have played a part in the aboriginal offender's conduct, and the types of sentencing procedures and sanctions which may be appropriate in the circumstances for the offender because of his or her particular aboriginal heritage or connection (*Gladue*, at para. 66). In particular, given that most traditional aboriginal approaches place a primary emphasis on the goal of restorative justice, the alternative of community-based sanctions must be explored.

In the search for a fit sentence, therefore, the role of the sentencing judge is to conduct the sentencing process and impose sanctions taking into account the perspective of the aboriginal offender's community. As was noted in *Gladue*, it is often the case that imposing a custodial sentence on an aboriginal offender does not advance the remedial purpose of s. 718.2(e), neither for the offender nor for his community. This is particularly true for less serious or non-violent offences, where the goal of restorative justice will no doubt be given greater weight than principles of denunciation or deterrence.

However, the scope of s. 718.2(e), as it applies to all offenders, restricts the adoption of alternatives to incarceration to those sanctions that are "reasonable in the circumstances." Again, as was expressly stated in *Gladue*, the Court in no way intended to suggest that as a general rule, the greatest weight is to be given to principles of restorative justice, and less weight accorded to goals such as denunciation and deterrence. Indeed, such a general rule would contradict the individual or case-by-case nature of the sentencing process, which proceeds on the basis of inquiring whether, given the particular facts of the offence, the offender, the victim and the community, the sentence is fit in the circumstances.

I should take this opportunity to stress that the guidelines as set out in *Gladue*, and reiterated in the present appeal, are not intended to provide a single test for a sentencing judge to apply in determining a reasonable sentence in the circumstances. Section 718.2(e) imposes an affirmative duty on the sentencing judge to take into account the surrounding circumstances of the offender, including the nature of the offence, the victims and the community.

Notwithstanding what may well be different approaches to sentencing as between aboriginal and non-aboriginal conceptions of sentencing, it is reasonable to assume that for some aboriginal offenders, and depending upon the nature of the offence, the goals of denunciation and deterrence are fundamentally relevant to the offender's community. As held in *Gladue*, at para. 79, to the extent that generalizations may be made, the more violent and serious the offence, the more likely as a practical matter that the appropriate sentence will not differ as between aboriginal and non-aboriginal offenders, given that in these circumstances, the goals of denunciation and deterrence are accorded increasing significance.

E. Whether the Imposition of a Conditional Sentence Is Reasonable in the Circumstances of This Case

(1) Significance of the Goal of Restorative Justice in Sentencing Aboriginal Offenders Convicted of Serious Crimes

The appellant submits that in according greater weight to the goals of denunciation and deterrence based on the nature of his offence, the sentencing judge did not take into account, as required by s. 718.2(e), the paramount significance of restorative justice within aboriginal communities. The appellant also submits that on the same basis, the Court of Appeal was in error when it held that it would be unreasonable to conclude that a fit sentence for a non-aboriginal offender would not also be a fit sentence for an aboriginal offender. It is important to note, however, that consistent with the reasoning in *Gladue*, supra, the Court of Appeal was referring to "serious crimes," rather than offences in general, as follows (at p. 140):

> For serious crimes, it would not be reasonable to conclude that a fit sentence for a non-aboriginal person would not also be fit for an aboriginal person, and this point was made by Esson JA speaking for the majority in the British Columbia Court of Appeal decision of *R v. Gladue* (1997), 119 CCC (3d) 481 at p. 506, who stated, "To put it another way, the particular circumstances could not reasonably support a conclusion that the sentence, if a fit one for a non-aboriginal person, would not also be fit for an aboriginal person."

Let me emphasize that s. 718.2(e) requires a different methodology for assessing a fit sentence for an aboriginal offender; it does not mandate, necessarily, a different result. Section 718.2(e) does not alter the fundamental duty of the sentencing judge to impose a sentence that is fit for the offence and the offender. Furthermore, in *Gladue*, as mentioned the Court stressed that the application of s. 718.2(e) does not mean that aboriginal offenders must always be sentenced in a manner which gives greatest weight to the principles of restorative justice and less weight to goals such as deterrence, denunciation, and separation (at para. 78). As a result, it will generally be the case, as a practical matter, that particularly violent and serious offences will result in imprisonment for aboriginal offenders as often as for non-aboriginal offenders (*Gladue*, at para. 33). Accordingly, I conclude that it was open to the trial judge to give primacy to the principles of denunciation and deterrence in this case on the basis that the crime involved was a serious one.

Whether a crime is indeed serious in the given circumstances is, in my opinion, a factual matter that can only be determined on a case-by-case basis. I am not suggesting that there are categories of offences which presumptively exclude the possibility of a non-custodial sentence. Indeed, Lamer CJ specifically rejected such an approach in relation to the conditional sentencing regime (*Proulx*, supra, at para. 79). More generally, Sopinka J, in *McDonnell*, supra, at paras. 32-33, rejected a category-based approach to sentencing for the following reasons:

> In any event, in my view it can never be an error in principle in itself to fail to place a particular offence within a judicially created category of assault for the purposes of

sentencing. There are two main reasons for this conclusion. First, *Shropshire* and *M.(C.A.)*, two recent and unanimous decisions of this Court, clearly indicate that deference should be shown to a lower court's sentencing decision. If an appellate court could simply create reviewable principles by creating categories of offences, deference is diminished in a manner that is inconsistent with *Shropshire* and *M.(C.A.)*. In order to circumvent deference and to enable appellate review of a particular sentence, a court may simply create a category of offence and a "starting point" for that offence, and treat as an error in principle any deviation in sentencing from the category so created. ... If the categories are defined narrowly, and deviations from the categorization are generally reversed, the discretion that should be left in the hands of the trial and sentencing judges is shifted considerably to the appellate courts.

Second, there is no legal basis for the judicial creation of a category of offence within a statutory offence for the purposes of sentencing. As has been true since *Frey v. Fedoruk*, [1950] SCR 517, it is not for judges to create criminal offences, but rather for the legislature to enact such offences.

Furthermore, Lamer CJ reasoned that a categorical approach represents only a partial, and therefore unbalanced, application of the fundamental sentencing principle of proportionality contained in s. 718.1 (*Proulx*, supra, at para. 83). Moreover, s. 718.1 provides that "[a] sentence must be proportionate to the gravity of the offence and the degree of responsibility of the offender." Thus, in assessing the seriousness of a crime we are directed to consider the gravity of the offence and the offender's degree of responsibility.

In this case, the trial judge did refer to "guideline cases binding on this court," an apparent reference to case law which outlined "starting point" guidelines for establishing sentences for serious sexual assaults. The reference to a "starting point" does not, however, establish that the judge failed to consider the seriousness of the offence and the offender's degree of responsibility on the facts of the case. Independent of this reference it is clear that the trial judge determined that this was a serious crime, taking into account the gravity of the offence, the existence or absence of aggravating factors, and the lack of evidence of remorse:

> The maximum term provided by the *Criminal Code* is 10 years imprisonment. The sexual assault occurred when the 18-year-old victim was either asleep or unconscious from the effects of alcohol. The medical evidence indicated vaginal abrasions but did not establish penetration or intercourse. It was, in my view, in any event, a major, or at the very best, a near major sexual assault, as those terms have been used in the guideline cases binding on this court. The paramount sentencing factors for these kinds of offences are deterrence and denunciation.
>
> Mr. Wells here took complete advantage of an unconscious 18-year-old girl. His own admitted and involuntary intoxication is no excuse. He violated the victim's personal integrity in the basest of ways.

I cannot conclude that the trial judge misconstrued the seriousness of the crime. In addition, the judge's use of the words "near major" or "major" instead of "serious" does not constitute a reversible error. I find no error in principle, no overemphasis of the appropriate factors, nor a failure to consider a relevant factor, and, accordingly, defer to the trial judge's assessment of the particular circumstances of the offence and offender (*M.(C.A.)*, supra). Therefore, the trial judge made a reasonable determination as to the availability of a conditional sentence.

I would like to add at this point that the reasons in *Gladue*, supra, do not foreclose the possibility that, in the appropriate circumstances, a sentencing judge may accord the greatest weight to the concept of restorative justice, notwithstanding that an aboriginal offender has committed a serious crime. As was concluded in *Gladue*, at para. 81, the remedial purpose of s. 718.2(e) directs the sentencing judge not only to take into account the unique circumstances of aboriginal offenders, but also to appreciate relevant cultural differences in terms of the objectives of the sentencing process:

> The analysis for sentencing aboriginal offenders, as for all offenders, must be holistic and designed to achieve a fit sentence in the circumstances. There is no single test that a judge can apply in order to determine the sentence. The sentencing judge is required to take into account all of the surrounding circumstances regarding the offence, the offender, the victims, and the community, including the unique circumstances of the offender as an aboriginal person. Sentencing must proceed with sensitivity to and understanding of the difficulties aboriginal people have faced with both the criminal justice system and society at large. When evaluating these circumstances in light of the aims and principles of sentencing as set out in Part XXIII of the *Criminal Code* and in the jurisprudence, the judge must strive to arrive at a sentence which is just and appropriate in the circumstances. By means of s. 718.2(e), sentencing judges have been provided with a degree of flexibility and discretion to consider in appropriate circumstances alternative sentences to incarceration which are appropriate for the aboriginal offender and community and yet comply with the mandated principles and purposes of sentencing. In this way, effect may be given to the aboriginal emphasis upon healing and restoration of both the victim and the offender.

The generalization drawn in *Gladue* to the effect that the more violent and serious the offence, the more likely as a practical matter for similar terms of imprisonment to be imposed on aboriginal and non-aboriginal offenders, was not meant to be a principle of universal application. In each case, the sentencing judge must look to the circumstances of the aboriginal offender. In some cases, it may be that these circumstances include evidence of the community's decision to address criminal activity associated with social problems, such as sexual assault, in a manner that emphasizes the goal of restorative justice, notwithstanding the serious nature of the offences in question.

As Lamer CJ noted in *M.(C.A.)*, supra, at para. 92, sentencing requires an individualized focus, not only of the offender, but also of the victim and community as well:

> It has been repeatedly stressed that there is no such thing as a uniform sentence for a particular crime. ... Sentencing is an inherently individualized process, and the search for a single appropriate sentence for a similar offender and a similar crime will frequently be a fruitless exercise of academic abstraction. As well, sentences for a particular offence should be expected to vary to some degree across various communities and

regions in this country, as the "just and appropriate" mix of accepted sentencing goals will depend on the needs and current conditions of and in the particular community where the crime occurred.

In this respect, I note that the appellant introduced evidence of the availability of an aboriginal-specific alcohol and drug abuse treatment program. There was, however, an indication that this program would be inappropriate for the appellant as a sexual offender. In addition, there was no evidence of the existence of, or the appellant's participation in, an anti-sexual-assault program.

(2) Extent of the Sentencing Judge's Obligation To Inquire into the Circumstances of an Aboriginal Offender

As noted in *Gladue*, supra, at para. 83, it will be necessary in every case for the sentencing judge to take judicial notice of systemic or background factors that have contributed to the difficulties faced by aboriginal people in both the criminal justice system, and throughout society at large. In addition, the judge is obliged to inquire into the unique circumstances of aboriginal offenders.

At times, it may be necessary to introduce evidence of this nature. It is to be expected in our adversarial system of criminal law that counsel for both the prosecution and the accused will adduce this evidence, but even where counsel do not provide the necessary information, s. 718.2(e) places an affirmative obligation upon the sentencing judge to inquire into the relevant circumstances. In most cases, the requirement of special attention to the circumstances of aboriginal offenders can be satisfied by the information contained in pre-sentence reports. Where this information is insufficient, s. 718.2(e) authorizes the sentencing judge on his or her own initiative to request that witnesses be called to testify as to reasonable alternatives to a custodial sentence.

Having said that, it was never the Court's intention, in setting out the appropriate methodology for this assessment, to transform the role of the sentencing judge into that of a board of inquiry. It must be remembered that in the reasons in *Gladue*, this affirmative obligation to make inquiries beyond the information contained in the presentence report was limited to "appropriate circumstances," and where such inquiries were "practicable" (at para. 84). The application of s. 718.2(e) requires a practical inquiry, not an impractical one. As with any other factual finding made by a court of first instance, the sentencing judge's assessment of whether further inquiries are either appropriate or practicable is accorded deference at the appellate level.

[The appeal was dismissed.]

NOTE

For a discussion of *Wells*, *Proulx*, and *Gladue* in the the context of an aboriginal offender convicted of trafficking, see *R v. Laliberte* (2000), 31 CR (5th) 1 (Sask. CA).

CHAPTER SEVENTEEN

Preventive Detention and Preventive Supervision

I. INTRODUCTION

This chapter addresses the ways in which the sentencing provisions approach the issue of dangerousness. Generally, sentencing that focuses on those offenders who are perceived to be dangerous is referred to as "preventive detention." The emphasis is on confinement and control based on a perception of risk or fear of future crimes. In addition to sentencing, the *Criminal Code*, RSC 1985, c. C-46, as amended, addresses perceived dangerousness at a number of points in the criminal process. For instance, at the bail stage, s. 515(10)(b) permits detention before trial when there is a "substantial likelihood" that the accused person will commit further offences while on bail. Sections 810.01, 810.1, and 810.2 of the Code provide for a recognizance with preventive conditions when there are reasonable grounds to believe that an individual will commit a criminal offence. While, technically speaking, these recognizances operate outside of the customary charge–trial–conviction criminal justice paradigm, the recognizances provided for in ss. 810.01, 810.1, and 810.2 have been used to achieve post-sentence control over certain individuals. Accordingly, they are considered in this chapter.

As discussed in Chapter 2, it has long been a principle of Canadian sentencing law that the primary purpose of sentencing is the protection of society. Section 718(c) of the Code identifies the separation of the offenders from society where necessary as an objective of sentencing. Thus, operating within the framework of the various statutory *maxima* established by Parliament, a sentencing judge can impose a sanction with public protection as the primary goal. The discretionary life sentence (for offences like manslaughter and aggravated sexual assault) is sometimes used with preventive detention in mind (see *R v. Pontello* (1977), 38 CCC (2d) 267 (Ont. CA) and *R v. Mesgun* (1997), 121 CCC (3d) 439 (Ont. CA)).

The majority of this chapter focuses on part XXIV (Dangerous Offenders and Long-Term Offenders) of the *Criminal Code*, which establishes a specialized procedure for sentencing those offenders who are feared to pose a serious risk of reoffending. As set out below, the dangerous offender provisions create a special designation and provide for indeterminate detention for certain offenders. Long-term offenders, who are thought to be at lower risk for recidivism, are dealt with through extended supervision in the community.

The last section of this chapter considers recognizances under ss. 810.01, 810.1, and 810.2 of the Code. By and large, Canada has rejected the propriety of further detention following a determinate sentence (that is, post-sentence detention). At one time, certain criminal justice/ mental health personnel attempted to circumvent the inevitable release of dangerous sociopaths at warrant expiry by having them committed under mental health legislation (see *Starnaman v. Penetanguishine Mental Health Centre* (1995), 24 OR (3d) 701 (CA)). With the advent of ss. 810.1 and 810.2, this practice may have died a natural death.

II. DANGEROUS OFFENDERS

A. Background

Canada first enacted preventive detention legislation in 1947, when the habitual offender provisions were enacted (SC 1947, c. 55, s. 18). A "habitual offender" was someone who had previously been convicted at least three times of an indictable offence punishable by more than five years' imprisonment. The following year, Parliament added the designation of "criminal sexual psychopath" to the Code (SC 1948, c. 39, s. 43), defined as anyone who "by a course of misconduct in sexual matters has evidenced a lack of power to control his sexual impulses and who as a result is likely to attack or otherwise inflict injury on any person." Later, in 1961, the "criminal sexual psychopath" label was dropped in favour of the "dangerous sexual offender" (SC 1960-61, c. 43, s. 32).

These early preventive detention provisions attracted a good deal of attention in the influential Report of the Canadian Committee on Corrections, *Toward Unity: Criminal Justice and Corrections* (Ottawa: Queen's Printer, 1969), also known as the Ouimet report. After a study of a group of individuals designated habitual offenders, the report determined that a substantial proportion of this group did not pose a serious threat to the public. The legislation seemed to be catching persistent offenders who, while constituting a serious social nuisance, were not dangerous (at 253). The way it was applied also reflected a disturbing disparity among the provinces. A hugely disproportionate number of individuals were sentenced as habitual offenders in British Columbia, where prosecutorial authorities found these provisions to be a useful tool for getting rid of "undesirables" in the West and stemming the immigration of criminals from eastern Canada (Michael Jackson, "The Sentencing of Dangerous and Habitual Offenders in Canada" (1997), 9 FSR 257). The Ouimet committee recommended substantial amendments to the preventive detention provisions, aimed at ensuring that only those whose background and criminal record created a real apprehension of further violence would be imprisoned indefinitely.

In 1975, the Supreme Court of Canada also expressed concern about the operation of the habitual offender provisions in *Hatchwell v. The Queen*, [1976] 1 SCR 39. Hatchwell was declared to be a habitual offender after being convicted of break and enter and theft of car keys. In reversing his sentence as a habitual offender, Dickson J (as he then was) portrayed a 44-year-old individual with many convictions, the overwhelming majority of which related to property, automobiles in particular. There were no violent offences. As Dickson J said for the majority:

> Section 688 [now s. 753] of the Code has two arms. Where an accused has been convicted of an indictable offence, the Court may, upon application, impose a sentence of preventive

detention in lieu of any other sentence that might be imposed for the offence for which he was convicted, if (a) the accused is found to be a habitual criminal and (b) the Court is of the opinion that because the accused is a habitual criminal, it is expedient for the protection of the public to sentence him to preventive detention. There can be no doubt the appellant satisfies the habitual criminal criteria (s. 688(2)(a)) in that he, since the age of 18 years, on at least three separate and independent occasions has been convicted of an indictable offence for which he was liable to imprisonment for five years or more and he is leading persistently a criminal life. That leaves, therefore, for determination only the question whether the Crown has established, beyond a reasonable doubt, that because the appellant is a habitual criminal it is expedient for the protection of the public to sentence him to preventive detention.

...

Is Hatchwell a menace to society or just a nuisance? Should he be confined to prison for the rest of his life, subject only to annual review of his case by the Parole Board and release from custody only in the absolute discretion of that Board? These are not easy matters of decision for one must balance the legitimate right of society to be protected from criminal depredations and the right of the man to freedom after serving the sentence imposed on him for the substantive offence which he committed. Habitual criminal legislation and preventive detention are primarily designed for the persistent dangerous criminal and not for those with a prolonged record of minor offences against property. The dominant purpose is to protect the public when the past conduct of the criminal demonstrates a propensity for crimes of violence against the person, and there is a real and present danger to life or limb. In those cases the way is clear and the word "menace" seems particularly apt and significant. That is not to say that crimes against property can never be cause for the invocation of preventive detention legislation, for the legislation contains no such exclusion and society is undoubtedly entitled to reasonable protection against crimes involving loss of or damage to property. It would seem to me, however, that when one is dealing with crime of this type, seeking to distinguish between that which is menace and that which is nuisance, there is greater opportunity and indeed necessity to assess carefully the true nature and gravity of the potential threat. For it is manifest that some crimes affecting property are very serious and others are not.

There are no crimes of violence in the record of the appellant. This is not conclusive but it is important. There is no evidence of association with known criminals during periods of freedom from custody. During these sometimes brief periods, the appellant has been gainfully employed. One former employer spoke in laudatory terms of his ability and attitude as a worker and expressed willingness to re-employ him at any time. The appellant is emotionally unstable and immature. The great majority of crimes committed by him appear to proceed from an uncontrolled aberration or fixation about cars. They are not motivated by gain nor by any destructive urge, for in every case, according to the evidence, the property taken was recovered undamaged. The appellant simply drives the stolen vehicles, until such time as he is apprehended. Of late he has shown a preference for large tractor-trailer units. This sort of irrational, senseless conduct is no doubt of annoyance to everyone, incommoding owners and vexing authorities, but it would seem to me that it partakes more of the quality of a nuisance than of a menace. Hatchwell is a bane rather than a danger to society.

...

I would allow the appeal, set aside the sentence of preventive detention and remit the case to the Court of Appeal to pass sentence in respect of the substantive offence, after receiving any submissions as to sentence by or on behalf of the appellant.

Major changes to the preventive detention legislation were soon to follow *Hatchwell*. In 1977, the *Criminal Code* was amended to create the current "dangerous offender" regime (SC 1976-77, c. 53, s. 14). A number, but not all, of the changes recommended in the Ouimet report were incorporated into this new legislation. The general structure of the current provisions (set out below) is rooted in these amendments. However, a few major changes, some procedural and others substantive, have since been made to this legislative scheme.

Approximately 20 years after the enactment of the dangerous offender provisions, Parliament was prompted recalibrate this part of the *Criminal Code* once again. This new interest in preventive detention was the result of a few highly publicized cases involving crimes of catastrophic violence. The most significant was the death of Christopher Stephenson, a 10-year-old boy who was killed by Joseph Fredericks, a sexual offender who had recently been released from prison on mandatory supervision. The inquest into this murder was wide-ranging and transcended the terrible facts of the case. The jury heard evidence that suggested that, had different decisions been taken into Fredericks's situation, both by the prosecutor at the outset of the prosecution and then by the Correctional Service of Canada when Fredericks's mandatory supervision date arrived, the tragedy might have been avoided. The jury also heard evidence that portrayed the existing dangerous offender provisions as being inadequate, unable to deal with "mistakes" at the front end of the system. The jury was presented with the evidence of a justice official from the state of Washington who extolled the virtues of a "sexual predator" statute that had been passed in that jurisdiction. This type of measure, being a hybrid of criminal and mental health legislative power, permits the state, during the currency of a determinate sentence, to apply to have an individual detained indefinitely after a determinate sentence expires. In its sweeping recommendations, the jury recommended that justice officials in Canada develop similar legislation and that a federal–provincial task force be struck to facilitate this recommendation. See Verdict of the Coroner's Jury into the Death of Christopher Stephenson, Brampton, Ontario (January 22, 1993). A few years later, another coroner's jury made similar recommendations, even though the case had nothing to do with the release of dangerous offenders from prison. The case involved a murder committed by a psychiatric patient on temporary leave from a psychiatric hospital. See Verdict of the Coroner's Jury into the Death of Dennis Kerr, Brockville, Ontario (April 12, 1994).

Shortly afterward, the federal government did create a federal–provincial–territorial task force on high-risk offenders (see Report of the Federal/Provincial/Territorial Task Force on High-Risk Violent Offenders, *Strategies for Managing High-Risk Offenders* (January 1995)). The most significant proposal to emerge was a recommendation that Parliament pass legislation that would allow for an offender to be designated a "long-term" offender, who could be supervised in the community for up to 10 years. The task force also made recommendations to change certain features of the existing dangerous offender provisions. Parliament followed the recommendation to create the new category of "long-term offender" (SC 1997, c. 17, ss. 4-8). In terms of the dangerous offender provisions, Parliament went much further than the task force recommendations and made a few highly significant changes to the process.

For more on the history and background of preventative detention in Canada, see Allan Manson, *The Law of Sentencing* (Toronto: Irwin Law, 2000), chapter 10, "Preventive Detention."

B. The Provisions

The provisions of part XXIV relating to dangerous offenders are set out below. In these provisions, there is occasional reference to "long-term offenders." The provisions respecting the latter are set out separately later in this chapter, although some of the provisions below apply to both types of offenders. It is fair to say that there is a significant degree of procedural integration between the two designations, especially in terms of the specified set of antecedent offences and the requirement of a psychiatric assessment.

C. Criminal Code, Sections 752, 753, 755, 756, 758, and 761

752. In this Part,

"court" means the court by which an offender in relation to whom an application under this Part is made was convicted, or a superior court of criminal jurisdiction;

"serious personal injury offence" means

(a) an indictable offence, other than high treason, treason, first degree murder or second degree murder, involving

(i) the use or attempted use of violence against another person, or

(ii) conduct endangering or likely to endanger the life or safety of another person or inflicting or likely to inflict severe psychological damage upon another person,

and for which the offender may be sentenced to imprisonment for ten years or more, or

(b) an offence or attempt to commit an offence mentioned in section 271 (sexual assault), 272 (sexual assault with a weapon, threats to a third party or causing bodily harm) or 273 (aggravated sexual assault).

752.1(1) Where an offender is convicted of a serious personal injury offence or an offence referred to in paragraph 753.1(2)(a) and, before sentence is imposed on the offender, on application by the prosecution, the court is of the opinion that there are reasonable grounds to believe that the offender might be found to be a dangerous offender under section 753 or a long-term offender under section 753.1, the court may, by order in writing, remand the offender, for a period not exceeding sixty days, to the custody of the person that the court directs and who can perform an assessment, or can have an assessment performed by experts. The assessment is to be used as evidence in an application under section 753 or 753.1.

(2) The person to whom the offender is remanded shall file a report of the assessment with the court not later than fifteen days after the end of the assessment period and make copies of it available to the prosecutor and counsel for the offender.

753(1) The court may, on application made under this Part following the filing of an assessment report under subsection 752.1(2), find the offender to be a dangerous offender if it is satisfied

(a) that the offence for which the offender has been convicted is a serious personal injury offence described in paragraph (a) of the definition of that expression in section

752 and the offender constitutes a threat to the life, safety or physical or mental well-being of other persons on the basis of evidence establishing

(i) a pattern of repetitive behaviour by the offender, of which the offence for which he has been convicted forms a part, showing a failure to restrain his behaviour and a likelihood of his causing death or injury to other persons, or inflicting severe psychological damage on other persons, through failure in the future to restrain his or her behaviour,

(ii) a pattern of persistent aggressive behaviour by the offender, of which the offence for which he or she has been convicted forms a part, showing a substantial degree of indifference on the part of the offender respecting the reasonably foresee-able consequences to other persons of his or her behaviour, or

(iii) any behaviour by the offender, associated with the offence for which he or she has been convicted, that is of such a brutal nature as to compel the conclusion that the offender's behaviour in the future is unlikely to be inhibited by normal standards of behavioural restraint; or

(b) that the offence for which the offender has been convicted is a serious personal injury offence described in paragraph (b) of the definition of that expression in section 752 and the offender, by his or her conduct in any sexual matter including that involved in the commission of the offence for which he or she has been convicted, has shown a failure to control his or her sexual impulses and a likelihood of his causing injury, pain or other evil to other persons through failure in the future to control his or her sexual impulses.

(2) An application under subsection (1) must be made before sentence is imposed on the offender unless

(a) before the imposition of sentence, the prosecution gives notice to the offender of a possible intention to make an application under section 752.1 and an application under subsection (1) not later than six months after that imposition; and

(b) at the time of the application under subsection (1) that is not later than six months after the imposition of sentence, it is shown that relevant evidence that was not reasonably available to the prosecution at the time of the imposition of sentence became available in the interim.

(3) Notwithstanding subsection 752.1(1), an application under that subsection may be made after the imposition of sentence or after an offender begins to serve the sentence in a case to which paragraphs (2)(a) and (b) apply.

(4) If the court finds an offender to be a dangerous offender, it shall impose a sentence of detention in a penitentiary for an indeterminate period.

(4.1) If the application was made after the offender begins to serve the sentence in a case to which paragraphs (2)(a) and (b) apply, the sentence of detention in a penitentiary for an indeterminate period referred to in subsection (4) replaces the sentence that was imposed for the offence for which the offender was convicted.

(5) If the court does not find an offender to be a dangerous offender,

(a) the court may treat the application as an application to find the offender to be a long-term offender, section 753.1 applies to the application and the court may either find that the offender is a long-term offender or hold another hearing for that purpose; or

(b) the court may impose sentence for the offence for which the offender has been convicted.

(6) Any evidence given during the hearing of an application made under subsection (1) by a victim of an offence for which the offender was convicted is deemed also to have been given during any hearing under paragraph (5)(a) held with respect to the offender.

• • •

754(1) Where an application under this Part has been made, the court shall hear and determine the application except that no such application shall be heard unless

   (a) the Attorney General of the province in which the offender was tried has, either before or after the making of the application, consented to the application;

   (b) at least seven days notice has been given to the offender by the prosecutor, following the making of the application, outlining the basis on which it is intended to found the application; and

   (c) a copy of the notice has been filed with the clerk of the court or the magistrate, as the case may be.

(2) An application under this Part shall be heard and determined by the court without a jury.

(3) For the purposes of an application under this Part, where an offender admits any allegations contained in the notice referred to in paragraph (1)(b), no proof of those allegations is required.

(4) The production of a document purporting to contain any nomination or consent that may be made or given by the Attorney General under this Part and purporting to be signed by the Attorney General is, in the absence of any evidence to the contrary, proof of that nomination or consent without proof of the signature or the official character of the person appearing to have signed the document.

• • •

757. Without prejudice to the right of the offender to tender evidence as to his or her character and repute, evidence of character and repute may, if the court thinks fit, be admitted on the question of whether the offender is or is not a dangerous offender or a long-term offender.

758(1) The offender shall be present at the hearing of the application under this Part and if at the time the application is to be heard

   (a) he is confined in a prison, the court may order, in writing, the person having the custody of the accused to bring him before the court; or

   (b) he is not confined in a prison, the court shall issue a summons or a warrant to compel the accused to attend before the court and the provisions of Part XVI relating to summons and warrant are applicable with such modifications as the circumstances require.

(2) Notwithstanding subsection (1), the court may

   (a) cause the offender to be removed and to be kept out of court, where he misconducts himself by interrupting the proceedings so that to continue the proceedings in his presence would not be feasible; or

   (b) permit the offender to be out of court during the whole or any part of the hearing on such conditions as the court considers proper.

• • •

761(1) Subject to subsection (2), where a person is in custody under sentence of detention in a penitentiary for an indeterminate period, the National Parole Board shall, forthwith after the expiration of seven years from the day on which that person was taken into custody and not later than every two years after the previous review, review the condition, history and circumstances of that person for the purpose of determining whether he or she should be granted parole under Part II of the *Corrections and Conditional Release Act* and, if so, on what conditions.

(2) Where a person is in custody under a sentence of detention in a penitentiary for an indeterminate period that was imposed before October 15, 1977, the National Parole Board shall, at least once in every year, review the condition, history and circumstance of that person for the purpose of determining whether he should be granted parole under Part II of the *Corrections and Conditional Release Act* and, if so, on what conditions.

D. Applying the Provisions

Prior to the 1997 amendments to part XXIV, numerous decisions addressed the content of these provisions. Indeed, in *R v. Lyons* (1987), 61 CR (3d) 1 (SCC), the Supreme Court of Canada rejected a constitutional challenge to the dangerous offender regime in part XXIV. While it might seem more natural to address questions of constitutionality first, we have decided to delay the discussion of *Lyons* until the next part. Seeing first how the courts have actually applied the dangerous offender provisions provides a context for evaluating how the Supreme Court resolved the constitutional claim.

As the cases below demonstrate, the courts have struggled in applying these criteria, which on their face are quite broad. Employing a correct interpretive approach is vital in this context because, while s. 754 of the Code says that a judge *may* declare someone to be a dangerous offender if the criteria are met, the Court of Appeal for Ontario in *R v. Moore* (1985), 44 CR (3d) 137 (Ont. CA) held that the judge *must* make a dangerous offender designation in these circumstances. While this interpretation is somewhat peculiar, it was made at a time when a second discretion was built into these provisions. Section 753 provided that, upon a declaration that an individual is a dangerous offender, the judge could impose an indeterminate sentence or sentence the offender in the normal manner. The 1997 amendments removed this second discretion, and s. 753(4) now *requires* that the individual be sentenced to an indeterminate period of incarceration once an individual has been declared a dangerous offender. With discretion removed at both vital junctures—at the point of applying the criteria and at the point of imposing sentence—it is crucial that the criteria be applied properly.

When considering the following cases, be careful to note what branch of s. 753(1) of the Code is being applied. The two branches, which correspond to the bifurcated definition of "serious personal injury offence" in s. 752, call for different tests. Section 753(1)(a) relates to convictions for violent indictable offences punishable by 10 years or more. The question is whether the offender "constitutes a threat to the life, safety or physical or mental well-being of other persons." This is based on the application of the criteria in paragraph (1)(a).

The second, alternative branch for declaring an individual to be a dangerous offender is found in s. 753(1)(b). This follows conviction for certain categories of sexual offences and requires the court to consider whether (1) the offender's conduct in any sexual matter shows a "failure to control his or her sexual impulses," and (2) there is a likelihood of "causing injury, pain or other evil to other persons through failure in the future to control his or her sexual impulses."

Apart from the separate tests, is there a significant difference in the level of danger-ousness reflected in the two branches of s. 753? Is a more coherent, integrated test called for? Perhaps more important, irrespective of what branch the prosecutor proceeds on, what level of risk must be proved before it is appropriate to designate the individual a dangerous offender? Consider this last issue in particular as you read the following cases.

R v. Langevin
(1984), 11 CCC (3d) 336 (Ont. CA)

LACOURCIÈRE JA: This appeal raises broad questions respecting the application of the dangerous offender provisions of Part XXI of the *Criminal Code* and their con-stitutional validity in the light of the fundamental rights now protected by the *Canadian Charter of Rights and Freedoms*.

On May 12, 1980, the appellant pleaded guilty to the offence of rape, contrary to s. 144 of the Code, before The Honourable Judge F.G. Carter in the County Court Judge's Criminal Court in the County of Huron. After the conviction, the Crown filed an application to have the appellant declared a dangerous offender pursuant to s. 688 of the Code. Following remands for the nomination of a psychiatrist by the appellant and for psychiatric observation, Judge Carter heard the application on September 10, 1980. He found the appellant to be a dangerous offender and, following a remand, sentenced him to an indeterminate period of detention, in lieu of any other sentence that might be imposed for the offence of rape.

...

Pattern of Repetitive Behaviour: S. 688(a)(i)

Mr. Gold submitted that, with respect to s. 688(a)(i), the learned trial judge erred in concluding that there existed a "pattern of repetitive behaviour," there being an insuf-ficient number of repeated offences by the appellant as displayed in the reported cases under that paragraph.

In my opinion, this element is not based solely on the number of offences but also on the elements of similarity of the offender's behaviour. The offences committed were remarkably similar. Two young girls were grabbed from behind by the appel-lant, a stranger, and both were taken to a secluded place and ordered to undress. Both were forced into anal as well as vaginal intercourse. The younger girl was forced to fellate the appellant. Both were threatened to assure their co-operation and were released only after assurances not to tell anyone were extracted from them. In the circumstances, these two offences were properly found to establish a pattern of repet-itive behaviour.

As to the failure of the appellant to restrain his behaviour, the learned trial judge concluded as follows:

Having considered the offender's past behaviour, having heard and analyzed the evi-dence of the expert witnesses, and the other evidence adduced, I am compelled to con-clude that the Crown has established to my satisfaction that there is a likelihood of the offender "causing death or injury to other persons or inflicting severe psychological damage upon other persons, through failure in the future to restrain his behaviour," as required by s. 688(a)(i). Whether such failure to refrain his behaviour stems from an inability to maintain control, or a refusal to maintain control, and whether such loss of control is triggered by aggressiveness or sexual impulse, and whether with or without the aid of alcohol it leads, in considering s. 688(a)(i), to the same result.

I fully agree with this conclusion and with the able and comprehensive analysis of the evidence which supports the finding that the appellant showed a failure to restrain his behaviour as well as the likelihood—not the certainty or probability (see *R v. Carleton* (1981), 69 CCC (2d) 1 at p. 6, 23 CR (3d) 129 at p. 135, [1981] 6 WWR 148; affirmed 6 CCC (3d) 480*n*, 36 CR (3d) 393*n*, [1984] 2 WWR 384*n*)—of causing death, injury or severe psychological damage through failure in the future to restrain his behaviour. In this case there was a strong basis, on the facts and the expert opinions in respect of them, on which the finder of fact could be satisfied beyond a reasonable doubt of the existing likelihood of future conduct.

Although the finding that the appellant is a dangerous offender can be supported on s. 688(a)(i) alone, it is necessary to deal briefly with the other arguments to the effect that the Crown has failed to prove the elements of dangerousness set out in s. 688(a)(iii) and s. 688(b), respectively.

Behaviour of a "Brutal Nature": S. 688(a)(iii)

Mr. Gold submitted that the learned trial judge erred in concluding the Guelph rape satisfied the requirement of behaviour of a "brutal nature" as required by subpara. (iii). The submission is, basically, that any rape by definition contains severe physical and psychological abuse, but that the "brutal nature" requirement of subpara. (iii) requires a greater element of savagery evidenced by sadism, torture or mutilation. The learned trial judge concluded that the appellant's conduct towards the 12-year old victim was "coarse, savage and cruel" and, accordingly, so "brutal" as to compel the conclusion that the appellant's behaviour in the future was "unlikely to be inhibited by normal standards of behavioural restraint" in the words of the subparagraph. This conclusion was supported by the expert evidence. I am satisfied that the brutal nature of the conduct which must be established before the requirements of the subparagraph are satisfied does not necessarily demand a situation of "stark horror" as exemplified by *R v. Hill* (1974), 15 CCC (2d) 145, and *R v. Pontello* (1977), 38 CCC (2d) 262.

Conduct which is coarse, savage and cruel and which is capable of inflicting severe psychological damage on the victim is sufficiently "brutal" to meet the test.

Failure To Control Sexual Impulses: S. 688(b)

With respect to s. 688(b), it was submitted that there was insufficient evidence of the appellant's failure to control his sexual impulses in the rape of the [D.] girl or in the rape of the [G.] girl and that the appellant's problem, as characterized by Dr. Hill, was related to aggressiveness but not necessarily of a sexual nature. From the nature of the offences and on the evidence of Dr. Fleming and Dr. Arnold, the Crown properly established the likelihood of the appellant causing future injury, pain or other evil through failure in the future to control his sexual impulses. For these reasons, I would not interfere with the finding that the appellant is a dangerous offender.

Whether Sentence Is Appropriate

The remaining question, on the merits, is whether detention for an indeterminate period was an appropriate sentence. The learned trial judge considered the alternatives open to him and, after reviewing *R v. Hill*, supra, and other case-law, concluded that the only reasonable sentence, to protect the public, would be life imprisonment, if it were not for the admonition of this Court, speaking through MacKinnon ACJO, who said in *R v. Keefe* (1978), 44 CCC (2d) 193 at p. 199:

> In determining whether to impose what amounted to an indefinite sentence it was appropriate for the Court to consider the psychiatric evidence with respect to the likelihood of the commission of further offences involving violence. However, this Court has emphasized that the imposition of a life sentence is not to be used as an alternative to invoking the provisions of the Code dealing with preventive detention with all the attendant safeguards: *R v. Pontello*, supra, and *R v. Hutton* (1978), 39 CCC (2d) 281.

Accordingly, the learned trial judge was satisfied that the imposition of an indeterminate sentence would better protect the public as well as the offender, through the advantages of periodic review provided by s. 695.1 of the Code. Without expressing any opinion on the alternative of a sentence of life imprisonment contemplated by the sentencing judge, I am satisfied that the imposition of a sentence of detention for an indeterminate period was a fit sentence.

Apart from *R v. Lyons*, dealt with in the next section, the Supreme Court of Canada has said relatively little about the dangerous offender provisions. The following case of *R v. Currie* is one of the few times that the court has offered its views on the proper interpretive approach to part XXIV of the Code. The case concerns the second branch of the test in s. 753(1), which focuses on sexual offences. Currie had a long history of committing sexual offences. In terms of their seriousness, the antecedent offences for the more recent dangerous offender application were far less serious than the past offences. The Court of Appeal for Ontario quashed the trial judge's dangerous offender declaration on the basis that the trial judge should have considered the relative seriousness of the antecedent offences. The Supreme Court of Canada disagreed with this approach and restored the trial judge's decision.

R v. Currie
(1997), 115 CCC (3d) 205 (SCC)

LAMER CJ: This appeal is concerned with the propriety of a dangerous offender designation and the corresponding indeterminate sentence that was imposed by the trial judge after the respondent, Robert Currie, was convicted of sexually assaulting three young girls. At the conclusion of the hearing of this appeal, this Court held, without providing reasons at that time, that neither the designation nor the sentence should be overturned. Our reasons now follow.

I. Facts and Procedural Background

The respondent, Robert Currie, was charged with three counts of sexual assault, for a series of related incidents in which he sexually touched a number of young girls on November 5, 1988 in a Towers department store in Barrie, Ontario. During the first incident, the respondent approached a group of four girls in the Towers toy section, felt and squeezed the buttocks of three of them, and left the area. During the second, more invasive incident, the respondent followed a group of three sisters near the store's tobacco department. At first, he placed his hand on the eldest girl's breast. Immediately thereafter, he approached the girls from behind and, as the trial judge described, "swept his hand between the legs of two of them in an attempt to touch their genitals." The frightened girls notified store employees and security personnel who eventually apprehended the respondent outside the store and awaited the arrival of the police.

The respondent was convicted of all charges on April 12, 1989 before Tobias J. Prior to sentencing, the Attorney General for Ontario initiated dangerous offender proceedings pursuant to s. 753(b) of the *Criminal Code*, RSC, 1985, c. C-46. Section 753(b) essentially provides that the Crown may apply to have an offender declared a "dangerous offender" and sentenced to an indefinite term of imprisonment if: (a) he has been convicted of a "serious personal injury offence"; and (b) his failure to control his sexual impulses reveals "a likelihood of his causing injury, pain or other evil to other persons" in the future. A "serious personal injury offence" is defined in s. 752 of the *Criminal Code* to include all forms of sexual assault.

These sexual assaults were not isolated incidents. Part of the rationale for seeking to have the respondent declared a dangerous offender was his lengthy history of sexual offences that occurred in the Ottawa, Toronto and Hamilton regions between 1975-1988. As outlined in disturbing detail in the judgments below and in the pleadings filed before this Court, the respondent had been previously convicted of numerous sexual offences, some of which were extremely violent and highly degrading to the victims.

Robert Currie's criminal sexual activity began in and around Ottawa between September and November 1975. In separate incidents, the respondent stalked and sexually attacked four women. All four of the incidents were serious and frightening for the victims, but two were comparatively more severe. On September 30, 1975, the respondent followed a teenage girl into a field. He caught her, undressed her and forced her to perform fellatio and engage in repeated acts of sexual intercourse. When she resisted he pulled her hair and struck her in the face. On November 29, 1975, later on the same night that he had indecently assaulted another victim, the respondent stalked a young woman in Nepean. After approaching her from behind and striking her to the ground, he forced her into the deep snow of a deserted field. He then undressed his victim completely, repeatedly struck her in the face, forced her to perform fellatio, and forced her to submit to multiple acts of anal and vaginal intercourse. He had a hunting knife in his possession during the rape with which he threatened the victim after the attack. She was bleeding heavily when he abandoned her naked in the snow.

As a result of these attacks, on May 20, 1976, the respondent was convicted of indecent assault, rape, and possession of a weapon and sentenced to five years' imprisonment. Since that time, whenever he was at large, his sexually impulsive criminal behaviour continued. In 1979, while on parole in Toronto, the respondent stalked and attacked a woman. When she screamed in response to his attempt to touch her genitals, he jammed his fingers into her mouth, pushed her to the ground and kicked her. He fled the scene, but was immediately apprehended by police and subsequently convicted of indecent assault. In Hamilton in 1981 and 1982, while under intensive police surveillance, the respondent was observed following and stalking a number of women through the city streets. In one case, the girl sensed she was being followed and sought shelter on the porch of a nearby home. In another case, the respondent indecently assaulted a woman he had been following by putting his hand under her clothing between her legs in an effort to touch her genitals. When arrested by police for the latter incident, the respondent stated:

> It was me I did it. I couldn't help myself. I asked for help before but they released me. I needed help but they let me go. I was going to play hockey and I picked this girl up hitchhiking. She was wearing a bathing suit. I got all turned on. It was like she was asking for it. Not this one but the other one. How do you guys do it? I mean when you see these girls wearing bathing suits all day. I need help. I am always stalking women, little kids, and people. I can't stop. ... I can't help myself. ... I'm always thinking about women. ... I didn't mean to harm anybody. I guess I figure it's just a few seconds of being frightened and it's all over and nobody is hurt.

A. Psychiatric Evidence

To substantiate its dangerous offender application, the Crown elicited the testimony of a psychiatrist, Dr. Angus McDonald, who participated in a two-month team assessment of the respondent after the commission of the recent Towers department store sexual assaults—the so-called "predicate offences." Dr. McDonald evaluated the respondent as an obsessed and extremely temperamental "sexual deviate" who had a "biological anomaly in the wiring of his brain." As such he was "a very dangerous person to society." In making these findings, Dr. McDonald was influenced by the admission the respondent made to a psychometrist at the Penetanguishene Mental Health Centre in 1989, in which he stated:

> [The] stuff I was doing in '79, I got rid of that. I don't bruise them now but don't get me wrong. They had better give me sex if I want it because I often have a knife and I always have my hands.

By way of conclusion, Dr. McDonald gave the prognosis that the respondent "was not open to treatment any longer and posed a risk to women and female children."

The defence-appointed psychiatrist, Dr. Basil Orchard, acknowledged that the respondent suffered from an impulsive personality disorder and "a polymorphous sexual deviation" that includes "voyeurism, heterosexual pedophilia and hebephilia and impulsive sexual aggressiveness." Given this diagnosis, he admitted that there was a likelihood that the respondent would re-offend. Dr. Orchard did conclude, however, that the respondent was neither schizophrenic nor psychotic and that he had shown change toward less violent behaviour. He prognosticated that if there were future recurrences of the respondent's criminal behaviour, his conduct would tend toward "nuisance-type offences" rather than offences of a violent nature. In sum, he did not "find him particularly dangerous at the present time."

...

II. Issues

The fundamental disagreement in the judgments below on the suitability of designating Robert Currie a dangerous offender and imposing an indeterminate sentence raises, in my opinion, the following three issues on appeal to this Court:

(1) Must a trial judge, when evaluating a dangerous offender application under s. 753(b) of the *Criminal Code*, focus on the seriousness of the specific predicate offences that have led to the Crown's dangerous offender application?
(2) Were the dangerous offender designation and the corresponding indeterminate sentence reasonably supported by the evidence?
(3) Were the dangerous offender designation and the corresponding indeterminate sentence premised on any errors of law?

Given our holding at the conclusion of the hearing, it should come as no surprise that the Court resolves each of these issues in favour of the appellant. A thorough explanation is nonetheless warranted and should provide needed guidance for future dangerous offender application hearings.

III. Analysis

It is the stated opinion of this Court that Robert Currie was properly designated a dangerous offender and correctly sentenced to an indeterminate period of incarceration. That opinion is grounded in two basic legal propositions both of which I develop and apply below. Those propositions are: first, given the nature and structure of s. 753(b) of the *Criminal Code*, a presiding trial judge need not focus on the objective seriousness of a predicate offence in order to conclude that a dangerous offender designation is warranted. Second, a finding of dangerousness by a trial judge is a finding of fact, frequently based upon the competing credibility of experts, and as long as it is reasonable, it is a finding which should not be lightly overturned.

A. Must a Trial Judge Focus on the Seriousness of the Predicate Offences?

The Court of Appeal quashed the trial judge's designation of Robert Currie as a dangerous offender principally because it found the trial judge erred by failing to focus on the seriousness of the predicate offences. The respondent has relied upon that finding and insists that, when evaluating the likelihood of danger that an offender presents, the sentencing judge must consider the relative gravity of the predicate offences. Unless there is "some rational relationship between the predicate offences and the sentences," the respondent contends that the offender is being sentenced for his past criminality.

It is true that, when viewed in isolation, the predicate offences appear less serious than much of the respondent's past conduct. Indeed the appellant has admitted that "[t]he predicate offences in this case are properly characterized as offences of a less serious nature than the offender's earlier offences, and thankfully do not approach the gravity of the very violent earlier offences." However, that observation does not necessarily translate into a conclusion that the designation of Robert Currie as a dangerous offender was misplaced. Rather, once an individual has committed an offence specifically defined in the *Criminal Code* as a "serious personal injury offence," he or she has made it possible for the Crown to invoke the *Criminal Code*'s dangerous offender application process. If that process is invoked, it is incumbent upon the trial judge to evaluate the offender's potential danger to the public and this may or may not depend upon the specific nature and objective gravity of the predicate offence.

Section 753(b) of the *Criminal Code* makes this point abundantly clear. ... In short, there are two thresholds that the Crown must surpass in order for the dangerous offender application to be successful. The Crown must first establish that the offender has been convicted of a "serious personal injury offence." Then the focus of the inquiry shifts. The question then becomes whether there is a "likelihood" that the offender will cause "injury, pain or other evil to other persons through [his] failure in the future to control his sexual impulses."

There is no question in this appeal that the predicate sexual assaults committed by the respondent against the young girls in the Towers department store constituted "serious personal injury offences." Section 752(b) of the *Criminal Code* defines "serious personal injury offence" to include "an offence or attempt to commit an offence mentioned in section 271 (sexual assault)." However, the parties fundamentally disagree over the manner in which the trial judge applied the second standard. The respondent alleges that the trial judge erred because he did not take proper notice of the relative gravity of the predicate offences. He submits that an indeterminate sentence is disproportionate to the seriousness of sexual touching.

My problem with this argument is twofold. First, the language of s. 753(b) explicitly states that there is no requirement to focus on the specific nature of the predicate offence. Section 753(b) provides that the prospective dangerousness of the offender is measured by reference to "his conduct in any sexual matter including that involved in the commission of the offence for which he has been convicted" (emphasis added). "[A]ny sexual matter" can refer to the predicate offence, but it need not. As long as the offender's past conduct, whatever conduct that might be, demonstrates a present likelihood of inflicting future harm upon others, the designation is justified. Second, the respondent's position is inconsistent with the nature and structure of the dangerous offender statutory scheme created by Parliament. As I indicated above, a crucial element of s. 753(b) is the notion of the "serious personal injury offence." Parliament has said that there are certain types of offences, which are inherently serious, that can trigger a dangerous offender application. As this Court observed in *R v. McCraw*, [1991] 3 SCR 72, at p. 83, sexual assault, whatever form it may take, is one of them. Other offences, presumably less threatening to the personal safety of others, do not trigger s. 753.

As such, I would find it contradictory, as well as callous, to categorize the impugned predicate assaults as "nuisance-type offences." These sexual assaults, while not as violent or grave as some of the respondent's earlier offences, were nevertheless within the category of violent and grave. The predicate offences involved repeated sexual touching of young girls in public and at least two of the victims of the assaults have experienced serious psychological trauma and other side effects. If these sexual assaults were not serious, sexual assault would not be enumerated as a s. 752 offence. Nor would Parliament have ever seen fit to eliminate the distinction between rape and indecent assault—indeed it would have ensured that such a distinction endured.

By definition, therefore, arguments of proportionality do not withstand scrutiny. There may be, as the respondent asserts, an objective difference between the nighttime rape at knife point and the predicate offences, but this distinction is not reflected in s. 752 or 753 of the *Criminal Code*. Indeed the respondent is asking the Court to alter or even reduce the definition of "serious personal injury offence." This alteration would, as the appellant notes, effectively guarantee that an accused who has committed an arguably less serious sexual predicate offence would never be declared a dangerous offender. I cannot imagine that Parliament wanted the courts to wait for an obviously dangerous individual, regardless of the nature of his criminal record and notwithstanding the force of expert opinion as to his potential dangerousness, to commit a particularly violent and grievous offence before he or she can be declared a dangerous offender.

Does it defy reality, as the respondent submits, to treat all "serious personal injury offences" the same in applying s. 753(b)? In my opinion, it does not. This might be problematic if s. 753(b) were a one-stage test. Section 753(b) might not make sense if, for example, it were to provide, without qualification, that a trial judge may designate any person who commits a "serious personal injury offence" as a dangerous offender. But, it is crucial to recognize that the conviction for a "serious personal injury offence" merely triggers the s. 753(b) application process. There remains a second stage to s. 753(b), at which point the trial judge must be satisfied beyond a reasonable doubt of the likelihood of future danger that an offender presents to society before he or she can impose the dangerous offender designation and an indeterminate sentence.

Parliament has thus created a standard of preventive detention that measures an accused's present condition according to past behaviour and patterns of conduct. Under this statutory arrangement, dangerous offenders who have committed "serious personal injury offences" can be properly sentenced without having to wait for them to strike out in a particularly egregious way. For example, suppose a known sexual deviate has been convicted of repeated offences for stalking and sexually assaulting young girls in playgrounds. He operates by offering them candy, touching their private parts, and if the children seem to comply or submit to his criminal advances, by taking them away where he violently sexually assaults them. Now suppose that individual is at large in society and caught by a parent at a playground after having offered a child candy and improperly touching her. In this example, like the present case, the predicate offence is objectively less serious than a violent and invasive rape, but the trial judge need not justify the dangerous offender designation and an indeterminate sentence as a just desert for the isolated act of sexual touching. On the theory of s. 753(b), the offender has committed an inherently "serious personal injury offence." On a dangerous offender application, a trial judge is then entitled to consider his "conduct in any sexual matter" to determine if he presents a future danger to society. Otherwise, we would be saying that an offender's present condition is defined by the precise degree of seriousness of the predicate offences. That is equivalent to assuming that a dangerous individual will always act out, or be caught for that matter, at the upper limits of his dangerous capabilities.

Contrary to the respondent's submission, this holding is entirely consistent with *R v. Lyons*, [1987] 2 SCR 309. In *Lyons*, the accused was convicted of break and enter, unlawful use of a weapon in a sexual assault, unlawful use of a firearm in an indictable offence, and theft. He was subsequently designated a dangerous offender by the trial judge and sentenced to indeterminate detention. The question that arose on appeal to this Court was whether the dangerous offender provisions of the *Criminal Code* were consistent with the *Canadian Charter of Rights and Freedoms*. The Court upheld the constitutionality of the provisions, principally on the basis that a dangerous offender is not being sentenced for past or even future criminality. As La Forest J indicated at p. 328:

> The individual is clearly being sentenced for the "serious personal injury offence" he or she has been found guilty of committing, albeit in a different way than would ordinarily be done. It must be remembered that the appellant was not picked up off the street because of his past criminality (for which he has already been punished), or because of fears or suspicions about his criminal proclivities, and then subjected to a procedure in order to determine whether society would be better off if he were incarcerated indefinitely. Rather he was arrested and prosecuted for a very serious violent crime and subjected to a procedure aimed at determining the appropriate penalty that should be inflicted upon him in the circumstances.

In my opinion, despite the reference to a "very serious violent crime," *Lyons* does not require that all predicate offences fit that description. As La Forest J indicated at the hearing of this case, when he asserted that Thomas Lyons was arrested and prosecuted for a "very serious violent crime" he was merely referring to the particular facts in *Lyons*. He was not, I would add, stating that predicate offences need to be especially serious and violent to justify a dangerous offender designation. In fact, while specifically aimed at providing the constitutional justification for s. 753 (then s. 688), the above passage from *Lyons* serves to underline the very point of this case— that "serious personal injury offences" are inherently serious and there is thus no need to think that the offender is being punished for his "past criminality." As in *Lyons*, there is nothing in this case that suggests the respondent has been "picked up off the street." Nor is there any more reason here than there was in *Lyons* to suggest that he is being punished for anything other than the predicate offences.

There is, however, another subtle wrinkle to this issue, and I would be remiss if I did not address it. Although the respondent relies upon the judgment of the Ontario Court of Appeal, he has argued that it would be a mistake to conflate their respective positions. On the one hand, the Court of Appeal quashed the dangerous offender designation largely because it found that the trial judge "failed to consider the gravity of the predicate offences in isolation from his previous offences" (p. 451). On the other hand, the respondent submits that the trial judge made the related but opposite error—that he ignored the predicate offences.

This argument is conceptually different, but I find it no more persuasive. For one, the language of s. 753(b) of the *Criminal Code* would seem to suggest that once the offender has been found guilty of a "serious personal injury offence," the trial judge can ignore the nature of the predicate offence. Notwithstanding the unlikelihood of such a scenario, as long as some conduct of the accused "in any sexual matter" demonstrates a likelihood that his sexual urges will cause future "injury, pain or other evil," there is no conceptual need to pay any attention to the predicate offence. Second, and more importantly, there is every indication that the trial judge did not ignore the nature of the predicate offences. In fact, on this very subject he endorsed Dr. McDonald's conclusion that "[a]lthough the predicate offences may appear less serious from an assaultive aspect, they are more blatant, indicating a lessening of control on the part of the respondent." He later concluded that "the violence and the brutality of the respondent's early sexual assaults ... continue to be evidenced in the pattern of his subsequent sexual assaults, including that conduct which resulted in his conviction upon the predicate offences."

As much as our system of criminal justice seeks to sentence the offence, imposing a proper sentence is very much a function of the dual nature of the specific crime and the unique attributes of the offender. Insofar as this duality is concerned, the effectiveness of s. 753(b) should not go unnoticed. The "serious personal injury offence" requirement acts as a gatekeeper to ensure that the sentence is not disproportionate to the offence. At the same time, the manner in which s. 753(b) allows a trial judge to evaluate an offender's present condition ensures that the uniquely dangerous attributes of each offender and his or her patterns of conduct are given due consideration, whatever form they might take.

B. Were the Dangerous Offender Designation and the Corresponding Indeterminate Sentence Reasonably Supported by the Evidence?

On the basis of the language of s. 753(b) of the *Criminal Code* and the principles I have articulated above, I am satisfied that there was enough evidence before Tobias J for him to find that the respondent was a dangerous offender. The respondent's pattern of criminal sexual behaviour and the psychiatric evidence of the Crown-nominated psychiatrist are certainly sufficient proof, if accepted by a trier of fact, to justify such a conclusion.

In this respect, the role of an appellate court is to determine if the dangerous offender designation was reasonable. This standard of reasonableness is similar to the traditional standard employed by appellate courts in their review of verdicts under

s. 686(1)(a)(i) of the *Criminal Code*. Reasonableness is the appropriate standard of review in this case because, as much as dangerous offender status is a part of the post-conviction process, the application of general standards of sentence review is not warranted given the broad language of s. 759. Section 759(1) provides:

> 759(1) A person who is sentenced to detention in a penitentiary for an indeterminate period under this Part may appeal to the court of appeal against that sentence on any ground of law or fact or mixed law and fact.

Given this provision, I do not find the "manifestly wrong" or "demonstrably unfit" general sentencing standards developed and applied in cases such as *R v. Shropshire*, [1995] 4 SCR 227, *R v. M.(C.A.)*, [1996] 1 SCR 500, or *R v. McDonnell*, [1997] 1 SCR 948, to be applicable to this situation. However, it is equally true that s. 759 cannot be interpreted as calling for the equivalent of a trial de novo on the dangerous offender application. Some deference to the findings of a trial judge is warranted. After all, credibility should be assessed and findings of fact should be made by the trier of fact. The trier of fact is present when the testimony is being given and has the contemporaneous ability to assess each witness.

I should also point out that I am sympathetic to the submission of the respondent and the conclusion of the Ontario Court of Appeal below that, given their s. 759 jurisdiction to review the propriety of an indeterminate sentence, appellate courts are necessarily entitled to consider whether the finding of dangerousness itself was justified. In other words, as much as *R v. Langevin* (1984), 11 CCC (3d) 336 (Ont. CA), and *R v. Sullivan* (1987), 37 CCC (3d) 143 (Ont. CA), correctly held that s. 759 does not give appellate courts an explicit jurisdiction to overturn a dangerous offender designation, the facts upon which a dangerousness finding are based are necessarily relevant to determining whether an indeterminate sentence should be quashed. Hence the finding of dangerousness is properly before an appellate court.

Accordingly, absent an error of law (which I discuss below), the crucial question on appeal is whether the trial judge's findings were reasonable. I can only conclude that they were. For one, there was consensus at the application hearing that Robert Currie is a pedophile and hebephile with a long history of sexual offences, some of which were extremely violent. The Crown-nominated psychiatrist, Dr. McDonald, diagnosed the respondent as an obsessed and temperamental hypersexual individual who was extremely dangerous to women and female children. In Dr. McDonald's view, the respondent inherited a biological anomaly in the wiring of his brain which makes his deviate sexual impulses uncontrollable. While Dr. McDonald accepted that the respondent's predicate assaults were not as serious as some of the assaults he had committed in the past, he found that they were "ominous" and more blatant because they were committed in a very public place. This suggested, in his opinion, a lessening of the respondent's ability to control his deviate impulses and he expected the respondent's offences to increase in severity in the long term.

This evidence alone was sufficient to justify the dangerous offender designation, and I do not accept the respondent's objection that it was a product of over-generalization. Experts necessarily bring past experiences to bear on their opinions and, as the appellant submits, Dr. McDonald's opinion was based on an extensive assessment of the respondent. As a result, the trial judge was perfectly entitled to believe Dr. McDonald's diagnosis, and conclude from the respondent's lengthy criminal history that the commission of the predicate offences was part of a pattern of sexual deviation. See *Sullivan*, supra. However, the trial judge also had the benefit of the testimony of the defence-nominated psychiatrist. Although Dr. Orchard concluded that the predicate offences exhibited a declining danger, he did acknowledge the profound nature of the respondent's sexual problems and also recognized that there was a likelihood that the respondent would re-offend. In fact, Dr. Orchard himself indicated that the respondent exhibited "a lot of tendencies towards violence or dangerous behaviour."

Furthermore, the Crown adduced evidence, which I believe was properly put before the trial judge, of comments the respondent made to a psychometrist in 1989. Robert Currie stated at that time:

> [The] stuff I was doing in '79, I got rid of that. I don't bruise them now but don't get me wrong. They had better give me sex if I want it because I often have a knife and I always have my hands.

This evidence, the reliability and strength of which the trial judge was able to evaluate, and which he was not required to discuss in his reasons to avoid error (*R v. Burns*, [1994] 1 SCR 656, at pp. 662-65, and *R v. Barrett*, [1995] 1 SCR 752, at pp. 752-53), further supports the conclusion that the respondent is dangerous. In fact it is a chilling reminder, from the mouth of the offender himself, of his sexually impulsive and volatile nature.

In my opinion, therefore, it was entirely open to the trial judge to prefer the evidence of Dr. McDonald to that of Dr. Orchard. It was not, however, similarly open to the Court of Appeal to re-evaluate the psychiatric evidence and overturn the dangerous offender designation because of a mere difference of opinion. I cannot overemphasize the point that no appellate court should lightly disturb a finding of dangerousness which is so heavily dependent upon the relative credibility of expert witnesses. In saying this, I have not forgotten the broad language of s. 759. However, having observed both experts and evaluated their reports, Tobias J simply found the opinion of Dr. McDonald to be more credible. It was a reasonable conclusion amply supported by the evidence. It should not have been disturbed by the Court of Appeal.

The reason for this finding is simple. To an outside observer, the predicate assaults can be interpreted in any number of ways. They might, as the Court of Appeal and respondent believe, carry information that suggests that the respondent's condition was improving. By contrast, because they occurred in broad daylight in a crowded public place, they might indicate that the respondent's condition had become more blatant and reflected a lessening of self-control. Further still, the predicate assaults might even be interpreted as part of a pattern that the respondent displayed in his earlier offences. As I noted at the outset of these reasons, on November 29, 1975, on the very day the respondent committed an extremely violent and degrading rape, he had also committed a less violent and less intrusive indecent assault on another victim sometime earlier. It is therefore possible that, even though the predicate offences were less violent than past offences, Robert Currie might have committed more violent and aggressive sexual assaults that very day, had he not been reported by his young victims.

The point is, s. 753(b) entrusts trial judges with evaluating these sorts of patterns, and in this case, the trial judge concluded, in a perfectly reasonable fashion, that the predicate offences exemplified a lessening of self-control. It is plausible to interpret the respondent's pattern of conduct differently, but the *Criminal Code* does not invite either this Court or the Court of Appeal to do so. Unless the trial judge's findings were unreasonable, and absent an error of law, the designation made by the trial judge should stand.

C. Did the Trial Judge Commit an Error of Law?

The respondent alleged, and the Court of Appeal agreed, that the trial judge's conclusions were based upon at least two errors of law. First, Finlayson JA stated that the trial judge misconstrued the burden of proof in dangerous offender proceedings. Second, the Court of Appeal intimated that the trial judge abdicated his sentencing responsibility to the National Parole Board. With respect, I find both of these conclusions unsatisfactory.

(1) Erroneous Burden of Proof

As I stated above, the Court of Appeal's conclusion that the trial judge misconstrued the burden of proof is based upon the following passage in the trial judge's reasons:

> I have not been unmoved by the submissions of counsel for the respondent that the character of his behaviour has changed markedly over a period of 15 years from violent to harmless, with the result that the respondent cannot now be described as dangerous. Nonetheless, these submissions have failed to persuade me that the violence and the brutality of the respondent's early sexual assaults do not continue to be evidenced in the pattern of his subsequent sexual assaults, including that conduct which resulted in his conviction upon the predicate offences.

I cannot accept that this passage reflects an erroneous reversal of the burden of proof. In my opinion, when the passage is read in its entire context, it is obvious that when Tobias J said that the respondent's submission "failed to persuade me" he was really indicating that the respondent's submissions had failed to disturb his findings as regards the respondent's dangerousness. In my opinion, this is clearly confirmed by the passage that immediately followed his impugned comment:

> I am satisfied, therefore, beyond a reasonable doubt, upon a consideration of all of the evidence adduced upon this application, that the predicate offences for which the respondent has been convicted are serious personal injury offences as described in paragraph (b) of the definition of that expression in section 752 of the *Criminal Code*, and that the respondent by his conduct since the year 1975 in those sexual matters herein described, including the predicate offences, has shown a failure to control his sexual impulses, and that there is an existing likelihood of the respondent causing injury, pain or other evil to other persons through failure in the future to control his sexual impulses.
>
> In the result, I declare the respondent a dangerous offender.

The Court cannot forget that s. 753(b) does not require proof beyond a reasonable doubt that the respondent will re-offend. Such a standard would be impossible to meet. Instead, s. 753(b) requires that the court be satisfied beyond a reasonable doubt that there is a "likelihood" that the respondent will inflict harm, and the trial judge took explicit notice of this, citing *R v. Knight* (1975), 27 CCC (2d) 343 (Ont. HC); *R v. Dwyer* (1977), 34 CCC (2d) 293 (Alta. CA); *R v. Carleton* (1981), 69 CCC (2d) 1 (Alta. CA) (aff'd [1983] 2 SCR 58). See also *Langevin*, supra. I am thus unwilling to conclude, on the basis of a few misplaced words, that the trial judge either misunderstood or misapplied the burden of proof on this dangerous offender application.

(2) Abdication of Responsibility

The respondent also contends that in his reasons on sentence, the trial judge effectively surrendered his sentencing responsibilities by deferring to the judgment of the National Parole Board under s. 761(1) of the *Criminal Code*. ... While it is important to recognize that an indeterminate sentence does not automatically follow a dangerous offender designation, I do not interpret Tobias J's reference to the National Parole Board's intermittent power of review as an abdication of responsibility. Instead, I view it as a judicial reminder that, although it may be indeterminate, Robert Currie's sentence need not be permanent.

IV. Conclusion

As the Court indicated at the hearing, the trial judge properly designated the respondent, Robert Currie, a dangerous offender. He was not required to focus on the objective seriousness of the predicate offences and accordingly his decision was wholly reasonable and supported by the evidence. Moreover, absent an error of law, of which there was none, the dangerous offender determination is a finding of fact that is almost always based upon the competing credibility of expert witnesses. As such, it is a decision which should not be lightly disturbed.

For all of these reasons, the appeal is allowed and the Court of Appeal's sentence of time served is set aside. The decision of the trial judge to designate the respondent a dangerous offender and the corresponding decision to impose an indeterminate sentence are restored.

Finally, consider the following excerpt from *R v. Neve*. Lisa Neve was the second woman in Canadian history to be designated a dangerous offender. The prosecutor applied to have her declared a dangerous offender following a conviction for robbery. Consequently, the first branch of s. 753(1) of the Code was engaged. The trial judge found Neve to be a dangerous offender and sentenced her to an indeterminate period of detention. The Court of Appeal for Alberta dismissed Neve's appeal against conviction, but concluded that her designation as a dangerous offender could not stand. The excerpts from the reasons in the Court of Appeal highlight some important contextual considerations relating to the operation of the dangerous offender provisions as a whole. They also address the issue of risk of harm from both qualitative and quantitative perspectives.

R v. Neve
(1999), 137 CCC (3d) 97 (Alta. CA)

FRASER CJA:

...

We identify a number of errors in the course of our analysis of these issues. Without in any way minimizing the complexity of these issues or their cumulative effect, Neve's appeal from her designation as a dangerous offender can be summarized this simply. According to Crown records, since 1947 (the year in which predecessor dangerous offender legislation first came into effect in Canada) until July 31, 1997, 219 offenders were designated dangerous offenders in Canada, an average of approximately 4 per year. Other data indicates that between 1978 and 1986, that number increased to an average of 7 per year. In the end, the overarching question to be answered is whether the decision designating Neve a dangerous offender was reasonable. Or to put the matter another way: does Neve, having regard to all relevant circumstances, fall within that very small group of offenders whom Parliament intended be designated as dangerous offenders—and which has led, in all of Canada over a 50-year period, to an average of 4 to 7 criminals a year being detained as dangerous offenders? In our view, for reasons we explain in detail below, the answer to this question is no.

...

Before addressing each of these issues in turn, we propose to review the facts relating to the robbery. One cannot overemphasize the importance of context, and hence the facts, not only to the conviction appeal, but also to the dangerous offender appeal. Context weighs heavily at many stages of a dangerous offender proceeding. The dangerous offender legislation requires a court to focus on the person (and all relevant circumstances relating to what that person has done) and not simply on numbers of convictions. Parliament has not chosen to adopt a formulaic "three strikes and you are out" approach to dangerous offender designations in Canada. Instead, before imposing one of the most serious sanctions under Canadian criminal law, a court is required to conduct a contextual analysis, concentrating on the offender and on the qualitative, quantitative and relative dimensions of the crimes the offender has committed.

Understanding the facts relating to this robbery is vital for another reason. Once an offender has been convicted, the findings made at trial stand, both in the sentence proceedings in that case, and in any subsequent criminal proceedings. While this does not preclude a judge's interpreting facts relating to prior offences, including the predicate offence, in light of evidence adduced at a dangerous offender hearing, it does prevent a judge's doing so in a manner which results in contradictory findings to those made at trial. What this means is that although the purpose for which fact findings are used may change, the findings themselves cannot.

A. Background Information and Trial Judgment

When these events occurred, Neve was 18 years old. She had been a prostitute since she was 12. Neve and her friend, Kim, approached the complainant, another prostitute.

Neve and Kim believed that the complainant had beaten one of their pregnant friends causing her to miscarry. They asked the complainant if she would like to go for a drink. The complainant agreed. It was about midnight. The complainant climbed into a truck with Neve and Kim. They questioned the complainant about the assault on their friend. She denied any involvement.

Kim drove to a field by a greenhouse just outside northeast Edmonton near a major highway and parked the vehicle. The trial judge found that the complainant was told to take her clothes off. Neve threatened to cut off the complainant's hair. Kim threatened that she would break the complainant's arm if she did not take her clothes off. The complainant refused to do so. Neve and Kim then proceeded to tear the complainant's clothes off, using a knife to cut the clothing so that it could be more easily torn. The complainant, whose evidence was accepted by the trial judge, confirmed that her clothes were being held away from her when the knife was used. In the process, the complainant received what she variously conceded was a "little scratch," a "tiny nick" or a "small cut." The complainant expressly acknowledged that the knife was being used quite carefully to remove her clothing, so as not to hurt her.

· · ·

During examination-in-chief, the complainant testified that Kim struck her about five times in the face. Although the complainant mentioned in cross-examination that Neve also struck her, she could not remember any details whatever, including the effect on her. Even with respect to Kim, the complainant testified that she did not remember having any pain or injury as a result of what Kim did. In fact, the complainant testified:

Q Okay. Now, did you receive any—any injuries as a result of this incident, ma'am?

A Nothing other than just a small cut.

· · ·

Neve and Kim drove away after first circling in the parking lot. The complainant testified that she did not know what was done with her clothes when they were removed from her. She was left without them. It was May and the temperature was then about five degrees Centigrade. She wrapped herself in some fibreglass insulation which she found nearby and made her way to the main highway where, according to her testimony, she was picked up a little bit later by a passing motorist who testified that she was "very, very cold, and she looked somewhat confused."

· · ·

With the complainant's help, the police later apprehended Neve. At the time of her arrest, a knife was found in her jacket pocket. She was informed of her right to counsel, but declined to exercise it. Neve was apparently then under the influence of drugs. At no time was Neve informed of her right to remain silent. Nor was she cautioned about the consequences of choosing to make a statement.

Later, while in a police holding cell, Neve cut her wrists. She was taken to hospital where she was treated. She was then returned to the cell. She told one of the constables that he better not leave because she was going to do the same thing again. A police constable watched over her until 7:30 a.m. While there, he asked Neve some questions about the events which led to her arrest. (It is Neve's answers to these questions which Neve contends were wrongly admitted into evidence at the trial.) The constable asked her the name of the other assailant. Neve replied that it was Kim. Neve then went on to explain the nature of the grievance she had with the complainant. Specifically, the constable testified:

> She—she also told me in reference to the—the alleged assault that she did it to get even because the complainant had beat up one of her—her friends who was pregnant at the time and also that the complainant was yelling—was the type that was yelling and getting out of hand, getting out of control. That was another reason for—for what they did.

Neve later asked to speak to a lawyer. After she had used the phone, she told the constable that instead of calling counsel, she had phoned Kim to advise her to leave the City.

• • •

B. The Decision Below on Dangerous Offender Status

It is appropriate at this stage to outline in skeletal form only the approach which the sentencing judge took to the question of whether Neve should be declared a dangerous offender. After deciding that the robbery which Neve committed qualified as a "serious personal injury offence," the sentencing judge addressed whether Neve constituted a threat based on her past behaviour meeting the threshold dangerousness requirements under s. 753(a). He concluded that she was a threat, relying on both ss. 753(a)(i) and (ii).

In doing so, it is evident that the judge took into account not only Neve's criminal record but other actions by her for which no criminal charges had ever been laid (but in respect of which evidence was called at the dangerous offender hearing), her behaviour as testified to by her family, psychiatrists, police officers, associates and corrections workers, and her diaries and personal records. We note that at the beginning of the dangerous offender hearing, 25 exhibits were admitted with the consent of the defence, including Neve's files from Alberta Hospital and the Remand Centre, along with the court records and transcripts from other cases in which Neve was convicted or pled guilty.

Part of the sentencing judge's analysis also involved assessing the evidence of five psychiatrists and a psychologist, four of the psychiatrists testifying for the Crown, and one psychiatrist and a psychologist for the defence. The sentencing judge essentially adopted the Crown's expert evidence over that of the defence, relying on it in support of his finding that Neve should be declared a dangerous offender. However, while preferring the evidence of two of the Crown's experts, both of whom suggested that Neve was a psychopath, the sentencing judge did not go so far as to find her a psychopath. He concluded that she suffered from a severe antisocial personality disorder.

In determining an appropriate period of incarceration, the sentencing judge was satisfied that Neve did not intend to change her ways or accept treatment. Accordingly, he reasoned that an indeterminate sentence was the only realistic choice. But before taking this step, he found that a three-year sentence, consecutive to any sentence Neve was then serving, would have been appropriate for the robbery.

• • •

Not everyone who is a criminal or for that matter a danger to the public is a danger-ous offender. In the spectrum of offenders, the dangerous offender legislation is designed to target—and capture—those clustered at or near the extreme end. Were this other-wise, constitutionality might stumble. In other words, the dangerous offender legislation is not intended to be a process of general application but rather of exacting selection.

As an example of the relatively narrow band of offenders to whom this legislation is directed—and has been applied—it is instructive to note that between 1978 and 1986, an average of 7 persons per year were sentenced in Canada as dangerous offend-ers. On average, each offender committed 12.12 offences, 2.2 of which were non-sexual violent crimes and 3.53 of which were sexual crimes: see *Lyons*, supra, at 348, citing affidavit evidence in the companion case *R v. Milne*, [1987] 2 SCR 512.

During oral argument, we requested confirmation of the number of dangerous offenders in Canada and a brief description of the crimes for which they had been convicted. Apparently, this evidence was readily available. We do not suggest that in future cases, the Crown must call detailed evidence with respect to other dangerous offenders. However, the minimal information we requested, and which the Crown helpfully compiled, is of some assistance: see Supplementary Materials of the Crown Respondent (Dangerous Offender Criminal Records). We concede that this informa-tion does not provide the details necessary to permit an assessment of the relative degree of seriousness of the offences committed by those already designated as dan-gerous offenders (whether vis-à-vis Neve or each other). But by painting as it does a more comprehensive picture of the face of dangerous offenders in Canada, both today and historically, it does provide a backdrop, albeit a very general one, against which a court can undertake its evaluation of whether an offender fits into that scene.

We are not saying that the picture cannot be expanded, whether numerically or in terms of the kinds of offences, or offenders, that might typically attract a dangerous offender designation. Of course, the size of the group may increase. So too may the categories of offences which are considered sufficiently serious to warrant use of this sanction, particularly as society becomes less tolerant of crimes of violence and more aware of the potentially long-lasting and traumatic effects of personal violence on victims. However, what we are saying is that in interpreting the scope of the dangerous offender provisions, one should do so in a manner which preserves their constitutional validity: *Slaight Communications Inc. v. Davidson*, [1989] 1 SCR 1038; *Hills v. Canada (Attor-ney General)*, [1988] 1 SCR 513. Ensuring that the group does not include anyone who falls outside of the intended and actual sweep of the legislation will accomplish this.

· · ·

D. Neve and the Dangerous Offender Designation

In all these circumstances, we have concluded that the decision to designate Neve a dangerous offender was not reasonable. It is only by taking the global perspective we have described that it is possible to assess whether Neve, in view of her record, and the circumstances and context of the offences she has committed, belongs in that relatively small group such that the most severe sentence that can be imposed under the Code, short of life imprisonment, is strenuously required: *Lyons*, supra, at 339.

There is no doubt that Neve has a history of offending the law; and we cannot say that Neve will not reoffend. That risk exists and it is a real risk. Indeed, it would be naive to think otherwise. However, the question is not whether there is a possibility or even a probability of Neve's reoffending in the future. While this consideration certainly goes on the scale, the central question which must be addressed at this stage is whether, given her past record and the various factors that we have noted and assessed, Neve falls within the intended small group of dangerous offenders in Canada. In our view, she does not.

Neve is a criminal but the totality of the circumstances here do not warrant a dangerous offender designation at this stage in her life. Neve's life found her moving from one set of extreme circumstances to another: prostitution from a very young age; abuse from her pimp; foster homes; placement centres; and drug and alcohol abuse. When her actual criminal record is parsed out from her thoughts and fantasies, what we have is a young woman with a relatively short criminal record for violence, disposed to telling shocking stories of violence. Considering her within the population of criminals in Canada, it cannot be said at this time that she falls within that "very small group of offenders whose personal characteristics and particular circumstances militate strenuously in favour of preventative incarceration." *Lyons*, supra, at 339.

When all is said and done, the question here is not whether Neve is the most dangerous, or even one of the most dangerous, young women that the psychiatrists who testified have ever seen. Nor is it whether Neve is one of the most dangerous young offenders, male or female. We do not have different classes of offenders in this country where one reviews those in a specific class—young offenders or young women for example—and then chooses the worst in that class to advance into the dangerous offender group. (We are not suggesting by this comment that Neve is the worst or near the worst in any class of offenders in Canada.) Instead, the question is whether, relatively speaking compared to all other offenders in Canada—male and female, young and old, advantaged and disadvantaged—Neve falls into that small group of offenders clustered at or near the extreme end of offenders in this country. For reasons we have explained, Neve is not in that group.

E. Constitutional Considerations

Not long after the *Canadian Charter of Rights and Freedoms*, part I of the *Constitution Act, 1982*, RSC 1985, app. II, no. 44, came into force, challenges were made to the dangerous offender provisions. None of them was successful. The leading case on this point is the decision of the Supreme Court of Canada in *R v. Lyons*, infra. The arguments made in *Lyons* represent the typical complaints about preventive criminal justice measures: (1) Is it fair to punish someone for a crime he or she has not yet committed, instead of imposing punishment only for past wrongful acts? (2) Is indeterminate detention not a "cruel and unusual" sort of punishment? and (3) Given that social science tells us that our ability to predict dangerousness is quite weak, is it not arbitrary to detain someone indefinitely on this basis?

As you read through *Lyons*, consider whether the court's responses to these arguments are adequate. Should other, more compelling arguments have been advanced in this case?

R v. Lyons
(1987), 61 CR (3d) 1 (SCC)

LA FOREST J: The broad issues raised in this appeal are whether the dangerous offenders provisions of the *Criminal Code*, RSC 1970, c. C-34, Pt. XXI, ss. 687 to 695, contravene the rights guaranteed by the *Canadian Charter of Rights and Freedoms* to "liberty" and "not to be deprived thereof except in accordance with the principles of fundamental justice" (s. 7), "not to be arbitrarily detained or imprisoned" (s. 9), "to the benefit of trial by jury" (s. 11), and "not to be subjected to any cruel and unusual treatment or punishment" (s. 12), and if so whether they can be justified under s. 1 of the Charter as being "such reasonable limits prescribed by law as can be demonstrably justified in a free and democratic society."

Facts and Procedural History

On 23rd September 1983 the appellant, Thomas Patrick Lyons, was arraigned on an information containing four charges: unlawfully breaking and entering a dwelling-house contrary to s. 306(1)(b) of the *Criminal Code*; unlawfully using a weapon or imitation thereof in committing a sexual assault, contrary to s. 246.2(a) of the Code; unlawfully using a firearm while committing an indictable offence, contrary to s. 83(1)(a) of the Code; and unlawfully stealing property of a total value exceeding $200, contrary to s. 294(a) of the Code. These offences were alleged to have been committed approximately one month after the appellant's sixteenth birthday.

The appellant elected trial by a judge without a jury on all four charges and waived his right to a preliminary inquiry. He subsequently entered pleas of guilty to all courts in the indictment. O'Hearn Co. Ct. J of the County Court Judge's Criminal Court for District 1, Nova Scotia, requested a pre-sentence report and adjourned the matter of sentence.

Just before the sentence hearing on 4th November 1983, defence counsel was informed, for the first time, that the Crown might bring a dangerous offender application under Pt. XXI of the Code. At the commencement of the hearing, the Crown requested and was granted an adjournment to permit it to consider bringing such an application. The application was subsequently made. On 8th November 1983 consent to the application was obtained from the Deputy Attorney General of Nova Scotia, as required by s. 689(a)(a) of the Code.

At the commencement of the hearing of the application on 14th December 1983, an agreed-upon statement of facts was read into the record. Evidence, including expert psychiatric testimony, was tendered on behalf of both the Crown and the appellant.

Though O'Hearn Co. Ct. J had at the outset warned the Crown attorney that he would have an "uphill fight" owing to the age of the appellant, the judge in the end found, on the basis of medical and other evidence presented to him, that it had been established beyond a reasonable doubt that the appellant qualified as a dangerous offender under the provisions of the Code. In his view, it had been shown that the appellant had a "sociopathic personality" and had so little conscience that it did not govern his actions. He concluded that it could be said with "a high degree of confidence" that it was "very likely" that the appellant would constitute a danger to the psychological or physical health and lives of others owing to "his in-built, perhaps congenital indifference to the consequences to others, his lack of affect, his lack of feeling for others." He belonged, the judge stated, to a class of people who, though mentally able to understand the law and to conform their conduct to its dictates, are so irresponsive to the law that they must be deal with by extraordinary measures.

O'Hearn Co. Ct. J also considered and rejected the appellant's contentions that Pt. XXI of the Code was constitutionally invalid as offending against the guarantees embodied in ss. 7, 9 and 12 of the Charter, and proceeded to sentence the appellant to an indeterminate period of detention in a penitentiary.

The appellant's appeal to the Nova Scotia Supreme Court, Appeal Division, was unanimously dismissed for reasons given by Macdonald JA. On 31st January leave to appeal to this Court was granted.

The following constitutional questions were stated by the court on 26th March 1985:

1. Whether the provisions of Part XXI of the *Criminal Code of Canada*, dealing with an application for finding and sentencing, an individual as a dangerous offender, in whole or in part, infringe or deny the rights guaranteed by sections 7, 9, 11, and/or 12 of the *Canadian Charter of Rights and Freedoms*?
2. If so, then are the provisions of Part XXI of the *Criminal Code*, in whole or in part, justified on the basis of s. 1 of the *Canadian Charter of Rights and Freedoms* and therefore not inconsistent with the *Constitution Act, 1982*?

The appellant also argued that his rights under s. 7 of the Charter were violated by the Crown's failure to give him notice, before his election of a mode of trial and the entry of his plea, that it intended to bring, or contemplated bringing, a "dangerous offender" application under Pt. XXI of the Code.

History and Analysis of Pt. XXI

Part XXI of the *Criminal Code* establishes a scheme for the designation of certain offenders as "dangerous offenders" and for sentencing such persons to a penitentiary for an indeterminate period. It is the product of frequently-amended legislation that has existed in Canada, in one form or another, since 1947. It has its genesis in the *Prevention of Crime Act, 1908* (8 Edw. 7, c. 59), ss. 10 to 16, under which a person convicted of a crime was subject to a "further sentence" of not less than five or more than ten years as preventive detention if he or she was found to be an habitual criminal. During the debates in Parliament on that Act, its author, Lord Gladstone, "made it clear that it was intended to deal not with the generality of 'habituals' but only with that more limited body of 'professional criminals' or 'persistent dangerous criminals' engaged in the more serious forms of crime": Fox, *The Modern English Prison* (1934), London, at p. 168.

...

The present legislation, enacted in 1977, clearly pursues the historical purpose of protecting the public, but is now carefully tailored so as to be confined in its application to those habitual criminals who are dangerous to others. In brief, Pt. XXI provides that, where a person has been found guilty of a "serious personal injury offence," the court may, upon application, find the offender to be a dangerous offender and may thereupon impose a sentence of indeterminate detention in lieu of any other sentence that the offender might have received for the offence.

...

To trigger the operation of this procedure, it is necessary by virtue of the opening words of subs. (a) and subs. (b) that the accused have been found guilty of a "serious personal injury offence" ... . Two of the crimes of which the appellant was convicted fall within this definition.

In addition to having been convicted of a serious personal injury offence, s. 688(a) and (b) provides that for the offender to qualify as a dangerous offender it must also be established that he constitutes a threat to the life, safety or well-being of others on the basis of evidence of the dangerous and intractably persistent or brutal behaviour described in paras. (i) to (ii), or that the offender has shown an inability to control his sexual impulses and a likelihood that he will thereby cause injury, pain or other evil to other persons. The findings of the courts below that behaviour described in s. 688 existed was not contested here.

Owing to the nature of the findings that must be made, provision is made for psychological, psychiatric and criminological evidence (s. 690) as well as character evidence (s. 694). Indeed, the evidence of at least two psychiatrists is obligatory. As well, the judge is empowered to make directions and to remand the offender for the purposes of observation (s. 691).

Because of the serious implications of the procedure for the accused, a number of safeguards have been provided. Thus the consent of the provincial Attorney General is required and the offender must, following the application, be given at least seven days' notice of the basis on which it is made (s. 689). The offender is allowed to nominate one of the psychiatric witnesses (s. 690(2)) and failure to do so obliges the court to nominate one on his or her behalf (s. 690(3)). The offender also has a right to be present at the hearing (s. 693), and to appeal against sentence (s. 694(1)). As well, the Solicitor General of Canada is to be furnished with copies of the psychological, psychiatric and criminological evidence and of the observations of the court (s. 695). Finally, and importantly, provision is made for review of the sentence at the expiration of three years from its imposition and every two years thereafter (s. 695.1).

...

As already mentioned the case raises issues concerning ss. 7, 9, 11 and 12 of the Charter. Indeed, several s. 7 issues are raised, the most fundamental of which, and hence the one with which I propose to begin, being whether the imposition of preventive detention for an indeterminate period offends against the principles of fundamental justice. The remaining s. 7 issues focus not on the punishment itself, but on the fairness of the process by which the deprivation of liberty is occasioned. I therefore propose to discuss the issues raised by the appellant under the following headings:

1. Does Pt. XXI violate s. 7 of the Charter? Specifically, does it offend against principles of fundamental justice to impose preventive detention as punishment for committing a crime?

2. Does Pt. XXI violate s. 12 of the Charter?

3. Does Pt. XXI violate s. 9 of the Charter?
4. Does Pt. XXI violate s. 7 of the Charter in other respects? Are the procedures by which the deprivation of liberty is occasioned, the standard of proof required under Pt. XXI, or the use of psychiatric evidence in a Pt. XXI application fundamentally unfair to offenders sought to be designated as dangerous? (An aspect of the foregoing inquiry concerns the more discrete question whether s. 17(f) of the Charter requires that a Pt. XXI application be heard by a jury.)
5. Were the appellant's rights under s. 7 violated by the Crown's failure to give the appellant notice before his election and plea?

A. Does Pt. XXI by Imposing Indeterminate Detention Offend Against Fundamental Justice Under S. 7 of the Charter?

In *Ref re S. 94(2) of the Motor Vehicle Act*, [1985] 2 SCR 486, this court held that the phrase "principles of fundamental justice" sets out the parameters of the right not to be deprived of life, liberty and security of the person. These principles were stated to inhere in the basic tenets and principles not only of the judicial system but also of the other components of our legal system (at p. 512, per Lamer J). Hence, to determine whether Pt. XXI violates the principles of fundamental justice by the deprivation of liberty suffered by the offender, it is necessary to examine Pt. XXI in light of the basic principles of penal policy that have animated legislative and judicial practice in Canada and other common law jurisdictions.

The appellant submits that Pt. XXI results in a deprivation of liberty that is not in accordance with the principles of fundamental justice, in that it permits an individual to be sentenced for crimes which he or she has not committed or for crimes for which he or she has already been punished. If this statement correctly described what in fact occurs under Pt. XXI, it would indeed constitute a violation of s. 7. The reality, however, is quite different. What s. 688 does is to permit a judge to impose a sentence of indeterminate detention on an individual for having committed an offence, which sentence is "*in lieu of* any other sentence that might be imposed *for the offence for which the offender has been convicted*" (emphasis added). The individual is clearly being sentenced for the "serious personal injury offence" he or she has been found guilty of committing, albeit in a different way than would ordinarily be done. It must be remembered that the appellant was not picked up off the street because of his past criminality (for which he has already been punished), or because of fears or suspicions about his criminal proclivities, and then subjected to a procedure in order to determine whether society would be better off if he were incarcerated indefinitely. Rather he was arrested and prosecuted for a very serious violent crime and subjected to a procedure aimed at determining the appropriate penalty that should be inflicted upon him in the circumstances.

Thus the appellant's contention that he is being punished for what he might do rather than for what he has done, or, in more traditional terms, that he is being found guilty in the absence of a finding of the requisite *actus reus*, must be rejected. The punishment, as I noted, flows from the actual commission of a specific crime, the requisite elements of which have been proved to exist beyond a reasonable doubt.

Nor do I find it objectionable that the offender's designation as dangerous or the subsequent indeterminate sentence is based, in part, on a conclusion that the past violent, antisocial behaviour of the offender will likely continue in the future. Such considerations play a role in a very significant number of sentences. I accordingly agree with the respondent's submission that it cannot be considered a violation of fundamental justice for Parliament to identify those offenders who, in the interests of protecting the public, ought to be sentenced according to considerations which are not entirely reactive or based on a "just deserts" rationale. The imposition of a sentence which "is partly punitive but is mainly imposed for the protection of the public" (*Re Moore and R* (1984), 54 OR (2d) 3 (HC)) seems to me to accord with the fundamental purpose of the criminal law generally, and of sentencing in particularly, namely, the protection of society. In a rational system of sentencing, the respective importance of prevention, deterrence, retribution and rehabilitation will vary according to the nature of the crime and the circumstances of the offender. No one would suggest that any of these functional considerations should be excluded from the legitimate purview of legislative or judicial decisions regarding sentencing.

It is thus important to recognize the precise nature of the penological objectives embodied in Pt. XXI. It is clear that the indeterminate detention is intended to serve both punitive and preventive purposes. Both are legitimate aims of the criminal sanction. Indeed, when society incarcerates a robber for, say, ten years, it is clear that its goal is both to punish the person and to prevent the recurrence of such conduct during that period. Preventive detention in the context of Pt. XXI, however, simply represents a judgment that the relative importance of the objectives of rehabilitation, deterrence and retribution are greatly attenuated in the circumstances of the individual case, and that of prevention correspondingly increased. Part XXI merely enables the court to accommodate its sentence to the common sense reality that the *present* condition of the offender is such that he or she is not inhibited by normal standards of behavioural restraint, so that *future* violent acts can quite confidently be expected of that person. In such circumstances it would be folly not to tailor the sentence accordingly.

It is noteworthy that numerous examples exist, both in Canada and abroad, of ways in which the need to protect the public from the risk of convicted persons reoffending has been taken into consideration by the judiciary and legislature alike.

The case law criteria for imposing a life sentence closely parallel those embodied in Pt. XXI. Indeed, life sentences and Pt. XXI sentences are primarily imposed for the same purposes and on the same type of offender. In *R v. Hill* (1974), 15 CCC (2d) 145 (Ont. CA), Jessup JA stated, at pp. 147-48:

> When an accused has been convicted of a serious crime in itself calling for a substantial sentence and when he suffers from some mental or personality disorder rendering him a danger to the community but not subjecting him to confinement in a mental institution and when it is uncertain when, if ever, the accused will be cured of his affliction, in my opinion the appropriate sentence is one of life. Such a sentence in such circumstances amounts to an indefinite sentence under which the Parole Board can release him to the community when it is satisfied, upon adequate psychiatric examination, it is in the interests of the accused and of the community for him to return to society. The

policy expressed in my opinion is that of the Criminal Division of the English court of Appeal: *cf.* Thomas, *Principles of Sentencing*, at pp. 272-9.

...

It is true that the *Hill* principle, which amounts to judge-made dangerous offender law, has clearly been limited by subsequent decisions. However, the basis of the retrenchment has not been a rejection of the principle of indeterminate detention for dangerous offenders. Rather, it has been the concern that the *Hill* principle not be used to circumvent the provisions of Pt. XXI with its attendant safeguards for the offender. As Martin JA, for the Ontario Court of Appeal, observed in *R v. Crosby* (1982), 1 CCC (3d) 233 at 240:

> The Crown, in our view, properly invoked the dangerous offender legislation in this case. This court has said on more than one occasion that rather than sentence a person who has been convicted of a serious offence and who is a continuing danger to life imprisonment, the prosecution should proceed under the dangerous offender provisions, where the offender has greater protection.

...

From what I have said already, I do not think that it could seriously be argued that the penological objectives embodied in Pt. XXI themselves violate s. 7 of the Charter. However, it is clear that the present Charter inquiry is concerned also, if not primarily, with the *effects* of the legislation. This requires investigating the "treatment meted out," i.e., what is actually done to the offender and how that is accomplished. Whether this "treatment" violates constitutional precepts seems to me to be an issue more aptly discussed under ss. 9 and 12 of the Charter, because these provisions focus on specific manifestations of the principles of fundamental justice. For convenience, I shall begin with s. 12.

B. Does Pt. XXI Constitute Cruel and Unusual Punishment Under S. 12 of the Charter?

The appellant contends that Pt. XXI violates s. 12 of the Charter in that it imposes a punishment that is unusually severe and serves no valid penological purpose more effectively than a less severe punishment (e.g. a determinate sentence).

This issue was addressed in *Re Moore and R*, supra and *R v. Langevin* (1984), 39 CR (3d) 333 (Ont. CA). In *Re Moore*, Ewaschuk J appears to have been influenced by the fact that this court had, in *Ex parte Matticks*, [1973] SCR vi, 15 CCC (2d) 213 [Que.], upheld the previous habitual offender legislation under s. 2(b) of the *Canadian Bill of Rights*, RSC 1970, App. III, which provides that no law of Canada shall be construed or applied so as to "impose or authorize the imposition of cruel and unusual treatment or punishment." If that more Draconian legislation was valid, he reasoned, so must the present legislation be valid. The reasons given by Ewaschuk J for sustaining the legislation may be summarized thus: the legislation would be acceptable to a large segment of the population; the specificity of the statutory requirements ensured their application on a rational basis; the protection of society is an important social purpose; the legislation is not an affront to public standards of decency given the procedural safeguards built into the process; and finally, the legislation is tailored so as not to be disproportionate to the crime and the offender's potential to harm others. Although all punishment is in some degree degrading to human dignity, he concluded, Pt. XXI is not impermissibly, or cruelly and unusually, degrading to human dignity.

While I agree with much of this reasoning, it is unnecessary to examine it in any detail. For since that decision, this court, in *Smith v. R*, 25th June 1987, [now reported (sub nom. *R v. Smith*) [1987] 1 SCR 1045], has had the opportunity to review the scope and meaning of s. 12, and it is against the backdrop of that case that this issue must be decided. *Smith* dealt with whether s. 5(2) of the *Narcotic Control Act*, RSC 1970, c. N-1, in providing for a mandatory minimum sentence of seven years on all persons found guilty of importing a narcotic, offended the right of individuals not to be subjected to cruel and unusual treatment or punishment. A majority of this court held that s. 5(2) did violate s. 12 and was not sustainable under s. 1 of the Charter.

Lamer J, speaking for the majority, set out the parameters of the right not to be subjected to cruel and unusual treatment or punishment in the following terms:

> In my view, the protection afforded by s. 12 governs the quality of the punishment and is concerned with the effect that the punishment may have on the person on whom it is imposed. I would agree with Laskin CJC in *Miller*, ... where he defined the phrase "cruel and unusual" as a "compendious expression of a norm." The criterion which must be applied in order to determine whether a punishment is cruel and unusual within the meaning of s. 12 of the Charter is, to use the words of Laskin CJC in *Miller* at p. 688, "whether the punishment prescribed is so excessive as to outrage standards of decency." In other words, though the state may impose punishment, the effect of that punishment must not be grossly disproportionate to what would have been appropriate.
>
> In imposing a sentence of imprisonment, the judge will assess the circumstances of the case in order to arrive at an appropriate sentence. The test for review under s. 12 of the Charter is one of gross disproportionality, because it is aimed at punishments that are more than merely excessive. We should be careful not to stigmatize every disproportionate or excessive sentence as being a constitutional violation, and should leave to the usual sentencing appeal process the task of reviewing the fitness of a sentence. Section 12 will be infringed only where the sentence is so unfit having regard to the offence and the offender as to be grossly disproportionate.
>
> In assessing whether a sentence is grossly disproportionate, the court must first consider the gravity of the offence, the personal characteristics of the offender and the particular circumstances of the case in order to determine what range of sentences would have been appropriate to punish, rehabilitate or deter this particular offender or to protect the public from this particular offender. The other purposes which may be pursued by the imposition of punishment, in particular the deterrence of other potential offenders, are thus not relevant at this stage of the inquiry. This does not mean that the judge or the legislator can no longer consider general deterrence or other penological purposes that go beyond the particular offender in determining a sentence, but only that the resulting sentence must not be grossly disproportionate to what the offender deserves. If a grossly disproportionate sentence is "prescribed by law," then the purpose which it seeks to attain will fall to be assessed under s. 1. Section 12 ensures that individual offenders receive punishment that are appropriate, or at least not grossly disproportionate, to their

particular circumstances, while s. 1 permits this right to be overridden to achieve some important societal objective.

One must measure the effect of the sentence actually imposed. If it is grossly disproportionate to what would have been appropriate, then it infringes s. 12. The effect of the sentence is often a composite of many factors and is not limited to the quantum or duration of the sentence but includes its nature and the conditions under which it is applied. Sometimes by its length alone or by its very nature will the sentence be grossly disproportionate to the purpose sought. Sometimes it will be the result of the combination of factors which, when considered in isolation, would not in and of themselves amount to gross disproportionality. For example, 20 years for a first offence against property would be grossly disproportionate, but so would three months of imprisonment, if the prison authorities decide it should be served in solitary confinement. ...

The numerous criteria proposed pursuant to s. 2(b) of the *Canadian Bill of Rights* and the Eighth Amendment of the American Constitution are, in my opinion, useful as factors to determine whether a violation of s. 12 has occurred. Thus, to refer to the tests listed by Professor Tarnopolsky, the determination of whether the punishment is necessary to achieve a valid penal purpose, whether it is founded on recognized sentencing principles, and whether there exist valid alternatives to the punishment imposed, are all guidelines which, without being determinative in themselves, help to assess whether the punishment is grossly disproportionate.

It is clear from the foregoing that s. 12 is concerned with the relation between the effects of, and reasons for, punishment. At the initial stage of the inquiry into proportionality, those effects are to be balanced against the particular circumstances of the offence, the characteristics of the offender and the particular purposes sought to be accomplished in sentencing that person in the manner challenged. If, in light of these considerations, the punishment is found to be grossly disproportionate, a remedy must be afforded the offender in the absence of social objectives that transcend the circumstances of the particular case and are capable of justifying the punishment under s. 1 of the Charter.

Let us first consider the substantive ways in which the present legislation itself seeks to accommodate the conflicting interests, on the one hand, of society in seeking to protect itself from dangerous criminals and, on the other, of the offender in not being subjected to punishment grossly disproportionate to the offence and the circumstances of the individual case. It seems to me that the legislative criteria embodied in s. 688 for designating offenders as dangerous and for sentencing such persons tend, although not conclusively, to sustain the legislation as not constituting a violation of s. 12. I say "not conclusively" for, as will be seen, it is only when s. 688 is read in the context of the scheme as a whole that the legislation can be upheld.

First, the legislation applies only to persons convicted of a "serious personal injury offence" as defined in s. 687. These offences all relate to conduct tending to cause severe physical danger or severe psychological injury to other persons. Significantly, the maximum penalty for all these offences must be at least ten years' imprisonment. Secondly, it must be established to the satisfaction of the court that the offence for which the person has been convicted is not an isolated occurrence, but part of a pattern of behaviour which has involved violence, aggressive or brutal conduct, or a failure to control sexual impulses. Thirdly, it must be established that the pattern of conduct is very likely to continue and to result in the kind of suffering against which the section seeks to protect, namely, conduct endangering the life, safety or physical well-being of others or, in the case of sexual offences, conduct causing injury, pain or other evil to other persons. Also explicit in one form or another in each subsection of s. 687 is the requirement that the court must be satisfied that the pattern of conduct is substantially or pathologically intractable. Finally, the court has the discretion not to designate the offender as dangerous or to impose an indeterminate sentence, even in circumstances where all of these criteria are met.

It seems to me that, having concluded that the legislative objectives embodied in Pt. XXI are not only of substantial importance to society's well-being but, at least in theory, sufficiently important to warrant limiting certain rights and freedoms, one must equally conclude that the legislative classification of the target group of offenders meets the highest standard of rationality (and I use the word not as a term of art) and proportionality that society could reasonably expect of Parliament. Not only has a diligent attempt been made to carefully define a very small group of offenders whose personal characteristics and particular circumstances militate strenuously in favour of preventive incarceration, but it would be difficult to imagine a better-tailored set of criteria that could effectively accomplish the purposes sought to be attained.

However, the legislative classification of offenders as dangerous is only one aspect of the "means analysis" under s. 12. It is equally important to consider the constitutional validity, under s. 12, of the actual "treatment meted out." There can be no doubt that detention per se, and preventive detention in particular, is not cruel and unusual in the case of dangerous offenders, for the group to whom the legislation applies has been functionally defined so as to ensure that persons within the group evince the very characteristics that render such detention necessary.

It is argued, however, that it is not the detention itself but its *indeterminate quality* that harbours the potential for cruel and unusual punishment. And it is difficult to deny that the effects of an indeterminate sentence on a dangerous offender must be profoundly devastating. It has, for instance, been argued before the court that the imposition of an indeterminate sentence, because of its uncertainty, saps the will of an offender, removing any incentive to rehabilitate himself or herself. However, this is equally true of a "determinate" life sentence such as is provided for by s. 306(1)(b). Indeed, in view of the provisions regarding parole, it is possible, at least theoretically, that a dangerous offender could be released consequent on his first review, three years after the detention was imposed and well in advance of the seven or so years an offender serving a life sentence must serve before his or her first such review. This is, however, rather unrealistic. Evidence before the court indicated that between 1980 and 1986 only six dangerous offenders were granted day parole, two of whom had served 10 to 15 years, three 15 to 20 years, and one more than 20 years.

In truth, there is a significant difference between the effect of a Pt. XXI sentence and other, more typical sentences. When a person is imprisoned for an absolute and determinate period, there is at least the certainty that the incarceration will end at the termination of that period. The convicted person, during the term of sentence, can remain in a passive state, secure in the knowledge that he or she will be released thereafter. For the offender undergoing an indeterminate sentence, however, the sole hope of release is parole. The ordinary convict, it is true, can also choose to actively affect the length of his or her sentence by attempting to conform his or her behaviour to meet the expectations of the parole board. But, whatever the legal nature of the interest in the availability of parole may be in general, it seems to me that, as a *factual* matter, the availability of parole is not as important a factor in deciding whether a determinate sentence is cruel and unusual as it is in assessing the constitutionality of a Pt. XXI sentence.

This is so because in the context of a determinate sentencing scheme the availability of parole represents an additional super-added protection of the liberty interests of the offender. In the present context, however, it is, subsequent to the actual imposition of the sentence itself, the sole protection of the dangerous offender's liberty interests. Indeed, from the point of view of the dangerous offender, his or her detention is never complete until it is factually complete. In this sense, each opportunity for parole will appear to the dangerous offender as the sole mechanism for terminating his or her detention, for rendering it certain. Moreover, it is clear that an enlightened inquiry under s. 12 must concern itself first and foremost with the way in which the effects of punishment are likely to be experienced. Seen in this light, therefore, the parole process assumes the utmost significance, for it is that process alone that is capable of truly accommodating and tailoring the sentence to fit the circumstances of the individual offender.

In my opinion, if the sentence imposed under Pt. XXI was indeterminate, simpliciter, it would be certain, at least occasionally, to result in sentences grossly disproportionate to what individual offenders deserved. However, I believe that the parole process saves the legislation from being successfully challenged under s. 12, for it ensures that incarceration is imposed for only as long as the circumstances of the individual case require.

When an indeterminate sentence is imposed, Pt. XXI provides for periodic review, for the purposes of determining whether parole should be granted, of the "*condition, history and circumstances of that person*," after the first three years of detention and every two years thereafter. Section 695.1 provides as follows:

> 695.1(1) Subject to subsection (2), where a person is in custody under a sentence of detention in a penitentiary for an indeterminate period, the National Parole Board shall, forthwith after the expiration of three years from the day on which that person was taken into custody and not later than every two years thereafter, review the condition, history and circumstances of that person for the purpose of determining whether he should be granted parole under the *Parole Act* and, if so, on what conditions.
>
> (2) Where a person is in custody under a sentence of detention in a penitentiary for an indeterminate period that was imposed before the *Criminal Law Amendment Act, 1977* came into force, the National Parole Board shall, at least once in every year, review the condition, history and circumstances of that person for the purpose of determining whether he should be granted parole under the *Parole Act* and, if so, on what conditions.

The criteria in light of which an application for parole is considered are specified in s. 10(1)(a) of the *Parole Act*, RSC 1970, c. P-2:

10(1) the Board may

(a) grant parole to an inmate, subject to any terms or conditions it considers desirable, if the Board considers that

(i) in the case of a grant of parole other than day parole, the inmate has derived the maximum benefit from imprisonment.

(ii) the reform and rehabilitation of the inmate will be aided by the grant of parole, and

the release of the inmate on parole would not constitute an undue risk to society;

While the criteria embodied in s. 10(1)(a) do not purport to replicate the factual findings required to sentence the offender to an indeterminate term of imprisonment, they do afford a measure of tailoring adequate to save the legislation from violating s. 12. It must be remembered that the offender is being sentenced indeterminately because *at the time of sentencing* he was found to have a certain propensity. The sentence is imposed "in lieu of any other sentence" that might have been imposed and, like any other such sentence, must be served according to its tenor. *The offender is not being sentenced to a term of imprisonment until he is no longer a dangerous offender.* Indeed, s. 695.1 provides that the circumstances of the offender be reviewed for the purpose of determining whether *parole* should be granted and, if so, on what conditions; it does not provide that the label of dangerous offender be removed or altered. Finally, the very words of s. 695.1 of the Code and s. 10(1)(a) of the *Parole Act* establish an ongoing process for rendering the sentence meted out to a dangerous offender one that accords with his or her specific circumstances.

It may be argued that the legislation could be better tailored. For example, it might have been argued that the review process should focus solely on whether the offender continued to possess the characteristics that defined him or her as a proper subject of indeterminate detention. Indeed, one might say that to ask, as the Parole Board does, whether the individual has been reformed or rehabilitated is to pose a question that ex hypothesi cannot be answered affirmatively, for it was implicit in the designation of the offender as dangerous that he or she was not amenable to rehabilitation by usual means. However, this argument must be rejected for a number of reasons.

To begin with, the criteria actually used serve to emphasize the point made earlier in this judgment that sentencing, even under Pt. XXI, embodies a complex of penological objectives. I do not think it can be argued, as a matter either of logic or of common sense, that, by virtue of a decision to sentence an offender according to considerations based *primarily* on prevention, other equally valid, subsisting penal goals cease to be relevant. To reiterate, protecting society from the dangerous offender never wholly supplants the other legitimate objectives embodied in a Pt. XXI sentence.

Seen in this light, it would be preposterous to require of dangerous offenders only that they demonstrate to the parole board that they have ceased to be "dangerous" (in terms identical to those used in Pt. XXI), for this would require of them a lesser showing than is required of other convicts. It seems to me that, had s. 695.1 provided for a "dangerous offender review," rather than a parole review, but borrowed the identical criteria employed in the *Parole Act*, it would perhaps be more readily apparent that the review provided for does indeed accomplish the requisite tailoring sufficient to sustain the legislative scheme as a whole. Section 10(1)(a)(iii) requires the board to consider whether the release of the inmate would constitute an "undue risk" to society; if the accused continues to be dangerous, then by definition this criterion remains unsatisfied. Section 10(1)(a) also requires that the board be satisfied that the inmate has derived the maximum benefit from incarceration and that the inmate's reform and rehabilitation would be aided by release.

These criteria seem to me to be no less pertinent reflections of society's concerns in releasing dangerous offenders than they are in releasing other offenders. The fact that dangerous offenders may be less likely to satisfy these requirements is primarily a function of their dangerousness, not of the punishment imposed. Of course, the imposition of an indeterminate sentence may, like all sentences, sap the will of the offender to rehabilitate himself or herself. However, I would have thought the incentive to reform is far greater, at least theoretically, in the case of a dangerous offender. In this regard, I note that the availability of parole has been seen to validate mandatory life sentences in the context of similarly-motivated legislation in the United States: see *Solem v. Helm*, [100 S Ct. 3001 (1983)], per Powell J, for the majority.

Furthermore, I am not sure that to inquire into the presence or absence of less restrictive means is wholly compatible with the insistence of this court in *Smith*, supra, that s. 12 redress only punishment that is *grossly disproportionate* to the circumstances of any given case. The word "grossly," it seems to me, reflects this court's concern not to hold Parliament to a standard so exacting at least in the context of s. 12, as to require punishments to be perfectly suited to accommodate the moral nuances of every crime and every offender.

I would therefore conclude that Pt. XXI does not violate s. 12 of the Charter.

...

C. Does Part XXI Violate S. 9 of the Charter by Authorizing Arbitrary Detention or Imprisonment?

Counsel for the appellant contended that Pt. XXI violates the right of persons not to be arbitrarily detained or imprisoned, contrary to s. 9 of the Charter. He suggested that Pt. XXI results in arbitrary detention in the following respects: the test of "likelihood" under Pt. XXI is unconstitutionally vague; the labelling of persons as dangerous offenders is arbitrary, since it is based on inherently unreliable psychiatric evidence; and there are no guidelines with respect to the invocation of Pt. XXI such that the prosecutor has unfettered discretion as to when to make a dangerous offender application.

This court has not yet pronounced on the scope of s. 9 and the meaning of the words "arbitrarily detained or imprisoned," and I do not think this would be an appropriate case to do so. The issue was not strenuously argued by the parties or examined in depth in the courts below. More to the point, however, is that, in my view, even assuming that s. 9 were given the broadest possible interpretation, the appellant's submissions in this regard must fail.

There has been considerable controversy in the lower courts as to whether the ambit of protection afforded by s. 9 extends to imprisonment or detention specifically authorized under existing law or whether s. 9 is ipso facto satisfied when imprisonment is imposed in accordance with legislative requirements: see the cases canvassed in *R v. Konechny*, 38 CR (3d) 69 (BCCA), per Lambert JA, dissenting, at pp. 70-71. However, assuming that the right to attack a sentence under s. 9 is not foreclosed by the fact that it is legislatively prescribed, and that the statutory procedures have been judicially complied with (see *Re Mitchell and R* (1983), 42 OR (2d) 481 (sub nom. *Mitchell v. Ont. (AG)*), 6 CCC (3d) 193 (HC), per Linden J at p. 293), it seems to me that in no sense of the word can the imprisonment resulting from the successful invocation of Pt. XXI be considered "arbitrary." Indeed, when one fleshes out the specific submissions of the appellant in this regard they appear to be merely attempts to recast issues considered elsewhere in this judgment. For example, although the first two submissions made under this heading are directed to the alleged lack of proportionality or adequacy, in constitutional terms, of the legislative means to the objectives sought to be attained, they are not independently addressed to the arbitrary nature of the imprisonment. To the extent that these arguments reflect the appellant's concern that the procedure for the designation of offenders as dangerous is, in general terms, impermissibly unfair, I will address these arguments later under s. 7, where they properly belong. Similarly, to the extent that they belie a fear that punishment is being imposed without due concern for the circumstances of the particular offender, I have already addressed these arguments under s. 12.

However, even giving the word "arbitrary" its broadest signification, it is readily apparent that, not only is the incarceration statutorily authorized, but that the legislation narrowly defines a class of offenders with respect to whom it may properly be invoked, and prescribes quite specifically the conditions under which an offender may be designated as dangerous. If these criteria are themselves unconstitutional, it is because they otherwise fail adequately to safeguard the liberty of the individual, not because they are arbitrary. Indeed, as Ewaschuk J observed in *Re Moore*, supra, at p. 314, "the legislative criteria for finding a person a dangerous offender is [sic] perhaps the most detailed and demanding in the *Criminal Code*." Moreover, implicit in my discussion of the s. 12 issue is the common sense conclusion that the criteria in Pt. XXI are anything but arbitrary in relation to the objectives sought to be attained; they are clearly designed to segregate a small group of highly dangerous criminals posing threats to the physical or mental well-being of their victims.

As I see it, then, the sole issue left for consideration under s. 9 is whether the lack of uniformity in the treatment of dangerous persons that arises by virtue of the prosecutorial discretion to make an application under Pt. XXI constitutes unconstitutional arbitrariness. The appellant is not suggesting that prosecutors, in his case or generally, have exercised their discretion arbitrarily in this regard. Indeed, the affidavit evidence filed by the Crown in the companion case of *Milne v. R* [now reported post, p. 55 (sub nom. *R v. Milne*), [1987] 2 SCR 512] indicates that from 1978 to 1986 an average of only seven persons per year were sentenced under Pt. XXI. On average, each offender committed 12.12 offences, 2.2 of which were violent and 3.53 of which were sexual in nature. This suggests that the legislation has in general not been abused. I have no doubt that, if and when it is alleged that a prosecutor in a particular case was motivated by improper or arbitrary reasons in making a Pt. XXI application, a s. 24 remedy would lie. However, I do not think there is any warrant for presuming that the executive will act unconstitutionally or for improper purposes.

More important, however, is the fact that prosecutors always have a discretion in prosecuting criminals to the full extent of the law, an aspect of which involves making sentencing submissions. In this respect, I am in complete agreement with Crown counsel's submission that "it is the absence of discretion which would, in many cases, render arbitrary the law's application." As he notes:

> The absence of any discretion with respect to Part XXI would necessarily require the Crown to always proceed under Part XXI if there was the barest *prima facie* and the Court, upon making a finding that the offender is a dangerous offender, would always be required to impose an indeterminate sentence.

The foregoing also dispenses with the argument, not pursued here, that the judge ought not to have discretion with respect to whether he or she sentences an offender found to be dangerous to an indeterminate sentence. As Ewaschuk J stated in *Re Moore*, supra, at p. 310, the offender cannot be heard to complain of a discretion that can operate only to the offender's benefit. Indeed, it is apparent that one feature of s. 5(2) of the *Narcotic Control Act* that disturbed this court in *Smith*, supra, was the very fact that the imposition of sentence followed automatically upon conviction.

The remaining argument is that the prosecutorial discretion results in a geographical lack of uniformity and that this constitutes impermissible arbitrariness. However, the appellant is not arguing, as the accused did in *Morgentaler v. R*, SCC, 28th January 1988 (not yet reported), that this lack of uniformity is mandated by the terms of the legislation (which may or may not be a meritorious argument). Rather, this argument appears to recast the prosecutorial discretion argument. Moreover, variation among provinces in this regard may be inevitable, and indeed desirable, in a country where a federal statute is administered by local authorities. In any event, it may be observed parenthetically that, while the affidavit evidence suggests that dangerous offender applications are made more frequently in British Columbia (25 per cent of all such applications), and, perhaps surprisingly, never in Quebec, Newfoundland, Manitoba or Prince Edward Island, no attempt has been made to explain the significance of this data, for example, by relating it to the relevant population of offenders potentially coming within the provisions of Pt. XXI.

Having dealt with the broader issues, I now turn to the more specifically procedural issues raised by the appellant.

D. Are the Pt. XXI Procedures by Which This Deprivation of Liberty Is Occasioned and Reviewed Fundamentally Unfair?

(i) Does S. 11(f) of the Charter Require a Jury Hearing of a Pt. XXI Application?

Section 689(2) of the Code provides that an application under Pt. XXI shall be heard and determined by the court without a jury. The appellant submits that the procedure for designating an offender as dangerous is unfair and contrary to ss. 7 and 11(f) of the Charter, in particular, by denying the offender the right to the benefit of a jury's determination of dangerousness. I shall deal with the s. 11(f) issue first.

Section 11(f) of the Charter provides that:

> 11. Any person charged with an offence has the right ...
>
> (f) ... to the benefit of trial by jury where the maximum punishment for the offence is imprisonment for five years or a more severe punishment.

The key issue, for s. 11 purposes, is whether the Crown application to declare the offender a dangerous offender is equivalent to "charging" the offender with "an offence," for it is obvious that such offenders are liable to detention for periods much longer than five years.

…

There would seem to be no warrant for reconsidering the conclusion of this court that the "labelling" procedure does not constitute the charge of an offence. Nor do I think that a different conclusion can be justified for the purposes of s. 11 of the Charter. As I observed in *Schmidt v. R* (sub nom. *Can. v. Schmidt*), [1987] 1 SCR 500, the phrase "any person charged with an offence" in the opening words of the section must be given a constant meaning that harmonizes with the various paragraphs of the section. It seems clear to me that for the purposes of s. 11 it would be quite inappropriate to conclude that a convicted person is charged with an offence when confronted with a Pt. XXI application. How can it be said that the right to the presumption of innocence until proven *guilty* (s. 11(d)) and the right to bail (s. 11(e)), for example, could have any application in the context of the unique post-conviction proceeding mandated by Pt. XXI?

(ii) Does S. 7 of the Charter Require a Jury Hearing and Do the Pt. XXI Hearing and Review Procedures Otherwise Meet the Standard of Fairness Under That Section?

The conclusion that the appellant is not entitled to the benefit of trial by jury under s. 11(f) does not, however, conclusively decide the question whether he is entitled to a determination by a jury of the question of his dangerousness, or, more generally, whether the procedural incidents of the proceeding are constitutionally adequate to safeguard his liberty.

…

The cases to which I have referred dealt primarily with the use of hearsay evidence in such proceedings and with the question whether dangerousness could constitutionally be proved simply on a preponderance of evidence rather than beyond a reasonable doubt. Quite apart from the specific conclusions of the American courts respecting these matters, I would adopt the functional reasons given by those courts for viewing the "labelling" hearing to be the kind of hearing that attracts a high level of procedural protection for the offender. I find their approach to be more attuned to the distinctive nature of such inquiries, and more congruent with the reality of the very profound consequences that the labelling procedure harbours for the offender. Nevertheless, I would conclude that it is not required, as a constitutional matter, that the determination of dangerousness be made by a jury.

It is clear that, at a minimum, the requirements of fundamental justice embrace the requirements of procedural fairness: see, e.g., the comments to this effect of Wilson J in *Singh v. Can. (Min. of Employment & Immigration); Thandi v. Can. (Min. of Employment & Immigration); Mann v. Can. (Min. of Employment & Immigration)*, [1985] 1 SCR 177. It is also clear that the requirements of fundamental justice are not immutable; rather, they vary according to the context in which they are invoked.

Thus certain procedural protections might be constitutionally mandated in one context but not in another. Suffice it to say, however, that a jury determination is not mandated in the present context. The offender has already been found guilty of an offence in a trial at which he had the option of invoking his right to a jury. Moreover, the procedure to which he was subjected subsequent to the finding of guilt does not impact on his liberty to the same extent as that initial determination. Indeed, this is made clear by the same considerations that led this court, in [*Brusch v. The Queen* (1953), 105 CCC 340 (SCC)], to classify the proceedings as part of the sentencing process. While the legal classification of the proceeding as part of the sentencing process does not necessarily decide the question of the scope of the procedural protection to be afforded the offender, the functional, factual considerations animating that conclusion must be taken into account.

Finally, it is not insignificant that, unlike the situation in [*US v. Maroney*, 335 F2d 302 (1966)], the judge at such a hearing does retain a discretion whether or not to impose the designation or indeterminate sentence, or both.

It is noteworthy, too, that Pt. XXI provides considerable procedural protection to the offender. Section 689(1)(a) requires that the consent of the Attorney General be obtained either before or after the application is made. Section 689(1)(b) requires that "at least seven days notice be given to the offender by the prosecution, following the making of the application, outlining the basis on which it is intended to found the application." Moreover, the offender has the right to attend, present evidence and cross-examine witnesses, in addition to a right of appeal in the broadest terms on questions of fact, law or mixed fact and law.

It seems to me that s. 7 of the Charter entitles the appellant to a fair hearing; it does not entitle him to the most favourable procedures that could possibly be imagined. I do not think it can be argued that the procedure at a Pt. XXI application is unfair insofar as it denies to an offender the right to a jury's determination of his or her dangerousness.

...

(iii) Is the Standard of Proof Required Under Pt. XXI, or the Use of Psychiatric Evidence in a Pt. XXI Application, Fundamentally Unfair?

The appellant submits that Pt. XXI is fundamentally unfair in two other respects. He contends, first, that s. 688, in requiring proof that the offender constitutes a *threat* to the life, safety or physical or mental well-being of other persons, or that there is a *likelihood* of the offender causing injury, pain or other evil to other persons through a failure in the future to control his or her sexual impulses, is fundamentally unfair, in that the standard of proof required of the Crown is lower than that traditionally required in the criminal law process. Secondly, he argues that s. 690, by requiring that psychiatric evidence be tendered on an application under Pt. XXI, is fundamentally unfair to the extent that such evidence is an unreliable predictor of future conduct.

I do not believe that either of these submissions is valid. First, it is important to recognize exactly what is and what is not required to be proved on such an application. Subsection (a) and (b) of s. 688 both require proof that the offender represents a *threat* of some sort to society. It is nowhere required that it be proved that the offender *will* act in a certain way. Indeed, inherent in the notion of dangerousness is the risk, not the certainty, of harm.

The appellant asserts that a "likelihood" is ipso facto not susceptible of proof beyond a reasonable doubt. He cites in support the following statement of Isabel Grant, in her article "Dangerous Offenders" (1985), 9 *Dalhousie LJ* 347, at p. 360:

> How does one prove beyond a reasonable doubt that at some time in *some* setting, an individual is *likely* to endanger *some* person[?] Surely if we add "beyond a reasonable doubt" to a "future likelihood" the sum total can be no greater than a balance of probabilities, a standard we would never accept in a criminal trial.

However, as Holmes has reminded us, the life of the law has not been logic: it has been experience. The criminal law must operate in a world governed by practical considerations rather than abstract logic and, as a matter of practicality, the most that can be established in a future context is a likelihood of certain events occurring. To doubt this conclusion is, in actuality, to doubt the validity of the legislative objectives embodied in Pt. XXI, for to require certainty in such matters would be tantamount to rendering the entire process ineffective.

Moreover, I am not convinced, even as a matter of logic, that the appellant's submission is sound. It seems to me that a "likelihood" of specified future conduct occurring is the finding of fact required to be established; it is not, at one and the same time, the means of proving that fact. Logically, it seems clear to me that an individual can be found to constitute a *threat* to society without insisting that this require the court to assert an ability to predict the future. I do not find it illogical for a court to assert that it is satisfied beyond a reasonable doubt that the test of dangerousness has been met, that there exists a *certain* potential for harm. That this is really only an apparent paradox is aptly captured by Morden J in *R v. Knight* (1975), 27 CCC (2d) 343 at 356 (Ont. HC):

> I wish to make it clear that when I refer to the requisite standard of proof respecting likelihood I am not imposing on myself an obligation to find it proven beyond a reasonable doubt that certain events will happen in the future—this, in the nature of things would be impossible in practically every case—but I do refer to the quality and strength of the evidence of past and present facts together with the expert opinion thereon, as an existing basis for finding present likelihood of future conduct.

Having said the foregoing, it seems to me that when the appellant asserts that proof of a likelihood beyond a reasonable doubt still amounts merely to proof of a likelihood, it becomes apparent that what he is challenging is not the standard of proof but the fact that certain persons found to be "dangerous" will in fact not have been dangerous. This is the problem of "false positives," which I will address below.

I believe that the foregoing discussion also disposes of the contention that it is fundamentally unfair to the offender to require proof of dangerousness to be based in part on psychiatric evidence. Counsel for the appellant cited both academic and judicial authority recognizing the inability of psychiatrists, or anyone else, for that matter, to predict accurately future events. This is hardly a revelation. Indeed, the psychiatrists who testified at the hearing in the present case expressly disavowed any such claim.

It seems to me that the answer to this argument can be briefly stated. The test for admissibility is relevance, not infallibility. Judges at Pt. XXI hearings do not assume that psychiatrists can accurately predict the future; however, psychiatric evidence is clearly relevant to the issue whether a person is likely to behave in a certain way, and indeed is probably relatively superior in this regard to the evidence of other clinicians and lay persons; see Menzies, Webster and Sepejak, "The Dimensions of Dangerousness" (1985), 9 *L & Human Behaviour* No. 1.

• • •

Finally, the unreliability of psychiatric evidence also raises the problem of "false positives" (a statistical term representing the erroneous overprediction of future violence), discussed by Tobriner J for the majority of the California Supreme Court in *People v. Murtishaw*, 175 Cal. Rptr. 738 at 742-43:

> Numerous studies have demonstrated the inaccuracy of attempts to forecast future violent behaviour. Two commentators summarized the results as follows: "Whatever may be said for the reliability and validity of psychiatric judgments in general, there is literally no evidence that psychiatrists reliably and accurately can predict dangerous behaviour. To the contrary, such predictions are wrong more often than they are right." (Ennis & Litwack, *Psychiatry and the Presumption of Expertise: Flipping Coins in the Courtroom* (1974), 62 Cal. L Rev. 693, 737.) Professor Dershowitz in 1969 pointed to the skewed results characteristic of psychiatric forecasts: "it seems that psychiatrists are particularly prone to one type of error—over-predictions ... [F]or every correct psychiatric prediction of violence, there are numerous erroneous predictions." (Dershowitz, *The Psychiatrist's Power in Civil Commitment: A Knife That Cuts Both Ways* (Feb. 1969), Psych. Today, at p. 47.) Cocozza and Steadman in 1976 reviewed the various studies and reported that "Whether one examined the legal, behavioural science, or psychiatric literature on predictions of dangerousness, one constantly encounters conclusions similar to the one reached by Dershowitz that psychiatrists are generally inaccurate predictors." (Cocozza & Steadman, *op. cit.*, supra, 29 Rutgers L Rev. at p. 1085.) In 1978 Professor Monahan undertook a further review of studies of violence prediction and noted that the percentage of false positives (erroneous predictions that a subject would engage in violent behaviour) never fell below 54 percent and went as high as 99.7 percent. (Monahan, *The Prediction and Control of Violent Behavior* (1978), pp. 179-196, in Hearings Before the House Subcom. on Domestic and International Scientific Planning, 95th Cong., 2d Sess., pp. 175-252.)

This problem does not appear to undermine the utility and fairness of the scheme so much as to fortify the conclusion that the procedural protections accorded the offender, especially on review, ought to be very rigorous. In its *Report of the Committee on Mentally Abnormal Offenders*, the Butler Commission recognized the difficulties in assessing dangerousness but nevertheless recommended that the British Parliament enact dangerous offender legislation with reviewable indeterminate sentences. It stated, at p. 60:

> [t]he fact that we cannot quantify the probability of future dangerous behaviour with actuarial precision is often allowed to obscure the fact that we can point with some confidence to categories of people who are more likely than others of the same sex and age-group to act in this way. Some kinds of sexual offence seem to be very repetitive. ...

Men with several convictions of violence are considerably more likely than their peers to be convicted of violence in the future. Again, it is sometimes argued that even if there are good grounds—clinical or actuarial—for assigning the individual to a high risk group, he might be one of the minority in that group who in the event will not behave in accordance with probability. But this dilemma is inescapably involved in every decision which is based on probabilities. All that can be done is to weigh the unpleasantness of the consequences for the individual against the harm which he may do to others. If the harm is likely to be slight the decision should be in his favour: if great and highly probable—for example, if a sexual offence is accompanied by serious violence—the best we can do is to make sure that the precautions are as humane as possible.

Similarly, Floud and Young reject the notion that in enacting dangerous offender legislation Parliament unfairly sacrifices innocent persons in favour of the public good (at pp. 48-49):

This argument is misconceived. Errors of prediction do not represent determinable individuals. It is not that we have difficulty in identifying the subjects of predicted error with the methods available to us; it is that they are in principle indeterminable. There are no hidden individuals identifiable in principle, but not in practice, who certainly would or would not reoffend. In this sense there are no innocent or guilty subjects of predictive judgment. ... The question is not "how many innocent persons are to sacrifice their liberty for the extra protection that special sentences for dangerous offenders will provide?" But "what is the moral choice between the alternative risks: the risk of harm to potential victims or the risk of unnecessarily detaining offenders judged to be dangerous?" *The essential nature of the problem of preventing wilful harm is misrepresented by talk of balancing individual and social costs. The problem is to make a just redistribution of risk in circumstances that do not permit of its being reduced.* There is a risk of harm to innocent persons at the hands of an offender who is judged likely to inflict it intentionally or recklessly—in any case culpably—in defiance or disregard of the usual constraints. His being in the wrong by virtue of the risk he represents is what entitles us to consider imposing on him the risk of unnecessary measures to save the risk of harm to innocent victims. [Emphasis added.]

I agree with this reasoning. Accordingly, the appellant's submissions on this point fail.

NOTE

As mentioned above, the recent amendments to the dangerous offender provisions altered the regime in the following ways: (1) s. 753(4) removes the discretion to impose a fixed sentence on a prisoner declared to be a dangerous offender; (2) s. 752.1 no longer requires the assessment of two psychiatrists, substituting the requirement of just one report; (3) s. 753(2) allows a dangerous offender application to be made six months after the original imposition of sentence if new information arises; and (4) s. 761(1) delays the first parole review of dangerous offenders from three years to seven years. All of these changes were opposed by the Canadian Bar Association (see Canadian Bar Association (National Criminal Justice Section), *Submission on Bill C-55: Criminal Code Amendments High Risk Offenders* (February 1997)). Indeed, the Federal/Provincial/Territorial Task Force on High-Risk Offenders issued the following caution (supra, at 13):

At their meeting in March, 1994, Ministers [responsible for justice] agreed not to amend Part XXIV of the *Criminal Code*, but rather to make better use of it. The Task Force reiterates its position that a major departure from the Dangerous Offender structure along the lines, for example, of the draft legislation developed in 1993, would fun afoul of the Supreme Court of Canada's judgement in *R v. Lyons*. The Court stressed the importance of a well-tailored measure that will target specific high-risk offenders with a form of punishment that flows from the commission of a specific crime. A measure that would allow a Dangerous Offender application later in sentence, without clear evidence of a new offence, could conflict with the Charter protections against double punishment and arbitrary detention.

The Task Force does recommend a few changes to the Dangerous Offender rules in the area of assessment, as described below. These changes should strengthen, rather than weaken, the current system.

Note that the task force did recommend that the law be changed such that, when an offender is declared to be a dangerous offender, an indeterminate sentence is mandatory (supra, at 21).

Do you think the dangerous offender provisions as they exist today would survive a constitutional challenge like the one in *Lyons*? Have the numerous protections in the legislation relied on in the reasons of LaForest J been altered to such a degree that the legislation is now constitutionally infirm? Consider whether *Lyons* is still the authentic baseline or standard for determining the constitutionality of this type of legislation.

III. LONG-TERM OFFENDERS

A. Background

As discussed in the introduction to this chapter, the long-term offender provisions were enacted in 1997. They were created on the recommendation of the Federal/Provincial/Territorial Task Force on High-Risk Offenders. The provisions were designed to catch the type of offender who, while not worthy of the dangerous offender designation, still requires some form of preventive detention. Like the dangerous offender amendments, this measure arose from the government's (and the task force's) concern with "sexual predators." Remember that probation can be attached only to a sentence of imprisonment that is no longer than two years. The answer to this limitation was the creation of the long-term offender designation, which permits up to 10 years of supervision to be added onto a penitentiary sentence if the offender meets the "substantial risk" to reoffend standard in s. 753.1. Thus, the long-term offender designation is a middle ground between an indeterminate sentence and an ordinary fixed-term sanction.

B. The Provisions

753.1(1) The court may, on application made under this Part following the filing of an assessment report under subsection 752.1(2), find an offender to be a long-term offender if it is satisfied that

(a) it would be appropriate to impose a sentence of imprisonment of two years or more for the offence for which the offender has been convicted;

(b) there is a substantial risk that the offender will reoffend; and

(c) there is a reasonable possibility of eventual control of the risk in the community.

(2) The court shall be satisfied that there is a substantial risk that the offender will reoffend if

(a) the offender has been convicted of an offence under section 151 (sexual interference), 152 (invitation to sexual touching) or 153 (sexual exploitation), subsection 173(2) (exposure) or section 271 (sexual assault), 272 (sexual assault with a weapon) or 273 (aggravated sexual assault), or has engaged in serious conduct of a sexual nature in the commission of another offence of which the offender has been convicted; and

(b) the offender

(i) has shown a pattern of repetitive behaviour, of which the offence for which he or she has been convicted forms a part, that shows a likelihood of the offender's causing death or injury to other persons or inflicting severe psychological damage on other persons, or

(ii) by conduct in any sexual matter including that involved in the commission of the offence for which the offender has been convicted, has shown a likelihood of causing injury, pain or other evil to other persons in the future through similar offences.

(3) Subject to subsections (3.1), (4) and (5), if the court finds an offender to be a long-term offender, it shall

(a) impose a sentence for the offence for which the offender has been convicted, which sentence must be a minimum punishment of imprisonment for a term of two years; and

(b) order the offender to be supervised in the community, for a period not exceeding ten years, in accordance with section 753.2 and the *Corrections and Conditional Release Act*.

...

(4) The court shall not make an order under paragraph (3)(b) if the offender has been sentenced to life imprisonment.

(5) If the offender commits another offence while required to be supervised by an order made under paragraph(3)(b), and is thereby found to be a long-term offender, the periods of supervision to which the offender is subject at any particular time must not total more than ten years.

(6) If the court does not find an offender to be a long-term offender, the court shall impose sentence for the offence for which the offender has been convicted.

753.2(1) Subject to subsection (2), an offender who is required to be supervised by an order made under paragraph 753.1(3)(b) shall be supervised in accordance with the *Corrections and Conditional Release Act* when the offender has finished serving

(a) the sentence for the offence for which the offender has been convicted; and

(b) all other sentences for offences for which the offender is convicted and for which sentence of a term of imprisonment is imposed on the offender, either before or after the conviction for the offence referred to in paragraph (a).

(2) A sentence imposed on an offender referred to in subsection (1), other than a sentence that requires imprisonment of the offender, is to be served concurrently with the long-term supervision ordered under paragraph 753.1(3)(b).

(3) An offender who is required to be supervised, a member of the National Parole Board, or, on approval of that Board, the parole supervisor, as that expression is defined in subsection 134.2(2) of the *Corrections and Conditional Release Act*, of the offender, may apply to a superior court of criminal jurisdiction for an order reducing the period of long-term supervision or terminating it on the ground that the offender no long presents a substantial risk of reoffending and thereby being a danger to the community. The onus of providing that ground is on the applicant.

(4) The applicant must give notice of an application under subsection (3) to the Attorney General at the time the application is made.

753.3(1) An offender who is required to be supervised by an order made under paragraph 753.1(3)(b) and who, without reasonable excuse, fails or refuses to comply with that order is guilty of an indictable offence and liable to imprisonment for a term not exceeding ten years.

Note the sanctions for breach of long-term supervision that apply after the original sentence and the carceral warrant has expired. First, under s. 753.3(1), failure or refusal to comply without reasonable excuse is a new indictable offence subject to imprisonment. Second, under s. 135.1 of the *Corrections and Conditional Release Act*, the offender on long-term supervision can be suspended or returned to custody, or committed to a community-based residential facility or a mental health facility for up to 90 days.

C. Applying the Provisions

Judicial experience with the new provisions has been limited. Consider the interpretive issue addressed by the British Columbia Court of Appeal in *R v. McLeod*. Do you think the court's approach to what is properly characterized as an antecedent offence unduly expands the legitimate reach of the long-term offender provisions? Moreover, is the court's approach to the issue in s. 753.1(1)(b) of whether there is a "substantial risk" to reoffend too restrictive?

R v. McLeod
(1999), 136 CCC (3d) 492 (BC CA)

PROWSE JA:

Nature of Appeal

Mr. McLeod is appealing from the decision of a Provincial Court judge made April 26, 1998, designating him a long-term offender and sentencing him to a period of two years' imprisonment followed by seven years' supervision in the community on strict conditions. The Provincial Court judge also made an order under s. 100 of the *Criminal Code*, RSC 1985, c. C-46 (the "Code"), prohibiting Mr. McLeod from possessing firearms "except for the purpose of aboriginal hunting for sustenance and then only with the consent of his probation officer and on any conditions as set out by the probation officer."

Grounds of Appeal

Mr. McLeod submits that the learned sentencing judge erred in:

(1) finding Mr. McLeod to be a long-term offender despite the fact that Mr. McLeod had not been convicted of one or more of the sexual offences enumerated in s. 753.1(2)(a) of the Code;

(2) finding Mr. McLeod to be a long-term offender in the absence of the consent of the Attorney General to a long-term offender application, contrary to s. 754(1)(a) of the Code;

(3) imposing a lifetime weapons prohibition in the absence of a notice seeking greater punishment under s. 727 of the Code, or, alternatively, failing to exercise his discretion to impose a lesser prohibition.

In reply, the Crown submits that the learned sentencing judge erred in exceeding his jurisdiction by imposing conditions on the lifetime weapons prohibition.

Background

In October 1997, Mr. McLeod was charged on a four-count Information with: aggravated assault, use of a weapon during an assault; possession of a weapon for a purpose dangerous to the public peace; and uttering a threat to cause death or bodily harm. These charges arose out of an incident which occurred on September 29, 1997, in Fort St. John, BC.

Prior to Mr. McLeod's first appearance, Crown counsel and counsel for Mr. McLeod had discussions whereby Mr. McLeod agreed to plead guilty to two counts on the Information on the understanding that the Crown would stay the other charges and seek to have Mr. McLeod designated a long-term offender pursuant to s. 753.1 of the Code. Accordingly, on November 26, 1997, Mr. McLeod pleaded guilty to one count of assault causing bodily harm and one count of possession of a weapon for a purpose dangerous to the public peace. Thereafter, the sentencing judge ordered an assessment of Mr. McLeod pursuant to s. 752.1 of the Code.

The sentencing was adjourned to permit the assessment to be completed and to permit the Crown to seek the consent of the Attorney General to its proposed application to have Mr. McLeod designated a long-term offender. In the result, the Attorney General did not provide a consent to an application to have Mr. McLeod designated a long-term offender, but, rather, provided a consent to have Mr. McLeod designated a dangerous offender.

Thereafter, on March 20, 1998, Crown counsel filed his application to have Mr. McLeod designated a dangerous offender, together with a notice to Mr. McLeod in that regard. On March 24, the matter returned to court and the sentencing judge was advised that the Crown would be proceeding by way of a dangerous offender application. Counsel for Mr. McLeod objected, stating that Mr. McLeod's guilty plea was predicated upon the Crown proceeding by way of a long-term offender application. The sentencing judge dealt with this objection by finding that the Crown was bound by its plea bargain and then proceeding with the application before him as if it were an application for a long-term offender designation. As earlier noted, he determined that Mr. McLeod should be designated a long-term offender and subjected to the maximum period of post-incarceration supervision.

...

Discussion

1. Long-Term Offenders—Sexual Offences

...

(c) Analysis

...

In my view, the meaning of s. 753.1 is straightforward, whether read separately or in the larger context of Part XXIV of the Code. It provides that a court may find an offender to be a long-term offender if the three conditions set out in s-ss. 753.1(1)(a) to (c) are met:

(a) it would be appropriate to impose a sentence of imprisonment of two years or more for the offence for which the offender has been convicted;

(b) there is a substantial risk that the offender will reoffend; and

(c) there is a reasonable possibility of eventual control of the risk in the community.

Subsection 753.1(2)(a) simply provides that the court must find ("shall be satisfied") that there is a substantial risk the offender will reoffend if the conditions set out in that subsection are met. One of those conditions is that the offender has been convicted of the sexual offences set out in that subsection (which include sexual offences of a less serious nature than those caught within the definition of "serious personal injury offence" in s. 752). Thus, if an offender is convicted of one of the sexual offences delineated in s. 753.1(2)(a), the court must find that there is a substantial risk that the offender will reoffend; that is, that the second condition in s. 753.1(1)(b) has been met. Before the court can designate the offender a long-term offender, however, the court must still determine whether the other two conditions in s. 753.1(1)(a) and (c) have been satisfied.

I do not agree with the submission on behalf of Mr. McLeod that the effect of s. 753.1(2)(a) is to restrict the scope of s. 753.1(1) to apply only to offenders who are convicted of one or more of the sexual offences listed in s. 753.1(2)(a). If Parliament had intended to limit the designation of long-term offender to those convicted of sexual offences, it could have done so by simply adding that as a fourth condition to be satisfied under s. 753.1(1). Counsel for Mr. McLeod is, in effect, asking us to read a fourth condition into that subsection which does not otherwise exist.

Nor am I persuaded that the wording of s. 752.1(1) (set out at para. 10, supra) is of assistance in determining the scope of s. 753.1. The former section simply enables the court to order that an offender be remanded for assessment if the person is convicted of a serious personal injury offence as defined in s. 752 (which includes both sexual and non-sexual offences), or of one of the less serious sexual offences included in s. 753.1(2)(a). I am unable to find anything in s. 752 which limits the scope of s. 753.1 to sexual offenders.

Similarly, I am unable to find any other provision in Part XXIV of the Code which either directly or indirectly suggests that Parliament intended the long-term offender designation to apply only to sexual offenders. If recourse to Hansard were necessary to determine the mischief at which the long-term offender provisions were directed (and I do not find such recourse necessary), I would agree with Mr. McLeod's counsel that the primary focus of discussion in the House of Commons with respect to these provisions was directed to the supervision and control of sexual offenders when they return to the community upon completion of their sentences of two years or more. Paedophiles, in particular, were seen to present a particular concern. But, it is difficult to accept the proposition that Parliament intended that repeat offenders who did not meet the criteria for a dangerous offender designation under s. 753(1) could not be found to be long-term offenders unless they had committed one of the sexual offences listed in s. 753.1(2)(a). For example, if an offender repeatedly assaulted his or her spouse when intoxicated, but his or her actions did not fit within the definition of "serious personal injury offence" in s. 752, it is difficult to conceive that Parliament did not intend to provide the same protection to the public upon that offender's release into the community as in the case of a repeat offender who was convicted of "exposure" under s. 173(2) of the Code. (Exposure is one of the sexual offences set out in s. 753.1(2)(a).) While the sexual offender may be a higher profile offender in the community than the spouse-beater, I can find nothing in s. 753.1, read alone, or in the context of Part XXIV, which suggests that the long-term offender designation was not intended to protect the public from the latter by providing for his or her ongoing supervision in the community upon release from custody.

I also note that s. 753(5) provides that where the court finds that a person does not meet the criteria for a dangerous offender designation, the court may go on to determine whether the offender meets the criteria for a long-term offender designation based on the same predicate offences. Again, there is nothing in that section which indicates that the court can only go on to determine whether an offender meets the long-term offender criteria if the predicate offences are sexual offences.

In coming to these conclusions, I am mindful of the background and legislative history leading to the revisions to the dangerous offender provisions of the Code and the introduction of the long-term offender provisions. A key factor in that background was the *Report of the Federal/Provincial/Territorial Task Force on High Risk Violent Offenders: Strategies for Managing High Risk Offenders* (Victoria: Department of Justice, January 1995) (the "Report"). Amongst other things, the Report stressed that there was a need for legislation to deal with some categories of offenders (with an emphasis on paedophiles), who do not meet the criteria of dangerous offenders, but, who, nonetheless, are capable of harming numerous victims as a result of their chronic criminal behaviour. At p. 19 of the Report, which specifically deals with the proposed new classification of long-term offenders, the authors state as follows:

> A sentencing option providing for long term supervision would be aimed at cases where an established offence cycle with observable cues is present, and where a long term

relapse prevention approach may be indicated. The success of an LTS [long term supervision] scheme based on the relapse prevention model rests on several key factors.

  a. The measure should be focused on particular classes of offender. The inclination to make long-term supervision widely available should be resisted as costly, unwarranted in most cases, and as contributing to "net widening." The target group, and thus the expectations of the scheme, should be well defined;
  b. The criteria should selectively target those offenders who have a high likelihood of committing further violent or sexual crimes but who would not likely be found to be a Dangerous Offender.

. . .

It is evident when reading the Report in conjunction with Part XXIV of the Code, that the recommendations of the Task Force with respect to the long-term offender proposals were, for the most part, adopted in Bill C-55, *An Act to amend the Criminal Code* (high risk offenders), *the Corrections and Conditional Release Act, the Criminal Records Act, the Prisons and Reformatories Act and the Department of the Solicitor General Act*, SC 1997, c. 17. The provisions with which we are here concerned came into force on August 1, 1997. Thus, while paedophiles and other sexual predators may well have been the primary targets of the new long-term offender provisions, I can find nothing in the background or legislative history confining their application to sexual offenders.

I am also satisfied that the interpretation I have given to these provisions is in accordance with s. 12 of the *Interpretation Act*, as providing a "fair, large and liberal construction and interpretation" which best attains the object of these provisions, which is to provide increased protection to the public from repeat offenders who represent a risk to the community if left unsupervised after serving a federal custodial sentence.

(d) Conclusion

On the basis of my conclusion that the long-term offender provisions of the Code are not restricted in their application to those convicted of the sexual offences set out in s. 753.1(2)(a) of the Code, I would dismiss the first ground of appeal.

2. *Consent of the Attorney General*

Counsel for Mr. McLeod submits that the sentencing judge erred in designating Mr. McLeod a long-term offender in the absence of the consent of the Attorney General to an application for a long-term offender designation.

Counsel for the Crown points to the fact that the defence did not object at the time of sentencing to the sentencing judge proceeding as if he were dealing with a long-term offender application. Her principal argument with respect to this ground of appeal, however, is summarized in the following excerpt from her factum:

  48. As well, because s. 753(5) allows the court to treat a DO [dangerous offender] application as an LTO [long-term offender] application, by necessary implication the consent of the Attorney General to a DO proceeding must be sufficient for what is in

effect a lesser included proceeding. There is no mention of a further consent being filed in the event that the court finds itself under s. 753(5). The consent filed in this case therefore met the requirements of s. 754(1)(a).

While this submission has a certain pragmatic attraction, I am of the view that this issue is jurisdictional in nature and not amenable to the compromise solution fashioned by the sentencing judge. The only application before the sentencing judge was an application for a dangerous offender designation, together with the consent of the Attorney General to that application. While it is understandable that the sentencing judge was unwilling to proceed with the dangerous offender application given the previous position taken by the Crown, which had resulted in Mr. McLeod's guilty pleas, I am satisfied that it was not open to the court to override the Attorney General's election to proceed in this fashion by unilaterally treating the application as one under s. 753.1 of the Code.

Section 754 is explicit as to the nature of the consent required in circumstances such as these. ... As earlier noted, the only application before the court was the application for a dangerous offender designation. That is the only application to which the Attorney General had consented. In fact, when asked to consent to a long-term offender designation he had declined to provide it. If pressed to provide his consent to a long-term offender designation when the sentencing judge made it clear that he had no intention of proceeding with a dangerous offender proceeding, the Attorney General may well have deemed it appropriate to proceed by way of prohibition or mandamus. Thus, even if it were open to the court to infer that the Attorney General would have consented to a long-term offender application, I would not draw that inference in these circumstances.

Further, while it is true that in the circumstances set out in s. 753(5) of the Code a dangerous offender application may ultimately result in a long-term offender designation, there is no suggestion that s. 753(5) had any application in this case. I agree with the defence that if s. 753(5) applied, it would not have been necessary for the Crown to seek the further consent of the Attorney General to continue with the proceeding once it had been determined that the offender was not a dangerous offender and before the offender could be designated a long-term offender.

I would allow the appeal on this ground.

Conclusion

The options available to the Court of Appeal from a finding that an offender is a long-term offender are set out in s. 759(3.1) of the Code. It provides:

> (3.1) On an appeal against a finding that an offender is a long-term offender, the court of appeal may
>> (a) allow the appeal and
>>> (i) find that the offender is not a long-term offender and quash the order for long-term supervision, or
>>> (ii) order a new hearing; or
>> (b) dismiss the appeal.

Since the issues raised on this appeal did not deal with the merits of the finding that Mr. McLeod is a long-term offender, I would not accede to his counsel's request that we find that Mr. McLeod is not a long-term offender and quash the order for long-term supervision. Rather, I would order a new hearing under s. 759(3.1)(a)(ii) of the Code. At that hearing, if the Crown persists in seeking to proceed by way of a dangerous offender application, it is open to the defence to raise any arguments with respect to the propriety and legal consequences of the Crown's failure to adhere to its plea bargain that were available to it at the original hearing.

···

In the result, I would allow the appeal and remit the matter to the Provincial Court for a new hearing.

IV. PREVENTIVE RECOGNIZANCES

A. Background

Dangerous offender and long-term offender applications follow the conviction of an individual. Thus, a condition precedent to the operation of those provisions is a conviction for a "serious personal injury offence." We now turn our attention to preventive measures that may be employed in the absence of a trial and conviction.

Building on the use of common law peace bonds and the statutory peace bonds in s. 810 of the *Criminal Code*, in 1993[1] and 1997[2] Parliament created three new post-sentence preventive vehicles. The impetus for enacting these provisions came, at least in part, from a desire to address concerns about perceived dangerousness once a sentence has been completed. These provisions may be used to impose post-sentence supervision on individuals who are perceived to be dangerous.

While there are differences among the three provisions, they are similar in structure. Section 810.01 is triggered by fear that someone will commit a criminal organization offence. Section 810.1 can be triggered when someone fears on reasonable grounds that a sexual offence against a child will be committed. Section 810.2 addresses fear of a serious personal injury offence. All three of these mechanisms require applications to a court and may result in a recognizance lasting up to 12 months that includes specific conditions. Sections 810.01 and 810.2 require the consent of the provincial attorney general before an information may be received by a provincial court judge. Sections 810.01 and 810.1 require fear that a particular person or persons may be victimized; there is no such requirement in s. 810.2. A breach of any of these recognizances is a hybrid offence, which is punishable by up to two years' imprisonment when prosecuted by indictment.

---

1   SC 1993, c. 45, s. 11.

2   For s. 810.2, see SC 1997, c. 17, s. 9; for s. 810.01, see SC 1997, c. 23, s. 19.

B. The Provisions

When fear of criminal organization offence

810.01(1) A person who fears on reasonable grounds that another person will commit a criminal organization offence may, with the consent of the Attorney General, lay an information before a provincial court judge.

(2) A provincial court judge who receives an information under subsection (1) may cause the parties to appear before the provincial court judge.

(3) The provincial court judge before whom the parties appear may, if satisfied by the evidence adduced that the informant has reasonable grounds for the fear, order that the defendant enter into a recognizance to keep the peace and be of good behaviour for any period that does not exceed twelve months and to comply with any other reasonable conditions prescribed in the recognizance, including the conditions set out in subsection (5), that the provincial court judge considers desirable for preventing the commission of a criminal organization offence.

(4) The provincial court judge may commit the defendant to prison for a term not exceeding twelve months if the defendant fails or refuses to enter into the recognizance.

(5) Before making an order under subsection (3), the provincial court judge shall consider whether it is desirable, in the interests of the safety of the defendant or of any other person, to include as a condition of the recognizance that the defendant be prohibited from possessing any firearm, cross-bow, prohibited weapon, restricted weapon, prohibited device, ammunition, prohibited ammunition, or explosive substance, or all of these things, for any period specified in the recognizance, and where the provincial court judge decides that it is so desirable, the provincial court judge shall add such a condition to the recognizance.

...

(6) The provincial court judge may, on application of the informant, the Attorney General or the defendant, vary the conditions fixed in the recognizance.

...

Where fear of sexual offence

810.1(1) Any person who fears on reasonable grounds that another person will commit an offence under section 151, 152, 155 or 159, subsection 160(2) or (3), section 170 or 171, subsection 173(2) or section 271, 272 or 273, in respect of one or more persons who are under the age of fourteen years, may lay an information before a provincial court judge, whether or not the person or persons in respect of whom it is feared that the offence will be committed are named.

(2) A provincial court judge who receives an information under subsection (1) shall cause the parties to appear before the provincial court judge.

(3) The provincial court judge before whom the parties appear may, if satisfied by the evidence adduced that the informant has reasonable grounds for the fear, order the defendant to enter into a recognizance and comply with the conditions fixed by the provincial court judge, including a condition prohibiting the defendant from engaging in any activity that involves contact with persons under the age of fourteen years and prohibiting the defendant from attending a public park or public swimming area where persons under the age of fourteen years are present or can reasonably be expected to be present, or a daycare centre, schoolground, playground or community centre, for any period fixed by the provincial court judge that does not exceed twelve months.

(3.1) The provincial court judge may commit the defendant to prison for a term not exceeding twelve months if the defendant fails or refuses to enter into the recognizance.

...

Where fear of serious personal injury offence

810.2(1) Any person who fears on reasonable grounds that another person will commit a serious personal injury offence, as that expression is defined in section 752, may, with the consent of the Attorney General, lay an information before a provincial court judge, whether or not the person or persons in respect of whom it is feared that the offence will be committed are named.

(2) A provincial court judge who receives an information under subsection (1) may cause the parties to appear before the provincial court judge.

(3) The provincial court judge before whom the parties appear may, if satisfied by the evidence adduced that the informant has reasonable grounds for the fear, order that the defendant enter into a recognizance to keep the peace and be of good behaviour for any period that does not exceed twelve months and to comply with any other reasonable conditions prescribed in the recognizance, including the conditions set out in subsections (5) and (6), that the provincial court judge considers desirable for securing the good conduct of the defendant.

(4) The provincial court judge may commit the defendant to prison for a term not exceeding twelve months if the defendant fails or refuses to enter into the recognizance.

(5) Before making an order under subsection (3), the provincial court judge shall consider whether it is desirable, in the interests of the safety of the defendant or of any other person, to include as a condition of the recognizance that the defendant be prohibited from possessing any firearm, cross-bow, prohibited weapon, restricted weapon, prohibited device, ammunition, prohibited ammunition or explosive substance, or all such things, for any period specified in the recognizance, and where the provincial court judge decides that it is so desirable, the provincial court judge shall add such a condition to the recognizance.

(5.1) Where the provincial court judge adds a condition described in subsection (5) to a recognizance order, the provincial court judge shall specify in the order the manner and method by which

(a) the things referred to in that subsection that are in the possession of the defendant shall be surrendered, disposed of, detained, stored or dealt with; and

(b) the authorizations, licences and registration certificates held by the defendant shall be surrendered.

(5.2) Where the provincial court judge does not add a condition described in subsection (5) to a recognizance order, the provincial court judge shall include in the record a statement of the reasons for not adding the condition.

(6) Before making an order under subsection (3), the provincial court judge shall consider whether it is desirable to include as a condition of the recognizance that the defendant report to the correctional authority of a province or to an appropriate police authority, and where the provincial court judge decides that it is desirable for the defendant to so report, the provincial court judge may add the appropriate condition to the recognizance.

C. The Constitutionality of the Provisions

As noted above, the three types of preventive recognizances differ in some respects, but they are similar in a number of crucial ways. The following decision of the Court of

Appeal for Ontario in *Budreo* addresses the constitutionality of s. 810.1 (sexual offences) of the Code. It also confronts a number of interpretive issues that are easily applicable to the other recognizances in sections 810.01 (criminal organizations) and 810.2 (serious personal injury offences).

R v. Budreo
(2000), 46 OR (3d) 481 (CA)

LASKIN JA:

Introduction

[1] Section 810.1 of the *Criminal Code*, RSC 1985, c. C-46, enacted by Parliament in 1993, permits the court to impose a recognizance on any person likely to commit any one of a number of listed sexual offences against a child under 14 years of age and to prohibit that person for up to one year from engaging in activities or attending places—a public park, public swimming area, daycare centre, schoolground or playground—where children under 14 are likely to be present. ... A recognizance may be imposed though the person has not committed an offence and has no previous criminal record. If an informant fears on reasonable grounds that the person will commit one of the listed offences and a provincial court judge, after a hearing, is satisfied that the informant has reasonable grounds for the fear, then the person may be ordered to enter into a recognizance. The issue on this appeal is the constitutionality of s. 810.1.

[2] The appellant Wray Budreo is a paedophile. He has a long record of sexual offences against young boys. In November 1994, he was released from prison after serving a sentence for three convictions for sexual assault. The Crown immediately sought a recognizance under s. 810.1. The appellant brought an application to prohibit the provincial court judge, His Honour Judge Kelly, from holding the s. 810.1 hearing and for a declaration that s. 810.1 was unconstitutional because it violated ss. 7, 9, 11 and 15 of the *Canadian Charter of Rights and Freedoms*.

[3] In a lengthy and well-reasoned decision, Then J concluded that s. 810.1 was constitutional except in two respects. First, he declared "community centre," one of the places a person could be prohibited from attending under s. 810.1(3), to be inoperative because it was overly broad contrary to s. 7 of the Charter and could not be justified under s. 1. Second, he found that s. 810.1(2), which required the provincial court judge to cause the parties to appear before the court, infringed ss. 7 and 9 of the Charter and could not be justified under s. 1. To remedy this violation, however, Then J read down the word "shall" in s. 810.1(2) to read "may."

[4] The appellant Budreo appealed and was supported in his appeal by the intervenor, the Canadian Civil Liberties Association. In oral argument the appellant narrowed the focus of his appeal to three main issues. First, he submitted that s. 810.1 violated s. 7 of the Charter. In his submission, s. 810.1 deprived him of his liberty contrary to the principles of fundamental justice in three ways: s. 810.1 creates a status offence; it is impermissibly broad; and it is impermissibly vague. Second, he submitted that Then J erred in reading down "shall" to "may" in s. 810.1(2) and that

he should instead have declared the subsection inoperative. Third, he submitted that Then J erred in holding that a person subject to a s. 810.1 proceeding can be compelled to court by an arrest warrant under s. 507(4) of the Code and can be detained pending the hearing under s. 515. As part of this third submission the appellant asked us to reconsider this court's decision in *R v. Allen* (1985), 18 CCC (3d) 155, 8 OAC 16 (CA) in the light of the Charter.

[5] I would dismiss the appellant's appeal. Because I agree substantially with the reasons of Then J, I will limit my own reasons to summarizing the main points on which I rely, focusing on the specific arguments that were made before us.

Background Facts

[6] The appellant is 55 years old. He has been diagnosed as a paedophile. He has an extensive criminal record dating back to 1961, which includes many convictions for indecent assault and sexual assault committed against young boys. These convictions, in the main, have resulted from the "physical touching" of boys between five and 17 years of age. Of the appellant's 36 convictions, 26 have been for the physical touching of young males.

[7] On November 18, 1994, the appellant was released from the Kingston Penitentiary, after having served a six-year sentence for three counts of sexual assault. These sexual assault convictions concerned three incidents in which the appellant convinced the victims—young boys—to lay down in a park and then fondled their bare stomachs, and in two cases their genitals. In sentencing the appellant, Webber DCJ wrote, "Clearly, Mr. Budreo is a person who has a paedophiliac problem which has existed for many, many years and it appears that there is very little that has been done for him and there is very little that he has done for himself, except on a spasmodic and irregular basis."

[8] On his release, at the request of the Correctional Service of Canada, the appellant submitted to a psychiatric assessment under the *Mental Health Act*, RSO 1990, c. M.7 to determine whether he was certifiable. The psychiatrist with the Correctional Service who did the assessment declined to certify the appellant. The psychiatrist concluded that the appellant did not pose a sufficient risk of serious harm to himself or to members of the public, that he had made considerable gains toward rehabilitating himself, and that he was "well motivated." Doctors at the Clarke Institute of Psychiatry also concluded that the appellant did not pose a danger to himself or others and, thus, should not be admitted under the *Mental Health Act*.

[9] Since his release, the appellant has followed a treatment plan devised for him. The treatment plan consists of continued psychiatric counselling directed by a doctor at the Clarke Institute and monthly injections of the anti-androgen drug Luperon.

[10] Nonetheless, the appellant's release from prison sparked considerable publicity, most of it negative. The appellant had gone first to Peterborough and then to Toronto. He was under continuous police surveillance in both cities and press releases were issued to tell the public of his whereabouts.

[11] Within three days of his release, the Crown began proceedings under s. 810.1 of the *Criminal Code*. The Crown acknowledges that it sought a recognizance under

s. 810.1, not because the appellant had done anything improper or illegal since his release from prison, but because of his criminal record and his diagnosis as a paedophile.

[12] On November 20, 1994, Detective Wendy Leaver of the Metropolitan Toronto Police Service asked the appellant to agree to enter into recognizance under s. 810.1. The appellant was apparently unwilling to do so. The s. 810.1 application was then scheduled for November 22, 1994 and the appellant was told to obtain counsel.

[13] Detective Leaver swore an information under s. 810.1 in which she said she feared, on reasonable grounds, that the appellant would commit any one of a number of specified sexual offences against children under the age of 14. She said that her fear was based on the appellant's psychiatric reports between 1963 and 1993, his criminal record, numerous hospital and parole board reports and a conversation with the appellant's treating psychiatrist at the Clarke Institute, who considered the appellant a high-risk paedophile if he did not take Luperon.

[14] Detective Leaver attended before Judge Kelly on November 22, 1994. The appellant came to court voluntarily. Nonetheless, Detective Leaver asked the appellant to leave the courtroom, and once he had done so, arrested him under s. 507(4) of the *Criminal Code*.

[15] The appellant was then in custody. The Crown therefore proceeded with a show cause hearing before Judge Kelly to determine whether the appellant would be released on bail pending the s. 810.1 application. The appellant had met with a lawyer the evening before, but that lawyer had not been retained to conduct the show cause hearing. The lawyer did ask that the hearing be adjourned 48 hours and that, in the interim, the appellant be released from custody. The Crown opposed the adjournment. Judge Kelly refused the adjournment request, saying that he would grant it only if the appellant remained in custody. The lawyer then withdrew. The appellant, unrepresented, agreed to the conditions of his release on bail sought by the Crown.

[16] These conditions included that he not engage in any activity involving contact with persons under the age of 14 unless in the presence of and under the supervision of Reverend Hugh Kirkegaard and another adult; that he not be at or be within 50 metres of a public park, swimming area, daycare, school ground, playground, community centre or any other place where persons under 14 can reasonably be expected to be found, except in the presence of and under the supervision of Reverend Kirkegaard and another adult; that he continue to take Luperon (or Provera) at least once a month; and that he continue counselling or treatment at the Clarke Institute. The s. 810.1 hearing was adjourned to November 28, 1994.

[17] On November 28, 1994, Judge Kelly varied the appellant's bail conditions. At the same time, the appellant brought an application for prerogative relief to prevent Judge Kelly from proceeding with the s. 810.1 hearing and for a declaration that ss. 810.1 and 507(4) of the Code violated ss. 7, 9, 11 and 15 of the Charter. Pending the resolution of the constitutional issues, the s. 810.1 hearing has been adjourned.

[18] However, on December 13, 1994, the appellant's bail conditions were further varied by Hoilett J. Under the amended conditions, the appellant continues to be prohibited from activities involving contact with persons under 14 years of age unless in the presence of an adult who does not have a criminal record, he continues to be restricted in his movement in parks and community centres, and he continues to be

required to take counselling. The material in the record shows that the appellant was continuing his counselling at the Clarke Institute and was continuing to take Luperon.

[19] Fresh evidence filed on appeal showed that the appellant brought a further application to vary the conditions of his bail, which was opposed by the Crown. In a decision dated October 1, 1998, Keenan J refused the application. In his reasons, he noted that the appellant's bail conditions were virtually identical to the recognizance conditions under s. 810.1; that but for a single breach of the condition not to consume alcohol, the appellant had complied with all the conditions of his bail for four years; that he had co-operated with a Circle of Support and Accountability organized by volunteers of the Mennonite faith; and that, indeed, Detective Leaver had partici-pated in the Circle to supervise the appellant and assist in his treatment. Nonetheless, Keenan J could find "no basis for varying the recognizance of bail." I turn now to the constitutional issues in this appeal.

Discussion

First Issue—Does S. 810.1 Violate S. 7 of the Charter?

...

[22] To make out a violation of s. 7 the appellant must show first that s. 810.1 deprives him of his right to life, liberty or security of the person; and second, that this deprivation is contrary to the principles of fundamental justice.

[23] The Crown acknowledges that the appellant meets the first branch of the s. 7 test. Section 810.1 deprives the appellant of his liberty. The conditions in s. 810.1 prevent the appellant from going to many places that other Canadians can freely go to and thus prevent the appellant from participating fully in a community's activities. Although not as serious an intrusion on his freedom as detention or imprisonment, these conditions in s. 810.1 still restrict the appellant's "liberty" under s. 7 of the Charter. Whether these restrictions on the appellant's liberty are in accordance with the principles of fundamental justice is at the heart of this appeal. The appellant argues that s. 810.1 contravenes the principles of fundamental justice for three reasons: it creates an offence based on status; it is overbroad; and it is void for vagueness.

(i) Does S. 810.1 Create a Status Offence?

[24] The appellant submits that s. 810.1 creates an offence based on a person's status alone, that is based on a person's medical diagnosis or even on a person's past criminal record but without any current offending conduct. The appellant argues that s. 810.1 is punitive, that it punishes a person though that person may have done nothing wrong. An offence based on status alone, according to the appellant, is con-trary to the principles of fundamental justice.

[25] Accepting that a status offence contravenes fundamental justice, there are two answers to the appellant's submission. The main answer is that s. 810.1 does not create an offence. It is a preventive provision, not a punitive provision. It aims not to punish past wrongdoing but to prevent future harm to young children, to prevent

them from being victimized by sexual abusers. The second answer is that s. 810.1 is not about a person's status. It is about assessing the present risk of a person committing a sexual offence against young children.

[26] Whether s. 810.1 is punitive or preventive permeated the argument of this appeal. Indeed, characterizing s. 810.1 as punitive is central to the appellant's position. If s. 810.1 is punitive, if it creates an offence, then the appellant fairly argues that it contains inadequate constitutional safeguards. Then J, however, held that s. 810.1 was a preventive measure aimed at the protection of children, and I agree with him.

[27] The criminal justice system has two broad objectives: punish wrongdoers and prevent future harm. A law aimed at the prevention of crime is just as valid an exercise of the federal criminal law power under s. 91(27) of the *Constitution Act, 1867*, as a law aimed at punishing crime. Thus, the appellant has not argued, nor could he, that Parliament cannot validly pass a law to prevent future harm to children.

[28] What the appellant does argue is that the law Parliament did pass, s. 810.1, is more punitive than preventive, and thus creates an offence, based solely on a person's status. Some aspects of s. 810.1 are punitive or coercive: the availability of an arrest warrant; detention pending a hearing unless the defendant is released on bail; and jail on the defendant's refusal to enter into a recognizance. These coercive aspects, however, are necessary to preserve the integrity of the s. 810.1 proceedings. By themselves, they do not turn s. 810.1 into a punitive provision. Nor does the stigma that undoubtedly accompanies a s. 810.1 proceeding make the proceeding punitive. That stigma will attach whether the section is preventive or punitive.

[29] To characterize s. 810.1 as punitive, as creating an offence, the appellant would have to show that its purpose is "to mete out criminal punishment" or that it has a "true penal consequence." A true penal consequence, according to the Supreme Court of Canada in *R v. Wigglesworth*, [1987] 2 SCR 541 at p. 561, 52 CCC (3d) 385 is "imprisonment or a fine which by its magnitude would appear to be imposed for the purpose of redressing the wrong done to society at large."

[30] By these standards, s. 810.1 does not create an offence. Its purpose is not to punish crime but to prevent crime from happening. Its sanctions are not punitive, nor are they intended to redress a wrong; they are activity and geographic restrictions on a person's liberty intended to protect a vulnerable group in our society from future harm.

[31] As Then J observed, s. 810.1 is analogous to s. 810, the peace bond provision of the *Criminal Code*. Typically, s. 810 is used to protect an identified victim, a person already harmed, from further harm where evidence points to the likelihood of danger to the victim from continuing contact with another person. Courts have consistently held that s. 810 is a preventive measure, that it does not create an offence or mete out a criminal punishment. The appellant did not suggest otherwise. Nor indeed did the appellant suggest that s. 810 was unconstitutional. Instead, he sought to distinguish s. 810 by arguing that it is meant to address breaches of the peace between citizens, and thus it amounts to a private remedy to ensure that named individuals remain law abiding.

[32] I see nothing "private" in s. 810. It authorizes a recognizance order in the same way as does s. 810.1. Both are concerned with preventing victimization. The main differences between s. 810 and s. 810.1 are the group of likely victims and the

breadth of restrictions that may be imposed. A recognizance order under s. 810 aims to prevent harm to named individuals and the restrictions are tailored to prevent contact between those persons and the likely perpetrator. A recognizance order under s. 810.1 aims to prevent harm to a large group of children, identified only by their age, and the restrictions must necessarily be more extensive to prevent contact between this large group of children and the likely perpetrator. Section 810.1 is therefore broader than s. 810. But the two sections are similar enough that if s. 810 does not create an offence, it is hard to see how s. 810.1 does either.

[33] Moreover, I do not regard s. 810.1 as authorizing court-ordered restrictions on a person's liberty because of that person's status. Section 810.1 looks not to a person's status but to a person's present risk of future dangerousness. That risk will have to be assessed by looking at all relevant factors in a person's life, factors that are not immutable but will change over time.

[34] Thus, I conclude that s. 810.1 does not create a status offence. It is a preventive measure. Indeed, if the preventive aspect of the federal criminal law power is going to be used anywhere, I cannot think of a more important use than the protection of young children from likely sexual predators. However, although s. 810.1 is properly characterized as a preventive measure, to be constitutionally valid, it must be neither overbroad nor vague.

(ii) Is S. 810.1 Overbroad?

[35] The appellant submits that s. 810.1 is overbroad contrary to ss. 7 and 9 of the Charter. Because I do not think that s. 9 adds anything to the appellant's position, I will focus only on s. 7.

[36] That a law not be overbroad is now accepted as a principle of fundamental justice: [*R v. Heywood* (1994), 94 CCC (3d) 481 (SCC)]. "Overbreadth" looks at the means a legislature has chosen to achieve a legitimate objective. The means chosen must be sufficiently tailored or narrowly targeted to meet their objective. If the means chosen are too broad or too wide, if the law goes further than necessary to accomplish its purpose, the law becomes arbitrary or disproportionate. A person's rights will be limited without good reason. The principles of fundamental justice will be violated.

[37] I accept the legitimacy, and indeed the importance, of Parliament's objective in passing s. 810.1 of the *Criminal Code*. Children are among the most vulnerable groups in our society. The sexual abuse of young children is a serious societal problem, a statement that needs no elaboration. A sizeable percentage of the sexual offences against children—according to the record, approximately 30 per cent—occurs in public places, the very places specified in s. 810.1. The expert evidence shows that recidivism rates for sexual abusers of children are high and that keeping high-risk offenders away from children is a sound preventive strategy. Parliament thus cannot be faulted for its objective in enacting s. 810.1. The state should not be obliged to wait until children are victimized before it acts. The societal interest in protecting children from sexual abuse supports Parliament's use of the preventive part of its criminal law power.

[38] Even accepting the legitimacy of Parliament's purpose, the appellant submits that the means it has chosen in s. 810.1 to achieve that purpose are too broad. The

appellant focuses on four aspects of s. 810.1: the extent of the restrictions on his liberty, the imposition of these restrictions without a requirement of any previous offending conduct, the pre-hearing arrest and detention provisions to which he was subjected, and the extent of the procedural protections he was afforded. I will deal with each of these. Overall, however, I am not persuaded that s. 810.1 is overbroad. Parliament might have chosen other means to achieve its objective but the means that it did choose are reasonable and in accordance with the principles of fundamental justice.

1. Extent of Restrictions Does Not Make S. 810.1 Overbroad

[39] If a recognizance is ordered, a defendant may be restricted from participating in any activities or from attending a public park or public swimming area where children under 14 may reasonably be expected to gather or a daycare centre, schoolground or playground. In my view, these restrictions, although limiting a defendant's liberty, are not overbroad. I say that for three reasons. First, the restrictions stop short of detention or imprisonment. I think it fair to conclude that detention or imprisonment under a provision that does not charge an offence would be an unacceptable restriction on a defendant's liberty and would be contrary to the principles of fundamental justice. But as Then J observed, the restrictions contemplated by s. 810.1 permit a defendant to lead a reasonably normal life.

[40] Second, these restrictions on a defendant's liberty are proportional to the important societal interest in s. 810.1, the protection of young children. As McLachlin J observed in *R v. Seaboyer*, [1991] 2 SCR 577 at p. 603, 66 CCC (3d) 321, "the principles of fundamental justice reflect a spectrum of interests, from the rights of the accused to broader societal concerns. Section 7 must be construed having regard to those interests. ..." The defendant's right to liberty is not the only s. 7 interest at stake in s. 810.1. The societal interest in protecting young children from harm must also be taken into account. Section 810.1 attempts to balance these two interests: the interest of likely child sexual abusers in going where they please, including places where young children gather, and the interest of the state in ensuring that young children can go safely and securely to places typically associated with children's activities. In my view, s. 810.1 strikes a reasonable compromise between these two interests. It provides a measured intrusion into a defendant's liberty consistent with protecting young children from harm.

[41] Third, accepting Then J's deletion of community centres, the restrictions contemplated by s. 810.1 are narrowly targeted to meet Parliament's objective. The only places a defendant may be prohibited from going are where children under age 14 are or can reasonably be expected to be present; and the only activities a defendant may be prohibited from engaging in are those involving contact with children under 14. By limiting the scope of s. 810.1 in this way, I do not accept the submission of the provincial Crown that s. 810.1(3) authorizes the court to impose broader restrictions on a defendant's liberty than activities, areas or places where children are likely to be found. Section 810.1(3) provides that a judge may "order the defendant to enter into a recognizance and comply with the conditions fixed by the provincial court judge, including" the specified conditions. The specified conditions following the word "including" are examples of the kinds of conditions that can be imposed. The context of s. 810.1 and its overall purpose suggest that the word "including" is used to

limit the scope of the general term "conditions" to those conditions similar to the specified examples. On this interpretation, a judge could prohibit a defendant from going to a recreation hall where young children were likely to be present but could not, for example, require a defendant to take the drug Luperon, however desirable that may be. This interpretation, in my view, not only appropriately reflects the context and purpose of s. 810.1, it also accords with Charter values. A broader interpretation, permitting the judge to order a defendant to take a course of treatment or to take a particular drug, under a provision that does not create an offence would raise serious Charter concerns. Under the narrower interpretation I have adopted, the restrictions contemplated by s. 810.1 are not overbroad.

2. Lack of a Requirement of a Previous Criminal Record Does Not Make S. 810.1 Overbroad

[42] A recognizance order may be imposed on a defendant who has no previous criminal record, who has committed no overt sexual act, who has seemingly done nothing wrong. All that is required is for the presiding judge to be satisfied the informant has reasonable grounds for the fear that the defendant will commit a sexual offence against a child under 14. The appellant submits that without a triggering requirement of some previous offending conduct, s. 810.1 is overbroad because it applies to too many people. I do not accept this submission.

[43] What s. 810.1 is trying to measure is a defendant's present likelihood of future dangerousness or present risk of committing a sexual offence against children in the future. Predicting future dangerousness is not an exact science. However, the impossibility of making exact predictions does not render s. 810.1 overbroad and contrary to our principles of fundamental justice. La Forest J addressed this point in dealing with the dangerous offender legislation in *R v. Lyons*, [1987] 2 SCR 309 at pp. 364-65, 37 CCC (3d) 1:

> However, as Holmes has reminded us, the life of the law has not been logic: it has been experience. The criminal law must operate in a world governed by practical considerations rather than abstract logic and, as a matter of practicality, the most that can be established in a future context is a likelihood of certain events occurring. ...
>
> It seems to me that a "likelihood" of specified future conduct occurring is the finding of fact required to be established; it is not, at one and the same time, the means of proving that fact. Logically, it seems clear to me that an individual can be found to constitute a threat to society without insisting that this require the court to assert an ability to predict the future.

So too did Lamer CJC in dealing with the bail system in *R v. Morales*, [1992] 3 SCR 711 at p. 739, 77 CCC (3d) 91:

> The bail system has always made an effort to assess the likelihood of future dangerousness while recognizing that exact predictions of future dangerousness are impossible. The Report of the Canadian Committee on Corrections (Ouimet Report (1969)), one of the studies which led to the current bail system, recognized the impossibility of precise predictions at p. 110:
>
> > It has been argued that there is no accurate way of predicting the accused's behaviour pending trial. Even if a measure of predictability could be achieved, any

fact-finding process for determining this issue would be so time-consuming as
to nullify the purpose of bail.

We think the issued [sic] involved are no more difficult than others which courts
are constantly called upon to resolve in other areas of the law. Some reasonable
assessment of the probability of the accused's behaviour pending trial is not impossible. If the prosecution does not make out a reasonable cause for denial of bail,
it follows that it should be granted.

The bail system does not aim to make exact predictions about future dangerousness
because such predictions are impossible to make. However, *Lyons* demonstrates that it
is sufficient to establish a likelihood of dangerousness, and that the impossibility of
making exact predictions does not preclude a bail system which aims to deny bail to
those who likely will be dangerous.

[44] A previous criminal record for sexual assault against children will no doubt
be relevant to predicting future dangerousness in many cases. But insisting on a previous record before a recognizance can be ordered would undermine the preventive
purpose of s. 810.1. It would require a child to be victimized before the Crown could
act, even if the Crown had highly reliable evidence of dangerousness. If some previous offending conduct were required before a recognizance could be ordered, then
the Crown could not protect children from child sexual abusers known to medical
authorities but not yet charged or from sexual abusers who could not be charged
because the victim was too traumatized to testify or because the victim could not be
found. Instead of requiring some previous offending conduct, s. 810.1 invites the
presiding judge to consider all the relevant evidence on whether a defendant will
commit a sexual offence against children. I agree with Then J's summary of the kinds
of evidence likely to be led before the presiding judge (at p. 365):

> For instance, evidence may be led that the defendant has made a threat or sexual
> proposition to a specific child or a group of children. More common, no doubt, will
> be cases where evidence will be led at the hearing concerning the individual's gen-
> eral proclivity to abuse children sexually. This could be based on a relevant criminal
> record and past behaviour around children. Evidence of a diagnosed medical mental
> disorder that predisposes the defendant to be sexually attracted to children might
> weigh in favour of ordering a recognizance, just as evidence of continuing successful
> treatment will be in the defendant's favour. On the very wording of the section, no
> one factor can be determinative.

[45] This passage reflects a sensible approach to a proceeding under s. 810.1.
Requiring a criminal record or some other offending conduct as a condition of a recognizance order under s. 810.1 is at odds with the preventive purpose of the section. I
conclude that s. 810.1 is not overbroad because it fails to require any offending
conduct before a recognizance can be ordered.

3. The Pre-Hearing Provisions for Arrest and Bail Do Not Make
   S. 810.1 Overbroad

[46] The provisions for pre-trial arrest and bail—which, as I will discuss later in
these reasons, apply to a proceeding under s. 810.1—carry with them the possibility

of a sanction more severe—custody or detention—than any sanction that may be imposed as a result of a hearing under s. 810.1. That possibility, however, does not make the section overbroad. Pre-trial arrest or even pre-hearing detention may be necessary to secure the defendant's attendance at the hearing or to prevent harm to children pending a hearing because of a defendant's unwillingness to comply with reasonable terms of release. In short, as I have already said, pre-trial arrest and detention may be needed in some cases to ensure the integrity and viability of the s. 810.1 proceedings themselves.

4. Procedural Safeguards Are Sufficient To Not Make S. 810.1 Overbroad

[47] The procedural safeguards in s. 810.1 are adequate. Anyone subjected to a s. 810.1 application receives notice of the hearing. The hearing must meet the procedural fairness requirements of a summary conviction trial. No order can be made until after the hearing is completed. The presiding provincial court judge has discretion to limit the restrictions imposed. Any order made is not a lifelong injunction; it can last no longer than a year and may be renewed only after an entirely new hearing. A person subjected to a s. 810.1 order may appeal the order and may, at any time, seek to vary the conditions.

[48] I therefore conclude that s. 810.1 is not overbroad. Instead, it strikes a reasonable balance between the liberty interest of the defendant and the state's interest in protecting young children from harm. A defendant's liberty interest may be restricted only after a hearing complying with the requirements of natural justice and only to the extent needed to avoid unreasonably jeopardizing the safety and security of young children.

(iii) Is S. 810.1 Void for Vagueness?

[49] Like the overbreadth principle, the void for vagueness principle is also concerned with whether the legislature has used precise enough means to achieve its objective. But whereas overbreadth is concerned with whether the legislation is targeted sufficiently narrowly, vagueness is concerned with whether the legislation is defined with sufficient clarity. The rationale for the void for vagueness principle is that, unless a law sufficiently delineates the area of risk of unlawful conduct, citizens will not have the fair notice of the law to which they are entitled, and police officers and others will have too much discretion in deciding how and when to enforce the law. Thus, a law must provide "an intelligible standard according to which the judiciary must do its work" and "an adequate basis for legal debate, that is for reaching a conclusion as to its meaning by reasoned analysis applying legal criteria." Otherwise, the law will be impermissibly vague contrary to the principles of fundamental justice.

[50] The appellant submits that s. 810.1 does not sufficiently delineate an area of risk of unlawful conduct, and thus does not provide fair substantive notice to a citizen, because it allows for restrictions on liberty on an informant's fear on reasonable grounds. The appellant argues that the word "fear" should be contrasted with the word "belief," which is used in *Criminal Code* provisions authorizing an arrest or a search. "Fear," according to the appellant, can be irrational or emotional and is invariably subjective, while "belief" can be assessed objectively.

[51] I do not accept the appellant's argument. The word "fear" or "fears" should not be considered in isolation but together with the modifying words in s. 810.1(1) "on reasonable grounds." Fear alone connotes a state of belief or an apprehension that a future event, thought to be undesirable, may or will occur. But "on reasonable grounds" lends objectivity to the apprehension. In other words, the phrase "fears on reasonable grounds" in s. 810.1(1) connotes a reasonably based sense of apprehension about a future event, or as Then J put it, it "equates to a belief, objectively established, that the individual will commit an offence" (at p. 381).

[52] Moreover, although an informant's fear triggers an application under s. 810.1, under s-s. (3) a recognizance order can only be made if the presiding judge is satisfied by "evidence" that the fear is reasonably based. Section 810.1(3) therefore requires the judge to come to his or her own conclusion about the likelihood that the defendant will commit one of the offences listed in s-s (1). Although the "evidence" the judge relies on might include hearsay, a recognizance could only be ordered on evidence that is credible and trustworthy.

[53] Despite the need for the informant's state of belief to be objectively assessed and for the presiding judge to come to an independent conclusion, I acknowledge some imprecision in the phrase "fears on reasonable grounds." But some imprecision is to be expected because s. 810.1 requires a prediction about future dangerousness. So too does s. 810, which uses the same phrase. The phrase is not so imprecise that it fails to delineate an area of risk or fails to provide an adequate basis for legal debate. Moreover, it is surrounded by requirements in s. 810.1—the information, the summons, the hearing itself—that give the defendant fair notice of the conduct sought to be prevented; and if a recognizance is ordered, the defendant will have fair notice of the conditions imposed and, thus, will know how to comply. The threshold for declaring a law void for vagueness is appropriately high. Section 810.1 does not pass this threshold. I would not give effect to this ground of appeal.

Second Issue—Did Then J Err in Reading Down "Shall" to "May" in S. 810.1(2) of the Code?

[54] Section 810.1(2) provided that "a provincial court judge who receives an information under s-s. (1) shall cause the parties to appear before the provincial court judge." Then J held that, in the context of a preventive provision like s. 810.1, making the issuance of process on a defendant mandatory violated ss. 7 and 9 of the Charter and could not be justified under s. 1. In his view, "an automatic issuance of process, with the potential arrest of the defendant, is excessive and unwarranted." It provides "no control on obviously unfounded informations under which a person may be summonsed or arrested" (at pp. 399-401). Thus, it subjects the ordinary citizen to capricious or unjustifiable detention. In Then J's view, and relying on the Supreme Court's decision in *Baron v. Canada*, [1993] 1 SCR 416, 78 CCC (3d) 510, "a residual discretion is a constitutional requirement." The Crown does not take issue with Then J's holding that "shall" in s. 810.1(2) is unconstitutional.

[55] The appellant, however, takes issue with Then J's remedy. Having found that a discretion was a constitutional requirement, Then J applied s. 52 of the *Constitution*

Act, 1982, and read down "shall" to "may." The appellant submits that he should simply have declared the subsection inoperative.

[56] The Supreme Court refused to read down "shall" to "may" in *Baron* itself, and in *R v. Swain*, [1991] 1 SCR 933, 63 CCC (3d) 481. Then J distinguished *Baron* on the grounds that the Attorney General in that case had not asked for the remedy of reading down and that, unlike the provision challenged in *Baron*, s. 810.1(2) was not central to the legislative regime in s. 810.1. I think it fair to say, however, that when legislation expressly excludes a judicial discretion, courts have been reluctant to read one in as a constitutional remedy. Nonetheless, in my view, Then J was correct to read down "shall" to "may" in this case.

[57] In deciding on the appropriate remedy under s. 52 for a Charter breach, "the court must apply the measures which will best vindicate the values expressed in the Charter while refraining from intrusion into the legislative sphere beyond what is necessary." Before reading down or reading in, the court must ask "whether it is safe to assume that the legislature would have enacted the legislation in its altered form." Here, "may" in s. 810.1(2) appropriately vindicates Charter values. Giving the presiding judge a discretion whether to summons or arrest a defendant once an information is sworn is an important constitutional safeguard. Thus, the remedy of reading in "may," although explicitly altering the legislation, will "preserve statutory objectives within clear constitutional contours."

[58] Recent legislation shows that we can safely assume Parliament would have enacted s. 810.1(2) with the word "may." In 1997 Parliament added two new provisions to the *Criminal Code* similar to s. 810.1, and in each new provision used the word "may" instead of "shall." Section 810.01 authorizes a recognizance order against a person likely to commit "a criminal organization offence," and s. 810.2 authorizes a recognizance order against a person likely to commit "a serious personal injury offence." Sections 810.01 and 810.2 are worded similarly to s. 810.1 with necessary modifications for their context. Sections 810.01(2) and s. 810.2(2) are identical to s. 810.1(2) except that in place of "shall cause the parties to appear before the provincial court judge," in the two new provisions Parliament has used "may cause the parties to appear before the provincial court judge." Because Parliament itself has enacted s. 810.01 and s. 810.2 to conform to Then J's decision, we can safely assume that reading down "shall" to "may" does not unnecessarily intrude into the legislative domain. I would not give effect to this ground of appeal.

Third Issue—Do SS. 507(4) and 515 of the Criminal Code Apply to a Proceeding Under S. 810.1?

[59] In *R v. Allen*, this court held that what is now s. 507(4) of the Code, allowing for the issuance of a warrant for the arrest of the accused, applies to s. 810 of the Code. Section 507(4) provides:

> 507(4) Where a justice considers that a case is made out for compelling an accused to attend before him to answer to a charge of an offence, he shall issue a summons to the accused unless the allegations of the informant or the evidence of any witness or witness-

es taken in accordance with subsection (3) discloses reasonable grounds to believe that it is necessary in the public interest to issue a warrant for the arrest of the accused.

[60] In *Allen*, the accused argued that s. 507(4) applied to "a charge of an offence" and thus could not apply to a proceeding under s. 810, which did not create an offence. Goodman JA, writing for the court, rejected this argument. Section 507(4) is in Part XVI of the Code; s. 810 is in Part XXVII dealing with summary convictions. Section 795 of the Code, which is also in Part XXVII, states that the provisions of Part XVI "with respect to compelling the appearance of an accused before a justice … in so far as they are not inconsistent with the Part, apply, with such modifications as the circumstances require, to proceedings under this Part." In Goodman JA's view, s. 795 made s. 507(4) applicable to a proceeding under s. 810 even though s. 810 "does not create an offence" (at p. 158).

[61] Section 515, the provision permitting bail pending trial, also is in Part XVI of the Code; and s. 810.1 is in Part XXVII of the Code. Therefore, applying *Allen*, both ss. 507(4) and 515 apply to proceedings under s. 810.1.

[62] The appellant asked us to reconsider *Allen* on its own terms or in the light of the Charter. In my view, *Allen* was correctly decided. Applying provisions relating to a charge against an accused (ss. 507(4) and 515) to a proceeding commenced by the laying of an information (s. 810.1) is a modification contemplated by s. 795 of the Code. I am supported in this conclusion by the decision of the Saskatchewan Court of Appeal in *R v. Wakelin* (1992), 71 CCC (3d) 115, 97 Sask. R 275 (CA), which reached a similar result.

[63] *Allen*, however, was decided without reference to the Charter. The appellant submits that applying ss. 507(4) and 515 to a s. 810.1 proceeding violates s. 7 of the Charter. The argument has two branches: both permitting pre-hearing arrest and detention because of a fear of future misconduct and permitting a more severe sanction pending the hearing than could be ordered at the conclusion of the s. 810.1 hearing violates the principles of fundamental justice. I disagree.

[64] First, the presiding judge has a discretion whether to issue a warrant for the arrest of a defendant or to detain a defendant pending a hearing. If a defendant is released pending a hearing, the judge has discretion concerning the bail conditions to be imposed. The existence of this judicial discretion is, as I have already said, an important constitutional safeguard and procedural protection for the defendant. The presiding judge has ample authority to balance the interests of the defendant and the interests of the public pending a s. 810.1 hearing and to ensure that the hearing is held promptly. Second, and repeating what I said earlier, provision for pre-hearing arrest and detention is needed to preserve the integrity of the s. 810.1 proceedings. The court may need the power of arrest and detention to ensure the attendance of a defendant at the hearing or to protect children from the possibility of serious harm pending the hearing.

[65] Moreover, s. 810.1 is not rendered unconstitutional because, in a particular case, an arrest warrant may have been improvidently issued or inappropriate bail conditions may have been imposed pending the hearing. Support for this view may be found in the decision of this court in *R v. Finlay* (1985), 52 OR (2d) 632, 23 CCC (3d) 48 (CA), where it was argued that the provisions of former s. 178.13 of the

Criminal Code, which gave a judge the power to issue a wiretap authorization, were unconstitutional because the broadly-worded provision did not comply with minimum constitutional standards for search and seizure. Martin JA held that, properly interpreted, the provision complied with the Charter (at p. 70 CCC). The requirement that the authorization be granted only where to do so was in "the best interests of the administration of justice" imported the requirement that the judge be satisfied the granting of the authorization would further or advance the objectives of justice, and, therefore, imported a requirement to balance the state's interest in law enforcement and the individual's interest in privacy. These requirements, in turn, called on the judge to apply minimum constitutional standards under s. 8 of the Charter.

[66] The same analysis applies to the arrest and release procedure imported into s. 810.1. Under s. 507(4), the justice is to compel the defendant's attendance by means of a summons only, unless the allegations of the informant or the evidence "discloses reasonable grounds to believe that it is necessary in the public interest to issue a warrant for the arrest of the accused." Because a hearing under s. 810.1 can only result in the defendant being required to enter into a recognizance, the circumstances in which it would be "necessary in the public interest" to issue an arrest warrant will be limited to cases where that process is necessary to preserve the integrity of the s. 810.1 proceedings. The justice will require the informant to make out a case that the defendant will not otherwise attend court or that the defendant poses an imminent risk to the safety of children, which s. 810.1 is designed to protect.

[67] If the justice does issue an arrest warrant, s. 515 of the *Criminal Code* directs the justice to release the defendant on a simple undertaking without conditions, unless the prosecutor shows cause why some more intrusive order—such as a recognizance with conditions—is required. The discretion under s. 515 must be exercised judicially and bearing in mind the limited conditions that can be imposed following a successful s. 810.1 application.

[68] Finally, although s. 515 provides that the justice may order the detention of the defendant pending the s. 810.1 hearing, that discretion is circumscribed by the provisions of s. 515(10), which authorize detention only where necessary to ensure the defendant's attendance at court, for the protection or safety of the public or "any other just cause," including the maintenance of confidence in the administration of justice. Again, in the light of the limited consequences of a successful s. 810.1 application, only in unusual circumstances will the justice be entitled to order the detention of the defendant pending the hearing. Indeed, it will be a rare case where it would enhance confidence in the administration of justice to detain a defendant who is not alleged to have committed any crime and who can only be required to enter into a recognizance at the conclusion of the proceedings.

[69] So interpreted, these various provisions of the Code strike the appropriate balance between the public interest in the protection of children and the liberty interest of the defendant.

[70] For these reasons, I view ss. 507(4) and 515 in their application to s. 810.1 as being in accordance with the principles of fundamental justice. Therefore, I would not give effect to this ground of appeal.

The reasoning of the lower court decision (by Then J) in *Budreo* was applied in *R v. Baker*, [1999] BCJ no. 681 (SC), to reject a constitutional challenge to s. 810.2 (serious personal injury offence). This provision is somewhat wider than s. 810.1 because it is not necessary that a specified victim be named in the information or the subsequent recognizance.

CHAPTER EIGHTEEN

Parole and Early Release

I. INTRODUCTION

This chapter provides an overview of parole and early release in Canada. From a procedural perspective, these issues can be technical and complex. Rather than addressing the many issues in detail, we sketch the framework of early release and set out some aspects of the substantive discussions about its legitimacy and efficacy. We deal only with the federal context. Provinces have their own correctional statutes that govern temporary absences. In Ontario, Quebec, and British Columbia, there are provincial parole boards as well. For the most part, the elements are similar and sometimes identical, but one should consult the relevant provincial or territorial legislation when concerned about a non-federal prisoner.

For a discussion of the history of parole in Canada, see Cole and Manson, *Release from Imprisonment: The Law of Sentencing, Parole and Judicial Review* (Toronto: Carswell, 1990), 159-89. The major events in the history of federal early release are as follows:

1899   The enactment of the *Ticket of Leave Act*, providing for licences to be granted to prisoners by the governor general, on the advice of the minister of justice, that permitted the prisoner to be at large subject to re-commitment for breaching a term of the licence or committing a new offence.

1959   The establishment of the National Parole Board (NPB), which, pursuant to the terms of the *Parole Act*, was empowered to grant, suspend, and revoke parole.

1970   The provision of "mandatory supervision," which required federal prisoners who were released by reason of remission to be supervised subject to re-commitment for breaching a condition or committing a new offence; this applied only to penitentiary prisoners.

1986   The passage of the detention provisions, which empowered the NPB to detain a prisoner until the warrant expiry date if there were grounds to believe that an offence involving death or serious harm would be committed if he or she was released.

1992   The passage of the *Corrections and Conditional Release Act*, SC 1992, c. 20 (CCRA), which replaced both the *Penitentiary Act* and the *Parole Act*; among other important provisions, it replaced the remission-based release on mandatory supervision with statutory release after two-thirds of a sentence is served.

The CCRA includes a general statement of purpose and applicable principles:

100. The purpose of conditional release is to contribute to the maintenance of a just, peaceful and safe society by means of decisions on the timing and conditions of release that will best facilitate the rehabilitation of offenders and their reintegration into the community as law-abiding citizens.

101. The principles that shall guide the Board and the provincial parole boards in achieving the purpose of conditional release are

(a) that the protection of society be the paramount consideration in the determination of any case;

(b) that parole boards take into consideration all available information that is relevant to a case, including the stated reasons and recommendations of the sentencing judge, any other information from the trial or the sentencing hearing, information and assessments provided by correctional authorities, and information obtained from victims and the offender;

(c) that parole boards enhance their effectiveness and openness through the timely exchange of relevant information with other components of the criminal justice system and through communication of their policies and programs to offenders, victims and the general public;

(d) that parole boards make the least restrictive determination consistent with the protection of society;

(e) that parole boards adopt and be guided by appropriate policies and that their members be provided with the training necessary to implement those policies; and

(f) that offenders be provided with relevant information, reasons for decisions and access to the review of decisions in order to ensure a fair and understandable conditional release process.

102. The Board or a provincial parole board may grant parole to an offender if, in its opinion,

(a) the offender will not, by reoffending, present an undue risk to society before the expiration according to law of the sentence the offender is serving; and

(b) the release of the offender will contribute to the protection of society by facilitating the reintegration of the offender into society as a law-abiding citizen.

II. THE ELEMENTS OF PAROLE

The following discussion provides a clear picture of how the system works generally, but does not include a technical analysis of the relevant procedures. Although parole litigation has not been extensive, there is a small body of case law that should be consulted to obtain a more detailed account of these elements.

There are some basic definitions that appear throughout the CCRA to explain the different kinds of releases:

Full parole   This is defined by s. 99 simply as the "authority granted to an offender to be at large during the offender's sentence." Parole and its applicable conditions continues until warrant expiry unless it is suspended, cancelled, terminated, or revoked.

Day parole	Section 99 defines this as the authority granted by the NPB to an offender "to be at large during the offender's sentence in order to prepare the offender for full parole or statutory release, the conditions of which require the offender to return to a penitentiary, a community-based residential facility or a provincial correctional facility each night, unless otherwise authorized in writing."
Temporary absence	There are two types: escorted (ETA) and unescorted (UTA). For prisoners serving a life sentence for murder and dangerous offenders, the jurisdiction over UTAs is vested in the NPB. For most other prisoners, UTAs can be granted by the institution head (see CCRA, s. 116(2)). Again, with the exception of murderers, ETAs are granted by the institutional head for limited periods (usually less than 5 days, but up to 15 days, with the approval of the commissioner), or for an unlimited period for medical reasons (see CCRA, s. 17). Assuming that the prisoner does not present an undue risk, the statutory reasons for an ETA include "medical, administrative, community service, family contact, personal development for rehabilitative purposes, or compassionate reasons, including parental responsibilities." A common reason for an ETA, besides a medical reason, is to attend a family funeral.
Statutory release	This is the point, usually after serving two-thirds of a sentence, that a prisoner is entitled to be released pursuant to s. 127, unless the prisoner is subject to detention until warrant expiry under s. 130(3).

A. Eligibility

The law in effect on the date of sentencing determines the prisoner's eligibility for all forms of statutory release. For murder, this has usually been stipulated in the *Criminal Code*. For all other offences, eligibility has been established by the parole legislation in force at the time of the offence. Currently, the CCRA establishes the day parole eligibility date (DPED) and the full parole eligibility date (PED) as follows:

119(1) Subject to section 747 of the *Criminal Code*, the portion of a sentence of imprisonment that must be served before an offender may be released on day parole is

(a) one year, where the offender was, before October 15, 1977, sentenced to preventive detention;

(b) three years, where the offender was sentenced to detention in a penitentiary for an indeterminate period;

(c) where the offender is serving a sentence of imprisonment of two years or more, other than a sentence referred to in paragraph (a) or (b), the greater of

(i) the portion ending six months before the date on which full parole may be granted, and

(ii) six months; or

(d) one half of the portion of the sentence that must be served before full parole may be granted, where the offender is serving a sentence of imprisonment of less than two years.

(2) The Board is not required to review the case of an offender who applies for day parole if the offender is serving a sentence of imprisonment of less than six months.

120(1) Subject to sections 747 and 761 of the *Criminal Code* and to any order made under section 741.2 of that Act, the portion of a sentence of imprisonment that must be served before an offender may be released on full parole is the lesser of

(a) one third of the sentence of imprisonment, and

(b) seven years.

(2) The portion of a sentence of imprisonment for life, imposed otherwise than as a minimum punishment, that must be served before an offender may be released on full parole is seven years less any time spent in custody between the day on which the offender was arrested and taken into custody, in respect of the offence for which the sentence was imposed, and the day on which the sentence was imposed.

(3) The Board is not required to review the case of an offender who applies for full parole if the offender is serving a sentence of imprisonment of less than six months.

(4) Where an offender is serving a sentence of imprisonment in respect of which no order has been made under section 741.2 of the *Criminal Code* and another sentence of imprisonment in respect of which such an order has been made, the offender may be released on full parole after having served a period of imprisonment equal to the lesser of one half or ten years of that other sentence and, in addition,

(a) where the two sentences are to be served concurrently, one third of any portion of the first term that is not served concurrently with the other term; or

(b) where the two sentences are to be served consecutively, the lesser of

(i) one third of the first term, and

(ii) the portion of the term that would have had to be served before full parole could have been granted in the event that the two sentences were to have been served concurrently.

(5) No offender referred to in subsection (4) is required to serve more than one half of the sentence of imprisonment before becoming eligible for full parole.

Essentially, this scheme provides for full parole eligibility after serving one-third of a sentence and day parole eligibility six months before that date. Before 1992, the day parole eligibility date was one-sixth of the sentence. The prolongation to six months before full parole eligibility diminished the use of long periods of successive day paroles. The NPB also has authority over UTAs for lifers and prisoners serving a sentence for a schedule I or II offence (see ss. 116(1) and 107(1)(e)). Generally, eligibility for a UTA occurs at one-half of the parole eligibility period (see s. 115(1)(c)). No maximum security prisoners can qualify for a UTA (see s. 115(3)).

A person sentenced to imprisonment for life as a maximum sentence (that is, for an offence other than murder) is eligible for parole after serving seven years. For all life sentences, credit toward eligiblity begins when the prisoner is arrested for the offence, and includes any days in custody after that time. For all other offences, credit toward parole eligibility accumulates only after the sentence is imposed.

B. Increasing Parole Eligibility

Amendments to the *Criminal Code* in 1992 permit a trial judge, in certain circumstances, to increase the period of parole ineligibility up to one-half of the sentence. The following case discusses the relevant factors that a judge should consider before making an order under s. 743.5 of the Code (formerly s. 741.2).

R v. Goulet
(1995), 37 CR (4th) 373 (Ont. CA)

GRIFFITHS JA:

...

The *Corrections and Conditional Release Act*, SC 1992, c. 20, was proclaimed in force on November 1, 1992. This legislation replaced the *Penitentiary Act*, RSC 1985, c. P-5, and the *Parole Act*, RSC 1985, c. P-2, and now governs the Correctional Service of Canada and the National Parole Board. Section 203 amended the *Criminal Code* by adding s. 741.2 [now s. 743.6], which reads as follows:

> 741.2. Notwithstanding subsection 120(1) of the *Corrections and Conditional Release Act*, where an offender is sentenced, after the coming into force of this section, to a term of imprisonment of two years or more on conviction for one or more offences set out in Schedules I and II to that Act that were prosecuted by way of indictment, the court may, if satisfied, having regard to the circumstances of the commission of the offences and the character and circumstances of the offender, that the expression of society's denunciation of the offences or the objective of specific or general deterrence so requires, order that the portion of the sentence that must be served before the offender may be released on full parole is one half of the sentence or ten years, whichever is less.

Schedule I referred to in the section contains offences primarily involving violence, various sexual offences, and offences against children. Schedule II contains various drug offences under the *Narcotic Control Act*, RSC 1985, c. N-1, including trafficking.

Section 120(1) of the *Corrections and Conditional Release Act* provides that subject to certain statutory exceptions, a person sentenced to a term of imprisonment in a federal penitentiary is required to serve one-third of the sentence of imprisonment imposed or seven years, whichever is less, before becoming eligible for full parole.

Section 741.2 clearly operates as an exception to the general statutory provision governing parole eligibility and contemplates a further restriction on the offender's liberty beyond that which normally flows from the prison term imposed by the sentencing judge. An order made under s. 741.2 restricting eligibility for parole increases the punishment imposed by the sentence in a very real way. In making an order under s. 741.2 increasing parole ineligibility the sentencing judge is looking into the future and declaring that the offender should not even be considered for parole during some part of what would otherwise be his or her period of parole eligibility. A s. 741.2 order pre-empts the normal role of the Parole Board during the added period of parole ineligibility and replaces the case-by-case exercise of that expert tribunal's discretion with an absolute order made years before the effect of that order is felt. Both the nature and effect of an order made under s. 741.2 suggest to me that the section should not be invoked routinely.

Unfortunately, the wording of s. 741.2 provides the judge with very little guidance to determine when this exceptional authority over parole eligibility should be exercised. According to s. 741.2 there are two criteria which must be satisfied before the power to delay parole eligibility will be triggered. First, the sentence must be for two years or more, and it must be in relation to an offence set out in Schs. I or II. Second, parole eligibility may only be delayed where, having regard to the circumstances of the commission of the offences and the character and circumstances of the offender, the expression of society's denunciation of the offences or the objectives of specific or general deterrence so requires.

While the first criterion is straightforward, the second is more problematic. As Fish JA observed in the decision of the Court of Appeal for Quebec in *R v. Dankyi*, [1993] RJQ 2767, the criteria stipulated in this provision are "virtually indistinguishable from the established criteria for determining the appropriate sentence in the first place." Although the criteria governing the sentencing in the first place and the application of s. 741.2 in the second place may overlap, the presumption is that Parliament intended s. 741.2 to have some additional purpose. It then falls to the courts to give the section meaning and function.

In *Dankyi*, a sentence of eight years' imprisonment, with a s. 741.2 order, was imposed on a conviction of possession of heroin for the purpose of trafficking. One of the appellant's grounds of appeal was that an order under s. 741.2 should not stand in the absence of clear reasons warranting its application. This proposition was accepted by the Court of Appeal and the s. 741.2 order was set aside. Fish JA, delivering the reasons of the court, said at pp. 271-72:

> In my view, section 741.2 does not introduce a new general scheme of eligibility for parole. Rather, it provides a special rule for special cases. It is essentially analogous, in that regard, to section 744, which contains similar language and permits a judge, where the offender has been convicted of second degree murder, to increase within certain limits the normal period of ineligibility for parole.
>
> Section 741.2, unlike section 744, relates to offences for which the permitted sentences range in many instances, including the one that concerns us here, from probation to life imprisonment. This vast latitude assumes, and at the same time provides for, significant differences in gravity between separate occurrences of the same crime. It also permits judges to impose sentences that take into account the distinguishing characteristics of the individual offender.
>
> In this light, the conceptual foundation of section 741.2 of the *Criminal Code* appears to me elusive. It permits judges to increase the normal period of ineligibility for parole according to criteria stipulated in the provision. These statutory guidelines are virtually indistinguishable from the established criteria for determining the appropriate sentence in the first place.
>
> On any view of the matter, since the scope of permissible sentences is itself conceived to accommodate the best and the worst of cases, section 741.2 can only be justified as an exceptional measure reserved for particular circumstances requiring an additional form of denunciation, deterrence or incapacitation.

In *Leahy*, the Ontario Court of Appeal held unanimously that "the specific reasons of the trial Judge [for increasing the period of ineligibility for parole] should be clearly enunciated." That case dealt with second degree murder, where the sentence, as I have already noted, is fixed by law.

In cases governed by section 741.2, such as this one, there is no mandatory punishment and the sentence imposed therefore already reflects the aggravating and mitigating circumstances of the case, and the character of the individual offender. It is for that reason all the more important, in my view, that the trial judge clearly enunciate his or her specific reasons for increasing the ordinary period of ineligibility for parole.

I would respectfully agree with the foregoing reasoning.

The sentencing judge should first determine what is a fit sentence having regard to the accepted principles relating to sentencing which will, of course, include the possible rehabilitation of the accused. It is only after the sentencing judge has arrived at an appropriate sentence that he or she should then consider whether the particular circumstances of the offence, or the character and circumstances of the offender, require that the normal statutory powers of the Parole Board be circumscribed by a s. 741.2 order.

In my view, s. 741.2 should only be invoked as an exceptional measure where the Crown has satisfied the court on clear evidence that an increase in the period of parole ineligibility is "required." There should be articulable reasons for invoking s. 741.2 and, as suggested in *R v. Dankyi*, supra, the trial judge should give clear and specific reasons for the increase in parole ineligibility.

The circumstances of the offence will rarely provide much additional assistance under s. 741.2 where those circumstances have formed the primary basis for fixing the appropriate period of incarceration. If the offence is one of unusual violence, brutality or degradation, then the need to strongly express society's denunciation of the offence may make a s. 741.2 order appropriate. The section should not be invoked on the basis of more general concerns which are not specific to the particular offence such as the frequency of the commission of that type of offence in the community.

The distinguishing characteristics of the offender may provide more fruitful grounds for invoking s. 741.2 as an exceptional measure. Where the Crown has adduced clear evidence that the offender will not be deterred or rehabilitated within the normal period of parole ineligibility, an order under s. 741.2 will be appropriate. A history of prior parole violations, or violations of other forms of conditional release, or evidence that significant prior custodial sentences have had little impact would be appropriate factors to consider in applying s. 741.2.

In the recent decision of this court in *R v. Faulds* (1994), 20 OR (3d) 13, the court had an opportunity to discuss the application of s. 741.2. The appellants Faulds and Schweir pleaded guilty to the robbery of a Brinks truck. The trial judge sentenced each to ten years' imprisonment and ordered, pursuant to s. 741.2, that neither be eligible for parole until they had served one-half of their sentence. On appeal, this court held that the s. 741.2 orders could not stand since the section would have no application to offences occurring before the section came into force. However, this court held that had s. 741.2 been applicable, the trial judge's order would have been appropriate in the circumstances. It was noted that Schweir had an extensive criminal record, including four prior convictions of robbery in the eight years preceding the commission of this offence. It was obvious that significant penitentiary terms had not deterred him. In fact, he was on mandatory supervision at the time the offence was committed. Faulds also had a serious criminal record including four prior convictions for robbery and three prior weapons offences. He was on parole at the time the offence was committed. These were "professional criminals ready to engage in high risk criminal activity for a substantial gain."

It is impossible to precisely define the circumstances in which a s. 741.2 order would be justified. I would emphasize again that the section should not be an automatic feature of sentencing but should only be invoked in those cases where the Crown has adduced and can point to clear evidence of justification, as, for example, in *Faulds*.

Applying the Criteria to the Present Case

In the present case, the trial judge imposed a sentence of three years' imprisonment which we considered to be fit and proper for the reasons given by the trial judge. In doing so, the trial judge considered the dangerous and addictive nature of crack cocaine and the quantity involved in this offence. He also considered the age of the appellant (21 years) and his previous record. He was influenced by the fact that the use of crack cocaine was on the increase in the London area and that there had been a number of recent arrests involving crack cocaine and violence. All of these factors were relevant and appropriate in assessing the duration of the custodial sentence, but there was nothing exceptional in these circumstances to justify the imposition of a s. 741.2 order. It should be noted that the Crown did not ask for such an order. The trial judge brought it up on his own initiative.

While there was some evidence of violence, that is, the stabbing of James in the crack house, there was no evidence to connect the appellant with this incident. The offence for which he was convicted did not involve violence. The appellant had no prior record involving offences of violence. The evidence of violence in the community associated with crack trafficking had little relevance to the potential rehabilitation of the appellant. Favourable to the appellant on this issue was his wish to become involved in the substance abuse program while incarcerated, but there was no evidence as to how long such a program might take.

In my respectful view, the potential for rehabilitation and parole of the appellant was an issue best left to the parole authorities. This was not an appropriate case for the imposition of a s. 741.2 [now s. 743.6] order.

PROBLEM

In 1999, Smith is convicted of manslaughter. The victim was viciously beaten to death while Smith was severely intoxicated. Smith has a previous record for manslaughter in 1985, for which he was sentenced to 10 years' imprisonment. Since his release from that sentence, he was convicted on two occasions of assault causing bodily harm. Smith has been in custody for 2 years pending the trial. The Crown has submitted that the only appropriate sentence is a life sentence. The trial judge has questioned the applicable parole eligibility rule. First, if sentenced to life, when would Smith be eligible for parole? Second, can the judge use s. 743.6 to delay parole? See *R v. Shorting* (1995), 102 CCC (3d) 385 (Man. CA).

C. Parole by Exception

Although it rarely occurs, it is possible for some prisoners to be considered for parole before their eligibility date. This has become known as parole by exception.

121(1) Subject to section 102 and notwithstanding section 119 or 120 or any order made under section 741.2 of the *Criminal Code*, parole may be granted at any time to an offender
   (a) who is terminally ill;
   (b) whose physical or mental health is likely to suffer serious damage if the offender continues to be held in confinement;
   (c) for whom continued confinement would constitute an excessive hardship that was not reasonably foreseeable at the time the offender was sentenced; or
   (d) who is the subject of an order to be surrendered under the *Extradition Act* or the *Fugitive Offenders Act* and to be detained until surrendered.
(2) Subsection (1) does not apply to any offender who is
   (a) serving a sentence of life imprisonment imposed as a minimum punishment or commuted from a sentence of death; or
   (b) serving, in a penitentiary, a sentence of detention for an indeterminate period.

This provision does not apply to prisoners serving life sentences or indeterminate sentences. In May 2000, a subcommittee of the House of Commons Standing Committee on Justice and Human Rights released a review of the CCRA five years after its enactment ("the five-year review"). With respect to parole by exception, the subcommittee recommended that "offenders serving life sentences or indeterminate sentences who are terminally ill and who present, in the opinion of the NPB, no undue risk" should also be eligible for extraordinary consideration. However, any such decisions must be approved by the chair of the NPB (see Sub-committee on Corrections and Conditional Release Act of the Standing Committee on Justice and Human Rights, *A Work in Progress: The Corrections and Conditional Release Act* (Ottawa: Public Works Canada, 2000), 39-40.

D. Accelerated Parole

This mechanism was intended to fast-track non-violent offenders, and was first introduced in 1992 with the CCRA. Essentially, s. 125 of the CCRA and its related regulations provide that cases of first-time penitentiary prisoners who are not serving a sentence for murder, a life sentence, or an offence from the list that would qualify for detention, shall be sent to the NPB at least three months before the prisoners' full parole eligibility date (PED). The file is then reviewed without a hearing by the NPB. If the NPB is "satisfied that there are no reasonable grounds to believe that the offender, if released, is likely to commit an offence involving violence before the expiration of the offender's sentence," it orders that the offender be released on full parole at PED (see s. 126(2)). If the board does not order release, the prisoner must get reasons and is subsequently entitled to a hearing on reaching full parole eligibility.

This mechanism received substantial consideration by the House of Commons sub-committee, which conducted the five-year review of the CCRA.

Sub-committee on Corrections and Conditional Release Act of the Standing Committee on Justice and Human Rights, *A Work in Progress:*
The Corrections and Conditional Release Act
(Ottawa: Public Works Canada, 2000), 33-35

4.24 The Sub-committee repeatedly heard at its hearings that the conditional release programs most successful in reducing recidivism were those that relied on discretionary decisions by either the Correctional Service or the National Parole Board. In its brief, the Canadian Resource Centre for Victims of Crime stated:

> It is interesting to note that the conditional releases with the highest success rates are those that rely on the judgments of professionals and are based on proper risk assessments that focus on public safety, where the lowest success rates are for those releases by law, including statutory release and accelerated parole review.

4.25 While the Sub-committee notes the lower success rate among offenders released under accelerated parole review for day and full parole, it does not believe that accelerated parole review should be eliminated. In fact, it believes that two amendments should suffice to make accelerated parole review correspond to the Sub-committee's position on conditional release: tightening the eligibility criteria; and changing the risk of recidivism criterion to be taken into account by the National Parole Board in reviewing cases.

4.26 The Sub-committee considers it crucial to recognize a significant difference between the accelerated parole review procedure and statutory release. Unlike statutory release as it currently stands, accelerated parole review ensures that all eligible offenders' cases are carefully reviewed by the Correctional Service of Canada and the National Parole Board. Moreover, under the Act, if after reviewing a case the Board has reason to believe that the offender will commit a violent offence listed in Schedule I of the Act before the expiry of the warrant of committal, the Board is required to deny release under the accelerated parole review procedure.

4.27 Unlike the current conditions governing statutory release, accelerated parole review is not a right, but is a simplified case review procedure reserved for offenders considered non-violent who are serving a first federal term of incarceration.

4.28 Under section 125 of the Act, an offender eligible for accelerated parole review is:

- sentenced to a federal penitentiary for the first time;
- not serving a sentence for murder or aiding and abetting murder;
- not serving a life sentence;
- not convicted of an offence listed in Schedule I of the Act;
- not convicted of a criminal organization offence; and
- not subject to a court order making them ineligible for parole before serving at least half of their sentence (this condition includes offences listed in Schedule II of the Act).

4.29 Unlike other offenders, those who meet all these conditions are automatically streamed into a simplified review procedure for possible day or full parole, with no requirement for a hearing before the National Parole Board. They may also benefit from day parole, not six months before their full parole eligibility dates as is the case for offenders ineligible for accelerated parole review, but after serving six months or one-sixth of their sentences, whichever is longer. In reviewing these cases, the Board must also use the criterion of violent recidivism, not general recidivism, as is the case for offenders ineligible for accelerated parole review.

4.30 Although the Sub-committee considers it important to retain accelerated parole review, so first time federal offenders considered non-violent need not be subjected to the negative influence of some repeat offenders, it also considers two amendments to the accelerated parole review procedure essential. The Sub-committee believes offenders incarcerated for Schedule I or Schedule II offences should not be eligible. As well, the recidivism criterion taken into account by the National Parole Board in reviewing these cases should specify general recidivism, not violent recidivism. It is the Sub-committee's view that the Parole Board should grant parole only if it is convinced there are no reasonable grounds to believe that any offence will be committed before the expiry of the warrant of committal.

Recommendation 13

The Sub-committee recommends that the *Corrections and Conditional Release Act* be amended to ensure that the accelerated parole review procedure is not available to offenders incarcerated for offences listed in Schedule II to the Act, regardless of whether there has been a judicial determination of parole eligibility.

Recommendation 14

The Sub-committee also recommends that the *Corrections and Conditional Release Act* be amended to ensure that the National Parole Board, in reviewing the cases of offenders eligible for accelerated parole review and determining whether they should be released on day parole or full parole, takes into account the general recidivism criterion.

E. Statutory Release

Until 1992, all prisoners in Canada were entitled to earn remission at the rate of 15 days per month. If completely earned and not forfeited for disciplinary offences, this could amount to remission credits totalling approximately one-third of the prisoner's sentence. At the point when the days actually served in custody and the number of earned remission credits equalled the total sentence, the prisoner was entitled to be released. For provincial prisoners, this meant an unconditional release but federal prisoners were released on mandatory supervision. Provincial prisoners can still earn remission (see s. 6 of the *Prisons and Reformatories Act*, RSC 1985, c. P-20). However, in 1992, the CCRA abolished remission for federal prisoners and replaced it with "statutory release," which occurs after two-thirds of a sentence has been served.

127(1) Notwithstanding the *Prisons and Reformatories Act*, an offender sentenced, committed or transferred to penitentiary is entitled to be released on the date determined in accordance with this section and to remain at large, subject to this Act, until the expiration of the sentence according to law.

(2) Subject to subsections (4) and (5), the statutory release date of an offender sentenced to imprisonment for one or more offences committed before the day on which this section comes into force shall be determined by crediting against the sentence

(a) any remission, statutory or earned, standing to the offender's credit on that day; and

(b) the maximum remission that could have been earned on the balance of the sentence pursuant to the *Penitentiary Act* or the *Prisons and Reformatories Act*, as those Acts read immediately before that day.

(3) Subject to subsection (4), the statutory release date of an offender sentenced to imprisonment for one or more offences committed on or after the day on which this section comes into force is the day on which the offender completes two thirds of the sentence.

(4) The statutory release date of an offender sentenced to imprisonment for one or more offences committed before the day on which this section comes into force and for one or more offences committed on or after the day on which this section comes into force is the later of

(a) the day determined by crediting against the sentence the aggregate of

(i) any remission, statutory or earned, standing to the offender's credit on that day, and

(ii) the maximum remission that could have been earned on the balance of the sentence pursuant to the *Penitentiary Act* or the *Prisons and Reformatories Act*, as those Acts read immediately before that day, and

(b) the day on which the offender completes two thirds of the sentence.

(5) subject to subsections 130(7) and 138(2), the statutory release date of an offender who is on parole or who is subject to mandatory supervision under the *Parole Act* on the day on which this section comes into force, and whose parole or release subject to mandatory supervision is revoked on or after that day, is the day on which the offender completes two thirds of the unexpired portion of the sentence after being recommitted to custody pursuant to subsection 138(1).

(6) An offender who is entitled to be released on statutory release may choose to remain in custody for all or any portion of the sentence the offender is serving.

(7) an offender sentenced, committed or transferred (otherwise than pursuant to an agreement entered into under subsection 16(1) to penitentiary on or after August 1, 1970 who is released on statutory release is subject to supervision in accordance with this Act, but no other offender released under this section is subject to supervision.

Prisoners on statutory release are subject to compulsory conditions that are prescribed by regulation and any other conditions that the NPB "considers reasonable and necessary in order to protect society and to facilitate the offender's successful reintegration into society" (see s. 133(3)). Like prisoners on parole, the prisoner on statutory release can be returned to custody if the statutory release is suspended, terminated, cancelled, or revoked.

F. Detention

Probably the most significant change to the function of the NPB was the introduction of the detention provisions that permit the denial of release on statutory release. The history of this enactment goes back to the early 1980s when the NPB was criticized following a few high-profile offences that were committed by offenders who had been released on mandatory supervision. Although these releases were the result of the statutory process and not the result of the NPB's discretion, the media and the public do not always appreciate these distinctions. In response, the strategy of "gating" was devised. Because the *Parole Act* authorized the suspension and revocation of an offender on parole or mandatory supervision "to protect society," it was reasoned that a prisoner could be immediately suspended and recommitted to confinement based on a *prediction* of his or her post-release conduct. This metaphor of "gating" conveyed both a return to custody from the prison gate and also the negating of the expected release.

In late 1982, nine prisoners who were about to be released were immediately suspended at the penitentiary gates. A series of *habeas corpus* applications were commenced across the country, arguing that the NPB had no authority to deny anyone their release on mandatory supervision. When two of these cases reached the Supreme Court of Canada, a unanimous court agreed that the *Parole Act* only authorized suspension and revocation based on post-release conduct (see *R v. Moore* (1983), 33 CR (3d) 97 (SCC)).

Shortly after the Supreme Court decision, new legislation was introduced that would amend the *Parole Act* by using a predictive test similar to that found in the dangerous offender provisions of the *Criminal Code*. In 1985, the bill passed the House of Commons, but was rejected by the Senate. In the summer of 1986, Prime Minister Mulroney recalled Parliament and passed the amendment to the *Parole Act*. The extraordinary move of recalling Parliament during the summer had been taken in the past only to declare war or legislate an end to public sector strikes. On this occasion, the argument made was that there were 50 dangerous prisoners in custody who, without this legislation, would be released into the community. (Notwithstanding the apparent identification of 50 prisoners within the entire system as the reason for immediate legislative action, since 1986 the detention rate rose to a high of 484 prisoners in 1995-96. The rate has since dropped to 233 prisoners detained in 1998-99.)

In *R v. Cunningham*, infra, the Supreme Court confirmed the constitutional validity of the detention provisions. This case also marks the beginning of the "balancing" methodology of Charter analysis whereby the Supreme Court has asserted that the definition of rights encompassed by s. 7 of the *Canadian Charter of Rights and Freedoms*, part I of the *Constitution Act, 1982*, RSC 1985, app. II, no. 44, required balancing the rights of the individual with larger societal rights. (Up to this point, many observers had assumed that any balancing would occur within the strictures of s. 1.)

R v. Cunningham
(1990), 80 CCC (3d) 492 (SCC)

[In 1981, the prisoner had been sentenced to 12 years' imprisonment for manslaughter. He expected to be released on mandatory supervision on April 8, 1989. He had maintained good behaviour in prison. In 1988, his parole officer recommended him for parole and requested a community assessment because the appellant had indicated that he would be returning to his home community, not far from the scene of the crime. Subsequently, he was referred by the commissioner to the NPB for a detention hearing.]

McLACHLIN J:

...

His community, alerted to his release by the community assessment, evinced concern at his early release given the violence of the crime. Further assessments made in the six months preceding the early release date suggested that he remained homicidal when drunk. There was said to be a 50% chance of his returning to alcohol, and a 50% chance that if drunk he would commit an act of violence. There was also evidence that he was somewhat unstable and had not accepted his responsibility for the crime. While this evidence was brought forward in the six months preceding the anticipated release date, similar observations may be found in the prison records for preceding years. Following a detention hearing, the appellant was ordered to be detained until his sentence expired on February 13, 1993, subject to annual reviews. The appellant brought an action to the Supreme Court of Ontario for a writ of *habeas corpus*.

...

My conclusion is that while the appellant's liberty may be said to have been adversely affected by the changes to the *Parole Act*, the deprivation was not contrary to the principles of fundamental justice.

The first question is whether the appellant has suffered a deprivation of liberty which attracts the protection of s. 7 of the Charter. This raises two subsidiary questions: (1) has the appellant shown that he has been deprived of liberty?; (2) if so, is the deprivation sufficiently serious to attract Charter protection?

In my view, the appellant has shown that he has been deprived of liberty. The argument that because the appellant was sentenced to twelve years' imprisonment there can be no further impeachment of his liberty interest within the twelve-year period runs counter to previous pronouncements, and oversimplifies the concept of liberty. This and other courts have recognized that there are different types of liberty interests in the context of correctional law. In *Dumas v. LeClerc Institute*, [1986] 2 SCR 459, at p. 464, Lamer J (as he then was) identified three different deprivations of liberty: (1) the initial deprivation of liberty; (2) a substantial change in conditions amounting to a further deprivation of liberty; and (3) a continuation of the deprivation of liberty. In *R v. Gamble*, [1988] 2 SCR 595, at p. 645, this Court held by a majority, per Wilson J (Lamer and L'Heureux-Dubé JJ concurring) that the liberty interest involved in not continuing the period of parole ineligibility may be protected by s. 7 of the Charter:

> ... the continuation of the 25-year period of parole ineligibility deprives the appellant
> of an important residual liberty interest which is cognizable under s. 7 and which may
> be appropriately remedied by way of habeas corpus if found to be unlawful.

American authority is to the same effect. In *Greenholtz v. Inmates of Nebraska Penal and Correctional Complex*, 442 US 1 (1979), at pp. 9-10, the Supreme Court of the United States per Burger CJ held that an expectation of liberty created by a parole statute created a liberty interest in parole release that is protected by the Due Process Clause of the Fourteenth Amendment. This finding was affirmed in *Board of Pardons v. Allen*, 482 US 369 (1987). Notwithstanding a vigourous dissent by O'Connor J (Rehnquist CJ and Scalia J concurring) in that case, relying on *Board of*

Regents of State Colleges v. Roth, 408 US 564 (1972), this remains the law in the United States.

I do not find it useful to ask whether the liberty interest was "vested" or "not vested." The only questions which arise under the Charter are whether a protected liberty interest is limited, and if so, whether that limitation accords with the principles of fundamental justice. To qualify an interest as "vested" or "not vested" does not really advance the debate, except in the sense that a vested interest might be seen as being more important or worthy of protection than one which is not vested. In that event, I think it better to speak directly of the importance of the interest, rather than introducing the property law concept of vesting. At the same time, it is important to recognize that liberty interests may cover a spectrum from the less important to the fundamental. A restriction affecting the form in which a sentence is served, the issue here, may be less serious than would be an *ex post facto* increase in the sentence.

In the case at bar, the appellant was sentenced to twelve years and was required under his warrant of committal, both before and after the amendment of the *Parole Act*, to serve that sentence in its entirety. Thus the duration of the restriction of his liberty interest has not been affected. As Lamer J held for the Court in *Dumas*, supra, at p. 464, "In the context of parole, the continued detention of an inmate will only become unlawful if he has acquired the status of a parolee." The appellant had never acquired parolee status, and his sentence, contrary to his counsel's submissions, has not been increased.

However the manner in which he may serve a part of that sentence, the second liberty interest identified by Lamer J in *Dumas*, supra, has been affected. One has "more" liberty, or a better quality of liberty, when one is serving time on mandatory supervision than when one is serving time in prison. The appellant had a high expectation, contingent on his good behaviour, that he would be released on mandatory supervision on April 8, 1989, had the *Parole Act* not been amended; indeed, he would automatically have been released on mandatory supervision given his good behaviour. The effect of the 1986 amendment of the *Parole Act* was to reduce that expectation of liberty, in the sense that it curtailed the probability of his release on mandatory supervision. This resulted from the new power of the Commissioner to refer exceptional cases to the Parole Board based on events and information in the six months immediately preceding the presumptive release date. As the British Columbia Court of Appeal put it in *Re Ross and Warden of Kent Institution* (1987), 34 CCC (3d) 452 (BC CA), at p. 454: "The effect of the 1986 amendments ... is to alter the right of an inmate to serve a portion of his sentence on mandatory supervision by qualifying that right."

I conclude that the appellant has suffered deprivation of liberty. The next question is whether the deprivation is sufficiently serious to warrant Charter protection. The Charter does not protect against insignificant or "trivial" limitations of rights: *R v. Edwards Books and Art Ltd.*, [1986] 2 SCR 713, at p. 759 (per Dickson CJ); *R v. Jones*, [1986] 2 SCR 284, at p. 314; *Lavigne v. Ontario Public Service Employees Union*, [1991] 2 SCR 211, at p. 259; *Andrews v. Law Society of British Columbia*, [1989] 1 SCR 143, at pp. 168-69. It follows that qualification of a prisoner's expectation of liberty does not necessarily bring the matter within the purview of s. 7 of the Charter. The qualification must be significant enough to warrant constitutional protection. To require that all changes to the manner in which a sentence is served be in accordance with the principles of fundamental justice would trivialize the protections under the Charter. To quote Lamer J in *Dumas*, supra, at p. 464, there must be a "substantial change in conditions amounting to a further deprivation of liberty."

The change in the manner in which the sentence was served in this case meets this test. There is a significant difference between life inside a prison versus the greater liberty enjoyed on the outside under mandatory supervision. Such a change was recognized as worthy of s. 7 protection in *Gamble*, supra.

Having concluded that the appellant has been deprived of a liberty interest protected by s. 7 of the Charter, we must determine whether this is contrary to the principles of fundamental justice under s. 7 of the Charter. In my view, while the amendment of the *Parole Act* to eliminate automatic release on mandatory supervision restricted the appellant's liberty interest, it did not violate the principles of fundamental justice. The principles of fundamental justice are concerned not only with the interest of the person who claims his liberty has been limited, but with the protection of society. Fundamental justice requires that a fair balance be struck between these interests, both substantively and procedurally (see *Re BC Motor Vehicle Act*, [1985] 2 SCR 486, at pp. 502-3, per Lamer J; *Singh v. Minister of Employment and Immigration*, [1985] 1 SCR 177, at p. 212, per Wilson J; *Pearlman v. Manitoba Law Society Judicial Committee*, [1991] 2 SCR 869, at p. 882, per Iacobucci J). In my view the balance struck in this case conforms to this requirement.

The first question is whether, from a substantive point of view, the change in the law strikes the right balance between the accused's interests and the interests of society. The interest of society in being protected against the violence that may be perpetrated as a consequence of the early release of inmates whose sentence has not been fully served needs no elaboration. On the other side of the balance lies the prisoner's interest in an early conditional release.

The balance is struck by qualifying the prisoner's expectation regarding the form in which the sentence would be served. The expectation of mandatory release is modified by the amendment permitting a discretion to prevent early release where society's interests are endangered. A change in the form in which a sentence is served, whether it be favourable or unfavourable to the prisoner, is not, in itself, contrary to any principle of fundamental justice.

Indeed, our system of justice has always permitted correctional authorities to make appropriate changes in how a sentence is served, whether the changes relate to place, conditions, training facilities, or treatment. Many changes in the conditions under which sentences are served occur on an administrative basis in response to the prisoner's immediate needs or behaviour. Other changes are more general. From time to time, for example, new approaches in correctional law are introduced by legislation or regulation. These initiatives change the manner in which some of the prisoners in the system serve their sentences.

The next question is whether the nature of this particular change in the rules as to the form in which the sentence would be served violates the Charter. In my view, it does not. The change is directly related to the public interest in protecting society from persons who may commit serious harm if released on mandatory supervision.

Only if the Commissioner is satisfied on the facts before him that this may be the case can he refer the matter to the Parole Board for a hearing. And only if the Board is satisfied that there is a significant danger of recidivism can it order the prisoner's continued incarceration. Thus the prisoner's liberty interest is limited only to the extent that this is shown to be necessary for the protection of the public. It is difficult to dispute that it is just to afford a limited discretion for the review of parole applicants who may commit an offence causing serious harm or death. Substantively, the balance is fairly struck.

Nor does the procedure established under the Act and Regulations violate the principles of fundamental justice. The change was made by law. The new procedure provides for a hearing to consider whether the expectation of release on mandatory supervision was warranted. The prisoner is entitled to representation throughout. The material on which the matter may be referred for hearing is limited. Under s. 21.3(3) of the *Parole Act*, the reference together with the relevant information is to be submitted no later than six months before the presumptive release date. The only exception to this general rule is provided where either the behaviour of the inmate or information obtained within the six months warrants a review. There are also provisions for new hearings to review the detention in the future. These requirements provide safeguards against arbitrary, capricious orders and ensure that curtailment of release on mandatory supervision occurs only when it is required to protect the public and then only after the interests of the prisoner in obtaining the release have been fully and fairly canvassed.

...

I conclude that the appellant has not established that the changes to the *Parole Act* deprived him of his liberty contrary to the principles of fundamental justice. No violation of s. 7 having been made out, it is unnecessary to consider the arguments under s. 1 of the Charter.

I turn to the final issue: whether the Commissioner's referral of the appellant's case to the Parole Board was illegal and contrary to the law. Under s. 21.3(3), the Commissioner may refer an inmate's case to the Board no later than six months preceding his "presumptive release" on mandatory supervision. An exception to this general rule is permitted where, due to the inmate's behaviour or information received within the six month period, the Commissioner has reason to believe that the inmate is likely, prior to the expiration of his sentence, to commit an offence causing death or serious harm. The Commissioner must have formed the belief on the basis of "information obtained within those six months" (s. 21.3(3)(a)(ii)).

The Commissioner referred the appellant's case as a "Commissioner's Referral based upon new information," offering the opinion that "without treatment intervention there are reasonable grounds to believe that this inmate is likely to commit an offence causing death or serious harm prior to warrant expiry date." The Commissioner's memorandum included two psychiatric reports, a letter from the Crown prosecutor and an updated RCMP report. All this information was received within the six months before the presumptive release date. It is argued that the information relied on by the Commissioner, while nominally arising within the six-month period before the appellant's prospective date for release on mandatory supervision, in fact is no more than an update of information which was on the appellant's file before that period. It is true that references to the appellant's volatility, drinking problems, lack of acceptance of guilt and tendency to violence when drunk may be found in the files prior to the six-month period. But that should not, in my view, prevent the Commissioner from relying on new and revised reports to the same effect when they come to his attention within the six-month period before the prospective release date. Indeed, it would be an unusual case where information coming forward in the six-month pre-release period did not find its echoes and antecedents in the previous prison record, given the long-standing nature of the problems typically involved in these cases.

I would agree with the motions judge that an objective test is appropriate. The issue put before this Court was whether the information could be said to be "new" in the substantive sense, rather than merely the temporal sense. The motions judge, having considered all the material, concluded on an objective test that it had not been established that the Commissioner had acted illegally in the sense of not forming his opinion on the basis of information obtained within six months. My review of the record does not persuade me that he was wrong.

In my view, the Commissioner did not violate the Act by referring the appellant's case to the National Parole Board for reconsideration of his eligibility for release on mandatory supervision.

NOTE

Since the decision in *Cunningham*, the scope of the detention provisions has been expanded. The list of offences that can lead to detention now includes serious drug offences and sexual offences involving children. For the extensive lists, see schedules I and II to the Act and s. 129(9).

The significant elements of the current detention provisions are set out below. Note that they encompass two stages: referral by the Correctional Service or commissioner and the detention hearing before the NPB. The standard for detention is whether the NPB is satisfied that the offender is likely to commit an offence causing death or serious harm, a sexual offence involving a child, or a serious drug offence if released.

Corrections and Conditional Release Act
SC 1992, c. 20, as amended by SC 1995, c. 42, ss. 129-132

129(1) Before the statutory release date of an offender who is serving a sentence of two years or more that includes a sentence imposed for an offence set out in Schedule I or II or an offence set out in Schedule I or II that is punishable under section 130 of the *National Defence Act*, the Commissioner shall cause the offender's case to be reviewed by the Service.

(2) After the review of the case of an offender pursuant to subsection (1), and not later than six months before the statutory release date, the Service shall refer the case to the Board together with all the information that, in its opinion, is relevant to it, where the Service is of the opinion

(a) in the case of an offender serving a sentence that includes a sentence for an offence set out in Schedule I, that

(i) the commission of the offence caused the death of or serious harm to another person and there are reasonable grounds to believe that the offender is likely to commit an offence causing death or serious harm to another person before the expiration of the offender's sentence according to law, or

(ii) the offence was a sexual offence involving a child and there are reasonable grounds to believe that the offender is likely to commit a sexual offence involving a child before the expiration of the offender's sentence according to law; or

(b) in the case of an offender serving a sentence that includes a sentence for an offence set out in Schedule II, that there are reasonable grounds to believe that the offender is likely to commit a serious drug offence before the expiration of the offender's sentence according to law.

(3) Where the Commissioner believes on reasonable grounds that an offender who is serving a sentence of two years or more is likely, before the expiration of the sentence according to law, to commit an offence causing death or serious harm to another person, a sexual offence involving a child or a serious drug offence, the Commissioner shall refer the case to the Chairperson of the Board together with all the information in the possession of the Service that, in the Commissioner's opinion, is relevant to the case, as soon as is practicable after forming that belief, but the referral may not be made later than six months before the offender's statutory release date unless

(a) the Commissioner formed that belief on the basis of behaviour of the offender during the six months preceding the statutory release date or on the basis of information obtained during those six months; or

(b) as a result of any recalculation of the sentence under this Act, the statutory release date of the offender has passed or less than six months remain before that date.

(3.1) Where paragraph (3)(b) applies and the statutory release date has passed, the Commissioner shall, within two working days after the recalculation under that paragraph, make a determination whether a referral is to be made to the Chairperson of the Board pursuant to subsection (3) and, where appropriate, shall make a referral, and the offender is not entitled to be released on statutory release pending the determination.

(4) At the request of the Board, the Service shall take all reasonable steps to provide the Board with any additional information that is relevant to a case referred pursuant to subsection (2) or (3).

...

[Sections 129(5), (6), and (7), dealing with applicable procedures when the commissioner makes a referral to the NPB after the six months before statutory release, have been omitted.]

(8) The Commissioner may delegate to the correctional authorities of a province the powers of the Service and of the Commissioner under this section in relation to offenders who are serving their sentences in a correctional facility in that province.

(9) In this section and sections 130 and 132, "serious drug offence" means an offence set out in Schedule II; "sexual offence involving a child" means

(a) an offence under any of the following provisions of the *Criminal Code* that was prosecuted by way of indictment, namely,

(i) section 151 (sexual interference),

(ii) section 152 (invitation to sexual touching),

(iii) section 153 (sexual exploitation),

(iv) subsection 160(3) (bestiality in presence of child or inciting child to commit bestiality),

(v) section 170 (parent or guardian procuring sexual activity by child),

(vi) section 171 (householder permitting sexual activity by child),

(vii) section 172 (corrupting children),

(viii) subsection 212(2) (living off the avails of prostitution by a child), and

(ix) subsection 212(4) (obtaining sexual services of a child),

(b) an offence under any of the following provisions of the *Criminal Code* involving a person under the age of eighteen years that was prosecuted by way of indictment, namely,

(i) section 155 (incest),

(ii) section 159 (anal intercourse),

(iii) subsections 160(1) and (2) (bestiality and compelling bestiality),

(iv) section 271 (sexual assault),

(v) section 272 (sexual assault with a weapon, threats to a third party or causing bodily harm), and

(vi) section 273 (aggravated sexual assault),

(c) an offence under any of the following provisions of the *Criminal Code*, chapter C-34 of the Revised Statutes of Canada, 1970, as they read immediately before January 1, 1988, that was prosecuted by way of indictment, namely,

(i) section 146 (sexual intercourse with a female under 14),

(ii) section 151 (seduction of a female between 16 and 18), and

(iii) section 167 (householder permitting defilement),

(d) an offence involving a person under the age of eighteen years under any of the following provisions of the *Criminal Code*, chapter C-34 of the Revised Statutes of Canada, 1970, as they read immediately before January 1, 1988, that was prosecuted by way of indictment, namely,

(i) section 153 (sexual intercourse with step-daughter),

(ii) section 155 (buggery or bestiality),

(iii) section 157 (gross indecency), and

(iv) section 166 (parent or guardian procuring defilement), or

(e) an offence involving a person under the age of eighteen years under any of the following provisions of the *Criminal Code*, chapter C-34 of the Revised Statutes of Canada, 1970, as they read immediately before January 4, 1983, that was prosecuted by way of indictment, namely,

(i) section 144 (rape),

(ii) section 145 (attempt to commit rape),

(iii) section 149 (indecent assault on female), and

(iv) section 156 (indecent assault on male).

(10) In determining whether an offender is likely to commit an offence causing death or serious harm to another person, a sexual offence involving a child or a serious drug offence, it is not necessary to determine whether the offender is likely to commit any particular offence.

130(1) Where the case of an offender is referred to the Board by the Service pursuant to subsection 129(2) or referred to the Chairperson of the Board by the Commissioner pursuant to subsection 129(3) or (3.1), the Board shall, subject to subsections 129(5), (6) and (7), at the times and in the manner prescribed by the regulations,

(a) inform the offender of the referral and review, and

(b) review the case, and the Board shall cause all such inquiries to be conducted in connection with the review as it considers necessary.

(2) An offender referred to in subsection (1) is not entitled to be released on statutory release before the Board renders its decision under this section in relation to the offender.

(3) On completion of the review of the case of an offender referred to in subsection (1), the Board may order that the offender not be released from imprisonment before the expiration of the offender's sentence according to law, except as provided by subsection (5), where the Board is satisfied

(a) in the case of an offender serving a sentence that includes a sentence for an offence set out in Schedule I, or for an offence set out in Schedule I that is punishable under section 130 of the *National Defence Act*, that the offender is likely, if released, to commit an offence causing the death of or serious harm to another person or a sexual offence involving a child before the expiration of the offender's sentence according to law,

(b) in the case of an offender serving a sentence that includes a sentence for an offence set out in Schedule II, or for an offence set out in Schedule II that is punishable under section 130 of the *National Defence Act*, that the offender is likely, if released, to commit a serious drug offence before the expiration of the offender's sentence according to law,

(c) in the case of an offender whose case was referred to the Chairperson of the Board pursuant to subsection 129(3) or (3.1), that the offender is likely, if released, to commit an offence causing the death of or serious harm to another person, a sexual offence involving a child or a serious drug offence before the expiration of the offender's sentence according to law.

. . .

(4) Where the Board is not satisfied as provided in subsection (3) but is satisfied that

(a) at the time the case was referred to it, the offender was serving a sentence that included a sentence for an offence set out in Schedule I or II, or for an offence set out in Schedule I or II that is punishable under section 130 of the *National Defence Act*, and

(b) in the case of an offence set out in Schedule I or an offence set out in Schedule I that is punishable under section 130 of the *National Defence Act*, the commission of the offence caused the death of, or serious harm to, another person or the offence was a sexual offence involving a child, it may order that if the statutory release is later revoked, the offender is not entitled to be released again on statutory release before the expiration of the offender's sentence according to law.

...

[Section 131, dealing with the mandatory annual reviews of prisoners who have been detained under s. 130(3), has been omitted.]

132(1) For the purposes of the review and determination of the case of an offender pursuant to section 129, 130 or 131, the Service, the Commissioner or the Board, as the case may be, shall take into consideration any factor that is relevant in determining the likelihood of the commission of an offence causing the death of or serious harm to another person before the expiration of the offender's sentence according to law, including

(a) a pattern of persistent violent behaviour established on the basis of any evidence, in particular,

(i) the number of offences committed by the offender causing physical or psychological harm,

(ii) the seriousness of the offence for which the sentence is being served,

(iii) reliable information demonstrating that the offender has had difficulties controlling violent or sexual impulses to the point of endangering the safety of any other person,

(iv) the use of a weapon in the commission of any offence by the offender,

(v) explicit threats of violence made by the offender,

(vi) behaviour of a brutal nature associated with the commission of any offence by the offender, and

(vii) a substantial degree of indifference on the part of the offender as to the consequences to other persons of the offender's behaviour;

(b) medical, psychiatric or psychological evidence of such likelihood owing to a physical or mental illness or disorder of the offender;

(c) reliable information compelling the conclusion that the offender is planning to commit an offence causing the death of or serious harm to another person before the expiration of the offender's sentence according to law; and

(d) the availability of supervision programs that would offer adequate protection to the public from the risk the offender might otherwise present until the expiration of the offender's sentence according to law.

(1.1) For the purposes of the review and determination of the case of an offender pursuant to section 129, 130 or 131, the Service, the Commissioner or the Board, as the case may be, shall take into consideration any factor that is relevant in determining the likelihood of the commission of a sexual offence involving a child before the expiration of the offender's sentence according to law, including

(a) a pattern of persistent sexual behaviour involving children established on the basis of any evidence, in particular,

(i) the number of sexual offences involving a child committed by the offender,

(ii) the seriousness of the offence for which the sentence is being served,

(iii) reliable information demonstrating that the offender has had difficulties controlling sexual impulses involving children,

(iv) behaviour of a sexual nature associated with the commission of any offence by the offender, and

(v) a substantial degree of indifference on the part of the offender as to the consequences to other persons of the offender's behaviour;

(b) reliable information about the offender's sexual preferences indicating that the offender is likely to commit a sexual offence involving a child before the expiration of the offender's sentence according to law;

(c) medical, psychiatric or psychological evidence of the likelihood of the offender committing such an offence owing to a physical or mental illness or disorder of the offender;

(d) reliable information compelling the conclusion that the offender is planning to commit such an offence; and

(e) the availability of supervision programs that would offer adequate protection to the public from the risk the offender might otherwise present until the expiration of the offender's sentence according to law.

(2) For the purposes of the review and determination of the case of an offender pursuant to section 129, 130 or 131, the Service, the Commissioner or the Board, as the case may be, shall take into consideration any factor that is relevant in determining the likelihood of the commission of a serious drug offence before the expiration of the offender's sentence according to law, including

(a) a pattern of persistent involvement in drug-related crime established on the basis of any evidence, in particular,

(i) the number of drug-related offences committed by the offender,

(ii) the seriousness of the offence for which the sentence is being served,

(iii) the type and quantity of drugs involved in any offence committed by the offender,

(iv) reliable information demonstrating that the offender remains involved in drug-related activities, and

(v) a substantial degree of indifference on the part of the offender as to the consequences to other persons of the offender's behaviour;

(b) medical, psychiatric or psychological evidence of such likelihood owing to a physical or mental illness or disorder of the offender;

(c) reliable information compelling the conclusion that the offender is planning to commit a serious drug offence before the expiration of the offender's sentence according to law; and

(d) the availability of supervision programs that would offer adequate protection to the public from the risk the offender might otherwise present until the expiration of the offender's sentence according to law.

G. Suspension and Revocation

Suspension and revocation are the major instruments of conditional release supervision. They permit designated officers to suspend a release and return an offender to custody if satisfied that it is "necessary and reasonable ... in order to prevent a breach of condition or to protect society." Once the offender has been returned to custody, the case is reviewed and the suspension can be cancelled or the case can be referred to the NPB to determine whether the release should be terminated or revoked. Both result in return to confinement under s. 138(1), but there are some differences in consequences that arise from the fact that termination is usually a result of "circumstances beyond the offender's control (see s. 135(5)(b)). For example, after a revocation, there is no obligation to conduct a parole review for one year, even if the prisoner is eligible (see s. 138(5)). Also, what are known as "one-shot statutory releases" are not affected by termination, but are triggered by revocation (see ss. 130(4), 130(6), and 138(6)).

Before considering the following provisions, there are two cautions. First, note that the procedures and requirements that govern the processes of suspension, cancellation, termination, and revocation are technical and detailed; a careful search of case law should be conducted to find any judicial decisions that may impose specific interpretations on the statutory provisions. Second, amendments to the CCRA have returned to the era of automatic consequences for the commission of an offence while on conditional release. Section 135(9.1) provides for a revocation when a person on parole or statutory release is incarcerated for an additional sentence. There is only limited scope to be exempted from this provision. Section 135(9.2) creates an exception when the additional sentence is a concurrent one that arises from an offence committed before the release.

Corrections and Conditional Release Act
SC 1992, c. 20, as amended by SC 1995, c. 42, ss. 135-138

135(1) A member of the Board or a person, designated by name or by position, by the Chairperson of the Board or by the Commissioner, when an offender breaches a condition of parole or statutory release or when the member or person is satisfied that it is necessary and reasonable to suspend the parole or statutory release in order to prevent a breach of any condition thereof or to protect society, may, by warrant,

(a) suspend the parole or statutory release;

(b) authorize the apprehension of the offender; and

(c) authorize the recommitment of the offender to custody until the suspension is cancelled, the parole or statutory release is terminated or revoked or the sentence of the offender has expired according to law.

(2) A person designated pursuant to subsection (1) may, by warrant, order the transfer to penitentiary of an offender who is recommitted to custody pursuant to subsection (1) in a place other than a penitentiary.

(3) The person who signs a warrant pursuant to subsection (1) or any other person designated pursuant to that subsection shall, forthwith after the recommitment of the offender, review the offender's case and

(a) where the offender is serving a sentence of less than two years, cancel the suspension or refer the case to the Board together with an assessment of the case, within fourteen days after the recommitment or such shorter period as the Board directs; or

(b) in any other case, within thirty days after the recommitment or such shorter period as the Board directs, cancel the suspension or refer the case to the Board together with an assessment of the case stating the conditions, if any, under which the offender could in that person's opinion reasonably be returned to parole or statutory release.

(4) The Board shall, on the referral to it of the case of an offender serving a sentence of less than two years, review the case and, within the period prescribed by the regulations, either cancel the suspension or terminate or revoke the parole.

(5) The Board shall, on the referral to it of the case of an offender serving a sentence of two years or more, review the case and, within the period prescribed by the regulations, unless the Board grants an adjournment at the offender's request,

(a) cancel the suspension, where the Board is satisfied that, in view of the offender's behaviour since release, the offender will not, by reoffending before the expiration of the offender's sentence according to law, present an undue risk to society;

(b) where the Board is not satisfied as provided in paragraph (a), terminate the parole or statutory release of the offender if it was suspended by reason of circumstances beyond the offender's control or revoke it in any other case; or

(c) where the offender is no longer eligible for the parole or entitled to be released on statutory release, terminate or revoke it.

(6) If in the Board's opinion it is necessary and reasonable to do so in order to protect society or to facilitate the reintegration of the offender into society, the Board, when it cancels a suspension of the parole or statutory release of an offender, may

(a) reprimand the offender in order to warn the offender of the Board's dissatisfaction with the offender's behaviour since release;

(b) alter the conditions of the parole or statutory release; and

(c) order the cancellation not to take effect until the expiration of a specified period not exceeding thirty days after the date of the Board's decision, where the offender violated the conditions of parole or statutory release on the occasion of the suspension and on at least one previous occasion that led to a suspension of parole or statutory release during the offender's sentence.

(6.1) Where a person referred to in subsection (3) or the Board cancels a suspension under this section, the person or the Board, as the case may be, shall forward a notification of the cancellation of the suspension or an electronically transmitted copy of the notification to the person in charge of the facility in which the offender is being held.

(7) Independently of subsections (1) to (6), where the Board is satisfied that the continued parole or statutory release of an offender would constitute an undue risk to society by reason of the offender reoffending before the expiration of the sentence according to law, the Board may, at any time,

(a) where the offender is no longer eligible for the parole or entitled to be released on statutory release, terminate or revoke the parole or statutory release; or

(b) where the offender is still eligible for the parole or entitled to be released on statutory release,

(i) terminate the parole or statutory release, where the undue risk to society is due to circumstances beyond the offender's control, or

(ii) revoke the parole or statutory release, where the undue risk to society is due to circumstances within the offender's control.

(8) The Board may exercise its power under subsection (7) notwithstanding any new sentence to which the offender becomes subject after being released on parole or

statutory release, whether or not the new sentence is in respect of an offence committed before or after the offender's release on parole or statutory release.

(9) Where the Board exercises its power under subsection (7), it shall review its decision at times prescribed by the regulations, at which times it shall either confirm or cancel its decision.

(9.1) Where an offender whose parole or statutory release has not been terminated or revoked is incarcerated as a result of an additional sentence for an offence under an Act of Parliament, the parole or statutory release, as the case may be, is revoked on the day on which the offender is incarcerated as a result of the additional sentence.

(9.2) Subsection (9.1) does not apply where the additional sentence is to be served concurrently with, and is in respect of an offence committed before the commencement of, the sentence to which the parole or statutory release applies.

(9.3) Where an offender who is released on parole receives an additional sentence described in subsection (9.2) and the day determined in accordance with section 119, 120 or 120.2, as the case may be, on which the offender is eligible for parole is later than the day on which the offender received the additional sentence, the parole becomes inoperative and the offender shall be reincarcerated.

(9.4) Unless the lieutenant governor in council of a province in which there is a provincial parole board makes a declaration under subsection 113(1) that subsection (9.1) applies in respect of offenders under the jurisdiction of that provincial parole board, subsection (9.1) does not apply in respect of such offenders, other than an offender who

(a) is serving a sentence in a provincial correctional facility pursuant to an agreement entered into under paragraph 16(1)(a); or

(b) as a result of receiving an additional sentence referred to in subsection (9.1), is required, pursuant to section 743.1 of the *Criminal Code*, to serve the sentence in a penitentiary.

(9.5) Where an offender to whom subsection (9.1) does not apply who is on parole that has not been revoked or terminated receives an additional sentence, for an offence under an Act of Parliament, that is to be served consecutively with the sentence the offender was serving when the additional sentence was imposed, the parole becomes inoperative and the offender shall be reincarcerated until the day on which the offender has served, from the day on which the additional sentence was imposed, the period of ineligibility in relation to the additional sentence and, on that day, the parole is resumed, subject to the provisions of this Act, unless, before that day, the parole has been revoked or terminated.

(10) For the purposes of this Part, an offender who is in custody by virtue of this section continues to serve the offender's sentence.

(11) For the purposes of this Act, where a suspension of parole or statutory release is cancelled, the offender is deemed, during the period beginning on the day of the issuance of the suspension and ending on the day of the cancellation of the suspension, to have been serving the sentence to which the parole or statutory release applies.

· · ·

[Section 135.1, dealing with suspension and revocation in relation to long-term offenders, has been omitted.]

136. When the parole or statutory release of an offender is terminated or revoked or where it becomes inoperative pursuant to subsection 135(9.3) or (9.5), a member of the Board or a person designated, by name or by position, by the Chairperson of the Board or by the Commissioner may, by warrant, authorize the apprehension and recommitment to custody of the offender pursuant to section 137.

137(1) A warrant of apprehension issued under section 11.1, 18, 118, 135, 135.1 or 136 or by a provincial parole board, or an electronically transmitted copy of such a warrant, shall be executed by any peace officer to whom it is given in any place in Canada as if it had been originally issued or subsequently endorsed by a justice or other lawful authority having jurisdiction in that place.

(2) A peace officer who believes on reasonable grounds that a warrant is in force under this Part or under the authority of a provincial parole board for the apprehension of a person may arrest the person without warrant and remand the person in custody.

(3) Where a person has been arrested pursuant to subsection (2), the warrant of apprehension, or an electronically transmitted copy thereof, shall be executed within forty-eight hours after the arrest is made, failing which the person shall be released.

138(1) Where the parole or statutory release of an offender is terminated or revoked, the offender shall be recommitted to custody and shall serve the portion of the sentence that remained unexpired on the day on which the parole or statutory release was terminated or revoked.

(2) An offender whose parole or statutory release has been terminated is

(a) eligible for parole in accordance with section 120, 120.1, 120.2 or 120.3, as the case may be; and

(b) entitled to be released on statutory release in accordance with section 127.

(3) An offender whose parole or statutory release has been terminated is not liable to forfeit

(a) any remission with which the offender was credited pursuant to the *Prisons and Reformatories Act*; or

(b) any credits under the *Transfer of Offenders Act*.

(4) An offender whose parole or statutory release has been revoked is eligible for parole in accordance with section 120, 120.1, 120.2 or 120.3, as the case may be.

(5) Notwithstanding sections 122 and 123, the Board is not required to conduct a review for the purpose of parole of the case of an offender referred to in subsection (4) within one year after the date on which the offender's parole or statutory release is revoked.

(6) Subject to subsections 130(4) and (6), an offender whose parole or statutory release has been revoked is entitled to be released on statutory release in accordance with section 127.

III. THE PAROLE DEBATE

Over the years, the legitimacy, efficacy, and fairness of parole have been the subject of substantial debate in Canada. Aside from questions about whether parole decisions are made fairly or arbitrarily, there are some important intrinsic issues about a system of discretionary conditional release. The "truth in sentencing" advocates argue that parole distorts the judicially imposed sentence and that every day before warrant expiry should be served. Even more moderate critics like the Canadian Sentencing Commission supported the abolition of parole. However, the commission was content to retain remission-based release. Recently, the argument has been mooted that the reverse should occur: abolish statutory release and permit only discretionary-based release decisions. While reading the following materials—although they all antedate the CCRA and may refer to old *Parole Act* provisions—consider whether parole should be retained.

Canadian Sentencing Commission, *Sentencing Reform: A Canadian Approach*
(Ottawa: Supply and Services Canada, 1987) (footnotes omitted)

...

The purpose underlying the newly-created system of discretionary parole release was based on a rehabilitation-oriented model of justice. It is within this framework that the release criteria to guide the parole board in the exercise of its discretion were formulated.

...

Although parole was based on a model of rehabilitation, this model has never been implemented in Canada. According to this model, prison serves as a kind of maximum-security hospital and parole provides the necessary period for convalescence. Since treatment and recovery periods are difficult to quantify in advance, a true rehabilitation model can only be realized in the context of a system of indeterminate sentencing. Canada never adopted a system of indeterminate sentencing and hence, in adopting parole, only adopted part of the rehabilitation model. In the US, however, indeterminate sentencing and discretionary parole release together formed the package required for a real attempt at a rehabilitative model. It is disenchantment with this rehabilitation model that has led a number of US states, over the past 15 years, to abolish discretionary parole release as well as to create sentencing commissions to move toward a system of determinate sentencing. Some states that have abolished discretionary parole release have retained a parole board to release and supervise those inmates serving life sentences. In addition, parole boards have been retained to fulfill the discretionary release function for those inmates sentenced prior to the abolition of parole. Given the adoption of the Commission's recommendations, similar provisions must be made for Canada's Parole Board. So far 11 states have abolished discretionary parole release: Alaska, Arizona, California, Colorado, Connecticut, Illinois, Indiana, Maine, Minnesota, New Mexico and North Carolina. The problems created by adopting only one element of the rehabilitation model are illustrated in the above criteria for parole release. Under our current system of determinate sentencing, it is difficult to understand how one would determine whether an offender has derived "maximum benefit from imprisonment." We have seen in the historical chapter that one of the most frequently recurring themes in official reports on incarceration was that imprisonment had a debilitating rather than a rehabilitative effect on prisoners. Hence, some would argue it is hard to imagine any benefits accruing to someone who spends a number of years in a penitentiary. In addition, since it is impossible to predict accurately who will re-offend (or when, or why), the issues of risk to society and reform of the inmate are tenuous grounds upon which to release, suspend or revoke inmates on full parole.

2.1.3 Effects of Parole on the Meaning of the Sentence

a) Time Served in Custody

Terms of imprisonment in this country are substantially affected by parole release. While the relative merits of parole remain controversial, some characteristics and consequences of the system are clear enough. First, approximately one-third of eligible prisoners are granted release on full parole at some point in their sentences. The majority of all prisoners who are released on full parole were granted full parole upon their first application. Paroled prisoners serve an average of 40% of their sentence inside prison before obtaining release. Over three-quarters of those released on full parole serve less than half of their sentences in prison. (These statistics are all drawn from the 1981 *Solicitor General's Study of Conditional Release*). Tables (data from 1977 to 1981) provided by the Statistical Liaison Office of the National Parole Board corroborate the view that parole intervention in time actually served in prison is substantial. The following trends emerge:

- 95% of offenders convicted of offences against the person (excluding murder, attempted murder and manslaughter) who received sentences of over 10 years serve less than 10 years in prison;
- 70% of offenders convicted of attempted murder, second-degree murder and manslaughter who received sentences of over ten years served less than ten years in prison. This figure would actually be higher if it did not also encompass cases of second degree murder. Those convicted of second degree murder serve a mandatory period of at least 10 years before becoming eligible for parole. Hence, they automatically increase the percentage of offenders who serve ten years or more in prison.
- 98% of offenders convicted of drug offences and who received sentences of over 10 years served less than 10 years in prison.

These statistics make it clear that there is a substantial difference between the sentence a judge hands down and the length of time an offender actually serves in prison. Moreover, there is a great deal of variation in the parole release rates across different parts of the country. In 1978, for example, there was a 26% difference between the regions demonstrating the highest and lowest rates of parole (Solicitor General of Canada, 1986). These variations—as well as the indeterminate nature of parole—may lead offenders and public alike to perceive parole as inequitable.

b) Sentence Equalization

Another consequence of parole is that known as "sentence equalization": offenders serving longer sentences are more likely to get released on parole than are offenders sentenced to shorter terms. This leads to the result—paradoxical to some quarters such as the public—that the more serious offences (e.g., manslaughter and attempted murder) have higher parole release rates than less serious offences such as theft and fraud. This pattern is noted in a recent report (Hann and Harman, 1986) for the Ministry of the Solicitor General. These authors found that for the period of 1975/76 through 1981/82 parole release rates for manslaughter were between 51% and 64%. These percentages are approximately ten percentage points in excess of a less serious offence (robbery) and 20 to 30 percentage points above the release rates for break and enter.

· · ·

To summarize, it is clear that offenders convicted of more serious offences (such as manslaughter) serve a significantly smaller proportion of their sentences in custody than offenders convicted of much less serious crimes (such as fraud). As well, an offender convicted of a serious armed robbery may serve the same time in custody as a purse-snatcher. One consequence of this, as Mandel (1975) has pointed out, is to scramble the rankings of seriousness derived from the existing maximum penalty structure. Proportionality is lost in the shuffle from the sentence handed down by the judge to the early release of the offender on parole.

Another manifestation of the equalization effect can be seen in statistics of time served by parolees versus mandatory supervision releases. Thus, while inmates eventually released on parole were assigned, on average, much longer sentences than inmates released on mandatory supervision, the two groups ended up spending approximately the same amount of time in prison. This was noted by the *Solicitor General's Study of Conditional Release* (1981), and is also apparent from more recent data provided by the National Parole Board (1984).

The following statistics for manslaughter and robbery cases for the period 1982-83 illustrate the point. If one compares average sentence lengths of parole releases to mandatory supervision releases the difference is striking: those convicted of manslaughter and later released on parole were sentenced on average to 84 months. Those convicted on manslaughter and released on mandatory supervision were sentenced, on average, to 57 months. However, in terms of time served in prison the two groups are quite similar: 38 months for parolees, 41 months for those released on mandatory supervision.

The 1981 study of Conditional Release concluded: "Both sentence mitigation and sentence equalization, then, clearly appear to be effects of parole, despite the very firm National Parole Board position that they are not objectives" (p. 39). This effect seems undesirable for two reasons. First, because it violates the principle of proportionality, offering in effect a greater discount in time served to those convicted of more serious offences. This militates against equity and justice. Second, because it illustrates how the current system requires parole authorities to encroach upon the sentencing authority of the courts. This Commission is of the opinion that sentence equalization is a negative consequence of parole, and, thus, concurs with the position taken by the Goldenberg Committee (1974) in its report on parole in Canada.

2.1.4 Consideration of Parole and Remission by Sentencing Judges

The already murky waters of sentencing are clouded still further by judges considering, at time of sentencing, release on parole and remission. (Remission will be dealt with in greater detail in the next section). This consideration may take many forms. For example, it is possible that at least some judges are aware of the unstated yet clearly manifested policy to release higher proportions of serious offenders (for reasons of sentence mitigation and equalization) on full parole. If they are, judges may be increasing the lengths of sentences for certain offenders in anticipation of early release on full parole. Whether they follow this particular strategy or not, what evidence is there that judges are affected by the possibility of parole and remission? In the Commission's survey of sentencing judges (Research #6), only 35% of respondents stated that they never took parole into account at sentencing. Hogarth (1971) reported that two-thirds of judges in his sample admitted they sometimes adjusted their sentences in light of the possibility of parole being granted. To quote the *Solicitor General's Study of Conditional Release*: "In more candid moments, some judges will admit in effect to tripling the sentence in order to provide for a fixed period of 'denunciatory' imprisonment (prior to full parole eligibility), for a remission period, and for a 'parole' or 'rehabilitation' period" (p. 111).

The question of whether judges should consider parole and remission has generated an inconsistent response. The case law does not provide for a uniform approach to this question. There appears to be support in some provinces for the position that this is a valid consideration for judges in the determination of the sentence (see Campbell and Cole, 1986; Ruby 1980). Clearly, inconsistent application of a rule concerning the consideration of parole and remission can lead to unwarranted disparities in sentencing. Ruby (1980) sums it up: "Regardless of the merits of the discussion it would certainly be desirable that some measure of uniformity on this issue be attained, as a prisoner serving a lengthy term in Ontario will quite rightfully have a sense of grievance with regard to the consideration given there to his parole possibilities as compared to that of his fellows in other provinces" (p. 327).

2.1.5 Concerns: Lack of Equity, Clarity and Predictability

It is difficult to discuss concerns regarding equity and predictability as separate issues since by and large, if a process lacks one, it lacks all three. So, for example, problems of equity arise when full parole release is seen to lack clarity and predictability. Concerns with the operation of these principles in the current system of discretionary release have been raised in earlier chapters but some points bear repetition here.

Critics of parole have long argued that the criteria for parole release are too vague and broad to provide any real guidance to the decision-maker. One regrettable consequence is that parole decisions—both regarding release and revocation—are often seen to be arbitrary by inmates.

Previous government reports have alluded to negative reactions to parole on the part of offenders. The Sub-committee on the Penitentiary System in Canada (1977) noted that "inmates are under the impression that the Parole Board does not, in all circumstances, treat them fairly. The records contain many examples of inmates whose parole has been revoked because they arrived a few minutes late and who were also charged with being unlawfully at large" (p. 151). This same report also stated the following (in reference to the need for a mechanism other than revocation): "It is, therefore, extremely disconcerting to hear of inmates having their paroles suspended and revoked for essentially trivial reasons" (p. 151).

One of the recommendations (#64) of the 1977 Sub-Committee on the Penitentiary System in Canada acknowledged these perceptions:

> The appearance of arbitrariness in parole, especially in parole revocation without notice or reasons, is an unsettling factor in penitentiary life. There is also much resentment of the fact that mandatory supervision places discharges under conditions similar to parole for a period of time equal to that of their earned and statutory remission.
>
> The parole system should be reviewed with a view to lessening these arbitrary aspects.

Similar findings emerged from surveys of offenders conducted by this Commission. In one (Ekstedt, 1985), those who had experience with parole expressed reservations about the fairness of decisions. That the system is perceived to be arbitrary by those most critically affected by it lends a very real support to the concerns repeated in the literature. In addition to the perceived unfairness of a process grounded in wide discretion is the dilemma that some judges do and others do not consider the likelihood of full parole release in setting the length of a term of imprisonment. The practice of the Parole Board of effectively equalizing sentence lengths through parole release is further seen to undermine the sentence of the court.

There is no clear understanding on the part of offenders, criminal justice professionals, judges or the public as to the laws and practices surrounding discretionary parole release. The laws are complex, the practices vary and the result is that there is no shared understanding of what a sentence of imprisonment actually means. It is, in fact, not possible to predict with any accuracy the actual time in custody that most inmates will serve. Due to the wide discretion given to release authorities and the individualized nature of the release criteria, no convicted offender receiving a lengthy term of imprisonment can know how much time he or she faces in custody after hearing the sentence of the court.

Although general support was expressed for some form of early release, a recurring concern in submissions received by the Commission was the accountability of the releasing authority in the exercise of its discretion. Support was expressed for greater clarity in release criteria, guidelines for the releasing authority to ensure uniformity of approach and the need for some body to review early release decisions. Many groups and individuals stressed the need for better communication between judges who impose the sentence and the parole board and correctional authorities who ultimately administer it. The overall picture of a process fragmented by different approaches to sentencing emerged from the submissions.

The concerns expressed above primarily address the problems of discretionary parole release within the context of the existing sentencing structure. The concerns become even more pronounced when full parole release is considered within the context of the commission's proposals regarding principles of sentencing and its integrated set of recommendations. Proportionality and discretionary release on full parole are not natural allies. The reason for this is obvious—proportionality can only be drawn between two determinate quantities. The judge imposes a fixed term of imprisonment. This sentence is stated in open court and is subject to review by a higher court. The parole release date, of course, remains undetermined at the time of sentencing. In fact, in some cases the release decision is made on the basis of evidence that may not be revealed to the accused. The decision of the board is therefore not subject to public scrutiny or judicial review.

...

5. List of Recommendations

10.1   The Commission recommends the abolition of full parole, except in the case of sentences of life imprisonment.

10.2   The Commission recommends that earned remission be retained by way of credits awarded for good behaviour which may reduce by up to one-quarter the custodial portion of the sentence imposed by the judge.

10.3   The Commission recommends that all offenders be released without conditions unless the judge, upon imposing a sentence of incarceration, specifies that the offender should be released on conditions.

10.4   The Commission recommends that a judge may indicate certain conditions but the releasing authority shall retain the power to specify the exact nature of those conditions, modify or delete them or add other conditions.

10.5   The Commission recommends that the nature of the conditions be limited to explicit criteria with a provision that if the judge or the releasing authority wishes to prescribe an "additional" condition, they must provide reasons why such a condition is desirable and enter the reasons on the record.

10.6   The Commission recommends that where an offender, while on remission-based release, commits a further offence or breaches a condition of release, he or she shall be charged with an offence of violating a condition of release, subject to a maximum penalty of one year.

10.7   The Commission recommends that voluntary assistance programs be developed and made available to all inmates prior to and upon release from custody to assist them in their re-integration into the community.

10.8   The Commission recommends that a Sentence Administration Board be given the power to withhold remission release according to the criteria specified in the recently enacted legislation: *An Act to Amend the Parole Act and the Penitentiary Act*.

10.9   The Commission recommends that all inmates be eligible to participate in a day release program after serving two-thirds of their sentence, with the exception of those who meet the requirements for withholding remission release.

10.10   The Commission recommends that the granting of special leave according to explicit criteria remain at the discretion of the prison administration. Inmates shall be eligible for special leave passes immediately upon being placed in custody.

10.11   The Commission recommends that parole by exception be abolished and that cases where the inmate is terminally ill or where the inmate's physical or mental health is likely to suffer serious damage if he or she continues to be held in confinement shall be dealt with by way of the Royal Prerogative of Mercy.

10.12   The Commission recommends that the Sentence Administration Board should conduct the necessary review and forward submissions regarding clemency to the Solicitor General.

10.13   The Commission recommends that the Canadian immigration law should provide necessary authority for the deportation of convicted offenders in specified circumstances.

10.14   The Commission recommends that where a judge imposes a custodial sanction, he or she may recommend the nature of the custody imposed.

10.15   The Commission further recommends that federal and provincial governments provide the necessary resources and financial support for the establishment and maintenance of open custody facilities.

10.16   The Commission recommends that the mandatory life imprisonment sentence be retained for first and second degree murder and high treason.

10.17   The Commission recommends that inmates serving sentences for first degree murder or high treason be eligible for release on conditions after serving a minimum of 15 years up to a maximum of 25 years in custody. The court would set the date of eligibility for release within that limit.

10.18   The Commission recommends that inmates serving a life sentence for second degree murder be eligible for release on conditions after serving a minimum of ten years, and a maximum of 15 years in custody. The court would set the date of eligibility for release within that limit.

10.19   The Commission recommends that at the eligibility date, the inmate have the burden of demonstrating his or her readiness for release on conditions for the remainder of the life sentence.

10.20   The Commission recommends that the ineligibility period set by the court be subject to appeal.

M. Mandel, "Democracy, Class and the National Parole Board"
(1984-1985), 27 *Cr. LQ* 159 (footnotes omitted)

"Every individual is equal before and under the law and has the right to the equal protection and equal benefit of the law" proclaims the *Canadian Charter of Rights and Freedoms* (s. 15). Marxists have generally derided this sort of proclamation as completely incompatible with the enormous disparities in economic power and social class which exist in Canadian society. We have, indeed argued that, far from standing apart from these class divisions, the law is "superstructural," that is its precise function is to maintain the class structure ("relations of production") by providing norms and institutions which allow this structure to flourish. This is subtly, though importantly, different from merely saying that the law and legal institutions are there to protect the "status quo," because it specifies the aspect of the status quo protected, not the legal or democratic status quo of equal citizens but the productive relations status quo of massive inequality, of dominance and subordination. Individual interests are protected, but only according to their placement in the relations of production, that is as *class* interests.

Marxism has often called in aid of its point of view the persistent and severe over-representation of subordinate classes in institutions of legal repression such as prisons. For example, in Susan Binnie's study of Ontario reformatory inmates, "managerial, professional and technical" occupations had less than one-quarter of their strength in the ordinary population (3.87% to 17.8%), while "labourers" were over-represented by a factor of 2.6 (16.02% to 6.24%). And in Irvin Waller's sample of Ontario penitentiary releases, it was found that on "all three indicators of job functioning (longest job, level of skill and wage) before admission the ex-prisoner held a lower-order job than the average male, a finding now well documented in criminology." Unemployment rates (at arrest) of male prisoners admitted to the provincial institutions of five provinces in 1978 ranged from 60% to 75% and were from two to over four times the age-adjusted unemployment rate for each province. Finally, though all ethnic groups are represented in the prison population, the native peoples of Canada, unquestionably the economically worst off ethnic group, are over-represented by a factor of about six in Canada's prison population.

Thus the prison population is heavily skewed in favour of the economically marginal groups in the social structure. Lest it be thought that the under-representation of women is a contradiction of this, it should be pointed out that *among women*, the economically most marginal are also over-represented.

These data, striking as they are, are nevertheless ambiguous because they do not rule out the possibility that people are being treated equally by the law. It might be that crime itself varies in amount and seriousness by class and that the social skew in prison is due merely to an impartial law being applied to the same social skew in criminal behaviour.

In fact, analysis of the actual practices of the law and even the specific ideologies which are used to legitimate these practices reveals that this is not the case. I have argued elsewhere that the Canadian sentencing system departs substantially from democratic principles of equality before (and "under") the law and is as much concerned with the enforcement of the social relations of production, that is the class relations, as it is with the prevention of harm to individuals through crime and that it is this that, at least partly, accounts for the social skew in the prison population. Sentencing judges consistently tailor their sentences to the degree to which an offender fulfils his or her role in the productive system, whatever the offence, and to the degree to which offences, whatever their legal severity and the harm they do to individuals, oppose or protect the productive relations status quo. This is made possible by an institutional structure reposing great discretionary authority in sentencing courts and by a legal theory which both guides and legitimates the exercise of this discretion on the basis of "denunciation" and "rehabilitation."

Though sentencing thus contains many undemocratic elements, it also contains some democratic ones. As can be seen from the empirical studies which establish sentencing's class bias and from the law in the statutes and the cases, the legal nature of the offence does exert *some* control on the outcome. However, whatever democratic elements remain in sentencing are completely undermined by what Foucault has called "*the principle of the modulation of penalties.*" This principle comprehends all those variations in penalty which penal authorities administer, including the location of the prisoner on the infinitely graded continuum between minimum and super-maximum security, temporary absences, various forms of "remission" and the largest single modulator, the parole system. According to Foucault, the establishment of the penitentiary system in the context of the massive economic and political transformations which took place at the end of the eighteenth century brought with it a fundamental transformation in the judicial function, albeit under the cover of a relative stability in the law with respect to offences: Judges have been led "to judge something other than crimes"—namely the criminal—"to do something other than judge"—namely to rehabilitate—"and the power of judging has been transferred, in part to other authorities than the judges of the offence." This latter aspect Foucault calls a "fragmentation of the legal power to punish" and in Canada's case it has reposed enormous powers in the hands of parole authorities, who supervise virtually the entire length of virtually every prison sentence. One recent example will be instructive. This is the case of *McNamara (No. 2)* otherwise known as the "Hamilton Dredging Scandal."

This case involved charges of conspiracy to defraud the government of over five million dollars through a bid-rigging scheme which went on for five years among nine corporations and eleven corporate executives. The trial lasted more than 14 months and took up 197 court days earning it the title of "the longest criminal trial in Canadian history" and presumably the most expensive. *The Globe and Mail* reported that six of the accused were listed in the Canadian Who's Who and their lawyers were the best that money could buy. *The Globe* also reported this statement from one of the jurors:

> We realized they were very important businessmen and we wanted to be as fair as possible. It's just an awesome responsibility. It's an experience I won't forget.

In the result, only five persons and eight corporations were convicted. After further appeals, concluded another year and a half later, three human and one corporate convictions were quashed. The remaining seven corporations were fined six million dollars and the two humans, McNamara and Cooper, received prison terms of five years and three years respectively, taking into account their age (they were both 14 years older than when the conspiracies had started) and previous good character. About the latter, the trial judge said the following and the Court of Appeal agreed:

> All of the accused are persons of previous good character. All may be considered as first offenders. This does not reduce the seriousness of the offence, but is a factor when considering sentence. ...
>
> The evidence indicates that not only has [Cooper] been a person of good reputation but that he has contributed a great deal in public service to his community and is capable of making a great contribution in the future. Counsel for Mr. Cooper submitted that this is a proper case for a fine plus an order for community service. There is no doubt

Mr. Cooper would be of value to the community but I am afraid that the need for a deterrent sentence has a much higher priority.

Their appeals to the Supreme Court of Canada were dismissed a few months after and they finally went to prison.

The point of all this is that Cooper was out in six months in time for a winter holiday in Florida and the Caribbean and McNamara was out in ten months, both under the authority of the National Parole Board. When the facts became known, an NDP member stood up in the House of Commons and screamed that there was "one law for the rich, powerful friends of the Liberal Government and another law for the poor." Were the authorities embarrassed? Not at all. The National Parole Board chairman's response in a letter to the editor of *The Globe and Mail* is worth quoting in full:

Your editorial Privileged Parole (April 28) implies that the National Parole Board decides when an inmate is eligible for parole. The board decides *if* an inmate is to be released *when* he becomes eligible; the law and, in certain cases, the courts, set the date of possible release, not the board. Sydney Cooper and Harold McNamara were by law eligible for parole and the board, taking into account that they were first-time, non-violent offenders and that their release plans were sustained by excellent community support, decided to release them.

Ever since the 1899 *Ticket of Leave Act*, the question of political interference in parole decisions has been investigated, notably by the Archambault Commission (1938) and the Fauteux Committee (1956). To suggest that "powerful friends of the Liberal Government" receive special treatment and that there is a law for the poor and another for the rich, is completely contrary to fact.

The opprobrium attached to Mr. Cooper and Mr. McNamara during their trial and incarceration is the greatest deterrent to this type of non-violent crime. Releases on any type of parole are restricted by specific conditions. As a consulting engineer and chairman of the building committee of the Baycrest Centre for Geriatric Care in Toronto since 1978, Mr. Cooper was, in this rare instance, allowed to travel outside of his designated area for professional reasons.

The National Parole Board, in releasing Mr. Cooper and Mr. McNamara, is not condoning their crimes. All we are saying is that deserving, not privileged, inmates should be given the opportunity to return to society to lead productive and law-abiding lives.

W.R. Outerbridge
National Parole Board
Ottawa.

There are a few interesting things to note about this affair: (1) The chairman's attempt to disclaim responsibility for parole is dubious. Only about one-third of those eligible for *full parole* ever receive it and less than half of those receive it as soon as they are eligible. McNamara and Cooper were released on *day parole*, a privilege granted to only about half those again who receive parole. So the mechanism is highly selective. (2) The National Parole Board's interpretation of the day parole provisions, which in the case of certain prisoners is apparently full parole by another name, extends "normal eligibility" for parole from one-third of the sentence to one-sixth of the sentence. Even this can be eclipsed by a similarly broad interpretation of the pheonix-like "parole by exception" provisions. This means that the Parole Board's jurisdiction over the sentence is virtually total. (3) Though the courts in this case had justified the prison terms on the basis of the need for "general deterrence" of the offence, this is directly contradicted and almost completely wiped out by the Parole Board. (4) The "individual" factors of no criminal record and "good character" which were taken into account in mitigation of the original sentences are further intensified by the Parole Board, and to them is added the feature of "release plans sustained by excellent community support" which in this case is entirely dependent on the offenders' class status as wealthy business persons. (5) The Parole Board seems as interested in the "productive" as in the "law-abiding" future of the offenders.

This is perhaps an extreme case, but extreme cases often shed light on the general workings of the system. I want to emphasize two factors about this case which are characteristic of the general workings of the system. They are the complete substitution of individual preventive for general preventive concerns on the one hand, and the class nature of the individual preventive concerns on the other.

…

The Act evidently leaves to the Parole Board a great deal of freedom in making its determination. According to the board's chairman for the past 14 years, these statutory criteria "are wide enough to drive a truck through, and they are really not that much help. … But essentially, when you come right down to it, what the alchemy is by which you come to the decision of yes or no is a subjective judgment, sure. It is a value judgment made by the board members." Nevertheless, there seem to be a few regularities in this "value judgment" which can be inferred from the "General Guidelines" from the National Parole Board's current *Policy and Procedures Manual* (s. 104-6):

> 1.1 In making its decision, the Board generally considers, but is not limited to, the following guidelines:
>
> (a) The nature and gravity of the inmate's offence;
>
> (b) the inmate's history of law-violation, his past and present behaviour;
>
> (c) the inmate's total personality as it reflects the presence or absence of potential for serious harm to society;
>
> (d) the possibility that on release the offender would return to a life of criminal conduct and the possible effect on society if he did so;
>
> (e) the efforts made by the inmate during his imprisonment to improve himself through educational and vocational training and how well they demonstrate his desire to become a law-abiding citizen;
>
> (f) the inmate's plans for release and whether they are realistic enough to aid in his ultimate rehabilitation;
>
> (g) the extent of support available from family, friends and other contacts in the community;
>
> (h) whether employment possibilities exist;
>
> (i) how well the inmate appears to understand the circumstances that contributed to his criminal behaviour;

(j) how well he can identify his personal goals and his capacity to maintain his motivation;

(k) community response to a release.

At first sight this appears to be a bewildering set of criteria in which *everything* is considered relevant. However, on reflection and having regard to other sources, it is possible to discern a working model.

In the first place, the primary concern seems to be with individual prevention, that is with the extent to which the prospective parolee can be expected to offend against the law when released and, indeed, when the parole is finished. The references to the offence in items (a) and (k) seem perfunctory and are certainly outnumbered by other concerns. In order to assess this likelihood of future criminality the board deems literally everything relevant, but there is an emphasis on the prisoner's *attitude* which the board is to gauge from his or her behaviour in prison, plans for release and understanding of the crime. In addition to these attitudinal matters, the board also considers the concrete factors of the criminal record, and the social and economic environment into which the prisoner will be released.

The expressed goals and the concrete factors are easy to grasp, but the attitudinal factors require further investigation. Elsewhere in the manual, one is given some indication of what this means. Under "Police Reports," the board "wishes to know if the inmate was co-operative when apprehended" (s. 103-3: 2.2.2). From judges, the board wants an "impression of the inmate and his attitude and demeanour at the time of his sentencing" (s. 103-3: 2.3.2(b)). Sentencing courts generally consider "demeanour" in the sense of whether it is respectful or not. A disrespectful demeanour is said to show "lack of remorse," remorse being a mitigating factor. The required court-room demeanor has recently been characterized as "deferential." Indeed, the attitudinal references in the guidelines of the Parole Board seem designed to elicit *humility* from the prospective parolee: he or she must have made an effort to "improve," and his or he plans must be "realistic." Another aspect of this attitude seems to be how the prospective parolee explains his or her offence. The board seems concerned that the prisoner "accepts responsibility" for the offence.

...

This concern with "responsibility" pervades the prison system. The first "basic principle" of the Correctional Service of Canada, at least as endorsed by the Federal Corrections Agency Task Force Report, endorsed in turn by the then Solicitor-General is: "The offender is ultimately responsible for his criminal behaviour." And the whole goal of prison programmes is said to be to allow the offender "to demonstrate responsible conduct." The *MacGuigan Report* based its approach on the notion of "personal reformation" which it said "emphasises the personal responsibility of the prisoners interested." This was also endorsed by the Solicitor-General.

So the proper attitude is one that exhibits an acceptance of one's responsibility for the crime, an acceptance that it was "wrong" and a deferential and co-operative attitude with authority. What does all this mean concretely in the actual parole decision? Canadian empirical research into this question is somewhat more extensive than in the case of sentencing. Several very revealing studies have been undertaken.

In MacNaughton-Smith's study of approximately 800 National Parole Board decisions to grant or deny parole taken during the period 1962 to 1964, the factors that emerged as most important were the recommendation of the prison authorities, the parolee's proposed occupation and the criminal record. The institutional recommendation by itself was more important than any of the individual elements of institutional behaviour combined, some of which were entirely unrelated to parole granting (for example, formal discipline reports) and some of which were rather strongly related. These latter factors included, in order of importance: whether the prisoner received complete trades training, whether there was a favourable custodial report on his "industry" and whether he had a record of steady work. This suggests that the mere absence of rule-breaking behaviour is not enough to influence the decision and that, though certain definite, positive activities have an impact, there is something extra that cannot be captured in these terms which results in a favourable institutional recommendation. With respect to employment prospects on release, the question seems not to have been the nature of the job but whether or not there was one. Strongly but apparently only indirectly related to the parole decision was whether the applicant was employed at the time of the offence or not. The more extensive the criminal record and the greater the history of imprisonment, the lower was the chance of receiving parole, though the nature of the offences in the record did not seem to make any independent contribution. The legal type of the current offence did not seem to figure at all in factors strongly associated with parole. There were some weak associations between certain types of offences and parole, namely those convicted of murder and robbery were more likely to receive parole than others and those convicted of breaking and entering were less likely to receive parole. But this seemed entirely due to the strong effect of the length of the sentence, those with longer sentences being more likely to receive parole.

While MacNaughton-Smith's study was concerned with a mixture of "hard" and "soft" data, Demers' study of 541 parole decisions made by the National Parole Board during 1972 dealt mostly with hard data, including age, sex, race, socio-economic status, education, employment record, employment status on arrest, current offence type, aggregate sentence, number of previous convictions and previous institutional experience. When comparing this study with that of MacNaughton-Smith it should be noted that no attempt was made by Demers to gauge the impact of institutional behaviour or of the opinions of institutional authorities on the parole decision

Demers found that the strongest relationship of all was between the parole officer's recommendation and the decision, meaning that in most cases the recommendation and decision were the same. However, controlling for the officer's recommendation he found the remaining important factors to be: (1) whether there had been a previous parole violation (which reduced the chances of parole); (2) current offence a non-violent property offence (reduced); (3) drug offender (reduced); (4) age (younger offenders had a better chance of parole); and (5) education (the better educated had a better chance of parole). Demers also investigated the factors influencing the parole officer's recommendation, given its importance in determining the final result. Here three factors emerged as significant: employment history (the better it was, the greater the chance of parole), sex (women had a better chance of parole) and race (whites had a better chance of parole than natives).

Race seemed to play a completely independent role. It was not systematically related to such "legal" factors as current offence or criminal record or to any other variable. In short, it could not be explained away. It should be noted that the absence of race as a relevant factor in MacNaughton-Smith's study seems to have been due to the fact that information on this variable was lacking in over 75% of the cases. MacNaughton-Smith made no effort to study the effect of sex on parole decisions.

Socio-economic status seems to have made little difference to the parole decision in Demers' study, but as the author noted, the range was extremely small. The fact that employment history did have an impact is evidence that, with parole as with sentencing, it is the fact of a job and not the nature of the job that counts. It should also be noted that unlike MacNaughton-Smith, Demers did not study job prospects on *release*, which might explain the prominence of employment *history*, because the two appear to be very strongly related.

MacNaughton-Smith's and Demers' studies were largely corroborated by Nuffield's recently published study of 2,500 releases from federal penitentiaries during 1970-72. This was a study of the *proportion of sentence served before release* and thus would include questions of remission as well as of parole, but parole would still be the major factor involved. Another difference from the other studies is that the race variable was not included, nor were such matters as institution or parole officer recommendation. This may account for Nuffield's ability to explain so little of the variation in her sample. Perhaps her finding that the security rating of the prisoner's institution bore a strong direct relationship to the proportion of sentence served can be used as a proxy for institutional evaluation, thus providing indirect support for the importance of this factor.

Once again, prior penal record emerges as the most important factor in explaining the variation in the proportion of sentence served. This is followed by the demographic variables of age and employment status at arrest (the younger and employed serving smaller portions of their sentences). These are followed by length of aggregate sentence, which, as in the other studies, varied directly with chances of early release. Apart form this, the offence type was not related to early release.

An interesting aspect of Nuffield's study is her attempt to relate parole decision-making to the risk of recidivism, defined as re-arrest for an indictable offence within three years of release. The factors analyzed by Nuffield were able to account for only 7.7% of the variation, but they are at least very suggestive. Penal record is the most important factor in recidivism as in release, and aggregate sentence also figures prominently in the expected direction, indicating that if the Parole Board's goal is to select for early release those least likely to be re-arrested, it is on the right track with these variables. On the other hand, age, which was more important than aggregate sentence in predicting recidivism, went in the *opposite* direction from what the Parole Board would seem to expect, as the younger parolees were more likely to be re-arrested. Finally, employment status at arrest, to which the board seems to attach so much importance on the release decision, was only very weakly related to recidivism.

...

We owe to Foucault the insight that the penitentiary system "is not intended to eliminate offences but rather to distinguish them, to distribute them, to use them"; that the goal of the penitentiary invention was the "discipline" of offenders and not the prevention of crime; and that the task of the new penal technicians was "to produce bodies that were both docile and capable" through "perpetual assessment" and "permanent observation." However, Foucault is somewhat coy about the precise nature or object of that docility which remains for him an abstract "normalization." Melossi and Pavarini, on the other hand, in examining the same historical terrain from the point of view of material reality and not just expressed ideas, are more explicit. The penitentiary "is like a factory producing proletarians":

> The whole secret of the workhouse and the *Rasp-huis* lay, right from the very start, in the way they applied bourgeois *ideals* of life and society to the preparation of people, particularly poor people, proletarians, so that they would accept an order and discipline which would render them docile instruments of exploitation.

Thus is solved the apparent paradox in Paterson's often quoted aphorism: "It is impossible to train men for freedom in a condition of captivity." It turns out that they are not being trained for "freedom" at all but for the captivity of subjection to arbitrary personal power which is the worker's concrete situation in capitalism. In this way the penal system is put at the service of the oppressive social relations of production, the relations of inequality, of dominance and subordination which characterize Canada as they do all capitalist societies. Pushed aside, no matter how often repeated in Bills and Charters of Rights, are all of the bourgeois ideals of democracy which, as usual, find it impossible to co-exist with bourgeois reality.

F.E. Gibson, "The Renewal of Parole"
(1990), 32 *Canadian Journal of Criminology* 487

The past several years have been a time of intense public scrutiny and challenge for the National Parole Board. Growing public concern about crime and violence crystallized to some extent around national headlines about violent crimes committed by parolees, or by offenders on temporary absence or under mandatory supervision. Two major coroner's inquests, several inquiries and studies, and, of course, the Report of the Canadian Sentencing Commission (1987) raised fundamental questions about the purpose of parole and its relationship to other agencies of criminal justice and the community.

The past decade has also seen the National Parole Board under pressure to make the changes necessary to keep up with the evolution of Canadian jurisprudence. Not only has the common law concept of the "duty to act fairly" evolved and thereby exerted pressure on the decision making of the Board; but 1982 also saw the introduction of the *Canadian Charter of Rights and Freedoms* which will continue to shape the parole decision making process in Canada.

While draft amendments to the *Parole Act* (1988) and *Taking Responsibility*, the Report of the Standing Committee on Justice and Solicitor General (1988) strongly endorsed the concept of parole, they also contemplated major reform. Similarly, recent public opinion surveys indicate strong support for parole but equally strong demands for reform. The Board can expect continuing public scrutiny, continuing demands from community and victims groups to demonstrate its commitment and contribution to public protection, and continued demands from the courts and organizations representing offenders to demonstrate that its decision making is fair and consistent. These concerns, the increased public scrutiny and demands for accountability, have led to a very healthy process of reflection and renewal. The Board has clarified its purpose and the principles which must guide its decision making process.

Legal Mandate

The *Parole Act* gives the Board exclusive jurisdiction and absolute discretion to grant, deny, terminate, or revoke day parole and full parole for inmates in federal, territorial, and provincial prisons, except for cases under the jurisdiction of provincial parole boards. Ontario, Quebec, and British Columbia have parole boards with, generally speaking, jurisdiction over inmates serving a definite sentence of less than two years in their own provincial institutions.

Almost all offenders, except those serving life or indeterminate sentences, accumulate remission credits and are released to serve in the community the portion of the remission time left to their credit, subject to mandatory supervision. The adoption by Parliament of Bill C-67 in July 1986, authorized the Board to delay, until warrant expiry, the release of certain offenders considered to present an immediate and serious risk to commit a violent act causing death or serious harm. The Board may also prescribe conditions, including residence in an approved facility, on certain offenders with violence in their records who are being released.

Purpose of Parole

Within this framework, the Board undertook a fundamental review of its purpose, its mission. This review resulted in a reaffirmation of the Board's paramount commitment to public protection through facilitating the offender's safe reintegration into the community and promoting timely opportunities for rehabilitation.

The Board's mission statement provides that:

> The National Parole Board, as part of the Criminal Justice System, makes independent, quality conditional release decisions and clemency recommendations. The Board, by facilitating the timely reintegration of offenders as law-abiding citizens, contributes to the protection of society.

The mission sets out the business of the National Parole Board. It also rejects certain models or visions of parole.

The Parole Board is not in the business of punishing offenders or "resentencing." While Boards in some jurisdictions have this as an explicit part of their mandate, the National Parole Board plays a role in administering the sentence of the court in a manner that respects the sentence and contributes to public protection. Parole cannot be granted until the denunciatory portion of an offender's sentence—as determined in regulation as the parole eligibility date—has been served. After that point, structured, gradual release into the community with conditions necessary to manage risk and appropriate to the needs of the offender is possible only because the offender has time remaining under sentence. Similarly, the Board may revoke parole on the basis of a violation of the conditions of parole because the offender is still under sentence.

The National Parole Board is not a mechanism for controlling prison or penitentiary population. Again, one can find releasing bodies in other jurisdictions with an explicit mandate to reduce the number of prisoners to manageable levels. Parole in Canada explicitly rejects this approach. The *Parole Act* does not allow it. The National Parole Board's commitment to public protection does not allow it.

The commitment to public protection demands that parole decisions first be based on a careful assessment of risk, using the best available tools and information. But this does not mean that the Board simply acts as a filter for the correctional system, allowing only the best risks back into the community. Over 90% of all offenders currently incarcerated will re-enter the community—with or without parole. Criminologists and corrections practitioners have long recognized the potentially debilitating effects of incarceration and the difficulty many offenders have in making the transition from prison or penitentiary to the community. This is a critical stage for offenders. Gradual release with quality supervision and community-based support and programs, as provided through day or full parole, gives offenders a far greater chance of success than does "cold turkey" release on warrant expiry or even mandatory supervision, where conditions are legally restricted. Because release on mandatory supervision is generally not based on risk, it provides no incentive for offenders to participate in programs.

Some offenders are very clearly "bad risks" for release into the community and, until treatment and programs within the institution have substantially reduced the risk they pose, they should not be given parole. Some offenders are clearly "good risks" and can reintegrate into the community with only minimal control. But most offenders fall somewhere between. The Parole Board must then assess the risk each offender poses, satisfy itself that the risk can be managed, set the conditions necessary to manage the risk, and provide appropriate reassessment of the offender's progress within the institution or in the community. The National Parole Board is responsible for ensuring that the timing, conditions, and plans for release adequately address risk, the needs of the offender, and the capacity of the community to address those needs.

To reiterate, corrections and parole have a dual mandate: administer the sentence of the court; and use the time during which they are responsible for the offender to promote rehabilitation, facilitate the offender's safe reintegration into the community, and break the cycle of recidivism. The National Parole Board plays a crucial role in making or refusing release decisions in the interests of public safety.

Respect for and Sensitivity to Individuals

Over the past decade, the National Parole Board, like other administrative decision making bodies, has tried to keep pace with the rapid evolution in case law and, particularly, the implications of the Charter. As part of its process of renewal, the Board made a commitment to the principles of fairness, consistency, and respect for and sensitivity to individuals in its decision making process.

Its first "core value," articulated as part of the mission exercise, is intended to guide the Board in all of its activities:

> We recognize and respect the inherent dignity of individuals and the equal and inalienable rights of all members of society.

This core value goes beyond respect of the rights of offenders. In the past, many within the Board characterized the offender as "the client." The renewed understanding of our purpose has helped to change that focus. The community is our client and this demands that we be respectful of and sensitive to the impact of our decisions on all of those with an interest in our work, including victims and victims organizations, and the diverse communities we serve. Strengthened partnership and communication with victims and the community also contribute to quality decisions.

This value is reflected, as well, in the Board's increasing reliance on hearings. The hearing is a method to assess the offender in a non-adversarial way. Offenders are notified in advance of the information the Board will use in making its decision and are given the opportunity to respond. They are entitled to assistants to help them present their case to the Board and are informed, in writing, of the board's decision and reasons. Offenders also have access to a formal appeal process. The Board has committed itself to meeting the expanding natural justice requirements and strengthening procedural safeguards. Enabling offenders to be informed participants in the decision making process contributes to quality decisions. As well, the board is actively involved with CSC in finding the best way to obtain quality information from victims, and to provide to victims, as individuals, information that respects their interests and needs.

Implementing the Mission

The Board has always taken some measure of pride, or at least comfort, in the fact that the "success rate" of offenders on day and full parole is significantly greater than of those released on mandatory supervision. Unfortunately, little is heard by the public about our success stories, the many parolees who became successful contributors to their community and who sometimes turn their efforts to helping other offenders make the transition.

But the events of the past several years have reminded all of us in the corrections enterprise that our success rates do not and can never justify complacency. We have always known that our failures can have tragic human consequences. However rare statistically, these failures quite rightly receive intense media and public attention. This scrutiny serves to remind us that we will be and should be judged on the quality of each individual decision and the effectiveness of the implementation of each decision, that we must recognize and learn from our mistakes, that we must work constantly to improve the quality of corrections and parole.

In 1989, the National Parole Board committed itself to a strategy for implementing its mission. This strategy was based on three related themes: professionalism, openness, and accountability.

The Board has become more *professional*. On March 1, 1988, the Board implemented decision policies to structure the review process and guide the consideration for parole. These policies ensure that all Board decisions are based on common criteria, respect natural justice requirements, and focus on risk to society as the primary criterion for conditional release. In 1989, based upon the results of the board's monitoring of the policies and the experience of applying them, the decision policies were reviewed, and a number of revisions were made to refine and improve them.

Over the past two years, the Board has integrated its decision policies into its day to day operations. These policies have contributed to improved consistency and to the national character of the Board. As well, hearing assistants will be available to support members and remove some of the administrative burden associated with requirements, such as the taping of hearings and the procedural safeguards that are essential features of the duty to act fairly.

Board members received, and will continue to receive, extensive training on the application of the decision policies, on approaches to risk assessment, on the needs of victims, and on the special needs and circumstances of female offenders and aboriginal offenders. The Board is currently examining what kinds of multicultural training may be necessary. We are intensifying our work in these ares.

Openness means, in part, working closely with our partners in criminal justice. We are, for example, strengthening our relationships with our partners, the Courts, the prosecution, the police, and corrections agencies, particularly the Correctional Service of Canada. The missions of the Correctional Service of Canada and the National Parole Board both recognize that rehabilitation and reintegration promote the protection of society. There is a strong sense of partnership between CSC and NPB, as both agencies share the challenge of meeting their objectives within the current social and fiscal environment. The policies of the Board demand that offenders participate in programs prior to release on parole. The Correctional Service of Canada is responsible for the delivery of these programs and whatever other treatment may be necessary. While CSC produces or compiles most of the information by which an inmate's readiness for release can be assessed, it is the Board that makes the determination. The Board is responsible for the decision, and the CSC is responsible for the supervision of all inmates on conditional release. Both agencies are currently reviewing the case preparation and decision process in order to identify and eliminate overlap and duplication. This exercise has the potential not only to reduce costs and administrative burden, but also to contribute to correctional effectiveness, and quality decision making.

Of particular importance for the future is the relationship of sentencing and parole. Clearly, the question of whether parole serves to change or make uncertain rather than simply administer sentences has been at the base of many of the calls for both sentencing and parole reform. Questions have been raised, for example, about the appropriateness of current eligibility dates, about whether sentencing judges take parole into account in setting sentences, and about whether parole boards consider the reasons for sentence when deliberating about parole. Perhaps most important, greater communication and mutual understanding are necessary between sentencing judges and parole boards. They must work together to develop a framework which respects the unique mandates of each, but which ensures that sentencing and parole complement one another in their common pursuit of a just and safe society.

Openness also means strengthening our relationships with all elements of the community we serve, particularly victims and victims organizations. In 1989, at the First Canadian Organization for Victims of Crime Conference, the NPB released a handbook entitled *Victims: questions and answers on parole,* designed to answer those questions victims ask in the aftermath of their trauma. In the last two years, the Board has had increased interactions with victims. Victims and their organizations are demanding more information from various components of the criminal justice system throughout the various phases of criminal investigation, trial, sentence, and sentence administration. The publication of the handbook is recognition of the legitimate interest of victims to be informed of the NPB's policies and programs. The Board is continuing to work with victims and victims organizations to clarify and refine relationships and ensure the effective participation of victims and the community in the Board's policy development.

But most important, openness means openness to public scrutiny—to ensure that the Board is accountable. For example the report of the Standing Committee, *Taking Responsibility*, proposed that board hearings be open to the public. There is also a growing interest on the part of victims, police, media representatives and others to attend hearings, to understand the Board, how it operates and the reasons for its decisions. The Board has therefore undertaken a broad study of the hearing process. Its objectives are to ensure national consistency in the parole process; to eliminate any unnecessary expenditures; and to provide a framework to respond to the objectives of openness and accountability, recognizing the diversity of the offender population and the diverse communities to which they will return.

The Board has become more *accountable*. We have strengthened our capacity to monitor and review decisions. We can and must do more. We must continue to put in place the structures and processes necessary to demonstrate that each decision was made on the basis of sound information and was directed to protecting society, contributing to crime prevention by reducing recidivism, and respecting the needs of the community and the rights of the offender. Our business is decision making. It is against each individual decision that we should and will be measured. All that we do must be directed to improving the quality of those decisions.

The Board has come to understand more clearly and fully its role in contributing to a just, peaceful, and safe society. Its mission makes it part of the solution. Its commitment to openness, professionalism, and accountability will ensure that renewal continues in partnership with the community.

NOTE

The following recent data showing the NPB's activities will put the "parole debate" into context. When you consider the full parole granting rate in table 1, it is important to note that it includes the "accelerated parole release" (APR) category. Accordingly, the 1997-98 rate of 42 percent consists of an APR grant rate of 94 percent combined with a regular grant rate of only 23 percent (see National Parole Board, *Performance Monitoring Report* (July 2000)).

Table 1   Parole and Day Parole Granting, 1993-1998[a]

Type of release	Year	Granted	Denied	Total granted/ denied	Grant rate
Day parole	1993-94	4,350	2,331	6,681	65.1
	1994-95	3,895	2,596	6,491	60.0
	1995-96	3,162	2,216	5,378	58.8
	1996-97	2,698	1,396	4,094	65.9
	1997-98	3,651	1,461	5,112	71.4
Full parole	1993-94	2,589	4,203	6,792	38.1
	1994-95	2,205	4,376	6,581	33.5
	1995-96	1,954	3,715	5,669	34.5
	1996-97	1,746	2,624	4,370	40.0
	1997-98	1,976	2,731	4,707	42.0

[a] Solicitor-General Canada, *Corrections and Conditional Release Statistical Review*, 1998, at 61.

Table 2   Full Parole Outcomes, 1993-1998[a]

Federal full parole	1993-94		1994-95		1995-96		1996-97		1997-98	
	#	%	#	%	#	%	#	%	#	%
Successful completions	1,548	62.9	1,622	62.7	1,533	67.4	1,280	65.1	1,231	67.5
Revocations for breach of conditions	511	20.7	623	24.1	464	20.4	423	21.5	392	21.5
Revocations with non-violent offence	336	13.6	281	10.9	242	10.6	232	11.8	183	10.0
Revocations with violent offence	68	2.8	59	2.3	34	1.5	31	1.6	19	1.0
Total	2,463	100.0	2,585	100.0	2,273	100.0	1,966	100.0	1,825	100.0

[a] Solicitor-General Canada, *Corrections and Conditional Release Statistical Review*, 1998, at 69.

Table 3 Statutory Release Outcomes, 1993-1998[a]

Statutory release	1993-94 #	%	1994-95 #	%	1995-96 #	%	1996-97 #	%	1997-98 #	%
Successful completions	2,370	59.6	2,590	60.6	2,826	60.6	2,971	57.8	2,965	57.5
Revocations for breach of conditions	954	24.0	1,204	28.2	1,260	27.0	1,510	29.4	1,578	30.6
Revocations with non-violent offences	551	13.9	381	8.9	469	10.1	567	11.0	540	10.5
Revocations with violent offence	102	2.6	102	2.4	111	2.4	93	1.8	72	1.4
Total	3,977	100.0	4,277	100.0	4,666	100.0	5,141	100.0	5,155	100.0

[a] Solicitor-General Canada, *Corrections and Conditional Release Statistical Review*, 1998, at 71.

CHAPTER NINETEEN

The Judicial Review of Penitentiary and Parole Decision Making

I. INTRODUCTION

For many years, Canadian courts seemed to be following their American counterparts in adopting a "hands-off" approach to prison and parole issues. (For a detailed account of prisoners' efforts to obtain remedies, see the chapter entitled "The Prisoner Before the Courts" in Cole and Manson, *The Law of Parole, Sentencing and Judicial Review* (Toronto: Carswell, 1990), 39-108.) With respect to parole issues, *habeas corpus* was available, but only in a limited number of situations. First, the issue had to engage an arguable jurisdictional defect or illegality such that success meant release from custody. Second, the illegality had to be apparent without going behind the warrant (see *Mitchell v. The Queen*, [1976] 2 SCR 570). Looking at penitentiary issues, a narrow conception of the scope of *certiorari* (and prohibition, its temporal flip-side) was used to deny remedies to prisoners. In retrospect, actions for declaratory relief were likely available to prisoners, but these were not attempted. The probable reason was cost and delay. *McCann v. The Queen*, [1976] 1 FC 570 (FCTD), a successful action for a declaration under the *Canadian Bill of Rights* that long-term confinement in segregation at the BC Penitentiary constituted cruel and unusual punishment, demonstrates both the potential role and the enormous amount of time and money involved in such actions.

II. RELIEF IN THE NATURE OF CERTIORARI

The supervisory jurisdiction over federal decision makers was moved to the Federal Court when it was established in 1972. At the time, it was anticipated that the new s. 28 remedy in the *Federal Court Act* might apply to prisoners. This provision included a broad "review and set aside" power that applied to any decision required by law to be made on a judicial or quasi-judicial basis. However, any expectation that this would provide a remedy for prisoners was dashed in *Martineau and Butters v. Matsqui Institution Inmate Disciplinary Board*, [1978] 1 SCR 118, where the majority held that neither the commissioner's directives nor the incipient duty to act fairly placed penitentiary discipline decisions in this category of decisions required "by law" to be made on a judicial or quasi-judicial basis. In dissent, Laskin CJC was critical of the majority's conception of "law," and described it as "too nihilistic" for him to accept. Shortly afterward, the issue returned to the Supreme Court as a *certiorari* application under s. 18 of the *Federal Court Act* in what has been commonly called *Martineau (No. 2)*. In the interim, the Supreme Court had firmly rejected the traditional classification approach to judicial review and adopted the general duty to act fairly as the standard for procedural obligation owed by public and statutory decision makers (see *Re Nicholson and Haldimand-Norfolk Regional Board of Police Commissioners*, [1979] 1 SCR 311).

In *Martineau*, the defendant had been charged with the serious disciplinary offences of having two persons in a cell and committing an indecent act. He was convicted of an apparently included offence that was recorded as "being in an indecent position." He was convicted and sentenced to 15 days' dissociation. At his hearing, he was absent when some of the evidence against him was heard. The commissioner's directive dealing with disciplinary hearing procedures expressly stated that no finding should be made against an inmate for a serious or flagrant offence unless he or she has appeared at the hearing so that the evidence can be given in his or her presence. Martineau sought *certiorari* in the Federal Court—Trial Division. The Correctional Service disputed the court's jurisdiction to grant such relief. Although the court of first instance agreed that it had jurisdiction, on appeal to the Federal Court of Appeal, the arguments against remedial jurisdiction prevailed. Jackett CJ was content that disgruntled prisoners could satisfy their grievances by writing their member of parliament. On appeal to the Supreme Court, shortly after its acceptance of the duty to act fairly, the argument in favour of a remedy received a more welcome reception. The court allowed the prisoner's appeal unanimously. For the majority, Pigeon J accepted that *certiorari* was available to challenge disciplinary decisions on procedural grounds, but that its use should be restricted to "cases of serious injustice." The opinion of Dickson J has, in subsequent years, been accepted as more accurately explaining the proper scope of *certiorari* as an evolving remedy.

Martineau v. Matsqui Institution Disciplinary Board
(1979), 50 CCC (2d) 1 (SCC)

DICKSON J:

...

The appeal raises in general terms the question of the supervisory role, if any, of the Federal Court, Trial Division, in respect of disciplinary boards within Canadian penitentiaries. It also calls for consideration of three related issues of importance in Canadian administrative law.

First, it compels resolution of the continuing debate concerning the review jurisdiction of the Trial Division and Court of Appeal under, respectively, ss. 18 and 28 of the *Federal Court Act*, RSC 1970, c. 10 (2nd Supp.), an issue left open by this Court in earlier judgments. If the Court of Appeal lacks jurisdiction under s. 28 to entertain an application to review and set aside, then the question which must be asked, and to which this case must give the answer, is whether the impugned decision or order can be challenged by application for *certiorari* under s. 18 of the Act.

Second, the case calls for closer analysis of the duty to act fairly—the English "fairness doctrine"—than has hitherto been necessary.

Third, the appeal raises the question of the potential breadth of the common law remedy of *certiorari* in Canada.

...

It has been argued that s. 18 purports to transfer jurisdiction from provincial Courts to the Trial Division of the Federal Court and clothes the latter with exclusive jurisdiction to grant relief by way of *certiorari* against federal boards, commissions or other tribunals, but that s. 28 removes that jurisdiction from the Trial Division in respect of *certiorari*, despite the express words of s. 18. In other words, the terms of s. 28 completely exclude what s. 18 apparently granted. If that view be correct, and s. 18 is indeed sterile and without independent life, then a narrow reading of s. 28 will virtually deny Canadians recourse against federal tribunals. It is not disputed that the Inmate Disciplinary Board of Matsqui Institution is a federal board, commission or other tribunal.

...

Thus, *Howarth*, supra, distinguishes between ss. 18 and 28 review jurisdiction in the Federal Court, the new remedy under s. 28 not being exhaustive of Federal Court jurisdiction to review federal Government action. The consequence, as Mr. Justice Pigeon puts it, is that under the *Federal Court Act* "a distinction is made between two classes of orders of federal boards."

Further, a distinction is clearly drawn between the duty to act judicially and the duty to act fairly. Pigeon J rejects the argument that a duty to act fairly is relevant to the question of jurisdiction under s. 28, but the relevance of such an argument in the context of s. 18 is expressly left open.

...

Restrictive reading of s. 28 of the *Federal Court Act* need not, of necessity, lead to a reduction in the ambit for judicial review of federal Government action. Section 18 is available. Section 28 has caused difficulties, not only because of the language in which it is cast but, equally, because it tended to crystallize the law of judicial review at a time when significant changes were occurring in other countries with respect to the scope and grounds for review. Sections 18 and 28 of the *Federal Court Act* were obviously intended to concentrate judicial review of federal tribunals in a single federal Court. As I read the Act, Parliament envisaged an extended scope for review. I am therefore averse to giving the Act a reading which would defeat that intention and posit a diminished scope for relief from the actions of federal tribunals. I simply cannot accept the view that Parliament intended to remove the old common law remedies, including *certiorari*, from the provincial superior Courts, and vest them in the Trial Division of the Federal Court, only to have those remedies rendered barren through the interaction of ss. 18 and 28 of the Act. I would apply the principle laid down by Brett LJ in *R v. Local Government Board* (1882), 10 QBD 309 at p. 321, that the jurisdiction of a Court ought to be exercised widely when dealing with matters perhaps not strictly judicial, but in which the rights or interests of citizens are affected.

VI

The dominant characteristic of recent developments in English administrative law has been expansion of judicial review jurisdiction to supervise administrative action by public authorities. *Certiorari* evolved as a flexible remedy, affording access to judicial supervision in new and changing situations. In 1689 Chief Justice Holt could say, in *Re Cardiffe Bridge* (1689), 1 Salk. 146, 91 ER 135 "wherever any new jurisdiction is erected, be it by private or public Act of Parliament, they are subject to the inspections of this Court by writ of error, or by *certiorari* and *mandamus*." And in *Groenwelt v. Burwell et al.* (1694), 1 LD Raym. 454 at pp. 467-9, 91 ER 1202, Holt CJ, held again, in the context of the censors of the College of Physicians of London, that

> it is plain, that the censors have judicial power ... where a man has power to inflict imprisonment upon another for punishment of his offence, there he hath judicial authority ... for it is a consequence of all jurisdictions, to have their proceedings returned here by *certiorari*, to be examined here. ... Where any Court is erected by statute, a *certiorari* lies to it. ...

Nor has perception of *certiorari* as an adaptable remedy been in any way modified. The amplitude of the writ has been affirmed time and again: see, for example, the judgment of Lord Parker LJ in *R v. Criminal Injuries Compensation Board, Ex. p. Lain*, [1967] 2 QB 864 at p. 882:

> The position as I see it is that the exact limits of the ancient remedy by way of *certiorari* have never been and ought not to be specifically defined. They have varied from time to time being extended to meet changing conditions. At one time the writ only went to an inferior court. Later its ambit was extended to statutory tribunals determining a *lis inter partes*. Later again it extended to cases where there was no *lis* in the strict sense of the word but where immediate or subsequent rights of a citizen were affected. The only constant limits throughout were that it was performing a public duty.

Roskill LJ, in *Re Liverpool Taxi Owners' Ass'n*, [1972] 2 All ER 589 at p. 596 expressed the thought in these words:

> The long legal history of the former prerogative writs and of their modern counterparts, the orders of prohibition, *mandamus* and *certiorari* shows that their application has always been flexible as the need for their use in differing social conditions down the centuries had changed.

The principles of natural justice and fairness have matured in recent years. And the writ of *certiorari*, in like measure, has developed apace. The speeches in *Ridge v. Baldwin et al.*, [1964] AC 40, show the evolutionary state of administrative law.

Does *certiorari* lie to the Inmate Disciplinary Board? The usual starting point in a discussion of this nature is the "Electricity Commissioners" formula, found at p. 205 of *R v. Electricity Com'rs, Ex p. London Electricity Joint Committee Co. (1920), Ltd., et al.*, [1924] 1 KB 171 (CA), where Atkin LJ had this to say:

> Wherever any body of persons having legal authority to determine questions affecting the rights of subjects, and having the duty to act judicially, act in excess of their legal authority they are subject to the controlling jurisdiction of the King's Bench Division exercised in these writs.

Difficulty has arisen from the statement of Atkin LJ in part from the fact that his words have been treated as if they had been engraved in stone, and in part because it is not clear what Atkin LJ meant. How far, if at all, did he mean to limit the use of orders for *certiorari* and prohibition by the phrase "and having the duty to act judicially"? What did he mean by "judicially" in the context? It will be recalled that in the *Electricity Com'rs* case itself *certiorari* and prohibition issued to a group of administrators who were acting far more as part of the legislative than of the judicial process.

Rights of Subjects

The term "rights of subjects" has given concern, often being treated by Courts as the *sine qua non* of jurisdiction to permit review. There has been an unfortunate tendency to treat "rights" in the narrow sense of rights to which correlative legal duties attach. In this sense, "rights" are frequently contrasted with "privileges," in the mistaken belief that only the former can ground judicial review of the decision-maker's actions. *Lain*, supra, is invaluable on this branch of Lord Atkin's test. There the absence of any legal right on the part of the claimants to *ex gratia* payments from the criminal injuries compensation board would seem to pose an insuperable obstacle, but Ashworth J disposed of this impediment without trouble and in broadest language (p. 892):

> For my part I doubt whether Atkin LJ was propounding an all-embracing definition of the circumstances in which relief by way of *certiorari* would lie. In my judgment the words in question read in the context of what precedes and follows them, would be of no less value if they were altered by omitting "the rights of" so as to become "affecting subjects."

Lord Denning aptly summarized the state of the law on this aspect in *Schmidt v. Secretary of State for Home Affairs*, [1969] 2 Ch. 149 (CA). There, the Master of the Rolls stated [p. 170]:

> The speeches in *Ridge v. Baldwin* ... show that an administrative body may, in a proper case, be bound to give a person who is affected by their decision an opportunity of making representations. It all depends on whether he has some right or interest, or, I would add, some legitimate expectation, of which it would not be fair to deprive him without hearing what he has to say.

Professor Wade, in his book on *Administrative Law*, 4th ed. (1977), pp. 541-2, has captured the relevance of this requirement of the test in this passage:

> This requirement is really correlative to the idea of legal power, the exercise of which necessarily affects some person's legal rights, status or situation. The primary object of *certiorari* and prohibition is to make the machinery of government operate properly in the public interest, rather than to protect private rights. ... The requirement of a decision "affecting rights" is not therefore a limiting factor; it is rather an automatic consequence of the fact that power is being exercised.

When concerned with individual cases and aggrieved persons, there is the tendency to forget that one is dealing with public law remedies, which, when granted by the Courts, not only set aright individual injustice, but also ensure that public bodies exercising powers affecting citizens heed the jurisdiction granted them. *Certiorari* stems from the assumption by the Courts of supervisory powers over certain tribunals in order to assure the proper functioning of the machinery of Government. To give a narrow or technical interpretation to "rights" in an individual sense is to misconceive the broader purpose of judicial review of administrative action. One should, I suggest, begin with the premise that any public body exercising power over subjects may be amenable to judicial supervision, the individual interest involved being but one factor to be considered in resolving the broad policy question of the nature of review appropriate for the particular administrative body.

Duty To Act Judicially

Prior to the decision in *Ridge v. Baldwin*, supra, it was generally accepted that *certiorari* would only be granted when the nature of the process by which the decision was arrived at was a judicial process or a process analogous to the judicial process: *Nakkuda Ali v. Jayaratne*, [1951] AC 66, [1950] 2 WWR 927 (PC). This notion of a "super-added duty to act judicially," as a separate and independent precondition to the availability of natural justice, and inferentially, to recourse to *certiorari*, was unequivocally rejected by Lord Reid in *Ridge*, supra (p. 75):

> If Lord Hewart meant that it is never enough that a body simply has a duty to determine what the rights of an individual should be, but that there must always be something more to impose on it a duty to act judicially before it can be found to observe the principles of natural justice, then that appears to me impossible to reconcile with the earlier authorities.

In the *Electricity Commissioners* case itself, supra, Lord Reid observed, the judicial element was inferred from the nature of the power.

Perhaps the best expression of the significance of the decision in *Ridge v. Baldwin*, supra, is found in the reasons of Lord Widgery CJ in *R v. London Borough of Hillingdon, Ex p. Royco Homes Ltd.*, [1974] 2 All ER 643 at p. 649 (QBD), wherein he considered the availability of *certiorari* to review the grant of a planning permission by a local authority:

> Accordingly it may be that previous efforts to use *certiorari* in this field have been deterred by Atkin LJ's reference to it being necessary for the body affected to have the duty to act judicially. If that is so, that reason for reticence on the part of applicants was, I think, put an end to in the House of Lords in *Ridge v. Baldwin* ... in the course of his speech Lord Reid made reference to that oft-quoted dictum of Atkin LJ and pointed out that the additional requirement of the body being under a duty to act judicially was not supported by authority. Accordingly it seems to me now that that obstacle, if obstacle it were, has been cleared away and I can see no reason for this court holding otherwise than that there is power in appropriate cases for the use of the prerogative orders to control the activity of a local planning authority.

A flexible attitude toward the potential application of *certiorari* was furthered in another recent English case, this one in the Court of Appeal, in *R v. Barnsley Metropolitan Borough Council, Ex p. Hook*, [1976] 3 All ER 452.

In a *habeas corpus* case, *Re H.K. (An Infant)*, [1967] 2 QB 617, Lord Parker was of the opinion that the immigration officers who refused to admit a boy into the United

Kingdom were acting in an administrative and not in a judicial or quasi-judicial capacity: nevertheless, he held they must act honestly and fairly, otherwise their decision could be questioned by *certiorari*. And in the *Liverpool Taxi Owners* case, supra, Roskill LJ spoke of the power of the Courts to intervene in a suitable case when the function was administrative and not judicial or quasi-judicial (p. 596):

> The power of the court to intervene is not limited, as once was thought, to those cases where the function in question is judicial or quasi-judicial. The modern cases show that this court will intervene more widely than in the past. Even where the function is said to be administrative, the court will not hesitate to intervene in a suitable case if it is necessary in order to secure fairness.

Then there is the well-known passage in the speech of Lord Morris of Borth-y-Gest in *Furnell v. Whangarei High Schools Board*, [1973] AC 660 at p. 679 (PC), speaking for a Privy Council majority of three: "[n]atural justice is but fairness writ large and juridically. It has been described as 'fair play in action.' Nor is it a leaven to be associated only with judicial or quasi-judicial occasions." In the same case, the penultimate paragraph from the speech of Viscount Dilhorne and Lord Reid, dissenting, reads (p. 691):

> It is not in this case necessary to decide whether the function of the subcommittee is to be described as judicial, quasi-judicial or administrative. I am inclined to think that it is at least quasi-judicial, but if it be administrative, it was the duty of the sub-committee before they condemned or criticised Mr. Furnell "to give him a fair opportunity of commenting or contradicting what is said against him." That they did not do.

Professor John Evans, writing in 23 *McGill LJ* 132 at pp. 134-5 (1977), has noted:

> Recent English decisions have severed the availability of *certiorari* and prohibition from the requirement that the body must act "judicially" in the sense that it is bound by the rules of natural justice. It may be concluded, therefore, that there is nothing in the judgment of Pigeon J [in *Howarth*] to prevent the Trial Division from quashing decisions of a "purely administrative" nature or from developing procedural requirements derived from the "duty to act fairly."

In the view of another commentator, Professor Jones 21 *McGill LJ* 434 at p. 438 (1975):

> Certainly in England and in most other parts of the Commonwealth, the requirement for judicial review that the exercise of a statutory power must not only affect the rights of a subject, but also be subject to a superadded duty to act judicially, is now thoroughly discredited. In other words, the ratio of *Nakkuda Ali v. Jayaratne* in the Privy Council—and hence, one would have thought, of *Calgary Power v. Copithorne* in the Supreme Court of Canada—is no longer good law.

The authorities to which I have referred indicate that the application of a duty of fairness with procedural content does not depend upon proof of a judicial or quasi-judicial function. Even though the function is analytically administrative, Courts may intervene in a suitable case.

In the case at bar, the Disciplinary Board was not under either an express or implied duty to follow a judicial type of procedure, but the board was obliged to find facts affecting a subject and to exercise a form of discretion in pronouncing judgment and penalty. Moreover, the board's decision had the effect of depriving an individual of his liberty by committing him to a "prison within a prison." In these circumstances, elementary justice requires some procedural protection. The rule of law must run within penitentiary walls.

In my opinion, *certiorari* avails as a remedy wherever a public body has power to decide any matter affecting the rights, interests, property, privileges, or liberties of any person.

VIII

Fairness

The approach taken to the "fairness" doctrine by the Court in *Re Nicholson and Haldimand-Norfolk Regional Board of Com'rs of Police* (1978), 88 DLR (3d) 671, [1979] 1 SCR 311, 23 NR 410, notably its differentiation from traditional natural justice, permits one to dispense with classification as a precondition to the availability of *certiorari*. Conceptually, there is much to be said against such a differentiation between traditional natural justice and procedural fairness, but if one is forced to cast judicial review in traditional classification terms, as is the case under the *Federal Court Act*, here can be no doubt that procedural fairness extends well beyond the realm of the judicial and quasi-judicial, as commonly understood.

Once one moves from the strictures of s. 28 of the *Federal Court Act*, the judgment in *Nicholson*, supra, permits departure from the rigidity of classification of functions for the purposes of procedural safeguards. In finding that a duty of fairness rested upon the Police Commissioners in a dismissal case, Chief Justice Laskin, speaking for a majority of the Court, employed the English fairness cases to import that duty. While the cases were there used to establish minimal protection for the constable under the *Judicial Review Procedure Act, 1971* (Ont.), c. 48, the same cases have been employed in England to extend the reach of *certiorari* to decisions not strictly judicial or quasi-judicial. After referring to the emergence of a notion of fairness "involving something less than the procedural protection of traditional natural justice," the Chief Justice had this to say (p. 681 DLR, p. 325 SCR):

> What rightly lies behind this emergence is the realization that the classification of statutory functions as judicial, quasi-judicial or administrative is often very difficult, to say the least; and to endow some with procedural protection while denying others any at all would work injustice when the results of statutory decisions raise the same serious consequences for those adversely affected, regardless of the classification of the function in question: see, generally, Mullan, "Fairness: The New Natural Justice," 25 *Univ. of Tor. LJ* 281 (1975).

The Chief Justice also quoted a passage from Lord Denning's judgment in *Selvarajan v. Race Relations Board*, [1976] 1 All ER 12 (CA), in which the Master of the Rolls summed up his earlier decisions and formulated the "fundamental rule" (p. 19):

> that, if a person may be subjected to pains or penalties, or be exposed to prosecution or proceedings, or deprived of remedies or redress, or in some such way adversely affected

by the investigation and report, then he should be told the case made against him and be afforded a fair opportunity of answering it.

Of particular interest in the passage is the absence of reference to "rights." The imprecise "rights/privileges" dichotomy is utterly ignored.

IX

One matter remains—the so-called "disciplinary exception." There are authorities (see *R v. Army Council, Ex p. Ravenscroft*, [1917] 2 KB 504; *Dawkins v. Lord Rokeby* (1871), 8 QB 255; *Re Armstrong and Whitehead* (1973), 11 CCC (2d) 327, [1973] 2 OR 495) which hold that review by way of *certiorari* does not go to a body such as the armed services, police, or firemen, with its own form of private discipline and its own rules. Relying on this analogy, it is contended that disciplinary powers are beyond judicial control and that this extends to prison discipline. I do not agree.

In *Fraser v. Mudge et al.*, [1975] 3 All ER 78 (CA), it was held that the *English Prison Act, 1952*, requiring the Home Secretary to give an inmate charged with an offence a proper opportunity of presenting his case, did not entitle the inmate to legal representation at the hearing, but Lord Denning MR observed that those who heard the case had the duty to act fairly. Judicial review was not precluded.

There is the more recent case of *R v. Board of Visitors of Hull Prison, Ex. p. St. Germain et al.*, [1979] 1 All ER 701. The central issue in that case was whether *certiorari* would go to quash a disciplinary decision of a board of visitors, the duties of which embraced inquiry into charges against inmates. The Divisional Court found that disciplinary procedures within the prison were judicial, but invoked the "disciplinary exception," and held that the actions of the board of visitors were not amenable to the review by way of *certiorari*. A unanimous Court of Appeal disagreed, however, holding that adjudication by boards of visitors in prisons were, indeed, amenable to *certiorari*. The Court rejected the submission that prisoners have no legally enforceable rights. Megaw LJ concluded that the observance of procedural fairness in prisons is properly a subject for review. Shaw LJ held that despite deprivation of his general liberty a prisoner remains invested with residuary rights appertaining to the nature and conduct of his incarceration. Waller LJ accepted the proposition of Lord Reid in *Ridge v. Baldwin et al.*, [1964] AC 40, that deprivation of rights or privileges are equally important and applied that proposition to the context of prison discipline.

• • •

The Supreme Court of the United States in *Wolff v. McDonnell* (1978), 418 US 539, was called upon to consider what "due process," assured by the Fourteenth Amendment of the *American Constitution*, required in a prison setting. The Court, speaking through Mr. Justice White, held that where the prisoner was in peril of losing good time, or being placed in solitary confinement, he was entitled to written notice of the charge and a statement of fact findings and to call witnesses and present documentary evidence where it would not be unduly hazardous to institutional safety or correctional jails. However, there was no constitutional right to confront and cross-examine witnesses or to counsel.

It seems clear that although the Courts will not readily interfere in the exercise of disciplinary powers, whether within the armed services, the police force or the penitentiary, there is no rule of law which necessarily exempts the exercise of such disciplinary powers from review by *certiorari*.

The authorities, in my view, support the following conclusions:

1. *Certiorari* is available as a general remedy for supervision of the machinery of Government decision-making. The order may go to any public body with power to decide any matter affecting the rights, interests, property, privileges, or liberty of any person. The basis for the broad reach of this remedy is the general duty of fairness resting on all public decision-makers.

2. A purely ministerial decision, on broad grounds of public policy, will typically afford the individual no procedural protection, and any attack upon such a decision will have to be founded upon abuse of discretion. Similarly, public bodies exercising legislative functions may not be amenable to judicial supervision. On the other hand, a function that approaches the judicial end of the spectrum will entail substantial procedural safeguards. Between the judicial decisions and those which are discretionary and policy-oriented will be found a myriad decision-making processes with a flexible gradation of procedural fairness through the administrative spectrum. That is what emerges from the decision of this Court in *Nicholson*, supra. In these cases, an applicant may obtain *certiorari* to enforce a breach of the duty of procedural fairness.

3. Section 28 of the *Federal Court Act*, that statutory right of review compels continuance of the classification process in the Federal Court of Appeal, with clear outer limits imposed on the notion of "judicial or quasi-judicial." No such limitation is imported in the language of s. 18, which simply refers to *certiorari*, and is therefore capable of expansion consistent with the movement of the common law away from rigidity in respect of the prerogative writs. The fact that a decision-maker does not have a duty to act judicially, with observance of formal procedure which that characterization entails, does not mean that there may not be a duty to act fairly which involves importing something less than the full panoply of conventional natural justice rules. In general, Courts ought not to seek to distinguish between the two concepts, for the drawing of a distinction between a duty to act fairly, and a duty to act in accordance with the rules of natural justice, yields an unwieldy conceptual framework. The *Federal Court Act*, however, compels classification for review of federal decision-makers.

4. An inmate disciplinary board is not a Court. It is a tribunal which has to decide rights after hearing evidence. Even though the board is not obliged, in discharging what is essentially an administrative task, to conduct a judicial proceeding, observing the procedural and evidential rules of a Court of law, it is, none the less, subject to a duty of fairness and a person aggrieved through breach of that duty is entitled to seek relief from the Federal Court, Trial Division, on an application for *certiorari*.

5. It should be emphasized that it is not every breach of prison rules of procedure which will bring intervention by the Courts. The very nature of a prison institution requires officers to make "on the spot" disciplinary decisions and

the power of judicial review must be exercised with restraint. Interference will not be justified in the case of trivial or merely technical incidents. The question is not whether there has been a breach of the prison rules, but whether there has been a breach of the duty to act fairly in all the circumstances. The rules are of some importance in determining this latter question, as an indication of the views of prison authorities as to the degree of procedural protection to be extended to inmates.

6.   A widening of the ambit of *certiorari* beyond that of a s. 28 application will, undoubtedly, at times, present a problem in determining whether to commence proceedings in the Court of Appeal or in the Trial Division. However, the quandary of two possible forums is not less regrettable than complete lack of access to the Federal Court.

7.   It is wrong, in my view, to regard natural justice and fairness as distinct and separate standards and to seek to define the procedural content of each. In *Nicholson*, supra, the Chief Justice spoke of a "notion of fairness involving something less than the procedural protection of the traditional natural justice." Fairness involves compliance with only some of the principles of natural justice. Professor de Smith, *Judicial Review of Administrative Action* (1973), 3rd ed. p. 208, expressed lucidly the concept of a duty to act fairly:

> In general it means a duty to observe the rudiments of natural justice for a limited purpose in the exercise of functions that are not analytically judicial but administrative.
>
>   The content of the principles of natural justice and fairness in application to the individual cases will vary according to the circumstances of each case, as recognized by Tucker LJ, in *Russell v. Duke of Norfolk et al.*, [1949] 1 All ER 109 at p. 118.

8.   In the final analysis, the simple question to be answered is this: Did the tribunal on the facts of the particular case act fairly toward the person claiming to be aggrieved? It seems to me that this is the underlying question which the Courts have sought to answer in all the cases dealing with natural justice and with fairness.

XI

I would allow the appeal, set aside the judgment of the Federal Court of Appeal, and restore the judgment of Mr. Justice Mahoney of the Federal Court, Trial Division. There should be no costs in this Court nor in the Federal Court of Appeal.

Appeal allowed.

The Standard of Review

Although it was important to ensure that penitentiary and parole decisions were amenable to judicial review and subject to the duty to act fairly, the issue of the applicable standard of review still remained. This has been an important issue in administrative law generally. Canadian courts started to articulate an approach of deference, but also recognized that not all decision makers and not all decisions warranted the same degree of deference. Recent cases like *Pushpanathan*, [1998] 1 SCR 982, and *Baker*, [1999] 2 SCR 817, have advanced this analysis substantially.

The following penitentiary case demonstrates how these issues apply to that specific context. The prisoner was serving a 12-year sentence for robbery and other related offences. He was originally confined at Kingston Penitentiary, but was transferred to Warkworth Institution, a medium-security penitentiary, in 1995. He was involuntarily transferred back to Kingston Penitentiary in 1996 on the basis of information received that he "may be contemplating or planning to escape." Subsequently, he became concerned that his institutional files contained erroneous information, including an indication that he had assaulted another prisoner when he was, in fact, the victim of the assault, and various references to escapes or planned escapes. He pursued a grievance, attempting to have the erroneous information removed. It moved through all levels up to the commissioner, but the prisoner received no relief except an assurance that his objections would be recorded in his file. Representing himself, he brought a judicial review application challenging the various decisions that had been made about his file and his complaint.

Tehrankari v. Correctional Service of Canada
[2000] FCJ no. 495

LEMIEUX J: The central questions in this judicial review application, pursuant to section 18.1 of the *Federal Court Act*, by Allen Tehrankari (the "applicant"), an inmate in Kingston Penitentiary, a maximum security prison operated by the Correctional Service of Canada ("CSC" or "Service"), is the scope of the obligation contained in section 24 of the *Corrections and Conditional Release Act*, 40-41 Elizabeth II, c. 20, assented to on June 18, 1992 (the "Act"), as it relates to the CSC and in what circumstances can this Court intervene when a request for correction is refused. Section 24 of the Act reads:

24(1) The Service shall take all reasonable steps to ensure that any information about an offender that it uses is as accurate, up to date and complete as possible.

(2) Where an offender who has been given access to information by the Service pursuant to subsection 23(2) believes that there is an error or omission therein,

(a) the offender may request the Service to correct that information; and

(b) where the request is refused, the Service shall attach to the information a notation indicating that the offender has requested a correction and setting out the correction requested. ...

24(1) Le Service est tenu de veiller, dans la mesure du possible, à ce que les renseignements qu'il utilise concernant les délinquants soient à jour, exacts et complets.

(2) Le délinquant qui croit que les renseignements auxquels il a eu accès en vertu du paragraphe 23(2) sont erronés ou incomplets peut demander que le Service en effectue la correction; lorsque la demande est refusée, le Service doit faire mention des corrections qui ont été demandées mais non effectuées.

The decision sought to be reviewed was made by the Commissioner of the CSC on July 23, 1998 at the final grievance level prescribed by section 90 of the Act and sections 74 to 80 of the *Corrections and Conditional Release Regulations*, SOR/92-620.

...

The applicant could not, in this judicial review proceeding, challenge decisions which relate back to 1995 and 1996 and, in particular, decisions involving involuntary transfer, the raising of his security level and administrative segregation which could have been challenged at the appropriate time where he would have been entitled, subject to some exceptions, to the information which CSC was relying on to make those decisions (see sections 28 to 45 of the Act). The applicant cannot, through a review from the Commissioner's decision in this matter, make a collateral attack on past decisions which he had an opportunity to challenge directly at the appropriate time subject to the time limits prescribed under section 18 of the *Federal Court Act*.

However, at the hearing, the applicant refocussed the issue properly on the interpretation of section 24 of the Act and counsel for the respondent joined issue on this point. In the circumstances, I will proceed on a limited basis and limit any remedies to the application of the section.

(2) The Prison Context

Any remedy flowing from this proceeding must take into account the prison context is a special one. For example, in *Cardinal v. Director of Kent Institution*, [1985] 2 SCR 643, Le Dain J pointed out the minimal or essential requirements of procedural fairness in the circumstances must be "fully compatible with the concern that the process of prison administration, because of its special nature and exigencies, should not be unduly burdened or obstructed by the imposition of unreasonable or inappropriate procedural requirements. There is nothing to suggest that the requirement of notice and hearing by the Director, where he does not intend to act in accordance with a recommendation by the Segregation Review Board for the release of an inmate from segregation, would impose an undue burden on prison administration or create a risk to security" (see page 660). My colleague Nadon J in *Cartier v. Canada (Attorney General)*, [1998] 165 FTR 209 (FCTD) expressed the same caution about the special prison context when interpreting the scope of subsection 27(3) of the Act which provides for certain information not to be disclosed where the Commissioner has reasonable grounds to believe that disclosure of the information would jeopardize the safety of any person or the security of the penitentiary.

(3) Standard of Review

A word needs to be said about the standard of review applicable in this case keeping in mind the type of decision made and the decision-maker (see *Baker v. Canada (Minister of Citizenship and Immigration)*, [1999] 2 SCR 817). In *Baker*, supra, L'Heureux-Dubé J pointed out it was held in *Pushpanathan v. Canada (Minister of Citizenship and Immigration)*, [1998] 1 SCR 982, a decision which related to the determination of a question of law in that case (the interpretation of the exclusion provisions in section 2 of the *Immigration Act* as they relate to the definition of Convention refugee) made by the Immigration and Refugee Board, was subject to a standard of review of correctness but on other questions, the standard of review varied.

In *Baker*, supra, the Supreme Court of Canada enumerated the four factors to be examined to assess the standard of review on these questions.

The first factor to be examined is the presence or absence of a privative clause in the Act. There is no privative clause contained in the Act insulating the decisions of the Commissioner taken in the grievance process.

The second factor is the expertise of the decision-maker. The decision-maker here is the Commissioner of the Correctional Service or his or her delegate. There can be no doubt, that in matters related to prison administration, the Commissioner has expertise relative to the Courts which leads to substantial deference in decisions taken by the Commissioner in matters of internal prison management.

The third factor is the purpose of the provision, in particular, and the Act as a whole. Parliament in sections 3 and 4 of the Act, has said what the purpose of the Federal Correctional Service is and what are the applicable principles which shall guide it in achieving that purpose. Section 3 provides:

> 3. The purpose of the federal correction system is to contribute to the maintenance of the just, peaceful and safe society
>
>> (a) carrying out sentences imposed by the Courts through the safe and humane custody and the supervision of offenders and
>>
>> (b) assisting the rehabilitation of offenders and their reintegration into the community as law-abiding citizens through the provision of programs in penitentiaries and in the community. ...

> 3. Le système correctionnel vise à contribuer au maintien d'une société juste, vivant en paix et en sécurité, d'une part, en assurant l'exécution des peines par des mesures de garde et de surveillance sécuritaires et humaines, et d'autre part, en aidant au moyen de programmes appropriés dans les pénitenciers ou dans la collectivité, à la réadaptation des délinquants et à leur réinsertion sociale à titre de citoyens respectueux des lois.

In terms of the principles that guide the Service, section 4 provides:

> 4. The principles that shall guide the Service in achieving the purpose referred to in section 3 are
>
>> (a) that the protection of society be the paramount consideration in the corrections process;
>>
>> (b) that the sentence be carried out having regard to all relevant available information, ... and information obtained from victims and offenders;
>>
>> (c) that the Service enhance its effectiveness and openness through the timely exchange of relevant information with other components of the criminal justice system, and through communication about its correctional policies and programs to offenders, victims and the public; ...
>>
>> (e) that offenders retain the rights and privileges of all members of society, except those rights and privileges that are necessarily removed or restricted as a consequence of the sentence; ...

(g) that correctional decisions be made in a forthright and fair manner, with access by the offender to an effective grievance procedure; …

4. Le Service est guidé, dans l'exécution de ce mandat, par les principes qui suivent:

a) la protection de la société est le critère prépondérant lors de l'application du processus correctionnel;

b) l'exécution de la peine tient compte de toute information pertinente dont le Service dispose, … des renseignements obtenus au cours du procès ou dans la détermination de la peine ou fournis par les victimes et les …

c) il accroît son efficacité et sa transparence par l'échange, au moment opportun, de renseignements utiles avec les autres éléments du système de justice pénale ainsi que par la communication de ses directives d'orientation générale et programmes correctionnels tant aux délinquants et aux victimes qu'au grand public; …

e) le délinquant continue à jouir des droits et privilèges reconnus à tout citoyen, sauf de ceux dont la suppression ou restriction est une conséquence nécessaire de la peine qui lui est infligée; …

g) ses décisions doivent être claires et équitables, les délinquants ayant accès à des mécanismes efficaces de règlement de griefs … .

The particular provision involved is section 24 which mandates the Service to take all reasonable steps to ensure that any information about an offender that it uses is as accurate, up-to-date and complete as possible conditioned by a provision which says that where an offender believes there is an error or omission in the information, the offender may request the Service to correct that information and, if the request is refused, the Service must attach to the information a notation indicating the offender has requested a correction and setting out the correction requested.

As I view it, section 24 of the Act is part of an offender's "rights package" established by Parliament in 1992 when the Act was passed to modernize previous legislation, i.e. the *Penitentiaries Act* and the *Parole Act*, a modernization which was compelled by decisions of the Supreme Court of Canada and lower courts on prisoners' rights.

The signal given by Parliament in section 24, in the form of a statutory duty imposed on the Service, is that the "information banks" reflected in various reports maintained about offenders should contain the best information possible: exact, correct information without relevant omissions and data not burdened by past stereotyping or archaisms related to the offender. In Parliament's view, the quality of the information prescribed by section 24 leads to better decisions about an offender's incarceration and, in this manner, leads to the achievement of the purposes of the Act. Section 24 of the Act, however, is not concerned with the inferences or assessments drawn by the Service from file information. Section 24 cannot be used to second guess decisions by the CSC provided the information base on which those conclusions are drawn comply with this provision. Section 24 deals with primary facts; this point will be expanded on later.

The precise decision which section 24 gives rise to is the decision by the Service whether or not to rectify the record of an offender who believes the information about him/her is inaccurate. Such a decision, limited to primary facts, does not involve considerable choices by the CSC and turns on the application of proper legal principles and involves the rights and interests of an offender.

The fourth factor is the nature of the problem in question especially whether it relates to the determination of law or facts. The decision whether to correct the record involves an appreciation of the facts in an offender's files but must be based on a correct interpretation of what the law requires.

To conclude on this point, I would apply a correctness standard if the question involved is the proper interpretation of section 24 of the Act; however, I would apply the standard of reasonableness simpliciter if the question involved is either the application of proper legal principles to the facts or whether the refusal decision to correct information on the offender's file was proper. The patently unreasonable standard applies to pure findings of fact. ... (Subsection 18.2(4) of the *Federal Court Act*, RSC 1985, c. F-7.)

I find the applicant has made out his case on the balance of probabilities; the information he complained of in his files did not meet the standards required by section 24.

(3) On What Basis Can the Refusal To Correct Be Reviewed?

Paragraph 24(2)(b) provides "where the request is refused, the Service shall attach to the information a notation ... ." Do these words preclude this Court reviewing the CSC's decision not to correct because the only remedy provided by the Act in such a case is a notation to be attached to the offender's file?

Properly construed, these words enable the CSC to correct or refuse to correct the information—because there is this choice, the CSC exercises a discretion when making the decision to correct or not. (See *Baker v. Canada (MCI)*, supra, at paragraph 52.) If so, such a discretion is reviewable on proper principles governing the review of discretionary decisions such as bad faith, improper purpose, irrelevant consideration and error of law. (See *Maple Lodge Farms Ltd. v. Government of Canada*, [1982] 2 SCR 2 at pp. 7-8.)

F. Conclusion

Under section 24 of the Act, the CSC must take reasonable steps to ensure that any information in an offender's files is as accurate, up-to-date and complete. For reasons given, I have found the specific information in the applicant's files which the applicant complained of do not comply with the standards of the section. The applicant requested correction but the CSC refused the request.

I find the Commissioner, in exercising his discretion to refuse to correct the information requested, committed a number of reviewable errors.

First, he did not properly interpret the scope of the CSC's obligations in terms of the accuracy, completeness and up-to-date nature of the information. This misinterpretation led him to conclude some of the information on file was valid or justified. Second, he failed to appreciate the nature and limits of the discretion inherent in a decision to refuse to correct information. Parliament simply did not intend inaccurate information remain on file counterbalanced only by an offender's correction request noted on file. The CSC, in the circumstances, was obligated to consider why a correction was not appropriate. Third, whatever appreciation the Commissioner had on the scope of the discretion to refuse a correction, such refusal had to be based on proper considerations which were lacking in this case. To refuse to correct misinformation on the grounds the Service exercised its option to increase the applicant's security level or to justify inaction to correct on the basis the information was still relevant for administrative purposes amount to, in my view, improper considerations.

I conclude the applicant succeeds in this judicial review application. The question remains as to the appropriate remedy.

I am sensitive to the fact the information the applicant sought to have corrected in his files is dated in 1997 and that the CSC has a continuous process of reevaluating offenders. Indeed, a file correction relating to one item the applicant complained of here was made in the applicant's OSLRD file (see page 85 of the applicant's record) but this information does not seem to have been reflected in other files (see applicant's record, page 86).

I am also sensitive to what was said by Le Dain J in *Cardinal*, supra, regarding imposing burdens on the CSC. As I see it, the case management officer is the point person with the offender. The application record reveals the CMO interfaces on a daily basis with an offender.

In the circumstances, the CMO is required to review the offender's current files and determine whether they should be corrected in accordance with these reasons. What should be reviewed is limited to those matters in the applicant's original complaint. The applicant is to be advised of the results of the CMO's review and proposed action.

G. Disposition

For all these reasons, this judicial review is allowed, the decision of the Commissioner is set aside, and the matter remitted for reconsideration on the basis of these reasons.

NOTE

The issue of expertise is an important one that should not be answered too quickly. Is Lemieux J suggesting that all internal prison decision makers are experts regardless of the nature of the decision? Is he overemphasizing the prison context in a way that would tilt the balance in favour of administrative decision making? What about parole decisions? Because board members deal with release issues on a daily basis, does that make them experts, especially when the central issue is now one of assessing risk? We accept that the clinical predictions of forensic psychiatrists can be wrong as often as they are right, so why should we give more deference to the National Parole Board?

III. HABEAS CORPUS

At least since the Magna Carta, forms of *habeas corpus* have been available to enforce liberty and free illegally detained prisoners. Blackstone described *habeas corpus* as applicable to "all manner of illegal confinement." By virtue of this remedy, superior courts became the repository of the liberty rights of all prisoners. Yet, in the mid-20th century in Canada, it started to lose its vigour as a remedy to protect liberty. As mentioned above, the majority of the Supreme Court in *Mitchell v. The Queen*, [1976] 2 SCR 570, had held that a court could not go behind a warrant to find a jurisdictional defect or illegality. This was a case where a parolee attempted to argue that his committal breached the due process guarantee of the *Canadian Bill of Rights* because he was given no reasons for his suspension and no opportunity to respond to any allegations against him before he was revoked and recommitted to custody. One of the decisions had held that the usual practice of seeking *certiorari* in aid of *habeas corpus* to enable a court to examine affidavit material was no longer available since *certiorari* jurisdiction had been transferred to the Federal Court. Accordingly, it was argued, one could not obtain *certiorari* in aid from a superior court. In dissent, Laskin CJC pointed out the distinction between *certiorari* to quash and *certiorari* to bring up the record that had been missed by some of his colleagues. Although the *Mitchell* decision was a blow to *habeas corpus*, it came just before the Supreme Court adopted the duty to act fairly. How would a parolee ever raise a fairness argument if he or she could not use an affidavit or transcript to go behind a warrant of committal?

Another issue that arose was in respect of involuntary transfers to a higher security institution. If made unfairly or without jurisdiction, the decision could be challenged. However, was *habeas corpus* an available vehicle for this purpose, or was it necessary to seek *certiorari* in the Federal Court? Certainly, *habeas corpus* was a cheaper and more expeditious remedy. Aside from the issue of extrinsic material, it was also argued that an involuntary transfer was not the proper subject matter of *habeas corpus* because it would not result in complete liberty, but merely a transfer back to the original place of confinement.

These issues came together in a trilogy of cases decided by the Supreme Court in the mid-1980s: *Cardinal v. Kent Institution*, [1985] 2 SCR 643; *Morin v. National Special Handling Unit Review Committee*, [1985] 2 SCR 662; and *R v. Miller*, [1985] 2 SCR 613. The lead decision on the role of *habeas corpus* was the *Miller* case, which dealt with an inmate's transfer from Matsqui Institution in British Columbia to the special handling unit, located then at Millhaven Institution in Ontario. Although initially denied *habeas corpus* relief, the Ontario Court of Appeal reversed and supported a modern approach to the remedy. The Crown appealed to the Supreme Court.

R v. Miller
[1985] 2 SCR 613

LE DAIN J: According to the respondent's affidavit in support of his application for *habeas corpus* with *certiorari* in aid, he was an inmate in Matsqui penitentiary on June 2, 1981, when a "disturbance" occurred in the dining area where he was employed. He claimed that he was not in the dining area at the time and that he was not responsible in any way for the disturbance. He was, nevertheless, placed in administrative segregation in Matsqui on June 5th and in segregation in Kent Institution and Millhaven, to which he was subsequently transferred, on July 11th and July 23rd respectively. On July 29, 1981, he was placed in the special handling unit at Millhaven.

Confinement in a special handling unit is reserved for particularly dangerous inmates, as indicated by s. 5 of Commissioner's Directive 274 of December 1, 1980, which defines "Special Handling Unit" as follows:

"Special Handling Unit" (SHU) is a facility established to deal exclusively with inmates who, in addition to requiring maximum security, have been identified as being particularly dangerous.

According to the directive, a special handling unit programme of confinement consists of four phases, the first of which is a period of assessment in administrative segregation. According to the respondent's affidavit, which describes the nature of the confinement in the various phases in considerable detail, in the first phase consisting of administrative segregation the inmate is cut off from all association with other inmates and is confined to his cell for all but one hour of the day. In subsequent phases of the programme limited association with other inmates and somewhat longer periods outside the cell are permitted, but speaking generally, it may be said that confinement in a special handling unit is a significantly more restrictive form of detention than the normal one in a penitentiary, involving the loss or denial of several privileges or amenities enjoyed by the general inmate population.

According to the respondent's affidavit, he was advised by letter about two weeks after he was placed in the special handling unit that he had been put there because of his involvement in the disturbance at Matsqui and specifically because he had broken windows in the kitchen and had manufactured an explosive device. The respondent states that he was never given an opportunity to confront the evidence, if any, of his involvement in the incident at Matsqui on which the decision to confine him in the special handling unit was based. He was never charged with a disciplinary offence arising out of that incident nor was any criminal charge laid against him. He was not given a psychological examination, and there was nothing in his background or in the nature of the offences of which he was convicted to suggest that he was a particularly dangerous inmate. In October, 1981, he attended a hearing of the National Special Handling Unit Review Committee, but he was not informed of the evidence against him nor given any opportunity to meet it. He was told that he could only secure his release from the special handling unit into normal association with the general population of the penitentiary by good behaviour. In the respondent's submission there was no basis nor justification whatever for placing him in the special handling unit.

In his application for *habeas corpus* with *certiorari* in aid the respondent contended that confinement in the special handling unit at Millhaven is not authorized by statute or regulation and is therefore unlawful, and further or alternatively, that his confinement in the special handling unit was carried out in a manner that denied him procedural fairness. The respondent conceded that he was lawfully required to be detained in a penitentiary. His mandatory supervision release date was July 3, 1983, and we were informed at the hearing of the appeal that he had been released.

...

The question whether a provincial superior court has jurisdiction to issue *certiorari* in aid of *habeas corpus* to review the validity of a detention imposed by federal authority arises, as has been indicated, because of the terms of s. 18 of the *Federal Court Act*, which confers on the Trial Division of the Federal Court of Canada an exclusive original jurisdiction to issue *certiorari* against any federal board, commission or other tribunal.

...

On the question of jurisdiction to issue *certiorari* in aid of *habeas corpus* I am in respectful agreement with the conclusion of Laskin CJC in *Mitchell*, essentially for the reasons given by him, which I understand to be the importance of making the *habeas corpus* jurisdiction of the provincial superior courts an effective one and the distinction between *certiorari* to quash and *certiorari* in aid, regarded as a procedural or evidentiary device to make *habeas corpus* more effective. With reference to this distinction Laskin CJC said at pp. 246-7 CCC, p. 83 DLR, p. 578 SCR:

> It is quite clear to me that there is a marked difference between *certiorari*, used to quash a conviction or an order by its own strength, and *certiorari* in aid of *habeas corpus* to make the latter remedy more effective by requiring production of the record of proceedings for that purpose.

One must approach this issue, I think, from the same point of departure as was adopted by Laskin CJC that the provisions of the *Federal Court Act* indicate a clear intention on the part of Parliament to leave the jurisdiction by way of *habeas corpus* to review the validity of a detention imposed by federal authority with the provincial superior courts. While s. 18 of the *Federal Court Act* confers an exclusive and very general review jurisdiction over federal authorities by the prerogative and extraordinary remedies, to which specific reference is made, it deliberately omits reference to *habeas corpus*. That this was not an oversight but a well-considered decision is indicated by s. 17(5) of the Act, which expressly confers exclusive jurisdiction on the Federal Court with respect to an application for *habeas corpus* by a member of the Canadian Forces serving outside Canada. I agree with Laskin CJC that because of its importance as a safeguard of the liberty of the subject *habeas corpus* jurisdiction can only be affected by express words. One may think of reasons why it was thought advisable to leave the *habeas corpus* jurisdiction with respect to federal authorities with the provincial superior courts, including the importance of the local accessibility of this remedy. The important thing, as I see it, is that the decision to create this exception to the exclusive review jurisdiction of the Federal Court, with whatever problems arising from concurrent or overlapping jurisdiction it might cause, is really determinative of the question of jurisdiction to issue *certiorari* in aid. There can be no doubt that *certiorari* in aid is important, if not essential, to the effectiveness of *habeas corpus*. This was emphasized by both Anderson JA, with whom the other members of the British Columbia Court of Appeal agreed on this issue in *Cardinal* and *Oswald*, and by Cory JA in the case at bar. In many cases it may not be possible for a court to determine whether there has been an absence or excess of jurisdiction if the record of the tribunal which imposed or authorized the detention is not brought before it. The importance of *habeas corpus* itself, and by implication the importance of maintaining it as a fully effective remedy is, as Laskin CJC observed, given particular emphasis by its inclusion as a guaranteed right in s. 2(c)(iii) of the *Canadian*

Bill of Rights. To this recognition may now be added the constitutional guarantee of the right to *habeas corpus* in s. 10(c) of the *Canadian Charter of Rights and Freedoms*. Because of the clear intention to leave the *habeas corpus* jurisdiction over federal authorities with the provincial superior courts and the importance of *certiorari* in aid to the effectiveness of *habeas corpus*, it cannot, in my opinion, have been intended that the reference to *certiorari* in s. 18 of the *Federal Court Act* should have the effect of undermining or weakening the *habeas corpus* jurisdiction of the provincial superior courts by the exclusion or denial of *certiorari* in aid. Certainly such a construction is to be avoided if at all possible. It can be avoided by application of the distinction emphasized by Laskin CJC between *certiorari* as an independent and separate mode of review having as its object to quash the decision of an inferior tribunal and *certiorari* as an ancillary procedure used to serve an essentially evidentiary purpose. A very full discussion of this distinction, with reference to many of the decisions in which it has been noted and applied, is to be found in Cromwell, "*Habeas Corpus* and Correctional Law," 3 *Queen's LJ* 295 at pp. 320-3 (1977). Applying the distinction to the reference to *certiorari* in s. 18 of the *Federal Court Act*, it is reasonable to conclude, because of the association in that section of *certiorari* with the other prerogative and extraordinary remedies, that the reference is to the independent remedy of *certiorari* to quash. It is unlikely that Parliament intended to confer an exclusive jurisdiction to issue *certiorari* in aid when it had clearly withheld the jurisdiction to issue *habeas corpus*. For these reasons I conclude that a provincial superior court has jurisdiction to issue *certiorari* in aid of *habeas corpus* to review the validity of a detention authorized or imposed by a federal board, commission or other tribunal as defined by s. 2 of the *Federal Court Act*, and that accordingly the Ontario Court of Appeal did not err in concluding as it did on this issue.

III

In view of this conclusion on the question of jurisdiction to issue *certiorari* in aid of *habeas corpus* it may not be strictly necessary to deal with the question which was treated as an alternative issue by the British Columbia Court of Appeal in *Cardinal* and *Oswald* and by the Ontario Court of Appeal in the case at bar—whether on *habeas corpus* without *certiorari* in aid a court may consider affidavit or other extrinsic evidence to determine whether there has been an absence or excess of jurisdiction. It is well established that affidavit evidence is admissible on *certiorari* to show jurisdictional error. Both Courts of Appeal were led, however, by their analysis of this question to reach a conclusion on it at variance with that of Ritchie J in *Mitchell*, without much explicit consideration of the jurisprudence of this Court on which the opinion of Ritchie J purported to be based. Moreover, this question may well be an issue in the *Morin* appeal. For these reasons it is probably desirable that it be dealt with here in order to remove the uncertainty which now necessarily exists concerning it.

...

In *Re Shumiatcher* (1961), 131 CCC 259, 31 DLR (2d) 2, [1962] SCR 38, the relevant issue was whether the court could look at certain solemn declarations which the applicant for *habeas corpus* was charged with having induced a person to make, knowing them to be false, and thereby being a party, by virtue of s. 22(1) of the *Criminal Code*, to the offence defined by s. 114 (now s. 122). The application for *habeas corpus* challenged the validity of the committal for trial on the ground that the person making the solemn declarations was not a person permitted, authorized or required by law to make them, within the meaning of s. 114. The solemn declarations made reference to a statement of claim. Judson J framed the issue as follows, at p. 265 CCC, p. 9 DLR, p. 45 SCR:

> This brings me to the question of what use may be made of this material on a motion for *habeas corpus* before a Judge of this Court.
>
> The Crown's submission is that I am limited to looking at the warrant of committal and that I cannot look at these declarations and the statement of claim any more than I can look at the evidence—seven or eight volumes of it—given on the preliminary hearing.

After quoting from the judgments of this Court in *Re Trepanier* (1885), 12 SCR 111; *Ex parte Macdonald* (1896), 3 CCC 10, 27 SCR 683, and *Goldhar v. The Queen* (1960), 126 CCC 337, 25 DLR (2d) 401, [1960] SCR 431, with reference to *habeas corpus* against a warrant of committal after conviction, and observing that this Court did not have jurisdiction to issue *certiorari* in aid of *habeas corpus*, Judson J concluded on this issue as follows, at p. 267 CCC, pp. 10-1 DLR, p. 47 SCR:

> In my opinion the jurisdiction of this Court is similarly limited in an inquiry into a committal for trial. In the absence of power to issue a writ of *certiorari* in aid of *habeas corpus*, a Judge of this Court has no power to look at the evidence at the preliminary hearing or to receive affidavit evidence relating to it.
>
> My jurisdiction is limited to a consideration of the warrant of committal and the other material that I have referred to—the recognizances and the order of Judge Hogarth. I cannot look at evidence, whether a transcript of the evidence at the preliminary hearing or evidence sought to be introduced by way of affidavit identifying a portion of such evidence.
>
> I am founding my reasons on this branch of the case entirely on that principle and I am expressing no opinion on the point on which I heard full argument—whether there does exist, by virtue of provincial legislation, permission to take a declaration of this kind.

In *Goldhar*, the issues raised on the application for *habeas corpus* were the regularity on its face of a calendar of sentences as a certificate of the appellant's conviction and the applicable maximum penalty, having regard to a change that had taken place in the law. Fauteux J (as he then was), with whom Taschereau, Abbott and Judson JJ concurred, expressed the rationale for the exclusion of extrinsic evidence on an application for *habeas corpus* as follows, at pp. 347-8 CCC, pp. 409-10 DLR, p. 439 SCR:

> The question, which counsel for the appellant admittedly sought to be determined by way of *habeas corpus* proceedings, is stated in the reasons for judgment of other members of the Court. In my view, it is one which would require the consideration of the evidence at trial and which, in this particular case, extends beyond the scope of matters to be inquired under a similar process. To hold otherwise would be tantamount to convert the writ of *habeas corpus* into a writ of error or an appeal and to confer, upon every one having authority to issue the writ of *habeas corpus*, an appellate jurisdiction over the

orders and judgments of even the highest Courts. It is well settled that the functions of such a writ do not extend beyond an inquiry into the jurisdiction of the Court by which process the subject is held in custody and into the validity of the process upon its face.

I agree with the view that the appellant has been convicted and sentenced by a Court of competent jurisdiction, that the calendar is a certificate regular on its face that the appellant has been so convicted and sentenced and that, with the material before him, Martland J rightly dismissed the application for a writ of *habeas corpus*.

The above passage, in my respectful opinion, reflects the true distinction or criterion respecting the consideration of extrinsic evidence on an application for *habeas corpus*—the distinction between issues going to the merits and issues going to jurisdiction. The issues in both *Shumiatcher* and *Goldhar* were clearly issues going to the merits. The same is true of *Re Trepanier*, where the applicant alleged that the convicting magistrate erred on the facts in convicting him. He sought a writ of *habeas corpus* with *certiorari* in aid to bring up the record of the proceedings to ascertain whether there was sufficient evidence to convict. This was clearly an attempt to employ *habeas corpus* to review the merits of a conviction. Ritchie CJ said at p. 113:

> The jurisdiction of the magistrate being unquestionable over the subject-matter of complaint and the person of the prisoner, and there being no ground for alleging that the magistrate acted irregularly or beyond his jurisdiction, and the conviction and warrant being admitted to be regular, the only objection being that the magistrate erred on the facts and that the evidence did not justify the conclusion as to the guilt of the prisoner arrived at by the magistrate, I have not the slightest hesitation in saying that we cannot go behind the conviction and inquire into the merits of the case by the use of the writ of *habeas corpus*.

In the subsequent case of *Re Sproule* (1886), 12 SCR 140, the issues were jurisdictional but the Court held that extrinsic evidence could not be considered on *habeas corpus* to contradict the record of a superior court that is regular on its face. The conviction and sentence by the court of *oyer* and *terminer* and general jail delivery had been confirmed by the Supreme Court of British Columbia and Ritchie CJ spoke in terms of the conclusive character of the record of a superior court as follows at p. 191:

> I venture to propound without fear of successful contradiction, that by the law of England and of this Dominion, where the principles of the common law prevail, that if the record of a superior court contains the recital of facts requisite to confer jurisdiction, which the records in this case did, it is conclusive and cannot be contradicted by extrinsic evidence; and if the superior courts have jurisdiction over the subject-matter and the person, as the court of *oyer* and *terminer* and general gaol delivery and the Supreme Court of British Columbia had in this case, the records of their judgments and sentences are final and conclusive, unerring verity, and the law will not, in such a case, allow the record to be contradicted.

and he emphasized the distinction in this respect between the records of inferior courts and those of superior courts as follows at p. 193:

> And I venture humbly, and with all respect, to suggest that the difficulty in this case has arisen from a misapprehension of what can, and what cannot, be done under a writ of

habeas corpus, but more especially from not duly appreciating the distinction between the validity and force of records of courts of inferior, and of courts of superior, jurisdiction, but treating records of superior and inferior courts as being of the same force and effect.

Re Sproule was applied by this Court in *Ex parte Macdonald*, supra, and *Ex parte Henderson* (1929), 52 CCC 95, [1930] 1 DLR 420, [1930] SCR 45, where there were jurisdictional issues involved, in support of the more general or unqualified proposition that the court was limited on *habeas corpus* to an examination of the warrant of committal in determining whether there had been an absence or excess of jurisdiction.

Thus the true basis of this Court's jurisprudence with respect to the admission or consideration of extrinsic evidence on an application for *habeas corpus* consists of two principles: the principle that extrinsic evidence must not be permitted to convert an application for *habeas corpus* into an appeal on the merits, and the principle that the record of a superior court is conclusive as to the facts on which the court's jurisdiction depends and cannot be contradicted by extrinsic evidence. It has been suggested that the court was particularly concerned about the first principle when it was exercising an original jurisdiction in respect of *habeas corpus*, and that this may have led to the broad and unqualified expression of the rule respecting the consideration of extrinsic evidence on *habeas corpus* that is to be found in some of its decisions: see Sharpe, *The Law of Habeas Corpus* (1976), p. 51, note 2. With respect to the second principle, I agree with the suggestion in Sharpe, "*Habeas Corpus* in Canada," 2 *Dal. LJ* 241 at p. 261 (1975), that it should apply only to the records of superior courts or courts of general common law jurisdiction. In *Mitchell v. The Queen* (1975), 24 CCC (2d) 241, 61 DLR (3d) 77, [1976] 2 SCR 570, neither of these principles was applicable. As I have indicated, the grounds of attack were clearly jurisdictional, and the record, dependent as it was on the proceedings and decisions of an inferior tribunal, was not of the character entitled to be treated as conclusive of the facts of jurisdiction. In my respectful opinion, the view expressed in *Mitchell* that the affidavit evidence could not be considered went beyond the true basis of the court's jurisprudence on this question. In fact, two members of the majority in the result (Martland and de Grandpré JJ), as well as the minority (Laskin CJC, Spence and Dickson JJ), did consider the affidavit evidence in deciding whether there had been an absence or excess of jurisdiction in ordering the detention.

As the British Columbia and Ontario Courts of Appeal pointed out in *Cardinal* and *Oswald* and in the case at bar, it may only be possible to establish jurisdictional error on *habeas corpus* by affidavit evidence, even where the record is brought up by *certiorari* in aid. This is particularly true of a violation of natural justice or a denial of procedural fairness. This is a compelling reason, in my opinion, for confining the rule against consideration of extrinsic evidence on an application for *habeas corpus* within its proper boundaries.

Support for a broader approach to the admission or consideration of extrinsic evidence on *habeas corpus* to determine issues of jurisdiction may be found in the decision of the House of Lords in *Schtraks v. Government of Israel et al.*, [1964] AC 556, which was relied on by the Courts of Appeal in *Cardinal* and *Oswald* and the case at bar. There it was held that fresh evidence was admissible on an application for *habeas corpus* to show that the magistrate lacked jurisdiction to make the committal order in an extradition case because the offence was of a political character. Lord Hodson appears to have held in effect that the rule concerning the admission of affidavit evidence on *habeas corpus* is the same as it is on *certiorari*, as suggested by the following passage at pp. 605-6:

> Proceeding by *habeas corpus* is analogous to that by *certiorari* to remove a conviction, see Short and Mellor's *Crown Practice* (1908), p. 319. Affidavits are not admissible to controvert facts found by the judgment of a court of competent jurisdiction, though they may be received to show some extrinsic collateral matter essential to jurisdiction or to show total want or excess of jurisdiction.

I am therefore of the opinion that, subject to the limitation arising from the conclusive character of the records of courts of superior or general common law jurisdiction, a court may on an application for *habeas corpus* without *certiorari* in aid consider affidavit or other extrinsic evidence to determine whether there has been an absence or excess of jurisdiction.

IV

I turn to the question whether *habeas corpus* will lie to determine the validity of the confinement of an inmate of a penitentiary in a special handling unit and to obtain his release from such confinement, if it is found to be unlawful, into normal association with the general population of the penitentiary.

This issue turns on the view that one takes of the proper role of *habeas corpus* and the extent to which it should be adapted to the reality of the various forms of confinement or detention within penal institutions. An important policy consideration, in the context of the exclusive review jurisdiction of the Federal Court, is the extent to which the use of *habeas corpus* to determine the validity of a particular form of detention amounts to an indirect assumption of the Federal Court's review jurisdiction with respect to the administrative decisions of federal correctional authorities.

Those who oppose the resort to *habeas corpus* to challenge the validity of a particular form of confinement or detention in a penal institution contend that it fails to meet two essential conditions of the traditional availability of this remedy: (a) that there be a deprivation of liberty, and (b) that what is sought is the complete liberty of the applicant and not merely his or her transfer to another form of detention or restraint of liberty. This view of the traditional role of *habeas corpus* is reflected in the decisions in *Ex parte Rogers* (1843), 7 Jur. 992, and *R v. Governor of Wandsworth Prison, Ex parte Silverman* (1952), 96 Sol. J 853. In *Rogers* a prisoner applied for *habeas corpus* to obtain his release from a part of a prison "where the confinement was stricter and the food more scanty" to the place in the prison where he had been confined before the transfer. In dismissing the application Denman CJ, with whom Williams, Coleridge and Wightman JJ concurred, said:

> It is quite clear that we cannot entertain this application. The object of the writ of *habeas corpus* is, generally, to restore a person to his liberty, not to pronounce a judgment as to the room or part of a prison in which a prisoner ought to be confined.

In *Silverman*, a prisoner in preventive detention complained that he was not receiving the special treatment which the applicable statute required to be provided, and he sought by an application for *habeas corpus* to be transferred to a place where such treatment was provided. In dismissing the application for *habeas corpus* Hilberry J is reported to have held that if a writ of *habeas corpus* were issued,

> the only question would be whether the applicant should be released or not; and the prison governor's return would state that he was being detained under a sentence of preventive detention, which would be a perfectly good answer.

These cases were relied on by Hugessen ACJ, as he then was, in *Berrouard v. The Queen*, an unreported judgment of November 30, 1981, and related unreported decisions (referred to by the Quebec Court of Appeal in *Morin*) in dismissing applications for *habeas corpus* to challenge the validity of confinement in what appears from the expressions used to have been a special handling unit. I quote from an English version of what he said, as reported in *Re Morin and Yeomans et al.* (1982), 1 CCC (3d) 438 at p. 441, 142 DLR (3d) 582 at p. 585, [1982] Que. CA 464:

> These six motions for *habeas corpus* each raise the same point of law. In each case, the applicant alleges that he is at present serving a sentence and that he has been unjustifiably transferred into a special detention unit, or a special segregation unit.
>
> An essential pre-condition to the granting of the remedy of *habeas corpus* is the privation of the subject's liberty: *Massella v. Langlais* (1955), 112 CCC 1, [1975] 4 DLR 346, [1955] SCR 263. Similarly, in a motion for *habeas corpus*, the principal object of this remedy is the obtaining of liberty for the subject: *R v. Governor of Wandsworth Prison; Ex p. Silverman* (1952), 96 Sol. Jo. 853 (Queen's Bench Div. Ct., Hilberry, Streatfeild and McNair JJ); *Ex parte Rodgers* (1843), 7 Jur. 992 (Court of Queen's Bench, Denman CJ, Williams, Coleridge and Wightman JJ). I have read with much interest the judgment of my colleague Chief Justice McEachern, of the Supreme Court of British Columbia, in *Cardinal* and *Oswald v. Attorney-General*, an unreported judgment delivered on December 30, 1980. With all respect which I have for my colleague, I am not in agreement with his position that the writ of *habeas corpus* can be used to modify the conditions of detention since, even if the writ is granted, the prisoner's detention will continue after the final judgment is delivered. This is also our case.
>
> It accordingly follows that I am in agreement with the decision of my colleague Mr. Justice Jean-Paul Bergeron in the *Morin v. Yeomans* case, an unreported judgment delivered on November 18, 1981.

In *Morin*, which, as I have said, was a case of *habeas corpus* without *certiorari* in aid, Bergeron J referred to the conclusion of McEachern CJSC in *Cardinal* and *Oswald* that *habeas corpus* would lie to determine the validity of a particular form of detention in a penitentiary and said he could not agree with it. He held that judicial review of the administrative decisions of the federal correctional authorities fell within the exclusive jurisdiction of the Federal Court by way of *certiorari*. In his view, the conditions of detention of a person who was otherwise lawfully imprisoned under a valid warrant of committal could not give rise to *habeas corpus*. In dismissing the appeal from the judgment of Bergeron J, the Quebec Court of Appeal noted that the appellant had taken proceedings by way of *certiorari* in the Federal Court to challenge the validity of his confinement in the special handling unit and that there would therefore be the danger of conflicting judgments if it were held that the Superior Court had jurisdiction to issue *habeas corpus* to determine the same issue. The Court of Appeal concluded that proceedings to challenge administrative action within federal penitentiaries was within the exclusive jurisdiction of the Federal Court. Thus it would appear that the Superior Court and the Court of Appeal in *Morin* were influenced in the view which they took of the proper application of *habeas corpus* by the implications of a concurrent or overlapping review jurisdiction with respect to the administrative decisions of the federal correctional authorities.

The British Columbia courts in *Cardinal* and *Oswald* and the Ontario Court of Appeal in the case at bar applied the notion of a "prison within a prison" in holding that *habeas corpus* would lie to determine the validity of confinement in administrative segregation or a special handling unit, and if such confinement be found unlawful, to order the release of the inmate into the general population of the penitentiary. The concept of a "prison within a prison" is referred to by Sharpe, *The Law of Habeas Corpus*, p. 149, where he speaks in favour of such an application of *habeas corpus*, and by Dickson J, as he then was, in *Martineau v. Matsqui Institution Disciplinary Board (No. 2)* (1979), 50 CCC (2d) 353, 106 DLR (3d) 385, [1980] 1 SCR 602, where, with reference to the decision of the disciplinary board which sentenced the inmate for a disciplinary offence to 15 days in the penitentiary's special corrections unit, he said at p. 373 CCC, p. 405 DLR, p. 622 SCR:

> Moreover, the board's decision had the effect of depriving an individual of his liberty by committing him to a "prison within a prison." In these circumstances, elementary justice requires some procedural protection. The rule of law must run within penitentiary walls.

This statement reflects the perception that a prisoner is not without some rights or residual liberty (see also *Solosky v. The Queen* (1979), 50 CCC (2d) 495 at p. 510, 105 DLR (3d) 745 at p. 760, [1980] 1 SCR 821 at p. 839) and that there may be significant degrees of deprivation of liberty within a penal institution. The same perception is reflected in the reasons for judgment of McEachern CJSC and Anderson JA in *Cardinal* and *Oswald* and Cory JA in the case at bar on this issue. In effect, a prisoner has the right not to be deprived unlawfully of the relative or residual liberty permitted to the general inmate population of an institution. Any significant deprivation of that liberty, such as that effected by confinement in a special handling unit, meets the first of the traditional requirements for *habeas corpus*, that it must be directed against a deprivation of liberty.

Moreover, the principle that *habeas corpus* will lie only to secure the complete liberty of the subject is not invariably reflected in its application. There are applications of *habeas corpus* in Canadian case-law which illustrate its use to release a person from a particular form of detention although the person will lawfully remain under some other restraint of liberty. Examples are the use of *habeas corpus* to recover the custody of children (*Stevenson v. Florant* (1926), 46 CCC 362, [1926] 4 DLR 897, [1927] AC 211; affirming, [1925] SCR 532; *Dugal v. Lefebvre* (1934), 62 CCC 178, [1934] 4 DLR 552, [1934] SCR 501); to release a person on parole where the parole has been unlawfully revoked (*Re Cadeddu and The Queen* (1982), 4 CCC (3d) 97, 146 DLR (3d) 629, 40 OR (2d) 128; *Re Swan and The Queen* (1983), 7 CCC (3d) 130, 150 DLR (3d) 626, 35 CR (3d) 135); and to transfer an inmate from an institution in which he has been unlawfully confined to another institution (*Re Bell and Director of Springhill Medium Security Institution et al.* (1977), 34 CCC (2d) 303, 38 CRNS 1, 19 NSR (2d) 216; *R v. Frejd* (1910), 18 CCC 10, 22 OLR 566). In all of these cases the effect of *habeas corpus* is to release a person from an unlawful detention, which is the object of the remedy. The use of *habeas corpus* to release a prisoner from an unlawful form of detention within a penitentiary into normal association with the general inmate population of the penitentiary is consistent with these applications of the remedy.

An enlarged approach to the concept of custody for purposes of *habeas corpus* is reflected in American case-law. Formerly American courts took the view that *habeas corpus* would only lie where a favourable judgment would result in immediate release from all forms of detention: *McNally v. Hill* (1934), 293 US 131. Since then the concept of custody has been greatly expanded to permit a wider use of *habeas corpus* for the protection of prisoners' rights. In *Jones v. Cunningham* (1963), 371 US 236, where *habeas corpus* was held to be available to an applicant who was not in physical custody but on parole, the Court said at p. 243 that *habeas corpus* is "not now and never has been a static, narrow, formalistic remedy; its scope has grown to achieve its grand purpose—the protection of individuals against erosion of their right to be free from wrongful restraints upon their liberty." In *Peyton v. Rowe* (1968), 391 US 54, *habeas corpus* was allowed to challenge the validity of a sentence yet to be served. In *Johnson v. Avery* (1969), 393 US 483, *habeas corpus* was allowed to challenge the validity of a condition of confinement in the form of a prison regulation which limited the access of illiterate inmates to the courts by forbidding their fellow prisoners from serving as jailhouse lawyers. It was held that the unlawful regulations made the custody unlawful. In *Wilwording v. Swenson* (1971), 404 US 249, the United States Supreme Court reversed the Missouri courts which had held that *habeas corpus* would not lie where the object was not to secure the release of the petitioners from the penitentiary altogether but to challenge their living conditions and disciplinary measures. The Supreme Court affirmed the approach it had adopted in *Johnson v. Avery*. It should be noted, however, that in *Preiser v. Rodriguez* (1973), 411 US 475, Stewart J, speaking for the majority, expressed himself in terms which might suggest that the question was regarded as still being open. He said at p. 499: "This is not to say that *habeas corpus* may not also be available to challenge such prison conditions. See *Johnson v. Avery*, 393 US 483 (1969); *Wilwording v. Swenson*, supra, at 251. When a prisoner is put under additional and unconstitutional restraints during his lawful custody, it is arguable that *habeas corpus* will lie to remove the restraints making the custody illegal. See Note, Developments in the Law—*Habeas Corpus*, 83 *Harv. L Rev.* 1038, 1084 (1970)." The note to which Stewart J referred approved the approach adopted in the leading case of *Coffin v. Reichard* (1944), 143 F2d 443 (6th Cir.), where it was said at p. 445: "A prisoner is entitled to the writ of *habeas corpus* when, though lawfully in custody, he is deprived of some right to which he is lawfully entitled even in his confinement, the deprivation of which serves to make his imprisonment more burdensome than the

law allows or curtails his liberty to a greater extent than the law permits." After referring to *Coffin* the note states at pp. 1085-6:

> No other circuit purports to follow *Coffin*. Most courts instead believe that *habeas* juris-
> diction is lacking when the petitioner is not asking for the invalidation of a custody
> imposed by sentence, on the theory that the petitioner is not seeking a present or future
> release. But this fails to recognize that the lawfulness of a custody depends, not merely
> upon the legal basis for some kind of custody, but upon the lawfulness of the specific
> type and manner of confinement in question. Where the specific detention abridges
> federally protected interests—by placing petitioner in the wrong prison, denying him
> treatment, imposing cruel and unusual punishment, impeding his access to the courts,
> and so on—it is an unlawful detention and *habeas* lies to release the petitioner therefrom.
> It is immaterial that the petitioner might then be placed in a different, lawful custody or
> that his being sentenced to a term of confinement might itself be lawful. The custody
> requirement, and the corresponding insistence on discharge from custody, do not pre-
> vent *habeas corpus* from being an appropriate remedy for the review of unlawful prison
> administration.

Since that note was written the point of view expressed in it has been adopted by
federal courts of appeal. See, for example, the following cases recognizing the availability of *habeas corpus* to challenge the validity of various forms of segregated
confinement in a prison on the ground of a violation of due process: *McCollum v.
Miller* (1982), 695 F2d 1044 (7th Cir.); *Krist v. Ricketts* (1974), 504 F2d 887 (5th
Cir.); *Bryant v. Harris* (1972), 465 F2d 365 (7th Cir.); *Dawson v. Smith* (1983), 719
F2d 896 (7th Cir.), and *Streeter v. Hopper* (1980), 618 F2d 1178 (5th Cir.).

After giving consideration to the two approaches to this issue, I am of the opinion
that the better view is that *habeas corpus* should lie to determine the validity of a
particular form of confinement in a penitentiary notwithstanding that the same issue
may be determined upon *certiorari* in the Federal Court. The proper scope of the
availability of *habeas corpus* must be considered first on its own merits, apart from
possible problems arising from concurrent or overlapping jurisdiction. The general
importance of this remedy as the traditional means of challenging deprivations of
liberty is such that its proper development and adaptation to the modern realities of
confinement in a prison setting should not be compromised by concerns about conflicting jurisdiction. As I have said in connection with the question of jurisdiction to
issue *certiorari* in aid of *habeas corpus*, these concerns have their origin in the legislative judgment to leave the *habeas corpus* jurisdiction against federal authorities
with the provincial superior courts. There cannot be one definition of the reach of
habeas corpus in relation to federal authorities and a different one for other authorities. Confinement in a special handling unit, or in administrative segregation as in
Cardinal and *Oswald* is a form of detention that is distinct and separate from that
imposed on the general inmate population. It involves a significant reduction in the
residual liberty of the inmate. It is in fact a new detention of the inmate, purporting to
rest on its own foundation of legal authority. It is that particular form of detention or
deprivation of liberty which is the object of the challenge by *habeas corpus*. It is
release from that form of detention that is sought. For the reasons indicated above, I

can see no sound reason in principle, having to do with the nature and role of *habeas corpus*, why *habeas corpus* should not be available for that purpose. I do not say that *habeas corpus* should lie to challenge any and all conditions of confinement in a penitentiary or prison, including the loss of any privilege enjoyed by the general inmate population. But it should lie in my opinion to challenge the validity of a distinct form of confinement or detention in which the actual physical constraint or deprivation of liberty, as distinct from the mere loss of certain privileges, is more restrictive or severe than the normal one in an institution.

A. Refining the Scope of Habeas Corpus: Steele v. Mountain Institution

Steele v. Mountain Institution, [1990] 2 SCR 1385, a unanimous judgment written by Cory J, confirmed *habeas corpus* relief for a prisoner who had been imprisoned for almost 37 years as a "criminal sexual psychopath," a predecessor to the modern dangerous offender designation. Steele was 18 years old when he was given that designation after his conviction for attempted rape. His counsel argued that, in the absence of any indicia of dangerousness, it was cruel and unusual punishment in violation of s. 12 of the *Canadian Charter of Rights and Freedoms*, part I of the *Constitution Act, 1982*, RSC 1985, app. II, no. 44, to continue his confinement. Over the years, Steele had been released on parole, but parole privileges had been revoked for breach of conditions. Instead of returning to the National Parole Board, he brought his case to court.

Steele v. Mountain Institution
[1990] 2 SCR 1385

CORY J: Theodore Steele, the respondent, has attained the age of 55. For almost 37 of those years he has been detained in an institution. In my view the issue raised on this appeal is whether the Parole Board erred in refusing to release him on parole with the result that his continuing imprisonment constitutes cruel and unusual punishment.

The period of incarceration has been long indeed. When the respondent entered prison, Mr. St. Laurent was Prime Minister and General Eisenhower was President. He remained incarcerated through the Cuban missile crisis, the assassination of President Kennedy, the Vietnam War, the FLQ crisis, the Watergate scandal, the Iran/Iraq War, the easing of tension between the Soviet Union and the United States, and the enactment of the *Canadian Charter of Rights and Freedoms*. An era has passed.

...

It will be remembered that it was determined by Paris J, and upheld by the Court of Appeal, that although the indeterminate continuing detention of a dangerous offender had been held in *Lyons*, supra, to be constitutional, nevertheless, in certain rare cases such as this one, the continuing detention of an offender would constitute cruel and unusual punishment in violation of s. 12 of the Charter. If this position is correct it would mean that while the parole review process would work effectively in the vast majority of cases, there would be the occasional case in which even the most responsible and careful application of the parole review process could not prevent a continuing detention from becoming cruel and unusual punishment.

I must, with respect, differ from that conclusion. It seems to me to fly in the face of the decision of this Court in *Lyons*, supra, where this Court observed at p. 363 that "the fairness of certain procedural aspects of a parole hearing may well be the subject of constitutional challenge, at least when the review is of the continued incarceration of a dangerous offender." In my view the unlawful incarceration of Steele was caused, not by any structural flaw in the dangerous offender provisions, but rather by errors committed by the National Parole Board. These errors are apparent upon a review of the record of Steele's treatment by the Board over the long years of his detention.

In 1948, provisions for the indeterminate sentencing of "criminal sexual psychopaths" were enacted. The same group of amendments to the Code provided for a review of the condition, history and circumstances of the offender's detention once every three years by the Minister of Justice. In 1958, the National Parole Board was created by the *Parole Act*, SC 1958, c. 38. At this time the authority for conducting the review of the sentences of criminal sexual psychopaths was transferred to the Parole Board. Section 8(a) of the *Parole Act* established the following criteria for granting parole:

> 8. The Board may
>> (a) grant parole to an inmate if the Board considers that the inmate has derived the maximum benefit from imprisonment and that the reform and rehabilitation of the inmate will be aided by the grant of parole;

These criteria remained in effect until 1968 when they were replaced by the provisions of s. 16(1) cited above. These provisions require the Board to grant parole where: (i) the inmate has derived the maximum benefit from imprisonment; (ii) the inmate's reform and rehabilitation will be aided by the grant of parole; and (iii) the inmate's release would not constitute an undue risk to society.

In reviewing the indeterminate sentences of dangerous offenders, it is fundamentally important that the Board consider these criteria. As La Forest J stated in *Lyons* at pp. 340-41:

> ... in the context of a determinate sentencing scheme the availability of parole represents an additional, superadded protection of the liberty interests of the offender. In the present context, however, it is, subsequent to the actual imposition of the sentence itself, the sole protection of the dangerous offender's liberty interests. ...
>
> Seen in this light, therefore, the parole process assumes the utmost significance for it is that process alone that is capable of truly accommodating and tailoring the sentence to fit the circumstances of the individual offender.

It is only by a careful consideration and application of these criteria that the indeterminate sentence can be made to fit the circumstances of the individual offender. Doing this will ensure that the dangerous offender sentencing provisions do not violate s. 12 of the Charter. If it is clear on the face of the record that the Board has misapplied or disregarded those criteria over a period of years with the result that an offender remains incarcerated far beyond the time he or she should have been properly paroled, then the Board's decision to keep the offender incarcerated may well violate s. 12. In my opinion, this is such a case.

First, Steele's imprisonment had long ago reached the point at which he had derived "the maximum benefit from imprisonment." During his incarceration governments have changed, wars have begun and ended and a generation has grown to maturity. He has been in prison longer than the vast majority of the most cruel and callous murderers. Indeed, it is uncertain whether imprisonment provided Steele with any benefit at all. During the first 20 years of his detention there were no facilities in British Columbia that could provide the psychiatric treatment Steele needed. By the time it was available, Steele was a middle-aged institutionalized offender who, not surprisingly, viewed the treatment program as a means of gaining his release rather than as an opportunity for rehabilitation.

Throughout the period of his imprisonment, numerous observers expressly stated not only that Steele had received the maximum benefit from imprisonment, but also that continued detention would cause him to deteriorate. As early as 1960, Dr. P. Middleton warned that any treatment facilities available in the penitentiary would not offset "the pernicious effects of association" with other inmates. Others who made this same point include: Dr. D.C. MacDonald, Deputy Warden W.H. Collins and Field Representative P.D. Redecopp in 1964; Dr. J.C. Bryce in 1968; Mr. Lee Pulos in 1970; Field Parole Officer William F. Foster and Mr. Pulos, again, in 1972; Dr. Milton H. Miller and Dr. A. Saad in 1974; and Dr. W.J. Ross in 1981. Even Dr. Noone, who testified for the Crown in this application, acknowledged the detrimental effects of indeterminate sentencing for dangerous offenders. While some observers expressed the opinion that Steele should not be released, not one of them appears to have argued that continued incarceration had been or would be beneficial for Steele.

The second criterion has also long been satisfied. Steele has deteriorated in the prison environment. Many, indeed the great majority of those psychiatrists and psychologists who assessed him, expressed the opinion that his rehabilitation could only be facilitated and attained by his gradual, supervised release into the community. It appears that the Parole Board acknowledged this in its decisions to grant Steele limited freedom between 1968 and 1970 and between 1980 and 1987. During both of these periods the Board permitted Steele to undertake a programme of escorted passes that resulted in brief stays in a half-way house environment. These periods of relative freedom were terminated when Steele infringed his parole conditions by drinking alcohol and breaking curfew. Unfortunately, despite assessments by observers suggesting that these parole violations were merely adjustment problems, the Board seems to have presumed that Steele was incapable of benefitting from an association with the community outside the prison.

There remains then the third and most important criterion, namely whether the offender constitutes an undue risk to society. If an inmate's release continues to constitute an undue risk to the public, then his or her detention can be justifiably maintained for a lifetime. There can be no doubt that in the ordinary course of events the assessment as to whether or not an inmate's release would pose an undue risk to the community is best left in the discretion of the experts who participate in the Parole Board review decisions. However, in light of the inordinate length of Steele's period of incarceration, it is appropriate to consider whether the Board erred in its evaluation that Steele did in fact constitute a danger to the community.

Of the psychiatrists and psychologists who interviewed Steele and whose reports were provided to the Parole Board, sixteen expressed a recommendation as to whether or not he should be paroled. Thirteen of the sixteen recommended that he should be released on some form of supervised parole. Two stated that he should not be released. One psychologist changed his mind over the course of several years from a position which cautioned against parole to one of arguing in favour of parole. Those recommending release were: Dr. MacDonald in 1956 and 1964; Dr. Middleton in 1960; Dr. Bryce in 1968; Dr. Lipinski in 1970 and 1972; Dr. Bulmer in 1970; Mr. Pulos in 1970 and 1972; Mr. P. DesLauriers in 1972; Dr. Robert Halliday in 1973; Dr. Miller, Dr. Saad, Mr. F.M. Van Fleet and Mr. K.S. Oey in 1974; and Dr. Tyhurst in 1979 and 1985. Those counselling against release were: Dr. Eaves in 1979 and 1980; and Dr. Noone in 1985 and 1988. Dr. W.J. Ross considered that Steele was not "a good risk" when he first assessed him in 1978; however, by 1981 he was recommending that Steele be released on gradual parole.

On the application, Paris J heard testimony from three psychiatric experts. Of those, Dr. Marcus and Dr. Koopman testified that Steele was not dangerous and should be released. Dr. Noone stated that Steele remained an untreated sexual psychopath who should not be released. After carefully reviewing the evidence in extensive detail, Paris J concluded that Steele's release would not endanger the public.

Upon the evidence presented to this Court, the careful reasons and conclusion of Paris J on this issue are in my view preferable to those of the Parole Board which as will be demonstrated did not properly exercise its jurisdiction.

It is difficult to find any evidence of acts committed by Steele during the past two decades that would suggest that he remained an undue risk to society. His parole violations resulted not from a tendency to repeatedly engage in violent or sexually deviant behaviour, but from the difficulties he had in abiding by parole curfew restrictions and abstaining from drinking alcohol. The nature of these problems was described by Dr. Marcus in these words:

> He finds it very hard to adhere to inflexible rules such as those that are imposed when he is on parole. ... His personality style is always to stretch the clock. ... It is a similar attitude which has led Mr. Steele into situations where he has been in breach of parole conditions relating to meeting curfews. Here again Mr. Steele holds the view that he is now 53 years old and after a lifetime in prison he should not be held to requirements which treat him in a somewhat childlike [manner]. It is precisely this attitude which has made him a bad parole prospect in terms of meeting all the expectations and rules imposed by his Parole Officer. Yet, in my opinion, what must be kept firmly in mind in the context of assessing the degree of risk of harm to others that Mr. Steele poses at the present time, is that Mr. Steele in the course of these recent infractions did not repeat the pattern either of his original offence nor of his re-offending while on parole in 1962.

The problems inherent in requiring chronic alcoholics to meet rigid drinking restrictions have been well documented in the *Report of the Inquiry into Habitual Criminals in Canada*, vol. 1 (1984), where Judge Leggett wrote at p. 83:

> Many of the habitual criminals are alcoholic. This disease has been a significant factor in the "revolving-door syndrome" of these individuals. When released on parole, a condition to abstain from alcohol is frequently included as a condition to such release. While some of the habitual criminals have been able to abide by this condition and

successfully complete parole, many others have not. Those who have failed to abide by such conditions have found themselves, sooner or later, re-incarcerated as a result of the revocation of their parole.

Steele may have a problem with alcohol and in dealing with rigid discipline. But those factors in themselves cannot justify his continued detention. If breaches of a domestic curfew and the consumption of alcohol were the sole criteria for liberty then a significant proportion of our society should be incarcerated for an indefinite period. That is not to say that breaches of the conditions of parole should not be seriously considered. However, all the circumstances of the breach and any explanations as to the reasons for its occurrence should also be taken into account.

The statutory criteria should be applied to the individual inmate and considered in light of all the relevant circumstances. One of those circumstances will be length of the term served. The passage of several decades in prison may not in itself justify parole. However, it may well serve as an indication that the inmate is no longer dangerous. Surely with the passage of very long periods of time sexual appetite might reasonably be expected to decline to an extent that it may at least be controlled, if not extinguished. As well, a lengthy incarceration with the concomitant institutionalizing effect upon the inmate may serve to explain and perhaps to some extent excuse certain breaches of discipline.

In my view the evidence presented demonstrates that the National Parole Board has erred in its application of the criteria set out in s. 16(1)(a) of the *Parole Act*. The Board appears to have based its decision to deny parole upon relatively minor and apparently explicable breaches of discipline committed by Steele, rather than focussing upon the crucial issue of whether granting him parole would constitute an undue risk to society. As a result of these errors, the parole review process has failed to ensure that Steele's sentence has been tailored to fit his circumstances. The inordinate length of his incarceration has long since become grossly disproportionate to the circumstances of this case.

It will only be on rare and unique occasions that a court will find a sentence so grossly disproportionate that it violates the provisions of s. 12 of the Charter. The test for determining whether a sentence is disproportionately long is very properly stringent and demanding. A lesser test would tend to trivialize the Charter.

As well, it should not be forgotten that there is in place a method whereby appellate courts can review sentences to ensure that they are appropriate. In *R v. Smith*, [1987] 1 SCR 1045, Lamer J set out the strict test for reviewing a sentence under s. 12 of the Charter. At page 1072 he wrote:

> The test for review under s. 12 of the Charter is one of gross disproportionality, because it is aimed at punishments that are more than merely excessive. We should be careful not to stigmatize every disproportionate or excessive sentence as being a constitutional violation, and should leave to the usual sentencing appeal process the task of reviewing the fitness of a sentence. Section 12 will only be infringed where the sentence is so unfit having regard to the offence and the offender as to be grossly disproportionate.

The history of the offence and the offender which I have set out makes it apparent that the sentence is now "so unfit having regard to the offence and the offender as to be grossly disproportionate." This is one of those rare cases where the sentence continuing Steele's detention after 37 years in prison violates s. 12 of the Charter.

It is necessary to make a further comment. As I have made clear above, the continuing detention of a dangerous offender sentenced pursuant to the constitutionally valid provisions of the *Criminal Code* will only violate s. 12 of the Charter when the National Parole Board errs in the execution of its vital duties of tailoring the indeterminate sentence to the circumstances of the offender. This tailoring is performed by applying the criteria set out in s. 16(1) of the *Parole Act*. Since any error that may be committed occurs in the parole review process itself, an application challenging the decision should be made by means of judicial review from the National Parole Board decision, not by means of an application for *habeas corpus*. It would be wrong to sanction the establishment of a costly and unwieldly parallel system for challenging a Parole Board decision. As well, it is important that the release of a long term inmate should be supervised by those who are experts in this field. I agree with the comments of Locke JA:

> In the case of persons subject to an indeterminate sentence who have spent many years in prison, it is highly desirable that their release, if and when it occurs, should be conditional, should be subject to supervision by those experienced in the parole or probation fields, and should be accompanied by the sort of assistance which will increase their likelihood of adjusting to the change in environment and, if possible, becoming self-sufficient and useful members of society. Under the present statutory and administrative arrangements, it seems that this can be achieved only in association with release by the parole board, in the exercise of its discretion under s. 761 of the *Criminal Code*.

However, in view of Steele's age and the length of his detention, it would be unfair to require him to commence new proceedings by way of judicial review from the National Parole Board decision. In these highly unusual circumstances, I would confirm Steele's release on the basis of the application for *habeas corpus*. I further agree with the position taken by the Court of Appeal that since his release cannot be regulated through normal parole procedures, it is appropriate, in the interest of public safety, to maintain the conditions placed by the Court of Appeal upon his release.

NOTE

In total, 13 judges examined Steele's case and all agreed that he was entitled to be released as a result of a breach of s. 12 of the Charter. This serves as an important example of the potential use of *habeas corpus* to bring forward a Charter claim. Moreover, one must note the characterization of a liberty interest as provided in *R v. Miller*, above, where Le Dain J held that *habeas corpus* was aviable to challenge "a significant reduction in the residual liberty of the inmate," which can, in some circumstances, relate to the conditions of confinement. Along with cases like *R v. Gamble*, [1988] 2 SCR 595, which dealt with s. 7 and parole ineligibility for first-degree murder after a conviction under the wrong law, there appeared to be a renaissance in the use of *habeas corpus* as an accessible and effectual remedy.

However, the final paragraph in the judgment of Cory J in *Steele* has blunted this progress. His admonition about establishing a "costly and unweildly parallel system for challenging a Parole Board decision" was made in the context of a life-time indeterminate sentence. This was a case where it was legitimate to ask whether there was any need to supervise Steele in the community. This is the key to Cory J's comments. Clearly, a court does not have supervisory resources. However, given that the relief is sought under s. 24(1) of the Charter, the court is empowered to do what is "appropriate and just." In *Steele*, that meant imposing conditions on his release. Although there may be some preventive detention cases that raise a procedural fairness argument that might better be dealt with by way of judicial review that returns the matter to the National Parole Board, cases that engage fundamental questions about the legality of confinement, like *Steele*, should not be barred from access to *habeas corpus*.

Regrettably, some superior courts have been persuaded that the final paragraph in *Steele* means that no parole issue should be dealt with by way of *habeas corpus* and that all issues should be raised by judicial review in the Federal Court. This elevates Cory J's comment in *Steele* from a caution raised in the context of indeterminate sentences to a complete denial of *habeas corpus* relief in a much larger class of cases. Do you think this is what Cory J intended? Is this consistent with the role of *habeas corpus* as explained in *Miller*? In *R v. Pearson* (1992), 17 CR (4th) 1 (SCC), a case dealing with the constitutionality of reverse-onus bail provisions, Lamer CJC referred to *Steele* and said that just as "*habeas corpus* should not become a costly and unwieldy parallel system of parole review, it should not become a costly and unwieldy parallel system of bail review." Still, he accepted that *habeas corpus* was an available remedy in *Pearson* because of its particular Charter dimensions.

B. The Timing of Habeas Corpus

Another Supreme Court of Canada decision brought a pragmatic examination of the issue of timing. Historically, it had been accepted that one could not use *habeas corpus* to challenge a form of confinement until that confinement had commenced—that is, the remedy did not lie until the custody commenced. This made some practical sense because the jailer's return to a *habeas corpus* application was usually the warrant of committal, and this generally accompanied the prisoner. Beyond this practical point, is there any reason to deny *habeas corpus* in a situation where the allegedly illegal custody is certain and imminent?

Idziak v. Minister of Justice (1992), 17 CR (4th) 161 (SCC) was an extradition case. The minister's decision to surrender Idziak was challenged on s. 7 Charter grounds. Counsel for the government of Canada, on behalf of the requesting state, argued that *habeas corpus* could not be used to attack the warrant of committal because it had not yet been executed. The Supreme Court held that there would be no point in forcing a person to wait until after he or she had been extradited and subjected to the impugned confinement before he or she could bring *habeas corpus* to challenge it. As long as the future confinement was not speculative, *habeas corpus* was an appropriate remedy to seek. The existence of the warrant that would result in a loss of residual liberty was sufficient.

The ruling in *Idziak* became important in a totally unrelated context. After the Arbour Inquiry into the Prison for Women, the Correctional Service followed its plan to close the Prison for Women (P4W) in favour of smaller, regional facilities. Unfortunately, the

Edmonton institution was opened prematurely, and incidents, such as walk-aways and a homicide, resulted. Consequently, the commissioner announced the policy that no maximum-security women prisoners would be transferred to the new facilities. But where would they go? In the Prairies and the Maritimes, any women already in the new facilities who were classified as maximum security were transferred to nearby men's institutions, and housed there in separate units. A handful of women prisoners were kept at the P4W, pending its closure. In the spring of 1997, it was announced that the P4W was finally being closed and the remaining women would be moved to a range at Kingston Peniten-tiary, a male maximum-security institution, which had been painted pink and was being prepared for them. Although the actual date of the transfer was kept secret for security reasons, every prisoner was given written notice that the transfer would take place within the next few weeks. The prisoners, with the support of the Canadian Association of Elizabeth Fry Societies, commenced a *habeas corpus* application challenging the legality of their transfer to a male institution. The challenge raised a number of s. 15 Charter arguments and was supported by volumes of social science and expert opinion about the distinct nature of women's confinement and the confinement of aboriginal women, in particular. On the first appearance in court, counsel for the prisoners argued that an order should issue prohibiting the imminent transfer until the legailty of the confinement issue had been resolved. The Correctional Service argued that the *habeas corpus* application was premature until the prisoners had been transferred and any legal questions should be raised by judicial review in the Federal Court. The presiding judge rejected this position and ordered that the prisoners not be transferred until the s. 15 challenge had been resolved. (Clearly, if the transfer had gone ahead, P4W would have immediately ceased to exist as a penitentiary, and it would have been impossible to return the prisoners to that form of confinement.) The presiding judge also decided that the case raised difficult factual issues and that it should proceed as a trial and not as an application. The Correc-tional Service appealed this interlocutory ruling to the Ontario Court of Appeal. The appeal was heard on December 12, 1997, a few weeks before the trial was set to begin. The right to seek *habeas corpus* prior to the transfer was confirmed in a brief oral judgment.

Beaudry et al. v. Commissioner of Corrections, Warden of Prison for Women and Warden of Kingston Penitentiary
[1997] OJ no. 5082 (CA)

BROOKE, ROBINS, and MOLDAVER JJA: Applying the rationale of the decisions of the Supreme Court of Canada in *Miller v. The Queen*, *Gamble v. The Queen*, and *Idziak v. Canada (Minister of Justice)*, we are of the opinion that the judge below did not err in holding that the applicants, that is the respondents in this appeal, are enti-tled to seek relief by way of *habeas corpus* even though they are not yet in the Region-al Treatment Centre.

We make no decision as to the remedies, if any, that may be available to the appli-cants and leave such issues to the trial of this matter which we are advised is sched-uled to proceed on January 5, 1998.

The appeal is dismissed.

NOTE

A few days after the Court of Appeal decision, *supra*, the matter ended without trial in a consent judgment, which provided that the prisoners would not be sent to Kingston Penitentiary. In 2000, the P4W was finally closed.

IV. PAROLE DECISIONS AND THE CHARTER

As demonstrated above in the cases of *Cunningham* and *Steele*, parole decisions implicate a prisoner's liberty interest and can raise issues under ss. 7, 9, and 12 of the Charter. However, in such cases, the question will be for the court to scrutinize whether the National Parole Board has respected or violated the prisoner's Charter rights. A different question is whether the National Parole Board is empowered to scrutinize whether another state agency had respected a prisoner's Charter rights. In other words, can a prisoner argue that material placed in front of the National Parole Board cannot be considered because it was obtained in violation of the prisoner's rights?

The majority and minority decisions in *Mooring*, *infra*, reflect two very different perspectives on the decision-making role of the National Parole Board. It is also significant to note that the Supreme Court did not comment on using *habeas corpus* to raise this issue.

National Parole Board et al. v. Mooring
(1996), 104 CCC (3d) 97 (SCC)

[Mooring was on mandatory supervision when he was arrested and charged with various offences arising from the police seizure of a stolen gun and what could have been housebreaking equipment from his van. These charges were stayed, apparently because Crown counsel believed that the search of the applicant's van violated the Charter and that evidence concerning the search would not be admissible at trial. However, the National Parole Board revoked his mandatory supervision, relying upon this evidence. Mooring's *habeas corpus* application was dismissed. The judge held that the Parole Board was entitled to take into account evidence that may have been obtained in violation of the Charter. This was reversed on appeal to the BC Court of Appeal. The majority held that the Parole Board was a court of competent jurisdiction within the meaning of s. 24 of the Charter, with the ability to exclude evidence where such evidence was obtained by a Charter violation. The board appealed to the Supreme Court.]

SOPINKA J (L'Heureux-Dubé, Gonthier, Cory, and Iacobucci JJ concurring): This appeal concerns the National Parole Board's decision to revoke the respondent's parole based in part on evidence gathered in a manner that may have violated the respondent's constitutional rights. Specifically, the court must determine whether or not the board is a "court of competent jurisdiction" for the purpose of making an order excluding evidence under s. 24(2) of the *Canadian Charter of Rights and Freedoms*. If the board is not a court of competent jurisdiction, the court must determine what practice the board should follow when faced with information that has been gathered in a manner that would be excluded by a court of competent jurisdiction.

...

A. Is the National Parole Board a "Court of Competent Jurisdiction"?

In my view, the National Parole Board is not a court of competent jurisdiction within the meaning of s. 24 of the Charter. I have arrived at this conclusion based on a review of previous decisions of this court, as well as on an examination of the basic structure and function of the Parole Board.

Previous decisions of this court have considered the definition of the phrase "court of competent jurisdiction" in s. 24 of the Charter. In *Mills v. The Queen* (1986), 26 CCC (3d) 481, 29 DLR (4th) 161, [1986] 1 SCR 863, for example, the court was faced with the issue of whether or not a preliminary inquiry judge was a court of competent jurisdiction within the meaning of s. 24. Although Lamer J (as he then was) disagreed with the majority on the final disposition of that case, a majority of the court accepted Lamer J's definition of a "court of competent jurisdiction" (at p. 515 CCC, p. 195 DLR):

—A court of competent jurisdiction in an extant case is a court that has jurisdiction over the person, the subject-matter and has, under the criminal or penal law, jurisdiction to grant the remedy.

Subsequent decisions of this court have reaffirmed the three-tiered test of *Mills*: see, for example, *Cuddy Chicks Ltd. v. Ontario (Labour Relations Board)* (1991), 81 DLR (4th) 121, [1991] 2 SCR 5, 50 Admin. LR 44, and *Tetreault-Gadoury v. Canada (Employment and Immigration Commission)* (1991), 81 DLR (4th) 358, [1991] 2 SCR 22, 50 Admin. LR 1. In each case it was held that a court or tribunal will only be a "court of competent jurisdiction" where the body in question has jurisdiction over the parties, the subject-matter, and the remedy sought by the complainant.

Most recently, this court applied the three-tiered test of *Mills* in *Weber v. Ontario Hydro* (1995), 125 DLR (4th) 583, [1995] 2 SCR 929, 30 Admin. LR (2d) 1. Writing for a majority of the court, McLachlin J made the following observations (at p. 606, paras. 65-6):

It is thus Parliament or the legislature that determines if a court is a court of competent jurisdiction; as McIntyre J puts it [in *Mills*], the jurisdiction of the various courts of Canada is fixed by Parliament and the legislatures, not by judges. Nor is there magic in labels; it is not the name of the tribunal that determines the matter, but its powers. (It may be noted that the French version of s. 24(1) uses "tribunal" rather than "cour.") The practical import of fitting Charter remedies into the existing system of tribunals, as McIntyre J notes, is that litigants have "direct" access to Charter remedies in the tribunal charged with deciding their case.

It follows from *Mills* that statutory tribunals created by Parliament or the legislatures may be courts of competent jurisdiction to grant Charter remedies, provided they have jurisdiction over the parties and the subject-matter of the dispute and are empowered to make the orders sought.

Clearly then, decisions of this court have established that jurisdiction over the parties, the subject-matter and the remedy are necessary conditions for a statutory tribunal to be considered a court of competent jurisdiction within the meaning of s. 24.

Even assuming that the Parole Board has jurisdiction over the parties and the subject-matter, I am satisfied, on the basis of (i) the structure and function of the board, and (ii) the language of the board's constituting statute, that it is not empowered to make the order sought.

The Parole Board acts in neither a judicial nor a quasi-judicial manner: *Mitchell v. The Queen* (1975), 24 CCC (2d) 241 at p. 257, 61 DLR (3d) 77 at p. 93, [1976] 2 SCR 570. The elements of a parole hearing are described by David Cole and Allan Manson in *Release from Imprisonment* (Toronto: Carswell, 1990). The authors point out that several elements of the hearing distinguish Parole Board proceedings from those which take place before a traditional court. For example, counsel appearing before the Parole Board serve an extremely limited function. According to Cole and Manson (at p. 428):

> Although counsel is present as an advocate, since the hearing is inquisitorial there is no one against whom counsel can act as an adversary. Indeed, counsel should recall throughout that as far as the Board is concerned, the only occasion on which he may speak, as outlined in the Regulation, is at the end of the hearing when he is given an opportunity to address the Board on behalf of the client.

In addition, the traditional rules of proof and evidence do not apply in post-suspension proceedings before the board. As Cole and Manson point out (at p. 431):

> While the Board will consider legal defences or mitigating circumstances where a new charge has been laid, in the post-suspension hearing context Board members do not regard themselves as constrained by the formal rules of the criminal law respecting the admissibility of evidence, the presumption of innocence, or the necessity for proof beyond a reasonable doubt.

Other differences between parole hearings and more traditional court proceedings include (1) the board lacks the power to issue subpoenas, (2) "evidence" is not presented under oath, and (3) the panel presiding over the hearing may have no legal training.

In the decision currently under review, the appeal division of the board described its function in the following terms:

> The function of the Board at a post-suspension review is quite distinct from that of the courts. The Board must decide whether the risk to society of [the respondent's] continued conditional release is undue. In making that determination, the Board will review all information available to it, including any information indicating a return to criminal activity in the community.
>
> This applies whether or not the charges in court have been withdrawn, stayed or dismissed.

Clearly then, the Parole Board does not hear and assess evidence, but instead acts on information. The Parole Board acts in an inquisitorial capacity without contending parties—the state's interests are not represented by counsel, and the parolee is not faced with a formal "case to meet." From a practical perspective, neither the board itself nor the proceedings in which it engages have been designed to engage in the balancing of factors that s. 24(2) demands.

In the risk assessment function of the board, the factors which predominate are those which concern the protection of society. The protection of the accused to ensure a fair trial and maintain the repute of the administration of justice which weighs so heavily in the application of s. 24(2) is overborne by the overriding societal interest. In assessing the risk to society, the emphasis is on ensuring that all reliable information is considered provided it has not been obtained improperly. As stated by Dickson J, as he then was, in *R v. Gardiner* (1982), 68 CCC (2d) 477 at pp. 513-14, 140 DLR (3d) 612 at p. 648, [1982] 2 SCR 368, in relation to sentencing proceedings:

> One of the hardest tasks confronting a trial judge is sentencing. The stakes are high for society and for the individual. Sentencing is the critical stage of the criminal justice system, and it is manifest that the judge should not be denied an opportunity to obtain relevant information by the imposition of all the restrictive evidentiary rules common to a trial. Yet the obtaining and weighing of such evidence should be fair. A substantial liberty interest of the offender is involved and the information obtained should be accurate and reliable.

These principles apply *a fortiori* to proceedings before the Parole Board in which the subject has already been tried, convicted and sentenced. As stated by the Supreme Court of the United States in *Morrissey v. Brewer*, 408 US 471 (1972) at p. 489:

> We emphasize there is no thought to equate this second stage of parole revocation to a criminal prosecution in any sense. It is a narrow inquiry; the process should be flexible enough to consider evidence including letters, affidavits, and other material that would not be admissible in an adversary criminal trial.

Like the basic structure and function of the Parole Board, the language of the board's enabling statute makes it clear that the board lacks the ability or jurisdiction to exclude relevant evidence. The language of the *Corrections and Conditional Release Act* confers on the board a broad inclusionary mandate. Not only is it not bound to apply the traditional rules of evidence, but it is required to take into account "all available information that is relevant to a case." No mention is made of any power to apply exclusionary rules of evidence. Indeed, such a provision would conflict with its duty to consider "all available information that is relevant."

I conclude from the foregoing that the board does not have jurisdiction over the remedy sought. It is not, therefore, a court of competent jurisdiction within the meaning of s. 24 of the Charter.

I am supported in this conclusion by the decisions of the US circuit courts. The US Supreme Court has not specifically dealt with the applicability of the exclusionary rule to parole proceedings, although the logical extension of the statement in *Morrissey* to which I refer above would suggest that the rule does not apply. The issue has been dealt with by 10 of the federal circuit courts. Except for the Fourth Circuit, all have held the rule inapplicable. In the Fourth Circuit, which is the exception, the Court of

Appeals refused to apply the exclusionary rule in state probation proceedings: see *Grimsley v. Dodson*, 696 F2d 303 (1982). One circuit, the Second Circuit, admits of an exception in the case of warrantless searches.

In *United States v. Winsett*, 518 F2d 51 (9th Cir. 1975), it was held that a board's mandate to consider "all reliable evidence" was inconsistent with allowing the board to exclude relevant evidence. The statement in *Pratt v. United States Parole Commission*, 717 F Supp. 382 (EDNC 1989), is typical of the reasoning in these cases (at p. 387):

> this parole revocation proceeding is a far cry from a full blown criminal prosecution. Constitutional protections vindicated by the exclusionary rule do not apply with full force in the minimum due process environment of the parole revocation hearing. Societal costs thought worthy of paying for the operation [of] the rule have already been exacted. Nothing is served by exacting that full measure of costs a second time. The very special needs of supervision … would be sacrificed if parole authorities were prohibited from weighing the full extent of petitioner's conduct by reason of the exclusionary rule. The parole revocation decision must meet the preponderance of proof standard … after those tenets of minimum due process have been followed. Nowhere does the beyond-a-reasonable-doubt burden apply. The right to a trial by jury does not apply. The parolee does not even enjoy the right to a judicial decision maker. Neither, in my view, does a parolee have the right to insist on strict adherence to fourth amendment standards. And, for the reasons set out above, in my view the exclusionary rule does not apply either.

See also *United States ex rel. Sperling v. Fitzpatrick*, 426 F2d 1161 (2d Cir. 1970), and *United States v. Bazzano*, 712 F2d 826 (3d Cir. 1983). In each case, the courts have held that policy considerations favour denying parole or probation boards the authority to exclude relevant information. In my view, many of these policy considerations are equally relevant in the Canadian context. As a result, I conclude that the Parole Board is not a court of competent jurisdiction for the purposes of excluding relevant evidence under s. 24(2) of the Charter.

B. Procedures Where Evidence Is Gathered Improperly

Having found that the National Parole Board is not a court of competent jurisdiction within the meaning of s. 24 of the Charter, it remains to be determined what procedures the board must follow when faced with evidence that has been gathered in a manner violating the rights of the parolee.

The law is well settled that statutory tribunals such as the Parole Board are bound by a duty of fairness in deciding upon the rights or privileges of individuals. For example, in *Cardinal v. Director of Kent Institution* (1985), 23 CCC (3d) 118, 24 DLR (4th) 44, [1985] 2 SCR 643, it was held that a prison director was required to act fairly in determining whether or not to segregate a prisoner from the rest of the prison population. Writing for a unanimous court, Le Dain J held (at p. 126 CCC, pp. 51-2 DLR) that:

> This Court has affirmed that there is, as a general common law principle, a duty of procedural fairness lying on every public authority making an administrative decision which is not of a legislative nature and which affects the rights, privileges or interests

of an individual: *Re Nicholson and Haldimand-Norfolk Regional Board of Com'rs of Police* (1978), 88 DLR (3d) 671, [1979] 1 SCR 311, 23 NR 410; *Martineau v. Matsqui Institution Disciplinary Board (No. 2)*, (1979), 50 CCC (2d) 353, 106 DLR (3d) 385, [1980] 1 SCR 602; *A-G Can. v. Inuit Tapirisat of Canada et al.* (1980), 115 DLR (3d) 1, [1980] 2 SCR 735, 33 NR 304.

Clearly, the Parole Board's decision to revoke a parolee's conditional release has a profound effect on the rights of the parolee. The board's decision will conclusively determine whether the applicant is released into the community or retained in the confines of a prison or penitentiary. As a result, in making that decision to grant or revoke parole, the board is required to act fairly.

The duty of the Parole Board to act fairly can also be found in the board's constituting statute, the *Corrections and Conditional Release Act*. For example, s. 4(g) of that Act provides that all correctional decisions must be "made in a forthright and fair manner, with access by the offender to an effective grievance procedure." Similarly, s. 101(f) of the Act provides that the Parole Board must pursue a "fair and understandable conditional release process." Finally, s. 147(1)(a) of the Act provides that an appeal of the board's decision lies in all cases where the board "failed to observe a principle of fundamental justice." Clearly, these provisions impose upon the board a duty to act in accordance with the principles of fairness.

What is the content of the board's "duty to act fairly"? The content of the duty of fairness varies according to the structure and the function of the board or tribunal in question. In the parole context, the Parole Board must ensure that the information upon which it acts is reliable and persuasive. To take an extreme example, information extracted by torture could not be considered reliable by the board. It would be manifestly unfair for the board to act on this kind of information. As a result, the board would be under a duty to exclude such information, whether or not the information was relevant to the decision. Wherever information or "evidence" is presented to the board, the board must make a determination concerning the source of that information, and decide whether or not it would be fair to allow the information to affect the board's decision.

In determining whether or not it would be fair to consider a particular piece of information, the board will often be guided by decisions of the courts regarding the exclusion of relevant evidence. For instance, where incriminating statements are obtained from the offender, the law of confessions based on an admixture of reliability and fairness will be pertinent although not binding. The board may, in appropriate circumstances, conclude that reliance on a coerced confession is unfair. Decisions concerning s. 24(2) of the Charter will also be relevant to the board's final decision. However, cases decided under s. 24(2) should not be determinative of the board's decision to exclude relevant information based on the principles of fairness. Obviously, different considerations will often apply in the parole context. For example, s. 101(a) of the *Corrections and Conditional Release Act* requires "that the protection of society be the paramount consideration in the determination of any case." This will accordingly be a guiding principle where the board is required to rule on the admissibility of a particular piece of information. The board's expertise and experience concerning the protection of society will aid the board in arriving at a decision.

Should the board fail to abide by the principles of fairness in making those decisions, an appeal lies to the appeal division under s. 147(1)(a) of the *Corrections and Conditional Release Act*. The board's decision is also subject to judicial review.

As a statutory tribunal, the board is also subject to the dictates of s. 7 of the Charter. In this regard, it must comply with the principles of fundamental justice in respect to the conduct of its proceedings. This does not mean that it must possess or exercise a power to exclude evidence that has been obtained in a manner that contravenes the Charter. If this were so, it would tend to make the inclusion of s. 24(2) of the Charter superfluous. While the principles of fundamental justice are not limited to procedural justice, it does not follow that a tribunal that applies the rules of fairness and natural justice does not comply with s. 7. If the myriad of statutory tribunals that have traditionally been obliged to accord nothing more than procedural fairness were obliged to comply with the full gamut of principles of fundamental justice, the administrative landscape in the country would undergo a fundamental change. The statement in *Reference re: Section 94(2) of the Motor Vehicle Act* (1985), 23 CCC (3d) 289, 24 DLR (4th) 536, [1985] 2 SCR 486, to the effect that the principles of fundamental justice involve more than natural justice meant that the court was empowered in appropriate circumstances to invalidate substantive law and was not limited to judicial review of the procedural practices of a statutory body.

It is a basic tenet of our legal system that the rules of natural justice and procedural fairness are adjusted by reference to the context in which they are administered. This is one of the basic tenets of our legal system to which Lamer J (as he then was) referred in *Reference re: Section 94(2) of the Motor Vehicle Act* as the source of the principles of fundamental justice. In my opinion, adherence by the board to the practice and procedures outlined above constitutes full compliance with the principles of fundamental justice and, therefore, with s. 7 of the Charter.

C. Disposition

I would allow this appeal on the ground that the National Parole Board is not a court of competent jurisdiction. I would accordingly set aside the judgment of the British Columbia Court of Appeal. Ordinarily, I would remit the respondent's case to the Parole Board, to be dealt with in accordance with these reasons. However, since the respondent's sentence has already expired, the Parole Board is *functus officio*.

MAJOR J (McLachlin J concurring, dissenting):

I. Introduction

I have read the reasons of my colleague Justice Sopinka which set out the facts and statutory provisions relevant to this appeal. With respect, I do not agree with his conclusion that the National Parole Board lacks the jurisdiction under s. 24(2) to exclude evidence which has been obtained in a manner that infringes Charter rights. Nor do I agree that more than a decade after the introduction of the Charter, the application of the common law doctrine of procedural fairness by the Parole Board is sufficient to protect the constitutional rights of parolees.

In my view, the National Parole Board is a "court of competent jurisdiction" within the meaning of s. 24 of the Charter. I have reached this conclusion based on an examination of the previous decisions of this court, the statutory provisions which govern the Parole Board and the application of basic Charter principles.

As a "court of competent jurisdiction" for the purposes of granting an exclusionary remedy under s. 24(2), the National Parole Board can determine whether to exclude from its consideration information which was obtained in contravention of Charter rights where the admission of such evidence would bring the administration of justice into disrepute. As a result, in a parole determination or revocation hearing, the parolee has a direct opportunity to raise a breach of Charter rights and to seek an effective remedy.

The National Parole Board has the jurisdiction and the responsibility to consider whether a breach of Charter rights has occurred according to the legal tests established in the jurisprudence of this court for determining violations of these rights.

The National Parole Board must then determine, under s. 24(2), whether the admission of the evidence in a parole granting or revocation hearing would bring the administration of justice into disrepute. In the context of the National Parole Board, the administration of justice means the administration of the parole process.

Although the National Parole Board has the jurisdiction to exclude evidence, it also has a mandate to admit a broad range of evidence in keeping with its paramount goal of protecting the public from recidivist offenders. In light of its legislated mandate, it will be an unusual case where the National Parole Board will exclude evidence under the s. 24(2) test of bringing the administration of the parole process into disrepute.

...

I agree with this description of Charter rights and the role of s. 24 in guaranteeing that Charter rights are actually enforced. If the Charter is to remain a "vibrant and vigorous instrument for the protection of the rights and freedoms of Canadians" there must be an effective remedy where there has been a violation.

Following *Mills*, a trilogy of cases determined that where the enabling statute grants the power to determine questions of law, an administrative tribunal has the power and responsibility not to apply provisions of that enabling statute which are incompatible with the Charter: *Douglas/Kwantlen Faculty Assn. v. Douglas College* (1990), 77 DLR (4th) 94, [1990] 3 SCR 570, 50 Admin. LR 69; *Cuddy Chicks Ltd. v. Ontario (Labour Relations Board)* (1991), 81 DLR (4th) 121, [1991] 2 SCR 5, 50 Admin. LR 44; *Tetreault-Gadoury v. Canada (Employment and Immigration Commission)* (1991), 81 DLR (4th) 358, [1991] 2 SCR 22, 50 Admin. LR 1. In these cases the court affirmed the correctness of the three-pronged test enunciated by Lamer J in *Mills* for determining a "court of competent jurisdiction": jurisdiction over the parties, the subject-matter and the remedy sought by the complainant. It was not necessary, however, to determine whether the tribunals in question were courts of competent jurisdiction under s. 24 of the Charter. The power and responsibility not to apply statutory provisions which are unconstitutional was found to flow from s. 52(1) of the *Constitution Act, 1982*, which declares every law which is inconsistent with the Charter to be of no effect.

Of particular relevance to this appeal are the comments of La Forest J, who wrote the majority judgment in each of the trilogy of cases, about the advantages of having constitutional issues determined by an administrative tribunal. This question is discussed in detail in *Douglas/Kwantlen Faculty Assn. v. Douglas College*. At p. 125,

La Forest J notes that the primary advantage of having tribunals determine constitutional questions is to ensure that a citizen can rely on Charter guarantees when the tribunal is in a position to determine the rights of that citizen:

> [I]f there are disadvantages to allowing arbitrators or other administrative tribunals to determine constitutional issues arising in the course of exercising their mandates, there are clear advantages as well. First and foremost, of course, is that the Constitution must be respected. The citizen, when appearing before decision-making bodies set up to determine his or her rights and duties, should be entitled to assert the rights and freedoms guaranteed by the Constitution.

In *R v. Seaboyer* (1991), 66 CCC (3d) 321 at pp. 412-13, 83 DLR (4th) 193 at pp. 284-5, [1991] 2 SCR 577, McLachlin J noted that it is this right of a Canadian citizen to rely on Charter guarantees when there is a final determination of "rights and duties" which helps to explain why the arbitrator in *Douglas College* was held to be able to determine constitutional questions but the preliminary inquiry judge in *Mills* was not:

> The position of a judge or magistrate on a preliminary inquiry is readily distinguished from the position of the arbitrator in *Douglas College*. The legislation governing the arbitrator in that case conferred on him wide powers to decide both questions of fact and law and to finally resolve the dispute between the parties. That task could not be achieved without deciding the Charter issue. As La Forest J put it in *Douglas College*, at p. 125: "The citizen, when appearing before decision-making bodies set up to determine his or her rights and duties, should be entitled to assert the rights and freedoms guaranteed by the Constitution." The contrary is true for a judge on a preliminary inquiry, whose only task is to determine whether prosecution in other proceedings is warranted. The rights of the accused need not and should not be resolved at this initial stage. The lack of power in a preliminary inquiry judge to decide constitutional questions does not prevent an accused from asserting his or her Charter rights; it merely defers the process until the accused is before the decision-making body charged with the task of fully determining the accused's "rights and duties"—the trial court.

Thus, the decisions in the trilogy of cases are consistent with the principle enunciated by Lamer J in *Mills* that where there is a Charter right there must also be a Charter remedy.

In *Douglas College*, La Forest J also noted a number of other advantages which flow from allowing tribunals to determine constitutional questions. By raising Charter issues before the tribunal, the Charter issue can be dealt with in the context in which it arises without necessitating duplicate, expensive and time-consuming application to a court. A specialized tribunal in reaching its decision sifts the facts and compiles a record for the benefit of a reviewing court. Also the expertise and specialized competence of the tribunal can be of invaluable assistance in constitutional interpretation in order to ensure the primacy of the Constitution.

In the recent case of *Weber v. Ontario Hydro* (1995), 125 DLR (4th) 583, [1995] 2 SCR 929, 30 Admin. LR (2d) 1, this court addressed the question of whether an administrative tribunal could be a court of competent jurisdiction for the purposes of granting a remedy under s. 24 of the Charter. The issue in that case was whether a labour arbitrator had the jurisdiction to award damages under s. 24 of the Charter for surveillance by the employer which allegedly breached the rights guaranteed by ss. 7 and 8. The majority held that a labour tribunal is a court of competent jurisdiction for the purpose of granting damages pursuant to s. 24.

In holding that a labour tribunal is a court of competent jurisdiction, McLachlin J for the majority applied the three-pronged test for the definition of a court of competent jurisdiction established in *Mills* and relied on the advantages of having tribunals decide constitutional issues which are set out in *Douglas College*. McLachlin J noted that the question of whether a tribunal is a court of competent jurisdiction is answered by examining the enabling statute since it is Parliament and not judges who establish jurisdiction. She also held that there is no magic in labels and that the fact that a body is labelled a "tribunal" rather than a "court" is not determinative. At p. 606, paras. 65-6, she concluded:

> It is thus Parliament or the legislature that determines if a court is a court of competent jurisdiction; as McIntyre J puts it, the jurisdiction of the various courts of Canada is fixed by Parliament and the legislatures, not by judges. Nor is there magic in labels; it is not the name of the tribunal that determines the matter, but its powers. (It may be noted that the French version of s. 24(1) uses "tribunal" rather than "cour.") The practical import of fitting Charter remedies into the existing system of tribunals, as McIntyre J notes, is that litigants have "direct" access to Charter remedies in the tribunal charged with deciding their case.
>
> It follows from *Mills* that statutory tribunals created by Parliament or the legislatures may be courts of competent jurisdiction to grant Charter remedies, provided they have jurisdiction over the parties and the subject-matter of the dispute and are empowered to make the orders sought.

It is also important to note that the majority of the court in *Weber* rejected the argument that only a court of law in the traditional sense with legally trained judges should be regarded as a court of competent jurisdiction. Iacobucci J, in dissent, summarized the view which was not accepted at p. 592, para. 16:

> In short, the choice of the word "court" in s. 24(1) reflects an intention to confer the ability to decide questions of remedies for Charter violations on those institutions which are conceptually "courts." It is the characteristics of a "court": the rules of procedure and evidence, the independence and legal training of its judges, the possibility of hearing from a third party intervener such as an Attorney General or an *amicus curiae*, which make it the most suitable forum to hear a s. 24(1) application.

In my opinion, the recent decision of this court in *Weber* is correct and is consistent with earlier case law. While the trilogy of tribunal cases did not decide the issue of whether tribunals are courts of competent jurisdiction for the purposes of s. 24, it did decide that where a tribunal has the power to consider questions of law, it can and must also make determinations about the constitutional validity of the provisions of its enabling statute. In those cases this court clearly rejected the view that the lack of legal training on the part of tribunal members precludes them from making constitutional determinations. As La Forest J noted in *Cuddy Chicks*, at pp. 129-30:

It must be emphasized that the process of Charter decision-making is not confined to abstract ruminations on constitutional theory. In the case of Charter matters which arise in a particular regulatory context, the ability of the decision-maker to analyze competing policy concerns is critical. Therefore, while board members need not have formal legal training, it remains that they have a very meaningful role to play in the resolution of constitutional issues. The informed view of the board, as manifested in a sensitivity to relevant facts and an ability to compile a cogent record, is also of invaluable assistance.

The considerations which animated this court's decisions in the trilogy of tribunal cases apply with equal force when considering whether a tribunal has the jurisdiction to grant Charter remedies under s. 24. Of primary importance is the ability of the citizen to rely upon and assert Charter rights in a direct manner in the normal procedural context in which the issue arises.

It is also axiomatic to the earlier case law that in order to protect the vibrancy and vigour of Charter protections, the citizen must have access to a meaningful remedy for Charter violations where there is to be a final determination of his or her rights and duties.

Given that administrative tribunals, such as the Parole Board in this case, have jurisdiction to impose punitive sanctions, it would be an unusual result if they lacked the ability to grant individuals Charter remedies, not at large but within the parameters of their legislated jurisdiction.

There is no reason in principle why any of the practical advantages enunciated by La Forest J in the trilogy should apply with any less force to a tribunal granting a remedy under s. 24 than to a tribunal declining to enforce a constitutionally invalid statutory provision. If anything, tailoring a specific Charter remedy for a specific applicant before a tribunal is more suited to a tribunal's special role in determining rights on a case-by-case basis in the tribunal's area of expertise. It has less serious ramifications than determining that a statutory provision will not be applied on Charter grounds.

...

Sopinka J concludes that even assuming the Parole Board has jurisdiction over the parties and the subject-matter he is satisfied that the board is not empowered to make the order sought. By relying on factors such as the lack of an adversarial process, the lack of formal rules of evidence and the lack of legal training of Parole Board members he finds that the Parole Board is not a court of competent jurisdiction. My colleague resurrects the requirement that a "court of competent jurisdiction" must be a traditional court. The majority of the court in *Weber* rejected this view. Moreover, the factors relied on by Sopinka J have never been accepted as reasons for limiting a tribunal's power to determine constitutional issues.

The *Weber* case is consistent with the prior case law of this court which holds that the test for a "court of competent jurisdiction" is to be determined by an examination of the statute to see whether the tribunal in question has been granted jurisdiction over the parties, the subject-matter and the remedy sought. It is therefore necessary to turn to an examination of the statute which governs the National Parole Board to determine whether it meets this tripartite test.

It is indisputable that the National Parole Board has jurisdiction over the party and the subject-matter. The party is an offender eligible for parole and the subject-matter is the granting or revocation of parole. Section 107(1) of the *Corrections and Conditional Release Act* grants the Parole Board the exclusive jurisdiction and absolute discretion to finally determine whether parole should be granted or revoked:

> 107(1) Subject to this Act, the *Prisons and Reformatories Act*, the *Transfer of Offenders Act* and the *Criminal Code*, the Board has exclusive jurisdiction and absolute discretion
>
> (a) to grant parole to an offender;
>
> (b) to terminate or to revoke the parole or statutory release of an offender, whether or not the offender is in custody under a warrant of apprehension issued as a result of the suspension of the parole or statutory release;
>
> (c) to cancel a decision to grant parole to an offender, or to cancel the suspension, termination or revocation of the parole or statutory release of an offender.

The more difficult question on this appeal is whether the National Parole Board has been granted jurisdiction over the remedy sought. Some care should be taken to appropriately define the remedy sought by the respondent in this case.

As Lambert JA pointed out in the reasons for the majority in the British Columbia Court of Appeal (93 CCC (3d) 415, 35 CR (4th) 92, 24 CRR (2d) 329), the test would not lead anywhere if the remedy was considered to be applying the Charter in order to exclude evidence at a parole hearing: that remains the question and not the answer. The majority of this court in *Weber* rejected the view that enabling legislation must expressly confer the jurisdiction to grant a Charter remedy before this stage of the test is met. Such an approach would require that any adjudicative bodies pre-existing the Charter would be barred from applying it unless their constituting statutes were amended.

This view is clearly untenable and inconsistent with the result in *Mills*. Provincial courts are a ready example of bodies entitled to grant Charter remedies without their constituting statutes being amended.

On the other hand, I would respectfully reject the definition of remedy chosen by Lambert JA, who held (at p. 437) that "the remedy is the granting of parole." This approach defines the remedy at too great a level of abstraction and seems to mix the remedy and subject-matter. I accept the argument of the appellants that to define the remedy in this manner is tantamount to saying that every tribunal which can make an order of some nature has Charter jurisdiction.

In my view, the correct approach lies between these two extremes. The remedy to be considered under the third stage of the *Mills* test is the specific remedy which the applicant seeks under the Charter for the breach of a Charter right. However, the question to be determined is not whether the legislation grants the jurisdiction to direct this remedy under the Charter but rather simply whether it grants the jurisdiction to grant this sort of remedy.

For example, in *Mills* the remedy sought under the Charter was a stay of proceedings in order to remedy pre-trial delay. A preliminary inquiry judge is not a court of competent jurisdiction because he does not have the power under the *Criminal Code* to grant a stay of proceedings. On other hand, a trial judge has the jurisdiction to grant this sort of remedy and thus is a court of competent jurisdiction although there is no specific legislative authorization in the *Criminal Code* to grant Charter remedies. Likewise in *Weber*, a labour arbitration board was found to be a court of competent jurisdiction to award damages under s. 24(1) because an award of damages lies within the sphere of remedies that this kind of board is authorized to grant. A specific legislative jurisdiction to grant Charter damages was not required.

In this case the respondent seeks to have evidence excluded under s. 24(2) of the Charter. The remedy sought is the exclusion of evidence. Therefore, the final stage in the application of the *Mills* test is whether the legislation which governs the National Parole Board either expressly or implicitly grants the jurisdiction to exclude evidence. In my view, it does.

In deciding what information to consider in parole determination deliberations, the National Parole Board must strike a balance between the inclusion and the exclusion of information. Thus, although the board has the jurisdiction to exclude evidence on a limited number of grounds, it also has a broad inclusionary mandate. The board's statutory obligation to include a broader range of information than would be considered under the traditional rules of evidence is fully in keeping with its role of public protection and as a watchguard against recidivism by parolees.

Section 101 provides that the National Parole Board should take into consideration all available information that is relevant to the case:

> 101. The principles that shall guide the Board and the provincial parole boards in achieving the purpose of conditional release are
>
>   (b) that parole boards take into consideration all available information that is relevant to a case, including the stated reasons and recommendations of the sentencing judge, any other information from the trial or the sentencing hearing, information and assessments provided by correctional authorities, and information obtained from victims and the offender

In argument, the appellants emphasized the fact the statute uses the term "information" which is broader than the term "evidence" and my colleague relies on the fact that the board is not bound by formal rules of evidence. Neither of these considerations resolves the issue of whether the board is entitled to exclude evidence. Evidence is simply a subset of the term "information" and there may be exclusion beyond that provided for in formal evidentiary rules.

In my opinion, the statute expressly contemplates a power to exclude information from its consideration since it restricts the board to a consideration of relevant information. In *Seaboyer*, at pp. 389-90 CCC, pp. 261-2 DLR, McLachlin J held that it is a principle of fundamental justice that a finder of fact consider only what is relevant and, with limited exceptions, all that is relevant. She also noted that this relevancy principle underlies the formal rules of evidence:

> It is fundamental to our system of justice that the rules of evidence should permit the judge and jury to get at the truth and properly determine the issues. This goal is reflected in the basic tenet of relevance which underlies all our rules of evidence: see *R v. Morris* (1983), 7 CCC (3d) 97, [1983] 2 SCR 190, and *R v. Corbett* (1988), 41 CCC (3d) 385,

[1988] 1 SCR 670, 64 CR (3d) 1. In general, nothing is to be received which is not logically probative of some matter requiring to be proved and everything which is probative should be received, unless its exclusion can be justified on some other ground.

The governing statute also requires that the board exclude evidence which it deems to be unreliable or inaccurate. Section 147(1)(d) of the *Corrections and Conditional Release Act* provides for an appeal of the board's decision to the appeal division on the ground that the board "based its decision on erroneous or incomplete information."

As noted by Sopinka J the duty to not consider information which is unreliable or unpersuasive also arises from the common law doctrine of procedural fairness which applies to a statutory tribunal such as the Parole Board: see *Cardinal v. Director of Kent Institution* (1985), 23 CCC (3d) 118 at p. 126, 24 DLR (4th) 44 at pp. 51-2, [1985] 2 SCR 643. In *R v. Gardiner* (1982), 68 CCC (2d) 477 at p. 514, 140 DLR (3d) 612 at p. 648, [1982] 2 SCR 368, Dickson J, as he then was, stated in relation to sentencing proceedings which, like parole hearings, involve a relaxation of formal evidentiary rules: "A substantial liberty interest of the offender is involved and the information obtained should be accurate and reliable."

The governing statute contemplates that the board must exclude from its consideration any information which is irrelevant or which is unreliable. Thus, although it is not bound by formal evidentiary rules, the board is bound to observe the two guiding principles which inform the traditional rules of evidence: relevance and reliability. The statutory requirement that the board must exclude from its consideration information which is irrelevant or unreliable establishes that the board has jurisdiction to exclude evidence. Therefore, the board has jurisdiction over the remedy sought by the respondent in this case, and the third stage of the *Mills* test is met.

The fact that the National Parole Board meets the three requirements of the *Mills* test is sufficient to establish that the board is a court of competent jurisdiction to grant a remedy under s. 24 of the Charter. It is worth noting that the governing statute also contemplates that the board must apply the Charter. Section 147(1) provides:

> 147(1) An offender may appeal a decision of the Board to the Appeal Division on the ground that the Board, in making its decision,
>> (a) failed to observe a principle of fundamental justice;
>> (b) made an error of law;
>> (c) breached or failed to apply a policy adopted pursuant to subsection 151(2).

The legislation requires that the Parole Board has to observe the principles of fundamental justice in making its decision. This echoes the wording of s. 7 of the Charter, which guarantees the right not to be deprived of liberty except in accordance with the principles of fundamental justice.

It is appropriate that the Parole Board, which can substantially interfere with a liberty interest by granting, denying or revoking parole, should be required to apply the principles of fundamental justice. The principles of fundamental justice require more than the common law doctrine of procedural fairness relied on by Sopinka J.

The legislation also permits review for errors of law, which implicitly recognizes that the board can determine issues of law. The capacity of a statutory tribunal to decide questions of law has been held by this court in the trilogy of tribunal cases to be determinative of whether a tribunal can decide Charter issues which arise in the exercise of its statutory mandate.

Finally, an appeal is allowed for failure to apply policies adopted under s. 151(2). The policy adopted under s. 151(2) in relation to appeals sets out the mandate of the appeal division in terms which require it to ensure compliance with the Charter:

> The Appeal Division reviews decisions of the Board, upon the appeal of a decision by the offender pursuant to s. 147(1) of the *Corrections and Conditional Release Act*. The Appeal Division, through its review process, and decision-making authority, and the issuance of Appeal Division Reports, contributes to the quality of conditional release decisions by ensuring that decisions and decision-making processes are fair and equitable and comply with the legislation, the *Charter of Rights and Freedoms*, the Board's policies and procedures, and principles of the National Parole Board Mission Statement.

The application of the *Mills* test leads to the conclusion that the board is a court of competent jurisdiction for the purposes of granting a remedy under s. 24(2) and an examination of the governing statute demonstrates a legislative intention that Charter principles apply to the determination of the liberty interests of parolees. It remains only to consider policy issues.

As discussed earlier, the policy considerations raised by Sopinka J (that the board does not use an adversarial process, that formal rules of evidence do not apply and that not all board members have legal training) have been rejected by this court as inadequate reasons for preventing a statutory tribunal from determining constitutional issues. On the other hand, the advantages of having a tribunal decide such issues, set out by La Forest J in *Douglas College*, apply in support of recognizing the Parole Board as a court of competent jurisdiction.

Recognition of the Parole Board as a court of competent jurisdiction would enable the Charter issue to be dealt with in the context in which it arises without, as previously noted, necessitating an expensive and time-consuming application to a court. The Parole Board's determination would find facts and compile a record for the benefit of a reviewing court. The expertise and specialized competence of the tribunal could be of invaluable assistance in constitutional interpretation particularly on the question of when the admission of unconstitutionally obtained evidence in the parole determination process might bring the administration of justice into disrepute.

However, the overriding policy consideration which militates in favour of finding that the Parole Board is a court of competent jurisdiction is the fact that the Parole Board has the exclusive jurisdiction to finally determine the liberty interests of a parolee. I agree with Lambert JA who concluded that if the Parole Board is not a court of competent jurisdiction then the parolee is deprived of Charter protection with respect to unconstitutionally obtained evidence, at p. 440:

> Counsel for the National Parole Board has firmly maintained that the National Parole Board is not a court of competent jurisdiction under s. 24 of the Charter. If he is right, then when the National Parole Board refuses to consider whether to grant the Charter remedy of exclusion of evidence that is relevant and admissible, because it was obtained in the course of a Charter breach, then that refusal cannot be a jurisdictional

error or an error in law. Accordingly, on that approach there can be no remedy whatever for a breach of a prisoner's Charter rights leading to a loss of statutory release. The reason is that if the National Parole Board is not a court of competent jurisdiction neither the Supreme Court of British Columbia nor the Federal Court, Trial Division, can say that there was an error in jurisdiction or an error in law in the National Parole Board failing to consider a question that it is not empowered to consider.

That result, on the basis of the reasoning of counsel for the National Parole Board, would put the prisoner beyond the protection of the Charter in relation to evidence improperly obtained.

In my view, it is wholly inconsistent with the principles of Charter interpretation enunciated by this court on numerous occasions for a Charter right to exist without a citizen having access to a Charter remedy.

If the Charter is to be a robust and vigorous instrument for the protection of the rights of all Canadians and if Charter guarantees are to be meaningful and respected there must be access to a Charter remedy where rights have been violated. The broad and liberal interpretation of the Charter espoused by this court requires at a minimum respect for what Lamer J in *Mills* (at p. 518 CCC, p. 198 DLR) termed "the basic proposition that there should always be a court of competent jurisdiction to award such relief as is just and appropriate in the circumstances." Access to a remedy should not be denied to a citizen simply because he is already under detention by the state. The Charter's benefits apply to everyone, including prisoners: see *Weatherall v. Canada (Attorney-General)* (1993), 83 CCC (3d) 1 sub nom. *Conway v. Canada (Attorney-General)*, 105 DLR (4th) 210, [1993] 2 SCR 872.

The proposition that there must be a Charter remedy where rights have been violated applies with particular force to a tribunal which has the power to finally determine issues which substantially affect the liberty of an individual. The role of the National Parole Board cannot be compared to that of a preliminary inquiry judge whose only role is to determine whether there is a sufficiency of evidence to proceed to trial. Nor can it be compared to that of a statutory tribunal whose mandate is limited to the granting of civil remedies such as damages. It is much more directly analogous to that of a trial court judge, who, subject to appeal for errors of law or jurisdiction, can finally determine the liberty interest of an individual.

Sopinka J seeks to minimize the impact of finding that the National Parole Board cannot grant a Charter remedy by noting that the parolee still enjoys the protection of the common law guarantee of procedural fairness. With respect, it cannot be assumed that the common law doctrine of procedural fairness is co-extensive with the guarantee of the "principles of fundamental justice" in the Charter which is echoed in the *Corrections and Conditional Release Act*.

Procedural fairness is simply one aspect of the doctrine of natural justice which is applied at common law to administrative tribunals. This court has consistently refused to restrict the substantive guarantee of fundamental justice in s. 7 to the procedural realm. In *Reference re: Section 94(2) of the Motor Vehicle Act* (1985), 23 CCC (3d) 289, 24 DLR (4th) 536, [1985] 2 SCR 486, this court was unanimous in finding that " 'fundamental justice,' as the term is used in the Charter, involves more than natural justice (which is largely procedural) and includes as well a substantive element": per McIntyre J at p. 293 CCC, p. 541 DLR. As Lamer J writing for the majority elaborated at pp. 301-2 CCC, pp. 548-50 DLR:

> I am of the view that it would be wrong to interpret the term "fundamental justice" as being synonymous with natural justice as the Attorney-General of British Columbia and others have suggested. To do so would strip the protected interests of much, if not most, of their content and leave the "right" to life, liberty and security of the person in a sorely emaciated state. Such a result would be inconsistent with the broad, affirmative language in which those rights are expressed and equally inconsistent with the approach adopted by this Court toward the interpretation of Charter rights in *Law Society of Upper Canada v. Skapinker* (1984), 11 CCC (3d) 481, 9 DLR (4th) 161, [1984] 1 SCR 357, per Estey J and *Hunter v. Southam Inc.*, supra.
>
> The principles of fundamental justice are to be found in the basic tenets of our legal system. They do not lie in the realm of general public policy but in the inherent domain of the judiciary as guardian of the justice system. Such an approach to the interpretation of "principles of fundamental justice" is consistent with the wording and structure of s. 7, the context of the section, i.e., ss. 8 to 14, and the character and larger objects of the Charter itself. It provides meaningful content for the s. 7 guarantee all the while avoiding adjudication of policy matters.
>
> Thus, it seems to me that to replace "fundamental justice" with the term "natural justice" misses the mark entirely.

In the context of the admission of evidence, procedural fairness looks only to the use of evidence in the proceedings (i.e., issues of reliability and relevancy), whereas the principles of fundamental justice require an examination of whether constitutional guarantees were respected in the manner in which the evidence was obtained.

Moreover, the mere fact that protections found in the common law may be substantially co-extensive with Charter protections is not sufficient justification for denying a citizen the opportunity to obtain a just and appropriate remedy for a Charter breach.

The Charter provides significant protections to Canadians and governs every aspect of the interaction between the state and the individual in Canada. The view that a citizen must be content with the protections offered by the common law in spite of Charter guarantees is a reactionary approach to constitutional rights which has not been endorsed by this court.

Our constitutional jurisprudence has developed on the basis that the Charter should be given a broad and purposive interpretation. It is consistent with this view that a generous approach be taken to granting Charter remedies. Generally speaking, it is preferable to find tribunals capable of granting constitutional remedies where those lie within their statutory mandate. In the event that a tribunal errs in this regard, a court can correct the error. As La Forest J points out, statutory tribunals "can expect no curial deference with respect to constitutional decisions": *Cuddy Chicks*, at p. 130.

...

I therefore conclude that the majority of the British Columbia Court of Appeal was correct to hold that the National Parole Board is a court of competent jurisdiction for the purposes raised on this appeal and would dismiss the appeal.

Remedy

I am in agreement with both parties that Lambert JA, on behalf of the court below, misconceived the nature of *certiorari* in aid of *habeas corpus* believing it to be necessary to quash the decision of the National Parole Board. Only the Federal Court has jurisdiction to grant *certiorari* as a remedy with respect to a decision of the National Parole Board. *Certiorari* in aid of *habeas corpus* is the means by which a reviewing court may obtain the evidentiary record for the purpose of determining an application for *habeas corpus*: see *Re Cardinal and The Queen* (1982), 67 CCC (2d) 252, 137 DLR (3d) 145, [1982] 3 WWR 593 (BC CA) at pp. 269-70; reversed on other grounds 23 CCC (3d) 118, 24 DLR (4th) 44, [1985] 2 SCR 643 (sub nom. *Cardinal v. Director of Kent Institution*).

This appeal arose from an application for *habeas corpus*. Once it is determined that the respondent was unlawfully detained owing to the failure of the National Parole to exercise its jurisdiction to determine the constitutional issue raised by the respondent, the respondent is entitled to request the court to grant a writ of *habeas corpus* to relieve him from unlawful detention. However, the court retains the discretion at common law not to issue a writ of *habeas corpus* but rather to direct that the constitutional challenge be remitted back to the tribunals for a determination on the merits: *R v. Pearson* (1992), 77 CCC (3d) 124 at p. 148, [1992] 3 SCR 665, 17 CR (4th) 1, per Lamer CJC. In my view, in most instances the appropriate remedy would be an order remitting the matter back to the National Parole Board for a further hearing.

Disposition

In the particular circumstances of this case in which the respondent's sentence has already expired, I agree with Sopinka J that the National Parole Board is *functus officio*. I would therefore uphold that portion of the order of the British Columbia Court of Appeal which granted the writ of *habeas corpus*.

NOTE

Lamer CJC and La Forest J concurred with the decision of Sopinka J in two short opinions. The concurring decision of Lamer CJC is interesting. Essentially, he observed that the crucial distinction is whether the tribunal is empowered to accept and exclude evidence. This has substantial implications for the original decision in *Mills* because a justice at a preliminary inquiry has clear authority to exclude evidence. Accordingly, Lamer CJC concluded that the decision in *Mooring* effectively reversed *Mills* such that a justice at a preliminary inquiry should be considered a "court of competent jurisdiction" for s. 24 Charter purposes.

Before considering whether you agree with the views expressed by Sopinka J or Major J, can you articulate an argument for denying the state's use of illegally obtained evidence in a criminal trial, but permiting the same evidence to be used to recommit the person if he or she happens to be a parolee?

V. JUDICIAL REVIEW AND THE PAROLE BOARD'S APPEAL DIVISION

Administrative law has always recognized that statutory review mechanisms that provide a parallel avenue of review should preclude the usual judicial review jurisdiction until that avenue has been exhausted. This is not simply a mechanical exhaustion of remedies issue but a question whether there is an alternative remedy. A statutory avenue should be pursued as long as it provides the individual with a comparable opportunity for review. Section 147 of the *Corrections and Conditional Release Act*, SC 1992, c. 20, established the "Appeal Division."

Section 147(1) provides that an offender can appeal a decision on the ground that the board

(a) failed to observe a principle of fundamental justice;

(b) made an error of law;

(c) breached or failed to apply a policy adopted pursuant to s. 151(2);

(d) based its decision on erroneous or incomplete information; or

(e) acted without jurisdiction or beyond its jurisdiction, or failed to exercise its jurisdiction.

Pursuant to s. 147(4), the Appeal Division can affirm the original decision, affirm but order a new review, or "reverse, cancel or vary the decision." However, s. 147(5) provides:

The Appeal Division shall not render a decision under subsection (4) that results in the immediate release of an offender from imprisonment unless it is satisfied that

(a) the decision appealed from cannot reasonably be supported in law, under the applicable policies of the Board, or on the basis of the information available to the Board on its review of the case; and

(b) a delay in releasing the offender would be unfair.

Does s. 147 sufficiently empower the Appeal Division to qualify it as an alternative remedy? Can the Appeal Division entertain claims under the Charter? Do the restrictions in s. 147(5), above, make the Federal Court—Trial Division a more effective vehicle, or are they similar to the discretion that a court would exercise in determining, after an error had been found, whether a remedy should be granted? In this context, it is important to note that the subject matter is liberty—an issue high on the list of interests potentially at stake.

The trend in Federal Court decisions, as illustrated by *Mackie*, infra, favours the requirement that the offender appeal to the Appeal Division before seeking judicial review.

Re Mackie and Warden of Drumheller Institution
[1997] FCJ no. 1000 (TD)

HARGRAVE, PROTHONOTARY (Reasons for Order): The Respondents' motion is to strike out the Originating Notice of Motion on the grounds that the Applicant, a prison inmate with a statutory release date of 18 July 1997, but ordered detained by the National Parole Board (the "Board") pursuant to section 130 of the *Corrections and*

Conditional Release Act, SC 1992, c. 20, has an adequate alternative remedy and thus cannot succeed on his judicial review application in this Court. Indeed, the Applicant has availed himself of the alternate remedy by filing an appeal of the Board's decision with the Appeal Division of the Board under section 147(1) of the Act, but believes he can obtain a quicker remedy from this Court. It is interesting that the Applicant began his appeal to the Appeal Division of the Board on 30 May 1997, two weeks after beginning this judicial review application.

Delay is, according to the Applicant, a main reason for proceeding in the Federal Court: had the Board not detained the Applicant, he would be on parole as of 18 July 1997. However, the Applicant's material indicates that the Appeal Division of the Board will not take up his case until perhaps October 1997, or a little later. I would point out, assuming the application were to proceed in this Court with a fairly minimal extension within which the Respondents might file their affidavits and with the Applicant filing his material without any waiting time, the Applicant might be in a position to apply for a hearing date in the latter half of August. In the normal course of events the Applicant would have to wait between one and three months for a one day hearing date and from two to four months for a date for a two day judicial review hearing. At best the Applicant might obtain a short judicial review hearing by the end of September, as opposed to perhaps sometime in October before the Appeal Division of the Board.

The time difference in which the remedies might be obtained is only one factor in determining whether this proceeding ought to be allowed to go forward. However, to begin, there is the issue of whether the Respondent can strike out the Originating Notice of Motion.

In *David Bull Laboratories (Canada) Inc. v. Pharmacia Inc.* (1995), 176 NR 48 the Federal Court of Appeal considered, without deciding the point, whether an originating notice of motion might be struck out under Rule 419. Rule 419 is limited to actions. The Court of Appeal touched on Rule 5, the gap rule, but pointed out that there was not necessarily a gap in the Federal Court Rules for "... the direct and proper way to contest an originating notice of motion which the respondent thinks to be without merit is to appear and argue at the hearing of the motion itself" (page 52). While the Court of Appeal did not have to decide whether an originating notice of motion could be struck out, Mr. Justice Strayer commented: "This is not to say that there is no jurisdiction in this court either inherent or through rule 5 by analogy to other rules, to dismiss in summary manner a notice of motion which is so clearly improper as to be bereft of any possibility of success. (See e.g. *Cynamid Agricultural de Puerto Rico Inc. v. Commissioner of Patents* (1983), 74 CPR (2d) 133 (FCTD); and the discussion in *Vancouver Island Peace Society et al. v. Canada (Minister of National Defence) et al.*, [1994] 1 FC 102; 64 FTR 127, at 120-121 FC (TD)). Such cases must be very exceptional and cannot include cases such as the present where there is simply a debatable issue as to the adequacy of the allegations in the notice of motion." (pages 54 and 55)

In *Canadian Pasta Manufacturers' Association v. Aurora Importing & Distributing Ltd.*, an unreported 23 April 1997 decision in proceeding A-252-97, the Federal Court of Appeal struck out a judicial review proceeding with the words "we are all of opinion that this application for judicial review could not possibly succeed."

The test for striking out, from *David Bull Laboratories*, that an originating notice of motion must be "… so clearly improper as to be bereft of any possibility of success" is, if possible, an even more stringent test than is to be applied in striking out an action under Rule 419. To make a regular thing of interlocutory motions to strike out judicial review proceedings would be a waste of time and resources. But alternately, it would be an equally irresponsible waste of time and resources, paid for in a large part by the taxpayer, to allow a futile judicial review proceeding, which will not lead to any practical result, to proceed beyond a motion to strike out.

Here the Applicant submits he ought to be allowed to have parallel proceedings, an appeal under the *Corrections and Conditional Release Act* and this judicial review, primarily because the latter may be more convenient and expedient. But convenience and expedience are not the test. Nor is the test whether one forum is better than the other. I must ask myself whether a forum consisting of the Appeal Division of the Board, constituted under *Corrections and Conditional Release Act*, is an adequate forum: see *Canadian Pacific Ltd. v. Matsqui Indian Band* (1995), 26 Admin. LR (2d) 1 at 29 (SCC).

There is a recent case very much on point, a decision of Mr. Justice McKeown, in *Fehr v. The National Parole Board*, (1995) 93 FTR 161 and specifically his consideration of proceeding T-769-94, beginning at page 171 of the Fehr decision. In that instance Ms. Fehr, a penitentiary inmate whose day parole had been revoked on the ground that while free on parole she was an undue risk to society, had not exhausted all appeal procedures under the *Corrections and Conditional Release Act*, namely by first appealing to the Appeal Division of the Board.

Mr. Justice McKeown recognizes that the existence of an alternate statutory appeal remedy does not automatically preclude an application to the Court for *certiorari*, for it is at the discretion of the Court whether to hear such a case and here he refers to *Harelkin v. University of Regina*, [1979] 2 SCR 561. He concludes that the Applicant ought to have pursued an appeal to the Appeal Division of the Board before coming to the Court as the legislation setting up that appeal provided an adequate alternate remedy to *certiorari*. In the *Fehr* case the Applicant sought a review of the Parole Board's decision, together with *certiorari*, the same remedy sought in the present instance by Mr. Mackie.

Mr. Justice McKeown did qualify his reasoning to some degree by pointing out that, while the appeal route is to avoid a multiplicity of proceedings, an applicant still might have judicial review when the statutory remedy is not broad enough to cover all of the issues which are properly for appeal: "The purpose of having an appeal route is to avoid a multiplicity of proceedings before the court. As such, where an appeal route exists, it should, in general, be pursued to the extent that it may be, before seeking judicial review. I wish to make clear, however, that a decision may only be appealed to the extent provided for in the legislation. Judicial review may still be available for issues which may not be properly appealed" (page 171).

In the present instance the jurisdiction of the Appeal Board is broad. It is set out clearly in section 147(1) of the Act: "(1) An offender may appeal a decision of the Board to the Appeal Division on the ground that the Board, in making its decision, (a) failed to observe a principle of fundamental justice; (b) made an error of law;

(c) breached or failed to apply a policy adopted pursuant to subsection 151(2); (d) based its decision on erroneous or incomplete information; or (e) acted without jurisdiction or beyond its jurisdiction, or failed to exercise its jurisdiction."

Mr. Mackie's grounds for appeal, set out in the motion for judicial review, may be summarized as an error on the part of the Board in law and in jurisdiction by applying legislation retrospectively and failing to observe the principles of natural justice and procedural fairness, all clearly within the Appeal Board's mandate.

The merits of the Applicant's case, which may well be substantial, are not at issue. Rather it is the adequacy of the Applicant's alternate remedy. Assessment of this alternate remedy is not a matter of working in a factual vacuum, which is sometimes the case in an interlocutory proceeding, for the issues and facts are clear. Mr. Mackie has a remedy by way of an appeal to the Appeal Division of the National Parole Board. The grounds of the appeal are clearly set out in his Originating Notice of Motion. The faults alleged on the part of the Board which initially heard his case are clearly within the statutory scope of the Appeal Board.

There is no prejudice to require the Applicant to complete the appeal, which he has begun, before the Appeal Board under the *Corrections and Conditional Release Act*, as a precondition to coming to this Court. He presently has a completely adequate remedy before the Appeal Board. It is an appeal to a specialized and expert Board. If that remedy is not as quick as might be the situation in the Federal Court, the likely difference in time to a hearing is marginal. I am reinforced in this view by the fact that not only has the Applicant this alternate remedy, but also he has in fact commenced that parallel remedial process. Mr. Mackie's situation is similar to that of the applicant in the *Fehr* decision, an application for *certiorari* and review in which there was an adequate alternative remedy of appeal to the same Appeal Board. This being the situation the present judicial review proceeding is futile. It is plain and obvious that it could not possibly succeed: it is so clearly improper to have and indeed to have subsequently commenced a parallel alternative remedy that this judicial review application is bereft of any chance of success. It is therefore struck out.

William McInnes is one of Australia's most popular writers, delighting readers with his memoirs *A Man's Got to Have a Hobby* and *That'd Be Right*, his novels *Cricket Kings*, *The Laughing Clowns* and *The Birdwatcher*, and his insight into Australian life since the 1940s, written with Essential Media and Entertainment, *The Making of Modern Australia*. In 2011, with his wife Sarah Watt he co-wrote *Worse Things Happen at Sea*, which was named the best non-fiction title in the ABIA and the Indie Awards in 2012. In 2014, he wrote *Holidays*, his unique perspective on the Australian obsession with taking a hard-earned break.

Also an award-winning actor, William has won two Logies and an AFI Award for Best Actor for his role in the film *Unfinished Sky*. He received critical and public acclaim for his leading role in the film *Look Both Ways*, written and directed by Sarah Watt, and recently starred in the ABC television series *The Time of Our Lives* and *Hello Birdie*.

William McInnes grew up in Queensland and lives in Melbourne with his two children.

Also by William McInnes

A Man's Got to Have a Hobby

Cricket Kings

The Making of Modern Australia

(with Essential Media & Entertainment)

That'd Be Right

Worse Things Happen at Sea (with Sarah Watt)

The Laughing Clowns

The Birdwatcher

Holidays

WILLIAM McINNES
full bore

hachette
AUSTRALIA

hachette
AUSTRALIA

Published in Australia and New Zealand in 2016
by Hachette Australia
(an imprint of Hachette Australia Pty Limited)
Level 17, 207 Kent Street, Sydney NSW 2000
www.hachette.com.au

10 9 8 7 6 5 4 3 2 1

National Library of Australia
Cataloguing-in-Publication data:

McInnes, William, 1963– author.
Full bore / William McInnes.

978 0 7336 3552 6 (paperback)

Contains biographical information.
McInnes, William, 1963–
Sports – Social aspects – Australia – Anecdotes.
Popular culture – Australia – Anecdotes.

306.0994

Cover design by Christabella Designs
Cover photographs: (front cover) William at Redcliffe, photographed by Sarah Watt, courtesy of
William McInnes; (back cover) courtesy Calum Robertson/Newspix
Text design by Bookhouse, Sydney
Typeset in 12.35/18.4 pt Bembo Std by Bookhouse, Sydney
Printed and bound in Australia by McPherson's Printing Group

To Mrs Stone – a wonderful teacher

Contents

Chapter 1

It Began in an Auction House

It began in an auction house. I was sitting on a plastic seat. I had been sitting on that plastic seat for two hours, trying to look interested in what was going on around me.

I was there as a part of a television series about the fascinating stories and people that can be found at auction houses. They were fascinating initially but after an age of sitting, nodding and staring at heavy characterless pieces of Edwardian furniture, the shine had come off a bit.

For the tenth time, I nodded for the cameras and proclaimed how interesting a set of drawers, which had the charm and warmth of the Monolith from *2001: A Space Odyssey*, was. The owner of the drawers, a pleasantly abrasive widow, told me how her doctor husband had been passionate about this type of furniture.

I switched off a bit and my mind wandered. The plastic seats we were sitting on were the same as the ones I had sat on at high school during an English class about mime.

It wasn't just the seats that took my mind in this direction though. One of the bidders at the auction was loosely throwing out his right arm and then letting it fall with every bid, as though he were fishing. It looked for the entire world as if he were a member of that long-ago mime class.

Squashed in the classroom on our plastic seats, it was almost a point of honour, and a wise move in the interests of self-preservation, not to put too much effort into the mime exercise.

Our long-nosed teacher was as bored as us. She, after all, had seen it all before – or so she thought. She only roused herself if somebody spoke. 'It is mime. Silence!' she would bellow. Or if a student did something that was deemed, in her words, 'lewd and indecent'. Then she would scream, 'Noooooooooo!'

One boy dropped to the floor and then started to rub his bottom back and forth. At first the teacher seemed a bit stunned and then, not quite sure of what was going on but certain that it was lewd, she screamed, 'Noooooooooooo!' She summoned the boy to the front. 'You will tell the deputy head what you did here today, Martin,' she said.

After a moment's pause for thought, deciding she couldn't trust Martin to pass on the message accurately, the long-nosed teacher told him to wait while she wrote a note. She folded it, gave it to Martin and told him to give it to the deputy head.

He left the room then reappeared at the door a few moments later to protest, having rather sensibly read the note on the verandah.

'I wasn't strangling one, I was my dog with worms.'

The long-nosed teacher looked at him blankly.

Martin elaborated. 'I wasn't miming strangling one – a poo. I was miming my dog, Dexter, with worms.'

'Silence! It is mime!' was the long-nosed teacher's response. Martin the Strangler went off to his fate and we went back to mime.

A boy nearby me was doing a low-rent, generic form of fishing, throwing out an arm loosely, letting it fall and then rotating his other hand in little circles, winding in the line. It was the go-to mime effort when nothing else could be found in the creative cupboard.

Occasionally the pretend fishing rod would jerk with the imaginary fish on the end of the line, but more often than not it was the basic cast and reeling-in mime. Martin the Strangler had been trying to imaginatively stir the pot a bit, but heaven help anybody who wanted to be truly creative, like the poor sod who painted his face with sandshoe whitener and tried to be a falling snowflake to the strains of Queen's 'Bohemian Rhapsody'.

He'd even brought along a cassette player.

Why he thought a snowflake would be falling in subtropical 1970s Brisbane is anyone's guess. But he did his best at floating down and melting and, of course, never lived it down. It didn't help that the long-nosed

3

teacher said, after he had melted, 'Well done, Lawrence, very imaginateeeve.' For some reason she drew out the last syllable as if she were a Mexican cantina-owner from a bad John Wayne film.

Lawrence was never allowed to forgeeet it. Whether standing in a lunchtime line at the tuckshop, or even detention in a hopeless maths class, he would always be referred to as Snowflake, usually with an accompanying push or thump.

It must have, quite frankly, been awful for him. Although it always got a laugh from me.

I sat and thought a bit and looked again at the woman selling the *Space Odyssey* drawers.

She seemed forlorn all of a sudden. 'Oh, I do miss my husband terribly,' she said softly.

I looked at her and all her *Space Odyssey* furniture and couldn't even begin to comprehend what it must have been like to sit and watch piece after piece of her husband's belongings offered up to strangers. It wasn't the Monolith that was moving on, it was a piece of her life, her husband.

She sat like that for a moment longer, then she smiled tightly and said, 'Oh bugger this, I'm off out the back for a smoke.'

•

The auction included toys and collectables from the late nineteenth century to the 1980s. I had a go bidding for a die-cast Mr Whippy van but was soon outbid by a gaggle of determined middle-aged men in stone-washed jeans and tipped hair. They stared balefully at each other as they battled over a set of 1960s Corgi toy cars.

One of these men was the miming fisherman bidder. His rather rakish bidding was at odds with his intense stare. During a tea break I sidled up to him as he made a cup of instant coffee with grim-faced determination.

'You did well with the Mr Whippy,' I said.

He gave me a curt nod of the head.

'You collect them, do you, mate?'

He gave me a quick look. 'Not just Mr Whippy vans, mate. I have a wider interest,' he said, as if to collect just tiny Mr Whippy vans would be somehow suspect.

'Did you have them when you were a kid?'

He smiled. 'No, mate. Couldn't afford them. Got Matchbox models but not the die-cast ones. Wanted them, but never got them.'

I asked when he started collecting them.

'When I got on, made a bit of money and the kids had left home. My wife told me to get a hobby.'

I nodded. I was going to go back to my plastic seat but the fishing mime bidder went on. 'Every birthday when I would get a Matchbox car, my mum would give me a little cuddle and say, "Maybe next year." As if she was saying sorry that she couldn't afford to get one of the Corgis. Never bothered me but I always remember it. I collect them now, and I remember Mum. Funny.'

He bought four more Corgi models with his fishing mime bidding. After the last purchase he said to me, 'Another one for Mum,' and laughed.

Inspired, I bid on a baggy green Australian cricket cap that had once been worn by captain Kim Hughes. Just to say I had bid, really. When bidding quickly rose to an astronomical amount, I panicked, wondering which child I'd have to sell to pay for it, but then I thought of my father, with whom I'd watched Kim Hughes's tearful resignation press conference. Hughes didn't even get through it; trying to be full of bravado he suddenly descended into a blubbing blond mess and scuttled out of the room broken-hearted. A golden boy who came a cropper. A leader who couldn't, or wasn't, allowed to lead the team he was given.

'Too much talent and not enough mongrel,' my father said of Kim. 'He's no Ian Chappell.' Actually, there wasn't much pity for Kim from my father, just a bit of perplexed fatalism. 'That's not on,' said my father when Kim started crying, and he looked about to see if my mother was anywhere near. 'Not up to speed, that. It's only a bloody game. No reason to sob, you silly sod. Weak as piss, son, weak as water.'

Thousands of dollars on a sobbing sod's baggy green. But I suppose a baggy green is a baggy green. Eventually I was put out of my misery by an agent for an institutional collector, who looked about as interested in what he had purchased as a stick insect might be.

Next was a signed photo of an old cricketer called Maurice Leyland. The photo was very beige and hailed from another, more gentlemanly time. Maurice was a generous-shaped man who in the photo had a shy smile on his face and his hands shoved deep in his voluminous cricket whites.

'He looks like he's enjoying himself!' said the auctioneer. 'I wonder what he's up to way down there. At the bottom of his pockets.'

His words just hung in the air until the bidding began.

I was determined to take something home from the auction, and Maurice was it, although he didn't stay long. Later, I wrote about buying him in all his beige-framed, deep-pocketed glory in a newspaper column and received the oddest response. It was from a Brisbane woman, who was a relative of Maurice's. She wondered if it were too rude to ask if she might be able to purchase Maurice so he could hang on the walls of his family's house. I posted Maurice to her with a note saying the pleasure had been all mine and that I could think of nothing better than Maurice smiling shyly and doing whatever he was doing in his pockets in the home of some of his kin.

As I looked at Maurice's photo and his signature, I thought of all the stuff that's been made. All those bits and pieces. Where do they all go? Some were here but all the rest were just out in the great 'There'.

A day later I was browsing at an op shop stall. The oppie, like the entire suburb, was in a state of transition. So much so that the church, which used to be next to the op shop,

7

had been deconsecrated and had itself become the op shop. The altar area had been left open as a welcoming place where anybody might like to come and sit a while.

The op shop staff was being turned over as much as the contents of the undies drawer. All the cheery, chatty old ladies had given way to a younger set of charity workers. Gone was the cheeky aged Scottish woman who would whoop with joy when somebody bought something she never thought anyone would find interest in. ('Well! Would youuuuu ever have thourrrrrrrrt! Somebody has taken the Barry Manilow t-shirt!' she would sing joyfully. Barry didn't even appear on the shirt, it was just a shirt that she thought he would have worn.) In her place were a couple who drifted about like early morning hot-air balloons, endowed with a self-proclaimed great deal of good taste and style. Or an enthusiastic but prickly volunteer, who would either be full of good cheer or have abrupt and aggressive character advice. 'You arrogant turd,' she advised me as I flipped through the record stacks once.

I looked up and saw her glowering at me.

'Yeah, you,' she said again.

Perhaps it was the disdainful way I was flipping through the platoon of Kamahl records. Above her, in a golden frame smiling beatifically, was the photo of another op shop volunteer who had died a few years earlier. A kind-natured, round old woman who used to give my son and other toddlers Monte Carlo biscuits from her special bickie box under the front counter. Two faces of the op shop, past and present, before me. The transition could be a tricky trip.

Now, I peered in through the door and saw no sign of the prickly woman. I decided to push my luck and enter but tried to be discreet by sifting through the old vinyl collection in my most humble manner.

I decided that I couldn't live without the classic recording of *Love is a Piano Accordion*. Two models, supposedly in the throes of deep love, clung to each other like a mixture of two drowning people or awkward cousins at a bad wedding. Maybe they were cousins. Drowning awkward accordion cousins.

Still trying to browse drenched with humility, I picked up a little Ladybird book entitled *A First Book of Saints*. Well, the pictures were nice and it had all the old faves: Pat, Francis, Christopher and Joan.

I looked at these things. These bits of flotsam and jetsam from the tide of time. I wondered to whom the shyly smiling Maurice Leyland had signed his 'Best Wishes', as well as what on earth he was up to in his trousers.

I looked through the little Ladybird book and found that it had belonged to 'Roberta of the 3rd Glenroy Brownie Pack'. How did Roberta get on? What did she see and where did she go? Did she ever think about her little book of saints? Who, I wondered, was her favourite saint? The pick of Roberta.

As for the cousins on *Love is a Piano Accordion*, they just gave me a laugh.

I thought of the face of the old woman at the auction when she remembered just how much she missed her husband, not really his monolithic heavy furniture.

And I remembered Snowflake. Decades after that fateful mime class I was walking through Sydney's CBD on the way to a meeting.

I thought I was headed through a door of a hotel lobby in George Street, but instead I marched into a very clean, large glass wall to the side of the entrance. My face hitting the glass sounded like a deep gong summoning monks from a cavernous Himalayan retreat. I reeled back, my eyes watering, and looked up to see a greasy imprint of what presumably was my nose festooning the glass.

And as my eyes adjusted I saw a man doubled over in mirth. Laughing as if he would break in two. I stared and he laughed more. I wondered if he recognised me. I think he did and I think that's why he laughed more.

He had changed a bit since he took that tape recorder into mime class and painted his face with sandshoe whitener. Now he was dressed in the uniform of an air steward.

Snowflake. Laughing at me. Somehow it seemed just. And it also seemed human. That these memories, these things, bits and pieces, which had belonged to other people, go round and round, that some of them were now with me. Maybe they're just crap, nothing of note, but maybe they are more. Maybe they remind us how brief and transient we all are. And maybe they remind us just what fun we have while we're here.

These bits and pieces of stuff all have stories – stories of where they came from, stories of the people who they belonged to.

And that is what this book is about.

Chapter 2

Matchbox Memories

It somehow seemed right that we ended up banging on about the Brisbane Rugby League competition of the 1970s during a round of golf that my old friend PB, my son and I were engaged in because the game was a form of time travel anyway.

My double-digit scores were channelling Malcolm Fraser's 1980s double-digit unemployment and inflation. I put it down to the fact that my left knee had given up the ghost and I was walking with an awkward gait. Someone who looked and behaved a lot like me also had a very animated conversation with a four-wood and then an even more animated interaction between the four-wood and a tree. My son laughed and said it was like playing golf with Basil Fawlty.

'You look like you're selling double tickets,' PB said and laughed.

My son was a bit perplexed by this old-coot talk, so busied himself with playing a more-than-useful golf shot.

Double sellers. Every suburban footy ground had them. Blokes who'd prowl about the sidelines with vinyl bags, usually suspended under beer guts of varying sizes. These double sellers were 'great clubmen' and were out and about in all kinds of weather raising money for their teams. They were a sort of in-between creature, breaking the demarcation line of spectator and player, with a heightened role in the game. The roped area would signify where the crowd could not pass, but the double seller existed in between the rope and the touchline and seemed to operate on another plane, not on the level of the players or even the referee, but certainly above the two touch judges, or 'touchies' as sneeringly referred to by the crowd.

Redcliffe's double seller was a fellow with grey hair and a moustache who often had a faraway look in his eyes, as if he were looking past today and into tomorrow. He was a heavy smoker and his voice was very deep and loud, almost operatic. This was at odds with how he moved, bellowing along with a mistimed swaggering gait as if his lower half was not quite in unison with the rest of him. Uncle Reg said the double seller's carburettor was misfiring, but as I had little practical knowledge of cars and engineering at the time, this meant almost nothing to me. However, I could see by the way the double seller walked that, mechanically, he had a problem.

Yet the double seller always got to where he was going, and did what he had to do. 'Eight for ten, sixteen for twenty! First point scorers!' And he would pull for the first point scorers from his pouch.

It was a harmless form of gambling. You'd purchase a ticket and receive two numbers corresponding to the players on the ground. If your numbered player scored, you'd win. This much I understood; what happened next lost me. While you watched the game and waited for the first scorers, the double seller would continue to bellow their cryptic cry. 'Eight for ten, sixteen for twenty!' I had no idea what the chant meant and still don't. PB tried to explain it to me that day on the golf course, but no matter how much he tried to make me understand I still couldn't fathom it.

It didn't really matter because it was a long time ago. A long time.

But if we stopped and thought for a bit, both PB and I could reel off game after game and many of the characters who ran across the 1970s Brisbane Rugby League fields — even my son knew some of the players because he had heard me bang on about them on many occasions. PB's and my celebration of the BRL is odd in itself, because PB played soccer and I, outside a couple of midweek Commonwealth Bank Cup games in high school, played rugby union.

What was it about the mid-1970s rugby league that seemed so memorable? It was a different Brisbane back then. A little rougher, maybe, a bit more of a small town. But a town that was a little richer in the way its people interacted. Every suburb had its own character, its own politics, and footy was a way in which these idiosyncrasies were played out before the city's people.

This was never better demonstrated than by some of the playing grounds. Purtell Park was Wests Panthers' home ground in the leafy suburb of Bardon. It may have been one of the 'nicer' areas to live in but the ground was a shocker, with a slope so pronounced it was an advantage for players to have one leg shorter than the other.

My father thought the players on Purtell Park all moved like Groucho Marx, the comedian who walked with an exaggerated, bent-over scuttling crouch. So after a while Purtell Park became known as Groucho's Paddock.

Bishop Park was Norths' oval and had a unique and cosy feel, encapsulated in its nickname of Bash-up Park. 'You want to take out your teeth when you watch football there,' said my mother. 'No good endangering the gob enamel.'

Neumann Oval was nestled in Albion under Cloudland Dance Hall and was the home of one of the best-named sporting teams: the Fortitude Valley Diehards. Redcliffe had the showgrounds with its rickety green timber grandstand and besser-block clubhouse. Corbett Park was the Brothers' home ground, located in the Grange, with a scaffolding stand that wasn't as big as Redcliffe's rickety green thing but a lot steadier. For whatever reason, it was known to us as Home on the Grange.

Wynnum Manly's Kougari Oval was so far from anywhere that you needed a cut lunch and a passport to make the journey comfortable.

'It's the jet set at Wynnum this weekend, young Mac,' said Ken McCrohan, the proprietor of the BP service station on the corner of Duffield Road, as I stood at the counter deciding which flavour chewing gum I would buy. Ken had played for Redcliffe and Australia in the sixties so I knew that he knew how the BRL worked.

I went to the Kougari Oval game with my mother, half-expecting to see people dressed up in jet-set fashions. If not quite like the glamorous people in Peter Stuyvesant 'passport to smoking pleasure' cinema ads then at the very least dressed like people from the 'Society' pages of the Saturday *Courier Mail*. Like the couple celebrating their wedding anniversary with a delightful matching pantsuit combination as they enjoyed the seafood buffet at Neptune's Valley seafood restaurant. The only way you could tell them apart was that one of them had a moustache that draped from his lip like a stage curtain.

Before we left, I asked my mother if I should wear long socks with my shorts because we were going to Kougari Oval. She looked at me with a frown and said, 'Whatever for, you stupid boy?' I told her about Ken McCrohan's jet set and she laughed. 'You'd be lucky to see anybody at Wynnum who knows how to wear thongs, let alone long socks,' she said.

'They have problems with the laces,' my father added.

There was always a healthy competition between Redcliffe and Wynnum – the two teams from either end of the bay – so I took my parents' banter with a grain of salt and made sure I had a pair of long socks just in case.

The only people who were close to being dressed up at Kougari Oval were the double sellers; they had leather pouches instead of vinyl ones slung under their tummies. Still, it didn't take long for Kougari and the whole area of Wynnum Manly to become known as the Jet Set.

Yes, Brisbane was undoubtedly smaller and more contained back then. It defined itself by its own measures – and the Brisbane Rugby League competition was one of them. I thought the Presidents Cup and the Peter Scott Memorial Shield were some of the most prized sporting trophies in the world. And the Kirks Cup, the BRL's grand final trophy, was the greatest of them all.

I am slightly amazed that I can remember these titles – then again, why wouldn't I? They seemed pretty important when I was nine. The Presidents Cup was played between the two top teams on the ladder after the first round, and the Peter Scott Memorial Shield was played between the two top teams after the second round. Big news in Brizzy.

Brisbane in the 1970s was a split society; one part sought to cling to its past but another began to seriously challenge for the future. The Joh Bjelke-Petersen governments were keen on infrastructure development but not on social and political evolution. So Joh, in his cultivated bumbling way, would point to the cranes that dotted the Brisbane skyline and challenge people to say that it wasn't development, as all the while, under the cover of night, heritage buildings were demolished, despite the protests of citizens attempting to save parts of the city's history. At the same time authorities would try to preserve a particular brand of law and order that wasn't putting too fine a point on respecting everybody's idea of civil rights.

Counter to this was a burgeoning arts and music scene that went hand in glove with a greater social and political awareness of the world beyond the city borders. It was part of an unstoppable tide that would flow over Joh and his fellow travellers, but in the meantime under the 1970s umbrella of a city in evolution, there was a whole world of daggy endeavour.

Daggy adventures in the old Brisbane included the Warana Festival, a collection of floats and people sweating underneath papier-mâché costumes; and Mater Prize Home outings, where on a given weekend a good number of Brisbane's population would slowly walk through a new home that would be raffled for the Mater Hospital charity. Or the Monday morning *Courier Mail* sports results, where a parade of truly odd Queensland games and pastimes might be seen. The cribbage, euchre and croquet results were there, along with vigoro scores.

Vigoro was the greatest mystery – a cricket-like game played by 'the ladies', with a soft rubber ball and a paddle bat. There was a large woman from Margate whom I would see packing her car around eight or eight-thirty on a Saturday morning as I came back from the beach after fishing. She always wore a swirling pleated skirt and a white short-sleeved shirt, sunglasses and very red lipstick. She was preparing to head off into the mythical place of 'girls' sport' – Downey Park, the home of hockey and netball and her particular pastime of vigoro. My mother knew her as 'Oh Desley, down the road!' and we would always be informed, via Mum's declarations from the *Courier Mail*, of how 'Desley had done at Downey'.

The BRL was one of the other grand pillars of dag from this time. Despite occasional intrusions courtesy of the yearly pastings by New South Wales in the interstate series, it was a universe unto itself. It couldn't last, of course, and didn't, but I think the mid-1970s was probably the height of the BRL. Everything was, for want of a better term, so wonderfully Brisbane and homemade.

The club songs are a perfect example. All were sung to familiar tunes like 'Waltzing Matilda', 'Lili Marlene' and 'When the Saints Go Marching In'. Memorable efforts were Wynnum Manly's song to the tune of 'Men of Harlech', Redcliffe's dirge-like version of 'Click Go the Shears' and Wests Panthers' imbecilic ditty to the tune of 'Alexander's Ragtime Band'. The two beauties of the BRL club songs were those of Brothers, or, to be more accurate Past Brothers, my second team, which was sung to the tune of an Irish shanty. It included the rather dubious lyrics, 'When the season is done and the playing is over/It's Brothers the premiers rolling in clover.'

'Sounds like a police charge sheet,' my father would helpfully add in his clarion voice whenever the song was played at Corbett Park. Nothing, though, could compare to Norths Devils' anthem sung to 'March of the Toreadors' from Bizet's *Carmen*. 'The other team will hide/From Satan's side/Norths will shout with pride/Stand up and cheer/Stand up and cheer/Stand up and cheeeeeeeeeeer!'

This last is a particular favourite of mine for no other reason than once when I was wandering through uptown New York, I heard it being sung rather loudly by a gentleman who was being helped into a town car after what must have been a very good night out. Amid the rest of the noise of that night, it stood out like a dog's balls. I was stupefied but very appreciative of the efforts of whoever it was who had travelled from Albert Bishop Park, Nundah, to Harlem.

•

And then I remembered another celebration of the 1970s BRL universe: the matchboxes.

As we wandered on the golf course, I asked PB if he remembered the matchboxes. He looked at me and then he laughed. '4IP Colour Radio!' He remembered them, all right. In 1975, a collection of matchboxes featuring club crests and players was produced by somebody as a way of cashing in on the popularity of the code. It was probably the radio station 4IP, which would promote itself by whatever means available. They'd even turn up to Mater Prize Homes openings in a Mini Moke with a couple of local radio personalities handing out station stickers and the odd balloon, regaling us with their cries of '4IP good guys giveaways!'. Their voices bore no relation to what they actually looked like – which was a random assortment of blokes at the bus stop.

And why wouldn't they get on the bandwagon of commemorative matchboxes? It was startling to see such a bold marketing step and it seemed rather modern and daring to have at your fingertips such a basic necessity as matches, decorated with team colours and identities. It only lasted one season but they were memorable.

Take the Bevan Bleakley matchbox from the 1975 Brisbane Rugby League series, produced by the Australian Match Manufacturing Co Pty Ltd and 'League Action Live on Colour Radio 4IP'. The immortal description of the Redcliffe Dolphins' flaming red-headed Bevan: 'Truck driver, fierce front rower who plays full bore for eighty minutes.' I wondered why on earth Bevan had been selected for the honour of having his face stuck on a box of matches. We all thought he was terrific – but, really, he was as rough as guts and a bit of a wild man at heart. Then it dawned on me that there wouldn't have been that many red-headed tearaways pounding around on the footy fields of Brisbane. In fact, I could only think of one other red-headed player – the rather unfortunately named Gary Prickett, so why wouldn't a Redcliffe ranga be thought a good ambassador for red-headed matches?

My mother had kept a set of BRL matches, constantly refilling the Bevan box, using it again and again until the flint sides of the box had almost worn out. 'Come on Bevan, light up for Iris,' she would say and Bevan's matches would explode into flame and light the wooden stove in the kitchen or the homemade barbecue in the backyard. 'Well done, Bevan!' my father would cry out in answer and invariably give my mother a bear hug.

Bevan was a particular favourite in our house, not just because he was *full bore* but because you always heard Bevan Bleakley stories. Like the time he was prevented from entering the Settler's Inn bar at the back of the Moreton Bay Hotel by the then proprietor, Artie Beetson, because Bevan wasn't dressed appropriately. Thongs and Stubbies weren't allowed, not even by Artie's casual standards. Bevan was not going to argue with Artie but he was also not going to be deterred when it came to a bit of socialising. The story was that he wrapped himself from the waist down in toilet paper and fronted up. Apparently Artie Beetson laughed and let him in.

'Bevan's a thinking man's boofhead, all right,' my mum said rather proudly when told the story. There were other players, too, on other matchboxes, with photos so hopelessly unposed they looked like they'd come straight from the pages of somebody's family photo album.

Each matchbox had a photo of the player's head and, underneath, his name and titbits of information that somehow seemed gloriously small town and almost like a fable. Of sorts. Another Redcliffe tough nut, Rod Halley, was billed as a concrete worker and a crash-tackling forward whose nickname was 'Kamikaze'.

Really, you couldn't make it up.

Tony Trent, a Norths second rower, had a head of hair that basically told the story of the 1970s decade so beautifully that no words were needed. It was all there in that continent of hair follicles – the optimism, the sprawling development, rebellious directions, inflation, a hint of disco and even a sniff of the oil crisis. And in keeping with the unposed nature of the whole matchbox exercise, Tony's photo caught him almost mid-blink so his eyes were slits and he had a happy gormless grin on his long, lantern-jawed face.

His matchbox description was a variation on a theme, his occupation being listed as 'transport contractor'. Which basically meant, I suppose, that he was a truck driver. He was also at home in the forwards or the backs; he was 'versatile, with a capital V,' said my father, as if Tony were some ancient philosopher. Versatile. My father, inspired by Versatile's matchbox photo and encouraged by my mother, would refer to Tony Trent as 'you eyeless bugger'.

Norths certainly had all the hairstyles covered. Steve Calder was an attacking second rower and cost clerk who had a basin cut only a mother could love. He looked like a cross between a pageboy from the *Prince Valiant* comic strip and a stormtrooper. But a Wynnum Manly player named Bob Clapham, sales representative, took the hair stakes by a country mile. He had a moustache that looked like a walrus and his hair was a mountainous fountain of black. He looked very happy with himself, as if he was a fusion between some extreme glam-rock guitarist and a baron freshly arrived home from a riotous good night out at Charles II's Restoration court.

John Eales, Easts, taxation officer, a Rothman's Gold Medal Winner in 1973 and a smart back who could trigger attacking moves in a flash, caused a certain amount of consternation. This wasn't because of his footballing ability or his rather pleasant photograph on the matchbox.

One evening while my father and I were fishing off Woody Point jetty, a man nearby us was trying to light a rather lugubrious-looking pipe.

My father was busy taking in the view of the bay, watching the water and having the odd chat while I lost various bits and pieces of bait which had been dredged up from the freezer after my mother had defrosted it.

'Christ knows what that might be,' she'd said. 'You couldn't even give it to the dogs and you can't put it in the bin.' She'd thought for a moment and then said to my father, pointing at me, 'Take that thing fishing.'

The thing being me.

So there I was, threading a series of dubious-looking substances onto a rusty hook and casting them into the water where they presumably either dissolved with unknown consequences or sent cross-eyed any fish that were silly enough to have a nibble.

My father looked over at the man, who had been tossing in a crab net, trying to light his pipe. 'Having trouble, brother? You'd better change the flint.'

A few other people laughed and the pipe-smoker smiled. 'No, it's this bugger makes me fidgety. The tax man.' And he shook the box of matches.

'Oh, that bastard from Easts,' said someone from the dark. And my father muttered, 'Time to cross yourself or touch wood,' and a man with a towelling hat decided to do both.

The pipe-smoker nodded. 'The small businessman's lament.'

A man with an Alvey side-cast reel dug into his Stubbies shorts front pocket, pulled out another matchbox and tossed it to the pipe-smoker.

'Here, have a go with Dauthy,' he said. Dauthy, also known as Ian Dauth; Brothers, mechanic; Brisbane Representative; among the top point-scorers, great winger and a fine kick.

And John Eales, the smiling handsome tax man from Stones Corner, was popped back into the pipe-smoker's dry fishing bucket as he flicked a match and then sucked on his pipe, and a cloud of pleasant-smelling Borkum Riff tobacco shrouded his head and drifted across the jetty.

There were a few laughs and a couple of cries of, 'Well done, Dauthy!' as if Ian Dauth had dobbed one over the goal posts from the sidelines with his high-stepping kicks.

•

The names and faces on those matchboxes come from a more insular and homogeneous era, before Australia's multi-racial society became the norm. In that way, the 1970s BRL comp seems even more remote and distant: the names are usually Anglo-Australian with few syllables.

Though of course there were some exceptions, notably the wonderfully named John Ribot de Bresac, who sounded like he had stepped out of the pages of *The Scarlet Pimpernel* and revolutionary France. Instead of being an adventurous baronet rescuing aristos from the guillotine and making the ladies swoon, Ribot de Bresac was an electrician, a lock, a promising forward and capable kicker.

He also had an uneven mullet that he soon cut after the matchbox photo was taken, added a moustache to his upper lip, and became known as Johnny Ribot, which sounds like a character Elvis Presley might have played in one of his entertainingly ghastly movies.

This name change was prompted, perhaps, by the creative interpretations of his Gallic hyphenated names. One afternoon at Lang Park somebody from the outer roared out, 'Give it to Johnny Reebo-de-ball-sack!'

'You remember John Payne?' I asked PB. John Payne — who never got his melon on a matchbox but did do a print ad for the Permanent Building Society wearing his rep jersey — was an honest toiler who came up from Sydney and played with a fair bit of dash for Easts and then Norths. He also played for Queensland and then Australia.

'I remember him,' PB said. 'I saw him sitting in a change room after a game. Blood streaming from his knees and elbows, just sitting absolutely ragged, with a can of beer in his hand.

'I was going to go up to him and tell him how well he'd played – they had gotten done, Easts, but he had played so well I thought I should go tell him. As I got near he just looked at me, as if to say, "Not now, son, not now."'

I had forgotten PB was one of the chosen ones, a ball boy for the senior grades. He was another of those half creatures of the touchline, bringing the balls in from the sidelines, or even more theatrically handing over the little container of sand for the place kicks.

The aura associated with being a ball boy was never more palpably evident than one afternoon at the Redcliffe showgrounds when PB came off after delivering the sand.

He heard his voice called out by Kim Dicker.

'Kim Dicker!' I repeated.

'Yes, mate, Kim Dicker,' PB said. If you had known Kim Dicker, you too would have said her name like that, with that note of unrequited longing that middle-aged men can strike. She was one of those people who still loomed large in the memory.

'What did she want?' I asked.

PB smiled. 'She called me over and said I looked like I needed an Escort.'

'An Escort?'

'Yeah, an Escort cigarette. So she gave me one.'

'She gave you a durrie?'

'Yes.'

'In your ball boy uniform?'

'Yes, white jumper and red V on the front.'

'What did you do with the Escort?'

'Stuck it behind my ear and ran over to the mound of sand between the showgrounds and the hockey club to refill the bucket.'

'A ball boy running the sand with an Escort behind your ear?'

PB nodded. 'Golden days.'

I thought for a bit. Being a ball boy *and* having Kim Dicker offer you a durrie seemed almost unfair; they were things that didn't come the way of many people that often in life. Kim Dicker thought you were worth giving an Escort to: it was akin to Shakespeare writing you a sonnet or Manet painting *Olympia* for Victorine Meurent. I asked him, 'Did Kim Dicker say anything else to you?'

'Nah.'

Then, in an attempt at kindness, PB said, 'Mate, it was just the uniform.'

That mollified me somewhat, but still – Kim Dicker. The ball boy uniform. As well as getting close enough to Kim Dicker for her to actually speak to him, PB would have gotten up close to those big men who take the sand, suck in deep breaths and mould a little sand platform for the toe-poking torpedo place kick.

Men like John Payne. He was a good player, Payney. The last time I'd heard his name was at a function I had attended at the Broncos Leagues Club in 2015. It was a Men of League do, a charity organisation filled with old familiar faces from the distant days of John Payne.

In front of me at this function was Bob Green, an amiable roguish man in his late sixties who used to be described by journalists as 'the Wests Panthers hard man' or 'enforcer'. He used to have a snappy mo-and-beard combo, which had a hint of the court of Philip II of Spain. Now, clean-shaven and sporting a comb-over, he was straight-faced as he said, 'I never did a dirty or illegal thing in my career,' and then erupted into a wheezy peal of laughter. He was laughing together with a matchbox face, the pageboy stormtrooper Steve Calder from Norths, who now wore his grey hair close-cropped. I was standing not too far away, beer in hand, towering over both of them.

It was a collision of past and present that caused a slight recalibration in the way one perceives oneself. If these old men around me used to be young men I watched playing when I was a boy, where does that leave me? Standing with a beer in my hand watching two old footy players laughing at each other, getting on with life. I suppose that is what I am doing too, in a roundabout way.

But then I saw something else. Men of League is one of those organisations that doesn't forget life can throw up all sorts of things at people. Life can be a grand ride, following a set and planned course, but it can also be a bit rough, a bit unexpected. It can be a mixed bag. Still, it's just life.

And life had happened to John Payne; he had gotten old and needed a bit of a hand. Men of League did their best to extend one and sorted out some accommodation for him in an aged-care facility. Just making sure that a player like John Payne – who gave his all on a long-ago Sunday afternoon game – wasn't forgotten.

•

League has changed a lot. No more torpedo place kicks, or kicking duels or proper heaving messy scrums or even double sellers.

Groucho's Paddock lost its slope and became Purtell Park, and Corbett Park, our Home on the Grange, was razed when the Brothers Club folded. It's now a residential townhouse complex.

We have all changed, I think. When I was a kid watching the double seller who saw into tomorrow stalking up and down the sidelines, I never thought I would be walking with the same gait as him on a lovely afternoon of golf.

That amiable form of gambling he was involved in looks more than quaint now in the shadow of the multimillion-dollar betting industry that drapes itself over all sorts of sports. 'Please gamble responsibly' comes the almost comedic phrase from various spruikers of the gaming industry. And they try to say it straight-faced after a frenetic greasing of the odds and betting specials that are used as berley to lure the punters to click on their phones with a wager. As if betting on a game is a completely integral part of sport, just another facet of enjoying the spectacle. Rugby league today is more a part of the entertainment business than a sport. The players look like they come out of some sports laboratory when compared to the matchbox heroes.

Funnily enough, it was one of the matchbox heroes that helped to change the game. The promising lock John Ribot de Bresac transformed into John Ribot and became the administrator of the Brisbane Broncos and then the chief of Super League, the breakaway league competition run by the News Corporation when it failed to gain the television rights for the game.

This particular matchbox hero was responsible for the corporatisation and market-driven focus of the game.

I saw him once at an opening night for *The Phantom of the Opera* that I took my hard-of-hearing mother-in-law to. ('It's the best way to enjoy this show,' she said, as she took out her hearing aids, 'just enjoy the costumes.') I couldn't help myself. Standing behind him, I leant forward and said softly in his ear, 'Johnny Reebo-de-ball-sack.'

He threw back his head and laughed. 'Did I play against you?' he said as he turned to me.

'No,' I said. 'But I saw you play.'

'Who'd you go for?'

'Redcliffe.'

He smiled. 'Oh, the peninsula, good old Dolphins!' He

had ended up playing there for a few years. 'Golden days,' he said as we parted.

I watched as he went back into the theatre and thought how ironic it was that he was instrumental in changing those golden days.

Modern players are fitter, faster, come from all over the globe, are better paid and generate blaring headlines and hype almost every day as befitting their professional entertainer status. The matchbox faces, by contrast, all had occupations outside their rugby league identities. Sales reps, concreters, transport operators (truck drivers, please, who was old Tony Trent fooling?), teachers and so on. They were the blokes down the road who had a life in between the weekends, things to do as well as running around in shorts and long socks for an hour and a half on a Saturday or Sunday arvo.

Men like Bevan Bleakley.

I remember buying a Bevan Bleakley matchbox on eBay when I was waiting for a delayed plane in an airport lounge, surfing mindlessly on the net. I have a habit of occasionally typing in a name from the 1970s BRL just to see what pops up. Well, up came Bevan's matchbox melon shot and his mug. I laughed in delight. It was like seeing an old friend, old Bevan on the screen, with his great granite face exploding in a huge smile. Then I was quiet for a few moments and I pressed the 'buy' button.

In the quiet, I thought of my parents. And of dear old *full bore* Bevan Bleakley. I used to love watching him play. I thought of how, when I was young, I must have thought that my parents would never be anything but big and loud and loving. How I could never have comprehended that they would one day be just a memory. If we are lucky, the memories will be good ones; it's nothing to get too sad about during a game of 1970s golf, but it is something to think about.

I got ready to play another Basil Fawlty fairway shot and, mid-swing, my son and my friend PB yelled in unison: 'Eight for ten, sixteen for twenty!' I took out a divot from the turf that was big enough for an in-ground pool. And I laughed.

And then I asked PB what it – 'Eight for ten, sixteen for twenty!' – means. Again.

Chapter 3

Little Golden Books and Coffee

If you want to find a place where memories and stuff collide, a place that shows you just how much changes and how much is eerily the same, then the local café or coffee shop is a gold mine.

Coffee. Coffee shops. People don't drink coffee in the home so much now; to get proper coffee you go out. Just like my son and I were doing. We went to a nice coffee shop, one of our favourites.

Coffee used to come in blends in glass jars, tins and little envelopes from places like caravan park kiosks and the Red Cross stall at the Redcliffe Hospital Outpatients clinic. With brands like Pablo, Nescafé, Bushells, International Roast, Douwe Egberts and the dreaded Caterer's Blend.

I asked my father what that blend was. 'Anything some sweaty bloke who picks his nose sweeps up off the floor and puts in a bucket. Stick with tea.'

And it was always instant. Like some magic trick. A spoonful from whatever was your choice of jar into the bottom of a cup, add hot water, milk, sugar. Instant coffee. 'Anything instant can't be any good,' rattled my father. 'Nothing that works that fast can be any good. Except a good fart to clear the pipes to get you going in the morning.'

This advice was shared well out of my mother's hearing.

Still, coffee – instant or not – could well and truly get a hold of a person.

One friend of my mother's would drop by and have coffee and a catch-up; this necessitated a jar of Maxwell House being kept in the cupboard for use on these occasions. 'She does love her Maxwell House,' said my mother. 'She calls it her Miracle in a Cup.'

'That,' my father said from his chair by the front window, 'is a bit rich. Miracles! Nobody in the Bible worth his or her salt would drink instant bloody coffee, not even if it was Maxwell House. Not even bloody Herod.'

The idea of people from the Bible behaving like the rest of us was sort of novel. Perhaps when Gabriel dropped over for a catch-up and told Mary what she could expect for Christmas, she got the Maxwell House out of the cupboard.

Or maybe something else.

'Would they drink Bonox?' my sister Corby piped up. She was always up for a bit of fun.

'Coffee, tea or Bonox' was a catchcry from a television commercial that was annoying enough to seep down into the psyche.

Bonox was sort of a grown-ups' drink, which is why it tasted so odd, or at least that was my theory. It came in a jar or in cubed form and was even more dreaded than Caterer's Blend. You dissolved it in a cup of hot water to produce a murky brown cup of heat. We sometimes had it foisted upon us in a plastic mug when it made a guest appearance on primary school soup days, which were a Wednesday during winter.

Usually you had pea and ham or chicken soup but it was eight ball time when, along with a piece of buttered white bread, came a cup of brown stain and a furtive look from the mothers who filled in on soup day.

Somebody had forgotten to get the orders for the tins of the usual soup.

'Bonox – there must be something in it!' was another advertising phrase for the brown murk.

This was meant to describe its hearty, health-giving properties. If it was good for Gran and then Mum and Dad, then there must be something in it.

My father wasn't shy in giving his assessment of Bonox and its commercial. 'There's something in it, all right – boiled-up arseholes, hoof and tripe. Bonox, my arse.' As was his hobby, he sometimes appropriated a word from some other part of life to dismiss something he thought sub-par. Bonox joined the list that included banjo players, pie cans, Barabbas and tripehound. 'That's a lot of bloody steaming Bonox!' could apply to school reports, the weather segment on the news or a prime ministerial statement.

All the same, my sister's question of whether people in the Good Book imbibed Bonox was still to be answered. 'Well, when you think about it, Bonox is as basic and primitive as you can get, so you can't count it out,' said my mum.

'Bonox! Bonox? No,' said my father.

'Well, you don't know, Colin.' Mum smiled. 'People got up to all sorts of things in the Bible. Maybe on a cold night.'

'Bonox in the Bible? Nobody would touch that broth with a ten-foot barge pole – not in the part that counts, anyway.' This, I knew, meant the New Testament.

'But some mad old coot in sandals from the Old Testament might have had a sip.' My parents laughed and my father winked at my sister and me.

I had no idea what was going on, but they were having fun and that was lovely. So Bonox was good for something after all.

'They all drank tea, for Christ's sake,' our father assured us.

'But was that all they drank?' I asked.

'Oh, they had wine of course,' my father began to expand on his topic. 'And Jesus had the odd shandy on his birthday.' This made some sort of sense.

'John the Baptist was fond of stout, but look what happened to him. Lost his head and that's why Baptists don't drink.' I nodded without knowing why and my father finished, 'And St Peter, of course, well, he was a four-ex man and a good bloke all round.' He thought for a bit and added, 'But old Joseph would drink anything that went round, that's why he believed Mary.'

'Colin!' my mother shouted.

Under his breath he added, 'Why wouldn't the poor sod want a gargle?' And then, for my mother's benefit, he said loudly, 'Just having a chat, love.' And then he looked at us and said, 'Just stick to tea.'

•

Coffee was a bit too modern, a bit too American for my father ever to really take to it; this was a man who was suspicious of tea bags. Tea to him was loose leaf and brewed in a pot. Even on picnics, when tea bags or a tin of instant coffee would make things more practical, my father insisted on making real tea. This was the kind of tea he'd made when he worked on building the concrete platforms that bedded the huge utility poles carrying the electrical wires that powered the state.

We had driven to a picnic spot that was next to a pleasant enough river, with some nice trees and a huge utility pole towering above.

'Helped put that there,' said Dad, looking at the tower with his neck craned back, as we gathered around a public barbecue to prepare for lunch.

Lunch invariably meant a billy of tea being brewed – a billy being a pot with a lid and no spout, filled with steaming hot water and some loose-leaf black tea. The tea would be allowed to brew, steaming like a device from some mad scientist's laboratory, and then, with some mysterious wisdom known only to him, my father would declare the tea brewed. It would be poured awkwardly into white enamel tin cups.

'You can't beat this,' my father would say as hot liquid would splatter everywhere, fingers were scalded and cups were dropped with a yelp and a whine which made parents yell.

If the tea wasn't spilt, you would hold the enamel cup trying not to whimper as the heat became almost too much to bear, and when you finally came to drink it, a flotilla of tea leaves would have to be sifted through your teeth.

It was a drink from another era, although on the trip to the electricity tower my father added a bit of bushcraft that took the brewing process to a new level.

He picked up a tea towel, carefully folded it over a few times and wrapped it around the billy's handle and said casually, 'Show you a trick to get a good cup of tea.'

My mother looked up from distributing egg sandwiches and said with a slightly anxious note, 'Colin?'

'I know what I'm about, love.' He stood, carefully, positioning his legs wide apart and staggering them slightly with his front leg bent at the knee.

'Watch yourself,' he said with a look at us, and then to himself, 'Here we go.' He slowly started to turn his stiffened right arm around in a full circle, and the steaming billy went with it.

'Colin!' my mother said again.

'It's right, don't bend the elbow, that's the trick!' grunted my father. He kept rotating his arm and then for a bit of fun, I think, he went faster and faster. The billy became a blur.

'Colin!' my mother shouted.

'It's right!' my father yelled back happily.

'It looks like you're about to take off!'

My father giggled and was about to speak to my mother when something did take off – the billy.

'Christ almighty!' yelled my father and staggered forward in little steps, the handle of the billy still wrapped in the tea towel clutched in his hand sans the billy.

'Lift-off!!' cried my mother and we kids ran screaming in all directions while the billy soared up into the air with a graceful arc, courtesy of the handle giving out at the bottom of one of my father's great swings, and landed in the carpark with a thud as it spat tea everywhere.

After that, tea bags, and occasionally coffee, were taken on the picnics.

Yet it was the fact coffee seemed to be evolving that began to fascinate even my father.

After a chat and a fuel fill-up at Ken McCrohan's BP servo on the corner, my father came back with news of a new development. The Café-Bar. A beige plastic contraption with a row of chunky rectangular handles that would turn and dispense the makings of a coffee. Sugar, coffee and hot water. Then, more remarkably, there were the handles that let you add soup or chocolate powder.

'It's all pretty jet age,' my father said. 'You don't need milk, they've got whitener. Top shelf – for coffee,' he added.

It wasn't long before a Café-Bar was in Dad's shed and it was as if there amongst his drills, leads, jars of screws and nails something that belonged to NASA had found a home.

Whitener. This was an odd substance called Coffee-mate. Powdered non-dairy sweetener that would add instant flavour to whatever instant coffee was plopped into the cup.

My father soon referred to it as a 'touch of eyebrow' because of a TV advertisement where a pair of bored office workers bemoan another boring Monday morning with another boring cup of coffee to start the work day. Then a singing co-worker extols the virtues of Coffee-mate, so rich and creamy. They all break into song, including a dark-haired man with a moustache who sings, 'We've never had it before' and raises his eyebrow so much that, Ken McCrohan told my father, he could wipe his arse with it.

Coffee-mate could only be bought in chemists. We were told this by the obligatory deep-toned voice-over; the implication being that if it was only available at chemists it must be good for you.

My father wasn't too sure about this. 'You know, you buy all sorts of crap from chemists,' and he nodded to my mother. 'Not too sure about the old Coffee-mate.'

'Non-dairy whitener and sweetener' was a marketing department's way of describing a dehydrated collection of corn syrups, soybean oils, phosphoric acid and extracts from seaweeds and non-lactose milk proteins.

Coffee might have been jet age, but still, it could be a bit too modern for its own good. My father reverted to milk. And soon he went back to tea, donating his Café-Bar to the show society.

Now, coffee has become such an essential part of Australian life that it's almost impossible to imagine a day without it.

Flat whites, long blacks, lattes, cappuccinos, mochas, macchiatos, and on and on it goes.

You can get almost any coffee almost anywhere in Australia, even though sometimes the acceptance of types of coffee may reflect a certain reluctance to embrace a more complex social make-up.

In the Northern Territory a group of us sat in a coffee shop waiting to begin filming for a television show. We were waiting for a rainstorm to pass and ordered a coffee.

Two cappuccinos, one latte, a long black and a soy latte.

We sat chatting and looking out at the rain until the waiter came with the coffees. 'Here you go,' she said. 'Long black, the two caps, the normal latte.' This term 'normal' should have given us a hint something was up. She paused and then continued, happily placing the last coffee down on the table. 'The gay latte.'

'The gay latte?' I said.

'Well that's what we call 'em.' And she smiled and went about her business.

We looked at each other and shrugged.

•

You could get soy lattes in the coffee shop my son and I were visiting. We walked in and smelt the reassuring aroma of coffee, a warm, welcoming smell that I found hard to believe had been a part of all my son's life but not really all of mine.

Just below the shelf where customers could purchase a series of travel drinking cups with the café's name monogrammed on them, was a collection of old jars and tins – a sort of decoration and homage, I suppose, to the heritage of coffee.

This was apt.

Coffee used to mean empty glass containers that would hang around in sheds and pantries for years, though not for decoration. They could contain all sorts of things, from bolts, nuts, nails and cooking ingredients to homemade jams and chutneys.

And sometimes contents even more exotic.

Coming back from the beach with my father one afternoon we were stopped by Mrs Rhona Finlayson, the lady who lived at the top of the street which led to the beach, and who had a bore-water pump and a rather heavy-looking concrete flamingo in her front yard.

My parents said that the flamingo had gout. That's why its ankles were so big. And so, whenever any of us passed we would say, 'Hello Gouty!' to the concrete bird.

Mrs Finlayson called out to my father. 'Col, I've got something to show you.'

Usually, Mrs Rhona Finlayson calling out to either of my parents was a good thing. It meant she would chat and give us a Cottee's lime cordial and Iced VoVos. But not that arvo.

We stopped not far from Gouty and Mrs Rhona Finlayson came over and held out a Pablo coffee jar. The blue sombrero was on the lid, but inside there was no coffee. Just what I took to be little blue-green rocks.

Mrs Finlayson rattled them around and said, 'There, that there's my gallstones.'

'Well done, Rhona!' said my father. 'You've got a squadron of them!'

She held them out to me. I saw the little stones in the glass and in the background the head of Gouty the flamingo.

'These things, these were in me! Right there,' and she pointed in the direction of her abdomen. 'Little swines of things.'

I didn't know what to think. And this feeling was compounded by my father muttering as we walked off, 'It's a bucket of laughs getting old, sunshine.'

•

We were in the café, my son and I, for breakfast. I'm big but he's bigger. Fitter and leaner and ready for the breakfast which the café's menu called Gluttony. It was a good café with nice people and glorious food. And small tables. You can't have everything. We settled our large and eager frames around, over and under the dinky tables and picked up the menus.

The contents of the menu hadn't changed, but the format had. Instead of laminated paper, the café's delights were encased within a series of Little Golden Book covers.

It wasn't unknown for coffee shops to use retro kitsch. A café nearby used old album covers. Another, laminated period magazine covers.

Now we had Little Golden Book covers. Little Golden Books have been around since 1941 when they were created to be durable and easily affordable. They were so successful that the brand passed through a number of corporate hands because they turned so much coin.

They were sold at supermarkets, sometimes even at corner shops, were colourful, easily read, and even though they were so very American, this didn't seem to stop them floating about almost everywhere in the world. They would turn up in the most unlikely spots.

Like the Rockhampton Base Hospital Outpatients ward in the 1980s during my university days. I came across *The Saggy Baggy Elephant* there in a pile of magazines and books stuck on a table next to a row of plastic chairs. I had to do something with myself so I rummaged through the pile of reading matter and settled on Saggy Baggy.

I was in the Outpatients after heroically trying to recreate Jack Nicholson's performance from *Easy Rider* as a pillion passenger on a friend's motorbike after a reasonable session at the Students' Club.

'For God's sake, hang on,' he shouted.

I assured him I would do so and then I started to wave my arms up and down à la the film character, a seedy country lawyer who found a bit of freedom on the back of Peter Fonda's chopper motorbike as they travelled across America.

Unlike dear old Jack in *Easy Rider*, I managed to fall from the Suzuki 250 and land with a resounding thump on my sizeable arse. I was suitably dressed for such an incident – wearing nothing but a pair of Stubbies, a rugby jumper, thongs and helmet. My mate gallantly gave me a lift to the Base Hospital and, between guffaws, deposited me at the door.

Along the way, I balanced on the back of his bike and waved occasionally to the motorists who tooted in appreciation of my grand and bloodied arse being presented to the passing public.

I gave my mate the thumbs up and waddled into the hospital to present myself and my bare red buttocks, framed by the tattered remnants of the Stubbies shorts.

I nonchalantly stood and flipped through *The Saggy Baggy Elephant*. A story of a worried little elephant that felt he didn't belong because he didn't fit into his skin. Well, lucky Saggy Baggy, I thought, to have an excess of skin.

A man holding a hanky to his bloody head stared dully at my arse and me.

I held up Saggy Baggy. 'Great book, this!'

He just stared and breathed heavily.

As I stood swaying, I noticed that somebody had been at work with a texta on the illustrations of *The Saggy Baggy Elephant*.

Occasionally he was cross-eyed, or wearing glasses and finally a lion that Saggy Baggy was having a chat with was anatomically very excited about the conversation.

Saggy Baggy can have that effect.

46

My name was called and a lovely nurse tried to be as kind as possible.

I took the book with me as we entered a cubicle and presented it to her. 'Here, I thought you might like this.'

She looked at me and at the book, laughed a little and then said, 'Thanks.' She then set about her business of picking bits of gravel out of my bloodied arse.

I heard a cough and turned to see an old head poking through a curtain partition. From that head came a voice as rough as somebody who gargles with Drano.

'Yep. You win, young fella. Thought I was dumb but you take the cake. I Supa-glued me bum to a bit of wood. But you got no bum at all. You'd be the dumbest I've seen.'

'Saggy Baggy Elephant,' said the nurse. 'What a way to make a living.'

And she burst into a delightful peal of laughter.

•

I looked at the cover of *The Saggy Baggy Elephant* on a menu and smiled a little. My son looked at me and tilted his head in question. I decided not to share my Saggy Baggy Outpatients tale, but instead picked up *Scuffy the Tugboat*, the story of a little tugboat who finds his way into a big harbour.

I had been read this book as a child. I had read this book to my son.

I held it up. 'I read this to you when you were little.'

My son looked at me. 'Yeah. I loved it.'

I looked at him.

'I loved when you read me the coffee list and the all-day breakfasts.'

'Up yours,' I said. He laughed.

Then he reminded me that another coffee shop, near the high school he attended, used to have similar menus encased in Little Golden Books. That café fronted onto a side street that was clogged with the morning rush hour. People dropped their kids at the school and then tried to make their way into the stream of cars and trams and buses on the busy main road.

Sometimes people's tempers and thoughts about the day ahead would get the better of them and they'd attempt to push and nudge into the stream from the narrow side street.

The cars were nearly always swollen big things, like the one I drove, but I wasn't in a hurry to get anywhere when my son and I sat and had breakfast at this café. He was in his senior year and had later starts on certain days and so on those mornings we would sit at the side windows, he in his blazer and uniform and me in whatever I had thrown on, and we would watch the antics of the drivers and cheer the regulars we picked out in the traffic crush.

Chuffer was a man I recognised in that roundabout way of parents who know each other with an unnamed recognition from Saturday sport. Know the face, not the name. Sometimes you might even say hello. But no name.

Chuffer had smoked at those games but back then he was just another father hanging around at Saturday sport. On those Saturdays he'd half skulk off around to a tree or wander a little way off and light up, nursing his smoke in a curled hand, but I can't remember him smoking in the manner he did when in traffic. There, sitting in his car, he would demolish the cigarette with great long, inhaling breaths, making the smoke glow like the end of ET's fingers.

In fact, his fingers would glow so much, smoke would stream from them.

People have a tendency to feel they suddenly become invisible once they sit in their cars. Something about a car makes people imagine they are by themselves. So they indulge in personal activities that make spectating from a café with a Little Golden Book menu quite enjoyable. To an extent.

Sometimes things became a bit gruesome. In between hoovering his durrie, Chuffer would send an excavating finger up either nostril, as great puffs of smoke streamed around him and out of the car.

'He's a machine,' said my son admiringly.

In other little worlds on four wheels, ears were being cleaned with all manner of items scrounged from a furtive search around the confines of the car.

'He's going to use the pen!' I told my son as we looked at a man in a European sedan.

'No, no,' my son answered, as if it was beyond comprehension that anybody would be capable of such an act.

But sure enough, in the pen dipped as if the ear was an inkwell.

My son stared and burst into laughter. He was almost an adult at that stage, the time at his school nearing an end, and he sat next to me watching the grown-ups go about their day.

People like Chuffer, going knuckle-deep in a nostril as they worry about how late they'll be for wherever they are supposed to be.

Another favourite, in a BMW SUV, was a woman we knew as Flicker De Niro. She flicked her head from one side to another to clear her hair from her eyes and then when she tried to insinuate her car into a space where it would never fit, jutted her chin and started vigorously pointing with her finger in the direction of the unfortunate commuter who, holding hands up in astonishment behind his steering wheel as if he was begging forgiveness, stared back at her as if she were Robert De Niro at his most fearsome.

Flicker De Niro.

There was also 'Come on, come on', a man who sat furtively behind the steering wheel of a wagon talking to himself. It took us a couple of breakfasts to work out what he was saying. 'I think he's saying, "Come on",' said my son.

'Yeah?'

The man in the wagon wound the windows down and it became obvious. 'Come on, COME on, COME ON!' he shrieked as nobody went anywhere in the traffic.

And there was always a collection of multi-taskers. People checking their hair, applying lipstick, eyeliner, emailing or texting on their phone, sipping on a takeaway coffee and all the while – usually without a hand on the wheel – motoring forward.

My son looked at these grown-ups. Adults. Going to where they were going, behaving like this. Not a bad lesson to learn about people, I think.

But now, waiting for our breakfast in one of our favourite coffee shops, my son reminded me of one time when we sat in the other café watching the traffic. I had picked up a Little Golden Book menu and begun reading it to him in the repetitive, simple form of text that the Little Golden Books dealt in.

A man next to us, who was ordering a coffee, stared at us, especially at my son in his school blazer. My son gave him the thumbs up. We laughed. I kept on pretending to read. The man stared, gathered his coffee and left. He walked past the side windows and looked at my son again, who gave him a double thumbs up.

Now, back in one of our favourite coffee shops, my son nodded his head to me.

'You remember him, Dad?' my son asked as he held the menu in his hand.

I nodded. 'Yeah, sort of.'

'He was a teacher at school. I think he actually thought you were reading a Little Golden Book to me.'

'Oh bullshit.'

'No,' my son assured me. 'He took my history class once and spoke very s-l-o-w-l-y t-o m-e-e-e-e.'

I looked at my son. He looked at me.

'So thanks for that, Dad.'

I waved the book at him.

'You know this book, *Little Toot*, and this book.'

My son looked at me.

'I can't remember it,' he said.

'You liked it.'

'I'm so hungry,' he said. 'Do you think they would ever write a Little Golden Book about Chuffer and Flicker De Niro?'

I looked at him.

'*Chuffer and Flicker Stuck in Traffic?*'

I laughed.

I looked at him and said again, 'Do you remember when I read this to you? Seriously?'

He smiled and shook his head.

I unbound myself from the table and put back *Scuffy the Tugboat* and then picked up other Little Golden Books I remembered.

I held up one called *Sooty*. About a dog in a fire station. 'You remember Sooty?'

My son shook his head.

'You liked that one, I think.'

My son shrugged.

'And this one, you really liked this one.'

I held up a *Fairy Princess's Birthday*.

He stared back at me.

'You loved this one.'

He laughed and shook his head. 'Up yours. I'm starving,' he said.

Then I held up a book about dogs. A Little Golden Book about different breeds of dogs. I remembered this book.

'The dog book!' my son yelled and laughed.

I nodded. 'The one with the spotted dog on the fire engine.'

'The Dalmatian!' my son said. I gave it to him. 'And the German shepherd and the blind man.'

It looked very small in his hands. 'I don't know if a book with dogs on its cover makes that suitable a menu,' he said.

I nodded.

'I liked this book,' he said.

'My mum put on different voices for the different dogs,' I told him.

'So did you,' he said.

I nodded.

'You spoke like a German for the German shepherd.'

'Zat's right,' I said.

'Dag.' He smiled.

I thought about that blind man and the Alsatian in the Little Golden Book. The blind man with his hat and heavy coat walking through the city. I remember as a boy feeling half sorry and half happy for the man because he had the dog.

Although there were a few things I couldn't work out. Firstly, why the city and people looked so different from Redcliffe. The cars seemed odd, odder even than the creatures that roamed around the streets of the peninsula.

Odder than things like Nissan Cedrics, or Hillman Minxs and the chocolate allsorts Volkswagens of my mother.

And instead of the Kingswoods and Premiers, the taxis were yellow bubble things driven by men in uniforms and peaked caps.

And the dog. The seeing-eye dog was an Alsatian, not the usual labrador we saw in supermarkets and outside newsagents with a slot in its head where you made a donation to the Blind Society.

Alsatians were things like the mad animal that lived next door to us at Redcliffe in the fire station, or wolf-like police dogs from the black-and-white images of the civil rights protest marches in the sixties in America's south, or like M'lady.

Oh, M'lady. M'lady and drip-filter coffee.

I looked up at the café's heritage display. I saw the coffee filter papers.

In one of the years I spent at drama school I had the pleasure of spending a month or two in a house that I shared with two other students.

One was a woman in third year who behaved like she was in a 1950s English movie matinee on a wet Sunday afternoon, and the other was an Irish girl in my year with whom I engaged in serious drinking duels, which she unfailingly won hands down.

And M'lady. A large lifeboat of an Alsatian that belonged to Movie Matinee. It wasn't unusual to find M'lady snout-first, rummaging through the bin eating whatever she could find. She would fart and wheeze her way throughout the house, and as the place wasn't really that big the atmosphere within the rooms became quite close.

It was a dark house with two bedrooms and another space like a large cupboard. That was my room. It was as wide as I was tall, and had a unique feel. This was because Movie Matinee, whose place it sort of was, insisted that the fan from the laundry be constantly on to keep the fumes of the bleach in the laundry cupboard and the ammonia blocks in the toilet bearable, but really a lot of the atmosphere in that house came down to M'lady.

The fan also had another effect. My cell was right next to the laundry so it was a bit like being in a steerage cabin on an old steamer, right next to the din of the engines.

Movie Matinee had a few interesting qualities. She ate a lot of salads with beans and alfalfa and would drink drip-filter coffee by the gallon. She had a habit of talking to people indirectly through M'lady.

'M'lady, M'lady,' she would declare as I lay in a foetal position in my cell, 'has somebody forgotten to pay the rent and put in housekeeping money? M'lady, I hope they remember, *this* morning!'

I would somehow manage to contort my head to face Movie Matinee, who would be standing in the laundry with high-waist jeans stroking M'lady's head, and the oafish animal would stare up at her and then make some noise that sounded like something had exploded deep within its stomach. The belly would heave and travelling up from its girth would come a half belch and half bark.

'Yes, M'lady, yes,' agreed Movie Matinee.

She often caught M'lady in the bins, inside in the cupboard under the sink or outside in the yard. The dog was a recidivist offender and thrived on cracking takeaway containers and slurping up the leftovers, chewing pizza boxes and licking anything that remained on the inside of tins.

And this gourmand also had a surprising taste for filtered coffee grounds. Once when we all returned home at roughly the same time, the floors of the dark house, from the front door to the engine room of the laundry, were covered with chewed filter paper and coffee remains, combined with a few extra interesting bits and pieces.

'Agh! It's eating the coffee,' said Irish as if she was denouncing a witch. 'A dog that eats coffee!'

I saw the great head of M'lady chewing another filter cup filled with coffee grounds.

I laughed.

Movie Matinee wasn't amused.

'So some people think it's funny, M'lady! Some people should know better. It's not your fault you think they're tacos!'

I stopped laughing and looked at what Movie Matinee held in her hands.

A sodden circle of fat filter paper.

Irish spoke from behind me, 'Well, look, they sort of do resemble tacos.' And she exploded into laughter.

'Some people should close the cupboard door properly, shouldn't they, M'lady!' yelled Movie Matinee.

The coffee filter hissed. The dog belch-barked and I was warned by a glare from Movie Matinee.

My days were numbered. The end came at the start of a week when Irish got a glint in her eye and asked, 'Thirsty?' like a challenge to a duel. I knew a Movie Matinee and M'lady double act wouldn't be far away.

Irish and I would sit down at the kitchen table and go at whatever we thought could drown the other person. Irish handled casks of white wine like a six-shooter in an old Western, and wasn't far behind with red wine. She declared beer off limits because Australian stuff was too fizzy and upset her stomach, but any spirits were fair game. I more than matched her when it came to dark spirits and she told me after we worked through a bourbon and a rum on successive nights, 'Oh yes, you've got some Irish in you.' I took this as not so much a statement of kinship but perhaps a calling of a truce in the battle of the bottle.

Then Irish moved on to white spirits. I had a crack at keeping up, but she slaughtered me.

While we were sipping in the kitchen, M'lady would wander in, maybe drop a fart and wander off.

'Ah, that fecking dog,' said Irish. 'M'lady. What a name for an animal like that. It's not as if the fecking thing is a duchess or something. M'lady!'

It was indeed an odd choice, especially considering that M'lady was actually a M'lud, a male.

'It's got a complex, that's for sure, poor sod of a thing,' said Irish.

Movie Matinee was off performing in a third-year show. Even so, the drip-filter coffee contraption simmered away, occasionally hissing to remind us to keep ourselves nice and remember Matinee's rules.

'Oh that awful bloody thing,' sneered Irish, looking at the filter. 'Tasteless. TASTELESS!'

She stared at the machine and smiled. That was when it went pear-shaped.

'Fancy a coffee?' she said.

How many cups we had I don't know, but it was black and warm and was vodka and then gin based. Even shots of tequila made it through the hissing system.

Perhaps this impaired the process of placing the liquor-sodden coffee remains safely in the bin and out of reach of M'lady, or perhaps we may have let the dog have its tacos. I don't know. I didn't put up much of a fight as the dog and us became completely rat-arsed.

'Oh, she loves her tacos!' chortled Irish.

Poor old M'lady. He/she got distinctly wobbly and it was only when Irish saw the time, and there was a prolonged hiss from the coffee filter, that we started trying to be sensible.

'Jeeesus, she'll be home soon. Try and sober the dog up, I'll try and clean up.'

Sober the dog up?

I was going to ask for instructions as to how that might be achieved but I found it hard to articulate the question and, in any case, Irish was already well into cleaning mode. She whirled around in some mad dance, making as much mess as cleaning. What she picked up in one part of the room ended up somewhere else, in the opposite corner, on the ceiling, stuck to the window.

I decided to take M'lady for a walk. How I got as far as the driveway or how long it took us to get there I'm not sure, but it was the most apt case of the blind leading the blind.

Reaching the end of the hallway seemed miracle enough because the noises from me and the smells emitting from the dog were indescribable.

I was attempting to walk out onto the road when the headlights of Movie Matinee's car illuminated M'lady and me in a sad tableau.

I tried to wave as the lights came nearer. I tried to pat the dog's head but only managed to grab its tail and steady myself from falling over. M'lady made a unique noise.

Movie Matinee got out of the car and stood under a streetlight. We stared at each other and then M'lady let out a long constant stream of pee.

When she finally finished, I said, 'Too many tacos.'

I left the house that weekend, never to return.

Now that deserves a Little Golden Book.

In the café, I looked at the dog book.

It had been in the hands of three generations of our family. My mother's, my son's and mine.

Now it was a menu holder. In a good café where nobody drinks filtered coffee, or uses a Café-Bar.

And where people like my son breakfast quite frequently. Nobody used to go out for breakfast when I was a kid. Breakfast was one of those at-home things, almost automatically functionary, which you did inside.

Like pulling hairs out of your nose or some such thing. If you wanted to dress it up, you might have a special cereal like Frosties or Rice Bubbles.

But no, there we were, ordering our long blacks and waiting for our breakfasts. And trying not to get in the way, even though we were seated.

The café was so full that one man was flattening himself against a wall as he was trying to pay.

'Well, do you think some people care about anybody else?' a woman with a three-wheeled pram trying to get out said. The words were put in the manner of a rhetorical question, which a high school teacher had tried her best to teach me about in debating. 'The rhetorical question is a very powerful debating weapon. A question which in itself is a statement, it demands no answer.'

We were seated in the teacher's staff room while she tried to give us a few final pointers for the debate. As she was doing this she was slowly pressing down on a Bodum coffee plunger.

'These things are French, you know,' she said to no one in particular. 'Very finicky, the French.'

I had never seen one before in my life.

'You go too slow, it takes forever. You go too fast, it's a *Bridge on the River Kwai*.'

We three boys didn't know what she was talking about.

'Remember, the rhetorical question —' She stopped and then yelled, 'Oh bug—' Stopped herself again and then slowly and with great control muttered, 'What have I done?' in the manner of Alec Guinness from the climax of *Bridge on the River Kwai* when he realises he has been duped by his captors and he throws himself on the detonating plunger.

She turned to us with coffee spreading across her waist and said, 'Not too quick, not too quick.'

I wrote that down, as well as making a note on the importance of the rhetorical question.

Unfortunately, I combined her advice in a debate against a girls' college who cleaned us up spectacularly. I asked so many questions that they all sounded the same and I asked them so slowly that I came across like a hard-of-hearing tourist who either wasn't quite right or had little English.

Now in the café, the three-wheeled mum dropped the question that needed no answer in the direction of the man flattening himself against the wall. He tried valiantly to make space for her as she attempted to manoeuvre between the man and our table.

It seemed we were taking up too much room. The fact that the pram was as big as a Panzer tank and would barely contain itself on the Monash Freeway let alone a caffeine hotspot didn't really seem to register on the three-wheeled mum.

Her friends, a clutch of three-wheeled mums, were finishing their coffees and talking about cattle exports to Indonesia. They weren't holding back.

'Well I'm not responsible; we're vegos. We don't eat meat.'

'I know what a vegetarian is,' said her friend.

Another of the circle pushed away the remains of a sausage roll that a child had left behind.

'How can you condone what the farmers do?'

'You can't just say that.'

'Well, who else is to blame?'

'People just don't care,' said the departing three-wheeled mum as she wheeled over the spread-eagled man's foot.

He didn't seem to expect or want an apology.

'See you at yoga,' she said over her shoulder and the other three-wheelers waved.

I imagined my big son in a three-wheeler and it was beyond comprehension. If he got up a little too early, I used to take him for an early morning walk, carrying him in a sling around my shoulders, and he hung, usually asleep, on my chest.

It had seemed a pretty new thing back then in our neighbourhood, but now baby carriers were everywhere. Back then I would get a takeaway coffee from the bakery on the corner and sip it while we walked around the footy oval in the early morning dew. I could feel him move against me sometimes, a little wriggling bundle. Feel him breathe.

And I would drink my coffee. I looked at my son in our favourite coffee shop and wondered if I should tell him that sometimes the smell and the taste of coffee make me think of him. Only occasionally, but when it does it makes me think how much I loved him then and love him now.

He suddenly looked at me.

'You know, one of the saddest things is a truck filled with sheep or cattle being driven through the city. Saw one the other day on the way to uni. The smell of pee and shit. All locked up. All that city noise and smells that those animals aren't used to. Sad.' He'd been listening to the three-wheeled mums. He half laughed. 'I still want my Gluttony with bacon and sausage. But it's sad.'

I looked at him.

'I am starving,' he said again, 'but it doesn't mean I don't think about it.'

Conversations over coffee, a good old catch-up and no Maxwell House anywhere to be seen. Some customers used the coffee shop as if it were a confessional. A woman ordered a skinny latte and began the exercise of oversharing.

In the time it took the barista to make a takeaway skinny latte, I found out more about her than a stranger should know.

Firstly, her latest waxing was distressing. At first she liked it but then Adam, whoever Adam was, said it could have been better. But as if that wasn't enough, she was worrying whether she should have bought the investment apartment on the Gold Coast. Her adviser had said it was good but Adam thought that Southbank was more strategic, that Melbourne was always going to be a growing city and that oversupply in a place like the Gold Coast would be the first to take a hit when the crash came.

I wondered whether that was before or after Adam had seen the results of her waxing.

Getting a coffee used to be simpler.

'Well, it can be tough knowing how to go about things,' said the barista. 'But if you don't go about things, you don't do anything. Do you?'

A rhetorical question, I thought.

The skinny latte waxer looked at him and then smiled rather graciously. 'Oh, thank you,' she said and she took her coffee and was probably just as appreciative of the words as the caffeine.

Our coffees came, good coffees. I took a sip and thought I should tell my son about the early morning walks with him in a sling.

But instead I sat and waited. Out came our breakfasts. I put *Scuffy the Tugboat* and the dog book away.

We looked at out breakfasts.

Then my son looked up and smiled at me. And he said slowly, 'I remember Scuffy. The little tugboat. He got lost in a stream and then ended up in the harbour, with all the big ships and then he got picked up in a net by a fisherman.'

I looked at my son.

'And the fisherman gave him back to the little boy who had lost him in the stream. I remember you reading it.' Then my son looked at his breakfast. 'Scuffy ended up where he began.'

'Lucky him,' I said.

'I liked that story,' said my son. He smiled.

I sipped my coffee.

We began to eat.

And it was good.

Chapter 4

Snap, Crackle and Pop, Part I

Just before we went into the house, my good friend turned to me and said with a look and tone that should usually be used when addressing unruly labradors, 'Behave yourself.'

I nodded and added a half whingey, 'Yes, yes,' and pressed the doorbell. If I'd had a tail, I would have wagged it.

She shook her head. She wasn't sure about this labrador.

We were there for a dinner party. It was described as a 'gathering' in the email my good friend had forwarded to me. A gathering at the home of a couple she knew well and I was acquainted with.

What was the gathering in aid of? I asked. My good friend didn't know, but she thought it might be just for a general catch-up.

As we stood at the door I looked at the front yard: very neat, very clean, very simple. There must be a word that people who knew about design would use to describe it. I tried to think of what it might be, and the word came to mind: brutalism. Straight white paths, crushed white and black stones and, here and there, severe, tortured-looking plants. Brutal and neat.

'Is it a housewarming thing?' I asked my good friend, and she looked at me and shook her head.

'No, they've been here for years.'

I stared at the garden again. 'Shit, they must be neat.'

My good friend looked up at me, 'Just behave yourself.'

The door opened and a pleasant and very neat-looking woman smiled and welcomed us into a hallway that seemed almost a continuation of the paths outside. The floor fell away slightly along one side and, in the depression, lay a line of crushed rock. Instead of tortured plants, there was a piece of tortured sculpture.

There was some laughter from around the corner at the end of the hallway and then we were greeted by a pleasant and even neater man. He said hello and kissed my good friend on the cheek. 'Welcome to our home; make yourselves comfortable,' he said and ushered us into a large, empty living area where another seven or so people sat or stood.

It was a little awkward because there wasn't anywhere to sit down. It wasn't that it was an unpleasant house; it was just that it was so clean and ordered. Brutally clean and ordered.

My good friend jabbed me a bit with her elbow and indicated we should go over and say hello to our fellow guests. I thought half enviously that the neat and pleasant people could find almost anything they wanted in this house inside of a few minutes. Well inside.

I thought of the stuffed glovebox of a house that is my home, with its maze of rooms and buildings out the back, and its rather haphazard arrangements. Of the walls covered with paintings, prints, photographs and bric-a-brac. John Wayne commemorative plates, a talking model of the Robot from *Lost in Space* that sits on top of the toilet cistern and says, 'Danger! Danger, Will Robinson!' when the toilet is flushed.

Next to it is a Dalek that doesn't do anything at all except be a Dalek, and that is probably enough to do. There's other claptrap that has no meaning except to the people who live in our house, like a small, dented tin of salmon above the back doors. The tin is dented because I threw it at my son as he ran laughing through the carpark of the local supermarket.

Seeing me waddling towards my car with the shopping, he had lain in wait to frighten me. He leapt out from behind a corner, yelling. I had shrieked, tripped and dropped the shopping, he exploded into laughter and then I screamed and, picking up a tin which had rolled out of a split plastic bag, hurled it at him. He turned back to see the tin flying through the air and bent his head out of the way as if he was avoiding a bouncer in cricket. The tin kept on going, hit a car and then was retrieved by my son, who gave an acknowledgement of 'Good effort, big guy!'

We'd both burst out laughing. It was that sort of a home.

And so I would go to the useful drawer to try and find something that I needed around the house.

The useful drawer. This drawer was under the glass cabinet and was where everything that was deemed half useful was shoved. Stuff like prehistoric mobile phones, prehistoric phone chargers that of course don't match the phones, drill bits, batteries from the last century, pens from various hotels, and bits that might fit pieces but when you try, you find out they don't.

Not that long before I found myself at the neat and pleasant couple's house, I had gone to the useful drawer with the intention of looking for some gaffer tape. When I had finally gotten the drawer open, after loosening and disentangling two letter openers – one from Ireland and the other from a theme park in Hong Kong, which had stabbed into the top of the drawer, jamming it shut – I came across an old View-Master slide reel for People of the World.

Why this should be in the useful drawer was questionable, but I quickly forgot about the gaffer tape and held up the reel to the light to try and make some sense of it. 'Pole throwing in Sweden' and 'Fisherman from France' followed Queen Elizabeth and Prince Philip and an Egyptian shepherdess. Strange three-dimensional images that were vaguely educational in a weird photo-album way (especially Soviet tots and German hikers).

I remembered being quite fascinated by slide presentations at school as they were basically opportunities for sleep or zoning out. But on the odd occasion, when the blinds were pulled down and the room darkened and the images flashed up on the screen that was pulled down over the blackboard, the whole process took on a more epic quality.

Especially when a rather irascible but pleasant teacher who stood a few times for the DLP in state elections and held to a clear demarcation line between religion and education, showed our class 'Science in Farming'.

The teacher and his wife had spawned a squadron of children and clearly didn't believe in birth control or a looser style of life. He was forever wandering about during lunch breaks at the back of the science building by the bike racks, talking to himself and rolling cigarettes from Havelock fine cut tobacco. He rolled and smoked so much he ended up having tobacco stains on his middle and forefingers to such an extent that they looked like burnished gold. This earned him the nickname of The Midas Touch and then in turn Mr Goldfingers.

His interpretation of some images that the slide show could throw up was slightly at odds with what the makers, the Department of Primary Industry, had intended.

A series of rather nonplussed animals were intermingled with people wearing large boots, white coats, hairnets and glasses.

On one slide, a smiling bearded man had his arm shoulder-deep in a cow's arse.

There were titters.

'A novel approach to milking,' said Mr Goldfingers as he tried to move the slide projector along quickly. When the same slide appeared after Mr Goldfingers had gone back two spaces to a close-up shot of a cow with soft brown eyes and then back again to the bearded, shoulder-deep milker, Mr Goldfingers said with a straight face, 'People will go to any lengths to find loose change.'

The other startling moment was when a series of ewes were shown arranged in a rack, lying on their backs with their legs in the air. Not far away was another person in a white coat, hairnet and large plastic goggles, pointing towards the ewes.

There were no descriptive words, save for the lamentably bare, 'Sheep in a clinic'. Mr Goldfingers added in a matter-of-fact tone, 'Good eating there. Chops, chops and chops.'

About four years later, at a senior party held in somebody's home, I did a bit of business with one of the many Goldfingers daughters, who seemed not to share too much of her father's reticence in engaging with the more social aspects of life.

As we explored each other behind the shed in the shadow of the banana trees, I couldn't help myself and said, in between smooches and our hands Burke and Wills-ing around various crevices and parts of our anatomy, 'People will go to any lengths to find loose change.'

Back at my useful drawer, I finally finished fiddling with the slide reel, having identified a mounted police officer standing guard outside some suitably imposing civic building, and placing the reel carefully back where I had found it – beneath a plastic basket holding batteries – I went back out to my study and then remembered why I wanted gaffer tape and proceeded to search for it again.

I never found it and subsequently went up to the hardware store and bought three rolls.

Later that day, when I went to put on a load of washing, I picked up a laundry powder container and there behind it was a little wall of gaffer tape rolls. During the next week, I came across little outposts of gaffer tape. One in a sock drawer, one on top of the fridge and two beside the back of the TV.

I looked around the bare room where we had been invited to make ourselves comfortable. No, I didn't think the neat and pleasant couple would take long to find whatever they wanted.

'Now, who'd like what to drink?' asked the neat and pleasant man standing before us. His chinos were ironed and a part of me wondered why because I wore the same sort of chinos, mainly for the reason that they had the boldly descriptive term of 'non-iron' on the wash label.

But he ironed his, and he looked neat. Mine had let the non-iron team down, with crinkled areas like a relief map up and down the legs.

I wondered vaguely where our iron had gone and had a feeling that I had seen a hint of checkered cord winding behind the castle of gaffer tape that I should try to remember I had in the laundry cupboard.

Then, as I lifted my eyes from the neat and pleasant man's chinos, past his linen shirt – ironed – and then up to his smiling head, I saw along the way, perched on his shoulder, a cockatiel.

'Oh, hello, Memo,' said the neat man's wife. 'Memo, everyone,' and she smiled a nice smile and waved a hand of introduction towards the small parrot.

'Memo, you want to say hello?' said the neat man.

The bird shuffled about; whistled a bit and bobbed its head up and down. 'He's dancing and he's such a flirt!'

Memo must have had its wings clipped because it just paraded up and down the man's shoulders, whistling.

We gave our orders, a white wine for my good friend and a beer for me. The neat man went off, chatting to his bird, to fetch our drinks and while he was gone a tall, bald man who was a senior police officer leant over to me and whispered, 'That bird has the neatest birdcage known to man, not a piece of shit on the bottom of it.'

I looked at him and he nodded.

'I've known him,' – him being the neat and pleasant man with the pleasant wife and natty bird on his shoulder – 'since we were in junior school. Hasn't changed a bit. Always neat, not a thing out of place.'

I nodded.

Then I saw something hanging in a frame on the wall. This was of note mainly because there was nothing else adorning any other part of the house.

I walked over towards it and my good friend gave me another look, but I nodded my head a little in the time-honoured middle-aged man manner indicating everything was okay – this labrador wasn't up for mischief, just a bit of a look-see.

At first I thought it might be an old advertisement ripped from a magazine but on closer inspection I saw it was a game of snakes and ladders. I realised it was off the back of a breakfast cereal pack: Rice Bubbles, with the three little elfin kitchen workers who were created to represent the taste and nature of the breakfast cereal. Snap, Crackle and Pop.

The idea was you could hear the goodness of the cereal, crackling away with freshness, as you poured the milk in, and then as you munched away it would snap and pop in your mouth. Of course, if you left it too long it became a soggy mess, but for the first few minutes it would pop in the bowl. Especially if you obeyed the advertisements and put your ear to the bowl, then you'd certainly hear something.

This adherence to the marketing campaign's suggestion led to the time-honoured elder sibling expression of love – the Rice Bubbles dunk. One would, especially if one was the youngest, be encouraged to place one's ear to the bowl and prove the ads correct, then while you'd be listening a friendly hand would push the side of your face into the bowl.

It was only ever done once, but I think the result was the same: you either cried, like I did, or stoically took it on the chin, or rather the side of your face, and got on with eating the Rice Bubbles.

Being the youngest I never had a chance to continue this tradition – until I had a child of my own. On the occasions that my young son had Rice Bubbles, usually as a holiday treat, it was all I could do to contain the urge to dunk him after I had suggested he place his ear to the bowl to listen to the crackling.

Perhaps it was because he genuinely seemed to enjoy this secret of the breakfast bowl that I could never betray his trust with the face-plunge. Although something about his character always suggested to me he would have taken it on the chin and tucked into the Rice Bubbles.

And it might have been better to dunk him, because for a fair while after being repeatedly encouraged by me to listen to the bowl of noise, he quite understandably came to think that listening to your bowl of food was a part of the routine of breakfast.

When he lowered his ear to a plate of Vegemite toast for the third morning in a row while staying with his grand-mother, this was explained by my wife to her mother as 'some Queensland thing'.

The little characters on the Rice Bubbles packet all smiled broadly and usually had their arms outstretched in welcome. Snap was dressed as a chef and was blond, then Crackle was a red-haired oddity in a red-striped sleeping hat, while Pop was some half-military, half-cooking type.

The breakfast cereal had been around so long its characters had become euphemisms for all sorts of stuff.

Old coots sitting at the Ambassador's bar in Redcliffe would mutter about having a bit of snap, crackle and pop in a glass on a hot day, while I remember staggering around a nightclub in Darlinghurst early one morning when a large man in a white linen suit erupted from a toilet bellowing, 'Snap, crackle and pop!' then proceeded to collapse near the wash basins.

Rice Bubbles: all things to all people. Birthday parties were always marked with chocolate crackles, a mixture of cocoa, Rice Bubbles and copha. They were one of those treats that promised so much more than they delivered, because the first one was smashing and drove you to another. The ultimate effect of crackle overload was gagging on copha and a rather entertaining attack of the squirts.

On a hot day the chocolate crackles' use-by date was reached with terrifying speed; the things dissolving into oily pools of sodden Rice Bubbles in the little crinkle-cut paper baking cups.

All things considered, Rice Bubbles were a go-to part of a couple of generations' childhoods, but framing the back of a packet and putting it on a wall seemed a little peculiar. It wasn't as if Snap, Crackle and Pop were cute and entertaining, more like an insipid, almost obnoxious, marketing concept that even had a bit of a whiff about them when you peered at their smiling little faces at breakfast time.

And there were better cereal characters; Tony the Tiger from Frosties was friendlier, but the cereal was basically a chance to rot your teeth with sugar-frosted cornflakes.

And there was Toucan Sam from Froot Loops, which were different coloured weeties rings that tasted like a mixture of cordial and some vaguely medicinal mouthwash.

King Willie from Weeties was a round little monarch for puffed wheat, and Coco the Monkey from Coco Pops was so wrong on so many levels, especially when the television advertisements were flogged to young minds and the Coco character spoke about the cereal as a 'cruncheee' chocolate milkshake in high-pitched broken English.

Rice Bubbles were fairly bland in the taste and character departments, so if it wasn't for the visceral memory of a face-plunge as some guiding lesson in life, there was, I thought, no way the neat and pleasant man could possibly want to frame the characters because he liked them.

But then again, he did have a cockatiel on his shoulder, I thought as he returned with our drinks. I tried to remember the last time I had seen an adult with a parrot on their shoulder, outside an old pirate movie.

I recalled a tourist at the Currumbin Wildlife Sanctuary screaming, 'Jesus, Mary and Joseph' repeatedly as she was engulfed by a flock of parrots while she held a plate of birdseed. And her husband yelling, 'Smile, for Christ's sake!'

But those weren't birds that the woman owned so I rustled around a bit in my head and, as memories are wont to do, I found a man and parrot – but before I arrived there, the first station I stopped at was an evening when I had felt mopey.

Everybody feels a bit mopey sometimes, often for no reason – even large middle-aged males can become a bit sooky.

Various methods can be employed to deal with this: having a gargle with some tipple water, eating food like dim sims or hectic homemade hamburgers, or watching something on TV.

I chose the latter.

The last time I had felt mopey I'd watched an adaptation of Jane Austen's *Persuasion*. I don't particularly care for the rest of her work, but there's something spookily, wonderfully romantic about *Persuasion*.

But you don't want to watch it too much – abusing any mopey treatment isn't wise and, really, there should be a disclaimer about the effects of watching too many cinematic or television adaptations of Jane Austen, or any period drama for that matter.

My other go-to audiovisual mopey treatments weren't appealing either. Watching Wallabies highlights on loop from YouTube had just become annoying. It was almost unbelievable to see the evidence of the decline of a once-competent and belligerent scrum and backs that ran straight without reverting to bad Riverdance footwork. So I trawled for something sooky to watch. Nothing in the digital cupboard. I asked my daughter to recommend a film that was a good mopey tonic.

She looked at me with that look teenagers reserve for fathers. It's not quite describable but every father knows it.

She shrugged her shoulders. '*Jaws*?'

I shook my head.

'*Ten Things I Hate About You?*'

I thought a bit then shook my head.

'Grease?'

I thought about it. 'Yeah!'

My daughter gave me that look again and sighed. 'I'm having a shower.'

Grease. I saw it once and kind of liked it so I thought it might be a good mopey tonic. A musical parody about high school love in the 1950s, it's almost as if it's someone's dream of being a high school student again.

Everybody playing the students looked nearly middle-aged and the grown-ups looked like they belonged to Moses' Probus Club – assuming Moses had a Probus Club.

Olivia Newton-John has a scene with John Travolta where she displays the most frightening passive aggressive manner I have ever seen. I nearly screamed. My son asked what was wrong; I had to admit that I had witnessed the ghost of many girls I had known. I tried to explain but I didn't make sense. Then I started laughing. He shook his head and walked off. Anyway. It wasn't that bad, but it certainly wasn't a mopey tonic.

I ended up skipping to the end where Olivia Newton-John is struggling around in black leotards and high heels, like a drunk trying to be a vamp to please John Travolta, who is trying to please her by being a sporty jock who stopped smoking.

The ending is the pair of them dressed up in their vampy best driving through the sky.

Still, the evening turned out okay. I stumbled across a good mopey tonic, a Gene Hackman and Tommy Lee Jones flick where they Hackmanned and Lee Jones-ed to the hilt.

I told my good friend the next day that I had watched *Grease*. She delivered the adult version of the look my daughter had given me.

'That film,' she said, 'is sort of fun but it's the best argument against school reunions.'

'Why?' I asked.

'Because they are all so old it looks like a school reunion nightmare.'

I thought this a bit strong. Nothing wrong with school reunions really, a fascinating mixture of fun and horror seeing what time has done to people.

But then I remembered sitting with my mate PB on the hill at Redcliffe's Dolphin Oval watching a game of league when I saw a man who had once been a year ahead of us at school walking with a parrot on his shoulder.

A full-on parrot.

He was barefoot, with way too many beads and a rather too nonchalant meandering manner.

Someone in the crowd said loudly, 'Now that's a bloke who peaked at high school.'

I tried hard to remember him at school, and came up only with the image of him at little lunch (no matter how hard the teachers tried to tell us it was morning recess, it was always known as little lunch) on a sports day, wearing his grey sports shorts with a green and gold stripe up the sides rather too high-hitched for them to be comfortable, and screaming out that he had chocolate crackles, fresh from a home economics class, to eat.

To peak at high school. They should make a musical out of that. Maybe they have – it's called *Grease*.

I was informed that our old school chum was a chandler, a person who deals in supplies for ships, presumably for the yachts in the marinas that dot the Sunshine and Gold coasts.

So perhaps he had some link to the sea which made a parrot on the shoulder acceptable, but the neat and pleasant man looked to me to be squarely at home in his neat and pleasant home in a neat and pleasant suburb with no nautical reason for wandering about with a bird on his shoulder.

I realised, as I thought about this, that my good friend, the neat and pleasant man and the bird on his shoulder were all looking at me.

My friend's look was the most worrisome. Like a good labrador I dropped whatever it was that I might have had in my mouth and smiled. I had to say something. What? If I mentioned the bird I would look like I was being a bit judgemental, and why do that? These people were nice. And what would my good friend say? So I said, 'Do you like *Grease*?'

Even the bird looked as if it thought I was a two-sip screamer.

Then my new chum, the senior police officer, piped up. Almost in the manner of someone throwing a life buoy to a man overboard.

'*Grease*? It was on the other night. Didn't mind when Olivia Newton-John tarted herself up at the end, in the black slacks.'

There was a small pause.

'Who,' I asked, trying not to laugh, 'says slacks?'

'Well, come on, the first time I saw it I was thirteen, and it's not a great message to send, but you know, I grew up in Bendigo.'

His wife laughed.

'What's not a great message? Wearing tight *slacks*?' she asked.

'No, chuffing on the ciggy and . . . you know.'

'No, I don't, Nathan.'

'Slutting it up to get John Travolta. Well, that's a dry gully she went up.'

'Nathan!' said the senior police officer's wife.

'Well, just saying.'

My good friend looked at me as if to say, 'You started this.'

The pleasant man smiled a bit, trying to make the best of things and I finally nodded to the Rice Bubbles packet to change the subject.

'Why the old Rice Bubbles in the frame?' I hoped it sounded casual.

The neat man smiled a little and said, 'Why do you think?'

'You liked Snap, Crackle and Pop?' I got the most obvious one out of the way.

He frowned a little. 'Pardon?'

'The three little pixies who made Rice Bubbles.' It was my chum, the senior police officer.

'Nathan, they weren't pixies.'

'They were actually strange figures,' said a woman with

red hair. 'I mean, one was a cook, but the other two were sort of odd.'

'Well, they're here,' I pointed to the back of the packet in the frame.

'Oh yeah, they are peculiar things, aren't they?'

'Well, no I didn't keep it because of them,' the pleasant man said.

'See, they're pixies!' said the senior police officer, pointing up at the frame.

'Nathan, they're elves. How on earth do you ever arrest anybody?'

'Pixies, elves, whatever, if they commit a crime, I arrest them.'

People laughed, but not the pleasant man. His bird scuttled along his shoulder.

'Memo,' he said, almost telling the bird off.

Then the woman with the red hair had a realisation.

'You kept it because it was the pack that you got the toy in to complete a set.'

'Oh bullshit!' I exclaimed in wonder.

'You didn't get a full set, did you?' the senior police officer asked me.

The red-headed woman was smiling at us. 'Yeah, you two get it.' She turned back to the pleasant man. 'What set was it? Where is it?'

The pleasant man stared. The bird made some sort of noise and bobbed up and down.

'I didn't.'

We stared back.

'I didn't get a set,' he said.

'Oh,' said the red-headed woman and then looked at the packet in the frame and frowned.

The bird shuffled up and down again and the pleasant man had had enough.

'I'm putting Memo back in his cage.'

When he had gone, the red-headed woman turned and said, like a TV detective pondering a mystery, 'Why would he keep the back of a Rice Bubbles packet if he didn't get the set?'

Nobody had the answer. I looked to the senior police officer.

'How long have you known him?'

'Years, went to school together.'

'In Bendigo?'

'Yeah,' he said. 'I never even knew it was a Rice Bubbles packet, just thought it was a bit of art in a frame.'

'Nathan,' said his wife, smiling, 'isn't it basically your job to notice things?'

He just nodded and laughed back. 'Yeah.'

We looked again at the back of the Rice Bubbles packet in the frame, all of us quiet for a few seconds. I think we all thought the same thing.

We were all roughly the same age and knew how precious a complete set of cereal toys would be – a complete set. We would have kept the packet that we found the last toy in.

Cereal box toys were a marketing ploy almost as old as the idea of boxed cereal itself. W.K. Kellogg was the first to hit upon the idea of rewarding brand loyalty by baiting the consumer with a toy.

At first, in the early 1900s, the customer had to write away for the toy but in the post World War II period, when it became cheaper to mass-produce products, toys were placed inside the packets of cereal.

The early toys were nearly always military themed: submarines, tanks and little plastic soldiers. In the sixties, they were space themed: capsules and space men made from different coloured plastic.

In time a more fantastic sort of creation could be found inside the cereal packets – odd little space creatures, dogs of the world, pirates, walking camels and cows and elephants.

Not all cereals had toys – the 'healthier' cereals, such as almost anything produced by Sanitarium, seemed keen to educate the consumer. Their marketing efforts were nearly always based around cards of animals – native to Australia, or other exotic creatures from around the world.

There'd be a suitable 'Wild Kingdom' shot of a big cat in long grass and on the other side of the card would be some printed information to entertain you as you digested the contents of the cereal pack. Sadly, nobody really cared if you ended up with a complete set of educational cards.

On the occasions when toys were even vaguely educational they weren't so tempting. Anything from Nabisco was crap, including the odd lumpy-looking figurines of the world's 'national dress'. This effort took clichés and generalisations to a new height, with lots of conical hats for Asian nationalities, a Spanish matador, and a dancing German in small pants, a funny hat and his knee tilted at an alarming angle. My father said he looked like 'a very happy Teuton out for a happy night'.

My mother told him to watch himself, but added that the little German obviously hadn't been much of a threat in the war.

'Yes,' my father agreed. 'Von Hungry Bum is a very happy little camper, isn't he?' Courtesy of the lumpy moulding of the Nabisco novelties, the German indeed had, as my brother first noted, a hungry bum, where his shorts disappeared snugly up his buttocks.

'Ready for action all right,' said my father, and my mother simply said, 'Colin!' in a tone that shut him up.

Apart from Von Hungry Bum, the toys included the infamous Dutch national dress figure. Infamous because these figurines for some reason so fascinated my mother that she cut out the back of a Nabisco cereal packet and then sticky-taped the figurines we collected onto the corresponding illustrations on the packet.

All except the 'Dutch Cow' were trussed to the packet and, no matter how many packets were bought, and no matter how much we ate of the wretched rice puffs, no 'Dutch Cow' appeared.

'Oh Christ, it's another bloody Von Hungry German,' cried my mother as she rummaged in the packet for the figurine and produced the sad little figure with the bad neck. Thai and Scottish dancers, and people with bowls of fruit on top of their heads were all doubled and sometimes tripled up, but never was the 'Dutch Cow' unearthed from the cereal. When the series run ended, the only comment my mother made was, 'Trust the bloody Dutch.'

But the conspiracy was bigger than just the Dutch. It seemed almost impossible to get a complete set of any series of toys. And if the lumpy efforts from Nabisco could drive my mother to distraction, they could certainly intoxicate younger minds.

And that, of course, was the desired effect.

The good stuff was in the fun cereals, the ones that were of dubious nutritional quality – the Coco Pops, Frosties and Froot Loops gang. The list of essential vitamins contained inside sounded like a Melbourne Cup field – niacin leading out, followed by riboflavin, thiamin and, booting along on the inside at a steady pace, folate.

And almost all the fun cereals were kept for special occasions, such as birthdays or holidays. I chose Frosties for my birthday and the whole idea was to finish the packet on that particular day before anybody else could get near them.

My sister Rhian sorted me out on my eighth birthday when she replaced the wax packet containing my leftover Frosties with a packet of shredded wheat. I was so incoherently enraged that my mother thought I was in the grip of a sugar-drenched delirium and pronounced that that was the last Frosties birthday. 'The boy can't handle the sugar!'

'He's just like Uncle Ivor with gin,' agreed my aunt, who the year before had given me something very special and much sought after – a variety pack with small packets of all the cereals. The problem was trying to keep track of those packets, as in a large family this highly prized breakfast bullion could be pinched within a minute and, instead of wolfing down a hit of Froot Loops or Coco Pops, you would be left with the arid Sultana Bran or Special K.

But of all the fun cereals, Rice Bubbles were the most ubiquitous because, even if they weren't exactly healthy, they seemed relatively harmless when compared to the other sugar-drenched cereals.

And so a simple plastic bit of temptation drove little people to all sorts of desperation. Once, while shopping with my mother, I went after a chance to get the piano-playing clam from King Neptune's Orchestra and ripped open the top of a Rice Bubbles pack to see if I could pry one loose. A mistake for young players; the toys were not only inside the cardboard pack but also deep within the wax paper membrane containing the rice bubbles.

'You stupid boy, I'll have to buy the bloody thing now!' And my mother had to throw two packs of Nabisco cereal back on the shelf and forgo her forlorn search for the 'Dutch Cow'.

I thought my mother's actions were admirable and honest but flew in the face of the evidence of quite a few ripped breakfast cereal packets there on the shelves with the telltale little-fingered tears at the corners.

Those breakfast cereal break and enters didn't just end at the supermarket shelf for, once home, cereal crime continued.

Over the bowl, the packet would be shaken to empty the contents and ideally there among the rice bubbles would be your crazy critter, whacky walker, or dog of the world.

And, like half-crazed prospectors from the goldfields with all eyes on the bowl, the tension around the breakfast table would become too much and there would erupt shrieks, recriminations and accusations that too much cereal was being shaken into the bowl.

'You've got to leave some room for milk!' was the more frequent and most useless form of attack.

Ultimately, hands were thrust into the packet on the sly and went mining for the toy, or one simply poured the whole packet out into a bigger bowl or onto the table, took the toy and then tried fretfully to place the cereal back into the packet. If you were caught committing either of these cereal crimes then undoubtedly a clip across the ear awaited you, but it was worth risking it for the toy.

A friend of mine enjoyed the novelty of finding a toy so much that he began to recycle objects in the cereal. At first he slipped in toys already recovered from the cereal but he quickly branched out into increasingly eclectic 'toys': a yoyo, a pencil sharpener and a bottle top from a XXXX longneck, which aroused suspicion but he assured his mum that it was from 'beers of the world'. The game was up when he took his father's dental plate and placed it in the cereal for whoever was lucky enough to unearth it. When it was unearthed one wet morning his father was irate. 'A bloody week I've been without my plate, Neville!'

His sisters were disgusted and his mother lay into him like a cane cutter but, Neville assured me, it was all sorts of worth it.

Especially when his father complained his teeth tasted of Froot Loops.

At tuckshop all the mothers listened to the story of Neville's inventiveness and how Neville's dad still smelt of Froot Loops when he gave his wife a kiss goodbye in the morning.

'You,' said my mother pointing right at me, 'don't get any ideas from that silly friend of yours.' For a few days she was on cereal watch until she was satisfied nothing had been added à la Neville.

Neville's dad, who had been a handy rugby league player and a fairly imposing sort of a human, was thereafter called Mr Froot Loops, and my father would often take my mum on an after-dinner stroll to check out what Froot Loops' real estate business had to offer in the way of property and land.

Whether or not this breakfast cereal criminality lay the groundworks for future careers in crime would be an interesting case study, but undeniably some toys created an itch that just had to be scratched.

I couldn't care less for Daffy Dawgs, which were a variety of professions in the guise of dumb-looking dogs, but I was fairly keen on the Dogs of the World series. I wanted to see if our mongrel – a kelpie – ever got a look-in, but no, all that came from the bowels of the packet were Scottish terriers, corgis and Great Danes. Not even a labrador.

But King Neptune's Orchestra was the series I really wanted. For some reason instrument-playing shellfish and fish fascinated me; the whole concept was quite surreal when compared to the rather boring Snap, Crackle and Pop figures on the outside of the pack. It was as if there was a bit of Daliesque surreal humour wrapped in Disney cute.

And then there was the girl with the warts. A pretty girl who could run faster than any other boy in grade five. She had warts on her thumb, which she tried to hide, and if boys like me wanted to tease her because we had no way of speaking sensibly to her, even though that's what we all wanted desperately to do, we would stare and rub our own thumb in the spot where her warts were and make her blush.

She had a Critter King she kept inside her pencil case and would place on her desk as she prepared for the day.

One day I had rubbed my thumb at her in class, and made her look away and wrap her hand in a little hanky. That afternoon as I was walking home I saw her standing with her mum in the Woolies carpark. She was crying and holding out her thumb. Her mum cuddled her and I stood and watched a while, then walked on home.

The next day as she prepared her desk, I scuttled past and popped down another in the series of Crater Critters, Mr Upsy Downsy, an odd orange ball with an upside-down face and a little black top hat you could take on and off. Quite highly prized in the world of breakfast cereal toys.

I didn't know whether she had seen it, until, just before the teacher began the class, she turned and looked at me. I stared back and then nodded.

She gave me the loveliest smile. I blushed and hardly said a word to her again. I never rubbed my thumb at her again, and King Critter and Upsy Downsy stood together on her desk for that whole year.

I stood looking at the Rice Bubbles packet in the frame and I thought of her. Where she had gone and what had become of her. I wondered how long she had kept King Critter and Upsy Downsy. And her warts, I wonder how she got on with them.

'I know what you're thinking about.' It was my new chum, the senior police officer, sounding just like a police officer. I thought, I doubt it, mate, but I wasn't going to admit to thinking about thumb warts and a lovely smile.

'Captain Cutlass?' said the senior police officer. 'The purple one.'

I thought for a bit and then laughed. Captain Cutlass was the last in a series of cereal box novelty pirates and the purple ones were as rare as hen's teeth.

The senior police officer laughed with me. 'I never got close to getting the set of pirates but everyone knew that the purple Captain Cutlass was one to get a hold of.' He looked at the framed packet with me and slowly said, 'The purple Captain Cutlass. Sounds a bit like *The Maltese Falcon*, a bit of a mystery.'

I nodded.

'*The Mystery of the Purple Captain Cutlass* – very Agatha Christie.'

I thought for a moment. 'Do you read any of those mystery novels? Crime books?'

He rolled his eyes. 'Oh Christ no. Get too much of that sort of palaver at work.'

He stopped for a bit and then winked, 'But I would read *The Mystery of the Purple Captain Cutlass.*'

'Nathan, you are such a dag,' said his wife warmly and they walked off back to where the pleasant woman stood showing my good friend a small, tortured statue.

I looked back at Snap, Crackle and Pop. And I thought to myself, I knew what he meant.

Chapter 5

Snap, Crackle and Pop, Part II

I was still looking at the Rice Bubbles packet when the neat and pleasant man came back without his bird. When I turned I saw that he had kindly gotten another drink for me.

I also saw that I was the only one still looking at the frame; everyone else, including my good friend, had gathered around the other end of the room.

I took my drink and thanked the pleasant man and he took my empty bottle and smiled.

'Still looking at the packet?'

I admitted that I was. 'I was thinking about the toys inside. Funny how a bit of plastic can make you remember so much.'

He nodded. 'I can vaguely remember those toys but that isn't why I put the packet in the frame.'

'Oh,' I said.

He nodded again. 'And I didn't keep it because I liked the – things.'

'Snap, Crackle and Pop,' I said, helping him a little.

'Hmmm. Yeah, you know their names.'

It was said quite pleasantly but suddenly I felt a little uncomfortable, as though perhaps a middle-aged man shouldn't be on a first-name basis with a breakfast cereal.

'Spent a lot of mornings with them,' I said.

He nodded again, and then pointed the empty beer bottle at the frame. 'It was the game.'

I looked at him.

'The game, that's why I kept it.'

I looked at the packet in the frame.

'The game?'

He nodded.

'Snakes and ladders?' I tried to sound pleasant. I don't know if I did.

He nodded again.

I nodded.

He looked at me.

I looked at him. Then at the game.

Snakes and ladders.

A basic board game, made up of a grid of squares. If you landed on a square with the head of a snake in it, you had to follow the snake's body to its tail.

On the other hand, if your marker arrived on a square with the bottom rung of a ladder, you would follow the ladder up, getting a leg-up with your journey through the game.

Its origins reside in a game of chance and morals: the snakes being the sinful areas of human activity leading to falling down the race of life, while the ladders are the opportunities and good fortune that can come one's way.

It's all very haphazard and full of chance, and was popular with kids because it was so easy. When you really think about it, snakes and ladders relies so much on the roll of the dice and happenstance that it isn't a bad introduction to gambling. But the neat and pleasant man didn't seem to be the sort of person who took a fancy on the punt.

So he liked snakes and ladders. This, I had to confess, struck me as odd.

The game was always found in the more suspect show bags at the Redcliffe Show, as a novelty space-filler in between odd-looking chocolate creatures that were rip-off Bertie Beetles or Caramello Koalas. (The chocolate creatures were lumpy and had the distinct taste and appearance of repeatedly melted and reset product.)

I was never really sold on snakes and ladders and perhaps my failure to embrace the game, and board games in general, was because of the connection to the disappointment with the odd choccies in the show bags, something I like to call the Redcliffe Show Bag Syndrome.

A show bag is supposed to be a delight – a little bit of magic for a kid. Expectations are raised and when the harsh reality of the suspect Redcliffe show bags sets in, it creates a sense of betrayal and cynicism towards the promise of good things in general.

It can apply to all sorts of things, from politicians promising some special vision like Kevin Rudd or Malcolm Turnbull, to diet plans and faith or lifestyle gurus who promise to deliver a new and improved you. Sooner or later they all fall foul of the Redcliffe Show Bag Syndrome.

And along with the syndrome I had a lacklustre relationship with the whole idea of board games, thanks to a birthday present I received from my nanna, or Nanny, as my mother called her mother. It was a combined 'holiday' game set which contained dominos, draughts, bingo, chess, and snakes and ladders.

All the pieces were quickly lost but Nanna did try and play with me one afternoon when she visited us.

I had, I admit, almost no interest but I sat down and vagued out while Nanna nattered away.

She asked me what I'd like to play and I said checkers.

'You're not American, are you? It's draughts!' she said.

As half the pieces had gone missing, we had to use milk bottle tops from the craft box that my mother kept under the stairs. This craft box was a forerunner of my useful drawer and was one of the efforts my mother made to wrangle the heaving home she and my father had created. Why she kept milk bottle tops at first seemed a bit of a mystery but in fact they came in handy on any number of occasions: Christmas decorations, a fly deterrent made by threading fishing line through the foil and hanging the string of bottle tops in doorways and nearly decapitating people when they rushed in or out of the doors ('Oh Christ, I've bottle-topped myself again!' my mum herself cried when trotting in with the shopping one rainy day) and, of course, as emergency checkers replacements.

Checkers or draughts, with or without milk bottle tops, is pretty basic but I tried to lose as quickly as I could so I could go off and watch the telly or generally buggerise around elsewhere.

This infuriated my nanna, who muttered that I was a 'Dreadful boy' over and over as I put a milk bottle top in my mouth.

I tried to tell her that the milk bottle top in my mouth was a fresh one, just off the bottle and I was licking the cream off the bottom, but all I managed to do was cough a bit, and then I pushed it out between my lips and tried to smile. This was of course an outright lie; I was up to something other than playing checkers or draughts or whatever you may like to call it.

For some reason known only to me and my tiny brain, I had been putting as many milk bottle tops in my mouth as I could manage, because I thought it was more of an interesting challenge than spending time playing a board game with my grandmother.

I wasn't quite sure how many I had in my mouth, but it was quite a stack and I had to admit it was sort of fascinating.

Then, a milk bottle top fell out of my mouth. Nanna looked at me and shook her head. I thought she might be understanding about the fact that my gob was full with blue and gold milk bottle tops, but then maybe she might not – she was old, after all.

I was never really sure what her age was, but she always seemed so very old to me and a bit worn out by life. And who can blame her for being slightly grumpy when she had to deal with a ball of idiocy like myself. Her youngest grandchild not only couldn't play draughts, he didn't make much sense when he tried to speak. I had a mouth full of foil and just hummed and made strange singing sounds in response to her encouragement in my board game tutelage.

I looked on as she started to pack up the draughts game, all the while mumbling about there not being enough bottle tops.

Then she stopped and decided to go on to snakes and ladders, turning over the board and placing two milk bottle top markers on the starting square. During the game, I confounded her by what she took to be my inability to count the number of squares I should move after rolling the dice – I was concentrating on not swallowing any milk bottle tops. I had, I decided, overreached in my gob-stuffing.

'It's snakes and bleeding ladders and you still can't get it right, you dreadful boy.'

I sneezed and, not wanting to give away the trove of milk bottle tops in my gob, I kept my mouth firmly shut. As a result of the pressure, a loosened golly flew out from my nose, landing on the board and looking, as I pointed out quite wittily I thought, like a snake had poo-ed itself.

Although I did notice that my voice sounded very strange and simple and I could tell that I had dribbled a bit.

Nanna sighed and muttered again that I was a dreadful boy. And I hadn't any idea, and couldn't even play snakes and ladders. She got up and went into the kitchen to make a cup of tea and to mutter again to her daughter about me.

My mother laughed and said, 'He couldn't possibly be that hopeless,' and came marching out to where I sat, with the bottle top that had fallen out now back in my mouth.

'What is it you are doing to that milk bottle top? *My* milk bottle top,' she said.

I took one out of my mouth and she demanded to know what I had done to Nanna.

I didn't think I had done anything because Nanna always seemed kind of grumpy but I suspected the problem may have had something to do with my rather listless engagement with the game we were playing. What I was sure of was I didn't want my mother to know I had another milk bottle top – one of her milk bottle tops – in my mouth. So I sort of hummed.

My mother looked at me and then back at her mother and looked like she thought that perhaps I very well might have been that hopeless.

She rearranged the snakes and ladders board and said, 'Come on, play.' Like some gambler with a six-gun on their hip from an old Western movie that she liked. She liked them almost as much as she did board games.

My mother had a certain look that let me know she knew I was up to something, just like when the gambler cowboy with the six-gun on his or her hip was about to call somebody out for cheating.

I stared back like a rabbit and began to play.

'Count out the squares,' she said, looking at me.

I looked back.

'Count them,' she said, almost morphing into some concoction of John Wayne, Henry Fonda and Mum.

I rolled the dice.

And DukeFondaMum narrowed her eyes.

Nanna had come to stand beside Mum like some deputy. She looked down at me, with a cup of tea in her hand.

I tried to count to four and sounded like a novelty circus act where some faintly exotic animal tries to speak like a human.

I landed on a ladder.

'What did you land on?' asked DukeFondaMum.

'Adddggh,' I heard myself say. I coughed.

'What have you got in your mouth, you dreadful boy?' said Deputy Nanna.

I coughed again and milk bottle tops frisbee-ed out from my gob.

'My milk tops,' roared DukeFondaMum and her hand shot out to my mouth. 'Milk tops!'

I'm sure when the makers of the holiday board game pack came up with the concept they had such a scene of family fun in mind. A mother roaring at her son while scouring his mouth with her fingers, fishing for milk bottle tops, while a scowling grandmother stands there saying, 'Dreadful boy.'

Snakes and ladders was abandoned after my mother had made sure my mouth was cleared and made me clean the bottle tops and then my mouth. She looked at me incredulously. 'What a thing to do! Eight milk tops in your mouth!'

My father, when he was told, nodded his head and said, 'Typical.'

After that, my mother riffed on a theme from Nanna and morphed it into 'You stupid boy.'

The epithet 'stupid boy' was lifted from the TV series *Dad's Army*, which was based around the adventures of a hopeless home guard unit in World War II England.

The platoon's commander was a pompous bank manager, Captain Mainwaring, and he used this phrase when talking to an idiot young volunteer called Frank Pike. Pike was a bit simple and that was why he found himself in the volunteer unit.

My mother had collected enough evidence to have a sound guess at my own behaviour and so gleefully applied the phrase to her own 'little Pike'. Namely me. It was taken by both of us in good humour and, in time, the whole of our family adopted this title for me.

It was just the way a big family handled its internal workings and there was nothing like a knockabout sensibility to express a bit of warmth and affection. Right up until the end of her life, my mother maintained a unique way of expressing herself.

In hospital, nearing her death, each of us, her two sons and three daughters, would take turns sitting with her.

Sometimes she would be asleep and we would let her be and just sit beside her bed in case she might wake.

On one occasion I walked into her room and a sister on a pastoral visit sat beside her. I thought my mum was sleeping, but the sister smiled up at me and waved a little and then said to my mother gently, 'Iris, your son is here.'

My mother didn't move.

'Iris?' said the sister again, just as gently but a little louder.

I looked down at my mum, a big wonderful woman, not always perfect, sometimes shy and prone to quick judgement but always there whenever any of her children might have needed her.

The woman whose arms had held me, whose voice had soothed me and whose love had surrounded me all my life, now diminished and stricken in her bed.

'Iris,' said the sister once again. 'Your son.'

My mother's mouth opened slightly and she said, 'Is it the fat one or the stupid one?'

The look on the sister's face I will always remember, it was all she could do not to laugh, a hint of a smile was there as she said just as quietly and gently, while keeping her eyes on me, 'I'm not sure, Iris.'

My mum's head slowly turned and one eye opened and took me in and then she sighed. 'Bound to happen, the stupid one's gotten fat.'

I laughed. And said I loved her. And asked if she wanted a game of snakes and ladders.

My mother smiled a little and said, 'Hello, you stupid boy.'

•

Standing there with the pleasant man and his framed snakes and ladders, I thought of my mum for a moment. What a cracking piece of humanity she was and I had to laugh again at her and the sister on her pastoral visit.

The pleasant man looked at me and I told him I was just remembering how I played snakes and ladders once with my mum.

He nodded. 'Ever play with your dad?'

My dad? Once on a rainy weekend my mum told him that he should stop pacing around the house and do something like read a book or play a game with the kids.

He chose us. He was a happy volcano of a man who always seemed to have something else on his mind and so when he played a game with us it was always a bit of an event. His favourite game was something he called 'thump snap'.

The old game of snap with a twist.

Thump snap, as played by my father, was incredibly loud, fast and very entertaining. He would roar and cheer and slam his hands down on the cards, then try and have blindfolded versions, which he called 'Helen Keller Rummy' – the house shaking as he thumped the table and roared, 'Snap!' The neighbourhood dogs would bark and soon anybody in the house, not just those playing, would be yelling out 'Snap!'

Games with my father were played at cyclonic speed and you would invariably win against him because he really couldn't be bothered playing.

So in snakes and ladders, when he landed on a ladder he would make up some rule about it being upside down and he'd go back to the start. Almost every dice throw not made by him was a double or treble score and the game was over before it began, always ending with his big hand shaking yours and him saying, 'The better man wins, by Christ, you're a magician,' and he would scoot off and do what he really wanted to do, which was to bang a nail into something, chat with the neighbours, dance in the kitchen with Mum or sit with the dog.

It never struck me as cheating or not trying, just a fun thing that a father would do. My father's true gift was wandering around our house in search of jobs he could do and then finding us playing a game, which would inevitably be in the way, or a chance to give a character assessment to one of his children.

Corby had a board game called Green Ghost that had to be played in the dark as it was set in a haunted house with bits and pieces that glowed in the dark. This included a large, podgy green ghost who rotated with a ratcheting sound to warn players how many spaces you could move.

If you didn't want to play at night, then rooms and spaces had to be blanketed out to create a dark enough setting for the game. In subtropical southeast Queensland, a game of Green Ghost could become quite a steamy experience. If it was in the girls' room, blankets would be hung over the windows and any crack was closed up with towels, causing my father to dub the room the Sweat Lodge. The close atmosphere would make my father mutter about 'those mad buggers growing mushrooms out of their arses it's so bloody close in there', which helped transform Green Ghost into Mushroom Bums.

And there was a game called Mystery Date that belonged to my eldest sister Laurie that my father detested and I adored. Basically, the board game's excitement centred on a plastic door in the middle of the game that opened and revealed the identity of your mystery date – a series of young men who could take you out on an evening's fun.

It was an American game with no nod to Australia whatsoever, and made by Milton Bradley which, my father said, was 'as yank as a name can be'. Yet my father gave us the gift of assigning personalities to all the would-be suitors the door opened to reveal. The fellow in a white dinner jacket was a Young Liberal called Trevor; the bloke with a bowling ball was a DLP bastard; the ski date was a deluded fool called Enoggera Man; and the slovenly, dishevelled grub, who was to be avoided, was called George Georges after the left-wing Labor senator from Queensland. My father was from the right of the Labor Party and thought that while old George Georges wasn't a bad bloke, he was just bloody hopeless.

My father became slightly alarmed when he came across me playing on my own one day and I informed him that I was trying to open the door on the bowling date man.

He looked at me.

'Him? The DLP bastard?'

I nodded.

'In Christ's name, why?'

'I like him.'

My father stared.

'I like the bowling man.'

My father considered this and then said loudly to the rest of the house, 'The DLP bastard? Are you all there? Iris!' he yelled to my mother downstairs.

'What?' she yelled back.

'Is your son all there?' Meaning me.

I thought I was having a bit of fun and said, 'Don't you want me to go out with the bowling man?'

'You can go out with a drunken llama if you want but nobody in this house goes out with a DLP bastard – unless it's out the back of a shed to dust them up!'

Whenever any game was played, it always seemed better when it descended into an all-out opera.

My family wasn't alone in this regard. At university I knew a girl whose dad was a surgeon and his trick at family gatherings was to attempt to play a game called Operation when he had imbibed one too many recreationals.

Operation was a game where the player had to remove novelty objects from corresponding holes in a prone patient. Things like ice-cream cones and frogs and pails of water. If they touched the patient then the nose would glow red and a beeping sound was made.

Watching a skilled health professional giggling as he set off the game's alarm, and then barking for a more powerful anaesthetic was interesting, to say the least.

'Is the anaesthetic for the patient or for you?' said his wife.

'Me please!' he laughed and then, as another alarm went off, 'God, I was never any good at this, was I?' His brother was a solicitor and would watch and yell that there was another malpractice case won and so everyone could have another drink of 'something fizzy' to celebrate.

It was, the box said, a game of skill and patience and fun for the whole family. This phrase, 'fun for the whole family', was found on almost all games, and was supposedly the magic elixir for tightening the bonds of family. Spending time together.

'Time together' is both satisfying and incredibly frustrating, especially during that floating time after Christmas and before New Year; the traditional 'board game' season. It's also a slightly fraught idea, depending upon how people are travelling at Christmas. Sometimes the last thing you need to do is spend more time with a sibling, in-law or partner who, for any number of reasons, may well be giving you the right royal irrits. Maybe all you want to do is zone out and watch the cricket or sneak off and hop on the computer to catch up on a bit of work you assured everyone was already finished.

'We're supposed to be spending time *together*,' somebody will say.

This is where the concept is fraught, because time together can mean sitting down and attempting to complete a communal activity. Which is good theoretically, but in practice it can be as cohesive as a bad day at the United Nations.

One summer we spent time doing a communal jigsaw, a country scene from the Austrian Alps. It started with promise, a few pieces here and there, slotted in occasionally during the day and then late at night.

Then some competitive gene kicked in and it became a free-for-all. Arguments over which piece of a snow-capped peak had been put in where and by whom; accusations that a piece of barn had been repeatedly forced into a roof when it was in fact a piece of fence.

Time together can quickly turn feral.

Board games can turn adults into whining children and can break strong spirits. It's almost as if they are specially designed to create the least communal a spirit as possible. I find the best thing to do is to not read the rule book and muddle along.

'For Christ's sake,' a girlfriend's father said once when somebody wanted to read the rules for Monopoly before we began playing. 'Do we have to waste time going through that lot of rubbish? Most Australians go about their business without reading the Constitution and laws of governance!'

As a result, the games of Monopoly that family played were akin to a blueprint for the global financial disaster. Recriminations abounded for years.

A board game–based grudge runs through many homes. 'A feud for the whole family!' should be an added line on the box just to give people fair warning.

Whether it be based around a Trivial Pursuit gripe or the way a word was created illegally for a Scrabble win, these grudges fester away for years. I know this as a fact. As a child one Christmas, I was given an exciting game of aerial warfare tactics called Flight Manoeuvres. I was taken with it because a RAAF Dassault Mirage, complete with a red kangaroo inside roundels, graced the box. The object of the game was to capture the opposing team's troop carrier.

The box promised family fun but what happened instead was that everyone who played ended up screaming blue murder at each other and yelling, 'You're lying about your troop carrier!'

Of course people would lie about where their troop carrier was because the idea was to win, but as a kid I thought yelling and screaming at each other was the whole point.

Certainly my mother was impressed with the game. 'I'm going to burn the bleeding bloody thing.'

We revisited this spirit of 'spending time together' recently with a board game called Articulate. 'The fast talking description game!' That's what is printed on the box. Basically you pull out a card and are given something to describe along with parameters guiding how you are allowed to describe it. And a timer filled with white sand gives you a time limit.

It's a good game, a fun game. And of course nobody really read the rules, which ensured that the game resembled a particularly appalling question time or a bad police interview. After a point, questions were just repeatedly yelled like a scene from *1984*.

I mean, really, how do you successfully describe 'insobriety' or where the Cotswolds are, without screaming? The reassuring and startling thing is that, like some deep-seated behavioural instinct from a wildlife documentary, you know that the same time next year you'll be 'spending time together'.

•

We stood, the pleasant man and I, looking at the game of snakes and ladders.

'I suppose it's all about spending time together, isn't it?' I said, half joking.

The pleasant man smiled and pointed to the frame, 'That game was the first time I beat my father at anything, the first time.'

I looked at him. He nodded.

'It meant a lot to me; my father really set a standard, I guess. And when I beat him, I felt that I could do just about anything. It gave me a buzz.'

I thought for a bit and tried to say as neutrally as possible, 'Beating your dad at snakes and ladders?' but I couldn't hide a hint of incredulity in my voice.

He smiled.

I couldn't help myself. 'When did you play? This game against your father?'

He looked a little taken aback but kept smiling. 'It was a weekend, in winter.'

'What did he say when you won?'

He smiled a little wider. 'Well, that is what made it so special. He shook my hand and said, "The better man won."'

'He didn't,' I said.

'Yeah, meant a lot.'

I could have told the pleasant man that my old man had done exactly the same thing and that perhaps there was a set manner in which parents behaved with their children. I had done the same thing with my children and carried on like a loon when they had beaten me at some board game.

I remembered how my daughter would spend hours playing a game called Rummy Cub with my mother, her Nanna Mac. How my mother would play with such loud enjoyment and when she was beaten by my little girl, she would theatrically pronounce, 'Oh, the gloves are off now' and whisper things like 'Clever clogs' and 'Smart little swine of a thing, aren't we!'

And how my daughter giggled at her Nanna Mac and how she laughs today when she talks about those nights playing Rummy Cub.

I remembered my own nanna, how old and grumpy I thought she was making me play a board game I wasn't really interested in. Perhaps she wanted to try and spend time with her youngest grandchild, try and get to know him better. Maybe work out what sort of a person he might grow into because a part of her knew she wouldn't be around to know first-hand.

I remembered once coming back from school sport and finding my aunt and grandmother in the backyard with my mum and two of my sisters. They had been laughing at something, all of them, and I looked to Nanna standing swaying slightly with a hoola hoop in her old hands.

'Oh,' she said, 'devil of a thing, Bottle Tops.' And her old face lit up in a smile. It took me a while to work out that she was calling me Bottle Tops, which was pretty funny.

'Is your dad still alive?' I asked the pleasant man.

He shook his head. 'No, no. He's dead. He died in a car accident when I was a kid.'

I looked at the frame. A kid. Maybe it happened not long after he had, on a rainy weekend, played a game of snakes and ladders, which amazingly his son had won.

'That is a good thing to have hanging on a wall,' I said to the pleasant man.

'Thanks,' he said. 'Thanks for asking.' And we headed over to where the rest of the guests were.

My good friend looked at me and whispered, 'Are you behaving yourself?'

And I wagged my tail.

Chapter 6

At Home in the Kitchen with the Dogs

I got home late the other night and mooched into the kitchen looking for something to munch on. The house was quiet, everyone else was asleep, including the dogs outside. They hadn't shown any interest in getting up and padding over to the doors to say hello, which was a bit unusual, but not unknown.

All asleep.

There was a time when, if I had been away from my home, I'd hear little voices shriek in delight when I stepped up to the front door and there'd be a dog barking and then legs, both little humans' and a friendly hound's, skittling up the hall to be there when I opened that door.

It's a sound that I can hear still somewhere in my mind's eye (some may like to call it my soul) and a sound that makes me happy. Once you have experienced that sound, it can never be unheard. It doesn't matter that I don't hear it every night because it is as present as the first time I heard it and felt it. It is tucked away in my kitbag of sensations and feelings, and it tells me I am home.

Another way of feeling at home is standing in the kitchen and mooching.

The kitchen is where stuff always happens, where something is made, offered and shared, the engine room of a home if you like. A place where you'll find a sense of belonging. Even late at night, when everybody else is asleep.

I looked down at a pile of books that had been plonked on the corner of the big kitchen bench.

They were cookbooks, bound for the op shop donation bin. For some reason, on a recent morning when I had been making a coffee in the kitchen, I had decided it'd be a good idea to go through the bookcase containing the recipes and cookbooks. That is why they were in bags on the bench en route to the op shop.

The cookbook bookcase hardly sees any custom and a particular area deep in my brain had decided it was time to rationalise that section of the house. I put this down to the fact that my method of making a cup of coffee is based around having something to listen to. Usually the radio but sometimes a selected piece of music. That morning I felt, of all things, like listening to an old spoken-word album by a man called Tex Morton. He was an old trans-Tasman country and western performer from the 1950s through to the early 1980s who could turn his hand to almost any part of the performing arts.

Aunty Rita liked his 'talking poetry' and when we would stay with her occasionally, she would plonk on some Tex to set 'a bit of a tone' as she liked to say. He had a very deep, growly voice with a hint of an American accent that added to his 'cowboy' character. It always sounded a little odd, especially when he was performing something distinctly Australian. But it was also fun to hear transpacific vowels reciting Australian verse, as if an Australian golfer who spent time plying his trade in America was having a crack at Banjo Paterson ballads as well as describing how he blew up on the back nine.

It was Tex's doggerel ballads that were the most fun, and they ranged from all over the world, always accompanied by a whining, trembling organ in the background. Things like 'Dangerous Dan McGrew', about a crazed miner in 1890s Yukon, who comes into a bar and has a barney with Dangerous Dan, basically over their shared love of a woman called Lou.

Aunty Rita would always say with a wink as Tex cranked up with his musical accompaniment, 'Oh I do like a trembling organ, don't you?'

Apparently not only Aunty Rita liked the poem, so did American President Ronald Reagan, who recited it to Queen Elizabeth II and Margaret Thatcher. Although whether there were any trembling organs involved wasn't recorded.

Tex's talking poetry was a listening favourite at Aunty Rita's, especially Dangerous Dan McGrew, with a nice glass of something warm at night.

'Glass of old smoky puts you right there in the saloon, don't you think?' Aunty Rita would say with a very satisfied sigh.

One morning I asked her if we could listen to the Dan poem. She smiled, popped it on and said coffee would be the go instead of old smoky; after all, miners did love their coffee.

And she went to her kitchen, rustled around and came back with 'the makings' of brekky and we listened to old Tex. Her kitchen was a magical solace for such a small space. I remember cups with birds on them and a square box with a handle and a little bottom drawer that was a pepper grinder. And a big tin biscuit box, which had an image of a strange-looking blonde girl in braids with tiny teeth in her smiling mouth, cuddling a medicated-looking cocker spaniel.

'Half strangling the poor thing, more like it,' Aunty Rita said. It was a fascinating and quite terrifying image and when Aunty Rita would hand out Scotch Fingers and Mint Slices she would add, 'Not too many now or I'll give you the cocker spaniel treatment.'

And even though she insisted that a coffee would be the thing to set the tone in the morning, the fact that she never drank coffee didn't register with me at the time. She was just playing along, having fun with one of her nephews.

I think it was the magpies singing in the pine tree at the front of my home as I woke that made me want to set a bit of a tone for the day with dear old Tex. Aunty Rita used to have a couple of half-tame maggies on her land at Deception Bay and their warbling call in the morning and in the evening would bookend the day. It so happened I had acquired a Tex Morton album in my travels and so hunted for it through all the other rather dubious works of vinyl I have collected. I discovered an overspill between the records and cookbooks. Tex, in his slouched fedora, pencil-thin moustache and rather sizeable stomach, smiling with a guitar that it seemed he could barely reach, was sandwiched in between two *Women's Weekly* soft-cover international cuisine cookbooks, an Indian and a Malaysian. This rather irritating delay in hearing once again about how Dangerous Dan McGrew met his fate in that saloon determined the need for cookbook rationalisation.

On the cluttered shelves, there were a fair few 'celebrity' chef efforts, some of whom I couldn't even recall, even though the books' cover blurbs assured me that the faces were famous personalities. Drive-time hosts, French cooks, bluff middle-aged fellows with hats standing behind a barbecue in the middle of nowhere and Esther Dean, queen of the no-dig garden.

Many were Poms.

Given the questionable quality of English cuisine and dietary habits, I found this quite odd. So many people from the Old Dart who had made Australia their home seemed to live on platefuls of bland stodge so it never sat quite right when someone with an English accent rabbited on about good food.

I never got over the conversation my mother had had at Coles New World supermarket on the Friday shop with a friend – a woman who sounded like she was a character from the TV series *All Creatures Great and Small*, a show about vets in the Yorkshire Dales in the 1930s.

I barely deciphered a word but understood enough of what was going into the All Creatures' shopping trolley as we stood at the delicatessen section.

'God, you're not buying tripe, are you?'

All Creatures assured us she was.

Tripe, onion, Pecks devilled ham paste and cream with crumbly cheese.

'It's crackin',' she smiled.

My mother and I nearly gagged and on our way home Mum, who was Welsh, kept repeating, 'The Bloody Poms. How could they?'

There were many English efforts among our cookbooks.

Nigella Lawson when she was out and about for the first time, along with the Two Fat Ladies whom my father-in-law adored – 'They eat so much butter!' he would shout as if that in some way validated his own love of butter.

And Jamie Oliver in a number of incarnations – from punk novelty to crusading apron-wearer; Keith Floyd looking jolly and happy with a lopsided grin and a big bucket of wine before cancer got him; even Gordon Ramsay when he was novel; and a couple of Rick Stein efforts with him unkempt, scruffy and totally in love with what was on his plate. They had to stay.

Most, however, made their way into a donation bag, especially the interestingly titled *Jamie's 15 Minute Meals*.

This may have been the case for Mr Oliver but for most people they tended to take a bit longer. I can remember a mate embarking on a fifteen-minute recipe of Jamie's which turned into what seemed like fifteen hours of screaming, stomping and groaning in the kitchen.

'This Pommy bastard does this on purpose – it's an imperial plot to drive us all mad,' my mate moaned. We ended up eating fish and chips down on the beach. How very English.

A lot of the books had the feel of last-minute Christmas presents. Especially the two copies of Matthew Hayden's cookbook, one bought by my mother and one by my mother-in-law the same year. Old Haydos had a boom time that Christmas.

And even though they tried to swallow Tex Morton, I had to keep those two *Women's Weekly* cookbooks and a raft of other *Weekly* efforts; it seemed wrong to turf them. Call me old-fashioned, but whoever took the photos for the *Weekly* was a magician; just looking at the pages was enough to make me feel full.

We had a history, the *Weekly* cookbooks and I. In a share house where I occasionally occupied a room there was a couple who followed a rather enthusiastic alternative lifestyle. They had a unique ragtag collection of philosophies with which to live by, a little bit of Buddhism, a scattering of Hare Krishna, a pinch of anarchy and a certain elasticity which added up to a rather eccentric view of life.

The two of them had a habit of farewelling their faeces before flushing the toilet, which was a bit disconcerting at first as the house wasn't that big and noise travelled. The idea, they said when I finally asked why they did this, was one of respect. 'It's right to say thanks for what was a part of us, for what it gave us and to wish it well.'

It was harmless but sometimes a little alarming. The two of them, dubbed Vego One and Vego Two, had differing styles when it came to turd sayonaras. Vego One had a quiet whispery manner and was prone to very long Nelly Melba farewells to what he had just dropped.

Vego Two was much louder and more to the point. 'Ta ta, thanks for that,' or 'See ya' and a booming, 'Now you take care of yourself.' So one sounded like he was whispering a mad long incantation while the other like he was at the football.

They were very energetic vegetarians and not shy about telling meat-eaters what they thought about the digestion of 'other souls'.

'You know you're eating a soul,' said Vego Two as he saw me polishing off a bag of chicken-flavoured chips.

I sort of shrugged my shoulders. 'Mate, I don't know how much actual chicken would be in these things, they're chock full of all sorts of crap. Salt, spices, probably chemicals.'

He stared at me. 'Perhaps they're not in there alone.'

I looked at him and he nodded. The thing with the vegos was that I was never quite sure if they were genuine or taking the mickey, but they were entertaining to say the least.

Vego Two would often ask me what I was eating. If I said it was some meat he would inform me about the damage it would do to me. It became a bit of a game after a while.

'What are you eating, Will?'

'A chop.'

'A soul died in fear and you are digesting fear. It will affect you.'

'How?'

'It will make you aggressive.'

'If I eat fear?'

'Yes, fear makes you aggressive.'

'What makes you say that?'

In the background, I could hear Vego One muttering his mournful goodbyes to a poo. He was going on for ages. Vego Two could hear too.

'That is a long goodbye,' I said.

Vego Two nodded and said, straight-faced, 'Must be a big one.'

Once, another housemate and I were eating, of all things, tofu burgers from a school fete around the corner.

Vego Two appeared in the back garden and asked us what we were eating. Before I could answer, my other housemate said, 'Hamburger with the lot.' I stopped eating and looked at him and he nodded at me to indicate I should go along with it. Vego Two went to town, saying so many species mixed into a mass-produced bun spelled trouble. After Vego Two had gone, I asked my other housemate why he had lied about what we were eating.

'It gives the poor sod something to do. I mean, shit, have you seen his porn?'

I hadn't.

'He keeps a stash in a cupboard in the laundry.'

This I found hard to believe but my fellow carnivorous housemate assured me it was true. Later on, when I was on the way out for the evening, Vegos One and Two were having a bit of a set-to in the way that couples do, not overly loud but a bit pointed here and there as I tried to get out of the way.

'Well,' Vego One said, 'why don't you just go out and look at your dirty books then.' It was one of those oxygen-sucking moments that makes anyone who isn't involved in the argument wish they weren't there.

Still, once you've heard something like that you can't help but remember it. The next time I was in the laundry I couldn't help but have a bit of a look around for the 'dirty books'.

They weren't that hard to find. There wasn't much else in the laundry besides an old washing machine, a sink and two shelves. I had seen the books before, on the top shelf and just let them be, although I did think it was an odd place to keep cookbooks. Well, one person's cookbooks were another's dirty books.

A few days later, I went into the laundry to put on a load of washing and found Vego Two with a bowl of vegetables. He was eating and staring into a *Women's Weekly* soft-cover cookbook, which was propped up on the washing machine. *Festive Celebrations*. The page was open on a roast chicken spread with what looked like some sausage rolls around the dish and some bacon draped over the gold and crispy skin.

Vego Two was just staring at the golden chook, chewing methodically. He slowly half turned to me without really taking his eyes off the festive food spread.

'They your dirty books?' I asked.

Vego Two nodded, still staring at the festive fowl and friends. Not taking his eyes off the book, he said slowly, his mouth half full of food, 'Makes this taste better.'

It was odd, especially when I realised that Vego Two had the same look on his face as he had when he watched me eating meat.

I told my other meat-eating housemate this and he said I should feel flattered.

I had to admit, the festive chook did look good and whoever took the photo would have been proud that it elicited such passion from Vego Two.

So, no, I couldn't throw out the *Women's Weekly* cookbooks, and even though a few tomes were so old they were printed by companies long since evaporated by mergers and economic rationalism, like Hamlyn, or they used imperial measurements, they stayed simply because they were owned by previous generations of my family. And because some of the recipes were easier to follow and less fussy and ornate than the ones created by the celebrities.

What really caught my attention, though, were the cookbooks and recipes of a more exotic origin.

Politics in Queensland is always interesting and volatile to say the least and this was borne out by some guest chefs from the *Redcliffe Neighbourhood Centre Cookbook*, a Christmas gift from my mum in the mid-1990s. Two leaders of the Opposition, two Members of the House of Representatives for the seat of Petrie and a premier who was no longer premier at printing, a case of a spate of elections getting in the way of a deadline. All in all, the late Wayne Goss, the first premier in the cookbook, created a pretty respectable beef casserole.

Teresa Gambaro, plying her trade as the second MHR for Petrie in those days, faxed in (yes faxed! It was that long ago) this beauty: 'Coat one side of a barramundi in cajun powder and fry fillet in oil.' To the point, and would definitely give Jamie Oliver a run for a fifteen-minute meal.

Amid cakes and sweets, Barry Bolton, then Mayor of Redcliffe, old man of my great mate PB and all-round good egg, gave as his choice of dessert, a gin fizz. Good on you, Barry.

And there was *Entertaining with the Country Club 1957 to 82* from my children's great-grandmother from Young in New South Wales. Inside was a note, 'Grandma recommends Judy's Chicken'. And then in brackets, 'And a good Scotch'. A folder of loose-leafed collected recipes, beginning with the startling 'Fish Finger Pizzas'. Tips for cooking with chillies from some fellow called Bill Brooks. 'Try to wear rubber gloves. Don't rub your eyes or mouth and don't pick your butt! It will smart.' Fair enough, Bill.

On the subject of warnings, a torn piece of lined writing paper with the scrawled capitals 'NEVER AGAIN' was stuck over the recipe for the dire White Christmas. Just to make sure, the ingredient copha had an annotated exclamation mark in red ink added to the recipe every time it appeared in the instructions.

Then there was an inexcusable collection of Spam suggestions, from Spam burgers to Spamwiches and three ideas called Spam Goes Hawaiian. The accompanying photographs looked like a crime scene but I must admit I have a history with Spam.

The cookbook was the last one I used from the shelf on a night when I was baching at home. It was sadly old school. A Bledisloe Cup test and then a marvellously, entertainingly awful Roger Moore James Bond movie on telly made it a perfect night in front of the box by myself.

I decided not to go the takeaway option but instead, spurred on by a recipe suggestion – I am sure the photographer must have been a relative of the *Women's Weekly* food snapper – I went down the Spam burger path, along with a six-pack of gargle fizz.

I decided to take the healthy option when I came to purchasing the tinned treat, picking up a tin of Spam Lite. I also picked up two egg rings, as described in the recipe suggestion, along with beetroot, cheese slices, lettuce and red onion. What good the Spam Lite did me was doubtful but an All Blacks thumping never worried me less and I was convinced that Roger Moore was the greatest thespian the world had ever seen.

Lord knows what was in that tin.

And then there was the recipe I gave to the kids' primary school for a fundraising cookbook.

Suzy's Evil Pasta.

Suzy was a friend I had met in drama school. She came from a family of four daughters and her father was a marvellous, roguish journalist who used to edit a now-defunct Sydney daily tabloid. When he couldn't fill the paper, he would wrangle one of his daughters into appearing on page three in whatever set of bathers was available. Including a leopard-print bikini his eldest daughter wore, which threw him into paroxysms of outrage, yelling, 'What would you wear something like that for? It's indecent!'

Suzy, who never answered her dad's page three emergency calls, was a model before she went to drama school. She had worked extensively in America and it was there that she came across a heart-poundingly excessive pasta recipe, courtesy of a Swedish model she always said would be a good partner for me.

'She's tall and grumpy and really yells a lot.'

'Really,' I said.

'There might be a problem though, William.'

'What's that?'

'She's a lesbian.'

'I see.'

'Yeah – I think.'

I never met the grumpy Swede but her pasta sauce nearly did me in. Prosciutto ham, garlic, broccoli, blue cheese and cream.

There is a fellow who lives down the road who used to be a parent from the primary school and availed himself of Suzy's pasta sauce recipe as a once-a-month treat. I see him occasionally and he yells out, 'Suzy's sauce – still evil!' and he laughs and gives me two thumbs up.

Still mooching in the kitchen, I looked at the clock. Nearly midnight, it's a Cinderella snack that's needed, something quick, no fuss and magical. Not much of an ask, is it? Only one place to go: the fridge. Leftovers. I remembered there was a fairly healthy leftover takeaway serving of chicken vindaloo that was biding its time on the shelves.

I opened the fridge and surveyed its fairly well stocked paddock, but no Cinderella vindaloo. My son must have got to it before me. So I sifted through the contents of the fridge. There was a lot to go through but nothing ready-made. It all seemed too much trouble.

I peered into the freezer. Walt peered back. Don't want any part of him. Walt was a brown trout that was caught in the rivers of northern Tasmania by my son the week before the first Ashes Test in 2013. Somehow we never got around to doing anything with him and so he just stayed in there, looking not all that worse for wear wrapped in a sleeping bag of cling wrap.

That was how he (or she, for all any of us really knew) was christened Walt. I had to explain to my daughter who

Walt Disney was, how he created the Disney Studios, how he was the driving force behind *Snow White*, *Cinderella*, Goofy and Mickey Mouse, and *Lady and the Tramp* and all the rest of those films, as well as the Disneyland theme parks.

'He must have been a nice guy,' was what my daughter said. 'Is that why we called the trout Walt? Because of all the animated animals?'

I didn't think Walt the trout was all that animated but I did say that Walt Disney was all right. I didn't think it necessary to go into his supposed right-wing beliefs and habits.

As a youngster I used to hang out for him to appear on the TV on a Sunday night, in his grey suit in his office introducing all the old animation stories and dodgy live action stuff that was a supposed highlight of a kid's week.

I told my daughter that Walt the trout cryogenically snoozing the days away was like the urban myth that Walt Disney's body was supposedly frozen in a vault in Disneyland awaiting technological advances to wake him up down the track.

My daughter nodded, went off and Googled Walt Disney and then wanted to know if he was a racist and anti-Semitic and had ruined people's careers during the Red witch hunts of the 1950s.

I told her a person could be a lot of things, some good and some bad. My daughter nodded, and said, 'Cop-out, Dad.' And then added that Walt Disney had been cremated and his ashes interred in a cemetery.

I said I didn't know that, and my daughter said that urban myths were pretty stupid but that calling the trout Walt was funny and left it at that.

I said hello to Walt, as we all did when we went looking for something in the freezer, and added the question, 'Were you a good 'un or a bad 'un, Walt?' But Walt wasn't up for a chat. And the freezer wasn't giving me much help with a Cinderella snack.

Then, for no reason I could think of, I started humming the theme music to the Disney ride Space Mountain, said so long to Walt and shut the freezer door. I stopped humming and wandered over to a cupboard and opened it, looked and then started humming the theme to Space Mountain again. Perhaps it had something to do with a can of Golden Circle sweet corn I saw in the cupboard or perhaps it was just a good tune.

One day, if you are lucky enough, you might find yourself in a Disney Franchise Park somewhere and discover three minutes of senseless and enjoyable mayhem. Space Mountain. Best ride going around.

Complete with a cracking tune.

It was fresh in the memory for me as we'd found ourselves haring around the Hong Kong Space Mountain on a recent holiday.

My mind went straight to some of the amazing meals we had in dear old Hong Kong.

The fried rice, softer and subtler, the Cantonese chicken with casings of chillies falling about the dish like the spent shotgun cartridges from some old Arnie Schwarzenegger action movie from the eighties. And the cabbage. What they could do with cabbage made my eyes water.

It's a global world these days so it's surprising when something grabs your attention and takes you to a place that in some strange way defines you. Gives you a sense of what you are and where you might have come from. Gives you a sense of belonging.

What did this to me? A can of sweet corn kernels, the same brand as the one in my cupboard, only this particular can was in Hong Kong.

I was waiting for the traffic lights to change so I could cross the street and get back into the air-conditioned hotel I was staying in.

Hong Kong – very humid, very close, very busy. I bent my head slightly, wiping my brow. And saw it, a can of sweet corn. Not just any can of sweet corn. It was a can of Golden Circle sweet corn.

Golden Circle.

A flurry of memories and images. Little postcards, if you like. Of people and places. The Golden Circle cannery at Northgate, with its own railway station, Bindha, for the workers.

'Bin-dere? Bin-where? Bin-dha!' It was the wonky joke always muttered by somebody when you caught the train in to Brisbane from the north side.

It smelt sticky and sweet.

I remember our train stopping at the station one day and a woman making her way out of the carriage with the long bench seats, nodding to a workmate on the platform, then breaking out with a dreadful song called '9 to 5' by Sheena Easton and then dissolving into giggles.

On the year seven school excursion to the Golden Circle cannery, a guide ushered us into an area with the words, 'This is where all the excitement is!' We dutifully turned our heads to rows of expressionless, gloved and hair-netted people wreaking havoc on pineapples. A boy, who grew up to be a dental surgeon, said in an awed whisper, 'Boy, they are good with their hands.'

I wonder if he ever thinks of those knives and pineapples when he's with his patients.

The interesting thing when your mind and memory are jolted unexpectedly is the way you always drift back to the people associated with the trigger. It's not surprising, really, it's people and their stories that make up the history of a place.

I thought of this not so long ago, after a day sifting through an archive collection of buildings, names, places and endless faces. I was working on a project about the history of Brisbane as told through its changing population and, as I walked out into the city streets, it was odd being confronted by the living Brisbane.

All the stories being lived out around me after I'd spent the day sifting through bits and pieces of lives lived. Including a pamphlet from 1947 extolling the virtues of the products of the Golden Circle Northgate Cannery. It featured the

'Pineapple Girl', a tinted figure of a woman holding her hand out indicating a massive pineapple with the cannery superimposed upon it. She looked like she had fallen into a vat of fake tan and the whole effect was slightly surreal.

A history, I decided as I clambered aboard a CityCat, is a melding of both place and people that makes someone feel they belong. We headed off past the South Bank arts precinct and under the row of graceful bridges that cross the river, as the city's skyline began to shine in the darkening sky. Up towards the University of Queensland and past the units that dot the river's banks, I saw streams of flying foxes gliding through the sky in front of a big rising moon. They seemed so close to the verandahs of those units, almost as if the units' occupants could reach out and touch them.

A silhouetted figure standing on the edge of a verandah suddenly waved through the flying foxes, out into the night. A long slow wave to somebody somewhere. A bit like the Pineapple Girl's welcoming wave to the cannery.

A mum and her young daughter were sitting not far from me at the back of the CityCat and the mum directed the girl's eyes towards the waving figure. The little girl giggled and waved back. The mum waved back. And then the deckhand. And then me.

I don't know how long I looked at that bloody can of Golden Circle sweet corn kernels in Hong Kong, thinking of that moment on the back of the CityCat.

The lights changed and I crossed the road with teeming crowds and peeled off into the rarefied chill of the hotel.

I got into a lift with a yawning aircrew, a family on holiday and a trio on business. We all had our stories, this lift full of people.

I laughed. Because I bet nobody else's included a tin of corn, but you can never tell, really.

•

Standing in front of an open cupboard dreaming about food from another hemisphere wasn't doing me any good. So I stopped humming, and looked past the tin of corn.

Then I saw it at the back of the cupboard. A biscuit box.

There is something about biscuit boxes that is quite evocative, perhaps because they are always a treat to share with people, like Aunty Rita's strangled spaniel biscuit box. Or perhaps it was just because of where that box had come from.

The neighbourhood's local handyman, Mr Leonard, had given us that box of biscuits. There have been better handymen, because this fellow was so incapacitated by a life of hard work that he had to be constantly rescued from misadventure while trying to help people.

The old lady from three houses down came across to my house in her nightie and Hush Puppy slippers early one evening to ask if I could help Mr Leonard. He'd done his back while attempting to secure the barge boards around the bottom of her house to keep the cats from getting in under.

I went across to find a smiling Mr Leonard on all fours with his head resting close to the ground. He gave a small nod of welcome.

'Back's gone again. Do you think you'd be able to help me up, son?'

He wasn't very heavy. It was never too much of a problem helping him when the alert went out. He was a generous man, always dropping things off he thought people might find useful, such as the box of biscuits with an alpine scene on it.

'Hello, son, would you like these? Box of bickies, good ones, I should think. Too much for me. Made in Europe.'

I couldn't turn him down, so I asked him in for a cup of tea and, of course, a biscuit.

'Oh no, no. That'd be a waste. You save them for yourselves.'

And he disappeared across the street. He was a lovely man. Was.

He's been dead about fifteen years. And the biscuits – the writing tells me on the back of the box – were made in Yugoslavia.

It doesn't even exist anymore. A quick Google and I see it came to an end in 1992, so Lord knows how long these things have been floating around cupboards. They're older than my daughter.

The biscuits are long gone; it is just the box now. I can't quite understand how it has managed to stay intact through four house renovations.

I told my son this once years ago. He told me we should clean the cupboards a bit more. I tried not to throw anything sharp at him and advised loudly that if he had any thoughts about cleaning, he could apply them to his room – a landscape of odd smells, darkness and mystery. I half expected to find Kurtz from *Heart of Darkness* in there. The horror, the horror.

I settled down and told my son about Mr Leonard. He couldn't remember him. I told him about the friendliest neighbourhood handyman who was also about the least effective. And I told him about the old lady in her Hush Puppy slippers. Then we talked about Yugoslavia. How it came about, how it ended. All the troubles that intolerance, hate and suspicion can cause.

He said, 'Lucky we're Australian.'

He walked to the front windows and asked me to point to the houses that were the homes of the Hush Puppy lady and Mr Leonard. He looked at Mr Leonard's old place.

'I can remember the girl who could really kick the footy. And then the guy with the motorbikes. Can't remember Mr Leonard.'

People come, people go. He was quiet for a bit, then turned to me.

'We should clean out the cupboards more, but please don't throw the box away.'

I wasn't sure if he was serious but I walked to the kitchen and put it up at the back of the cupboard.

And there it still sits in the corner, Mr Leonard's box of bickies. I can't begin to tell anybody exactly why, but it just seems so at home in the kitchen.

•

I looked down at one of man's best friends. Always waiting, loyally there to serve. The microwave. I wondered what I could whack in it. I thought of the ornamental tins of Irish stew, bought as a joke by a mate as homage to the shared father-and-son snacks of our youth.

I remember my dad, on those odd occasions when we found ourselves alone at home on the weekends, usually after coming home from the footy, ripping open one of his tins of Tom Piper Irish stew and dolloping spoonfuls in between two slices of the finest packaged white bread, adding some cheese and then squeezing them into a jaffle iron.

What was plonked on the plate was a bit of a culinary train smash but sort of fun, if for no other reason than it would be accompanied by my father repeating with a flourish, 'Deeply suspicious, but highly delicious!'

In the days of my youth, it was a novelty for my father to go anywhere near the kitchen to prepare food for the family. Those were the days when generations of fathers would sit at the table and say, 'Why would you want to eat out? Heaven's a home-cooked dinner.'

Probably because hardly any of them would be doing the cooking. The one time my father came close to taking us to a restaurant was after a Redcliffe victory at Lang Park when he nearly stopped at the Chicken A-Go-Go takeaway on Sandgate Road, just down from Holloway's corner, on the way home.

We slowed, nearly stopped and for a moment I thought I'd enter the palace with the dancing chook with the long-beaded necklace and mini skirt. But Chicken A-Go-Go was a no-go.

We moved on. 'Bugger it,' said my father. 'If there's no Irish stew, we'll fry up some camp pie at home.'

I whined. Others groaned.

'That's the food that won the war,' my father assured us.

Camp pie was a rung below Spam but two above bully beef. So much stuff seemed to come from cans and tins. Sausages and vegetables and the deeply suspicious Irish stew.

Today in almost every suburb are restaurants of almost every nationality and those diverse culinary tastes are also at home in pantries and kitchens across Australia. Succeeding waves of immigration to Australia were quickly reflected in the food. Greek, Lebanese, Italian and other parts of the Mediterranean and Middle East in the years after World War II produced Australia's love affair with kebabs, pizza and pastas. In the sixties, seventies and beyond, the Asian cuisines of Thailand, Vietnam and Indonesia made their presence felt. African restaurants now abound. The diversity goes on.

It wasn't always like that. Once a Chinese restaurant had to serve Chinese and Australian meals. Each Chinese selection looked different but the 'Aussie' stuff was steak and chips. And if you wanted home-cooked Chinese food you'd go with something out of a tin, like Kan Tong Chinese meals, which tasted about as authentic as a tin of beans.

It's been fun learning about food. Discovering the different varieties of pasta. Discovering spaghetti didn't just come from a tin. (Although tinned spaghetti did taste good on a white bread sandwich with a glass of Quik.) Discovering different ways of eating sushi and sashimi, and realising that Chinese cuisine didn't just mean a couple of dim sims and a chow mein. The glory of a Fortitude Valley yum cha. Learning that Indian cuisine didn't actually demand the vegetables be cubed and covered in sultanas. Curry didn't come out of a tin with a man called Clive on it. A Clive of India curry night.

Australians have arguably become the most diverse food aficionados in the world. It's an example of that great Australian spirit of having a go, giving things a crack and along the way changing a little and enjoying the ride.

Still, there's always a part of me that thinks I missed out a bit with Chicken A-Go-Go.

It was then that I saw the note on the bench. 'Dad, there's no dog food.' Not only was I mooching in search of a Cinderella snack, it was Mother Hubbard time. Not a thing in the cupboard for the dogs. I looked and saw them through the glass doors. Ray and Delilah, two delightfully mad kelpies. They were awake now and doing their hungry/ we're glad to see you/throw something for us to chase/we didn't dig up the new garden bed again look. Just being lovely hounds.

I whistled softly and they came in the dog door into the kitchen and stood, then sat, then stood, then sat and quivered.

I stood looking at the produce before me. What could they eat? I didn't feel like a run to the late-night supermarket. What to do?

I decided to set a bit of a tone and went over to the records and put on old Tex Morton and his talking poetry.

With Tex rhyming away about Dangerous Dan McGrew, I thought, why not go old school? What did the dogs of my childhood eat? When they ate dog food it was usually something called Dinky Di or Chum.

'So chunky you could carve it,' I said to the cupboard, in a bad Scottish accent. It was the tagline to the TV ad for Chum. Dinky Di never had a tagline, or TV ad for that matter – it wasn't that sort of product.

But it was good enough for our dogs.

I remembered that on occasion they had butcher's bones and pet mince, but more often than not they had what we had – our table scraps and leftovers, if there were any, mixed in with a bit of dry dog food from the bin by the sink.

In our home, we also kept the dry dog food in a bin by the sink. I checked it was empty and found myself staring down at a few pieces of dry dog food lying near an ornamental *Young and the Restless* coffee mug, which was the dog food server. *The Young and the Restless* was a convoluted American soap that had been on television for years, but could also describe the state of Ray and Delilah.

I looked in the cupboard again, took out some pasta, a few tins of some fish called sprats, and some vegies out of the fridge. Sprats: they sounded like a family from Kallangur, north of Brisbane. Doug, Karen, Enoch and Monica Sprats. Enoch Sprats would play on the wing for the Broncos. Perhaps

Doug Sprats would have been on a box of 4IP matches from the seventies. Played for Valleys.

Ray and Delilah danced a little.

When did the pet food industry take off? I thought as Tex Morton intoned the final moments of Dangerous Dan McGrew.

There are boutique pet shops, like the one around the corner from our home, selling unimaginable stuff, like holistic dog food and vitamin supplements. Up the road a way, a huge pet barn squats, full of novelties turning a coin. Jut-jawed TV vets smiling on the labels offering free pet insurance.

I picked up the note about the dog food situation and saw that 'R and D have been walked at the dog park'. The dog park, what an evolution of a meeting place that had become. Once it was just a park.

The local dog park used to have two tennis courts on it but they went to ruin after organised sport became unfashionable and so it was decided that the space would become a dog park.

There is something about that particular dog park.

I was there the evening before and not for the first time the character of the place fascinated me. A house that bordered the park had two of the noisiest dogs known to modern man in the backyard. They would bark at the passing parade of dogs in the park like it was the end of the world.

Those dogs inside that fence never once set a paw inside the park, which seemed the strangest and saddest state. Walking around, you would hear them bark, madly, aimlessly.

Other than that, the park was full of the usual suspects. An old bloke with an even older dog he called Tugboat waddling around together on a two-can trip. This was in reference to the two cans of Vic Bitter the old fellow would quietly sip as he and Tugboat did the tour of the park. When he was finished he would stand by the bin and squash the cans before popping them in. Nigel, an elegant grey striped whippet, hunched quivering between the legs of his elegant, quivering owner, a bald man in a turtleneck jumper.

The man always seemed nervous that Nigel was about to explode into a mad dash around the park, which would erupt into a volcanic canine game of chasey. Ray and Delilah saw Nigel and stopped dead in their tracks and just stared, sussing out if Nigel was up for a chase.

'Oh, here they are,' said Nigel's owner. 'The two with whippet fever.'

I laughed. Ray and Delilah certainly had whippet fever. And so did a big Alsatian – or was it a German shepherd? – which was jumping on top of Mango, a rather noisy beagle, and looked as if it was trying to push him to Bundaberg and back.

The Alsatian's owner had picked him up from an animal shelter and, in a bid to make him less aggressive, had given him a softer name. Donna. It was the name of his second wife, he told me. He'd also given me a business card, which revealed he was a real estate agent and a reiki healer.

The renaming settled the reason why Donna was trying to push Mango to Bundaberg and back in such an aggressive manner.

'It's all about dominance,' said the reiki real estate agent. 'They're just testing each other out.' It seemed to me that the testing was all one way because, despite his barking, Mango wasn't getting a look-in.

I asked what Donna's name was before his rechristening. 'His name was Sabre,' he whispered.

'Sabre!' I almost laughed. From Sabre to Donna. A big leap, even for an Alsatian. Or was it a German Shepherd?

'Shush, please,' said Donna's owner. 'I don't want him to hear his old name.'

Somehow I don't think Donna, who used to be known as Sabre, really cared. He was tired of Mango and was eyeing off Ray and Delilah.

A psychiatrist with a drawling, well-rounded voice and her architect husband, with a designer safety pin adorning his glasses, walked towards me with their dogs, Valentine and Kock. Yes, Kock. Valentine was something called a pharaoh hound and Kock was a Basenji – an African breed that supposedly didn't bark.

The psychiatrist with the well-rounded voice spoke to her dogs, growling to Valentine and then making a noise sounding like she was being strangled to Kock.

The dog park had a hardcore group of regulars who would catch up by making a small circle in the middle of the park, so it looked like a meeting of chieftains. Some people even brought chairs to make the experience a bit more comfortable. They would sit in the circle and chat while their dogs did dog stuff, unconcerned by whatever their owners thought.

Dog parks, apparently, are just as much of a meeting place for people as for dogs. A friend of mine told me at a barbecue that she was asked by her social enhancer – apparently there is such a profession; I thought it was something that came in a bottle – whether she had a dog.

My friend said yes.

'Well,' said the social enhancer, 'let your dog do the hard work for you. A dog park is a hotbed for meeting people.'

My friend told me she took her dog to lots of dog parks and never met anybody of real consequence. 'The dog was a dud. Stupid, skittish terrier thing I inherited from my sister when she went overseas. It never stopped yapping and wouldn't sniff any other dog's bum. Its bloody name was Minsie. Minsie! Useless.'

'Dog park dating doesn't work?' I asked.

My friend was quiet and then laughed. 'Oh, it works. I borrowed my brother's labrador, chocolate, failed as a guide dog because it was too friendly and its name . . .' she paused and then let out a triumphant shout. 'Fred!'

'Fred?' I repeated.

She laughed and nodded her head. 'Fred! Yes.'

'Good?'

'Fred was fan-fucking-tastic. I ended up with a phone full of numbers and ultimately him,' and she pointed to a nice-looking man standing over by a garden bed talking about mulch.

'What sort of dog does – um?' I nodded my head in the direction of the mulch talker.

'Fred,' she answered. And she wiggled her eyebrows. 'Same name as the labby!'

I nodded my head. 'So what sort of dog does Fred have?' I asked.

She looked at me. 'Oh, he doesn't have a dog.'

'No dog?'

'No.'

'What was he doing at the dog park?'

She let out a raucous peal of laughter. 'God, William, what do you think?'

I stared and shrugged my shoulders.

'You old fossil. He was trying to hook up with somebody.'

'At a dog park? With no dog?'

She laughed.

'Isn't that against the rules?'

'What rules?'

'Dog park rules.'

She laughed again. I thought for a moment and said, 'Would you let Fred go off to a dog park by himself?'

She shot me a look and laughed again. 'God, William, you are such an old fart. God love you.'

And she called over Fred, the dog-less dog park patron, who, it seemed, was very nice.

So perhaps some of the chieftains in the middle of the dog park were on the prowl. Maybe it was a different sort of circle. Maybe they were playing spin the bottle. Or dog bone.

They were probably just engaging in a bit of chitchat; maybe some of them had followed the advice of their own social enhancers. The funny thing was that, even though they probably all had dogs, some of them had a very hands-off attitude to their animals, concentrating more on the circle work.

Social connection didn't end at the circle. A Facebook page was advertised on the dog park gate and I told my son to go online and see what it was like.

It turned out that people posted about events and get-togethers, and the goings and comings of the community.

And then it got a bit odd. Some posts were made in the guise of dogs from the park. Some of them I knew. Like Jerry the German Shepherd (or Alsatian? Which one is it again?). 'Jerry is very grouchy today and perhaps should ask his owner about having certain bits and pieces removed to calm him down.' I didn't know whether that was referring to the dog or the owner.

I tapped my son's shoulder. 'What do they say about Ray and Delilah?'

'Oh Dad, don't be pathetic.'

'Come on!'

'If you want to know, you go on Facebook and find out.'

'I don't do Facebook.'

My son groaned. 'It says "Ray and Delilah are antisocial, indulged psychopaths."'

'What?' I roared.

My son laughed. 'You goose, you'd believe anything.'

'What does it say?'

'That Ray and Delilah are raucous and full of energy.'

'That means they're out of control and badly behaved.'

'What?' he said.

'It's code. It's like a school report, full of euphemisms.'

My son stared.

'"Must try harder" means you are on a detention and "a pleasure to have in the class —"'

My son interrupted, 'That's what my reports said.'

'— means you are an antisocial, indulged psychopath.'

My son stared and then shook his head. 'Goose.'

The dog park could be a weird little universe, especially when politics became involved, like when the architect had a go at me about Clive Palmer.

He raised his eyebrows above his safety pin and smiled to me.

'Well, what is it about your lot up north?'

'Oh yes!' said Donna's owner. 'What about Clive Palmer! What is it with you Queenslanders?'

Donna took a liking to Valentine and tried to give it the Bundaberg treatment, but Valentine took exception.

'You really are quite a strange lot. You have all those thugs in suits and then you've got Bob Katter!' said the psychiatrist, in between growls to Valentine.

The architect smiled.

The reiki real estate agent giggled. Donna went all Sabre on Valentine, and Kock started joining in and the psychiatrist started growling and making the strangling sound and the architect started yelling out, 'Kock! Kock! KOCK!'

No one thought it even vaguely silly.

Then the whippet finally took off and the whole park fell into whippet fever. Ray and Delilah ran after it, followed by dogs of all sizes and shapes. Like some crazy cartoon animation, maybe by Walt the trout's namesake, a small brigade of dogs ran and ran and ran in circles after Nigel the whippet. Owners yelled, whistled and growled and the dogs went faster.

'What are they doing?' cried one man.

'They're just being dogs, mate,' said an old man and he started to laugh, his belly heaving. 'Look at the mad buggers go!'

In the kitchen, I looked down at the two whippet-fever hounds, lovely, raucous Ray and Delilah.

I cooked the pasta, chucked in the vegies and sprats, Enoch the flying Bronco and all, and Tex Morton was finishing up an old anonymous poem – 'You may think you're important down here while you exist, But after you're gone. You'll never be missed.' I looked around my kitchen – at the books, my daughter's scribbled note, at the fridge with Walt in the freezer – and thought of all the stories.

The record player's needle started to scrape and lift and there was a gentle hiss of static. The two dogs looked up at me, I smiled down at them, filled their two bowls with the old-school Mother Hubbard goulash I had made and said to them gently, 'I'd miss you two hounds, I know that much.'

They looked up and I laughed. I put their bowls down and said, 'Deeply suspicious, but highly delicious.'

The dogs wolfed it down, then leapt up and down for a pat and a scratch.

I stood in the kitchen, feeling warm and home. I didn't open any other doors. I didn't need a Cinderella snack. Sometimes you don't need food. Good memories fill you up.

Chapter 7

Noise in Cars

Crawling slowly through the rows of cars at the airport carpark with my 'friend' after returning from an overnight trip to Sydney, I saw something I looked upon with a certain envy.

It was a Commodore station wagon. The soon to be discontinued old Commodore is nice enough in itself but that wasn't what was causing the envy.

It was what the car was doing.

Like any airport carpark, the place was chock full and there's no more frustrating exercise than prowling around a multi-level edifice in a motor vehicle, with the wheels squeaking plaintively, searching for a space to park in.

You are tempted by the small car space squeezed next to a pylon with the jagged marks of other attempted parking efforts left gouged in the concrete like the notches in a gunfighter's belt. Things become desperate.

But not for the driver in the Commodore. Moving at a comfortable pace, the car sauntered past a small car space, stopped and easily reverse-parked into the bay.

It was so effortless that I couldn't believe it.

I wasn't the only one who was impressed.

'Did you see that park?' my friend asked after a moment.

'Yeah,' I said. I almost wanted to applaud. When the driver skipped out of the car I had to let her know what I thought of her skill.

I gave the highest accolade available in carpark parlance.

'Good park,' I said with a nod.

'Thank you,' said the pleasant woman who walked off to catch a plane.

'Is that sort of skill taught or is it something that runs in a family? Just something lodged in someone's genetic make-up?'

'I think you might be overthinking this,' said my friend.

'Did you see that park?' I almost yelled. 'How does someone park like that?'

I make no pretence at being a good driver. And I come from a long line of questionable drivers. My father used to love shouting out and waving to his mates on the Redcliffe Peninsula as he drove around, always gesticulating with his hands and arms.

I asked him once if he shouldn't hold onto the wheel with his hands a bit more.

'That's what your knees were made for, Cabbagehead,' he said as he gripped the wheel between his knees and demonstrated what he wanted to do to referee Bernie Pramberg's neck after a Redcliffe Dolphins loss to Norths. Meanwhile the ute drifted to all points of the compass.

But parking was like an opera in my family. Back in the seventies and eighties there was no such thing as the cursed blessing of park assist, that beeping sound like a submarine's sonar. Instead, my parents provided their own vocal accompaniment to parking.

'Yes! Yes! Blooooooody hell! Why are these spaces so small?'

Or the immortal cry, 'Right, right, good, goooooooood, bugger me, bugger me, *buuuuugger meee!*'

Park assist is agonising really, it not only beeps like the end of the world is about to happen as you slowly reverse, it's also a chorus of parking ineptitude.

I have to stop, get out and see what the car is about to hit and I swear the only thing that the car will actually hit is its shadow.

It's worse when you are slowly attempting to park next to a car with people in it. They sit mesmerised, staring at you and your vehicle as the park assist beeps frenetically. A soundtrack of inanity.

But there was nothing funnier than seeing people trying to direct someone into a park in the days of yore. Men were the worst. I remember a school trip to Brisbane where we watched a pair of blokes trying to park a van in Elizabeth Street. One stood behind the van, slowly beckoning the driver into a park, standing behind the jerkily reversing vehicle shouting, 'You're right, you're right, you're right —'

While the driver was screaming, 'What! What! What?' The mad call and response was stopped with a scream of 'STOP! Christ almighty!' And then thumping on the back of the van.

Good parking. Making one of life's mundanely torturous tasks into a thing of grace. I am a hopeless driver and so it is simply beyond me.

In fact, I was so hopeless I had lost my car in the carpark. That was why I was with my friend. We had spent three-quarters of an hour trying to find a silver Volvo; in fact, we had spent our entire relationship trying to find that silver Volvo wagon.

I had gotten off a plane earlier and walked to the carpark and stood. And looked. And swore. And stood. And stalked.

Not for the first time, I realised that parking a car can be a fraught exercise, even if the vehicle is capable of parking itself, because the whole process is rendered pointless if you can't remember where you put the bloody thing. You must be able to follow the basic rule of parking: you have to be able to find the car again.

The day before, I had arrived at the airport in a tizz, running late, found a park and gleefully managed to sneak in and run off to hop on a plane.

It was somewhere, I told myself as I tried to find it, somewhere. I had been convinced it was on level four in the purple section, but it was nowhere to be seen.

I had happily told a fellow passenger on my flight that I didn't have to wait for any luggage and so I could scoot off straight away.

Instead, I stood on level four and watched him drive off, farewelling me with an almost childlike flexing of his fingers.

I had no option but to make the carpark walk of shame and get help from the machine with a big orange button. I had seen people standing there in humiliation as I drove past and now I was one of them, a lost soul in the carpark.

'Press for help' was written underneath the button. I pressed and the button made a small sound and then sneezed. Then it spoke. Like a Dalek.

The machine said, 'Excuse me for that. How can I help?'

I told the machine I couldn't remember where my car was.

The machine asked what my registration number was and I stood a while and had to admit that I didn't know what my rego was either.

The machine said slowly in Dalek tones, 'You don't know what your rego is?' It sounded a bit like a parent talking to a hopeless child.

My pride got the better of me and I blurted out that my car was a silver Volvo wagon.

The machine almost sighed. 'A Volvo wagon. All right, someone will come and help you.'

I added, 'It's a dirty silver Volvo with an untidy collection of clothes and stuff in the back. The general flotsam and jetsam of life.'

The machine sighed this time. 'All right, someone will come and help.'

I said thank you but the machine didn't respond. I stood and nodded my head. I had also discovered, I thought, that there were quite a few dirty silver Volvo wagons with the flotsam and jetsam of life turfed into the back of them on level four. Each time, I had forlornly run up to them with expectation, before realising that the rubbish in the back wasn't mine.

It was like an old romantic film set in wartime where a character haplessly wanders along a steam-filled platform in a train station trying to make out her returned hero in uniform, running up to one brave soldier after another, thinking it is her beloved, only to be left alone on the platform.

The poor cow in the film didn't even have the orange button and the Dalek to ask for help, so I should count my lucky stars.

It was surprising that silver Volvo wagons were so popular and then I realised that Volvos still looked like Volvos. By and large, boxy, solid, tanks.

That may sound slightly unhinged, but try walking around a carpark to find a particular car amongst a collection of mostly anonymous-looking designs. No wonder a Volvo stands out.

Take the Commodore so beautifully parked by the pleasant woman: it was fairly amorphous and didn't look that different from a current model Ford, or Toyota, or any other car brand. It didn't look anything like the Holdens of my youth, big floating boats of cars that I was never completely sold on, mainly because of an experience in my early teens.

Once, a parent of a footy teammate gave me a lift in their Holden Premier. It was very clean and smelt of air freshener, and the back seat was covered in a plastic seat protector, which was a bit sticky and hot beneath our legs. I asked my teammate why it was on. My teammate looked to the front of the car and asked simply, 'Dad?', as if he had never been too sure why the bubbly plastic was on the vinyl seats.

The friendly, if rather fastidious, parent turned with a smile and said: 'We love our Holden and we don't want your footy dirt rubbing off on the seat.'

The father also had a Technicolor mole the size of Uluru on his chin, with three long hairs sprouting from it.

I have never forgotten the connection between the mole and make of car and consequently I've never been able to feel entirely at home in a Holden. My loss. But you should have seen those hairs. Wafting about like tentacles on a sea anemone searching through the tidal water for prey.

I shivered a little in the airport carpark, thinking of them, and then was startled by a man in a large four-wheel drive. He was speaking to me through a loudhailer attached to the roof of his car.

'Are you the gentleman who has lost his Volvo wagon?'

I stared at him, wondering why on earth he was using the loudhailer as he was only about two metres from me.

He repeated the question slowly and I, equally as slowly, nodded my head. He asked me to step into the car. I walked over and sat in the vehicle, and that is how I came to be slowly crawling around the big carpark.

We, my friend and I, had seen the woman park her Commodore on level two after we'd driven to the top of the seven-level carpark and were making our way down in search of my silver Volvo wagon.

My friend wore a uniform with epaulettes and the parking company's name on them, and cargo pants tucked into boots. As we went down each floor he said into his radio handpiece, 'Mobile retrieve to base, negative on the silver Volvo wagon, progressing to next level.'

He was very nice, if officious, but gave me the distinct feeling he should have been flying something instead of drifting through the parking bays. Perhaps it was because he had a model of the USS *Enterprise* from *Star Trek* on his dashboard.

'Relax, mate,' he said. 'You're not the first person to have misplaced a car. It'll turn up.'

I nodded. And felt like an absolute arsepart. How could I, even as a self-confessed bad driver, have come to this: sitting next to a man who was kindly, if somewhat eccentrically, helping me try and find my misplaced car.

I sighed and apologised.

The carpark man assured me it was okay. 'Listen, just listen to the radio a bit and don't worry.'

He flicked a switch and 'When Will I See You Again' by an American group called The Three Degrees came on.

The carpark man laughed. 'What are the chances? That song! And you!'

I looked at him. He looked at me and he laughed again.

'I mean, you not being able to find your car. When will I see you again!'

I tried a smile and then said, I must admit a bit sookily, 'Yeah, I suppose.'

The carpark man took that in and then turned off the radio. 'Look,' he said, 'why don't you see if that Volvo over there is yours?'

I said I didn't think it was, although it was the same model and it certainly seemed messy enough. It was worth a shot.

I got out and walked towards the car. It did sort of look like mine and I walked on, hoping that it wasn't the railway platform scene from the wartime romance again.

I pressed my key's 'unlock' button and saw no yellow flash of lights. I turned back to the carpark man.

He spoke to me through the loudhailer again. 'Try the handle. Go on.'

I turned and reached out for the door handle. The car's alarm exploded, and so did I.

I screamed and staggered back with a middle-aged, frightened foxtrot.

The man laughed through his loudhailer.

'Works every time.' He smiled and then waved me back over to the car.

I started to laugh.

'Works every time,' he repeated when I got back in the car. 'You looked like you might need a bit of a laugh. Here, have a listen.'

And we rolled off listening to the theme of *Star Trek* while the little model of the starship *Enterprise* bobbled on the dash. I looked at the carpark Captain Kirk and he said, as he checked the cars in the bays, 'Just a bit of fun.'

'Is this the radio or your own music?' I asked.

His eyes still on the bays, he smiled a little and said, 'Just a bit of stuff I stuck together, music to find cars by. Just a bit of noise in a car.'

I was going to ask if he had his whole finding-a-car routine worked out, from The Three Degrees to a bit of *Star Trek* and a prank or two.

But then we saw the Commodore sleekly reverse and park in a space that seemed too small. And I started to bang on about parking.

A little while later, on the ground floor, just as we were about to head upstairs again, I saw it. A silver Volvo wagon, half parked across the line.

'That'd be your Volvo then?' said the carpark Captain Kirk.

I nodded.

Captain Kirk said, 'Winner, winner, chicken dinner.'

I thanked him, he waved and went off with *Star Trek* still playing in his car, boldly going to explore the universe of the carpark.

But who was I to judge his taste in music? It was just noise in a car.

•

Trying to hail a cab in the middle of a city drenching the other week, I ended up under an awning with a few other people, waiting for the rain to abate.

Then I heard the sound of someone half humming, half singing a tune I recognised.

The person humming walked slowly past us. It was a woman. Probably older than myself, although I couldn't really be sure. She wasn't dressed for the wet and looked soaked to the bone but I had that sense that wherever she might be physically didn't really matter to her.

She walked on past and into the rain, humming.

A couple, who looked like they had been up to a bit of shopping, laughed.

'How on earth would she know that?' said the woman.

'I don't think she would have seen *A Room with a View*,' said the man.

The woman laughed. A few other people joined in.

I looked but didn't say anything.

The tune the woman hummed was used in the 1986 film of EM Forster's *A Room with a View*, which was a dreamy romantic story of love in Edwardian England.

It's a Puccini tune called 'Oh My Beloved Father', and it is so warmly evocative that even in that half-hummed and mumbled version it was unmistakable. Hearing it was quite unexpected and lovely.

Music is one of humankind's most wonderful creations and classical music, for want of a better term, is some of the best. You only have to hear a live concert from a full symphony orchestra to understand what a complex and marvellous beast classical music can be. How the various sections of the orchestra stand out and then blend together to form a great wave of sound that surges over you or upon which you are carried to wherever your imagination and heart take you.

And that's the thing, classical music, perhaps more than most, taps into the emotions and minds of people. It has such scope, range and power it may be seen as rarefied art. So rarefied it has its own aficionados and devotees who believe its secrets are only known, appreciated and understood by them.

So people laugh a little and ask how a person walking aimlessly in the rain could be humming a piece of Puccini. As if she had no right.

I'm not sure if they even knew the title of the tune, or that there are people who really know their music, who would consider themselves purists, to whom Puccini is a sort of populist musical theatre showman. Not a serious composer, just a fellow who could give his audiences a nice tune they could hum after the show.

But if you told Giacomo Puccini someone would be humming his music nearly a hundred years after he composed the tune, I'm sure he'd be over the moon.

•

I made my daughter watch *The Way We Were* with Robert Redford and Barbra Streisand and when the song 'The Way We Were' played she nodded her head in approval at both Robert and the song.

'Classical,' she said, pointing at Redford when he was in his prime, staring after La Streisand at the end.

It made me think of how some songs are so intertwined with a movie scene you can't get the film or the song out of your head. *Casablanca*, Humphrey Bogart, Ingrid Bergman and 'As Time Goes By'. Pat Swayze, Demi Moore, that weird clay thing and 'Unchained Melody'. And it can also be the music alone: what would *Jaws* be without that John Williams' rip-off of Stravinsky? Or *The Dam Busters* without that triumphant march tune? Or *Star Wars* without John Williams' ripping tune?

Even when the film is ordinary or the song is awful it still sticks. Think of *Flashdance* and *Top Gun*.

But in real life, the soundtrack often just doesn't match the scene.

I was in an airport lounge and the TV monitor was tuned to, of all things, parliamentary question time.

The TV, however, was muted and the sound came from a digital device behind me, which was playing an old moaning, orgasmic ditty by Donna Summer called 'Love to Love You Baby'.

Not familiar with it? Type it into your search engine and then close your eyes and picture question time. You'll certainly look at our federal leaders differently.

Tony Abbott was doing his strange nodding head movement and odd tongue poke while Bill Shorten was disappearing into yet another ill-fitting suit while Ms Summer was singing about laying close together and loving her baby. And moaning. In tune.

It was, to say the least, entertainingly disconcerting.

It made me think of other odd life soundtrack moments.

Not to be too personal about it but while I went about the business of having a vasectomy on a Saturday morning, performed by the appropriate professional who was dressed as if he was eager for his Saturday afternoon round of golf, I had the snip to the tune of 'Can You Feel the Love Tonight' followed by 'The Way We Were'.

At the funeral of an elderly neighbour we waited for the service to begin to the tune of the Bee Gees' 'Stayin' Alive'. Maybe it was her sense of humour but nobody else seemed to be in on the joke.

During a one-day international between the Aussies and the Kiwis the incoming batsmen were welcomed to the pitch with their choice of theme music. It was all quite new, especially to Glenn McGrath, who stalked out at the end of the Australian innings to the tune of Racey's 'Lay Your

Love on Me'. It was courtesy of his fast-bowling colleague Damien Fleming, who got in first to stitch up his mate.

Years ago when I was a kid, before life became so much more 'connected', my father ascended our home's steepling roof on a Sunday afternoon in his t-shirt and Stubbies to wrangle the TV antenna to get a better picture for the rousing cowboy adventure we were watching, *The Sons of Katie Elder.*

While John Wayne, Dean Martin and co came in and out of focus, and static buzz filled the lounge room, we stood in the backyard staring and shouting advice to Dad as he teetered on the roof with the antenna.

Suddenly the movie's rip-snorting theme music by Elmer Bernstein roared from the telly. We looked up as the music filled the afternoon, giving Dad and his suburban backyard heroics a soundtrack.

'Much better than John Wayne,' said my mother as she smiled up at her husband.

Quite right.

But it's the noise in cars that is really evocative.

Sooner or later we all encounter one of those days when the world just seems to be a rather awful place, where news of some awful calamity or misfortune, or a piece of almost unimaginable evil makes you feel down.

It might sound trite and simple-minded, but on those days it's important to remind yourself that life can be fun.

Driving home with my daughter one day, the radio news bulletin was about the heartbreaking killing of a young woman in Melbourne. I switched the radio off but the awfulness was still complete. I thought about the woman's family and her friends. And her fear. In a way I felt ashamed that another man could be capable of committing such an act.

My daughter said something. I didn't hear. I kept driving and she said something again so I nodded.

Music began to play. The music from my daughter's phone was booming through the car's system. Music collected from her life. I drove along with traffic on the freeway and I travelled even further.

The first three songs were all Beatles; she sang along with them. 'Love Me Do', 'The Ballad of John and Yoko' and 'Revolution'. 'This is really good, this one,' she said as 'Revolution' howled away.

When I was young, maybe around four or five, my brother got a copy of The Beatles' White Album for Christmas. He played it for most of the morning, until it was replaced by a warbling Andy Williams and his white teeth and Christmas carols. But I remembered listening to 'Revolution'.

'Really good,' said my daughter, bopping away beside me in her school uniform.

It is a great song.

Next was Florence and the Machine. Then a UK Squeeze song, 'Another Nail in My Heart'. I sang along with her. She laughed and then clicked ahead a bit and it was dear old Mental As Anything with 'If You Leave Me Can I Come Too?'. I laughed.

'Your mum and I loved this song,' I told her.

'I know,' she said.

Then a group I didn't know.

I said this to my daughter and she laughed. 'Of Monsters and Men.'

She clicked again and let me have a Dean Martin. 'On an Evening in Roma'.

We sang along, the way my mother and I used to.

'You can hear his smile,' said my daughter.

Nearly home, another click and the Ramones exploded in the big Swedish car with their version of 'Spiderman'.

I laughed and was happy. Then I thought that perhaps the father of the murdered young woman had laughed like this with his daughter. Maybe they had sung songs together. Maybe he had been buoyed by her.

My daughter started to get out of the car as we arrived home and I said her name.

She looked back.

I tried to tell her that I loved her. I got as far as 'I . . .' and stopped. I thought, I am going to cry.

She smiled and said, 'I know.' She ran inside.

•

A little while later, I was driving my daughter to school and she decided to play, 'A bit of the old David Bowie.'

Her brother likes Dave too.

'Bit of a talent, wasn't he, Dad?'

I have to agree.

It's something special when your children pick up a bit of music that you thought you were clever in purloining from your siblings and they run with it.

The first time I saw David Bowie I was very young; he was on a TV show called *GTK* – Get To Know. It was an ABC effort of the 1970s, giving something to the youngsters for about ten minutes every weeknight at six thirty. After it came *Bellbird*, a soapie set in a country town, and then, excitements of excitement, *To Market To Market*, a rundown of what was charting in fruit and vegetable markets.

David Bowie was wearing a large hat and speaking in an English accent that sounded smart but not poncy; he was saying there was a fly in the milk he was drinking.

In those days the only music you had in the car was what was on the radio, so when my father drove me down to primary school in his truck on a wet day, we listened to Major Tom's first incarnation in 'Space Oddity'. Old David sang about tin cans and blue planets and nothing he, Major Tom, or anybody really, could do.

'Well, I'll be buggered,' said my father. 'Is that the skinny bloke? Not bad.'

It was some of the highest praise my father could offer.

And that's the thing about old David. Long after that rainy day he continued to come up with music that appealed to people from across all spectrums.

The first time I came out in public as an old David admirer was in a lost and lamented place of magic called The Record Market.

You could buy all sorts of stuff there, from speeches of Winston Churchill and Adolf Hitler to 45s by The Riptides, The Sex Pistols or Sandy Scott TV specials and countless compilation albums that were flogged with a hypnotic shrieking monotone, promising 'Twenty Original Artists and Twenty Original Hits'.

Or, as was bandied around, 'All the hits and none of the shit.'

There were Christmas albums, songs of faith albums, country and western albums, novelty albums and the unforgettable Ripsnorter collections, unique to Australia, that were marketed with the bizarrely memorable cartoon drawing of a pig in high heels, jeans and lipstick. It evolved into a series: ripped jeans with the names of the artists written down the side of a partially exposed female buttock.

Seventies marketing at its finest.

Still, Ripsnorter records were valued enough to become big-ticket birthday and Christmas gifts, and sometimes even offerings of love.

A friend was given the Ripsnorter album with the exposed buttock by a would-be suitor and on the album cover, written in texta below the list of artists, was an invitation to a date.

She went.

Old David was warbling away on the store's stereo about 'Changes'.

I stood listening in a rugby top and banana-yellow Stubbies board shorts with a face full of pimples, feeding myself a thickshake. 'What a great song,' I declared.

The woman behind the counter looked sort of surprised and sort of relieved and sort of horrified that somebody like me had the faculties to appreciate old David.

Once old David was seen as a bit dangerous and odd; a changeling. A girl I was keen on said he was androgynous. I nodded, thinking it meant he could kick with both feet. I wouldn't have put it past him.

Well played, old David.

Chapter 8

The World Moves Too Fast

I was standing in the checkout line when the woman at the checkout summed it up, 'The world is moving too fast.'

It was early February and somebody had just told her the Easter eggs had arrived on the shelves that morning.

Forget about Easter, I was certain that only the other day it was Christmas. Maybe that's what happens when you get along in years, everything blends into the next big moment on the calendar year.

The self-serve checkouts weren't functioning, so the queues at the registers were swelling. Standing in line waiting, slowly shuffling forward, I looked around at the shelves.

Toothy rabbits, cross-eyed bunnies in shiny foil uniforms, boxes of eggs of all shapes and sizes and, not far away under the specials sign, trays of hot cross buns, out in February.

A little girl moved away from her mum, who was carrying a baby boy in a sling, and picked out a chocolate bunny.

When I was a child, eggs and bunnies didn't make an appearance until the week before Easter and hot cross buns only appeared magically a few days before Holy Thursday.

I was never a fan of the hot cross bun. I once asked my mum for a cream bun instead, a big yellowy thing with a mountain of cream in the valley of the bun, topped with sickly sweet jam. I got a right going-over.

'It's not the point if you like it or not. You don't get what you want all the time, that's not what Easter's about.'

In the checkout line I wondered what Easter was about. Of course I knew it was about Christ, how he died on the cross and rose again. We'd been taught that.

But what did it mean to me? It was a holiday, and then it was about Easter eggs. And the interesting fact that Easter egg chocolate had a different taste from normal chocolate. There were also the weird sugar eggs my nanna liked. Like china, they shattered into hard little pieces you were supposed to enjoy eating.

I used to like the Humpty Dumpty eggs with Smarties inside. You'd rattle the egg and hear the Smarties bouncing around and then crack the egg open and count who had the most inside the egg. My sister Corby got sixty-five one year.

The little girl's mum gently took the bunny away.

'Why is it called an Easter bunny, Mummy?'

'Because they come out at Easter,' said the mum.

Or early February.

'What's Easter? What's Easter, Mummy?'

'It's about spending time with your family and doing as you are told,' said the mum.

I'm about as religious as a house brick but even I thought Jesus Christ should get a mention. But maybe it's hard to explain the religious aspects to a little girl.

I saw a copy of *Cleo* magazine in the magazine rack. It was being wound up after forty-four years of publication.

The rack used to be almost half a shopping aisle long but now it was quite a modest tiered shelf, half full of shaving blades. A sign of the changing times. Magazines and newspapers were thinning out. What you once had to hold and flip through in your hands you could now access on your phone or tablet via the net.

The magazines weren't getting much of a look-over, but the stationery was, especially the 'Back to School' specials that were plonked where the drinks fridge usually stood between the register line and the mag rack. A little girl was holding two pencil cases with characters from the Disney film *Frozen* on them. Her sister, a bit older, was saying to her, 'You don't need them, you don't. You're in prep.'

The little sister clutched the two pencil cases grimly and said nothing.

I remembered when my daughter had started school. Her first day, in a uniform three sizes too big that she had worn around the house on holidays to practise. She would get dressed up in her uniform, with her hat and her backpack, kiss her mum and me goodbye, walk to the front door, open it, then step outside. Then she'd walk back in, go to her bedroom, take the uniform off and get back into her civvies. She had her school shoes, socks and backpack set out just so, in preparation for the first trip to school.

I remembered walking her up to school. She was wearing the big, green broad-brimmed hat that barely stayed on her head and, just before she walked into the assembly hall, holding my hand so tight I thought she might break something, she looked up at me and gave me a little smile.

Then she let go and disappeared into the lines of children who all looked like green-topped mushrooms in their big hats. I looked at my hand, at the marks her little nails had made and, by the time I had made it halfway back down the street, the marks had disappeared and I felt a little odd. Not sad, but as if some part of my life was changing, as if something had left.

Now she is in her final year of high school and wears her uniform like a veteran grunt dragging herself back into battle for one last mission.

I thought about my son's first day. Now he's finished a uni degree.

The woman behind me in the queue had a handle on things. Her grandkids were piling up erasers, pencils and pens.

'No more workbooks now! The school gives you those.' She laughed a little. 'And you don't need any stickers; you're not allowed to decorate things anymore.'

She turned to me. 'The best thing about school this time of year was what you tried to stick on your exercise books.'

I laughed. I remembered at primary school you were allowed to decorate your exercise books, with terms and conditions delivered by various teachers. 'This is a privilege to show what the subject means to you. Not a chance to be silly or rude. Please remember this.'

Usually it meant wrapping the books in paper and then placing a cut-out from a magazine or perhaps a collector's card from a breakfast cereal – a Sanitarium one usually, they were the serious cereals after all – that reflected the subject the exercise book was dedicated to.

I'm not sure how some of my efforts got past the starting post. One book was wrapped in the department store Barry and Roberts' blue and white wrapping paper with no photo on the front. But on the blue paper was the store name printed in a faux handwritten style. So along with my name in grade four scrawl was, 'Barry and Roberts'. Which might have been a bit confusing.

My father used to say to me that 'Your mates Barry and Roberts sound like two happy bachelors! Must be a good book,' and he'd laugh while my mother told him to shush.

Better still was when I attached photos to subjects. I always preferred brown paper as the backdrop to a variety of illustrations to advertise my dedication to the pursuit of learning. So, for example, my grade six science book had an illustration of a baboon smoking a pipe while drinking from a tankard. On my English and written expression book was a view, taken from the back, of pigs feeding at a trough, which basically presented a pig's arse on my workbook. My special notes book was an anxious-looking sailor grabbing hold of a rope on board a clipper ship, and on my maths book was a helicopter rescuing an astronaut from the sea. This was the only time that any of my exercise book covers elicited a response from one of my teachers. All that my year seven teacher Mr Henzley said was, 'Quite apt.'

The woman behind me in the checkout queue smiled. 'I was given a week's lunch detention by the nuns when I put a picture of The Eagles on my biology exercise book. All that hair, dull stares and pouting. A week's detention.'

Then she said after a moment, 'Poor old Glenn Frey.'

He was gone now. David Bowie had died too. And Alan Rickman.

I never liked The Eagles, and I would never in a million years have put any of The Eagles on anything I owned at school.

But sometimes the world turns quickly.

In about year ten in the late seventies exercise books appeared with photos on the cover, so there was no longer any need to decorate them.

One was of a hang-glider soaring through the sky and another was of a cowboy, I think, sitting on the edge of the Grand Canyon, staring out at its majesty.

They were particularly pointed choices for school work-books. Flying high and soaring to new heights of learning or contemplating the vastness of the world before the student.

At my dear old school those metaphors were sorted out with a bit of pen work. Extra details were added, usually to do with defecation, spitting or other bodily functions. Although I always thought the best alteration to the Grand Canyon cover was the cowboy trying to fish, with a fishing rod and a short line with a worm on it. Hopeless.

I started laughing at the memory.

The woman in the queue looked at me. 'You can laugh, but when the nuns gave you lunch detention, they meant it.'

Then she too laughed.

I thought of my daughter. I couldn't remember her decorating exercise books, or my son for that matter; they just had workbooks, sometimes with the school crest, sometimes not.

Though my daughter had stickers on her laptop. One of Anne Boleyn. One of Malala Yousafzai. One of JFK, Lincoln and Martin Luther King. And one of her own designs.

I thought of *Cleo*. My sisters all read it; my mother was suspicious of it. My father made that harrumphing sound fathers of his generation made.

Especially when he caught me flipping through it.

'It's the magazine with the nude coots in it, for God's sake,' he said to my mother. 'What does your bloody son want it for?'

The *Cleo* centrefolds. A series of rather modest fold-out images of men naked, or almost naked save for a strategically placed hand or some other decency preserver. They never really showed their 'bad jams' as my parents called genitals and the only centrefold I remember clearly was the hapless

QIT first grade rugby team. Packing a scrum, starkers. Bums to the camera.

'Oh, wake up,' said my mother. 'He's looking at the underwear advertisements.'

My father stared.

'For women.'

My father nodded. Then made that harrumphing sound.

It was true. Underwear advertisements and the fashion pages extolling swimsuits were surprisingly plentiful in a magazine supposedly intent on empowering women, and they were enough to keep me peeking through the pages.

And why not? They were in colour, on quality paper and there were more of them when compared to the shots of women in bathers that were dotted occasionally in the pages of the *Courier Mail* and the *Sunday Sun*.

Cleo and the other 'young woman's' magazine, *Cosmopolitan*, usually had quite a few shiny pages dedicated to women in swimmers – the August issue always got me interested – and underwear ads all year round that wouldn't have been out of place in lad mags of the same vintage.

One ad showed a model eating a banana in the sand in a gold one-piece. I had no idea why at the time. I was about thirteen and had an inkling of what I might be looking at but had no real concept of the details involved.

Maybe she was just sticking half a banana down her mouth because she was hungry. At the very least it was good to see she ate well.

Even more ridiculous in hindsight was the excitement with which we boys greeted the illustrated underwear advertisements in newspapers. We used to talk about them at school, pretending we thought they were funny, but in the library we looked at them on the sly quite a bit. There'd be a couple of pages full of pencil drawings of female figures in bras and weird-looking long undies, like bicycle shorts, with lines criss-crossing at all angles. The figures were thin and angular and didn't look like any of the mums at the tuckshop or sport.

They were just drawings, so it seemed okay that they didn't look like real women. But when I really thought about it the models didn't look like any of the mums either.

'They're not supposed to look like mums,' said a friend.

The newspaper ads also had a few men in undies. Just as thin and angular and always with a moustache, and with a pipe in their mouth. And hands on their hips.

Even the *Redcliffe Herald* had a few ads on the odd occasion, when the happy bachelors Barry and Roberts had a sale on, and what was noticeable about these drawings was that the men had bigger pipes. And sometimes they were holding fishing rods or golf clubs and the other hand was on a hip. The intention, I can see now, was to imply how comfortable and supportive the undies were to a man who was going about the activities that men do, like sport and pipe-smoking. Getting out and about and living, with hands, or a hand, on a hip.

These drawings also fascinated me because they were in the same style as those of comic strips and magazines.

In newspapers the comics were usually adjacent to the television program listing and weather forecast, towards the back of the paper, and there was a mixture of kids' and adult-themed strips.

Some – like 'The Potts', 'Fred Basset', 'The Wizard of Id' and 'Hägar the Horrible' – didn't look anything like the undies ads, but the ones that were supposedly directed at the 'older' readers were dead-set ringers. There was one called 'Air Hawk' about a bloke called Jim Hawk who was a flying doctor's pilot and a former intelligence agent who lived in Alice Springs and was still up for danger and a bit of espionage. He flew about in a Nomad aircraft that I knew was an Australian designed and built plane because we were always putting pictures of it in projects or hearing about it in lecturettes about Australian Industry.

Once, a girl asked a question during a lecturette, which was unheard of, but as she was new we put it down to her not knowing how things were done at Humpybong Primary. The fact that she probably wanted to learn something only dawned on me in the checkout line.

'Why,' she had asked, pointing to the Nomad aircraft, 'is a plane with propellers so special? Shouldn't a modern plane have jets?'

'Well,' said the teacher, 'that's just being picky. How can Australia make a plane with jets? The Nomad is very good at what it does.'

And it was good enough to allow Jim Hawk to do stuff, which was all pretty tame because even though he was a man of mystery and adventure, you can only get up to so much in three or four panels in a newspaper.

What made Jim Hawk a particular favourite was the suggestion of what he might look like in his adventures were he to be drawn à la the undies ads. Jim, somehow balancing a golf club, fishing rod, pipe and the controls of a Nomad all the while with a hand on his hip.

Comics for adults seemed silly. I noticed a few magazines on the rack near the checkout queue had actors in comic-book costume on the covers, spruiking the latest Marvel Superhero franchise release.

Well, there you go, I thought, the more things change.

There were other comics where the undies theory created even more fun. Commando war comics could bring me and my brother to tears, especially the immortal 'Ten Tough Paratroopers'. This particular effort detailed a deadly mission for ten paratroopers and had the added bonus of an accompanying poem when each paratrooper bit the dust.

So when only six tough paratroopers are left and they all have to jump into a stream to escape the dastardly '*schweinhund*-ing' Nazis (everything was a *schweinhund* zis and a *schweinhund* zat!), we are informed they take a DIVE.

One silly sod comes up for air right in the middle of a *schweinhund*-ing picnic, gets his last rights and so then there are five.

For tough paratroopers, the illustrations were eerily similar to some of the *Redcliffe Herald*'s 'corset wear' drawings.

For a while I subscribed to an English magazine called *Tiger and Scorcher* with a collection of characters that were beyond surreal and which I thought, even at the age of twelve, hilarious.

'Roy of the Rovers' was about a captain–coach of a soccer team called Melchester Rovers, who was a two-hands-on-hips character and always seemed to spend way too much time being drawn in communal baths celebrating a win with his teammates, one of whom was called Tubby and the other Blackie. Enough said.

'Hot Shot Hamish' was about a giant Scottish player; 'Skid Solo' was a Formula One driver; 'Martin's Marvellous Mini' was about two besties and their rally car. 'Billy's Boots' concerned itself with a boy who found a famous sportsman's footwear, which gave the boy the sportsman's prowess. The sportsman's name was Dead Shot Keen.

This was topped by a creation Salvador Dali could only have hoped to aspire to: a Native American wrestler called Johnny Cougar who had wrestling adventures in England with his 'manager' Sandy, a burly man with spectacles. Johnny spoke in his dialogue bubble in broken English and had a unique dietary program. 'By Manitou, Cougar heap like bangers and mash. Give much energy in ring!' said old Johnny with a rather questionable look on his face.

Johnny was always drawn wearing his jocks with his hand on his hip. Even when he was tucking into his bangers and mash.

There was, of course, no mention of women or girls in these comics, save for the occasional mother figure or perhaps a photo of some odd English sports star on a page, such as a show jumper and her horse from an Olympics, or Sue Barker, the tennis player who was 'engaged' to Cliff Richard. Good luck with that, Sue.

The lack of women in the comics' pages didn't mean, though, that you didn't think about them in a different way. My friend Burps, with whom I did traffic duty out the front of our school, blurted out a confession as we held our red flags to signal it was time for the pedestrians to cross.

Traffic duty consisted of two boys holding out flags to form a gate over the zebra crossing; the gate would open to let people cross and then close to let traffic pass.

Burps had seemed a bit preoccupied on traffic duty since his mother, who helped in the office, had walked through the crossing gate with a frosty, 'Jeffrey,' by way of acknowledgement. I had no idea why he was called Burps; I had never heard him belch in all the time I had known him. No burp, fart, hiccup or any bodily function sound had ever been emitted by him, which was odd, for amongst us boys these sounds were highly regarded.

All I know is that at school he was known almost universally as Burps. So it always came as a shock to hear his given name. Especially in the chilly tones of his mother. It meant something was up.

I looked at him and he looked away and spat between his teeth, a skill many of us were quite jealous of.

It was a sign he didn't want to talk, so I let him be. But the next time the flagged gate closed he spoke.

'Mum gave me a belt last night.'

'Yeah?'

He nodded.

'What happened?'

'The Channel Seven weather girl.'

I looked at him, but then the gate opened. Obviously Burps didn't want to talk in front of the parents and students on the zebra crossing.

When the gate closed he continued. He was brief and to the point.

'Weather came on when we were having tea, Mum asked me to get the potatoes and give them to Nan. I was holding the mash and Nan couldn't hold the spoon because she couldn't get her glasses on.'

The gate opened, Burps stopped. The Channel Seven weather girl was the light at the end of the bulletin. Two men in yellow suits, like they were in a show band, read the news. One was a moonlighting, narrow-eyed teacher who spoke like he was trying to sound English and who was also a rugby referee on the weekends, while the other man had lots of hair and a generous mid-1970s mo. Both, serious-faced, bellowed in odd, rounded voices.

Then came the weather with Caroline. She smiled as if the whole thing was a bit of a joke as she pointed to a tiny weather map with temperature figures and wind gusts marked in texta. She always wore normal clothes, like jumpers and leather jackets, rather than the citrus jackets of the men. And she had the nicest natural voice and a lovely laugh. But what she had to do with Burps's nan and mashed potato, I couldn't work out.

The gates closed. Burps went on.

'The mash was hot but Mum said to wait for Nan to get her glasses on. I looked at the telly and the weather. Had to take my mind off the mashed spuds. And then she, the weather girl, looked at me square in the eyes and . . .' He paused. 'I cracked a stiffy.'

I looked at him.

'Right in front of Nanna, just when she got her glasses on. Mum went to town on me. "Not in front of Nan," she yelled.'

The gates opened and he added, 'Had me footy shorts on, nowhere to hide.'

Cracking a stiffy in front of your family. I winced. Apparently Burps's mum was upset enough as it was, but when Burps tried to hide his stiffy with the mash, his nan missed the bowl and poked him in the thigh with her spoon and he dropped the mash on the table.

Burps's nan yelled at him for being clumsy and then screamed louder at the sight of what was going on in his footy shorts.

The next time the gates closed I asked what else happened. Burps took a deep breath and said, 'We're not allowed to watch Channel Seven anymore.' He made a sound with his nose, got ready to spit and, just before he did, muttered, 'Got to watch Channel Two.'

The ABC, just a bleary-looking bloke with glasses in a bad suit and a pointer doing the weather; no danger of wayward mashed–potato serving there.

In the checkout queue, another kid was trying to grab a bunny and was told off by his father, who dragged him up towards the dairy section, the boy howling, 'Bunny, bunnyyyyyyyy!' as he went.

The little girl still had the two *Frozen* pencil cases. 'Nanna,' cried her sister, 'she doesn't need them!'

Growing up can be a bit fraught now and then and I wondered what happened to that weather presenter and her lovely laugh.

It didn't matter that those stupid comic books didn't have that many women in them because soon we'd left behind stuff like Johnny Cougar the surrealistic wrestler and come across other magazines that were chock full of girls.

In adolescence there were lads' mags and adult mags, all with varying degrees of explicitness. Most were quite tame by today's standards but still . . .

At my son's year nine school meeting, the head of year told the assembled parents, 'You would be surprised at what a teenage boy can look at on the internet and even more surprised at how adept he can be at hiding where he's been.'

Anything is possible on the ocean of the internet. Once, in the early part of this century, I walked into the local municipal library and spotted a group of boys bunched around a screen in the computer room.

I stopped then stepped back and, through the window, I saw they were laughing at a pornographic image. I tapped on the window, they turned, I pointed at them and they smiled. A couple gave me the thumbs up. I banged on the window and they clicked off the image and then just stared at me.

And I left it at that. What do you say?

The checkout line moved forward and I heard a woman behind me say, 'Oh I might as well, and it's the last one.'

She left the queue, grabbed the last ever *Cleo* and said to her partner, 'Last ever sealed section.'

The sealed section. Readers would have to tear the pages open to gaze upon the contents that were deemed too thought-provoking to be exposed during an idle flip-through at the magazine stand.

That section had a bit to answer for. Quite a lovely young woman with whom I enjoyed a lovely time when I was at drama school decided one weekend, on the advice of *Cleo*'s sealed section, to embark upon a creative and fun way of spicing up our 'relationship'.

She didn't use that word to describe what we were engaged in because I am sure it would have made both of us shudder but nonetheless she thought the idea the sealed section came up with might be pursued.

We set aside a Saturday night and she told me of the plan. We were to share a bottle of fine champagne and each choose a video.

I had no money at the time, so fine champagne meant either Spumante or a six-pack of Emu Bitter. She told me to shush up, she would get the champagne. I said okay, and the movies?

She smiled.

I nodded.

She shrugged her shoulders and smiled.

I stared.

Not for the first time somebody remarked on a certain denseness to my perception.

'You know, an erotic movie.'

I nodded.

'The magazine said it would be fun and exciting.'

I didn't say anything. I just nodded. And she smiled.

Saturday came and we settled down. The champagne was pretty good. It looked sort of French, even if it wasn't, and I had brought some flowers I had picked up from a supermarket.

I don't know if they were suggested in the magazine's sealed section, but I thought I should contribute something.

She said thank you and we had a glass or two of champagne.

'Let's show each other our videos,' she said.

She knew something was up by the way I nodded.

'What did you get?' she asked.

'What did *you* get?'

She showed me what she had got.

'Where did you get that from?' My voice was sort of incredulous. After all, Perth in the 1980s wasn't exactly seedy red-light central.

'I got it from my dad's shed.' And she smiled and shrugged her shoulders.

'What's yours?' She gave me a kiss.

I showed her my film.

She stared. She didn't smile.

Where Eagles Dare. An implausible war story about Clint Eastwood and Richard Burton versus the German army in the Austrian Alps. Sort of *The Sound of Music,* but with no songs and a lot more German uniforms.

It was my turn to shrug. 'Sorry, I couldn't think of anything and the guy at the video shop said all the good bits were cut out of the ones on the shelves.'

She stared at me.

'Although he did suggest *Last Tango in Par—*'

'No,' she said definitely. 'No.'

'Yeah, well, that's what I thought,' I said.

She told me we should watch what she had found in her dad's shed.

After watching a bit, we finished the champagne.

'What are we supposed to do with that?' I asked.

She smiled. 'Not much,' she said.

And she turned it off.

'Oh Dad,' was all she said, then laughed. 'And no,' she told me, 'we're not watching that war thing.'

We ended up watching what was left of *Hey Hey It's Saturday.*

The sealed section didn't stop there. In a coffee shop around the corner from my home I sat with my kids and hordes of toddlers waiting for a long black, flipping through a magazine with a not-so-sealed section entitled 'What he REALLY thinks about when he's masturbating!'

I found myself becoming acquainted with Matt, an office administrator who spoke about what he actually did at his workstation. Really. Then he would realise he was procrastinating and get back to work.

Procrastinating? No, *Matt*, you were surfing porn and masturbating. At work.

Surely Matt and his workstation flipping were the creation of a journalist? Or maybe not. Maybe people could be that odd.

Another time, I was in a very pleasant town in a beautiful if secluded part of the country for a charity event. It was raining and cold so I went inside a coffee shop for a coffee to warm me up. There were quite a few ferns and indoor plants and a couple of movie posters; one of an Isabelle Adjani film called *Queen Margot*, which featured a photo of her looking beyond beautiful. I studied it quite happily and waited for someone to come and serve me.

There was a bell and I rang it.

'Just a tick,' said a voice from a back room.

I waited and looked at the other poster, one for *Rocky III*, with Sylvester Stallone all oiled up in his boxing gear staring dumbly into space.

Then a voice came from behind a large indoor plant in the corner. 'Who do you like more? The queen or Rocky?'

I looked for a bit and saw a fellow sitting at a table.

'Oh, I think I'd take Isabelle over old Sly,' I said.

He nodded.

The voice from the back room sang out again. 'Look, sorry, I'll just be a tick.'

I assured the voice I was in no hurry.

The man at the table spoke again. 'You in town for the charity do?'

I said I was.

'Good for you,' he said and added, 'staying long?'

I told him I was just there for the weekend.

'Good for you.'

There was a silence and the rain on the roof sounded quite lovely.

'Bit wet,' the man at the table said.

'Yeah,' I agreed.

'You want to see my box?' He got up and walked over to where I stood.

'Sorry?' I said.

'My box. My cock box.'

The rain fell on the roof.

I turned my rather sizeable frame towards him and said, in my best conservative old-fart manner, 'Why would I want to do that?'

He didn't really need an invitation. He had a box, a bit like a shoebox, that he plonked down on the counter, removed the lid and proceeded to show me the contents. My parents would have called the images he showed me 'bad jams' of the male type.

I looked at him; he was just a man. In a cardigan and chinos. Showing me a box of bad jams. He was, I thought, 'not all there'. He'd stop soon. Maybe it was his idea of a joke. They were just bits and pieces of people.

He flipped through them, old-school porn surfing, a bit like those series of still images of Don Bradman hitting a four off a cover drive, the flipping making it appear as if he were moving. Although Don was more correct in his stroke play and his size didn't deviate. This man's collection was all over the shop, a strobing set of male bad jams was not something you saw every day.

No wonder, I thought, that the *Cleo* centrefolds didn't show too much back in the day. There is something to be said for leaving the rest to the imagination.

'Oh well, there you go, mate,' I said as he finished flipping through his cock box collection.

'Here, meet some of the locals.' He pulled out a couple of Polaroids with a name and a date on top. Dale. The rain fell on the roof.

'And here's Lance; not much to show there,' he said.

The rain fell.

'And meet Maurie.'

The rain fell.

'I see you've got quite a lot of Maurie.'

The rain fell.

'Oh, he prefers Maur-reeece.'

'Well, good for him. Ta ta, mate.'

'You had enough then?' he asked.

'Mate, no more, not on an empty stomach.' And I turned and walked outside.

As I made it through the door I heard the voice from the back room say, 'Can I help . . . Oh, Graham, did you show him that box of yours?'

I walked off into the rain, thinking to myself, well, that was something. Later that night, halfway through the charity event at the community hall, I turned to a man from the shire council and began to tell him about my coffee shop encounter.

'I was out and about today, just in the main street.'

'Oh yeah? Meet any of the locals? Bloody hell, they are a funny old box of chocolates around here, I can tell you that much for nothing.'

I smiled and thought it only polite to get his name again before I started to recount my meeting with Graham and his box of cocks.

'What was your name again, sorry?' I asked.

'Maurie,' he said. 'Although my friends call me Maur-reeece.'

And he smiled.

I didn't mention Graham. Or his box.

A funny box of chocolates, all right. I still couldn't quite believe it as I stood at the checkout line and looked down at the odd, buck-toothed chocolate rabbits.

I looked at the self-serve checkouts standing idle. They were always a problem at this particular supermarket.

I remembered another time when the too-calm automated voice from the machine was telling people to 'Clear the bagging area.' Over and over.

'Sort this out,' said a young man in a natty work suit to the woman from the supermarket whose job it was to patrol the self-service checkouts. 'Come on, sort this out.'

He spoke to her as you might a dog. She was old enough to be his mother.

Young natty suit swore. At the woman or the machine, nobody knew.

Another man at another checkout muttered to the auto-mated female voice, 'Stupid cow, shut up, you cow.'

'Clear the bagging area,' said the voice calmly.

'Of what?' he whined.

It might have been funny on another night.

The supermarket woman dealing with natty suit's shopping told the other man that she'd be over in a minute.

'Sort me first,' said natty suit.

'That girl at the defence academy in Canberra,' said a man in front of me, nodding to the headline of a newspaper on the stand.

The banner headline blared the latest instalment of the scandal that had engulfed the defence academy when a young female cadet had consensual sex with another cadet but the act, unknown to her, was recorded and Skyped to other cadets.

Like all sensational news events it was hard to tell what was fact and what was rumour and assumption but the latest headline was eye-catching. The paper claimed the female cadet had been ordered to apologise to her fellow cadets for going to the media regarding the allegations.

'Sorry?' the man's wife said distractedly as she was trying to find her shopping loyalty rewards card.

'The one who got filmed when she had it off with another cadet,' said the man.

'What about her?' said his wife.

'She's going to have to apologise to the academy. That's what the paper reckoned they said. Good for them.'

His wife didn't say anything.

'She can't sign on for the army and let her mates down when things get tough,' he said.

'Clear the bagging area,' said the machine.

'I'd like to bloody clear you,' said the man at the checkout.

'That girl should be kicked out of the forces,' the man in front continued. 'You can't betray fellow soldiers. Women in the forces just cause trouble.' It sounded like he was taking his anger about waiting out on the cadet.

That cadet was somebody's sister. Someone's daughter. I wondered if the man had a daughter. If he had, what would 'betrayal' mean then?

I should have asked him but I didn't. I wanted to go home. And I felt I'd let down the young cadet. And my daughter. All the women I knew.

'I'm really in a hurry,' said natty suit. 'Sort it.'

'Mate,' I heard myself finally say, 'put a lid on it.'

Natty suit looked a little wounded. He was about to say something but the supermarket woman spoke.

'This is the problem. Your magazine's barcode is torn.' She held up a soft-porn lads' mag.

Natty suit looked at her. 'I won't have it then,' he said sookily.

A silence. Then:

'Please clear the bagging area.'

That was four years ago. The world may move too fast, but sometimes it doesn't seem to move at all.

Chapter 9

In the Bottle Shop with Beards

It was a Saturday night and I popped in to a bottle shop to pick up my occasional bottle of medicinal Irish gargle water.

The bottle shop was quite full, people picking up a wine to have with dinner or mulling over the beers and ciders banked up in the fridges. Just a normal night, but then I noticed that something wasn't quite right.

I was the only man there who didn't have a beard.

Beards. Everywhere. The guy in front with the wine, the two guys together with Mexican beer, a bunch of mates debating what beer to take to Athol's – I bet Athol had a beard; his name just lent itself to one – the tall, good-looking bloke with the tall, good-looking girlfriend. All beard-wearers. Well, not the tall, good-looking girlfriend but, you know, give them time.

The two young men behind the counter had beards too, and a fresh-from-work tradie who'd just entered and looked like a merino sheep was glued to his face.

The younger guys' beards were more ornate or, as a friend of mine put it, 'manscaped'.

When did beards become so popular?

When I was a kid not many grown-ups had beards.

Maybe the ghostly sea captain in the TV show *The Ghost and Mrs Muir*, but he also wore weird turtleneck jumpers, so he was a ghost with some bad fashion sense. Then there were the blokes on religious instruction posters at school. A fine collection of holy beards.

I worked out a theory about beards and Christianity. The good guys usually had clean, neat beards and the bad guys were either clean-shaven, and in very fetching Roman armour, or had long, messy, dark beards. In fact, the bad guys always looked exactly the same.

I was asked to hold up one of the posters once, which was a pretty rare honour, especially for me. The posters had a piece of varnished dowel at the top and bottom and would be unfurled with a great flourish by our instructor.

I can remember being chosen to hold up something to do with Jesus and the tax department. Lots of long beards there, but the tax collector who was paying attention to Jesus, who stood there pointing, had a short, neat beard. Hey presto, here's St Matthew!

But that was in the old days. Indeed, one of my father's

seminal pieces of democratic advice was to 'never vote for a bloke with a beard because the bugger is hiding something'.

And outside of the freaky old guy who caught the Red Bus to Kallangur on Saturday from the bus stop by the jetty, I can't remember too many real-life grown-ups wearing beards.

There were a few teachers at high school who had beards but they weren't great ambassadors for facial hair. The Big Swede was a maths teacher who taught logarithms like a cop from a bad movie. He'd bang the table and ask me a question and when I answered he'd stare at me and then tell me he didn't believe me.

He wore patent leather shoes and short shorts. He was scary at first but after a while the tough-cop stuff just withered. You can only bad-cop for so long.

We had an English teacher, who happened to be English, and was also the owner of a very hearty growth of facial hair. He was also a pathological fantasist who had been everything and everywhere, and created a sort of Wilbur Smith hero persona for himself. Outdoorsman, hunter, adventurer and also a man of mystery and danger.

In class, for no reason, he would break into a story about one of his adventures.

'When I was in the commandos,' came out when we were supposed to be studying a Judith Wright poem, 'I hiked with a broken leg over ten miles of Arctic terrain.' Or the priceless advice when a kid had problems understanding what an adverb was and how it might be used in sentence construction. 'When I was on safari in Kenya, we had a hunter with the same problem as you.' He stroked his beard and said slowly, 'A crack shot with deadly concentration and ice-cold nerves. But no adverb sense.'

Why a hunter on safari would need to understand how an adverb is a word that can add descriptive power to modify a verb is not easy to imagine.

The English teacher was sort of harmless and almost entertaining but he would stroke his beard so often, trying to appear wise and mysterious, that it looked like he was stroking a cat. Or trying to make sure the beard didn't fall off.

There was another teacher – a poor sod with Coke-bottle-lens glasses and a tight perm – who cringed in the corner like a shellshock victim. He taught Citizenship Education. What a great name for a subject: 'Citizenship Education'. It sounds Orwellian and our bearded hero was less Big Brother and more Winston Smith after O'Brien and his rat in a cage had finished with him. The idea that such a quivering mess could be capable of teaching us anything about citizenship was a bit of a stretch.

A boy called Peter Wallace came up with a theory that the Citizenship Education teacher grew a beard because he thought it might make him appear older and give him a bit more authority. The problem, however, was the beard had a sort of permed look and, like his hair, made him seem tortured and a bit desperate. A thoughtful lad, Peter also observed the similarity between the teacher's beard and that of pubic hair.

'When you think about it, a beard is just the same as pubes. Only out of control and run wild. Why would you want to show your pubes off in public?'

'That,' he said, indicating the teacher's beard, 'is pube-lic hair?'

The teacher subsequently earned the happy title of Mr Pubeface and I must admit that this rather graphically entertaining description, and the lasting impression made by the Citizenship Education teacher's spectacular lack of success, has always made me look at beards in a particular light.

It's true that in my youth there were other adults who sported beards. Greg Chappell had one later in his career; AB, Allan Border, did too, but that was just a phase, facial hair being cheaper than sunblock, I suppose.

And they don't have a blade of face-grass now.

Beards. When did they regain popularity?

Bald guys with beards never count – they're just compensating.

A friend grew one occasionally and said, 'Cheaper than a tattoo and if it looks like crap, just give it the Gillette treatment, no skin grafts needed.'

True. But then if tattoos don't interest you, why would beards be the go? Tattoos are also beyond me, although it doesn't mean I don't appreciate them on some level.

Pulling into a fast-food chain carpark to answer a phone call, I saw a human being held together by a network of ink. Celtic-cum-Polynesian-cum-axes and weeping skulls. Then when he returned with his paper bag of takeaway gold, on the top of his arm – from the shoulder to elbow – was the most painstakingly lifelike rendition of Audrey Hepburn posing from *Breakfast at Tiffany's*. Sunglasses, cigarette in holder, pearls. Beneath her were the words 'Moon River'.

As if his tatts had been designed by some dysfunctional civic planning committee.

The second memorable tattoo encounter was with a bikini-clad woman walking in front of me as I staggered along a beach for a run.

Over the top of one buttock was the word 'Family' and over the other the word 'Friends'.

Choosing to display these words on these parts of her anatomy was mysterious. It didn't seem likely her family and friends would be looking there that much, well, maybe on the beach.

When I was a young fellow, tatts were something that indicated a certain type of person. Rough trade, bikies, would-be toughs or bad actors on *Homicide* had them. People from the other side of the tracks.

Obviously I haven't kept up with social trends – tatts are everywhere, in fact they're all over the tracks.

They seem particularly popular amongst the young. It makes sense in a way – their bodies are firm, tatts look flashy. The problem is a body doesn't stay that way. You see enough Christmases, you'll understand. Gravity takes hold. Things sag. Nothing sadder than a saggy tatt.

Except when a tatt suddenly appears on an older body when sag is setting in. Emerging from a dip at the beach, I bumped into a similarly middle-aged actor friend sporting inked green barbed wire with roses entwined around his unremarkable bicep.

'You've got a tatt,' I said incredulously.

'A tattoo,' my acting chum corrected. 'A Christmas present. Listen, Will, it's something different, just a bit of individual expression.'

I stared.

He laughed. 'Will, not everyone is as conservative as you, you old fart.'

Fair enough. But his tattoo was as individualistic as a lemming parade. Maybe a Christmas tatt is now on the mid-life crisis must-have list. Along with a Harley-Davidson, fast red cars, blondes and all the other clichés. I don't know.

Maybe people just want to have one – good on them. Maybe it's culturally important. Okay. Maybe it's a fashion. But not all fashion is good. I once wore a skivvy and Stubbies shorts to a party in 1989. Me, conservative?

But I could take off my fashion tragedy. Imagine a lifetime of skivvy and Stubbies tattoos.

Perhaps a conversation one Sunday lunch when I was a boy had a lot more impact on me than I care to admit.

My brother was engaged in a favourite pastime of us children: trying to annoy our father. The whole point was to get him roaring, and a number of methods were employed. Telling him you wanted to marry a Baptist would wind him up for some reason. Even better was one of my sister's preferred modes of provocation. She chose simply to sit and stare at my father as he ate.

On this occasion it was a slightly half-arsed attempt over tomato and cheese sandwiches. My brother was talking about how he saw a man called Neil who sometimes hired from my father's hire business. My father called Neil 'The Thinker' because he was always telling my father he was, 'Thinking of doing stuff.'

'Thinkin' about goin' over to Straddie, Col.'

'Thinkin' about gettin' a new ute, Col.'

'Thinkin' about havin' Chinese tonight, Col.'

He'd also said he was 'Thinkin' of getting a tattoo.'

My father reached for the salt and said The Thinker wouldn't be getting any tatts.

'But I might get one,' said my brother.

'Why would – why would you say that?'

'Because a tatt would look good.'

My father sighed. Then he pointed a sandwich at my brother and said, 'The only blokes allowed to have a tattoo are returned men and pirates.'

A returned man was such an old-fashioned thing for him to have said, even then; a returned man was somebody who had served in the armed forces.

'Dad, you're a returned man,' said my sister Corby.

My brother hopped in, 'Does that mean you've got a tattoo?'

My father took a mouthful of his sanger and chewed, looking at the table. He swallowed and said, 'Too right I do.'

We all stared. Surely he must be joking. 'Just above my arse,' he said. 'It says, "Exit only".'

I still wasn't sure but my mother laughed and added, 'Maybe you should have got the other sign you love.'

'Wrong Way Go Back!' roared my father. It was one of his favourite moments of the day when he saw the road sign that seemed to be unique to southeast Queensland, where the rapid spread of highways and new roadworks didn't always go to plan. The junction where Anzac Avenue joined the Bruce Highway was a delight, with three signs declaiming 'Wrong Way Go Back' as false starts and half-finished entrances dotted the area.

'That's a lot of letters there, love,' said my father thoughtfully. 'Bit painful. And very Old Testament, Wrong Way Go Back.'

Every time I see a tattoo, I think of that phrase. I still hear my father and mother laughing.

I never went down the tatt avenue but I did try to grow a beard once at uni as part of a beard-growing competition to raise funds for a charity.

It looked like I had stuck my face in a bowl of congealed gravy. My father wanted to know why I'd done it. 'Oh, something to do.'

He looked at me, called me an arsepart and harrumphed off, muttering to the dog about silly bloody pie cans.

And I got paid to grow a beard for a film nobody went to see. But young fellows seem to really be taken by them. When did it start?

I have noticed my son, now at uni, has one. In my own family, a beard-wearer. I asked him why a beard was a look with young blokes today.

He looked up from the couch, scratched a bit and said, 'Dunno. I'm just growing it for something to do.'

This encouraged me to yell at nothing in particular and make harrumphing sounds, before stomping around the backyard and muttering things to the dogs, who took absolutely no interest.

So, not wanting to appear too much of an old coot, I tried not to let the mystery of the pubeface get to me too much.

•

Unlike Hipsters with their deeply suppressed emotions, perhaps a result of the fact their demographic is named after a type of underwear, old coots like me are still capable of exclaiming in surprise when we see something truly remarkable.

There is a particular exclamation which is reserved for truly awesome moments. It sounds a bit like when you stand under a cold shower, but with a metaphysical tone.

I emitted the sound the other night when that bloke Felix Baumgartner, an Austrian daredevil, sorry, *the* Austrian

Daredevil, shuffled out of his balloon capsule and stood looking down at the Earth for what seemed like an age, then let go and tumbled through the atmosphere.

I got that feeling at the back of my knees reserved for really startling moments, like a call from my accountant regarding audits.

But when he stood there I felt very human. Frail. Scared and a little amazed. God knows what the Austrian Daredevil thought.

And when he fell. Procreate me!

My children and I yelled. I can't begin to imagine what the Austrian Daredevil did inside his bubble helmet.

Although it was weird that it was all dressed up like an old moon shot video. These sorts of things used to be run by NASA and were vaguely connected to governments. Now it's a soft drink company who sent up somebody in a balloon and created an 'oh wow' moment.

My son made a bigger noise than my daughter when the daredevil jumped and I wasn't far behind. The dogs barked.

'Have you ever seen anything like that in your life?' asked my daughter.

I just made a lesser cold shower metaphysical sound.

And then up popped the Austrian Daredevil at a press conference. He looked completely normal. Well, obviously he was fit; you don't get flabby daredevils, Austrian or otherwise, but he looked like one of those dads who would turn up at a working bee in the days of kindy and primary school. You know, the ones who are fit and sort of good at everything.

But then I thought, how would his kids feel when he turns up at the working bee? 'My dad is the Austrian Daredevil. He's the one jumping off things.'

Then I wondered if that was what he put on his passport.

Occupation: the Austrian Daredevil.

I tried to answer my daughter's question. Had I ever seen anything like that before?

There was dear old Evel Knievel, a somewhat shady stuntman who would walk around in white leathers bedecked with stars, and who wore a weird half-cape that he would flap out when he was doing something impressive. His hair and manner screamed oiled-up hillbilly. He was unique in the sense that he set a world record for having the most broken bones and was famous just as much for his motorcycle prangs as his successful feats of daring.

These usually consisted of jumping over buses or cars and falling off, although he did try to jump the Snake River Canyon in a rocket made in a shed somewhere, but he was mad.

Then there was José Canga and his French Canadian Hell Drivers who drove old EH Holdens over the goalposts at the old Redcliffe Showgrounds. He was pretty good value, and did fantastic things with an EH, but he wasn't in the Austrian Daredevil class.

I went to school with Ricky Kiel, who had a go at eating a cake of soap at lunchtime. He got about three-quarters of the way through before bubbles starting coming out his mouth and I think he had to go off to hospital. He would also occasionally try and ride bicycles off the jetty at Redcliffe.

Then I remembered a daredevil to match Felix.

Me.

Fuelled by cans of orange Tarax and clothed only in an immodest pair of Stubbies board shorts, I climbed to the top of the Centenary Pool high tower, stood and peered down at the world below like Felix. Some kids started a 'Jump, jump' chant. The dreaded public outing of having lost your bottle. I was a lanky streak of white encased in the dubious canary-yellow Stubbies, shaking and staring at the blue below and listening to the chant.

Felix didn't have to cop that.

'Jump! Jump! Jump!'

And then I jumped. And in that awful moment before I screamed, I heard a strangely satisfying collective gasp and a voice said, 'Fuck me, he did it!'

I jumped, and tried to chuck a bomb dive. And ended up with my testicles way further north of the equator than they had any right to be. To top it off, I received a clip behind the ear from a guy dressed in white with a nametag that read STAFF and was banned from the pool.

As I walked to the change room, a little boy eating an ice-cream gave me the thumbs up and I gave him my version of the 'nod', the slow acknowledgement with a nod of the head that I had seen footy players do when congratulated on some bit of paddock bravery. And why not?

A bomb dive from the high tower at Centenary Pool. In yellow Stubbies.

Beat that, Austrian Daredevil.

But sometimes the moment of disbelief and awe at something you watch or experience doesn't have to be a Daredevil moment. And perhaps it's not awe that you experience, but a perspective on time and what it is to share the world with what seem to be random strangers.

I was in a supermarket once, wandering aimlessly with a trolley thinking, not for the first time, that I really should get a shopping list together. More efficient than grazing up and down the aisles, but then I wouldn't have met the old bloke.

He was dressed in a suit and tie and was staring at the refrigerated shelves.

It was the tie that stood out. Canary yellow. The colour of my Daredevil Stubbies. And incongruously, it was marked with the Playboy Bunny motif in white, smack dab in the middle of the tie.

I looked for a little too long and the man smiled absently.

'Good tie,' I said.

'Present from my grandchildren. I think they thought it might be funny. But you know, it's a happy colour.'

'On a formal shop?' I asked.

He looked at me. Smiled a little, then said, 'Just been to the church across the road for its hundredth anniversary today.'

'Oh yeah?' I said, and I stared at the shelves too.

He nodded. 'Got married there in 1951 and my daughter got married there in 1976.'

'And the grandkids?'

He shook his head. 'No, they didn't bother.'

'Oh?' I say.

'Can't say I blame them, even I seem to have lost my faith along the way.'

'Really?'

He nodded, paused and then added, 'And the full-cream milk. Where do they put it?'

I looked at the range of milks and had no answer. There was every strain of milk product except for full cream.

'Lost me faith and lost the milk. Don't know what's worse,' he said.

We both stood and stared.

'There.' I pointed. A row of full cream.

'Right in front of me!' he said. 'Well, that's a sign. Got the milk, now for me faith.'

'Where will you look?' I asked.

He turned slightly and said, 'I have to get washing powder and tomatoes.' He had a think, and then smiled. 'I feel good about the fruit and vegies. I'll look there. Least I can do. Good luck to you, son.'

I looked back at the milk and the full cream seemed to have disappeared again. I laughed.

Then a day later at the beach, I was flopping about trying to regain some movement in my right knee, which after years of suburban jock-dom had finally given up the ghost on a recent trip to Japan.

On a lift to the top of a ski field my brother had suggested we take this opportunity to re-enact the cable car scene from the hoary old World War II adventure *Where Eagles Dare*, my erotic movie choice from the planned night of passion in Perth all those years ago.

Which of us was Richard Burton and which Clint Eastwood wasn't clear, but something happened to my knee.

Now, a month or so later, my erotic knee still hurt.

It was a very hot day and plonking myself in the water was so lovely I started singing a pleasantly idiotic song from a Disney film, about bobbing along on the bottom of 'The Beautiful Briny Sea'.

I heard a laugh. It was a woman, breaststroking along rather gracefully.

She stopped. She had a lovely laugh, and smile.

'First swim of the summer for me,' she said. 'Always wonder why it takes me so long to get in.'

I nodded.

'I took my children to see that film in the cinema. The film you sang that song from. *Bedknobs and Broomsticks*,' she said.

I thought to myself, hardly anybody uses the word 'cinema' anymore, and the way she said it was quite lovely.

And she looked as if she was remembering.

Then she started to sing the song.

We both sang it.

And she laughed.

'Oh, that's lovely.' She smiled and swam off, humming.

I looked after her. And noticed my knee wasn't bothering me anymore.

•

A while later, on a Sunday night at our beach house, putting out the rubbish bins, I saw what I took to be three generations of a family – grandfather, son and grandson – walking along the track.

Stopping not far from me, the little boy looked up in the night sky, littered with stars.

'What are they? Those things,' he said.

'What do you think, Dad?' said the boy's father to the grandfather.

The old man looked up.

Then he looked to me and said, 'Any thoughts?'

I looked up and shook my head.

We all stood staring at the sky.

The little boy spoke.

'Whatever they are, they're pretty good sparklers.'

'Well, that's good enough for me,' said the grandfather. Good enough for us all. Random moments with strangers.

•

I looked around the bottle shop and saw that besides being the only bare-faced customer I was also the only bare-headed one. Just like the different beers in the fridge, there were a number of head garment choices on display, but they all seemed to be for decoration: tiny little trilbies and beanies with way too much styling.

Almost every winter a beanie has been plonked on my noggin. And if I had ever conceived of a beanie etiquette, I would have contended that the perfect instruction for placing a beanie upon your head would be to 'plonk' it.

But now it seems the beanie has become a fashion item with a right and wrong way to wear it. A younger beanie-wearer, who of course was also wearing a beard, pointed this out to me. Not a full beard but a neat sculptured affair that assured me he knew what he was talking about.

It happened when I was standing with a younger colleague in front of those fashionable big glass doors that theatre companies like to have these days and we saw our reflection.

There we were, two men dressed for winter. Him with fingerless gloves, coloured scarf, satchel carrier bag and grey beanie.

Me with my middle-aged podge, bad knees, cardigan, chinos and loafers, and plonked-on beanie.

He laughed at the reflection.

I asked if he was laughing at me.

'Yes,' he admitted with a very fetching smile. 'It's the beanie.'

I asked him what was wrong with my beanie. A beanie to me is a functional piece of winter attire that you plonk on your head if it's cold at the footy, on a walk, out fishing or on your way to work. You pull it down over your ears and take it off when you're not cold anymore. My younger colleague was a nice man and didn't want to be rude but I encouraged him to be free with his opinions.

'Well, you look like you're off to burgle something, either that or you're a cross between a fisherman and someone who wants to go and watch a game of rugby.'

'Yeah, well, I'm wearing a beanie,' I said, slightly incredulously.

The manicured beard smiled. 'A beanie can be a style statement.'

I looked at him and his style statement.

It was like a slightly baggy windsock or maybe an elf's hat from a pantomime. A beanie as a style statement. I still miss the little pompom on top of the beanies of my childhood but I make do with the utilitarian black woollen job I now wear. Functionality rather than stylishness.

The world changes. We both walked on, him in his style statement and me in my beanie.

The beanies in the bottle shop were, I realised, much more style statement than beanie, so I looked at the beers in the fridge. There were so many to choose from.

Back in the day, beer used to be simple. It was either XXXX or XXXX. Draught or bitter. People pretended to drink Carlton, which was okay because they made Crown, which was the best beer in Australia.

This was obvious because for years the only time I ever saw a Crownie was at weddings or at the best and fairest award night if a sporting team had had a really good year.

Pilsner was an old coot's beer but okay, and then there was the much-derided Brisbane Bitter. It was an attempt to create Victoria Bitter up north; only it didn't taste like Vic. It didn't really taste like anything, even the ads were tasteless. A group of bike-riding models in unfortunate 1980s 'sportswear' engaging in a bike race for no apparent reason other than to get doused by buckets of water. Then suddenly there was some guy with a beard drinking Brisbane Bitter.

Very few people made their own beer back then; there was a Dutch bloke who drove a Leyland P76 and occasionally hired painter's trestles from my father's mostly homemade hire business.

'Old Dutchy' lived in Deception Bay and would frequent a home-brew shop in Burpengary. I knew this because I heard him nattering to my father about how his home-brew was 'Vantashtic, abshoulootly vantashtic! Real daste to it.'

At dinner I said maybe we should brew our own beer. My father wasn't impressed.

'Listen, you, there's a certain sort that makes home-brew.'

I looked at my father.

'Like Dutch blokes with beards who drive a P76 and live out at Decepo Bay – the rest of us go to the pub.'

It's funny though, because back in the day people used to do a lot of stuff themselves that they don't do now. Like try and fix their cars. Depending on what particular suburb you lived in, it wasn't that unusual to find a block and tackle and a car's engine hanging from it, while 'stuff' was done to the vehicle in a front or backyard. There were quite a few block and tackles in Redcliffe gardens – like huge ornate, post-industrial sculptures. You'd never try and fix a car yourself today, but lots of people are giving home-brew a crack.

People like my eldest sister who makes a stout that is a cracking drop.

And there's a couple around the corner who have a whole new food world going on: chooks in the garden, a beehive in the corner and a home-brew set up in the shed. Pale ales and Belgian blondes are their go.

A part of the attraction of home-brewing is the little community that springs up with the fermentation of a home-made drop. My grand mate PB has a clutch of brewers who gather at his place whenever they bottle the 'next batch'.

I went once. PB hovered about, a Jedi of the backyard, Old Home-Brew Kenobi with his padawans: Sid, Dan, Young Tristan, Crando, Daryl and the man who is known as the Legend of the Flying Corona.

A man occasionally called Rodney.

Apparently Rod bottled something or other in an old Corona bottle and, while it was fermenting, it took off. Literally. Embedding itself in the ceiling.

'Yeah, bit of a fizz in that little number,' admitted the Flying Corona.

There were mutterings of not sterilising and cleaning bottles properly but they were brushed aside by Old Home-Brew Kenobi.

'Well, all we know is it happened,' he said in Obi-Wan tones.

Then they all got back to banging on about triples, and pale ales and kölsches and whatever.

And they were, as I remember, all wearing hats.

I thought about another time I went to PB's for a barbecue. It was a warmish Sunday and I'd decided to walk. I wore a hat; seemed sensible enough.

I've gotten to the point in my life where, along with a lawyer, accountant, GP, dentist and a physiotherapist – I also have a dermatologist.

The first question she asked was where I grew up.

'Queensland,' I said.

She looked as if she had won the lottery.

So that's why I always have a hat handy. Plonked on top of my middle-aged, well-fed face. I can remember hats, 'slip slop slap' ads and smothering myself in sunscreen. And still I ended up with a dermatologist.

But I always liked wearing hats. As a kid I used to wear buckets and empty ice-cream tubs as hats apparently, and on the first day of school, my new grey school hat was pinched by a kid named Paulga.

Maybe he thought it was his; I was certain it was mine. But even today I still remember the look on his face. He loved that hat and he hated me.

I thought of him as I walked in the heat. I hoped he got a hat in the end. Because he looked demented when the teacher saw my name written in that school hat.

I put Paulga out of mind and waddled along with my dermatologist's-delight complexion.

I passed a few people, and not that many had hats. Instead they wore sunglasses, very long shorts and tattoos.

There were a few baseball caps, but everyone had them back to front, like Lleyton Hewitt. Not much protection from the sun but I suppose people wear hats for all sorts of reasons. Fashion.

Baseball hats backwards just look silly, but then I am about as fashionable as Y-fronts so I can't really talk.

One only has to look at some of the bizarre states of headwear at Melbourne's Spring Racing Carnival – especially on Melbourne Cup Day – to know high-fashion fascinators can be simply ridiculous. Birds have had quite useful feathers plucked to be stuck disastrously on top of some glammed-up, toothy racegoer's tortured hair.

There was a time when people wore terry-towelling hats, ridiculous things offering about as much sun protection as a knotted hanky, and necessitating zinc cream be slathered across lips and noses.

And berets. I played golf with a bloke who insisted on wearing a beret. He ended up looking like a piece of beetroot from a tin of Golden Circle.

Hats were fashionable up until the late 1950s, and depending on who you ask, the reasons for their decline range from John F Kennedy appearing hatless in public and showing off his fine head of tousled hair to the fact there aren't as many birds crapping from above, so protection from bird droppings isn't as necessary.

I hope birds are plentiful enough around Caulfield to get a couple of dropping shots back for feathered friends stuck on a fascinator-clad Melbourne Cup guest.

The hat I was wearing was a Panama or, as a friend says, a ponce-top.

I walked into the local bottle-o and somebody yelled out, 'Got a new book out, Will, trying to look like a writer, are we?'

When I arrived at PB's, I was greeted by the sight of everyone wearing hats. Apparently the barbecue had a theme: silly hat.

PB and Rod were wearing junior cricket caps. PB's suspiciously pristine Margate cap was up against Rod's suitably worn Scarborough maroon effort.

Scarborough was my old team and, as I made a note to find my old cap, I was asked if I had come as Tony Greig. 'You could do a pitch inspection!'

In front of the beer fridge, I laughed at the memory and the young man with the manscaped beard turned and looked at me. He was with his tall, beardless girlfriend.

'Good to see the contents of the beer fridge can make you happy. Just imagine how you'll feel when you have one.'

I nodded. 'Well, I'll see.' And I picked up a six-pack.

'The anticipation is the best part of getting something you like,' said the tall young woman. 'Like that man with the shoes.'

Her boyfriend laughed. 'Oh, that was beautiful. Wasn't it?'

I looked at them and they both smiled.

'That old guy that sits on the bench by the cleaners was in the op shop this morning and he'd found some shoes but he didn't have enough money for them. But he was so excited.'

Her boyfriend laughed.

She continued. 'So Harvey,' she indicated her boyfriend, 'bought them for him, and the old guy said he wasn't going to wear them home, he just wanted to carry them home, these new shoes that fit.'

'Well done you, Harvey,' I said.

He shrugged a little self-consciously and his girlfriend laughed and pinched his chin. 'Yeah, well done, Harvey.'

It was Patrice, the mother of a friend of mine, who put footwear in a unique perspective. 'You ever feel bad about things, you feel like a bit of a pick-me-up – go out and buy a new pair of shoes. That'll do the trick.'

I asked my friend what his mum meant.

He looked a bit blank, had a think, then said, 'I guess she meant you should start building up from the bottom.'

Perhaps there's a point there. Most people spend a lot of their life on their feet so it's important to get things right.

On one level footwear is a basic functional piece of clothing, like undies. Only, hopefully, not as prone to smelling as much, but one never knows.

But like anything connected to us humans, footwear becomes much more.

A symbol of status and fashion.

The first serious piece of footwear I can remember owning was a pair of thongs. Status and fashion eat your heart out.

They were blue and seemed like all I needed to be happy. Indeed, whenever I see a pair of thongs I get a little wistful.

Beach, summer, ease. I loved them.

But even these humble icons of the feet have been turned into a brand competition.

Last summer at the beach my daughter needed some thongs. Fair enough. We spent ages going through basic rubber thongs branded with different names until I yelled, 'They're just thongs!'

People turned and pitied my ignorance.

They're not called thongs anymore. They're Havaianas, Kustom, Roxy, Rip Curl and on and on.

My love of thongs probably led to my affair with the much-maligned Crocs.

I love a pair of Crocs; weird, clunky bits of foamy whatever they are, they were originally designed as a spa shoe. Well, that says it all. My mother called them 'formal thongs' and I have committed many footwear sins with Crocs.

I wore them once to an awards ceremony, simply because I forgot I had them on. Too comfortable by half.

A word to the wise: they're not very functional in wet weather, especially when you run out with the bin in early morning drizzle trying to catch the rubbish truck.

Slipping is an understatement. I went Torvill and Dean-ing down the footpath as if the bin and I were going for gold in the pairs figure-skating.

But shoes can be strangely meaningful. I once had a pair of Bata Scouts. Now that was a day. They weren't top-shelf because they didn't have the compass in the heel but they had animal prints on the soles. It never dawned on me that the fact there was no compass in the heel indicated they were knock-offs, but it didn't matter – they meant the world to me.

School shoes came to me rather later than most because at dear old Humpybong Primary nobody really wore shoes; naked feet were the go for years.

Shoes can give out signals. I always remember reading *The Second Sex* by Simone de Beauvoir where she opined that men love high heels on women because it put women on a platform for display but didn't enable them to move with speed and comfort, only teeter as an adornment.

And, you know, who would argue? There's a current TV ad for a brand of shoes with some gormless-looking git with a beard and various women in high heels and underpants, which crudely bears out that point.

If politicians want to appear 'of the people' they almost always choose to wear R.M. Williams elastic-sided boots. These fine comfortable boots cost a bomb but have that outback, pioneering feel about them. They also don't have laces to struggle with, so perhaps that's why our nation's leaders favour them.

And I can't deny the feeling that a new pair of football boots used to give me.

They smelt fresh. And even though I always longed for Adidas's mythical three stripes, I adored the possibility that a new Barry Muir football boot gave.

I knew I'd play like a busted arse but a new boot had that promise of possibility.

And the old bloke by the cleaners with his new shoes bought by Harvey, happy as a king.

Dear old Patrice, perhaps she had a point. And perhaps I was wrong thinking I had people sussed with generalisations and clichés.

Harvey and his partner and the old man with his new shoes just show that people can always surprise.

Chapter 10

Keeping Track of Time

At a hairdresser I heard a sound that took me to all sorts of places. An alarm clock. Somebody was having a colour put in their hair and the alarm rang for the developer to be washed out of the newly tinted follicles.

That alarm clock sound, an antiquated metallic ring, was the sound of time having passed, of a part of a life lived, even if it is at the hairdresser.

I have had a tricky relationship with the timepieces of my life.

I am one of those people who swear a lot at clocks because whenever I look at one I realise I am meant to be somewhere else.

Daylight savings, and the difference in various time zones, at least give me an excuse and a couple of days' grace when it comes to being late.

It's rather entertaining when you witness a fellow tribe member of the Clock Abusers Society in action. I saw a rather irritated man jogging through Melbourne airport staring at his wristwatch muttering repeatedly, 'You bloody bugger, you bloody bugger!'

The alarm bell in the hairdressers took me back to the trampolines at Suttons Beach in my childhood.

Ten cents for ten minutes. I'd clamber up onto the trampoline and try and bounce as much as possible until the tinny alarm bell would ring.

The trampolines were a bit problematic. I was always hanging out to get on them but once on I'd get a bit freaked out and simply bounce up and down like a loon. The fact that you always had an audience who were pretty free with their critical appraisals of trampoline performance didn't help matters.

A kid with epically bad teeth told me I should fart so I could maybe bounce higher, which I thought a bit rich because he was even worse at jumping than me.

I remember watching a girl gyrate her body into all sorts of bouncing forms and thought I'd never seen anything as lovely. But even for her, the tinny bell tolled.

School clocks were also a nightmare. Solid, institutional-looking things, telling the time agonisingly slowly. Especially when you were waiting to get out of the class or for some dire lesson to end. I remember sitting in high school zoning out completely while a desperate mathematics teacher tried to talk me through some equation that was a combination of numerals and letters. The whole idea of combined numerals and letters was completely horrible to me and all I could hear, as he worked his mouth furiously, was the sound of a mower down on the school oval. And the clock behind his increasingly irritated and frenetic head. The time it told was ten to three. Ten to three and the sound of mowing, the groundsman going round and round in circles, the drone and the clock on ten to three.

I was told to stand. I did so. The clock was still at ten to three. The teacher more frenetic. I remember that he had recently separated from his wife. He was even more intense than Mr Goldfingers puffing away on his Havelock roll-your-owns. Somebody, I think a quiet boy who took his religion very seriously, said he thought he'd seen the maths teacher crying once.

It was still ten to three and the mower kept going round the oval and the teacher, in retrospect, was indulging in a bit of workplace therapy.

A vein stood out on his forehead and he stopped yelling.

The sound of mowing. The Sound of Mowing. Now there's a name for a musical. Maria, the Baron and five young von Trapps mowing across the Austrian Alps.

Then, it stopped. The mowing. The teacher was staring at me. 'Well? Well?' he shouted.

I looked at the clock. It hadn't changed.

'Well??'

I looked at him and said, 'Ten to three.'

The range of emotions that registered across his face was quite moving, even to a pimply twerp like myself as a teenager. The poor man tried to incorporate 'ten to three' somewhere into the mathematical problem he was shrieking about. He mouthed the words and tried to make sense of them. He looked at the board. He looked back at me.

'Ten to three?' he repeated.

I nodded my head and said slowly, 'Yeah. That's about it. Ten to three.'

When he screamed, two teachers from nearby rooms sent students into our maths class to see if everything was all right.

And then the mower started again.

To this day, when I sit somewhere and time seems to take forever, I hear the sound of mowing and that scream. And think to myself, Ten to three.

•

Even when timepieces are combined with another instrument of modern life they can still be annoying. Like the clock radio.

When I think of the clock radio I think of Aunty Rita. We were sitting down together enjoying a steak and kidney pie one day waiting for her clock radio to sound the alarm.

Aunty Rita had a cow that needed to be turned every half an hour or so because it couldn't stand and the alarm signalled it was cow-turning time. The numbers on the clock turned over like an old cricket scoreboard with someone manually changing the score and when the score reached thirty, the alarm went off.

Instead of the dull buzz of the clock's alarm, the alarm switch was set to the radio and it warbled into life.

The voice of Bertie Higgins singing 'Key Largo' rang out. Bertie Higgins sounds like a comic relief character from an Agatha Christie novel, an amateur sleuth fresh off the links in tweed cap and plus-fours, solving crimes in between swilling gin fizzes. But no, Bertie was a somewhat seedy-looking unit in a white suit and floral shirt singing about 'larve' in the Florida Keys.

'Oh I do love this song,' said Aunty Rita and we sang the inane chorus to the poor Friesian as we rolled her over.

Bertie warbled away to his baby about how they had it all and, for the sake of a rhyme, he likened him and his baby to Bogie and Bacall – Hollywood movie stars Humphrey Bogart and Lauren Bacall.

Talk about overreaching. The video clip shows Bertie on a speedboat, wearing a floral shirt and sporting a shiny shoulder-length mullet and a beard. Even worse, when you looked a little more closely at Bertie, his beard had a distinct 'religious instruction' feel to it. Not long and unruly, but short and cropped. Almost as if Bertie was a disciple gone bad. So that's what Judas had done with his thirty pieces of silver. He hadn't got the guilts over how he'd completely burnt Jesus and gone off and done himself in; instead he'd gotten himself a career in 1980s easy-listening seedy crooning.

So there was Bertie Judas, his floral shirt and a thin glinting gold neck chain, with a nameless woman in sunglasses and a bathing suit accompanying him. His baby on a bouncing boat.

Still, both my aunt and I sang the chorus to the cow.

And the stricken creature softly mooed.

A religion teacher once tried to engage a class of us with the hip, up-to-date gadget of the seventies when discussing how Christ rose after his crucifixion.

'You know, Jesus got up from his tomb, and he did it without the help of a clock radio. That's pretty cool, hey?'

I wondered if Jesus had to turn a cow or he got up to the chorus of Bertie Higgins going off his melon about Bogie and Bacall.

Once when I was working in Sydney I had a series of early morning starts and needed to get out of bed as quickly as possible. For some people, like me, getting out of bed can be as torturous and as noisy as an opera with lots of high notes and a fair amount of tragedy and implausible plots thrown in for good measure.

The alarm sound on the clock radio was a harsh metallic beeping that I had managed to sleep through twice, so I had to set the alarm to something that would get me up and on my way.

Alan Jones.

Perfect. I awoke to the dulcet tones of the Sydney radio shock jock's morning editorial, which half the time was a right royal spray ripping some politician or public figure a new one.

It was like a cross between being told off by a particularly frenetic housemaster and a bilious rugby coach, which I suppose is sort of what he was. I felt like I should put my mouthguard in to get on with the day.

On one occasion I awoke to Jones doing an advertisement for a North Sydney colonic irrigation business. I think it was the quickest I had ever gotten out of bed.

I also have form with clocks as presents. I received a rather humorous backhander from an actress who's become a fixture of megaplex screens around the globe.

A *Thunderbirds Are Go* clock.

She thought it was a suitable gift because my acting style reminded her of the wooden marionette Tracy boys of International Rescue. Then she was told by a couple of the crew that I had done the *Thunderbirds* run down the stairs as a bet between them and me.

When I was seventeen I received a quartz Seiko digital watch and it seemed so space age and modern I assumed it was waterproof and promptly went swimming with it on.

Modern didn't mean waterproof, but because it was a birthday present and sort of cool I wore the dead digital watch like a dill.

That was my one sad attempt to make the tool of time a fashion accessory.

It's funny how things run in families: my daughter, at seventeen, chose to wear an old *Star Wars* wristwatch featuring Obi-Wan Kenobi and his lightsaber, not because it told the time, which it no longer did, but because it was 'kind of fun'.

Watches these days may be tarted up as jewellery and bits of high fashion with sports and movie stars flogging them on the back of glossy magazines and billboards but they are still basically tools of time. When you're an actor though, a watch can be a real peril.

I was filming a television drama where the scene involved me not being able to find my young son at a train station. My character was also late for an appointment so I was meant to be running along the station platform, looking at my watch, displaying fear and anger at the same time. The director told me it was all supposed to encapsulate the modern struggle between career and family. 'It's a metaphor for the modern male condition, yes?'

It sounded like a tutorial for a humanities elective at university but I nodded and assured the director I would metaphor away with all my might.

'Look at your watch and search the platform for your son, I want to see the gradual panic, the fear take over anger.'

I nodded again.

The actor's nod is a dangerous thing, it is ten percent saying, 'Yes I understand your direction and what you want me to do' and ninety percent saying, 'I'd like a coffee, can we just do it so I can go home, I wonder if I left the stove on, how soon is too early to have a beer, look at that pigeon over there, I shouldn't have eaten that extra bacon sandwich . . .'

I stopped nodding and away I went for about an hour running up and down the platform trying to be angry and frightened and capture the condition of the modern Australian male. And in between takes, nodding at the director.

When I saw the scene later in the studio, I just stared in disbelief. For some reason instead of just looking at my watch, I went to Watch Acting 101.

My arm shot out and bent at the elbow, my wrist then doubled up to my face so I could tell the time, then the movement was reversed.

I remembered I had been arsing about at the time and had done it as a joke for one take. For some reason that was what had been picked to be used in the scene.

I protested.

'Apparently the other shots were soft,' said the studio tech trying not to laugh. I groaned. I knew what he was talking about. That awful moment all actors are confronted with one day. The MEM. The Motion Embarrassment Moment. When you see yourself running.

Anybody can stand still and walk on screen but running is a real eye-opener.

You can't fake running. I used to be able to run. In a film called *Look Both Ways* I ran so much that an American film critic spent a paragraph describing my classic middle-distance runner stride and stuff all about my acting performance.

But age catches up. I knew my knees were shot, but the day we filmed the scene on the station platform I had inserts in and had taken my glucosamine that morning – and I thought I moved okay.

Perhaps it was the heeled boots I wore. Or the fitted shirt. I stared at the vision on the screen of a large man, in a tight shirt, with odd arm movements teetering along, looking like he was trying desperately to get to the toilet.

I turned to the tech and said, 'Well, I think I've captured the condition of the modern Australian male.'

He laughed a little too willingly; my actor's ego sensed that this particular scene had been the source of some humour and concern.

I told myself it didn't really matter that much. And then I turned my eyes to the screen where I was frozen in mid awkward gait. At worst I looked like someone trying to arthritically goosestep across the platform while doing a series of odd 'hail Caesar' type movements with my arm.

And at best I looked like the participants in the 1973 Redcliffe RSL fathers' 100-metre 'dash' at the annual Christmas party.

Except those gallant hobbling contestants ran that way because of the courage and endeavour they'd shown fighting for our nation and defeating fascism and national socialism on various battlegrounds of world conflict.

I ran that way because I was a fat old ham. Or a well-fed fascist running late for a train.

Running on screen, there should be an award for it. It's hard to pull off.

When did you ever see Laurence Olivier run? Did Marlon Brando ever sprint? Don't expect Cate Blanchett to jog anywhere soon on screen. Russell Crowe won't even have a go. And he's a bloke who'll have a crack at just about anything. Okay, he ran in *Gladiator*, but Ridley Scott looked after him.

Leonardo DiCaprio can run, sprinting everywhere in *Body of Lies*, but our Russ had the right idea in that film – he just wandered around in a dressing-gown with a cup of coffee.

Running is hard. Just ask Tom Cruise. He must have an overabundance of self-esteem because he runs in almost every film. Runs and shouts.

Big mistake.

A director friend of mine called it the tiny man's curse.

'Old Tom is like Daniel Craig, they pump their arms and lift their knees too much. They think they're running like Mal Meninga, but they're acting running. They're like a cross between Munchkins on a Stairmaster and one of those bunnies with a Duracell battery up its bum.'

Just for the record, my director friend was a very handy football player and still has functioning knees so he may have been a bit hard on the boys.

When you see an actor embrace bad running it's quite enjoyable. Liam Neeson cut a swathe through a lot of nasty, sweaty fellows with beards in *Taken*, but when you see him running he looks pretty timid, especially when he chucks in a bit of dodgy watch acting.

And dear old Roger Moore in some of his Bond efforts confirms he's the Bradman of bad running.

He slopped away from a temple in a pair of white slippers and a dubious karate outfit, which looked like a pair of

Peter Alexander pyjamas. He is a real thigh chafer, a bit like watching Graham Gooch run in to bowl his occasional medium pacers.

Even in a pair of caramel flares and a sports coat, old Roger looked gloriously ordinary running across a fleet of rubber alligators.

Yes, there should be an award and I can't think of anyone better to name it after. Get your nominations in for the most prestigious award for bad running on screen – The Roger.

•

An exhibition of Hollywood costumes at the Australian Centre for the Moving Image emphasised time and its passing in surprising ways.

The first costume was Scarlett O'Hara's green velvet dress from *Gone With the Wind*. I thought of my mother. Not because she was anything like Scarlett O'Hara but simply because she loved the movie. She loved the scene with this dress made from curtains and how cranky Scarlett got when Rhett Butler laughed at her.

'For a bloke with bad teeth he was lovely,' said Mum.

I stood for a moment in front of the dress, feeling quite sad. Missing my mum in this world. Then I laughed and was filled with warmth that she'd been the woman she was.

Next, I came face to face with John Wayne's outfit from *The Searchers*. The first time I saw this film was on a rainy Sunday. I was very young and eating baked beans on toast at the moment when John Wayne scowled at two settlers' children captured and brought up by Native Americans. 'Hard to believe they're white,' said another character.

'They ain't,' whispered John Wayne and stared at the children.

He looked ferocious. I was scared. My father, who was sitting nearby sipping on a Sunday arvo frothy, said slowly, 'Who'd have thought that fat bastard could act as good as that.' Then he looked at me and smiled. 'It's only pretend.'

I walked over and joined the swarm of people looking at Marilyn Monroe's dress from *Some Like It Hot*.

'Poor girl, poor girl,' said a woman to her friend. 'I used to think she was so big. And booby.'

'Everybody did,' said her friend.

'But that dress, it's as tiny as anything. The poor girl was the size of a sparrow.'

They paused. Then the woman's friend spoke.

'It's a little bit like an op shop. Isn't it?'

'How do you mean?'

'All these old clothes. Belonging to so many dead people.'

'Oh, well, that's put it in a new light.'

'But what lovely memories.'

Her friend was silent for a moment, then said, 'At least it doesn't smell like an op shop.' Still looking at Marilyn Monroe's dress, she added, 'Poor, poor girl.'

It was surprising to see the size of some of the costumes and, therefore, the size of some of the actors.

John Wayne's costume was immense, but surprisingly so was Tom Hanks's from *Saving Private Ryan*. Keanu Reeves's *Matrix* outfit was even larger.

Brad Pitt's *Fight Club* outfit looked startlingly petite while Daniel Craig's Bond dinner suit took the cake.

Two old fellows stood looking up at it. 'By God, look at the size of that, he's tiny!'

'No Sean Connery.'

'They've gone from a second rower down to a halfback.'

And they growled off together, banging on about their favourite James Bond movies.

It struck me as odd that people would feel such a connection, and an emotional one, to a movie costume or the actor who wore it. But perhaps it wasn't what they saw before them; it was the memories of where they were, who they were with and how they felt when they saw the film.

I remembered my father talking about Bing Crosby dying and how awkward it felt when one of your touchstones passed away.

Sometimes when you meet someone you have admired on the screen the impact they have on you can take you by surprise.

Wendy Hughes was a glorious actor who seemed to be as smart as she was gorgeous.

I first saw her in the 1978 movie *Newsfront*. If you haven't seen it then find it, watch and wonder at an Australia past.

It was the last scene in *Newsfront* that completely had me.

Bill Hunter walked away from his Americanised brother, refusing to sell film he had shot at the 1956 Olympics for propaganda purposes.

As he stalked off down a tunnel to obscurity, Wendy Hughes gave a wonderful, unexplainable look of love and admiration towards him and said in her warm, lovely Australian voice, 'He's just old-fashioned.'

At the age of thirteen, I thought her beautiful and smart and strong, and I hoped somewhere in my adolescent dreams that someday someone would say something like that about me.

I didn't think a lot more about it, even though I noticed Wendy Hughes over the years in various television shows and films, and even sat behind her at an awards show once.

But somehow that moment on screen buried itself deep in my mind. Perhaps it was that look she gave, perhaps it was the film. Perhaps it was just a moment.

At a friend's party one New Year's Eve I met Wendy Hughes. 'Met' is too big a word. We were introduced as we both headed in different directions.

Wendy Hughes. Nineteen seventy-eight was a long time ago by then, but when she turned to me and said hello, I just stared, a little in shock. And then said, like a loon, 'Good evening.'

Wendy Hughes laughed and looked a bit surprised at the formal phrase, especially on New Year's Eve.

My friend said, 'You've got to forgive William, he's from Queensland.'

Wendy Hughes looked at me, smiled, and said, 'He's just old-fashioned.'

I don't mind admitting, I nearly cried.

We never spoke another word to each other. But when I heard of her death, I remembered both times she had said that line. 'He's just old-fashioned.'

I wandered around the exhibition one more time and I stopped by the costume of Tom Hanks from *Saving Private Ryan*. I looked at my watch to check the time and I noticed the costume had a watch attached. It was an old-style silver wristwatch.

I stood there looking at it and I thought of Nabbo.

Or rather Mr Donald MacNab.

Nabbo was the deputy head at Humpybong Primary School. I was a ratbag. Our paths used to cross a little too often for both our liking. Of all the teachers who ever inflicted punishment upon me, Nabbo seemed the most pained by it.

Almost as if giving me the cuts hurt him as much as it hurt my fingers.

I would go into his office and he would sigh and look at his wristwatch, a silver one, and touch it with the index finger of his other hand. He did this quite often, as if he was always conscious of time passing, of making time matter. Perhaps he had better things to do than deal with little boofheads like me.

Then he'd shake his head slowly and go about the business of being a deputy head.

He was very neat, wore his hair short and always seemed to be dressed in a white shirt and tie and dark trousers, occasionally adding a green jumper in winter.

He was calm, kind – a gentleman. He was always quietly reassuring and being presented before him was the best result when caught perpetrating some primary school crime.

There were some interesting teachers at Humpybong, like a man who was almost an albino who, according to rumour, was supposed to eat white mice sandwiches in his old Zephyr car at lunchtime. Another man who would wander out on the verandah during class and get out his makings, roll a durrie and puff on it while keeping an eye on his class through the smoke.

And then there was Mrs O'Halloran. She was one of the most fearsome teachers because she actually thought it was reasonable for students to try and learn. Her students loved her but one day when our teacher had gone home ill and Mrs O'Halloran came into our classroom to oversee us, I found her demands a little unsettling. She asked me the square root of nine.

I had no idea of square, spherical, triangular or any form of roots.

'Square root of nine!' she yelled.

I freely admit I panicked.

I randomly trawled for some scrap of knowledge to satisfy her – but my mathematics cupboard wasn't going to open. I searched for anything that could pass as knowledge. I came up with facts about apples that I'd gained from one of my sister's old school projects, then added some Captain Cook titbits and finally rounded off with a half blue ditty that I had no idea was half blue.

Mrs O'Halloran's face went beet-red and I was sent outside to find my brain.

I staggered out into the playground and stood staring across Moreton Bay.

My name was called. It was Nabbo.

What did I think I was doing out of class?

I told him I was trying to find my brain.

Nabbo winced.

'Mrs O'Halloran?'

'Yes, sir.'

He pursed his lips slightly and half shook his head.

Then this wonderful man walked over, stood beside me for a while, sighed, looked at his silver watch, tapped it with his other hand, sighed again and then patted me softly on the shoulder.

'Well, good luck with that one, son. I'm sure it's there somewhere.'

I heard of his death a week before I went to the exhibition. He'd lived an extraordinary ordinary life. I discovered he'd volunteered for duty in World War II, trained in Canada as a RAAF navigator in the bombing squadrons and served until his plane was shot down and landed in neutral Sweden. He was imprisoned, and then ended up as an intelligence liaison officer in the British Embassy.

But I never knew any of that when I was at Humpybong Primary. I never considered him flying thousands of feet in the sky, through flak, battling enemy aircraft; never thought that as he checked his instruments and worked out positions, that he might check his watch and sigh and tap the face with the index finger of his other hand.

Never considered that while he was our deputy head, perhaps he was remembering his war years. His comrades. His enemies. Even what those bombs that he dropped had destroyed.

But I'll always remember him the day I tried to find my brain and the kindness he showed.

I looked at the silver wristwatch on the model, a part of a costume from a make-believe movie hero. I looked at my own watch again, and just for Nabbo, the type of man who would never have a costume in a Hollywood movie exhibition, I sighed and tapped it with the index finger of my other hand.

Chapter 11
Afternoon Telly

Spring. It means birthdays. My son's, my niece's, my sister's and mine. It means the respective parents all had productive festive seasons. The other thing that September means is magpies. Angry magpies.

Apparently it's just the males getting toey around the mating season – swooping down upon anything that looks like it might be passing through their little patch of earth. Whatever it is, maggies have a tendency to do their blob completely in the first month of spring.

It's such an annual event that it should be given some sort of recognition. Maybe a Festival of the Swoop.

The beginning of the season is also heralded by photos in the local paper of unsuspecting joggers, walkers or cyclists being swooped upon by aggressive maggies. Photographers lie in wait in their favourite spots to capture the moments and gleefully publish images of grimacing and shrieking members of the public.

PB sent me a Redcliffe 'best of', which are too wonderful for words. Living in southeast Queensland, you grow up with the sudden appearance of feathers and beak above you, but I first became aware of the true poignant power of the Festival of the Swoop one afternoon in primary school.

I had been kept in for after-school detention with Bradley Phie. What crime we had committed against the order of Humpybong Primary School is lost in the mists of time but I do remember we had kept each other amused with burps, underarm farts and a few raspberry tones blown on crooked arms in the library for half an hour. As we left detention, we spoke about what we would watch on the telly that arvo.

Bradley Phie was all for *Mister Ed*, the talking horse. I laughed. *Mister Ed* was old school. *I Dream of Jeannie*, that was the go. A scantily clad genie called Jeannie in a little bottle was way better than a talking horse.

When we reached Langdon Park, Bradley said he would wait for a while by the side.

I asked him why.

Bradley said he wanted to be alone and think.

This came as a surprise. I shrugged my shoulders.

'What you going to think about?'

He looked off into the sky and, after a pause, he said solemnly, 'Mister Ed.'

Then he nodded.

'See ya,' he said, and he almost laughed.

I was thinking that if I hurried I still might be able to make it home in time to catch *I Dream of Jeannie*. I must have been nearly ten and even though Mister Ed was fun, the relationship he had with Wilbur, his architect owner, was sort of odd because Wilbur seemed to be closer to Ed than to his wife, whose name nobody could remember.

Besides, the sight of a half-naked woman materialising from a plume of smoke streaming from a tall bottle that had been rubbed vigorously by a man in a military uniform had kind of caught my attention. And to top it all off, the lovely Jeannie would bow and coo 'Master! What is it that you wish?' to the officer.

Ah yes, the good old days of wholesome entertainment.

I sort of got the gist of what was going on but my middle sister, Rhian, used to encourage me to rub a long-necked brass decorative bottle on the shelves at home to see if I could make a Jeannie appear.

Always open to suggestion, I went to work caressing the bulbous bottom of the bottle, but then my sister would encourage me to rub it like Major Nelson from the TV show and so I would put my best efforts into replicating what I had seen.

Major Nelson, who was a rather highly strung astronaut, prone to screaming when his Jeannie appeared, would rub the bottle rather energetically, so I followed suit.

'Rub it faster!' yelled my sister. I obeyed.

'Now scream like Major Nelson!'

I attacked the neck of the brass bottle and rubbed so fast that smoke might have appeared. At the same time I screamed in a high-pitched tone.

Then, satisfied, my sister would yell to a handy adult, 'He's doing it!'

My mother would roar into action. 'Is he at the bloody bottle again? Why do you encourage him?'

My sister laughed.

'Don't give Cabbagehead any ideas, for Christ's sake – he'll be blind by the time he's ten,' offered my father.

'Colin!'

'Well, look at him, will you? He's off to the races.'

'Here,' my mother snapped. 'Give me that bottle, you stupid boy.' And she would hold the bottle in front of me and point a warning finger as I heaved breathlessly. 'No bottle for you, this is going on the high shelves.'

And so it would sit, on the top of the bookcase, waiting, while my sister laughed. She did, however, pay me a compliment in later life when she rang one mid-morning on a weekend to say she just wanted to let me know that she was proud that I seemed to have turned out to be relatively well-adjusted and quite a decent man.

'What brought that on?' I asked.

'I just turned the TV on and *I Dream of Jeannie* was on.' And then she laughed. 'Go on, rub the bottle like Major Nelson!' and she howled down the line.

'Yes, thanks for that,' was all I could offer.

I had serious form with *I Dream of Jeannie* and, wanting to get my fix, I left Bradley alone and marched off across the park.

It didn't take long before the first magpie got me. There were two, I think, but it felt like there was a whole squadron on my tail. I ran shrieking this way and that. I panicked and my legs wanted to go off in different directions to the rest of me. It must have been quite a show.

Was this punishment for my thoughts about the contents of the steaming bottle? Should I have just said that I liked *Mister Ed*? How impure is a talking horse? I could have kept my seedy *I Dream of Jeannie* thoughts a secret.

Bradley Phie collapsed in laughter. 'Master! Master,' he called out, imitating Jeannie.

Stitched up by the old magpie swoop, camouflaged successfully with the temptation of afternoon telly.

•

I Dream of Jeannie was one of a number of television sitcoms that for some reason were thought to be suitable entertainment for schoolkids in the late afternoon.

There was a raft of this late-afternoon entertainment, all about ten to fifteen years out of date by the time it was screened. All of the sitcoms seemed to be based on the premise that the shows were as silly and inane as possible, and almost all were devoid of children which meant the adults were required to behave childishly. The men were all puerile idiots, more like mid-teenagers than the astronauts, lawyers, architects, professors or advertising men they supposedly portrayed. All professionals and all new can-do careerists of the postwar West. Whereas even though women could have magical powers, they spent most of their time in the kitchen or, in Jeannie's case, the bottle.

Yet there were moments from these shows that stayed with me long after those afternoon telly sessions.

There was one episode of *I Dream of Jeannie* where Roger, the astronaut friend of Major Nelson, somehow got his hands on the next day's newspaper with the next day's news.

How did he use this glimpse into the future? To subvert history and change the course of the world for good? No, Roger headed for the racing results and proceeded to make a killing, picking all the winners for that day's races. I remember looking at the screen and thinking, *if only.*

Behind me, my father, home early from work, muttered, 'If only.'

I turned to see him standing and looking at the telly. 'You don't have to be Irish to see the glory of this, sunshine. If only.'

Years later at a Melbourne Cup barbie, I helped the hosts cut up the newspaper with the names of the horses running that year for the sweep.

The male host, whom I knew slightly, stopped and stared at the newspaper. 'If only I had Roger's newspaper.'

I didn't really need to ask but I did anyway. '*I Dream of Jeannie?*'

He nodded. 'The one with the paper from tomorrow. Every Cup Day I think of it. Bizarre, really.'

'Did your parents like that episode?' I asked.

He rolled his eyes. 'Oh my God, I don't think they ever had a bet on anything in their lives, not even on Cup Day, but I can remember them saying, "If only".'

Those afternoon telly shows became a part of my mind simply because they were repeated so many times and so would reappear at a moment's recall. On a flight to Canberra one Saturday winter's morning, we were diverted to Wagga because of bad fog. Wagga has quite a serviceable airport and is a lovely part of the world. But when one is confined to a tiny airline terminal lounge together with the passengers on another Canberra-bound flight, all huddling together waiting for the flights to resume, the experience can be a little too much.

There was a television high in the corner of the little terminal and it was tuned to the local regional station. It was showing a camping show about a man in a big hat with a big ute pulling a big caravan around Australia.

You couldn't really hear the television so nobody paid much attention as the big-hatted man, who also sprouted a beard, nodded and winked at the camera. It felt as if it was the end of whatever it was he was doing for that week.

I looked away and heard a man sigh. He had been on my plane and he was working on his tablet. He tapped a few times and then swore softly.

He tapped a few more times and then left a phone message for a business associate that he would have to meet them on the Monday morning instead as his flight was cancelled.

He hung up and groaned again, then leant back in his seat and closed his eyes.

Everybody had to be somewhere and right now the only thing any of us had in common was that we were all late.

I heard someone in the next row say, 'This is the one where Peter is Benedict Arnold.'

Before I even turned to look at the television I knew it was *The Brady Bunch*, another staple of afternoon telly that was being rerun, forty-plus years after it was created, on a winter's Saturday morning in Wagga.

The show was about a blended family, a widower with three sons and a widow with three daughters, and how they all shared a big house with a clinker chimney, and a bustling maid. It was about how they all got on together as a typical family. A typical American family.

In real life the bustling maid was a religious fanatic, Mr Brady was gay and some of the Brady kids would come to work stoned off their melons.

But it was just another piece of wholesome afternoon telly accepted as a staple of the day.

It was insane, really, that I could remember this episode about the middle son, Peter, not wanting to be Benedict Arnold in the school play. Arnold was a figure from America's War of Independence with the British and was so reviled a character that, according to Brady lore at least, if you were a bit on the nose and untrustworthy, someone would call you 'A Benedict Arnold'.

What interest Australians would have in this minor piece of America's history is doubtful, it probably went in one ear and out the other, or perhaps it lodged there as seemingly useless bits of knowledge can and waited for a question on trivia night to reach in and mine it.

I looked at the TV and saw Peter grumpy and I knew why. He was sloping into the kitchen and the bustling maid, Alice, was a little worried.

I said, without thinking, 'Not everybody can be George Washington.'

The man beside me, who had had to reschedule his meeting to Monday, laughed.

I looked at him and he had opened his eyes and was now looking at the television. 'Old Alice has got it figured and . . .' he waited for a moment, 'here's the song.'

The show had gone into its hypnotic simplistic theme song and around the terminal people sang bits and pieces of the song. There was laughter and a few groans.

'*The Brady Bunch*, shit, can the day get any worse?'

The man next to me laughed again, 'I know this song better than the national anthem.'

I looked at him.

'Well at least I know all the words to the Brady one; how many people know all the verses to "Advance Australia Fair"?' he said, smiling.

It was my turn to laugh. It was probably true.

'Yes. The old Bradys,' as if they were a family that grew up around the corner.

We watched for a moment and the man said to me, 'Do you know I had this theory that I would try to have relationships with girls who were like the Bradys?'

'Really?'

'Yes. It was insane. Marcia, the smart pretty eldest; Jan, the hardworking middle daughter; and Cindy, the cute youngest. With a speech impediment.' He shook his head. 'Insane.'

As conversations in airports go this was turning out to be a bit more entertaining than usual.

'How did that work out for you?' I asked.

'Crap really, the Marcias were all a bit boring, some of the Jans were okay but hard work and the Cindys just felt like The Elephant Man after a while.' He shook his head. 'You try finding someone with an attractive lisp. I even had a thing for an older woman.'

'Because of Mrs Brady?'

'No,' he laughed. 'The parents were off limits. Because of Alice.'

'Alice?' I nearly shouted.

A couple of people turned their heads and a few laughed quietly.

'Yeah, the crazy God-botherer. I thought she was soothing and kind. Instead of a lunatic, with that seedy butcher Sam bringing her brown paper bags of meat.'

'You had an Alice period?'

'Look, mate,' he laughed. 'It took me two decades to work out I was gay. I went up a lot of dry gullies.'

We both laughed.

'Nothing for Greg or Peter or the other one?'

'Bobby,' he said, giving the name of the youngest Brady boy. He shook his head, smiling, 'No, I didn't really know what was going on with myself there, but you know in hindsight, I suppose Peter was the nicest.'

'Benedict Arnold,' I said.

He laughed. He paused for a bit and then shook his head again. 'Although I ended up with a partner called Jan.'

'Is he a middle child?' I asked.

'As a matter of fact he is.'

'What about you?' he asked me. 'Do you reckon you used this sort of stuff as a form guide for life?'

Now that's a question, I thought.

'I don't know, maybe.' I had a bit of a think. 'I was more of your *I Dream of Jeannie* type.'

'Oh yeah,' he said rather analytically. 'I can see that.'

I nodded.

'The episode with the paper. The race results.'

I shrugged my shoulders.

'I can definitely see that.'

He was still for a moment. 'Bloody hell, you've got a whole dossier on me and we've only been chatting for about ten minutes.'

'Power of *The Brady Bunch*,' I said.

He nodded and then looked up to the TV. 'I like Peter the best, I think, he seemed the most normal.'

•

The actors from those afternoon telly shows became so familiar in their roles that they were still referred to by those character names, even if they went on to appear in other shows.

Wandering back from the beach one morning with the dogs, I started thinking about The Professor. And when I say The Professor, I mean a bloke called Russell Johnson who played The Professor in *Gilligan's Island*.

I had seen on a news site that he had died, the news heralded by the headline, 'The Professor Dies'.

He was a very old man and had lived a long and full life. He had died surrounded by his family, and I suppose that's not a bad way to go. No need for undue sadness because, as Clint Eastwood growls in *Unforgiven*, 'We all have it coming.'

That's just the way life is.

But for endless afternoons after school, for countless childhoods, he was The Professor from *Gilligan's Island*, a show that was completely barking mad. The show's premise was that the characters were all castaways on an island and every time they tried to escape, they were brought undone by Gilligan. He was a big-eared guy who would run around, howling inanities, maniacally creating all sorts of unintentional chaos amongst the motley characters, one of whom was The Professor – our friend Russell Johnson.

Along with the sooky millionaire, Thurston Howell the Third, who seemed to be a heightened template of Malcolm Turnbull in later years, The Professor was my favourite. He was always inventing inconceivable claptrap – but I remember one episode when, during a talent contest, The Professor was trying to blow pepper into the faces of the other island blokes. He looked a hoot and my father gave a heady tribute to Russell Johnson. 'Doesn't look like a bad sort of a bloke, I'd have a beer with him.'

Praise from a grown-up.

Russell Johnson kept thousands of fan letters, not through vanity but because so many kids watching the show took up science and medicine in part because of his character.

'That's quite humbling and not a bad thing to have achieved in your life,' he said.

At his funeral a neurosurgeon and an astrophysicist from NASA came and spoke, saying how much his portrayal had inspired them.

I patted my dogs and realised why I'd thought about The Professor. I shared his work not only with strangers – like the neurosurgeon – but also with my family, my friends. People I loved and still love. He was a touchstone that made me remember them, made me smile.

I had the same feeling upon hearing about the death of Gerry Anderson, even though he wasn't an actor and never appeared on screen, and even though you had to be of a certain age, I couldn't help sparing a quiet thought for old Gerry.

He created a series of puppet shows that were supposedly at the cutting edge of entertainment. Called 'Supermarionation', the shows featured wooden puppets with bushy eyebrows, huge heads and tiny wobbly limbs controlled by embarrassingly visible strings.

Most of the puppets were based on a physical resemblance to now almost-forgotten movie stars of the time: James Garner, Sean Connery and Steve McQueen.

Oddly, the Thunderbirds and their friends make me think of newsreaders with their plastic veneer made-up faces.

The shows were simplistic boys' own futuristic adventures. *Stingray* took place under the sea, *Fireball XL5* was a bewilderingly large-eyed and disconcertingly wobbly space adventurer, and *Captain Scarlet* was a military officer of the future who would die but come back to life. The most memorable show, *Thunderbirds*, was about the Tracy family, a group of sons and their father, who lived on an island with palm trees and flew around the globe in startling machines averting disaster and saving lives.

They called themselves International Rescue, an organisation run by the father, a puppet with the gravitas of a newsreader like Walter Cronkite. He didn't do much except growl sonorously and sit behind a desk. Of his wife and the mother of his five sons there was no mention. Interestingly, none of the Tracy boys looked like each other but when I was a kid this lack of familial similarity and lack of female presence never struck me as suspicious. Another mind might have thought differently about the boys of Tracy Island, but for me, they were just saving the world.

A gay props man I worked with once had a habit of sighing loudly when things got a bit too much on set. One day he rolled his eyes and said wistfully, 'Oh my God, get me to Tracy Island and those Tracy boys.'

I exchanged looks with another actor who whispered, 'Mate, that's my childhood arvos he's mucking around with.'

To even things up, there was International Rescue's English operative, the spectacularly single Lady Penelope.

Personality tests could be applied to which Tracy Thunderbird you related. Scott was the noisy go-to guy. Virgil was the all-purpose all-rounder. Weird John was up in Space. Then there was almost albino Alan from the rocket, and introverted nutbag Gordon from the submarine. All the heroes had American accents, because it was the age of America. Before the Vietnam conflict became contaminated, before the space race had lost its excitement. The fact that the characters were voiced by barely disguised English actors, with a couple of notable Australians in the form of Bud Tingwell and Brisbane's own Ray Barrett, added to the fun.

Then there was Brains, an inventor and technological wizard who created the machines in which the Tracy boys saved, if not quite the world, then bits and pieces of it.

This character had large horn-rimmed glasses, an odd close-cropped haircut – even for a puppet it was odd – and a stuttering, hesitant way of speaking.

One afternoon my Aunty Rita had come in to Redcliffe to shop and sat having a cup of tea with my mum while I stared at the Thunderbirds on the telly. Brains was trying to explain in his quivering manner something to the patriarch Jeff Tracy about an important discovery he had made.

'Oh, he sounds like he's up been up to no good in a library,' said Aunty Rita.

'What do you mean?' asked my mother.

'Well, as if he's gone off to the reference section and is having a bit too much fun with himself. All that panting and muttering. Like that man from Burpengary who got banned.'

'Rita!' exclaimed my mother.

'He was terribly bright but not quite right in the head.'

'Well, he should have got out and played a bit more sport,' advised my mother.

'Should have gone for a good long walk.'

'Always the bright ones. Would you like another Monte Carlo?'

I wasn't quite sure what they were talking about. I knew my aunt was always a keen correspondent with all the comings and goings and juicy rumours fresh around Deception Bay and surrounds. And I knew somehow it was connected to what was on the telly, so I asked rather gormlessly, 'Does Brains come to Burpengary?'

There was a pause, then my mother said, 'No, just another fellow.'

'Yes,' said Aunty Rita. 'I don't think poor old Brains could get up to much strife with what he's got to show.'

'Rita!' yelled my mother. And then I heard them explode in laughter; maybe the Thunderbirds weren't quite as space-age as I might have thought.

The boys of Tracy Island and International Rescue never cured diseases, ended famines, stopped wars or eradicated poverty. They just flew model planes emitting streams of talcum powder.

It was silly, delightful fun and the show's charm was that it knew this. But really, the mad glory of the show was how it stayed with you. *Thunderbirds* was already a decade old when I first watched it but I was still fascinated.

Nearly twenty years after its creation, at uni after a too-good night out, someone had the idea of a *Thunderbirds* streak. We all disrobed and did a 100-metre Supermario-nation race.

'Well, I suppose we've got a little bit more to show than the Tracy boys,' somebody said.

'Speak for yourself,' came a reply.

'Get Set! Thunderbirds Are Go!'

•

Most of the men had been there for most of the night. We were in the small sports bar of a hotel way up north in Western Australia and it was football finals time. None of the teams we barracked for were playing, but it was something to watch as we sipped the evening away. Little clumps of men, maybe about twelve of us all up, some sitting together, most by themselves. We each had different reasons for being in that part of Australia; a fair few wore fluoro work clothes and outfits from their daytime occupations – practical, hands-on nation-building jobs, by the looks of them.

I mooched in later than most after a hard day flogging my books at a fairly lovely resort and pulled up a seat and watched the telly too.

Nobody really spoke to each other, apart from a few exchanges about what the Hawks were doing to the Dockers and what the Dockers were doing to themselves.

'Can't think outside the plan,' said a man with a red beard and a fair amount of dust on his clothes.

'Too defensive, got no attack,' said someone in the shadows at the end of the bar.

A pause and the Hawthorn players walked calmly off in a bunch talking to each other as if they were planning the construction of some major piece of infrastructure.

'They're like fucking engineers on a site visit. All business,' said a man with a tough face, neat black beard and immaculate tatts. A few fellow patrons laughed and nodded.

I thought to myself, I bet the Hawthorn players would love to be described like that, by these blokes in a pub. As if they were recognisable types in these men's world – if not one of the boys, then one of the bosses.

The game we were watching was a replay of a match played earlier in the night, and everybody knew the score, but they watched anyway. Late on a Friday night, tired from a week's work and a bit fizzed from a session in the sports bar. We kept watching as the Hawks methodically solved any minor on-site problems posed by the Fremantle Dockers, until it was time for last drinks.

Some more drinks were ordered but nobody looked like they were in a hurry to leave.

The barman was the youngest in the room, somewhere around the late twenties. The ages of the other men ranged from mid-thirties up to late fifties.

'Chance for one more?' I asked.

The barman looked at his watch and nodded. 'Yeah, but after that it's time. Time, gents.'

Nobody said anything for a bit and then the bloke from the shadows at the end of the bar said clearly and deliberately, 'Not until you put the video on.'

The barman made my drink and shook his head. 'Of course, the video.'

I looked at him as I took my drink. He laughed a little. 'The video?'

He glanced at me and smiled. 'You'd be about the right age for the video, I think.'

I took a sip of my last drink. 'Righto then,' I said.

Sam Mitchell, the Hawthorn champion, was being interviewed after the game and spoke about team efforts; enjoying success and why nights like this were what the game and life were all about. He didn't say anything else; in fact the stocky little footy player with a pleasant manner disappeared altogether.

The screen went blue and then, after a little while, silvery, glittery things appeared against a grey background. I realised it was black and white.

And then the camera pulled out and I recognised instantly what it was we were watching.

'Jesus,' I said. *'Adventure Island.'*

The barman chuckled quietly. 'Thought you were the right age.'

Adventure Island. An old kids' show from the late 1960s and early 1970s made by the Australian Broadcasting Commission as it was named back in the day. It was a show for little kiddies, set on a magical island where kids were invited by Sue the Narrator to join in the adventures of the residents. Two dreary pandas who were a couple called The Pandas; a whingey, funny Clown; Mrs Flowerpots, who ran a shop; and Lisa, who was, I think, some sort of maid who had very black hair and was very thin with black eyes that I always thought were a bit too close together. She skipped and sang all the time.

There were also a couple of funny bumbling baddies who were always up to no good.

It was the Friday closing segment of the show that we were watching now, dredged up by some search engine from the depths of the internet. The maid and Sue the Narrator, with her gorgeous brown eyes and dimple, would walk down a lane saying goodbye to all the characters. The Pandas, then the Clown and Mrs Flowerpots would do a dance and the Clown would go into his caravan and then Mrs Flowerpots, who even back then as a kid I knew was a bloke in drag, would bang on for a bit to Sue and the maid and then disappear into 'her' shop.

All the while, Lisa the Maid had been singing a soft sweet song of farewell to all the kids watching. She sang about how sad it was that the folk on Adventure Island had to say goodbye to us all, but that they'd be back on Monday and they'd be thinking of us. They just had to go because Time was something none of us could borrow.

When the song finished the maid skipped off into the darkness, then Sue the Narrator gazed into the camera, said a little poem, smiled endearingly at us all, clicked her fingers and disappeared.

The camera pulled out, the lane went dark, and two prop wrought-iron gates swung closed.

A choir sang the chorus of the song and a hovering compass appeared as a harp's strings trembled over the image of the compass. Then, blackness.

Adventure Island.

We were allowed to watch it for the last twenty minutes occasionally on a Friday afternoon at Infants school, a practice that was, I think, pretty widespread across the country. Even in those days there was a surprising touch of melancholy to the week's end of the show, as if in a roundabout way we always knew and understood that Time was finite.

Nevertheless, sitting in a little bar with a group of pissed and half-pissed men forty or so years later and watching the closing credits was an oddly emotional experience. A lot had happened to all of us in the interim. Once we had been young boys watching the ending of the show for the first time.

We had all grown older; eventually we had found ourselves congregated loosely in that bar on that particular night.

Time is something you cannot borrow. How many little children's dreams and expectations had life bumped around, with compromises, broken hearts and personal ups and downs? How many goodbyes were said and unsaid?

The tough guy with the neat black beard and immaculate tatts let out a deep sigh and his shoulders shuddered. He bowed his head and rubbed his eyes. Breathed deeply and then stood up.

'You right, mate?' said the man covered in dust.

The tough-looking guy nodded and made a 'yeah' sort of sound. 'Just thinking about . . . just thinking about shit.'

He took a deep breath, laughed a little ruefully and then stood up to leave.

The voice from the shadows of the bar said softly, echoing the song's sentiments, 'We'll be thinking of you.'

I sat and sipped my drink.

The barman shook his head. 'Bizarre, how that thing gets to people.'

I nodded. 'What did you think of Sue?' I asked.

'Mate, she is gorgeous,' said the barman. 'So gorgeous. Weird video, man, but sort of sweet.'

I sipped my drink. 'Never liked the Pandas,' I said.

The voice from the shadows of the bar laughed. 'What was wrong with the Pandas?'

'Did you notice how the Pandas walked the same way Hawthorn players do when they're solving on-site problems?'

I didn't really know if they did, but it made the voice from the shadows and the barman laugh.

I finished my drink and went back to my hotel room. Catching up with afternoon telly, especially in middle age, can be a bit disconcerting sometimes.

•

A friend's uncle said the only good thing that ever came out of Japan was the LandCruiser.

Everything else produced in that complex and amazing country, according to Uncle Noel (who never seemed complete without an Escort cigarette hanging from his lips), was 'Just cheap tripe. Made in Japan rubbish!'

Everybody's entitled to his or her opinions and Uncle Noel, now long gone, was always willing to share his. The moon landing was a fake, you couldn't trust Tupperware because it was a religious plot organised by Americans, and menthol cigarettes emasculated the smoker.

But I could never accept that everything made in Japan was rubbish.

I mean, my father liked Makita power tools. 'You get a bloody hat with the thing, now that's handy!' and the most reliable television of my youth was a Panasonic.

But it was cartoons that showed the real worth of Japan.

The Japanese cartoons shown on telly in the afternoons were a series of strange science-fiction animations about little boys with superpowers. Astro Boy was kitted out in what looked like a bad pair of swimming togs and gumboots. He had a round face and big round brown eyes and spoke very quickly with an American accent, a trait shared by all the Japanese cartoon characters. It was a hectic American dubbing that sounded like someone calling a race.

Astro Boy was a bit of a worry with his bathers, but Prince Planet was okay. He came from a suburb somewhere in the vastness of space and ended up fighting crime and evil-doers on Earth. He had the added bonus that set Japanese cartoons apart – a singable theme song.

I'm sure I wasn't the only kid who made a medallion like Prince Planet's out of cardboard, texta-ed a star and a big P in the middle and went running around the yard. I added the novel touch of putting my mother's Yardley talc down the back of my pants to create the effect of jet exhaust.

My father returned home from work wearing his Makita cap and stared in stupefaction as I screamed about the yard with talcum exhaust streaming from my arse.

It was, I think, the first time I can remember my father saying to my mother, 'For Christ's sake, what is that bloody son of yours doing?'

And my mother shot back, 'Oh and you had nothing to do with it, I suppose?'

She pointed to me when she said 'it'. Thus began the long pastime of my parents, divvying up responsibility for their youngest and possibly their most idiotic child.

Kimba the White Lion was a talking lion from the African jungle who sounded like both Astro Boy and Prince Planet.

He hung out with a pretty stupid antelope and a cranky mandrill that was a bit scary. The mandrill behaved a bit like the odd man I would sometimes see at a bus stop I passed on the way to school. He would watch me, or anyone who passed, and yell, 'No bus no, no bus!' and point at the timetable. And as people walked by he would continue to wave and shout at nothing in particular.

'He's all right,' my mother would tell me, 'just not quite right in the head. Don't go thinking you're any better.'

Like Prince Planet, Kimba also had a pretty good theme song, but the best song of all belonged to Gigantor. The space-age robot. He never said anything and was one of the weirdest-looking heroes. Pot-bellied, with a pointy nose and a wavy piece of metal for hair, he wore what looked like a pair of slippers on his feet as he flew around the world at the beck and call of boy wonder Jimmy Sparks, who controlled Gigantor with a little lunchbox with two handles.

And you'd be surprised to learn that he sounded exactly like Astro Boy, Prince Planet and Kimba the White Lion.

The other characters in *Gigantor* were also quite memorable: Inspector Blooper; Bob Brilliant, the scientist; and Dick Strong, a super-secret agent.

I'm not making it up.

I loved Gigantor. I told my mum he reminded me of Gough Whitlam. There was something pretty out there about them both. My mum just shook her head, but seemed relieved I had stopped rubbing the brass bottle.

Whatever her thoughts, *Gigantor*, undeniably, had the best theme song, which was proof that Japan didn't make rubbish.

Years later at uni, I won enough money to pay the rent on my digs by singing the *Gigantor* song in a pub talent contest. Silly rhymes about Might and Right and Space Age and being bigger than big! I added a few Gigantor dance moves that the patrons at the bar approved of.

You beauty.

Gigantor came to Australia for an episode – on holiday! And even though Gigantor's holiday experience in our continent had a bit more to do with a politically incorrect Western movie shoot 'em up between cowboys and 'Indians', there was in that cultural mash-up a novelty that someone, or something, from overseas chose to come to Australia.

What's not to love about the big bloke?

In Kobe, Japan, there's a twenty-metre statue of Gigantor built to symbolise the city's recovery from the awful 1995 earthquake.

In Japan on holiday one Christmas we visited the plaza where the big statue stands. It was supposed to be a centre for tourist traffic and shopping but most of the shops were empty and people didn't seem to be paying much notice to the statue of Gigantor, looking like he'd been caught in an aerobics pose. I looked at him there in Kobe, my brother striking the same pose beneath him. I laughed. I thought of 'Uncle' Noel and how he got it wrong about that made in Japan rubbish.

My brother and I hobbled around Tokyo after our families, but we got tired of trying to fit into a series of tiny 'cat cafés' so my niece and my daughter could pat a roomful of tabbies and sip on a pretty ordinary coffee. Having a cup of instant coffee, sweetened with condensed milk, while being clawed by cats in a humid, closed kitty-littered room was a bit too much of a stretch for us.

'Christ, it's like having a sniff of the local cat lady,' I said.

'Too much, too much,' agreed my brother.

You could see by the looks on the faces of the cage attendants that they weren't too keen on having two large, middle-class Australian males stumbling about their tiny little universe. I felt something brewing when my daughter and niece insisted on taking the tiny lift on another trip to another cat café.

'I don't think we'll fit.'

'Just get in, fuck you,' said my brother in suitable big brother tones.

My son followed me into the lift and then my brother shuffled in.

The lift seemed to think seriously about the prospect of lifting not one but three large Australians up a small flight of stairs.

'It won't go,' said my son.

My brother groaned and shuffled out, only to have the lift doors close quickly upon his sizeable arse.

Hearing a large man bellow in shock is pretty funny. When that man is wearing a bright yellow Smurf beanie and a large purple puffer jacket, it is quite hysterical.

The lift released my brother and he turned with a surprising amount of dignity and said calmly, in almost Shakespearean pentameter à la Richard the Third calling for his horse, 'My arse, my arse, the lift grabbed my arse.'

We gave up on the café cats and headed back to the street. Then my brother simply said, 'Gigantor.'

'What?' I asked.

He pointed to a model of the space-age robot in a toyshop and quoted a line from the *Gigantor* theme song pertaining to Gigantor's size.

I answered with a corresponding line about Gigantor's strength. We shuffled into the shop and bought one each.

My space-age robot sits on top of my bookshelf in my study at home, with his clunky hands on his pudding hips. Once, when I was sitting thinking about something or other, I noticed him amongst all the other stuff stuck there and I quoted a few words of the theme song.

And was, to my delight, answered by my daughter, who had come to ask me something. She rounded off the theme song, put her hands on my shoulders and said, 'Hey, Daddy-oh, ready to fight for right against wrong?'

Now, sharing a part of your childhood afternoon telly with your daughter: that is a gift.

Chapter 12

In the Dark of the Night and the Bright of the Morning

In the dark of the night, when you should be asleep, it's good to have German springs.

Buying a bed's important. You'll spend a great deal of time in it, so best to get it right. It's also a sign of being a grown-up – for years you accept what's been provided by parents, then when you leave home all sorts of adventures can happen. In a Perth house I struck gold with a room complete with a lovely-looking bed, only to be haunted by the words of the vacating tenant, who took recreational habits to new heights. His nickname was Himalaya because he was always so high.

Himalaya gazed at the bed and sighed in a wistful voice drenched in excess, 'Adventures that darling has seen. Safe travels in her. But remember to hold on.'

I asked what he meant, he smiled and lay down, and promptly collapsed on the bed. I slept on the floor for weeks.

A friend swears a good bed is more important than a husband. 'I should know,' she assured me. 'I've had three husbands and only one bed – it's never let me down.'

So, in a bedding store I was determined to get it right. I was approached by a salesperson with a nametag identifying him as Chris.

Could he help me?

I nodded.

And he was off. Speaking very quickly and enthusiastically. 'You're big, a very large individual.'

I admitted I was.

In an instant I was lying on a bed. His face was above me.

Chris asked and answered his own questions. 'Good bed? It is. The reason? Springs.'

I looked at him.

'German springs. They'll last for years.'

The bed was big and firm.

'Do you remember that ad with the steamroller?' I asked for no reason in particular.

Chris nodded enthusiastically.

'Yes – the big bloke with the moustache in PJs sleeping on the street *and* the steamroller goes down one side of the mattress *and* he doesn't wake up!' He clapped. 'Same company makes this bed!'

'You seem to like your job,' I said. He had hairy nostrils.

'It's only my weekend job.'

His real job? An astrophysicist.

I looked up at his hairy nostrils. 'Really?'

'Oh yes,' he said. 'What I love.'

To Chris, the whole idea of astronomy was about to change with the James Webb Space Telescope replacing the Hubble. Potentially we may have to rethink our knowledge of the universe.

'Now that's exciting!' he said.

Perhaps, but I thought how sometimes the sky unnerves me.

'Don't you ever get frightened looking at the stars?' I asked. 'By that feeling of randomness?'

He laughed. 'Randomness? What's more exciting than working out where we came from? The responsibility of knowledge is pretty cool.'

He had a point. But it was nearly Easter and I couldn't help myself.

'You have any faith?'

'As in religion?' he laughed. 'Science and religion aren't the happiest of companions. Even though there's a Vatican Observatory and Pope Gregory XIII used astronomy to come up with a Gregorian calendar – look how they treated Galileo.'

To Chris, religion couldn't change, but a faith based on science's constant search for knowledge could. 'What about you?'

'Pardon?' I said.

'What about you, do you have a faith?'

'I don't know,' I said.

Chris got out his phone. 'Here, look at this,' he said, like he was showing a photo of his children. 'It's beautiful. It's NGC 4945, the Spiral Galaxy.'

I looked at a galaxy light years away, a little uneasily. It was a bit like staring at eternity, though to Chris it was probably the possibility of knowledge.

In search of a bed, I was getting a lesson in metaphysics.

Then I looked more closely at the galaxy. The image was black sparkled with silver and a flash of colour.

'Mate, it looks a bit like an old toilet tile from a pub,' I said.

Chris stared at the image. 'God, it does a bit. I'll never look at NGC 4945 the same way again.'

I ended up buying the bed and the German springs have proved to be worth the investment. I lay in it last night. In the dark of the night. And I couldn't sleep. I was thinking about next door.

The old lady who'd lived next door had moved out about four months before. She seemed very old, her age accentuated because she'd been a part of the neighbourhood ever since my wife and I moved into the house next to hers.

For some time after we moved into our home she would talk quite happily to us over the fence or in the street, little neighbourhood chitchat. And she would smile widely and be effusive in her hellos and goodbyes.

She didn't seem to like that many of the people in the street where we lived. People weren't what they seemed, she said, they say one thing and mean another.

Occasionally she would even mind our son when he was a toddler so we could go to the movies. She would give him chocolate coins and let him watch television as long as it was Channel Seven because she liked *Wheel of Fortune*.

She would get cranky, my son said, when she got the words wrong. 'You've got to have a good vocabulary,' she would say, 'but you've also got to have a good imagination.'

Then we started to extend the house and we became people in the street that said one thing and meant another. She wouldn't chat to us anymore, and she and her daughter would never say hello or even acknowledge us, even if we were parking our cars at the same time, or putting out the rubbish bins on Monday night.

Once when I stomped out into the backyard after an argument, which I invariably lost, my wife came out to generously offer peace terms but I hadn't finished sulking.

She gave me a little bit of extra advice to go on with and was about to head back inside when we both heard a scrabbling noise, then a whisper and then an oath. I walked over to the fence and the noises stopped. I stayed there for a while and they started again and I could hear the unmistakable sounds of the old lady muttering and growling under her breath.

I got an outdoor chair, placed it against the fence, stood on the chair and looked over the fence.

The old lady was there. She had come outside to listen to our argument; she must have followed it through her house and out to the kitchen and then outside to where she found herself stuck. In between her shed and the fence.

I asked her if she needed help and she said quite happily, 'No, no. It's all right, thank you. I'm just . . . I'm just . . . no, it's all right, all fine and dandy.'

I went inside but went back out to check if she was all right for the following half an hour or so until she freed herself.

Last night, lying in my bed, in the dark of night, I couldn't sleep. I thought about the old lady. It had been four months since she'd left to enter an aged-care facility because things became a bit too much for her.

She'd lived with her daughter in that house for years until her daughter died from cancer. Her other daughter, who lived interstate, did what she could, but it's hard sometimes, life.

The old lady often locked herself out and asked us for help. At all hours. Sometimes it would be about her rubbish bins – someone had moved them, could we come and look? Someone had come down the side path. There were always noises and shadows; someone had been fiddling with the lock. Why?

Some people in the street, she thought.

The world was closing in on the old lady.

She would knock on the front door; you couldn't see her through the glass panels she had become so tiny.

She stood, looking up, then smiled. 'I'm sorry, I should say, I'm so sorry.' And she would ask why her television wasn't on Channel Seven.

One of us would pop over and try and help.

'I always watch Channel Seven, someone has been changing the station.'

I would walk through her house, full of trinkets and ornaments, a little cabinet filled with cheap china dogs: spaniels with big eyes and labradors and Scottish terriers. The house smelt of age, of an old life. I walked through to the kitchen, where her television sat on the bench, blazing static vision and noise. I would press a button and then Channel Seven would come on.

'Where's the wheel?' she said once.

'*Wheel of Fortune?*'

'Yes,' she said.

I said I didn't know, maybe it had been on earlier in the afternoon, though I didn't think it had been on for a decade.

The old lady stood in her kitchen and looked at me. Behind her was a beautiful 1940s poster for the WRNS, the Women's Royal Naval Service or the Wrens. A young woman in an elegant, sharp uniform, snapping to attention and saluting, with a smile, to the horizon. In the corner of the frame were service medals.

'Were you in the Wrens?' I asked.

She stared and then said, 'Here's Channel Seven.' Then she looked at me. 'And how are the docks going, William? Busy?'

I said I didn't work on the docks.

She sighed a little and pointed to the television, then to me. 'Still play-acting? How's it going?'

I was about to answer when she suddenly yelled, 'My God, look at you! You've let yourself go, William. You look like John Wayne, in those films just before he died.'

I paused. Then said goodnight.

I couldn't help myself and when I was being driven to my play-acting job I Googled John Wayne's last films.

'Christ alive!' I half yelled. There was John Wayne, a great hulk of a man in a bad suit who looked like an exploded potato wearing a toupée, scowling into the camera.

'Bad news?' asked the driver. We stopped at an intersection and I showed him the image on my phone.

The driver looked, and asked, 'Is that you?'

'Fuck off!' I said. We both laughed. And I thought to myself, she can sort out Channel Seven herself.

But the next time she knocked on the door I went over. She couldn't find her torch. She often asked if we had a torch she could borrow because she couldn't find hers. I'd pop up to the local supermarket and buy her one. Lost count of how many I bought.

A few nights later I went over again to help her with her television and she said she couldn't understand why she had so many torches.

I looked at a drawer full of torches.

I told her, 'It's wise to keep some spares handy.'

She smiled and nodded. Then she asked how my wife was.

My wife had died four years ago. I told her my wife was good.

She nodded.

'I feel so old,' she said and she just stared. 'I'm an old fool,' she said. I gave her another torch and she put it in the drawer.

Sometimes in the backyard I would hear her over the fence. Making a soft noise as if she was listening to what might be going on over my side of the fence.

'You all right?'

'Yes,' she would say, 'fine and dandy. Just dandy.'

On one such morning I said good morning over the fence and asked if all was okay over there.

She said yes, but she thought someone was watching her or watching her house.

I took a sip of my coffee and told her to just sing out if she needed anything. Then I patted Foss.

Foss was a housewarming gift for our place at the beach, but he hadn't made his way down there yet. Foss was a large fibreglass gorilla, straight out of a David Attenborough documentary. He was in a position of reflective pose and was given to me by my good friend because his boofheaded reflection and healthy gorilla gut reminded her of me.

Why? You'd have to ask her, but as housewarming gifts went, the gorilla was a beauty. He was plonked in the garden and was immediately given a series of names. Kong and King then David, in honour of the great man himself, then Sigourney (Weaver) or Bryan (Brown) because of the old eighties film *Gorillas in the Mist* and then he was finally christened Foss. Foss for Dian Fossey who was the inspiration for the film.

So Foss sat in the garden, making me think of other objects which had been made to adorn gardens.

Like the carved black tyre swans that seemed to be everywhere in the gardens of my childhood until they all disappeared, becoming as extinct as the dinosaurs. Or the concrete Mexican sombreros in which a cactus or some other half-exotic plant was stuck.

And then there were the homemade statues of Mr Gale, a man who lived in Plume Street for a while.

He created a unique front yard double act of an angry-looking Viking and a smiling Marie Antoinette figure. Then he added a swagman that looked a bit too real for my mother's taste, especially in the rain. I remember Mr Gale talking to my father on Suttons Beach about how he loved making his concrete figures.

'Well, good for you,' my father said, 'all we've got is some odd little gnomes.'

Mr Gale died quite young and I don't know if any of his statues still stand, but I hope they do.

But the go-to image of garden statues has got to be gnomes.

Our homemade efforts had noses that were as big as the funny drooping beanie-type hats that pointed out from the back of their heads. The whole effect was a little bit macabre but definitely full of character. These days, gnomes can be bought almost anywhere, mass-produced and evenly finished.

The other great thing about garden statues was the grand adventures they could go on. Lots of people – including me, I admit – have occasionally engaged in pinching a gnome and taking him on a bit of a holiday with accompanying photos of the little man's travels, and then returning him to the garden from whence he came. The practice, I believe, has been given a new millennium–derived name: Game of Gnomes.

And what goes around comes around. The morning after I had proudly placed Foss in the garden, I awoke to find him missing.

I needn't have worried.

It became apparent he'd gone on holiday around a fair few gardens, all evidenced by images delivered to my mobile phone, until Foss was returned safely home.

Nice to see some garden traditions remain.

The old lady had said she felt like somebody was watching her; I looked down at Foss's unblinking eyes and took another mouthful of coffee, dressed in my robe.

A robe sounds regal. Like a monarch stalking about his grounds, or some hairy bloke from *Game of Thrones*, wrapped in ermine and fur. Or biblical, if you remember the countless screenings of the old Easter TV favourite, *The Robe*, where a young, handsome Richard Burton and his plummy booming voice tell of Christ's robe, gambled for and won by a Roman centurion at the foot of Christ's Crucifixion.

A tale of faith and redemption.

281

Well, that ain't my robe. There is nothing redemptive about my robe and nothing regal about it, either.

My robe covers up a lot of sins and indulgences. It is also a sign that I've reached a stage of life where one of the great satisfactions is hoisting myself out of bed and creaking about in a garment that, if you wanted to be polite, would be described as a dressing-gown.

But why be polite: it's a robe, a cotton-towelling thing drawn together with a sash. Violently vertically striped, with pockets as deep as a mineshaft. An article of clothing made for just mooching about.

Occasionally, as with pyjamas, the robe makes a fleeting appearance in the public world. Nothing too outrageous; even I have my limits. Just the usual examples – prowling under the cover of darkness with a few bags of rubbish to squeeze into other bins in the neighbourhood, or wheeling out the bins when the council rubbish trucks are heard coming early in the morning; and to harrumph into the car and give my daughter a lift to the train station. Although, sadly, one day she forgot her lunch and a prolonged presence in public occurred. I roared down the railway platform in my crocs and robe, unshaven, with an unmade early morning head, screaming out her name and brandishing a container of salad, juice and a couple of bits of fruit.

Satisfyingly, I got a few back slaps and a smattering of applause.

This is just to point out that I do not unleash the glory of the robe on other members of the human race lightly.

So it was a rather surprising moment in the garden when a representative of my fellow human beings commented on my robe.

I was scratching and patting the dogs when I turned and shrieked.

A drone, about the size of a takeaway pizza box, was hovering just above head height. It wobbled and drifted over to the outdoor furniture and landed. The bottom of my robe started to quack and vibrate. It was my mobile, down in the mineshaft pockets. The quacking ringtone was courtesy of my daughter, who changes the ringtone as often as she can.

I rummaged about in the mineshaft, grabbed the phone and answered it.

It was a mate with whom I used to play cricket. I hadn't seen him for a while. I said hello, and he told me I had a good robe.

I said a bit dumbly, 'What?'

And he repeated, 'Looking good, Will, in your robe.' And he laughed.

It transpired that he had moved on from sub district cricket, as I had, and found a new pastime. He was involved in the local drone club. It was his drone that was now squatted on the outdoor table, his drone that had given me a start.

I looked at the drone.

'Can you see me?' I said.

'Yes,' he said.

His drone had a camera.

'Where are you?'

'Out the front of your house.'

I invited him in for a coffee. He asked if I was interested in becoming the patron of the local drone club.

I told him I didn't think I was.

He asked me to think about it. 'Great family fun, mate.'

Seriously. Drones. A drone club.

Drones were evolved remote-controlled things, a progression from model boats and the weird buzzy model planes people used to fiddle about with in Humpybong Creek years ago. Odd people who'd always shout and point too much. But they could never see me in my robe, in my backyard. And now here was an old mate, peering at me with his drone.

The old lady next door had said she thought someone was watching her, watching her house. It was a bizarre world, sometimes.

Her house now stood empty; a gardener would come occasionally to keep the lawn in shape and I would collect any mail that might come.

Then the other day I heard the sound of things being broken and the dull thump of something hitting metal.

I looked to see a big skip in the old lady's driveway being filled with her belongings. The sound of unwanted chairs, tables, books, ornaments and garden statues being placed into the skip sounded like a sad and mournful bell.

That night I read Philip Larkin's poem 'Aubade'. It's a terrifyingly beautiful poem about the inevitability of death. Set just before dawn in the between world of night and day, a man lies awake thinking about how the new day brings him only closer to death. The day brings light and the routines with which we try to distract ourselves from the inevitable fate.

It's a bit grim but it is beautiful, and it never does anyone any harm to think about the fragility and finite nature of life.

Then people might appreciate it more.

The night after I read Larkin's poem, I awoke, of all times, just before dawn. I sat alone in my room

I thought of the skip piled high with tangible ornaments of that old lady's life.

How many pieces of the routine of her life were lying there? I saw her collection of china dogs, some broken. A pair of spaniel's eyes lying on top of a two-year-old EZ2See calendar.

And that empty house, waiting to become somebody's new home.

That is no bad thing, I thought, new people making a new home. Life rolling on. Someday it will happen to the house that is my home.

I thought of these things. Of all the things in my home, where they had been and where they had come from. I thought of people I have loved and who have left this life we have.

Philip Larkin's words were hanging in the air. It can be quite lonely when you think these thoughts. But then there is always Dean Martin. My parents adored him. There was one song I discovered from the old rum pot American crooner, forever dressed in a dinner jacket with a cigarette never far from his fingers. He had a hoary television show where he'd sit on a couch and croon.

The song I loved to watch was 'A Hundred Years From Today'. My son asked why I liked it so much, that song, that clip of Dean Martin singing. We were visiting my sister in Queensland, whose home was the house where I grew up.

'Why do you, Will?' she said in a tone that big sisters use to little brothers.

I thought for a bit and then said, 'It's a moment, a bit of time where a man is happy and content with everything. Life. Death. The bag of being human.'

My sister looked quite surprised. 'That is quite a good answer,' she said. And she went and got me one of her good stouts.

That song, the way Martin sings it, his laughter before he sings at some off-camera and unheard joke, even him fagging on as he croons about love and mortality isn't so different from Philip Larkin's beautiful poem, or the coldness of life's belongings piled in a skip. Existentialism, mixed with humanism all dressed up in a smooth lounge singer. Life goes on until it stops. Philip Larkin is a genius but Deano has the right take on the whole thing: a wink, a smile, and sharing our time with people we love.

And just to make sure I understood, I looked outside my bedroom window and I saw movement in the banksia.

It was a bird. An eastern yellow robin, a pretty little native bird. I watched and remembered. When that banksia was planted. And why. The little bird hopped from frond to frond and its colours stood out against the pollen-tipped crimson red of the banksia.

There'd been a bit of an argument about whether it was a good idea to plant that banksia – not a major one but the sort of 'just wait and see when it grows' argument.

A gardening argument. Sometimes they can get fairly heated, gardening arguments, especially when unilateral decisions are made.

The neighbours across the road bunged on a show when a pretty little tree was given a bit of a pruning by another neighbour, Joss. Pruning is too kind a word; it was as if the shady little tree suddenly joined the marines because there was basically no foliage left apart from a few shoots at about knee level.

The look on the neighbour's face was priceless. She proceeded to let rip with both barrels.

Then there was laughter and now 'Joss's haircut' has become a part of our street's folklore.

Gardens have changed a lot since I was a child, but, at its heart, the relationship people have with a garden hasn't. In the garden where I grew up were two massive Moreton Bay figs at either end of the yard that framed the back shed.

And mulberry trees, a few rangy gums and a mango tree and a lemon tree that was called the outside toilet.

A world of fruit, branches and leaves that gave a reason for all sorts of wildlife to hare around. Fruit bats and parrots.

Sounds like most people's nightmare nowadays.

And every garden in my childhood seemed to have a lawn, a carpet of grass that was half couch, half buffalo and occasionally a few bindis to keep things interesting and young feet honest.

There were often little vegie plots with tomatoes, zucchinis and beans, but it was the odd, fascinating incidentals of edible vegetation that pointed to a sparser way of life. Like *Monstera deliciosa* – a long, thin conical 'thing' with hexagonal little pods, which were fleshy and chewy. Then the even more gothic chokos. Choko vines were usually strung along a back fence, and heavy green fruit with stiff bristles bulged here and there.

Once on our way to Suttons Beach we walked past a garden that had a flotilla of chokos hanging on a vine. Their proud owner, an old man, looked up and muttered, 'What do you think of them? What do you think of me Martian testicles?'

I can't say that I ever rushed to the table if chokos were up for offer after that. But gardens always seemed a lovely place, where your parents would chat together as they'd water the garden with a hose in the evenings. Their time.

Or where you would leap through the diamond spray of the sprinkler as it reached out to the outer reaches of the garden.

A place where things grew. Where little plans came to fruition and where parts of a person's personality lived.

Like my mother-in-law. She was a quiet, determined woman who loved her garden and would always bring little bunches of flowers and cuttings from her garden to decorate Christmas tables and birthday parties.

On the day of her funeral service, one of her daughters had snuck back into that garden, which had been sold and the property was waiting for demolition to make way for townhouses.

She had brought back a little bundle of flowers and soft-textured cuttings. We all knew, without asking, from where they had come.

It was the same sort of bundle of flowers that my mother-in-law had placed gently on the coffin of my wife, her daughter.

I looked at the bird in the banksia and remembered. How my wife had planted the tree, and how I had thought it would be better somewhere else. We had argued. The old lady next door had listened.

And I remembered how, after we had made up, my wife had smiled with her playful wise eyes and said, 'Just wait till it grows. You can watch the birds in the morning.'

I remembered. And smiled. And in the bright of the morning I played Dean Martin.

Chapter 13

It Ends, I Think, in an Auction House

It ends, I think, in an auction house. A big barn run by a dreadlocked son and his mum and a group of friends. It's a place that deals in collectables and what people who know about such things call 'pop culture ephemera'.

To others it's a shed full of crap; delicious, odd crap.

Military uniforms, gowns that were supposedly just the things to wear to dinner parties and special nights out from decades past but would get you arrested on a Saturday night now.

Countless bootleg recordings of Rolling Stones records that a man in a booming Scottish voice successfully bid on with a 'Yes!'

A collection of dental tooth implants that somebody bought to make brooches and cufflinks from; a box of antique mobile phones was bought by a collector.

I looked through that box and found a couple of phone models that I owned; now they're antiques.

One was an orange flip-out phone I unknowingly took for an impromptu bomb off a jetty with my son in Tathra and another model was the same as one I left on the roof of a cab.

At the time, I had been having a rather one-way conversation with a television executive who was trying to convince me to appear in a show he was producing.

He was a nice enough man, enthusiastic and full of energy, and he would ask a question and then proceed to answer it. I had been on the phone to him since I landed at Sydney airport.

When the taxi pulled up outside my hotel, I got out and put the phone on the roof as I pulled my bag out, then shut the door and stepped back to see the taxi drive off into the city and the evening.

With my phone still on the roof, presumably with the producer asking and answering questions.

I looked at the phone as it disappeared and simply thought, Oh well.

I bumped into the producer at an awards show later in the year, and he clapped me on the back, saying to people nearby, 'Well, look at you. Do you know how long I tried to convince him to do that show? An hour and a half! And he still said no. But I tell you, always good to talk to you, Will. Always.'

I said the same to him and, as I wandered back to my seat, I worked out that from the airport to my hotel in a cab would have taken twenty-five minutes at the most. For over an hour in that phone conversation, he had amused himself.

There was a collection of breakfast cereal toys that made up a lot for auction. I saw the unmistakable milky figures of the Nabisco national dress of the world collection, but even as I looked I half knew there wouldn't be any 'Dutch Cow' to be seen. There was a purple Captain Cutlass and a bowler-hatted Upsy Downsy, the sort I had put on the desk of the girl with the wart on her finger.

Another lot consisted of prehistoric transistors and cameras and gee-whiz implements like those from K-Tel, whose every product had an O'matic attached to it. Hair-O'matic, Veg-O'matic and Brush-O'matic – as if, my mother used to say, they came from some mad Irish clan like our father.

Also up for offer was a set of Pokémon trading cards; my son would have given his all for them when he was eight and nine.

Pokémon were fictional creatures created by a Japanese video game designer in the mid-1990s. When I saw those cards I could hear my son screaming with his friends as they sat on the trampoline, 'Pikachu, Pikachu, Pikachu!'

They were so important to him, the thing most filling his mind on that afternoon, and they were completely lost on me.

Then, looking at a collection of old *Life* magazines, I looked up for some reason and saw it. And I knew, even as I glanced at it, that it was hers.

292

A print, from a limited run, a print of a seagull flying.

It was the work of my wife, a series she had created years before she had even met me, before I had opened the front door of a share house and there she was in the doorway waiting. She'd come to visit a housemate.

She wore Wayfarers sunglasses, a green dress, and black boots. Behind her was her S series Valiant. She flipped up her Wayfarers, and smiled, at me.

She had done the print, I think, when she lived at Pittwater, with a big studio that would sometimes flood but which was worth it, she said, because it taught her never to take things for granted. Those things could always change. And besides, she loved a bit of random nature.

The print was high up on the wall, set apart from the other paintings and hangings. I looked in the catalogue and saw it was not mentioned or numbered, and then one of the staff, standing next to me, said quietly, 'It's lovely, isn't it?'

I turned to her and she indicated with a nod of her head that she was talking about the print of the seagull.

It takes a while for people to see it, she told me, but once they do they look for it whenever they come in. 'It glows up there. So lovely.'

I asked if she knew who the artist was.

'No, I don't, but I know it's lovely. And it's not for sale. It's something that makes you happy, takes you away to a lovely place.'

I nodded.

'Anyway, that's what people say they feel when they see it. And that's pretty neat, don't you think?' And she went about her business.

In this barn full to the brim with items for auction, there's so much stuff; some collectable stuff, some valuable stuff and some just stuff. Everyday stuff.

But it all has a story if you look. It can tell of people's lives and hopes and dreams.

And sometimes, you can see something that makes people happy and takes them to a lovely place.

Acknowledgements

I would like to acknowledge, in no particular order of importance, the following people: Robert 'Bowtie' Watkins, Karen Ward, Deonie Fiford, Anna Egelstaff, all at Hachette, Bernadette Foley, Bevan Bleakley, Rick McCosker, Paleface Adios, Peter Bolton, Clem McInnes, Stella McInnes, Amanda Higgs, Ray and Delilah.

hachette
AUSTRALIA

If you would like to find out more about Hachette Australia,
our authors, upcoming events and new releases you can visit
our website, Facebook or follow us on Twitter:

hachette.com.au
facebook.com/HachetteAustralia
twitter.com/HachetteAus